OPERATIONS MANAGEMENT

NINTH EDITION

Nigel Slack

Alistair Brandon-Jones

Pearson

Harlow, England • London • New York • Boston • San Francisco • Toronto • Sydney • Dubai • Singapore • Hong Kong
Tokyo • Seoul • Taipei • New Delhi • Cape Town • São Paulo • Mexico City • Madrid • Amsterdam • Munich • Paris • Milan

PEARSON EDUCATION LIMITED
KAO Two
KAO Park
Harlow
CM17 9SR
United Kingdom
Tel: +44 (0)1279 623623

First published under the Pitman Publishing imprint 1995 (print)
Second edition (Pitman Publishing) 1998 (print)
Third edition 2001 (print)
Fourth edition 2004 (print)
Fifth edition 2007 (print)
Sixth edition 2010 (print)
Seventh edition 2013 (print and electronic)
Eighth edition 2016 (print and electronic)
Ninth edition 2019 (print and electronic)

ISBN: 978-1-292-25396-1 (print)
      978-1-292-25399-2 (PDF)
      978-1-292-25398-5 (ePub)

British Library Cataloguing-in-Publication Data
A catalogue record for the print edition is available from the British Library

Library of Congress Cataloging-in-Publication Data
Names: Slack, Nigel, author. | Brandon-Jones, Alistair.
Title: Operations management / Nigel Slack, Alistair Brandon-Jones.
Description: Ninth edition. | Harlow, England; New York: Pearson, 2019.
Identifiers: LCCN 2018059217| ISBN 9781292253961 (print) | ISBN 9781292253992
    (pdf) | ISBN 9781292253985 (epub)
Subjects: LCSH: Production management. | Manufacturing processes. | Industrial management.
Classification: LCC TS155 .S562 2019 | DDC 658.5—dc23LC record available at https://urldefense.
    proofpoint.com/v2/url?u=https-3A__lccn.loc.gov_2018059217&d=DwIFAg&c=0YLnzTkWOdJlub_
    y7qAx8Q&r=wtkxc2wc_pdG3u4VJ_y_HvFT4KYqFU-SxO1DssK0Al0&m=V0PiMd0EbVkgxs5Wwmdv2E
    3zM_AZd3xyja3TEjz25dM&s=_v363uqbzOz-M9Ebf-1rclfjyyakgg1Fhy_3jhuhrXE&e=

10 9 8 7 6 5 4 3 2 1
23 22 21 20 19

Cover image: © Shutterstock Premier/IM_Photo

Print edition typeset in 9.25/12 Charter ITC Std by Pearson CSC
Printed in Slovakia by Neografia

NOTE THAT ANY PAGE CROSS REFERENCES REFER TO THE PRINT EDITION

OPERATIONS MANAGEMENT

BRIEF CONTENTS

CONTENTS

PART ONE

DIRECTING THE OPERATION — 2

Companion Website

For open-access **student resources** specifically written to complement this textbook and support your learning, please visit **www.pearsoned.co.uk/slack**

Lecturer Resources

For password-protected online resources tailored to support the use of this textbook in teaching, please visit **www.pearsoned.co.uk/slack**

Guide to 'operations in practice', examples, short cases and case studies

Chapter	Location	Company/example	Region	Sector/activity	Company size
1 Operations management		Pret a Manger	Global	Hospitality	Medium
		Torchbox	UK	Web design	Small
		MSF	Global	Charity	Large
		Adidas			
		Ski Verbier Exclusive	Europe	Hospitality	Small
		Hewlett Packard		Manufacturing	Large
		To be a great operations manager…	Global	N/A	N/A
		Concept Design Services	General	Design/ manufacturing/ distribution	Medium
2 Operations performance		Novozymes	Europe	Pharmaceutical	Large
		Patagonia	Global	Garments	Large
		Quality Street	Global	Confectionery	Large
		The Golden Hour	General	Healthcare	N/A
		Travelling by rail			
		Mymuesli	German	Web retail	Small
		Aldi	Europe	Retail	Large
		The Penang Mutiara	Malaysia	Hospitality	Medium
		IKEA			
3 Operations strategy		Dow Corning			
		SSTL	UK/Space	Aerospace	Medium
		Micraytech – Part 1			
		Micraytech – Part 2			
		Tesco			
		Micraytech – Part 3			
		Amazon	Global	Web retail	Large
		Micraytech – Part 4			
		Nokia	Global	Telecomm	Large
		McDonald's	Global	Hospitality	Large
4 Product and service innovation		Dyson			
		Auto industry			
		IKEA			
		The circular economy	Global	Design/retail	Large
		Apple iPhone	Global	Sustainability	Various
		Toyota	Global	Design	Large
		Dreddo Dan's	Global	Snack food	Large

Chapter	Location	Company/example	Region	Sector/activity	Company size
5 The structure and scope of operations		Aalsmeer flower auction Hollywood studios Dubai airport Rolls-Royce Rana Plaza ARM and Intel Samsung Surgery and shipping	USA Global India/ Global	Creative Design and Design/ manufacturing Healthcare/ transportation	Large Large Large
6 Process design		Changi airport Fast food Ecover Sands Film Studio Space4 housing London Underground Sainsbury's Action Response	Singapore Global Europe UK UK UK UK	Air travel Hospitality Manufacturing Creative Construction Retail Charity	Large Large Large Small Medium Large Small
7 The layout and look of facilities		Ducati Quiet and interaction in laboratory layout Factory flow helps surgery Supermarket layout Customer flow in retail operations Office cubicles The event hub	UK Various UK	Healthcare Design Policing	Medium Various Medium
8 Process technology		Technology or people? Go figure Marmite Legacy versus fintech UK mail Rampaging robots Rochem	Various UK UK	Various Food Food processing	Various Large Medium
9 People in operations		W. L. Gore Exoskeleton device Michelin High customer contact jobs Music while you work Technology and surveillance at work Grace faces (three) problems	Global Global UK	Manufacturing Various Legal	Large Various Medium

Chapter	Location	Company/example	Region	Sector/activity	Company size
10 Planning and control		Joanne manages the schedule	UK	Retail	Medium
		Operations control at Air France	Global	Airline	Large
		Can airline passengers be sequenced?	General	Airports	Various
					Various
		The hospital triage system	Global	Healthcare	
		Sequencing and scheduling at London's Heathrow airport			Medium
		The life and times of a chicken sandwich (Part 1)	UK	Food processing	
		Ryanair			
		subtext Studios Singapore			
11 Capacity management		Rise of the gig economy			
		Demand forecasting in baseball			
		Signal technology			
		Surge pricing			
		Demand management			
		United Airlines			
		Heathrow			
12 Supply chain management		Apple	Global	Technology	Large
		The North Face	Global	Garment manufacture	Large
		The tsunami effect	Asia	Various	Various
		Levi Strauss	Global	Garment manufacture	Large
		KFC			
		Wimbledon			
		Maersk and IBM			
		Supplying fast fashion	Global	Garment design/ manufacture/retail	Large
13 Inventory management		National Health Service	UK	Public sector	Large
		Blood and Transplant service	Global	Power generation	Large
		Energy inventory			
		Cost of too much stock			
		Mountains of grit	South Africa	Wholesale	Small
		Flame electrical			
		Mr Ruben's bakery	Global	Retail	Large
		Amazon			
		Toilet roll delay			
		Supplies4medics	Europe	Retail	Medium

Chapter	Location	Company/example	Region	Sector/activity	Company size
14 Planning and control systems		Butcher's pet care	UK	(Dog) food production	Medium
		SAP and its partners	Global	Systems developers	
		The life and times of a chicken salad sandwich (Part 2)	UK	Food production	Medium
		What a waste	USA	Recycling	Large
		Psycho Sports	N/A	Manufacturing	Small
15 Lean operations		Lean construction		Domestic food preparation	N/A
		Toyota	Global	Auto production	Large
		Autonomy at Amazon			
		Pixar adopts lean	USA	Creative	Large
		Waste reduction in airline maintenance	N/A	Air transport	N/A
		KONKEPT			
		Boeing and Airbus			
		Jamie's 'lean' cooking	UK	Domestic food preparation	Large
16 Improvement		Sonae Corporation	Portugal	Retail	Large
		The checklist manifesto	N/A	Healthcare	Various
		6Wonderkinder	Germany	App developer	Small
		Improvement at Heineken	Netherlands	Brewer	Large
		SixSigma at Wipro	India	Outsourcers	Large
		Triumph motorcycles			
		Learning from Formula 1	UK	Transport	Various
		Schlumberger's InTouch technology			
		Ferndale Sands Conference Centre			
17 Quality management		TNT Express	Global	Transport	Large
		Victorinox	Switzerland	Manufacturing	Large
		Four Seasons	Global	Hospitality	Large
		Virgin Atlantic			
		Magic Moments	UK	Photography	Small
		Testing cars (close) to destruction			
		What a giveaway			
		IKEA			
		Ryanair	Europe	Airline	Large
		Fat finger syndrome	Global	Finance	Various
		Deliberate defectives	Canada	Manufacturing	Large
		Quality systems			
		Preston plant	Canada	Manufacturing	Medium

Chapter	Location	Company/example	Region	Sector/activity	Company size
18 Managing risk and recovery		‹644› Merlin ‹648› Internet of Things ‹652› It's the exception that proves the rule The rise of the MicroMort ‹660› OVH Slagelse Industrial Services	N/A Denmark	Various Manufacturing	Various Medium
19 Project management		Crossrail Ocado Halting the growth of malaria Vasa's first and last voyage Berlin Brandenburg Airport The BBC's DMI The Scottish Parliament Building United Photonics	Global Sweden UK Malaysia	Healthcare Military Construction Development	Large N/A Large Large

PREFACE

Operations may not run the world, but it makes the world run

Operations management is *everywhere*. Every time you experience a service and every time you buy a product, you are benefiting from the accomplishments of the operations managers who created them. Operations management is concerned with creating the services and products upon which we all depend. And all organizations produce some mixture of services and products, whether that organization is large or small, manufacturing or service, for profit or not for profit, public or private. And, if you are a manager, remember that operations management is not confined to the operations function. All managers, whether they are called Operations or Marketing or Human Resources or Finance, or whatever, manage processes and serve customers (internal or external). This makes at least part of their activities 'operations'.

Operations management is also *important*. Thankfully, most companies have now come to understand the importance of operations. This is because they have realized that, in the short term, effective operations management gives the potential to improve both efficiency and customer service simultaneously. Even more important, operations management can provide the capabilities that ensure the survival and success of an enterprise in the long term.

Operations management is also *exciting*. It is at the centre of many of the changes affecting the business world – changes in customer preference, changes in supply networks, changes in how we see the environmental and social responsibilities of enterprises, profound changes in technologies, changes in what we want to do at work, how we want to work, where we want to work, and so on. There has rarely been a time when operations management was more topical or more at the heart of business and cultural shifts.

Operations management is also *challenging*. Promoting the creativity that will allow organizations to respond to so many changes is becoming the prime task of operations managers. It is they who must find the solutions to technological and environmental challenges, the pressures to be socially responsible, the increasing globalization of markets and the difficult-to-define areas of knowledge management.

The aim of this book

This book provides a clear, authoritative, well-structured and interesting treatment of operations management as it applies to a variety of businesses and organizations. The text provides both a logical path through the activities of operations management and an understanding of their strategic context.

More specifically, this text is:

▶ *Strategic* in its perspective. It is unambiguous in treating the operations function as being central to competitiveness.
▶ *Conceptual* in the way it explains the reasons why operations managers need to take decisions.
▶ *Comprehensive* in its coverage of the significant ideas and issues which are relevant to most types of operation.
▶ *Practical* in that the issues and challenges of making operations management decisions *in practice* are discussed. The 'Operations in practice' feature, which starts every chapter, the short cases that appear through the chapters and the case studies at the end of each chapter, all explore the approaches taken by operations managers in practice.
▶ *International* in the examples that are used. There are over 120 descriptions of operations practice from all over the world.
▶ *Balanced* in its treatment. This means we reflect the balance of economic activity between service and manufacturing operations. Around 75 per cent of examples are from organizations that deal primarily in services and 25 per cent from those that are primarily manufacturing.

Who should use this book?

This book is for anyone who is interested in how services and products are created.

▶ *Undergraduates* on business studies, technical or joint degrees should find it sufficiently structured to provide an understandable route through the subject (no prior knowledge of the area is assumed).

- ▶ *MBA students* should find that its practical discussions of operations management activities enhance their own experience.
- ▶ *Postgraduate students* on other specialist Master's degrees should find that it provides them with a well-grounded and, at times, critical approach to the subject.

Distinctive features

Clear structure

The structure of the book uses the '4 Ds' model of operations management that distinguishes between the strategic decisions that govern the *direction* of the operation, the *design* of the processes and operations that create products and services, planning and control of the *delivery* of products and services, and the *development,* or improvement of operations.

Illustrations-based

Operations management is a practical subject and cannot be taught satisfactorily in a purely theoretical manner. Because of this we have used short 'Operations in practice' cases that explain some of the issues faced by real operations.

Worked examples

Operations management is a subject that blends qualitative and quantitative perspectives; worked examples are used to demonstrate how both types of technique can be used.

Critical commentaries

Not everyone agrees about what is the best approach to the various topics and issues within operations management. This is why we have included 'critical commentaries' that pose alternative views to the one being expressed in the main flow of the text.

Summary answers to key questions

Each chapter is summarized in the form of a list of bullet points. These extract the essential points that answer the key questions posed at the beginning of each chapter.

Case studies

Every chapter includes a case study suitable for class discussion. The cases are usually short enough to serve as illustrations, but have sufficient content also to serve as the basis of case sessions.

Problems and applications

Every chapter includes a set of problem-type exercises. These can be used to check out your understanding of the concepts illustrated in the worked examples. There are also activities that support the learning objectives of the chapter that can be done individually or in groups.

Selected further reading

Every chapter ends with a short list of further reading that takes the topics covered in the chapter further, or treats some important related issues. The nature of each piece of further reading is also explained.

Teaching and learning resources for the ninth edition

New for the ninth edition

In the 9th edition we have retained the extensive set of changes that we made in the 8th edition. In addition, we have retained the '4Ds' structure (direction, design, delivery and development) that has proved to be exceptionally popular. Needless to say, as usual, we have tried to keep up to date with the (increasingly) rapid changes taking place in the (wonderful) world of operations.

Specifically, the 9th edition includes the following key changes:

▶ An extended and refreshed set of 'Problems and applications' questions that will help you practise analysing operations. They can be answered by reading the chapter. Model answers for the first two questions can be found on the companion website for this book. Answers to all questions are available to tutors adopting the text.

▶ The long-standing case study in Chapter 2 on the Mutiara Hotel has been replaced by a new case that examines some of the innovative changes at Ikea as it faces challenges to its traditional operating practices.

▶ The process technology chapter has been re-designed to reflect the ongoing rapid development of new technologies that are having an often significant impact on all types of operation. In addition, most chapters have new 'Operations in practice' examples of the application of new technologies.

▶ We have extended and refreshed the popular 'Operations in practice' examples throughout the book.

There are now more than 130 of the examples, over 40 per cent of which are new to this book.

▶ We have strengthened even further the emphasis on the idea that 'operations management' is relevant to every type of business and all functional areas of the organization.

▶ Many new ideas in operations management have been incorporated, including surge pricing, digital twins, servitization, B2B and B2C relationships, line of sight in internal process networks, Net Promoter Scores, process mining, the Gartner hype cycle and primary capability analysis for new technologies, work–life balance, the use of blockchain in supply chains, human and system planning and control system integration, knowledge management, the circular economy, quality of experience, service guarantees and cyber security. However, we have retained the emphasis on the foundations of the subject.

▶ The book has been visually redesigned to aid learning.

▶ A completely new instructor's manual is available to lecturers adopting this textbook, together with PowerPoint presentations for each chapter and a Test-bank of assessment questions. Visit www.pearsoned. co.uk/slack to access these. Most importantly, a set of online resources to enable students to check their understanding, practise key techniques and improve their problem-solving skills now accompanies the book. Please see below for details of MyLab Operations Management.

Making the most of this book

All academic textbooks in business management are, to some extent, simplifications of the messy reality that is actual organizational life. Any book has to separate topics which in reality are closely related, in order to study them. For example, technology choice impacts on job design, which in turn impacts on quality management; yet, for simplicity, we are obliged to treat these topics individually. The first hint therefore in using this book effectively is to look out for all the links between the individual topics. Similarly, with the sequence of topics, although the chapters follow a logical structure, they need not be studied in this order. Every chapter is, more or less, self-contained. Therefore, study the chapters in whatever sequence is appropriate to your course or your individual interests. But because each part has an introductory chapter, those students who wish to start with a brief 'overview' of the subject may wish first to study Chapters 1, 6, 10 and 16 and the chapter summaries of selected chapters. The same applies to revision – study the introductory chapters and summary answers to key questions.

The book makes full use of the many practical examples and illustrations that can be found in all operations. Many of these were provided by our contacts in companies, but many also come from journals, magazines and newspapers. So if you want to understand the importance of operations management in everyday business life, look for examples and illustrations of operations management decisions and activities in newspapers and magazines. There are also examples which you can observe every day. Whenever you use a shop, eat a meal in a restaurant, borrow a book from the library or ride on public transport, consider the operations management issues of all the operations for which you are a customer.

The case exercises and study activities are there to provide an opportunity for you to think further about the ideas discussed in the chapters. Study activities can be used to test out your understanding of the specific points and issues discussed in the chapter and discuss them as a group, if you choose. If you cannot answer these, you should revisit the relevant parts of the chapter. The case exercises at the end of each chapter will require some more thought. Use the questions at the end of each case exercise to guide you through the logic of analysing the issue treated in the case. When you have done this individually try to discuss your analysis with other course members. Most important of all, every time you analyse one of the case exercises (or any other case or example in operations management) start off your analysis with the two fundamental questions:

▶ How is this organization trying to compete (or satisfy its strategic objectives if a not-for-profit organization)?

▶ What can the operation do to help the organization compete more effectively?

Ten steps to getting a better grade in operations management

We could say that the best rule for getting a better grade is to be good. We mean really, really good! But, there are plenty of us who, while fairly good, don't get as good a grade as we really deserve. So, if you are studying operations management, and you want a really good grade, try following these simple steps:

Step 1 Practise, practise, practise. Use the 'Key questions' and the 'Problems and applications' to check your understanding. Use the 'Study plan' feature in MyLab Operations Management and practice to master the topics that you find difficult.

Step 2 Remember a few **key models,** and apply them wherever you can. Use the diagrams and models to describe some of the examples that are contained within the chapter. You can also use the revision pod casts on MyLab Operations Management.

Step 3 Remember to use both **quantitative and qualitative analysis.** You'll get more credit for appropriately mixing your methods: use a quantitative model to answer a quantitative question and vice versa, but qualify this with a few well-chosen sentences. Both the chapters of the book, and the exercises on MyLab Operations Management, incorporate qualitative and quantitative material.

Step 4 There's always a *strategic* **objective** behind any operational issue. Ask yourself, 'Would a similar operation with a different strategy do things differently?' Look at the 'Operations in practice' pieces in the book.

Step 5 Research widely around the topic. Use websites that you trust – we've listed some good websites at the end of the book and on MyLab Operations Management. You'll get more credit for using references that come from genuine academic sources.

Step 6 Use **your own experience.** Every day, you're experiencing an opportunity to apply the principles of operations management. Why is the queue at the airport check-in desk so long? What goes on behind the scenes of your favourite restaurant? Use the videos on MyLab Operations Management to look further at operations in practice.

Step 7 Always answer the question. Think 'what is really being asked here? What topic or topics does this question cover?' Find the relevant chapter or chapters, and search the key questions at the beginning of each chapter and the summary at the end of each chapter to get you started.

Step 8 Take account of the three tiers of accumulating marks for your answers.

(a) First, demonstrate your knowledge and understanding. Make full use of the text and MyLab Operations Management to find out where you need to improve.
(b) Second, show that you know how to illustrate and apply the topic. The case studies and 'Operations in practice' sections, combined with those on MyLab Operations Management, give you hundreds of different examples.
(c) Third, show that you can discuss and analyse the issues critically. Use the critical commentaries within the text to understand some of the alternative viewpoints.

Generally, if you can do (a), you will pass; if you can do (a) and (b), you will pass well; and if you can do all three, you will pass with flying colours!

Step 9 Remember not only **what** the issue is about, but also **understand why!** Read the text and apply your knowledge on MyLab Operations Management until you really understand why the concepts and techniques of operations management are important, and what they contribute to an organisation's success. Your new-found knowledge will stick in your memory, allow you to develop ideas, and enable you to get better grades.

Step 10 Start now! Don't wait until two weeks before an assignment is due. Log on (www.pearson.com/mylab/operations-management), read on, and GOOD LUCK!

Nigel Slack and Alistair Brandon-Jones

Nigel Slack is an Emeritus Professor of Operations Management and Strategy at Warwick University, and an Honorary Professor at Bath University. Previously he has been Professor of Service Engineering at Cambridge University, Professor of Manufacturing Strategy at Brunel University, a University Lecturer in Management Studies at Oxford University and Fellow in Operations Management at Templeton College, Oxford. He worked initially as an industrial apprentice in the hand-tool industry and then as a production engineer and production manager in light engineering. He holds a Bachelor's degree in Engineering and Master's and Doctor's degrees in Management, and is a Chartered Engineer. He is the author of many books and papers in the operations management area, including *The Manufacturing Advantage* published by Mercury Business Books (1991), *Making Management Decisions* (1991) published by Prentice Hall, *Service Superiority* (with Robert Johnston, 1993) published by EUROMA, *The Blackwell Encyclopedic Dictionary of Operations Management* (with Michael Lewis) published by Blackwell, *Operations Strategy,* now in its fifth edition (with Michael Lewis, 2017) published by Pearson, *Perspectives in Operations Management (Volumes I to IV* with Michael Lewis, 2003) published by Routledge, *Operations and Process Management,* now in its fifth edition (with Alistair Brandon-Jones, 2018) published by Pearson, *Essentials of Operations Management,* now in its second edition (with Alistair Brandon-Jones, 2018) also published by Pearson, and *The Operations Advantage* published by Kogan Page (2017). He has authored numerous academic papers and chapters in books. He also acts as a consultant to many international companies around the world in many sectors, especially financial services, transport, leisure and manufacturing. His research is in the operations and manufacturing flexibility and operations strategy areas.

Alistair Brandon-Jones is a Full (Chaired) Professor in Operations and Supply Management at the University of Bath School of Management, Visiting Professor at Hult International Business School, DTU in Denmark, and NOVA in Portugal. Between 2014 and 2017, he was Associate Dean for Post-Experience Education, responsible for MBA, EMBA, EngDoc, DBA and DBA South Africa. He was formerly a Reader at Manchester Business School, an Assistant and Associate Professor at Bath School of Management, and a Teaching Fellow at Warwick Business School. He holds a Bachelor's degree in Management Science (2000) and a PhD (2006) from Warwick Business School. In addition to *Operations Management,* his other books include *Operations and Process Management* (with Nigel Slack), the fifth edition published in 2018, *Essentials of Operations* (with Nigel Slack), the second edition published in 2018, and *Quantitative Analysis in Operations Management* (with Nigel Slack), published in 2008, alongside a number of translations and adaptations of these books around the world. Alistair is an active empirical researcher, focusing on e-enabled operations and supply, professional service operations, and healthcare operations, and supported by funding from the Design Council, Economic and Social Research Council (ESRC), Engineering and Physical Sciences Research Council (EPSRC), Welsh Assembly Government and Local Government Association. He has published this research extensively in world-leading journals including *Journal of Operations Management, International Journal of Operations and Production Management, International Journal of Production Economics* and *International Journal of Production Research.* He has also disseminated his research through various practitioner publications, conferences, workshops and white papers. Alistair has consulting and executive development experience with organizations around the world, in various sectors including petrochemicals, health, financial services, manufacturing, defence and government. In addition, he has won numerous prizes for teaching excellence and contributions to pedagogy, including from Times Higher Education, Association of MBAs (AMBA), Production Operations Management Society (POMS), University of Bath, University of Manchester and University of Warwick.

ACKNOWLEDGEMENTS

During the preparation of the ninth edition of this book (and previous editions) we have received an immense amount of help from friends and colleagues in the Operations Management community. In particular everybody who has attended one of the regular 'faculty workshops' deserves thanks for the many useful comments. The generous sharing of ideas from these sessions has influenced this and all the other OM books that we prepare. Our thanks go to everyone who attended these sessions and other colleagues who have helped us. It is, to some extent, invidious to single out individuals – but we are going to.

We thank Pär Åhlström of Stockholm School of Economics, James Aitken of University of Surrey, Erica Ballantyne of Sheffield University, Yongmei Bentley of the University of Bedfordshire, Helen Benton of Anglia Ruskin University, Ran Bhamra of Loughborough University, Tony Birch of Birmingham City University, Abhijeet Ghadge of Heriot Watt University, Eamonn Ambrose of University College Dublin, Andrea Benn of the University of Brighton, Briony Boydell of the University of Portsmouth, John K. Christiansen of Copenhagen Business School, Philippa Collins of Heriot-Watt University, Paul Coughlan of Trinity College Dublin, Stephen Disney of Cardiff University, Doug Davies of the University of Technology, Sydney, Tony Dromgoole of the Irish Management Institute, J.A.C. de Haan of Tilburg University, Ioannis Dermitzakis of Anglia Ruskin University, Carsten Dittrich of the University of Southern Denmark, David Evans of Middlesex University, Ian Evans of Sunderland University, Margaret Farrell of Dublin Institute of Technology, Andrea Foley of Portsmouth University, Paul Forrester of Keele University, Andrew Gough of Northampton University, Ian Graham of Edinburgh University, Alan Harle of Sunderland University, Catherine Hart of Loughborough Business School, Graeme Heron of Newcastle Business School, Steve Hickman of the University of Exeter, Chris Hillam of Sunderland University, Ian Holden of Bristol Business School, Mickey Howard of Exeter University, Kim Hua Tan of the University of Nottingham, Stavros Karamperidis of Heriot Watt University, Tom Kegan of Bell College of Technology, Hamilton, Xiaohong Li of Sheffield Hallam University, John Maguire of the University of Sunderland, Charles Marais of the University of Pretoria, Peter McCullen of the University of Brighton, Roger Maull of Exeter University, Bart McCarthy of Nottingham University, Lynne Marshall of Nottingham Trent University, John Meredith Smith of EAP, Oxford, Joe Miemczyk of ESCP Business School Europe, Michael Milgate of Macquarie University, Keith Millar of Ulster University, Keith Moreton of Staffordshire University, Phil Morgan of Oxford Brooks University, Adrian Morris of Sunderland University, Nana Nyarko of Sheffield Hallam University, John Pal of Manchester Metropolitan University, Gary Priddis of University of Brighton, Sofia Salgado Pinto of the Católica Porto Business School, Gary Ramsden of the University of Lincoln, Steve Robinson of Southampton Solent University, James Rowell of the University of Buckingham, Frank Rowbotham of the University of Birmingham, Hamid Salimian of the University of Brighton, Sarah Schiffling of the University of Lincoln, Andi Smart of Exeter University, Nigel Spinks of the University of Reading, Rui Soucasaux Sousa of the Católica Porto Business School, Alex Skedd of Northumbria Business School, Martin Spring of Lancaster University, Dr Ebrahim Soltani of the University of Kent, R. Stratton of Nottingham Trent University, Ali Taghizadegan of the University of Liverpool, Dr Nelson Tang of the University of Leicester, Meinwen Taylor of South Wales University, David Twigg of Sussex University, Helen Valentine of the University of the West of England, Arvind Upadhyay of the University of Brighton, Andy Vassallo of the University of East Anglia, Vessela Warren of the University of Worcester, Linda Whicker of Hull University, John Whiteley of Greenwich University, Bill Wright of BPP Professional, Ying Xie of Anglia Ruskin University, Maggie Zeng of the University of Gloucestershire and Li Zhou of the University of Greenwich.

Our academic colleagues in the Operations Management Group at Warwick Business School, Bath University also helped, both by contributing ideas and by creating a lively and stimulating work environment. At Warwick, thanks go to, Vikki Abusidualghoul, Hayley Beer, Nicola Burgess, Mehmet Chakkol, Max Finne, Emily Jamieson, Mark Johnson, Pietro Micheli, Giovanni Radaelli, Ross Ritchie, Rhian Silvestro and Chris Voss. At Bath, thanks go to Maria Battarra, Emma Brandon-Jones, Emily Collins, Gunes Erdo-gan, Emmanuel Fragniere, Vaggelis Giannikas, Andrew Graves, Joanne Hinds, Jooyoung Jeon, Adam Joinson, Jas Kalra, Richard Kamm, Ana Levordashka, Michael Lewis, Sheik Meeran, Kate Muir, Ibrahim Muter, Fotios Petropoulos, Lukasz Piwek, Jens Roehrich, Brian Squire, Tommy Van Steen, Christos Vasilakis, Baris Yal-abik and Dimitris Zisis.

Our late friend and colleague, Bob Johnston, con-tributed both expertise and wisdom to earlier editions of this book. We still miss his intelligence, insight and support.

We were lucky to receive continuing professional and friendly assistance from a great publishing team. Especial thanks to Catherine Yates, Carole Drummond, Natalia Jaszczuk and Rufus Curnow.

Finally, to our families, who both supported and tolerated our nerdish obsession, thanks are inadequate, but thanks anyway to Angela and Kathy, and Emma and Noah.

Nigel Slack and Alistair Brandon-Jones

PUBLISHER'S ACKNOWLEDGEMENTS

Images

(key: b-bottom; c-centre; l-left; r-right; t-top)

5 **Alamy:** P. T. Photography/Alamy Stock Photo; 8 **Shutterstock:** (tl)Jenson/Shutterstock; (tl2)Alexander Raths /Shutterstock; (bl2) ESBProfessional/Shutterstock 8 **123RF:** (cl)Hongqi Zhang; 8 **Alamy:** (bl1)MARKA/ Alamy Stock Photo; 10 **Alamy:** Laura Beach/Cultura Creative (RF)/Alamy Stock Photo; 11 **Alamy:** André Quillien/Alamy Stock Photo; 12 **Alamy:** (bl)Jemastock/ Alamy Stock Vector; 12 **Alamy:** (bc)Frank Nikol. DieKleinert/Alamy Stock Photo; 12 **Shutterstock:** (br) Studio_G/Shutterstock; 13 **Alamy:** Suzanne Plunkett/ Alamy Stock Photo; 24 **Shutterstock:** Haveseen/Shutterstock; 25 **Getty Images:** Alain LE BOT/Gamma-Rapho/ Getty Images 28 **123RF:** Pablo Hidalgo/123RF; 32 **123RF:** Guasor/123RF; 40 **Shutterstock:** Francis J Dean/Shutterstock; 43 **Getty Images:** George Frey/Getty Images News/Getty Images; 48 **Shutterstock:** (bl1) Hadrian/Shutterstock; Blaz Kure/Shutterstock; 48 **Shutterstock:** (br1)Blaz Kure/Shutterstock; 48 **Shutterstock:** (bl2)Michael Rolands/Shutterstock; 48 **Shutterstock:** (br2)Buruhtan/Shutterstock; 49 **Alamy:** Urbanbuzz/ Alamy Stock Photo; 51 **Shutterstock:** JaneHYork/Shutterstock; 53 **Shutterstock:** Blend Images/Shutterstock; 55 **Shutterstock:** CKP1001/Shutterstock; 57 **Alamy:** Quantum Images/Alamy Stock Photo; 67 **Shutterstock:** Cate_89/Shutterstock; 73 **Shutterstock:** Yuriy Golub/ Shutterstock; **123RF:** Andrey Armyagov/123RF; 80 **Shutterstock:** AC Rider/Shutterstock; 84 **Alamy:** World History Archive/Alamy Stock Photo; 85 **Shutterstock:** Alastair Wallace/Shutterstock; 87 **Shutterstock:** Dainis Derics/Shutterstock; 89 **Shutterstock:** Eric Broder Van Dyke/Shutterstock; 91 **123RF:** Anzebizjan/123RF; 95 **Alamy:** Frank Sorge/Agencja Fotograficzna Caro/ Alamy Stock Photo; 103 **Alamy:** Rafael Ben Ari/Alamy Stock photo; 111 **Getty Images:** Rachel Murray/Getty Images Entertainment/Getty Images; 113 **Shutterstock:** Zavatskiy Aleksandr/Shutterstock; 116 **Shutterstock:** Anton_Ivanov/Shutterstock; 119 **Shutterstock:** Jim Holden/Shutterstock; 120 **Shutterstock:** Denys Prykhodov/Shutterstock; 132 **Getty Images:** Junko Kimura. Staff/Getty Images AsiaPac/Getty Images; 137 **123RF:** Ivan Traimak/123RF; 145 **Shutterstock:** Twobee/Shutterstock; 148 **123RF:** Ktsdesign/123RF; 153 **123RF:** Jakub Gojda/123RF; 156 **Shutterstock:** Matheus Obst/ Shutterstock; 159 **Alamy:** Zakir Hossain Chowdhury/ NurPhoto/ZUMA Press, Inc/Alamy Stock Photo; 162 **Shutterstock:** Scorpp/Shutterstock; 166 **Shutterstock:** Andrey_Popov/Shutterstock; 170 **Shutterstock:** Zivica Kerkez/Shutterstock; 178 **Alamy:** Urbanmyth/Alamy Stock Photo; 181 **Shutterstock:** Jax10289/Shutterstock; 183 **Alamy:** Ed Brown/Alamy Stock Photo; 184 **123RF:** Dinis Tolipov/123RF; 185 **123RF:** Belchonock/123RF; 185 **Getty Images:** (bc) Lionel Bonaventure/Afp/Getty Images; 186 **Shutterstock:** (tl) Supergenijalac/Shutterstock; 186 **Shutterstock:** (cl) Liunian/Shutterstock; 186 **Shutterstock:** (bl) Jacob Lund/Shutterstock; 187 **123RF:** (tl) Lightfieldstudios/123RF; 187 **123RF:** (bl) Iakov Filimonov/123RF; 191 **Shutterstock:** Dobrovizcki/Shutterstock; 201 **Alamy:** Ellen Isaacs/Alamy Stock Photo; 210 **123RF:** Juliet514/123RF; 216 **Alamy:** (tr)Fiorani Fabio/Agenzia Sintesi/Alamy Stock Photo; 216 **Shutterstock:** (br) Colormaker/Shutterstock; 227 **123RF:** Tele52/123RF; 230 **Getty Images:** Monkeybusinessimages/iStock/Getty Images; 231: **UNP:** Jon Super/UNP; 237 **Shutterstock:** Vs148/Shutterstock; 240 **Shutterstock:** Graham Taylor/Shutterstock; 249 **Shutterstock:** Shevs/Shutterstock; 254 **123RF:** Nataliya Dvukhimenna/123RF; 264 **Shutterstock:** TippaPatt/Shutterstock; 266 **Alamy:** TomBham/Alamy Stock Photo; 269 **Shutterstock:** Alexander Limbach/Shutterstock; 272 **Shutterstock:** Eckehard Schulz/Shutterstock; 278 **Alamy:** (tr) Ashley Cooper/Alamy Stock Photo; 278 **Getty Images:** (br) Manfred Segerer/Ullstein Bild/Getty Images; 288 **Lockheed Martin Corporation:** Lockheed Martin Corporation; 291 **Alamy:** (br)Dpa picture alliance archive/Alamy Stock Photo; 291 **Shutterstock:** (cr)Mauritz Antin/Epa/Shutterstock; 292 **Shutterstock:** Jason Salmon/Shutterstock; 296 **Getty Images:** Emmanuel Aguirre/Photographer's Choice RF/Getty Images; 298 **123RF:** Dmitriy Shironosov/123RF; 300 **Shutterstock:** Africa Studio/Shutterstock; 303 **Shutterstock:** StockLite/Shutterstock; 319 **Getty Images:** Dasril Roszandi/ NurPhoto/Getty Images; 323 **Alamy:** David Kilpatrick/ Alamy Stock Photo; 331 **Shutterstock:** 06Photo/Shutterstock; 333 **Getty Images:** Rick Madonik/Toronto Star/Getty Images; 336 **Shutterstock:** A Periam Photography/Shutterstock; 339 **Shutterstock:** ProKasia/ Shutterstock; 349 **Shutterstock:** Dragon Images/Shutterstock; 357 **123RF:** DaisyDaisy/123RF; 366 **123RF:** Levgen Onyshchenko/123RF; 369 **Shutterstock:**

Text

257 Unilever UK: Unilever UK, Reproduced with kind permission of Unilever PLC and group companies; **289 University of California Press :** Hackman, J. Richard, Greg R. Oldham, Robert Janson, and Kenneth Purdy, A new strategy for job enrichment, *California Management Review*, Vol. 17 (3), republished with permission of University of California Press. Permission conveyed through Copyright Clearance Center, Inc., © 1975, University of California Press; **296, 297 Elsevier Inc.:** Republished with permission of Elsevier, from Beauregard, T. Alexandra and Henry, Lesley C. (2009) Making the link between work-life balance practices and organizational performance. *Human Resource Management Review*, 19. pp. 9–22.; **311 Southern Management Association Annual:** Barnes, Frank C. (1983) 'Principles of Motion Economy: Revisited, Reviewed, and Restored', *Proceedings of the Southern Management Association Annual Meeting* (Atlanta, GA 1983), p 298. © 1983, Southern Management Association Annual; **415 Crown copyright:** The UK government Department for Environment, Food and Rural Affairs, Procuring the Future Sustainable Procurement National Action Plan: Recommendations from the Sustainable Procurement Task Force, 2006. Contains public sector information licensed under the Open Government Licence v3.0. © 2006 Crown copyright; **417 Harvard Business Publishing:** Fisher, Marshall, What is the right supply chain for your product? *Harvard Business Review*, March–April, pp. 105–116, reprinted by permission of Harvard Business Review. © 1997, Harvard Business Publishing; **423 Harvard Business Publishing:** Kraljic Peter, Purchasing must become supply management, *Harvard Business Review*, September 1983, reprinted by permission of Harvard Business Review. © 1983, Harvard Business Publishing; **432 Warwick Business School:** Professor Mark Johnson, Warwick Business School, The 50,000-mile journey of Wimbledon's tennis balls, 3 July 2017. © 2017, Warwick Business School; **473 Times Newspapers Limited:** Murad Ahmed, Amazon knows what you want, *The Times*, 28 January 2004. © 2004, Times Newspapers Limited; **487 The Institution of Engineering and Technology:** Allan K., My way – IT at Butcher's Pet Care, The Institution of Engineering and Technology © 2009; **501 Emerald Group Publishing Limited:** Republished with permission of Emerald Group Publishing Limited from Sherry Finney and Martin Corbett (2007) ERP implementation: a compilation and analysis of critical success factors, *Business Process Management Journal,* vol. 13 no. 3, 2007, pp. 329–347.; **502 IDG Communications, Inc.:** Kanaracus, Chris, Waste Management sues SAP over ERP implementation, in InfoWorld From IDG, MAR 27, © 2008, IDG Communications, Inc.; **502:** Turbit Neville (2005) ERP Implementation – The Traps, The Project Perfect White Paper Collection, www.projectperfect.com.au. Retrieved from: http://www.projectperfect.com.au/downloads/Info/info_erp_imp.pdf; **527 McKinsey & Company:** Applying Lean in Offices, Hospitals, Planes and Trains, Presentation at The Lean Services Summit, Amsterdam, 24 June (2004) p. 30, McKinsey & Company, www.mckinsey.com. © 2004 McKinsey & Company; **535 Stockholm School of Economics:** Example written and supplied by Janina Aarts and Mattia Bianchi, Department of Management and Organization, Stockholm School of Economics; **539 Sergio Rattner:** Rattner, Sergio, what is the Theory of Constraints, and How Does it Compare to Lean Thinking? The Lean Enterprise Institute, 2009. © 1999 Sergio Rattner; **540 Springer:** C.A. Voss and A. Harrison, Strategies for implementing JIT, in, Just-in-Time Manufacture, IFS/Springer-Verlag (Voss, C.A. (ed.) 1987) Copyright © 1987 Springer; **550 Católica Porto Business School:** Case by Professors Rui Soucasaux Sousa and Sofia Salgado Pinto, Católica Porto Business School, Portugal, Adapted, with permission. © Católica Porto Business School; **555 The Financial Times Ltd:** Vasagar, Jeevan, Experiment with a bit of anarchy, 28 January 2014. © 2014, The Financial Times Ltd; **578 Oxford University Press:** "Definition of *knowledge* in English" *OED Online,* Oxford University Press, December 2018, https://en.oxforddictionaries.com/definition/knowledge, Accessed 12 February 2019; **591: The Institution of Engineering and Technology:** Adapted from Vitaliev V (2009) The much-loved knife, The Institution of Engineering and Technology © 2009; **594, American Marketing Association:** Parasuraman, A., Zeithaml, V.A. and Berry, L.B., A conceptual model of service quality and implications for future research, *Journal of Marketing*, Vol. 49, Fall, pp. 41–50, © 1985, American Marketing Association; **615 EFQM:** The EFQM Excellence Model, retrieved from: http://www.efqmmiddleeast.org/efqm-model.html. Used with permission. © 2018, EFQM; **678 Routledge:** D'Herbemont, O. and César, B., Managing sensitive projects: A lateral approach, English version by Cutrin, T. and Etcheber, P. © 1998, Routledge; **679 Mattia Bianchi:** Example written and supplied by Mattia Bianchi, Department of Management and Organization, Stockholm School of Economics.

PART ONE

Directing the operation

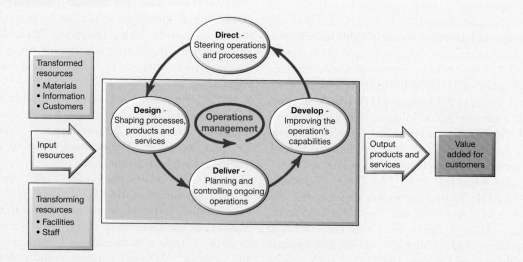

This part of the book introduces the idea of 'operations' and the operations function. It also examines the fundamental activities and decisions that shape the overall direction and strategy of the operations function. The chapters in this part are:

▶ **Chapter 1 Operations management**

This introduces the common ideas that describe the nature and role of operations and processes in all types of organization.

▶ **Chapter 2 Operations performance**

This identifies how the performance of the operations function can be judged.

▶ **Chapter 3 Operations strategy**

This examines how the activities of the operations function can have an important strategic impact.

▶ **Chapter 4 Product and service innovation**

This looks at how innovation can be built into the product and service design process.

▶ **Chapter 5 The structure and scope of operations**

This describes the major decisions that determine how, and the extent to which an operation adds value through its own activities.

Operations management

KEY QUESTIONS

What is operations management?

Why is operations management important in _all_ types of organization?

What is the input–transformation–output process?

What is the process hierarchy?

How do operations and processes differ?

What do operations managers do?

INTRODUCTION

Operations management is about how organizations create and deliver services and products. Everything you wear, eat, sit on, use, read or knock about on the sports field comes to you courtesy of the operations managers who organized its creation and delivery. Every book you borrow from the library, every treatment you receive at the hospital, every service you expect in the shops and every lecture you attend at university – all have been created by operations managers. While the people who supervised their creation and delivery may not always be called 'operations managers', that is what they really are. And that is what this book is concerned with – the tasks, issues and decisions of those operations managers who have made the services and products on which we all depend. This is an introductory chapter, so we will examine what we mean by 'operations management', how operations processes can be found everywhere, how they are all similar yet different, and what it is that operations managers do (see Figure 1.1).

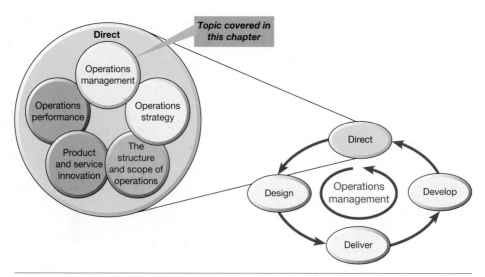

Figure 1.1 This chapter examines operations management

What is operations management?

Operations management is the activity of managing the resources that create and deliver services and products. The operations function is the part of the organization that is responsible for this activity. Every organization has an operations function because every organization creates some type of services and/or products. However, not all types of organization will necessarily call the operations function by this name. (Note in addition that we also use the shorter terms 'the operation' or 'operations' interchangeably with the 'operations function'.) Operations managers are the people who have particular responsibility for managing some, or all, of the resources that comprise the operations function. Again, in some organizations, the operations manager could be called by some other name. For example, he or she might be called the 'fleet manager' in a distribution company, the 'administrative manager' in a hospital, or the 'store manager' in a supermarket.

> **Operations principle**
>
> All organizations have 'operations' that produce some mix of services and products.

OPERATIONS IN PRACTICE  Pret a Manger[1]

Described by the press as having 'revolutionized the concept of sandwich making and eating', Pret a Manger opened its first shop in London. Now it has over 440 shops: most in the UK, but also in the US, Hong Kong, France, China and Dubai. It says that its secret is to focus continually on the quality of its food and of its service, avoiding the chemicals and preservatives common in most 'fast' food. Pret says that it sells food that can't be beaten for freshness. At the end of the day, it gives almost everything it hasn't sold to charity. The Pret Foundation Trust works with homeless charities to ensure that its unsold sandwiches go to people who need them, rather than to waste, with 87 per cent of its unsold food being re-distributed. Pret a Manger shops have their own kitchens where fresh ingredients are delivered every morning, with food prepared throughout the day. The team members who are serving on the tills at lunchtime will have been making sandwiches in the kitchen that morning. This flexibility helps to level out workloads throughout the day. But it does require staff who can make the switch between preparation and service smoothly. 'We

are determined never to forget that our hardworking people make all the difference. They are our heart and soul', says Pret. 'When they care, our business is sound. If they cease to care, our business goes down the drain. In a retail sector where high staff turnover is normal, we're pleased to say our people are much more likely to stay around! We work hard at building great teams. We take our reward schemes and career opportunities very seriously. We don't work nights (generally), we wear jeans, we party!' Pret also invests heavily in training through its 'Pret Academies' and its online training resources.

Keeping staff committed is important to a company like Pret that takes pride in its customer service. 'We'd like to think we react to our customers' feelings (the good, the bad, the ugly) with haste and absolute sincerity', it says. 'Pret customers have the right to be heard. Do call or email. Our UK Managing Director is available if you would like to discuss Pret with him. Alternatively, our CEO hasn't got much to do; hassle him!' More formally, customer feedback is a key ingredient of weekly management meetings. Staff are rewarded for being nice to customers; they collect bonuses for delivering outstanding customer service. Each Pret outlet is regularly visited by a secret shopper who scores the shop on such performance measures as speed of service, product availability and cleanliness. In addition, the mystery shopper rates the 'engagement level' of the staff. At a more strategic level, environmental sustainability issues have always been important to Pret. Its sustainability strategy has five key elements: using fewer resources, sustainable farming, healthy food, a positive contribution to society and embedding an awareness of sustainability within its values.

If you want a flavour of some of the issues involved in managing a modern successful operation, look at the 'Operations in practice' example on Pret a Manger. It illustrates how important the operations function is for any company whose reputation depends on creating high-quality, sustainable and profitable products and services. Its operations, like its products and services, are innovative, it focuses very much on customer satisfaction, it invests in the development of its staff, and it plays a positive role in fulfilling its social and environmental responsibilities. All of these issues are (or should be) high on the agenda of any operations manager in any operation. Of course, exactly what is involved in producing and delivering products and services will depend to some extent on the type of organization. Table 1.1 shows just some of the activities of the operations function for various types of organization.

Operations in the organization

The operations function is central to the organization because it creates and delivers services and products, which is its reason for existing. The operations function is one of the three core functions of any organization. These are:

▶ the marketing (including sales) function – which is responsible for communicating the organization's services and products to its markets in order to generate customer requests;
▶ the product/service development function – which is responsible for coming up with new and modified services and products in order to generate future customer requests;
▶ the operations function – which is responsible for the creation and delivery of services and products based on customer requests.

In addition, there are the support functions which enable the core functions to operate effectively. These include, for example, the accounting and finance function, the technical function, the human resources function and the information systems function. Remember that although different organizations may call their support functions by different names, almost all organizations will have the three core functions.

In practice, however, there is not always a clear division between functions. This leads to some confusion over where the boundaries of the operations function should be drawn. In this book, we use a relatively broad definition of operations. We treat much of the product/service development, technical and information systems activities and some of the human resource, marketing, and accounting and finance activities as coming within the sphere of operations management. We view the operations function as comprising all the activities necessary for the day-to-day fulfilment of customer requests within the constraints of environmental and social sustainability. This includes sourcing services and products from suppliers and delivering services and products to customers.

Table 1.1 Some activities of the operations function in various organizations

Internet service provider	Fast food chain	International aid charity	Furniture manufacturer
▶ Maintain and update hardware	▶ Locate potential sites for restaurants	▶ Provide aid and development projects for recipients	▶ Procure appropriate raw materials and components
▶ Update software and content	▶ Provide processes and equipment to produce burgers etc.	▶ Provide fast emergency response when needed	▶ Make sub-assemblies
▶ Respond to customer queries	▶ Maintain service quality	▶ Procure and store emergency supplies	▶ Assemble finished products
▶ Implement new services	▶ Develop, install and maintain equipment	▶ Be sensitive to local cultural norms	▶ Deliver products to customers
▶ Ensure security of customer data	▶ Reduce impact on local area, and packaging waste		▶ Reduce environmental impact of products and processes

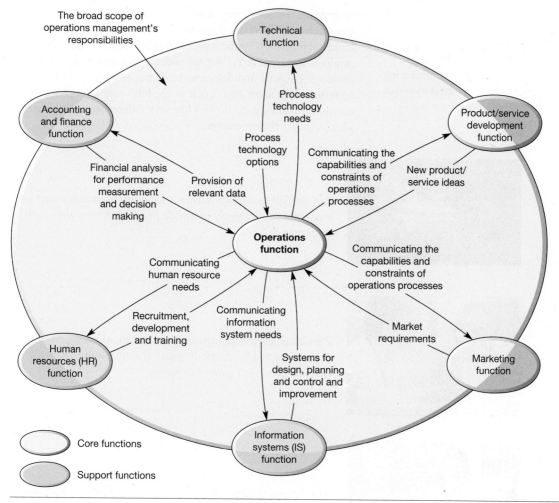

Figure 1.2 The relationship between the operations function and other core and support functions of the organization

Figure 1.2 illustrates some of the relationships between operations and other functions in terms of the flow of information between them. Although not comprehensive, it gives an idea of the nature of each relationship. Note that the support functions have a different relationship with operations than the core functions. Operations management's responsibility to support functions is primarily to make sure that they understand operations' needs and help them to satisfy these needs. The relationship with the other two core functions is more equal – less of '*this is what we want*' and more '*this is what we can do currently – how do we reconcile this with broader business needs?*'

> **Operations principle**
> Operations managers need to cooperate with other functions to ensure effective organizational performance.

Why is operations management important in *all* types of organization?

In some types of organization, it is relatively easy to visualize the operations function and what it does, even if we have never seen it. For example, most people have seen images of an automobile assembly line. But what about an advertising agency? We know vaguely what they do – they create the advertisements that we see on the web, in magazines and on television – but what is their operations function? The clue lies in the word 'create'. Any business that creates something must use resources to do so, and so must have an operations activity. Also, the automobile plant and the advertising agency do have one important element in common; both have a higher objective – to make a profit from creating and delivering their products or services. Yet not-for-profit organizations also use their resources to create and deliver services, not to make a profit, but to serve society in some way. Look at the following examples of what operations management does in five very different organizations and some common themes emerge.

Automobile assembly factory – *Operations management uses machines to efficiently assemble products that satisfy current customer demands*

Physician (general practitioner) – *Operations management uses knowledge to effectively diagnose conditions in order to treat real and perceived patient concerns*

Management consultant – *Operations management uses people to effectively create the services that will address current and potential client needs*

Disaster relief charity – *Operations management uses our and our partners' resources to speedily provide the supplies and services that relieve community suffering*

Advertising agency – *Operations management uses our staff's knowledge and experience to creatively present ideas that delight clients and address their real needs*

Start with the statement from the 'easy to visualize' automobile plant. Its summary of what operations management does is: '*Operations management uses machines to efficiently assemble products that satisfy current customer demands*'. The statements from the other organizations are similar, but use slightly different language. Operations management uses, not just machines but also '*knowledge*', '*people*', '*our and our partners' resources*' and '*our staff's knowledge and experience*', to efficiently (or effectively, or creatively) assemble (or produce, change, sell, move, cure, shape, etc.) products (or services or ideas) that satisfy (or match or exceed or delight) customer (or client or citizens' or society) demands (or needs or concerns or even dreams).

Whatever terminology is used there is a common theme and a common purpose to how we can visualize the operations activity in any type of organization; small or large, service or manufacturing, public or private, profit or not-for-profit. Operations management uses '*resources* to *appropriately create outputs* that *fulfill defined market requirements*' (see Figure 1.3). However, although the essential nature and purpose of operations management is the same in any type of organization, there are some special issues to consider, particularly in smaller organizations and those whose purpose is to maximize something other than profit.

Operations management in the smaller organization

Operations management is just as important in small organizations as it is in large ones. Irrespective of their size, all companies need to create and deliver their service and products efficiently and effectively. However, in practice, managing operations in a small or medium-size organization has its own set of problems. Large companies may have the resources to dedicate individuals to specialized tasks but smaller companies often cannot, so people may have to do different jobs as the need arises. Such an informal structure can allow the company to respond quickly as opportunities or problems present themselves. But decision making can also become confused as individuals' roles overlap. Small companies may have exactly the same operations management issues as large ones but they can be more difficult to separate from the mass of other issues in the organization. However, small operations can also have significant advantages; the 'Operations in practice' example on Torchbox illustrates this.

Operations management uses...

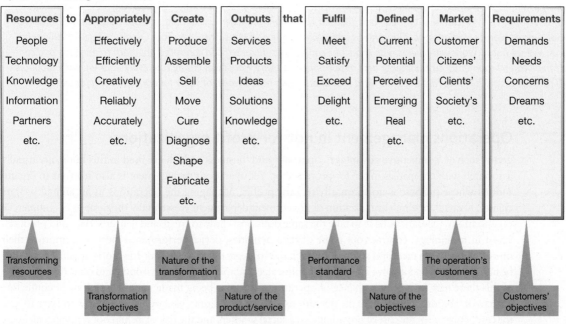

Resources	to	Appropriately	Create	Outputs	that	Fulfil	Defined	Market	Requirements
People		Effectively	Produce	Services		Meet	Current	Customer	Demands
Technology		Efficiently	Assemble	Products		Satisfy	Potential	Citizens'	Needs
Knowledge		Creatively	Sell	Ideas		Exceed	Perceived	Clients'	Concerns
Information		Reliably	Move	Solutions		Delight	Emerging	Society's	Dreams
Partners		Accurately	Cure	Knowledge		etc.	Real	etc.	etc.
etc.		etc.	Diagnose	etc.			etc.		
			Shape						
			Fabricate						
			etc.						

Transforming resources — Transformation objectives — Nature of the transformation — Nature of the product/service — Performance standard — Nature of the objectives — The operation's customers — Customers' objectives

Figure 1.3 Operations management uses resources to appropriately create outputs that fulfil defined market requirements.

Torchbox: award-winning web designers[2]

We may take it for granted, yet browsing websites, as part of your studies, your job, or your leisure, is an activity that we all do – probably every day, probably many times each day. All organizations need to have a web presence if they want to sell products and services, interact with their customers, or promote their cause. And, not surprisingly, there is a whole industry devoted to designing websites. In fact, taken over the years, web development has been one of the fastest growing industries in the world. But it's also a tough industry. Not every web design company thrives, or even survives beyond a couple of years. To succeed, web designers need technology skills, design capabilities, business awareness and operational professionalism. One that has succeeded is Torchbox, an independently-owned web design and development company based in Oxfordshire. Employing around 50 people, it provides 'high-quality, cost-effective, and ethical solutions for clients who come primarily, but not exclusively, from the charity, non-governmental organisations and public sectors'.

Co-founder and Technical Director Tom Dyson has been responsible for the technical direction of all major developments. *'There are a number of advantages about being a relatively small operation',* he says. *'We can be hugely flexible and agile, in what is still a dynamic market. But at the same time, we have the resources and skills to provide a creative and professional service. Any senior manager in a firm of our size cannot afford to be too specialised. All of us here have their own specific responsibilities; however, every one of us shares the overall responsibility for the firm's general development. We can also be clear and focused on what type of work we want to do. Our ethos is important to us. We set out to work with clients who share our commitment to environmental sustainability and responsible, ethical business practice; we take our work, and that of our*

clients, seriously. If you're an arms dealer, you can safely assume that we're not going to be interested.'

Nevertheless, operational effectiveness is also essential to Torchbox's business. *'We know how to make sure that our projects run not only on time and to budget',* says Olly Willans, a co-founder and the firm's Creative Director, *'but we also like to think that we provide an enjoyable and stimulating experience – both for our customers' development teams and for our staff too. High standards of product and service are important to us: our clients want accessibility, usability, performance and security embedded in their web designs, and of course, they want things delivered on-time and on-budget. We are in a creative industry that depends on fast-moving technologies, but that doesn't mean that we can't also be efficient.'* Torchbox uses a 'kanban' approach (fully explained in Chapter 15) to control its operations. *'Using sound operations management techniques helps us constantly to deliver value to our clients',* says Tom Dyson. *'We like to think that our measured and controlled approach to handling and controlling work helps ensure that every hour we work produces an hour's worth of value for our clients and for us.'*

Operations management in not-for-profit organizations

Terms such as 'competitive advantage', 'markets' and 'business', which are used in this book, are usually associated with companies in the for-profit sector. Yet operations management is also relevant to organizations whose purpose is not primarily to earn profits. Managing the operations in an animal welfare charity, hospital, research organization or government department is essentially the same as in commercial organizations. Operations have to take the same decisions – how to create and deliver service and products, invest in technology, contract out some of their activities, devise performance measures, improve their operations performance, and so on. However, the strategic objectives of not-for-profit organizations may be more complex and involve a mixture of political, economic, social or environmental objectives. Because of this there may be a greater chance of operations decisions being made under conditions of conflicting objectives. So, for example, it is the operations staff in a children's welfare department who have to face the conflict between the cost of providing extra social workers and the risk of a child not receiving adequate protection. Nevertheless, the vast majority of the topics covered in this book have relevance to all types of organization, including non-profit, even if the context is different and some terms may have to be adapted.

MSF operations provide medical aid to people in danger[3]

Médecins Sans Frontières (MSF) is an independent humanitarian organization providing 'medical aid where it is most needed, regardless of race, religion, politics or gender and raising awareness of the plight of the people we help in countries around the world'. Its core work takes place in crisis situations – armed conflicts, epidemics, famines and natural disasters such as floods and earthquakes. Its teams deliver both medical aid (including consultations with a doctor, hospital care, nutritional care, vaccinations, surgery, obstetrics and psychological care) and material aid (including food, shelter, blankets, etc.). Each year, MSF sends doctors, nurses, logisticians, water-and-sanitation experts, administrators and other professionals to work alongside locally hired staff. It is one of the most admired and effective relief organizations in the world. But no amount of fine intentions can translate into effective action without superior operations management. As MSF says, it must be able to react to any crisis with 'fast

response, efficient logistics systems, and efficient project management'.

Its response procedures are continuously being developed to ensure that it reaches those most in need as quickly as possible. The process has five phases: proposal, assessment, initiation, running the project and closing. The information that prompts a possible mission can come from governments, humanitarian organizations, or MSF teams already present in the region. Once the information has been checked and validated, MSF sends a team of medical and logistics experts to the crisis area to carry out a quick evaluation. When approved, MSF staff start the process of selecting personnel, organising materials and resources and securing project funds. Initiating a project involves sending technical equipment and resources to the area. Thanks to its pre-planned processes, specialised kits and the emergency stores, MSF can distribute material and equipment within 48 hours, ready for the response team to start work as soon as they arrive. Once the critical medical needs have been met, MSF begins to close the project with a gradual withdrawal of staff and equipment. At this stage, the project closes or is passed onto an appropriate organization. MSF will also close a project if risks in the area become too great to ensure staff safety. Whether it is dealing with urgent emergencies, or a long-running programme, everything MSF does on the ground depends on efficient logistics. Often, aircraft can be loaded and flown into crisis areas within 24 hours. But, if it is not a dire emergency, MSF reduces its costs by shipping the majority of material and drugs by sea.

The new operations agenda

Changes in the business environment have had a significant impact on the challenges faced by operations managers. Some of them are in response to changes in the nature of demand. Many (although not all) industries have experienced increased cost-based competition while simultaneously their customers' expectations of quality and variety have increased. What is technological possible is also changing rapidly, as are customers' attitude to social and environmental issues. At the same time, political, legal and regulatory structures have changed. In response, operations managers have had to adjust their activities to cope, especially in the following areas:

▶ *New technologies* – In both manufacturing and service industries, process technologies are changing so fast that it is difficult to predict exactly what their effect will be, only a few years in the future. Certainly, they are likely to have a dramatic effect, radically altering the operating practices of almost all types of operation.

▶ *Different supply arrangements* – Markets have become more global, often meaning a demand for a higher variety, or customized products and services. Also, globalized supply markets are opening up new options in how operations source input goods and services. Very few businesses have not considered purchasing from outside their own geographic area. But while bringing opportunities for cost savings, a bigger supply market also brings new problems of long supply chains, supply vulnerability and reputational risk.

▶ *Increased emphasis on social and environmental issues* – Generally, customers have been developing an increased ethical and environmental sensitivity. This is leading to operations having to change the way they create their products and services, and be more transparent about it. Similarly, there is a greater expectation about the ethical treatment of all an operation's stakeholders, including customers, the workforce, suppliers and society in general.

Operations principle

Operations management is at the forefront of coping with, and exploiting, developments in business and technology.

Figure 1.4 identifies just some of the operations responses in these three areas. (If you don't recognize some of the terms in Figure 1.4, don't worry, we will explain them throughout the book.) These responses form a major part of a *new agenda* for operations. Of course, the issues in Figure 1.4 are not comprehensive, nor are they universal. But very few operations functions will be unaffected by at least some of them. Also, you will find 'Operations in practice' examples at several points in this book that look at various aspects of these three areas.

Developments in:

- The business and competitive environment
- Technological possibilities
- Social and environmental attitudes
- Global political environment
- Regulatory and legal environment

Adoption of *new technologies*, for example:

- Internet
- Algorithmic decision making
- Artificial intelligence
- 3D printing
- Robotics
- 'Big data' analysis

Adoption of different *supply arrangements*, for example:

- Global operations networks
- Partnership relationships
- Business ecosystem analysis
- Reputational risk management

Increased emphasis on *social and environmental issues*, for example:

- Triple bottom line performance
- Environmentally sensitive design
- Flexible working patterns
- Energy saving

Figure 1.4 Changes in the business environment are shaping a new operations agenda

How Adidas coped with shrinking fashion cycles

There is a vast industry involved in designing, making and distributing trainers (sneakers). It is an industry where supply chains are complex, and involve an extensive network of specialized operations, each focusing on the individual components that make up the shoes. A single part could have crossed back and forwards between several different countries before being assembled into the finished product, usually by hand. Most of the making is done in Asia, where labour costs are low compared with Western countries and where there is an immense and interconnected network of specialist manufacturers employing thousands of people. Most well-known brands have tended to concentrate on the design, marketing and distribution. Adidas, like most of its rivals, subcontracted the 'making' part of the total process (it had not run or owned its own manufacturing operations since the 1990s) but the network of suppliers it employs spreads over more than 1,000 facilities in 63 countries. Yet, like other similar companies, Adidas faces some problems with its Asian outsourcing model. First, growing affluence in the area has resulted in rising costs. Second, the longer and more complex a supply network, the more difficult it is to oversee every single operation that contributes to the finished shoe, which opens any company to reputational damage if a supplier employs unacceptable working practices (although Adidas has a particularly thorough set of 'workplace standards' to which all suppliers must conform). Finally, this globalised and complex supply chain means a long lead-time between conceiving a new trainer and it eventually arriving in the shops. And it is this last point that can be the most problematic, particularly for fashionable trainers with a short 'fashion life'. From the initial design for a new trainer, through prototype creating and testing, to placing orders on suppliers, setting up the production process, ramping up production, and finally sending the trainers to the shops, can take as long as 18 months. Even orders to replenish stocks can take two to three months. But fashion cycles for trainers are getting shorter, with some designs lasting only one to three years.

Faced with this tension between slow lead-times on one hand and short fashion cycles on the other, Adidas developed its 'Speedfactory' operation, the first one of which was located in Ansbach, Germany, halfway between Munich and Frankfurt (the second one is near Atlanta in the US). The Speedfactory is totally automated, and designed to be able to accommodate new technologies, such as 3D printing, as they become appropriate. And because almost all the stages of manufacturing are done on the same site, it makes Adidas considerably faster and more flexible, especially in producing limited runs of fashionable products. Speedfactory can produce shoes in days, which also gives the company the ability to replenish the fastest selling products during the same season. Each Speedfactory can make around 500,000 pairs of trainers a year (small compared to over 400 million that Adidas makes using its traditional supply chain). But Speedfactory is not intended to compete with its Asian subcontractors; it complements them. For shoe designs with relatively high and predictable volumes, the traditional Asian supply networks still dominate. But for local (European and US) markets with high-end, fashion-oriented trainers for environmentally sensitive customers, the Speedfactory is a fast and flexible addition to Adidas' traditional supply.

Note how the 'Operations in practice' example of Adidas demonstrates how one company is being innovative in tackling the challenges inherent in the 'new operations agenda' that we identified earlier in the chapter. It is an example of how changes in market requirements prompted a response that involves new technologies (including automation and 3D printing), a rethinking of how supply was to be organised (bringing some, albeit limited, work back to Europe and the US), and consideration of environmental sustainability issues (reduced transportation and less waste from 3D printing).

What is the input–transformation–output process?

All operations create and deliver service and products by changing *inputs* into *outputs* using an 'input–transformation–output' process. Figure 1.5 shows this general transformation process model that is the basis of all operations. Put simply, operations are processes that take in a set of input resources which are used to transform something, or are transformed themselves, into outputs of services and products. And although all operations conform to this general input–transformation–output model, they differ in the nature of their specific inputs and outputs. For example, if you stand far enough away from a hospital or a car plant, they might look very similar, but move closer and clear differences do start to emerge. One is a service operation delivering 'services' that change the physiological or psychological condition of patients; the other is a manufacturing operation creating and delivering 'products'. What is inside each operation will also be different. The hospital contains diagnostic, care and therapeutic processes whereas the motor vehicle plant contains metal forming machinery and assembly processes. Perhaps the most important difference between the two operations, however, is the nature of their inputs. The hospital transforms the customers themselves. The patients form part of the input to, and the output from, the operation. The vehicle plant transforms steel, plastic, cloth, tyres and other materials into vehicles.

> **Operations principle**
>
> All processes have inputs of transforming and transformed resources that they use to create products and services.

Inputs to the process

One set of inputs to any operation's processes are transformed resources. These are the resources that are treated, transformed or converted in the process. They are usually a mixture of the following:

▶ **Materials** – operations which process materials could do so to transform their *physical properties* (shape or composition, for example). Most manufacturing operations are like this. Other operations process materials to change their *location* (parcel delivery companies, for example). Some, like retail operations, do so to change the *possession* of the materials. Finally, some operations *store* materials, such as warehouses.

▶ **Information** – operations which process information could do so to transform their *informational properties* (that is, the purpose or form of the information); accountants do this. Some change the *possession* of the information: for example, market research companies sell information. Some *store* the information, such as archives and libraries. Finally, some operations, such as telecommunication companies, change the *location* of the information.

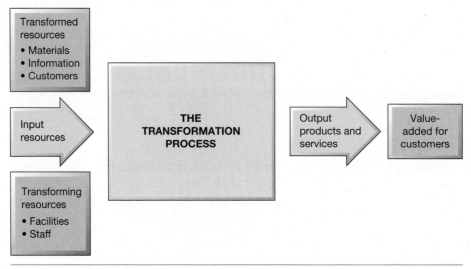

Figure 1.5 All operations are input–transformation–output processes

▶ **Customers** – operations which process customers might change their *physical properties* in a similar way to materials processors: for example, hairdressers or cosmetic surgeons. Some *store* (or more politely *accommodate*) customers: hotels, for example. Airlines, mass rapid transport systems and bus companies transform the *location* of their customers, while hospitals transform their

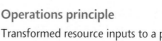
physiological state. Some are concerned with transforming their *psychological state:* for example, most entertainment services such as music, theatre, television, radio and theme parks. But customers are not always simple 'passive' items to be processed. They can also play a more active part in many operations and processes. For example, they create the atmosphere in a restaurant; they provide the stimulating environment in learning groups in education, they provide information at check-in desks, and so on. When customers play this role, it is usually referred to as 'co-production' because the customer plays a vital part in the provision of the product/service offering.

Some operations have inputs of materials *and* information *and* customers, but usually one of these is dominant. For example, a bank devotes part of its energies to producing printed statements by processing inputs of material, but no one would claim that a bank is a printer. The bank also is concerned with processing inputs of customers at its branches and contact centres. However, most of the bank's activities are concerned with processing inputs of information about its customers' financial affairs. As customers, we may be unhappy with badly printed statements and we may be unhappy if we are not treated appropriately in the bank. But if the bank makes errors in our financial transactions, we suffer in a far more fundamental way. Table 1.2 gives examples of operations with their dominant transformed resources.

The other set of inputs to any operations process are transforming resources. These are the resources which act upon the transformed resources. There are two types which form the 'building blocks' of all operations:

▶ facilities – the buildings, equipment, plant and process technology of the operation;
▶ staff – the people who operate, maintain, plan and manage the operation. (Note we use the term 'staff' to describe all the people in the operation, at any level.)

The exact nature of both facilities and staff will differ between operations. To a five-star hotel, its facilities consist mainly of 'low-tech' buildings, furniture and fittings. To a nuclear-powered aircraft carrier, its facilities are 'high-tech' nuclear generators, and sophisticated electronic equipment. Staff will also differ between operations. Most staff employed in a factory assembling domestic refrigerators may not need a very high level of technical skill. In contrast, most staff employed by an accounting company are, hopefully, highly skilled in their own particular 'technical' skill (accounting). Yet

Table 1.2 Dominant transformed resource inputs of various operations

Predominantly processing inputs of materials	Predominantly processing inputs of information	Predominantly processing inputs of customers
▶ All manufacturing operations	▶ Accountants	▶ Hairdressers
▶ Mining companies	▶ Bank headquarters	▶ Hotels
▶ Retail operations	▶ Market research companies	▶ Hospitals
▶ Warehouses	▶ Financial analysts	▶ Mass rapid transports
▶ Postal services	▶ News services	▶ Theatres
▶ Container shipping line	▶ University research units	▶ Theme parks
▶ Trucking companies	▶ Telecoms companyies	▶ Dentists

Operations principle

All processes have transforming resources of facilities (equipment, technology, etc.) and people.

although skills vary, all staff can make a contribution. An assembly worker who consistently misassembles refrigerators will dissatisfy customers and increase costs just as surely as an accountant who cannot add up. The balance between facilities and staff also varies. A computer chip manufacturing company, such as Intel, will have significant investment in physical facilities. A single chip fabrication plant can cost in excess of $5 billion, so operations managers will spend a lot of their time managing their facilities. Conversely, a management consultancy firm depends largely on the quality of its staff. Here operations management is largely concerned with the development and deployment of consultant skills and knowledge.

Outputs from the process

Operations create products and services. Products and services are different. Products are usually tangible things whereas services are activities or processes. A car or a newspaper or a restaurant meal is a product, whereas a service is the activity of the customer using or consuming that product. Some services do not involve products. Consultancy advice or a haircut is a process (although some products may be supplied in support of the service, such as a report or a hair gel). Also, while most products can be stored, at least for a short time, service only happens when it is consumed or used. So, accommodation in an hotel room for example will perish if it is not sold that night, a restaurant table will remain empty unless someone uses it that evening.

Most operations produce both products and services

Some operations create and deliver just services and others just products, but most operations combine both elements. Figure 1.6 shows a number of operations (including some described as examples in this chapter) positioned in a spectrum from 'pure' products to 'pure' service. Crude oil producers are concerned almost exclusively with the product which comes from their oil wells. So are aluminium smelters, but they might also deliver some services such as technical advice. Services in these circumstances are called 'facilitating services'. To an even greater extent, machine tool manufacturers deliver facilitating services such as technical advice and applications engineering. The services delivered by a restaurant are an essential part of what the customer is paying for. It is both a manufacturing operation which creates and delivers meals and a provider of service in the advice, ambience and service of the food. An information systems provider may create software 'products', but primarily it is providing a service to its customers, with facilitating products. Certainly, a management consultancy, although it produces reports and documents, would see itself primarily as a service provider. Finally, pure services solely create and deliver services, such as a psychotherapy clinic. Of the 'Operations in practice' examples in this chapter, Adidas produces tangible products. Pret a Manger both creates and 'serves' its products. Médecins Sans Frontières supplies physical aid in emergencies, but also intangible advice and medical help. Hotels such as Formule 1 and especially Ski Verbier Exclusive are close to being pure services, although they both have some tangible elements such as food. Torchbox's customers receive no physical product but are paying for the design and functionality of the website designs

Operations principle

Most operations produce a mixture of tangible products and intangible services.

Product or service?

Increasingly the distinction between services and products is difficult to define. Nor is it particularly useful. Not only do most businesses produce a combination of products and services, but also the outputs from their operations are increasingly seen as a combined 'package'. One buys a vehicle from a motor dealer (a product), but part of the decision to buy that vehicle could have been based on the ongoing (at least for a few years) servicing and financing deal. This idea of thinking about integrated

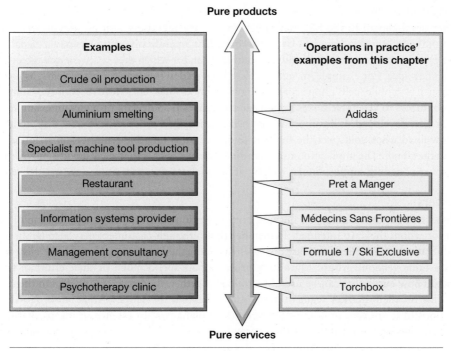

Figure 1.6 The output from most operations is a mixture of products and services. Some general examples are shown here together with some of the operations featured as 'Operations in practice' examples in this chapter.

products and services (often termed simply 'offerings') is powerful. Indeed, we would argue that *all* operations are service providers which may create and deliver products as part of the offering to their customers. This is why operations management is important to all organizations. Whether they see themselves as manufacturers or service providers is very much a secondary issue.

Operations principle

Whether an operation produces tangible products or intangible services is becoming increasingly irrelevant. In a sense, all operations produce service for their customers.

Servitization

A term that is often used to indicate how operations, which once considered themselves exclusively producers of products, are becoming more service-conscious is 'servitization' (or servitisation). Servitization involves (often manufacturing) firms developing the capabilities they need to provide services and solutions that supplement their traditional product offerings.[4] The best-known example of how servitization works was when Rolls-Royce, the aero engine manufacturer, rather than selling individual engines, offered the option of customers being able to buy 'power-by-the-hour'. What this meant was that many of its customers in effect bought the power the aero engine delivers, with Rolls-Royce pro-

Operations principle

Servitization involves firms developing the capabilities to provide services and solutions that supplement their traditional product offerings.

viding both the physical engines and all of the support (including maintenance, training, updates and so on) to ensure that they could continue to deliver power. This may sound like a small change, but the effects were important. First, Rolls-Royce became a provider of service (the power to make the aircraft fly) as opposed to a manufacturer of technically complex products. Second, it means that what customers really want (the reliable provision of power) and the objectives of the company are more closely aligned. Third, it provides an opportunity for companies to earn additional revenue from new services.

Subscription services

A further development to the idea that all outputs from operations can be seen as services is the concept of the 'subscription model'. Using this model, an operation's customers pay a (usually) fixed amount each agreed time period, usually a month or year, for which they receive a pre-agreed service. It is not a new idea. For example, magazines have been sold in this way for many years, as have some services such as mobile (cell) phone contracts, gym memberships, etc. More recently, consumer offerings, from razors to vegetable boxes, have been sold this way. Software provides an example of how offerings have developed. It has moved from being primarily a product (sold on a disk) to an intangible download when sold over the Internet to an even less tangible rental or subscription service based 'in the cloud'. The implication for operations management is that such services move from 'one off' supply to ongoing supply, similar to how utilities (electricity, gas, water, etc.) are delivered.

Customers

Any discussion about the nature of outputs from operations must involve consideration of the customers for whom they are intended. Remember that although customers may also be an input to many operations (see earlier), they are also the reason for their existence. Nor should 'customers' be seen as a homogeneous group. Marketing professionals spend much of their effort in trying to understand how customers can be usefully grouped together, the better to understand their various needs. This is called 'market segmentation', and is beyond the scope of this book. However, the implications of it are very important for operations managers. In essence, it means that different customer groups may want different things from an operation, even if they want the same product or service. We shall discuss this issue further in Chapter 3.

B2B and B2C

One distinction between different types of customer is worth describing at this point, because we shall be using the terminology at other points in the book. That is between Business to Business (B2B) and Business to Consumer (B2C) operations. B2B operations are those that provide their products or services to other businesses. B2C operations provide their products or services direct to the consumers who (generally) are the ultimate users of the outputs from the operation. Serving individual customers and serving other businesses are very different. This means that the operations serving these two types of customer will be faced with different kinds of concerns, and probably be organised in different ways. Yet an understanding of customers is always important (whether business customers, or consumers). Without them, there would be no operation. It is critical that operations managers are aware of customers' needs, both current and potential. This information will determine what the operation has to do and how it has to do it (the operation's strategic performance objectives), which in turn defines the service/product offering to be designed, created and delivered.

> **Operations principle**
> An understanding of customer needs is always important, whether customers are individuals or businesses.

What is the process hierarchy?

So far we have discussed operations management, and the input–transformation–output model, at the level of 'the operation'. For example, we have described the sandwich shop, the web designer, the disaster relief operation and the sports shoe manufacturer. But look inside any of these operations. One will see that all operations consist of a collection of processes (although these processes may be called 'units' or 'departments') interconnecting with each other to form a network. Each process acts as a smaller version of the whole operation of which it forms a part, and transformed resources flow in between them. In fact, within any operation, the mechanisms that actually transform inputs into outputs are these processes. A 'process' is an arrangement of resources and activities that transform inputs into outputs that satisfy (internal or external) customer needs. They are the 'building blocks' of all operations, and they form an 'internal network' within an operation. Each process is,

Table 1.3 Some operations described in terms of their processes

Operation	Some of the operation's processes
Airline	Passenger check-in assistance, baggage drop, security / seat check, board passengers, fly passengers and freight around the world, flight scheduling, in-flight passenger care, transfer assistance, baggage reclaim, etc.
Department store	Source merchandise, manage inventory, display products, give sales advice, sales, aftercare, complaint handling, delivery service, etc.
Police service	Crime prevention, crime detection, information gathering / collating, victim support, formally charging / detaining suspects, managing custody suites, liaising with court / justice system, etc.
Ice cream manufacturer	Source raw materials, input quality checks, prepare ingredients, assemble products, pack products, fast freeze products, output quality checks, finished goods inventory, etc.

at the same time, an internal supplier and an internal customer for other processes. This 'internal customer' concept provides a model to analyse the internal activities of an operation. It is also a useful reminder that, by treating internal customers with the same degree of care as external customers, the effectiveness of the whole operation can be improved. Table 1.3 illustrates how a wide range of operations can be described in this way.

Operations principle

A process perspective can be used at three levels: the level of the operation itself, the level of the supply network, and the level of individual processes.

Within each of these processes is another network of individual units of resource such as individual people and individual items of process technology (machines, computers, storage facilities, etc.). Again, transformed resources flow between each unit of transforming resource. Any business, or operation, is made up of a network of processes and any process is made up of a network of resources. But also, any business or operation can itself be viewed as part of a greater network of businesses or operations. It will have operations that supply it with the services and products it needs, and unless it deals directly with the end consumer, it will supply customers who themselves may go on to supply their own customers. Moreover, any operation could have several suppliers and several customers, and may be in competition with other operations creating similar services or products to itself. This network of operations is called the 'supply network'. In this way, the input–transformation–output model can be used at a number of different 'levels of analysis'. Here we have used the idea to analyse businesses at three levels: the process, the operation and the supply network. But one could define many different 'levels of analysis', moving upwards from small to larger processes, right up to the huge supply network that describes a whole industry.

This idea is called the 'hierarchy of operations' or the 'process hierarchy', and is illustrated for a business that makes television programmes and videos in Figure 1.7. It has inputs of production, technical and administrative staff, cameras, lighting, sound and recording equipment, and so on.

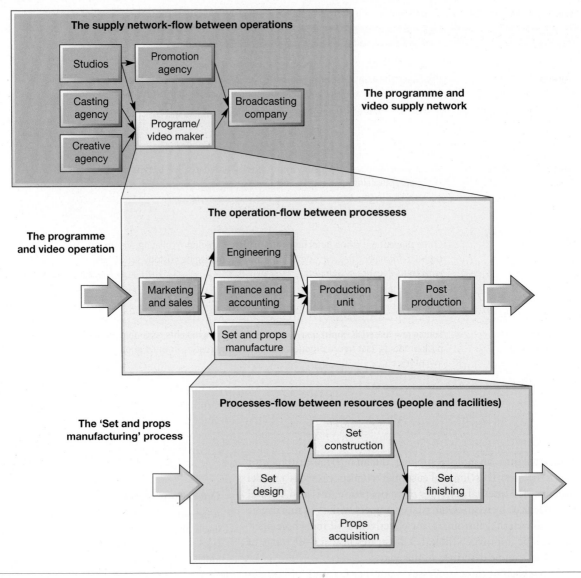

Figure 1.7 Operations and process management requires analysis at three levels: the supply network, the operation and the process

It transforms these into finished programmes, promotional music videos, etc. At a more macro level, the business itself is part of a whole supply network, acquiring services from creative agencies, casting agencies and studios, liaising with promotion agencies, and serving its broadcasting company customers. At a more micro level within this overall operation there are many individual processes; workshops manufacturing the sets; marketing processes that liaise with potential customers; maintenance and repair processes that care for, modify and design technical equipment; production units that shoot the programmes and videos; and so on. Each of these individual processes can be represented as a network of yet smaller processes, or even individual units of resource. So, for example, the set manufacturing process could comprise four smaller processes: one that designs the sets, one that constructs them, one that acquires the props, and one that finishes (paints) the set.

Operations management is relevant to all parts of the business

The example in Figure 1.7 demonstrates that it is not just the operations function that manages processes; all functions manage processes. For example, the marketing function will have processes that create demand forecasts, processes that create advertising campaigns and processes that create marketing plans. These processes in the other functions also need managing, using similar principles to those within the operations function. Each function will have its 'technical' knowledge. In marketing, this is the expertise in designing and shaping marketing plans; in finance, it is the technical knowledge of financial reporting. Yet each will also have a 'process management' role of producing plans, policies, reports and services. The implications of this are very important. Because all managers have some responsibility for managing processes, they are, to some extent, operations managers. They all should want to give good service to their (often internal) customers, and they all will want to do this efficiently. So, operations management is relevant for all functions, and all managers should have something to learn from the principles, concepts, approaches and techniques of operations management. It also means that we must distinguish between two meanings of 'operations':

Operations principle

All parts of the business manage processes, so all parts of the business have an operations role and need to understand operations management principles.

▶ 'Operations' as a function, meaning the part of the organization which creates and delivers services and products for the organization's external customers;
▶ 'Operations' as an activity, meaning the management of the processes within any of the organization's functions.

Table 1.4 illustrates just some of the processes that are contained within some of the more common non-operations functions, the outputs from these processes and their 'customers'.

Business processes

Whenever a business attempts to satisfy its customers' needs it will use many processes, both in its operations and in its other functions. Each of these processes will contribute some part to fulfilling customer needs. For example, the television programme and video production company, described previously, creates and delivers two types of 'product'. Both of these involve a slightly different mix of processes within the company. The company decides to re-organize its operations so that each product is created from start to finish by a dedicated process that contains all the elements necessary for its production, as in Figure 1.8. So, customer needs for each product are entirely fulfilled from

Operations principle

Processes are defined by how the organization chooses to draw process boundaries.

Table 1.4 Some examples of processes in non-operations functions

Organizational function	Some of its processes	Outputs from its processes	Customer(s) for its outputs
Marketing and sales	▶ Planning process ▶ Forecasting process ▶ Order-taking process	▶ Marketing plans ▶ Sales forecasts ▶ Confirmed orders	▶ Senior management ▶ Sales staff, planners, operations ▶ Operations, finance
Finance and accounting	▶ Budgeting process ▶ Capital approval processes ▶ Invoicing processes	▶ Budgets ▶ Capital request evaluations ▶ Invoices	▶ Everyone ▶ Senior management, requesters ▶ External customers
Human resources management	▶ Payroll processes ▶ Recruitment processes ▶ Training processes	▶ Salary statements ▶ New hires ▶ Trained employees	▶ Employees ▶ All other processes
Information technology	▶ Systems review process ▶ Help desk process ▶ System implementation project processes	▶ System evaluation ▶ Systems advice ▶ Implemented working systems and aftercare	▶ All other processes in the business

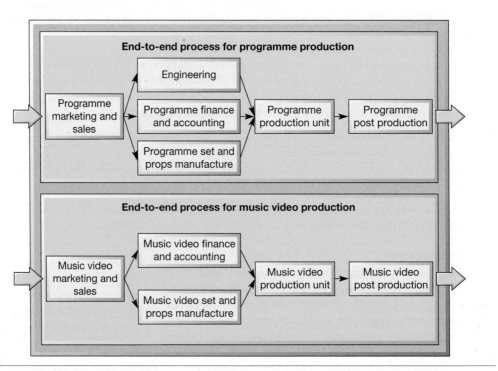

Figure 1.8 The television and video company divided into two 'end-to-end' business processes, one dedicated to creating programmes and the other dedicated to creating music videos

within what is called an 'end-to-end' business process. These often cut across conventional organizational boundaries. Reorganizing (or 're-engineering') process boundaries and organizational responsibilities around these business processes is the philosophy behind business process re-engineering (BPR), which is discussed further in Chapter 16.

How do operations and processes differ?

Although all operations processes are similar in that they all transform inputs, they do differ in a number of ways, four of which, known as the four Vs, are particularly important:

▶ The volume of their output.
▶ The variety of their output.
▶ The variation in the demand for their output.
▶ The degree of visibility that the creation of their output has for customers.

The volume dimension

Let us take a familiar example. The epitome of high-volume hamburger production is McDonald's, which serves millions of burgers around the world every day. Volume has important implications for the way McDonald's operations are organized. The first thing you notice is the repeatability of the tasks people are doing and the systemization of the work, where standard procedures are set down specifying how each part of the job should be carried out. Also, because tasks are systematized and repeated, it is worthwhile developing specialized fryers and ovens. All this gives *low unit costs*. Now consider a small local cafeteria serving a few 'short order' dishes. The range of items on the menu may be similar to the larger operation, but the volume will be far lower, so the repetition will also be far lower and the number of staff will be lower (possibly only one person), and therefore individual staff are likely to perform a wider range of tasks. This may be more rewarding for the staff, but less open to systemization. Also, it less feasible to invest in specialized equipment. So the cost per burger served is likely to be higher (even if the price is comparable).

The variety dimension

A taxi company offers a relatively high-variety service. It is prepared to pick you up from almost anywhere and drop you off almost anywhere. To offer this variety it must be relatively *flexible*. Drivers must have a good knowledge of the area, and communication between the base and the taxis must be effective. However, the cost per kilometre travelled will be higher for a taxi than for a less customized form of transport such as a bus service. Although both provide the same basic service (transportation), the taxi service has a higher variety of routes and times to offer its customers, while the bus service has a few well-defined routes, with a set schedule. If all goes to schedule, little, if any, flexibility is required from the bus operation. All is standardized and regular, which results in relatively low costs compared with using a taxi for the same journey.

The variation dimension

Consider the demand pattern for a successful summer holiday resort hotel. Not surprisingly, more customers want to stay in summer vacation times than in the middle of winter. At the height of 'the season' the hotel could be full to its capacity. Off-season demand, however, could be a small fraction of its capacity. Such a marked variation in demand means that the operation must change its capacity in some way: for example, by hiring extra staff for the summer. The hotel must try to predict the likely level of demand. If it gets this wrong, it could result in too much or too little capacity. Also, recruitment costs, overtime costs and under-utilization of its rooms all have the effect of increasing the hotel's costs of operation compared with a hotel of a similar standard with level demand. A hotel which has relatively level demand can plan its activities well in advance. Staff can be scheduled, food can be bought and rooms can be cleaned in a *routine* and *predictable* manner. This results in a high utilization of resources and unit costs which are likely to be lower than those hotels with a highly variable demand pattern.

The visibility dimension

Visibility is a slightly more difficult dimension of operations to envisage. It means how much of the operation's activities its customers experience, or how much the operation is exposed to its customers. Generally, customer-processing operations are more exposed to their customers than material- or information-processing operations. But even customer-processing operations have some choice as to how visible they wish their operations to be. For example, a retailer could operate as a high-visibility 'bricks and mortar', or a lower visibility web-based operation. In the 'bricks and mortar', high-visibility operation, customers will directly experience most of its 'value-adding' activities. Customers will have a relatively *short waiting tolerance,* and may walk out if not served in a reasonable time. Customers' perceptions, rather than objective criteria, will also be important. If they perceive that a member of the operation's staff is discourteous to them, they are likely to be dissatisfied (even if the staff member meant no discourtesy), so high-visibility operations require staff with good customer contact skills. Customers could also request services or products which clearly would not be sold in such a shop, but because the customers are actually in the operation they can ask what they like! This is called 'high received variety'. This makes it difficult for high-visibility operations to achieve high productivity of resources, so they tend to be relatively high-cost operations. Conversely, a web-based retailer, while not a pure low-contact operation, has far lower visibility. Behind its website, it can be more 'factory-like'. The *time lag* between the order being placed and the items ordered by the customer being retrieved and dispatched does not have to be minutes, as in the shop, but can be hours or even days. This allows the tasks of finding the items, packing and dispatching them to be *standardized* by staff who need few customer contact skills. Also, there can be relatively *high staff utilization*. The web-based organization can also centralize its operation on one (physical) site, whereas the 'bricks and mortar' shop needs many shops close to centres of demand. Therefore, the low-visibility web-based operation will have lower costs than the shop.

> **Operations principle**
>
> The way in which processes need to be managed is influenced by volume, variety, variation and visibility.

OPERATIONS IN PRACTICE

Two very different hospitality operations

Ski Verbier Exclusive[5]

It is the name of the company that gives it away; Ski Verbier Exclusive Ltd is a provider of 'up-market' ski holidays in the

Swiss winter sports resort of Verbier. With 23 years' experience of organising holidays , it looks after luxury properties in the resort that are rented from their owners for letting to Ski Verbier Exclusive's clients. The properties vary in size and the configuration of their rooms, but the flexibility to reconfigure the rooms to cater for the varying requirements of client groups is important. *'We are very careful to cultivate as good a relationship with the owners, as we are with our clients that use our holiday service'*, says Tom Avery, joint founder and director of the company. *'We have built the business on developing these personal relationships, which is why our clients come back to us year after year* [40% to 50% of clients are returners]. *We pride ourselves on the personal service that we give to every one of our clients; from the moment they begin planning their ski holiday, to*

the journey home. What counts is experience, expertise, obsessive eye for detail and the understated luxury of our chalets combined with our ability to customise client experience.' And client requests can be anything from organizing a special mountain picnic complete with igloos, to providing an ice sculpture of Kermit the Frog for a kids' party. The personal concierge service begins from the moment the client books. The company's specialist staff have all lived and worked in Verbier and take care of all details of the trip well in advance, from organizing airport transfers to booking a private ski instructor, from arranging private jet or helicopter flights to Verbier's local airport, to making lunch reservations in the best mountain restaurants. *'We cater for a small, but discerning market'*, says Tom. *'Other companies may be bigger, but with us it's our personal service that clients remember.'* However, snow does not last all the year round. The company's busiest period is mid-December to mid-April. That is when all the properties that the company manages are full. The rest of the year is not so busy, but the company does offer bespoke summer vacations in some of its properties. These can be either self-catering, or with the full concierge service that clients get in the ski season. *'We adapt to clients' requirements,'* says Tom. *'That is why the quality of our staff is so important. They have to be good at working with clients, be able to judge the type of relationship that is appropriate, and be committed to providing what makes a great holiday. That's why we put so much effort into recruiting, training and retaining our staff.'*

Formule 1

Hotels are high-contact operations – they are staff-intensive and have to cope with a range of customers, each with a variety of needs and expectations. So, how can a highly successful chain of affordable hotels avoid the crippling costs of high customer contact? Formule 1, a subsidiary of the French Accor group, manages to offer outstanding value by adopting two principles not always associated with hotel operations – standardization and an innovative use of technology. Formule 1 hotels are usually located close to the roads, junctions and cities that make them visible and accessible to prospective customers. The hotels themselves are made from state-of-the-art volumetric prefabrications. The prefabricated units are arranged in various configurations to suit the characteristics of each individual site. All rooms are 9 square metres in area, and are designed to be attractive, functional, comfortable and soundproof. Most important, they are designed to be easy to clean and maintain. All have the same fittings, including a double bed, an additional bunk-type bed, a wash basin, a storage area, a working table with seat, a wardrobe and a television set. The reception of a Formule 1 hotel is staffed only from 6.30 am to 10.00 am and from 5.00 pm to 10.00 pm. Outside these times an automatic machine sells rooms to credit card users, provides access to the hotel, dispenses a security code for the room and even prints a receipt. Technology is also evident in the washrooms. Showers and toilets are automatically cleaned after each use by using nozzles and heating elements to spray the room with a disinfectant solution and dry it before it is used again. To keep things even simpler, Formule 1 hotels do not include a restaurant, as they are usually located near existing ones. However, a continental breakfast is available, usually between 6.30 am and 10.00 am, and of course on a 'self-service' basis!

Mixed high- and low-visibility processes

Some operations have both high- and low-visibility processes within the same operation. In an airport, for example: some activities are totally 'visible' to its customers, such as information desks answering people's queries. These staff operate in what is termed a 'front-office environment'. Other parts of the airport have little, if any, customer 'visibility', such as the baggage handlers. These rarely seen staff perform the vital but low-contact tasks, in the back-office part of the operation.

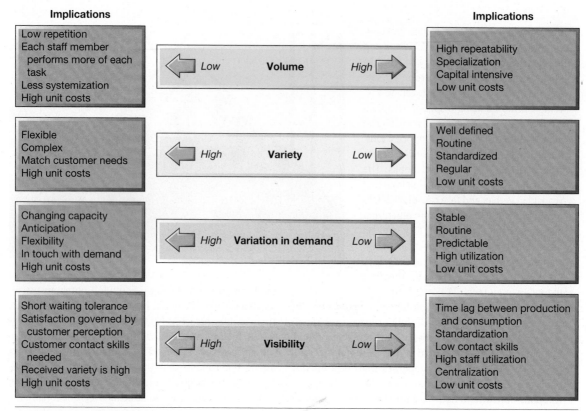

Figure 1.9 A typology of operations

The implications of the four Vs of operations processes

All four dimensions have implications for the cost of creating and delivering services and products (see Figure 1.9). Put simply, high volume, low variety, low variation and low customer contact all help to keep processing costs down. Conversely, low volume, high variety, high variation and high customer contact generally carry some kind of cost penalty for the operation. This is why the volume dimension is drawn with its 'low' end on the left, unlike the other dimensions, to keep all the 'low cost' implications on the right. To some extent the position of an operation on the four dimensions is determined by the demand of the market it is serving. However, most operations have some discretion in moving themselves on the dimensions. Figure 1.9 summarizes the implications of such positioning.

 Operations principle

Operations and processes can (other things being equal) reduce their costs by increasing volume, reducing variety, reducing variation and reducing visibility.

Worked example

Figure 1.10 illustrates the different positions on the dimensions of the Ski Verbier Exclusive operation and the Formule 1 hotel chain (*see* the 'Operations in practice' example on 'Two very different hospitality operations'). At the most basic level, both provide the same basic service. They accommodate people. Yet they are very different. Ski Verbier Exclusive provides luxurious and bespoke vacations for a relatively small segment of the ski holiday market. Its variety of services is almost infinite in the sense that customers can make individual requests in terms of food and entertainment.

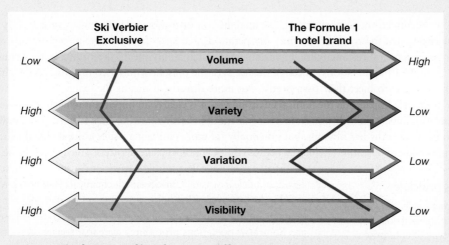

Figure 1.10 The four Vs profiles of two very different hospitality operations

Variation is high with four months of 100 per cent occupancy, followed by a far quieter period. Customer contact, and therefore visibility, is also very high (in order to ascertain customers' requirements and provide for them). All of this is very different from the Formule 1 branded hotels, whose customers usually stay one night, where the variety of services is strictly limited, and business and holiday customers use the hotel at different times, which limits variation. Most notably, though, customer contact is kept to a minimum. Ski Verbier Exclusive has very high levels of service, which means it has relatively high costs. Its prices therefore are not cheap. Certainly not as cheap as Formule 1, which has arranged its operation in such a way as to provide a highly standardized service at minimal cost.

What do operations managers do?

The exact details of what operations managers do will, to some extent, depend on the way an organization defines the boundaries of the function. Yet there are some general classes of activities that apply to all types of operation irrespective of whether they are service, manufacturing, private or public sector, and no matter how the operations function is defined. We classify operations management activities under the four headings: direct, design, deliver and develop.

▶ *Directing* the overall strategy of the operation. A general understanding of operations and processes and their strategic purpose and performance, together with an appreciation of how strategic purpose is translated into reality, is a prerequisite to the detailed design of operations and process. This is treated in Chapters 1 to 5.
▶ *Designing* the operation's services, products and processes. Design is the activity of determining the physical form, shape and composition of operations and processes together with the services and products that they create. This is treated in Chapters 6 to 9.
▶ Planning and control process *delivery*. After being designed, the delivery of services and products from suppliers and through the total operation to customers must be planned and controlled. This is treated in Chapters 10 to 15.
▶ *Developing* process performance. Increasingly it is recognized that in operations, or any process, managers cannot simply routinely deliver services and products in the same way that they always have done. They have a responsibility to develop the capabilities of their processes to improve process performance. This is treated in Chapters 16 to 19.

Operations management impacts environmental sustainability

Earlier, we identified the importance of sustainability on operations management practice. It is worth re-emphasizing that many of the activities of operations managers have a huge impact on their organization's environmental sustainability. Environmental sustainability means (according to the Brundtland Report from the United Nations) 'meeting the needs of the present without compromising the ability of future generations to meet their own needs'. Put more directly, it means the extent to which business activity negatively impacts on the natural environment. It is clearly an important issue, not only because of the obvious impact on the immediate environment of hazardous waste, air, and even noise, pollution, but also because of the less obvious, but potentially far more damaging issues around global warming.

It is important to operations managers because the pollution-causing disasters which make the headlines seem to be the result of a whole variety of causes – oil tankers run aground, nuclear waste is misclassified, chemicals leak into a river, or gas clouds drift over industrial towns. But in fact they all have something in common. They were all the result of an operations-based failure. Somehow operations procedures were inadequate. Less dramatic in the short term, but perhaps more important in the long term, is the environmental impact of products which cannot by recycled and processes which consume large amounts of energy. In fact, many of operations management's environmental issues are concerned with waste. Operations management decisions in product and service design significantly affect the utilization of materials both in the short term as well as in long-term recyclability. Process design influences the proportion of energy and labour that is wasted as well as materials wastage. Planning and control may affect material wastage (packaging being wasted by mistakes in purchasing, for example), but also affects energy and labour wastage. Improvement, of course, is dedicated largely to reducing wastage. Here environmental responsibility and the conventional concerns of operations management coincide. Reducing waste, in all its forms, may be environmentally sound but it also saves cost for the organization.

> **Operations principle**
>
> Operations management activities will have a significant effect on the sustainability performance of any type of enterprise.

> **Operations principle**
>
> Operations management activities can be grouped into four broad categories: directing the overall strategy of the operation, designing the operation's products, services and processes, planning and controlling delivery, and developing performance.

The model of operations management

We can now combine two ideas to develop the model of operations and process management that will be used throughout this book. The first is the idea that *operations* and the *processes* that make up both the operations and other business functions are transformation systems that take in inputs and use process resources to transform

HP's recycling activities[6]

HP (Hewlett Packard) began recycling hardware as far back as 1987, when it was the only major computer manufacturer to operate its own recycling facility. Since then it has recovered over billions of kilograms of products for reuse or recycling. Its recycling programme seeks to reduce the environmental impact of its products, minimizing waste going to landfills by helping customers discard products conveniently in an environmentally sound manner. Recovered materials, after recycling, have been used to make products, including auto body parts, clothes hangers, plastic toys, fence posts and roof tiles.

HP has developed a standard for management of hardware at the end of its useful life to ensure hardware is responsibly recycled or recovered. It also helps other electronics recyclers to work effectively with its products by providing disassembly instructions to them. More than 75 per cent of its Inkjet cartridges and 24 per cent of its LaserJet toner cartridges are manufactured with what is known as 'closed loop' recycled plastic. This

▶

them into outputs. The second idea is that the resources both in an organization's operations as a whole and in its individual processes need to be managed in terms of how they are *directed*, how they are *designed*, how *delivery* is planned and controlled and how they are *developed* and improved. Figure 1.11 shows how these two ideas go together. This book will use this model to examine the more important decisions that should be of interest to all managers of operations and processes.

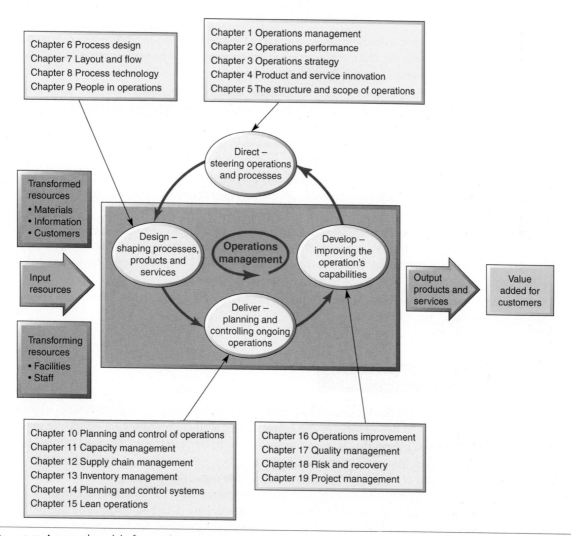

Figure 1.11 A general model of operations management

To be a great operations manager you need to . . .

So, you are considering a career in operations management, and you want to know, 'is it for you?' What skills and personal qualities will you need to make a success of the job as well as enjoying yourself as you progress in the profession? Well, the first thing to recognize is that there are many different roles encompassed within the general category of 'operations management'. Someone who makes a great risk control system designer in an investment bank may not thrive as a site manager in a copper mine. A video game project manager has a different set of day-to-day tasks when compared with a purchasing manager for a hospital. So, the first skill you need is to understand the range of operations-related responsibilities that exist in various industries; and there is no better way to do this than by reading this book! However, there are also some generic skills that an effective operations manager must possess. Here are some of them. How many of them do you share?

▶ *Enjoys getting things done* – Operations management is about doing things. It takes energy and/or commitment to finishing tasks. It means hitting deadlines and not letting down customers, whether they are internal or external.

▶ *Understands customer needs* – Operations management is about adding value for customers. This means fully understanding what 'value' means for customers. It means 'putting yourself in the customer's place'; knowing what it is like to be the customer, and knowing how to ensure that your services or products make the customer's life better.

▶ *Communicates and motivates* – Operations management is about directing resources to produce services or products in an efficient and effective manner. This means articulating what is required and persuading people to do it. Interpersonal skills are vital. Operations managers must be 'people people'.

▶ *Learns all the time* – Every time an operations manager initiates an action (of any kind) there is an opportunity to learn from the result. Operations management is about learning, because without learning there can be no improvement, and improvement is an imperative for all operations.

▶ *Committed to innovation* – Operations management is always seeking to do things better. This means creating new ways of doing things, being creative, imaginative and (sometimes) unconventional.

▶ *Knows their contribution* – Operations management may be the central function in any organization, but it is not the only one. It is important that operations managers know how they can contribute to the effective working of other functions.

▶ *Capable of analysis* – Operations management is about making decisions. Each decision needs to be evaluated (sometimes with very little time). This involves looking at both the quantitative and the qualitative aspects of the decision. Operations managers do not necessarily have to be mathematical geniuses, but they should not be afraid of numbers!

▶ *Keeps cool under pressure* – Operations managers often work in pressured situations. They need to be able to remain calm no matter what problems occur.

Critical commentary

The central idea in this introductory chapter is that all organizations have operations processes which create and deliver services and products, and all these processes are essentially similar. However, some believe that by even trying to characterize processes in this way (perhaps even by calling them 'processes') one loses or distorts their nature and depersonalizes or takes the 'humanity' out of the way in which we think of the organization. This point is often raised in not-for-profit organizations, especially by 'professional' staff. For example, the head of one European 'Medical Association' (a doctors' trade union) criticized hospital authorities for expecting a *sausage factory service based on productivity targets'*. No matter how similar they appear on paper, it is argued, a hospital can never be viewed in the same way as a factory. Even in commercial businesses, professionals, such as creative staff, often express discomfort at their expertise being described as a 'process'.

Summary answers to key questions

What is operations management?

▶ Operations management is the activity of managing the resources that are devoted to the creation and delivery of service and products. It is one of the core functions of any business, although it may not be called 'operations management' in some industries.

▶ Operations management is concerned with managing processes. And all processes have internal customers and suppliers. But all management functions also have processes. Therefore, operations management has relevance for all managers.

Why is operations management important in *all* types of organization?

▶ Operations management uses the organization's resources to create outputs that fulfil defined market requirements. This is *the* fundamental activity of any type of enterprise.

▶ Operations management is increasingly important because today's changing business environment requires new thinking from operations managers, especially in the areas of new technology, supply networks and environmental sustainability.

What is the input–transformation–output process?

▶ All operations can be modelled as input–transformation–output processes. They all have inputs of transforming resources, which are usually divided into 'facilities' and 'staff', and transformed resources, which are some mixture of materials, information and customers.

▶ Most operations create and deliver a combination of services and products, rather than being a 'pure' service or product operation.

What is the process hierarchy?

▶ All operations are part of a larger supply network which, through the individual contributions of each operation, satisfies end customer requirements.

▶ All operations are made up of processes that form a network of internal customer–supplier relationships within the operation.

▶ End-to-end business processes that satisfy customer needs often cut across functionally based processes.

How do operations and processes differ?

▶ Operations and processes differ in terms of the volume of their outputs, the variety of outputs, the variation in demand for their outputs, and the degree of 'visibility' they have.

▶ High volume, low variety, low variation and low customer 'visibility' are usually associated with low cost.

What do operations managers do?

▶ Responsibilities can be classed in four categories – direct, design, deliver and develop.
  — Direct includes understanding relevant performance objectives and setting an operations strategy.
  — Design includes the design of the operation and its processes and the design of its services and products.
  — Delivery includes the planning and controlling of the activities of the operation.
  — Develop includes the improvement of the operation over time.

▶ Increasingly operations managers have a responsibility for an operations environmental performance.

Design house partnerships at Concept Design Services

'I can't believe how much we have changed in a relatively short time. From being an inward- looking manufacturer, we became a customer- focused 'design and make' operation. Now we are an integrated service provider. Most of our new business comes from the partnerships we have formed with design houses. In effect, we design products jointly with specialist design houses that have a well-known brand, and offer them a complete service of manufacturing and distribution. In many ways we are now a 'business-to-business' company rather than a 'business-to-consumer' company.' (Jim Thompson, CEO, Concept Design Services (CDS))

CDS had become one of Europe's most profitable homeware businesses. Originally founded in the 1960s, the company had moved from making industrial mouldings, mainly in the aerospace sector, and some cheap 'homeware' items such as buckets and dustpans, sold under the 'Focus' brand name, to making very high-quality (expensive) stylish homewares with a high 'design value'.

The move into 'Concept' products

The move into higher-margin homeware had been masterminded by Linda Fleet, CDS's marketing director, who had previously worked for a large retail chain of paint and wallpaper retailers.

'Experience in the decorative products industry had taught me the importance of fashion and product development, even in mundane products such as paint. Premium-priced colours and new textures would become popular for one or two years, supported by appropriate promotion and features in lifestyle magazines. The manufacturers and retailers who created and supported these products were dramatically more profitable than those who simply provided standard ranges. Instinctively, I felt that this must also apply to homeware. We decided to develop a whole coordinated range of such items, and to open up a new distribution network for them to serve up-market stores, kitchen equipment and specialty retailers. Within a year of launching our first new range of kitchen homeware under the Concept brand name, we had over 3,000 retail outlets signed up, provided with point-of-sale display facilities. Press coverage generated an enormous interest which was reinforced by the product placement on several TV cookery and 'lifestyle' programmes. We soon developed an entirely new market and within two years Concept products were providing over 75 per cent of our revenue and 90 per cent of our profits. The price realization of Concept products is many times higher than for the Focus range. To keep ahead we launched new ranges at regular intervals'.

The move to the design house partnerships

'Over the last four years, we have been designing, manufacturing and distributing products for some of the more prestigious design houses. This sort of business is likely to grow, especially in Europe where the design houses appreciate our ability to offer a full service. We can design products in conjunction with their own design staff and offer them a level of manufacturing expertise they can't get elsewhere. More significantly, we can offer a distribution service which is tailored to their needs. From the customer's point of view the distribution arrangements appear to belong to the design house itself. In fact they are based exclusively on our own call centre, warehouse and distribution resources.'

The most successful collaboration was with Villessi, the Italian designers. Generally it was CDS's design expertise which was attractive to 'design house' partners. Not only did CDS employ professionally respected designers, they had also acquired a reputation for being able to translate difficult technical designs into manufacturable and saleable products. Design house partnerships usually involved relatively long lead times but produced unique products with very high margins, nearly always carrying the design house's brand.

'This type of relationship plays to our strengths. Our design expertise gains us entry to the partnership but we are soon valued equally for our marketing, distribution and manufacturing competence.' (Linda Fleet, Marketing Director)

Manufacturing operations

All manufacturing was carried out in a facility located 20 km from Head Office. Its moulding area housed large injection-moulding machines; most with robotic material handling capabilities. Products and components passed to the packing hall, where they were assembled and inspected. The newer, more complex products often had to move from moulding to assembly and then back again for further moulding. All products followed the same broad process route but with more products needing several progressive moulding and assembly stages, there was an increase in 'process flow re-cycling' which was adding complexity. One idea was to devote a separate cell to the newer and more complex products until they had 'bedded in'. This cell could also be used for testing new moulds. However, it would need investment in extra capacity that would not always be fully utilized. After manufacture, products were packed and stored in the adjacent distribution centre.

'When we moved into making the higher margin Concept products, we disposed of most of our older, small injection-moulding machines. Having all larger machines allowed us to use large multi-cavity moulds. This increased productivity by allowing us to produce several products, or components, each machine cycle. It also allowed us to use high-quality and complex moulds which, although cumbersome and more difficult to change over, gave a very high-quality product. For example, with the same labour we could make three items per minute on the old machines, and 18 items per minute on the modern ones using multi moulds. That's a 600 per cent increase in productivity. We also achieved high dimensional accuracy, excellent surface finish, and extreme consistency of colour. We could do this because of our expertise derived from years making aerospace products. Also, by standardising on single large machines, any mould could fit any machine. This was an ideal situation from a planning perspective, as we were often asked to make small runs of Concept products at short notice.' (Grant Williams, Operations Manager)

Increasing volume and a desire to reduce cost had resulted in CDS subcontracting much of its Focus products to other (usually smaller) moulding companies.

'We would never do it with any complex or Design House partner products, but it should allow us to reduce the cost of making basic products while releasing capacity for higher margin ones. However there have been quite a few "teething problems". Coordinating the production schedules is currently a problem, as is agreeing quality standards. To some extent it's our own fault. We didn't realise that subcontracting was a skill in its own right. And although we have got over some of the problems, we still do not have a satisfactory relationship with all of our subcontractors.' (Grant Williams, Operations Manager)

Planning and distribution services

The distribution services department of the company was regarded as being at the heart of the company's customer service drive. Its purpose was to integrate the efforts of design, manufacturing and sales by planning the flow of products from production, through the distribution centre, to the customer. Sandra White, the Planning Manager, reported to Linda Fleet and was responsible for the scheduling of all manufacturing and distribution, and for maintaining inventory levels for all the warehoused items.

'We try to stick to a preferred production sequence for each machine and mould so as to minimise set-up times by starting on a light colour, and progressing through a sequence to the darkest. We can change colours in 15 minutes, but because our moulds are large and technically complex, mould changes can take up to three hours. Good scheduling is important to maintain high plant utilisation. With a higher variety of complex products, batch sizes have reduced and it has brought down average utilization. Often, we can't stick to schedules. Short-term changes are inevitable in a fashion market. Certainly, better forecasts would help . . . but even our own promotions are sometimes organized at such short notice that we often get caught with stock-outs. New products in particular are difficult to forecast, especially when they are "fashion" items and/or seasonal. Also, I have to schedule production time for new product mould trials; we normally allow 24 hours for the testing of each new mould received, and this has to be done on production machines. Even if we have urgent orders, the needs of the designers always have priority.' (Sandra White, Planning Manager)

Customer orders for Concept and design house partnership products were taken by the company's sales call centre located next to the warehouse. The individual orders would then be dispatched using the company's own fleet of medium and small distribution vehicles for UK orders, but using carriers for the continental European market. A standard delivery timetable was used and an 'express delivery' service was offered for those customers prepared to pay a small delivery premium. However, a recent study had shown that almost 40 per cent of express deliveries were initiated by the company rather than customers. Typically, this would be to fulfil deliveries of orders containing products out of stock at the time of ordering. The express delivery service was not required for Focus products because almost all deliveries were to five large customers. The size of each order was usually very large, with deliveries to customers' own distribution depots. However, although the organization of Focus delivery was relatively straightforward, the consequences of failure were large. Missing a delivery meant upsetting a large customer.

Challenges for CDS

Although the company was financially successful and very well regarded in the homeware industry, there were a number of issues and challenges that it knew it would have to address. The first was the role of the design department and its influence over new product development.

New product development had become particularly important to CDS, especially since it had formed alliances with design houses. This had led to substantial growth in both the size and the influence of the design department, which reported to Linda Fleet.

'Building up and retaining design expertise will be the key to our future. Most of our growth is going to come from the business which will be brought in through the creativity and flair of our designers. Those who can combine creativity with an understanding of our partners' business and design needs can now bring in substantial contracts. The existing business is important, of course, but growth will come directly from these people's capabilities.' (Linda Fleet, Marketing Director)

But not everyone was so sanguine about the rise of the design department.

'It is undeniable that relationships between the designers and other parts of the company have been under strain recently. I suppose it is, to some extent, inevitable. After all, they really do need the freedom to design as they wish. I can understand it when they get frustrated at some of the constraints which we have to work under in the manufacturing or distribution parts of the business. They also should be able to expect a professional level of service from us. Yet the truth is that they make most of the problems themselves. They sometimes don't seem to understand the consequences or implications of their design decisions or the promises they make to the design houses. More seriously they don't really understand that we could actually help them do their job better if the cooperated a bit more. In fact, I now see some of our design house partners' designers more than I do our own designers. The Villessi designers are always in my factory and we have developed some really good relationships.' (Grant Williams, Operations Manager)

The second major issue concerned sales forecasting, and again there were two different views. Grant Williams was convinced that forecasts should be improved.

'Every Friday morning we devise a schedule of production and distribution for the following week. Yet, usually before Tuesday morning, it has had to be significantly changed because of unexpected orders coming in from our customers' weekend sales. This causes tremendous disruption to both manufacturing and distribution operations. If sales could be forecast more accurately, we would achieve far high utilization, better customer service and, I believe, significant cost savings.' (Grant Williams, Operations Manager)

However, Linda Fleet saw things differently.

'Look, I do understand Grant's frustration, but after all, this is a fashion business. By definition it is impossible to forecast accurately. In terms of month-by-month sales volumes we are in fact pretty accurate, but trying to make a forecast for every week and every product is almost impossible to do accurately. Sorry, that's just the nature of the business we're in. In fact, although Grant complains about our lack of forecast accuracy, he always does a great job in responding to unexpected customer demand.'

Jim Thompson summed up his view of the current situation.

'Particularly significant has been our alliances with the Italian and German design houses. In effect we are positioning ourselves as a complete service partner to the designers. We have a world-class design capability together with manufacturing, order processing, order-taking and distribution services. These abilities allow us to develop genuinely equal partnerships which integrate us into the whole industry's activities'. (Jim Thompson, CEO)

Linda Fleet also saw an increasing role for collaborative arrangements.

'It may be that we are seeing a fundamental change in how we do business within our industry. We have always seen ourselves as primarily a company that satisfies consumer desires through the medium of providing good service to retailers. The new partnership arrangements put us more into the "business to business" sector. I don't have any problem with this in principle, but I'm a little anxious as to how much it gets us into areas of business beyond our core expertise.' (Linda Fleet, Marketing Director)

The final issue which was being debated within the company was longer term, and particularly important.

'The two big changes we have made in this company have both happened because we exploited a strength we already had within the company. Moving into Concept products was only possible because we brought our high-tech precision expertise that we had developed in the aerospace sector into the homeware sector where none of our new competitors could match our manufacturing excellence. Then, when we moved into design house partnerships we did so because we had a set of designers who could command respect from the world-class design houses with whom we formed partnerships. So what is the next move for us? Do we expand globally? We are strong in Europe but nowhere else in the world. Do we extend our design scope into other markets, such as furniture? If so, that would take us into areas where we have no manufacturing expertise. We are great at plastic injection moulding, but if we tried any other manufacturing processes, we would be no better than, and probably worse than, other firms with more experience. So what's the future for us?' (Jim Thompson, CEO).

QUESTIONS

1 Why is operations management important in CDS?

2 Draw a four Vs profile for the company's products / services.

3 What would you recommend to the company if it asked for your advice in improving its operations?

Problems and applications

All chapters have 'Problems and applications' questions that will help you practise analysing operations. They can be answered by reading the chapter. Model answers for the first two questions can be found on the companion website for this book.

1 Quentin Cakes make about 20,000 cakes per year in two sizes, both based on the same recipe. Sales peak at Christmas time when demand is about 50 per cent higher than in the quieter summer period. Its customers (the stores that stock its products) order its cakes in advance through a simple Internet-based ordering system. Knowing that Quentin Cakes some surplus capacity, one of its customers has approached the company with two potential new orders.

   The *Custom Cake* option – this would involve making cakes in different sizes where consumers could specify a message or greeting to be 'iced' on top of the cake. The consumer would give the inscription to the store, which would e-mail it through to the factory. The customer thought that demand would be around 1,000 cakes per year, mostly at celebration times such as Valentine's Day and Christmas.

   The *Individual Cake* option – this option involves Quentin Cakes introducing a new line of about 10–15 types of very small cakes intended for individual consumption. Demand for this individual-sized cake was forecast to be around 4,000 per year, with demand likely to be more evenly distributed throughout the year than its existing products.

   The total revenue from both options is likely to be roughly the same and the company has only capacity to adopt one of the ideas. But which one should it be?

2 Re-read the 'Operations in practice' example on Pret a Manger. (a) Do you think Pret a Manger fully understands the importance of its operations management? (b) What kind of operations management activities at Pret a Manger might come under the four headings of direct, design, deliver and develop?

3 Here are two examples of how operations try to reduce the negative effects of having to cope with high levels of variety. Research each of them (there is plenty of information on the web) and answer the following questions. (a) What are the common features of these two examples? (b) What other examples of standardization in transport operations can you think of?

   Example 1 – The Bombay Tiffin Box Suppliers Association (search under dabbawalas) operates a service to transport home-cooked food from workers' homes to office locations in downtown Bombay. Workers from residential districts must ride commuter trains to work. They can be conservative diners, who may also be constrained by cultural taboos on food handling by caste. Their workers, known as dabbawalas, pick up the food in the morning in a regulation tin 'tiffin' box, deposited at the office at lunch time, and returned to the home in the afternoon. The dabbawalas take advantage of public transport to carry the tins, usually using otherwise under-utilized capacity on commuter trains in the mid-morning and afternoon. Different colours and markings are used to indicate to the (sometimes illiterate) dabbawalas the process route for each tin.

   Example 2 – Ports have had to handle an infinite variety of ships and cargoes with widely different contents, sizes and weights, and, while in transit or in storage, protect them from weather and pilferage. Then the transportation industries, in conjunction with the International Standards Organization (ISO), developed a standard shipping container design. Almost overnight the problems of security and weather protection were solved. Anyone wanting to ship goods in volume only had to seal them into a container and they could be signed over to the shipping company. Ports could standardize handling equipment and dispense with warehouses (containers could be stacked in the rain if required). Railways and trucking companies could develop trailers to accommodate the new containers.

4 'My flight to Stockholm would be late landing. We were in a "stack" of planes circling above Brussels. Air traffic control had closed the runways for a short period at dawn, because of snow. Flights from

all over the world were now being allocated new landing slots. After a 20-minute delay, we landed on a recently cleared runway. Even then there was a further 'hold' on a taxiway while de-icing of the apron was being completed. All around the airport I could see the flashing beacons of the snow-clearing vehicles, catering suppliers' vans, aviation fuel trucks, baggage trailers, buses transporting crews and passengers, security police cars, and an assortment of other vehicles. Brussels airport always looks busy, with over 10 million passengers a year, but this morning the complexity and scale of the operations were particularly evident. About an hour late, we pulled up to the gate, and we disembarked into an icy-cold air bridge, leaving behind a particularly litter-strewn cabin. The team of cleaners and maintenance staff waiting just outside will have a hard time, with more mess and less time than usual to deal with it, as the airline will want a quick turnaround to get back on to schedule. We could just hear the sound of baggage and cargo being unloaded, catering vehicles arriving, fuel being loaded, and technicians checking over the engines. From the air bridge, we walked past the crowded seating areas, where groups were awaiting the signal from the gate staff to board their delayed flights. Anxious to get ahead of the crowd, we ran past the rows of cafés, bars and shops, hoping to avoid the morning queue for Passport Control. However, my next journey was to the First Aid room! I had apparently slipped on some spilt coffee that had not been cleaned up in the haste of the morning, and had fallen awkwardly, straining my ankle and smashing my duty-free brandy.

Suitably patched up, I hobbled with my colleagues and joined the queue for Passport Control, and eventually through to Baggage Reclaim. Passengers usually get there first, but the accident had changed all that. The video screens showed no reference to our flight arrival; the remaining bags had apparently been removed from the carousel and were being stored in an adjacent office. But we were reunited with our belongings, and hastened (slowly in my case) to the taxi rank. Yet there was no quick ride to the city because of a long queue, so we went to the station below, where a dedicated 'City Express' train departs every 20 minutes for the city.

After a successful day at our Brussels office, a taxi was called, and we were back at the airport in the evening rush hour. The departures check-in area has a huge electronic display which lists all departures. No queue at the check-in desk, so we had our boarding passes in only a couple of minutes. By this time, my injured leg was throbbing painfully, so the check-in staff arranged for a wheelchair and attendant to take me through Border Control and security checks. While my colleagues used the escalator, I took the slower route by lift, meeting outside the duty-free shops. We bought some Belgian chocolates and headed for a café-bar. After a welcome glass of specialty beer, we headed for the airline's executive lounge. De-icing crews were working on the parked aircraft and others were treating the runways. Concerned that we might be delayed and miss our connection, we checked with staff at the information desk. They confirmed that, although there could be some delays, our connecting flights would be held.'

(a) Identify all the processes and their activities which are mentioned. Classify them in accordance with their type. (b) Which of these processes were most affected by the severe weather? (c) Approximately how many different organizations are involved in delivering the goods and services described in this question? What are the implications of this?

5   Not all surgery conforms to our preconceptions of the individual 'super-craftsperson', aided by her back-up team, performing the whole operation from first incision to final stitch. Many surgical procedures are fairly routine. An example is the process that was adopted by one Russian eye surgeon. The surgical procedure in which he specializes is a revolutionary treatment for myopia (short-sightedness) called 'radial keratotomy'. In the process eight patients lie on moving tables arranged like the spokes of a wheel around its central axis, with only their eyes uncovered. Six surgeons, each with his or her 'station', are positioned around the rim of the wheel so that they can access the patients' eyes. After the surgeons have completed their own particular portion of the whole procedure, the wheel indexes round to take patients to the next stage of their treatment. The surgeons check to make sure that the previous stage of the operation was performed correctly and then go on to perform their own task. Each surgeon's activity is monitored on TV screens overhead and the surgeons talk to each other through miniature microphones and headsets. (a) Compare this approach to eye surgery with a more conventional approach. (b) What do you think are the advantages and disadvantages of this approach to eye surgery?

6   Write down five services that you have 'consumed' in the last week. Try and make these as varied as possible. Examples could include public transport, a bank, any shop or supermarket, attendance at an education course, a cinema, a restaurant, etc. Try and identify how these services are different and how they are similar.

Selected further reading

Anupindi, R. and Chopra, S. (2013) *Managing Business Process Flows,* **3rd edn, Pearson, Harlow.**
Takes a 'process' view of operations, it's mathematical but rewarding.

Barnes, D. (2007) *Operations Management: An international perspective,* **Cengage Learning.**
A text that is similar in outlook to this one, but with more of a (useful) international perspective.

Hall, J.M. and Johnson, M.E. (2009) When should a process be art, not science? *Harvard Business Review,* **March.**
One of the few articles that looks at the boundaries of conventional process theory.

Hammer, M. and Stanton, S. (1999) How process enterprises really work, *Harvard Business Review,* **November–December.**
Hammer is one of the gurus of process design. This paper is typical of his approach.

Jacobs, F.R. and Chase, R.B. (2012) *Operations and Supply Chain Management,* **3rd edn, McGraw-Hill/Irwin, New York.**
There are many good general textbooks on operations management. This takes a supply chain view, although written very much for an American audience.

Johnston, R., Clark, E. and Shulver, M. (2012) *Service Operations Management,* **4th edn, Pearson, Harlow.**
What can we say! A great treatment of service operations from the same stable as this textbook.

Slack, N. (2017) *The Operations Advantage,* **Kogan Page, London.**
More of a practical treatment of how operations management can contribute to strategic success. Aimed at practising managers.

Slack, N. and Lewis, M.A. (2017) *Operations Strategy,* **5th edn, Pearson, Harlow.**
A more strategic coverage of operations management.

2

Operations performance

KEY QUESTIONS

Why is operations performance vital in any organization?

How is operations performance judged at a societal level?

How is operations performance judged at a strategic level?

How is operations performance judged at an operational level?

How can operations performance be measured?

How do operations performance objectives trade off against each other?

INTRODUCTION

Operations are judged by the way they perform. However, there are many ways of judging performance and there are many different individuals and groups doing the judging. Also, performance can be assessed at different levels. In this chapter, we start by describing a very broad approach to assessing operations performance at a societal level that uses the 'triple bottom line' to judge an operation's social, environmental and economic impact. We then look at how operations performance can be judged in terms of how it affects an organization's ability to achieve its overall strategy. The chapter then looks at the more directly operational-level aspects of performance – quality, speed, dependability, flexibility and cost. Finally, we examine how performance objectives trade off against each other. On our general model of operations management, the topics covered in this chapter are represented by the area marked on Figure 2.1.

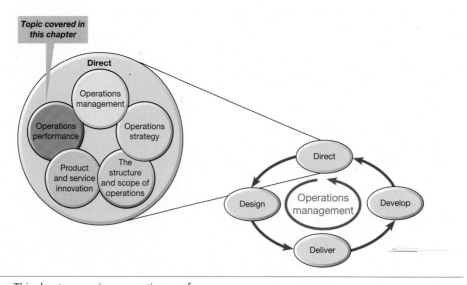

Figure 2.1 This chapter examines operations performance

Why is operations performance vital in any organization?

It is no exaggeration to view operations management as being able either to 'make or break' any business – not just because the operations function is large and, in most businesses, represents the bulk of its assets and the majority of its people, but because the operations function gives the power to compete by providing the ability to respond to customers and by developing the capabilities that will keep it ahead of its competitors in the future. But when things go wrong in operations, the reputational damage can last for years. We will deal with the nature of operations failures in Chapter 18, but the first point to make is that when operations do go wrong it is often the direct result of poor operations management. From parcel delivery failures that inconvenience an operation's customers, to air crashes that kill them, operations failures are both obvious and serious. Not that all operations failures have to be dramatic. One could argue that simply doing what has always been done is a failure to exploit opportunities to do things better. However, do not think that operations management is just about avoiding failure – its contribution to an organization's overall success is far greater than that.

Operations management can 'make' the organization in several ways. First, operations management is concerned with doing things better – better quality, better service, better responsiveness, better reliability, better flexibility, better cost and better use of capital invested in facilities. And it is this focus on 'better', on improvement, that can potentially make operations the driver of improvement for the whole organization. Second, through the continual learning that can come from its improvement activities, operations management can build the 'difficult to imitate' capabilities that can have a significant strategic impact. (We will deal further with this issue in the next chapter on operations strategy.) Third, operations management is very much concerned with 'process', with how things are done. And there is a relationship between process and outcome. Good operations management is the best way to produce good products and services.

Of course, operations managers will always face new challenges, not only when they have major new projects to manage, but also more generally as their economic, social, political and technological environment changes. Many of these decisions and challenges seem largely economic in nature. Can we generate an acceptable return if we invest in new technology? Other decisions have more of a 'social' aspect. How do we make sure that all our suppliers treat their staff fairly? Yet others have an environmental impact. Are we doing enough to reduce our carbon footprint? What is more, the 'economic' decisions also have an environmental and social aspect to them. Will a new product feature make end-of-life recycling more difficult? How do we make sure that suppliers treat their staff well, but still make a profit? And this is the great dilemma – how do operations managers try to be, simultaneously, economically viable while being socially and environmentally responsible?

> **Operations principle**
>
> Good operations performance is fundamental to the sustainable success of any organization.

OPERATIONS IN PRACTICE   Novozymes[1]

It is not surprising perhaps that a company whose products help other firms to operate more sustainably should itself be keen to stress its own environmental and social performance. This certainly is true for Novozymes, the Denmark-based company, whose worldwide production of enzymes, micro-organisms and biopharmaceutical ingredients help its customers in the household care, food and beverage, bioenergy, agriculture and pharmaceutical industries to *make more from less, while saving energy and generating less waste*'. Novozymes is the world leader in what it terms 'bioinnovation', particularly in the field of enzyme production and application. Enzymes are proteins that, in nature, initiate biochemical reactions in all living organisms. It is enzymes that convert the food in our stomachs to energy and turn the falling leaves in the forest to compost. Novozymes' operations find enzymes in nature and optimize them so that they can replace harsh chemicals, accelerate its customers' production processes and minimize the use of scarce resources. These enzymes are widely used in many industries, including laundry

▶

and dishwashing detergents, bread, beer and wine production, animal feed and biofuels.

How does Novozymes judge its own performance? It is a commercial company with investors who expect a return on their investment, but the company also strives to balance this with its environmental and social impact. In terms of its environmental performance, Novozymes has two aspects to monitor. The first is its products and services' impact on its customers' performance. The company conducts peer-reviewed life cycle assessment (LCA) studies to document the environmental impact of its biosolutions for its customers and advise them on ways to reduce their CO_2 emissions. As regards its own operations, Novozymes attempts to reduce the consumption of natural resources (including water usage) every year and mitigate the negative environmental impact of its production processes. Likewise, the improvement in energy efficiency is driven by continuous process optimizations and the implementation of energy-saving projects at its global production sites. But all production processes produce waste and by-products, so Novozymes seeks continual improvement in the amount of waste and by-products that is sent for landfill or incineration. This has the double effect of reducing the cost of waste treatment as well as minimizing the company's environmental footprint. As a result of these efforts, the Dow Jones Sustainability Index, a global sustainability benchmark, has ranked Novozymes among the top 3 per cent of companies in the chemical industry sector.

The company also track several aspects of its social performance. These include: employee satisfaction and

development, diversity and equal opportunities, occupational health and safety, compliance with human rights and labour standards, corporate citizenship efforts and business integrity. Perhaps most impressively, Novozymes sets long-term performance targets in key aspects of its performance that are integrated into incentive schemes throughout the organization. Long-term financial performance is measured conventionally through the rate of sales growth, profitability and the return on invested capital. But Novozymes also has a number of 5-year 'impact targets': for example, to reach 6 billion people, especially in emerging markets, with its products that enhance sustainability; to educate by providing knowledge of the potential of biology to 1 million people by training in factories, local-community outreach and involvement with universities and business schools; and to save the world 100 million tons of CO_2 a year through customers applying its products.

Performance at three levels

Looking at the example of how Novozymes monitors and reports its performance demonstrates that 'performance' is not a straightforward concept. First, it is multi-faceted in the sense that a single measure can never fully communicate the success, or otherwise, of something as complex as an operation. Second, performance can be assessed at different levels, from the broad, long-term, societal level of Novozymes' environmental monitoring, for example, to its more operational-level concerns over how it improves day-to-day efficiency and serves its individual customers. In the rest of this chapter we will look at how operations can judge its performance at three levels, illustrated in Figure 2.2.

▶ The broad, societal level, using the idea of the 'triple bottom line'.
▶ The strategic level of how an operation can contribute to the organization's overall strategy.
▶ The operational level, using the five operations 'performance objectives'.

How is operations performance judged at a societal level?

The decisions that are made within any operation and the way it goes about its day-to-day activities will affect a whole variety of 'stakeholders'. Stakeholders are the people and groups who have a legitimate interest in the operation's activities. Some stakeholders are internal, for example the

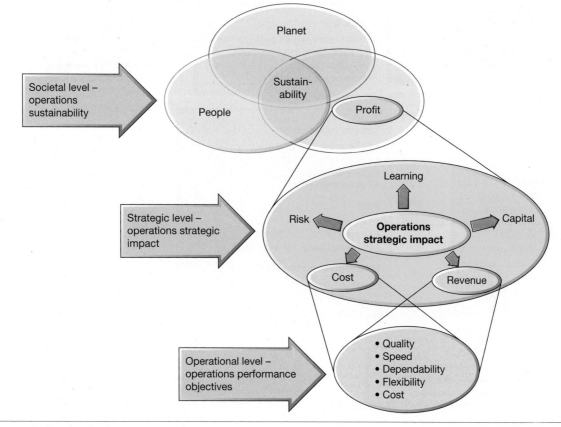

Figure 2.2 Three levels of operations performance

operation's employees; others are external, for example customers, society or community groups and a company's shareholders. Some external stakeholders have a direct commercial relationship with the organization, for example suppliers and customers; others do not, for example industry regulators. In not-for-profit operations, these stakeholder groups can overlap. So, voluntary workers in a charity may be employees, shareholders and customers all at once. However, in any kind of organization, it is a responsibility of the operations function to understand the (sometimes conflicting) objectives of its stakeholders and set its objectives accordingly. Figure 2.3 illustrates just some of the stakeholder groups who would have an interest in how an organization's operations function performs. But although each of these groups, to different extents, will be interested in operations performance, they are likely to have very different views of which aspect of performance is important. Nevertheless, if one is to judge operations at a broad societal level, one must judge the impact it has on its stakeholders.

> **Operations principle**
> All operations decisions should reflect the interests of stakeholder groups.

Corporate social responsibility (CSR)

This idea that operations should take into account their impact on a broad mix of stakeholders is often termed 'corporate social responsibility' (generally known as CSR). According to the UK government's definition: '*CSR is essentially about how business takes account of its economic, social and environmental impacts in the way it operates – maximizing the benefits and minimizing the downsides . . . Specifically, we see CSR as the voluntary actions that business can take, over and above compliance with minimum legal requirements, to address both its own competitive interests and the interests of wider society*'.[2] A more direct link with the stakeholder concept is to be found in the definition used by Marks and Spencer, the UK-based retailer: '*Corporate Social*

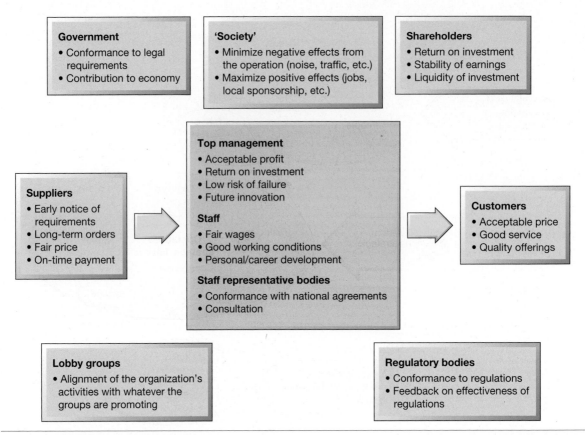

Government
- Conformance to legal requirements
- Contribution to economy

'Society'
- Minimize negative effects from the operation (noise, traffic, etc.)
- Maximize positive effects (jobs, local sponsorship, etc.)

Shareholders
- Return on investment
- Stability of earnings
- Liquidity of investment

Suppliers
- Early notice of requirements
- Long-term orders
- Fair price
- On-time payment

Top management
- Acceptable profit
- Return on investment
- Low risk of failure
- Future innovation

Staff
- Fair wages
- Good working conditions
- Personal/career development

Staff representative bodies
- Conformance with national agreements
- Consultation

Customers
- Acceptable price
- Good service
- Quality offerings

Lobby groups
- Alignment of the organization's activities with whatever the groups are promoting

Regulatory bodies
- Conformance to regulations
- Feedback on effectiveness of regulations

Figure 2.3 Stakeholder groups with typical operations objectives

Responsibility . . . is listening and responding to the needs of a company's stakeholders. This includes the requirements of sustainable development. We believe that building good relationships with employees, suppliers and wider society is the best guarantee of long-term success. This is the backbone of our approach to CSR'.[3]

The issue of how CSR objectives can be included in operations management's activities is of increasing importance, from both an ethical and a commercial point of view. It is treated several times at various points throughout this book.

The triple bottom line

One common term that tries to capture the idea of a broader approach to assessing an organization's performance is the 'triple bottom line'[4] (TBL, or 3BL), also known as 'people, planet and profit'. Essentially, it is a straightforward idea: simply that organizations should measure themselves not just on the traditional economic profit that they generate for their owners, but also on the impact their operations have on society (broadly, in the sense of communities, and individually, for example in terms of their employees) and the ecological impact on the environment. The influential initiative that has come out of this triple bottom line approach is that of 'sustainability'. A sustainable business is one that creates an acceptable profit for its owners, but minimizes the damage to the environment and enhances the existence of the people with whom it has contact. In other words, it balances economic, environmental and societal interests. This gives the organization its 'licence to operate' in society. The assumption underlying the triple bottom line (which is not universally accepted) is that a sustainable business is more likely to remain successful in the long term than one which focuses on economic goals alone. Only a company that produces a balanced TBL is really accounting for the total cost of running its operations.

> ✔ **Operations principle**
>
> Operations should judge themselves on the triple bottom line principle of people, planet and profit.

Patagonia and the triple bottom line[5]

In 2012, Yvon Chouinard – founder and owner of Patagonia Inc., the outdoor-clothing firm that designs, develops and markets clothing and gear for a wide range of outdoor sports – became the first business person to take advantage of a new law in California that gave businesses greater freedom to follow strategies which they believe benefit society as a whole rather than simply concentrating on maximizing profits. According to Mr Chouinard, Patagonia is one of the new 'benefit corporations' (usually called 'B Corps'). To meet the criteria as a B Corp, a firm should have a clear and unequivocal social and/or environmental mission, and a legal responsibility to respect the interests of workers, the community and the environment as well as its shareholders. In other words, Patagonia is operating according to triple bottom line principles. Patagonia's Mission Statement goes like this: *'Build the best product, cause no unnecessary harm, and use business to inspire and implement solutions to the environmental crisis'*. The company uses environmentally sensitive materials (organic cotton, recycled and recyclable polyester, and hemp among them) and both sponsors and participates in a host of environmental initiatives that range from promoting wildlife corridors to combating genetic engineering. The company tries to persuade its customers to give their used products charity or sell them. It even encourages customers to think carefully before purchasing a new garment. It once paid for a full-page advert in the *New York Times* showing a picture of its best-selling fleece jacket, with the headline, 'Don't Buy This Jacket.' The advert pointed out the cost to the environment of making the jacket and asked customers whether they really needed it.

Its employees enjoy generous healthcare, subsidized day care, flexible work schedules and paid time off for environmental internships. Many share the company's values and are active in environmental and community causes. And, like most clothing companies, Patagonia outsources its production. But it is important, it says, to work with suppliers *'that share our values of integrity and environmentalism. It really is true that you can't make good products in a bad factory, and we did business with some of the world's best. They were, for the most part, efficient and well run. The people who worked in them tended to have a lot of experience. Despite high employee turnover elsewhere in the garment industry, these factories were able to retain employees because they paid them fairly and treated them humanely.'* Transparency is also important. In an effort to understand the social and environmental impacts of its supply chain, Patagonia launched its *Footprint Chronicles,* in which it traces the environmental and social impact of products from design through fibre creation to construction to shipment to its warehouse.

The social bottom line (people) – the social account, measured by the impact of the operation on the quality of people's lives

The idea behind the social bottom line performance is not just that there is a connection between businesses and the society in which they operate – that is self-evident. Rather it is that businesses should accept that they bear some responsibility for the impact they have on society and balance the external 'societal' consequences of their actions with the more direct internal consequences, such as profit. At the level of the individual, social bottom line performance means devising jobs and work patterns which allow individuals to contribute their talents without undue stress. At a group level, it means recognizing and dealing honestly with employee representatives. In addition, businesses are also a part of the larger community and, it is argued, should be recognizing their responsibility to local communities by helping to promote their economic and social well-being. Some ways that operations can impact the social bottom line performance include the following:

▶ Customer safety from products and services
▶ Employment impact of an operation's location

- Employment implications of outsourcing
- Repetitive or alienating work
- Staff safety and workplace stress
- Non-exploitation of developing country suppliers.

The environmental bottom line (planet) – the environmental account, measured by environmental impact of the operation

Environmental sustainability (according to the World Bank) means *'ensuring that the overall productivity of accumulated human and physical capital resulting from development actions more than compensates for the direct or indirect loss or degradation of the environment'.*[6] Put more directly, it is generally taken to mean the extent to which business activity negatively impacts the natural environment. It is clearly an important issue, not only because of the obvious impact on the immediate environment of hazardous waste, air and even noise pollution, but also because of the less obvious, but potentially far more damaging, issues around global warming. Operations managers cannot avoid responsibility for environmental performance. It is often operational failures which are at the root of pollution disasters and operations decisions (such as product design) which impact on longer-term environmental issues. Some ways that operations can impact the environmental bottom line performance include the following:

- Recyclability of materials, energy consumption, waste material generation
- Reducing transport-related energy
- Noise pollution, fume and emission pollution
- Obsolescence and wastage
- Environmental impact of process failures
- Recovery to minimize impact of failures.

The economic bottom line (profit) – the economic account, measured by profitability, return on assets, etc., of the operation

The organization's top management represent the interests of the owners (or trustees, or electorate, etc.) and therefore are the direct custodians of the organization's economic performance. Broadly this means that operations managers must use the operation's resources effectively, and there are many ways of measuring this 'economic bottom line'. Finance specialists have devised various measures (such as return on assets etc.), which are beyond the scope of this book, to do this.

Some ways that operations can impact the financial bottom line performance include the following:

- Cost of producing products and services
- Revenue from the effects of quality, speed, dependability and flexibility
- Effectiveness of investment in operations resources
- Risk and resilience of supply
- Building capabilities for the future.

We will build on these 'economic bottom line' issues in the next section on judging operations performance at a strategic level.

Critical commentary

The dilemma with using this wide range of triple bottom line, stakeholders or CSR to judge operations performance is that organizations, particularly commercial companies, have to cope with the conflicting pressures of maximizing profitability, on the one hand, and the expectation that they will manage in the interests of (all or part of) society in general with accountability and

▶

transparency, on the other. Even if a business wants to reflect aspects of performance beyond its own immediate interests, how is it to do it? According to Michael Jensen of Harvard Business School, *'At the economy-wide or social level, the issue is this: If we could dictate the criterion or objective function to be maximized by firms (and thus the performance criterion by which corporate executives choose among alternative policy options), what would it be? Or, to put the issue even more simply: How do we want the firms in our economy to measure their own performance? How do we want them to determine what is better versus worse?'*[7] He also holds that using stakeholder perspectives gives undue weight to narrow special interests who want to use the organization's resources for their own ends. The stakeholder perspective gives them a spurious legitimacy which *'undermines the foundations of value-seeking behaviour'*.

How is operations performance judged at a strategic level?

Many (although not all) of the activities of operations managers are operational in nature. That is, they deal with relatively immediate, detailed and local issues. However, it is a central idea in operations management that the type of decisions and activities that operations managers carry out can also have a significant strategic impact. Therefore, if one is assessing the performance of the operations function, it makes sense to ask how it impacts the organization's strategic 'economic' position. We will examine in more detail the way that operations management can think about the strategic role. But, at a strategic level, there are five aspects of operations performance that we identified as contributing to the 'economic' aspect of the triple bottom line that can have a significant impact (see Figure 2.4).

Let us start by looking at how operations affect profit. At a simple (and simplistic) level, profit is the difference between the costs of producing products and services and the revenue the organization secures from its customers in exchange. (In public sector operations an equivalent, although difficult to measure, performance metric could be 'welfare per unit of expenditure'.)

Figure 2.4 Operations can contribute to financial success through low costs, increasing revenue, lowering risk, making efficient use of capital and building the capabilities for future innovation

Operations management affects costs

It seems almost too obvious to state, but almost all the activities that operations managers regularly perform (and all the topics that are described in this book) will have an effect on the cost of producing products and services. Clearly the efficiency with which an operation purchases its transformed and transforming resources, and the efficiency with which it converts its transformed resources, will determine the cost of its products and services. And for many operations managers it is *the* most important aspect of how they judge their performance. Indeed, there cannot be many, if any, organizations that are indifferent to their costs.

Operations management affects revenue

Yet cost is not necessarily always the most important strategic objective for operations managers. Their activities also can have a huge effect on revenue. High-quality, error-free products and services, delivered fast and on time, where the operation has the flexibility to adapt to customers' needs, are likely to command a higher price and sell more than those with lower levels of quality, delivery and flexibility. And operations managers are directly responsible for issues such as quality, speed of delivery, dependability and flexibility, as we will discuss later in the chapter.

The main point here is that operations activities can have a significant effect on, and therefore should be judged on, the organization's profitability. Moreover, even relatively small improvements in cost and revenue can have a proportionally even greater effect on profitability. For example, suppose a business has an annual revenue of €1,000,000 and annual costs of €900,000, and therefore a 'profit' of €100,000. Now suppose that, because of the excellence of its operations managers in enhancing quality and delivery, revenue increases by 5 per cent and costs reduce by 5 per cent. Revenue is now €1,050,000 and costs €855,000. So, profit is now €195,000. In other words, a 5 per cent change in cost and revenue has improved profitability by 95 per cent.

Net promoter score (NPS)

One popular method of measuring the underlying levels of customer satisfaction (an important factor in determining revenue) is the 'net promoter score' (NPS). This is computed by surveying customers and asking them how likely they are to recommend a company, service or product (on a scale of 1 to 10, where 1 = not at all likely, and 10 = extremely likely). Customers giving a score of 1 to 6 are called 'detractors', those giving a score of 9 or 10 are called 'promotors', those giving a score of 7 or 8 are called 'passives'. The NPS is calculated by ignoring passives and subtracting the number of detractors from the number of promoters. So, if 200 customers are surveyed, and 60 are promotors, 110 passives and 30 detractors, the NPS is calculated as follows:

$$NPS = 60 - 30 = 30$$

What is considered an acceptable NPS varies, depending on the sector and nature of competition, but as a minimum target, a positive (>0) score might be regarded as (just) acceptable. NPS is a simple metric that is quick and easy to calculate, but some see that as its main weakness. It is without any sophisticated scientific basis, nor does it provide an accurate picture of customer behaviour. For example, if the survey mentioned above had resulted in 115 promotors, 0 passives and 85 detractors, it would still give an NPS of 30. Yet here, customers are far more polarised. However, notwithstanding its failings, using NPS over time can be used to detect possible changes in customer attitudes.

Operations management affects the required level of investment

How an operation manages the transforming resources that are necessary to produce the required type and quantity of its products and services will also have a strategic effect. If, for example, an operation increases its efficiency so that it can produce (say) 10 per cent more output, then it will not need to spend investment (sometimes called capital employed) to produce 10 per cent more output. Producing more output with the same resources (or sometimes producing the same output with fewer resources) affects the required level of investment.

Operations management affects the risk of operational failure

Well-designed and run operations should be less likely to fail. That is, they are more likely to operate at a predictable and acceptable rate without either letting customers down or incurring excess costs. And if they ever do suffer failures, well-run operations should be able to recover faster and with less disruption (this is called resilience). This is fully treated in Chapter 18.

Operations management affects the ability to build the capabilities on which future innovation is based

Operations managers have a unique opportunity to learn from their experience of operating their processes in order to understand more about those processes. This accumulation of process knowledge can build into the skills, knowledge and experience that allow the business to improve over time. But more than that, it can build into what are known as the 'capabilities' that allow the business to innovate in the future. We will examine this idea of operations capabilities in more detail in the next chapter.

Operations principle

All operations should be expected to contribute to their business at a strategic level by controlling costs, increasing revenue, making investment more effective, reducing risks, and growing long-term capabilities.

How is operations performance judged at an operational level?

Assessing performance at a societal level, and judging how well an operation contributes to strategic objectives, are clearly important, particularly in the longer term, and form the backdrop to all operations decision making. But running operations at an operational day-to-day level requires a more tightly defined set of objectives. These are called operations 'performance objectives'. There are five of them and they apply to all types of operation. Imagine that you are an operations manager in any kind of business – a hospital administrator, for example, or a production manager in an automobile plant. What kinds of things are you likely to want to do in order to satisfy customers and contribute to competitiveness?

▶ You would want to do things right; that is, you would not want to make mistakes, and would want to satisfy your customers by providing error-free goods and services which are 'fit for their purpose'. This is giving a quality advantage.

▶ You would want to do things fast, minimizing the time between a customer asking for goods or services and the customer receiving them in full, thus increasing the availability of your goods and services and giving a speed advantage.

▶ You would want to do things on time, so as to keep the delivery promises you have made. If the operation can do this, it is giving a dependability advantage.

▶ You would want to be able to change what you do; that is, being able to vary or adapt the operation's activities to cope with unexpected circumstances or to give customers individual treatment. Being able to change far enough and fast enough to meet customer requirements gives a flexibility advantage.

▶ You would want to do things cheaply; that is, produce goods and services at a cost which enables them to be priced appropriately for the market while still allowing for a return to the organization; or, in a not-for-profit organization, give good value to the taxpayers or whoever is funding the operation. When the organization is managing to do this, it is giving a cost advantage.

The next part of this chapter examines these five performance objectives in more detail by looking at what they mean for four different operations: a general hospital, an automobile factory, a city bus company and a supermarket chain.

Operations principle

Operations performance objectives can be grouped together as quality, speed, dependability, flexibility and cost.

Why is quality important?

Quality is consistent conformance to customers' expectations, in other words 'doing things right', but the things which the operation needs to do right will vary according to the kind of operation. All operations regard quality as a particularly important objective. In some ways quality is the most visible part of what an operation does. Furthermore, it is something that a customer finds relatively easy to judge about the operation. Is the product or service as it is supposed to be? Is it right or is it wrong? There is something fundamental about quality. Because of this, it is clearly a major influence on customer satisfaction or dissatisfaction. A customer perception of high-quality products and services means customer satisfaction and therefore the likelihood that the customer will return. Figure 2.5 illustrates how quality could be judged in four operations.

Quality inside the operation

When quality means consistently producing services and products to specification it not only leads to external customer satisfaction, but makes life easier inside the operation as well.

Quality reduces costs The fewer mistakes made by each process in the operation, the less time will be needed to correct the mistakes and the less confusion and irritation will be spread. For example, if a supermarket's regional warehouse sends the wrong goods to the supermarket, it will mean staff time, and therefore cost, being used to sort out the problem.

Quality increases dependability Increased costs are not the only consequence of poor quality. At the supermarket, it could also mean that goods run out on the supermarket shelves with a resulting loss of revenue to the operation and irritation to the external customers. Sorting the problem out could also distract the supermarket management from giving attention to the other parts of the supermarket operation. This in turn could result in further mistakes being made. So, quality (like the other performance objectives, as we will see) has both an external impact, which influences customer satisfaction, and an internal impact, which leads to stable and efficient processes.

> **✓ Operations principle**
>
> Quality can give the potential for better services and products, and save costs.

Quality could mean . . .

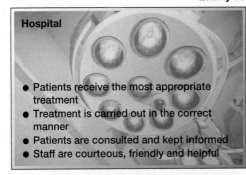

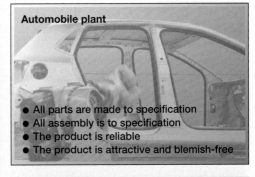

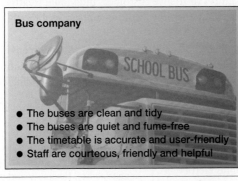

Figure 2.5 Quality means different things in different operations

Quality at Quality Street[8]

It has been a point of some debate for generations of children (and some adults): *'what is your favourite amongst the Quality Street assortment of chocolates?'* The world-famous brand of assorted chocolates is made in the same area of the UK where John Mackintosh first made this new type of sweet by mixing hard and soft caramel in 1890. But it was John Mackintosh's son who conceived and developed Quality Street in 1936. His idea (novel at the time) was to wrap each individual sweet separately and package them in a tin to preserve their quality. And Nestlé, which now owns the brand, has maintained this emphasis on quality. In fact, like all Nestlé products, Quality Street is made under the strict quality standards enshrined in the company's quality policy that outlines its commitment to *'build trust by offering products and services that match consumer expectation and preference'*. In other words, Nestlé understands that quality has a profound effect on how its products are viewed by consumers. As a food company (the largest in the world), it is also aware of its responsibility to comply with all food safety and regulatory requirements. *'I don't think most people are aware of the amount of work that goes into ensuring that the food they eat is safe'*, says John O'Brien, Head of the Food Safety and Integrity Research Programme at the Nestlé Research Center in Lausanne, Switzerland. *'Consumers rightly expect that the product they buy is safe to eat and contains what it says on the label'*, he said. *'But they also expect fewer preservatives on that label.'* Quality Street are free from artificial colours, flavourings and preservatives, and since 2009, the packaging has been completely recyclable. The coloured wrappers are biodegradable and can be composted with garden waste, while the foil wrappers and the tin container can be recycled in the same way as cans. Yet, while consumer perception and particularly safety is of paramount concern at Quality Street, high-quality operations also have an impact on costs. Nestlé's quality policy is to gain a zero-defect,

no-waste attitude by everyone in the company'. Its 'Quality Management System' is used globally to guarantee compliance with quality standards and to create value for consumers. It is audited and verified by independent certification bodies to prove conformity to internal standards, laws and regulatory requirements. 'Quality by design' is built in during product development and the company's 'Supplier Code' sets minimum standards that it asks its suppliers, employees, agents and subcontractors to respect at all times. In the factory, it applies internationally recognized good manufacturing practices (GMP) that cover all aspects of manufacturing, including standard operating procedures, people management and training, equipment maintenance and handling of materials.

And the favourite Quality Street? Well several variants have been and gone, including Malt Toffee, Fruits of the Forest Cream, Almond Octagon and Gooseberry Cream. But of the 12 Quality Streets you will find in each tin today, one (admittedly unscientific) study claimed it was the Strawberry Cream.

Why is speed important?

Speed means the elapsed time between customers requesting products or services and their receiving them. Figure 2.6 illustrates what speed means for the four operations. The main benefit to the operation's (external) customers of speedy delivery of goods and services is that the faster they can have the product or service, the more likely they are to buy it, or the more they will pay for it, or the greater the benefit they receive (see the 'Operations in practice' case 'App saves two minutes of the "The Golden Hour"').

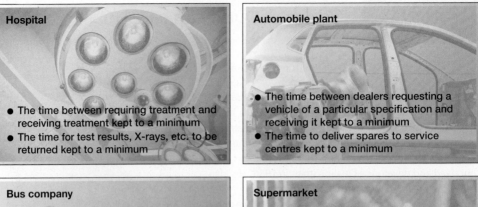

Hospital

- The time between requiring treatment and receiving treatment kept to a minimum
- The time for test results, X-rays, etc. to be returned kept to a minimum

Automobile plant

- The time between dealers requesting a vehicle of a particular specification and receiving it kept to a minimum
- The time to deliver spares to service centres kept to a minimum

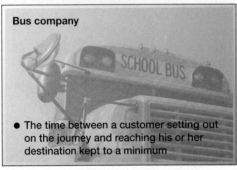

Bus company

- The time between a customer setting out on the journey and reaching his or her destination kept to a minimum

Supermarket

- The time taken for the total transaction of going to the supermarket, making the purchases and returning kept to a minimum
- The immediate availability of goods

Figure 2.6 Speed means different things in different operations

Speed inside the operation

Inside the operation, speed is also important. Fast response to external customers is greatly helped by speedy decision making and speedy movement of materials and information inside the operation. And there are other benefits.

Speed reduces inventories Take, for example, the automobile plant. Steel for the vehicle's door panels is delivered to the press shop, pressed into shape, transported to the painting area, coated for colour and protection and moved to the assembly line where it is fitted to the automobile. This is a simple three-stage process, but in practice material does not flow smoothly from one stage to the next. First, the steel is delivered as part of a far larger batch containing enough steel to make possibly several hundred products. Eventually it is taken to the press area, pressed into shape and again waits to be transported to the paint area. It then waits to be painted, only to wait once more until it is transported to the assembly line. Yet again it waits by the trackside until it is eventually fitted to the automobile. The material's journey time is far longer than the time needed to make and fit the product. It actually spends most of its time waiting as stocks (inventories) of parts and products. The longer items take to move through a process, the more time they will be waiting and the higher inventory will be. This is an important idea which will be explored in Chapter 15 on lean operations.

Speed reduces risks Forecasting tomorrow's events is far less of a risk than forecasting next year's. The further ahead companies forecast, the more likely they are to get it wrong. The faster the throughput time of a process, the later forecasting can be left. Consider the automobile plant again. If the total throughput time for the door panel is six weeks, door panels are being processed through their first operation six weeks before they reach their final destination. The quantity of door panels being processed

> **Operations principle**
>
> Speed can give the potential for faster delivery of services and products, and save costs.

will be determined by the forecasts for demand six weeks ahead. If instead of six weeks, they take only one week to move through the plant, the door panels being processed through their first stage are intended to meet demand only one week ahead. Under these circumstances it is far more likely that the number and type of door panels being processed are the number and type that eventually will be needed.

It is often called 'The Golden Hour'. It is the hour immediately following traumatic injury in which medical treatment to prevent irreversible internal damage and optimize the chance of survival is most effective. 'The Golden Hour' was first described by Dr R. Adams Cowley, who recognized that the sooner trauma patients reached definitive care – particularly if they arrived within 60 minutes of being injured – the better their chance of survival. So, few services have more need of speed than the emergency services. In responding to road accidents especially, every second is critical. Making full use of 'The Golden Hour' means speeding up three elements of the total time to treatment: the time it takes for the emergency services to find out the details of the accident, the time it takes them to travel to the scene of the accident, and the time it takes to get the casualty to appropriate treatment. That is why the London Air Ambulance service was delighted when a new tablet app saved its emergency team two minutes in responding to emergencies. Rather than having to take all the details of an emergency before they rushed to their helicopter, the app together with enhanced mobile communication allows them to set off immediately and receive the details on their tablet when they are in the air. But is getting airborne two minutes sooner really significant? It is, when one considers that, if starved of oxygen, a million brain cells can die every minute. It allows the service's advanced trauma

doctors and paramedics to perform procedures to relieve pain, straighten broken limbs, even perform open-chest surgery to restart the heart, often within minutes of injury. Including trauma medics in the team, in effect, brings the hospital to the patient, wherever that may be. When most rescues are only a couple of minutes' flying time back to the hospital, speed can really save lives. However, it is not always possible to land a helicopter safely at night (because of possible overhead wires and other hazards), so conventional ambulances will always be needed, both to get paramedics quickly to accident victims and to speed them to hospital.

Why is dependability important?

Dependability means doing things in time for customers to receive products or services exactly when they are needed, or at least when they were promised. Figure 2.7 illustrates what dependability means in the four operations. Customers might only judge the dependability of an operation after the product or service has been delivered. Initially this may not affect the likelihood that customers will select the service – they have already 'consumed' it. Over time, however, dependability can override all other criteria. No matter how cheap or fast a bus service is, if the service is always late (or unpredictably early) or the buses are always full, then potential passengers will be better off calling a taxi.

Dependability inside the operation

Inside the operation internal customers will judge each other's performance partly by how reliable the other processes are in delivering material or information on time. Operations where internal dependability is high are more effective than those which are not, for a number of reasons.

Dependability saves time Take, for example, the maintenance and repair centre for the city bus company. If the centre runs out of some crucial spare parts, the manager of the centre will need to spend time trying to arrange a special delivery of the required parts, and the resources allocated to service the buses will not be used as productively as they would have been without this disruption. More seriously, the fleet will be short of buses until they can be repaired and the fleet operations

Dependability could mean . . .

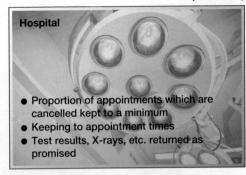

Hospital
- Proportion of appointments which are cancelled kept to a minimum
- Keeping to appointment times
- Test results, X-rays, etc. returned as promised

Automobile plant
- On-time delivery of vehicles to dealers
- On-time delivery of spares to service centres

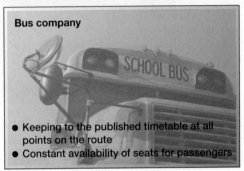

Bus company
- Keeping to the published timetable at all points on the route
- Constant availability of seats for passengers

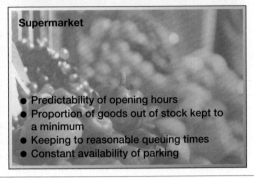

Supermarket
- Predictability of opening hours
- Proportion of goods out of stock kept to a minimum
- Keeping to reasonable queuing times
- Constant availability of parking

Figure 2.7 Dependability means different things in different operations

manager will have to spend time rescheduling services. So, entirely due to the one failure of dependability of supply, a significant part of the operation's time has been wasted coping with the disruption.

Dependability saves money Ineffective use of time will translate into extra cost. The spare parts might cost more to be delivered at short notice and maintenance staff will expect to be paid even when there is no bus to work on. Nor will the fixed costs of the operation, such as heating and rent, be reduced because the buses are not being serviced. The rescheduling of buses will probably mean that some routes have inappropriately sized buses and some services could have to be cancelled. This will result in empty bus seats (if too large a bus has to be used) or a loss of revenue (if potential passengers are not transported).

What does dependability mean when travelling by rail?[10]

When the operator of a private railway firm that serves the Tokyo suburbs issued an apology after one of its trains departed 20 seconds ahead of schedule, it made headlines around the world. Passengers on the 9.44.40 am Tsukuba Express from Minami Nagareyama station, just north of Tokyo, were oblivious to the 20 second early departure when the train (which had arrived on time) pulled away at 9.44.20 am. In most parts of the world such a small error would not be any cause for comment (except perhaps to congratulate the company for being so close to the scheduled time), but the company that operates the Tokyo service clearly felt different. In a formal statement they said that they 'deeply apologise for the severe inconvenience imposed upon our customers.' They said that the conductor on the train had not properly checked the train's timetable. In future, they said, the crew had been instructed to 'strictly follow procedure to prevent a recurrence'. But what about any passengers who may have missed the train because it left 20 seconds early? Not to worry – another train arrived 4 minutes later (and left on time).

The story prompted news outlets to focus on how rail services in various countries performed in terms of their dependability (punctuality, as it would usually be called by rail operators). Japan is indeed one of the best on-time performing countries. The Japanese high-speed bullet train arrives a mere 54 seconds behind schedule on average. If a Japanese train is five minutes late or more, passengers are given a certificate that they can give to their boss or teacher as an excuse for being late. Perhaps predictably for a country famous for its clocks and watches, the Swiss operator SBB rates as among the most punctual in Europe with 88.8 per cent of all passengers arriving on time and customer satisfaction surpassing the company's target of 75 per cent. Other national rail networks with good dependability records include Sweden, Denmark, Germany and France. But comparisons are complicated by different definitions of exactly what 'on time' means. A Swiss train is late if it arrives more than three minutes after the advertised time. But, in the UK it can be up to five minutes late (10 minutes if it's a longer journey) and still be recorded as 'on time'. In fact, there are a wide range of 'lateness' standards used throughout the world. In Ireland, a train is 'on time' if it's less than 10 minutes late (or five minutes for Dublin's Dart network). Trains in the USA are allowed 10 minutes' leeway for journeys up to 250 miles, and up to 30 minutes for

journeys of more than 550 miles. In Australia, each rail company has its own definitions of punctuality. In Victoria, trains have between five and 11 minutes' flexibility. Queensland's trains have either four or six minutes, depending on the route. Also, countries measure different types of punctuality. In the UK punctuality is measured when the train arrives at its final destination. In Switzerland, they monitor the punctuality of individuals (how late did each passenger arrive at whichever station they wanted to get off?).

Dependability gives stability The disruption caused to operations by a lack of dependability goes beyond time and cost. It affects the 'quality' of the operation's time. If everything in an operation is always perfectly dependable, a level of trust will have built up between the different parts of the operation. There will be no 'surprises' and everything will be predictable. Under such circumstances, each part of the operation can concentrate on improving its own area of responsibility without having its attention continually diverted by a lack of dependable service from the other parts.

> **Operations principle**
> Dependability can give the potential for more reliable delivery of services and products, and save costs.

Why is flexibility important?

Flexibility means being able to change the operation in some way. This may mean changing what the operation does, how it is doing it, or when it is doing it. Specifically, customers will need the operation to change so that it can provide four types of requirement:

▶ product/service flexibility – the operation's ability to introduce new or modified products and services;

▶ mix flexibility – the operation's ability to produce a wide range or mix of products and services;

▶ volume flexibility – the operation's ability to change its level of output or activity to produce different quantities or volumes of products and services over time;

▶ delivery flexibility – the operation's ability to change the timing of the delivery of its services or products.

Figure 2.8 gives examples of what these different types of flexibility mean to the four different operations.

Mass customization

One of the beneficial external effects of flexibility is the increased ability of operations to do different things for different customers. So, high flexibility gives the ability to produce a high variety of products or services. Normally high variety means high cost (see Chapter 1). Furthermore, high-variety operations do not usually produce in high volume. Some companies have developed their

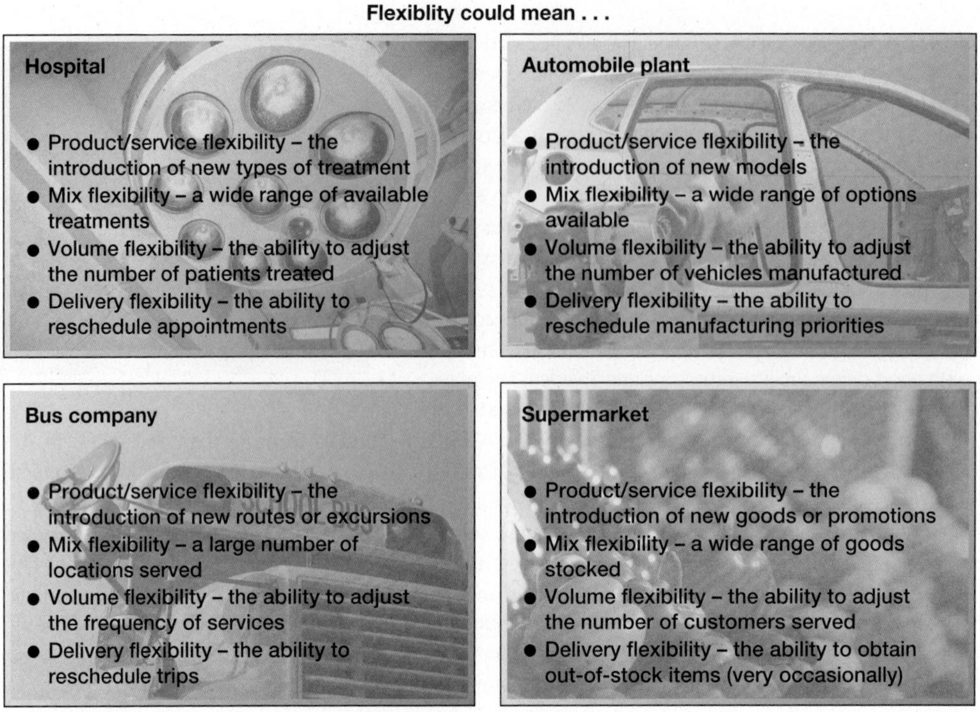

Hospital

- Product/service flexibility – the introduction of new types of treatment
- Mix flexibility – a wide range of available treatments
- Volume flexibility – the ability to adjust the number of patients treated
- Delivery flexibility – the ability to reschedule appointments

Automobile plant

- Product/service flexibility – the introduction of new models
- Mix flexibility – a wide range of options available
- Volume flexibility – the ability to adjust the number of vehicles manufactured
- Delivery flexibility – the ability to reschedule manufacturing priorities

Bus company

- Product/service flexibility – the introduction of new routes or excursions
- Mix flexibility – a large number of locations served
- Volume flexibility – the ability to adjust the frequency of services
- Delivery flexibility – the ability to reschedule trips

Supermarket

- Product/service flexibility – the introduction of new goods or promotions
- Mix flexibility – a wide range of goods stocked
- Volume flexibility – the ability to adjust the number of customers served
- Delivery flexibility – the ability to obtain out-of-stock items (very occasionally)

Figure 2.8 Flexibility means different things in different operations

flexibility in such a way that products and services are customized for each individual customer. Yet they manage to produce them in a high-volume, mass production manner which keeps costs down. This approach is called mass customization. Sometimes this is achieved through flexibility in design. For example, Dell is one of the largest volume producers of personal computers in the world, yet allows each customer to 'design' (albeit in a limited sense) their own configuration. Sometimes flexible technology is used to achieve the same effect. Another example is Paris Miki, an upmarket eyewear retailer which has the largest number of eyewear stores in the world, which uses its own 'Mikissimes Design System' to capture a digital image of the customer and analyse facial characteristics. Together with a list of customers' personal preferences, the system then recommends a particular design and displays it on the image of the customer's face. In consultation with the optician the customer can adjust shapes and sizes until the final design is chosen. Within the store the frames are assembled from a range of pre-manufactured components and the lenses ground and fitted to the frames. The whole process takes around an hour. Another example is the mymuesli case.

OPERATIONS IN PRACTICE	566 quadrillion individual muesli mixes –now that's flexible[11]

Three university students, Hubertus Bessau, Philipp Kraiss and Max Wittrock, in the small city of Passau, Germany, came up with the concept of mymuesli – the first web-based platform where you can mix your own organic muesli online, with a choice of 75 different ingredients. This makes it possible to create 566 quadrillion individual muesli mixes – and you can even name your own muesli mix. *'We wanted to provide customers with nothing else*

▶

but the perfect muesli', they say. *'Of course, the idea of custom-mixing muesli online might sound wacky . . . but think about it – it's the breakfast you were always looking for.'* All muesli is mixed in the Passau production site according to strict quality standards and hygiene law requirements. Ingredients are strictly organic, without additional sugar, additives, preservatives or artificial colours. On visiting the website customers first have to pick a muesli base. After this, they add other basics and ingredients such as fruit, nuts and seeds and extras. And the company will deliver it direct by courier to your door! The chosen name is printed on the can to make it even more personal. One of mymuesli's great assets is the multitude of eccentric and exotic ingredients sourced from around the world. Philipp Kraiss, one of the company founders, is constantly on the lookout for 'new, crazy and tasty' muesli ingredients. The company has now expanded its operations to the UK. *'We seriously hope that mymuesli will find just as many friends here in the UK as in Germany and Austria'*, says Max Wittrock, another of the three founding members.

Agility

Judging operations in terms of their agility has become popular. Agility is really a combination of all the five performance objectives but particularly flexibility and speed. In addition, agility implies that an operation and the supply chain of which it is a part (supply chains are described in Chapters 5 and 12) can respond to the uncertainty in the market. The term is particularly common in software development, where it indicates the ability to produce working, quality software in short, fast increments with development teams able to accept and implement fast, changing requirements. Used more generally, agility means responding to market requirements by producing new and existing products and services fast and flexibly.

Flexibility inside the operation

Developing a flexible operation can also have advantages to the internal customers within the operation.

Flexibility speeds up response Fast service often depends on the operation being flexible. For example, if the hospital has to cope with a sudden influx of patients from a road accident, it clearly needs to deal with injuries quickly. Under such circumstances a flexible hospital which can speedily transfer extra skilled staff and equipment to the accident and emergency department will provide the fast service which the patients need.

Flexibility saves time In many parts of the hospital, staff have to treat a wide variety of complaints. Fractures, cuts or drug overdoses do not come in batches. Each patient is an individual with individual needs. The hospital staff cannot take time to 'get into the routine' of treating a particular complaint; they must have the flexibility to adapt quickly. They must also have sufficiently flexible facilities and equipment so that time is not wasted waiting for equipment to be brought to the patient. The hospital's time is being saved because it is flexible in 'changing over' from one task to the next.

Flexibility maintains dependability Internal flexibility can also help to keep the operation on schedule when unexpected events disrupt the operation's plans. For example, if the sudden influx of patients to the hospital requires emergency surgical procedures, routine operations will be disrupted. This is likely to cause distress and considerable inconvenience. A flexible hospital might be able to minimize the disruption by possibly having reserved operating theatres for such an emergency, and being able to bring in medical staff quickly who are 'on call'.

> **Operations principle**
> Flexibility can give the potential to create new, wider variety, differing volumes and differing delivery dates of services and products, and save costs.

Why is cost important?

To the companies that compete directly on price, cost will clearly be their major operations objective. The lower the cost of producing their goods and services, the lower can be the price to their customers. Even those companies which do not compete on price will be interested in keeping costs low. Every euro or dollar removed from an operation's cost base is a further euro or dollar added to its profits. Not surprisingly, low cost is a universally attractive objective. The case on everyday low prices at Aldi describes how one retailer keeps its costs down.

The ways in which operations management can influence cost will depend largely on where the operation's costs are incurred. The operation will spend its money on staff (the money spent on employing people), facilities, technology and equipment (the money spent on buying, caring for, operating and replacing the operation's 'hardware') and materials (the money spent on the 'bought-in' materials consumed or transformed in the operation). Figure 2.9 shows typical cost breakdowns for the hospital, car plant, supermarket and bus company.

> **Operations principle**
>
> Cost is always an important objective for operations management, even if the organization does not compete directly on price.

Keeping operations costs down

All operations have an interest in keeping their costs as low as is compatible with the levels of quality, speed, dependability and flexibility that their customers require. The measure that this is most frequently used to indicate is productivity. Productivity is the ratio of what is produced by an operation (its output) to what is required to produce it (its input):

$$\text{Productivity} = \frac{\text{Output from the operation}}{\text{Input to the operation}}$$

Often partial measures of input or output are used so that comparisons can be made. So, for example, in the automobile industry productivity is sometimes measured in terms of the number of cars produced per year per employee. This is called a single-factor measure of productivity:

$$\text{Single-factor productivity} = \frac{\text{Output from the operation}}{\text{One input to the operation}}$$

Cost could mean . . .

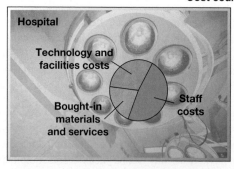

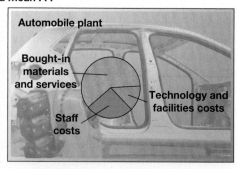

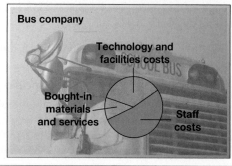

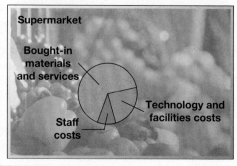

Figure 2.9 Cost means different things in different operations

Everyday low prices at Aldi

Aldi is an international 'limited assortment' supermarket specializing in 'private label', mainly food products. It has carefully focused its service concept and delivery system to attract customers in a highly competitive market. The company believes that its unique approach to operations management makes it *'virtually impossible for competitors to match our combination of price and quality'*. And it has proved especially successful in meeting the increasingly price-conscious behaviour of customers. How has it done this? By challenging the norms of retail operations. Its operations are kept deliberately simple, using basic facilities to keep down overheads. Most stores stock only a limited range of goods (typically around 700 compared with 25,000 to 30,000 stocked by conventional supermarket chains). The private label approach means that the products have been produced according to Aldi quality specifications and are only sold in Aldi stores. Without the high costs of brand marketing and advertising, and with Aldi's formidable purchasing power,

prices can be 30 per cent below their branded equivalents. Other cost-saving practices include open-carton displays, which eliminate the need for special shelving, no grocery bags to encourage recycling as well as saving costs, multiple bar codes on packages (to speed up scanning) and using a 'cart rental' system which requires customers to return the cart to the store to get their coin deposit back.

This allows different operations to be compared excluding the effects of input costs. One operation may have high total costs per car but high productivity in terms of number of cars per employee per year. The difference between the two measures is explained in terms of the distinction between the cost of the inputs to the operation and the way the operation is managed to convert inputs into outputs. Input costs may be high, but the operation itself is good at converting them to goods and services. Single-factor productivity can include the effects of input costs if the single input factor is expressed in cost terms, such as 'labour costs'. Total factor productivity is the measure that includes all input factors.

$$\text{Multi-factor productivity} = \frac{\text{Output from the operation}}{\text{All inputs to the operation}}$$

Improving productivity One obvious way of improving an operation's productivity is to reduce the cost of its inputs while maintaining the level of its outputs. This means reducing the costs of some or all of its transformed and transforming resource inputs. For example, a bank may choose to relocate its call centres to a place where its facility-related costs (for example, rent) are cheaper. A software developer may relocate its entire operation to India or China where skilled labour is available at rates significantly less than in European countries. A computer manufacturer may change the design of its products to allow the use of cheaper materials. Productivity can also be improved by making better use of the inputs to the operation. For example, garment manufacturers attempt to cut out the various pieces of material that make up the garment by positioning each part on the strip of cloth so that material wastage is minimized. All operations are increasingly concerned with cutting out waste, whether it is waste of materials, waste of staff time, or waste through the under-utilization of facilities.

A health-check clinic has five employees and 'processes' 200 patients per week. Each employee works 35 hours per week. The clinic's total wage bill is £3,900 and its total overhead expenses are £2,000 per week. What is the clinic's single factor labour productivity and its multi-factor productivity?

$$\text{Labour productivity} = \frac{200}{50} = 40 \text{ patients/employee/week}$$

$$\text{Labour productivity} = \frac{200}{5 \times 35} = 1.143 \text{ patients/labour hour}$$

$$\text{Multi-factor productivity} = \frac{200}{(3,900 + 2,000)} = 0.0339 \text{ patients/£}$$

Cost reduction through internal effectiveness Our previous discussion distinguished between the benefits of each performance objective externally and internally. Each of the various performance objectives has several internal effects, but *all of them* affect cost, so one important way to improve cost performance is to improve the performance of the other operations objectives (see Figure 2.10):

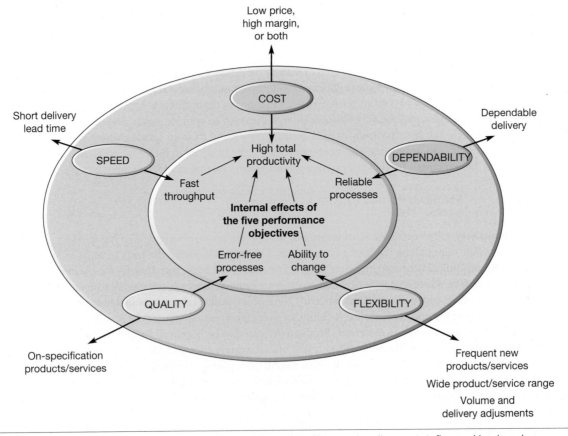

Figure 2.10 Performance objectives have both external and internal effects. Internally, cost is influenced by the other performance objectives

- High-quality operations do not waste time or effort having to redo things, nor are their internal customers inconvenienced by flawed service.
- Fast operations reduce the level of in-process inventory between micro operations, as well as reducing administrative overheads.
- Dependable operations do not spring any unwelcome surprises on their internal customers. They can be relied on to deliver exactly as planned. This eliminates wasteful disruption and allows the other micro operations to operate efficiently.
- Flexible operations adapt to changing circumstances quickly and without disrupting the rest of the operation. Flexible micro operations can also change over between tasks quickly and without wasting time and capacity.

Worked example

Slap.com is an Internet retailer of speciality cosmetics. It orders products from a number of suppliers, stores them, packs them to customers' orders, and then dispatches them using a distribution company. Although broadly successful, the business is very keen to reduce its operating costs. A number of suggestions have been made to do this. These are as follows:

- Make each packer responsible for his or her own quality. This could potentially reduce the percentage of mis-packed items from 0.25 per cent to near zero. Repacking an item that has been mis-packed costs €2 per item.
- Negotiate with suppliers to ensure that they respond to delivery requests faster. It is estimated that this would cut the value of inventories held by slap.com by €1,000,000.
- Institute a simple control system that would give early warning if the total number of orders that should be dispatched by the end of the day actually is dispatched in time. Currently 1 per cent of orders is not packed by the end of the day and therefore has to be sent by express courier the following day. This costs an extra €2 per item.

Because demand varies through the year, sometimes staff have to work overtime. Currently the overtime wage bill for the year is €150,000. The company's employees have indicated that they would be willing to adopt a flexible working scheme where extra hours could be worked when necessary in exchange for having the hours off at a less busy time and receiving some kind of extra payment. This extra payment is likely to total €50,000 per year.

If the company dispatches 5 million items every year and if the cost of holding inventory is 10 per cent of its value, how much cost will each of these suggestions save the company?

Analysis

Eliminating mis-packing would result in an improvement in quality. Currently 0.25 per cent of 5 million items are mis-packed. This amounts to 12,500 items per year. At €2 repacking charge per item, this is a cost of €25,000 that would be saved.

Getting faster delivery from suppliers helps reduce the amount of inventory in stock by €1,000,000. If the company is paying 10 per cent of the value of stock for keeping it in storage, the saving will be €1,000,000 × 0.1 = €100,000.

Ensuring that all orders are dispatched by the end of the day increases the dependability of the company's operations. Currently, 1 per cent are late; in other words, 50,000 items per year. This is costing €2 × 50,000 = €100,000 per year which would be saved by increasing dependability.

Changing to a flexible working hours system increases the flexibility of the operation and would cost €50,000 per year, but it saves €150,000 per year. Therefore, increasing flexibility could save €100,000 per year.

So, in total, by improving the operation's quality, speed, dependability and flexibility, a total of €325,000 can be saved.

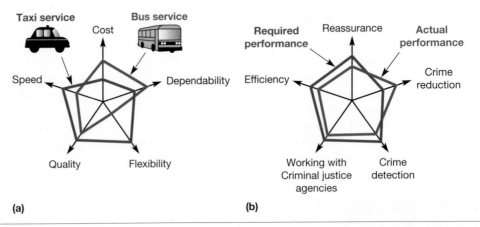

Figure 2.11 Polar representations of (a) the relative importance of performance objectives for a taxi service and a bus service, and (b) a police force's targets and performance

The polar representation of performance objectives

A useful way of representing the relative importance of performance objectives for a product or service is shown in Figure 2.11(a). This is called the polar representation because the scales which represent the importance of each performance objective have the same origin. A line describes the relative importance of each performance objective. The closer the line is to the common origin, the less important is the performance objective to the operation. Two services are shown, a taxi and a bus service. Each essentially provides the same basic service, but with different objectives. The differences between the two services are clearly shown by the diagram. Of course, the polar diagram can be adapted to accommodate any number of different performance objectives. For example, Figure 2.11(b) shows a proposal for using a polar diagram to assess the relative performance of different police forces in the UK.[12]

How can operations performance be measured?

Having defined the three levels of operations performance, any business will need to measure how well, or badly, it is doing. This is performance measurement. It is the process of *quantifying action,* where measurement means the process of quantification and the performance of the operation is assumed to derive from actions taken by its management. Some kind of *performance measurement* is a prerequisite for judging whether an operation is good, bad or indifferent. Without performance measurement, it is impossible to exert any control over an operation on an ongoing basis, or to judge whether any improvement is being made.

Performance measurement, as we are treating it here, concerns three generic issues:

▶ What factors should be included as performance measures?
▶ Which are the most important performance measures?
▶ What detailed measures should be use?

What factors should be included as performance measures?

Earlier in this chapter we explained how operations performance could be described at three levels: the societal level that included consideration of social and environmental factors as well as economic ones; the strategic level that included consideration of risk, capital and innovation capability issues as well as profitability; and the operational level that included the more directly operations-related factors of quality, speed, dependability, flexibility and cost. There are two important points to make here. First, sometimes these measures are aggregated into 'composite' measures that combine several measures, such as 'customer satisfaction', 'overall service level' or 'operations agility'. These more

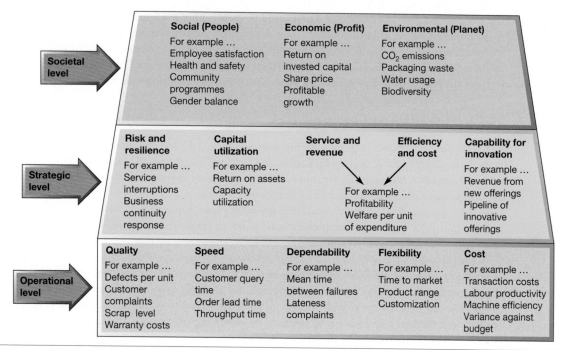

Figure 2.12 Performance measures at the three levels

aggregated 'composite' performance measures help to present a picture of the overall performance of a business, although they may include some influences outside those that operations performance improvement would normally address (customer satisfaction may partly be a function of how a service is advertised, for example). Second, all of the factors at each level can be broken down into more detailed measures. Figure 2.12 gives examples of this. These more detailed performance measures are usually monitored more closely and more often, and although, by themselves, they provide a limited view of an operation's performance, taken together they do provide a more descriptive and complete picture of what should be and what is happening within the operation. In practice, most organizations will choose to use performance measures from all three levels.

Which are the most important performance measures?

One of the problems of devising a useful performance measurement system is trying to achieve some balance between having a few key measures on the one hand (straightforward and simple, but may not reflect the full range of organizational objectives), or, on the other hand, having many detailed measures (complex and difficult to manage, but capable of conveying many nuances of performance). Broadly, a compromise is often reached by making sure that there is a clear link between the operation's overall strategy, the most important (or 'key') performance indicators (often called KPIs) that reflect strategic objectives, and the bundle of detailed measures that are used to 'flesh out' each key performance indicator. Obviously, unless strategy is well defined then it is difficult to 'target' a narrow range of key performance indicators.

What detailed measures should be used?

The five performance objectives – quality, speed, dependability, flexibility and cost – are really composites of many smaller measures. For example, an operation's cost is derived from many factors which could include the purchasing efficiency of the operation, the efficiency with which it converts materials, the productivity of its staff, the ratio of direct to indirect staff, and so on. All of these measures individually give a partial view of the operation's cost performance, and many of them overlap in terms of the information they include. However, each of them does give a perspective on the cost performance of an operation that could be useful either to identify areas for improvement or to monitor the extent of improvement. If an organization regards its 'cost' performance as unsatisfactory, disaggregating it into 'purchasing efficiency', 'operations efficiency', 'staff productivity', etc. might explain the root cause of the poor performance. The 'operational' level in Figure 2.12 shows some of the partial measures which can be used to judge an operation's performance.

The balanced scorecard approach

Arguably, the best-known performance measurement approach, and one used by many organizations, is the 'balanced scorecard' devised by Kaplan and Norton: '*The balanced scorecard retains traditional financial measures. But financial measures tell the story of past events, an adequate story for industrial age companies for which investments in long-term capabilities and customer relationships were not critical for success. These financial measures are inadequate, however, for guiding and evaluating the journey that information age companies must make to create future value through investment in customers, suppliers, employees, processes, technology, and innovation.*'[13]

In the three-level framework used here, it lies across the strategic and operational levels. As well as including financial measures of performance, in the same way as traditional performance measurement systems, the balanced scorecard approach also attempts to provide the important information that is required to allow the overall strategy of an organization to be reflected adequately in specific performance measures. In addition to financial measures of performance, it also includes more operational measures of customer satisfaction, internal processes, innovation and other improvement activities. In doing so it measures the factors behind financial performance which are seen as the key drivers of future financial success. In particular, it is argued that a balanced range of measures enables managers to address the following questions (see Figure 2.13):

▶ How do we look to our shareholders (financial perspective)?
▶ What must we excel at (internal process perspective)?
▶ How do our customers see us (the customer perspective)?
▶ How can we continue to improve and build capabilities (the learning and growth perspective)?

> **Operations principle**
>
> Multi-dimensioned performance measurement approaches, such as the balanced scorecard, give a broader indication of overall performance.

The balanced scorecard attempts to bring together the elements that reflect a business's strategic position, including product or service quality measures, product and service development times, customer complaints, labour productivity, and so on. At the same time, it attempts to avoid performance reporting becoming unwieldy by restricting the

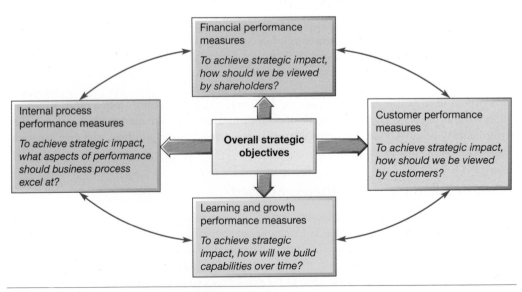

Figure 2.13 The measures used in the balanced scorecard

number of measures and focusing especially on those seen to be essential. The advantages of the approach are that it presents an overall picture of the organization's performance in a single report, and, by being comprehensive in the measures of performance it uses, encourages companies to take decisions in the interests of the whole organization rather than sub-optimizing around narrow measures.

How do performance objectives trade off against each other?

Earlier we examined how improving the performance of one objective inside the operation could also improve other performance objectives. Most notably better quality, speed, dependability and flexibility can improve cost performance. But externally this is not always the case. In fact, there may be a 'trade-off' between performance objectives. In other words, improving the performance of one performance objective might only be achieved by sacrificing performance in another. So, for example, an operation might wish to improve its cost efficiencies by reducing the variety of products or services that it offers to its customers. '*There is no such thing as a free lunch*' could be taken as a summary of this approach. Probably the best-known summary of the trade-off idea comes from Professor Wickham Skinner, who said: '*most managers will readily admit that there are compromises or trade-offs to be made in designing an airplane or truck. In the case of an airplane, trade-offs would involve matters such as cruising speed, take-off and landing distances, initial cost, maintenance, fuel consumption, passenger comfort and cargo or passenger capacity. For instance, no one today can design a 500-passenger plane that can land on an aircraft carrier and also break the sound barrier. Much the same thing is true in [operations].*'[14]

But there are two views of trade-offs. The first emphasizes 'repositioning' performance objectives by trading off improvements in some objectives for a reduction in performance in others. The other emphasizes increasing the 'effectiveness' of the operation by overcoming trade-offs so that improvements in one or more aspects of performance can be achieved without any reduction in the performance of others. Most businesses at some time or other will adopt both approaches. This is best illustrated through the concept of the 'efficient frontier' of operations performance.

> **Operations principle**
>
> In the short term, operations cannot achieve outstanding performance in all their operations objectives.

Trade-offs and the efficient frontier

Figure 2.14(a) shows the relative performance of several companies in the same industry in terms of their cost efficiency and the variety of products or services that they offer to their customers. Presumably all the operations would ideally like to be able to offer very high variety while still having very high levels of cost efficiency. However, the increased complexity that a high variety of product or service offerings brings will generally reduce the operation's ability to operate efficiently. Conversely, one way of improving cost efficiency is to limit severely the variety on offer to customers. The spread of results in Figure 2.14(a) is typical of an exercise such as this. Operations A, B, C, D have all chosen a different balance between variety and cost efficiency. But none is dominated by any other operation in the sense that another operation necessarily has 'superior' performance. Operation X, however, has an inferior performance because operation A is able to offer higher variety at the same level of cost efficiency and operation C offers the same variety but with better cost efficiency. The convex line on which operations A, B, C and D lie is known as the 'efficient frontier'. They may choose to position themselves differently (presumably because of different market strategies) but they cannot be criticized for being ineffective. Of course, any of these operations that lie on the efficient frontier may come to believe that the balance they have chosen between variety and cost

> **Operations principle**
>
> Operations that lie on the 'efficient frontier' have performance levels that dominate those which do not.

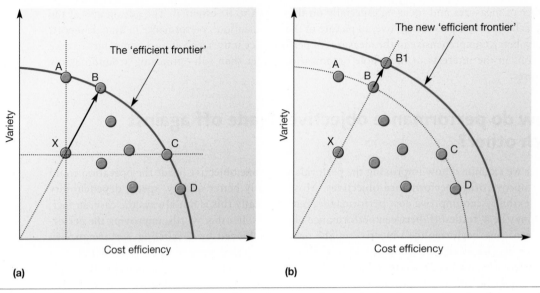

Figure 2.14 The efficient frontier identifies operations with performances that dominate other operations' performance

efficiency is inappropriate. In these circumstances, they may choose to reposition themselves at some other point along the efficient frontier. By contrast, operation X has also chosen to balance variety and cost efficiency in a particular way but is not doing so effectively. Operation B has the same ratio between the two performance objectives but is achieving them more effectively.

However, a strategy that emphasizes increasing effectiveness is not confined to those operations that are dominated, such as operation X. Those with a position on the efficient frontier will generally also want to improve their operations effectiveness by overcoming the trade-off that is implicit in the efficient frontier curve. For example, suppose operation B in Figure 2.14(b) wants to improve both its variety and its cost efficiency simultaneously and move to position B1. It may be able to do this, but only if it adopts operations improvements that extend the efficient frontier. For example, one of the decisions that any supermarket manager has to make is how many checkout positions to open at any time. If too many checkouts are opened then there will be times when the checkout staff do not have any customers to serve and will be idle. The customers, however, will have excellent service in terms of little or no waiting time. Conversely, if too few checkouts are opened, the staff will be working all the time but customers will have to wait in long queues. There seems to be a direct trade-off between staff utilization (and therefore cost) and customer waiting time (speed of service). Yet even the supermarket manager might, for example, allocate a number of 'core' staff to operate the checkouts but also arrange for those other staff who are performing other jobs in the supermarket to be trained and 'on call' should demand suddenly increase. If the manager on duty sees a build-up of customers at the checkouts, these other staff could quickly be used to staff checkouts. By devising a flexible system of staff allocation, the manager can both improve customer service and keep staff utilization high.

Operations principle

An operation's strategy improvement path can be described in terms of repositioning and/or overcoming its performance trade-offs.

This distinction between positioning on the efficient frontier and increasing operations effectiveness by extending the frontier is an important one. Any business must make clear the extent to which it is expecting the operation to reposition itself in terms of its performance objectives and the extent to which it is expecting the operation to improve its effectiveness in several ways simultaneously.

Summary answers to key questions

Why is operations performance vital in any organization?

▶ Operations management can either 'make or break' any business. In most businesses, it represents the bulk of its assets.

▶ The positive effects of a well-run operation include a focus on improvement, the building of 'difficult to imitate' capabilities, and an understanding of the processes that are the building blocks of all operations.

▶ The negative effects of a poorly run operation include failures that are obvious to customers (and expensive for the organization), a complacency that leads to the failure to exploit opportunities for improvement.

How is operations performance judged at a societal level?

▶ Operations decisions affect a variety of 'stakeholders'. Stakeholders are the people and groups who have a legitimate interest in the operation's activities.

▶ This idea that operations should take into account the impact on a broad mix of stakeholders is termed 'corporate social responsibility' (CSR).

▶ Performance at the societal level often uses the idea of the triple bottom line (TBL, or 3BL, also known as 'people, planet and profit'). It includes the social bottom line, the environmental bottom line and the economic bottom line.

▶ The social bottom line incorporates the idea that businesses should accept that they bear some responsibility for the impact they have on society and balance the external 'societal' consequences of their actions with the more direct internal consequences, such as profit.

▶ The environmental bottom line incorporates the idea that operations should accept that they bear some responsibility for the impact they have on the natural environment.

▶ The economic bottom line incorporates the conventional financial measures of performance derived from using the operation's resources effectively.

How is operations performance judged at a strategic level?

▶ The type of decisions and activities that operations managers carry out can have a significant strategic impact.

▶ In particular, operations can affect economic performance in five ways:

— It can reduce the costs.

— It can achieve customer satisfaction through service.

— It can reduce the risk of operational failure.

— It can reduce the amount of investment that is necessary.

— It can provide the basis for *future* innovation.

How is operations performance judged at an operational level?

▶ The five 'performance objectives' that are used to assess the performance of operations at an operational level are quality, speed, dependability, flexibility and cost.

- Quality is important because: By 'doing things right', operations seek to influence the quality of the company's goods and services. Externally, quality is an important aspect of customer satisfaction or dissatisfaction. Internally, quality operations both reduce costs and increase dependability.

- Speed is important because: By 'doing things fast', operations seek to influence the speed with which goods and services are delivered. Externally, speed is an important aspect of customer service. Internally, speed both reduces inventories by decreasing internal throughput time and reduces risks by delaying the commitment of resources.

- Dependability is important because: By 'doing things on time', operations seek to influence the dependability of the delivery of goods and services. Externally, dependability is an important aspect of customer service. Internally, dependability within operations increases operational reliability, thus saving the time and money that would otherwise be taken up in solving reliability problems and also giving stability to the operation.

- Flexibility is important because: By 'changing what they do', operations seek to influence the flexibility with which the company produces goods and services. Externally, flexibility can produce new products and services (product/service flexibility), produce a wide range or mix of products and services (mix flexibility), produce different quantities or volumes of products and services (volume flexibility), produce products and services at different times (delivery flexibility). Internally, flexibility can help speed up response times, save time wasted in changeovers, and maintain dependability.

- Cost is important because: By 'doing things cheaply', operations seek to influence the cost of the company's goods and services. Externally, low costs allow organizations to reduce their price in order to gain higher volumes or, alternatively, increase their profitability on existing volume levels. Internally, cost performance is helped by good performance in the other performance objectives.

How can operations performance be measured?

- It is unlikely that for any operation a single measure of performance will adequately reflect the whole of a performance objective. Usually operations have to collect a whole bundle of partial measures of performance.

- The balanced scorecard (BSC) is a commonly used approach to performance measurement and incorporates measures related to: How do we look to our shareholders (financial perspective)? What must we excel at (internal process perspective)? How do our customers see us (the customer perspective)? How can we continue to improve and build capabilities (the learning and growth perspective)?

How do operations performance objectives trade off against each other?

- Trade-offs are the extent to which improvements in one performance objective can be achieved by sacrificing performance in others. The 'efficient frontier' concept is a useful approach to articulating trade-offs and distinguishes between repositioning performance on the efficient frontier and improving performance by overcoming trade-offs.

IKEA looks to the future[15]

For decades, IKEA has been one of the most successful retail operations in the world, with much of its success founded on how it organizes its design, supply and retail service operations. With over 400 giant stores in 49 countries, IKEA has managed to develop its own standardized way of selling furniture. Its so-called 'big box' formula has driven IKEA to the global No. 1 position in furniture retailing. 'Big box' because the traditional IKEA store is a vast blue-and-yellow maze of a showroom (on average around 25,000 square metres) where customers often spend around two hours – far longer than in rival furniture retailers. This is because of the way it organizes its store operations. IKEA's

philosophy goes back to the original business, started in the 1950s in Sweden by the late Ingvar Kamprad. He was selling furniture, through a catalogue operation, and because customers wanted to see some of his furniture, he built a showroom on the outskirts of Stockholm and set the furniture out as it would be in a domestic setting. Also, instead of moving the furniture from the warehouse to the showroom area, he asked customers to pick the furniture up themselves from the warehouse, an approach that became fundamental to IKEA's ethos; what has been called the 'we do our part, you do yours' approach.

IKEA's 'big box' stores

IKEA offers a wide range of Scandinavian designs at affordable prices, usually stored and sold as a 'flat pack' which the customer assembles at home. *'It was an entirely new concept, and it drove the firm's success',* says Patrick O'Brien, Retail Research Director at retail consultancy GlobalData. *'But it wasn't just what IKEA was selling that was different, but how it was selling it.'* The stores were located and designed around one simple idea – that finding the store, parking, moving through the store itself, and ordering and picking up goods should be simple, smooth and problem-free. Catalogues are available at the entrance to each store showing product details and illustrations. For young children, there is a supervised children's play area, a small cinema, a parent and baby room and toilets, so parents can leave their children in the supervised play area for a time. Parents are recalled via the loudspeaker system if the child

has any problems. Customers may also borrow pushchairs to keep their children with them.

Parts of the showroom are set out in 'room settings', while other parts show similar products together, so that customers can make comparisons. Given the volume of customers, there are relatively few staff in the stores. IKEA say they like to allow customers to make up their minds. If advice is needed, 'information points' have staff who can help. Every piece of furniture carries a ticket indicating its location in the warehouse from where it can be collected. Customers then pass into an area where smaller items are displayed that can be picked directly, after which they pass through the self-service warehouse where they can pick up the items they viewed in the showroom. Finally, customers pay at the checkouts, where a conveyor belt moves purchases up to the checkout staff. The exit area has service points and a large loading area allowing customers to bring their cars from the car park and load their purchases. Within the store a restaurant serves, among other things, IKEA's famous Swedish meatballs. IKEA's fans say they can make a visit to the store a real 'day out'.

But not everyone is a fan

Yet not all customers (even those who come back time after time) are entirely happy with the traditional IKEA retail experience. Complaints include:

▶ It can be a long drive to reach one of their stores (unless you are 'lucky' enough to live near one).

- The long 'maze-like' journey that customers are 'encouraged' to take through the store is too prescriptive.

- There are too few customer-facing staff in the store.

- There are long queues at some points in the store, especially at checkouts, and at busy times such as weekends.

- Customers have to locate, pick off the shelves, and transport, sometimes heavy, products to the checkouts.

- IKEA designs can be 'bland' (or 'clean and aesthetically pleasing', depending on your taste).

- The furniture has to be assembled once you get it home, and the instructions are confusing.

Although many are

However, the impressive growth and success of IKEA over the years indicates that the company is doing many things right. The reasons customers give for shopping at IKEA include the following.

- Everything is available under one roof (albeit a very big roof).

- The range of furniture is far greater than at other stores.

- The products are displayed both by category (e.g. all chairs together) and in a room setting.

- Availability is immediate (competitors often quote several weeks for delivery).

- There is a kids' area and a restaurant so visiting the store is 'an event for all the family'.

- The design of furniture is 'modern, clean and inoffensive' – they fit anywhere.

- For the quality and design, the products are very good 'value for money'.

Was a new approach needed?

For decades, IKEA's unique retailing operations, combined with an excellent supply network and a customer-focused design philosophy, was an effective driver of healthy growth. However, there were indications that the company was starting to ask itself how it could solve some of the criticisms of its retail operations. 'We had to move away from conversations that began, "I love IKEA, but shopping at an IKEA store is not how I want to spend my time"' (Gillian Drakeford, IKEA's UK boss). It needed to counter the complaints by some customers that its stores were understaffed, that the navigation of stores was too prescriptive, and that queues were too long. 'We have had a great proposition for 60 years, but the customer had to fit around it. But the world has changed and to remain

relevant we need to have a proposition that fits around the customer' (Gillian Drakeford).

IKEA was also realising that its 'big box' stores were under threat from a decline in car ownership (in 1994, 75 per cent of 21–29-year-olds held driving licences in the UK; by 2017 that had dropped to 66 per cent). Also, customers were increasingly wanting their flat-pack furniture to be delivered, rather than having to drive to an IKEA store to collect it. Ideally, they also wanted to order it online. IKEA did have an online presence, but compared with its competitors it was relatively underdeveloped. Not only that, but not all customers wanted to assemble their own furniture.

'The entire premise that IKEA developed was that consumers would be willing to drive their cars 50 kilometres to save some money on something that looks amazing,' said Ray Gaul, a retail analyst at Kantar Retail. 'Young people like IKEA, but they can't or don't want to drive to IKEA.' However, the traditional 'big box' strategy was still popular with many customers, and sales from its stores continued to grow. Yet, in most markets, there were plenty of potential customers who could not reach an IKEA store within a reasonable drive (assumed to be around two-and-a-half hours). And some degree of rethinking IKEA's operating model seemed to be required. Torbjorn Loof, chief executive of Inter IKEA (who manage the IKEA concept) summarised their commitment to a rethink. 'We have been successful on a long journey. But it is clear that one era is ending and another beginning.'

Smaller stores to complement the larger ones

From 2015, IKEA opened several smaller-footprint stores in Europe, Canada, China, and Japan. But not all were the same. As a deliberate strategy, each was slightly different. This allowed the company to test alternative ways of locating, designing and managing its new ventures. Should they have cafés? How big should they be? Should they carry a range of products, or focus on a single category? Should they be located in shopping malls or on the high street? So, a 'pop-up' IKEA store in central Madrid offered only bedroom furnishings. A store in Stockholm focused on kitchens. It allowed customers to cook in the store, and book a 90-minute consultation to plan their kitchen. A small store in London stocked a range of product categories, but had no café (only a coffee machine), and in place of a supervised kids' play area, computer games were provided. Other new stores were, in some ways, similar to traditional stores, but smaller, with fewer car parking spaces and less inventory, and acted as order-and-collection points. In some, customers could get expert advice on larger purchases, such as kitchens or bathrooms. Often in the smaller stores, only a few items could be purchased and taken home instantly. Rather, customers could use touchscreens to order products and arrange for delivery or pickup at a convenient time. 'For me, it's a test lab for penetrating city centres,' said one senior IKEA executive. 'About 70 per cent of the people shopping there wouldn't go to a [traditional IKEA] store.'

TaskRabbit

In 2017 IKEA bought TaskRabbit, whose app was one of the leaders in what was becoming known as the 'gig' economy. Using its app, over 60,000 independent workers or 'taskers' (at the time of acquisition) offered their services to customers wanting to hire someone to do tasks such as moving or assembling furniture. 'In a fast-changing retail environment, we continuously strive to develop new and improved products and services to make our customers' lives a little bit easier. Entering the on-demand, sharing economy enables us to support that,' IKEA chief Jesper Brodin said in a statement. 'We will be able to learn from TaskRabbit's digital expertise, while also providing IKEA customers additional ways to access flexible and affordable service solutions to meet the needs of today's customer.'

Web-based retailing

Arguably, the most significant retailing development in this period was the growth in online shopping. However, IKEA was slow to move online. Partly, this was because there was internal reluctance to interfere with its successful 'big box' retail operations that encouraged customers to spend a long time in store and make impulse-purchases. However, it became clear that the company needed to become fully committed to 'multi-channel' retail operations, including online sales. But it was also clear that there would not be a total shift to online sales. The idea was to offer both physical and digital options for customers who wanted to use both channels, and to win new customers online who would never make the journey to its 'big box' superstores. Some retail experts warned that the new strategy carried the same risks faced by all firms going online. According to Marc-André Kamel of consultants Bain & Company, 'customers are not shifting entirely to e-commerce, but wish to mix and match channels'. And, although IKEA had little choice but to invest in online channels, the danger was that it could raise costs, especially as the company was also planning significant bricks-and-mortar expansion in new markets such as India, South America and South-East Asia.

Third-party sales

Another break with traditional IKEA practice came when it announced that it would consider selling its products through independent 'third-party' online retailers. Torbjörn Lööf, CEO of Inter IKEA, said the decision to supply online retailers was an important part of the broader overhaul of their operations. '[It] is the biggest development in how consumers meet Ikea since the concept was founded', he told the Financial Times.

Sustainability

IKEA was among the world's biggest users of wood (estimated as around 1 per cent of all wood used), and some environmental groups condemned what they saw as the 'disposable' nature of its furniture. Responding to this criticism, IKEA appointed a Chief Sustainability Officer – the first time that sustainability was directly represented in the senior management team, and a recognition of the growing role of sustainability in determining how IKEA was perceived. It also recognized the ability of sustainability to drive business innovation. IKEA, like an increasing number of companies, accepted that they lived in a world of finite resources and recognise that consumption needed to reflect this. Because of this realisation, IKEA, were seeking new ways to meet people's needs and aspirations whilst staying within the limits of our planet. They saw the emerging circular-economy business model as a great opportunity to develop their business further. This was preferable to viewing sustainability as a risk to their business. Sooner or later, other companies would start creating business models that disrupted the IKEA way of selling home furnishings. In one initiative in Belgium IKEA offered their customers five options to give furniture a second life: selling old IKEA-furniture in the store (at the price paid to the customer who supplied it), renewing it by repainting or reassembling, repairing by offering replacement parts, returning old furniture through their transport service, and donating it to social organisations. Some commentators questioned the idea of selling longer-lasting products and trading pre-owned items without a mark-up, as being bad for business. However, IKEA disagreed on the grounds that people may sometimes come to IKEA with a bit of a guilty conscience, wanting to buy stuff, but unable to completely forget the consequences. In fact, they believed that their actively welcomed the move. When they started buying back our furniture at Aalborg they actually saw an increase in revenue.

QUESTIONS

1 In the traditional IKEA 'big box' stores, what is the relative importance of the operational performance objectives (quality, speed, dependability, flexibility, cost), compared with a conventional high-street furniture store?

2 What trade-offs are customers who go to these big stores making?

3 How does the strategy of increasing IKEA's online presence impact on these trade-offs?

4 An IKEA executive was reported as saying that in some parts of the world 'we have reached the point of "peak stuff"'. It was interpreted by some as a warning that consumer appetite for home furnishings had reached a crucial turning point. What are the implications of this for IKEA?

Problems and applications

All chapters have Problems and applications' questions that will help you practise analysing operations. They can be answered by reading the chapter. Model answers for the first two questions can be found on the companion website for this book.

1   The environmental services department of a city has two recycling services – newspaper collection (NC) and general recycling (GR). The NC service is a door-to-door collection service that, at a fixed time every week, collects old newspapers that householders have placed in reusable plastic bags at their gate. An empty bag is left for the householders to use for the next collection. The value of the newspapers collected is relatively small; the service is offered mainly for reasons of environmental responsibility. By contrast the GR service is more commercial. Companies and private individuals can request a collection of materials to be disposed of, using either the telephone or the internet. The GR service guarantees to collect the material within 24 hours unless the customer prefers to specify a more convenient time. Any kind of material can be collected and a charge is made depending on the volume of material. This service makes a small profit because the revenue both from customer charges and from some of the more valuable recycled materials exceeds the operation's running costs. How would you describe the differences between the performance objectives of the two services?

2   Xexon7 is a specialist artificial intelligence (AI) development firm that develops algorithms for various online services. As part of its client service it has a small (10-person) help-desk call centre to answer client queries. Clients could contact them from anywhere in the world at any time of the day or night with a query. Demand at any point in time was fairly predictable, especially during the (European) daytime. Demand during the night hours (Asia and the Americas) was considerably lower than in the daytime and also less predictable. *'Most of the time we forecast demand pretty accurately and so we can schedule the correct number of employees to staff the work stations. There is still some risk, of course. Scheduling too many staff at any point in time will waste money and increase our costs, while scheduling too few will reduce the quality and response of the service we give'* (Peter Fisher, Help Desk Manager). Peter was, overall, pleased with the way in which his operation worked. However, he felt that a more systematic approach could be taken to identifying improvement opportunities. *'I need to develop a logical approach to identifying how we can invest into improving things like sophisticated diagnostic systems. We need to both reduce our operating costs and maintain, and even improve, our customer service.'* What are the trade-offs that must be managed in this type of call centre?

3   The health clinic described in the worked example earlier in the chapter has expanded by hiring one extra employee and now has six employees. It has also leased some new health monitoring equipment which allows patients to be processed faster. This means that its total output is now 280 patients per week. Its wage costs have increased to £4,680 per week and its overhead costs to £3,000 per week. What are its single-factor labour productivity and its multi-factor productivity now?

4   A publishing company plans to replace its four proof-readers who look for errors in manuscripts with a new scanning machine and one proof-reader in case the machine breaks down. Currently the proof-readers check 15 manuscripts every week between them. Each is paid €80,000 per year. Hiring the new scanning machine will cost €5,000 each calendar month. How will this new system affect the proofreading department's productivity? (Proof-readers work 45 weeks per year.)

5   Look again at the figures in the chapter which illustrate the meaning of each performance objective for the four operations. Consider the bus company and the supermarket, and in particular consider their external customers. Draw the relative required performance for both operations

on a polar diagram. Consider the internal effects of each performance objective. For both operations, identify how quality, speed, dependability and flexibility can help to reduce the cost of producing their services.

6   Visit the websites of two or three large oil companies such as Exxon, BP, Shell or Total. Examine how they describe their policies towards their customers, suppliers, shareholders, employees and society at large. Identify areas of the company's operations where there may be conflicts between the needs of these different stakeholder groups. Discuss or reflect on how (if at all) such companies try and reconcile these conflicts.

Selected further reading

Bourne, M., Kennerley, M. and Franco, M. (2005) Managing through measures: a study of the impact on performance, *Journal of Manufacturing Technology Management,* vol. 16, issue 4, 373–395.
What it says on the tin.

Gray, D., Micheli, P. and Pavlov, A. (2015) *Measurement Madness,* Wiley, New York.
Lots of examples of how companies can misuse performance measurement.

Kaplan, R.S. and Norton, D.P. (2005) The balanced scorecard: measures that drive performance, *Harvard Business Review,* July–August.
The latest pronouncements on the balanced scorecard approach.

Neely, A. (2012) *Business Performance Measurement: Unifying Theory and Integrating Practice,* Cambridge University Press, Cambridge.
A collection of papers on the details of measuring performance objectives.

Pine, B.J. (1993) *Mass Customization,* Harvard Business School Press, Boston, MA.
The first substantial work on the idea of mass customization. Still a classic.

Savitz, A.W. and Weber, K. (2006) *The Triple Bottom Line: How Today's Best-Run Companies Are Achieving Economic, Social and Environmental Success – and How You Can Too,* Jossey-Bass, San Francisco.
Good on the triple bottom line.

Waddock, S. (2003) Stakeholder performance implications of corporate responsibility, *International Journal of Business Performance Management,* vol. 5, nos 2–3, 114–124.
An introduction to stakeholder analysis.

3

Operations strategy

INTRODUCTION

In the long term, the major (and some would argue, only) objective of operations is to provide the organization with some form of strategic advantage. That is the reason why the management of processes, operations and supply networks must be aligned with overall strategy. While it will always be necessary to make adjustments to accommodate circumstances, simply reacting to current, possibly short-term, issues can lead to constant changes in direction and the operation becoming volatile and unstable. That is why all organizations need the 'backdrop' of a well-understood strategic direction, so they know (at least, roughly) where they are heading and how they could get there. Once the operations function has understood its role in the business and after it has articulated its performance objectives, it needs to formulate a set of general principles that will guide its decision-making. This is the operations strategy of the company. Many *enduringly* remarkable enterprises, from Apple to Zara, use their operations resources to gain long-term strategic success. Such firms have found that it is the way they manage their operations that sets them apart from their competitors. Yet, the concept of 'strategy' itself is not straightforward and neither is operations strategy. This chapter considers four perspectives, each of which goes partway to illustrating the forces that shape operations strategy. It then examines how these perspectives can be reconciled and how the *process* of operations strategy can be organized effectively. Figure 3.1 shows the position of the ideas described in this chapter in the general model of operations management.

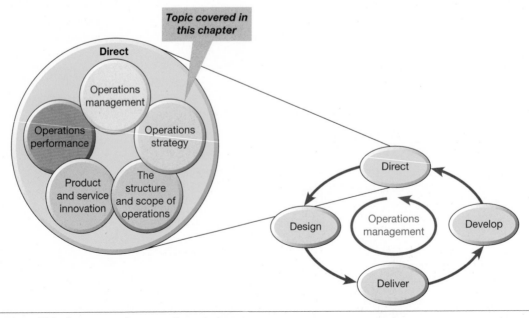

Figure 3.1 This chapter examines operations strategy

Dow Corning's operations strategy[1]

For years, Dow Corning was a silicon business with a market position built on service and technical excellence. Customers had been willing to pay top prices for pioneering technology, premium products and customized service. Yet, as the market matured it became clear that some customers were becoming increasingly price sensitive. The premium price strategy was under attack both from large competitors that had driven down costs and from smaller competitors, with lower overheads. Dow Corning was 'stuck in the middle'. In response, Dow Corning decided to undertake detailed analysis of its market and segment customers based on the key factors motivating them to make purchases. Its work revealed four key groups of customers:

▶ *Innovative solution seekers* – customers who wanted innovative silicone-based products.
▶ *Proven solution seekers* – customers needing advice on existing proven products.
▶ *Cost-effective solution seekers* – customers who may even pay premium prices for a product, if it could take costs out of their business by improving their productivity.
▶ *Price seekers* – experienced purchasers of commonly used silicone materials wanting low prices and an easy way of doing business with their supplier.

Each of these segments held a distinct message for Dow Corning's operations. For *innovative solution seekers,* there was a need to collaborate more closely with customers' R&D personnel in order to develop new products. To target *proven solution seekers,* the operations function took a more internal approach, working closely with the Dow Corning sales team. The aim was to help them understand its product range in more detail to improve conversion in the sales process. For *cost-effective solution seekers,* the focus was once again on working closely with the sales staff, but in this case the knowledge transfer was more bi-directional. The key was to build a stronger understanding of customers' processes and help better match their requirements with appropriate offerings. Finally, for the *price seeker* segment the focus was firmly on bringing down the costs of manufacturing and delivery. This last group was the most challenging for Dow Corning. Its sales to this segment were small and declining, but the segment represented around 30 per cent of the total market for silicones and was expected to grow significantly. Dow Corning's solution? Create a new offering, called Xiameter. This was a 'no-frills', low-price, restricted-range, minimum-order-quantity service, without any technical advice, that could only be accessed on the web (drastically cutting the costs of selling). Delivery times were sufficiently long to fit individual orders into the operation's existing manufacturing schedule.

The development of the Xiameter offering provides a good example of the sequence that organizations can follow in seeking to align the requirements of the market with the capabilities of its operations. The sequence looks something like this:

▶ *Segment the market:* This allowed Dow Corning to identify the differing requirements of different customer groups.
▶ *Assess current performance:* Dow Corning reviewed its performance for *each market segment* before making any decisions about how it might change direction.
▶ *Decide which segments to serve:* Dow Corning decided that, while it was weak in the price seeker segment, it was worth pursuing ways in which it might compete.
▶ *Determine what is necessary for the business to compete:* For price seekers, Dow Corning would need to supply at low cost, and abandon its technical advice service, because most customers in this segment were not willing to pay for it.
▶ *Determine what operations has to do:* For Xiameter to be successful, it would need to emphasize its 'no frills' service (hence the new Xiameter brand), and reduce excess sales overheads (hence web-based sales). Most critically, for this high-volume, low-variety operation to work, customers would need to be prevented from asking for anything that would increase costs (hence limited product range, minimum order quantities and delivery times that do not disrupt production schedules).

What is strategy and what is operations strategy?

Surprisingly, 'strategy' is not particularly easy to define. Linguistically the word derives from the Greek word '*strategos*' meaning 'leading an army'. And although there is no direct historical link between Greek military practice and modern ideas of strategy, the military metaphor is powerful. Both military and business strategy can be described in similar ways, and include some of the following:

▶ Setting broad objectives that direct an enterprise towards its overall goal.
▶ Planning the path (in general rather than specific terms) that will achieve these goals.
▶ Stressing long-term rather than short-term objectives.
▶ Dealing with the total picture rather than stressing individual activities.
▶ Being detached from, and above, the confusion and distractions of day-to-day activities.

From this perspective, strategic decisions are those that are widespread in their effect on the organization, define the position of the organization relative to its environment, and move the organization closer to its long-term goals. But 'strategy' is more than a single decision; it is the *total pattern of the decisions* and actions that influence the long-term direction of the business. Thinking about strategy in this way helps us to discuss an organization's strategy even when it has not been explicitly stated. Observing the total pattern of decisions gives an indication of the *actual* strategic behaviour.

These points relating to *strategy* apply equally to *operations strategy*. Operations strategy is defined as the 'pattern of decisions and actions that shape the long-term vision, objectives and capabilities of the operation and its contribution to the overall strategy of the business'.[2] At first, the term 'operations strategy' sounds like a contradiction. How can 'operations', a subject that is generally concerned with the day-to-day creation and delivery of products and services, be strategic? 'Strategy' is usually regarded as the opposite of those day-to-day routine activities. But, as we have indicated previously, '*operations*' is not the same as '*operational*'. 'Operations' are the resources that create products and services, and it is clear that they can have a real strategic impact. 'Operational' is the opposite of strategic, meaning day-to-day, detailed and often localized. So, one can examine both the operational *and* the strategic aspects of operations. It is also conventional to distinguish between the 'content' and the 'process' of operations strategy. The *content* of operations strategy is the specific decisions and actions that set the operations role, objectives and activities. The *process* of operations strategy is the method that is used to make the specific 'content' decisions.

> ✅ **Operations principle**
> Operations is not the same as operational; it does have a strategic role.

Using operations strategy to articulate a vision for the contribution of operations

Most businesses expect their operations strategy to improve operations performance over time. In doing this, operations should be progressing from a state where they contribute very little to the competitive success of the business through to the point where they are directly responsible for its competitive success. The 'vision' of an operation is a clear statement of how operations intend to contribute value for the business. It is not a statement of what the operation wants to *achieve* (those are its objectives), but rather an idea of what it must *become* and what contribution it should make. A common approach to summarizing operations contribution is the seminal Hayes and Wheelwright four-stage model.[3] The model traces the progression of the operations function from what is the largely negative role in 'stage 1' operations to a position where it is the central element of competitive strategy in 'stage 4'. Figure 3.2 illustrates the four steps involved in moving from stage 1 to stage 4.

> ✅ **Operations principle**
> Operations strategy should articulate a 'vision' for the operations function's contribution to overall strategy.

Stage 1: Internal neutrality

This is the very poorest level of contribution by the operations function and the effect is to harm the organization's ability to compete effectively. In stage 1, the operations function is inward-looking and, at best, reactive with very little positive to contribute towards competitive success. Its vision is

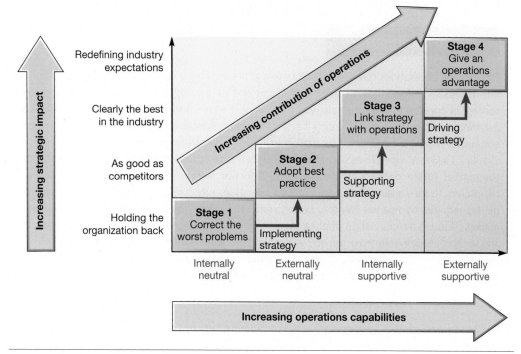

Figure 3.2 Hayes and Wheelwright's four-stage model of operations contribution sees operations as moving from implementation of strategy, through to supporting strategy, and finally to driving strategy

to be 'internally neutral', so as to stop holding the organization back in any way. It attempts to achieve this by 'avoiding making mistakes'.

Stage 2: External neutrality

The first step of breaking out of stage 1 is for the operations function to begin comparing itself with similar companies or organizations in the outside market. This may not immediately take it to the 'first division' of companies in the market, but at least it is measuring itself against its competitors' performance and trying to implement 'best practice'. In stage 2, the vision of the operations function is to become 'externally neutral' with operations in the industry.

Stage 3: Internally supportive

Stage 3 operations have typically reached the 'first division' of their markets. For such operations, the vision becomes to be clearly and unambiguously the very best in the market. They achieve this by gaining a clear view of the company's competitive or strategic goals and supporting it by developing appropriate operations resources. The operation is trying to be 'internally supportive' by providing a credible operations strategy.

Stage 4: Externally supportive

Stage 3 used to be viewed as the limit of the operations function's contribution. Yet the model captures the growing importance of operations management by suggesting a further stage. The difference between stages 3 and 4 is subtle, but important. A stage 4 operations function is one that is providing *the* foundation for an organization's competitive success. It is forecasting likely changes in markets and supply, and it is developing the operations-based capabilities which will be required to compete in future market conditions. Stage 4 operations are innovative, creative and proactive and are driving the company's strategy by being 'one step ahead' of competitors – what Hayes and Wheelwright call being 'externally supportive'.

The four perspectives on operations strategy

Different authors have slightly differing views and definitions of operations strategy. However, between them, four 'perspectives' emerge as shown in Figure 3.3.[4]

The idea that operations can have a leading role in determining a company's strategic direction is not universally accepted. Both stage 4 of Hayes and Wheelwright's four-stage model and the concept of operations 'driving' strategy not only imply that it is possible for operations to take such a leading role, but are explicit in seeing it as a 'good thing'. A more traditional stance taken by some authorities is that the needs of the market will always be pre-eminent in shaping a company's strategy. Therefore, operations should devote all their time to understanding the requirements of the market (often defined by the marketing function within the organization) and devote themselves to their main job of ensuring that operations processes can actually deliver what the market requires. Companies can only be successful, they argue, by positioning themselves in the market (through a combination of price, promotion, product design and managing how products and services are delivered to customers) with operations very much in a 'supporting' role. In effect, they say, Hayes and Wheelwright's model should stop at stage 3. The issue of an 'operations resource' perspective on operations strategy is discussed later in the chapter.

▶ Operation strategy should align with what the whole group or business wants – sometimes called the 'top-down' perspective.
▶ Operations strategy should translate the enterprise's intended market position so as to provide the required objectives for operations decisions – sometimes called the 'outside-in' perspective.
▶ Operations strategy should learn from day-to-day activities so as to cumulatively build strategic capabilities – sometimes called the 'bottom-up' perspective.
▶ Operations strategy should develop the business's resources and processes so that its capabilities can be exploited in its chosen markets – sometimes called the 'inside-out' perspective.

None of these four perspectives alone gives a comprehensive picture, but together they provide some idea of the pressures that go into forming the content of an operations strategy. In the next four sections of this chapter, we will treat each perspective in turn, before examining how these can be reconciled effectively.

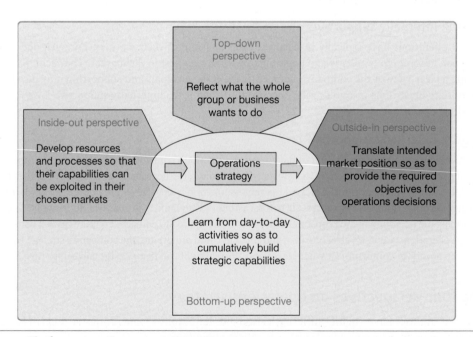

Figure 3.3 The four perspectives on operations strategy

Changing the economics of space exploration[5]

You don't think of space satellites as cheap items; and of course, they aren't. They are usually extremely expensive. In the early days of space missions, this meant that only superpowers could afford to develop and launch them. The conventional wisdom was that space was such a hostile environment that satellites would have to be constructed using only specially developed components that could endure the severe conditions encountered in space. Yet in the late 1970s this assumption was challenged by Sir Martin Sweeting, who then was studying for his PhD at the University of Surrey in the UK. The aerospace research team in the Electrical Engineering Department had built its first satellite (called UoSAT-1) using commercial off-the-shelf components. It was about as big as two microwave ovens, weighing in at 72 kg. By contrast, some of the huge satellites being launched by government space agencies were as large as a London double-decker bus. It was launched in 1981 with the help of NASA, which had been persuaded to provide a free launch, piggybacking on a mission to put a large scientific satellite into orbit. The team followed this up with a second satellite (UoSAT-2) that they built in just six months and launched in 1984. A year later Surrey Satellite Technology Limited (SSTL) was formed as a spin-out company from the university to transfer the results of its research into a commercial enterprise. The firm's vision was to open up the market for space exploration by pioneering the use of small and relatively cheap, but reliable, satellites built from readily available off-the-shelf components, at the time a revolutionary idea. Now, SSLT is the world's leading small satellite company. Its 500 staff have launched over 40 satellites.

It achieved this success partly because it was an early player in the market, having the vision to see that there would be a market for small satellites. However, in addition, it developed an operations strategy that was innovative in finding ways of keeping the cost of building the satellites down to a minimum. SSTL pioneered the low-cost, low-risk approach to delivering operational satellite missions within short development timescales and with the capability that potential customers wanted. In the early 1980s, Sir Martin Sweeting speculated that it would be possible to use programmable technology to build small satellites that were 'intelligent' when compared with conventional large and expensive hard-wired satellites. This allowed the satellite to be reprogrammed from the ground. Particularly important was the company's use of commercial off-the-shelf technology. It enabled SSTL to keep costs as low as realistically possible by, in effect, exploiting the, often enormous, investments by consumer-electronics companies and others who had developed the complex components for their products. Even if this sometimes limited what a satellite could do, it provided the scale economies that would be impossible if they were designing and making customized components from scratch. 'We were being parasitic, if you like,' admitted Sir Martin.

However, not all commercially available components made for terrestrial use were up to coping with conditions in space. Reliability is essential in a satellite. Even though off-the-shelf components and systems became increasing reliable, they were rigorously tested to make sure that they were up to the severe conditions found in space. Knowing which components can be used and which cannot is an important piece of knowledge. Yet, although individual components and systems are often bought off-the-shelf, the company does most of its operations activities itself. This allows SSTL to provide a complete in-house design, manufacture, launch and operation service as well as a range of advice, analysis and consultancy services. 'What distinguishes us is our vertically integrated capability, from design and research to manufacturing and operations,' says Sir Martin. 'We don't have to rely on suppliers, although of course we buy in components when that is advantageous.'

How does operations strategy align with business strategy (top-down)?

A top-down perspective often identifies three related levels of strategy – corporate, business and functional.

▶ A *corporate strategy* should position the corporation in its global, economic, political and social environment. This will consist of decisions about what types of business the group wants to be in, what parts of the world it wants to operate in, how to allocate its cash between its various businesses, and so on.

▶ Each business unit within the corporate group will also need to put together its own *business strategy*, which sets out its individual mission and objectives. This business strategy guides the business in relation to its customers, markets and competitors, and also the strategy of the corporate group of which it is a part.

▶ The operations, marketing, product/service development and other functions will then need to consider how best they should organize themselves to support the business's objectives. These *functional strategies* need to consider what part each function should play in contributing to the strategic objectives of the business.

So, the 'top-down' perspective on operations strategy is that it should take its place in this 'hierarchy of strategies'. As such, the role of operations is largely one of implementing or 'operationalizing' higher-level strategy. For example, a Printing Services Group has a company that prints packaging for consumer products. The group's management figures that, in the long term, only companies with significant market share will achieve substantial profitability. Its corporate objectives therefore stress market dominance. The consumer packaging company decides to achieve volume growth, even above short-term profitability or return on investment. The implication for operations strategy is that it needs to expand rapidly, investing in extra capacity (factories, equipment and labour) even if it means excess capacity in some areas. It also needs to establish new factories in all parts of its market to offer relatively fast delivery. The important point here is that different business objectives would probably result in a very different operations strategy. Figure 3.4 illustrates this strategic hierarchy, with some of the decisions at each level and the main influences on the strategic decisions.

> **Operations principle**
>
> Operations strategies should reflect top-down corporate and/or business objectives.

Although this rather neat relationship between the levels of corporate, business and operations strategy may seem a little 'theoretical', it is still a powerful idea. What it is saying is that in order to understand strategy at any level, one has to place it in the context of what it is trying to do (the level above) and how it is trying to do it (the level below). At any level, a good top-down perspective should provide clarity and connection. It should clarify what an operations strategy should be prioritizing, and give some guidance on the strategy to be achieved.

Correspondence and coherence

Developing a functional strategy from a business strategy is not always straightforward. There are ambiguities to clarify and conflicts to be reconciled. Inevitably, business strategy consists of aggregated and approximate objectives. It cannot spell out every detail of how a function should interpret its objectives. Yet there should be a clear, explicit and logical connection between each functional strategy and the business strategy. Moreover, there should also be a clear, explicit and logical connection between a functional strategy and the decisions taken *within* the function. In other words, there should be *correspondence* between different levels of strategy. But *correspondence* is not all that is required. Operations strategy must also be *coherent*, both with other functional strategies and within itself. Coherence means that the choices that are made across or within functions should not pull it in different directions. All decisions should complement and reinforce each other in the promotion of the business's and the operation's objectives. Figure 3.5 illustrates these two ideas of correspondence and coherence.[6]

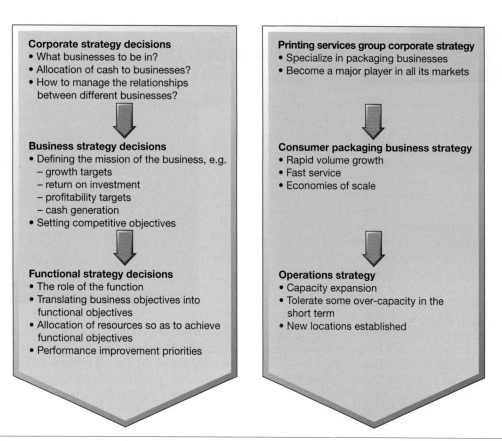

Corporate strategy decisions
- What businesses to be in?
- Allocation of cash to businesses?
- How to manage the relationships between different businesses?

Business strategy decisions
- Defining the mission of the business, e.g.
  - growth targets
  - return on investment
  - profitability targets
  - cash generation
- Setting competitive objectives

Functional strategy decisions
- The role of the function
- Translating business objectives into functional objectives
- Allocation of resources so as to achieve functional objectives
- Performance improvement priorities

Printing services group corporate strategy
- Specialize in packaging businesses
- Become a major player in all its markets

Consumer packaging business strategy
- Rapid volume growth
- Fast service
- Economies of scale

Operations strategy
- Capacity expansion
- Tolerate some over-capacity in the short term
- New locations established

Figure 3.4 The top-down perspective of operations strategy and its application to the Printing Services Group

The concepts of the 'business model' and the 'operating model'

Two concepts have emerged over the last few years that are useful in understanding the top-down perspective on operations strategy – the 'business model' and the 'operating model'. The relationship between these two concepts is shown in Figure 3.6.

A *business model* is the plan that is implemented by a company to generate revenue and make a profit (or fulfil its social objectives if a not-for-profit enterprise). It includes the various parts and organizational functions of the business, as well as the revenues it generates and the expenses it incurs. In other words, what a company does and how it makes money from doing it. It often includes such elements a:[7] the *value proposition* of what is offered to the market, the *target customer segments* addressed by the value proposition, the *distribution channels* to reach customers, the *core capabilities* needed to make the business model possible and the *revenue streams* generated by the business model. The idea of the business model is broadly analogous to the idea of a 'business strategy', but implies more of an emphasis on *how* to achieve an intended strategy as well as exactly *what* that strategy should be.

In contrast, the concept of an *operating model* is more operational in nature and there is no universally agreed definition. Here, we define it as a 'high-level design of the organization that defines the structure and style which enables it to meet its business objectives'.[8] Ideally, an operating model should provide a clear, 'big picture' description of what the organization does and how it does it. It defines how the critical work of an organization is carried out. It should provide a way to examine the business in terms of the key relationships between business functions, processes and structures that are required for the organization to fulfil its mission. It can include such elements as: key performance indicators (KPIs), with an indication of the relative importance of performance objectives, new investments and intended cash flows; who is responsible for products, geographies, assets, specific processes, systems and technologies etc; and the structure of the organization.

Note that an operating model reflects the idea that we proposed in Chapter 1 – that all managers are operations managers and all functions can be considered as operations because they comprise

Innovation at Micraytech[9] (Part 1, top-down)

Micraytech is a metrology systems company that develops integrated measurement systems for large international clients in several industries, and is part of the Micray Group that includes several high-tech companies. It has grown through a strategy of providing products with a high degree of technical excellence and innovation together with an ability to customize its systems and offer technical advice to its clients. The Group has set ambitious growth targets for the company over the next five years and has relaxed its normal 'return on sales' targets to help it achieve this. As part of this strategy, Micraytech attempted to be the first in the market with all appropriate new technical innovations. From a top-down perspective, its operations function, therefore, needed to be capable of coping with the changes which constant product innovation would bring. It developed processes that were flexible enough to develop and assemble novel components and systems while integrating them with software innovations.

The company's operations function realized that they needed to organize and train their staff to understand the way technology is developing so that they could put in place the necessary changes to the operation. It also needed to develop relationships with both existing and potentially new suppliers who could respond quickly when supplying new components. So, the top-down logic here is that everything about the operation – its processes, staff, systems and procedures – must, in the short term, do nothing to inhibit and, in the long term, actively develop the company's competitive strategy of growth through innovation.

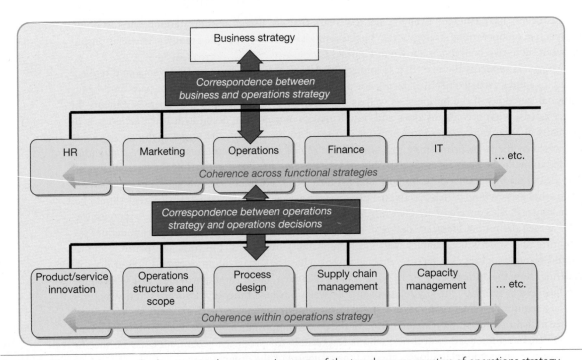

Figure 3.5 Correspondence and coherence are the two requirements of the top-down perspective of operations strategy

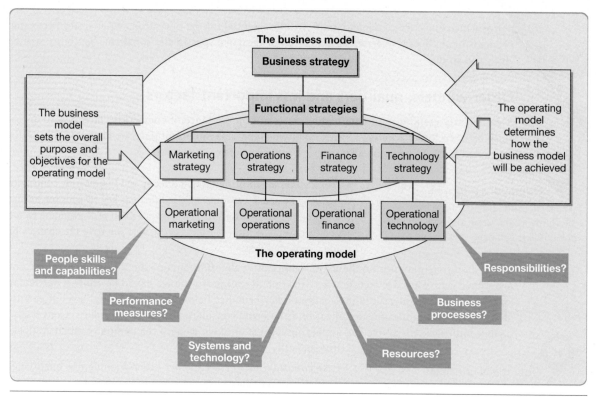

Figure 3.6 The concepts of the 'business model' and the 'operating model' overlap – with the operating model indicating how processes, resources, technology, people, measures and responsibilities are to be organized to support the business model

processes that deliver some kind of service. An operating model is like an operations strategy, but applied across all functions and domains of the organization. Also, there are clear overlaps between the 'business model' and the 'operating model', although an operating model focuses more on how an overall business strategy is to be achieved.

How does operations strategy align with market requirements (outside-in)?

Any operations strategy should reflect the intended market position of the business. No operation that continually fails to serve its markets adequately is likely to survive in the long term. Organizations compete in different ways, so the operations function should therefore respond by providing the ability to perform in a manner that is appropriate for the intended market position. This is called a market (or outside-in) perspective on operations strategy.

How market requirements influence operations strategy performance objectives

Operations adds value for customers and contributes to competitiveness by being able to satisfy the requirements of its customers. The most useful way to do this is to ensure that operations is achieving the right priority between its 'operational' performance objectives, discussed in the previous chapter – quality, speed, dependability, flexibility and cost. Whatever competitive factors are important to customers should influence the priority of each performance objective. For example, a customer emphasis on fast delivery will make speed important to the operation. When it is important that products or services are delivered exactly when they are promised, the performance objective of dependability will be essential for the operation. When customers value products or services that have been adapted or designed specifically for them, flexibility will be vital, and so on.

Order winners, qualifiers and less important factors

A particularly useful way of determining the relative importance of competitive factors is to distinguish between 'order winning', 'order qualifying' and 'less important' factors. Figure 3.7 illustrates their relative effects on competitiveness (or attractiveness to customers).

> **Operations principle**
>
> The relative importance of the five performance objectives depends on how the business competes in its market.

Order winners are those things that directly and significantly contribute to winning business. Customers regard them as key reasons for buying the product or service. Raising performance in an order-winning factor will either result in more business or at least improve the chances of gaining more business.

Order qualifiers may not be the major competitive determinants of success, but are important in another way. They are factors where the operation's performance has to be above a particular level just to be considered by the customer. Performance below this 'qualifying' level of performance often disqualifies the organization from being considered by many customers. Conversely, further improvement above the qualifying level is unlikely to gain the company much competitive benefit.

> **Operations principle**
>
> Competitive factors can be classified as 'order winners', 'qualifiers' or 'less important'.

Less important factors are neither order winning nor qualifying. They do not influence customers in any significant way. They are worth including in any analysis only because they may be of importance in other parts of the operation's activities.

The impact of product/service differentiation on market requirements

If, as is likely, an operation differentiates its services based on different customer segments, it will need to determine the performance objective for each segment. For example, Table 3.1 shows two customer segments in the banking industry. Here the distinction is drawn between the customers who are looking for banking services for their private and domestic needs (current accounts, overdraft facilities, savings accounts, mortgage loans, etc.) and those corporate customers who need banking services for their (often large) organizations. These latter services would include such things as letters of credit, cash transfer services and commercial loans.

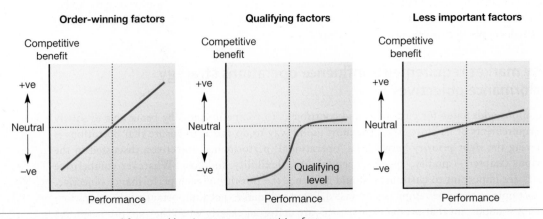

Figure 3.7 Order-winning, qualifying and less important competitive factors

Table 3.1 Different banking services require different performance objectives

	Retail banking	Corporate banking
Products	Personal financial services such as loans and credit cards	Special services for corporate customers
Customers	Individuals	Businesses
Range of services offered	Medium but standardized, little need for special terms	Very wide range, many need to be customized
Changes to service design	Occasional	Continual
Delivery	Fast decisions	Dependable service
Quality	Means error-free transactions	Means close relationships
Volume per service type	Most services are high volume	Most services are low volume
Profit margins	Most are low to medium, some high	Medium to high
Competitive factors		
Order winners	Price	Customization
	Accessibility	Quality of service
	Ease of transaction	Reliability/trust
Qualifiers	Quality	Ease of transaction
	Range	Price
Less important		Accessibility
Internal performance objectives	Cost	Flexibility
	Speed	Quality
	Quality	Dependability

The impact of product/service life cycle on market requirements

One way of generalizing the behaviour of both customers and competitors is to link it to the life cycle of the products or services that the operation is producing. The exact form of product/service life cycles will vary, but generally they are shown as the sales volume passing through four stages – introduction, growth, maturity and decline. The implication of this for operations management is that products and services will require different operations strategies in each stage of their life cycle, as shown in Figure 3.8.

Introduction stage

When a product or service is first introduced, it is likely to be offering something new in terms of its design or performance, with few competitors offering the same thing. The needs of customers are unlikely to be well understood, so operations management needs to develop the flexibility to cope with any changes and be able to give the quality to maintain product/service performance.

Growth stage

As volume grows, competitors may enter the growing market. Keeping up with demand could prove to be the main operations preoccupation. Rapid and dependable response to demand will help to keep demand buoyant, while maintaining quality levels can ensure that the company keeps its share of the market as competition starts to increase.

Innovation at Micraytech (Part 2, outside-in)

The Micray Group saw a major growth opportunity for Micraytech by continually incorporating technological innovations in its product offerings. However, Micraytech's Marketing management knew that this could be achieved by focusing on one or both of two distinct markets. The first is the market for 'individual metrology devices'. These are 'stand-alone' pieces of equipment bought by all types of industrial customers and had traditionally been the company's main market. The second market was for 'integrated metrology systems'. These were larger, more complex, more expensive (and higher margin) offerings that were customized to individual customers' requirements. The two types of offering had overlapping, but different characteristics. 'Individual metrology devices' competed on their technical performance and reliability, together with relatively short delivery times compared with competitors. The 'integrated metrology systems' offerings currently accounted for only a small part of the company's sales, but it was a market that was forecast to grow substantially. The customers for these systems were larger manufacturers that were investing in more automated

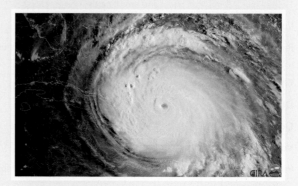

technologies and required metrology systems that could be integrated into their processes. From an 'outside-in' perspective, if it was to take advantage of this emerging market, Micraytech would have to learn how to work more closely with both its direct customers and the firms that were supplying its customers with the automated technologies. In addition to Micraytech's traditional technical skills, it would have to increase its software development, data exchange and client liaison skills.

Sales volume	Introduction into market	Growth in market acceptance	Maturity of market, sales level off	Decline as market becomes saturated
Customers	Innovators	Early adopters	Bulk of market	Laggards
Competitors	Few/none	Increasing numbers	Stable numbers	Declining numbers
Likely order winners	Product/service specification	Availability	Low price Dependable supply	Low price
Likely qualifiers	Quality Range	Price Range	Range Quality	Dependable supply
Dominant operations performance objectives	Flexibility Quality	Speed Dependability Quality	Cost Dependability	Cost

Figure 3.8 The effects of the product/service life cycle on operations performance objectives

Maturity stage

As demand starts to level off, some early competitors may have left the market and the industry may be dominated by a few larger companies. So, operations will be expected to get the costs down in order to maintain profits or to allow price cutting. Because of this, cost and productivity issues, together with dependable supply, are likely to be the operation's main concerns.

Decline stage

After time, sales will decline with more competitors dropping out of the market. There might be a residual market, but unless a shortage of capacity develops, the market will continue to be dominated by price competition. So, operations objectives continue to be dominated by cost.

> **Operations principle**
>
> Operations strategy objectives will change depending on the stage of the business's services and products.

OPERATIONS IN PRACTICE

Tesco learns the hard way[10]

When market conditions change, it usually means that operations strategy should change. But it can take time before changes become obvious, and even longer to react. This was a lesson that Tesco, the UK's biggest, and one of its most successful, retailers learned, when, by 2014, it had slumped to a £6.4bn loss. Although it was still comfortably the market leader in grocery sales, its lead over rivals had worsened. Like-for-like sales (sales in its stores and online, while removing the effect of new stores opening) were down nearly 4 per cent; significant in the retail world. Tesco had not seen numbers this bad for 20 years. Why, asked its detractors, had the company not realized that its strategy was failing? One critic described Tesco as being 'like a juggernaut with a puncture and a worrying rattle in the engine'. Some of Tesco's problems at this time were beyond its control and a result of competitor activity. Waitrose (an up-market supermarket, with a good reputation for quality) was serving the top end of the market, while German discount stores Aldi and Lidl were attracting more cost-conscious customers. However, some problems were of Tesco's own making, caused by its operations strategy failing to respond fast enough to market requirements. The strategy of building large, out-of-town superstores was continued, even though a sharper monitoring of consumer behaviour would have revealed that such large-capacity units had lost their attraction as families cut down on weekly trips to the supermarket and opted instead for home deliveries, and topping up their groceries with trips to local stores. In fact, Philip Clarke, then Tesco's chief executive, admitted that he ought to have moved faster to cut back on planned superstore openings in response to clear radical

changes in shopping habits. *'Hindsight is a wonderful thing. It's never really there when you need it'*, said Mr Clarke. *'I probably should have stopped more quickly that* [superstore] *expansion, I probably should have made the reallocation* [to small, local stores] *faster'*.

This episode in Tesco's (largely successful) history provided important lessons. Making significant changes in operations strategy can be extremely disruptive and costly in the short run, but necessary in the long run, even when the long-term consequences of a major change are unknowable (although better demand forecasting, can help – see Chapter 11). Understandable then that in the face of such uncertainty, organizations, especially those with large inflexible investments, often delay change. However, having made major changes in its corporate, business and functional strategies, Tesco did recover in terms of like-for-like sales.

How does operations strategy align with operational experience (bottom-up)?

The 'top-down' perspective provides an orthodox view of how functional strategies *should* be formulated. However, while it is a convenient way of thinking about strategy, it does not represent the way strategies *are* formulated in most cases. When any group is reviewing its corporate strategy, it will take into account the circumstances, experiences and capabilities of the various businesses that form the group. Similarly, when reviewing their strategies, organizations will consult the individual functions about their capabilities and constraints and incorporate the ideas that come from each function's day-to-day experience. This is the *bottom-up* perspective, illustrated in Figure 3.9.

The bottom-up perspective accounts for the fact that in many cases organizations move in a particular strategic direction because their on-going experience at an operational level convinces them that it is the right thing to do. The 'high level' strategic decision making, if it occurs at all, may simply confirm the general consensus around a given strategic direction and provide the resources to make it happen effectively. This is sometimes called the concept of 'emergent strategies'.[11] It sees strategy making, at least partly, as a relatively unstructured and fragmented process to reflect the fact that the future is at least partially unknown and unpredictable.

> **Operations principle**
>
> Operations strategy should reflect bottom-up experience of operational reality.

For example, suppose the printing services company described previously succeeds in its expansion plans. However, in doing so it finds that having surplus capacity and a distributed network of factories allows it to offer an exceptionally fast service to customers. It also finds that some customers are willing to pay considerably higher prices for such a responsive service. Its experiences lead the company to set up a separate division dedicated to providing fast, high-margin printing services to those customers willing to pay. The strategic objectives of this new division are not concerned with high-volume growth but with high profitability.

The reinforcing effect of top-down and bottom-up perspectives on operations strategy

The top-down and bottom-up perspectives are often seen as being diametrically opposite ways of looking at operations strategy, but they are not. In fact, the two perspectives can be mutually reinforcing.

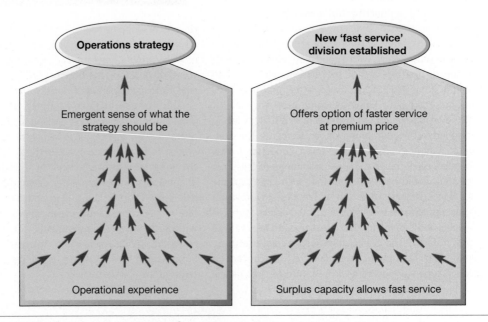

Figure 3.9 The 'bottom-up' perspective of operations strategy

Innovation at Micraytech (Part 3, bottom-up)

Over time, as its operations strategy developed, Micraytech discovered that continual product and system innovation was having the effect of dramatically increasing its costs. Although it was not competing on low prices, and nor was it under pressure from the Group to achieved high rates of return on sales, its rising costs were impacting profitability to an unacceptable degree. In addition, there was some evidence that continual updating of product and system specifications was confusing some customers. Partially in response to customer requests, the company's system designers started to work out a way of 'modularizing' their system and product designs. This allowed one part of the system to be updated for those customers who valued the functionality that the innovation could bring, without interfering with the overall design of the main body of the system of which the module was a part. Over time, this approach became standard design practice within the company. Customers appreciated the extra customization, and modularization reduced operations costs. Note that this strategy emerged from the company's experience and

was therefore an example of a pure 'bottom-up' approach. Initially, no top-level board decision was taken to initiate this practice. Nevertheless, it emerged as the way in which the company's design engineers learned from their experience and used that learning to build their knowledge of how to lower some of the costs of innovation.

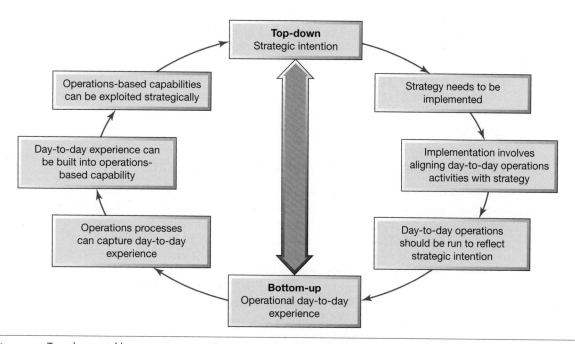

Figure 3.10 Top-down and bottom-up perspectives on operations strategy can reinforce each other

Figure 3.10 shows how this can work. The top-down perspective sets the overall direction and objectives for operations decisions and activities. In order to implement top-down strategy, the day-to-day activities of the operation must be aligned with the strategy. So, a way of judging operational day-to-day activities of an operation is to check that they fully reflect the overall top-down strategy of the organization. But, as we have illustrated earlier, the experience gained from day-to-day activities can be accumulated and built into capabilities that an organization could possibly exploit strategically. (We will expand this idea of 'capabilities' in the next section.)

How does operations strategy align with operations resources (inside-out)?

The final perspective of operations strategy is the operations resources (or 'inside-out') perspective. Its fundamental idea is that long-term competitive advantage can come from the capabilities of the operation's resources and processes, and these should be developed over the long term to provide the business with a set of capabilities or competences (we use the two words interchangeably).[12] So, the way an organization inherits, acquires or develops its operations resources will, over the long term, have a significant impact on its strategic success. They can form the basis of the businesse's ability to engage in unique and/or 'difficult to imitate' activities. Furthermore, the impact of an organization's 'operations resource' capabilities will be at least as great as, if not greater than, that which it gets from its market position. So, understanding and developing the capabilities of operations resources, although often neglected, is a particularly important perspective on operations strategy.

> **Operations principle**
>
> The long-term objective of operations strategy is to build operations-based capabilities.

Strategic resources and sustainable competitive advantage

The idea that building operations capabilities is a particularly important objective of operations strategy is closely linked with the 'resource-based view' (RBV) of the firm.[13] This holds that organizations with 'above-average' strategic performance are likely to have gained their sustainable competitive advantage because of their core competences (or capabilities). This means that the way an organization inherits, or acquires, or develops its operations resources will, over the long term, have a significant impact on its strategic success. The RBV differs in its approach from the more traditional view of strategy that sees companies as seeking to protect their competitive advantage through their control of the market. For example, they may do this by creating *barriers to entry* through product differentiation, or making it difficult for customers to switch to competitors, or controlling the access to distribution channels (a major barrier to entry in gasoline retailing, for example, where oil companies own their own retail stations). By contrast, the RBV sees firms being able to protect their competitive advantage through *barriers to imitation*: that is, by building up 'difficult-to-imitate' resources.

Understanding existing capabilities and constraints

An operations resource perspective must start with an understanding of the resource capabilities and constraints within the operation. It must answer the simple questions: what do we have and what can we do? An obvious starting point here is to examine the transforming and transformed resource inputs to the operation. However, trying to understand an operation by listing its resources alone is like trying to understand an automobile by listing its component parts. To understand the automobile, we need to describe how the component parts form its internal mechanisms. Within the operation, the equivalents of these mechanisms are its *processes*. Yet, even a technical explanation of the mechanisms does not convey its style or 'personality'. Something more is needed to describe these. In the same way, an operation is not just the sum of its processes; it also has *intangible* resources. An operation's intangible resources include such things as:

► its relationship with suppliers and the reputation it has with its customers;
► its knowledge of and experience in handling its process technologies;
► the way its staff can work together in new product and service development;
► the way it integrates all its processes into a mutually supporting whole.

These intangible resources may not be as evident within an operation, but they are important and often have real value. And both tangible and intangible resources and processes shape its capabilities.

The central issue for operations management, therefore, is to ensure that its pattern of strategic decisions really does develop appropriate capabilities.

Developing operations strategy from a resource-based perspective isn't just about understanding capabilities, it also requires the identification of *constraints*. No organization can merely choose which part of the market it wants to be in without considering its ability to deliver services and products in a way that will satisfy that market. For example, a small translation company offers general translation services to a wide range of customers who wish documents such as sales brochures to be translated into another language. It operates an informal network of part-time translators who enable the company to offer translation into or from most of the major languages in the world. Some of the company's largest customers want to purchase their sales brochures on a 'one-stop shop' basis and have asked the translation company whether it is willing to offer a full service, organizing the design and production, as well as the translation, of export brochures. This is a very profitable market opportunity; however, the company does not have the resources, financial or physical, to take it up. From a market perspective, it is good business, but from an operations resource perspective, it is not feasible.

> **Operations principle**
>
> Resource-based thinking requires identification of both operations capabilities and constraints.

While the operations resource perspective may identify *constraints* to satisfying some markets, it can also identify *capabilities* that can be exploited in other markets. For example, the same translation company has recently employed two new translators who have translation software skills, so now the company can offer a new 'fast response' service which has been designed specifically to exploit the capabilities within its operations resources. Here, the company has chosen to be driven by its resource capabilities rather than the obvious market opportunities.

Strategic resources and sustainable competitive advantage

The 'resource-based' explanation of why some companies manage to gain sustainable competitive advantage is that they have accumulated better or more appropriate resources. Put simply, 'above average' competitive performance is more likely to be the result of the core capabilities (or competences) inherent in a firm's resources than its competitive positioning in its industry. And resources can have a particularly influential impact on strategic success if they exhibit some or all of the following properties.[14]

OPERATIONS IN PRACTICE — Amazon's operations capabilities

As a publicly stated ambitious target it takes some beating – *'Amazon.com strives to be the Earth's most customer-centric company'*. Founded by Jeff Bezos, the Amazon.com website started as a place to buy books, giving its customers what at the time was a unique customer experience. Its initial success was followed by continued growth, based on a clear strategy of technological innovation. It may not be glamorous, but Amazon focused on what have been called 'the dull-but-difficult tasks' such as tracking products, managing suppliers, storing inventory and delivering boxes. 'Fulfilment By Amazon' allows other companies to use Amazon's logistics capability, including the handling of returned items, and gives them access to Amazon's 'back-end' technology. But perhaps the most revealing insight into Amazon's ability to dominate its markets is illustrated by the success of Amazon Web Services (AWS).

AWS is Amazon's cloud computing business, providing cloud-based, on-demand computing power for small and

larger high-profile customers such as Spotify's digital music service and Netflix's video streaming service. AWS's large and efficient operations can be better value than smaller companies could achieve, which is why prominent retailers work with AWS to power their e-commerce offerings. Offering business-to-business services is also good for Amazon. The problem with online retailing, said Bezos, is its seasonality. To deal with peak times, such as Christmas, Amazon has far more computing capacity than it needs for the rest of the year. At low points, it may be using only a fraction of its total capacity. Hiring out that spare capacity is an obvious way to bring in extra revenue. However, Amazon soon realized that its experience of operating cloud computing services was, in itself, a capability upon which services could be sold. The important point is that AWS provides business-to-business services that can make its customers' operations ultra-efficient. And this is based on the company's core competence of leveraging its processes and technology. However, some observers immediately criticized Amazon's apparent redefinition of its strategy. *'Why not'*, they said, *'stick to what you know, focus on your core competence of internet retailing?'* Bezos's response was clear. *'We **are** sticking to our core competence. The only thing that's changed is that we are exposing it for (the benefit of) others'.* At least for Jeff Bezos, Amazon is not so much an internet retailer as a provider of internet-based technology and logistics services.

▶ *They are scarce* – Unequal access to resources, so that not all competing firms have scarce resources such as an ideal location, experienced engineers, proprietary software, etc., can strengthen competitive advantage. So, for example, if a firm did not have the good foresight (or luck) to acquire a strategic resource (such as a supply contract with a specialist supplier) when it was inexpensive, it will have to try and acquire it after it has become expensive (because other firms are also now wanting it).

▶ *They are not very mobile* – Some resources are difficult to move out of a firm. For example, if a new process is developed in a company's Stockholm site and is based on the knowledge and experience of the Stockholm staff, the process will be difficult (although not totally impossible) to sell to another company based elsewhere in Europe (or even Sweden if the staff do not want to move). As a result, the advantages that derive from the process's resources are more likely to be retained over time.

▶ *They are difficult to imitate or substitute for* – These two factors help define how easily a resource-based advantage can be sustained over time. It is not enough only to have resources which are unique and immobile. If a competitor can copy these resources or, less predictably, replace them with alternative resources, then their value will quickly deteriorate. However, the less tangible the resources are and the more connected with the tacit knowledge embedded within the organization, the more difficult they are for competitors to understand and to copy.

Structural and infrastructural decisions

A distinction is often drawn between the strategic decisions which determine an operation's structure and those which determine its infrastructure. An operation's structural decisions are those which we have classed as primarily influencing design activities, while infrastructural decisions are those which influence the workforce organization and the planning and control, and improvement activities. This distinction in operations strategy has been compared to that between 'hardware' and 'software' in computer systems. The hardware of a computer sets limits to what it can do. In a similar way, investing in advanced technology and building more or better facilities can raise the potential of any type of operation. Within the limits that are imposed by the hardware of a computer, the software governs how effective the computer actually is in practice. The same principle applies with operations. The best and most costly facilities and technology will only be effective if the operation also has an appropriate infrastructure which governs the way it will work on a day-to-day basis. Figure 3.11 illustrates some typical structural and infrastructural decisions.

> **Operations principle**
>
> The long-term objective of operation strategy is to build operations-based capabilities.

How are the four perspectives of operations strategy reconciled?

As we stressed earlier, none of the four perspectives alone can give a full picture of any organization's operations strategy. But together they do provide a good idea of how its operations are contributing strategically. Figure 3.12 shows how the four perspectives can be brought together, using the example

Innovation at Micraytech (Part 4, inside out)

The modular approach to product design (described in Part 3) proved to be a big success for Micraytech. However, it posed two challenges for the company's operations. First, the technical aspects of integrating some of the more sophisticated modules proved difficult. This only affected a small proportion of customers, but they were the ones that were willing to pay premium prices for their systems. The only potential solution was to attempt to develop the interface modules that would allow previously incompatible modules to be integrated. When this solution was first proposed the relevant skills were not present in the company. It had to recruit specialist engineers to start on the design of the interfaces. During this design process, the company realized that it could potentially open up a new market. As the firm's Chief Operating Officer (COO) put it, *'If we designed the interfaces carefully, we could not only integrate all of our own in-house modules, we could also integrate other firms' instruments into our systems.'* This led to the second set of challenges; to develop relationships with possible suppliers, who might very well be competitors in some markets, so that they were willing to supply their equipment for inclusion in Micraytech's systems. Not only this, but also the firm had to ensure that the internal processes of its sales engineers consulting with clients, its design department designing the system to meet clients' needs, and its procurement managers

negotiating with equipment suppliers, all operated seamlessly. *'The success that we have enjoyed can be put down to two key capabilities. The first was to buy in the engineering skills to create technically difficult interfaces. That led to us understanding the value that could be gained from a seamless internal and external supply chain. Both of these capabilities are not totally impossible for other firms to copy, but they would be very difficult for them to get to our level of excellence'* (COO, Micraytech). Here, we see a clear example of the operations-resource perspective dominating the direction of Micraytech's overall business strategy.

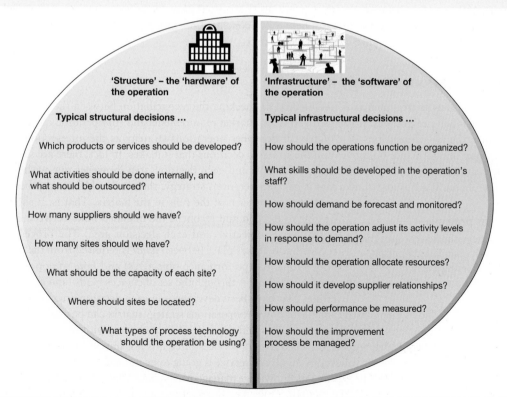

'Structure' – the 'hardware' of the operation

Typical structural decisions …

Which products or services should be developed?

What activities should be done internally, and what should be outsourced?

How many suppliers should we have?

How many sites should we have?

What should be the capacity of each site?

Where should sites be located?

What types of process technology should the operation be using?

'Infrastructure' – the 'software' of the operation

Typical infrastructural decisions …

How should the operations function be organized?

What skills should be developed in the operation's staff?

How should demand be forecast and monitored?

How should the operation adjust its activity levels in response to demand?

How should the operation allocate resources?

How should it develop supplier relationships?

How should performance be measured?

How should the improvement process be managed?

Figure 3.11 Typical structural and infrastructural operations strategy decisions

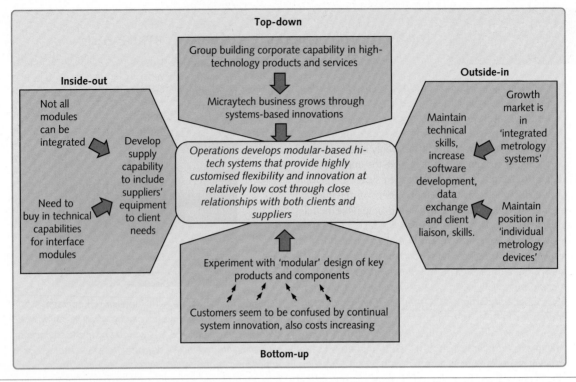

Figure 3.12 Top-down, outside-in, bottom-up, and inside-out perspectives of the Micraytech operations strategy

of Micraytech operations strategy that we have covered across this chapter. In this case, the four perspectives seem to be reasonably compatible, with its operations strategy fitting together from whichever perspective is chosen. In other words, each perspective is 'reconciled' with the others. This is one of the conditions for an effective operations strategy – the four perspectives must be reconciled. Here, we look at three models that can help this reconciliation – the operations strategy matrix, the 'line of fit' and the importance–performance matrix.

The operations strategy matrix

The operations strategy matrix is one method of checking the reconciliation between the inside-out and outside-in perspectives. It brings together (a) market requirements and (b) operations resources to form the two dimensions of a matrix. It describes operations strategy as the intersection of a company's performance objectives and the strategic decisions that it makes. In fact, there are several intersections between each performance objective and each decision area (however one wishes to define them). If a business thinks that it has an operations strategy, then it should have a coherent explanation for each of the cells in the matrix. That is, it should be able to explain and reconcile the intended links between each performance objective and each decision area. The process of reconciliation takes place between *what* is required from the operations function (performance objectives) and *how* the operation tries to achieve this through the set of choices made (and the capabilities that have been developed) in each decision area.

> **Operations principle**
>
> An operation's strategy should articulate the relationship between operations objectives and the means of achieving them.

Figure 3.13 shows a simplified example of how the operations strategy matrix can be used. A parcel courier service competes primarily on its quality and dependability of service, with price (cost) and innovation also being fairly important. The range of services offered is not unimportant, but not of prime concern. The company believes its quality of service is going to be influenced largely by investment in 'track and trace' technology and its knowledge management system (that allows improvements in its processes to be recorded and shared). Other key intersections are as illustrated in the figure.

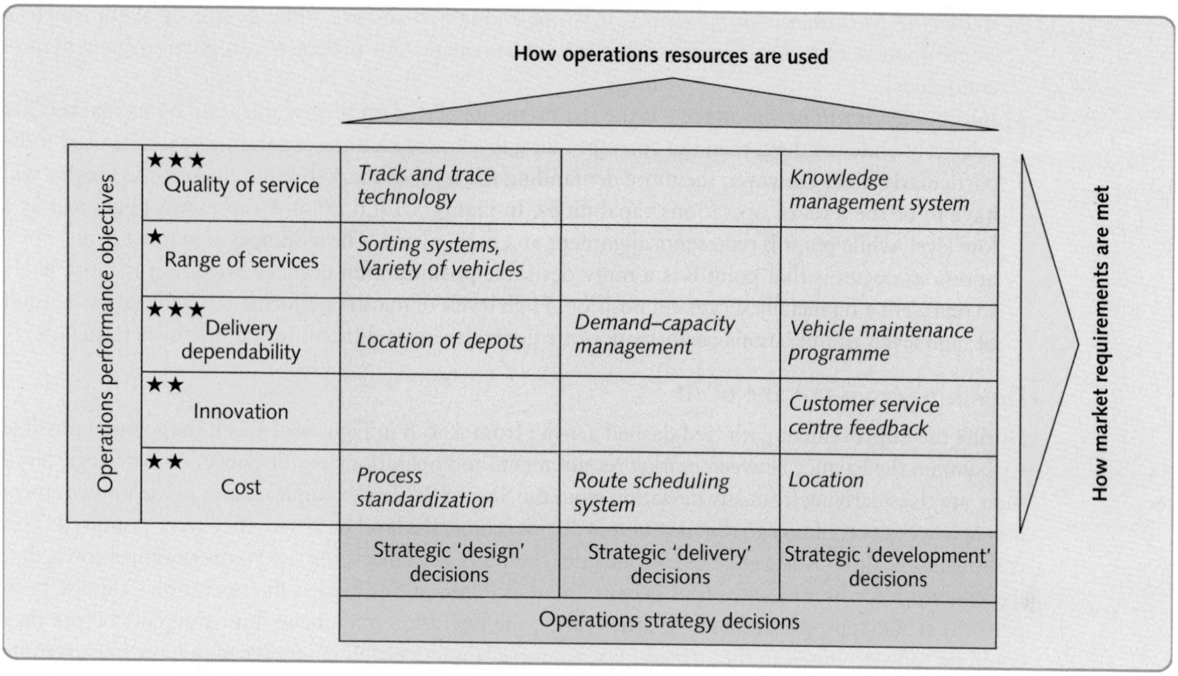

How operations resources are used

	Operations performance objectives	Strategic 'design' decisions	Strategic 'delivery' decisions	Strategic 'development' decisions
★★★ Quality of service		Track and trace technology		Knowledge management system
★ Range of services		Sorting systems, Variety of vehicles		
★★★ Delivery dependability		Location of depots	Demand–capacity management	Vehicle maintenance programme
★★ Innovation				Customer service centre feedback
★★ Cost		Process standardization	Route scheduling system	Location

How market requirements are met

Operations strategy decisions

Figure 3.13 The operations strategy matrix defines operations strategy by the intersections of performance objectives and operations decisions – in this case for a parcel delivery courier

Note that not all cells are occupied. This is not because there is no relationship between the performance objectives and the decisions that these cells represent; it is that the decisions are not seen as being particularly important in the context of the whole strategy.

The 'line of fit' between market requirements and operations capabilities

The operations strategy matrix is a good model for testing whether market requirements and the operations capability perspectives fit together. It makes explicit the specific aspects of market requirements (quality, speed, dependability, flexibility, cost, etc.) and the decisions that support operations capability (design, delivery and development). The disadvantage is that it gives little sense of the dynamics of reconciliation – how the balance between market requirements and the operations capability changes over time. This is where the 'line of fit' model is useful. It is based on the idea that, ideally, there should be a reasonable degree of alignment, or 'fit', between the requirements of the market and the capabilities of the operation. Figure 3.14 illustrates the concept of fit diagrammatically. The vertical dimension represents the (outside-in) nature of market requirements that reflect the intrinsic needs of customers or their expectations. This includes such factors as the strength of the brand or reputation, the degree of differentiation and the extent of market promises. Moving along this dimension indicates a broadly enhanced level of market performance. The horizontal scale represents the level of the organization's operations capabilities. This includes its ability to achieve its competitive objectives and the effectiveness with which it uses its resources. Moving along the dimension indicates a broadly enhanced level of operations capabilities and therefore operations performance.

> **Operations principle**
> Operations strategy should aim for alignment or 'fit' between an operation's performance and the requirements of its markets.

While the line of fit model is conceptual rather than a practical tool, it does illustrate some ideas around the concept of strategic improvement. In terms of the framework illustrated in Figure 3.14(a), improvement means three things.

1 *Achieving 'alignment'* – This means achieving an approximate balance between 'required market performance' and 'actual operations performance'. The diagonal line in Figure 3.14(a) therefore represents a 'line of fit' with market requirements and operations capabilities in balance.

2 *Achieving 'sustainable' alignment* – It is not enough to achieve some degree of alignment to a single point in time. Equally important is whether operations processes can adapt to new market conditions.

3 *Improving overall performance* – If the requirements placed on the organization by its markets are relatively undemanding, then the corresponding level of operations capabilities will not need to be particularly high. However, the more demanding the level of market requirements, the greater will have to be the level of operations capabilities. In Figure 3.14(a) point A represents alignment at a low level, while point B represents alignment at a higher level. The assumption in most firms' operations strategies is that point B is a more desirable position than point A because it is more likely to represent a financially successful position. High levels of market performance, achieved as a result of high levels of operations performance, are generally more difficult for competitors to match.

Deviating from the line of fit

During the improvement path (red dashed arrow) from A to B in Figure 3.14(a) it may not be possible to maintain the balance between market requirements and operations performance. At a strategic level, there are risks deriving from any deviation from the 'line of fit'. For example, delays in the improvement to a new website could mean that customers do not receive the level of service they were promised. This is shown as position X in Figure 3.14(b). Under these circumstances, the risk to the organization is that its reputation (or brand) will suffer because market expectations exceed the operation's capability to perform at the appropriate level. At other times, the operation may make improvements before they could be fully exploited in the market. For example, the same online retailer may have improved its website so that it can offer extra services, such as the ability to customize products, before those products have been stocked in its distribution centre. This means that, although an improvement to its ordering processes has been made, problems elsewhere in the company prevent the improvement from giving value to the company. This is represented by point Y on Figure 3.14(b).

Using the importance–performance matrix to determine operations strategy improvement priorities

One can use the idea of comparing market and operations perspectives at a more focused and disaggregated level to provide direct guidance to operations managers. So, rather than ask generally, 'what are the market requirements for our products and/or services?' one asks 'how important are

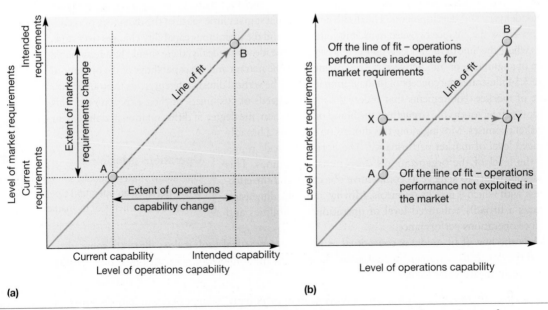

(a)   (b)

Figure 3.14 In operations improvement, there should be 'fit' between market requirements and operations performance. Deviation from the line of 'fit' can expose the operation to risk

Nokia's failure to adapt[15]

Only a few years ago Nokia was the king of the mobile phone business – and it was a good business to be in, with double-digit growth year on year. The company was omnipresent and extremely powerful, a pioneer that had supplied the first mass wave of the expanding mobile phone industry. It dominated the market in many parts of the world and the easily recognizable Nokia ring-tone echoed everywhere from boardrooms to shopping malls. So why did this, once dominant, company eventually sink to the point where it was forced to sell its mobile communications business to Microsoft? The former Nokia CEO, Jormal Ollila, admitted that Nokia made several mistakes, but the exact nature of those mistakes is a point of debate among business commentators. Julian Birkinshaw, a Professor at London Business School, dismisses some of the most commonly cited reasons. Did it lose touch with its customers? Well, yes, but by definition that must hold for any company whose sales drop so drastically in the face of thriving competitors. Did it fail to develop the necessary technologies? No. Nokia had a prototype touchscreen before the iPhone was launched, and its smartphones were technologically superior to anything Apple, Samsung, or Google had to offer for many years. Did it not recognize that the basis of competition was shifting from the hardware to the ecosystem? (A technology ecosystem in this case is a term used to describe the complex system of interdependent components that work together to enable mobile technology to operate successfully.) Not really. The 'ecosystem' battle began in the early 2000s, with Nokia joining forces with Ericsson, Motorola and Psion to create Symbian as a platform technology that would keep Microsoft at bay.

Where Nokia struggled was in relying on an operations strategy that failed to allocate resources appropriately and

could not implement the changes that were necessary. As far as resource allocation was concerned, Nokia saw itself primarily as a hardware company rather than a software company. Its engineers were great at designing and producing hardware, but not the programs that drive the devices. They underestimated the importance of software (including, crucially, the apps that run on smartphones). Largely, it was hardware rather than software experts who controlled its development process. By contrast, Apple, had always emphasized that hardware and software were equally important. Yet while it was losing its dominance, Nokia was well aware of most of the changes occurring in the mobile communications market and the technology developments being actively pursued by competitors. Arguably, it was not short of awareness, but it did lack the capacity to convert awareness into action. The failure of big companies to adapt to changing circumstances is one of the fundamental puzzles in the world of business, says Professor Birkinshaw.

the competitive factors that characterize a product or service?' The intention is to gain an understanding of the relative importance to customers of the various competitive factors. For example, do customers for a particular product or service prefer low prices to a wide range? The needs and preferences of customers shape the *importance* of operations objectives within the operation. Similarly, rather than ask generally, 'what are our operations capabilities?' one asks 'how good is our operation at providing the required level of performance in each of the competitive factors?' But how good is our performance against what criteria? Strategically the most revealing point of comparison is with competitors. Competitors are the points of comparison against which the operation can judge its performance. From a competitive viewpoint, as operations improves its performance, the improvement which matters most is that which takes the operation past the performance levels achieved by its competitors. The role of competitors then is in determining achieved *performance*. (In a not-for-profit context, 'other similar operations' can be substituted for 'competitors'.)

Both importance and performance have to be brought together before any judgement can be made as to the relative priorities for improvement. Just because something is particularly important to its

> **Operations principle**
>
> Improvement priorities are determined by importance for customers and performance against competitors or similar operations.

customers does not mean that an operation should necessarily give it immediate priority for improvement. It may be that the operation is already considerably better than its competitors at serving customers in this respect. Similarly, just because an operation is not very good at something when compared with its competitors' performance, it does not necessarily mean that it should be immediately improved. Customers may not particularly value this aspect of performance.

▶ *Judging importance to customers* – Earlier, we introduced the idea of order winning, qualifying and less important competitive factors, and one could take these three categories as an indication of the relative importance of each performance factor. But usually one needs to use a slightly more discriminating scale. One way to do this is to take our three broad categories of competitive factors – order winning, qualifying and less important – and to divide each category into three further points representing strong, medium and weak positions. Figure 3.15(a) illustrates such a scale.

▶ *Judging performance against competitors* – At its simplest, a competitive performance standard would consist merely of judging whether the achieved performance of an operation is better than, the same as, or worse than that of its competitors. However, in much the same way as the nine-point importance scale was derived, we can derive a more discriminating nine-point performance scale, as shown in Figure 3.15(b).

The priority for improvement that each competitive factor should be given can be assessed from a comparison of their importance and performance. This can be shown on an importance–performance matrix that, as its name implies, positions each competitive factor according to its scores or ratings on these criteria. Figure 3.16 shows an importance–performance matrix divided into zones of improvement priority (see later).

The first zone boundary is the 'lower bound of acceptability', shown as line AB in Figure 3.16. This is the boundary between acceptable and unacceptable performance. When a competitive factor is rated as relatively unimportant (8 or 9 on the importance scale), this boundary will in practice be low. Most operations are prepared to tolerate performance levels which are 'in the same ball-park' as their

(a) Importance scale for competitive factors		
Rating	**Description**	
1	Provides a crucial advantage to customers	High
2	Provides an important advantage to customers	
3	Provides a useful advantage to customers	
4	Needs to be up to good industry standard	
5	Needs to be up to median industry standard	
6	Needs to be within close range of rest of industry	
7	Not usually important but could become so	
8	Very rarely considered by customers	
9	Never considered by customers	Low

(b) Performance scale for competitive factors		
Rating	**Description**	
1	Considerably better than similar organizations	Good
2	Clearly better than similar organizations	
3	Marginally better than similar organizations	
4	Sometimes marginally better than similar organizations	
5	About the same as similar organizations	
6	Slightly worse than the average of similar organizations	
7	Usually marginally worse than similar organizations	
8	Generally worse than most similar organizations	
9	Consistently worse than most similar organizations	Poor

Figure 3.15 Nine-point scales for judging importance and performance

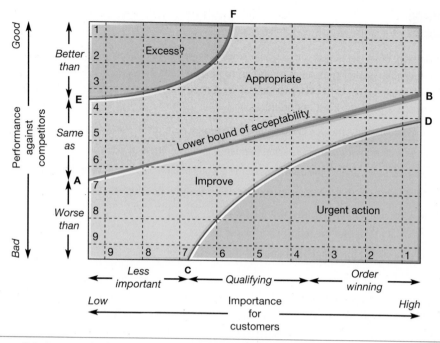

Figure 3.16 Priority zones in the importance–performance matrix

competitors (even at the bottom end of the rating) for unimportant competitive factors. They only become concerned when performance levels are clearly below those of their competitors. Conversely, when judging competitive factors that are rated highly (1 or 2 on the importance scale) they will be markedly less sanguine at poor or mediocre levels of performance. Minimum levels of acceptability for these competitive factors will usually be at the lower end of the 'better than competitors' class. Below this minimum bound of acceptability, there is clearly a need for improvement; above this line there is no immediate urgency for any improvement. However, not all competitive factors falling below the minimum line will be seen as having the same degree of improvement priority. A boundary approximately represented by line CD represents a distinction between an urgent priority zone and a less urgent improvement zone. Similarly, above the line AB, not all competitive factors are regarded as having the same priority. The line EF can be seen as the approximate boundary between performance levels which are regarded as 'good' or 'appropriate' on the one hand and those regarded as 'too good' or 'excess' on the other. Segregating the matrix in this way results in four zones which imply very different priorities:

▶ *The 'appropriate' zone* – competitive factors in this area lie above the lower bound of acceptability and so should be considered satisfactory.
▶ *The 'improve' zone* – lying below the lower bound of acceptability, any factors in this zone must be candidates for improvement.
▶ *The 'urgent-action' zone* – these factors are important to customers but performance is below that of competitors. They must be considered as candidates for immediate improvement.
▶ *The 'excess?' zone* – factors in this area are 'high performing', but not important to customers. The question must be asked, therefore, whether the resources devoted to achieving such performance could be used better elsewhere.

How can the process of operations strategy be organized?

An operations strategy is the starting point for operations improvement. It sets the direction in which the operation will change over time. It is implicit that the business will want operations to change for the better. However, unless an operations strategy gives some idea as to *how* improvement will happen, it is not fulfilling its main purpose. This is where considering the *process* of operations strategy comes in. It is concerned with the method that is used to determine what an operations strategy should be and how it should be

Worked example

EXL Laboratories is a subsidiary of an electronics company. It carries out research and development as well as technical problem-solving work for a wide range of companies, including companies in its own group. It is particularly keen to improve the level of service which it gives to its customers. However, it needs to decide which aspect of its performance to improve first. It has devised a list of the most important aspects of its service:

▶ *The quality of its technical solutions* – the perceived appropriateness by customers.

▶ *The quality of its communications with customers* – the frequency and usefulness of information.

▶ *The quality of post-project documentation* – the usefulness of the documentation which goes with the final report.

▶ *Delivery speed* – the time between customer request and the delivery of the final report.

▶ *Delivery dependability* – the ability to deliver on the promised date.

▶ *Delivery flexibility* – the ability to deliver the report on a revised date.

▶ *Specification flexibility* – the ability to change the nature of the investigation.

▶ *Price* – the total charge to the customer.

EXL assigned a score to each of these factors using the 1–9 scale that we described in Figure 3.15. After this EXL turned its attention to judging the laboratory's performance against competitor organizations. Although it has benchmarked information for some aspects of performance, it has to make estimates for the others. Both these importance and performance scores are shown in Figure 3.17.

EXL Laboratories plotted the importance and performance ratings it had given to each of its competitive factors on an importance–performance matrix. This is shown in Figure 3.18. It shows that the most important aspect of competitiveness – the ability to deliver sound technical solutions to its customers – falls comfortably within the appropriate zone. Specification flexibility and delivery flexibility are also in the appropriate zone, although only just. Both delivery speed and delivery dependability seem to be in need of improvement as each is below the minimum level of acceptability for their respective importance positions. However, two competitive factors, communications and cost/price, are clearly in need of immediate improvement. These two factors should therefore be assigned the most urgent priority. The matrix also indicates that the company's documentation could almost be regarded as 'too good'.

The matrix may not reveal any total surprises. The competitive factors in the 'urgent-action' zone may be known to be in need of improvement already. However, the exercise is useful for two reasons:

▶ It helps to discriminate between many factors which may be in need of improvement.

▶ The exercise gives purpose and structure to the debate on improvement priorities.

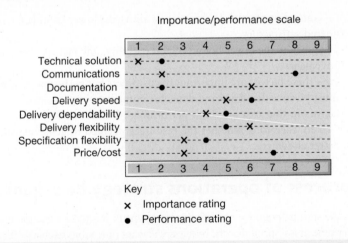

Figure 3.17 Rating 'importance to customers' and 'performance against competitors' on the nine-point scales for EXL Laboratories

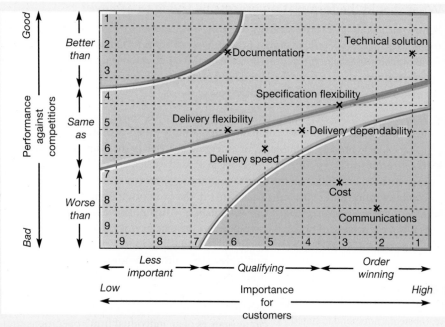

Figure 3.18 The importance–performance matrix for EXL Laboratories

implemented. This is a complex and difficult thing to achieve in practice. And although any simple step-by-step model of how to 'do' operations strategy will inevitably be a simplification of a messy reality, we shall use a four-stage model to illustrate some of the elements of 'process'. This stage model is shown in Figure 3.19 and divides the process of operations strategy into *formulation, implementation, monitoring and control*.[16] The four stages are shown as a cycle because strategies may be revisited depending on the experience gained from trying to make them happen.

Operations strategy formulation

The formulation of operations strategy is the process of clarifying the various objectives and decisions that make up the strategy, and the links between them. Unlike day-to-day operations management, formulating an operations strategy is likely to be only an occasional activity. Some firms will have a regular (e.g. annual) planning cycle and operations strategy consideration may form part of this. However, the extent of any changes made in each annual cycle is likely to be limited. In other words, the 'complete' process of formulating an entirely new operations strategy will be a relatively infrequent event. There are many 'formulation processes' which are, or can be, used to formulate operations strategies. Most consultancy companies have developed their own frameworks, as have several academics.

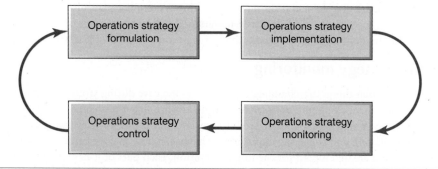

Figure 3.19 The stages of the process of operations strategy

What should the formulation process be trying to achieve?

Before putting an operations strategy together, it is necessary to ask the question, 'what should it be trying to achieve?' Clearly, it should provide a set of actions that, with hindsight, have provided the 'best' outcome for the organization. But 'the best' is a judgement that can only be applied in hindsight. Yet, even if we cannot assess the 'goodness' of a strategy in advance, we can check it out for some attributes that could stop it being a success, as follows.

▶ *Is operations strategy comprehensive?* – In other words, does it include all important issues? Business history is littered with companies that simply failed to notice the potential impact of, for instance, new process technology, or emerging changes in their supply network.

▶ *Is operations strategy coherent?* – As we discussed earlier, coherence is when the choices made in each decision area all direct the operation in the same strategic direction, with all strategic decisions complementing and reinforcing each other in the promotion of performance objectives.

▶ *Does operations strategy have correspondence?* – Again, as we discussed earlier, correspondence is when the strategies pursued correspond to the true priority of each performance objective.

▶ *Does operations strategy identify critical issues?* – The more critical the decision, the more attention it deserves. Although no strategic decision is unimportant, in practical terms some decisions are more critical than others. The judgement over exactly which decisions are particularly critical is very much a pragmatic one that must be based on the particular circumstances of an individual firm's operations strategy. However, the key is that they must be identified.

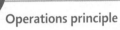

Operations principle

Operations strategies should be comprehensive, coherent, correspond to stated objectives and identify the critical issues.

Operations strategy implementation

Operations strategy implementation is the way that strategies are operationalized or executed. It means attempting to make sure that intended strategies are actually achieved. It is important because no matter how sophisticated the intellectual and analytical underpinnings of a strategy, it remains only a document until it has been implemented. But the way one implements any strategy will very much depend on the specific nature of the changes implied by that strategy and the organizational and environmental conditions that apply during its implementation. However, strategy practitioners typically point to three key issues that are important in achieving successful implementation.

▶ *Clarity of strategic decisions* – There is a strong relationship between the formulation stage and the implementation stage of operations strategy. The crucial attribute of the formulation stage is clarity. If a strategy is ambiguous it is difficult to translate strategic intent into specific actions. With clarity, however, it should be easier to define the intent behind the strategy, the few important issues that need to be developed to deliver the intent, the way that projects should be led and resourced, who will be responsible for each task, and so on.

▶ *Motivational leadership* – Leadership that motivates, encourages and provides support is a huge advantage in dealing with the complexity of implementation. Leadership is needed to bring sense and meaning to strategic aspirations, maintain a sense of purpose over the implementation period, and, when necessary, modify the implementation plan in the light of experience.

▶ *Project management* – Implementation means breaking a complex plan into a set of relatively distinct activities. Fortunately, there is a well-understood collection of ideas of how to do this. It is called 'project management' and a whole chapter is devoted to this subject (Chapter 19).

Operations strategy monitoring

Especially in times when things are changing rapidly, as is the case during strategic change, organizations often want to track ongoing performance to make sure that the changes are proceeding as planned. Monitoring should be capable of providing early indications (or a 'warning bell' as some call it) by diagnosing data and triggering appropriate changes in how the operations strategy is being implemented. Having created a plan for the implementation, each part of it has to be monitored to ensure that planned activities are indeed happening. Any deviation from what should be happening (that is, its plans) can then be rectified through some kind of intervention in the operation.

Operations strategy control

Strategic control involves the evaluation of the results from monitoring the implementation. Activities, plans and performance are assessed with the intention of correcting future action if that is required. In some ways, this strategic view of control is similar to how it works operationally (which is discussed in Chapter 10), but there are differences. At a strategic level, control can be difficult because strategic objectives are not always clear and unambiguous. Ask any experienced managers and they will acknowledge that it is not always possible to articulate every aspect of a strategic decision in detail. Many strategies are just too complex for that. So, rather than adhering dogmatically to a predetermined plan, it may be better to adapt as circumstances change. And, the more uncertain the environment, the more an operation needs to emphasize this form of strategic flexibility and develop its ability to learn from events.

Summary answers to key questions

What is strategy and operations strategy?

▶ Strategy is the total pattern of decisions and actions that position the organization in its environment and that are intended to achieve its long-term goals.

▶ Operations strategy concerns the pattern of strategic decisions and actions that set the role, objectives and activities of the operation. It can be used to articulate a vision for the (potential) contribution of operations to organizational success (i.e. moving from stage 1 to stage 4 of the Hayes and Wheelwright model of operations contribution).

▶ Operations strategy has content and process. The content concerns the specific decisions that are taken to achieve specific objectives. The process is the procedure that is used within a business to formulate its strategy.

▶ There are four key perspectives on operations strategy – the 'top-down', market requirement ('outside-in'), 'bottom-up' and operations resources ('inside-out').

▶ It is important to engage with a wide range of stakeholders, within and outside of the organization, when developing operations strategy.

How does operations strategy align with business strategy (top-down)?

▶ The 'top-down' perspective views strategic decisions at a number of levels. Corporate strategy sets the objectives for the different businesses that make up a group of businesses. Business strategy sets the objectives for each individual business and how it positions itself in its marketplace. Functional strategies set the objectives for each function's contribution to its business strategy.

▶ It is important to consider *correspondence* between these different levels of strategy and *coherence* both with other functional strategies and within itself.

▶ The concepts of the 'business model' and 'operating model' are useful in understanding the top-down perspective on operations strategy.

How does operations strategy align with market requirements (outside-in)?

▶ A 'market requirements' (outside-in) perspective of operations strategy sees the main role of operations as satisfying markets. From this perspective, operations performance objectives and operations decisions should be primarily influenced by a combination of customers' needs and competitors' actions.

▶ Market requirements are influenced by product/service differentiation and the stage that a product or service is within its lifecycle.

How does operations strategy align with operational experience (bottom-up)?

▶ The 'bottom-up' view of operations strategy emphasizes the 'emergent' view of strategy development based on day-to-day operational experience. While the 'top-down' perspective may describe how operations strategy (and other function strategies) *should* be developed, it often doesn't describe how it *is* developed.

▶ Top-down and bottom-up perspectives are in fact complementary. In one direction, top-down perspectives can be used to judge the extent to which operational day-to-day activities reflect the higher-level strategies. In the other direction, experience gained from day-to-day activities can be accumulated and built into capabilities that can then be exploited strategically.

How does operations strategy align with operations resources (inside-out)?

▶ The 'operations resource' perspective (inside-out) of operations strategy is based on the resource-based view (RBV) of the firm and sees the operation's core competences (or capabilities) as being the main influence on operations strategy.

▶ An operations resource perspective should start by understanding existing capabilities and constraints within the operation.

▶ Identifying strategic decision areas can help support capability building for operations and their extended supply networks.

▶ Strategic resources (also called capabilities or competences) are critical in generating sustainable competitive advantage. These resources are valuable, rare, costly to imitate and organized in a way to allow the organization to capture their value.

How are the four perspectives of operations strategy reconciled?

▶ Combined, the four perspectives give a good idea of how the content of operations strategy is developed and how operations excellence can act as a key source of competitive advantage. Among the models to support this activity are the operations strategy matrix, the 'line of fit' and the importance–performance matrix.

How can the process of operations strategy be organized?

▶ Formulating operations strategy is often called 'the process' of operations strategy and is made up of four stages – formulation, implementation, monitoring and control.

▶ Formulation is the process of clarifying the various objectives and decisions that make up the strategy, and the links between them. Implementation is the way that strategy is operationalized. Monitoring involves tracking on-going performance and diagnosing data to make sure that the changes are proceeding as planned and providing early indications of any deviation from plan. Control involves the evaluation of the results from monitoring so that activities, plans and performance can be assessed with the intention of correcting future action if required.

McDonald's: half a century of growth[17]

It's loved and it's hated. It is a shining example of how good-value food can be brought to a mass market. It is a symbol of everything that is wrong with 'industrialized', capitalist, bland, high-calorie and environmentally unfriendly commercialism. It is the best-known and most loved fast food brand in the world with more than 37,000 restaurants in 119 countries, providing jobs for 1.7 million staff and feeding 69 million customers per day (yes, per day!) or nearly 1 per cent of the entire world's population. It is part of the homogenization of individual national cultures, filling the world with bland, identical, 'cookie cutter', Americanized and soulless operations that dehumanize its staff by forcing them to follow rigid and over-defined procedures. But whether you see it as friend, foe, or a bit of both, McDonald's has revolutionized the food industry, affecting the lives both of the people who produce food and of the people who eat it. It has also had its ups (mainly) and downs (occasionally) as markets, customers and economic circumstances have changed. Yet, even in the toughest times it has always displayed remarkable resilience. What follows is a brief (for such a large corporation) summary of its history.

Starting small

Central to the development of McDonald's is Ray Kroc, who by 1954 and at the age of 52 had been variously a piano player, a paper cup salesman and a multi-mixer salesman. He was surprised by a big order for eight multi-mixers from a restaurant in San Bernardino, California. When he visited the customer, he found a small but successful restaurant run by two brothers Dick and Mac McDonald. They had opened their 'Bar-B-Que' restaurant 14 years earlier, and by the time Ray Kroc visited the brothers' operation it had a self-service drive-in format with a limited menu of nine items. He was amazed by the effectiveness of their operation. Focusing on a limited menu including burgers, fries and beverages had allowed them to analyse every step of the process of producing and serving their food. Ray Kroc was so impressed that he persuaded the brothers to adopt his vision of creating McDonald's restaurants all over the USA, the first of which opened in Des Plaines, Illinois in June 1955. However, later, Kroc and the McDonald brothers quarrelled, and Kroc bought the brothers out. Now with exclusive rights to the McDonald's name, the restaurants spread, and in five years there were 200 restaurants through the USA. Yet through this, and later, expansions, Kroc insisted on maintaining the same principles that he had seen in the original operation. *'If I had a brick for every time I've repeated the phrase Quality, Service, Cleanliness and Value, I think I'd probably be able to bridge the Atlantic Ocean with them'* (Ray Kroc).

Priority to the process

Ray Kroc had been attracted by the cleanliness, simplicity, efficiency and profitability of the McDonald brothers' operation. They had stripped fast food delivery down to its essence and eliminated needless effort to make a swift assembly line for a meal at reasonable prices. Kroc wanted to build a process that would become famous for food of consistently high quality using uniform methods of preparation. His burgers, buns, fries and beverages should taste just the same in Alaska as they did in Alabama. The answer was the 'Speedee Service System'; a standardized process that prescribed exact preparation methods, specially designed equipment and strict product specifications. The emphasis on process standardization meant that customers could be assured of identical levels of food and service quality every time they visited any store, anywhere. Operating procedures were specified in minute detail. Its first operations manual prescribed rigorous cooking instructions such as temperatures, cooking times and portions. Similarly, operating procedures were defined to ensure the required customer experience: for example, no food items were to be held more than 10 minutes in the transfer bin between being cooked and being served. Technology was also automated. Specially designed equipment helped to guarantee consistency using 'fool-proof' devices. For example, the ketchup was dispensed through a metered pump. Specially designed 'clam shell' grills cooked both sides of each meat patty simultaneously for a pre-set time. And when it became clear that the metal tongs used by staff to fill French-fry containers were awkward to use efficiently, McDonald's engineers devised a simple aluminium scoop that made the job faster and easier.

For Kroc, the operating process was both his passion and the company's central philosophy. It was also the foundation of learning and improvement. The company's almost compulsive focus on process detail was not an end in itself. Rather it was to learn what contributed to consistent high-quality service in practice and what did not. McDonald's always saw learning as important. It founded 'Hamburger University', initially in the basement of a restaurant in Elk Grove Village, Illinois. It had a research and development laboratory to develop new cooking, freezing, storing and serving methods. Also, franchisees and operators were trained in the analytical techniques necessary to run a successful McDonald's. It awarded degrees in 'Hamburgerology'. But learning was not just for headquarters. The company also formed a 'field service' unit to appraise and help its restaurants by sending field service consultants to review their performance on a number of 'dimensions' including cleanliness, queuing, food quality and customer service. As Ray Kroc said, *'We take the hamburger business more seriously than anyone else. What sets McDonald's apart is the passion that we and our suppliers share around producing and delivering the highest-quality beef patties. Rigorous food safety and quality standards and practices are in place and executed at the highest levels every day.'*

No story illustrates the company's philosophy of learning and improvement better than its adoption of frozen fries. French fried potatoes had always been important. Initially, the company tried observing the temperature levels and cooking methods that produced the best fries. The problem was that the temperature during the cooking process was very much influenced by the temperature of the potatoes when they were placed into the cooking vat. So, unless the temperature of the potatoes before they were cooked was also controlled (not very practical), it was difficult to specify the exact time and temperature that would produce perfect fries. But McDonald's researchers discovered that, irrespective of the temperature of the raw potatoes, fries were always at their best when the oil temperature in the cooking vat increased by three degrees above the low temperature point after they were put in the vat. So, by monitoring the temperature of the vat, perfect fries could be produced every time. But that was not the end of the story. The ideal potato for fries was the Idaho Russet, which was seasonal and not available in the summer months. At other times an alternative (inferior) potato was used. One grower, who, at the time, supplied a fifth of McDonald's potatoes, suggested that he could put Idaho Russets into cold storage for supplying during the summer period. Unfortunately, all the stored potatoes rotted. Not to be beaten, he offered another suggestion. Why don't McDonald's consider switching to frozen potatoes? But the company was initially cautious about meddling with such an important menu item. However, there were other advantages in using frozen potatoes. Supplying fresh potatoes in perfect condition to McDonald's rapidly expanding chain was increasingly difficult. Frozen potatoes could actually increase the quality of the company's fries if a method of satisfactorily cooking them could be found. Once again McDonald's developers came to the rescue. They developed a method of air-drying the raw fries, quick frying and then freezing them. The supplier, who was a relatively small and local suppler when he first suggested storing Idaho Russets, grew its business to supply around half of McDonald's US business.

Throughout its rapid expansion McDonald's focused on four areas – improving the product, establishing strong supplier relationships, creating (largely customized) equipment and developing franchise holders. But it was strict control of the menu that provided a platform of stability. Although its competitors offered a relatively wide variety of menu items, McDonald's limited itself to ten items. As one of McDonald's senior managers at the time stressed, *'It wasn't because we were smarter. The fact that we were selling just ten items* [and] *had a facility that was small, and used a limited number of suppliers created an ideal environment.'* Capacity growth (through additional stores) was also managed carefully. Well-utilized stores were important to franchise holders, so franchise opportunities were located only where they would not seriously undercut existing stores.

Securing supply

McDonald's says that it has been the strength of the alignment between the company, its franchisees and its suppliers (collectively referred to as the System) that has been the explanation for its success. But during the company's early years suppliers proved problematic. McDonald's approached the major food suppliers, such as Kraft and Heinz, but without much success. Large and established suppliers were reluctant to conform to McDonald's requirements, preferring to focus on retail sales. It was the relatively small companies that were willing to risk supplying what seemed then to be a risky venture. And as McDonald's grew, so did its suppliers, who also valued the company's less adversarial relationship. One supplier is quoted as saying, *'Other chains would walk away from you for half a cent. McDonald's was more concerned with getting quality. McDonald's always treated me with respect even when they became much bigger and didn't have to.'* Furthermore, suppliers were always seen as a source of innovation. For example, one of McDonald's meat suppliers, Keystone Foods, developed a novel quick-freezing process that captured the fresh taste and texture of beef patties. This meant that every patty could retain its consistent quality until it hit the grill. Keystone shared its technology with other McDonald's meat suppliers and today the process is an industry standard. Yet, supplier relationships were also rigorously controlled. McDonald's routinely analysed its suppliers' products.

Fostering franchisees

McDonald's revenues consisted of sales by company-operated restaurants and fees from restaurants operated by franchisees. McDonald's views itself primarily as a franchisor and believes franchising is *'important to delivering great, locally-relevant customer experiences and driving profitability'*. However, it also believes that directly operating restaurants is essential to providing the company with real operations experience. Of the 36,000 restaurants in 117 countries, approximately 80 per cent were operated by franchisees. But where some restaurant chains concentrated on recruiting franchisees that were then left to themselves, McDonald's expected its franchisees to contribute their experiences for the benefit of all. Ray Kroc's original concept was that franchisees would make money before the company did. So he made sure that the revenues that went to McDonald's came from the success of the restaurants themselves rather from initial franchise fees.

Initiating innovation

Ideas for new menu items have often come from franchisees. For example, Lou Groen, a Cincinnati franchise holder, had noticed that in Lent (a 40-day period when some Christians give up eating red meat on Fridays and instead eat only fish or no meat at all) some customers avoided the traditional hamburger. He went to Ray Kroc with his idea for a 'Filet-o-Fish': a steamed bun with a shot of tartar sauce, a fish fillet and cheese on the bottom bun. But Kroc wanted to push his own meatless sandwich, called the hula burger: a cold bun with a piece of pineapple and cheese. Groen and Kroc competed on a Lenten Friday to see whose sandwich would sell more. Kroc's hula burger failed, selling only six sandwiches all day, while Groen sold 350 Filet-o-Fish. Similarly, the Egg McMuffin was introduced by franchisee Herb Peterson, who wanted to attract customers into his McDonald's stores all through the day, not just at lunch and dinner. He came up with idea for the signature McDonald's breakfast item because he was reputedly *very partial to eggs Benedict and wanted to create something similar'.*

Other innovations came from the company itself. When poultry became popular, Fred Turner, then the Chairman of McDonald's, had an idea for a new meal: a chicken finger-food without bones, about the size of a thumb. After six months of research, the food technicians and scientists managed to reconstitute shreds of white chicken meat into small portions that could be breaded, fried, frozen then reheated. Test-marketing the new product was positive, and in 1983 they were launched under the name Chicken McNuggets. These were so successful that within a month McDonald's became the second largest purchaser of chicken in the USA. Some innovations came as a reaction to market conditions. Criticized by nutritionists who worried about calorie-rich burgers and shareholders who were alarmed by flattening sales, McDonald's launched its biggest menu revolution in 30 years in 2003 when it entered the prepared salad market. It offered a choice of dressings for its grilled chicken salad with Caesar dressing (and croutons) or the lighter option of a drizzle of balsamic dressing. Likewise, moves towards coffee sales were prompted by the ever-growing trend set by big coffee shops like Starbucks.

Problematic periods

Food, like almost everything else, is subject to swings in fashion. Not surprising then that there have been periods when McDonald's has had to adapt. The period from the early 1990s to the mid 2000s was difficult for parts of the McDonald's Empire. Growth in some parts of the world stalled. Partly this was due to changes in food fashion, nutritional concerns and demographic changes. Partly it was because competitors were learning to either emulate McDonald's operating system, or focus on one aspect of the traditional 'quick service' offering, such as speed of service, range of menu items, (perceived) quality of food, or price. Burger King promoted itself on its 'flame-grilled' quality. Wendy's offered a fuller service level. Taco Bell undercut McDonald's prices with its 'value pricing' promotions. Drive-through specialists sped up service times. Also, 'fast food' was developing a poor reputation in some quarters, and as its iconic brand, McDonald's was taking much of the heat. Similarly, the company became a lightning rod for other questionable aspects of modern life that it was held to promote, from cultural imperialism, low skilled jobs (called 'McJobs' by some critics), abuse of animals and the use of hormone-enhanced beef, to an attack on traditional (French) values (in France). A French farmer called Jose Bové (who was briefly imprisoned) got other farmers to drive their tractors through, and wreck, a half-built McDonald's.

Similarly, in 2015 McDonald's closed more stores in its US home market than it opened – for the first time in its 60-year history. Partly this was a result of the increase in so-called 'fast casual' dining, a trend that combined the convenience of traditional McDonald's style service with food that was seen as healthier, even if it was more expensive. Smaller rivals, such as Chipotle and Shake Shack, had started to take domestic market share.

Surviving strategies

Over recent years the company's strategy has been to become 'better, not just bigger', focusing on 'restaurant execution', with the goal of 'improving the overall experience for our customers'. In particular it has, according to some analysts, 'gone back to basics', a strategy used by McDonald's Chief Executive Officer, Steve Easterbrook, when he was head of the company's British operation, where he redesigned the outlets to make them more modern, introduced coffee and cappuccinos, worked with farmers to raise standards and increased transparency about the supply chain. At the same time, he participated fully and forcefully with the company's critics in the debate over fast food health concerns. But some analysts believe that the 'burger and fries' market is in terminal decline, and the McDonald's brand is so closely associated with that market that further growth will be difficult.

QUESTIONS

1 How has competition to McDonald's changed over its existence?

2 What are the main operations performance objectives for McDonald's?

3 What are the most important structural and infrastructural decisions in McDonald's operations strategy, and how do they influence its main performance objectives?

Problems and applications

All chapters have 'Problems and applications' questions that will help you practise analysing operations. They can be answered by reading the chapter. Model answers for the first two questions can be found on the companion website for this book.

1   ZNR Financial, a large accountancy corporation, is looking to assess the operations functions in three of its locations around the world. The ZNR Malaysia operations is marginally better than the operations of many of its competitors in the region, but still behind the very best players. The function is also viewed positively by other functions in the organization and its 'voice is heard' when it comes to strategy conversations. Arguably, ZNR Japan operations continues to provide the basis on which ZNR Japan competes – it recently developed advanced AI software to enable the company to access new larger corporate clients who, in addition to basic accountancy services, value the customer intelligence that working with ZNR Japan can offer them. ZNR Hong Kong operations is now clearly better than most of its competitors and has an active voice in the strategic direction of the firm. Recently, the operations team worked closely with marketing to respond to a key client's request to develop more automated processing of high-volume, low-variety work on its behalf. The initiative has proved successful, so marketing is becoming increasingly keen to build on this internal 'win-win' relationship. Where would you position the three ZNR operations functions on the Hayes and Wheelwright model of operations contribution?

2   Giordano is one of the most widespread clothes retailers. It is based in Hong Kong and employs more than 8,000 staff in over 2,000 shops. But when it was founded, up-market shops sold high-quality products and gave good service. Cheaper clothes were piled high and sold by sales assistants more concerned with taking the cash than smiling at customers. The company questioned why they could not offer value and service, together with low prices. To do this, they raised the wages of their salespeople by over 30 per cent, and gave all employees 60 hours of training. New staff were allocated a 'big brother' or 'big sister' from experienced staff to help them develop their service quality skills. Even more startling by the standards of their competitors, they brought in a 'no-questions asked' exchange policy irrespective of how long ago the garment had been purchased. Staff were trained to talk to customers and seek their opinion on products and the type of service they would like. This was fed back to the company's designers for incorporation into their new products. Their operating principles were summarized in its 'QKISS' list. Quality (do things right), Knowledge (keep experience up-to-date and share knowledge), Innovation (think 'outside of the box'), Simplicity (less is more), Service (exceed customers' expectations). (a) In what way did an appreciation of competitors affect the market position of the Giordano operation? (b) What are the advantages of sales staff talking to the customers?

3   Carry out an importance–performance analysis for an amusement park. In doing this, think about the competitive factors (i.e. the key ingredients) for this offering, their level of importance and their performance using the scale shown in Figure 3.15. Then map these onto an importance–performance matrix, as shown in Figure 3.16.

4   The Managing Partner of The Branding Partnership (TBP) was describing her business. *'It is about four years now since we specialized in the small to medium firms' market. Before that we also used to provide brand consultancy services for anyone who walked in the door. However, within the firm, I think we could focus our activities even more. There seem to be two types of assignment that we are given. About 40 per cent is relatively routine. Typically, these assignments are conventional market research and focus group exercises. These activities involve a relatively standard set of steps that can be carried out by relatively junior staff. Of course, an experienced consultant is needed to make some decisions. Customers expect us to be relatively inexpensive and fast in delivering the service. Nor do*

they expect us to make simple errors; if we did this too often we would lose business. Fortunately, our customers know that they are buying a "standard package". However, specialist agencies have been emerging over the last few years and they are undercutting us on price. Yet I still feel that we can operate profitably in this market. The other 60 per cent of our work is for clients who require more specialist services, such as assignments involving major brand reshaping. These assignments are complex, large, take longer and require significant branding skill and judgement. It is vital that clients respect and trust the advice we give them in all "brand associated" areas such as product development, promotion, pricing and so on. Of course, they assume that we will not be slow or unreliable, but mainly it's trust in our judgement backed up by hard statistics that is important to the client. This is popular work with our staff. It is both interesting and very profitable.' (a) How different are the two types of business described? (b) It has been proposed that she split the firm into two separate businesses: one to deal with routine services and the other to deal with more complex services. What would be the advantages and disadvantages of doing this?

5 DSD designs, makes and supplies medical equipment to hospitals and clinics. Its success was based on its research and development culture. Around 50 per cent of manufacturing was done in-house. Its products were relatively highly priced, but customers were willing to pay for its technical excellence and willingness to customize equipment. Around 70 per cent of all orders involved some form of customization from standard 'base models'. Manufacturing could take three months from receiving the specification to completing assembly, but customers were more interested in equipment being delivered on time rather than immediate availability. According to its CEO, *'manufacturing is really a large laboratory. The laboratory-like culture helps us to maintain our superiority in leading edge product technology and customization. It also means that we can call upon our technicians to pull out all the stops in order to maintain delivery promises. However, I'm not sure how manufacturing, or indeed the rest of the company, will deal with the new markets and products which we are getting into.'* The new products were 'small black box' products that the company had developed. These were devices that could be attached to patients, or implanted. They took advantage of sophisticated electronics and could be promoted directly to consumers as well as to hospitals and clinics. The CEO knew their significance. *'Although expensive, we have to persuade health care and insurance companies to encourage these new devices. More problematic is our ability to cope with these new products and new markets. We are moving towards being a consumer company, making and delivering a higher volume of more standardized products where the underlying technology is changing fast. We must become faster in our product development. Also, for the first time, we need some kind of logistics capability. I'm not sure whether we should deliver products ourselves or subcontract this. Manufacturing faces a similar dilemma. On one hand, it is important to maintain control over production to ensure high quality and reliability; on the other hand, investing in the process technology to make the products will be very expensive. There are subcontractors who could manufacture the products, they have experience in this kind of manufacturing but not in maintaining the levels of quality we will require. We will also have to develop a "demand fulfilment" capability to deliver products at short notice. It is unlikely that customers would be willing to wait the three months our current customers tolerate. Nor are we sure of how demand might grow. I'm confident that growth will be fast but we will have to have sufficient capacity in place not to disappoint our new customers. We must develop a clear understanding of the new capabilities that we will have to develop if we are to take advantage of this wonderful market opportunity.'* What advice would you give DSD? Consider the operational implications of entering this new market.

6 During manoeuvres in the Alps, a detachment of soldiers got lost. The weather was severe and the snow was deep. In these freezing conditions, after two days of wandering, the soldiers gave up hope and became reconciled to a frozen death on the mountains. Then, to their delight, one of the soldiers discovered a map in his pocket. Much cheered by this discovery, the soldiers were able to escape from the mountains. When they were safe back at their headquarters, they discovered that the map was not of the Alps at all, but of the Pyrenees. What is the relevance of this story to operations strategy?

Selected further reading

Braithwaite, A. and Christopher, M. (2015) *Business Operations Models: Becoming a Disruptive Competitor,* **Kogan Page, London.**
Aimed at practitioners, but authoritative and interesting.

Hayes, R.H., Pisano, G.P., Upton, D.M. and Wheelwright, S.C. (2005) *Pursuing the Competitive Edge,* **Wiley, Hoboken, NJ.**
The gospel according to the Harvard school of operations strategy. Articulate, interesting and informative.

Slack, N. (2017) *The Operations Advantage,* **Kogan Page, London.**
Apologies for self-referencing again! This book is written specifically for practitioners wanting to improve their own operations – short and to the point.

Slack, N. and Lewis, M. (2017) *Operations Strategy,* **5th edn, Pearson Education, Harlow.**
A book that takes a really deep dive into all aspects of operations strategy, with lots of cases and practical guidance.

4

Managing product and service innovation

KEY QUESTIONS

What is product and service innovation?

What is the strategic role of product and service innovation?

What are the stages of product and service innovation?

How should product and service innovation be resourced?

INTRODUCTION

Customers value innovation, and the businesses that provide it can succeed to a greater degree than their competitors which are content to provide the same offerings to their customers, created in the same old way. Companies such as Google, Amazon, Netflix, Nike, Airbnb, Apple and Dropbox have all been successful because they challenged the idea of what their markets wanted. Their products and services have been continually updated, altered and modified. Some changes are small, incremental adaptations to existing ways of doing things. Others are radical, major departures from anything that has gone before. The innovation activity is about successfully delivering change in its many different forms. Being good at innovation has always been important, but what has changed in recent years is the sheer speed and scale of innovation in industries all over the world. Innovation processes are also increasingly complex, with inputs from different individuals and departments within an organization, and a wide variety of external sources.

While operations managers may not always have full responsibility for service and product innovation, they're always involved in some way, if only to provide the information and advice upon which successful service or product development depends. However, increasingly operations managers *are* expected to take a greater and more active part in product and service innovation. Unless a product, however well designed, can be produced to a high standard, and unless a service, however well conceived, can be

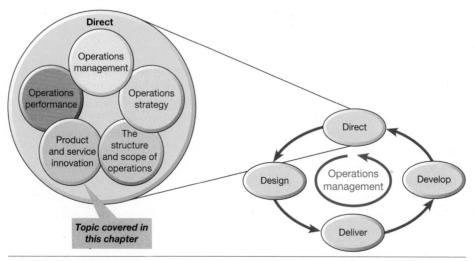

Figure 4.1 This chapter examines product and service innovation

implemented, they will never generate full benefits. In this chapter, we examine what is meant by product and service innovation; the strategic role of innovation; the key stages in the innovation process; and aspects of resources that must be considered to support innovation. Figure 4.1 shows where this chapter fits into the overall operations model.

What is product and service innovation?

There are a number of terms that we shall use in this chapter that have similar meanings, and are defined by different authorities in different ways, or overlap to some extent, and yet are related to each other. Specifically, we explore three related terms of creativity, innovation and design.

Creativity, innovation and design

The study of product and service innovation, what influences it and how to manage it, is a huge subject. However, a repeating theme in most innovation research is 'creativity'. Creativity is the ability to move beyond conventional ideas, rules or assumptions, in order to generate significant new ideas. It is a vital ingredient in innovation. It is seen as essential not just in product and service innovation, but also in the design and management of operations processes more generally. Partly because of the fast-changing nature of many industries, a lack of creativity (and consequently of innovation) is seen as a major risk.

The term 'innovation' is notoriously ambiguous and lacks either a single definition or measure. It is . . . 'a new method, idea, product, etc.' (*Oxford English Dictionary*), 'change that creates a new dimension of performance' (Peter Drucker, a well-known management writer), 'the act of introducing something new' (the *American Heritage Dictionary*), or 'a new idea, method or device' (*Webster Online Dictionary*). What runs through all these definitions is the idea of novelty and change. Innovation goes further than 'creativity' or 'invention' as it implies the process of transforming ideas into something that is not simply novel, but also has the potential to be practical and provide a commercial return.

'Design' is the process that transforms innovative ideas into something more concrete. Innovation creates the novel idea; design makes it work in practice. A design must deliver a solution that will work in practice and is an activity that can be approached at different levels of detail. Figure 4.2 illustrates the relationship between creativity, innovation and design as we use the terms here. These concepts are intimately related, which is why we treat them in the same chapter. First we will look at some of the basic ideas that help to understand innovation.

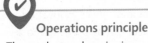

Operations principle

The product and service innovation process must consider three related issues of creativity, innovation and design.

The innovation S-curve

When new ideas are introduced in services, products or processes, they rarely have an impact that increases uniformly over time. Usually performance follows an S-shaped progress, as illustrated in Figure 4.3. In the early stages of the introduction of new ideas, although often large amounts of resources, time and effort are needed to introduce the idea, relatively small performance improvements are experienced. However, with time, as experience and knowledge about the new idea grows, performance increases. As the idea becomes established, extending its performance further becomes increasingly difficult (Figure 4.3(a)). When an idea reaches its mature, 'levelling-off' period, it is vulnerable to new ideas being introduced which, in turn, move through their own S-shaped progression. This is how innovation works; the limits of one idea being reached prompt newer, better ideas, with each new S-curve requiring some degree of re-design (see Figure 4.3(b)).

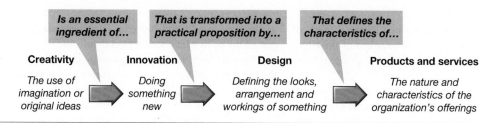

Figure 4.2 The relationship between creativity, innovation and design

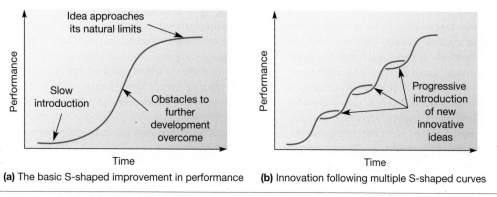

(a) The basic S-shaped improvement in performance

(b) Innovation following multiple S-shaped curves

Figure 4.3 The S-shaped curve of innovation

OPERATIONS IN PRACTICE	Dyson Innovation blows (and sucks) away the opposition[1]

In 2016, Dyson, the technology company, released its latest product – the Dyson Supersonic, a £299 hairdryer that marked the company's first move into the beauty sector and a major departure from its current range of products. Sir James Dyson's 'labour of love' took four years and cost £50 million to develop. The price of the product was significantly more than other high-end hairdryers and yet it was a phenomenal success, blitzing demand forecasts. According to Dyson, the priority was to *'alleviate the frustrations with conventional hairdryers which are unwieldy, tend to have weak airflow, and have the ability to damage your hair'*. The product was much lighter than traditional models, largely because the motor used in the Dyson product was so much smaller than traditional hairdryers. Steve Courtney, the project's senior engineer commented that *'bulky motors have held back hairdryer design. Developing our smallest, lightest digital motor meant we could change that.'* In addition, the new product overcame the issues of hair damage caused by

high temperatures of many traditional hairdryers. The Dyson Supersonic operated at a maximum temperature of 150 degrees compared to around 230 degrees for its leading competitors. In addition, Dyson's team of aero-acoustic engineers reduced the sound of the hairdryer significantly by pushing one of the key motor tones beyond the audible range for humans.

Whilst Dyson's products may seem diverse (vacuum cleaners, hand dryers, fans, hairdryers, heaters and humidifiers), they share similarities in terms of the technology use to generate airflow. And this technological innovation started its journey back in 1978, when a young James Dyson noticed how the air filter in the spray-finishing room of a company where he had been working was constantly clogging with power particles (just like a vacuum cleaner bag clogs with dust). So he designed and built an industrial cyclone tower, which removed the powder particles by exerting centrifugal forces. The question intriguing him was, *'Could the same principle work in a domestic vacuum cleaner?'* Five years and *five thousand* prototypes later he had a working design, since praised for its uniqueness and functionality. However, existing vacuum cleaner manufacturers were not as impressed – two rejected the design outright. So Dyson started making the product himself. Over the years, Dyson engineers have taken their vacuum technology further, developing core separator technology to capture even more microscopic dirt. Dirt now goes through three stages of separation. Firstly, dirt is drawn into a powerful outer cyclone. Centrifugal forces fling larger debris such as pet hair and dust particles into the clear bin at 500g (the maximum g-force the human body can take is 8g). Second, a further cyclonic stage, the core separator, removes dust particles as small as 0.5 microns from the airflow – particles so small you could fit 200 of them on this full stop. Finally, a cluster of smaller, even faster cyclones generate centrifugal forces of up to 150,000g – extracting particles

as small as mould and bacteria. Dyson cleaners now outsell the rivals who once rejected them.

Other designs, like the Dyson Supersonic, built on these early innovations. The Dyson Airblade is an electric hand dryer that dries hands quicker (around 10 seconds) and uses less electricity than conventional hand dryers. The Dyson Air Multipliers are a range of fans and fan heaters that work very differently to conventional fans and electric heaters. They don't have fast-spinning blades that chop the air and cause uncomfortable buffeting. Instead, they use Air Multiplier™ technology to draw in air and amplify it up to 18 times, producing an uninterrupted stream of smooth air. Sir James said the heater was part of the company's effort to turn itself into a *'broadline technology company'* rather than being seen as only an appliance maker. *'I would not limit the company to particular areas of technology or markets. We are developing a range of technologies to improve both industrial and consumer products so that the people using them get a better experience than with the comparable items that currently exist.'*

Alongside the success of the Dyson Supersonic, the company also saw an explosion in revenues from China (244 per cent), South Korea (100 per cent) and Japan (30 per cent), driven largely by sales of its cordless vacuum cleaners. The firm also announced a £330 million investment into its operations in Singapore aimed at improving both manufacturing and R&D capabilities, and opened a technology laboratory in China. Its biggest surprise, though, was its announcement in 2018 of a £2.8 billion investment in the development of three electric vehicles – a venture that auto industry commentators agreed was significant largely because of Dyson's proven success in its innovation processes.

Incremental or radical innovation

An obvious difference in how the pattern of new ideas emerges in different operations or industries is the rate and scale of innovation. Some industries, such as telecommunications, enjoy frequent and often significant innovations. Others, such as house building, do have innovations, but they are usually less dramatic. So, some innovation is radical, resulting in discontinuous, 'breakthrough' change, while other innovations are more incremental, leading to smaller, continuous changes. Radical innovation often includes large technological advancements that may require completely new knowledge and/or resources, making existing services and products obsolete and therefore non-competitive. Incremental innovation, by contrast, is more likely to involve relatively modest technological changes and to build upon existing knowledge and/ or resources, so existing services and products are not fundamentally changed. This is why established companies may favour incremental innovation: because they have the experience to have built up a significant pool of knowledge (on which incremental innovation is based). In addition, established companies are more likely to have a mindset that emphasizes continuity, perhaps not even recognizing potential innovative opportunities. New entrants to markets, however, have no established position to lose, nor do they have a vast pool of experience. As such, they may be more likely to try for more radical innovation.

What is the strategic role of product and service innovation?

Product and service innovation is a risky business. Not every idea is transformed, or is capable of being incorporated, into the design of a successful product or service. Sometimes this is because an innovative idea is just too challenging, at least with realistically available technology, or under prevailing market conditions. Sometimes the development cost is out of the reach of the business that had the original idea. Ideas may be abundant, but resources are limited. Yet despite the obstacles to successful innovation, almost all firms strive to be innovative. The reason is that there is overwhelming evidence that innovation can generate significant payback for the organizations that manage the incorporation of innovative ideas in the design of their products and services. What matters is the ability to identify the innovations and manage their transformation into effective designs so that they can sustain competitive advantage and/or generate social payback. As such, good design takes innovative ideas and makes them practical. So the design activity has one overriding objective: to provide products, services and processes which will satisfy the operation's customers. Remember, an organization's products and services are how markets judge it – they are its 'public face'. *Product* designers try to achieve aesthetically pleasing designs that exceed customers' expectations. They also try to design a product that performs well and is reliable during its lifetime. Further, they should design the product so that it can be manufactured easily and quickly. Similarly, *service* designers try to put together a service that exceeds customer expectations. Yet at the same time the service must be within the capabilities of the operation and be delivered at reasonable cost. Effective product and service innovation processes add value to any organization by:

▶ driving and operationalizing innovation, increasing market share and opening up new markets;
▶ differentiating products and services, making them more attractive to customers, while increasing consistency in the company's range, and helping to ensure successful product launches;
▶ strengthening branding, so that products and services embody a company's values;
▶ reducing the overall costs associated with innovation, through more efficient use of resources, reduced project failure rate and faster time to market.

OPERATIONS IN PRACTICE — Innovation partnerships in the auto industry[2]

Innovation alliances and shared products are becoming increasingly common in the auto industry, mainly to keep down escalating development costs and to share the considerable investment needed to meet new regulatory requirements for carbon dioxide emissions and safety standards. BMW and Toyota are one such example, with a technology development partnership for a variety of projects including fuel cell systems, powertrain electrification, lightweight materials, and a joint sports car vehicle platform used for the BMW Z4 Roadster and Toyota Supra. The collaborative undertaking was designed to bring together the development expertise, knowledge and financial resources of two of the most successful automobile companies in what they called '*a mid-to-long-term collaboration on next-generation environment-friendly technologies*'. BMW's chairman at the time, Norbert Reithofer, emphasized the strategic importance of the

partnership: '*Toyota is the leading provider of environment-friendly technology in the volume segment and the BMW Group is the most innovative and sustainable manufacturer of premium automobiles. We are now joining forces to further develop environment-friendly technologies and to expand our innovation leadership in each of our segments.'* Akio Toyoda, president of Toyota, said the deal was *'a great joy and a thrill'* and that he looked forward to allying his company to one that *'makes cars that are fun to drive. Both companies will bring their wide-ranging knowledge, starting with that concerning environmental technologies, to the table and make ever-better cars.'* The new sports car platform brings together Toyota's world-class manufacturing expertise and BMW's engineering talents and understanding of high-performance engines. *'We could do a sports car by ourselves. But if you look at the whole package . . . it makes sense. Both companies can have benefits. Sports cars are all about volumes because they can be relatively small',* said Herbert Diess, BMW board member and head of development.

However, not all alliances have been successful. Two years before the announcement of the Toyota–BMW deal, a partnership between VW and Suzuki broke up acrimoniously. The original intention was for the largest European carmaker, VW, to share development of a small car with Suzuki – the fourth player in the Japanese market. The jointly developed model was supposed to be aimed at growing markets such as India through Suzuki's leading position in that country. However, the deal fell apart. There were claims, which it denied, that VW was not doing as much sharing of its technology as Suzuki had envisaged, while VW argued that a deal between Suzuki and Fiat for diesel engines was a contractual breach. Suzuki had formed an alliance with Fiat some years earlier to make diesel engines in Asia and then extended the deal by sourcing diesel engines from Fiat for cars built in Hungary (Suzuki denied that the deal broke the agreement). After the break-up, industry analysts said the partnership had failed to benefit either company. Part of the problem seemed to be a lack of strategic fit. Volkswagen was a very big company trying to become the world's biggest auto company, while Suzuki was a relatively small company trying to focus on specific regional markets. But there were also different, and contrasting, corporate cultures that inhibited cooperation. Some saw Volkswagen as wanting to be the lead player in the partnership and Suzuki, with a reputation for valuing its independence, refusing to play the role of junior partner.

The process of design

At its most basic level, the innovation activity is a process that involves many of the same design issues common to other operations processes. As such, it is a process that conforms to the input–transformation–output model described in Chapter 1. Although organizations will have their own particular ways of managing innovation and design, the design *process* itself is essentially very similar across a whole range of industries. In general, the better the design process is managed, the better the service and product offering. Figure 4.4 illustrates the design activity as an input–transformation–output diagram. The transformed resource inputs will consist mainly of information in the form of market forecasts, market preferences, technical data and potential design ideas. It is these ideas and information that will be transformed in the design process into the final design. The process of transforming resource inputs includes the operations and design managers who manage the process, together with specialist technical staff with the specific knowledge necessary to solve design problems. It also may include suppliers, other collaborators and even especially interested customer groups (sometimes called 'lead users') who are brought in to provide their expertise. Transforming resources may also include computer-aided design (CAD) equipment and software.

Operations principle

The design activity is a process that can be managed using the same principles as other processes.

Performance objectives for the product and service innovation process

The performance of the design process can be assessed in much the same way as we would consider the products and services that result from it, namely in terms of quality, speed, dependability, flexibility and cost. Because product and service design has such an influence on sustainability, we include it alongside our normal operational-level objectives. These performance objectives have just as much relevance for innovation as they do for the on-going delivery of offerings once they are introduced to the market.

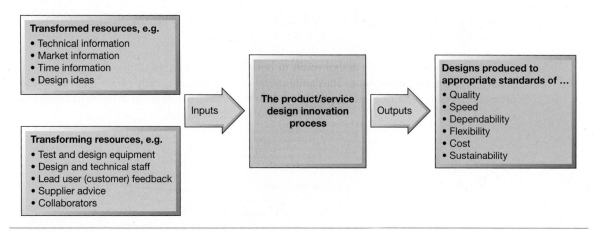

Figure 4.4 The product and service design innovation activity as a process

What does quality mean for the innovation process?

Design quality is not always easy to define precisely, especially if customers are relatively satisfied with existing service and product offerings. Many software companies talk about the 'I don't know what I want, but I'll know when I see it' syndrome, meaning that only when customers use the software are they in a position to articulate what they do or don't require. Nevertheless, it is possible to distinguish high- and low-quality designs (although this is easier to do in hindsight) by judging them in terms of their ability to meet market requirements. In doing this, the distinction between the specification quality and the conformance quality of designs is important. No business would want a design process that was indifferent to 'errors' in its designs, yet some are more tolerant than others. For example, in pharmaceutical development the potential for harm is particularly high because drugs directly affect our health. This is why the authorities insist on such a prolonged and thorough 'design' process (more usually called 'development' in that industry). Although withdrawing a drug from the market is unusual, it does occasionally occur. Far more frequent are the 'product recalls' that are relatively common in, for example, the automotive industry. Many of these are design related and the result of 'conformance' failures in the design process. The 'specification' quality of design is different. It means the degree of functionality, or experience, or aesthetics, or whatever the product or service is primarily competing on.

Operations principle

Innovation processes can be judged in terms of their levels of quality, speed, dependability, flexibility, cost and sustainability.

What does speed mean for the innovation process?

The speed of design matters more to some industries than others. For example, design innovation in construction and aerospace happens at a much slower pace than in clothing or microelectronics. However, rapid product or service innovation or 'time-based competition' has become the norm for an increasing number of industries. Sometimes this is the result of fast-changing consumer fashion. Sometimes a rapidly changing technology base forces it. Yet, no matter what the motivation, fast design brings a number of advantages.

▶ Early market launch – an ability to innovate speedily means that service and product offerings can be introduced to the market earlier and thus earn revenue for longer, and may command price premiums.

▶ Starting design late – alternatively, starting the design process later may have advantages, especially where either the nature of customer demand or the availability of technology is uncertain and dynamic, so fast design allows design decisions to be made closer to the time when service and product offerings are introduced to the market.

▶ Frequent market stimulation – rapid innovations allow frequent new or updated offerings to be introduced into the market.

Delays in the speed of the design result in both more expenditure on the design and delayed (and probably reduced) revenue. The combination of these effects usually means that the financial break-even point for a new offering is delayed far more than the original delay in its launch (see Figure 4.5).

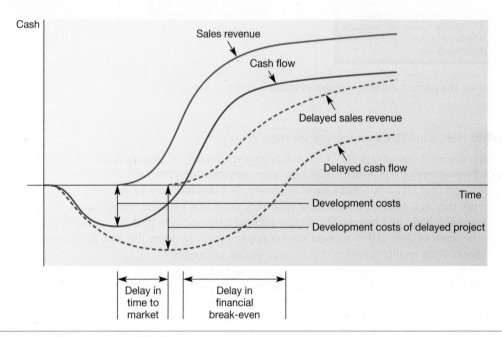

Figure 4.5 Delay in time to market of new innovations not only reduces and delays revenues, it also increases the costs of development. The combination of both of these effects usually delays the financial break-even point far more than the delay in the launch

IKEA's slow development process[3]

Most companies are obsessed with reducing the time to market (TTM) of their design process. Short TTM means lower development costs and more opportunities to hit the market with new designs. Some auto companies have reduced the design time for their products to less than three years, while a new smartphone (a far more dynamic market) can be developed in as little as six months. So why does IKEA, the most successful homeware retailer ever, take five years to design its kitchens? Because, with the huge volumes that IKEA sells, development costs are small compared with the savings that can result from product designs that bring down the final price in their stores.

'It's five years of work into finding ways to engineer cost out of the system, to improve the functionality,' IKEA's Chief Executive Peter Agnefjäll said of the company's 'Metod' kitchen (which means 'Method' in English). Metod is a complex product. It has over a thousand different components. The kitchen is a product of IKEA's 'democratic design' process that ensures designs that will work in homes anywhere in the world – an important consideration when you sell about one million kitchens a year. Also, unlike some big-ticket purchases, consumer taste in home furnishing does not shift rapidly. *'We still hang paintings above the sofa and tend to have a TV in the corner,'* says IKEA Creative Director Mia Lundström. But even if trends do not materialize overnight, it is still important to spot emerging consumer preferences. A research team visits thousands of homes annually and compiles reports that look as far as a decade into the future. So without the imperative to change its designs too frequently, product cost becomes a key driver. Rather than buy prefabricated components from outside sources, IKEA will develop its own if it will keep costs down.

What does dependability mean for the innovation process?

Rapid innovation processes that cannot be relied on to deliver dependably create significant challenges for organizations. Design schedule slippage can extend design times (speed effects), but worse, a lack of dependability adds to the uncertainty surrounding the innovation process. Unexpected technical difficulties, such as suppliers who themselves do not deliver solutions on time, or markets that change during the innovation process itself, all contribute to an uncertain and ambiguous design environment. Professional project management (see Chapter 19) of the innovation process can help to reduce uncertainty and prevent (or give early warning of) missed deadlines, process bottlenecks and resource shortages. Disturbances to the innovation process may be minimized through close liaison with suppliers as well as market or environmental monitoring. Nevertheless, unexpected disruptions will always occur, especially for the most innovative product and service designs. This is why flexibility within the innovation process is one of the most important ways in which dependable delivery of new service and product offerings can be ensured.

What does flexibility mean for the innovation process?

Flexibility in the innovation process is the ability to cope with external or internal change. The most common reason for external change is that markets, or specific customers, change their requirements. Although flexibility may not be needed in relatively predictable markets, it is clearly valuable in more fast-moving and volatile markets, where one's own customers and markets change, or where the designs of competitors' offerings dictate a matching or leapfrogging move. Internal changes include the emergence of superior technical solutions. In addition, the increasing complexity and interconnectedness of service and product components in an offering may require flexibility. A bank, for example, may bundle together a number of separate services for one particular segment of its market. Privileged account holders may obtain special deposit rates, premium credit cards, insurance offers, travel facilities and so on together in the same package. Changing one aspect of this package may require changes to be made in other elements. So extending the credit card benefits to include extra travel insurance may also mean the redesign of the separate insurance element of the package. One way of measuring innovation flexibility is to compare the cost of modifying a design in response to such changes against the consequences for profitability if no changes are made. The lower the cost of modifying an offering in response to a given change, the higher is the level of flexibility.

What does cost mean for the innovation process?

The cost of innovation is usually analysed in a similar way to the on-going cost of delivering offerings to customers. These cost factors are split up into three categories: the cost of buying the inputs to the process, the cost of providing the labour in the process and the other general overhead costs of running the process. In most in-house innovation processes the latter two costs outweigh the former.

What does sustainability mean for the innovation process?

The sustainability of a product or service is the extent to which it benefits the 'triple bottom line' – people, planet and profit. The design innovation process is particularly important in ultimately impacting on the ethical, environmental and economic wellbeing of stakeholders. Organizations increasingly consider sustainability in the design process. For example, some innovation activity is particularly focused on the ethical dimension of sustainability. Banks have moved to offer customers ethical investments that seek to maximize social benefit as well as financial returns. Such investments tend to avoid businesses involved in weaponry, gambling, alcohol and tobacco, for example, and favour those promoting worker education, environmental stewardship and consumer protection. Other examples of ethically focused innovations include the development of 'fair-trade' products. Similarly, garment manufacturers may establish ethical trading initiatives with suppliers; supermarkets may ensure animal welfare for meat and dairy products; and online companies may institute customer complaint charters.

Product or service innovation may also focus on the environmental dimension of sustainability. Critically examining the components of products towards a change of materials in the design could significantly reduce the environmental burden. Examples include the use of organic cotton or bamboo in clothing; wood or paper from managed forests used in garden furniture, stationery and flooring; recycled materials for carrier bags; and natural dyes in clothing, curtains and upholstery. Other innovations may be more focused on the use stage of an offering. The MacBook Air, for example, introduced an advanced power management system that reduced its power requirements. In the detergent industry, Unilever and Procter & Gamble have developed products that allow clothes to be washed at much lower temperatures. Architecture firms are increasingly designing houses that can operate with minimal energy or use sustainable sources of energy such as solar panels. Some innovations focus on making product components within an offering easier to recycle or re-manufacture once they have reached the end of their life. For example, some food packaging has been designed to break down easily when disposed of, allowing its conversion into high-quality compost. Mobile phones are often designed to be taken apart at the end of their life, so valuable raw materials can be re-used. For example, in 2018 Apple debuted a new robot, named Daisy, capable of disassembling 200 iPhones per hour in order to recover the various precious materials contained within. In the automotive industry, over 75 per cent of materials are now recycled.

Design innovation is not just confined to the initial conception of a product; it also applies to the end of its life. This idea is often called 'designing for the circular economy'. The circular economy (also called closed-loop or take-back economy) is proposed as an alternative to the traditional linear economy (or make-use-dispose, as it is termed). The idea is to keep products in use for as long as possible, extract the maximum value from them while in use and then recover and regenerate products and materials at the end of their service life. But the circular economy is much more than a concern for recycling as opposed to disposal. The circular economy examines what can be done right along the supply and use chain so that as few resources as possible are used, then products are recovered and regenerated at the end of their conventional life. This means designing products for longevity, reparability, ease of dismantling and recycling.

OPERATIONS IN PRACTICE	Product innovation for the circular economy[4]

Typical of the companies that have adopted the idea of the circular economy is Newlife Paints. It 'remanufactures' waste water-based paint back into a premium grade emulsion. All products in its paint range guarantee a minimum 50 per cent recycled content, made up from waste paint diverted from landfill or incineration. The idea for the company began to take root in the mind of industrial chemist, Keith Harrison. His garage was becoming a little unruly, after many years of do-it-yourself projects. Encouraged by his wife to clear out the mess, he realized that the stacked-up tins of paint represented a shocking waste. It was then that his search began for a sensible and environmentally responsible solution to waste paint. *'I kept thinking I could do something with it, the paint had an*

▶

intrinsic value. It would have been a huge waste just to throw it away.' Keith thought somebody must be recycling it, but no one was, and he set about finding a way to reprocess waste paint back to a superior grade emulsion. After two years of research, Keith successfully developed his technology, which involves removing leftover paint from tins and blending and filtering them to produce colour-matched new paints. The company has also launched a premium brand, aimed at affluent customers with a green conscience, called Reborn Paints, the development of which was partly funded by Akzo Nobel, maker of Dulux Paints. Although Keith started small, he now licenses his technology to companies such as the giant French transnational waste company Veolia. *'By licensing we can have more impact and spread internationally,'* he says.

What are the stages of product and service innovation?

Fully specified designs rarely spring, fully formed, from a designer's imagination. The design activity will generally pass through several key stages. It moves from the concept generation stage, to a screening stage, to a preliminary design stage that produces a design to be evaluated and prototyped before reaching the final design.

To create a fully specified service or product offering, potential designs tend to pass through a sequence of stages in the innovation process, shown in Figure 4.6. Although in practice designers will often recycle or backtrack through the stages and the sequence of stages will differ to some extent, most will use a stage model similar to this one. The innovation process starts with a general idea or 'concept' and progresses through to a fully defined specification for the offering incorporating various service and product components. In between these two states, the offering may pass through stages such as concept screening, preliminary design (including consideration of standardization, commonality, modularization and mass customization), evaluation and improvement, prototyping and final design.

> **Operations principle**
>
> Design processes involve a number of stages that move an innovation from a concept to a fully specified state.

Concept generation

Concept generation is where innovative ideas become the inspiration for new service or product concepts. And innovation can come from many different sources, both from within the organization and from outside.

Figure 4.6 The stages of product/service design innovation

Ideas from research and development – Many organizations have a formal research and development (R&D) function. As its name implies, its role is twofold. Research develops new knowledge and ideas in order to solve a particular problem or to grasp an opportunity. Development utilizes and operationalizes the ideas that come from research. And although 'development' may not sound as exciting as 'research', it often requires as much creativity and even more persistence. One product has commemorated the persistence of its development engineers in the product's name. Back in 1953 the Rocket Chemical Company set out to create a rust-prevention solvent and degreaser to be used in the aerospace industry. It took them 40 attempts to get the water displacing formula worked out. So that is what they called the product. WD-40 literally stands for Water Displacement, 40th attempt.

Ideas from staff – The contact staff in a service organization or the salesperson in a product-oriented organization could meet customers every day. These staff may have good ideas about what customers like and do not like. They may have gathered suggestions from customers or have ideas of their own. One well-known example – which may be urban myth – is that an employee at SwanVestas, the matchmaker, suggested having one instead of two sandpaper strips on the matchbox. It saved a fortune!

When Apple introduced its first-generation iPhone, the world of smartphones was changed forever. It was arguably one of the most influential products ever to be launched in the consumer technology market and set the benchmark for smartphones that came after it. Millions of iPhones have been sold over the last decade, making Apple one of the world's most valuable companies. However, the way that Apple managed the innovation process for its iPhone remained something of a secret for years after the product's launch. Originally visualized as a tablet computer, work on the iPhone was initiated partly because of the success of the firm's earlier product, the iPod music player. It was the profound effect that the iPod had on the music industry that encouraged Apple to consider what other markets it could challenge. Yet, it was a technological breakthrough, multi-touch display, which allowed the company to change course. As Steve Jobs said later, '*I had this idea about having a glass display, a multi-touch display you could type on. I asked our people about it. And six months later they came back with this amazing display.* [When] *we got inertial scrolling working and some other things, I thought, "My God, we can build a phone with this" and we put the tablet aside, and we went to work on the phone.*' But making the multi-touch display a working proposition was challenging for Apple's engineering team. They had to create an entirely new way in which users could interact with their phones. There were many novel unsolved problems to overcome. Every single part of the design had to be rethought to adapt to touch. For example, engineers had to make scrolling work on the iPhone not only when a user's finger moved up and down, but also when a user's thumb moved in an arc across the screen. And there were many other obstacles to overcome, some of which seemed almost insurmountable. Sir Jonathan Ive, Senior Vice-President of Design at Apple, has admitted that issues with the touchscreen were so difficult that it brought the project to the brink of being aborted. '*There were multiple times when we nearly shelved it because there were fundamental problems that we couldn't solve,*' said Sir Jonathan. '*I would put the phone to my ear and my ear dialled a number. The challenge is that you have to then detect all sorts of ear shapes, chin shapes, skin colour and hairdos. We had to develop technology, basically a number of*

▶

sensors, to inform the phone that "this is now going up to an ear, please deactivate the touchscreen"'.

Security during development was obsessively tight. For example, the senior Apple executive in charge of developing what would later become known as the iOS operating system was told that he could choose anyone he wanted from within Apple to join the embryonic iPhone team, but he was not allowed to hire anybody from outside the company. He could not even convey to potential team members exactly what they would be working on, just that it was a new and exciting project and that they would have to *'work hard, give up nights, and work weekends for years'.* When the development team formed, they were located on a separate and secured floor on Apple's campus. The development area was 'locked down' with extensive use of badge readers and cameras. Team members might have to show their badges five or six times to gain access.

The aesthetics of the iPhone were treated as being just as important as the iPhone technology. This was the responsibility of Apple's secretive industrial design group. Apple designer, Christopher Stringer, said that their objective was to create a *'new, original, and beautiful object* [that was] *so wonderful that you couldn't imagine how*

you'd follow it'. The design group, Stringer explained, comprised 16 'maniacal' individuals who shared one singular purpose – to *'imagine products that don't exist and guide them to life'.* They worked closely together, often gathering around a 'kitchen table' where team members exchanged ideas, often in a 'brutally honest' way. To the designers, even the tiniest of details were important. They often would create up to 50 designs of a single component before moving on to computer-aided design modelling and the creation of physical mock-ups.

The fact that the Apple designers overcame several technology and production bugs during the iPhone's development is partly a testament to its design team's belief, both in their technological skills and in their understanding of what people will buy. Apple avoids conducting market research when designing its products, a policy introduced by Steve Jobs, its late chief executive. *'We absolutely don't do focus groups,'* said Ive. *'That's designers and leaders abdicating responsibility. That's them looking for an insurance policy, so if something goes wrong, they can say, well this focus group says that only 30 per cent of people are offended by this and, look, 40 per cent think it's OK. What a focus group does is that it will guarantee mediocrity.'*

Ideas from competitor activity – Most organizations follow the activities of their competitors. A new idea from a competitor may be worth imitating, or better still, improving upon. Taking apart a competitor's service or product to explore potential new ideas is called 'reverse engineering'. Some aspects of services may be difficult to reverse engineer (especially 'back-office' services), as they are less transparent to competitors.

Ideas from customers – Marketing, the function generally responsible for identifying new service or product opportunities, may use market research tools for gathering data from customers in a structured way to test out ideas or check services or products against predetermined criteria. Ideas may also come from customers on a day-to-day basis; from complaints, or from every-day transactions. Organizations are increasingly developing mechanisms to facilitate the collection of this form of information. At a group level, crowdsourcing is the process of getting work or funding, or ideas (usually online) from a crowd of people.

Open sourcing – using a development community

Not all 'products' or services are created by professional, employed designers for commercial purposes. An open community, including the people who use the products, develops many of the software applications that we all use. If you use Google, Wikipedia or Amazon, you are using open-source software. The basic concept of open source software is simple. Large communities of people around the world, who have the ability to write software code, come together and produce a software product. The finished product is not only available to be used by anyone or any organization for free, but is regularly updated to ensure it keeps pace with the necessary improvements. The production of open source software is very well organized and, like its commercial equivalent, is continuously supported and maintained. However, unlike its commercial equivalent, it is absolutely free to use. Over the last decade, the growth of open source has been phenomenal with many organizations transitioning over to using this stable, robust and secure software. Open source has been the biggest change in software development for decades and is setting new open standards in the way software is used. The open nature of this type of development also encourages compatibility between products. BMW, for example, was reported to be developing an open-source platform for vehicle electronics. Using an open-source approach, rather than using proprietary software, BMW can allow providers of 'infotainment' services to develop compatible, plug-and-play applications.

Crowdsourcing

Closely related to the open sourcing idea is that of 'crowdsourcing'. Crowdsourcing is the process of getting work or funding, or ideas (usually online) from a crowd of people. Although in essence it is not a totally new idea, it has become a valuable source of ideas largely through the use of the Internet and social networking. For example, Procter & Gamble, the consumer products company, asked amateur scientists to explore ideas for a detergent dye whose colour changed when enough has been added to dishwater. Other uses of the idea involve government agencies asking citizens to prioritize spending (or cutting spending) projects.

'Lead users' and 'harbingers of failure'

Although the marketing function is generally responsible for identifying new service or product opportunities, often using formal structured market research tools, ideas may come less formally: for example, listening to customers on a day-to-day basis from everyday transactions or from complaints. A particularly useful source of customer-inspired innovation, especially for products and services subject to rapid change, is so-called 'lead users'. Lead users are users who are ahead of the majority of the market on a major market trend, and who also have a high incentive to innovate. Producers seeking user innovations to manufacture try to source innovations from lead users – because these will be most profitable to manufacture. These are the customers who, unlike most customers, have the real-world experience needed to problem solve and provide accurate data to inquiring market researchers. As these lead users will be familiar with both the positives and negatives of the early versions of products and services, they are a particularly valuable source of potentially innovative ideas.

By contrast, another category of customer may be valuable because of their ability to consistently make bad purchase decisions. One study claims that the same group of consumers has a tendency to purchase all kinds of failed products, time after time, flop after flop. These are the 'harbingers of failure'. As one of the authors of the study put it, *'These harbingers of failure have the unusual property that they keep on buying products that are taken from the shelves. These star-crossed consumers can sniff out flop-worthy products of all kinds. If you're the kind of person who bought something that really didn't resonate with the market, say, coffee-flavoured Coca-Cola, then that also means you're more likely to buy a type of toothpaste or laundry detergent that fails to resonate with the market.'*

Concept screening

Concept screening is the first stage of implementation where potential innovations are considered for further development against key criteria. It is not possible to translate all concepts into viable product or service packages. Organizations need to be selective. For example, DuPont estimates that the ratio of concepts to marketable offerings is around 250-to-1. In the pharmaceuticals industry, the ratio is closer to 10,000-to-1. The purpose of concept screening is to take initial concepts and evaluate them for their feasibility (can we do it?), acceptability (do we want to do it?) and vulnerability (what are the risks of doing it?). Concepts may have to pass through many different screens, and several functions might be involved. Table 4.1 gives typical feasibility, acceptability and vulnerability questions for marketing, operations and finance functions.

During concept screening a key issue to consider is deciding how big the innovation should be and where it should focus – innovation to the customer offering as opposed to innovation to the process of

> **Operations principle**
>
> The screening of designs should include feasibility, acceptability and vulnerability criteria.

Table 4.1 Some typical evaluation questions for marketing, operations and finance

Evaluation criteria	Marketing	Operations	Finance
Feasibility	Is the market likely to be big enough?	Do we have the capabilities to deliver it?	Do we have access to finance to develop and launch it?
Acceptability	How much market share could it gain?	How much will we have to reorganize our activities to deliver it?	How much financial return will there be on our investment?
Vulnerability	What is the risk of it failing in the marketplace?	What is the risk of our being unable to deliver it acceptably?	How much money could we lose if things do not go to plan?

delivery. The vast majority of innovation is continuous or incremental in nature. Here the emphasis is on steady improvement to existing offerings and to the processes that deliver them. This kind of approach to innovation is very much reflected in the lean and total quality management perspectives. On the other hand, some innovation is discontinuous and involves radical change that is 'new to the world'. Discontinuous innovation is relatively rare – perhaps 5–10 per cent of all innovations could be classified as such – but creates major challenges for existing players within a market. This is because organizations are often unwilling to disrupt current modes of working in the face of a barely emerging market, but by the time the threat has emerged more fully it may be too late to respond. Clayton Christensen refers to this problem as the Innovator's Dilemma,[6] which supports the ideas of the renowned economist Joseph Schumpeter that innovation should be a process of 'creative destruction'.

The design funnel

Applying these evaluation criteria progressively reduces the number of options which will be available further along in the design activity. For example, deciding to make the outside casing of a camera case from aluminium rather than plastic limits later decisions, such as the overall size and shape of the case. This means that the uncertainty surrounding the design reduces as the number of alternative designs being considered decreases. Figure 4.7 shows what is sometimes called the design funnel, depicting the progressive reduction of design options from many to one. But reducing design uncertainty also impacts on the cost of changing one's mind on some detail of the design. In most stages of design, changing a decision is bound to incur some sort of rethinking and recalculation of costs. Early on in the design activity, before too many fundamental decisions have been made, the costs of change are relatively low. However, as the design progresses the interrelated and cumulative decisions already made become increasingly expensive to change.

Preliminary design

Having generated an acceptable, feasible and viable service or product concept, the next stage is to create a preliminary design. The first task in this stage of design is to define exactly what will go into the service or product. For service-dominant offerings this may involve documentation in the form of job instructions or 'service blueprints'. For product-dominant offerings, preliminary design involves defining product specifications (McDonald's has over 50 specifications for the potatoes used for its fries) and the bill of materials, which details all the components needed for a single product. For example, the components for a remote 'presentation' mouse may include the presentation mouse itself, a receiver unit and packaging. All these three items are made up of components, which are, in turn, made up of other components, and so on. A 'component structure', shown in Figure 4.8, is the diagram that shows how these components all fit together to make the final product.

At this stage, there are significant opportunities to reduce cost through design simplification. The most elegant product and service innovations are often the simplest. However, when an operation delivers a variety of services or products (as most do) the range can become complex, which in turn

The whole process-based approach to innovation could be interpreted as implying that all new offerings are created in response to a clear and articulated customer need. While this is usually the case, especially for services and products that are similar to (but presumably better than) their predecessors, more radical innovations are often brought about by the innovation itself creating demand. Customers don't usually know that they need something radical. For example, in the late 1970s people were not asking for microprocessors, they did not even know what they were. An engineer in the USA improvised them for a Japanese customer who made calculators. Only later did they become the enabling technology for the PC and after that the innumerable devices that now dominate our lives. Similarly, fly-by-wire, digital cameras, Maersk's super-slow container ships, sushi on conveyor belts and the iPad are all examples of innovations that have been 'pushed' by firms rather than 'pulled' by pre-existing customer demand.

Nor does everyone agree with the dominant rational model in which possible design options are progressively reduced stage by stage through the optimization of known constraints and objectives. For some this neat model of the innovation, which underlies much business and engineering design literature, fails to accurately reflect the creativity, arguments and chaos that sometimes characterize real innovation projects. First, they argue, managers do not start out with an infinite number of options. No one could process that amount of information – and anyway, designers often have some set solutions in their mind, looking for an opportunity to be used. Second, the number of options being considered often increases as time goes by. This may actually be a good thing, especially if the activity was unimaginatively specified in the first place. Third, the real process of innovation involves cycling back, often many times, as potential solutions raise fresh questions or become dead ends, and as requirements and constraints evolve. In summary, the idea of the design funnel does not describe the process of innovation nor does it necessarily even describe what *should* happen. The action-centric or co-evolution perspective of innovation represents the antithesis of the rational model. It posits that offerings are designed through a combination of emotion and creativity; that the process by which this is done is generally improvised; and that the sequencing of innovation stages is in no way universal.

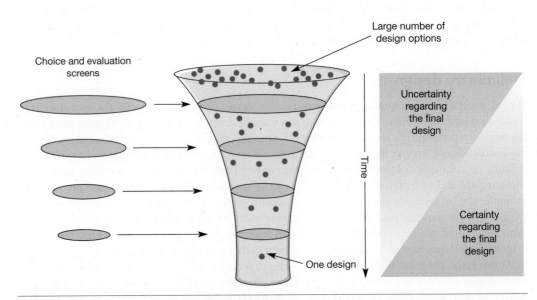

Figure 4.7 The design funnel – progressively reducing the number of possibilities until the final design is reached

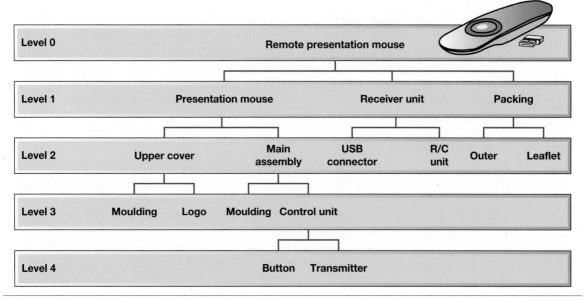

Figure 4.8 Component structure of a remote mouse

increases costs. Designers adopt a number of approaches to reduce design complexity. These include standardization, commonality, modularization and mass customization.

Standardization

Operations sometimes attempt to overcome the cost penalties of high variety by standardizing their products, services or processes. Often it is the operation's outputs that are standardized. Examples of this are fast-food restaurants, discount supermarkets or telephone-based insurance companies. Perhaps the most common example of standardization is the clothes which most us of buy. Although everybody's body shape is different, garment manufacturers produce clothes in only a limited number of sizes. The range of sizes is chosen to give a reasonable fit for most body shapes. Many organizations have significantly improved their profitability by careful variety reduction aimed at offering choice only where it is really valued by the end customer.

Commonality

Using common elements within a service or product can also simplify design complexity. Standardizing the format of information inputs to a process can be achieved by using appropriately designed forms or screen formats. The more different services and products can be based on common components, the less complex it is to produce them. For example, the European aircraft maker, Airbus, has designed its aircraft with a high degree of commonality. This meant that 10 aircraft models ranging from the 100-seat A318 through to the world's largest aircraft, the A380, feature virtually identical flight decks, common systems and similar handling characteristics. In some cases, such as the entire A320 family, the aircraft even share the same 'pilot-type rating', which enables pilots with a single licence to fly any of them. The advantages of commonality for the airline operators include a much shorter training time for pilots and engineers when they move from one aircraft to another. In addition, when up to 90 per cent of all parts are common within a range of aircraft there is a reduced need to carry a wide range of spare parts.

Modularization

The use of modular design principles, seen in computers for example, involves designing standardized 'sub-components' of a service or product, which can be put together in different ways. These standardized modules, or sub-assemblies, can be produced in higher volume, thereby reducing their cost. The package holiday industry can assemble holidays to meet a specific customer requirement, including pre-designed and purchased air travel, accommodation, insurance and so on. Similarly, in education there is an increasing use of modular courses, which allow 'customers' choice but ensure each module has economical student volumes.

Mass customization

Flexibility in design can allow the ability to offer different things to different customers. Normally high variety means high cost, but some companies have developed their flexibility in such a way that customized offerings are produced using high-volume processes and thus costs are minimized. This approach is called mass customization. For example, Paris Miki, an up-market eyewear retailer that has the largest number of eyewear stores in the world, uses its own 'Mikissimes Design System' to capture a digital image of the customer and analyse facial characteristics. Together with a list of customers' personal preferences, the system then recommends a particular design and displays it on the image of the customer's face. In consultation with the optician, the customer can adjust shapes and sizes until the final design is chosen. Within the store the frames are assembled from a range of pre-manufactured components and the lenses ground and fitted to the frames. The whole process takes around an hour.

Design evaluation and improvement

The purpose of this stage in the innovation process is to take the preliminary design and subject it to a series of evaluations to see if it can be improved before the service or product is tested in the market. There are a number of techniques that can be employed at this stage to evaluate and improve the preliminary design. Perhaps the best known is quality function deployment (QFD).

Quality function deployment

The key purpose of QFD is to try to ensure that the eventual innovation actually meets the needs of its customers. It is a technique that was developed in Japan at Mitsubishi's Kobe shipyard and used extensively by Toyota and its suppliers. It is also known as the 'house of quality' (because of its shape) and the 'voice of the customer' (because of its purpose). The technique tries to capture what the customer needs and how it might be achieved. Figure 4.9 shows a simple QFD matrix used in the design of a promotional USB data storage stick. The QFD matrix is a formal articulation of how the company sees the relationship between the requirements of the customer (the *whats*) and the design characteristics of the new product (the *hows*).

▶ The *whats,* or 'customer requirements', are the list of competitive factors which customers find significant. Their relative importance is scored, in this case on a 10-point scale, with *price* scoring the highest.
▶ The competitive scores indicate the relative performance of the product, in this case on a 1 to 5 scale. Also indicated are the performance of two competitor products.
▶ The *hows,* or 'design characteristics' of the product, are the various 'dimensions' of the design, which will operationalize customer requirements within the service or product.
▶ The central matrix (sometimes called the relationship matrix) represents a view of the interrelationship between the *whats* and the *hows*. This is often based on value judgements made by the design team. The symbols indicate the strength of the relationship. All the relationships are studied, but in many cases, where the cell of the matrix is blank, there is none.
▶ The bottom box of the matrix is a technical assessment of the product. This contains the absolute importance of each design characteristic.
▶ The triangular 'roof' of the 'house' captures any information the team has about the correlations (positive or negative) between the various design characteristics.

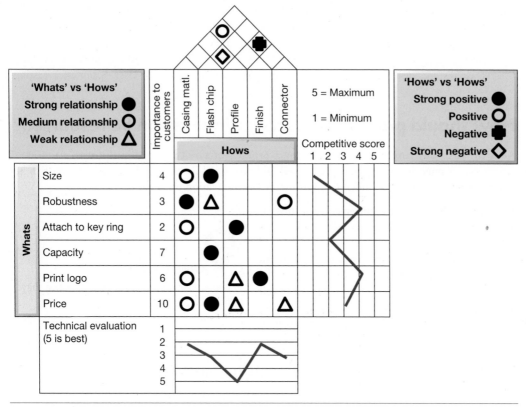

Figure 4.9 QFD matrix for a promotional USB data storage stick

Prototyping and final design

At around this stage in the design activity it is necessary to turn the improved design into a prototype so that it can be tested. It may be too risky to launch a product or service before testing it out, so it is usually more appropriate to create a 'prototype' (in the case of a product) or 'trial' (in the case of a service). Product prototypes include everything from clay models to computer simulations. Service trials may include computer simulations but also the actual implementation of the service on a pilot basis. Many retailing organizations pilot new services and products in a small number of stores in order to test customers' reaction to them. Virtual reality-based simulations allow businesses to test new services and products as well as visualize and plan the processes that will produce them. Individual component parts can be positioned together virtually and tested for fit or interference. Even virtual workers can be introduced into the prototyping system to check for ease of assembly or operation.

Alpha and beta testing

A distinction that originated in the software development industry, but has spread into other areas, is that between the alpha and beta testing of a product or service. Most software products include both alpha *and* beta test phases, both of which are intended to uncover 'bugs' (errors) in the product. Not surprisingly alpha testing comes before beta testing. Alpha testing is essentially an *internal* process where the developers or manufacturers (or sometimes an outside agency that they have commissioned) examine the product for errors. Generally, it is also a private process, not open to the market or potential customers. Although it is intended to look for errors that otherwise would emerge when the product is in use, it is in effect performed in a virtual or simulated environment, rather than in 'the real world'. After alpha testing, the product is released for beta testing. Beta testing is when the product is released for testing by selected customers. It is an *external* 'pilot-test' that takes place in 'the real world' (or near real world, because it is still a relatively short trial with a small sample) before commercial production. By the time a product gets to the beta stage, most of the worst defects should have been removed, but the product may still have some minor problems that may only become evident with user participation. This is why beta testing is almost always performed at the user's premises without any of the development team present. Beta testing is also sometimes called 'field testing', pre-release testing, customer validation, Customer Acceptance Testing, or User Acceptance Testing.

How should product and service innovation be resourced?

As is the case with any type of process, for a product or service innovation process to function effectively, it must be appropriately designed and resourced. In this section, we examine five key questions that should be considered in resourcing the innovation process:

▶ What are the capacity requirements for innovation?
▶ Should innovation be carried out in-house or out sourced?
▶ What technology can be used to support the innovation process?
▶ What organizational structure is most suitable for the innovation process?
▶ How can the innovation process be compressed?

Operations principle

For innovation processes to be effective they must be adequately resourced.

Understanding capacity requirements for innovation activities

In general, capacity management involves deciding on the appropriate level of capacity needed by a process and how it can be adjusted to respond to changes in demand. In the case of innovation, demand is the number of new designs needed by the business. The chief difficulty is that, even in very large companies, the rate of new innovation is not constant. This means that product and service design processes are subjected to uneven internal 'demand' for designs, possibly with several new offerings being introduced to the market close together, while at other times little innovation is needed. This poses a resourcing problem because the capacity of an innovation activity is often difficult to flex. The expertise necessary for innovation is embedded within designers, technologists, market analysts and so on. Some expertise may be able to be hired in as and when it is needed, but much design resource is, in effect, fixed.

Such a combination of varying demand and relatively fixed design capacity means some organizations are reluctant to invest in innovation processes because they see them as an under-utilized resource. A vicious cycle can develop in which companies fail to invest in innovation resources because many skilled design staff cannot simply be hired in the short term, resulting in innovation projects overrunning or failing to deliver appropriate solutions. This in turn may lead to the company losing business or otherwise suffering in the market place, which makes the company even less willing to invest in innovation resources.

Understanding whether innovation activities should be outsourced

Just as there are supply networks that deliver services and products, there are also networks that connect suppliers and customers in the innovation process. These networks are sometimes called 'design (or development) networks'. Innovation processes can adopt any position on a continuum of varying degrees of design engagement with suppliers, from retaining all the innovation capabilities in-house, to outsourcing all the innovation work. Between these extremes are varying degrees of internal and external capability. Figure 4.10 shows some of the more important factors that will vary depending on where an innovation process is on the continuum. Resources will be easily controlled if they are kept in-house because they are closely aligned with the company's normal organizational structures, but control should be relatively loose because of the extra trust present in

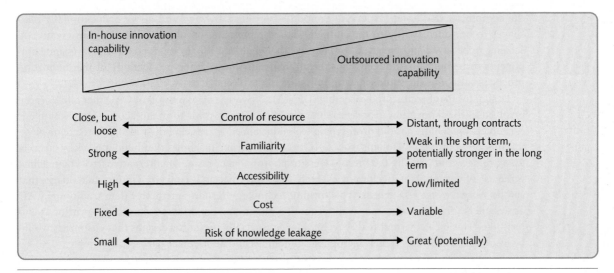

Figure 4.10 Implications of innovation in-house–outsourced continuum

working with familiar colleagues. Outsourced innovation work often involves greater control, with penalty clauses for delays often used in contracts.

The overall cost of in-house versus outsourced innovation will vary, depending on the firm and the project. An important difference, however, is that external innovation tends to be regarded as a variable cost. The more external resources are used, the more these variable costs will be. In-house innovation is more of a fixed cost. Indeed a shift to outsourcing may occur because fixed design costs are viewed as too great. From an open innovation perspective (discussed earlier in the chapter), it is argued that firms should be willing to buy in or license inventions for other organizations, rather than relying solely on innovations generated internally. Similarly, it may be beneficial to give access to under-used proprietary innovations through joint ventures, licensing, or spin-offs. However, a major inhibitor to open innovation is the fear of knowledge leakage. Firms become concerned that experience gained through collaboration with a supplier of design expertise may be transferred to competitors. There is a paradox here. Businesses usually outsource design primarily because of the supplier's capabilities, which are themselves an accumulation of specialist knowledge from working with a variety of customers. Without such knowledge 'leakage', the benefits of the supplier's accumulated innovation capabilities would not even exist.

Understanding what technologies to use in the innovation process

Technology has become increasingly important in innovation activities. Simulation software, for example, is now common in the design of everything from transportation services through to chemical factories. These allow developers to make design decisions in advance of the actual product or service being created. They allow designers to work through the experience of using the service or product and learn more about how it might operate in practice. They can explore possibilities, gain insights and, most importantly, explore the consequences of their decisions. Innovation technologies are particularly useful when the design task is highly complex, because they allow developers to reduce their own uncertainty of how services or products will work in practice. Technologies also consolidate information on what is happening in the innovation process, thus presenting a more comprehensive vision within the organization.

Computer-aided design

The best-known innovation technology is computer-aided design (CAD). CAD systems store and categorize component information and allow designs to be built up on screen, often performing basic engineering calculations to test the appropriateness of proposed design solutions. They provide the computer-aided ability to create a modified product drawing and allow conventionally used shapes to be added swiftly to the computer-based representation of a product. Designs created on screen can be saved and retrieved for later use that enables a library of standardized parts and components to be built up. Not only can this dramatically increase the productivity of the innovation process, it also aids the standardization of parts in the design activity.

Design for manufacture and assembly (DFMA) software is an extension of CAD that allows those involved in the innovation process to integrate their designs prior to manufacture. One example is 3-D object modelling, a rapid prototyping technique aimed at reducing the time taken to create physical models of products. Designs from CAD are created using machines that build models by layering up extremely thin (usually 0.05 mm) layers of photopolymer resin. An alternative to 3-D modelling is the use of virtual reality technologies. Here CAD information is converted into virtual images that can be viewed using 3-D glasses. This form of technology is more interactive than traditional CAD as designers (or customers) can 'walk around' a design and get a better sense of what it looks and feels like. This means virtual reality technology is especially useful for designs that customers would be inside, such as sports venues, aeroplanes, buildings and amusement parks, for example.

Digital twins

Michael Grieves of Florida Institute of Technology's Centre for Lifecycle and Innovation Management popularized the term 'digital twin'. It is the combination of data and intelligence that represents the structure, context and behaviour of a physical system of any type, offering an interface that allows one to understand past and present operations, and make predictions about the future.[7] In other words, digital twins are powerful digital 'replicas' that can be used instead of the physical reality of a product. Using the digital twin rather than the real product can significantly improve its operational performance without the expense of working on the real thing.[8] Not only that, but the use of the digital twin can extend throughout the product's life to provide valuable information to its user and evidence on how it is actually performing. So, for example, digital twins could monitor and simulate possible future scenarios and predict the need for repairs and other problems before they occur. This allows design improvements to be made before a product is used by customers as well as during its life.

Knowledge management technologies

In many professional service firms, such as management consultancies, design involves the evaluation of concepts and frameworks that can be used in client organizations to diagnose problems, analyse performance and construct possible solutions. They may include ideas of industry best practice, benchmarks of performance within an industry and ideas that can be transported across industry boundaries. However, such firms are often geographically dispersed and staff may spend most of their time in client organizations. This creates a risk for such companies of 'reinventing the wheel' continually. Most consultancy companies attempt to tackle this risk by using knowledge management routines based on their intranet capabilities. This allows consultants to put their experience into a common pool, contact other staff within the company who have skills relevant to a current assignment, and identify previous similar assignments. In this way information is integrated into the on-going knowledge innovation process within the company and can be tapped by those charged with developing new innovations.

Understanding what organizational structure to use in the innovation process

The total process of developing concepts through to market will almost certainly involve personnel from several different areas of the organization. Different functions will all have some part to play in making the decisions that shape the final design. Yet any product or service innovation project will also have an existence of its own. It will have a project name, an individual manager or group of staff who are championing the project, a budget and, hopefully, a clear strategic purpose. The organizational question is which of these two ideas – the various organizational functions that contribute or the innovation project itself – should dominate the way in which the innovation activity is managed?

Figure 4.11 illustrates the various alternative organizational structures for innovation processes.

▶ Functional organization – The innovation project is divided into segments and assigned to relevant functional areas and/or groups within functional areas. The project is coordinated by functional and senior management.

▶ Functional matrix (or lightweight project manager) – A person is formally designated to oversee the project across different functional areas. This person may have limited authority over the functional staff involved and serves primarily to plan and coordinate the project. Functional managers retain primary responsibility for their specific segments of the project.

▶ Balanced matrix – A person is assigned to oversee the project and interacts on an equal basis with functional managers. This person and the functional managers work together to direct innovation activities and approve technical and operational decisions.

▶ Project matrix (or heavyweight project manager) – A manager is assigned to oversee the project and is responsible for its completion. Functional managers' involvement is limited to assigning personnel as needed and providing advisory expertise.

▶ Project team (or tiger team) – A manager is given responsibility of a project team composed of a core group of personnel from several functional areas assigned on a full-time basis. The functional managers have no formal involvement.

Although there is no clear 'winner' among the alternative organizational structures, there is increasing support for structures towards the project rather than functional end of the continuum. Some authorities argue that heavyweight project manager structures and dedicated project teams are the

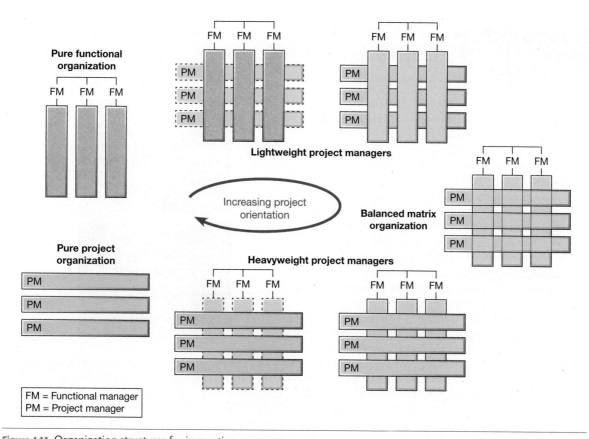

Figure 4.11 Organization structures for innovation processes

most efficient forms of organization in driving competitiveness, shorter lead-times and technical efficiency.

Perhaps of more interest is the suitability of the alternative structures for different types of innovation. Matrix structures are generally deemed to be appropriate for both simple and highly complex projects. Dedicated project teams, on the other hand, are seen as appropriate for projects with a high degree of uncertainty, where their flexibility becomes valuable. Functionally based structures, with resources clustered around a functional specialism, help the development of technical knowledge. Some organizations do manage to capture the deep technological and skills development advantages of functional structures, while at the same time coordinating between the functions so as to ensure satisfactory delivery of new service and product ideas.

Understanding how to compress the innovation process

Every product and service innovation has, eventually, to be created. This is why it is a mistake to separate the design of services and products from the design of the processes that will deliver them. Merging these two processes is usually called simultaneous (or interactive) design. Its key benefit is to reduce the time taken for the whole innovation activity. As noted earlier, reducing time to market (TTM) can give an important competitive advantage.

Here, we examine three key methods that can significantly reduce time to market for innovations:

▶ integrating the design of the offering and the design of the process,

---

OPERATIONS IN PRACTICE   Toyota's approach to organizing innovation

Like many aspects of its business, Toyota's approach to organizing its product and service innovation goes against the project matrix and project (tiger) team forms of coordination that are seen as best-practice by many other multi-national firms. Instead, Toyota has retained a strong functionally based organization to develop its offerings. It adopts highly formalized development procedures to communicate between functions and places strict limits on the use of cross-functional teams. But what is really different is its approach to devising an organizational structure for innovation that is appropriate for Toyota. The argument that most companies have adopted to justify cross-functional project teams goes something like this: *'Problems with communication between traditional functions have been the main reasons for failing to deliver new innovation ideas to specification, on time and to budget. Therefore let us break down the walls between the functions and organize resources around the individual development projects. This will ensure good communication and a*

market-oriented culture.' Toyota and similar companies, on the other hand, have taken a different approach. Their argument goes something like this: *'The problem*

▶ simultaneous development of the various stages in the overall process,
▶ early resolution of design conflict and uncertainty.

Integrating the design of the offering and design of the process

What looks like an elegant offering on paper may prove difficult to create and deliver on an on-going basis. Conversely, a process designed for one set of services or products may be incapable of creating different ones. It clearly makes sense to design offerings and operations processes together. For services, organizations have little choice but to do this because the process of delivery is usually part of the offering. However, it is useful to integrate the design of the offering and the process regardless of the kind of organization. The fact that many businesses do not do this is only partly because of their ignorance or incompetence. There are real barriers to doing it. First, the time scales involved can be very different. Offerings may be modified, or even redesigned, relatively frequently. The processes that will be used to create and deliver an offering may be far too expensive to modify every time the offering changes. Second, the people involved with the innovation on one hand, and on-going process design on the other, are likely to be organizationally separate. Finally, it is sometimes not possible to design an on-going process for the creation and delivery of services and products until they are fully defined.

Yet none of these barriers is insurmountable. Although on-going processes may not be able to be changed every time there is a change to the offering, they can be designed to cope with a range of potential services and products. The fact that design staff and operations staff are often organizationally separate can also be overcome. Even if it is not sensible to merge the two functions, there are communication and organizational mechanisms to encourage the two functions to work together. Even the claim that on-going processes cannot be designed until the nature of the offering is known is not entirely true. There can be sufficient clues emerging from innovation activities for process design staff to consider how they might modify on-going processes. This is a fundamental principle of simultaneous design, considered next.

Simultaneous development

We described the design innovation process as essentially a set of individual, predetermined stages, each with a clear starting and an ending point. The implicit assumption is that one stage is completed before the next one commences. Indeed, this step-by-step, or sequential, approach has traditionally been the typical form of product/service development. It has some advantages. The process is easy to manage and control because each stage is clearly defined. In addition, each stage is completed before the next stage is begun, so each stage can focus its skills and expertise on a limited set of tasks. However, the main problem of the sequential approach is that it is both time-consuming and costly. When each stage is separate, with a clearly defined set of tasks, any difficulties encountered during the design at one stage might necessitate the design being halted while responsibility moves back to the previous stage. This sequential approach is shown in Figure 4.12(a).

Yet often there is really little need to wait until the absolute finalization of one stage before starting the next. For example, perhaps while generating the concept, the evaluation activity of screening and selection could be started. It is likely that some concepts could be judged as 'non-starters' relatively early on in

Operations principle

Effective simultaneous development reduces time to market.

the process of idea generation. Similarly, during the screening stage, it is likely that some aspects of the design will become obvious before the phase is finally complete. Therefore, the preliminary work on these parts of the design could be commenced at that point. This principle can be taken right through all the stages, one stage commencing before the previous one has finished, so there is simultaneous or concurrent work on the stages (see Figure 4.12(b)). (Note that simultaneous development is often called simultaneous (or concurrent) engineering in manufacturing operations.)

Early resolution of design conflict and uncertainty

Characterizing product or service innovation as a whole series of decisions is a useful perspective. Importantly, a design decision, once made, need not irrevocably shape the final offering. In some cases, changing designs makes sense: for example, as new information emerges suggesting a better alternative. In addition, early decisions are often the most difficult to make because of the high level of uncertainty surrounding what may or may not work as a final design. This is why the level of debate, and even disagreement, over the characteristics of an offering can be at its most heated in the early stages of the process. One approach is to delay decision making in the hope that an obvious 'answer' will emerge. The problem with this is that, if decisions to change are made later in the innovation process, these changes will be more disruptive than if they are made earlier. Conversely, if the design team manages to resolve conflict early in the design activity, this will reduce the degree of uncertainty within the project and reduce the extra cost and, most significantly, time associated with either managing this uncertainty or changing decisions already made. Figure 4.13 illustrates two patterns of design changes through the life of the total design, which imply different time-to-market performances.

> **Operations principle**
>
> The design process requires strategic attention early, when there is most potential to affect design decisions.

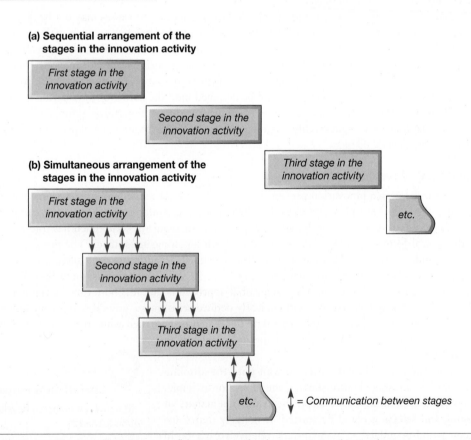

Figure 4.12 (a) Sequential arrangement of the stages in the design activity (b) Simultaneous arrangement of the stages in the design activity

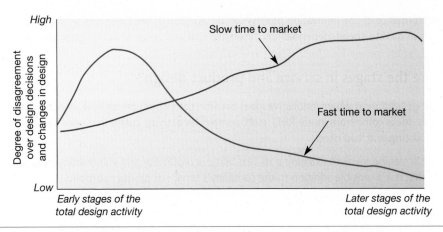

Figure 4.13 Early conflict resolution saves greater disruption later in the innovation process

There are two key implications of this. First, it is worth trying to reach consensus in the early stages of the innovation process even if this seems to be delaying the total process in the short term. Second, strategic intervention into the innovation process by senior management is particularly needed during these early stages. Unfortunately, there is a tendency for senior managers, after setting the initial objectives of the innovation process, to 'leave the details' to the technical experts. They may only become engaged with the process again in the later stages as problems start to emerge that need reconciliation or extra resources.

Summary answers to key questions

What is product and service innovation?

▶ We explore three related terms of 'creativity', 'innovation' and 'design'. 'Creativity' is the ability to move beyond conventional ideas, rules or assumptions, in order to generate significant new ideas. 'Innovation' is the act of introducing something new with potential to be practical and give commercial return. 'Design' is the process that transforms innovative ideas into something more concrete. A design delivers a solution that will work in practice.

▶ The innovation S-curve describes the impact of an innovation over time, slow at first, increasing in impact, then slowing down before levelling off.

▶ Incremental and radical innovations differ in how they use knowledge. Radical innovation often requires completely new knowledge and/or resources, making existing services and products obsolete. Incremental innovation builds upon existing knowledge and/or resources.

What is the strategic role of product and service innovation?

▶ Despite the obstacles to successful innovation, almost all firms strive to be innovative given the significant payback for the organizations that manage to incorporate innovative ideas in the design of their products and services.

▶ The innovation activity is a process that involves many of the same design issues common to other operations processes. As such, it is a process that conforms to the input–transformation–output model described in Chapter 1.

▶ The performance of the innovation process can be assessed in the same way as any process, namely in terms of quality, speed, dependability, flexibility, cost and, more broadly, sustainability.

What are the stages in service and product design?

▶ *Concept generation* is where innovative ideas become the inspiration for new service or product concepts. Ideas come from inside R&D, staff, competitor activity, customers, open sourcing, crowdsourcing and lead users.

▶ *Concept screening* involves examining its feasibility, acceptability and vulnerability in broad terms to ensure that it is a sensible addition to the company's service or product portfolio.

▶ *Preliminary design* involves the identification of all the component parts of the service or product and the way they fit together. Designers adopt a number of approaches to reduce design complexity, including standardization, commonality, modularization and mass customization.

▶ *Design evaluation and improvement* involves re-examining the design to see if it can be done in a better way, more cheaply or more easily. The best-known tool for this is quality function deployment (QFD).

▶ *Prototyping and final design* involves providing the final details which allow the service or product to be created or delivered. The outcome of this stage is a fully developed specification for the package of services and products, as well as a specification for the processes that will make and deliver them to customers.

How should product and service innovation be resourced?

▶ To be effective, the innovation process must be appropriately resourced. Issues to consider include understanding capacity requirements, deciding how much of the innovation process to outsource, and determining technology needs, organizational structure and methods to compress the innovation process.

▶ Organizations must understand the demand for innovation (i.e. number of new designs in a given period) and match this with their capacity for innovation.

▶ Organizations must determine whether all innovation activity should take place in-house or whether there are benefits in outsourcing some or all this activity to a third party.

▶ There are many technologies available to support the innovation process, including computer-aided design (CAD); design for manufacture and assembly (DFMA) software, such as 3-D modelling and virtual reality; digital twins; and knowledge management technologies.

▶ Selecting an appropriate organizational structure can support the innovation process. Typically, structures towards the project rather than functional end of the continuum (project matrix or project team) are seen as beneficial.

▶ The innovation process can often be compressed by integrating the design of the offering and the design of the process; adopting simultaneous development of the various stages in the overall process; and early resolution of design conflict and uncertainty.

Developing 'Savory Rosti-crisps' at Dreddo Dan's

'Most people see the snack market as dynamic and innovative, but actually it is surprisingly conservative. Most of what passes for innovation is in fact tinkering with our marketing approach, things like special offers, promotion tie-ins and so on. We occasionally put new packs round our existing products and even more occasionally we introduce new flavours in existing ranges. Rarely though does anyone in this industry introduce something radically different. That is why "Project Orlando" is both exciting and scary.'

Monica Allen, the Technical Vice-President of PJT's Snack Division, was commenting on a new product to be marketed under PJT's best-known brand 'Dreddo Dan's Surfer Snacks'. The Dreddo Dan's brand made use of surfing and outdoor 'action-oriented youth' imagery, but in fact was aimed at a slightly older generation who, although aspiring to such a life style, had more discretionary spend for the premium snacks in which the brand specialized. Current products marketed under the brand included both fried and baked snacks in a range of exotic flavours. The project, internally known as Project Orlando, was a baked product that had been 'in development' for almost three years but had hitherto been seen very much as a long-term development, with no guarantee of it ever making it through to market launch. PJT had several of these long-term projects running at any time. They were allocated a development budget, but usually no dedicated resources were associated with the project. Less than half of these long-term projects ever even reached the stage of being test marketed. Around 20 per cent never got past the concept stage, and less than 20 per cent ever went into production. However, the company

viewed the development effort put into these 'failed' products as being worthwhile because it often led to 'spin-off' developments and ideas that could be used elsewhere. Up to this point 'Orlando' had been seen as unlikely ever to reach the test marketing stage, but that had now changed dramatically.

'Orlando' was a concept for a range of snack foods, described within the company as 'savoury potato cookies'. Essentially they were inch discs of crisp, fried potato with a soft dairy cheese-like filling. The idea of incorporating dairy fillings in snacks had been discussed within the industry for some time but the problems of manufacturing such a product were formidable. Keeping the product crisp on the outside yet soft in the middle, while at the same time ensuring microbiological safety, would not be easy. Moreover, such a product would have to be capable of being stored at ambient temperatures, maintain its physical robustness and have a shelf life of at least three months.

Bringing Orlando products to market involved overcoming three types of technical problem. First, the formulation and ingredient mix for the product had to maintain the required texture yet be capable of being baked on the company's existing baking lines. The risk of developing an entirely new production technology for the offering was considered too great. Second, extruding the mixture into baking moulds while maintaining microbiological integrity (dairy products are difficult to handle) would require new extrusion technology. Third, the product would need to be packaged in a material that both reflected its brand image but also kept the product fresh through its shelf life. Existing packaging materials were unlikely to provide sufficient shelf life. The first of these problems had, more or less, been solved in PJT's development laboratories. The second two problems now seemed less formidable because of a number of recent technological breakthroughs made by equipment suppliers and packaging manufacturers. This had convinced the company that Orlando was worth significant investment and it had been given priority development status by the company's board. Even so, it was not expected to come to the market for another two years and was seen by some as potentially the most important new product development in the company's history.

The project team

Immediately after the board's decision, Monica had accepted responsibility to move the development forward. She decided to put together a dedicated project team to oversee the development. *'It is important to have representatives from all relevant parts of the company. Although the team will carry out much of the work themselves, they will still need the cooperation and the resources of their own departments. So, as well as being part of the team, they are also gateways to expertise around the company.'* The team consisted of representatives from marketing, the development kitchens (laboratories), PGT's technology centre (a development facility that served the whole group, not just the snack division), packaging engineers, and representatives from the division's two manufacturing plants. All but the manufacturing representatives were allocated to the project team on a full-time basis. Unfortunately, manufacturing had no one who had sufficient process knowledge and who could be spared from their day-to-day activities.

Development objectives

Monica had tried to set the objectives for the project in her opening remarks to the project team when they had first come together.

'We have a real chance here to develop an offering that not only will have major market impact, but will also give us a sustainable competitive advantage. We need to make this project work in such a way that competitors will find it difficult to copy what we do. The formulation is a real success for our development people, and as long as we figure out how to use the new extrusion method and packaging material, we should be difficult to beat. The success of Orlando in the marketplace will depend on our ability to operationalize and integrate the various technical solutions that we now have access to. The main problem with this type of offering is that it will be expensive to develop and yet, once our competitors realize what we are doing, they will come in fast to try and out-innovate us. Whatever else we do, we must ensure that there is sufficient flexibility in the project to allow us to respond quickly when competitors follow us into the market with their own "me-too" products. We are not racing against the clock to get this to market, but once we do make a decision to launch we will have to move fast and hit the launch date reliably. Perhaps most important, we must ensure that the crisps are 200 per cent safe. We have no experience in dealing with the microbiological testing which dairy-based food manufacture requires. Other divisions of PJT do have this experience and I guess we will be relying heavily on them.' (Monica Allen)

Monica, who had been tasked with managing the, now much expanded, development process had already drawn up a list of key decisions she would have to take.

▶ How to resource the innovation project – The division had a small development staff, some of whom had been working on Project Orlando, but a project of this size would require extra staff amounting to about twice the current number of people dedicated to the innovation process.

▶ Whether to invest in a pilot plant – The process technology required for the new project would be unlike any of the division's current technology. Similar technology was used by some companies in the frozen food industry and one option would be to carry out trials at these (non-competitor) companies' sites. Alternatively, the Orlando team could build their own pilot plant which would enable them to experiment in-house. As well as the significant expense involved, this would raise the problem of whether any process innovations would work when scaled up to full size. However, it would be far more convenient for the project team and allow them to 'make their mistakes' in private.

Table 4.2 Preliminary 'profit stream' projections for the Project Orlando offering, assuming launch in 24 months' time

Time period*	1	2	3	4	5	6	7
Profit flow ($ million)	???10	???20	50	90	120	130	135

*6-month periods

▶ How much development to outsource – Because of the size of the project, Monica had considered outsourcing some of the innovation activities. Other divisions within the company might be able to undertake some of the development work and there were also specialist consultancies that operated in the food processing industries. The division had never used any of these consultancies before but other divisions had occasionally done so.

▶ How to organize the innovation activities – Currently the small development function had been organized around loose functional specialisms. Monica wondered whether this project warranted the creation of a separate department independent of the current structure. This might signal the importance of this innovation project to the whole division.

Fixing the budget

The budget to develop Project Orlando through to launch had been set at $30 million. This made provision to increase the size of the existing innovation team by 70 per cent over a 20-month period (for launch 2 years from now). It also included enough funding to build a pilot plant which would allow the team the flexibility to develop responses to potential competitor reaction after the launch. So, of the $30m around $18m was for extra staff and contracted-out innovation work, $7.5m for the pilot plant and $4.5m for one-off costs (such as the purchase of test equipment, etc.). Monica was unsure whether the budget would be big enough.

'I know everyone in my position wants more money, but it is important not to under fund a project like this. Increasing our development staff by 70 per cent is not really enough. In my opinion we need an increase of at least 90 per cent to make sure that we can launch when we want. This would need another $5m, spread over the next 20 months. We could get this by not building the pilot plant, I suppose, but I am reluctant to give that up. It would mean begging for test capacity in other companies' plants, which is never satisfactory from a knowledge-building viewpoint. Also it would compromise security. Knowledge of what we were doing could easily leak to competitors. Alternatively, we could subcontract more of the research, which may be less expensive, especially in the long run, but I doubt if it would save the full $5m we need. More important, I am not sure that we should subcontract anything, which would compromise safety, and increasing the amount of work we send out may do that. No, it's got to be the extra cash or the project could overrun. The profit projections for the Orlando products look great [see Table 4.2], but delay or our inability to respond to competitor pressures would depress those figures significantly. Our competitors could get into the market only a little after us. Word has it that Marketing's calculations indicate a delay of only six months could not only delay the profit stream by the six months but also cut it by up to 30%.'

Monica was keen to explain two issues to the management committee when it met to consider her request for extra funding: first, that there was a coherent and well-thought-out strategy for the innovation project over the next two years; second, that saving $5m on Project Orlando's budget would be a false economy.

QUESTIONS

1 How would you rank the innovation objectives for the project?

2 What are the key issues in resourcing this innovation process?

3 What are the main factors influencing the resourcing decisions?

4 What advice would you give Monica?

Problems and applications

All chapters have 'Problems and applications' questions that will help you practise analysing operations. They can be answered by reading the chapter. Model answers for the first two questions can be found on the companion website for this book.

1   One product where customers value a very wide range of product types is domestic paint. Most people like to express their creativity in the choice of paints and other home decorating products that they use in their homes. Clearly, offering a wide range of paint must have serious cost implications for the companies that manufacture, distribute and sell the product. Visit a store that sells paint and get an idea of the range of products available on the market. How do you think paint manufacturers and retailers could innovate so as to increase variety but minimize costs?

2   '*We have to get this new product and fast*', said the Operations Director. '*Our competitors are close behind us and I believe their products will be almost as good as ours when they launch them*'. She was talking about a new product that the company hoped would establish them as the leader in the market. The company had put together a special development team together with their own development laboratory. They had spent £10,000 on equipping the laboratory and the cost of the development engineers would be £20,000 per quarter. It was expected that the new product would be fully developed and ready for launch within six quarters. It would be sold through a specialist agency that charged £10,000 per quarter and would need to be in place two quarters prior to the launch. If the company met its launch date, it was expected that it could charge a premium price that would result in profits of approximately £50,000 per quarter. Any delay in the launch would result in profits being reduced to £40,000 per quarter. If this development project were delayed by two quarters, how far would the break-even point for the project be pushed back?

3   Innovation becomes particularly important at the interface between offerings and the people who use them. Consider two types of website:
    (a) those which are trying to sell something, such as Amazon.com, and
    (b) those which are primarily concerned with giving information, for example reuters.com or nytimes.com
    What constitutes good innovation for these two types of website? Find examples of particularly good and particularly poor web design and explain the issues you've considered in making the distinction between them.

4   According to the Ellen MacArthur Foundation, a circular economy is '*one that is restorative and regenerative by design, and which aims to keep products, components and materials at their highest utility and value at all times, distinguishing between technical and biological cycles*'. Also see the example earlier in this chapter. What do you see as the main barriers to a more widespread adoption of the idea?

5   A janitor called Murray Spangler invented the vacuum cleaner in 1907. One year later he sold his patented idea to William Hoover, whose company went on to dominate the market. Now, the Dyson vacuum cleaner has jumped from nothing to a position where it dominates the market. The Dyson product dates back to 1978 when James Dyson designed a cyclone-based cleaner. It took 5 years and 5,000 prototypes before he had a working design. However, existing vacuum cleaner manufacturers were not as impressed – two rejected the design outright. So Dyson started making his new design himself. Within a few years Dyson cleaners were outselling the rivals who had once rejected them. The aesthetics and functionality of the design help to keep sales growing in spite of a higher retail

price. To Dyson, good design *'is about looking at everyday things with new eyes and working out how they can be made better. It's about challenging existing technology.'*

(a) What was Spangler's mistake?

(b) What do you think makes 'good design' in markets such as the domestic appliance market?

(c) Why do you think the two major vacuum cleaner manufacturers rejected Dyson's ideas?

(d) How did design make Dyson a success?

6 It sounds like a joke, but it is a genuine product innovation. It's green, it's square and it comes originally from Japan. It's a square watermelon. Why square? Because Japanese grocery stores are not large and space cannot be wasted. Similarly, a round watermelon does not fit into a refrigerator very conveniently. There is also the problem of trying to cut the fruit when it keeps rolling around. So an innovative Japanese farmer solved the problem with the idea of making a cube-shaped watermelon that could easily be packed and stored. There is no genetic modification or clever science involved in growing watermelons. It simply involves placing the young fruit into wooden boxes with clear sides. During its growth, the fruit naturally swells to fill the surrounding shape. (a) Why is a square watermelon an advantage? (b) What does this example tell us about product design?

Selected further reading

Christensen, C.M. (1997) *The Innovator's Dilemma.* **Boston, MA: Harvard Business School Press.**
Ground-breaking booking on disruptive innovation that has had a major influence on innovation theory over the last 20 years.

Kahney, L. (2014) *Jony Ive: The Genius Behind Apple's Greatest Products,* **Penguin, London.**
Inside the mind of one of the world's great designers.

Reason, B., Løvlie, L. and Brand Flu, M. (2016) *Service Design for Business: A Practical Guide to Optimizing the Customer Experience,* **John Wiley & Sons, Chichester.**
A book that looks at the 'entire service experience' and is very readable.

Rose, D. (2015) *Enchanted Objects: Innovation, Design, and the Future of Technology,* **Scribner Book Company, New York.**
An interesting book examining how technology is and will continue impact on design.

Tidd, J. and Bessant, J. (2013) *Managing Innovation: Integrating Technological, Market and Organizational Change,* **5th edn, John Wiley & Sons, Chichester.**
The definitive textbook in the area of innovation.

5

The structure and scope of operations

KEY QUESTIONS

What is the structure and scope of operations?

How should the network be configured?

How much capacity should operations have?

Where should operations be located?

How vertically integrated should the network be?

What activities should be in-house and what should be outsourced?

INTRODUCTION

No operation exists in isolation – it is part of a larger and interconnected network of other operations, referred to as the *supply network*. It will include the operation's suppliers and customers. It will also include suppliers' suppliers and customers' customers, and so on. At a strategic level, operations managers are involved in deciding both the structure and scope of these supply networks. *Structure decisions* involve deciding the overall configuration of the supply network, the amount of capacity needed within the network and where operations should be located. *Scope decisions* involve deciding the extent to which an operation does the activities performed by the network itself, as opposed to requesting a supplier do them on its behalf. The structure and scope of an operation's supply network is critical because it helps in understanding competitiveness, identifies of significant links in the network, and support is a longer-term perspective on operations issues. Figure 5.1 places the structure and scope of operations in the overall model of operations management.

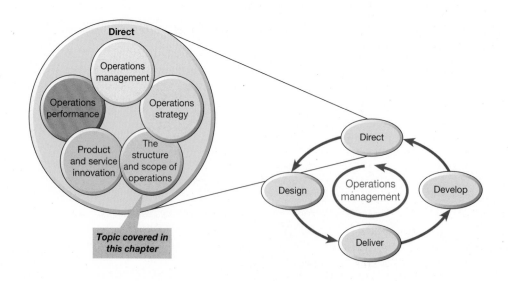

Figure 5.1 This chapter examines the structure and scope of operations

What is the structure and scope of operations?

The structure of an operation's supply network relates to its shape and form. The scope of an operation's supply network relates to the extent to which an operation decides to do the activities performed by the network itself, as opposed to requesting a supplier to do them. So, before we examine these two elements, first we need to establish what we mean by 'supply network' and why it is important that operations understands its position within it.

Supply networks

The supply network includes the chains of suppliers providing inputs to the operation, the chains of customers who receive outputs from the operation, and sometimes other operations that may at times compete and other times cooperate. Materials, parts, information, ideas and sometimes people all flow through the network of customer–supplier relationships formed by all these operations. On its supply side an operation has its first-tier suppliers of parts, or information, or services. These suppliers themselves have their own suppliers (second-tier suppliers) who in turn could also have suppliers, and so on. However, some second-tier suppliers may also supply an operation directly, thus missing out a link in the network. On the demand side of the network, 'first-tier' customers are the main customer group for the operation. These customers might not be the final consumers of the operation's products or services; they might have their own set of customers ('second-tier' customers). Again, the operation may at times supply second-tier customers directly. The suppliers and customers who have direct contact with an operation are called its immediate supply network, whereas all the operations that form the network of suppliers' suppliers and customers' customers, etc., are called the total supply network. Along with the forward flow of transformed resources (materials, information and customers) in the network, each customer–supplier linkage will feed back orders and information. For example, when stocks run low, retailers place orders with distributors, which likewise place orders with the manufacturer, which will in turn place orders with its suppliers, which will replenish their own stocks from their own suppliers. So flow is a two-way process with items flowing one way and information flowing the other.

Figure 5.2 illustrates the total supply network for two different operations. First is a plastic homeware (kitchen bowls, etc.) manufacturer. On the demand side it supplies products to wholesalers which supply retail outlets. However, it also supplies some retailers directly, bypassing a stage in the network – not an uncommon situation. As products flow from suppliers to customers, orders and information flow the other way from customers to suppliers. Yet it is not only manufacturers that are part of a supply network. The flow of physical materials may be easier to visualize, but service operations also sit within supply networks. One way to visualize the supply networks of some service operations is to consider the downstream flow of information that passes between operations. Most financial service supply networks can be thought about like this. However, not all service supply networks deal primarily in information. For example, the second illustration in Figure 5.2 shows the supply network centred on a shopping mall. It has suppliers that provide security services, cleaning services, maintenance services and so on. These first-tier suppliers will themselves receive services from recruitment agencies, consultants, etc. First-tier customers of the shopping mall are the retailers that lease retail space within the mall, who themselves serve retail customers. This is a supply network like any other. What is being exchanged between operations is the quality, speed, dependability, flexibility and cost of the services each operation supplies to its customers. In other words, there is a flow of 'operations performance' through the network. And although visualizing the flow of 'performance' through supply networks is an abstract approach to visualizing supply networks, it is a unifying concept. Broadly speaking, all types of supply network exist to facilitate the flow of 'operations performance'.

The importance of a supply network perspective

Understanding the nature of the supply network and the operations role within it is critical in understanding competiveness, identifying significant links in the network, and shifting towards a longer-term perspective.

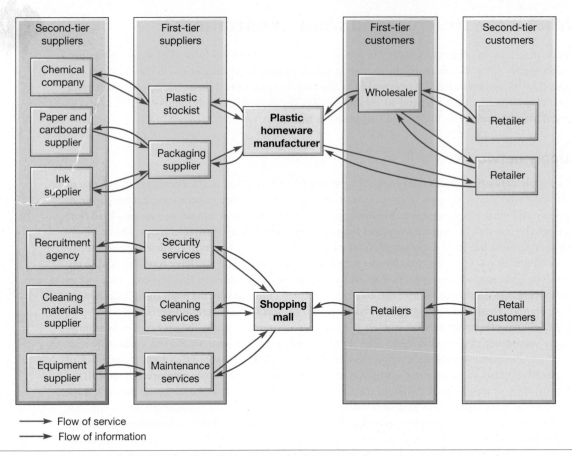

Figure 5.2 Supply network for a plastic homeware company and a shopping mall

Understanding competitiveness

Immediate customers and immediate suppliers, quite understandably, are the main concern for companies. Yet sometimes they need to look beyond these immediate contacts to understand *why* customers and suppliers act as they do. Any operation has only two options if it wants to understand its ultimate customers' needs at the end of the network. It can rely on all the intermediate customers and customers' customers, etc., which form the links in the network between the company and its end customers. Alternatively, it can look beyond its immediate customers and suppliers. Relying on one's immediate network is seen as putting too much faith in someone else's judgement of things which are central to an organization's own competitive health.

Identifying significant links in the network

Not everyone in a supply network has the same degree of influence over the performance of the network as a whole. Some operations contribute more to the performance objectives that are valued by end customers. So an analysis of networks needs to understand the downstream and the upstream operations that contribute most to end-customer service. For example, the important end customers for domestic plumbing parts and appliances are the installers and service companies that deal directly with consumers. They are supplied by 'stock holders', who must have all parts in stock and deliver them fast. Suppliers of parts to the stock holders can best contribute to their end customers' competitiveness partly by offering a short delivery lead time but mainly through dependable delivery. The key players in this example are the stock holders. The best way of winning end-customer business in this case is to give the stock holder prompt delivery, which helps keep costs down while providing high availability of parts.

Flower the world – Aalsmeer Flower Auction[1]

Located around 10 miles from Amsterdam in a small town called Aalsmeer is the flower capital of the world and home to the world's largest flower auction. Aalsmeer started trading flowers around 1880 and in 1912 two auction houses were developed to cater for the increasing trade in flowers. As the flower market boomed, fuelled largely by significant increases in exports, Aalsmeer found it needed somewhere much bigger to sort, store, sell and export its plants and flowers. So, in 1968 the Central Aalsmeer Auction merged with Bloemenlust Auction to form the Aalsmeer Flower Auction (Bloemenveiling Aalsmeer), which has continued to expand to the present day. At the Aalsmeer Flower Auction, every day, from 4 till 11 in the morning, over 40 million flowers and plants from across the globe – Europe, Kenya, Columbia, Ethiopia, Ecuador and others – are traded in a space covering 10.6 million square feet (the second largest building in the world). Annually, the Aalsmeer Flower Auction sells around 12.5 billion items, representing over 50 per cent of world trade in flowers, and has an annual turnover of €4.6 billion.

At first sight, the operations appear to be extraordinarily complex. There are around 20,000 species of plants and flowers from classic Dutch tulips to more exotic plants such as kangaroo paws, birds of paradise and rare orchids. Within the building, small 'trains' of crates containing these products are driven (or increasingly cycled for improved worker health) between quality check, sorting, auction rooms and despatch in a dizzying display where crashes seem inevitable but rarely happen. Within the auction rooms, there is similar frenzied activity where 120,000 transactions take place in a matter of hours each day from when trading starts at 7 am. Products are then shipped via lorry for local markets and airfreight for markets worldwide via the nearby Schiphol Airport within 24 hours. Of course, there is method in the madness! The processes within the Aalsmeer Flower Auction and across its network of operations are carefully coordinated. Given the criticality of speed and quality in delivering competitive advantage, this is vital. For example, standardization of containers that hold the wide variety of flowers and plants has dramatically reduced *operational variety* while still allowing for a huge range of products to flow through the giant floral hub. Similarly, simplification of the auction process, which uses a 'Dutch reverse auction' whereby the prices start from high to low, allowing for a single bid as opposed to multiple 'bidding-up', not only speeds up the trading activity but also reduces any *variability* in this process stage.

Looking beyond the auction itself, Royal Flora Holland, which operates the Aalsmeer Flower Auction, plays an extremely active role in coordinating its network of operations. Partnership agreements with suppliers, sharing of information (including more accurate demand forecasts), live tracking of products and their condition during transportation, training of farmers around new methods to improve product quality, shared R&D, and visits to both suppliers and buyers are all used to continually improve the competitiveness of Royal Flora Holland's *entire network*. However, as with all dominant players in markets, things change. Increasing costs of transportation, concerns over the sustainability of shipping flowers around the world, increased use of direct shipping from suppliers to key customers (an example of disintermediation covered later in this chapter), and the move of many growers from Europe to warmer and lower-cost climates in Africa over the last decade have all placed pressures on Royal Flora Holland's network. To counter these challenges, the organization has successfully expanded its customer markets in Russia and Eastern Europe, expanded its work on sustainability initiatives such as the Netherlands' Green Ports and further increased the level of value-added services offered to its members, such as market intelligence, training and IT support. In addition, it now manages direct shipment for some of its products (for example, roses from Kenya) on behalf of some large clients, such as the German discount chain Lidl and UK supermarket Tesco, using fixed price contracts rather than the daily price fluctuations of the auction clock.

Taking a longer-term perspective

There are times when circumstances render parts of a supply network weaker than its adjacent links. High street music stores, for example, have been largely displaced by music streaming and downloading services. A long-term supply network view would

> **Operations principle**
> A supply network perspective helps to make sense of competitive, relationship and longer-term operations issues.

involve constantly examining technology and market changes to see how each operation in the supply network might be affected.

Structure and scope

So what do we mean by the structure and scope of an operation's supply network? The first point to make is that structure and scope are strongly related (which is why we treat them together). For example, look again at the supply network for the shopping mall in Figure 5.2. Suppose that the company that runs the mall is dissatisfied with the service that it is receiving from the firm that supplies security services. Also suppose that it is considering three alternatives. Option 1 is to switch suppliers and award the security contract to a competitor of the current security services supplier. Option 2 is to accept an offer from the company that supplies cleaning services to supply both security and cleaning services. Option 3 is to take over responsibility for security itself, hiring its own security staff who would be put on the mall's payroll. These options are illustrated in Figure 5.3. The first of these options changes neither the structure nor the scope of this part of the supply network. The shopping mall still has three suppliers and is doing exactly what it did before. All that has changed is that the mall's security services are being provided by another (hopefully better) supplier. However, option 2 changes the structure of the supply network (the mall now has only two suppliers, the combined cleaning and security supplier, and the maintenance supplier), but not the scope of what the mall does – it does exactly what it did before). Option 3 changes both the structure of the network (again, the mall has only two suppliers: cleaning and maintenance services) and the scope of what the mall does (it now also takes on responsibility for security itself).

So, decisions relating to structure and scope are often interrelated. But, for simplicity, we will treat them separately in this chapter. The second point to make is that both structure and scope decisions actually comprise a number of other 'constituent' decisions. These are shown in Figure 5.4. The structure of an operation's supply network is determined by three sets of decisions.

▶ How should the network be configured?
▶ What physical capacity should each part of the network have? – The long-term capacity decision.
▶ Where should each part of the network be located? – The location decision.

The scope of an operation's activities within the network is determined by two decisions.

▶ The extent and nature of the operation's vertical integration.
▶ The nature and degree of outsourcing it engages in.

The final point to make here is that structure and scope decisions are undeniably strategic. Different approaches to the structure and scope of operations define how different organizations do business

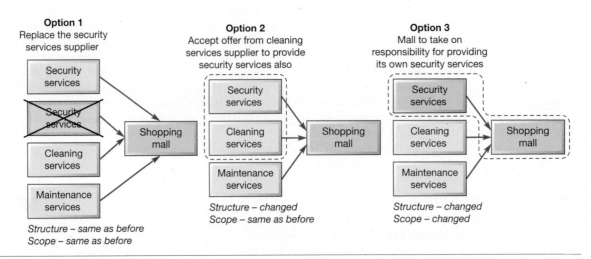

Figure 5.3 Three options for the shopping mall's supply network

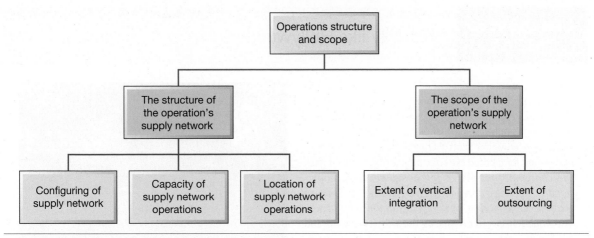

Figure 5.4 What determines an operation's structure and scope?

even when they are in similar markets. There are few decisions that are more strategic than which other businesses you are going to trade with (structure) and how much of the total activities in the supply network you are going to take responsibility for (scope). However, both structure and scope also have a more operational aspect. As we illustrated in Figure 5.3, an operation such as the shopping mall can change its supply arrangements in a relatively short-term manner, for example by simply changing its suppliers. We will treat the more operational day-to-day aspects of structure and scope in Chapter 12 on supply chain management.

How should the network be configured?

Configuring a supply network means determining its overall pattern, shape or arrangement of the various operations that make up the supply network. Even when an operation does not directly own, or even control, other operations in its network, it may still wish to change the shape of the network so as to change the nature of the relationships. Reconfiguring a supply network sometimes involves parts of the operation being merged – not necessarily in the sense of a change of ownership of any parts of an operation, but rather in the way responsibility is allocated for carrying out activities. A number of trends are reshaping networks in many industries. The most common example of network reconfiguration is the trend over the last decade to reduce the number of direct suppliers that organizations work with. The complexity of dealing with many hundreds of suppliers is both expensive and can prevent operations from developing close relationships with its suppliers. Other configuration trends include the disintermediation of some parts of the network, and a greater tolerance of other operations being both competitors and complementors at different times (co-opetition), the development of business ecosystems and the increasing use of a triadic as opposed to dyadic perspective in supply networks.

Disintermediation

One trend in some supply networks is that of companies within a network bypassing customers or suppliers to make contact directly with customers' customers or suppliers' suppliers. 'Cutting out the middle men' in this way is called disintermediation. An obvious example of this is the way the Internet has allowed some suppliers to 'disintermediate' traditional retailers in supplying goods and services to consumers. So, for example, many services in the travel industry that used to be sold through retail outlets (travel agents) are now also available direct from the suppliers. The option of purchasing the individual components of a vacation through the websites of the airline, hotel, car-hire operation, etc. is now extremely easy for consumers. Of course, they may still wish to purchase a service package

Virtually like Hollywood

Could that most ephemeral of all industries, Hollywood's film making business, hold messages about scope and structure for even the soberest of operations? It is an industry whose complexity most of us do not fully appreciate. The American writer Scott Fitzgerald said, *'You can take Hollywood for granted like I did, or you can dismiss it with the contempt we reserve for what we don't understand . . . not half a dozen men have ever been able to keep the whole equation of* [making] *pictures in their heads'.* The 'equation' involves balancing the artistic creativity and fashion awareness necessary to create a market for its products, with the efficiency and tight operations practices which get films made and distributed on time. But although the form of the equation remains the same, the way its elements relate to each other has changed profoundly. The typical Hollywood studio once did everything itself. It employed everyone from the carpenters, who made the stage, through to the film stars. The film star Cary Grant (one of the biggest in his day) was as much of an employee as the chauffeur who drove him to the studio, though his contract was probably more restrictive. The finished products were rolls of film that had to be mass produced and physically distributed to the cinemas of the world. No longer. Studios now deal almost exclusively in ideas. They buy and sell concepts, they arrange finance, they cut marketing deals and, above all, they manage the virtual network of creative and not so creative talent that goes into a film's production. A key skill is the

ability to put together teams of self-employed film stars and the small, technical specialist operations that provide technical support. It is a world that is less easy for the studios to control. The players in this virtual network, from film stars to electricians, have taken the opportunity to raise their fees to the point where, in spite of an increase in cinema attendance, returns are lower than at many times in the past. This opens opportunities for the smaller, independent studies. One way to keep costs low is by using inexpensive, new talent. Technology could also help this process. Digital processes allow easier customization of the 'product' and also mean that movies can be streamed direct to cinemas and direct to individual consumers' homes.

from travel agents, which can have the advantage of convenience. Nevertheless the process of disintermediation has developed new linkages in the supply network.

Co-opetition

One approach to thinking about supply networks sees any business as being surrounded by four types of players: suppliers, customers, competitors and complementors. Complementors enable one's products or services to be valued more by customers because they also can have the complementor's products or services, as opposed to when they have yours alone. Competitors are the opposite; they make customers value your product or service less when they can have their product or service, rather than yours alone. Competitors can also be complementors and vice versa. For example, adjacent restaurants may see themselves as competitors for customers' business. A customer standing outside and wanting a meal will choose between the two of them. Yet in another way they are complementors. Would that customer have come to this part of town unless there was more than one restaurant to choose from? Restaurants, theatres, art galleries and tourist attractions generally all cluster together in a form of cooperation to increase the total size of their joint market. It is important to distinguish between the way companies cooperate in increasing the total size of a market and the way in which they then compete for a share of that market. Customers and suppliers, it is argued, should have 'symmetric' roles. Harnessing the value of suppliers is just as important as listening to the needs of customers. Destroying value in a supplier in order to create it in a customer does not increase the value of the network as a whole. So, pressurizing suppliers will not necessarily add value. In the long-term it creates value for the total network to find ways of increasing value for suppliers as well as customers. All the players in the network, whether they are customers, suppliers, competitors or complementors, can be both friends and enemies at different times. The term used to capture this idea is 'co-opetition'.

Business ecosystems

An idea that is closely related to that of co-opetition in supply networks is that of the 'business ecosystem'. Like supply networks, business ecosystems include suppliers and customers. However, they also include stakeholders that may have little or no direct relationship with the main supply network yet interact with it by complementing or contributing significant components of the value proposition for customers. Many examples come from the technology industries. The innovative products and services that are developed in the technology sectors cannot evolve in a vacuum. They need to attract a whole range of resources, drawing in expertise, capital, suppliers, and customers to create cooperative networks. For example, the app developers that develop applications for particular operating system platforms may not be 'suppliers' as such, but the relationship between them and the supply network that supplies the mobile device is mutually beneficial. Building an ecosystem of developers around a core product can increase its value to the end customer and by doing so increase the usage of the core product. Such an ecosystem of complementary products and services can also create significant barriers to entry for new competitors. Any possible competitors would not only have to compete with the core product, but also have to compete against the entire ecosystem of complementary products and services.

The terminology used to describe business ecosystems is obviously based on that used to describe 'natural' biological systems, where elements in the 'ecosystem' affect and are affected by the others. This creates a constantly evolving set of relationships where, if they are to survive, business must be flexible, adaptable and preferably innovative. For an ecosystem to thrive, the different elements (businesses in this case) must communicate, establish trust, share information, collaborate, experiment and develop in a mutually supportive symbiotic manner. The comparison with the natural biological ecosystem is also important because it emphasizes that the relationships between things matter and that, to some extent, everything in a supply network touches everything else.

The triadic perspective on supply networks

The supply networks that were illustrated in Figure 5.2 are of course huge simplifications compared to reality. There are many operations, all interacting in different ways, to produce end products and services. Because of this, and to understand them better, supply network academics and professionals often choose to focus on the individual interaction between two specific operations in the network. This is called a 'dyadic' (simply meaning 'two') interaction, or dyadic relationship, and the two

Critical commentary

The idea of widening the discussion of supply networks to include the 'business ecosystem' concept, described earlier, is also not without its critics. Some see it as simply another management 'buzzword', indistinguishable from the longer-established idea of the supply network. Other critics believe that the ecosystem metaphor is just a way for business to appear 'green'. They claim that the metaphor is used to suggest that the commercial relationships, on which almost all supply networks are based, have developed and are run using 'natural' values and therefore should be left to operate free from societal or government interference.

operations are referred to as a 'dyad'. So if one wanted to examine the interactions that a focal operation had with one of its suppliers and one of its customers, one would examine the two dyads of 'supplier – focal operation', and 'focal operation – customer' (see Figure 5.5(a)). For many years most discussion (and research) on supply networks was based on dyadic relationships. This is not surprising as all relationships in a network are based on the simple dyad. However, more recently, and certainly when examining service supply networks, many authorities make the point that dyads do not reflect the real essence of a supply network. Rather, they say, it is triads, not dyads, that are the basic elements of a supply network (see Figure 5.5(b)). No matter how complex a network, it can be broken down into a collection of triadic interactions. The idea of triads is especially relevant in service supply networks. Operations are increasingly outsourcing the delivery of some aspects of their service to specialist providers, which deal directly with customers on behalf of the focal firm (more usually called the 'buying operation', or just 'buyer' in this context). For example, Figure 5.5(b) illustrates the common example of an airline contracting a specialist baggage handling company to provide services to its customers on its behalf. Similarly internal services are increasingly outsourced to form internal triadic relationships. For example, if a company outsources its IT operations, it is forming a triad between whoever is purchasing the service on behalf of the company, the IT service provider, and the employees who use the IT services.

Thinking about supply networks as a collection of triads rather than dyads is strategically important. First, it emphasizes the dependence of organizations on their suppliers' performance when they outsource service delivery. A supplier's service performance makes up an important part of how the buyer's performance is viewed. Second, the control that the buyer of the service has over service delivery to its customer is diminished in a triadic relationship. In a conventional supply chain, with a series of dyadic relationships, there is the opportunity to intervene before the customer receives the product or service. However, products or services in triadic relationships bypass the buying organization and go directly from provider to customer. Third, and partially as a consequence of the previous point, in triadic relationships the direct link between service provider and customer can result in power gradually transferring over time from the buying organization to the supplier that provides the service. Fourth, it becomes increasingly difficult for the buying organization to understand what

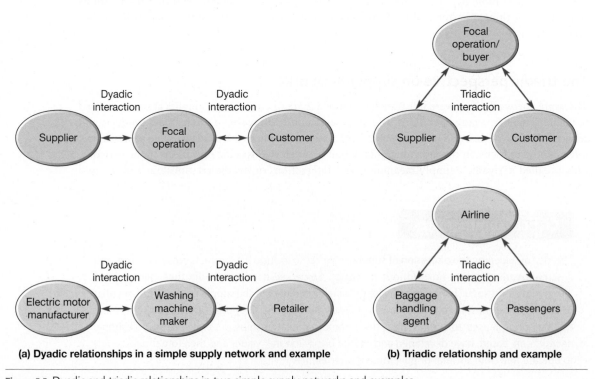

(a) Dyadic relationships in a simple supply network and example

(b) Triadic relationship and example

Figure 5.5 Dyadic and triadic relationships in two simple supply networks and examples

is happening between the supplier and customer at a day-to-day level. It may not even be in the supplier's interests to be totally honest in giving performance feedback to the buyer. In academia, this is referred to as the principal–agent problem, where the principal here is the buyer and the agent is the supplier. Finally, this closeness between supplier and customer, if it excludes the buyer, could prevent the buyer from building important knowledge. For example, suppose a specialist equipment manufacturer has outsourced the maintenance of its equipment to a specialist provider of maintenance services. This reduces the ability of the equipment manufacturer to understand how its customers are using the equipment, how the equipment was performing under various conditions, how customers would like to see the equipment improved, and so on. The equipment manufacturer may have outsourced the cost and trouble of providing maintenance services, but it has also outsourced the benefits and learning that come from direct interaction with customers.

How much capacity should operations have?

The next set of 'structure' decisions concerns the size or capacity of each part of the supply network. Here we treat capacity in a general long-term sense. The specific issues involved in measuring and adjusting capacity in the medium and short terms are examined in Chapter 11.

The amount of capacity an organization will have depends on its view of current and future demand. When an organization has to cope with changing demand, a number of capacity decisions need to be taken. These include choosing the optimum capacity for each site and timing the changes in the capacity of each part of the network. Important influences on these decisions include the concepts of economy and diseconomy of scale.

The optimum capacity level

Most organizations need to decide on the size (in terms of capacity) of each of their facilities. A chain of truck service centres, for example, might operate centres that have various capacities. The effective cost of running each centre will depend on the average service bay occupancy. Low occupancy because of few customers will result in a high cost per customer served because the fixed costs of the operation are being shared between few customers. As demand, and therefore service bay occupancy, increases, the cost per customer will reduce.

> **Operations principle**
> Most operations exhibit economy of scale effects where operating costs reduce as the scale of capacity increases.

The blue curves in Figure 5.6 show this effect for the service centres of 5-, 10- and 15-bay capacity. As the nominal capacity of the centres increases, the lowest cost point at first reduces. This is because the fixed costs of any operation do not increase proportionately as its capacity increases. A 10-bay centre has less than twice the fixed costs of a 5-bay centre. Also the capital costs of constructing the operations do not increase proportionately to their capacity. A 10-bay centre costs less to build than twice the cost of a 5-bay centre. These two factors, taken together, are often referred to as economies of scale – a universal concept that applies (up to a point) to all types of operation. However, economies of scale do not go on forever. Above a certain size, the lowest cost point on curves such as that shown in Figure 5.6 may increase. This occurs because of what are called diseconomies of scale, two of which are particularly important. First, complexity costs increase as size increases. The communications and coordination effort necessary to manage an operation tends to increase faster than capacity. Although not seen as a direct cost, this can nevertheless be very significant. Second, a larger centre is more likely to be partially underutilized because demand within a fixed location will be limited. The equivalent in operations that process physical items is transportation costs. For example, if a manufacturer supplies the whole of its European market from one major plant in Denmark, all supplies may have to be brought in from several countries to the single plant and all products shipped from there throughout Europe.

> **Operations principle**
> Diseconomies of scale increase operating costs above a certain level of capacity, resulting in a minimum cost level of capacity.

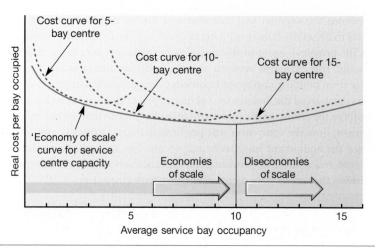

Figure 5.6 Unit cost curves for individual truck service centres of varying capacities

Operating at very high levels of capacity utilization (occupancy levels close to capacity) can mean longer customer waiting times and reduced customer service. There may also be less obvious cost penalties of operating centres at levels close to their nominal capacity. For example, long periods of overtime may reduce productivity levels as well as costing more in extra payments to staff; utilizing bays at very high utilization reduces maintenance and cleaning time that may increase breakdowns, reduce effective life, and so on. This usually means that average costs start to increase after a point that is often lower than the theoretical capacity of the operation. In addition, while large-scale operations usually have a cost advantage over smaller units, there are potentially significant advantages that can be exploited by small-scale operations. These include:

▶ more responsive to change and an ability to act more like entrepreneurs in launching new products and services;
▶ more flexibility in decision making, with greater levels of autonomy granted to individuals than in most large-scale operations;
▶ greater market sensing given proximity to changing markets with more, but smaller, units of capacity.

Timing changes in capacity

Changing the capacity of any operation in a supply network is not just a matter of deciding on its optimum capacity. The operation also needs to decide when to bring new capacity 'on-stream'. For example, Figure 5.7 shows the forecast demand for a manufacturer's new product. In deciding *when* new capacity is to be introduced the company can mix the three strategies.

▶ Capacity is introduced to generally *lead* demand – timing the introduction of capacity in such a way that there is always sufficient capacity to meet forecast demand.
▶ Capacity is introduced to generally *lag* demand – timing the introduction of capacity so that demand is always equal to or greater than capacity.
▶ Capacity is introduced to sometimes lead and sometimes lag demand, but inventory built up during the 'lead' times is used to help meet demand during the 'lag' times. This is called 'smoothing with inventory'.

Each strategy has its own advantages and disadvantages. These are shown in Table 5.1. The actual approach taken by any company will depend on how it views these advantages and disadvantages. For example, if the company's access to funds for capital expenditure is limited, it is likely to find the delayed capital expenditure requirement of the capacity-lagging strategy relatively attractive. Of course, the third strategy, smoothing with inventory, is only appropriate for operations that produce products that can be stored. Customer-processing operations such as hotels cannot satisfy demand in one year by using rooms that were vacant the previous year.

Dubai International Airport is now the world's busiest airport in terms of international travellers with 88.2 million passengers in 2017. It is also the third busiest overall, only behind Beijing Capital and Hartsfield-Jackson Atlanta. The United Arab Emirates (UAE) acts a key hub in international travel, with over 125 million passengers going through its three main airports – Dubai, Abu Dhabi and Sharjah. The story of Dubai International Airport started in 1959, when the then-ruler of Dubai, Sheikh Rashid bin Saeed Al Maktoum, ordered its construction. Like many others in the country, he believed that strengthening the aviation sector was essential in supporting sustainable development for the UAE. Just one year later the first flights were landing, albeit on a runway of compacted sand, followed soon after by a new asphalt runway and numerous extensions to the terminal facilities. As successive governments invested heavily in the airport, it became increasingly attractive to international carriers, fuelling the growth in passengers numbers. In 1990 there were 4.35 million passenger movements, by 2002 this figure had reached 15.9 million, by 2010 it had risen to 47.1 million, and this figure has been nearly doubled to the present day. The economy of scale effects are evident – more passengers lead to more investment (take the recent announcement of a major technology investment to support 'seamless' transfer and dramatically reduce waiting at passport control), while more investment leads to increased numbers of passengers wanting to use the airport, either point-to-point or as a hub for an onward destination. This virtuous cycle continues, at least for now. Emirates Airlines, Dubai Airport's main carrier, now operates the world's largest fleet of Airbus A380s, with over 100 of the world's biggest passenger planes (seating capacity 555–868 passengers depending on the configuration). Much of the reason it was able to justify such a large investment – each plane costs around $300–$400 million and the improvements to existing facilities to accommodate the

A380s were around $3.5 billion – is the now huge scale of its operations out of Dubai International. Qantas Airlines also flies A380s daily from Sydney and Melbourne to London via Dubai.

Dubai International Airport's success has driven the addition of new routes by home carriers Emirates and flydubai as well as increased frequency on existing routes. Alongside this 'home-grown' expansion, new carriers from around the globe continue to join Dubai International Airport, as it becomes an increasingly attractive destination and hub option. Further investments are intended in both process and technology to support growth up to 118 million in the coming years – clearly the Dubai government doesn't feel it has reached a point where diseconomies of scale are at play just yet! And Dubai International Airport isn't just interested in passengers – it is currently in the process of developing a major centre to handle imports and exports of flowers and plants. When completed, it will run a fully automated operation, capable of processing around 300,000 tonnes of product per annum whilst maintaining ambient temperatures of 2 to 4°C. For Royal Flora Holland (see earlier 'Operations in practice' example), this could be a major new threat to its dominance in the world trade of flowers and plants.

Break-even analysis of capacity expansion

An alternative view of capacity expansion can be gained by examining the cost implications of adding increments of capacity on a break-even basis. Figure 5.8 shows how increasing capacity can move an operation from profitability to loss. Each additional unit of capacity results in a *fixed-cost break* that is a further lump of expenditure,

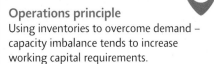

Operations principle
Using inventories to overcome demand – capacity imbalance tends to increase working capital requirements.

which will have to be incurred before any further activity can be undertaken in the operation. The operation is unlikely to be profitable at very low levels of output. Eventually, assuming that prices are greater than marginal costs, revenue will exceed total costs. However, the level of profitability at the point where the output level is equal to the capacity of the operation may not be sufficient to absorb all the extra fixed costs of a further increment in capacity. This could make the operation unprofitable in some stages of its expansion.

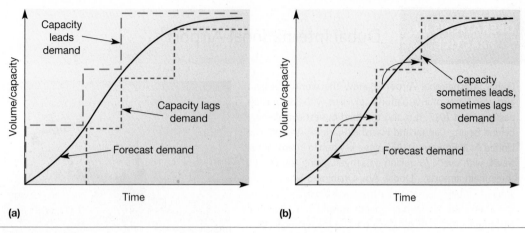

Figure 5.7 (a) Capacity-leading and capacity-lagging strategies, (b) Smoothing with inventories means using the excess capacity in one period to produce inventory that supplies the under-capacity period

Table 5.1 Arguments for and against leading, lagging and smoothing capacity strategies

Advantages	Disadvantages
Capacity-leading strategies	
Always sufficient capacity to meet demand, therefore revenue is maximized and customers satisfied	Utilization of the plants is always relatively low, therefore costs will be high
Most of the time there is a 'capacity cushion' that can absorb extra demand if forecasts are pessimistic	Risks of even greater (or even permanent) over-capacity if demand does not reach forecast levels
Any critical start-up problems with new operations are less likely to affect supply	Capital spending on capacity will be early
Capacity-lagging strategies	
Always sufficient demand to keep the operation working at full capacity, therefore unit costs are minimized	Insufficient capacity to meet demand fully, therefore reduced revenue and dissatisfied customers
Over-capacity problems are minimized if forecasts prove optimistic	No ability to exploit short-term increases in demand
Capital spending on the operation is delayed	Under-supply position even worse if there are start-up problems with the new operations
Smoothing with inventory strategies	
All demand is satisfied, therefore customers are satisfied and revenue is maximized	The cost of inventories in terms of working capital requirements can be high. This is especially serious at a time when the company requires funds for its capital expansion
Utilization of capacity is high and therefore costs are low	Risks of product deterioration and obsolescence
Very short-term surges in demand can be met from inventories	

Where should operations be located?

The location of each operation in a supply network is both a key element in defining its structure, and also will have an impact on how the network operates in practice. If any operation in a supply network gets the location wrong, it can have a significant impact, not just on its own profits, but also on those of others in the network. For example, siting a data centre where potential staff with appropriate skills will not live will affect its performance, and the service it gives its customers.

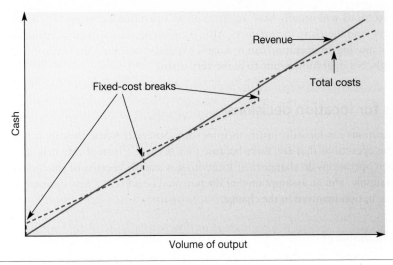

Figure 5.8 Repeated incurring of fixed costs can raise total costs above revenue

Worked example

A specialist graphics company is investing in a new machine, which enables it to make high-quality prints for its clients. Demand for these prints is forecast to be around 100,000 units in year 1 and 220,000 units in year 2. The maximum capacity of each machine the company will buy to process these prints is 100,000 units per year. The machines have a fixed cost of €200,000 per year and a variable cost of processing of €1 per unit. The company believes it will be able to charge €4 per unit for producing the prints.

Question
What profit is the company likely to make in the first and second years?

$$\text{Year 1 demand} = 100{,}000 \text{ units; therefore company will need one machine}$$
$$\text{Cost of manufacturing} = \text{Fixed cost for one machine} + \text{Variable cost} \times 100{,}000$$
$$= €200{,}000 + (€1 \times 100{,}000)$$
$$= €300{,}000$$
$$\text{Revenue} = \text{Demand} \times \text{Price}$$
$$= 100{,}000 \times €4$$
$$= €400{,}000$$
$$\text{Therefore, Profit} = €400{,}000 - €300{,}000$$
$$= €100{,}000$$
$$\text{Year 2 demand} = 220{,}000; \text{therefore company will need three machines}$$
$$\text{Cost of manufacturing} = \text{Fixed cost for three machines} + \text{Variable cost} \times 220{,}000$$
$$= (3 \times €200{,}000) + (€1 \times 220{,}000)$$
$$= €820{,}000$$
$$\text{Revenue} = \text{Demand} \times \text{Price}$$
$$= 220{,}000 \times €4$$
$$= €880{,}000$$
$$\text{Therefore, Profit} = €880{,}000 - €820{,}000$$
$$= €60{,}000$$

Note – the profit in the second year will be lower because of the extra fixed costs associated with the investment in the two extra machines.

Location decisions will usually have an effect on an operation's costs as well as its ability to serve its customers (and therefore its revenues). Also, location decisions, once taken, are difficult to undo. The costs of moving an operation can be hugely expensive and the risks of inconveniencing customers very high. No operation wants to move very often.

Reasons for location decisions

Not all operations can logically justify their location. Some are where they are for historical reasons. Yet even the operations that are 'there because they're there' are implicitly making a decision not to move. When operations do change their location, it is usually because of changes in demand and/or changes in supply, and an assumption that the potential benefits of a new location will outweigh any cost and disruption involved in the change.

Changes in demand

Customer demand shifting may prompt a change in location. For example, as garment manufacturers moved to Asia, suppliers of zips, threads, etc. started to follow. Changes in the volume of demand can also prompt relocation. To meet higher demand, an operation could expand its existing site, or choose a larger site in another location, or keep its existing location and find a second location for an additional operation; the last two options will involve a location decision. High-visibility operations may not have the choice of expanding on the same site to meet rising demand. A dry cleaning service may attract only marginally more business by expanding an existing site because it offers a local, and therefore convenient, service. Finding a new location for an additional operation is probably its only option for expansion.

Changes in supply

The other stimulus for relocation is changes in the cost, or availability, of the supply of inputs to the operation. For example, a mining or oil company will need to relocate as the minerals it is extracting become depleted. The reason why so many software companies located in India was the availability of talented, well-educated, but relatively lower-cost staff.

Rolls-Royce in Singapore[3]

When the aero engine manufacturer Rolls-Royce chose Seletar in Singapore to host its almost £400 million Asian expansion it did so for a number of reasons. First, the location had access to the skills and infrastructure to support technically complex manufacturing. Second, the company was no stranger to the region; it already serviced Singapore Airlines' engines at a special plant near Changi airport. Third, Asia is where the demand is. The world's fastest-growing airlines are in China, Singapore, Indonesia, India and the Gulf. Fourth, the generous tax incentives offered by the Singaporean government played a part, as did the construction of a road from Seletar to Changi airport so that engines could be loaded on to the cargo planes that fly them to Rolls-Royce's customers in Toulouse and Seattle. Yet, says the company, although important, these incentives were not as important as the 'soft' factors that make

Singapore so attractive: in particular, the City State's universities and colleges, which produce the highly skilled scientists, engineers and staff who are vital to producing

products that cannot be allowed to fail. Says Jonathan Asherson, 'We think that the focus in Asia, from an education and training perspective, will continue to be in areas of technology and engineering. The talent pipeline that we need as an industry and company will remain solid. That will influence the thinking around our investments. You need to develop technologies and business models that adapt to increasing pressure on costs, increasing pressure on reliability and the environment. We've worked with government agencies around developing work skills, qualifications, and developing curricula for the polytechnics and universities, where we work with them to predict the requirement and work on how that pipeline of talent can be built. Singapore is quite flexible and nimble where they see the high multiplier effect of, for example, high-value-added manufacturing.'

Evaluating potential changes in location

Evaluating possible locations is almost always a complex task because the number of location options, the criteria against which they could be evaluated and the comparative rarity of a single location that clearly dominates all others, make the decision strategically sensitive. Furthermore, the decision often involves high levels of uncertainty. Neither the relocation activity itself nor the operating characteristics of the new site might be as assumed when the decision was originally made. Because of this, it is useful to be systematic in terms of (a) identifying alternative options, and (b) evaluating each option against a set of rational criteria.

> **Operations principle**
> An operation should only change its location if the benefits of moving outweigh the costs of operating in the new location plus the cost of the move itself.

Identify alternative location options

The first relocation option to consider is not to. Sometimes relocation is inevitable, but often staying put is a viable option. Even if seeking a new location seems the obvious way forward, it is worth evaluating the 'do nothing' option, if only to provide a 'base case' against which to compare other options. In addition to the 'do nothing' option, there should be a number of alternative location options. It is a mistake to consider only one location, but seeking out possible locations can be a time-consuming activity. Increasingly, for larger companies, the whole world offers possible locations. The implication of the globalization of the location decision has been to increase both the number of options and the degree of uncertainty in their relative merits. The sheer number of possibilities makes the location decision impossible to 'optimize'. Rather, the process of identifying location options usually involves selecting a limited number of sites that represent different attributes. For example, a distribution centre, while always needing to be close to transport links, could be located in any of several regions and could be either close to population centres, or in a more rural location. The options may be chosen to reflect a range of both these factors. However, this assumes that the 'supply' of location options is relatively large, which is not always the case. In many retail location decisions, there are a limited number of High Street locations that become available at any point in time. Often, a retailer will wait until a feasible location becomes available and then decide whether to either take up that option or wait and take the chance that a better location becomes available soon. In effect, the location decision here is a sequence of 'take or wait' decisions.

Set location evaluation criteria

Although the criteria against which alternative locations can be evaluated will depend on circumstances, the following five broad categories are typical.

▶ *Capital requirements* – The capital or leasing cost of a site is usually a significant factor. This will probably be a function of the location of the site and its characteristics. For example, the shape of the site and its soil composition can limit the nature of any buildings erected there. Access to the site is also likely to be important, as are the availability of utilities, etc. In addition, the cost of the move itself may depend on which site is eventually chosen.

▶ *Market factors* – Location can affect how the market (in general or an individual customer) perceives an operation. Locating a general hospital in the middle of the countryside may have many advantages for its staff, but it clearly would be very inconvenient for its patients. Likewise, restaurants, stores, banks, petrol filling stations and many other high-visibility operations must all evaluate how alternative locations will determine their image and the level of service they can give. The same arguments apply to labour markets. Location may affect the attractiveness of the operation in terms of staff recruitment and retention. For example, 'science parks' are usually located close to universities because they hope to attract companies that are interested in using the skills available at the university. But not all locations necessarily have appropriate skills available immediately. Staff at a remote call centre in the western islands of Scotland, used to a calm and tranquil life, were stunned by the aggressive nature of many callers to the call centre, some being reduced to tears by bullying customers. They had to be given assertiveness training by the call centre management.

▶ *Cost factors* – Two major categories of cost are affected by location. The first is the costs of producing products or services. For example, labour costs can vary between different areas in any country, but are likely to be a far more significant factor when international comparisons are made, when they can exert a major influence on the location decision, especially in some industries such as clothing, where labour costs as a proportion of total costs are relatively high. Other cost factors, known as community factors, derive from the social, political and economic environment of the site. These include such factors as local tax rates, capital movement restrictions, government financial assistance, political stability, local attitudes to 'inward investment', language, local amenities (schools, theatres, shops, etc.), the availability of support services, the history of labour relations and behaviour, environmental restrictions and planning procedures. The second category of costs relate to both the cost of transporting inputs from their source to the location of the operation and the cost of transporting products and services from the location to customers. Whereas almost all operations are concerned to some extent with the former, not all operations are concerned with the latter, either because customers come to them (for example, hotels), or because their services can be 'transported' at virtually no cost (for example, some technology help desks). For supply networks that process physical items, however, transportation costs can be very significant.

▶ *Future flexibility* – Because operations rarely change their location, any new location must be capable of being acceptable, not only under current circumstances, but also under possible future circumstances. The problem is that no one knows exactly what the future holds. Nevertheless, especially in uncertain environments, any evaluation of alternative locations should include some kind of scenario planning that considers the robustness of each in coping with a range of possible futures. Two types of flexibility of any location could be evaluated. The most common is to consider the potential of the location for expansion to cope with increased activity levels. The second is the ability to adapt to changes in input or output factors. For example, suppliers or customers may themselves relocate in the future. If so, could the location still operate economically?

▶ *Risk factors* – Closely related to the concept of future flexibility is the idea of evaluating the risk factors associated with possible locations. The risk criteria can be divided into 'transition risk' and 'long-term risk'. Transition risk is simply the risk that something goes wrong during the relocation process. Some possible locations might be intrinsically more difficult to move to than others. For example, moving to an already congested location could pose higher risks to being able to move as planned than moving to a more accessible location. Long-tem risks could again include damaging changes in input factors such as exchange rates or labour costs, but can also include more fundamental security risks to staff or property.

How vertically integrated should an operation's network be?

The scope of an operation's control of its supply network is the extent that it does things itself as opposed to relying on other operations to do things for it. This is often referred to as 'vertical integration' when it is the ownership of whole operations that is being decided, or 'outsourcing' when individual activities are being considered. We will look at the 'outsourcing' decision in the next section. The virtual integration decision involves an organization assessing the wisdom of acquiring suppliers

The Rana Plaza disaster[4]

Many firms have shrunk their 'span of ownership' within their supply network. This is why the idea of 'outsourcing' non-core activities has been so well accepted over the last few decades. Focusing on a relatively narrow range of activities clearly has advantages. However, outsourcing activities also carries risks, often linked to a loss of control over suppliers. The Rana Plaza disaster provides an appalling example of the effect of this. On 24 April 2013 the Rana Plaza clothing factory near Dhaka in Bangladesh collapsed, killing at least 1,100 people. Many well-known clothing brands were sourcing products, either directly or indirectly, from the factory. It was claimed that local police and an industry association had issued a warning that the building was unsafe, but the owners had responded by threatening to fire people who refused to carry on working as usual. Understandably, there was an immediate call for tighter regulation and oversight by the Bangladeshi authorities and for the predominantly western retailers who sourced from the Rana Plaza, and similar unsafe factories, to accept some of the responsibility for the disaster and change their buying policies. Campaigning organizations including 'Labour Behind the Label', 'War on Want' and 'Made in Europe' urged retailers to be more transparent about their supply chains. They also called for compensation to be paid. But a year after the tragedy the compensation initiative that intended to raise $40m had raised only $15m, despite being backed by the UN's International Labour Organisation. Less than half the brands linked to clothes making at the building had made donations. Benetton and Matalan said they preferred to support other funds that assisted victims, while the French retailer Auchan claimed that it had no official production taking place in the building when it collapsed so it did not need to contribute towards compensation. Other contributions were relatively small. Walmart, the largest retailer in the world, offered to contribute about $1m compared to more than $8m from the far smaller Primark. The Bangladeshi authorities also came in for international criticism. For years they had made only relatively weak attempts to enforce national building regulations, especially if the landlords involved were politically well connected. After the disaster, they promised to apply the laws more rigorously, but such promises had been made before.

So, what are the options for western retailers? One option is to carry on as before and simply source garments from wherever is cheapest. Doing so would obviously be ethically questionable, but would it also carry a reputational cost? Or would consumers not enquire too deeply about where garments came from if they were cheap enough? Alternatively, retailers could quit sourcing from Bangladesh until its standards improve. But that may be difficult to enforce unless they took on the responsibility to police the whole supply chain right back to the cotton growers. It would also damage all Bangladeshi firms, even those that try to abide by safety rules. This in turn could also be damaging to the retailers' reputations. The third option is to stay and try to change how things are done in the country. Even before the Rana Plaza disaster retailers had met with some interested parties and governments to develop a strategy to improve safety in Bangladesh's 5,000 factories. Also some individual retailers had launched initiatives. Walmart had launched a fire-safety training academy and Gap had announced a plan to help factory owners upgrade their plants. However, individual initiatives are no substitute for properly coordinated safety improvements.

or customers, as well as the direction of integration, the extent of integration, and the balance among the vertically integrated stages. The decision as to whether to vertically integrate is largely a matter of a business balancing the advantages and disadvantages as they apply to that business.

In reality, different companies, even in the same industry, can make very different decisions over how much and where in the network they want to be. Figure 5.9 illustrates the (simplified) supply network for the wind turbine power generation industry. Original equipment manufacturers (OEMs) assemble the wind turbine nacelle (the nacelle houses the generator and gearbox). Towers and blades are often built to the OEM's specifications, either in-house or by outside suppliers. Installing wind turbines involves assembling the nacelle, tower and blades on site, erecting the tower and connecting to the electricity network. The extent of vertical integration varies by

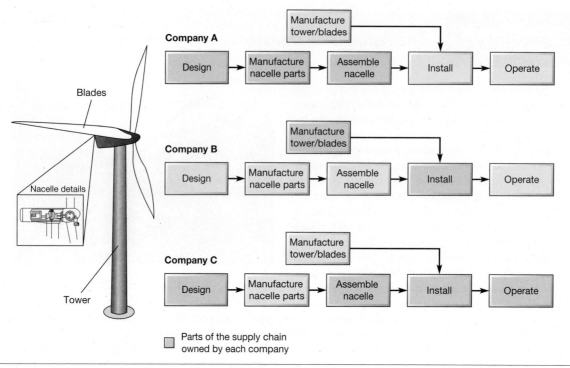

Figure 5.9 Three companies operating in the wind power generation industry with different vertical integration positions

company and component. The three companies illustrated in Figure 5.9 have all chosen different vertical integration strategies. Company A is primarily a nacelle designer and manufacturer that also makes the parts. Company B is primarily an installer that also makes the tower and blades (but buys in the nacelle itself). Company C is primarily an operator that generates electricity and also designs and assembles the nacelles as well as installing the whole tower (but it outsources the manufacture of the nacelle parts, tower and blades).

An organization's vertical integration strategy should consider three key elements – the direction of integration, the extent of integration and the balance amoung vertically integrated stages. Figure 5.10 illustrates these three aspects of vertical integration.

The direction of integration

If a company decides that it should control more of its network, should it expand by buying one of its suppliers or should it expand by buying one of its customers? The strategy of expanding on the supply side of the network is called backward or 'upstream' vertical integration and expanding on the demand side is called forward or 'downstream' vertical integration. Backward vertical integration, by allowing an organization to take control of its suppliers, is often used either to gain cost advantages or to prevent competitors gaining control of important suppliers. Forward vertical integration, on the other hand, takes an organization closer to its markets and allows more freedom to make contact directly with its customers, and possibly sell complementary products and services.

The extent of the process span of integration

Some organizations deliberately choose not to integrate far, if at all, from their original part of the network. Alternatively some organizations choose to become very vertically integrated. Take many large international oil companies, such as Exxon, for example. Exxon is involved with exploration and extraction as well as the refining of the crude oil into a consumable product – gasoline. It also has operations that distribute and retail the gasoline (and many other products) to the final customer.

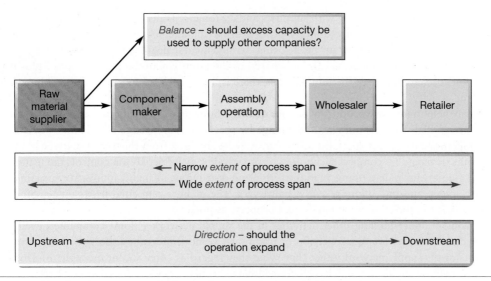

Figure 5.10 The direction, extent and balance of an operation's vertical integration

This path (one of several for its different products) has moved the material through the total network of processes, all of which are owned (wholly or partly) by the one company.

The balance among the vertically integrated stages

This is not strictly about the ownership of the network; it concerns the capacity and, to some extent, the operating behaviour of each stage in the network which is owned by the organization. It refers to the amount of the capacity at each stage in the network that is devoted to supplying the next stage. So a totally balanced network relationship is one where one stage produces only for the next stage in the network and totally satisfies its requirements. Less than full balance in the stages allows each stage to sell its output to other companies or buy in some of its supplies from other companies.

Advantages of vertical integration

Although extensive vertical integration is no longer as popular as it once was, there are still companies that find it advantageous to own several sequential stages of their supply network. Indeed very few companies are anywhere close to 'virtual', with no vertical integration of stages whatsoever. What then are the reasons why companies still choose to vertically integrate? Most justifications for vertical integration fall under four categories. These are:

▶ **It secures dependable access to supply or markets** – The most fundamental reasons for engaging in some vertical integration is that it can give more secure supply or bring a business closer to its customers. In some cases there may not even be sufficient capacity in the supply market to satisfy the company. It therefore has little alternative but to supply itself. Downstream vertical integration can give a firm greater control over its market positioning. For example, Apple has always adopted a supply network model that integrates hardware and software, with both its hardware and software designed by Apple.

▶ **It may reduce costs** – The most common argument here is that '*We can do it cheaper than our supplier's price*'. Such statements are often made by comparing the marginal direct cost incurred by a company in doing something itself against the price it is paying to buy the product or service from a supplier. But costs saving should also take into account start-up and learning costs. A more straightforward case can be made when there are technical advantages of integration. For example, producing aluminium kitchen foil involves rolling it to the required thickness and then 'slitting' it into the finished widths. Performing both activities in-house saves the loading and unloading activity and the transportation to another operation. Vertical integration also reduces the 'transaction costs' of dealing with suppliers and customers. Transaction costs are expenses, other than price, which are incurred in the process of buying and selling, such as searching for and selecting suppliers, setting up monitoring arrangements, negotiating contracts, and so on. However, if transaction costs can be lowered to the point where the purchase price plus transaction costs are less than the internal cost, there is little justification for the vertical integration of the activity.

▶ **It may help to improve product or service quality** – Sometimes vertical integration can be used to secure specialist or technological advantage by preventing knowledge getting into the hands of competitors. The exact specialist advantage may be anything from the 'secret ingredient' in fizzy drinks through to a complex technological process. For example, Dyson controls the majority of its value stream in developing, manufacturing and distributing its highly innovative vacuum cleaners, dryers, fans and, more recently, hairdryers. The main reason cited by its owner, Sir James Dyson, is to protect as much intellectual property as possible.

▶ **It helps in understanding other activities in the supply network** – Some companies, even those which are famous for their rejection of traditional vertical integration, do choose to own some parts of the supply network other than what they regard as core. So, for example, McDonald's, the restaurant chain, although largely franchising its retail operations, does own some retail outlets. How else, it argues, could it understand its retail operations so well?

OPERATIONS IN PRACTICE

Contrasting strategies on structure and scope: ARM versus Intel[5]

Nothing better illustrates the idea that there is more than one approach to competing in the same market than the contrasting business models of ARM and Intel in the microchip business. At one point, ARM's chip designs were to be found in almost 99 per cent of mobile devices in the world, while Intel dominates the PC and server markets. Yet ARM and Intel are very different companies, with different approaches to the structure and scope of their operations and, some claim, very different prospects for their future. They are certainly of a different size. In revenue terms Intel is around 50 times bigger than ARM. More interestingly, Intel is vertically integrated, both designing and manufacturing its own chips, while ARM is essentially a chip designer, developing intellectual property. It then licenses its processor designs to manufacturers such as Samsung, which in turn rely on sub-contracting 'chip foundry' companies to do the actual manufacturing (ironically, including Intel).

Intel's integrated supply network monitors and controls all stages of production, from the original design concept right through to manufacturing. Keeping on top of fast-changing and hugely expensive operations requires very large investments (it can cost around $5 billion to build a new chip-making plant). It is Intel's near-monopoly (therefore high volume) of the server and PC markets that helps it to keep its unit prices high, which in turn gives it the ability to finance the construction of the latest

semiconductor manufacturing equipment before its competitors. And having the latest manufacturing technology is important, as it can mean faster, smaller and cheaper chips with lower power consumption. As one industry source put it, *'Intel is one of the few companies left with the financial resources to invest in state-of-the-art manufacturing research and development. Everyone else – including all the ARM licensees – have to make do with shared manufacturing, mainstream technology, and less-aggressive physics.'*

By contrast, ARM's supply network strategy was a direct result of its early lack of cash. It did not have the money to invest in in its own manufacturing facilities (or to take the risk of subcontracting manufacturing), so it

▶

focused on licensing its 'reference designs'. Reference designs provide the 'technical blueprint' of a microprocessor that third parties can enhance or modify as required. This means that partners can take ARM reference designs and integrate them in flexibly to produce different final designs. And over the years a whole 'eco-system' of tools has emerged to help developers build applications around the ARM design architecture. The importance of ARM's supply 'eco-system' should not be underestimated. It is an approach that allows ARM's partners to be part of ARM's success rather than cutting them out of the revenue opportunities.

Disadvantages of vertical integration

The arguments against vertical integration tend to cluster around a number of observed disadvantages of those companies that have practised vertical integration extensively. These are as follows:

▶ **It creates an internal monopoly** – Operations, it is argued, will only change when they see a pressing need to do so. Internal supply is subject to reduced competitive forces that keep operations motivated to improve. If an external supplier serves its customers well, it will make higher profits; if not, it will suffer. Such incentives and sanctions do not apply to the same extent if the supplying operation is part of the same company.

▶ **You cannot exploit economies of scale** – Any activity that is vertically integrated within an organization is probably also carried out elsewhere in the industry. But the effort it puts into the process will be a relatively small part of the sum total of that activity within the industry. Specialist suppliers that can serve more than one customer are likely to have volumes larger than any of their customers could achieve doing things for themselves. This allows specialist suppliers to reap some of the cost benefits of economies of scale, which can be passed on in terms of lower prices to their customers.

▶ **It results in loss of flexibility** – Heavily vertically integrated companies by definition do most things themselves. This means that a high proportion of their costs will be fixed costs. They have, after all, invested heavily in the capacity that allows them to do most things in-house. A high level of fixed costs relative to variable costs means that any reduction in the total volume of activity can easily move the economics of the operation close to, or below, its break-even point.

▶ **It cuts you off from innovation** – Vertical integration means investing in the processes and technologies necessary to create products and services in-house. But, as soon as that investment is made the company has an inherent interest in maintaining it. Abandoning such investments can be both economically and emotionally difficult. The temptation is always to wait until any new technology is clearly established before admitting that one's own is obsolete. This may lead to a tendency to lag in the adoption of new technologies and ideas.

▶ **It distracts you from core activities (loss of focus)** – The final, and arguably most powerful, case against vertical integration concerns any organization's ability to be technically competent at a very wide range of activities. All companies have things that they need to be good at. It is far easier to be exceptionally good at something if the company focuses exclusively on it rather than being distracted by many other things. Vertical integration, by definition, means doing more things, which can distract from the (few) particularly important things.

What activities should be in-house and what should be outsourced?

Outsourcing is the activity of taking activities that could or have been carried out in-house and moving them to outsourced suppliers. Theoretically, 'vertical integration' and 'outsourcing' are almost the same thing, with the difference between them one of scale. Vertical integration is a term that is usually (but not always) applied to whole operations. So, buying a supplier because you want to deny its products to a competitor, or selling the part of your business that services your products to a specialist servicing company that can do the job better, is a vertical integration decision. Outsourcing usually applies to smaller sets of activities that have previously been performed in-house. Deciding to ask a specialist laboratory to perform some quality tests that your own quality control department used to do, or having your call (contact) centre taken over and run by a larger call centre company, are both outsourcing decisions.

Outsourcing (also known as the 'do-or-buy' or 'make-or-buy' decision) has become an important issue for most businesses. This is because, although most companies have always outsourced some of their activities, a larger proportion of direct activities are now being bought from suppliers. In addition, many indirect and administrative processes are now being outsourced. This is often referred to as business process outsourcing (BPO). Financial service companies in particular are outsourcing some of their more routine back-office processes. In a similar way many processes within the Human Resource function, from simple payroll services through to more complex training and development processes, are being outsourced to specialist companies. The processes may still be physically located where they were before, but the outsourcing service provider manages the staff and technology. The reason for doing this is often primarily to reduce cost. However, there can sometimes also be significant gains in the quality and flexibility of service offered.

Making the outsourcing decision

Outsourcing is rarely a simple decision. Operations in different circumstances with different objectives are likely to take different decisions. Yet the question itself is relatively simple, even if the decision itself is not: 'Does in-house or outsourced supply in a particular set of circumstances give the appropriate performance objectives that the operation requires to compete more effectively in its markets?' For example, if the main performance objectives for an operation are dependable delivery and meeting short-term changes in customers' delivery requirements, the key question should be: 'How does in-house supply or outsourcing give better dependability and delivery flexibility performance?' This means judging two sets of opposing factors – those that give the potential to improve performance, and those that work against this potential being realized. Table 5.2 summarizes some arguments for in-house supply and outsourcing in terms of each performance objective.

> **Operations principle**
> Assessing the advisability of outsourcing should include how it impacts on relevant performance objectives.

Incorporating strategic factors into the outsourcing decision

Although the effect of outsourcing on the operation's performance objectives is important, there are other factors that companies take into account when deciding if outsourcing an activity is a sensible option. For example, if an activity has long-term strategic importance to a company, it is unlikely to outsource it. For example, a retailer might choose to keep the design and development of its website in-house even though specialists could perform the activity at less cost because it plans to move into web-based retailing at some point in the future. Nor would a company usually outsource an activity where it had specialized skills or knowledge. For example, a company making laser printers may have built up specialized knowledge in the production of sophisticated laser drives. This capability may allow it to introduce product or process innovations in the future. It would be foolish to 'give away' such capability. After these two more strategic factors have been considered, the company's operations performance can be taken into account. Obviously if its operation's performance is already superior to any potential supplier, it would be unlikely to outsource the activity. But also even if its performance is currently below that of potential suppliers, it may not outsource the activity if it feels that it could significantly improve its performance. Figure 5.11 illustrates this decision logic.

> **Operations principle**
> Assessing the advisability of outsourcing should include consideration of the strategic importance of the activity and the operation's relative performance.

Table 5.2 How in-house and outsourced supply may affect an operation's performance objectives

Performance objective	'Do it yourself' In-house supply	'Buy it in' Outsourced supply
Quality	The origins of any quality problems are usually easier to trace in-house and improvement can be more immediate but can be some risk of complacency.	Supplier may have specialized knowledge and more experience, also may be motivated through market pressures, but communication more difficult.
Speed	Can mean synchronized schedules which speeds throughput of materials and information, but if the operation has external customers, internal customers may be low priority.	Speed of response can be built into the supply contract where commercial pressures will encourage good performance, but there may be significant transport/delivery delays.
Dependability	Easier communications can help dependability, but if the operation also has external customers, internal customers may receive low priority.	Late delivery penalties in the supply contract can encourage good delivery performance, but organizational barriers may inhibit communication.
Flexibility	Closeness to the real needs of a business can alert the in-house operation to required changes, but the ability to respond may be limited by the scale and scope of internal operations.	Outsource suppliers may be larger and have wider capabilities than in-house suppliers and more ability to respond to changes, but may have to balance conflicting needs of different customers.
Cost	In-house operations do not have to make the margin required by outside suppliers, so the business can capture the profits which would otherwise be given to the supplier, but relatively low volumes may mean that it is difficult to gain economies of scale or the benefits of process innovation.	Probably the main reason why outsourcing is so popular. Outsourced companies can achieve economies of scale and they are motivated to reduce their own costs because these directly impact on their profits, but transaction costs of working with a supplier need to be taken into account.

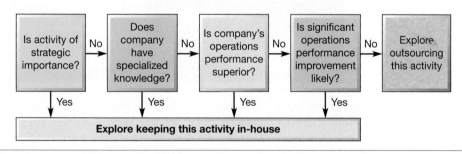

Figure 5.11 The decision logic of outsourcing

Outsourcing and offshoring

Two supply network strategies that are often confused are those of outsourcing and offshoring. Outsourcing means deciding to buy in products or services rather than perform the activities in-house. Offshoring means obtaining products and services from operations that are based outside one's own country. Of course, one may both outsource and offshore as illustrated in Figure 5.12. Offshoring is very closely related to outsourcing and the motives for each may be similar. Offshoring to a lower - cost region of the world is usually done to reduce an operation's overall costs, as is outsourcing to a supplier that has greater expertise or scale or both.

	Outsourcing	Offshore outsourcing
Company does not own the assets	Domestic supplier delivers products and/or services	Overseas supplier delivers products and/or services
Company owns the assets	**Domestic operations** Focal operation performs activities itself	**Offshore operations** Focal operation's overseas operation delivers products and/or services
	Within domestic markets	International markets

Ownership of operations (left axis label)

Location of operations (bottom axis label)

Figure 5.12 Offshoring and outsourcing are related but different

---

Samsung's subcontracted success

One of the best-known cautionary tales that illustrates the inherent dangers involved in subcontracting is that of how General Electric lost its microwave oven business. Although Japanese domestic appliance manufacturers, such as Matsushita and Sanyo, dominated the global microwave industry at the beginning of the 1980s, General Electric (GE) was enjoying reasonable success in the US market with its purpose-designed microwave oven plant in Maryland. However, it soon came under price pressures from Japanese competitors. What seemed an obvious solution was to subcontract the production of some of its more basic models, where margins were relatively small. GE explored the idea of subcontracting these models to one of its main rivals, Matsushita, even though giving one of its main competitors such an advantage was considered risky. GE also found a small, but go-getting, Korean company that was already selling very simple (and very cheap) models in the USA. GE decided to continue making the top of the range models itself, subcontract its cheaper models to Matsushita, but also place a small order of 15,000 units of its cheaper models to the Korean company, partly to see whether they could cope with the order. Of course it also made sense for GE to send their own engineers to help the Korean company and ensure that quality standards would be maintained. The GE engineers found that, although the Korean company had little knowledge, it was very willing to learn. Eventually the Koreans' production line started producing reasonable quality products, still at very low prices. Over time, the Korean company was given more and more orders by GE, which found that it was making more profit from the Korean-sourced products than those coming out of its own plant in the USA. This became particularly important as the market continued to mature and costs came under increased pressure. The Maryland plant attempted to cut its own costs but this proved especially difficult with so much of its volume now subcontracted to the Korean company. In the end the Maryland plant was closed and GE withdrew entirely from the microwave oven (indeed the whole domestic appliance) market. And the Korean company? It was called Samsung, and within 10 years of starting to make them it became the world's largest manufacturer of microwave ovens.

Probably the most controversial issue in supply network design is that of outsourcing. In many instances there has been fierce opposition to companies outsourcing some of their processes. Trade unions often point out that the only reason that outsourcing companies can do the job at lower cost is that they either reduce salaries, reduce working conditions, or both. Furthermore, they say, flexibility is only achieved by reducing job security. Employees who were once part of a large and secure corporation could find themselves as far less secure employees of a less benevolent employer with a philosophy of permanent cost cutting. Even some proponents of outsourcing are quick to point out the problems. There can be significant obstacles, including understandable resistance from staff who find themselves 'outsourced'. Some companies have also been guilty of 'outsourcing a problem'. In other words, having failed to manage a process well themselves, they ship it out rather than face up to why the process was problematic in the first place. There is also evidence that, although long-term costs can be brought down when a process is outsourced, there may be an initial period when costs rise as both sides learn how to manage the new arrangement.

Globalization, 're-shoring' and technology

Almost since the start of the industrial revolution, businesses across the world have been forging ever-closer relationships. Especially in the last few decades, the use of geographically dispersed suppliers to outsource at least some activities has become routine. This has been driven partly by labour cost differentials, partly by cheap and efficient IT connecting businesses, partly by trade deals, and partly by reduced transport costs. This is 'globalization', where products, raw materials, money, technology and ideas move (relatively) smoothly across national boundaries. Apple and others can design their products in California and assemble them in China. A French aerospace company can direct the activities of its Brazilian suppliers almost as effectively as if they were in the next town. Bill Clinton, the ex-president of the USA called globalization *'the economic equivalent of a force of nature, like wind or water. It pushes countries to specialize and swap, making them richer, and the world smaller.'*

But increasingly some economists and business commentators question whether the boom in globalized operations is over. Some cite protectionist pressures in some developed countries. Others see rising wages in (previously) less developed countries as reducing cost differentials. In addition, the operations-related advantages of sourcing from suppliers closer to home can be significant. Reducing reliance on complicated international supply chains can save transport and inventory costs, is less polluting, and is potentially less prone to reputational risk if far-off suppliers misbehave. It can also increase supply flexibility. For example, the Spanish fast fashion brand, Zara, manufactures some of its 'steady selling' items in low-cost factories in Asia, but makes the vast majority of its (less predictable demand) garments closer to its markets so that it can respond quickly to changing fashions (see the case study at the end of Chapter 12). Developments in technology could reinforce this so-called 're-shoring' (also referred to as 'back-shoring', 'home-shoring' and 'on-shoring') process. Automation may encourage a trend towards 'radical insourcing' where developed countries no longer need to outsource production to countries where wages are low (see the 'Operations in practice' example on Adidas in Chapter 1).

In other cases, problems with poor quality and unreliable delivery have led companies to re-think their geographically dispersed supply networks, including General Electric, Caterpillar, Ford and Apple. In services, customer frustrations based on perceived communication problems have led a number of companies to reverse off shoring decisions for their call centres, including United Utilities, British

Telecom, Santander Bank and PowerGen. It also appears that, in many case, shareholders approve of such re-shoring decisions. A recent study analysing the stock price effects of re-shoring announcements by US firms,[6] showed an average 0.45 per cent uplift in stock returns in the aftermath of an announcement – for the firms in the study, that represents an average increased market value of $322.57 million!

Summary answers to key questions

What is the structure and scope of operations?

▶ A supply network includes the chains of suppliers providing inputs to the operation and the chains of customers who receive outputs from the operation

▶ Understanding the nature of the supply network and the operations role within it is critical in understanding competiveness, identifying significant links in the network, and shifting towards a longer-term perspective.

▶ The 'structure' of an operation's supply network relates to the shape and form of the network. It involves decisions around network configuration, capacity levels for each part of the network, and the location of each part of the network.

▶ The 'scope' of an operation's supply network relates to the extent that an operation decides to do the activities performed by the network itself, as opposed to requesting a supplier to do them. This involves deciding the extent of vertical integration and the degree of outsourcing.

How should the network be configured?

▶ Configuring a supply network means determining its overall pattern, shape or arrangement of the various operations that make up the supply network.

▶ Changing the shape of the supply network may involves reducing the number of suppliers to the operation so as to develop closer relationships, and bypassing or disintermediation of operations within the network.

▶ All the players in the network, whether they are customers, suppliers, competitors or complementors, can be both friends and enemies at different times. The term used to capture this idea is 'co-opetition'.

▶ An idea that is closely related to that of co-opetition is that of the 'business ecosystem'. Like supply networks, business ecosystems include suppliers and customers, but they also include stakeholders that have little direct relationship with the main network, yet interact by complementing or contributing significant components of value for end customers.

▶ Operations are increasingly outsourcing the delivery of some aspects of their service to specialist providers, which deal directly with customers on behalf of the focal firm. This marks a shift from a 'dyadic' perspective to a 'triadic' perspective.

How much capacity should operations have?

▶ The amount of capacity an organization will have depends on its view of current and future demand. Key long-term capacity decisions include choosing the optimum capacity for each site and timing the changes in the capacity increase (or decrease) of each part of the network.

▶ When deciding the optimum capacity level, the concepts of economy and diseconomy of scale are critical.

▶ When deciding the timing of capacity change, organizations can consider a mix of three strategies – capacity introduced to *lead* demand, capacity introduced to *lag* demand and capacity smoothing, where inventory is used in lead periods to meet demand in lag periods.

Where should operations be located?

▶ The location of each operation in a supply network is both a key element in defining its structure, and also will have an impact on how the network operates in practice.

▶ Key reasons for location decisions include changes in demand and/or changes in supply.

▶ Evaluating potential changes in location involves two key steps:

— identifying alternative location options;

— setting location evaluation criteria, including capital requirements, market factors, cost factors, future flexibility and risk factors.

How vertically integrated should the network be?

▶ The scope of an operation's control of its supply network is the extent to which it does things itself as opposed to relying on other operations to do things for it. This is often referred to as 'vertical integration' when it is the ownership of whole operations that is being decided, or 'outsourcing' when individual activities are being considered.

▶ An organization's vertical integration strategy can be defined in terms of the direction of integration, the extent of the process span of integration, and the balance among the vertically integrated stages.

▶ Advantages of vertical integration may include securing access to supply or markets; reducing costs; improving product or service quality; and improved understanding of supply network activities.

▶ Disadvantages of vertical integration may include the creation of an internal monopoly; lack of economies of scale; potential loss of flexibility; and isolation from innovation.

What activities should be in-house and what should be outsourced?

▶ Outsourcing is the activity of taking activities that could be or have been carried out in-house and moving them to outsourced suppliers. It is also known as the 'do-or-buy' or 'make-or-buy' decision.

▶ Making the outsourcing decision involves comparing the relative impact on key performance objectives of doing an activity in-house versus using an outsourced supplier. It also requires incorporation of other strategic factors, such as long-term competitive advantage and risk.

▶ There is a key difference between outsourcing and off shoring. Outsourcing means deciding to buy in products or services rather than perform the activities in-house. Off-shoring means obtaining products and services from operations that are based outside one's own country.

▶ While globalization is a key trend that has led to geographically dispersed networks of operations, the last decade has seen some reversing of this trend, often referred to as re-shoring.

Just outside Rotterdam in the Netherlands, Frank Jansen, the Chief Operating Officer of Aarens Electronic (AE) was justifiably proud of what he described as *'the most advanced machine of its type in the world, which will enable us to achieve new standards of excellence for our products requiring absolute cleanliness and precision'* and *'a quantum leap in harnessing economies of scale* [and] *new technology to provide **the** most advanced operation for years to come'.* The Rotterdam operation was joining AE's two existing operations in the Netherlands. The company offered precision custom coating and laminating services to a wide range of customers, among the most important being Phanchem, to which it supplied dry photoresist imaging films, a critical step in the manufacturing of microchips. Phanchem then processed the film further and sold it direct to microchip manufacturers.

The Rotterdam operation

The decision to build the Rotterdam operation had been taken because AE believed that a new low-cost operation using 'ultra-clean' controlled environment technology could secure a very large part of Phanchem's future business – perhaps even an exclusive agreement to supply 100 per cent of its needs. When planning the new operation three options were presented to AE's Executive Committee.

A   Expand an existing site by building a new machine within existing site boundaries. This would provide around 12 to 13 million square metres (MSM) per year of additional capacity and require around €19 million in capital expenditure.

B   Build a new facility alongside the existing plant. This new facility could accommodate additional capacity of around 15 MSM per year but, unlike option A, would also allow for future expansion. Initially this would require around €22 million of capital.

C   Set up a totally new site with a much larger increment of capacity, probably around 25 MSM per year. This option would be the most expensive at around €30 million.

Frank Jansen and his team initially favoured option B, but in discussion with the AE Executive Committee, opinion shifted towards the more radical option C. *'It may have been the highest-risk option but it held considerable potential and it fitted with the AE Group philosophy of getting into high-tech specialized areas of business. So we went for it'* (Frank Jansen). The option of a very large, ultra clean, state-of-the-art facility also had a further advantage – it could change the economics of the photoresist imaging industry. In fact, global demand and capacity did not immediately justify investing in such a large increase in capacity. There was probably some overcapacity in the industry. But a large-capacity, ultra-clean type operation could provide a level of quality at such low costs that, if there were overcapacity in the industry, it would not be AE's capacity that would by lying idle.

Designing the new operation

During discussions on the design of the new operation, it became clear that there was one issue that was underlying all the team's discussions – how flexible should the process be? Should the team assume that they were designing an operation that would be dedicated exclusively to the manufacture of photoresist imaging film, and ruthlessly cut out any technological options that would enable it to manufacture other products, or should they design a more general-purpose operation that was suitable for photoresist imaging film, but could also make other products? It proved a difficult decision. The advantages of the more flexible option were obvious. *'At least it would mean that there was no chance of me being stuck with an operation and no market for it to serve in a couple of years' time'* (Frank Jansen). But the advantages of a totally dedicated operation were less obvious, although there was a general agreement that both costs and quality could be superior in an operation dedicated to one product.

Eventually the team decided to focus on a relatively non-flexible, focused and dedicated large machine. *'You can't imagine the agonies we went through when we decided not to make this a flexible machine. Many of us were not comfortable with saying, "This is going to be a photoresist machine exclusively, and if the market goes away we're in real trouble." We had a lot of debate about that. Eventually we more or less reached a consensus for focus but it was certainly one of the toughest decisions we ever made'* (Frank Janssen). The capital cost savings of a focused facility and operating costs savings of up to 25 per cent were powerful arguments, as was the philosophy of total process dedication. *'The key word for us was **focus**. We wanted to be quite clear about what was needed to satisfy our customer in making this single type of product. As well as providing significant cost savings to us it made it a lot easier to identify the root* causes of any problems because we would not have to worry about how it might affect other products. It's all very clear. When the line was down we would not be generating revenue! It would also force us to understand our own performance. At our other operations, if a line goes down, the people can be shifted to other responsibilities. We don't have other responsibilities here – we're either making it or we're not' (Frank Janssen).

When the Rotterdam operation started producing, the team had tweaked the design to bring the capacity at start-up to 32 MSM per year. Notwithstanding some initial teething troubles it was, from the start, a technical and commercial success. Within six months a contract was signed with Phanchem to supply 100 per cent of its needs for the next ten years. Phanchem's decision was based on the combination of manufacturing and business focus that the Rotterdam team has achieved, a point stressed by Frank Janssen. 'Co-locating all necessary departments on the Rotterdam site was seen as particularly important. All the technical functions and the marketing and business functions are now on site.'

Developing the supply relationship

At the time of the start-up, products produced in Rotterdam were shipped to Phanchem's facility near Frankfurt, Germany, almost 500 km away. This distance caused a number of problems including some damage in transit and delays in delivery. However, the relationship between AE and Phanchem remained sound helped by the two companies' cooperation during the Rotterdam start-up. 'We had worked closely with them during the design and construction of the new Rotterdam facility. More to the point, they saw that they would certainly achieve cost savings from the plant, with the promise of more savings to come as the plant moved down the learning curve' (Frank Janssen). The closeness of the relationship between the two companies was a result of their staff working together. AE engineers were impressed by their customer's willingness to help out while they worked on overcoming the start-up problems. Similarly AE had helped Phanchem when it needed extra supplies at short notice. As Frank Janssen said, 'partly because we worked together on various problems the relationship has grown stronger and stronger'.

In particular the idea of a physically closer relationship between AE and Phanchem was explored. 'During the negotiations with Phanchem for our 100 per cent contract there had been some talk about co-location but I don't think anyone took it particularly seriously. Nevertheless there was general agreement that it would be a good thing to do. After all, our success as Phanchem's sole supplier of coated photoresist was tied in to their success as a player in the global market – what was good for Phanchem was good for AE' (Frank Janssen). Several options were discussed within and between the two companies. Phanchem had, in effect, to choose between four options:

- Stay where it was near Frankfurt.
- Relocate to the Netherlands (which would give easier access to port facilities) but not too close to AE (an appropriate site was available 30 km from Rotterdam).
- Locate to a currently vacant adjacent site across the road from AE's Rotterdam plant.
- Co-locate within an extension that could be specially built onto the AE plant at Rotterdam.

Evaluating the co-location options

Relatively early in the discussions between the two companies, the option of 'doing nothing' by staying in Frankfurt was discounted. Phanchem wanted to sell its valuable site in the centre of Frankfurt. The advantages of some kind of move were significant. The option of Phanchem moving to a site 30 km from Rotterdam was considered but rejected because it had no advantages over locating even closer to the Rotterdam plant. Phanchem also strongly considered building and operating a facility across the road from the Rotterdam plant. But eventually the option of locating in a building attached to AE's Rotterdam operation became the preferred option. Co-location would have a significant impact on Phanchem's competitiveness by reducing its operating costs, enabling it to gain market share by offering quality film at attractive prices, thus increasing volume for AE. The managers at the Rotterdam plant also looked forward to an even closer operational relationship with the customer. 'Initially, there was some resistance in the team to having a customer on the same site as ourselves. No one in AE had ever done it before. The step from imagining our customer across the road to imagining them on the same site took some thinking about. It was a matter of getting use to the idea, taking one step at a time' (Frank Janssen).

The customer becomes a paying guest

However, when Frank and the Rotterdam managers presented their proposal for extending the plant to the AE board the proposal was not well received. 'Leasing factory space to our customer seemed a long way from our core business. As one Executive Committee member said, we are manufacturers; we aren't in the real estate business. But we felt that it would be beneficial for both companies' (Frank Janssen). Even when the proposal was eventually accepted, there was still concern over sharing a facility. In fact the Executive Committee insisted that the door between the two companies' areas should be capable of being locked from both sides. Yet the construction and commissioning of the new facility for Phanchem was also a model of cooperation. Now, all visitors to the plant are shown the door that had to be 'capable of being locked from both sides' and asked how many times they think it has been locked. The answer, of course, is 'never'.

QUESTIONS

1 What were the key structure and scope decisions taken by Aarens Electronic?

2 What were the risks involved in adopting a process design that was 'totally dedicated' to the one customer's needs?

3 What were the advantages and disadvantages of each location option open to Phanchem, and why do you think it eventually chose to co-locate with AE?

Problems and applications

All chapters have 'Problems and applications' questions that will help you practise analysing operations. They can be answered by reading the chapter. Model answers for the first two questions can be found on the companion website for this book.

1   Consider the music business as a supply network. How did music downloads and streaming affect each artist's sales? What implications has online music transmission had for traditional music retailers?

2   A data centre is *'a facility composed of networked computers and storage that businesses or other organizations use to organize, process, store and disseminate large amounts of data. A business typically relies heavily upon the applications, services and data contained within a data centre, making it a focal point and critical asset for everyday operations'.*[7] These facilities can contain network equipment, servers, data storage and back-up facilities, software applications for large companies, and more. Very few businesses (or people) do not rely on them. And determining their location is a crucial decision for those operations running them. In fact such businesses usually have a set method for choosing data centre location.

   Visit the websites of the types of business that run data centres (such as Intel, Cisco or SAP) and devise a set of criteria that could be used to evaluate potential sites.

3   A company that produces concrete paving slabs is introducing a new range of 'textured' non-slip products. To do this it must invest in a new machine. Demand is forecast to be around 10,000 units per month for the first year and approximately 24,000 units per month after that. The machines that produce these products have a capacity of 10,000 units per month. They have a fixed cost of £20,000 per month and a variable cost of processing of £1 per unit. The company has forecast that it will be able to charge £4 per unit. It has been suggested that it would make higher profits if sales were restricted to 20,000 units per month in the second year. Is this true?

4   The Fast and Efficient (FAC) transport group is reviewing its fleet maintenance operations. *'Our lease on our current maintenance and repair facilities site will expire in a year, and we need to decide how to operate in the future. Currently we have the one site with 5 repair bays. This can cope with our fleet of 40 trucks. But demand is growing and within two or three years we hope to be operating around 55–60 trucks. So we will have to choose a site (or sites) that allows for this increase. And that leads me to the next issue – should we stick to operating one central site, or should we plan to have two sites, one for the North and one for the South of our region?'*

   As far as FAC's operations managers could forecast, the costs of having one or two sites would be as follows.

   One site − Fixed cost of establishing the site   = €300,000
                               Variable cost of servicing trucks = €14,000 per truck per year
   Two sites − Fixed cost of establishing the sites (for both) = €500,000
                               Variable cost of servicing trucks = €10,000 per truck per year

   (they will be out of action for less time because sites would be closer)

   At what level of demand (in terms of the number of trucks operated by the company) will the two-site proposal be cheaper?

5   How could universities adopt the practice of outsourcing more?

6   'Globalization is very much a "mixed blessing". There is little doubt that it has lifted millions out of poverty, but it has also led to the destruction of traditional cultures in developing countries and many jobs in the developed world.' Draw up lists of what you see as the advantages and disadvantages of globalization.

Selected further reading

Chopra, S. and Meindl, P. (2014) *Supply Chain Management: Strategy, planning and operations,* **6th edn, Prentice Hall, NJ.**
A good textbook that goes into more detail on the strategic structure and scope issues covered in this chapter and the more operational issues covered in the supply chain management chapter.

Cullen, S.K., Lacity, M. and Willcocks L.P. (2014) *Outsourcing – All You Need To Know,* **White Plume Publishing, Boston, MA.**
A practical guide to outsourcing, with lots of examples across sectors and countries, from an experienced team of authors

Kim, Y., Yi-Su, C. and Linderman, K. (2015) Supply network disruption and resilience: A network struc-tural perspective, *Journal of Operations Management,* **vol. 33–34, January, pp. 43–59.**
A more in-depth article examining the effect of different structural networks on the likelihood of disruptions.

Moore, J.F. (2013) *Shared Purpose: A Thousand Business Ecosystems, A Connected Community, and the Future,* **CreateSpace Independent Publishing Platform, California.**
A short but sweet progress report on a study of ARM Holdings (see example in the chapter) and its 1,000-plus community of partners from the founder of the business ecosystems idea.

Oshri, I., Kotlarsky, J. and Willcocks, L.P. (2015) *The Handbook of Global Outsourcing and Offshoring,* **3rd edn, Palgrave Macmillan, Basingstoke.**
A clear and applied guide to the key steps in outsourcing and off shoring decisions

Steger, M.B. (2017) *Globalization: A Very Short Introduction,* **OUP, Oxford.**
A very good overview of globalization and its effects. It covers not only business issues, but also political, cultural, ideological and environmental perspectives.

PART TWO

Designing the operation

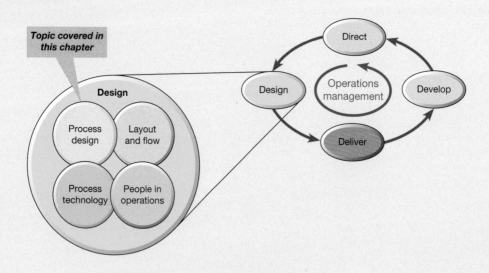

Topic covered in this chapter

Design

- Process design
- Layout and flow
- Process technology
- People in operations

Direct

Operations management

Design

Develop

Deliver

This part of the book looks at how the resources and processes of operations are designed. By 'design' we mean how the overall form, arrangement and nature of transforming resources impact on the flow of transformed resources as they move through the operation. And that is the order in which we treat the four key issues that concern the design of operations. The chapters in this part are:

▶ **Chapter 6 Process design**

This examines various types of process, and how these 'building blocks' of operations are designed.

▶ **Chapter 7 The layout and look of facilities**

This looks at how different ways of arranging physical facilities affect the nature of flow through the operation.

▶ **Chapter 8 Process technology**

This describes how the effectiveness of operations is influenced by the fast-moving developments in process technology.

▶ **Chapter 9 People in operations**

This looks at the elements of human resource management that are traditionally seen as being directly within the sphere of operations management.

6

Process design

KEY QUESTIONS

What is process design?

What should be the objectives of process design?

How do volume and variety affect process design?

How are processes designed in detail?

INTRODUCTION

In Chapter 1 we described how all operations consist of a collection of processes (though these processes may be called 'units' or 'departments') that interconnect with each other to form an internal network. Each process acts as a smaller version of the whole operation of which they form a part, and transformed resources flow between them. We also defined a process as 'an arrangement of resources and activities that transform inputs into outputs that satisfy (internal or external) customer needs'. They are the 'building blocks' of all operations, and as such they play a vital role in how well operations operate. This is why process design is so important. Unless its individual processes are well designed, an operation as a whole will not perform as well as it could. And operations managers are at the forefront of how processes are designed. In fact, all operations managers are designers. When they purchase or rearrange the position of a piece of equipment, or when they change the way of working within a process, it is a design decision because it affects the physical shape and nature of their process, as well as its performance. This chapter examines the design of processes. Figure 6.1 shows where this topic fits within the overall model of operations management.

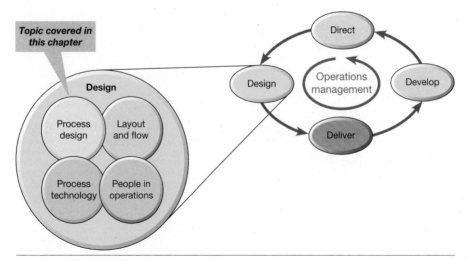

Figure 6.1 This chapter examines process design

What is process design?

To 'design' is to conceive the looks, arrangement and workings of something *before it is created*. In that sense, it is a conceptual exercise. Yet it is one that must deliver a solution that will work in practice. Design is also an activity that can be approached at different levels of detail. One may envisage the general shape and intention of something before getting down to defining its details. This is certainly true for process design. At the start of the process design activity it is important to understand the design objectives, especially when the overall shape and nature of the process is being decided. The most common way of doing this is by positioning it according to its volume and variety characteristics. Eventually the details of the process must be analysed to ensure that it fulfils its objectives effectively. Yet, it is often only through getting to grips with the detail of a design that the feasibility of its overall shape can be assessed. But don't think of this as a simple sequential process. There may be aspects concerned with the objectives, or the broad positioning, of the process that will need to be modified following its more detailed analysis.

Process design and product/service design are interrelated

Often we will treat the design of services and products, on the one hand, and the design of the processes that make them, on the other, as though they were separate activities. Yet they are clearly interrelated. It would be foolish to commit to the detailed design of any product or service without some consideration of how it is to be produced. Small changes in the design of products and services can have profound implications for the way the operation eventually has to produce them. Similarly, the design of a process can constrain the freedom of product and service designers to operate as they would wish (see Figure 6.2). This holds good whether the operation is producing products or services. However, the overlap between the two design activities is generally greater in operations that produce services. Because many services involve the customer in being part of the transformation process, the service, as far as the customer sees it, cannot be separated from the process to which the customer is subjected. Overlapping product and process design has implications for the organization of the design activity, as we discussed in Chapter 4. Certainly, when product designers also have to make or use the things that they design, it can concentrate their minds on what is important. For example, in the early days of flight, the engineers who designed the aircraft were also the test pilots who took them out on their first flight. For this reason, if no other, safety was a significant objective in the design activity.

> **Operations principle**
> The design of processes cannot be done independently of the services and/or products that are being created.

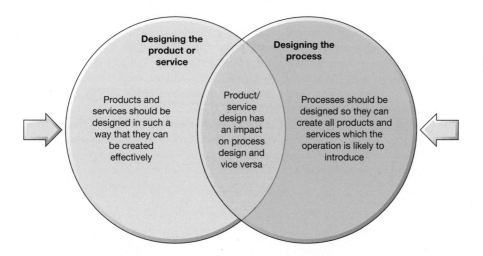

Figure 6.2 The design of products/services and the design of processes are interrelated and should be treated together

Airports are complex operations – really complex. Their processes handle passengers, aircraft, crew, baggage, commercial cargo, food, security, restaurants and numerous customer services. The operations managers, who oversee the daily operations of an airport, must cope with Aviation Administration rules and regulations, a huge number of airport service contracts, usually thousands of staff with a wide variety of specialisms, airlines with sometimes competing claims to service priority, and customers, some of whom fly every week and others who are a family of seven with two baby strollers who fly once a decade. Also, their processes are vulnerable to disruptions from late arrivals, aircraft malfunction, weather, the industrial action of workers two continents away, conflicts, terrorism and exploding volcanoes in Iceland. Designing the processes that can operate under these conditions must be one of the most challenging operations tasks. So, to win prizes for 'Best Airport' customer service and operating efficiency year after year has to be something of an achievement. Which is what the sixth busiest international airport, Changi airport in Singapore, has done. As a major air hub in Asia, Changi serves more than 100 international airlines flying to some 300 cities in about 70 countries and territories worldwide. It handles almost 60 million passengers (that's roughly 10 times the size of Singapore's population). A flight takes off or lands at Changi roughly once every 90 seconds.

When Changi opened its new Terminal 4, it increased the airport's annual passenger handling capacity to around 82 million. Every stage of the customers' journey through the terminal was designed to be as smooth as possible. The aim of all the processes within and around the terminal was to provide fast, smooth and seamless flow for passengers. Each stage in the customer journey was provided with enough capacity to cope with anticipated demand. A new overhead bridge was built across the airport boulevard connecting T4 with Singapore's highway system to enable the movement of cars, buses and airside vehicles. Two new car parks accommodate up to 1,500 vehicles. The terminal was connected to the new car parks via sheltered links. Once passengers arrive at the two-storey terminal building they pass through kiosks and automated options for self-check-in, self-bag tagging and self-bag-drops. Their bags are transported to the aircraft via an advanced and automated baggage handling system. Similarly, automated options,

including face recognition technology, are used at immigration counters and departure-gates. Biometric technology and 'fast and seamless travel' (FAST) services help to speed passenger throughput and increase efficiency. After security checks, passengers find themselves in 15,000 m² of shopping, dining and other retail spaces, featuring local, cultural and heritage-theme restaurants. This space also features a 300-metre-long Central Galleria, which is a glazed open space that visually connects the departure, check-in, arrival and transit areas across the terminal. The emphasis on the aesthetic appeal of the terminal is something that Changi considered important. It already boasts a butterfly garden, orchid and sunflower gardens as well as a koi pond.

The feelings of passengers using the terminal were an important part of its design. Architecturally, the design of T4 aimed to be functional, and yet have its own distinct character, while ensuring that the design and layout are passenger-centric and user-friendly. And with so many different companies involved in the day-to-day operation of the airport it was vital to include as many stakeholders as possible during the design. Workshops were conducted with various stakeholders, including airlines, ground handlers, immigration and security agencies, retail and food and beverage operators as well as other users to ensure that the T4 design met the needs of each party. The objective was to ensure that T4 could deliver a seamless and refreshing experience for travellers, and also be a place where staff would feel proud and motivated to work.

Process networks

In Chapter 1 we used the 'hierarchy of networks' to illustrate how any operation is both made up of networks (of processes) and a part of networks (of other operations). This idea is of more than

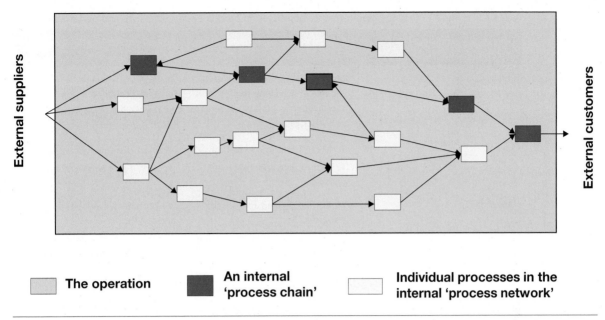

Figure 6.3 A process network within an operation showing an internal 'process chain'

academic interest. It is essential in making all networks, including process networks, work effectively. Figure 6.3 shows a simplified internal process network for one business. It has many processes that transform items and transfer them to other internal processes. Through this network there are many 'process chains': that is, threads of processes within the network. And thinking about processes as part of a network has a number of advantages. First, understanding how and where a process fits into the internal network helps to establish appropriate objectives for the process. Second, one can check to make sure that everyone in a process has a clear 'line of sight' forward through to end customers, so that the people working in each process have a better chance of seeing how they contribute to satisfying the operation's customers. Even more important, one can ask the question, 'how can each process help the intermediate processes that lie between them and the customer, to operate effectively?' Third, a clear 'line of sight' backwards through to the operation's suppliers makes the role and importance of suppliers easier to understand. Finally, reversing the question, not understanding how process chains interact can reduce the effectiveness of the whole operation, and increase the risk of disruption spreading. Process chains can become channels for disruption when things go wrong.

What should be the objectives of process design?

The whole point of process design is to make sure that the performance of the process is appropriate for whatever it is trying to achieve. For example, if an operation competes primarily on its ability to respond quickly to customer requests, its processes will need to be designed to give fast throughput times. This would minimize the time between customers requesting a product or service and them receiving it. Similarly, if an operation competes on low price, cost-related objectives are likely to dominate its process design. In other words, some kind of logic should link what the operation as a whole is attempting to achieve, and the performance objectives of its individual processes. As when we examined product and service design innovation in Chapter 4, we will include 'sustainability' as an operational objective of process design, even though it is really a far broader societal issue that is part of the organization's 'triple bottom line' (see Chapter 2). This is illustrated in Table 6.1.

> **Operations principle**
> The design of any process should be judged on its quality, speed, dependability, flexibility, cost and sustainability performance.

Table 6.1 The impact of strategic performance objectives on process design objectives and performance

Operations performance objective	Typical process design objectives	Some benefits of good process design
Quality	▶ Provide appropriate resources, capable of achieving the specification of products or services ▶ Error-free processing	▶ Products and services produced 'on-specification' ▶ Less recycling and wasted effort within the process
Speed	▶ Minimum throughput time ▶ Output rate appropriate for demand	▶ Short customer waiting time ▶ Low in-process inventory
Dependability	▶ Provide dependable process resources ▶ Reliable process output timing and volume	▶ On-time deliveries of products and services ▶ Less disruption, confusion and rescheduling within the process
Flexibility	▶ Provide resources with an appropriate range of capabilities ▶ Change easily between processing states (what, how, or how much is being processed?)	▶ Ability to process a wide range of products and services ▶ Low cost/fast product and service change ▶ Low cost/fast volume and timing changes ▶ Ability to cope with unexpected events (e.g. supply or a processing failure)
Cost	▶ Appropriate capacity to meet demand ▶ Eliminate process waste in terms of: ▶ excess capacity ▶ excess process capability ▶ in-process delays ▶ in-process errors ▶ inappropriate process inputs	▶ Low processing costs ▶ Low resource costs (capital costs) ▶ Low delay/inventory costs (working capital costs)
Sustainability	▶ Minimize energy usage ▶ Reduce local impact on community ▶ Produce for easy disassembly	▶ Lower negative environmental and societal impact

'Micro' process objectives

Operations performance objectives translate directly to process design objectives as shown in Table 6.1. But, because processes are managed at a very operational level, process design also needs to consider a more 'micro' and detailed set of objectives. These are largely concerned with flow through the process. When whatever is being 'processed' enters a process, it will progress through a series of activities where it is 'transformed' in some way. Between these activities it may dwell for some time in inventories, waiting to be transformed by the next activity. This means that the time that a unit spends in the process (its throughput time) will be longer than the sum of all the transforming activities that it passes through. Also, the resources that perform the processes activities may not be used all the time because not all items will necessarily require the same activities and the capacity of each resource may not match the demand placed upon it. So, neither the items moving through the process, nor the resources performing the activities may be fully utilized. Because of this the way that items leave the process is unlikely to be exactly the same as the way they arrive at the process. It is common for more 'micro' performance flow objectives to be used that describe process flow performance. For example:

▶ Throughput rate (or flow rate) is the rate at which items emerge from the process, i.e. the number of items passing through the process per unit of time.
▶ Cycle time is the reciprocal of throughput rate: it is the time between items emerging from the process. The term 'takt time' is the same, but is normally applied to 'paced' processes like moving belt assembly lines. It is the 'beat' or tempo of working required to meet demand.[1]
▶ Throughput time is the average elapsed time taken for inputs to move through the process and become outputs.
▶ 'Work-in-progress' or process inventory is the number of items in the process, as an average over a period of time.
▶ The utilization of process resources is the proportion of available time that the resources within the process are performing useful work.

Operations principle

Process flow objectives should include throughput rate, throughput time, work-in-progress and resource utilization, all of which are interrelated.

Fast (but not too fast) food drive-throughs

There is some dispute about who established the first drive-through (or drive-thru, if you prefer). Some claim it was the In-N-Out in California. Other claimants include the Pig Stand restaurant in Los Angeles, where Royce Hailey first promoted the drive-through service, allowing customers to simply drive by the back door of the restaurant where the chef would come out and deliver the restaurant's famous 'Barbequed Pig' sandwiches, and Red's Giant Hamburg in Springfield, Missouri. What became apparent though, as the drive-through idea began to spread (and include services other than fast food such as banks), was that their design could have a huge impact on their efficiency and profitability. Today, drive-through processes are slicker, and far, far, faster, although most stick to a proven formula with orders generally placed by the customer using a microphone and picked up at a window. It is a system that allows drive-throughs to provide fast and dependable service. In fact, there is strong competition between drive-throughs to design the fastest and most reliable process. For example, some Starbucks drive-throughs have strategically placed cameras at the order boards so that servers can recognize regular customers and start making their order – even before it's placed. Other drive-throughs have experimented with simpler menu boards and see-through food bags to ensure greater accuracy. There is no point in being fast if you don't deliver what the customer ordered. These details matter. It has been estimated that sales increase 1 per cent for every six seconds saved at a drive-through. One experiment in making drive-through process times slicker was carried out by a group of McDonald's restaurants. On California's central coast 150 miles from Los Angeles, a call centre took orders remotely from 40 McDonald's outlets around the country. The orders were then sent back to the restaurants and the food was assembled only a few metres from where the order was placed. Although saving only a few seconds on each order, it could add up to extra sales at busy times of the day. A good drive-through process should also help customers to contribute to speeding things up. So, for example, menu items must be easy to read and understand.

This is why what are often called 'combo meals' (burger, fries and a cola) can save time at the ordering stage. By contrast, complex individual items or meals that require customization can slow down the process. This can become an issue for drive-through operators when fashion moves towards customized salads and sandwiches. Yet there are signs that above a certain speed of service, other aspects of process performance become more important. As one drive-through chief operations manager points out, *'you can get really fast but ruin the overall experience, because now you're not friendly'.*

Standardization of processes

One of the most important process design objectives, especially in large organizations, concerns the extent to which process designs should be standardized. By standardization in this context we mean 'doing things in the same way', or more formally, 'adopting a common sequence of activities, methods and use of equipment'. It is a significant issue in large organizations because, very often, different ways of carrying out similar or identical tasks emerge over time in the various parts of the organization. But, why not allow many different ways of doing the same thing? That would give a degree of autonomy and freedom for individuals and teams to exercise their discretion. The problem is that allowing numerous ways of doing things causes confusion, misunderstandings and, eventually, inefficiency. In healthcare processes, it can even cause preventable deaths. For example, the Royal College of Physicians in the UK revealed that there were more than 100 types of charts that were used for monitoring patients' vital signs in use in UK hospitals.[2] This leads to confusion, they said. Potentially, thousands of hospital deaths could be prevented if doctors and nurses used a standardized bed chart. Because hospitals can use different charts, doctors and nurses have to learn how to read new ones when they move. They recommended that there should be just one chart and one process for all staff who check on patients' conditions. Professor Derek Bell said: '*Developing and adopting a standardized early warning system will be one of the most significant developments in healthcare in the next decade.*'

Standardization is also an important objective in the design of some services and products, for similar reasons (see Chapter 4). The practical dillema for most organizations is how to draw the line between processes that are required to be standardized, and those that are allowed to be different.

> **Operations principle**
>
> Standardizing processes can give some significant advantages, but not every process can be standardized.

Environmentally sensitive process design

With the issues of environmental protection becoming more important, process designers have to take account of 'green' (sustainability) issues. In many developed countries, legislation has already provided some basic standards. Interest has focused on some fundamental issues:

▶ *The sources of inputs* to a product or service. (Will they damage rainforests? Will they use up scarce minerals? Will they exploit the poor or use child labour?)

▶ *Quantities and sources of energy* consumed in the process. (Do plastic beverage bottles use more energy than glass ones? Should waste heat be recovered and used in fish farming?)

▶ *The amounts and type of waste material* that are created in the manufacturing processes. (Can this waste be recycled efficiently, or must it be burnt or buried in landfill sites?)

▶ *The life of the product itself.* If a product has a long useful life, will it consume fewer resources than a short-life product?

▶ *The end-of-life of the product.* (Will the redundant product be difficult to dispose of in an environmentally friendly way?)

Designers are faced with complex trade-offs between these factors, although it is not always easy to obtain all the information that is needed to make the 'best' choices. To help make more rational decisions in the design activity, some industries are experimenting with *life cycle analysis*. This technique analyses all the production inputs, the life cycle use of the product and its final disposal, in terms of total energy used and all emitted wastes. The inputs and wastes are evaluated at *every* stage of a service or product's creation, beginning with the extraction or farming of the basic raw materials. The short case 'Ecover's ethical operation design' demonstrates that it is possible to include ecological considerations in all aspects of product and process design.

> **Operations principle**
>
> The design of any process should include consideration of ethical and environmental issues.

Ecover's ethical operation design[3]

Ecover cleaning products, such as washing liquid, are famously ecological. In fact, it is the company's whole rationale. *'We clean with care',* says Ecover, *'whether you're washing your sheets, your floors, your hands or your dishes, our products don't contain those man-made chemicals that can irritate your skin'.* But it isn't just the company's products that are based on an ecologically sustainable foundation. Ecover's ecological factories in France and Belgium also embody the company's commitment to sustainability. Whether it is the factory roof, the use of energy or the way it treats the water used in the production processes, Ecover points out that it does its best to limit environmental impact. For example, the Ecover factory operates entirely on green electricity – the type produced by wind generators, tidal generators and other natural sources. What is more, it makes the most of the energy it does use by choosing energy efficient lighting, and then only using it when needed. And, although the machinery it uses in the factories is standard for the industry, it keeps its energy and water consumption down by choosing low-speed appliances that can multi-task and don't require water to clean them. For example, the motors on its mixing machines can mix 25 tonnes of Ecover liquid while 'consuming no more electricity than a few flat irons'. And it has a 'squeezy gadget that's so efficient at getting every last drop of product out of the pipes, they don't need to be rinsed through'. Ecover say that they *'hate waste, so we're big on recycling. We keep the amount of packaging used in our products to a minimum, and make sure whatever cardboard or plastic we do use can be recycled, re-used or re-filled. It's an*

ongoing process of improvement; in fact, we've recently developed a new kind of green plastic we like to call "Plant-astic" that's 100% renewable, reusable and recyclable – and made from sugarcane.'

Even the building is ecological. It is cleverly designed to follow the movement of the sun from east to west, so that production takes place with the maximum amount of natural daylight (good for saving power and good for working conditions). The factory's frame is built from pine rather than more precious timbers and the walls are constructed using bricks that are made from clay, wood pulp and mineral waste. They require less energy to bake, yet they're light, porous and insulate well. The factories' roofs are covered in thick, spongy Sedum (a flowering plant, often used for natural roofing) that gives insulation all year round. In fact, it's so effective, that they don't need heating or air conditioning – the temperature never drops below 4°C and never rises above 26°C.

How do volume and variety affect process design?

In Chapter 1 we saw how processes range from those producing at high volume (for example, credit card transaction processing) to a low volume (for example, funding a large complex take-over deal). Also, processes can range from producing a very low variety of products or services (for example, in an electricity utility) to a very high variety (for example, in an architects' practice). Usually the two dimensions of volume and variety go together – but in a reversed way. So, low-volume processes often produce a high variety of products and services, and high-volume processes often produce a narrow variety of products and services. Thus, there is a continuum from low volume–high variety through to high volume–low variety, on which we can position processes. And within a single operation there could be processes with very different positions on this volume–variety spectrum. So, for example, compare the approach taken in a medical service during mass medical treatments, such as large-scale immunization programmes, with that taken in transplant surgery where the treatment is designed specifically to meet the needs of one person. In other words, no one type of process design is best for all types of requirement in all circumstances – different products or services with different volume–variety positions require different processes.

Operations principle

The design of any process should be governed by the volume and variety it is required to produce.

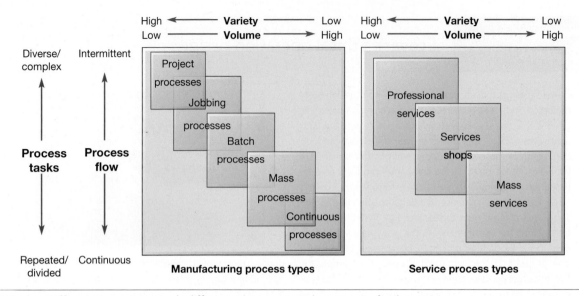

Figure 6.4 Different process types imply different volume–variety characteristics for the process

Process types

The position of a process on the volume–variety continuum shapes its overall design and the general approach to managing its activities. These 'general approaches' to designing and managing processes are called process types. Different terms are used to identify process types depending on whether they are predominantly manufacturing or service processes, and there is some variation in the terms used. For example, it is not uncommon to find the 'manufacturing' terms used in service industries. Figure 6.4 illustrates how these 'process types' are used to describe different positions on the volume–variety spectrum.

Project processes

Project processes deal with discrete, usually highly customized products, often with a relatively long time-scale between the completion of each item, where each job has a well-defined start and finish. Project processes have low volume and high variety. Activities involved in the process can be ill-defined and uncertain. Transforming resources may have to be organized especially for each item (because each item is different). The process may be complex, partly because the activities in such processes often involve significant discretion to act according to professional judgement. Examples of project processes include software design, movie production, most construction work and large fabrication operations such as those manufacturing turbo generators.

The major construction site shown in the picture is a project process. Each 'item' (building) is different and poses different challenges to those running the process (civil engineers).

Service shops

Service shops have levels of volume and variety (and customer contact, customization and staff discretion), between the extremes of professional and mass services (see next paragraph). Service is provided via mixes of front- and back-office activities. Service shops include banks, high street shops, holiday tour operators, car rental companies, schools, most restaurants, hotels and travel agents.

The health club shown in the picture has front-office staff who can give advice on exercise programmes and other treatments. Although every client has a unique fitness programme, certain activities (for example, safety issues) have to follow defined processes.

Mass services

Mass services have many customer transactions, involving limited contact time and little customization. Staff are likely to have a relatively defined division of labour and have to follow set procedures. Mass services include supermarkets, a national rail network, an airport, telecommunications service, library, television station, the police service and the enquiry desk at a utility. For example, one of the most common types of mass service are the call centres used by almost all companies that deal directly with consumers. Coping with a very high volume of enquiries requires some kind of structuring of the process of communicating with customers. This is often achieved by using a carefully designed enquiry process (sometimes known as a script).

> **Operations principle**
>
> Process types indicate the position of processes on the volume–variety spectrum.

This is the 'back office' of part of a retail bank (the type that we all use). It is a call centre that deals with many thousands of calls every day. Staff are required to follow defined processes (scripts) to make sure customers receive a standard service.

The product–process matrix

The most common method of illustrating the relationship between a process's volume–variety position and its design characteristics is shown in Figure 6.5. Often called the 'product–process' matrix,[5] it can in fact be used for any type of process, whether producing products or services. The underlying idea of the product–process matrix is that many of the more important elements of process design are strongly related to the volume–variety position of the process. So, for any process, the tasks that it undertakes, the flow of items through the process, the layout of its resources, the technology it uses, and the design of jobs, are all strongly influenced by its volume–variety position. This means that most processes should lie close to the diagonal of the matrix that represents the 'fit' between the process and its volume–variety position. This is called the 'natural' diagonal, or the 'line of fit'.

Although the idea of process types can be useful, it is in many ways simplistic. In reality, there is no clear boundary between process types. For example, many processed foods are manufactured using mass production processes but in batches. So, a 'batch' of one type of cake (say) can be followed by a 'batch' of a marginally different cake (perhaps with different packaging), followed by yet another, etc. Essentially this is still a mass process, but not quite as pure a version of mass processing as a manufacturing process that only made one type of cake. Similarly, the categories of service processes are likewise blurred. For example, a specialist camera retailer would normally be categorized as a service shop, yet it also will give, sometimes very specialized, technical advice to customers. It is not a professional service like a consultancy, of course, but it does have elements of a professional service process within its design. This is why the volume and variety characteristics of a process are sometimes seen as being a more realistic way of describing processes. The product–process matrix adopts this approach.

Moving off the natural diagonal

A process lying on the natural diagonal of the matrix shown in Figure 6.5 will normally have lower operating costs than one with the same volume–variety position that lies off the diagonal. This is because the diagonal represents the most appropriate process design for any volume–variety position. Processes that are on the right of the 'natural' diagonal would normally be associated with lower volumes and higher variety. This means that they are likely to be more flexible than seems to be warranted by their actual volume–variety position. That is, they are not taking advantage of their ability to standardize their activities. Because of this, their costs are likely to be higher than they would be with a process that was closer to the diagonal. Conversely, processes that are on the left of the diagonal have adopted a position that would normally be used for higher volume and lower variety processes. Processes will therefore be 'over-standardized' and probably too inflexible for their

Sands Film Studio, jobbing costume makers[4]

Every film or television programme that is set in any period, other than the present day, needs costumes for its actors. And most films have a lot of characters, so that means a lot of costumes. Look at Sands Film Studios in London and you will see a well-established and permanent costume-making workshop. You will also see a typical 'jobbing' process. Sands Films provides a wide range of wardrobe and costume services. Its customers are the film, stage and TV production companies, each of which has different requirements and time constraints. And because each project is different and has different requirements, the workshop's jobs go from making a single simple outfit to providing a wide variety of specially designed costumes and facilities over an extended production period. The facilities include most normal tailoring processes such as cutting, dyeing and printing, and varied specialist services such as corset and crinoline making as well as millenary (hats). During the design and making process actors often visit the workshop, which has been called an 'Aladdin's cave' of theatrical costumes. '*This is really where the actors come face to face with their character for the first time, and it's a fascinating process to watch*', Olivier Stockman, the company's Managing Director, says. Making a costume can only start once a project has been approved and a costume designer appointed, although discussions with the workshop may have started prior to that. When the budget and the timing have been agreed, the designer can start to present ideas and finished designs to the workshop. And although the processes in the workshop are well established, each costume requires different skills and so has a different route through the stages.

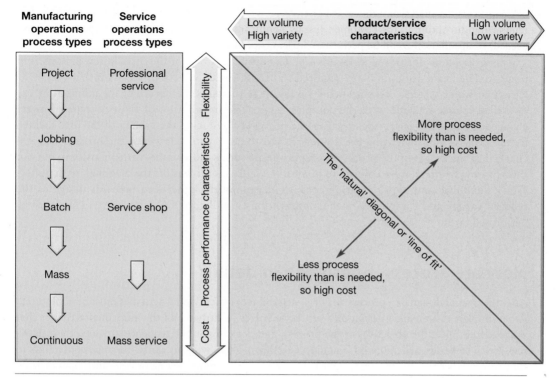

Figure 6.5 Deviating from the 'natural' diagonal on the product–process matrix has consequences for cost and flexibility

Source: Based on Hayes and Wheelwright

volume–variety position. This lack of flexibility can also lead to high costs because the process will not be able to change from one activity to another as readily as a more flexible process.[6] So, a first step in examining the design of an existing process is to check if it is on the natural diagonal of the product–process matrix. The volume–variety position of the process may have changed without any corresponding change in its design. Alternatively, design changes may have been introduced without considering their suitability for the processes volume–variety position.

> **Operations principle**
>
> Moving off the 'natural diagonal' of the product-process matrix will incur excess cost.

Example

The 'meter installation' unit of a water utility company installed and repaired water meters. Each installation job could vary significantly because the requirements of each customer varied and because meters had to be fitted into different water pipe systems. When a customer requested an installation, a supervisor would survey the customer's water system and inform the installation team. An appointment would then be made for an installer to visit the customer's location and install the meter. Then the company decided to install a new 'standard' remote-reading meter to replace the wide range of existing meters. This new meter was designed to make installation easier by including universal quick-fit joints that reduced pipe cutting and jointing during installation. As a pilot, it was also decided to prioritize those customers with the oldest meters and conduct trials of how the new meter worked in practice. All other aspects of the installation process were left as they were. However, after the new meters were introduced the costs of installation were far higher than forecast and the installers were frustrated at the waste of their time and the now relatively standardized installation job. So the company decided to change its process. It cut out the survey stage of the process because, using the new meter, 98 per cent of installations could be fitted in one visit, minimizing disruption to the customer. Just as significantly, fully qualified installers were often not needed, so installation could be performed by less expensive labour.

This example is illustrated in Figure 6.6. The initial position of the installation process is at point A. The installation unit was required to install a wide variety of meters into a very wide variety of water systems. This needed a survey stage to assess the nature of the job and the use of skilled labour to cope with the complex tasks. The installation of the new type of meter changed the volume–variety position for the process by reducing the variety of the jobs tackled by the process and increasing the volume it had to cope with. However, the process was not changed so the design of the process was appropriate for its old volume–variety position, but not the new one. In effect, it had moved to point B in Figure 6.6. It was off the diagonal, with unnecessary flexibility and high operating costs. Redesigning the process to take advantage of the reduced variety and complexity of the job (position C on Figure 6.6) allowed installation to be performed far more efficiently.

How are processes designed in detail?

After the overall design of a process has been determined, its individual activities must be configured. At its simplest this detailed design of a process involves identifying all the individual activities that are needed to meet the objectives of the process, and deciding on the sequence in which these activities are to be performed and who is going to do them. There will, of course, be some constraints to this. Some activities must be carried out before others and certain people or equipment can only do some activities. Nevertheless, for a process of any reasonable size, the number of alternative process designs is usually large. Because of this, process design is often done using some simple visual approach such as process mapping.

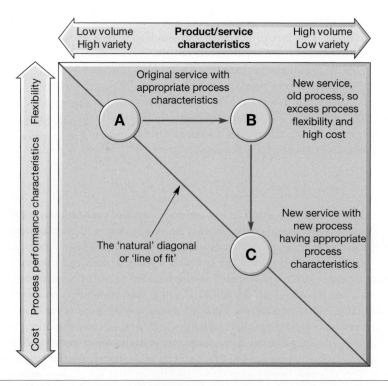

Figure 6.6 A product–process matrix with process positions from the water meter example

Space4 housing processes[7]

Productivity in house building is a problem. While most industries have made, sometimes spectacular, productivity gains, house building has actually been getting less productive. To add to the problem, a combination of population growth and rapid urbanization means that in many countries, demand for housing is rising rapidly. But some companies are trying to remedy this by adopting new production methods. Space4 is one of these. It is a division of Persimmon, which is the UK's largest house builder. Its huge building in Birmingham (UK) contains what some believe could be the future of house building. It is more like the way you would expect an automobile to be made. It has a production line whose 90 operators, many of whom have automobile assembly experience, are capable of producing the timber-framed panels that form the shell of the new homes at a rate of a house every hour. The automated, state-of-the-art electronic systems within the production process control all facets of the operation, ensuring that scheduling and operations are timely and accurate. There is a direct link between the computer-aided design (CAD) systems that design the houses and the manufacturing processes that make them, reducing the time between design and manufacture. The machinery itself incorporates automatic predictive and preventative maintenance routines that minimize the chances of unexpected breakdowns. But not everything about the process relies on automation. Because of their previous automobile assembly experience, staff are used to the just-in-time, high-efficiency culture of modern mass production. After production, the completed panels

are stacked in 3-metre piles and are then fork lifted into trucks where they are dispatched to building sites across the UK. Once the panels arrive at the building site, the construction workforce can assemble the exterior of a 1,200 sq ft (average size) new home in a single day. Because the external structure of a house can be built in a few hours, and enclosed in a weatherproof covering, staff working on the internal fittings of the house, such as plumbers and electricians, can have a secure and dry environment in which to work, irrespective of external conditions. Furthermore, the automated production process uses a type of high-precision technology which means there are fewer mistakes in the construction process on site. This means that the approval process from the local regulatory authority takes less time. This process, says Space4, speeds up the total building time from 12–14 weeks to 8–10 weeks.

Process mapping

Process mapping simply involves describing processes in terms of how the activities within the process relate to each other. There are many techniques which can be used for *process mapping* (or process blueprinting, or process analysis, as it is sometimes called). However, all the techniques identify the different *types of* activity that take place during the process and show the flow of materials or people or information through the process.

Process mapping symbols

Process mapping symbols are used to classify different types of activity. And although there is no universal set of symbols, used all over the world for any type of process, there are some that are commonly used. Most of these derive either from the early days of 'scientific' management around a

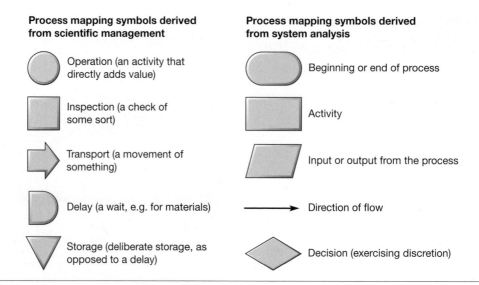

Process mapping symbols derived from scientific management

⬭ Operation (an activity that directly adds value)

▢ Inspection (a check of some sort)

⇨ Transport (a movement of something)

⬗ Delay (a wait, e.g. for materials)

▽ Storage (deliberate storage, as opposed to a delay)

Process mapping symbols derived from system analysis

⬭ Beginning or end of process

▢ Activity

▱ Input or output from the process

⟶ Direction of flow

◇ Decision (exercising discretion)

Figure 6.7 Some common process mapping symbols

century ago (see Chapter 9) or, more recently, from information system flowcharting. Figure 6.7 shows the symbols we shall use here.

These symbols can be arranged in order, and in series or in parallel, to describe any process. For example, Figure 6.8 shows one of the processes used in a theatre lighting operation. The company hires out lighting and stage effects equipment to theatrical companies and event organizers. Customers' calls are routed to the store technician. After discussing their requirements, the technician checks the

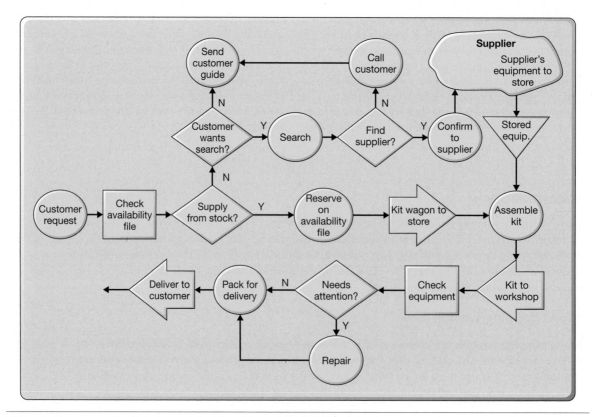

Figure 6.8 Process map for 'enquire to delivery' process at stage lighting operation

equipment availability file to see if the equipment can be supplied from the company's own stock on the required dates. If the equipment cannot be supplied in-house, customers may be asked whether they want the company to try and obtain it from other possible suppliers. This offer depends on how busy and how helpful individual technicians are. Sometimes customers decline the offer and a 'Guide to Customers' leaflet is sent to the customer. If the customer does want a search, the technician will call potential suppliers in an attempt to find available equipment. If this is not successful the customer is informed, but if suitable equipment is located it is reserved for delivery to the company's site. If equipment can be supplied from the company's own stores, it is reserved on the equipment availability file and the day before it is required a 'kit wagon' is taken to the store where all the required equipment is assembled, taken back to the workshop, checked, and if any equipment is faulty it is repaired at this point. After that it is packed in special cases and delivered to the customer.

> **Operations principle**
>
> Process mapping is needed to expose the reality of process behaviour.

Different levels of process mapping

For a large process, drawing process maps at this level of detail can be complex. This is why processes are often mapped at a more aggregated level, called high-level process mapping, before more detailed maps are drawn. Figure 6.9 illustrates this for the total *'supply and install lighting'* process in the stage lighting operation. At the highest level the process can be drawn simply as an input–transformation–output process with materials and customers as its input resources and lighting services as outputs. No details of how inputs are transformed into outputs are included. At a slightly lower or more detailed level, what is sometimes called an outline process map (or chart) identifies the sequence of activities but only in a general way. So, the process of *'enquire to delivery'* that is shown in detail

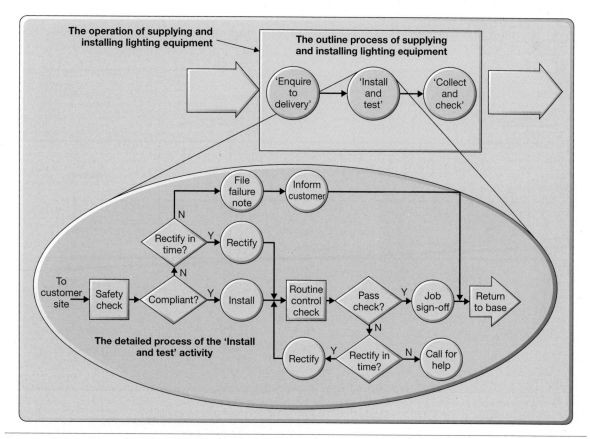

Figure 6.9 The 'supply and install' operations process mapped at three levels

in Figure 6.8 is here reduced to a single activity. At the more detailed level, all the activities are shown in a 'detailed process map' (the activities within the process 'install and test' are shown).

Although not shown in Figure 6.9, an even more micro set of process activities could be mapped within each of the detailed process activities. Such a micro detailed process map could specify every single motion involved in each activity. Some quick service restaurants, for example, do exactly that. In the lighting hire company example, most activities would not be mapped in any more detail than that shown in Figure 6.9. Some activities, such as 'return to base', are probably too straightforward to be worth mapping any further. Other activities, such as 'rectify faulty equipment', may rely on the technician's skills and discretion to the extent that the activity has too much variation and is too complex to map in detail. Some activities however may need mapping in more detail to ensure quality or to protect the company's interests. For example, the activity of safety checking the customer's site to ensure that it is compliant with safety regulations will need specifying in some detail to ensure that the company can prove it exercised its legal responsibilities.

Mapping visibility in process design

Processes with a high level of customer 'visibility' cannot be designed in the same way as processes that deal with inanimate materials or information. 'Processing' people is different. As we discussed in Chapter 1, operations and processes that primarily 'transform' people present a particular set of issues. Material and information are processed, but customers *experience* the process. In processes where customers see, at least, part of the process, it is sometimes useful to map them in a way that makes the degree of visibility of each part of the process obvious. This allows those parts of the process with high visibility to be designed so that they enhance the customer's perception of the process. Figure 6.10 shows yet another part of the lighting equipment company's operation: 'the collect and check' process. The process is mapped to show the visibility of each activity to the customer. Here four levels of visibility are used. There is no hard and fast rule about this; many processes simply distinguish between those activities that the customer *could* see and those that they couldn't. The boundary between these two categories is often called the 'line of

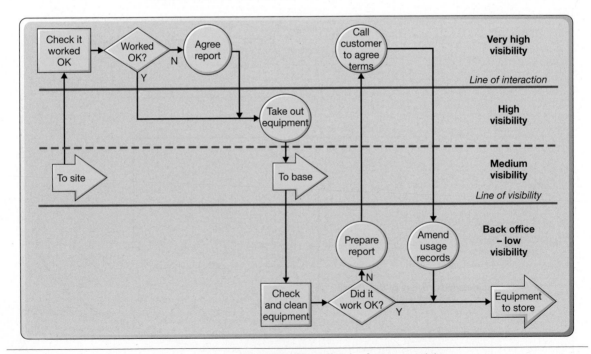

Figure 6.10 The 'collect and check' process mapped to show different levels of process visibility

visibility'. In Figure 6.10 three categories of visibility are shown. At the very highest level of visibility, above the 'line of interaction', are those activities that involve direct interaction between the lighting company's staff and the customer. Other activities take place at the customer's site or in the presence of the customer but involve less or no direct interaction. Yet further activities (the two transport activities in this case) have some degree of visibility because they take place away from the company's base and are visible to potential customers, but are not visible to the immediate customer.

Visibility, customer experience and emotional mapping

When customers experience a process, it results in the customer feeling emotions, not all of which are necessarily rational. Most of us have been made happy, angry, frustrated, surprised, reassured or furious as customers in a process. Nor is the idea of considering how processes affect customer emotions confined to those processes that are intended to engage the emotions: for example, entertainment-type organizations such as theme parks. Any high customer contact product (or more likely, service) always creates an experience for the customer. Moreover, customer experience will affect customer satisfaction, and therefore has the potential to produce customer loyalty, influence expectations and create emotional bonds with customers. This is why many service organizations are seeing how customers experience their processes (the so-called 'customer journey') at the core of their process design.

Designing processes with a significant experience content requires the systematic consideration of how customers may react to the experiences that the process exposes them to. This will include the sights, sounds, smells, atmosphere and general 'feeling' of the service. The concept of a 'servicescape', which is discussed in the next chapter, is strongly related to consideration of engaging customers so that they connect with the process in a personal way. One of the most common methods of designing such processes is to consider what are commonly called 'touch-points'. These have been described as, *'Everything the consumer uses to verify their service's effectiveness'*.[8] They are the points of contact between a process and customers, and there might be many different touch-points during the customer journey. It is the accumulation of all the experiences from every touch-point interaction that shapes customers' judgement of the process. The features of a process at the touch-points are sometimes called 'clues' (or 'cues'): these are the messages that customers receive or experience as they progress through the process. The emotions that result from these cues contain the messages that the customer will receive and therefore influence how a customer will judge the process. When designing processes, managers need to be concerned to ensure that all the messages coming from the clues at each stage of the process are consistent with the emotions that they want the customers to experience and do not give her wrong or misleading messages about the process. In the same way as process mapping indicates the sequence and relationship between activities, so emotional mapping can indicate the type of emotions engendered in the customer's mind as they experienced the process. Figure 6.11 is a simplified version of how this can work for a visit to an X-ray clinic for a simple medical investigation. There are many ways that emotions can be mapped and different diagrammatic representations can be used. In this case a simple scoring system has been used ranging from +3 (very positive) to −3 (very negative). At each stage, the reasons for the score are briefly noted.

> **Operations principle**
> The design of processes that deal with customers should consider the emotions engendered at each stage of the process.

Throughput time, cycle time and work-in-progress

So far, we have looked at the more conceptual (process types) and descriptive (process mapping) aspects of process design. We now move on to the equally important analytical perspective. And the first stage is to understand the nature of, and relationship between throughput time,

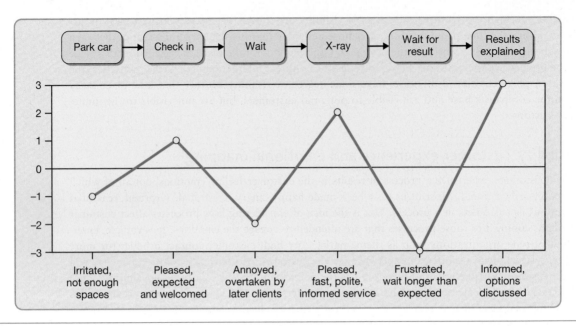

Figure 6.11 Customer experience map of a visit for an X-ray investigation

cycle time and work-in-progress. As a reminder, throughput time is the elapsed time between an item entering the process and leaving it, cycle time is the average time between items being processed and work-in-progress is the number of items within the process at any point in time. In addition, the work content for each item will also be important for some analysis. It is the total amount of work required to produce a unit of output. For example, suppose that in an assemble-to-order sandwich shop, the time to assemble and sell a sandwich (the work content) is two minutes and that two people are staffing the process. Each member of staff will serve a customer every two minutes; therefore, every two minutes, two customers are being served and so on average a customer is emerging from the process every minute (the cycle time of the process). When customers join the queue in the process they become work-in-progress (sometimes written as WIP). If the queue is ten people long (including that customer) when the customer joins it, he or she will have to wait ten minutes to emerge from the process. Or put more succinctly:

> **Operations principle**
>
> Process analysis derives from an understanding of the required process cycle time.

$$\text{Throughput time} = \text{Work-in-progress} \times \text{Cycle time}$$

In this case: 10 minutes' wait = 10 people in the system × 1 minute per person

Little's law

This mathematical relationship (throughput time = work-in-progress × cycle time) is called Little's law. It is simple but very useful, and it works for any stable process. Little's law states that the average number of things in the system is the product of the average rate at which things leave the system and average time each one spends in the system. Or, put another way, the average number of objects in a queue is the product of the entry rate and the average holding time. For example, suppose it is decided that in a new sandwich assembly and sales process, the average number of customers in the process should be limited to around ten and the maximum time a customer is in the process should be on average four minutes. If the time to assemble and sell a sandwich (from customer request to the customer leaving the process) in the new process has been reduced to 1.2 minutes, how many staff should be serving?

Putting this into Little's law:

$$\text{Throughput time} = 4 \text{ minutes}$$

$$\text{Work-in-progress, WIP} = 10$$

So, since:

$$\text{Throughput time} = \text{WIP} \times \text{cycle time}$$

$$\text{Cycle time} = \frac{\text{Throughput time}}{\text{WIP}}$$

$$\text{The cycle time for the process} = \frac{4}{10} = 0.4 \text{ minutes}$$

That is, a customer should emerge from the process every 0.4 minutes, on average. Given that an individual can be served in 1.2 minutes:

$$\text{The number of servers required} = \frac{1.2}{0.4} = 3$$

In other words, three servers would serve three customers in 1.2 minutes: that is, one customer in 0.4 minutes.

> **Operations principle**
>
> Little's law states that throughput time = work-in-progress × cycle time.

Worked example

Mike was totally confident in his judgement: *'You'll never get them back in time,'* he said. *'They aren't just wasting time, the process won't allow them to all have their coffee and get back for 11 o'clock.'* Looking outside the lecture theatre, Mike and his colleague Dick were watching the 20 business people who were attending the seminar queuing to be served coffee and biscuits. The time was 10.45 and Dick knew that unless they were all back in the lecture theatre at 11 o'clock there was no hope of finishing his presentation before lunch. *'I'm not sure why you're so pessimistic,'* said Dick. *'They seem to be interested in what I have to say and I think they will want to get back to hear how operations management will change their lives.'* Mike shook his head. *'I'm not questioning their motivation,'* he said, *'I'm questioning the ability of the process out there to get through them all in time. I have been timing how long it takes to serve the coffee and biscuits. Each coffee is being made fresh and the time between the server asking each customer what they want and them walking away with their coffee and biscuits is 48 seconds. Remember that, according to Little's law, throughput equals work-in-process multiplied by cycle time. If the work-in-process is the 20 managers in the queue and cycle time is 48 seconds, the total throughput time is going to be 20 multiplied by 0.8 minutes which equals 16 minutes. Add to that sufficient time for the last person to drink their coffee and you must expect a total throughput time of a bit over 20 minutes. You just haven't allowed long enough for the process.'* Dick was impressed. *'Err . . . what did you say that law was called again?' 'Little's law,'* said Mike.

Worked example

Every year it was the same. All the workstations in the building had to be renovated (tested, new software installed, etc.) and there was only one week in which to do it. The one week fell in the middle of the August vacation period when the renovation process would cause minimum disruption to normal working. Last year the company's 500 workstations had all been renovated within one working week (40 hours). Each renovation last year took on average 2 hours and 25 technicians had completed the process within the week. This year there would be 530 workstations to renovate but the company's IT support unit had devised a faster testing and renovation routine that would only take on average 1.5 hours instead of 2 hours. How many technicians will be needed this year to complete the renovation processes within the week?

Last year:

$$\text{Work-in-progress(WIP)} = 500 \text{ workstations}$$

$$\text{Time available}(T_t) = 40 \text{ hours}$$

$$\text{Average time to renovate} = 2 \text{ hours}$$

$$\text{Therefore throughput rate}(T_r) = 0.5 \text{ hours per technician}$$

$$= 0.5N$$

$$\text{where } N = \text{number of technicians}$$

$$\text{Little's law: WIP} = T_t \times T_r$$

$$500 = 40 \times 0.5N$$

$$N = \frac{500}{40 \times 0.5}$$

$$= 25 \text{ technicians}$$

This year:

$$\text{Work-in-progress(WIP)} = 530 \text{ workstations}$$

$$\text{Time available} = 40 \text{ hours}$$

$$\text{Average time to renovate} = 1.5 \text{ hours}$$

$$\text{Throughput rate}(T_r) = 1/1.5 \text{ per technician}$$

$$= 0.67N$$

$$\text{where } N = \text{number of technicians}$$

$$\text{Little's law: WIP} = T_t \times T_r$$

$$530 = 40 \times 0.67N$$

$$N = \frac{530}{40 \times 0.67}$$

$$= 19.88 \text{ (say 20) technicians}$$

Throughput efficiency

This idea that the throughput time of a process is different from the work content of whatever it is processing has important implications. What it means is that for significant amounts of time no useful work is being done to the materials, information, or customers that are progressing through the process. In the case of the simple example of the sandwich process described earlier, customer throughput time is restricted to 4 minutes, but the work content of the task (serving the customer) is only 1.2 minutes. So, the item being processed (the customer) is only being 'worked on' for 1.2/4 = 30 per cent of its time. This is called the throughput efficiency of the process.

$$\text{Percentage throughput efficiency} = \frac{\text{Work content}}{\text{Throughput time}} \times 100$$

In this case the throughput efficiency is very high, relative to most processes, perhaps because the 'items' being processed are customers who react badly to waiting. In most material and information transforming processes, throughput efficiency is far lower, usually in single percentage figures.

Value-added throughput efficiency

The approach to calculating throughput efficiency that is described above assumes that all the 'work content' is actually needed. Yet we have already seen from the Intel expense report example that changing a process can significantly reduce the time that is needed to complete the task. Therefore, work content is actually dependent upon the methods and technology used to perform the task. It may

Worked example

A vehicle licensing centre receives application documents, keys in details, checks the information provided on the application, classifies the application according to the type of licence required, confirms payment and then issues and mails the licence. It is currently processing an average of 5,000 licences every 8-hour day. A recent spot check found 15,000 applications that were 'in progress' or waiting to be processed. The sum of all activities that are required to process an application is 25 minutes. What is the throughput efficiency of the process?

$$\text{Work-in-progress} = 15,000 \text{ applications}$$

$$\text{Cycle time} = \text{time producing}$$

$$\frac{\text{Time producing}}{\text{Number produced}} = \frac{8 \text{ hours}}{5,000} = \frac{480 \text{ minutes}}{5,000} = 0.096 \text{ minutes}$$

From Little's law, throughput time = WIP × cycle time

$$\text{Throughput time} = 15,000 \times 0.096$$

$$= 1,440 \text{ minutes} = 24 \text{ hours} = 3 \text{ days of working}$$

$$\text{Throughput efficiency} = \frac{\text{Work content}}{\text{Throughput time}} = \frac{25}{1,440} = 1.74 \text{ per cent}$$

Although the process is achieving a throughput time of 3 days (which seems reasonable for this kind of process) the applications are only being worked on for 1.7 per cent of the time they are in the process.

be also that individual elements of a task may not be considered 'value-added'. In the Intel expense report example the new method eliminated some steps because they were 'not worth it': that is, they were not seen as adding value. So, value-added throughput efficiency restricts the concept of work content to only those tasks that are literally adding value to whatever is being processed. This often eliminates activities such as movement, delays and some inspections.

For example, if in the licensing worked example, of the 25 minutes of work content, only 20 minutes was actually adding value, then:

$$\text{Value-added throughput efficiency} = \frac{20}{1,440} = 1.39 \text{ per cent}$$

Workflow

When the transformed resource in a process is information (or documents containing information), and when information technology is used to move, store and manage the information, process design is sometimes called 'workflow' or 'workflow management'. It is defined as 'the automation of procedures where documents, information or tasks are passed between participants according to a defined set of rules to achieve, or contribute to, an overall business goal'. Although workflow may be managed manually, it is almost always managed using an IT system. The term is also often associated with Business Process Re-engineering (see Chapter 1 and Chapter 16). More specifically, workflow is concerned with the following:

▶ Analysis, modelling, definition and subsequent operational implementation of business processes
▶ The technology that supports the processes
▶ The procedural (decision) rules that move information/documents through processes
▶ Defining the process in terms of the sequence of work activities, the human skills needed to perform each activity and the appropriate IT resources

Process bottlenecks

A bottleneck in a process is the activity or stage where congestion occurs because the workload placed is greater than the capacity to cope with it. In other words, it is the most overloaded part of a process. And as such it will dictate the rate at which the whole process can operate. For example, look at the simple process illustrated in Figure 6.12. It has four stages and the total time to complete the work required for each item passing through the process is 10 minutes. In this simple case each of the four stages has the same capacity. In the first case (a) the 10 minutes of work is equally allocated between the four stages, each having 2.5 minutes of work. This means that items will progress smoothly through the process without any stage holding up the flow, and the cycle time of the process is 2.5 minutes. In the second case (b) the work has not been allocated evenly. In fact this is usually the case because usually it is difficult (actually close to impossible) to allocate work absolutely equally. In this case stage 4 of the process has the greatest load (3 minutes). It is the bottleneck, and will constrain the cycle time of the process to 3 minutes.

Bottlenecks reduce the efficiency of a process because, although the bottleneck stage will be fully occupied, the other stages will be underloaded. In fact the total amount of time invested in processing each item is four times the cycle time because, for every unit produced, all four stages have invested an amount of time equal to the cycle time. When the work is equally allocated between the stages, the total time invested in each product or service produced is $4 \times 2.5 = 10$ minutes. However, when work is unequally allocated, as illustrated, the time invested is $4 \times 3.0 = 12$ minutes. So, in total 2.0 minutes of time, 16.67 per cent of the total, is wasted. The activity of trying to allocate work equally between stages is called 'balancing', and the wasted time, expressed as a percentage, is called 'balancing loss'.

> **Operations principle**
>
> Allocating work equally to each stage in a process (balancing) smooths flow and avoids bottlenecks.

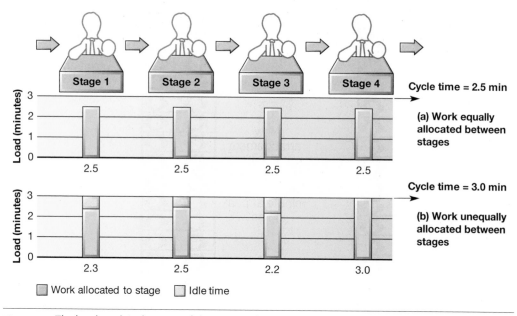

Stage 1 → Stage 2 → Stage 3 → Stage 4 →

Cycle time = 2.5 min

(a) Work equally allocated between stages

2.5 2.5 2.5 2.5

Cycle time = 3.0 min

(b) Work unequally allocated between stages

2.3 2.5 2.2 3.0

▢ Work allocated to stage   ▢ Idle time

Figure 6.12 The bottleneck is that part of the process that is the most overloaded relative to its capacity

Balancing work time allocation

Allocating work to process stages must respect the 'precedence' of the individual tasks that make up the total work content of the job that the process is performing. The most common way of showing task precedence is by using a 'precedence diagram'. This is a representation of the

> **Operations principle**
>
> Process design must respect task precedence.

London Underground tackles a bottleneck

Anyone who has travelled on a busy mass transport system like the London Underground knows how busy it can be, often with queues of passengers building up at various points as they move to or from their trains. One potential bottleneck for passengers on London Underground is the escalators. Traditionally, in London, passengers stand on the right side of the escalator, leaving the left side free for those who want to walk up or down. But in an attempt to reduce the bottleneck at the escalators, Transport for London, which runs the system, trialled a new arrangement that it believed would increase the capacity of its escalator at the Holborn station. Building new stations is expensive, so any way of increasing the capacity of existing ones is going to be attractive, and Holborn is a particularly busy station. The new (and radical, for Londoners) arrangement was to instruct passengers at peak times, not to walk, but to stand on both sides of the escalator. The decision was partly based on the fact that the escalators at Holborn are over 24 metres high. Apparently, height makes

a big difference to the willingness of passengers to walk up escalators. When they are only a few metres high, most people will walk up them. At 30 metres, only the very energetic walk. As shown in Figure 6.13, the trial was successful in that capacity increased significantly. However, experts warned that the increase in capacity would be far smaller at less busy times.

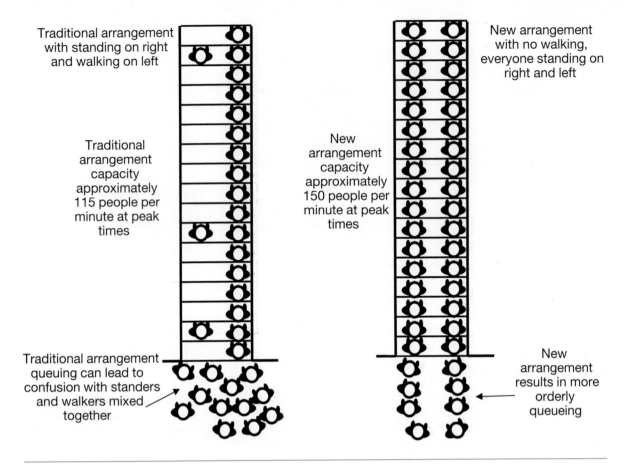

Figure 6.13 Requiring passengers to stand on both sides of the escalator makes it less of a bottleneck

ordering of the elements, where individual tasks are represented by circles connected by arrows, which signify the ordering of the tasks. Figure 6.14 in the following worked example illustrates how precedence diagrams can be used.

Arranging the stages

All the stages necessary to fulfil the requirements of the process may not be arranged in a sequential 'single line'. For example, suppose a mortgage application process requires four stages working on the task to maintain a cycle time of one application processed every 15 minutes. One possible arrangement of the four stages would be to arrange them sequentially, each stage having 15 minutes' worth of work. However, (theoretically) the same output rate could also be achieved by arranging the four stages as two shorter lines, each of two stages with 30 minutes' worth of work. Alternatively, following this logic to its ultimate conclusion, the stages could be arranged as four parallel stages, each responsible for the whole work content. Figure 6.15 shows these options.

This is a simplified example, but it represents a genuine issue. Should the process be organized as a single 'long thin', sequential arrangement, or as several 'short fat', parallel arrangements, or somewhere in between? (Note that 'long' means the number of stages and 'fat' means the amount of work allocated to each stage.) In any particular situation, there are usually technical constraints which limit

Karlstad Kakes (KK) is a manufacturer of speciality cakes, which has recently obtained a contract to supply a major supermarket chain with a speciality cake in the shape of a space rocket. It has been decided that the volumes required by the supermarket warrant a special production process to perform the finishing, decorating and packing of the cake. This line would have to carry out the elements shown in Table 6.2.

Table 6.2 The individual tasks that make up the total job of the finishing, decorating and packing of the cake

Task a – De-tin and trim	Task d – Clad in top fondant	Task g – Apply blue icing
Task b – Reshape	Task e – Apply red icing	Task h – Fix transfers
Task c – Apply base fondant	Task f – Apply green icing	Task i – To base and pack

Figure 6.14 shows the precedence diagram for the total job. The initial order from the supermarket is for 5,000 cakes a week and the number of hours worked by the factory is 40 per week. From this:

$$\text{The required cycle time} = \frac{40 \text{ hrs} \times 60 \text{ mins}}{5,000}$$

$$= 0.48 \text{ mins}$$

$$\text{The required number of stages} = \frac{1.68 \text{ mins (the total work content)}}{0.48 \text{ mins (the required cycle time)}}$$

$$= 3.5 \text{ stages}$$

This means four stages.

Working from the left on the precedence diagram, tasks a and b can be allocated to stage 1. Allocating task c to stage 1 would exceed the cycle time. In fact, only task c can be allocated to stage 2 because including task d would again exceed the cycle time. Task d can be allocated to stage 3. Either task e or f can also be allocated to stage 3, but not both or the cycle time would be exceeded. In this case, task e is chosen. The remaining tasks then are allocated to stage 4. The dotted lines in Figure 6.14 show the final allocation of tasks to each of the four stages.

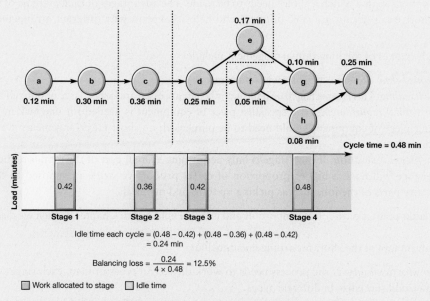

Figure 6.14 Precedence diagram for Karlstad Kakes with allocation of tasks to each stage

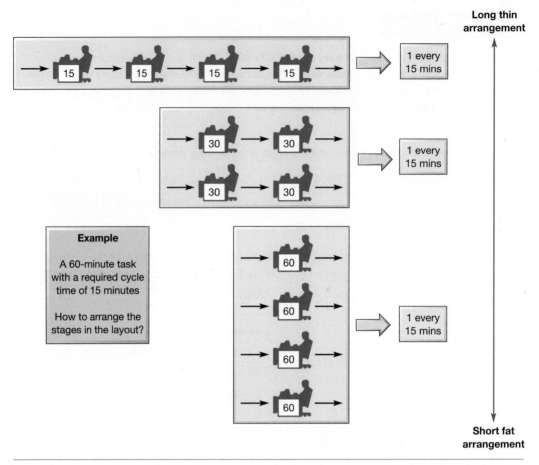

Figure 6.15 The arrangement of stages in a process can be described on a spectrum from 'long thin' to 'short fat'

either how 'long and thin' or how 'short and fat' the process can be, but there is usually a range of possible options within which a choice needs to be made. The advantages of each extreme of the long thin to short fat spectrum are very different and help to explain why different arrangements are adopted.

The advantages of the long thin arrangement include:

▶ *Controlled flow of items.* This is easy to manage.
▶ *Simple handling.* This is especially true if the items being processed are heavy, large or difficult to move.
▶ *Lower capital requirements.* If a specialist piece of equipment is needed for one task in the job, only one piece of equipment would need to be purchased; on short fat arrangements every stage would need one.
▶ *More efficient operation.* If each stage is only performing a small part of the total job, the person at the stage will have a higher proportion of direct productive work as opposed to the non-productive parts of the job, such as picking up tools and materials.

(This latter point is particularly important and is fully explained in Chapter 9 when we discuss job design.)

The advantages of the short fat arrangement include:

▶ *Higher mix flexibility.* If the process needs to work on several types of item, each stage or whole process could specialize in different types.
▶ *Higher volume flexibility.* As volume varies, stages can simply be closed down or started up as required; long thin arrangements would need rebalancing each time the cycle time changed.

- *Higher robustness*. If one stage breaks down or ceases operation in some way, the other parallel stages are unaffected; a long thin arrangement would cease operating completely.
- *Less monotonous work*. In the mortgage example, the staff in the short fat arrangement are repeating their tasks only every hour; in the long thin arrangement, it is every 15 minutes.

Low volume–high variety processes

Many of the ideas and analytical approaches described in this chapter derive largely from high volume–low variety processes. This does not mean that they cannot be used in low volume–high variety process design, but they often have to be modified or adapted in some way. For example, splitting activities into very small increments so that work can be balanced between stages (see earlier) is often neither possible or desirable when the variety of activities is very wide. This does not mean that trying to allocate work equally between work groups is not important, just that it will need to be done in a more approximate way. Even process mapping can be problematic. Some low volume–high variety processes are intrinsically difficult to describe as simple step-by-step sequential activities. There may be many alternative routes through a process than can be taken by whatever is being processed. Decisions about how to treat whatever is being processed may be a matter of judgement. The exact circumstances associated with processing something may not have occurred before. If it is information that is being processed, the information may be partial, uncertain or ambiguous.

From data mining to process mining

If a process has all or any of these conditions described above – in other words, if it is at the 'high variety–low volume' end of the volume–variety spectrum – one of the issues that process designers face is understanding exactly what really happens in the process. Not what is *supposed* to happen, but what actually happens in practice. This is where the (relatively) new technique of 'process mining' can be useful. Process mining is a combination of process analysis and data mining. It is often used where any official description of the process is questionable, over-simplified, or ambiguous (see Figure 6.16).

Data mining emerged as computer systems became common in business processes. It meant that individual companies began to store increasing amounts of data on their various transactions. As the volume of stored data grew, it became evident that within such vast data sets, it could be possible to discover potentially insightful connections and associations. The process of discovering interesting

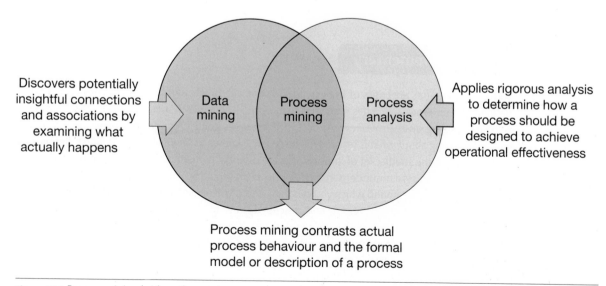

Discovers potentially insightful connections and associations by examining what actually happens

Data mining — Process mining — Process analysis

Applies rigorous analysis to determine how a process should be designed to achieve operational effectiveness

Process mining contrasts actual process behaviour and the formal model or description of a process

Figure 6.16 Process mining bridges the gap between conventional process analysis and data-centric analysis techniques

and useful patterns and relationships in large sets of raw data is called data mining (also called data discovery and knowledge discovery). It uses statistical analysis, algorithms and increasingly artificial intelligence tools together with database management to explore large databases. It is widely used in businesses that have frequent transactions with outside entities such as customers or suppliers (for example, credit-card-fraud detection analyses consumers' purchasing behaviour to detect anomalous, possibly fraudulent, behaviour).

Process mining has been described as the missing link between model-based process analysis (of the type treated elsewhere in this chapter) and the data-oriented analysis techniques used in data mining. Its objective is to understand how a process is actually performed. Operations managers may have a theoretical understanding of a process, but when there are a large number of possible conditions, and people in the process have some degree of discretion, actual behaviour may not be known with confidence. It is based on the use of 'event logs'. These are the basic records (or audit trail) that capture what happens in the use of an information system. They are like system files that are written within a program that reveal the nature, sequence and timing of events. After the data from these event logs have been cleaned and reformatted, they are subjected to a process-mining tool that can display (visually or otherwise) the process as it is actually performed in whatever detail is required. For example, suppose a customer calls an insurance help line to enquire about the progress of a claim. The call centre agent records the call, takes further details, and promises to get back to the customer after checking with colleagues. Other agents, perhaps from other departments, may also call the customer to gather further details. Eventually, after discussing the case, some kind of decision is made. Process mining can analyse the logs for this and other cases, and reveal how the process actually works. This can be used for further analysis, if required.

The effects of process variability

So far in our treatment of process design we have assumed that there is no significant variability either in the demand to which the process is expected to respond, or in the time taken for the process to perform its various activities. Clearly, this is not the case in reality. So, it is important to look at the variability that can affect processes and take account of it.

There are many reasons why variability occurs in processes. These can include the late (or early) arrival of material, information or customers, a temporary malfunction or breakdown of process technology within a stage of the process, the recycling of 'mis-processed' materials, information or customers to an earlier stage in the process, variation in the requirements of items being processed, etc. All these sources of variation interact with each other, but result in two fundamental types of variability.

Critical commentary

Some commentators are critics of the very idea of thinking in terms of 'processes'. They claim that defining jobs as processes incites managers to look on all activities as a machine-like set of routine activities, verging on the mindless. At best, it encourages going through the stages in a process without thinking about what is really involved (what is known as 'box ticking'). At worst, defining all activities into the straitjacket of 'process' kills the essential humanity of working life. The counter argument is that this is a misunderstanding of what is (or should be) meant by a 'process'. A process is simply a framework, around which you can think about who should do what, and when. It simply means that one has thought about, and described, how to do something. Processes need not necessarily be formal, highly constrained or detailed – though they might be. When a process is seen as being too rigid, it is usually because it has been designed inappropriately for its volume–variety position.

▶ Variability in the demand for processing at an individual stage within the process, usually expressed in terms of variation in the inter-arrival times of items to be processed.

▶ Variation in the time taken to perform the activities (i.e. process a unit) at each stage.

To understand the effect of arrival variability on process performance it is first useful to examine what happens to process performance in a very simple process as arrival time changes under conditions of no variability. For example, the simple process shown in Figure 6.17 comprises one stage that performs exactly 10 minutes of work. Items arrive at the process at a constant and predictable rate. If the arrival rate is one unit every 30 minutes, then the process will be utilized for only 33.33 percent of the time, and the items will never have to wait to be processed. This is shown as point A on Figure 6.17. If the arrival rate increases to one arrival every 20 minutes, the utilization increases to 50 per cent, and again the items will not have to wait to be processed. This is point B on Figure 6.17. If the arrival rate increases to one arrival every 10 minutes, the process is now fully utilized, but, because a unit arrives just as the previous one has finished being processed, no unit has to wait. This is point C on Figure 6.17. However, if the arrival rate ever exceeded one unit every 10 minutes, the waiting line in front of the process activity would build up indefinitely, as is shown as point D in Figure 6.17. So, in a perfectly constant and predictable world, the relationship between process waiting time and utilization is a rectangular function as shown by the red line in Figure 6.17.

> **Operations principle**
> Variability in a process acts to reduce its efficiency.

However, when arrival and process times are variable, then sometimes the process will have items waiting to be processed, while at other times the process will be idle, waiting for items to arrive. Therefore, the process will have both a 'non-zero' average queue and be underutilized in the same period. So, a more realistic point is that shown as point X in Figure 6.17. If the average arrival time

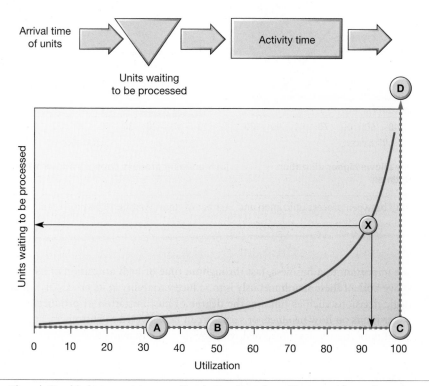

Figure 6.17 The relationship between process utilization and number of items waiting to be processed for constant, and variable, arrival and process times

were to be changed with the same variability, the blue line in Figure 6.17 would show the relationship between average waiting time and process utilization. As the process moves closer to 100 per cent utilization, the average waiting time will become longer. Or, to put it another way, the only way to guarantee very low waiting times for the items is to suffer low process utilization.

The greater the variability in the process, the more the waiting time–utilization relationship deviates from the simple rectangular function of the 'no variability' conditions that was shown in Figure 6.17. A set of curves for a typical process is shown in Figure 6.18(a). This phenomenon has important implications for the design of processes. In effect, it presents three options to process designers wishing to improve the waiting time or utilization performance of their processes, as shown in Figure 6.18(b). Either,

▶ Accept long average waiting times and achieve high utilization (point X)
▶ Accept low utilization and achieve short average waiting times (point Y), or
▶ Reduce the variability in arrival times, activity times, or both, and achieve higher utilization and short waiting times (point Z).

> **Operations principle**
>
> Process variability results in simultaneous waiting and resource under-utilization.

To analyse processes with both inter-arrival and activity time variability, queuing or 'waiting line' analysis can be used. This is treated in the supplement to Chapter 11. But do not dismiss the relationship shown in Figures 6.17 and 6.18 as some minor technical phenomenon. It is far more than this. It identifies an important choice in process design that could have strategic implications.

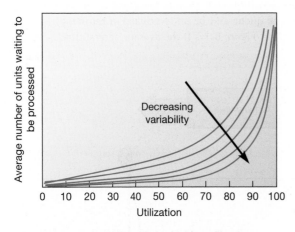

(a) Decreasing variability allows higher utilization without long waiting times

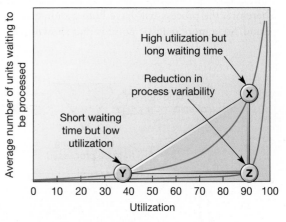

(b) Managing process capacity and/or variability

Figure 6.18 The relationship between process utilization and number of items waiting to be processed for variable arrival and activity times

Which is more important to a business, fast throughput time or high utilization of its resources? The only way to have both of these simultaneously is to reduce variability in its processes, which may itself require strategic decisions such as limiting the degree of customization of products or services, or imposing stricter limits on how products or services can be delivered to customers, and so on. It also demonstrates an important point concerned with the day-to-day management of process – the only way to absolutely guarantee 100 per cent utilization of resources is to accept an infinite amount of work-in-progress and/or waiting time.

Summary answers to key questions

What is process design?

▶ Design is the activity which shapes the physical form and purpose of both products and services and the processes that produce them.

▶ The design activity is more likely to be successful if the complementary activities of product or service design and process design are coordinated.

What should be the objectives of process design?

▶ The overall purpose of process design is to meet the needs of customers through achieving appropriate levels of quality, speed, dependability, flexibility and cost.

▶ The design activity must also take account of environmental issues. These include examination of the source and suitability of materials, the sources and quantities of energy consumed, the amount and type of waste material, the life of the product itself and the end-of-life state of the product.

How do volume and variety affect process design?

▶ The overall nature of any process is strongly influenced by the volume and variety of what it has to process.

▶ The concept of process types summarizes how volume and variety affect overall process design.

▶ In manufacturing, these process types are (in order of increasing volume and decreasing variety) project, jobbing, batch, mass and continuous processes. In service operations, although there is less consensus on the terminology, the terms often used (again in order of increasing volume and decreasing variety) are professional services, service shops and mass services.

How are processes designed in detail?

▶ Processes are designed initially by breaking them down into their individual activities. Often common symbols are used to represent types of activity. The sequence of activities in a process is then indicated by the sequence of symbols representing activities. This is called 'process mapping'. Alternative process designs can be compared using process maps and improved processes considered in terms of their operations performance objectives.

▶ The throughput time, work-in-progress and cycle time aspects of process performance are related by a formula known as Little's law: throughput time equals work-in-progress multiplied by cycle time.

▶ Variability has a significant effect on the performance of processes, particularly the relationship between waiting time and utilization.

The Action Response Applications Processing Unit (ARAPU)

Introduction

Action Response is a London-based charity dedicated to providing fast responses to critical situations throughout the world. It was founded by Susan N'tini, its Chief Executive, to provide relatively short-term aid for small projects until they could obtain funding from larger donors. The charity receives requests for cash aid usually from an intermediary charity and looks to process the request quickly, providing funds where and when they are needed. *'Give a man a fish and you feed him today, teach him to fish and you feed him for life. It's an old saying and it makes sense but, and this is where Action Response comes in, he might starve while he's training to catch fish'* (Susan N'tini).

Nevertheless, Susan does have some worries. She faces two issues in particular. First, she is receiving complaints that funds are not getting through quickly enough. Second, the costs of running the operation are starting to spiral. She explains: *'We are becoming a victim of our own success. We have striven to provide greater accessibility to our funds; people can access application forms via the internet, by post and by phone. But we are in danger of losing what we stand for. It is taking longer to get the money to where it is needed and our costs are going up. We are in danger of failing on one of our key objectives: to minimize the proportion of our turnover that is spent on administration. At the same time we always need to be aware of the risk of bad publicity through making the wrong decisions. If we don't check applications thoroughly, funds may go to the "wrong" place and if the newspapers gets hold of the story we would run a real risk of losing the goodwill, and therefore the funds, from our many supporters.'*

Susan held regular meetings with key stakeholders. One charity that handled a large number of applications for people in Nigeria told her of frequent complaints about the delays over the processing of the applications. A second charity representative complained that when he telephoned to find out the status of an application the ARAPU staff did not seem to know where it was or how long it might be before it was complete. Furthermore, he felt that this lack of information was eroding his relationship with his own clients, some of whom were losing faith in him as a result: *'trust is so important in the relationship'*, he explained.

Some of Susan's colleagues, while broadly agreeing with her anxieties over the organization's responsiveness and efficiency, took a slightly different perspective. *'One of the really good things about Action Response is that we are more flexible than most charities. If there a need and if they need support until one of the larger charities can step in, then we will always consider a request for aid. I would not like to see any move towards high process efficiency harming our ability to be open-minded and consider requests that might seem a little unusual at first'* (Jacqueline Horton, Applications Assessor).

Others saw the charity as performing an important counselling role. *'Remember that we have gained a lot of experience in this kind of short-term aid. We are often the first people that are in a position to advise on how to apply for larger and longer-term funding. If we developed this aspect of our work, we would again be fulfilling a need that is not adequately supplied at the moment'* (Stephen Nyquist, Applications Assessor).

The Action Response Applications Processing Unit (ARAPU)

Potential aid recipients, or the intermediary charities representing them, apply for funds using a standard form. These forms can be downloaded from the internet or requested via a special help line. Sometimes the application will come directly from an individual community leader but more usually it will come via an intermediary charity that is can help the applicant to complete the form. The application is sent to ARAPU, usually by fax or post (some are submitted online, but few communities have this facility).

ARAPU employs seven applications assessors with support staff who are responsible for data entry, coding, filing and 'completing' (staff who prepare payment, or explain why no aid can be given). In addition, a board of non-paid trustees meets every Thursday, to approve the assessors' decisions. The unit's IT system maintained records of all transactions, providing an update on the number of applications received, approved and declined, and payments allocated. These reports identified that the Unit received about 300 new applications per week and responded to about the same number (the Unit operates a 35-hour week). But while the Unit's financial targets were being met, the trend indicated that cost per application was increasing. The target for the turnaround of an application, from receipt of application to response, was 20 days, and although this was not measured formally, it was generally assumed that turnaround time was longer than this. Accuracy had never been an issue as all files were thoroughly assessed to ensure that all the relevant data were collected before the applications were processed. Productivity seemed high and there was always plenty of work waiting for processing at each section with the exception that the 'completers' were sometimes waiting for work to come from the committee on a Thursday. Susan had conducted an inspection of all sections' in-trays that had revealed a rather shocking total of about 2,000 files waiting within the process, not counting those waiting for further information.

Processing applications

The processing of applications is a lengthy procedure requiring careful examination by applications assessors trained to make well-founded assessments in line with the charity's guidelines and values. Incoming applications are opened by one of the four 'receipt' clerks who check that all the necessary forms have been included in the application; the receipt clerks take about 10 minutes per application. These are then sent to the coding staff, in batches twice a day. The five coding clerks allocate a unique identifier to each application and key the information on the application into the system. The coding stage takes about 20 minutes for each application. Files are then sent to the senior applications assessors' secretary's desk. As assessors become available, the secretary provides the next job in the line to the assessor.

About 100 of the cases seen by the assessors each week are put aside after only 10 minutes' 'scanning' because the information is ambiguous, so further information is needed. The assessor returns these files to the secretaries, who write to the applicant (usually via the intermediate charity) requesting additional information, and return the file to the 'receipt' clerks who 'store' the file until the further information eventually arrives (usually between 1 and 8 weeks). When it does arrive, the file enters the process and progresses through the same stages again. Of the applications that require no further information, around half (150) are accepted and half (150) declined. On average, those applications that are not 'recycled' take around 60 minutes to assess.

All the applications, whether approved or declined, are stored prior to ratification. Every Thursday the Committee of Trustees meets to formally approve the applications assessors' decisions. The committee's role is to sample the decisions to ensure that the guidelines of the charity are upheld. In addition, they will review any particularly unusual cases highlighted by the applications assessors. Once approved by the committee the files are then taken to the completion officers. There are three 'decline' officers whose main responsibility is to compile a suitable response to the applicant pointing out why the application failed and offering, if possible, helpful advice. An experienced declines officer takes about 30 minutes to finalize the file and write a suitable letter. Successful files are passed to the four 'payment' officers where again the file is completed, letters (mainly standard letters) are created and payment instructions are given to the bank. This usually takes around 50 minutes, including dealing with any queries from the bank about payment details. Finally, the paperwork itself is sent, with the rest of the file, to two 'dispatch' clerks who complete the documents and mail them to the applicant. The dispatch activity takes, on average, 10 minutes for each application.

The feeling among the staff was generally good. When Susan consulted the team, they said their work was clear and routine, but their life was made difficult by charities that rang in expecting them to be able to tell them the status of an application they had submitted. It could take them hours, sometimes days, to find any individual file. Indeed, two of the 'receipt' clerks now were working almost full time on this activity. They also said that charities frequently complained that decision making seemed slow.

QUESTIONS

1 What objectives should the ARAPU process be trying to achieve?

2 What is the main problem with the current ARAPU process?

3 How could the ARAPU process be improved?

Problems and applications

All chapters have 'Problems and application' questions that will help you practise analysing operations. They can be answered by reading the chapter. Model answers for the first two questions can be found on the companion website for this book.

1   Visit a branch of a retail bank and consider the following questions: (a) What categories of service does the bank seem to offer? (b) To what extent does the bank design separate processes for each of its types of service? (c) What are the different process design objectives for each category of service?

2   Revisit the 'Operations in practice' example that examines some of the principles behind supermarket process design. Then visit a supermarket and observe people's behaviour. You may wish to try and observe which areas they move slowly past and which areas they seem to move past without paying attention to the products. (You may have to exercise some discretion when doing this; people generally don't like to be stalked round the supermarket too obviously.) Try and verify, as far as you can, some of the principles that were outlined in the box. (a) What layout type is a conventional supermarket and how does it differ from a manufacturing operation using the same layout type? (b) What are the benefits of using customer tracking technology that traces the flow of customers through the shop?

3   One of the examples at the beginning of the chapter described 'drive-through' fast food processes. Think about (or better still, visit) a drive-through service and try mapping what you can see of the process (plus what you can infer from what may be happening 'behind the scenes').

4   *'It is a real problem for us',* said Angnyeta Larson. *'We now have only ten working days between all the expense claims coming from the departmental coordinators and authorizing payments on the next month's payroll. This really is not long enough and we are already having problems during peak times.'* Angnyeta was the department head of the internal financial control department of a metropolitan authority in southern Sweden. Part of her department's responsibilities included checking and processing expense claims from staff throughout the metropolitan authority and authorizing payment to the salaries payroll section. She had 12 staff who were trained to check expense claims and all of them were devoted full-time to processing the claims in the two weeks (10 working days) prior to the deadline for informing the salaries section. The number of claims submitted over the year averaged around 3,200, but this could vary between 1,000 during the quiet summer months up to 4,300 in peak months. Processing claims involved checking receipts, checking that claims met with the strict financial allowances for different types of expenditure, checking all calculations, obtaining more data from the claimant if necessary, and (eventually) sending an approval notification to salaries. The total processing took on average 20 minutes per claim. (a) How many staff does the process need on average, for the lowest demand, and for the highest demand? (b) If a more automated process involving electronic submission of claims could reduce the average processing time to 15 minutes, what effect would this have on the required staffing levels? (c) If department coordinators could be persuaded to submit their batched claims earlier (not always possible for all departments) so that the average time between submission of the claims to the finance department and the deadline for informing the salaries section was increased to 15 working days, what effect would this have?

5   The headquarters of a major creative agency offered a service to all its global subsidiaries that included the preparation of a budget estimate that was submitted to potential clients when making a 'pitch' for new work. This service had been offered previously only to a few of the group's subsidiary companies. Now that it was to be offered worldwide, it was deemed appropriate to organize the process of compiling budget estimates on a more systematic basis. It was estimated that the worldwide demand for this service would be around 20 budget estimates per week, and that, on average, the staff who would put together these estimates would be working a 35-hour week. The elements within the total task of compiling a budget estimate are shown in Table 6.3. (a) What is the required cycle time for this process? (b) How many people will the process require to meet the anticipated demand of 20 estimates per week? (c) Assuming that the process is to be designed on a 'long thin' basis, what elements would each stage be responsible for completing? And what would be the balancing loss for this process? (d) Assuming that instead of the long thin design, two parallel

Table 6.3 The elements within the total task of compiling a budget estimate

Element	Time (mins)	What element(s) must be done prior to this one?
A – obtain time estimate from creatives	20	None
B – obtain account handler's deadlines	15	None
C – obtain production artwork estimate	80	None
D – preliminary budget calculations	65	A, B, and C
E – check on client budget	20	D
F – check on resource availability and adjust estimate	80	D
G – complete final budget estimate	80	E and F

processes are to be designed, each with half the number of stations of the long thin design, what now would be the balancing loss?

6   At the theatre, the interval during a performance of *King Lear* lasts for 20 minutes and in that time 86 people need to use the toilet cubicles. On average, a person spends 3 minutes in the cubicle. There are 10 cubicles available. (a) Does the theatre have enough toilets to deal with the demand? (b) If there are not enough cubicles, how long should the interval be to cope with demand?

7   A gourmet burger shop has a daily demand for 250 burgers and operates for 10 hours. (a) What is the required cycle time in minutes? (b) Assuming that each burger has 7.2 minutes of work required, how many servers are required? (c) If the burger shop has a three-stage process for making burgers, stage 1 takes 2.0 minutes, stage 2 takes 3.0 minutes and stage 3 takes 2.2 minutes, what is the balancing loss for the process?

Selected further reading

Damelio, R. (2011) *The Basics of Process Mapping,* 2nd edn, Productivity Press, New York.
A practitioner book that is both very comprehensive and up-to-date.

Hammer, M. (1990) Reengineering work: don't automate, obliterate, *Harvard Business Review,* July–August.
This is the paper that launched the whole idea of business processes and process management in general to a wider managerial audience. Slightly dated but worth reading.

Harrington, H.J. (2011) *Streamlined Process Improvement,* McGraw Hill Professional, New York.
Practical and insightful.

Harvard Business Review (2011) *Improving Business Processes* (Harvard Pocket Mentor) Harvard Business School Press, Boston, MA.
A collection of HBR papers.

Hopp, W.J. and Spearman, M.L. (2011) *Factory Physics,* 3rd edn, Waveland Press Inc., Illinois.
Very technical so don't bother with it if you aren't prepared to get into the maths. However, some fascinating analysis, especially concerning Little's law.

Ramaswamy, R. (1996) *Design and Management of Service Processes,* Addison-Wesley Longman, Reading, MA.
A relatively technical approach to process design in a service environment.

Slack, N. (2017) *The Operations Advantage,* Kogan Page, London.
The chapter on 'internal processes' expands on some of the issues discussed here.

Sparks, W. (2016) *Process Mapping Road Trip: Improve Organizational Workflow in Five Steps,* Promptitude Publishing, Washington DC.
A practitioners' guide – straightforward and sensible.

7   The layout and look of facilities

KEY QUESTIONS

How can the layout and look of facilities influence performance?

What are the basic layout types and how do they affect performance?

How does the appearance of an operation's facilities affect its performance?

What information and analysis is needed to design the layout and look of facilities?

INTRODUCTION

The layout and look of an operation's facilities determines their physical positioning relative to each other and their aesthetic appearance. It involves deciding where to put all the facilities, desks, machines and equipment in the operation. Because people and facilities work together in most operations, this also impacts on how, and where, staff operate within the operation. It is also concerned with the physical appearance of an operation in a broader sense – an issue that is seen as increasingly important, given the effect it has on the people working in the operation and any customers who 'experience' the operation. Both the layout and look of facilities govern how safe, how attractive, how flexible and how efficient an operation is. They also determine how transformed resources – materials, information and customers – flow through an operation. For all these reasons, it is an important activity. It is it the first thing that most of us notice when we enter an operation. Also, relatively small changes – moving displays in a supermarket, the décor of a restaurant, the changing rooms in a sports centre, or the position of a machine in a factory – can affect flow through the operation, which, in turn, affects the costs and general effectiveness of the operation. Figure 7.1 shows the layout activity in the overall model of design in operations.

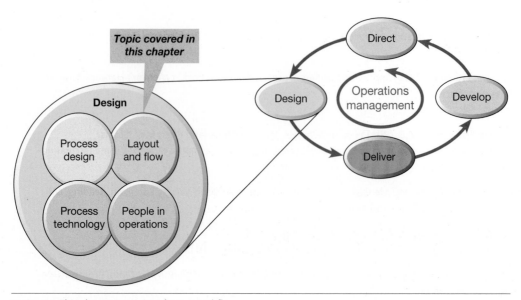

Figure 7.1 This chapter examines layout and flow

In this chapter we are going to do four things. First, we will look briefly at what operations managers are trying to achieve when they change the layout or look of their transforming resources. Second, we describe a number of recognized 'layout types'. These are derived largely from manufacturing, but we shall use non-manufacturing examples to demonstrate how they can also be used for a whole range of operations. Third, we look at how the physical appearance of operations influences their effectiveness both for their customers and for the staff working in them. Finally, we look at the information needed to decide on facilities' layout and look.

How can the layout and look of facilities influence performance?

The 'layout and look' of an operation or process means how its facilities are positioned relative to each other and how their general appearance is designed. These decisions will dictate the pattern and nature of how transformed resources progress through the operation or process. They also affect how both the people who staff the operation and, in high-visibility operations (where customers form part of the transformed resource), how customers judge their experience of being in the operation. Figure 7.2 shows how both layout and look of facilities affect some of the factors on which operations facilities are judged.

Layout and look are important decisions. If done badly, they can lead to over-long or confused flow patterns, long process times, inflexible operations, unpredictable flow, high costs, frustration for the people working in the operation and, in high-visibility operations, a poor customer experience. Nor are they always easy to change. A radical re-layout can cause disruption to on-going operations. So, operations managers can be reluctant to do it too often.

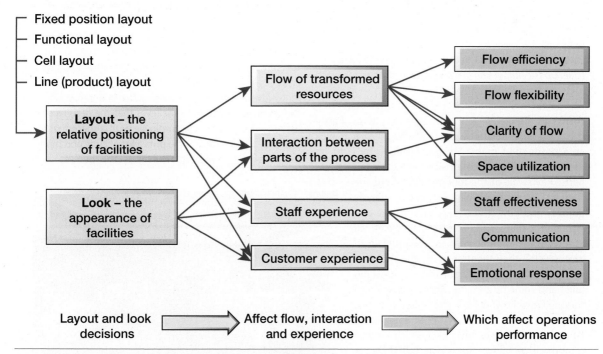

Figure 7.2 The layout and look of facilities involves the relative positioning of transforming resources within operations and processes, and their general appearance, which together dictate the nature and pattern of the flow of transformed resources and the experience of staff and, in high-visibility operations, customers

Ducati factory or Google office, they have to look good[1]

Don't be tempted to think that the principles of design that govern the layout and look of an engineering factory and the Head Office of a global high-tech company should be very different. Where facilities are located within the operation, and what they look like are important for both. Here are the two examples.

The Ducati factory in Bologna

Motorcycles have been built by Ducati at its current factory in Bologna continuously since 1946. But now, as well as producing 350 bikes every day in the busy season, the factory hosts visitors keen to see how the famous motorcycles are made. The assembly process starts in the 'supermarket' area of the factory. Each of the models made by Ducati has its own 'supermarket' zone. Here manufacturing trays are put together with exactly the right parts that will be needed for each of the subsequent stages in the assembly process. Because these 'kits' of parts exactly match the requirements for each product, any parts left in the tray at the end of assembly are an indication that something has gone wrong. Livio Lodi, who has worked in the Ducati factory for more than 26 years, is the official historian and curator of the Ducati museum on the site. He explain: 'With this new style of just-in-time production, we have been able to reduce over 85 per cent of the defects in the final product. Porsche engineers came to us here and explained the way to set up the production in a just-in-time philosophy which they got from Toyota originally.'

The factory has also become a tourist attraction thanks to the regular and popular factory tours. Partly it is a customer relations and marketing device as well as a production plant. So, the facilities have to be designed to accommodate visitors as well as motorcycle parts. Reviewers of the tour enthuse about the 'fantastic factory tour with wonderful friendly guides', and how it was 'very informative and knowledgeable', and 'interesting to see all aspects of the assembly of the wonderful Ducati motorcycle'; they mention how 'the museum was great and historic with some beautiful old bikes and some up to date winners'. Many visitors are Ducati owners, but the company shows the factory and the museum to everybody. Ducati say that they don't care which kind of motorcycle you have. But, if you ride a Ducati there, you can leave your bike inside the gates. If you don't ride a Ducati, you can leave it outside the entrance.

Google's revolutionary offices

Operations, and therefore operations layouts, are not confined to factories, warehouses, shops and other such workspaces. Many of us who work in operations actually work in offices. Financial services, Government, call centres and all the creative industries, all work for the most part sitting at their desks. (One estimate is that over 70 per cent of the UK's GDP is generated by people working in offices, although it is admittedly difficult to check.) So the layout of offices can affect operations performance for these industries just as much as layout can in a factory. And of all companies whose staff work in offices, Google, like many high-tech companies, is paying much more attention to its employees' work environment, the better to promote creativity and productivity. In fact, Google is famous for its innovative use of its workspaces. This is because Google thrives on creativity and it believes that the designs of its offices will provide every employee with a space that will encourage creativity. Google puts a lot of time and money into designing what it believes is the perfect work

environment – one that can mix business with pleasure in the sense that the staff can relax and unwind during their breaks. The layouts of Google's offices are designed to promote creativity and collaboration. How people move about the space and whom they meet and talk to are vital pieces of information that should contribute to any design. The information needs of the processes underlying activities are clearly an important driver of where the various departments of an organization are located. However, people sometimes are not fully aware how they are interacting with one another, or with the space where they work. So, in addition to examining the formal needs of people's jobs, it is valuable to examine employee behaviour. For example, where do people actually spend the majority of their time? Where and when do the most productive meetings happen? Where and when do people make phone calls? When is the office at its emptiest? When is it most full (and noisy)?

Elliot Felix led the team that wrote Google's global design guidelines for its offices. *'Google was doubling in size every year and building new locations everywhere',* he says. *'There was so much concern about what the ingredients of the offices should be and how they would all fit together cohesively for a consistent employee experience. We're never just talking about space. We're talking about culture, etiquette, and rituals. What a lot of people forget is that we imbue space with our values.'* There's a rule at Google that nobody should be located more than 100 metres away from food. There are eco-friendly kitchens complete with healthy food sited at strategic locations around the buildings (that is, in addition to the cafeteria). There are quiet places, such as libraries and sometimes aquariums, if you want somewhere quiet to relax or think through a problem. Some parts of the office look like an apartment, which appeals to those employees who like the idea of 'working from home' at the office. Designing these features in office buildings is partly a consequence of the long hours worked by many people in the high-technology industries. Offices must be equipped with areas for working and areas for relaxing (even if that means playing football, an approach championed by Google).

What makes a good layout?

As with most operations design decisions, what constitutes a 'good' design will depend partly on the strategic objectives of the operation. But whatever 'good' is for any specific operation, it will usually be judged against a common set of criteria, as indicated in Figure 7.2. These are:

▶ *The flow of transformed resources* – The route taken by transformed resources as they progress through an operation or process is governed by how its transforming resources are positioned relative to each other. Often the objective is to achieve high flow efficiency that minimizes distance travelled. But not always. For some customer transforming operations, supermarkets for example, layout objectives can include encouraging customers to 'flow' in particular ways that maximize sales. However, sometimes high flow efficiency can be achieved only by sacrificing flow flexibility – the ability of transformed resources to take many different routes. Additional objectives can include the clarity of the flow of materials and/or customers and an effective use of the space available in the operation.

▶ *The interaction between parts of the process* – The individual facilities or parts of a process can suffer or benefit from being positioned close to each other. Dirty processes should not be located near to other parts of the process where their pollution could reduce its effectiveness. Noisy processes should not be located near processes that require concentration (see the 'Operations in practice' example, 'Reconciling quiet and interaction in laboratory layout'). Conversely there may be a positive effect of locating parts of an operation close to each other, for example to encourage communication between staff (see the 'Operations in practice' example of Google's office layout).

▶ *Staff experience* – An obvious prerequisite for any layout in any type of operation is that it should not constitute any physical or emotional danger to staff. So, 'fire exits should be clearly marked with uninhibited access', 'pathways should be clearly defined and not cluttered', etc. Unnecessary movement, caused by poor layout, will take productive time away from value-adding tasks. But just as important is the 'look, touch, taste, smell and feel' of an operation that will influence the 'employee experience' and hence staff productivity and morale.[2]

▶ *Customer experience* – In high-visibility operations such as retail shops or bank branches, the layout and particularly the look of an operation can help to shape its image and the general experience of customers. Layout and look can be used as a deliberate attempt to establish a company's brand.

Reconciling objectives

As one can see, there are many and various objectives to attempt to achieve during the layout activity. Some, such as safety, security and staff welfare, are absolutely required. Others may have to be compromised, or traded off with other objectives. For example, two processes may have need of the same piece of equipment and could quite feasibly share it. This would mean good use of the capital used to acquire that equipment. But having both processes using it could mean longer and/or more confused process routes. Buying two pieces of equipment would underutilize them, but give shorter distance travelled. The 'Operations in practice' example 'Reconciling quiet and interaction in laboratory layout' is an example of how objectives have to be reconciled.

What are the basic layout types used in operations and how do they affect performance?

Most practical layouts are derived from only four basic layout types. These are:

▶ Fixed-position layout
▶ Functional layout
▶ Cell layout
▶ Line (sometimes called 'product') layout.

These layout types are loosely related to the process types described in Chapter 6. As Table 7.1 indicates, a process type does not necessarily imply only one particular basic layout.

Fixed-position layout

Fixed-position layout is in some ways a contradiction in terms, since the transformed resources do not move between the transforming resources. Instead of transformed resources flowing through an operation, the recipient of the processing is stationary and the facilities and people who do the

Table 7.1 Alternative layout types for each process type

Manufacturing process type	Potential layout types		Service process type
Project	Fixed position layout Functional layout	Fixed position layout Functional layout Cell layout	Professional service
Jobbing	Functional layout Cell layout		
Batch	Functional layout Cell layout	Functional layout Cell layouts	Service shop
Mass	Cell layout Product layout	Cell layout Product layout	Mass service
Continuous	Product layout		

Reconciling quiet and interaction in laboratory layout[3]

The layout of scientific laboratories is rarely straightforward. Not only can different areas of a laboratory require very different service needs (temperature, extraction, lack of vibration, etc.) but also two types of work in which all scientists engage can have different and opposing needs. On one hand, the development of new ideas is encouraged by free, and sometimes random, meetings between researchers. On the other hand, there are times when quiet reflection is vital to work through the implications of those same ideas. Moreover, different individuals have different preferred working patterns. The conversations, discussion and, sometimes noisy, debate between some researchers can both irritate and distract other staff who prefer quiet

to think and write up their work. Even in prestigious and high-profile research operations, this conflict can be difficult to reconcile. For example, some of the researchers working at the Francis Crick laboratory in central London complained that its open-plan layout, designed to encourage collaboration, made it difficult to concentrate on their work. Some people like the background noise, which can be similar to working in a café, while others prefer total silence, although many agree that the layout has been extremely successful in terms of promoting ad hoc meetings and has created new collaborations. Professor Alan Penn, who has been investigating how open-plan layouts (for example, those in advertising agencies or science

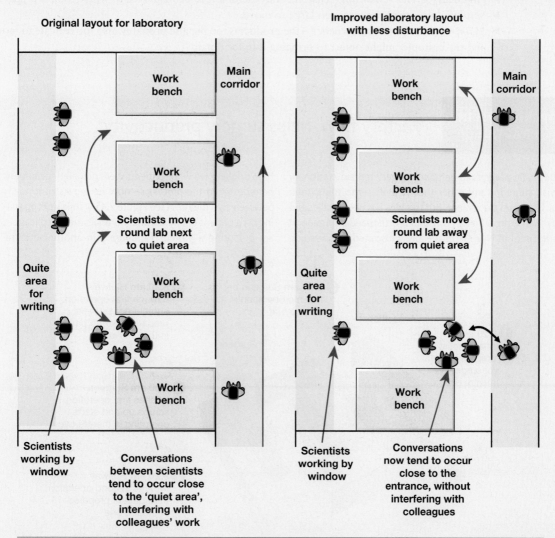

Figure 7.3 Example of an improved laboratory layout that reduces the degree of interference between different types of work (conversations and writing)

laboratories) affect behaviour, points out how designing laboratories with busy circulation spaces allows scientists from different research groups to effectively share ideas. People walking around can stop and join a conversation in the door of a laboratory. Conversations inside the laboratory, when they are next to where the relatively high-flow movement along the corridor occurs, lead to discussions between research groups.

Figure 7.3 illustrates how laboratory design can, to some extent, reduce the conflict between the benefits of interaction and the need for quiet. The conventional layout on the left allows potentially disruptive conversations to interfere with quiet areas. The marginally modified layout on the right encourages conversations to happen closer to the entrance, without interfering with colleagues.

processing move as necessary. This could be because the transformed resources are too large, too delicate or too inconvenient to move; for example:

▶ *Motorway construction* – the product is too large to move.
▶ *Open-heart surgery* – patients are too delicate to move.
▶ *High-class service restaurant* – customers would object to being moved to where food is prepared.
▶ *Shipbuilding* – the product is too large to move.
▶ *Mainframe computer maintenance* – the product is too big and probably also too delicate to move, and the customer might object to bringing it in for repair.

OPERATIONS IN PRACTICE

'Factory flow' helps surgery productivity[4]

Normally patients undergoing surgery remain stationary with surgeons and other theatre staff performing their tasks around the patient. But this idea has been challenged by John Petri, a French consultant orthopaedic surgeon at a hospital in Norfolk in the UK. Frustrated by spending time drinking tea while patients were prepared for surgery, he redesigned the process so now he moves continually between two theatres (see Figure 7.4). While he is operating on a patient in one theatre, his anaesthetist colleagues are preparing a patient for surgery in another theatre.

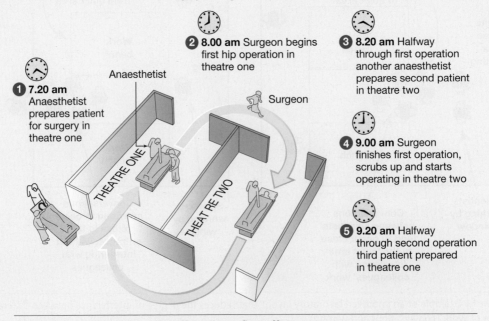

① 7.20 am Anaesthetist prepares patient for surgery in theatre one

Anaesthetist

② 8.00 am Surgeon begins first hip operation in theatre one

Surgeon

③ 8.20 am Halfway through first operation another anaesthetist prepares second patient in theatre two

④ 9.00 am Surgeon finishes first operation, scrubs up and starts operating in theatre two

⑤ 9.20 am Halfway through second operation third patient prepared in theatre one

Figure 7.4 Space utilization traded off to achieve flow efficiency

After finishing with the first patient, the surgeon 'scrubs up', moves to the second operating theatre and begins the surgery on the second patient. While he is doing this, the first patient is moved out of the first operating theatre and the third patient is prepared. This method of overlapping operations in different theatres allows him to work for five hours at a time rather than the previous standard three and a half hour session. *'If you were running a factory'*, says the surgeon, *'you wouldn't allow your most important and most expensive machine to stand idle. The same is true in a hospital.'* Currently used on hip and knee replacements, this layout would not be suitable for all surgical procedures. But since its introduction the surgeon's waiting list has fallen to zero and his productivity has doubled. *'For a small increase in running costs [reduced space utilization] we are able to treat many more patients [increased flow efficiency]'*, said a spokesperson for the hospital management. *'What is important is that clinicians . . . produce innovative ideas and we demonstrate that they are effective'.*

Functional layout

In functional layout, similar transforming resources are located together. This may be because it is convenient to group them together, or because their utilization is improved. It means that when transforming resources flow through the operation, they will take a route from activity to activity according to their needs. Different products or customers will have different needs and therefore take different routes. Usually this makes the flow pattern in the operation very complex. Examples of functional layouts include:

▶ *Hospital* – some processes (e.g. X-ray machines and laboratories) are required by several types of patient; some processes (e.g. general wards) can achieve high staff and bed utilization.
▶ *Supermarket* – some products, such as tinned goods, are convenient to restock if grouped together. Some areas, such as those holding frozen vegetables, need the common technology of freezer cabinets. Others, such as the areas holding fresh vegetables, might be together because that way they can be made to look attractive to customers.
▶ *Machining the parts which go into aircraft engines* – some processes (e.g. heat treatment) need specialist support (heat and fume extraction); some processes (e.g. machining centres) require the same technical support from specialist setter–operators, or need high utilization.

Like most functional layouts, a library has different types of user with different traffic patterns. The college library in Figure 7.5 has put its users into three categories, as follows (in fact very similar to the categories used by retail customers).[5]

▶ **Browsers** – who seek interesting or useful materials by surfing the Internet, browsing shelves and examining items, and moving around slowly while assessing the value of items.
▶ **Destination traffic** – who have a specific purpose or errand and are not deterred from it by surroundings or other library materials.
▶ **Beeline traffic** – who concentrate on goals unconnected with personal use of the library: for example, messengers, delivery staff, or maintenance workers.

Based on studies tracking these different types of customer, the library derived the following guide rules for the layout of its library.

▶ Position displays and services that need to be brought to users' attention at the front of the facility.
▶ To the right of the entrance should be: new acquisitions; items that might be selected on impulse and have no satisfactory substitutes; and items that require repeated exposure before users select them.
▶ On the left at the front should be items that probably will not be used unless there is maximum convenience for the user, such as reference books.
▶ The circulation desk should be on the left of the entrance, the last thing the user passes before leaving.

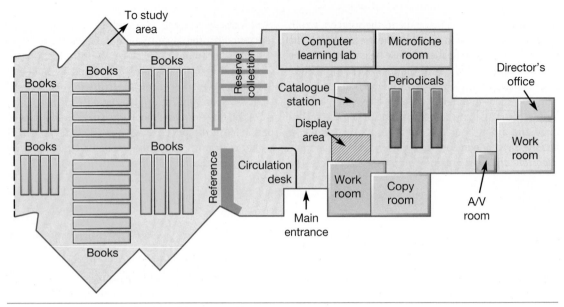

Figure 7.5 An example of a functional layout in a library

▶ The rear of the library should house items for which user motivation is strong, such as classroom-assigned materials and meeting rooms, or those which the user is willing to spend time and effort obtaining, such as microfiche printouts.

Cell layout

A cell layout is one where the transformed resources entering the operation are pre-selected (or pre-select themselves) to move to one part of the operation (or cell) in which all the transforming resources, to meet their immediate processing needs, are located. The cell itself may be arranged in either a functional or line (see next section) layout. After being processed in the cell, the transformed resources may go on to another cell. In effect, cell layout is an attempt to bring some order to the complexity of flow that characterizes functional layout. Examples of cell layouts include:

▶ *'Lunch' products area in a supermarket* – some customers use the supermarket just to purchase sandwiches, savoury snacks, cool drinks, yoghurt, etc. for their lunch. These products are often located close together so that customers who are just buying lunch do not have to search around the store.

▶ *Maternity unit in a hospital* – customers needing maternity attention are a well-defined group who can be treated together and who are unlikely to need the other facilities of the hospital at the same time that they need the maternity unit.

▶ *Some computer component manufacture* – the processing and assembly of some types of computer parts may need a special area dedicated to the manufacturing of parts for one particular customer who has special requirements such as particularly high quality levels.

Although the idea of cell layout is often associated with manufacturing, the same principle can be, and is, used in services. In Figure 7.6 the ground floor of a department store is shown, the predominant layout of which is a functional layout, with separate areas devoted to selling each type of goods. The exception is the 'shop-within-a-shop' area that is devoted to many goods that have a common sporting theme (sports clothes, sports shoes, sports bags, sports magazines, sports books, sports equipment, etc). They have been located in the 'cell' not because they are similar

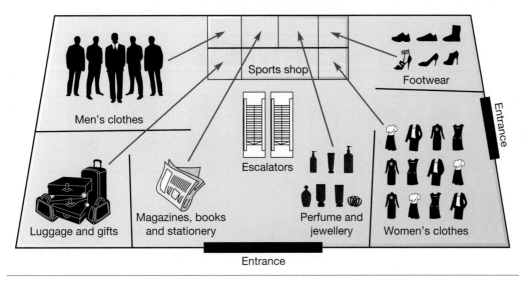

Figure 7.6 The floor plan of a department store showing the sports goods 'shop-within-a-shop cell' within the functional layout of the rest of the store

goods (shoes, books and drinks would not usually be located together) but because they are needed to satisfy the needs of a particular type of customer. The store management calculates that enough customers come to the store to buy 'sports goods' in particular to devote an area specifically to them.

Line (product) layout

Line layout involves locating the transforming resources entirely for the convenience of the transformed resources. Each product, piece of information or customer follows a prearranged route in which the sequence of activities required corresponds to the sequence in which facilities have been located. The transformed resources 'flow' along a 'line' according to their 'product' needs. This is why this type of layout is sometimes called flow or product layout. Flow is clear, predictable and therefore relatively easy to control. Usually, it is the standardized requirements of the product or service that lead to operations choosing line layouts. Examples of line layout include:

▶ *Mass-immunization programme* – all customers require the same sequence of clerical, medical and counselling activities.
▶ *Self-service cafeteria* – generally the sequence of customer requirements (starter, main course, dessert and drink) is common to all customers, but layout also helps control customer flow.
▶ *Automobile assembly* – almost all variants of the same model require the same sequence of processes.

But don't think that line layouts are not changing. Even Toyota, the best known of all automobile companies, which routinely uses this type of layout is rethinking the assembly line. The appreciation of the Japanese Yen has made it difficult for vehicles made in Japan to compete; and while Toyota, like other Japanese firms, has built factories in other parts of the world, if is still wants to manufacture in Japan, cost savings have to be made. Figure 7.7 shows just two of the ideas that Toyota is employing at its Miyagi factory in Japan to make assembly lines even more efficient. The top illustration shows how Toyota has positioned vehicles sideways rather than the conventional lengthways positioning. This is a simple idea, but it has the advantage of

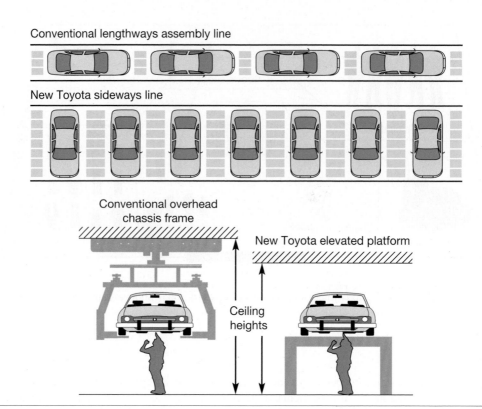

Figure 7.7 Contrasting arrangements in product (line) layout for automobile assembly plants

shortening the line by 35 per cent (which increases space utilization) and shortening the distance that workers have to walk between cars (which increases flow efficiency). The bottom illustration shows how, instead of the vehicle chassis hanging from overhead conveyor belts, they are positioned on raised platforms. This costs only half as much to construct and allows ceiling heights to be lowered, which is more space efficient and reduces heating and cooling costs by 40 per cent.

Mixed layouts

Many operations either design hybrid layouts that combine elements of some or all of the basic layout types, or use the 'pure' basic layout types in different parts of the operation. For example, a hospital would normally be arranged on functional layout principles – each department representing a particular type of function (the X-ray department, the surgical theatres, the blood-processing laboratory, and so on). Yet within each department, quite different layouts could be used. The X-ray department is probably arranged in a functional layout, the surgical theatres in a fixed-position layout and the blood-processing laboratory in a product layout.

 Operations principle

There are four basic layout types, fixed position, functional, cell and line, although layouts can combine elements of more than one of these.

Another example is shown in Figure 7.8. Here a restaurant complex is shown with three different types of restaurant and the kitchen which serves them all. The kitchen is arranged in a functional layout, with the various processes (food storage, food preparation, cooking processes, etc.) grouped together. The traditional service restaurant is arranged in a fixed-position layout. The customers stay at their tables while the food is brought to (and sometimes cooked at) the tables. The buffet restaurant is arranged in a cell-type layout with each buffet area having all the processes (dishes) necessary to serve customers with their starter, main course or dessert. Finally, in the cafeteria restaurant, all customers take the

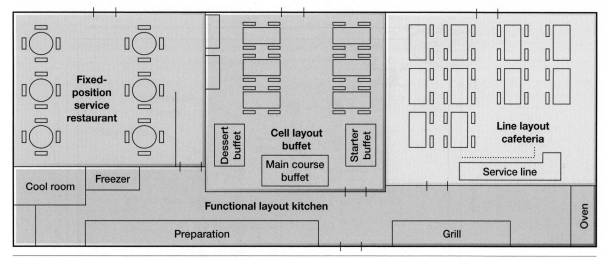

Figure 7.8 A restaurant complex with all four basic layout types

same route when being served with their meal. They may not take the opportunity to be served with every dish but they move through the same sequence of processes.

What type of layout should an operation choose?

The importance of flow to an operation will depend on its volume and variety characteristics. When volume is very low and variety is relatively high, 'flow' is not a major issue. For example, in telecommunications satellite manufacture, a fixed-position layout is likely to be appropriate because each product is different and because products 'flow' through the operation very infrequently, so it is just not worth arranging facilities to minimize the flow of parts through the operation. With higher volume and lower variety, flow becomes an issue. If the variety is still high, however, an entirely flow-dominated arrangement is difficult because there will be different flow patterns. For example, the library in Figure 7.5 will arrange its different categories of books and its other services partly to minimize the average distance its customers have to 'flow' through the operation. But, because its customers' needs vary, it will arrange its layout to satisfy the majority of its customers (but perhaps inconvenience a minority). When the variety of products or services reduces to the point where a distinct 'category' with similar requirements becomes evident but variety is still not small, cell layout could become appropriate, as in the sports goods cell in Figure 7.6. When variety is relatively small and volume is high, flow can become regularized and a line layout is likely to be appropriate, as in an assembly plant (see Figure 7.9).

>
> **Operations principle**
> Resources in low volume–high variety processes should be arranged to cope with irregular flow.

Although the volume–variety characteristics of the operation will narrow the choice down to one or two layout options, there are other associated advantages and disadvantages, some of which are shown in Figure 7.10. However, the type of operation will also influence the relative importance of these advantages and disadvantages. For example, a high-volume television manufacturer may find the low-cost characteristics of a product layout attractive, but an amusement theme park may adopt the same layout type primarily because of the way it 'controls' customer flow.

>
> **Operations principle**
> Resources in high volume–low variety processes should be arranged to cope with smooth, regular flow.

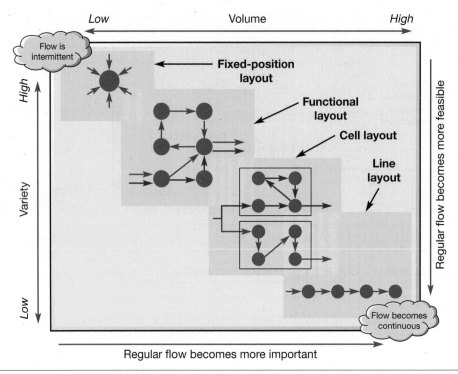

Figure 7.9 Different process layouts are appropriate for different volume–variety combinations

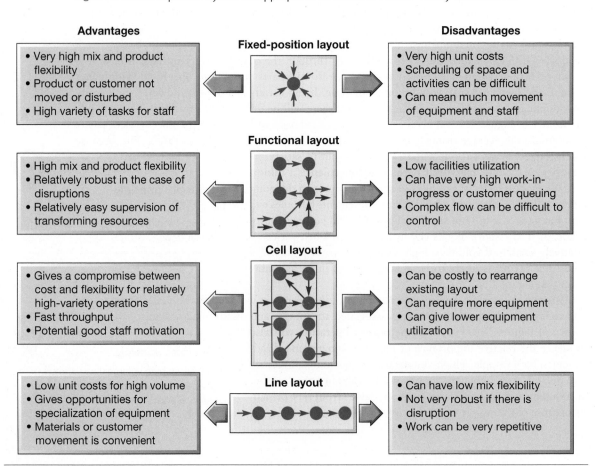

Figure 7.10 Some advantages and disadvantages of layout types

Supermarket layout

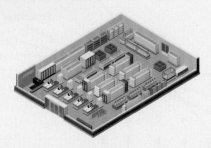

Successful supermarkets know that the design and layout of their stores has a huge impact on their profitability. This is why all big supermarket chains conduct extensive research into the most effective ways of laying out each part of their supermarkets and how best to position specific items. They must maximize their revenue per square metre and minimize the costs of operating the store, while keeping customers happy. At a basic level, supermarkets have to get the amount of space allocated to the different areas right and provide appropriate display and storage facilities. But it is not just the needs of the products that are being sold that are important; the layout must also take into consideration the psychological effect that the layout has on their customers. Aisles are made wide to ensure a relatively slow flow of trolleys so that customers pay more attention to the products on display (and buy more). However, wide aisles can come at the expense of reduced shelf space that would allow a wider range of products to be stocked. The actual location of all the products is a

critical decision, directly affecting the convenience to customers, their level of spontaneous purchase, and the cost of filling the shelves. Although the majority of supermarket sales are packaged tinned or frozen goods, the displays of fruit and vegetables are usually located adjacent to the main entrance, as a signal of freshness and wholesomeness, providing an attractive and welcoming point of entry. Basic products that figure on most people's shopping lists, such as flour, meat sugar and bread, may be spread out towards the back of the store and apart from each other so that customers have to walk along more aisles, passing higher-margin items as they search. High-margin items are usually put at eye level on shelves (where they are more likely to be seen) and low-margin products lower down or higher up. Some customers also go a few paces up an aisle before they start looking for what they need. Some supermarkets call the shelves occupying the first metre of an aisle 'dead space', not a place to put impulse-bought goods. But the prime site in a supermarket is the 'gondola-end', the shelves at the end of the aisle. Moving products to this location can increase sales 200 or 300 per cent. It is not surprising that suppliers are willing to pay for their products to be located here. The circulation of customers through the store must also be right, but this can vary depending on which country you live in. In the USA shoppers like to work their way through a supermarket anti-clockwise. By contrast, shoppers in the UK like to shop clockwise. The reason for this is a bit of a mystery. Some put it down to the different driving patterns of each country.

Cost analysis

Of all the characteristics of the various layout types, perhaps the most generally significant are the unit cost implications of layout choice. This is best understood by distinguishing between the fixed and variable cost elements of adopting each layout type. For any particular product or service, the fixed costs of physically constructing a fixed-position layout are relatively small compared with any other way of producing the same product or service. However, the variable costs of producing each individual product or service are relatively high compared to the alternative layout types. Fixed costs then tend to increase as one moves from fixed-position, through process and cell, to line layout. Variable costs per product or service tend to decrease, however. The total costs for each layout type will depend on the volume of products or services produced and are shown in Figure 7.11(a). This seems to show that for any volume there is a lowest-cost basic layout. However, in practice, the cost analysis of layout selection is rarely as clear as this. The exact cost of operating the layout is difficult to forecast and will probably depend on many often difficult to predict factors. Rather than use thin lines to represent the cost of layout as volume increases, broad bands, within which the real cost is likely to lie, are probably more appropriate (see Figure 7.11(b)). The discrimination between the different layout types is now far less clear. There are ranges of volume for which any of two or three layout

Operations principle

Different layout types have different fixed and variable costs which determine the appropriateness of layout for varying volume–variety characteristics.

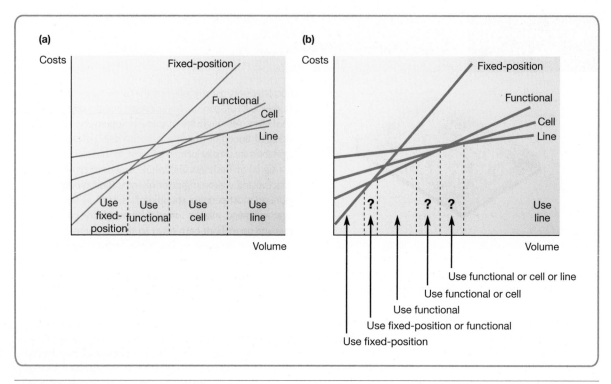

Figure 7.11 (a) The basic layout types have different fixed and variable cost characteristics which seem to determine which one to use. (b) In practice the uncertainty about the exact fixed and variable costs of each layout means the decision can rarely be made on cost alone

types might provide the lowest operating cost. The less certainty there is over the costs, the broader the cost 'bands' will be, and the less clear the choice will be. The probable costs of adopting a particular layout need to be set in the broader context of advantages and disadvantages shown in Figure 7.10.

How does the appearance of an operation's facilities affect its performance?

Traditionally, operations managers have focused on the more evident 'pattern of flow' issues associated with facilities layout. Yet the aesthetics of a layout (in other words, what it looks and feels like) are also important and are increasingly seen as being within the scope of what operations management should be concerned with. Organizations with high-visibility operations such as retailers, hospitals, or hotels have always understood that the look of their operations will affect customers' experience. Now, operations in most industries have come to understand the importance of aesthetics. Partly, this is because of the accumulating research evidence that the aesthetics of an operation can evoke positive or negative emotional response in people (whether they be customers or staff), and therefore affect their behaviour and well-being. Partly also, the approach of those technology companies that pioneered more relaxed and fluid working settings with the intention of encouraging casual encounters has started to influence other, less glamourous industries (see the 'Operations in practice' example on Ducati and Google earlier in the chapter).

The effect of workplace design on staff

There are some obvious and basic aspects of workplace design that will affect anyone working there. These are such things as: is it warm enough? Too warm? Sufficiently well lit to see adequately? Not too noisy? These are all factors that deal with the physiological aspects of working – how we fit in with our physical working environment. Clearly, people who are cold, or irritated by their noisy environment, or straining to see what they are doing, will probably not be feeling, or working, particularly well. We look at these issues in Chapter 9 when we consider 'ergonomics'. But there are other factors associated with the design of a workplace that could affect staff attitudes, motivation and behaviour. This is why in recent years many companies have devoted resources to what goes into their workplaces and what they look like. Increasingly, special meeting zones, cappuccino bars, fish tanks, relaxing bean bags, games consoles, hammocks, ping pong tables and other such features have been integrated into workspaces. Why is this?

The core of the argument for using these design features is that a workplace is more than simply the arrangement of facilities and the pattern of flow that it creates. It is also the furniture, the way space is used and even the colour of the paint on the walls. Some workplace designers would go further. The aesthetics of the workplace also reflects the culture of the organization. (There is no single authoritative definition of organizational culture, but generally it is taken to mean what it feels like to be part of an organization, 'the organization's climate'.[6]) Therefore, they argue, the appearance of a workplace should reflect the organization's culture. The key questions are 'what does that workplace say about our culture?' and 'how can we create an environment that further promotes our culture?' What works for one company may be counter-cultural at another.[7] The Google headquarters in California (known as the Googleplex) is often cited as a good example of a workplace that reflects the company's culture.

However, the proponents of improving the appearance of the working environment say that the idea is not simply to 'change the décor and therefore change the culture'. Workplace aesthetics is subtler than that. It can encourage desired behaviours, in particular when the workplace reflects the activities and needs of the people working there. So, for example, flexible modular systems of furniture made up of a number of components can be changed to meet different needs as they arise. Screens can enclose a workstation if more privacy is needed, tables can be moved around for meetings, and so on. A study by Herman Miller[8] (an office furniture manufacturer) identified seven workspace attributes that people value and which contribute to their satisfaction and (presumably) output. These were, in order of priority, a comfortable office, sufficient amount of work surface area, the flexibility to put their computer in the most suitable place, the capability to keep work within arm's reach, to contain sounds within the office, to keep out distracting noises from outside the office and to have 'visual privacy'.

> **Operations principle**
> Layout should take into consideration the aesthetic appearance of the workplace and type of facilities available to staff.

Critical commentary

The question of how much difference the aesthetics and components of the working environment make is not uncontentious. In fact, according to Thomas Davenport, an expert in 'knowledge working', there is little evidence that anyone worked more productively because of these features. *'There's no clear relationship between knowledge worker performance and various appealing features of the work environment, though they may help slightly with recruiting and morale.'*[9] There is also some evidence that open plan workplaces, casual meeting rooms, and more 'living-room-like spaces' are not universally popular with staff. Gensler, a design firm, surveyed more than 90,000 people across ten industries about their views on 'fluid', 'open-plan' working. It found a surprising amount of opposition, with many staff claiming that open-plan offices, in particular, make it difficult to concentrate because of excessive noise. What they actually valued were as few distractions as possible so that they could focus on their jobs.[10]

The Allen curve

Arranging the facilities in any workplace will directly influence how physically close individuals are to each other. And this, in turn, influences the likelihood of communication between individuals. So, what effects does placing individuals close together or far apart have on how they interact? The work of Thomas J. Allen at the Massachusetts Institute of Technology first established how communication dropped off with increased distance. In 1984 his book, *Managing the Flow of Technology*, presented what has become known as the 'Allen curve'. It showed a powerful negative correlation between the physical distance between

> **Operations principle**
>
> The likelihood of communication between people in their workplace falls off significantly as the distance between them increases. This is called the Allen curve.

Where did the office cubicle come from?[11]

Some people love them, many people loath them; the office cubicle is rarely viewed as a neutral arrangement. But originally the man who invented the concept, Robert Propst, a designer working for the office-furniture firm Herman Miller, hoped it would bring flexibility and independence to the office environment. What he was reacting against was the then common arrangement of row after row of desks (a bit like a university examination room), where office workers toiled from 9 to 5, usually with a passageway of private, closed-off offices reserved for managers. In 1968 Propst proposed what was the first modular office system, called the 'Action Office 2'. Using his system, space could be divided up by wall-like vertical panels that could be slotted together in various ways. His original idea was that each employee could have a clamshell arrangement that gave him or her both privacy and a view. This would be furnished with desks of different heights (to prevent back strain). In addition, areas for informal meetings and coffee could be created. Propst believed that the best way to arrange the 'walls' would be to join the panels at 120° angles. However, to his disappointment, office designers realized that they could squash more people into the available space if they arranged the 'walls' at 90° to form the classic cubicle. Propst also believed that people needed to stand as often as they sat (he was ahead of his time). So he created storage spaces located away from the cubicles to encourage workers to move about and encourage 'meaningful traffic'.

But cubicles were not universally popular. The unadorned open-plan arrangements were demotivating, but cubicles did not solve all their problems. Open-plan offices were noisy and distracting, but cubicles could be

just as bad. Cubicles failed to block unwanted noise, and at the same time could block natural light. Cubicles could even make people behave badly according to researchers at Cornell University, who found that employees in cubicles were more likely than those in open-plan offices to have loud (and long) conversations with visiting colleagues. This, they say, is possibly because cubicles 'mask the social cues such as facial expressions and body language that influence social interactions'. They also it easier to consume an antisocially smelly lunch or have loud conversations on the phone, oblivious to their colleagues' reactions. But cubicles are still being used in offices around the world. One explanation for this is that privacy is so valued that office planners try to create the illusion of it. This seems to be borne out by the way people personalize their cubicles with, amongst other things, pictures, flowers and rugs, even in some cases, curtains at the entrance, wallpaper, fairy lights and chandeliers.

colleagues and their frequency of communication. The 'Allen curve' estimated that we are four times as likely to communicate regularly with a colleague sitting two metres away from us as with someone 20 metres away (for example, separate floors marks a cut-off point for the regular exchange of certain types of technical information). As some experts have pointed out, the office is no longer just a physical place; email, remote conferencing and collaboration tools mean that colleagues can communicate without ever seeing each other. However, one study[12] showed that so-called distance-shrinking technology actually makes close proximity more important, with both face-to-face and digital communications following the Allen curve. Another study showed that engineers who shared a physical office were 20 per cent more likely to stay in touch digitally than those who worked elsewhere. Also, when they needed to collaborate closely, closely located colleagues e-mailed each other four times as frequently as colleagues in different locations.

The effect of workplace design on customers – servicescapes

If the appearance of an operation affects how its staff feel about working there, it certainly will also affect customers if they enter the workplace, as they do in 'high-visibility' operations. The term that is often used to describe the look and feel of the environment within an operation from a customer's perspective is its 'servicescape' (although it is sometimes also applied to how staff view their environment). There are many academic studies that have shown that the servicescape of an operation plays an important role, both positive and negative, in shaping customers' views.[13] The general idea is that ambient conditions, space factors and signs and symbols in a service operation will create an 'environmental experience' both for employees and for customers; and this environmental experience should support the service concept.

> **Operations principle**
>
> Layout should include consideration of the look and feel of the operation to customers and/or staff.

OPERATIONS IN PRACTICE

Servicescapes in bank branches

...but first, coffee

Although there is something of a question mark over the future of retail banks (several banks are axing many of their branches), they are keen to make sure that those that do remain have a warm and friendly feeling. This is why they pay so much attention to the décor and design of their branches. This even extends to their smell. When customers visit one South London branch of Lloyds Bank they are greeted by an attractive aroma. It is the fragrance of 'white tea and thyme', a scent carefully chosen to conjure up the right feeling in the bank's customers. Says the building's designer, Sarah Harrison, 'It gives that inviting feel, that welcoming feel. You can smell it on the High Street when the wind's blowing in the right direction.' But Lloyds is not only experimenting with perfume; there are other opportunities for 'designing' sensory experience. In one of its branches (in Manchester, UK) the impression has been described as of being in a 'high-tech giant's headquarters'. The traditional utilitarian furniture found in many traditional bank branches has been thrown out in favour of cool armchairs and free Wi-Fi. The branch also has its own coffee shop (partly because the aroma of coffee seems to lure potential new customers), stylish 'breakout pods' and the newest biometric technology. Lloyds' objective is to blend new technology with more traditional face-to-face expertise, so that their customers will find all they need in a bank, but in a reimagined setting.

The individual factors that influence this experience will then lead to certain responses (again, in both employees and customers). These responses can be put into three main categories:

▶ cognitive (what people think),
▶ emotional (what they feel), and
▶ physiological (what their bodies experience).

However, remember that a servicescape will contain not only objective, measurable and controllable stimuli but also subjective, immeasurable and often uncontrollable stimuli, which will influence customer behaviour. The obvious example is other customers frequenting an operation. As well as controllable stimuli such as the colour, lighting, design, space and music, other factors such as the number, demographics and appearance of one's fellow customers will also shape the impression of the operation.

What information and analysis is needed to design the layout and look of facilities?

Designing the layout and look of any operation's facilities will eventually move onto considering the details of the design. This means operationalizing the broad principles that governed the choice of whichever basic layout type was chosen and whatever aesthetic effect is wanted. But any detailed design should be based on the collection and manipulation of information regarding the nature and volume of the flow that the layout must accommodate, and the behaviour and preferences of staff and (if appropriate) customers.

Information for flow analysis of layouts

At a detailed level, layout can be complex. Often there are very many alternative ways to position facilities relative to each other. For example, in the very simplest case of just two work centres, there are only two ways of arranging these *relative to each other*. But there are six ways of arranging three centres and 120 ways of arranging five centres. This relationship is a factorial one. For N centres, there are factorial N ($N!$) different ways of arranging the centres, where:

$$N! = N \times (N - 1) \times (N - 2) \times \ldots \ (1)$$

So, for a relatively simple layout with, say, 20 work centres, there are $20! = 2.433 \times 10^{18}$ ways of arranging the operation. This is called 'combinatorial complexity' and it makes optimal layout solutions difficult to achieve in practice. Most layouts are designed by a combination of intuition, common sense, and systematic trial and error, a process that can be supported by using computer-aided design (CAD) software. Some of these treat the combinatorial complexity issue by using heuristic procedures. Heuristic procedures use what have been described as 'shortcuts in the reasoning process' and 'rules of thumb' in the search for a reasonable solution. They do not search for an optimal solution (though they might find one by chance) but rather attempt to derive a good suboptimal solution. However, both the information that is required, and how it is used, depends on the basic layout type that has been chosen.

> **Operations principle**
> Layouts are often combinatorially complex; there are many alternative layouts.

Information and analysis for the design of fixed-position layouts

In fixed-position arrangements the location of resources will be determined, not on the basis of the flow of transformed resources, but on the convenience of transforming resources themselves. The objective of the detailed design of fixed-position layouts is to achieve a layout for the operation which allows all the transforming resources to maximize their contribution to the transformation process by allowing them to provide an effective 'service' to the transformed resources. The detailed layout of some fixed-position layouts, such as building sites, can become very complicated, especially if the planned schedule of activities is changed frequently. Imagine the chaos on a construction site if heavy trucks continually (and noisily) drove past the site office, delivery trucks for one contractor had to cross other contractors' areas to get to where they were storing their own materials, and the staff who spent most time at the building itself were located furthest away from it. Although there are techniques which help to locate resources on fixed-position layouts, they are not widely used.

Information and analysis for the design of functional layout

Before starting the process of detailed design in functional layouts there are some essential pieces of information which the designer needs:

▶ the area required by each work centre;
▶ the constraints on the shape of the area allocated to each work centre;
▶ the degree and direction of flow between each work centre (for example, number of journeys, number of loads or cost of flow per distance travelled);
▶ the desirability of work centres being close together or close to some fixed point in the layout.

The degree and direction of flow are usually shown on a flow record chart like that shown in Figure 7.12 in the worked example. This information could be gathered from routing information, or where flow is more random, as in a library for example, the information could be collected by observing the routes taken by customers over a typical period of time.

Minimizing distance travelled

In most examples of functional layout, the prime objective is to minimize the costs to the operation which are associated with flow through the operation. This usually means minimizing the total distance travelled in the operation, as in Figure 7.13 in the worked example. The effectiveness of the layout, at this simple level, can be calculated from:

$$\text{Effectiveness of layout} = \Sigma F_{ij} \, D_{ij} \text{ for all } i \neq j$$

where

F_{ij} = the flow in loads or journeys per period of time from work centre i to work centre j

D_{ij} = the distance between work centre i and work centre j.

The lower the effectiveness score, the better the layout.

The steps in determining the location of work centres in a functional layout is illustrated in the worked example: Rotterdam Educational Group.

Rotterdam Educational Group (REG) is a company which commissions, designs and manufactures education packs for distance-learning courses and training. It has leased a new building with an area of 1,800 square metres, into which it needs to fit 11 'departments'. Prior to moving into the new building it has conducted an exercise to find the average number of trips taken by its staff between the 11 departments. Although some trips are a little more significant than others (because of the loads carried by staff), it has been decided that all trips will be treated as being of equal value.

Step 1 – Collect information

The areas required by each department together with the average daily number of trips between departments are shown in the flow chart in Figure 7.12. In this example the direction of flow is not relevant and very low flow rates (less than five trips per day) have not been included.

Step 2 – Draw schematic layout

Figure 7.13 shows the first schematic arrangement of departments. The thickest lines represent high flow rates between 70 and 120 trips per day; the medium lines are used for flow rates between 20 and 69 trips per day; and the thinnest lines for flow rates between 5 and 19 trips per day. The objective here is to arrange the work centres so that those with the thick lines are closest together. The higher the flow rate, the shorter the line should be.

Step 3 – Adjust the schematic layout

If departments were arranged exactly as shown in Figure 7.13(a) the building which housed them would be of an irregular, and therefore high-cost, shape. The layout needs adjusting to take into account the shape of the building. Figure 7.13(b) shows the departments arranged in a more ordered fashion which corresponds to the dimensions of the building.

Step 4 – Draw the layout

Figure 7.14 shows the departments arranged with the actual dimensions of the building and occupying areas which approximate to their required areas. Although the distances between the centroids of

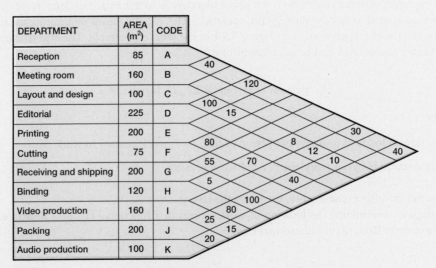

DEPARTMENT	AREA (m²)	CODE
Reception	85	A
Meeting room	160	B
Layout and design	100	C
Editorial	225	D
Printing	200	E
Cutting	75	F
Receiving and shipping	200	G
Binding	120	H
Video production	160	I
Packing	200	J
Audio production	100	K

Dimensions of the building = 30 metres × 60 metres

Figure 7.12 Flow information for Rotterdam Educational Group

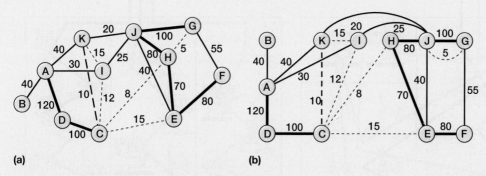

Figure 7.13 (a) Schematic layout placing centres with high traffic levels close to each other, (b) Schematic layout adjusted to fit building geometry

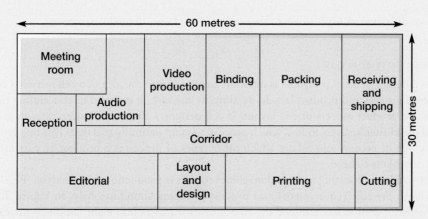

Figure 7.14 Final layout of building

departments have changed from Figure 7.14 to accommodate their physical shape, their relative positions are the same. It is at this stage that a quantitative expression of the cost of movement associated with this relative layout can be calculated.

Step 5 – Check by exchanging

The layout in Figure 7.14 seems to be reasonably effective but it is usually worthwhile to check for improvement by exchanging pairs of departments to see if any reduction in total flow can be obtained. For example, departments H and J might be exchanged, and the total distance travelled calculated again to see if any reduction has been achieved.

Information and analysis for the design of cell layout

Figure 7.15 shows how a functional layout has been divided into four cells, each of which has the resources to process a 'family' of parts. In doing this the operations management has implicitly taken two interrelated decisions regarding:

▶ the extent and nature of the cells it has chosen to adopt;
▶ which resources to allocate to which cells.

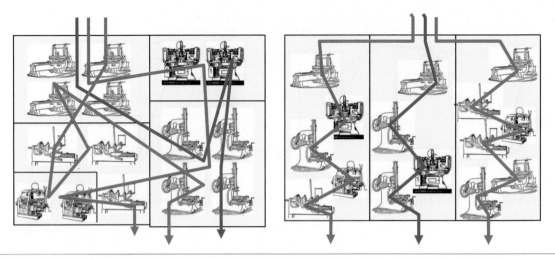

Figure 7.15 Cell layout groups the processes together which are necessary for a family of products/services

Production flow analysis[14]

The detailed design of cellular layouts is difficult, partly because the idea of a cell is itself a compromise between process and product layout. To simplify the task, it is useful to concentrate on either the process or product aspects of cell layout. If cell designers choose to concentrate on processes, they could use cluster analysis to find which processes group naturally together. This involves examining each type of process and asking which other types of processes a product or part using that process is also likely to need.

One approach to allocating tasks and machines to cells is production flow analysis (PFA), which examines both product requirements and process grouping simultaneously. In Figure 7.16(a) a manufacturing operation has grouped the components it makes into eight families – for example, the components in family 1 require machines 2 and 5. In this state the matrix does not seem to exhibit any natural groupings. If the order of the rows and columns is changed, however, to move the crosses as close as possible to the diagonal of the matrix which goes from top left to bottom right, then a clearer pattern emerges. This is illustrated in Figure 7.16(b) and shows that the machines could conveniently be grouped together in three cells, indicated on the diagram as cells A, B and C.

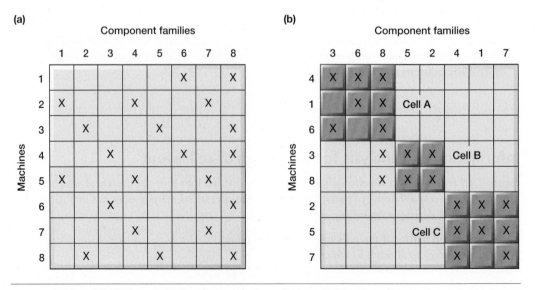

Figure 7.16 (a) and (b) Using production flow analysis to allocate machines to cells

Although this procedure is a particularly useful way to allocate machines to cells, the analysis is rarely totally clean. This is the case here where component family 8 needs processing by machines 3 and 8 which have been allocated to cell B. There are some partial solutions for this. More machines could be purchased and put into cell A. This would clearly solve the problem but requires investing capital in a new machine that might be under-utilized. Or, components in family 8 could be sent to cell B after they have been processed in cell A (or even in the middle of their processing route if necessary). This solution avoids the need to purchase another machine but it conflicts partly with the basic idea of cell layout – to achieve a simplification of a previously complex flow. Or, if there are several components like this, it might be necessary to devise a special cell for them (usually called a remainder cell) that will almost be like a mini-functional layout. This remainder cell does remove the 'inconvenient' components from the rest of the operation, however, leaving it with a more ordered and predictable flow.

Information and analysis for the design of line layout

The nature of the line layout design decision is a little different to the other layout types. Rather than 'where to place what', it is concerned more with 'what to place where'. Locations are frequently decided upon and then work tasks are allocated to each location. So the 'layout' activity is very similar to aspects of process design, which we discussed in Chapter 6. The main product layout decisions are as follows:

▶ What cycle time is needed?
▶ How many stages are needed?
▶ How should the task-time variation be dealt with?
▶ How should the layout be balanced?
▶ How should the stages be arranged ('long thin' layout to 'short fat' layout)?

Information and analysis for the design of the appearance of facilities

Traditionally, survey questionnaires and interviews have been used to assess both staff and customers' reaction to current and potential future workplace designs. Generally, indicators are developed for the questionnaires or interviews about both the level of satisfaction and the

---

OPERATIONS IN PRACTICE

Technology tracks customer flow in retail operations

Information is important to large retail operations. For years loyalty cards have been used to build profiles of shopper behaviour and preferences. Now technology is being used to refine the design and layout of shopping areas. Humans (known as 'trackers') are still used by some retailers to follow customers (discreetly) through stores to see how they flow between the various parts of a store, but it is technology that provides the greatest potential for understanding in-store flows. These technologies can include video surveillance, thermal sensing, lasers, face recognition and so-called device-based solutions.

Some of these technologies are sophisticated, but still being developed, such as face recognition linked with advanced artificial intelligence (AI) analysis. Others are more common with a proven track record, such as thermal imaging, which detects emissions from moving objects, and because it is not sensitive to light, can work in any space, no matter how well lit. But the technology that has, arguably, the most potential for capturing customer movement data is the use of sensors that pick up the unique identifier signals emitted by mobile phones as they automatically seek for Wi-Fi networks that they can join. (Bluetooth signals can also be used, but the advantage of Wi-Fi is that smartphones leave it on.) Data can be extracted from smartphone accelerometers, which can indicate where or when customers become engrossed in a display (because movement stops) or are checking out prices (phones are used frequently). However, some find the use of technology in this way a little creepy, and there are important issues of privacy involved in such customer surveillance. Data protection campaigners have warned that retailers could use phone tracking to identify and manipulate individual customers (to target ads at them, for example) without their knowledge – an issue that would be of interest to data privacy authorities. One privacy campaign group points out that the main problem is that people do not know that their phone is being used to monitor them. But others argue that if the data are used to generate only aggregated statistics, for example about surges in visitor numbers, it could be done in a privacy-friendly manner.

level of dissatisfaction. This is necessary because high levels of satisfaction do not automatically mean a low level of dissatisfaction. Different staff and/or customers can hold very different views about the positioning and appearance of layouts. More recently, some organizations have used remote recording to understand customers' and (sometimes) their staff's reaction to the layout and look of their operations.

Increasingly, it is tracking technology that is being used to collect data on customer movement (see the 'Operations in practice' example on 'Technology tracks customer flow in retail operations'). Using technology to monitor staff reaction has even more implications, especially ethically. It is treated in Chapter 9, People in operations.

Summary answers to key questions

How can the layout and look of facilities influence performance?

▶ The 'layout and look' of an operation or process means how its facilities are positioned relative to each other and how their general appearance is designed.

▶ These decisions will dictate the pattern and nature of the flow of transformed resources as they progress through the operation or process. They also affect how both the people who staff the operation and, in high-visibility operations (where customers form part of the transformed resource), how customers judge their experience of being in the operation.

▶ The objectives of layout include: minimizing (or sometimes maximizing) the flow of transformed resources, minimizing or maximizing aspects of the interaction between parts of the process, and enhancing the experience of both staff and, where appropriate, customers.

What are the basic layout types and how do they affect performance?

▶ There are four basic layout types. They are fixed-position layout, functional layout, cell layout and line layout.

▶ Partly the type of layout an operation chooses is influenced by the nature of the process type, which in turn depends on the volume–variety characteristics of the operation. Partly also the decision will depend on the objectives of the operation. Cost and flexibility are particularly affected by the layout decision.

▶ The fixed and variable costs implied by each layout differ such that, in theory, one particular layout will have the minimum costs for a particular volume level. However, in practice, uncertainty over the real costs involved in layout make it difficult to be precise about which is the minimum-cost layout.

How does the appearance of an operation's facilities affect its performance?

▶ The general appearance and aesthetics of a layout affects how staff view the operation in which they work, and how customers behave.

▶ The communication between people reduces with the distance between them. This is called the 'Allen curve'.

▶ In addition to the conventional operations objectives that will be influenced by the feel and general impression of the layout design, this is often called the 'servicescape' of the operation.

What information and analysis are needed to design the layout and look of facilities?

▶ In fixed-position layout, techniques are rarely used, but some, such as resource location analysis, bring a systematic approach to minimizing the costs and inconvenience of flow at a fixed-position location.

▶ In functional layout the detailed design task is usually (although not always) to minimize the distance travelled by the transformed resources through the operation. Either manual or computer-aided methods can be used to devise the detailed design.

▶ In cell layout the detailed design task is to group the products or customer types such that convenient cells can be designed around their needs. Techniques such as production flow analysis can be used to allocate products to cells.

▶ In line layout, the detailed design of product layouts includes a number of decisions, such as the cycle time to which the design must conform, the number of stages in the operation, the way tasks are allocated to the stages in the line and the arrangement of the stages in the line.

▶ Gathering information as the basis for the analysis of the appearance of facilities usually uses survey questionnaires and interviews to assess both staff and customers' reaction to current and potential future workplace designs. More recently, some operations have used remote recording to understand customers' and (sometimes) their staff's reaction to the layout and look of their operations.

CASE STUDY   The event hub

By Ross Richie, Warwick University

The 'event hub' was new, shiny and fitted with the latest equipment. Chief Superintendent Janice Walker was looking forward to using it as the 'Silver Commander' of the Joint Service Command (JSC) at the forthcoming 'event'. An 'event' is a term that is used to describe a wide range of public occasions, ranging from the management of a football match, a public protest or a Royal Wedding through to a critical incident such as a terrorist attack. The management of an event is a highly structured and well-practised activity, bringing together many different bodies that have an interest in it. These could include, for example, the ambulance service, the police, transport authorities, security services and local authorities, among others.

Although event command structures (who reports to whom) were clearly defined, the design of each event was unique. The operationalized command structure needed to be sufficiently flexible to cater for all the different bodies that are represented 'on the ground' (OTG). These are the ambulances you may see outside a football match or the lines of police officers escorting a demonstration. These OTG services have localized commanders, who have delegated tactical responsibility. They are called Bronze Commanders regardless of whether they belong to the ambulance, police or fire service, or any other body. Bronze Commanders all report to the Silver Commander.

The command hub

All of the OTG services and commanders report back into a centralized intelligence and decision-making command hub. It is often located away from the event, coordinated through a vast array of visual and audio communication networks. Within the hub there are representatives from each of the Bronze command units providing direct communication and command links to each of the OTG resources. Also in the hub, there is the single strategic commander – the 'Silver Commander'. In larger events, there may be as many as 80 different personnel in the command hub, coordinating between the Silver Commander and 15–20 OTG Bronze Commanders who, between them, manage more than 400 individual resources and assets.

The Silver Commander

Janice has acted as a Silver Commander before and knew that it was a highly pressured role, even though this time she would have a tactical advisor, a recorder (recording all decisions and actions), a communications officer and a runner in her support team. '*At some difficult phases of an event, you may be making several critical decisions every minute. Silver*

Commanders have to assimilate a wide range of intelligence from many sources, match this with your resources and their locations, communicate your decisions to the OTG Bronze Commanders, and do all this within strict policy and legislative constraints.'

In the upcoming event (a large protest march) Janice would have operational information inputs from:

▶ The Bronze command representatives

▶ Their communications officer (who summarizes radio communications)

▶ Intelligence feeds (from a specialist intelligence function)

▶ Any visual feeds, for example CCTV, policy logs, news and social media

She would also have advisory inputs from tactical, media and legal advisors. These advisory inputs were usually more discursive than the information coming from the OTG operational units. In the hub, the Bronze representatives would have support teams of their own. In this event, for example, the local authority planned to have five CCTV operators to support their function, whereas the ambulance service representation was only a single officer. Figure 7.17 shows the organizational 'chain of command' for the event.

Hub layout

The bodies and services represented in the hub had varying requirements. For example, some of the intelligence functions needed to be sure that their computer screens would not be overlooked by other functions that were not security cleared to an appropriate level because of the sensitivity and secrecy of their information (such as the local authority representatives). This meant that they had been located in the far corner of the hub. Yet the intelligence functions would

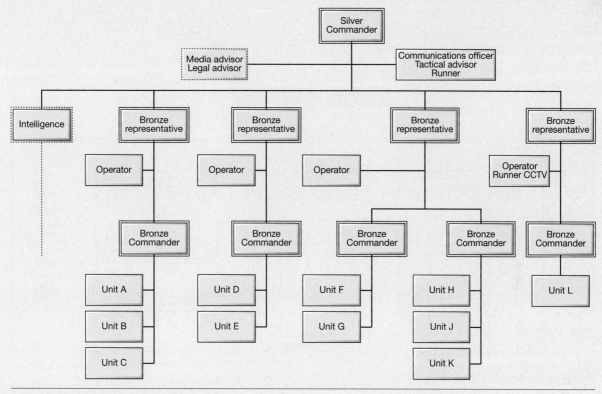

Figure 7.17 The chain of command for the event

also need to get operational updates from the ambulance service and local authority to direct their intelligence gathering efforts. Janice was worried that, because of this, there would be a high degree of travelling between different functions in the room.

The layout of the hub is shown in Figure 7.18. One of the greatest points of interest in the room was the mapping screen, where a screen placed on the wall had special-geographic information updated from all the OTG units. Both Bronze and Silver Commanders would probably need to view the real-time updates shown on this screen.

Janice, as Silver Commander, was allocated the only office in the hub. This was conventional practice because the Silver Commander needed a quiet place to go and consider his or her decisions and take confidential guidance from advisors.

Prior to the event, Janice had planned for 'update meetings' in the meeting room with 12 of her key personnel every 2 or 3 hours during the march. The meeting room was located 30 metres away from the hub, though in the same building. Also in the same building a secure area was provided for the wider intelligence functions. This was 10 metres away from the hub through two sets of locked doors. This provided a confidential area for the intelligence functions to operate without risk of information leakage.

Janice knew that events could be hectic, so in order to manage the busy room, and control the noise levels of the room, she had appointed a room manager who would sit in the centre of the room. The job of this officer would be to control movement within the room and intervene if noise levels became excessive.

What happened?

Janice was proved correct about it being hectic during the march. The first 2 hours of the protest went according to plan with good coordination within her team and between her team and the protest organizers. However, as the march progressed three things happened more or less concurrently. First, a splinter group from the march took a separate, non-agreed, route that required extra resources to police. Second, one of the people marching suffered a heart attack and needed emergency treatment and transport to the nearest hospital (difficult in the crowds). Third, an unexpected (and unauthorized), but small, counter-demonstration took place as the march passed a football stadium. And although the two sets of demonstrators were kept apart, there was raised tension and a need for extra monitoring of the situation. All of this resulted in an intense period of decision making and information gathering. Janice found herself continually moving between her office, their command

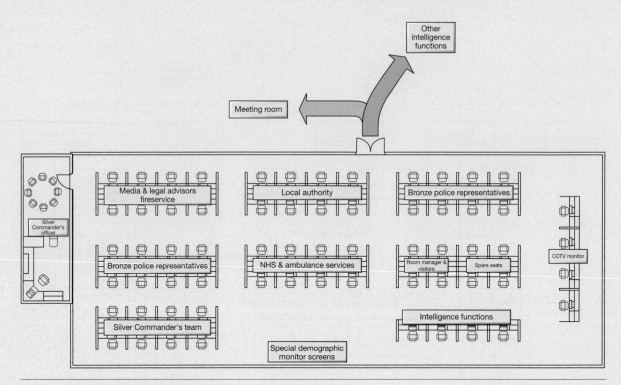

Figure 7.18 The layout of the command hub

teams and the screens, never spending more than a couple of minutes in one place. She was often followed by the tactical advisor, recorder and communications officer who had to run between her and their workstations because their computers and radios were fixed to the desk.

To try and reduce the travel of her staff, finally Janice abandoned her office and moved her chair over alongside her 'Silver Commander's team' area, close to the information screen. However, the general noise levels in the room were interrupting discussions, and Janice's update meetings were disturbing others in the room.

The move had a positive effect of unifying Janice and her team. However, now there was a constant flow of Bronze representatives and media advisors to and from the area where Janice was sitting. Yet this was preferable to the earlier disruption caused by Janice moving around the room. She also made a further decision, which was not to consult with the CCTV footage or the information screen, and moved her desk away from the screen area. 'It was information overload', said Janice. 'Using these boards, I don't need to micro-manage the

resources – this is what my extended chain of command is in place to do.'

After several hectic hours, the event concluded successfully, with no injuries or serious incidents, and with the operation being regarded as very successful. However, Janice had firm views on the new hub layout. 'The layout of the room hindered decision-making. The transfer of information on this kind of time-critical operation is vital. There must be a better way of setting out the hub. It would not require much capital to re-design the area to reflect what we do. It could be more like a production process that takes into account the common transfer processes between each function.'

QUESTIONS

1 What should an ideal design of an Event Centre be able to do?

2 Sketch out a layout for an Event Centre that would work better than the existing one.

Problems and applications

All chapters have 'Problems and applications' questions that will help you practise analysing operations. They can be answered by reading the chapter. Model answers for the first two questions can be found on the companion website for this book.

1   Revisit the 'Operations in practice' example 'Technology tracks customer flow in retail operations'. Then visit a supermarket and observe people's behaviour. You may wish to try and observe which areas they move slowly past and which areas they seem to move past without paying attention to the products. (You may have to exercise some discretion when doing this; people generally don't like to be stalked round the supermarket too obviously.) Try and verify, as far as you can, some of the principles that were outlined in the box. (a) What layout type is a conventional supermarket and how does it differ from a manufacturing operation using the same layout type? (b) Some supermarkets are using customer tracking technology that traces the flow of customers through the shop. What are the benefits of using this type of technology for supermarkets?

2   In an assembly operation for customized laboratory equipment the flow of materials through eight departments is as shown in Table 7.2. Assuming that the direction of the flow of materials is not important, construct a relationship chart, a schematic layout and a suggested layout, given that each department is the same size and the eight departments should be arranged four along each side of a corridor.

Table 7.2 Flow of materials between departments in standard container loads per day

		From							
		Dept 1	Dept 2	Dept 3	Dept 4	Dept 5	Dept 6	Dept 7	Dept 8
To	Dept 1		30						
	Dept 2	10		15	10				
	Dept 3		5		12	2		15	
	Dept 4		6			10	10		
	Dept 5				8		8	10	12
	Dept 6					2		30	
	Dept 7						13		2
	Dept 8				10	6		15	

3   The assembler of customised laboratory equipment negotiates a long-term arrangement to supply a simplified standard product to be sold to forensic laboratories worldwide. This product requires an assembly sequence that takes it, in order, from Departments 2 to 4 to 8 to 5. Estimates of demand indicate that the new product would account for 30 standard container loads per day. If this new product came to be seen as a permanent addition to the operation's work, how might the layout need to be changed?

4   A company that produces a wide range of specialist educational kits for 5–10-year-olds is based in an industrial unit arranged in a simple layout of six departments, each performing a separate task. The layout is shown in Figure 7.19, together with the results of an investigation of the flow of parts and products between each department. However, the company plans to revamp its product range. *'This new range will totally replace our existing products, and although I believe our existing layout is fine for the current product range, I think that we will need to reconfigure*

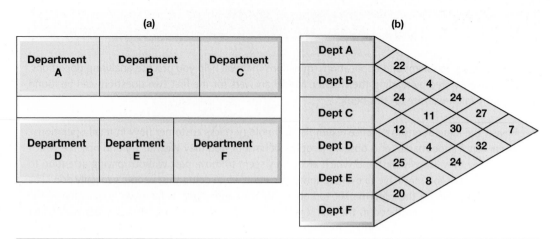

Figure 7.19 (a) The current layout of the educational kits producer, and (b) the current interdepartmental flow of parts and products (in pallet loads)

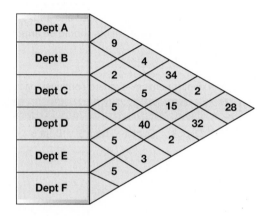

Figure 7.20 Estimated interdepartmental flow when the new product range is introduced

our layout when we make the transition to the new product range' (COO of the company). The estimate for the flow between the departments when the new product range is introduced is shown in Figure 7.20. (a) Is the COO right in thinking that the current layout is right for the current product range? (b) Assuming that the estimate of future interdepartmental flow is correct, how would you rearrange the factory?

5   A computer games developer is moving into new offices. The new office has a floor space of approximately 300 square metres in the form 20 metres by 15 metres. The company has six departments, as identified in Figure 7.21. This also shows the approximate area required by each department and the degree of closeness required between each department.

6   The operations manager of a specialist company assembling seabed monitors that record pollution levels had a dilemma. *'At the moment, we are producing around 40 seabed monitoring stations per year using what is basically a fixed-position layout. However, as volume increases over the next few years, we could move over to using a cell layout with two cells, one for use assembling monitors for tropical waters and one for colder waters. We know that the fixed costs associated with our current layout are €20,000 per year and the variable cost is €380 per unit. Using a cell layout, we think that the fixed cost per year will be €35,000 per year, but it could be as high as €40,000 or as low as €30,000 per year. We are clearer on*

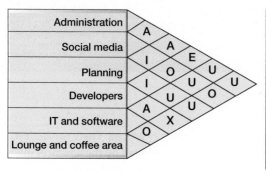

Department	Approximate area (sq. mtrs.)
Administration	35
Social media	35
Planning	45
Developers	80
IT and software	60
Lounge and coffee area	45

Code	Degree of closeness
A	Essential
E	Very important
I	Important
O	Neutral
U	Unimportant
X	Not desirable

Figure 7.21 The required areas and closeness for the six departments of the computer games developer

the variable cost, which we are fairly sure will be €60 per unit.' How much would the company's volume need to increase to be certain that the cell layout would be less costly?

Selected further reading

This is a relatively technical chapter and, as you would expect, most books on the subject are technical. Here are a few of the more accessible.

Karlsson, C. (1996) Radically new production systems, *International Journal of Operations and Production Management,* **vol. 16, no. 1, 8–19.**
An interesting paper because it traces the development of Volvo's factory layouts over the years.

Meyers, F.E. (2000) *Manufacturing Facilities Design and Material Handling,* **Prentice Hall, Upper Saddle River, NJ.**
Exactly what it says, thorough.

Plunkett, D. and Reid, O. (2014) *Detail in Contemporary Office Design (Detailing for Interior Design),* **Laurence King, London.**
An interior designer's take on how offices can look.

Rosenbaum, M.S. and Massiah, C. (2011) An expanded servicescape perspective, *Journal of Service Management,* **vol. 22, no. 4, 471–490.**
Academic but a good review of the research literature.

Van Meel, J., Martens, Y. and van Ree, H.J. (2010) *Planning Office Spaces: A Practical Guide for Managers and Designers,* **Laurence King, London.**
Exactly what the title says. A practical guide that includes both the 'flow' and the aesthetic aspects of office design.

White, J.A., White, J.A. Jnr and McGinnis, L.F. (1998) *Facility Layout and Location, An Analytical Approach,* **Prentice Hall Professional, Upper Saddle River, NJ.**
One for the practitioners but including many quantitative techniques.

Process technology

KEY QUESTIONS

What is process technology and why is it getting more important?

How can one understand the potential of new process technology?

How can new process technologies be evaluated?

How are new process technologies developed and implemented?

INTRODUCTION

There is a lot of new process technology around. There can be few, if any operations that have not been affected by the advances in process technology. And all indications are that the pace of technological development is not slowing down, in fact in many ways it is speeding up. This has important implications for operations managers because all operations use some kind of process technology, whether it is a simple cloud computing service or the most complex and sophisticated artificial intelligence driven automated factory. But this chapter is not particularly about specific technologies; there are too many of them, and they are changing too fast. Rather it is concerned with the questions that operations managers will need to ask, whatever the technology they are dealing with. All operations managers need to understand, in broad terms, what emerging technologies can do, how they do it, what advantages the technology can give, and what constraints it might impose on the operation. Figure 8.1 shows where the issues covered in this chapter relate to the overall model of operations management activities.

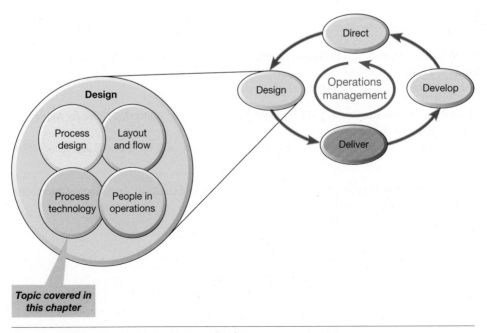

Figure 8.1 This chapter examines process technology

What is process technology and why is it getting more important?

The idea of harnessing technology to make operations more effective is not new. For example, the use of some form of automation to replace human work activities has been happening for at least the past 300 hundred years. What is new, is the sheer scope, sophistication and combination of technologies that are being deployed or developed to be part of operations activities in almost all parts of the economy. This has important implications, not only for how technology will be applied, but also for how operations are organized to make the most of new technologies' emerging capabilities. But even more important, some commentators argue, will be the rate and extent of change that operations managers will have to cope with. How operations managers deal with process technology is now one of the most important decisions that will shape the capabilities of operations.

Process technology versus product technology

Although the word 'technology' is frequently used in managerial conversation, what does this term actually mean? The *Oxford Dictionary* defines it as: 'The application of scientific knowledge for practical purposes, especially in industry.' In this chapter, we shall focus upon *process* technology as distinct from *product or service* technology. In manufacturing operations, it is a relatively simple matter to separate the two. For example, the product technology of a computer is embodied in its hardware and software. But the process technology that manufactured the computer is the technology that made and assembled all the different components. In service operations, it can be far more difficult to distinguish process from product/service technology. For example, theme parks such as Disney World use flight simulator technologies in some of their rides. These are large rooms mounted on a moveable hydraulic platform that, when combined with wide-screen projection, give a realistic experience of, say, space flight. But is it product/service or process technology? It clearly processes Disney's customers, yet the technology is also part of the product – the customers' experience. Product/service and process technologies are, in effect, the same thing.

The formal definition of process technology that we shall use here is 'the machines, equipment, and devices that *create* and/or *deliver* products and services'. Process technologies range from milking machines to exam marking software, from body scanners to bread ovens, from mobile phones to milling machines. In fact, process technology is pervasive in all types of operations. Without it, many of the products and services we all purchase would be less reliable, take longer to arrive and arrive unexpectedly, only be available in a limited variety, and be more expensive. Process technology has a very significant effect on quality, speed, dependability, flexibility and cost. That is why it is so important to operations managers, and that is why we devote a whole chapter to it.

Even when technology seems peripheral to the actual creation of goods and services, it can play a key role in *facilitating* the direct transformation of inputs to an operation. For example, the computer systems which run planning and control activities, accounting systems and stock control systems can be used to help managers and operators control and improve the processes. This type of technology is called indirect process technology. It is becoming increasingly important. Many businesses spend more on the computer systems which control their processes than they do on the direct process technology which acts on their material, information or customers.

> **Operations principle**
> Process technology is the machines, equipment and devices that create and/or deliver products and services.

It is worth noting, however, that the distinction between what is a 'product/service' technology and what is a 'process' technology can depend on context. What is one business's product/service technology is another's process technology. For example, the product/service technology that software firms embed in their planning and control systems is their customers' (indirect) process technology. Fanuc, the Japanese robot manufacturer, has a factory in Oshino, Japan, where its own industrial robots themselves produce industrial robots, supervised by a staff of only four workers per shift. The robots could be classed as *both* product and process technology.

What is 'new' in new technologies?

Why is new process technology becoming so important? Is process technology, and the way operations managers deal with it, really a more significant issue than it has always been? One can argue that it is, mainly for two reasons. The first is that most new process technologies have a greater capability than what they are replacing; in other words, new process technologies are capable of doing things that older technologies could not do, or do as well. Second, these increased capabilities have a greater scope of application; they can be applied in sectors of the economy, and in types of operation, where process technology used to be far less important.

New technologies often have increased capabilities

Even technologies, such as robots, that have become common place in many operations are becoming cheaper, more proficient and more adaptable. Algorithms used, for example, by banks to carry out routine transactions, or by parcel delivery companies to plan routes, can outperform human decision making. And when combined with artificial intelligence (AI) they can perform activities, such as medical diagnostics, previously presumed to require expert human judgement. At the same time, some technologies are becoming less expensive. Over a 20-year period, the cost of industrial robots has dropped by half while the cost of labour in developed economies has risen over 100 per cent. It is not surprising, then, that labour substitution accounts for some of the motive for adopting new technologies. But do not assume that it is always the main driver. Other performance benefits can be even more important, as we shall discuss later.

New technologies can increasingly be applied in all types of operation

The role and application of technology has always has been important for some operations. There used to be a simple division between those operations that used a lot of process technology, usually manufacturing operations, and those that used little or no process technology, usually service operations. But this is no longer true, and arguably has not been true for decades. High-volume services have for years understood the value of process technology. Online transactions for retail and other services are vital for their success. But now the scope and capabilities of so many technologies have expanded to the point where there are very few, if any, types of enterprise that are not actively using some kind of technology to support their operations processes. For example, in an airport, we check in and scan our passports using automated machines, progress through security with our bags (and sometimes ourselves) having been subjected to (semi-) automatic scanning, and obtain access to the gate by scanning our boarding card or phone image. Even when on the flight, the pilots may actively steer aircraft only for a few minutes before the autopilot takes over for the rest of the journey. But even relatively low-volume, high-variety professional services such as legal and medical services can benefit from new and value-adding technologies.

Operations principle

New process technologies can have increased capabilities and greater scope of application.

Process technology and transformed resources

One common method of distinguishing between different types of process technology is by what the technology actually processes – materials, information or customers. We used this distinction in Chapter 1 when we discussed inputs to operations and processes.

Material-processing technologies

These include any technology that shapes, transports, stores, or in any way changes physical objects. It obviously includes the machines and equipment found in manufacturing operations (robots, 3D printing, computer integrated manufacturing systems and so on), but also includes trucks, conveyors, packing machines, warehousing systems and even retail display units. In manufacturing operations, technological advances have meant that the ways in which metals, plastics, fabric and other materials are processed have improved over time. Generally, it is the

Technology or people? The future of jobs[1]

In his book, *The Power of Habit,* Charles Duhigg[2] relates a story to demonstrate that human beings are more predictable than we sometimes like to think. A man walked into a supermarket to complain to the manager. The supermarket had been sending direct mail to the man's daughter containing discount vouchers for baby clothes and equipment. 'She is only in high school', the father protested. The manager apologized profusely. 'It the fault of a new program that predicted pregnancy based on the buying behaviour of their customers', he said. It was obviously a mistake and he was very sorry. A few days later, the man again visited the supermarket and said that it was his turn to apologize. His daughter was indeed pregnant and due to give birth in a few months' time. The point of the story is that technology is increasing in sophistication to the extent that it is now capable of performing tasks that previously required skilled people making judgements based on insight and experience. Moreover, technology can often do those tasks better. A piece of software has replaced the marketing team trying to guess whom to sell baby clothes to. So technology is not only replacing people, but it is also 'climbing the skills ladder' all the time.

Of course, technological advances have always had an impact on the type of jobs that are in demand by businesses, and by extension, the type of jobs that are eliminated. So, much of the highly routine work of some mass manufacturing, or the type of standardized accounting processes that pay invoices, have been overtaken by the 'the robot and the spreadsheet'. Yet the type of work that is more difficult to break down into a set of standardized elements is less prone to being displaced by technology. The obvious examples of work that is difficult to automate are the type of management tasks that involve decision-making based on judgement and insight, teaching small children, diagnosing complex medical conditions, and so on. However, the future may hold a less certain future for such jobs. As the convenience of data collection and analysis becomes more sophisticated, and process knowledge increases, it becomes easier to break more types of work down into routine constituents, which allows them to be automated. However, the extent to which such automation will take hold is disputed. Carl Benedikt Frey and Michael Osborne, of the University of Oxford, maintain that the range of jobs that are likely to be automated is far higher than many assume, especially traditionally white-collar jobs such as accountancy, legal work, technical writing and (even) teaching. It is not simply that technology is getting cleverer; in addition, it can exploit the capability to access to far more data. Frey and Osborne even go so far as to estimate the probability that technology will mean job losses for certain jobs in the next two decades (bravely, because such forecasting is notoriously difficult). Amongst jobs most at risk are telemarketers (0.99, where 1.0 = certainty), accountants and auditors (0.94), retail salespersons (0.92), technical writers (0.89) and retail estate agents (0.86). Those jobs least likely to be replaced include actors (0.37), firefighters (0.17), editors (0.06), chemical engineers (0.02), athletic trainers (0.007) and dentists (0.004). Yet another study by the OECD (a group of relatively rich countries) claims these forecasts are too gloomy, and fewer people's jobs are likely to be destroyed by artificial intelligence and robots than has been suggested. However, many people will face a future in which their jobs may change significantly as technology affects the way processes are designed.

initial forming and shaping of materials at the start, and the handling and movement through the supply network that has been most affected by technology advances. Assembling parts to make products, although far more automated that once it was, presents more technical challenges.

Information-processing technology

Information-processing technology, or just information technology (IT), is the most common single type of technology within operations, and includes any device which collects, manipulates, stores or distributes information. Initially, it was the use of Internet-based technology that had the most obvious impact on operations – especially those that are concerned with buying and selling activity. Its advantage was that it increased both reach (the number of customers who could be reached and the number of items they could be presented with) and richness (the amount of detail which could be provided concerning both the items on sale and customers' behaviour in buying them). Subsequently, other types of information-processing technologies came to provide opportunities for process innovation, particularly those involving some form of analytical capability, such as algorithmic decision making, artificial intelligence (AI) and data mining, those involving communication or connectivity, such as blockchain, and those capable of processing visual information, such as augmented reality (AU).

Customer-processing technology

Although customer-processing operations were once seen as 'low-technology', now process technology is very much in evidence in many services. Increasingly the human element of service is being reduced with customer-processing technology being used to give an acceptable level of service while significantly reducing costs. There are three types of customer-processing technologies. The first category includes active interaction technology such as automobiles, online shopping, fitness equipment and self-checkout stations. In all of these customers themselves are using the technology to create the service. By contrast, aircraft, mass transport systems, moving walkways, elevators, cinemas, 'fitness' monitors and most theme park rides are passive interactive technologies; they 'process' (and sometimes control) customers (or aspects of a customer) in some way, but do not expect the customer to take a direct part in the interaction. Some customer-processing technology is 'aware' of customers but not the other way around: for example, security monitoring, or face recognition technologies in shopping malls or at national frontier customs areas. The objective of these 'hidden technologies' is to track customers' movements or transactions in an unobtrusive way.

Integrating technologies

Of course, some technologies process more than one type of resource, and/or are combinations of other technologies. These technologies are called 'integrating technologies'. For example, electronic point of sale (EPOS) technology integrates scanning and information technologies and processes shoppers, products and information. Perhaps the most-discussed of the more recent integrating technologies is 'industry 4.0'. This is the term for the automation and integration of manufacturing technologies. It is explained in more detail later.

How should operations managers manage process technology?

So, what are the responsibilities of operations managers as regards the management of process technology? It has always been an important issue to them because they are continually involved in the choice, installation and management of process technology. Now, with the increased potential of new technologies, how do operations managers decide on the best way of enabling their use, especially in circumstances where such technologies have not previously been appropriate? They should be able to do three things.

▶ First, they need to understand the technology to the extent that they are able to articulate what it should be able to do; not in the sense that they need to be experts in whatever constitutes the core science of the technology, but enough to understand its implications.

▶ Second, they should be able to evaluate alternative technologies, particularly as they affect the operations they manage, and share in the decisions of which technology to choose.

▶ Third, they must be able to manage – that is, develop, plan and implement – the technology so that it can reach its full potential in contributing to the performance of the operation as a whole.

Operations principle

Operations managers need to be able to understand, evaluate and manage new process technologies.

These are the three issues which this rest of this chapter deals with. They are illustrated in Figure 8.2.

Understanding the potential of new process technology

The first responsibility of operations managers is to gain an understanding of what a process technology can do. But 'understanding process technology' does not (necessarily) mean knowing the details of the science and engineering embedded in the technology. It means knowing enough about the principles behind the technology to be comfortable in evaluating some technical information, capable of dealing with experts in the technology and confident enough to ask relevant questions.

The four key questions

In particular the following four key questions can help operations managers to grasp the essentials of the technology.

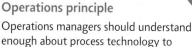

Operations principle

Operations managers should understand enough about process technology to evaluate alternatives.

▶ What does the technology do which is different from other similar technologies?
▶ How does it do it? That is, what particular characteristics of the technology are used to perform its function?
▶ What benefits does using the technology give to the operation?
▶ What constraints or risks does using the technology place on the operation?

For example, look at the worked example on QB House to think through these four key questions.

Emerging technologies – understand their primary capabilities

The four questions listed above are universal, in the sense that they can help to understand the implications for operations management of any new or emerging technology. But operations managers are not immune from more general public perceptions of the importance of new technologies, which is why it is worthwhile considering how technologies are seen.

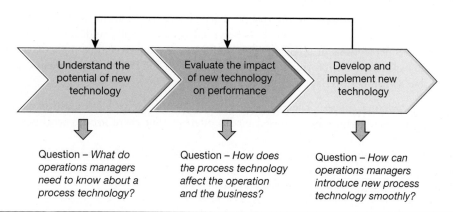

Figure 8.2 The three stages of process technology management

One day, in Japan, Kuniyoshi Konishi became so frustrated at having to wait to get his hair cut and then pay over 3,000 yen for the privilege, he decided that there must be a better way to offer this kind of service. *'Why not'*, he said, *'create a no-frills barber shop where the customer could get a haircut in ten minutes at a cost of 1,000 yen (€7)?'* He realized that a combination of technology and process design could eliminate all non-essential elements from the basic task of cutting hair. He achieved this in his chain of barbers called QB House. How is it done? First QB House's barbers never handle cash. Each shop has a ticket vending machine that accepts 1,000 yen bills (and gives no change!) and issues a ticket that the customer gives the barber in exchange for the haircut. Second, QB House does not take reservations. The shops don't even have telephones. Therefore, no receptionist is needed, or anyone to schedule appointments. Third, QB House developed a lighting system to indicate how long customers will have to wait. Electronic sensors under each seat in the waiting area and in each barber's chair track how many customers are waiting in the shop and different coloured lights are displayed outside the shop. Green lights indicate that there is no waiting, yellow lights indicate a wait of about 5 minutes and red lights indicate that the wait may be around 15 minutes. This system can also keep track of how long it takes for each customer to be served. Fourth, QB has done away with the traditional Japanese practice of shampooing its customers after the haircut to remove any loose hairs. Instead, the barbers use QB House's own 'air wash' system where a vacuum cleaner hose is pulled down from the ceiling and used to vacuum the customer's hair clean. The QB House system has proved so popular that its shops (now over 200) can be found not only in Japan but in many other South East Asian countries such as Singapore, Malaysia and Thailand. Each year almost 4,000,000 customers experience QB House's 10-minute haircuts.

Analysis

▶ *What does the technology do?* – Signals availability of servers, so managing customers' expectations. Avoids hairdressers having to handle cash. Speeds service by substituting 'air wash' for traditional shampoo.

▶ *How does it do it?* – Uses simple sensors in seats, ticket dispenser and air wash blowers.

▶ *What benefits does it give?* – Faster service with predictable wait time (dependable service) and lower costs, therefore less expensive prices.

▶ *What constraints or risks does it impose?* – Risks of customer perception of quality of service. It is not an 'indulgent' service. It is a basic, but value, service in which customers need to know what to expect and how to use it.

General perceptions of new technologies

Sometimes it is difficult to separate the reality of a new technology from the publicity and speculation that surrounds it, especially when its potential is not yet fully understood. One attempt to illustrate how perceptions of a technology's usefulness develop over time is the 'Gartner hype cycle' created by Gartner, the information technology research and consultancy company. It has five sequential (but sometimes overlapping) stages.

▶ *Stage 1 – 'technology trigger'*: The early stages of a technology; it probably exists in a theoretical or prototype stage (which has aroused media interest), but there are no working practical demonstrations.

▶ *Stage 2 – 'peak of inflated expectations'*: The technology has developed to the point where it is implemented by some more adventurous 'early adopter' operations. There is press coverage describing both successful and unsuccessful experiences.

- *Stage 3 – 'trough of disillusionment'*: The difficulties of using the technology in practical situations start to demonstrate its shortcomings. This results in something of a backlash, leading to disappointment and disillusionment with the technology.
- *Stage 4 – 'slope of enlightenment'*: Problems with the technology are slowly solved and its potential becomes more realistically understood. It is adopted by an increasing number of operations that learn how to implement it in their context.
- *Stage 5 – 'plateau of productivity'*: The technology, in its developed form, becomes widely adopted, probably with technical standards being shared by users and suppliers.

Classifying technologies by their primary capabilities

Any in-depth understanding of a technology calls for a knowledge of what, in general terms, it actually does. In other words, what is its 'primary capability? What is it better at than the technology that it replaces? Figure 8.3 shows some technologies that, at the time of writing, were new(ish). This is certainly not a fully comprehensive list. Some technologies are specialist, in the sense that their application is limited to one type of operation. Other technologies are (again, at the time of writing) still very much in their development stage. The intention is not to provide a comprehensive survey of technologies – that could be expanded into a whole book – nor is it to delve into technical details. Rather it is to demonstrate how operations managers have to look 'behind' the technology in order to start to understand what it is intended to do. The figure positions the technologies relative to five 'primary capabilities':

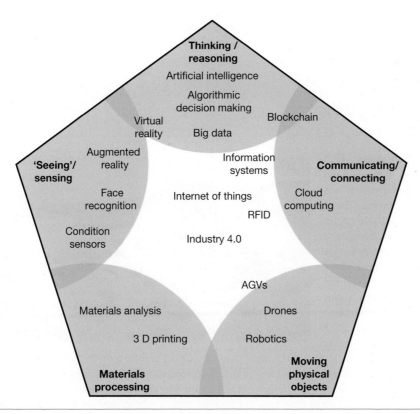

Figure 8.3 New and emerging technologies positioned relative to five 'primary capabilities': thinking/reasoning, seeing/sensing, communicating/connecting, moving physical objects, processing materials

▶ Technologies that can think, or reason
▶ Technologies that can see, or sense
▶ Technologies that can communicate, or connect
▶ Technologies that can move physical objects
▶ Technologies that can process materials

Technologies that can think, or reason

The best-known class of technology that attempts to replicate (and even surpass) human thinking is *artificial intelligence* (AI). This is an *'area of computer science that emphasizes the creation of intelligent machines that work and react like humans. Some of the activities computers with artificial intelligence are designed for include, speech recognition, learning, planning, and problem solving'*.[4] Since computers were developed, people have worked with, and been augmented by them. AI challenges this relationship as computers improve their capabilities to take more control. Somewhat less sophisticated, but more widely used (currently) in operations management is *algorithmic decision making*. An algorithm is a predefined sequence of instructions, or rules. Many of the models used in this book are algorithms that could be incorporated into decision-making routines. Algorithmic decision making may be combined with large data sets (often called 'big data').

Big data is a large volume of both structured and unstructured data whose analysis can reveal hidden patterns, correlations and other insights. Looking for relevant or pertinent information in big data sets is called data mining.

OPERATIONS IN PRACTICE

Go figure[5]

It was a significant event in the development of artificial intelligence (AI). Between 9 and 15 March 2016 a five-game match was played in the South Korean capital Seoul between arguably the best professional Go player called Lee Sedol and AlphaGo, a computer Go program developed by Google DeepMind. AlphaGo won the contest by 4 games to 1. Some commentators saw the event as a continuation of the 'man versus machine' chess battles that started when chess master Garry Kasparov lost to a computer named Deep Blue in a six-game match played in 1997. In fact, games like chess are a handy way to gauge a computer's evolution towards genuine artificial intelligence. This is where Go comes in. Although seemingly simple, it is a far more complex game than chess. Played all over East Asia, it is particularly popular with AI researchers in particular, for whom the idea of truly mastering Go has become something of an obsession. Why? Because compared with Go, teaching computers to master chess is easy. The size of a Go board means that the number of games that can be played on it is colossal: probably around 10^{170}, which is almost 100 orders of magnitude greater than the number of atoms in the observable universe

▶

(estimated to be around 10^{80}). As one of DeepMind's creators, Dr Demis Hassabis, points out, simply using raw computing power cannot master Go. Much more than chess, Go involves recognizing patterns that result from groups of stones surrounding empty spaces. Players can refer to seemingly vague notions such as 'light' and 'heavy' patterns of stones. *'Professional Go players talk a lot about general principles, or even intuition'*, says Dr Hassabis, *'whereas if you talk to professional chess players they can often do a much better job of explaining exactly why they made a specific move.'*

However, ideas such as 'intuition' are much harder to describe algorithmically than the formal rules of any game. That's why, before AlphaGo was developed, the best Go programs were little better than a skilled amateur. The breakthrough of AlphaGo was to combine some of the same ideas as the older programs with new approaches that focused on how the computer could develop its own 'instinct' about the best moves to play. It uses a technique that its makers have called 'deep learning' that allows the computer to develop an understanding of the instinctive rules of the game that experienced players can understand but cannot fully explain. It develops this learning by playing games against itself (or a slightly different version of itself) and analysing the vast amounts of data to sort out these 'intuitive' rules. However, as well as masses of data 'deep learning' also requires plenty of processing power. Yet it is the 'deep learning' that was being seen as the exciting development that would lead to further applications. Such an approach could help computers to do complex tasks like accurate face recognition or translate subtleties of meaning from one language to another. But, although the techniques used by AlphaGo are an important step in the progress to what in Dr Hassabis's view is the *'same sort of broad, fluid intelligence as a human being'*, they still lack some of the abilities that humans take for granted. Possibly the most important of these is the ability to apply lessons learned in one situation in another, what AI researchers call 'reasoning by analogy' or 'transfer learning'.

Technologies that can see, or sense

Some technologies exploit their ability to manipulate computer-generated or computer augmented visual information. For example, *augmented reality* technologies show an enhanced version of reality where live views of physical real-world environments are augmented with overlaid computer-generated images, thus supplementing one's perception of reality. *Virtual reality* goes further by using entirely computer-generated simulations, with which humans can interact in a seemingly real manner using special helmets and gloves fitted with sensors. Although both augmented and virtual reality technologies are used in entertainment operations, they are also valuable in surgery training, maintenance planning and process design. Both of these involve people using technology to view objects. *Face recognition* is the reverse of this. It uses still or video images of a scene to identify or verify one or more individuals using a stored database of faces, so that those people can be identified for (say) automatic charging for a service, or for security or advertising purposes. *Condition sensor* technologies are more intimate. They sense characteristics of people (e.g. fitness monitors), or materials (e.g. quality control sensors).

Technologies that can communicate, or connect

Arguably, the most significant capability that is increasingly built into many process technologies is the ability to network, connect or communicate with other elements in an operations process. For example, *cloud computing* applications allow dispersed groups of people to collaborate virtually, using shared information (in real time) and shared storage of information. *Blockchain* technology also relies on connected networks, but rather than 'share' it uses distributed databases in such a way that they maintain a shared list of records (called blocks), where each encrypted block of code contains the history of every block that came before it, with each transaction 'timestamped'. There is transparency within the network, but no single point where records could be hacked or corrupted. At a more technical level, communication between physical objects has been made significantly more effective through the use of *RFID* technologies. These devices use radio waves to automatically identify objects, collect data about them, and communicate it into *information systems* (integrated sets of components for collecting, storing and processing data, and for providing information and knowledge).

Technologies that can move physical objects

Robots are often credited with almost human-like abilities, but in fact are primarily used for handling materials, such as loading and unloading work pieces onto a machine, for processing where a tool is gripped by the robot, and for assembly where the robot places parts together. Some robots have some limited sensory feedback through vision control and touch control. A close relation of a robot is an *automated guided vehicle* (AGV). This is a materials-handling system that uses automated vehicles that are programmed to move between different stations (usually in a manufacturing or warehouse setting) without a driver. On a more airborne level, aerial *drones,* both guided and autonomous, are increasingly used in industrial applications. Non-military uses include safety and quality inspection, filming and journalism, search and rescue, precision agriculture and short-haul delivery.

Technologies that can process materials

The various developments in materials-processing technology tend to be too specialized and technical to grab popular attention. Nevertheless, plenty of new (or newish) processes are having a sometimes-significant effect on the economics and practice of materials-processing operations. Everything from miniaturization, to the use of lasers, to the creation of products with complex shapes and multi-functional materials, has opened novel processing opportunities. One technology that has received publicity is *3D printing,* also known as additive manufacturing. A 3D printer produces a three-dimensional object by laying down layer upon layer of material until the final form is obtained. But 3D printing is not a new technology as such. Since the 1990s it has been used to make prototype products quickly and cheaply prior to full production. Now it is increasingly used for finished products for real customers. Importantly, because the technology is 'additive' it reduces waste significantly. Sometimes as much as 90 per cent of material is wasted in machining some aerospace parts, for example.

Technologies with more than one primary capability

Some of the technologies described above have more than one primary capability, even if one of them is dominant. Virtual reality, for example, is a visual technology, but could not work without a relatively powerful thinking/reasoning capability. Automatic guided vehicles are concerned primarily with moving physical objects, but can frequently communicate, 'see' where they are going, and reason to work out alternative routes. Other important technologies combine even more primary capabilities. The *internet of things* (IoT) exploits the potential of RFID technology with its sensors and actuators, connects them using wireless networks and allows information systems and physical networks to merge. SAP, the developer of Enterprise Resource systems, describes the internet of things as: '*A world where physical objects are seamlessly integrated into the information network, and where the physical objects can become active participants in business processes. Services are available to interact with these "smart objects" over the Internet, query and change their state and any information associated with them, taking into account security and privacy issues.*'[6]

Perhaps the most developed of these technologies that combine several primary capabilities has become known as *Industry 4.0.* The name derives from the contention that there have been four industrial revolutions: first, mechanization through water and steam power; second, mass production and assembly lines powered by electricity; third, computerization and automation; and finally, fourth, smart factories combining digital, virtual and physical systems. The name Industry 4.0 was first publicly used in 2011 as 'Industrie 4.0' by a group of business people, political representatives and academics, meeting as an initiative to improve German manufacturing competitiveness. The German federal government formed a working group that published a vision for Industry 4.0 as: '*these Cyber-Physical Systems comprise smart machines, storage systems and production facilities capable of autonomously exchanging information, triggering actions and controlling each other independently. This facilitates fundamental improvements to the industrial processes involved in manufacturing, engineering, material usage and supply chain and life cycle management.*'

Love it or hate it, Marmite's energy recycling technology[7]

For those readers who live in regions of the world where Marmite is not a big seller, Marmite is 'a nutritious savoury spread that contains B vitamins, enjoyable in a sandwich, on toast, bread or even as a cooking ingredient'. It is not to everyone's taste, which is why it is advertised with the line '...you'll either love it or hate it'. But behind the clever advertising, Marmite, which is part of Unilever, the large food company, is a pioneer in recycling the leftovers from its production process into energy at the factory where it is made. The factory is in Burton upon Trent in the UK and every year around 18,000 tonnes of solidified Marmite deposit is left adhering to the surfaces of the machines and handling equipment that are used to produce the product. For years this residue was cleaned off and then either flushed into the sewerage system or sent to landfill sites. Then Unilever installed an anaerobic digester. This is a composter that contains microbes that feed on the waste. As they do this, they release methane, which is burned in a boiler that is connected to a generator that produces power. The system also captures the waste heat that comes

through the exhaust and helps heat the factory's water system (see Figure 8.4). But the Marmite example is just one part of Unilever's 'Sustainable Living Plan', first published in 2010. Since then it has published an update every year on the progress it is making globally and nationally towards meeting its Sustainable Living Plan targets.

Unilever publishes its performance as falling into three categories. The first is 'areas where we are making genuinely good progress'. These include sustainable sourcing, nutrition and eco-efficiency (including the Marmite project). The second category is 'areas where we have had to consider carefully how to reach our targets but are now ready to scale up', such a programme to increase the recycling rates of aerosols, encouraging more local councils to collect aerosols kerbside. 'However', the report admitted, 'we have more to do, working in partnership with industry, Government and NGOs to help to increase recycling and recovery rates'. The third category is 'areas where we are finding it difficult to make progress and will

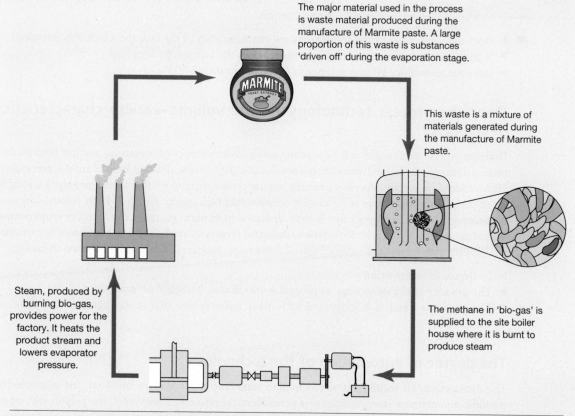

The major material used in the process is waste material produced during the manufacture of Marmite paste. A large proportion of this waste is substances 'driven off' during the evaporation stage.

This waste is a mixture of materials generated during the manufacture of Marmite paste.

The methane in 'bio-gas' is supplied to the site boiler house where it is burnt to produce steam

Steam, produced by burning bio-gas, provides power for the factory. It heats the product stream and lowers evaporator pressure.

Figure 8.4 Waste product recycling at Marmite

need to work with others to find solutions'. This includes targets that require consumer behaviour change, such as encouraging people to eat foods with lower salt levels or reducing the use of heated water in showering and washing clothes.

Amanda Sourry, Unilever UK and Ireland Chairman, said: 'The old view of growth at any cost is unacceptable; today the only responsible way to do business is through sustainable growth. It's for this reason that the Unilever Sustainable Living Plan is not just a bolt-on strategy, it's our blue-print for the future. Today's progress update shows that we've made some fantastic steps forward, particularly in the areas of sustainable sourcing, health and nutrition and reducing greenhouse gases. Just one year into the decade-long plan, we are proud of our achievements so far but there's still much more to do.'

How can new process technologies be evaluated?

The most common technology-related decision for operations managers is likely to be whether to adopt an alternative technology to whatever is currently being used. It is an important decision because process technology can have a significant effect on the operation's long-term strategic capability; no one wants to change expensive technologies too frequently. Yet, with the emergence of so many new process technologies with sometimes ambiguous capabilities, the evaluation process becomes both more difficult and more important. Added to this are new types of technological risk – security, obsolescence, implementation problems and the tendency of some organizations to get carried away with new technology for its own sake. But, whatever the difficulties, evaluation is necessary, so the characteristics of alternative technologies need to be evaluated so that they can be compared. Here we use three sets of criteria for evaluation.

Operations principle

Process technologies can be evaluated in terms of their fit with process tasks, their effect on performance and their financial impact.

▶ Does the technology fit the volume–variety characteristics of the task for which it is intended?
▶ What aspects of the operation's performance does the technology improve?
▶ Does the technology give an acceptable financial return?

Does the process technology fit the volume–variety characteristics of the task?

Different process technologies will be appropriate for different types of operations, not just because they process different transformed resources, but also because they do so at different levels of volume and variety. High variety–low volume processes generally require process technology that is *general purpose,* because it can perform the wide range of processing activities that high variety demands. High volume–low variety processes can use technology that is more *dedicated* to its narrower range of processing requirements. Within the spectrum from general purpose to dedicated process technologies, three dimensions in particular tend to vary with volume and variety. Figure 8.5 illustrates these three dimensions of process technology.

▶ Its degree of 'automation'
▶ The capacity of the technology to process work: that is, its 'scale' or 'scalability'
▶ The extent to which it is integrated with other technologies: that is, its degree of 'coupling' or 'connectivity'.

The degree of automation of the technology

To some extent, all technology needs human intervention. It may be minimal, for example the periodic maintenance interventions in a petrochemical refinery. Conversely, the person who operates the technology may be the entire 'brains' of the process, for example the surgeon using keyhole surgery techniques. The ratio of technological to human effort it employs is sometimes called

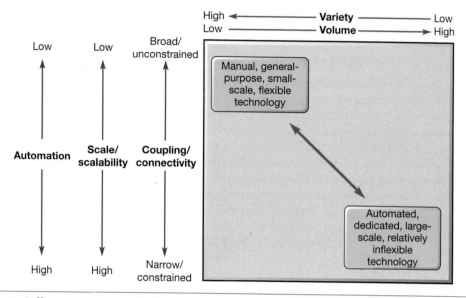

Figure 8.5 Different process technologies are important for different volume–variety combinations

the capital intensity of the process technology. Generally, processes that have high variety and low volume will employ process technology with lower degrees of automation than those with higher volume and lower variety. For example, investment banks trade in highly complex and sophisticated financial 'derivatives', often customized to the needs of individual clients, and each may be worth millions of dollars. The back-office of the bank has to process these deals to make sure that payments are made on time, documents are exchanged, and so on. Much of this processing will be done using relatively general-purpose technology such as spreadsheets. Skilled back-office staff are making the decisions rather than the technology. Contrast this with higher-volume, low-variety products, such as straightforward equity (stock) trades. Most of these products are simple and straightforward and are processed in very high volumes of several thousand per day by 'automated' technology.

The scale/scalability of the technology

There is usually some discretion as to the scale of individual units of technology. For example, the duplicating department of a large office complex may decide to invest in a single, very large, fast copier, or alternatively in several smaller, slower copiers distributed around the operation's various processes. An airline may purchase one or two wide-bodied aircraft or a larger number of smaller aircraft. The advantage of large-scale technologies is that they can usually process items more cheaply than small-scale technologies, but usually need high volume and can cope only with low variety. By contrast, the virtues of smaller-scale technology are the nimbleness and flexibility that is suited to high-variety, lower-volume processing. For example, four small machines can between them produce four different products simultaneously (albeit slowly), whereas a single large machine with four times the output can produce only one product at a time (albeit faster). Small-scale technologies are also more robust. Suppose the choice is between three small machines and one larger one. In the first case, if one machine breaks down, a third of the capacity is lost, but in the second, capacity is reduced to zero. The advantages of large-scale technologies are similar to those of large-capacity increments discussed in Chapter 5.

The equivalent to scale for some types of information-processing technology is *scalability*. By scalability we mean the ability to shift to a different level of useful capacity quickly and cost-effectively. Scalability is similar to absolute scale in so much as it is influenced by the same volume–variety characteristics. IT scalability relies on consistent IT platform architecture and the high process standardization that is usually associated with high-volume and low-variety operations.

The coupling/connectivity of the technology

Coupling means the linking together of separate activities within a single piece of process technology to form an interconnected processing system. Tight coupling usually gives fast process throughput. For example, in an automated manufacturing system, products flow quickly without delays between stages, and inventory will be lower – it can't accumulate when there are no 'gaps' between activities. Tight coupling also means that flow is simple and predictable, making it easier to keep track of parts when they pass through fewer stages, or information when it is automatically distributed to all parts of an information network. However, closely coupled technology can be both expensive (each connection may require capital costs) and vulnerable (a failure in one part of an interconnected system can affect the whole system). The fully integrated manufacturing system constrains parts to flow in a predetermined manner, making it difficult to accommodate products with very different processing requirements. So, coupling is generally more suited to relatively low variety and high volume. Higher variety processing generally requires a more open and unconstrained level of coupling because different products and services will require a wider range of processing activities.

> **Operations principle**
>
> Process technology in high-volume, low-variety processes is relatively automated, large-scale and closely coupled when compared to that in low-volume, high-variety processes.

How does the technology improve the operation's performance?

In Chapter 2, we identified the five operations performance objectives, on which an operation or process can be judged. So, a sensible starting point for evaluating the impact of any process technology on an operation is to assess how it affects its quality, speed, dependability, flexibility and cost performance. However, two refinements are necessary to the normal list of performance objectives. First, given that some process technologies can perform totally novel tasks (for example, 3D printing can create shapes and use materials in a novel manner), it is worth splitting the criterion of 'quality' into 'specification quality' (what can the technology do?) and 'conformance quality' (can it do it in an error-free manner?). Similarly, when considering the flexibility of technology, it is worth distinguishing between response flexibility (how easy is it to switch between tasks?) and range flexibility (how many different tasks can it perform?). In addition, again given the increased capabilities of some new process technologies, other criteria are worth including in any evaluation.

These assessment questions can be viewed as a starting point. The criteria should be adjusted depending on the operation for which the technology is intended. They are:

▶ What can the technology do? – Is it capable of doing something (or some things) that the previous technology could not do?

▶ How well can the technology do things? – Is it capable of doing things in an error-free manner?

▶ How fast can the technology do things? – Is it capable of doing things more rapidly?

▶ How reliably can the technology do things? – Is it capable of doing things with greater dependability?

▶ How flexibly (response) can the technology do things? – Is it capable of switching easily between tasks?

▶ What range of things can the technology do? – How many different tasks can it perform?

▶ How sustainable is the technology? – Does it have a positive environmental impact? (for example, see the 'Operations in practice' example on Marmite's energy recycling technology)

▶ Where can the technology do it? – Can it perform its tasks in alternative locations (for example, is it portable)?

▶ How safely can the technology do it? – Can it perform its tasks without harming people?

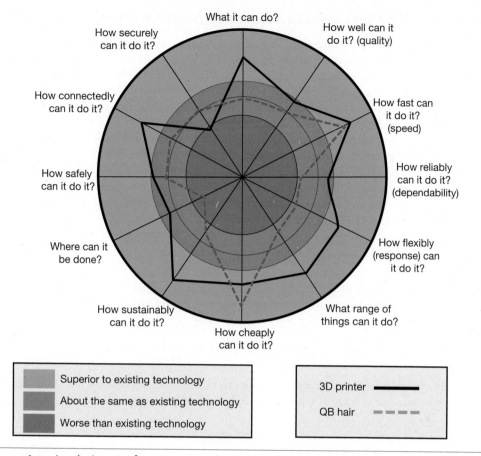

Figure 8.6 Assessing the impact of a processing technology on operations performance

▶ How connectedly can the technology do it? – Can it communicate or connect with other technologies?
▶ How securely can the technology do it? – Is it vulnerable to interference or hacking?

These criteria are shown on a 'polar' representation (see Chapter 2) in Figure 8.6. A technology being evaluated can be mapped on this type of diagram. In this representation, the evaluations are classed as 'worse than' (red), 'about the same' (orange), and 'better than' (green) compared with what the technology is replacing. It shows two examples of this. The first examines the QB House technology, described earlier. This shows that QB House has two advantages over conventional haircutting – it is (usually) faster and it is cheaper. However, there are fewer locations ('where can it be done?'), and the waiting time may be marginally less reliable. On all other criteria, it performs at more or less the same level as conventional hairdressers.

The second example shows the evaluation of a 3D printer to be used to produce prototype designs of biodegradable semi-rigid plastic packaging moulds. The performance of the proposed 3D printer is compared with the current method of producing the moulds using conventional machining techniques. It indicates that the new 3D technology would be superior in almost all respects, particularly in terms of its speed, flexibility, range, sustainability (because it wastes far less material), and its ability to connect with other technologies (particularly, in this case, the design system). However, this connectivity would make it less difficult to steal and replicate designs.

> **Operations principle**
>
> Process technology needs to be evaluated on a range of criteria that include its impact on the performance of the operation in which the technology will be used.

Does the technology give an acceptable financial return?

Assessing the financial value of investing in process technology is in itself a specialized subject. And while it is not the purpose of this book to delve into the details of financial analysis, it is important to highlight one important issue that is central to financial evaluation: while the benefits of investing in new technology can be spread over many years into the future, the costs associated with investing in the technology usually occur up front. So we have to consider the time value of money.[8] Simply, this means that receiving €1,000 now is better than receiving €1,000 in a year's time. Receiving €1,000 now enables us to invest the money so that it will be worth more than the €1,000 we receive in a year's time. Alternatively, reversing the logic, we can ask ourselves how much would have to be invested now to receive €1,000 in one year's time. This amount (lower than €1,000) is called the net present value of receiving €1,000 in one year's time.

For example, suppose current interest rates are 10 per cent per annum; then the amount we would have to invest to receive €1,000 in one year's time is:

$$€1,000 \times \frac{1}{(1.10)} = €909.10$$

So the present value of €1,000 in one year's time, *discounted for the fact that we do not have it immediately,* is €909.10. In two years' time, the amount we would have to invest to receive €1,000 is:

$$€1,000 \times \frac{1}{(1.10)} \times \frac{1}{(1.10)} = €1,000 \times \frac{1}{(1.10)^2} = €826.50$$

The rate of interest assumed (10 per cent in our case) is known as the discount rate. More generally, the present value of €x in n years' time, at a discount rate of r per cent, is:

$$[^*]\frac{x}{(1 + r/100)}n$$

Worked example

A warehouse stores and distributes spare parts. It is considering investing in a new 'retrieval and packing' system which converts sales orders into 'retrieval lists' and uses materials-handling equipment to automatically pick up the goods from its shelves and bring them to the packing area. The capital cost of purchasing and installing the new technology can be spread over three years, and from the first year of its effective operation, overall operations cost savings will be made. Combining the cash that the company will have to spend and the savings that it will make, the cash flow year by year is shown in Table 8.1.

However, these cash flows have to be discounted in order to assess their 'present value'. Here the company is using a discount rate of 10 per cent. This is also shown in Table 8.1. The effective life of this technology is assumed to be six years:

The total cash flow (sum of all the cash flows) = €1.38 million

However, the net present value (NPV) = €816,500

This is considered to be acceptable by the company.

Calculating discount rates, although perfectly possible, can be cumbersome. As any alternative, tables are usually used such as the one in Table 8.2.

So now the net present value is:

$$P = DF \times FV$$

Table 8.1 Cash flows for the warehouse process technology

Year	0	1	2	3	4	5	6	7
Cash flow (€000s)	−300	30	50	400	400	400	400	0
Present value (discounted at 10%)	−300	27.27	41.3	300.53	273.21	248.37	225.79	0

Table 8.2 Present value of €1 to be paid in future

Years	3.0%	4.0%	5.0%	6.0%	7.0%	8.0%	9.0%	10.0%
1	€0.970	€0.962	€0.952	€0.943	€0.935	€0.926	€0.918	€0.909
2	€0.942	€0.925	€0.907	€0.890	€0.873	€0.857	€0.842	€0.827
3	€0.915	€0.889	€0.864	€0.840	€0.816	€0.794	€0.772	€0.751
4	€0.888	€0.855	€0.823	€0.792	€0.763	€0.735	€0.708	€0.683
5	€0.862	€0.822	€0.784	€0.747	€0.713	€0.681	€0.650	€0.621
6	€0.837	€0.790	€0.746	€0.705	€0.666	€0.630	€0.596	€0.565
7	€0.813	€0.760	€0.711	€0.665	€0.623	€0.584	€0.547	€0.513
8	€0.789	€0.731	€0.677	€0.627	€0.582	€0.540	€0.502	€0.467
9	€0.766	€0.703	€0.645	€0.592	€0.544	€0.500	€0.460	€0.424
10	€0.744	€0.676	€0.614	€0.558	€0.508	€0.463	€0.422	€0.386
11	€0.722	€0.650	€0.585	€0.527	€0.475	€0.429	€0.388	€0.351
12	€0.701	€0.626	€0.557	€0.497	€0.444	€0.397	€0.356	€0.319
13	€0.681	€0.601	€0.530	€0.469	€0.415	€0.368	€0.326	€0.290
14	€0.661	€0.578	€0.505	€0.442	€0.388	€0.341	€0.299	€0.263
15	€0.642	€0.555	€0.481	€0.417	€0.362	€0.315	€0.275	€0.239
16	€0.623	€0.534	€0.458	€0.394	€0.339	€0.292	€0.252	€0.218
17	€0.605	€0.513	€0.436	€0.371	€0.317	€0.270	€0.231	€0.198
18	€0.587	€0.494	€0.416	€0.350	€0.296	€0.250	€0.212	€0.180
19	€0.570	€0.475	€0.396	€0.331	€0.277	€0.232	€0.195	€0.164
20	€0.554	€0.456	€0.377	€0.312	€0.258	€0.215	€0.179	€0.149

where
DF = the discount factor from Table 8.3
FV = future value

To use the table, find the vertical column and locate the appropriate discount rate (as a percentage). Then find the horizontal row corresponding to the number of years it will take to receive the payment. Where the column and the row intersect is the present value of €1. You can multiply this value by the expected future value, in order to find its present value.

Worked example

A healthcare clinic is considering purchasing a new analysis system. The net cash flows from the new analysis system are as follows.

Year 1: −€10,000 (outflow of cash)
Year 2: €3,000
Year 3: €3,500
Year 4: €3,500
Year 5: €3,000

Assuming that the real discount rate for the clinic is 9 per cent, using the net present value table (Table 8.3), demonstrate whether the new system would at least cover its costs. Table 8.3 shows the calculations. It shows that, because the net present value of the cash flow is positive, the new system will cover its costs, and will be (just) profitable for the clinic.

Table 8.3 Present value calculations for the clinic.

Year	Cash flow		Table factor		Present value
1	(€10,000)	×	1.000	=	(€10,000.00)
2	€3,000	×	0.917	=	€2,752.29
3	€3,500	×	0.842	=	€2,945.88
4	€3,500	×	0.772	=	€2,702.64
5	€3,000	×	0.708	=	€2,125.28
			Net present value	=	€526.09

OPERATIONS IN PRACTICE

Legacy versus fintech in financial services[9]

Fintech is the term that commentators in the financial service sector use to refer to innovation in all types of financial services. As Carolyn Wilkins, Senior Deputy Governor of the Bank of Canada announced, *'It is no exaggeration to say that we are in the midst of a defining moment for innovation in financial services. Some expect that new technology will cause a complete disruption of traditional financial institutions, giving businesses and households access to more convenient and customized services. Entrepreneurs are also finding applications well beyond finance, and these new technologies could transform other fields, such as humanitarian aid.'* Yet, arguably, what is more surprising is that this type of process technology was not *embraced* faster by the financial services industry. As one commentator put it, *'After all, money is mostly represented as an entry on a computer. It can be moved rapidly*

from one account to another with virtually no cost.' Moreover, finance firms as a whole spend more on IT, as a proportion of their revenues, than any other sector.

Three issues have (at the time of writing) inhibited the adoption of new fintech process technologies. And they all could apply to any 'disruptive' and industry-wide process technologies. The first is the traditional structure of the industry. According to Andrew Haldane, the Bank of England's chief economist, the international payments system still looks like a 'spaghetti junction', with money passing through several hands on the way from payer to recipient. Nor is it necessarily in the existing firm's interests to change the system. Each year huge revenues are earned by processing payments (around $1.7 trillion). The second reason is 'legacy'. IT systems in banks have grown for the most part incrementally, with updates and modifications over the years often 'patched' onto existing systems until a large part of firms' annual technology budget is consumed by maintaining, rather than re-designing, existing systems. The third issue is risk. Understandably, financial services firms are very much concerned with the reliability of any new technology, and new technologies are often unproven. A good example is distributed ledger technology (DLT) – the 'blockchain' technology behind the Bitcoin, the digital currency. Although many technology experts regarded a distributed ledger as being more secure (any hacker would have to crack several sites rather than a single, central register), doubts were expressed over the technology's ability to cope with the hundreds of thousands of transactions every second that the financial system needed to process.

How are new process technologies developed and implemented?

Developing and implementing process technology means organizing all the activities involved in making the technology work as intended. No matter how potentially beneficial and sophisticated the technology, it remains only a prospective benefit until it has been implemented successfully. So implementation is an important part of process technology management. Yet it is not always straightforward to make general points about the implementation process because it is very context dependent. That is, the way one implements any technology will very much depend on its the specific nature, the changes implied by the technology and the organizational conditions that apply during its implementation. In the remainder of this chapter we look at four particularly important issues that affect technology implementation: the way technology is planned over the long term, the idea of resource and process 'distance', the need to consider customer acceptability and the idea that if anything can go wrong, it will.

Technology planning in the long term – technology roadmapping

However, operations managers are involved with the development of process technologies, it is likely to be in consultation and collaboration with other parts of the firm. It is also likely to be in the context of some kind of formal planning process such as technology roadmapping. A technology roadmap (TRM) is an approach that provides a structure that attempts to assure the alignment of developments (and investments) in technology, possible future market needs, and the new development of associated operations capabilities. Motorola originally developed the approach in the 1970s so that it could support the development of its products and their supporting technologies. Bob Galvin, then Motorola's CEO, defined a TRM as: *an extended look at the future of a chosen field of inquiry composed from the collective knowledge and imagination of the brightest drivers of change in that field*. A TRM is essentially a process that supports technology development by facilitating collaboration between the various activities that contribute to technology strategy. It allows technology managers to define their firm's technological evolution in advance by planning the timing and relationships between the various elements that are involved in technology planning. For example, these 'elements' could include the business goals of the company, market developments or specific events, the component products and services that constitute related offerings, product/service and process technologies, the underlying capabilities that these technologies represent, and so on. Figure 8.7 shows the generic form of technology

'Wrong-shaped' parcels post a problem for UK Mail[10]

It was intended to be an investment in a 'transforming technology'. When UK Mail unveiled its £20 million investment in its new fully-automated sorting facility in Coventry in the Midlands of the UK, it expected that it would give it an edge over its competitors. Guy Buswell, the Chief Executive of UK Mail, said that the new hub would play a crucial role in the company's network. Aided by its new technology, the company, which competes with Royal Mail for parcel delivery business, had been expected to make healthy pre-tax profits. But that was before the new technology was brought into operation. In practice, the new state-of-the-art sorting equipment struggled to cope with the volume of 'irregular-shaped parcels' it was expected to process. This resulted in the operation having to divert a larger than expected proportion of its sorting to a manual process, which incurred extra operating costs. The setback was *'clearly very disappointing',* admitted

Guy Buswell, when the company announced its second profit warning in four months. The problems also hit the company's share price. The following year UK Mail announced that it would be acquired by Deutsche Post DHL Group.

roadmaps, while Figure 8.8 shows an example of a technology road map for the development of products/services, technologies and processes for a facilities management service.

The benefits of TRM are mainly associated with the way they bring together the significant stakeholders involved in technology strategy and various (and often differing) perspectives they have. The

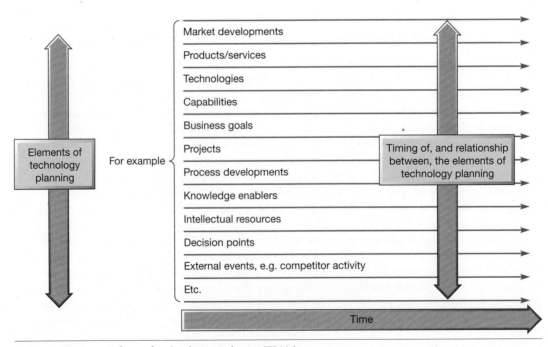

Figure 8.7 The generic form of technology roadmaps (TRMs)

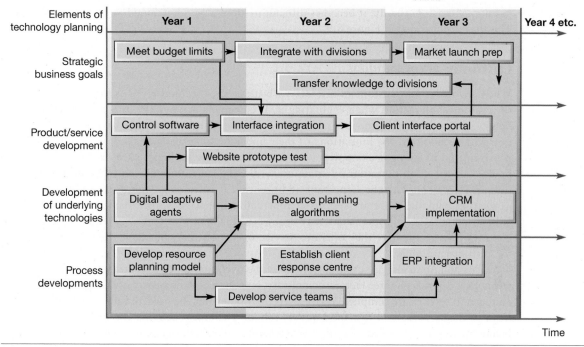

Elements of technology planning

| | Year 1 | Year 2 | Year 3 | Year 4 etc. |

Strategic business goals

Meet budget limits → Integrate with divisions → Market launch prep

Transfer knowledge to divisions

Product/service development

Control software → Interface integration → Client interface portal

Website prototype test

Development of underlying technologies

Digital adaptive agents → Resource planning algorithms → CRM implementation

Process developments

Develop resource planning model → Establish client response centre → ERP integration

Develop service teams

Time

Figure 8.8 Simplified example of a technology roadmap for the development of products/services, technologies and processes for a facilities management service

approach forms a basis for communication, and possibly consensus. After all, it does tackle some fundamental questions that concern any technology strategy. Why do we need to develop out technology? Where do we want to go with our technological capabilities? How far away are we from that objective? How can we get to where we want to be? In what order should we do things? By when should development goals be reached? Yet TRMs do not offer any solutions to any firm's technological strategic options; in fact, they need not offer options or alternative technology trajectories. They are essentially a narrative description of how a set of interrelated developments should (rather than will) progress. Because of this they have been criticized as encouraging over-optimistic projections of the future. Nevertheless, they do provide, at the very least, a plan against which technology strategy can be assessed.

Resource and process 'distance'

The degree of difficulty in the implementation of process technology will depend on the degree of novelty of the new technology resources and the changes required in the operation's processes. The less that the new technology resources are understood (influenced perhaps by the degree of innovation), the greater their 'distance' from the current technology resource base of the operation. Similarly, the extent to which an implementation requires an operation to modify its existing processes, the greater the 'process distance'. The greater the resource and process distance, the more difficult any implementation is likely to be. This is because such distance makes it difficult to adopt a systematic approach to analysing change and learning from mistakes. Those implementations which involve relatively little process or resource 'distance' provide an ideal opportunity for organizational learning. As in any classic scientific experiment, the more variables that are held constant, the more confidence you have in determining cause and effect. Conversely, in an implementation where the resource and process 'distance' means that nearly everything is 'up for grabs', it becomes difficult to know what has worked and what

Operations principle

The difficulty of process technology implementation depends on its degree of novelty and the changes required in the operation's processes.

has not. More importantly, it becomes difficult to know why something has or has not worked.[11] This idea is illustrated in Figure 8.9.

Customer acceptability

When an operation's customers interact with its process technology it is essential to consider the customer interaction when evaluating it. If customers are to have direct contact with technology, they must have some idea of how to operate it. Where customers have an active interaction with technology, the limitations of their understanding of the technology can be the main constraint on its use. For example, even some domestic technologies such as smart TVs cannot be used to their full potential by some owners. Other customer-driven technologies can face the same problem, with the important addition that if customers cannot use technologies such as internet banking, there are serious commercial consequences for a bank's customer service. Staff in manufacturing operations may require several years of training before they are given control of the technology they operate. Service operations may not have the same opportunity for customer training.

Walley and Amin[12] suggest that the ability of the operation to train its customers in the use of its technology depends on three factors: complexity, repetition and the variety of tasks performed by the customer. If services are complex, higher levels of 'training' maybe needed: for example, the technologies in theme parks and fast-food outlets rely on customers copying the behaviour of others. Frequency of use is important because the payback for the 'investment' in training will be greater if the customer uses the technology frequently. Also, customers may, over time, forget how to use the technology, but regular repetition will reinforce the training. Finally, training will be easier if the customer is presented with a low variety of tasks. For example, vending machines tend to concentrate on one category of product, so that the sequence of tasks required to operate the technology remains consistent. In other cases, the technology may not be trusted by customers because it is technology and not a person. Sometimes we prefer to put ourselves in the care of a person, even if their performance is inferior to a technology. For example, the use of robot technologies in surgery has distinct advantages over conventional surgery, but in spite of the fact that the surgeon is in control, it is viewed

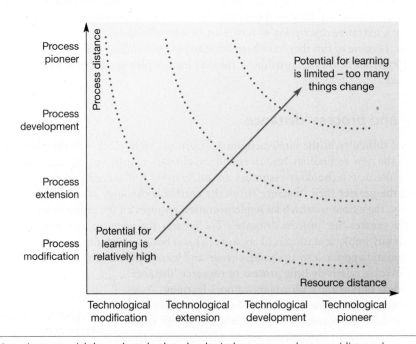

Figure 8.9 Learning potential depends on both technological resource and process 'distance'

with suspicion by some patients and physicians. When robot surgeons operate without any direct human control, rather than simply mirroring the movement of human surgeons, resistance is likely to be even greater. If, during the early adoption of a technology, there is some accident involving people, the resulting publicity can increase 'customer' resistance. For example, see the 'Operations in practice' case, 'Rampaging robots'.

Rampaging robots[13]

It is not a big problem (at least not at the moment), but it could become one as robot technologies start to mix directly with customers. Robots can be dangerous, and not just in a highly automated factory environment. (But factory robots can be dangerous. In 2015 a factory worker at a Volkswagen factory was picked up and killed by a robot. He was installing it when he was lifted up by the robotic arm and crushed against a metal plate, suffering fatal chest injuries.) It is the introduction of robotic technologies into the customer environment that could give rise to new areas of reputational risk for companies. For example, in

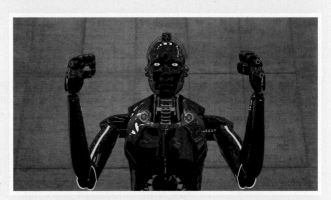

2016, a robot that was intended to guard against shoplifters accidentally ran over a 16-month-old boy at a shopping centre in Palo Alto, California – ironically, a town famous for high-tech industries. The 130 kg robot, which looks like R2-D2 from *Star Wars*, apparently did not sense that the child had fallen in its path and failed to stop before they collided. According to the boy's mother, '*The robot hit my son's head and he fell down — facing down — on the floor, and the robot did not stop and it kept moving forward.*'

It is an issue that was causing concern (or discussion) decades ago, before robots existed. The author and visionary Isaac Asimov devised his *Three Laws of Robotics* to protect humans.

1 Don't hurt a human being, or through inaction, allow a human being to be hurt.
2 A robot must obey the orders a human gives it unless those orders would result in a human being harmed.
3 A robot must protect its own existence as long as it does not conflict with the first two laws.

The robot's makers, Knightscope, said the incident was 'absolutely horrifying' and that the company would apologize directly to the family. It also pointed out that its fleet of similar robots had covered 25,000 miles on patrol duty and there had never been an incident like this before. Nevertheless, the Shopping Centre said it would temporarily take the robot out of service.

Other problems that have been raised by companies fearing legal liability and reputational risk include domestic devices like robot vacuum cleaners hurting pets or humans. A South Korean woman was sleeping on the floor when her robot vacuum 'ate' her hair. Also some 'automated' services could lead to customers confusing what's real and what isn't, resulting in customers revealing more than they intended. For example, 'Invisible Boyfriend' is a service that, for a monthly fee, sends 'pretend' romantic texts and voicemails to your phone – but not all customers realize it is not fully automated, and that there are human operators involved.

Anticipating implementation problems

The implementation of any process technology will need to account for the 'adjustment' issues that almost always occur when making any organizational change. By adjustment issues we

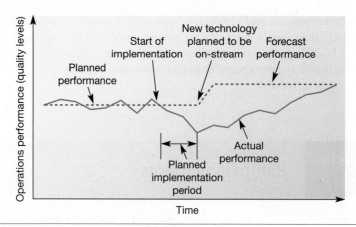

Figure 8.10 The reduction in performance during and after the implementation of a new process reflects 'adjustment costs'

mean the losses that could be incurred before the improvement is functioning as intended. But estimating the nature and extent of any implementation issues is notoriously difficult. This is particularly true because more often than not, Murphy's law seems to prevail. This law is usually stated as, 'if anything can go wrong, it will'. This effect has been identified empirically in a range of operations, especially when new types of process technology are involved. Specifically discussing technology-related change (although the ideas apply to almost any implementation), Bruce Chew of Massachusetts Institute of Technology[14] argues that adjustment 'costs' stem from unforeseen mismatches between the new technology's capabilities and needs and the existing operation. New technology rarely behaves as planned and as changes are made their impact ripples throughout the organization.

Figure 8.10 is an example of what Chew calls a Murphy curve. It shows a typical pattern of performance reduction (in this case, quality) as a new process technology is introduced. It is recognized that implementation may take some time; therefore allowances are made for the length and cost of a 'ramp-up' period. However, as the operation prepares for the implementation, the distraction causes performance actually to deteriorate. Even after the start of the implementation this downward trend continues and it is only weeks, indeed maybe months, later that the old performance level is reached. The area of the dip indicates the magnitude of the adjustment costs, and therefore the level of vulnerability faced by the operation.

Summary answers to key questions

What is process technology and why is it getting more important?

▶ Process technologies are the machines, equipment or devices that help operations to create or deliver products and services. Indirect process technology helps to facilitate the direct creation of products and services.

- Most new process technologies have a greater capability than what they are replacing, and many new technologies can be applied in all types of operation.
- One common method of distinguishing between different types of process technology is by what the technology actually processes – materials, information or customers.

How can one understand the potential of new process technology?

- Operations managers do not need to know the technical details of all technologies, but they do need to know the answers to four key questions: What does it do? How does it do it? What advantages does it give? What constraints does it impose?
- It can be difficult to separate the reality of a new technology from the publicity and speculation that surrounds it. The 'Gartner hype cycle' attempts to illustrate this using five sequential stages.
- An understanding of a technology calls for a knowledge of its 'primary capability'. That is, what is it better at than the technology it replaces: for example, its ability to think, or reason, see or sense, communicate or connect, move physical objects, or process materials.

How can new process technologies be evaluated?

- All technologies should be appropriate for the volume–variety characteristics of the task for which they are intended.
- All technologies should be evaluated by assessing the impact that the process technology will have on the operation's performance objectives (quality, speed, dependability, flexibility and cost) and other operational factors.
- All technologies should be evaluated financially. This usually involves the use of some of the more common evaluation approaches, such as net present value (NPV).

How are new process technologies developed and implemented?

- Implementing process technology means organizing all the activities involved in making the technology work as intended.
- A technology roadmap (TRM) is an approach that provides a structure that attempts to assure the alignment of developments (and investments) in technology, possible future market needs, and the new development of associated operations capabilities.
- The resource and process 'distance' implied by the technology implementation will indicate the degree of difficulty.
- Customer acceptability may be a barrier to implementation in customer-processing technologies.
- It is necessary to allow for the adjustment costs of implementation.

Rochem Ltd

Dr Rhodes was losing his temper. *'It should be a simple enough decision. There are only two alternatives. You are only being asked to choose a machine!'*

The Management Committee looked abashed. Rochem Ltd was one of the largest independent companies supplying the food-processing industry. Its initial success had come with a food preservative used mainly for meat-based products and marketed under the name of 'Lerentyl'. Other products were subsequently developed in the food colouring and food container coating fields, so that now Lerentyl accounted for only 25 per cent of total company sales, which were now slightly over £10 million.

The decision

The problem over which there was such controversy related to the replacement of one of the process units used to manufacture Lerentyl. Only two such units were used; both were 'Chemling' machines. It was the older of the two Chemling units which was giving trouble. High breakdown figures, with erratic quality levels, meant that output level requirements were only just being reached. The problem was: should the company replace the ageing Chemling with a new Chemling, or should it buy the only other plant on the market capable of the required process, the 'AFU' unit? The Chief Chemist's staff had drawn up a comparison of the two units, shown in Table 8.4.

The body considering the problem was the newly formed Management Committee. The committee consisted of the four senior managers in the firm: the Chief Chemist and the Marketing Manager, who had been with the firm since its beginning, together with the Production Manager and the Accountant, both of whom had joined the company only six months before.

What follows is a condensed version of the information presented by each manager to the committee, together with their attitudes to the decision.

The Marketing Manager

The current market for this type of preservative had reached a size of some £5 million, of which Rochem Ltd supplied approximately 48 per cent. There had, of late, been significant changes in the market – in particular, many of the users of preservatives were now able to buy products similar to

Table 8.4 A comparison of the two alternative machines

	CHEMLING	AFU
Capital cost	£590,000	£880,000
Processing costs	Fixed: £15,000/month	Fixed: £40,000/month
	Variable: £750/kg	Variable: £600/kg
Design	105 kg/month	140 kg/month
Capacity	98 ± 0.7% purity	99.5 ± 0.2% purity
Quality	Manual testing	Automatic testing
Maintenance	Adequate but needs servicing	Not known – probably good
After-sales services	Very good	Not known – unlikely to be good
Delivery	Three months	Immediate

Lerentyl. The result had been the evolution of a much more price-sensitive market than had previously been the case. Further market projections were somewhat uncertain. It was clear that the total market would not shrink (in volume terms) and best estimates suggested a market of perhaps £6 million within the next three or four years (at current prices). However, there were some people in the industry who believed that the present market only represented the tip of the iceberg.

Although the food preservative market had advanced by a series of technical innovations, 'real' changes in the basic product were now few and far between. Lerentyl was sold in either solid powder or liquid form, depending on the particular needs of the customer. Prices tended to be related to the weight of chemical used, however. Thus, for example, the current average market price was approximately £1,050 per kg. There were, of course, wide variations depending on order size, etc.

'At the moment I am mainly interested in getting the right quantity and quality of Lerentyl each month and although Production has never let me down yet, I'm worried that unless we get a reliable new unit quickly, it soon will. The AFU machine could be on line in a few weeks, giving better quality too. Furthermore, if demand does increase (but I'm not saying it will), the AFU will give us the extra capacity. I will admit that we are not trying to increase our share of the preservative market as yet. We see our priority as establishing our other products first. When that's achieved, we will go back to concentrating on the preservative side of things.'

The Chief Chemist

The Chief Chemist was an old friend of John Rhodes and together they had been largely responsible for every product innovation. At the moment, the major part of his budget was devoted to modifying basic Lerentyl so that it could be used for more acidic food products such as fruit. This was not proving easy and as yet nothing had come of the research, although the Chief Chemist remained optimistic.

'If we succeed in modifying Lerentyl the market opportunities will be doubled overnight and we will need the extra capacity. I know we would be taking a risk by going for the AFU machine, but our company has grown by gambling on our research findings, and we must continue to show faith. Also the AFU technology is the way all similar technologies will be in the future. We have to start learning how to exploit it sooner or later.'

The Production Manager

The Lerentyl Department was virtually self-contained as a production unit. In fact, it was physically separate, located in a building a few yards detached from the rest of the plant. Production requirements for Lerentyl were currently at a steady rate of 190 kg per month. The six technicians who staffed the machines were the only technicians in Rochem who did all their own minor repairs and full quality control. The reason for this was largely historical since, when the firm started, the product was experimental and qualified technicians were needed to operate the plant. Four of the six had been with the firm almost from its beginning.

'It's all right for Dave and Eric (Marketing Manager and Chief Chemist) to talk about a big expansion of Lerentyl sales; they don't have to cope with all the problems if it doesn't happen. The fixed costs of the AFU unit are nearly three times those of the Chemling. Just think what that will do to my budget at low volumes of output. As I understand it, there is absolutely no evidence to show a large upswing in Lerentyl. No, the whole idea (of the AFU plant) is just too risky. Not only is there the risk. I don't think it is generally understood what the consequences of the AFU would mean. We would need twice the variety of spares for a start. But what really worries me is the staff's reaction. As fully qualified technicians they regard themselves as the elite of the firm; so they should, they are paid practically the same as I am! If we get the AFU plant, all their most interesting work, like the testing and the maintenance, will disappear or be greatly reduced. They will finish up as highly paid process workers.'

The Accountant

The company had financed nearly all its recent capital investment from its own retained profits, but would be taking out short-term loans the following year for the first time for several years.

'At the moment, I don't think it wise to invest extra capital we can't afford in an attempt to give us extra capacity we don't need. This year will be an expensive one for the company. We are already committed to considerably increased expenditure on promotion of our other products and capital investment in other parts of the firm, and Dr Rhodes is not in favour of excessive funding from outside the firm. I accept that there might eventually be an upsurge in Lerentyl demand but, if it does come, it probably won't be this year and it will be far bigger than the AFU can cope with anyway, so we might as well have three Chemling plants at that time.'

QUESTIONS

1 How do the two alternative process technologies (Chemling and AFU) differ in terms of their scale and automation? What are the implications of this for Rochem?

2 Remind yourself of the distinction between feasibility, acceptability and vulnerability discussed in Chapter 4. Evaluate both technologies using these criteria.

3 What would you recommend the company should do?

Problems and applications

1   It is a new job, as yet without a formal title, but one commentator has called it being a 'robot wrangler'. They even proposed a possible job advert: *'Wranglers wanted for growing fleets of robots. Your responsibilities will include evaluating robot performance, providing real-time analysis and support for problems. You must be analytical, detail-oriented, friendly – and ready to walk. No advanced degree required.'* Elisabeth Reynolds at the Massachusetts Institute of Technology also sees a future for people overseeing robots. *'We use that term "autonomous" a lot when we think about robots, but in fact very few robots are purely autonomous,'* she says. Actual job adverts for this type of job use terms like technicians, monitors, handlers and operations specialists. Journalists have described the role as anything from robot chauffeurs to robot babysitters. Why would such a job be necessary? Isn't the role of new technologies to replace humans?

2   Modern aircraft fly on automatic pilot for most of their time. Most people are blissfully unaware that when an aircraft lands in mist or fog, it is a computer that is landing it. When auto pilots can do something better than a human pilot, it makes sense to use auto pilots. They can take control of the plane during the long and (for the pilot) monotonous part of the flight between take-off and landing. They can also make landings, especially when visibility is poor because of fog or light conditions. In fact, automatic landings when visibility is poor are safer than when the pilot is in control. On some flights, the auto pilot is switched on within seconds of the aircraft wheels leaving the ground and then remains in charge throughout the flight and the landing. As yet, commercial flights do not take off automatically, mainly because it would require airports and airlines to invest in extra guidance equipment which would be expensive to develop and install. Also, take-off is technically more complex than landing. Yet some in the airline industry believe that technology could be developed to the point where commercial flights can do without a pilot on the aircraft entirely. If it was developed, what would be the problems and benefits associated with introducing this type of technology?

3   The 'robot milkmaid' can milk between 60 and 100 cows a day. Computer-controlled gates activated by transmitters around the cows' necks allow the cows to enter. The machine then checks their health, connects them to the milking machine and feeds them while they are being milked. If illness is detected in any cow, or if the machine for some reason fails to connect the milking cups to the cow after five attempts, automatic gates divert it into special pens where the farmer can inspect it later. Finally, the machine ushers the cows out of the system. It also self-cleans periodically and can detect and reject any impure milk. Rather than herding all the cows in a 'batch' to the milking machine twice a day, the system relies on the cows being able to find their own way to the machine. Once they have been shown the way to the machine a few times, they go there of their own volition. The cows may make the journey to the machine three or more times per day. (a) What advantages do you think this technology gives? (b) Do you think the cows mind? (c) There is some anecdotal evidence that farmers still go to watch the process. Why do you think this is?

4   The International Frozen Pizza Company (IFPC) operates in three markets globally. Market 1 is its largest market where it sells 25,000 tons of pizza per year. In this market, it trades under the name 'Aunt Bridget's Pizza' and positions itself as making pizza 'just as your aunt Bridget used to make' (apparently, she was good at it). It is also known for innovation, introducing new and seasonal pizza toppings on a regular basis. Typically, it would be selling around 20 varieties of pizza at any one time. Market 2 was smaller, selling around 20,000 tons per year under its 'Poppet's Pizza' brand. Although less innovative than Market 1, it still sells around 12 varieties of pizza. Market 3 is the smallest of the three, selling 10,000 tons per year of relatively high-quality pizzas under its 'Deluxe Pizza' brand. Like Aunt Bridget's Pizza, Deluxe Pizza also sells a relatively wide product range for the size of its market. Currently, both markets 1 and 3 produce their products using relatively little process automation and rely on high numbers of people, to assemble their products. Market 2 had always been keen to adopt more automated technology and uses a mixture of

automated assembly and manual assembly. Now the management in Market 2 has developed an almost fully automated pizza assembly system (APAS). They claim that the APAS could reduce costs significantly and should be adopted by the other markets. Both Markets 1 and 3 are sceptical. *'It may be cheaper, but it can't cope with a high variety of products'* was their response. Use the volume–variety characteristics of the markets to explain the proposal by the management of Market 2.

5 Process technology can impact all of the operations performance objectives (quality, speed, dependability, flexibility and cost). Think through, and identify, how process technology could affect these performance objectives in the airline industry.

6 There have been a number of changes in medical process technology that have had a huge impact on the way healthcare operations manage themselves. In particular, telemedicine has challenged one of the most fundamental assumptions of medical treatment – that medical staff need to be physically present to examine and diagnose a patient. No longer; web-connected devices are now able to monitor an individual's health-related data and communicate the information to healthcare professionals located anywhere in the world. Medical staff are alerted to changing conditions as they occur, and provided with a status report of a person's health so that the appropriate care can be administered. Telemedicine generally refers to the use of communications and information technologies for the delivery of clinical care. Formally, telemedicine is the ability to provide interactive healthcare utilizing modern technology and telecommunications. It allows patients to virtually 'visit' with physicians, sometimes live using video links, sometimes automatically in the case of an emergency, sometimes where patient data are stored and sent to physicians for diagnosis and follow-up treatment at a later time. What do you think are the implications of telemedicine of how healthcare operations can be managed?

Selected further reading

Arthur, W.B. (2010) *The Nature of Technology: What It Is and How It Evolves,* **Penguin, Harmondsworth.**
Popular science in a way, but very interesting on how technologies evolve.

Brain (2001) *'How Stuff Works',* **Wiley, New York.**
Exactly what it says. A lot of the 'stuff' is product technology, but the book also explains many process technologies in a clear and concise manner without sacrificing relevant detail.

Brynjolfsson, E. and Mcafee, A. (2014) *The Second Machine Age: Work, Progress, and Prosperity in a Time of Brilliant Technologies,* **W.W. Norton, New York.**
This is one of the most influential recent books on how technology will change our lives.

Carr, N.G. (2000) Hypermediation: 'Commerce and Clickstream', *Harvard Business Review,* **January–February.**
Written in the height of the Internet boom, it gives a flavour of how Internet technologies were seen.

Chew, W.B., Leonard-Barton, D. and Bohn, R.E. (1991) Beating Murphy's Law, *Sloan Management Review,* **vol. 5, Spring.**
One of the few articles that treats the issue of why everything seems to go wrong when any new technology is introduced. Insightful.

Christensen, C.M. (2016) *The Innovator's Dilemma: When New Technologies Cause Great Firms to Fail,* **Harvard Business Review Press, Harvard, MA.**
The latest published version of a classic.

Tapscott, D. and Tapscott, A. (2016) *Blockchain Revolution: How the Technology Behind Bitcoin and Other Cryptocurrencies is Changing the World,* **Portfolio Penguin, London.**
A readable book outlining the uses and implications of Blockchain, but broad and generic rather than detailed.

People in operations

KEY QUESTIONS

Why are people issues so important in operations management?

How can the operations function be organized?

How do we go about designing jobs?

How are work times allocated?

INTRODUCTION

Operations management is often presented as a subject, the main focus of which is on technology, systems, procedures and facilities – in other words, the non-human parts of the organization. This is not true, of course. On the contrary, the manner in which an organization's human resources are managed has a profound impact on the effectiveness of its operations function. In this chapter we look especially at the elements of human resource management which are traditionally seen as being directly within the sphere of operations management. These are how operations managers contribute to human resource strategy, organization design, job design, and the allocation of 'work times' to operations activities. The more detailed (and traditional) aspects of these last two elements are discussed further in the supplement on work study at the end of this chapter. Figure 9.1 shows how this chapter fits into the overall model of operations activities.

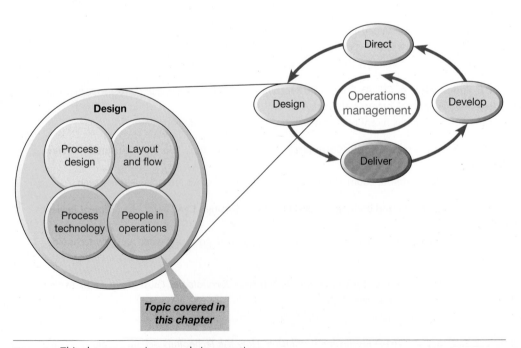

Figure 9.1 This chapter examines people in operations

Why are people so important in operations management?

To say that an organization's human resources are its greatest asset is something of a cliché. Yet it is worth reminding ourselves of the importance of the abilities, attitudes and culture of the people who make up the operations function. It is, after all, where most 'human resources' are to be found. It follows that it is operations managers who are most involved in the leadership, development and organization of human resources. In this chapter we examine some of the issues that most directly affect, or are affected by, operations management; these are illustrated in Figure 9.2. But the influence of operations management on the organization's staff is not limited to the topics that are covered in this chapter. Almost everything discussed in this book has a 'people' dimension. Yet, in some chapters, the human perspective is particularly important. In addition to this chapter, Chapters 16 and 17, for example, are concerned largely with how the contribution of the operation's staff can be harnessed. In essence the issues covered in this chapter define how people go about their working lives. It posi-tions their expectations of what is required of them, and it influences their perceptions of how they contribute to the organization. It defines their activities in relation to their work colleagues and it channels the flows of communication between different parts of the operation. But, of most importance, it helps to develop the culture of the organization – its shared values, beliefs and assumptions.

Operations principle

Human resources aspects are especially important in the operations function, where most 'human resources' are to be found.

Operations culture

What do we mean by culture in the context of the operations function? There is a wealth of academic or popular literature that treats the concept of organizational culture, but no single authoritative definition has emerged. Nevertheless, most of us know roughly what is meant by 'culture' in an organization. It is what it feels like to be part of it. What is assumed about how things get done rather than what is necessarily formally articulated. It is, in the words of one well-known writer on the subject, 'the way we do things around here' or 'the organization's climate'.[1] But the idea of 'organizational' culture can also apply to a single function like the operations function. In fact, there is considerable interest amongst researchers and practitioners in overcoming the cultural differences between different functions that can sometimes lead to what has been called 'cultural fragmentation'. Even though there may be elements of an organization's culture that are shared across all parts of the enterprise, different functions are very likely to have their own subcultures.

Believe, know and behave

Culture is difficult to explain. As was said of one organization with a particularly strong culture (a university as it happens), *'From the outside looking in, you can't understand it. From the inside looking out, you can't explain it.'* As far as the operations function is concerned, it is best summed up by what the operations team *believes,* what they *know* and how they *behave.* It is these three

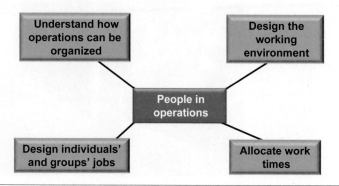

Figure 9.2 People in operations

W. L. Gore[2]

Most famous for its high-performance fabrics such as Gore-Tex, W. L. Gore also has an enviable reputation as being one of the best companies to work for wherever it operates. In a recent 'Best Companies to work for' list its associates (the company does not use the term 'employees') gave it the very top marks for 'feeling you can make a difference'. More than half of its staff have been with the firm for at least a decade, a consequence of its philosophy ('to make money and have fun'), and its unique organizational culture and job design practices. Few in the company have any formal job titles, or job descriptions. There are no managers, only leaders and associates, people are paid 'according to their contribution' and staff help to determine each other's pay. These ideas seem revolutionary yet are based on the company's founding principles from over 50 years ago. Started by Bill and Vieve Gore in the basement of their home in Delaware, it has now become a global business with facilities in more than 45 locations around the world. Its skilled staff develop, manufacture and sell a range of innovative products, virtually all of which are based on just one material (expanded polytetrafluoro-ethylene) which was discovered by Bob Gore (the founders' son), in 1969. It now has approximately 8,000 associates in its four main divisions (textiles, electronic, medical and industrial products) and annual revenues of over $2 billion.

Gore's approach to how it works with its staff is at the heart of the company's success. On almost every level Gore is different to other global companies. Associates are hired for general work areas rather than specific jobs, and with the guidance of their 'sponsors' (not bosses) and as they develop experience, they commit to projects that match their skills. Teams organize around opportunities as they arise with associates committing to the projects that they have chosen to work on, rather than having tasks delegated to them. Project teams are small, focused, multi-disciplined, and foster strong relationships between team members. Personal initiative is encouraged, as is 'hands-on' innovation, which involves those closest to a project in its decision making. There are, says Gore, no traditional organizational charts, no chains of command, no predetermined channels of communication. Instead, team members communicate directly with each other and are accountable to the other members of their team.

Groups are led by whoever is the most appropriate person at each stage of a project. Leaders are not appointed by senior management; they 'emerge' naturally by demonstrating special knowledge, skill or experience that advances a business objective. Everyone's performance is assessed using a peer-level rating system. Even the Group's CEO (one of the few people with a title), Terri Kelly, 'emerged' in this way. When the previous CEO retired, no shortlist of preferred candidates was interviewed; instead, along with board discussions, a wide range of associates were invited to nominate people they would be willing to follow. 'We weren't given a list of names – we were free to choose anyone in the company,' she says. 'To my surprise, it was me.'

The explicit aim of the company's culture is to 'combine freedom with cooperation and autonomy with synergy'. Everyone can earn the credibility to define and drive projects. Sponsors help associates chart a course in the organization that will offer personal fulfilment while maximizing their

contribution to the enterprise. Associates adhere to four basic guiding principles, originally expressed by Bill Gore:

▶ Fairness to each other and everyone with whom we come in contact.
▶ Freedom to encourage, help, and allow other associates to grow in knowledge, skill, and scope of responsibility.
▶ The ability to make one's own commitments and keep them.
▶ Consultation with other associates before undertaking actions that could impact the reputation of the company.

This degree of personal commitment and control by associates would not sit happily with a large 'corporate' style organization. It is no surprise, then, that Gore has unusual notions of economies of scale. Bill Gore believed in the need 'to divide so that you can multiply'. So when units grow to around 200 people, they are usually split up, with these small facilities organized in clusters or campuses. Ideally a dozen or so sites are close enough to permit good communication and knowledge exchange, but can still be intimate yet separate enough to promote a feeling of ownership. Bill Gore also believed that people come to work to be innovative and had a desire to invent great products. This, he said, *'would be the glue holding the company together'*, rather than the official procedures other companies rely on. And at Gore's Livingstone plant in Scotland the story of 'the breathable bagpipes' is used to illustrate this type of creative innovation generated from the company's culture of trust that allows people to follow their passion. The story goes that an associate who worked in Gore's filter bags department at Livingstone was also a keen exponent of his national instrument – the bagpipes. By day he'd be working on filter systems, in the evening he'd play his bagpipes. It occurred to him that the physical properties of the product he was putting together during the day could make a synthetic bag for the pipes he played in the evening. Traditionally, bagpipes have a bag made from sheepskin or cow leather which fills up with moisture and becomes a smelly health hazard. He recognized that if you added Gore-Tex, it would be breathable and it would be dry. He put a prototype together, tried it, and it worked. So he decided to spend time developing it, created a team to develop it further, and now almost all Scottish bagpipes have a Gore-Tex bag in them.

elements of operations culture, belief, knowledge and behaviour, which provide the foundations for how it contributes to the business and how capable it is to improve over time.[3]

▶ *What operations believe* – By 'operations belief', we mean what the people within the operations function accept as self-evident. For example, do operations believe that they have a responsibility to fully understand all other functions' strategies and their implications for operations? Do they develop capabilities within their operations resources and processes that offer a unique and long-lasting strategic advantage?
▶ *What operations should know* – What should the operations team know? Obviously, they should understand the underlying principles that govern how operations and processes work. Only with a thorough understanding of the objectives, concepts, tools and techniques of operations management will the operations function ever contribute fully to the success of any business.
▶ *How operations should behave* – The way operations managers should behave is not fundamentally different from any effective manager. The popular and academic literature has for decades been full of 'key behaviours' for effective leadership, and they don't seem to have changed much for years. 'Don't micromanage your team, empower them while still being available for advice.' 'Be a coach to your team.' 'Be clear and results-oriented, but help the team to see how they can achieve them.' 'Have a clear vision and strategy.' 'Always communicate, both ways – and listen to your team.' 'Support open discussion and listen to the team's concerns.' All of these might obvious, but they make good managerial sense.

How can the operations function be organized?

There are two issues here. The first is 'how should the total set of processes and resources that produce products and services be organized?' The second is 'how should operations managers, who make the decisions about operations, position themselves relative to the rest of the operations function'? We will look at the first issue by examining some common forms of organizational structures, and the second by examining the role of operations 'decision making'. First, though, it is worth looking at how 'organizations' can be described.

Perspectives on organizations[4]

How we illustrate organizations says much about our underlying assumptions of what an 'organization' is and how it is supposed to work. For example, the illustration of an organization as a conventional 'organogram' implies that organizations are neat and controllable with unambiguous lines of account-ability. But this is rarely the case. In fact, taking such a mechanistic view may be neither appropriate, nor desirable. Seeing an organization as though it was unambiguously machine-like is just one of several metaphors commonly used to understand organizations. One well-known analysis by Gareth Morgan proposes a number of 'images' or 'metaphors' which can be used to understand organizations, as follows.

> **Operations principle**
>
> There are many valid approaches to describing organizations. The process perspective is a particularly valuable one.

- ▶ **Organizations are machines** – The resources within organizations can be seen as 'components' in a mechanism whose purpose is clearly understood. Relations within the organization are clearly defined and orderly, processes and procedures that should occur usually do occur, and the flow of information through the organization is predictable. Such mechanical metaphors appear to impose clarity on what is actually messy organizational behaviour. But, where it is important to impose clarity (as in much operations analysis), such a metaphor can be useful, and is the basis of the 'process approach' used in this and similar books.
- ▶ **Organizations are organisms** – Organizations are living entities. Their behaviour is dictated by the behaviour of the individual humans within them. Individuals, and their organizations, adapt to circumstances just as different species adapt to the environment. This is a particularly useful way of looking at organizations if parts of the environment (such as the needs of the market) change radically. The survival of the organization depends on its ability to exhibit enough flexibility to respond to its environment.
- ▶ **Organizations are brains** – Like brains, organizations process information and make decisions. They balance conflicting criteria, weigh up risks and decide when an outcome is acceptable. They are also capable of learning, changing their model of the world in the light of experience. This emphasis on decision making, accumulating experience and learning from that experience is impor-tant in understanding organizations. They consist of conflicting groups where power and control are key issues.
- ▶ **Organizations are cultures** – An organization's culture is usually taken to mean its shared values, ideology, pattern of thinking and day-to-day ritual. Different organizations will have different cultures stemming from their circumstances and their history. A major strength of seeing organi-zations as cultures is that it draws attention to their shared 'enactment of reality'. Looking for the symbols and shared realities within an organization allows us to see beyond what the organization says about itself.
- ▶ **Organizations are political systems** – Organizations, like communities, are governed. The system of government is rarely democratic, but nor is it usually a dictatorship. Within the mechanisms of government in an organization are usually ways of understanding alternative philosophies, ways of seeking consensus (or at least reconciliation) and sometimes ways of legitimizing opposition. Individuals and groups seek to pursue their aims through the detailed politics of the organization. They form alliances, accommodate power relationships and manage conflict. Such a view is useful in helping organizations to legitimize politics as an inevitable aspect of organizational life.

Forms of organization structure

There are many different ways of defining 'organization structure'; here it is seen as the way in which tasks and responsibilities are divided into distinct groupings, and how the responsibility and coordi-nation relationships between the groupings are defined. Most organization designs attempt to divide an organization into discrete parts that are given some degree of authority to make decisions within their part of the organization. All but the very smallest of organizations need to delegate decision making in this way; it allows specialization so decisions can be taken by the most appropriate people. The main issue is what dimension of specialization should be used when grouping parts of the organization together. There are three basic approaches to this:

▶ Group resources together according to their *functional purpose* – so, for example, sales, marketing, operations, research and development, finance, etc.

▶ Group resources together by the *characteristics of the resources themselves* – this may be done, for example, by clustering similar technologies together (extrusion technology, rolling, casting, etc.). Alternatively, it may be done by clustering similar skills together (audit, mergers and acquisitions, tax, etc.). It may also be done according to the resources required for particular products or services (chilled food, frozen food, canned food, etc.).

▶ Group resources together by the *markets* which the resources are intended to serve – again this may be done in various ways. Markets may be defined by location, with distinct geographical boundaries (North America, South America, Europe and Middle East, South East Asia, etc.). Alternatively, markets may be defined by the type of customer (small firms, large national firms, large multinational firms, etc.).

There are an almost infinite number of possible organizational structures. However, some pure types of organization have emerged that are useful in illustrating different approaches to organizational design, even if, in their pure form, they are rarely found.

▶ **The U-form organization** – The unitary form, or U-form, organization clusters its resources primarily by their functional purpose. Figure 9.3(a) shows a typical U-form organization with a pyramid management structure, each level reporting to the managerial level above. Such structures can emphasize process efficiency above customer service and the ability to adapt to changing markets. But the U-form keeps together expertise and can promote the creation and sharing of technical knowledge. The problem then with the U-form organization is not so much the development of capabilities, but the flexibility of their deployment.

▶ **The M-form organization** – This form of organizational structure emerged because the functionally based structure of the U-form was cumbersome when companies became large, often with complex markets. It groups together either the resources needed for each product or service group, or alternatively, those needed to serve a particular geographical market, in separate divisions. The separate functions may be distributed throughout the different divisions (see Figure 9.3(b)), which can reduce economies of scale and operating efficiency. But it does allow each individual division to focus on the specific needs of its markets.

▶ **Matrix forms** – Matrix structures are a hybrid, usually combining the M-form with the U-form. In effect, the organization has simultaneously two different structures (see Figure 9.3(c)). In a matrix structure each resource cluster has at least two lines of authority, for example both to the division and to the functional groups. While a matrix organization ensures the representation of all interests within the company, it can be complex and sometimes confusing.

▶ **The N-form organization** – The 'N' in N-form stands for 'network'. In N-form organizations, resources are clustered into groups as in other organizational forms, but with more delegation of responsibility for the strategic management of those resources. N-forms have relatively little hierarchical reporting and control. Each cluster of resources is linked to the others to form a network, with the relative strength of the relationships between clusters changing over time, depending on circumstances (see Figure 9.3(d)). Senior management set broad goals and attempt to develop a unifying culture but do not 'command and control' to the same extent as in other organization forms.

Operations 'developers' – 'staff' and 'line' roles

Traditionally, it was common to distinguish between two types of role in organizations. People occupying classic 'staff' positions had a monitoring, planning, shaping and 'developing' role. They are the ones who are charged with building up the company's operations strategic capability. It is a task that needs some organizational 'space' to be performed effectively. It is certainly not a task that coexists

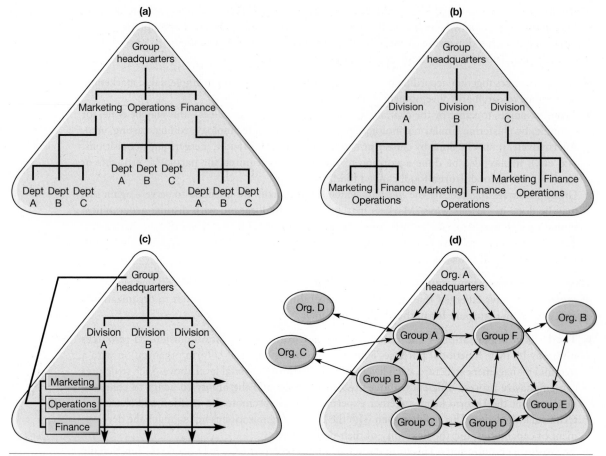

Figure 9.3 (a) U-form organizations give prominence to functional grouping of resources. (b) The M-form separates the organization's resources into separate divisions. (c) Matrix form structures the organization's resources so that they have two (or more) levels of responsibility. (d) N-form organizations form loose networks internally between groups of resources and externally with other organizations

easily with the hectic and immediate concerns of running an operation on a day-to-day basis. These people constitute what could be termed the 'operations developers' or 'central operations'. They perform what are called (slightly confusingly) 'staff' roles. By contrast, people occupying 'line' roles are those who run the day-to-day operations. Theirs is partly a reactive role, one that involves finding ways round unexpected problems: reallocating resources, adjusting processes, solving quality problems, and so on. They need to look ahead only enough to make sure that resources are available to meet targets. Theirs is the necessary routine. Knowing where the operation is heading, keeping it on budget and pulling it back on course when the unexpected occurs: no less valuable a task than the developer's but very different.

While these descriptions are clearly stereotypes, they do represent two types of operations task. The issue, for organizational design, is whether it is wise to separate them organizationally. It may cause more problems than it solves. Although it allows each to concentrate on their different jobs, it also can keep apart the two sets of people who have most to gain by working together. Here is the paradox: the development role does need freedom from the immediate pressures of day-to-day management but it is crucial that it understands the exact nature of these pressures. What makes the operation distinctive? Where do the problems occur? What improvements would make most difference to the performance of the operation? These questions can only be answered by living with the operation, not cloistered away from it. Similarly, the day-to-day operations manager has to interpret

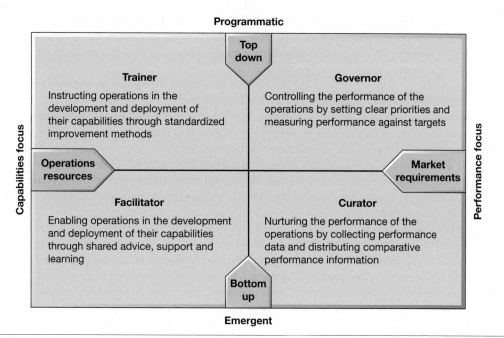

Figure 9.4 A typology of the operations developer's role

the workings of the operation, collect data, explain constraints and educate developers. Without the trust and cooperation of each, neither set of managers can be effective.

Four types of operations developer role

We can use the dimensions which define the perspectives on operations strategy described in Chapter 3 to examine the role that operations developers play within the operations function.

▶ *Top-down or bottom-up?* – If operations developers have a predominantly top-down view of the world, they are likely to take a programmatic approach to operations activities, emphasizing the implementation of overall company strategy. Conversely, if they take a bottom-up view, they are likely to favour a more emergent model of operations development where individual business operations together contribute to the overall building of operations expertise.

▶ *Market requirements or operations resource focus?* – If operations developers take a market requirements view of operations development, they are likely to focus on the explicit performance achieved by each part of the operations function and how far that performance serves to satisfy the operation's customers. An operations resource focus, on the other hand, emphasizes the way in which each part of the operation function develops its competences and successfully deploys them in its marketplaces.

We can use these two dimensions to define a typology of how the operations developer's role could work, as shown in Figure 9.4. It classifies operations developers into four pure types called governors, curators, trainers and facilitators – a typology. Although, in practice, the central operations function of most businesses is a combination of these pure types, usually one type predominates.

▶ *Operations developers as governors* – The term 'governor' is used to describe an agent of a central authority, interpreting operations strategy and arbitrating over any disputes. The term is also used to denote that the mechanism sets clear goals for each part of the operation, judges their performance and, if performance is not to target, wants to know the reason why.

▶ *Operations developers as curators* – Operations developers can be concerned primarily with performance against market requirements without being top-down. They may take a more emergent view by acting as the repository of performance data and ideas regarding operations practice for the company as a whole. The term 'curator' is used to capture this idea. Operations developers therefore will be concerned with collecting performance information, examples of best practice, and so on. They will also be concerned with disseminating this information so that operations managers in different parts of the business can benchmark themselves against their colleagues and, where appropriate, adopt best practice from elsewhere.

▶ *Operations developers as trainers* – Moving from the market requirements to the operations resources emphasis shifts the focus more to the development of internal capabilities. If the mindset of operations developers is top-down, their role becomes 'trainers', who develop clear objectives, usually derived from overall company strategy, and devise effect methods of developing the various parts of the overall operation. And because the needs of individual parts of the operation may differ, 'trainer' operations developers may devise improvement methodologies that can, to some extent, be customized.

▶ *Operations developers as facilitators* – In some ways this final type of operations developer role is the most difficult to operate effectively. They are again concerned with the development of operations capabilities but do so by acting as facilitators of change rather than instructors. Their role is to advise, support and generally aid the development and deployment of capabilities through a process of mentoring the various parts of the operation. They share responsibility with day-to-day operation managers in forming a community of operations practice. Implicit in this type of operations developer role is the acceptance of a relatively long-term approach to operations development.

How do we go about designing jobs?

Job design is concerned with how we structure each individual's jobs, the team to which they belong (if any), their workplace and their interface with the technology they use. In this section we deal with what is usually considered to be the central people-related responsibility of operations managers – job design. It is a huge topic and we can only deal with some of the influences on, and approaches to, job design.

The influences on job design that we deal with here are illustrated in Figure 9.5.

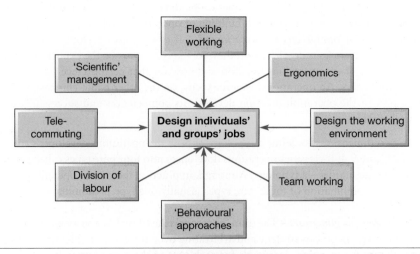

Figure 9.5 Some the influences on job design, work time allocation and the design of the working environment

The decisions of job design

Job design involves a number of separate yet related elements.

▶ **What tasks are to be allocated to each person in the operation?** Producing goods and services involves a whole range of different tasks which need to be divided between the people who staff the operation. Different approaches to the division of labour will lead to different task allocations.

▶ **What is the best method of performing each job?** Every job should have an approved (or best) method of completion. And although there are different ideas of what is 'best', it is generally the most efficient method but that fits the task, and does not unduly interfere with other tasks.

▶ **How long will it take and how many people will be needed?** Work measurement helps us calculate the time required to do a job, and therefore how many people will be needed.

▶ **How do we maintain commitment?** Understanding how we can encourage people and maintain job commitment is, arguably, the most important of the issues in job design. This is why behavioural approaches, including empowerment, teamwork and flexible working are at the core of job design.

▶ **What technology is available and how will it be used?** Many operational tasks require the use of technology. Not only does the technology need to be appropriately and designed, but so does the interface between the people and the hardware.

▶ **What are the environmental conditions of the workplace?** The conditions under which jobs are performed will have a significant impact on people's effectiveness. Although often considered a part of job design, we treat it separately in this chapter.

Task allocation – the division of labour

Any operation must decide on the balance between using specialists or generalists. This idea is related to the division of labour – dividing the total task down into smaller parts, each of which is accomplished by a single person or team. It was first formalized as a concept by the economist Adam Smith in his *Wealth of Nations* in 1776. Perhaps the epitome of the division of labour is the assembly line, where products move along a single path and are built up by operators continually repeating a single task. This is the predominant model of job design in most mass-produced products and in some mass-produced services (fast food, for example). There are some *real advantages* in division-of-labour principles:

▶ *It promotes faster learning.* It is obviously easier to learn how to do a relatively short and simple task than a long and complex one. This means that new members of staff can be quickly trained and assigned to their tasks when they are short and simple.

▶ *Automation becomes easier.* Dividing a total task into small parts raises the possibility of automating some of those small tasks. Substituting technology for labour is considerably easier for short and simple tasks than for long and complex ones.

▶ *Reduced non-productive work.* This is probably the most important benefit of division of labour. In large, complex tasks the proportion of time spent picking up tools and materials, putting them down again and generally finding, positioning and searching can be very high indeed. For example, one person assembling a whole motor car engine would take two or three hours and involve much searching for parts, positioning, and so on. Around half the person's time would be spent on these reaching, positioning, finding tasks (called non-productive elements of work). Now consider how a motor car engine is actually made in practice. The total job is probably divided into 20 or 30 separate stages, each staffed by a person who carries out only a proportion of the total. Specialist equipment and materials-handling devices can be devised to help them carry out their job more efficiently. Furthermore, there is relatively little finding, positioning and reaching involved in this simplified task. Non-productive work can be considerably reduced, perhaps to under 10 per cent, which would be very significant to the costs of the operation.

However, there are also serious drawbacks to highly divided jobs:

▶ *Monotony*. The shorter the task, the more often operators will need to repeat it. Repeating the same task, for example every 30 seconds, eight hours a day and five days a week, can hardly be called a fulfilling job. As well as any ethical objections, there are other, more obviously practical objections to jobs which induce such boredom. These include the increased likelihood of absenteeism and staff turnover, the increased likelihood of error and even the deliberate sabotage of the job.

▶ *Physical injury*. The continued repetition of a very narrow range of movements can, in extreme cases, lead to physical injury. The over-use of some parts of the body (especially the arms, hands and wrists) can result in pain and a reduction in physical capability. This is sometimes called repetitive strain injury (RSI).

▶ *Low flexibility*. Dividing a task up into many small parts often gives the job design a rigidity which is difficult to change under changing circumstances. For example, if an assembly line has been designed to make one particular product but then has to change to manufacture a quite different product, the whole line will need redesigning. This will probably involve changing every operator's set of tasks, which can be a long and difficult procedure.

▶ *Poor robustness*. Highly divided jobs imply materials (or information) passing between several stages. If one of these stages is not working correctly, for example because some equipment is faulty, the whole operation is affected. On the other hand, if each person is performing the whole of the job, any problems will only affect that one person's output.

Operations principle

There are both positive and negative effects of the division of labour, but it is still a significant factor in job design.

Designing job methods – scientific management

The term 'scientific management' became established in 1911 with the publication of the book of the same name by Fredrick Taylor (this whole approach to job design is sometimes referred to, pejoratively, as Taylorism). In this work he identified what he saw as the basic tenets of scientific management:[5]

▶ All aspects of work should be investigated on a scientific basis to establish the laws, rules and formulae governing the best methods of working.

▶ Such an investigative approach to the study of work is necessary to establish what constitutes a 'fair day's work'.

▶ Workers should be selected, trained and developed methodically to perform their tasks.

▶ Managers should act as the planners of the work (analysing jobs and standardizing the best method of doing the job) while workers should be responsible for carrying out the jobs to the standards laid down.

▶ Cooperation should be achieved between management and workers based on the 'maximum prosperity' of both.

The important thing to remember about scientific management is that it is not particularly 'scientific' as such, although it certainly does take an 'investigative' approach to improving operations. Perhaps a better term for it would be 'systematic management'. It gave birth to two separate, but related, fields of study, method study, which determines the methods and activities to be included in jobs, and work measurement, which is concerned with measuring the time that should be taken for performing jobs. Together, these two fields are often referred to as work study and are explained in detail in the supplement to this chapter.

Designing the human interface – ergonomic workplace design

Ergonomics is concerned primarily with the physiological aspects of job design. Physiology is about the way the body functions. It involves two aspects: first, how a person interfaces with his or her immediate working area; and second, how people react to environmental conditions. We

Critical commentary

Even in 1915, criticisms of the scientific management approach were being voiced. In a submission to the United States Commission on Industrial Relations, scientific management is described as:

▶ being in 'spirit and essence a cunningly devised speeding up and sweating system';

▶ intensifying the 'modern tendency towards specialization of the work and the task';

▶ condemning 'the worker to a monotonous routine';

▶ putting 'into the hands of employers an immense mass of information and methods that may be used unscrupulously to the detriment of workers';

▶ tending to 'transfer to the management all the traditional knowledge, the judgement and skills of workers';

▶ greatly intensifying 'unnecessary managerial dictation and discipline';

▶ tending to 'emphasize quantity of product at the expense of quality'.

Two themes evident in this early criticism do warrant closer attention. The first is that scientific management inevitably results in standardization of highly divided jobs and thus reinforces the negative effects of excessive division of labour previously mentioned. Second, scientific management formalizes the separation of the judgemental, planning and skilled tasks, which are done by 'management', from the routine, standardized and low-skill tasks, which are left for 'operators'. Such a separation, at the very least, deprives the majority of staff of an opportunity to contribute in a meaningful way to their jobs (and, incidentally, deprives the organization of their contribution). Both of these themes in the criticisms of scientific management lead to the same point: that the jobs designed under strict scientific management principles lead to low motivation among staff, frustration at the lack of control over their work, and alienation from the job.

will examine the second aspect of ergonomics later in this chapter. Ergonomics is sometimes referred to as human factors engineering or just 'human factors'. Both aspects are linked by two common ideas:

▶ There must be a fit between people and the jobs they do. To achieve this fit there are only two alternatives. Either the job can be made to fit the people who are doing it, or, alternatively, the people can be made (or perhaps less radically, recruited) to fit the job. Ergonomics addresses the former alternative.

▶ It is important to take a 'scientific' approach to job design: for example, collecting data to indicate how people react under different job design conditions and trying to find the best set of conditions for comfort and performance.

Anthropometric aspects

Many ergonomic improvements are primarily concerned with what are called the anthropometric aspects of jobs – that is, the aspects related to people's size, shape and other physical abilities. The design of an assembly task, for example, should be governed partly by the size and strength of the operators who do the job. The data which ergonomists use when doing this are called anthropometric data. Because we all vary in our size and capabilities, ergonomists are particularly interested in our range of capabilities, which is why anthropometric data are usually expressed in percentile terms. Figure 9.6 illustrates this idea. This shows the idea of size (in this case, height) variation.

Operations principle

Ergonomic considerations in job design can prevent excessive physical strain and increase efficiency.

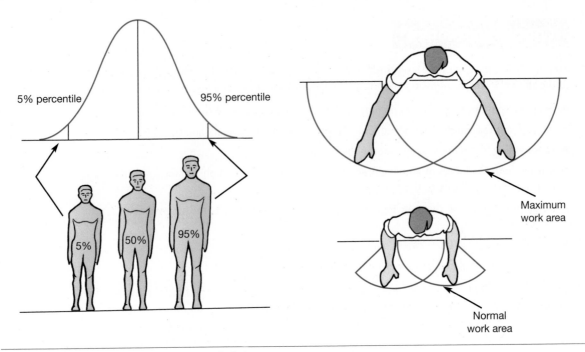

Figure 9.6 The use of anthropometric data in job design

Only 5 per cent of the population are smaller than the person on the extreme left (5th percentile), whereas 95 per cent of the population are smaller than the person on the extreme right (95th percentile). When this principle is applied to other dimensions of the body, for example arm length, it can be used to design work areas. Figure 9.6 also shows the normal and maximum work areas derived from anthropometric data. It would be inadvisable, for example, to place frequently used components or tools outside the maximum work area derived from the 5th percentile dimensions of human reach.

Exoskeleton devices take the strain[6]

Exoskeletons are not a new idea; since the 1960s they have been suggested for the enhancement of people's natural physical capabilities, usually for medical or military purposes. In the natural world, they are defined as 'a hard outer layer that covers, supports, and protects the body of an invertebrate animal such as an insect or crustacean'. But, in the context of physical work, it is usually taken to refer to a 'powered exoskeleton – a wearable powered mobile device that assists human movement or positioning to allow increased strength and/or endurance. Long the subject of science fiction, they are starting to be tested in industrial conditions. For example, typical of any automotive assembly lines, Ford requires its

▶

assembly employees to adopt positions that involve reaching overhead for long periods. This can result in aching back, neck and shoulders as well as general fatigue. This is why the company has partnered with California-based Ekso Bionics to trial an upper-body exoskeleton known as the EksoVest, which elevates and supports the arms. According to Marty Smets, an ergonomics expert at Ford who works on human systems and virtual manufacturing, Ford has been working on wearable robotics solutions since 2011, not to give their operatives superhuman strength, but to prevent injury. *'Right now, we're just using upper body supports, but we do have interest in other systems. Our goal right now is to just figure out how to integrate exoskeletons in our plants. Once we get them into our plants we can begin to replicate and figure out what the sweet spots are for application.'*

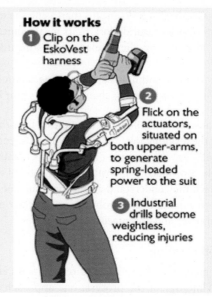

Designing for job commitment – behavioural approaches to job design

Jobs that are designed purely on division of labour, scientific management or even purely ergonomic principles can alienate the people performing them. Job design should also take into account the desire of individuals to fulfil their needs for self-esteem and personal development. This is where motivation theory and its contribution to the behavioural approach to job design is important. This achieves two important objectives of job design. First, it provides jobs that have an intrinsically higher quality of working life – an ethically desirable end in itself. Second, because of the higher levels of motivation it engenders, it is instrumental in achieving better performance for the operation, in terms of both the quality and the quantity of output. This approach to job design involves two conceptual steps: first, exploring how the various characteristics of the job affect people's motivation; second, exploring how individuals' motivation towards the job affects their performance at that job.

Typical of the models which underlie this approach to job design is that by Hackman and Oldham shown in Figure 9.7.[7] Here a number of 'techniques' of job design are recommended in order to affect particular core 'characteristics' of the job. These core characteristics of the job are held to influence various positive 'mental states' towards the job. In turn, these are assumed to give certain performance outcomes. In Figure 9.7 some of the 'techniques' (which Hackman and Oldham originally called 'implementing concepts') need a little further explanation:

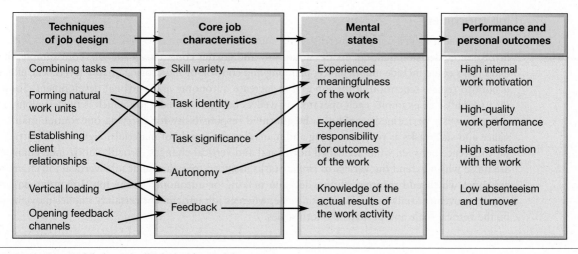

Figure 9.7 A typical 'behavioural' job design model

- Combining tasks means increasing the number of activities allocated to individuals.
- Forming natural work units means putting together activities which make a coherent whole.
- Establishing client relationships means that staff make contact with their internal customers directly.
- Vertical loading means including 'indirect' activities (such as maintenance).
- Opening feedback channels means that internal customers feedback perceptions directly.

Hackman and Oldham also indicate how these techniques of job design shape the core characteristics of the resulting job, and further, how the core characteristics influence people's 'mental states'. Mental states are the attitude of individuals towards their jobs: specifically, how meaningful they find the job, how much responsibility and control they feel they have over the way the job is done, and how much they understand about the results of their efforts. All of these mental states influence people's performance at their job in terms of their motivation, quality of work, satisfaction with their work, turnover and absenteeism.

Job rotation

If increasing the number of related tasks in the job is constrained in some way, for example by the technology of the process, one approach may be to encourage job rotation. This means moving individuals periodically between different sets of tasks to provide some variety in their activities. When successful, job rotation can increase skill flexibility and make a small contribution to reducing monotony. However, it is not viewed as universally beneficial either by management (because it can disrupt the smooth flow of work) or by the people performing the jobs (because it can interfere with their rhythm of work).

Job enlargement

The most obvious method of achieving at least some of the objectives of behavioural job design is by allocating a larger number of tasks to individuals. If these extra tasks are broadly of the same type as those in the original job, the change is called job enlargement. This may not involve more demanding or fulfilling tasks, but it may provide a more complete and therefore slightly more meaningful job. If nothing else, people performing an enlarged job will not repeat themselves as often, which could make the job marginally less monotonous. So, for example, suppose that the manufacture of a product has traditionally been split up on an assembly-line basis into 10 equal and sequential jobs. If that job is then redesigned so as to form two parallel assembly lines of five people, the output from the system as a whole would be maintained but each operator would have twice the number of tasks to perform. This is job enlargement. Operators repeat themselves less frequently and presumably the variety of tasks is greater, although no further responsibility or autonomy is necessarily given to each operator.

Job enrichment

Job enrichment means not only increasing the number of tasks, but also allocating extra tasks which involve more decision making, greater autonomy and greater control over the job. For example, the extra tasks could include maintenance, planning and control, or monitoring quality levels. The effect is both to reduce repetition in the job and to increase autonomy and personal development. So, in the assembly-line example, each operator, as well as being allocated a job which is twice as long as that previously performed, could also be allocated responsibility for carrying out routine maintenance and such tasks as record-keeping and managing the supply of materials. Figure 9.8 illustrates the difference between what are called horizontal and vertical changes. Broadly, horizontal changes are those which extend the variety of *similar* tasks assigned to a particular job. Vertical job changes are those which add responsibilities, decision making or autonomy to the job. Job enlargement implies movement only in the horizontal scale, whereas job enrichment certainly implies movement on the vertical scale and perhaps on both scales.

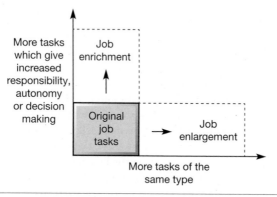

Figure 9.8 Job enlargement and job enrichment

Michelin calls it 'responsabilisation'[8]

This is how Édouard Michelin (then, a director of Michelin) put it back in 1928, *'The spirit of empowerment has always been one of our values and is part of the Michelin Group's "genetic code". One of our principles is to give responsibility to the person who carries out a given task because [they] know a lot about it.'* It is an approach to empowerment that survives today. In French, Michelin calls it 'responsabilisation', which roughly translates into English as a mixture of empowerment and accountability. It is an initiative that is part of the Group's efforts to streamline their organizational structures, increase responsiveness and efficiency, and encourage faster decision making. Team empowerment is seen as an essential part of this aim. *'Not only does it foster initiative and dialogue'*, says Michelin, *'it also enables decisions to be made close to operations and customers. Our Empowering Organizations are being developed throughout the Group, building trust-based relationships that encourage all employees to take part in our transformation. We are empowering front-line teams to organize themselves and find the right solutions to meet given objective in a framework defined by Management. In this way, managers are resuming their role as advisors, who develop people's capabilities and train their teams.'* In essence, 'responsabilisation' means shifting more operational responsibility to those people who work on the factory floor. This involves learning new skills: how to work effectively in teams, how to structure projects, how to manage conflicts and how to communicate in non-confrontational ways. Rather than issue direct instructions, team leaders act as coaches or, if any conflict arises, as referees. Workers in the teams allocate responsibility between themselves for tasks such as production scheduling, safety

procedures, quality control, and so on. After the company introduced the idea of greater worker autonomy in one of its factories, staff there said that they felt happier and more productive as a result. The company felt that it was such a success that it extended the practice to six factories in Europe and North America.

Empowerment

Empowerment is an extension of the *autonomy* job characteristic prominent in the behavioural approach to job design. However, it is usually taken to mean more than autonomy. Whereas autonomy means giving staff the *ability* to change how they do their jobs, empowerment means giving staff the *authority* to make changes to the job itself, as well as how it is performed. This can be designed into jobs to different degrees.[9] At a minimum, staff could be asked to contribute their suggestions for how the operation might be improved. Going further, staff could be empowered to redesign their jobs. Further still, staff could be included in the strategic direction and performance of the whole organization. The *benefits* of empowerment are generally seen as providing fast responses to customer needs (including dissatisfied customers), employees feeling better about their jobs and interacting with customers with more enthusiasm, promoting 'word-of-mouth' advertising and customer retention. However, there are *costs* associated with empowerment, including higher selection and training costs, perceived inequity of service and the possibility of poor decisions being made by employees.

OPERATIONS IN PRACTICE

Yahoo clamps down on telecommuting[10]

When Marissa Mayer, new the boss of Yahoo, ruled that employees of the company could no longer work from home, but must come into the office to work, it was met with horror throughout Silicon Valley, and beyond. The news also prompted a debate about how much freedom employees should be given to decide how, when and where they should do their jobs. Perhaps most surprising was that Ms Mayer's decision seemed to go against the trend, especially in high-tech companies, to allow and even encourage a degree of what had become known as 'telecommuting' (defined as 'the practice of working from home for a business and communicating through the use of personal computing and communication systems'). Surveys had recently shown that home-based working in some industries, especially information systems, engineering and science, was rising particularly quickly. Also, given that many of these technology firms produced the hardware and software that make working from home possible, it seemed only sensible to let their employees use them. As one headline read, 'The "9 to 5" mentality is dead'. And it's not surprising that telecommuting is popular; it has a number of advantages for firms. First, it is popular with (most) staff, so it helps retain (and gain access to a larger pool of) talent. It also is said to improve productivity by avoiding the sometimes distracting work environment. And, of course, because staff spend less time in the office, there can be substantial overhead savings.

This is possibly why Yahoo's decision was greeted with such criticism. 'An epic fail', 'hypocrite' and 'idiotic' were just some of the reactions. But it was not a fear that her employees were sitting around in their pyjamas all day that had prompted Yahoo's decision to send the memo to its

employees banning telecommuting. The leaked memo said that *'the habit has slowed the firm down and made it harder to have serendipitous meetings that can give birth to new ideas'* and it was the innovation that came from these meetings that the firm required. *'We can all feel the energy and buzz in our offices'*, the memo explained. Yahoo's defenders say that their staff are highly skilled people, such as designers and programmers, who needed more face time with colleagues. Quite simply, for Yahoo, the costs of telecommuting were greater than its benefits. And there are some widely accepted disadvantages of telecommuting. Working from home can be isolating, for staff and for managers who will need to put effort into keeping in touch. In fact, telecommuting can be difficult when employees require constant supervision. There is also the question of accountability. It is difficult to judge whether staff really are working rather than watching daytime TV. Nevertheless, a blanket ban on working from home is still unusual in high-tech industries. And within a year of Yahoo's original decision, there were some indications that, under certain circumstances, telecommuting was once more being permitted.

Team working

A development in job design which is closely linked to the empowerment concept is that of team-based work organization (sometimes called self-managed work teams). This is where staff, often with overlapping skills, collectively perform a defined task and have a high degree of discretion over how they actually perform the task. The team would typically control such things as task allocation between members, scheduling work, quality measurement and improvement, and sometimes the hiring of staff. To some extent most work has always been a group-based activity. The concept of teamwork, however, is more prescriptive and assumes a shared set of objectives and responsibilities. Groups are described as teams when the virtues of working together are being emphasized, such as the ability to make use of the various skills within the team. Teams may also be used to compensate for other organizational changes such as the move towards flatter organizational structures. When organizations have fewer managerial levels, each manager will have a wider span of activities to control. Teams which are capable of autonomous decision making have a clear advantage in these circumstances. The benefits of teamwork can be summarized as:

▶ improving productivity through enhanced motivation and flexibility;
▶ improving quality and encouraging innovation;
▶ increasing satisfaction by allowing individuals to contribute more effectively;
▶ making it easier to implement technological changes in the workplace because teams are willing to share the challenges this brings.

Flexible working

The nature of most jobs has changed significantly over the last 25 years. New technologies, more dynamic marketplaces, more demanding customers and a changed understanding of how individuals can contribute to competitive success have all had their impact. Also changing is our understanding of how home life, work and social life need to be balanced. Alternative forms of organization and alternative attitudes to work are being sought which allow, and encourage, a degree of flexibility in working practice which matches the need for flexibility in the marketplace. From an operations management perspective, three aspects of flexible working are significant: skills flexibility, time flexibility and location flexibility.

▶ *Skills flexibility* – A flexible workforce that can move across several different jobs could be deployed (or deploy themselves) in whatever activity is in demand at the time. In the short term staff at a supermarket may be moved from warehouse activities to shelf replenishment in the store to the checkout, depending on what is needed at the time. In the longer-term sense, multi-skilling means being able to migrate individuals from one skill set to another as longer-term demand trends

Critical commentary

Teamwork is not only difficult to implement successfully, but it can also place undue stress on the individuals who form the teams. Some teams are formed because more radical solutions, such as total reorganization, are being avoided. Teams cannot compensate for badly designed organizational processes; nor can they substitute for management's responsibility to define how decisions should be made. Often teams are asked to make decisions but are given insufficient responsibility to carry them out. In other cases, teams may provide results but at a price. The Swedish car maker Volvo introduced self-governing teams in the 1970s and 1980s which improved motivation and morale but eventually proved prohibitively expensive. Perhaps most seriously, teamwork is criticized for substituting one sort of pressure for another. Although teams may be autonomous, this does not mean they are stress-free. Top-down managerial control is often replaced by excessive peer pressure which is in some ways more insidious.

become obvious. So, for example, an engineer who at one time maintained complex equipment by visiting the sites where such equipment was installed may now perform most of his or her activities by using remote computer diagnostics and 'helpline' assistance. The implication of job flexibility is that a greater emphasis must be placed on training, learning and knowledge management. Defining what knowledge and experience are required to perform particular tasks and translating these into training activities are clearly prerequisites for effective multi-skilling.

▶ *Time flexibility* – Not every individual wants to work full-time. Many people, often because of family responsibilities, only want to work for part of their time, sometimes only during specific parts of the day or week (because of childcare responsibilities, etc.). Likewise, employers may not require the same number of staff at all times. They may, for example, need extra staff only at periods of heavy demand. Bringing both the supply of staff and the demand for their work together is the objective of 'flexible time' or flexi-time working systems. These may define a *core* working time for each individual member of staff and allow other times to be accumulated flexibly. Other schemes include annual hours schemes, one solution to the capacity management issue described in Chapter 11.

▶ *Location flexibility* – The sectoral balance of employment has changed. The service sector in most developed economies now accounts for between 70 and 80 per cent of all employment. Even within the manufacturing sector, the proportion of people with indirect jobs (those not directly engaged in making products) has also increased significantly. One result of all this is that the number of jobs which are not 'location-specific' has increased. Location-specific means that a job must take place in one fixed location. So a shop worker must work in a shop and an assembly line worker must work on the assembly line. But many jobs could be performed at any location where there are communication links to the rest of the organization. The realization of this has given rise to what is known as telecommuting, teleworking, 'flexible working', 'home working', mobile working, and creating the 'virtual office'. See the 'Operations in practice' example of telecommuting (or not) at Yahoo.

Work-related stress

The idea that there is a link between human resource strategy and the incidence of stress at work not new. Even some of the early scientific management pioneers accepted that working arrangements should not result in conditions that promoted stress. Now it is generally accepted that stress can seriously undermine the quality of people's working lives and, in turn, the effectiveness of the

Critical commentary

There is always a big difference between what is technically possible and what is organizationally feasible. Telecommuting does have its problems, especially those types of telecommuting that deny individuals the chance to meet with colleagues often face difficulties. Problems can include the following:

▶ *Lack of socialization* – offices are social places where people can adopt the culture of an organization as well as learn from each other. It is naïve to think that all knowledge can be codified and learnt formally at a distance.

▶ *Effectiveness of communication* – a large part of the essential communication we have with our colleagues is unplanned and face-to-face. It happens on 'chance meet' occasions, yet it is important in spreading contextual information as well as establishing specific pieces of information necessary to the job.

▶ *Problem-solving* – it is still often more efficient and effective informally to ask a colleague for help in resolving problems than formally to frame a request using communications technology.

▶ *It is lonely* – isolation amongst mobile or home workers is a real problem. For many of us, the workplace provides the main focus for social interaction. A computer screen is no substitute.

workplace. Here stress is defined as 'the adverse reaction people have to excessive pressures or other types of demand placed on them'.[11] In addition to the obvious ethical reasons for avoiding work-related stress, there are also business-related benefits, such as the following.

▶ Staff feel happier at work; their quality of working life is improved and they perform better.
▶ Introducing improvements is easier when 'stress' is managed effectively.
▶ Employment relations: problems can be resolved more easily.
▶ Attendance levels increase and sickness absence reduces.

Table 9.1 illustrates some of the causes of stress at work and what operations managers can do about it.

Work–life balance

A number of factors have made it increasingly difficult to separate work life from personal life. First is the general decline in the number of people working in operations where working times are very clearly delineated (usually those that employ routine, high-volume processes) towards operations where activities (and processes) are less formal and/or defined – and so are working times. Second, there is less distinction between what is clearly 'work' technologies (laptops, mobile devices, etc.) and personal devices, meaning that it is difficult to remain 'unconnected' from work emails, phone calls, etc. Third, as more people work from home, the discipline to set limited working hours is not always easy. Finally, some organizational cultures confuse 'working longer' with 'working better'. Ensuring that there is an appropriate split between work and personal life is usually taken to mean that work should not interfere unreasonably with family obligations and personal interests (although what exactly constitutes 'unreasonable' can be a cause of some disagreement). From an organization's perspective, the case for addressing work–life balance is usually made by stressing the following benefits.

▶ Employee retention is improved – staff who feel overloaded are more likely to seek alternative employment.

Table 9.1 Causes of stress at work and what could be done about it

Causes of stress	What can be done about it
Staff can become overloaded if they cannot cope with the amount of work or type of work they are asked to do	Change the way the job is designed, training needs and whether it is possible for employees to work more flexible hours
Staff can feel disaffected and perform poorly if they have no control or say over how and when they do their work.	Actively involve staff in decision making, the contribution made by teams, and how reviewing performance can help identify strengths and weaknesses
Staff feel unsupported: levels of sick absence often rise if employees feel they cannot talk to managers about issues that are troubling them	Give staff the opportunity to talk about the issues causing stress, be sympathetic and keep them informed
A failure to build relationships based on good behaviour and trust can lead to problems related to discipline, grievances and bullying	Check the organization's policies for handling grievances, unsatisfactory performance, poor attendance and misconduct, and for tackling bullying and harassment
Staff will feel anxious about their work and the organization if they don't know their role and what is expected of them	Review the induction process, work out an accurate job description and maintain a close link between individual targets and organizational goals
Change can lead to huge uncertainty and insecurity	Plan ahead so change is not unexpected. Consult with employees so they have a real input, and work together to solve problems

- ▶ Reputation – the promotion of a healthy work–life balance will develop a reputation that will help companies to attract more able staff.
- ▶ Health problems – staff 'burn-out' will eventually lead to a higher incidence of physical or mental health problems – an ethical as well as an economic (increased absenteeism) problem.
- ▶ Higher levels of staff performance – it is usually assumed that stressed or overloaded staff are less effective at getting work done, but this is disputed. Although some studies show that staff with a healthy work–life balance work more effectively, others say that there is 'insufficient evidence to support the notion that work–life practices enhance performance by means of reduced work–life conflict'.[12]

Many of the mechanisms for promoting better work–life balance are the measures that are described in this part of the chapter, such as various forms of flexible working, home working, job sharing, on-site child care, and so on.

The stress of high customer contact jobs[13]

Those jobs that are on the front line of dealing directly with customers (particularly a lot of customers, all the time, of all different types) can be particularly stressful. Not all customers will be reasonable, patient, courteous or even sane. The people who have these high customer contact roles need support, training and perhaps a special aptitude. And there is plenty of advice for staff who have to deal with customers who are angry because they feel that the level of service they have received is inadequate. Such advice usually includes such things as: acknowledge the (perceived) problem, try to put yourself in the position of the complainer, get the all facts

straight, and try to rectify the problem. It isn't easy, but if complaints can be resolved to the satisfaction of the customer, there can be significant benefits. Some surveys indicate that 90 per cent of customers whose complaints are resolved are happy to use the service again, and may even go on to become advocates for the service. Nevertheless, maintaining tolerance and politeness in the face of some particularly difficult customers can be more than, even experienced, staff can bear. That certainly was the case with Steven Slater, formerly an air steward on the US airline JetBlue. He was working on a New York flight when he had to arbitrate after a female passenger began arguing with a male passenger about space in the overhead luggage compartment during boarding. The female passenger swore at Mr Slater and pulled down the compartment door on his head. Later, when the plane landed, she seemingly refused to follow his request to remain in her seat and got up to take her bag from the overhead locker while the plane was still taxiing. Again, the woman allegedly swore at Mr Slater. It was then that his patience ran out in a particularly dramatic fashion. He went to the intercom and broadcast to the whole plane: *'To the passenger who just called me a motherf*****: F*** you. I've been in this business for 28 years and I've had it.'* He then collected his hand-luggage (and two beers from the trolley), opened the cabin door, activated the inflatable chute, announced, *'to those of you who have shown dignity and respect for 20 years, have a great ride'* and slid out of the (fortunately stationary) plane on to the runway. As a way to give up your job, it's not recommended. He was later arrested and charged with criminal mischief and reckless endangerment.

How should the working environment be designed?

The aspect of ergonomics that we examined earlier was concerned with how a person interfaces with the physical aspects of his or her immediate working area, such as its dimensions. But the subject also examines how people interface with their working environment. By this we mean the temperature, lighting, noise environment, and so on. It will obviously influence the way jobs are performed. Working conditions which are too hot or too cold, insufficiently illuminated or glaringly bright, excessively noisy or irritatingly silent will all influence the way jobs are carried out. Many of these issues are often covered by occupational health and safety legislation which controls environmental conditions in workplaces throughout the world. A thorough understanding of this aspect of ergonomics is necessary to work within the guidelines of such legislation.

> **Operations principle**
>
> Designing working environments is an important part of job design.

Working temperature

Predicting the reactions of individuals to working temperature is not straightforward. Individuals vary in the way their performance and comfort vary with temperature. Furthermore, most of us judging 'temperature' will also be influenced by other factors such as humidity and air movement. Nevertheless, some general points regarding working temperatures provide guidance to job designers:

▶ Comfortable temperature range will depend on the type of work being carried out; lighter work requires higher temperatures than heavier work.

▶ The effectiveness of people at performing vigilance tasks reduces at temperatures above about 29°C; the equivalent temperature for people performing light manual tasks is a little lower.

▶ The chances of accidents occurring increase at temperatures which are above or below the comfortable range for the work involved.

Illumination levels

The intensity of lighting required to perform any job satisfactorily will depend on the nature of the job. Some jobs which involve extremely delicate and precise movement, surgery for example, require very high levels of illumination. Other, less delicate jobs do not require such high levels.

Noise levels

The damaging effects of excessive noise levels are perhaps easier to understand than some other environmental factors. Noise-induced hearing loss is a well-documented consequence of working environments where noise is not kept below safe limits. When considering noise levels, bear in mind that the recommended (and often legal) maximum noise level to which people can be subjected over the working day is 90 decibels (dB) in the UK (although in some parts of the world the legal level is lower than this). Also bear in mind that the decibels unit of noise is based on a logarithmic scale, which means that noise intensity doubles about every 3 dB. In addition to the damaging effects of high levels of noise, intermittent and high-frequency noise can also affect work performance at far lower levels, especially on tasks requiring attention and judgement.

Ergonomics in the office

As the number of people working in offices (or office-like workplaces) has increased, ergonomic principles have been applied increasingly to this type of work. At the same time, legislation has been moving to cover office technology such as computer screens and keyboards. For example, European Union directives on working with display screen equipment require organizations to assess all workstations to reduce the risks inherent in their use, plan work times for breaks and changes in activity and provide information and training for users. Figure 9.9 illustrates some of the ergonomic factors which should be taken into account when designing office jobs.

Music while you work?[14]

Background music at work is not new. It has been used in the workplace for centuries. As far back as the industrial revolution orchestras and singers would be hired occasionally to perform for workers in the quieter factories. Later, in the 1940s, the BBC launched a radio program called *Music While You Work*. Broadcasting twice a day, it was made especially for factory workers. Artists who were booked for the show were told to 'play material with an upbeat rhythm that would keep the workers' attention', in the belief that it would improve productivity. But playing music at work is not always free. In the UK, for example, the law requires businesses that play any recorded music in public to get licences from the Performing Right Society (PRS),

which collects fees and pays royalties to composers and their publishers. Listening to a device through headphones, however, is free. But does music help or hinder?

Some bodies definitely think that it helps. Musicworks (which is an organization supported by the PRS, so it is not exactly independent) cites studies that show that music in the workplace promotes positive mood, can build team spirit, improves alertness and can reduce the number of workplace accidents. It can also, they say, cut the number of sick days and increase workplace productivity. One study by Teresa Lesiuk at the University of Miami found IT specialists who listened to music, completed tasks more quickly and came up with better ideas than those who didn't. But not everyone is convinced. *'If people need a high level of concentration, it could be a distraction,'* says Dr Carolyn Axtell, at the Institute of Work Psychology. *'When people choose to listen there can be positive effects – it can be relaxing and help manage other distractions such as noise. But when it's imposed, they can find it annoying and stressful.'* However, individuals can differ in their reaction to music and problems occur when colleagues clash. *'You can look away if you don't want to see something, but you can't close your ears,'* she says.

In another study researchers at London University studied the apparently common practice of surgeons playing music in the operating theatre (playlists ranged from gentle classical music through heavy metal, to electronic dance music). Patients didn't complain, being anaesthetized, but other members of the surgical team were not always happy. Music could damage communication in a surgical team, preventing team members from hearing instructions. Even worse, when sound levels are uneven and a new track blasts out unexpectedly, or when a surgeon turns up the volume when his or her favourite

song comes on, other team members can be disturbed. But notwithstanding the, sometimes conflicting, findings from researchers, some themes do emerge.

▶ How 'immersive' a task is makes a difference when evaluating music's effectiveness in increasing productive output. 'Immersive' refers to the variability and creative demand of the task. Creating an entirely original piece of work from scratch that demands a lot of creativity is 'immersive'. Performing more routine tasks such as answering emails is not. When the task is routine, clearly defined and repetitive, music is probably useful for most people.

▶ Music affects your mood. Apparently, it isn't the background noise of the music itself, but rather the improved mood that your favourite music creates that is the reason for the increase in productivity. In one study, information technology specialists who listened to music completed their tasks more quickly and came up with better ideas than those who didn't, because the music improved their mood.

▶ In open-plan offices where background chatter can be too much for some people to handle, headphones can help some people.

▶ Music does not help learning. It has a negative effect on absorbing and retaining new information, because it demands too much of your attention.

▶ Listening to music with lyrics, especially interesting and/or new lyrics, detracts from performing immersive tasks. Listening to lyrics activates the language centre of your brain, so trying to perform other language-related tasks is particularly difficult.

(Full disclosure: most of this book was written while listening to music.)

Figure 9.9 Ergonomics in the office environment

How are work times allocated?

Without some estimate of how long it takes to complete an activity, it would not be possible to know how much work to allocate to teams or individuals, to know when a task will be completed, to know how much it costs, to know if work is progressing according to schedule, and many other vital pieces of information that are needed to manage any operation. Without some estimate of work times, operations managers are 'flying blind'. At the same time, it does not need much thought before it becomes clear that measuring work times must be difficult to do with any degree of accuracy, or confidence. The time you take to do any task will depend on how skilled you are at the task, how much experience you have, how energetic or motivated you are, whether you have the appropriate tools, what the environmental conditions are, how tired you are, and so on. So, at best, any 'measurement' of how long a task will, or should, take will be an estimate. It will be our 'best guess' of how much time to allow for the task. That is why we call this process of estimating work times, 'work time allocation'. We are allocating a time for completing a task because we need to do so for many important operations management decisions. For example, work times are needed for:

▶ planning how much work a process can perform (its capacity);
▶ deciding how many staff are needed to complete tasks;
▶ scheduling individual tasks to specific people;
▶ balancing work allocation in processes (see Chapter 6);
▶ costing the labour content of a product or service;
▶ estimating the efficiency or productivity of staff and/or processes;
▶ calculating bonus payments (less important than it was at one time).

Notwithstanding the weak theoretical basis of work measurement, understanding the relationship between work and time is clearly an important part of job design. The advantage of structured and systematic work measurement is that it gives a common currency for the evaluation and comparison of all types of work. So, if work time allocation is important, how should it be done? In fact, there is a long-standing body of knowledge and experience in this area. This is generally referred to as 'work measurement', although as we have said, 'measurement' could be regarded as indicating a somewhat spurious degree of accuracy. Formally, work measurement is defined as 'the process of establishing the time for a qualified worker, at a defined level of performance, to carry out a specified job'. Although this is not a precise definition, generally it is agreed that a *specified job* is one for which specifications have been established to define most aspects of the job. A *qualified worker* is 'one who is accepted as having the necessary physical attributes, intelligence, skill, education and knowledge to perform the task to satisfactory standards of safety, quality and quantity'. Standard performance is 'the rate of output which qualified workers will achieve without over-exertion as an average over the working day provided they are motivated to apply themselves to their work'.

The techniques of work measurement

At one time, work measurement was firmly associated with an image of the 'efficiency expert', 'time and motion' man, or 'rate fixer', who wandered around factories with a stopwatch, looking to save a few cents or pennies. And although that idea of work measurement has (almost) died out, the use of a stopwatch to establish a basic time for a job is still relevant, and used in a technique called 'time study'. Time study and the general topic of work measurement is treated in the supplement to this chapter.

| OPERATIONS IN PRACTICE | Technology and surveillance at work[15] |

Monitoring and analysing how people work is not new. Work study has always been used to increase productivity by examining and evaluating methods of work. But, whereas traditionally observing how people go about their jobs has been performed 'up front' and been obvious to whoever is being examined, increasingly electronic surveillance technology is being used to track how we do our jobs. It is claimed to be a lot more effective, but a lot more controversial. Surveillance technologies range from simply requiring workers to tap in and out of their workplace (a method that has been used for over a century) to employee identification badges with integrated biometric measuring potential. These can track staff location, movements, interactions, the durations of any conversations, even the tone of voice being used in the conversation. Other technologies monitor whether you're at your desk, how often you are interrupted, what emails and phone calls are being made and even what speech patterns are being used.

All of this is in support of increasing productivity and devising new work methods, say its supporters. Not so, say its detractors. There are dangers inherent in such surveillance, especially as technology creates more opportunities for companies to monitor their employees in unprecedented ways. Certainly, not everyone likes to be monitored. One study[16] found (unsurprisingly) that the more people felt their privacy to be violated at work, the more dissatisfied they were. Also, when they believe the surveillance to be unnecessary or too intense, they are more likely to find ways to subvert, sabotage or trick the surveillance systems. Objections can be more formalized. For example, when journalists at *The Telegraph* (a UK newspaper) discovered that a tracking device had been added to their desks by senior management, their union objected and the sensors (which monitored body heat, indicating when employees were at their desk and how often they moved around) were removed. *'The right to be consulted on new procedures governing such data is enshrined in law,'* said the union's assistant general secretary. '[We] *will resist Big Brother-style surveillance in the newsroom.'* Nevertheless, surveillance can be deemed necessary. In 2018 the UK Food Standards Agency announced that closed-circuit television will be installed at all 900 meat-cutting plants it monitored under plans to improve hygiene and reduce the risk of food poisoning. It had discovered that several plants had breached food safety rules by altering use-by dates on meat or dropping meat on the floor and putting it back on to the production line.

As well as time study, there are other work measurement techniques in use. They include the following.

- *Synthesis from elemental data* is a work measurement technique for building up the time for a job at a defined level of performance by totalling element times obtained previously from studies of other jobs containing the elements concerned or from synthetic data.
- *Predetermined motion–time systems* (PMTS) are a work measurement technique whereby times established for basic human motions (classified according to the nature of the motion and the conditions under which it is made) are used to build up the time for a job at a defined level of performance.
- *Analytical estimating* is a work measurement technique which is a development of estimating whereby the time required to carry out the elements of a job at a defined level of performance is estimated from knowledge and experience of the elements concerned.
- *Activity sampling* is a technique in which a large number of instantaneous observations are made over a period of time of a group of machines, processes or workers. Each observation records what is happening at that instant and the percentage of observations recorded for a particular activity or delay is a measure of the percentage of time during which that activity or delay occurs.

Critical commentary

The criticisms aimed at work measurement are many and various. Among the most common are the following:

- All the ideas on which the concept of a standard time is based are impossible to define precisely. How can one possibly give clarity to the definition of qualified workers, or specified jobs, or especially a defined level of performance?
- Even if one attempts to follow these definitions, all that results is an excessively rigid job definition. Most modern jobs require some element of flexibility, which is difficult to achieve alongside rigidly defined jobs.
- Using stopwatches to time human beings is both degrading and usually counterproductive. At best it is intrusive, at worst it makes people into 'objects for study'.

- ▶ The rating procedure implicit in time study is subjective and usually arbitrary. It has no basis other than the opinion of the person carrying out the study.
- ▶ Time study, especially, is very easy to manipulate. It is possible for employers to 'work back' from a time which is 'required' to achieve a particular cost. Also, experienced staff can 'put on an act' to fool the person recording the times.

Summary answers to key questions

Why are people issues so important in operations management?

- ▶ Human resources are any organization's, and therefore any operation's, greatest asset. Often, most 'human resources' are to be found in the operations function.

What forms can organization designs take?

- ▶ One can take various perspectives on organizations. How we illustrate organizations says much about our underlying assumptions of what an 'organization' is. For example, organizations can be described as machines, organisms, brains, cultures or political systems.
- ▶ The relationship between the 'staff' and 'line' roles in operation can be modelled using the four perspectives on operations strategy that were discussed in Chapter 3.
- ▶ There are an almost infinite number of possible organizational structures. Most are blends of two or more 'pure types', such as the U-form, the M-form, matrix forms and the N-form.

How do we go about designing jobs?

- ▶ There are many influences on how jobs are designed. These include: the division of labour; scientific management; method study; work measurement; ergonomics; and behavioural approaches, such as job rotation, job enlargement and job enrichment, empowerment, team working and flexible working (including 'telecommuting').

How are work times allocated?

- ▶ The best-known method is time study, but there are other work measurement techniques including synthesis from elemental data, predetermined motion–time systems (PMTS), analytical estimating and activity sampling.

CASE STUDY   Grace faces (three) problems

Grace Whelan, Managing Partner of McPherson Charles, was puzzled. Three of her most successful teams seemed to be facing similar problems with their staff, even though each team had very different tasks, processes and types of staff. Every year the firm surveyed its entire staff in order to gauge their views, levels of satisfaction with their jobs and development needs. It was the results from the latest survey that surprised Grace. *'The results of the survey are really unanticipated. Only last year everything seemed fine. Now staff morale has evidently slumped in all three teams. Yet the partners who lead all of these teams are first class. Outstanding lawyers and good leaders.'*

McPherson Charles, based in Bristol in the West of England, had grown rapidly to be one of the biggest law firms in the region, with 21 partners and around 400 staff. Three years previously the firm had reorganized into 15 teams, each headed by a 'lead partner' and specializing in practising one type of law. It had proved to be a good organizational structure, which encouraged each team to organize themselves appropriately for the type of clients that they dealt with. In particular, three teams had flourished under this structure, 'family law', 'property' and 'litigation'. Now it was these very teams whose staff were showing signs of dissatisfaction.

Before the results of the survey were published to all staff, Grace knew that she would need to have worked out some kind of response to the issues raised. She decided to go and see each of the lead partners in the three teams. The first person she decided to talk to was Simon Reece, who led the family law team. Before doing so she explained what his team did.

Family law

'They are called the "family law" team but basically what they do is to help people through the trauma of divorce, separation and break up. Their biggest "high value" clients come to them because of word of mouth recommendation. Last year they had almost a hundred of these "high value" clients and they all valued the personal touch that they were able to give them, getting to know them well and spending time with them to understand the often "hidden" aspects of their case. Of course, not all their clients are the super-rich. About a third of the annual family law income comes from about 750 relatively routine divorce and counselling cases.'

Simon was blunt about the declining levels of staff satisfaction in his team. *'The problem is that working with the "high value" clients is just more fun and more rewarding than the routine "bread and butter" work. So my people who do that kind of work, usually the more experienced ones, don't want to take on the routine stuff. With "high value" cases you have to be able to untangle the personal issues from the business ones. Interviewing these clients cannot be rushed. They tend to be wealthy people with complex assets. We will often have to drop everything and go off half way round the world to meet and discuss their situation. There are no standard procedures, every client is different, and everyone has to be treated as an individual. So we have a team of individuals who rise to the challenge each time and give great service. By contrast, the routine work is a lot less interesting, yet sometimes very harrowing. The more junior staff who tend to take on the routine cases can sometimes feel themselves to be "second-class citizens". Many of them would like to get more experience with the complex high value work, but I can't take the risk of giving them that degree of responsibility, the work is too valuable. Also, frankly, the senior people who deal with the high value work don't want to give up their more glamorous work. I have been trying to make sure that everyone in my team who wants to has a mix of interesting and routine work over the year. It's the only way to develop them in the long term. You have to encourage them to exercise and develop their professional judgement. They are empowered to deal with any issues themselves or call on one of the more senior members of the team for advice if appropriate. It is important to give this kind of responsibility to them so that they see themselves as part of a team. But there are still tensions between senior and more junior staff. We are thinking about adopting an open-plan office arrangement centred around our specialist library of family case law, to try and encourage more cooperation.'*

Litigation

Grace was less concerned about the litigation team, led by Hazel Lewis. *'The litigation team has been our best success story. The have grown far faster than any other part of the firm, and a lot of that is down to Hazel. She provides a key service for our commercial client base. Their primary work consists of handling bulk collections of debt. The group has 17 clients of which 5 provide 85 per cent of total volume. They work closely with the accounts departments of the client companies and have developed a semi-automatic approach to debt collection. It's a great service that Hazel has largely automated.'*

Hazel had led the litigation team since it had been set up 4 years ago. As well as being the partner in charge of litigation, unusually she and her assistant were the only qualified lawyers in the team. *'Our problems in the litigation team are not really because of any internal tensions or disputes. Broadly, our people are happy with what they do and how they are supervised. The issue is just that we are so different from the rest of the firm. Apart from myself and Raymond [her assistant] everyone else in the team are either technicians who look after and develop the systems that we use, or people who have worked in processing or call centres, before they came to us. And between us we have developed a smart operation here. Our staff input data received from their clients into the system, from that point everything progresses through a pre-defined process, letters are produced, queries responded to and eventually debts collected, ultimately through court proceedings if necessary. Work tends to come in batches from clients and varies according to the time of year and client sales activities. At the moment things are fairly steady: we had almost 900 new cases to deal with last week. The details of each case are sent over by the client; our people input the data onto our screens and set up a standard diary system for sending letters out. Some people respond quickly to the first letter and often the case is closed within a week or so; other people ignore letters and eventually we initiate court proceedings. We know exactly what is required for court dealings and have a pretty good process to make sure all the right documentation is available on the day. Our problem is that the rest of the firm does not see us as being "proper lawyers", and they are right, we're not. But it does get difficult for our people, being looked down upon all the time. Our salary structure is different, our bonus scheme is different, and how we measure performance is different. But there is a solution. Because we have expanded so much, we need more space than is available in this building. I think that we should think about moving the litigation team. There is a great location out by the airport that could be expanded in the future if needed. There is really no reason for us to be located with the other teams.'*

Property

The 'property' team is one of the largest parts of the firm and is established in the local market with an excellent reputation for being fast, friendly and giving value for money. Most of their work is 'domestic', acting for individuals buying or selling their home, or their second home. Each client is allocated to a solicitor who becomes his or her main point of contact. But, given that they can have up to a hundred domestic clients a week, most of the work is actually carried out by the rest of the team of 'paralegal' staff (staff with qualifications less than a fully qualified lawyer) behind the scenes.

Kate Hutchinson, who led the property team, was proud of the process she and her team had set up. *'There is a relatively standard process to domestic property sales and purchases and we think that we are pretty efficient at managing these standard jobs. Our process has four stages, one dealing with land registry searches, one liaising with banks who are providing the mortgage finance, one who make sure surveys are completed and one section that finalizes the whole process to completion. We believe that this degree of specialization can help us achieve the efficiencies that are becoming important, as the market gets more competitive. Our particular problem is that increasingly we are also getting more complex "special" jobs. These are things like "volume re-mortgage" arrangements and rather complex "one-off" jobs, where a mortgage lender transfers a complex set of loan assets to another lender. These "special" jobs are always more complex than the domestic work and they are not popular with our staff. They don't always fit easily into our standard process, and they disrupt the routine of working. For example, sometimes there are occasions when fast completion is particularly important and that can throw us a bit.'*

Grace was more worried about the property team than Kate appeared to be. The firm had recently formed partnerships with two large speculative builders, which dealt in special 'plot sales' that would also be classed as non-standard 'specials' by Kate. Grace knew that all these 'specials' did involve a lot of work and could occupy several members of the team for a time. But they were an important source of revenue. Currently the team was dealing with up to 25 'specials' each week, and this would certainly increase. Grace suspected that Kate was mistaken to try and follow the same process with them as the normal domestic jobs. Maybe trying to do different things on the same process was the cause of the dissatisfaction in the team?

QUESTIONS

1 What are the problems amongst the staff of each of the three teams?

2 What are the individual 'services' offered by each of the three teams?

3 How would you describe each team's process in terms of the jobs of its staff?

4 What do you think each team leader should be doing to try and overcome their team's problems?

their main concerns was trying to balance the job with outside commitments, such as family and leisure. So, the Group introduced its flexible working policy, called 'Work Options'. It allowed staff to request a different working pattern from the conventional working day. Sometimes this simply involved starting and finishing earlier or later each day, while maintaining the same weekly hours. This could benefit the business. Varying staff's work patterns could mean staffing is more closely aligned with actual customer demand. Job sharing is also used. It suits two staff, who may not want full-time employment and the business can have two people's combined experience, skills and creativity. Job-sharing staff can also be more productive than full-time colleagues. Another form of flexible working is 'compressed working', where staff work a standard one or two weeks within a shorter time scale, for example by working some longer days a week, then taking extra time off to compensate. (a) What seem to be the main advantages and potential disadvantages of flexible working for staff, the company and customers? (b) How can a firm such as Lloyds try and overcome any clashes between the requirements of staff, the business and customers?

Selected further reading

Argyris, C. (1998) Empowerment: the emperor's new clothes, *Harvard Business Review,* **May–June.**
A critical but fascinating view of empowerment.

Bock, L. (2015) *Work Rules!: Insights from Inside Google that Will Transform How You Live and Lead,* **John Murray, London.**
With an agenda far wider than this chapter, it is nevertheless an absorbing book that gives an insight into an absorbing firm.

Dul, J. and Weerdmeester, B. (2008) *Ergonomics for Beginners: A Quick Reference Guide,* **3rd edn, CRC Press, Boca Raton, FL.**
Good, practical guidance on the removal from the workplace of physical and mental stresses caused by poor job or environmental design.

Hackman, R.J. and Oldham, G. (1980) *Work Redesign,* **Addison-Wesley, Reading, MA.**
Somewhat dated but, in its time, ground breaking and certainly hugely influential.

Herzberg, F. (1987) One more time: how do you motivate employees? (with retrospective commentary), *Harvard Business Review,* **vol. 65, no. 5, 109–120.**
An interesting look back by one of the most influential figures in the behavioural approach to job design school.

Lantz, A. and Brav, A. (2007) Job design for learning in work groups, *Journal of Workplace Learning,* **vol. 19, no. 5, 269–285.**
The title is self-explanatory.

Shorrock, S. (Editor) (2016) *Human Factors and Ergonomics in Practice.* **Routledge.**
An edited book, but with lots of examples of the real practice of human factors and ergonomics.

INTRODUCTION

A tale is told of Frank Gilbreth (the founder of method study) addressing a scientific conference with a paper entitled 'The Best Way to Get Dressed in the Morning'. In his presentation, he rather bemused the scientific audience by analysing the 'best' way of buttoning up one's waistcoat in the morning. Among his conclusions was that waistcoats should always be buttoned from the bottom upwards (to make it easier to straighten his tie in the same motion; buttoning from the top downwards requires the hands to be raised again). Think of this example if you want to understand scientific management and method study in particular. First of all, he is quite right. Method study and the other techniques of scientific management may often be without any intellectual or scientific validation, but by and large they work in their own terms. Second, Gilbreth reached his conclusion by a systematic and critical analysis of what motions were necessary to do the job. Again, these are characteristics of scientific management – detailed analysis and painstakingly systematic examination. Third (and possibly most important), the results are relatively trivial. A great deal of effort was put into reaching a conclusion that was unlikely to have any earth-shattering consequences. Indeed, one of the criticisms of scientific management, as developed in the early part of the twentieth century, is that it concentrated on relatively limited, and sometimes trivial, objectives.

The responsibility for its application, however, has moved away from specialist 'time and motion' staff to the employees who can use such principles to improve what they do and how they do it. Further, some of the methods and techniques of scientific management, as opposed to its philosophy (especially those which come under the general heading of 'method study'), can in practice prove useful in critically re-examining job designs. It is the practicality of these techniques which possibly explains why they are still influential in job design almost a century after their inception.

Method study in job design

Method study is a systematic approach to finding the best method. There are six steps:

1 Select the work to be studied.
2 Record all the relevant facts of the present method.
3 Examine those facts critically and in sequence.
4 Develop the most practical, economic and effective method.
5 Install the new method.
6 Maintain the method by periodically checking it in use.

Step 1 – Selecting the work to be studied

Most operations have many hundreds and possibly thousands of discrete jobs and activities which could be subjected to study. The first stage in method study is to select those jobs to be studied which will give the most return on the investment of the time spent studying them. This means it is unlikely that it will be worth studying activities which, for example, may soon be discontinued or are only performed occasionally. On the other hand, the types of job which should be studied as a matter of priority are those which, for example, seem to offer the greatest scope for improvement, or which are causing bottlenecks, delays or problems in the operation.

Step 2 – Recording the present method

There are many different recording techniques used in method study. Most of them:

▶ record the sequence of activities in the job;
▶ record the time interrelationship of the activities in the job; or
▶ record the path of movement of some part of the job.

Perhaps the most commonly used recording technique in method study is process mapping which was discussed in Chapter 4. Note that we are here recording the present method of doing the job. It may seem strange to devote so much time and effort to recording what is currently happening when, after all, the objective of method study is to devise a better method. The rationale for this is, first of all, that recording the present method can give a far greater insight into the job itself, and this can lead to new ways of doing it. Second, recording the present method is a good starting point from which to evaluate it critically and therefore improve it. In this last point the assumption is that it is easier to improve the method by starting from the current method and then criticizing it in detail than by starting with a 'blank sheet of paper'.

Step 3 – Examining the facts

This is probably the most important stage in method study and the idea here is to examine the current method thoroughly and critically. This is often done by using the so-called 'questioning technique'. This technique attempts to detect weaknesses in the rationale for existing methods so that alternative methods can be developed (see Table S9.1). The approach may appear somewhat detailed and tedious, yet it is fundamental to the method study philosophy – everything must be critically examined. Understanding the natural tendency to be less than rigorous at this stage, some organizations use pro forma questionnaires, asking each of these questions and leaving space for formal replies and/or justifications, which the job designer is required to complete.

Table S9.1 The method study questioning technique

Broad question	Detailed question
The purpose of each activity (questions the fundamental need for the element)	What is done? Why is it done? What else could be done? What should be done?
The place in which each element is done (may suggest a combination of certain activities or operations)	Where is it done? Why is it done there? Where else could it be done? Where should it be done?
The sequence in which the elements are done (may suggest a change in the sequence of the activity)	When is it done? Why is it done then? When should it be done?
The person who does the activity (may suggest a combination and/or change in responsibility or sequence).	Who does it? Why does that person do it? Who else could do it? Who should do it?
The means by which each activity is done (may suggest new methods)	How is it done? Why is it done in that way? How else could it be done? How should it be done?

Step 4 – Developing a new method

The previous critical examination of current methods has by this stage probably indicated some changes and improvements. This step involves taking these ideas further in an attempt to:

▶ eliminate parts of the activity altogether;
▶ combine elements together;
▶ change the sequence of events so as to improve the efficiency of the job; or
▶ simplify the activity to reduce the work content.

A useful aid during this process is a checklist such as the revised principles of motion economy. Table S9.2 illustrates these.

Steps 5 and 6 – Install the new method and regularly maintain it

The method study approach to the installation of new work practices concentrates largely on 'project managing' the installation process. It also emphasizes the need to monitor regularly the effectiveness of job designs after they have been installed.

Work measurement in job design

Basic times

Terminology is important in work measurement. When a *qualified worker* is working on a *specified job* at *standard performance,* the time he or she takes to perform the job is called the basic time for the job. Basic times are useful because they are the 'building blocks' of time estimation. With the basic times for a range of different tasks, an operations manager can construct a time estimate

Table S9.2 The principles of motion economy

Broad principle	How to do it
Use the human body the way it works best	▶ Work should be arranged so that a natural rhythm can become automatic. ▶ Motion of the body should be simultaneous and symmetrical if possible. ▶ The full capabilities of the human body should be employed. ▶ Arms and hands as weights are subject to the physical laws and energy should be conserved. ▶ Tasks should be simplified.
Arrange the workplace to assist performance	▶ There should be a defined place for all equipment and materials. ▶ Equipment, materials and controls should be located close to the point of use. ▶ Equipment, materials and controls should be located to permit the best sequence and path of motions. ▶ The workplace should be fitted both to the tasks and to human capabilities.
Use technology to reduce human effort	▶ Work should be presented precisely where needed. ▶ Guides should assist in positioning the work without close operator attention. ▶ Controls and foot-operated devices can relieve the hands of work. ▶ Mechanical devices can multiply human abilities. ▶ Mechanical systems should be fitted to human use.

Source: Adapted from Barnes, Frank C. (1983) 'Principles of Motion Economy: Revisited, Reviewed, and Restored', *Proceedings of the Southern Management Association Annual Meeting* (Atlanta, GA 1983), p. 298.

for any longer activity which is made up of the tasks. The best-known technique for establishing basic times is probably time study.

Time study

Time study is 'a work measurement technique for recording the times and rate of working for the elements of a specified job, carried out under specified conditions, and for analysing the data so as to obtain the time necessary for the carrying out of the job at a defined level of performance'. The technique takes three steps to derive the basic times for the elements of the job:

▶ observing and measuring the time taken to perform each element of the job;
▶ adjusting, or 'normalizing', each observed time;
▶ averaging the adjusted times to derive the basic time for the element.

Step 1 – Observing, measuring and rating

A job is observed through several cycles. Each time an element is performed, it is timed using a stopwatch. Simultaneously with the observation of time, a rating of the perceived performance of the person doing the job is recorded. Rating is 'the process of assessing the worker's rate of working relative to the observer's concept of the rate corresponding to standard performance. The observer may take into account, separately or in combination, one or more factors necessary to carrying out the job, such as speed of movement, effort, dexterity, consistency, etc.'. There are several ways of recording the observer's rating. The most common is on a scale which uses a rating of 100 to represent standard performance. If an observer rates a particular observation of the time to perform an element at 100, the time observed is the actual time which anyone working at standard performance would take.

Step 2 – Adjusting the observed times

The adjustment to normalize the observed time is:

$$\frac{\text{observed rating}}{\text{standard rating}}$$

where standard rating is 100 on the common rating scale we are using here. For example, if the observed time is 0.71 minutes and the observed rating is 90, then:

$$\text{Basic time} = \frac{0.71 \times 90}{100} = 0.64 \text{ mins}$$

Step 3 – Averaging the basic times

In spite of the adjustments made to the observed times through the rating mechanism, each separately calculated basic time will not be the same. This is not necessarily a function of inaccurate rating, or even the vagueness of the rating procedure itself; it is a natural phenomenon of the time taken to perform tasks. Any human activity cannot be repeated in *exactly* the same time on every occasion.

Standard times

The standard time for a job is an extension of the basic time and has a different use. Whereas the basic time for a job is a piece of information which can be used as the first step in estimating the time to perform a job under a wide range of conditions, standard time refers to the time *allowed* for the job under specific circumstances. This is because standard time includes allowances which reflect the rest and relaxation allowed because of the conditions under which the job is performed. So the standard time for each element consists principally of two parts, the basic time (the time taken by a qualified worker, doing a specified job at standard performance) and an allowance (this is added to the basic time to allow for rest, relaxation and personal needs).

Allowances

Allowances are additions to the basic time intended to provide the worker with the opportunity to recover from the physiological and psychological effects of carrying out specified work under specified conditions and to allow for personal needs. The amount of the allowance will depend on the nature of the job. The way in which relaxation allowance is calculated, and the exact allowances given for each of the factors which determine the extent of the allowance, varies between different organizations. Table S9.3 illustrates the allowance table used by one company which manufactures domestic appliances. Every job has an allowance of 10 per cent. The table shows the further percentage allowances to be applied to each element of the job. In addition, other allowances may be applied for such things as unexpected contingencies, synchronization with other jobs, unusual working conditions, and so on.

Figure S9.1 shows how average basic times for each element in the job are combined with allowances (low in this example) for each element to build up the standard time for the whole job.

Table S9.3 An allowances table used by a domestic appliance manufacturer

Allowance factors	Example	Allowance (%)
Energy needed		
Negligible	None	0
Very light	0–3 kg	3
Light	3–10 kg	5
Medium	10–20 kg	10
Heavy	20–30 kg	15
Very heavy	Above 30 kg	15–30
Posture required		
Normal	Sitting	0
Erect	Standing	2
Continuously erect	Standing for long periods	3
Lying	On side, face or back	4
Difficult	Crouching, etc.	4–10
Visual fatigue		
Nearly continuous attention		2
Continuous attention with varying focus		3
Continuous attention with fixed focus		5
Temperature		
Very low	Below 0°C	over 10
Low	0–12°C	0–10
Normal	12–23°C	0
High	23–30°C	0–10
Very high	Above 30°C	over 10
Atmospheric conditions		
Good	Well ventilated	0
Fair	Stuffy/smelly	2
Poor	Dusty/needs filter	2–7
Bad	Needs respirator	7–12

Element		Observation					Observation					Average basic time	Allowances	Element standard time
		1	2	3	4	5	6	7	8	9	10			
Make box	Observed time	0.71	0.71	0.71	0.69	0.75	0.68	0.70	0.70	0.70	0.68			
	Rating	90	90	90	90	80	90	90	90	90	90			
	Basic time	0.64	0.64	0.63	0.62	0.60	0.61	0.63	0.65	0.63	0.61	0.626	10%	0.689
Pack × 20	Observed time	1.30	1.32	1.25	1.33	1.33	1.28	1.32	1.32	1.30	1.30			
	Rating	90	90	100	90	90	90	90	90	90	90			
	Basic time	1.17	1.19	1.25	1.20	1.20	1.15	1.19	1.19	1.17	1.17	1.168	12%	1.308
Seal and secure	Observed time	0.53	0.55	0.55	0.56	0.53	0.53	0.53	0.55	0.49	0.51			
	Rating	90	90	90	90	90	90	90	90	100	100			
	Basic time	0.48	0.50	0.50	0.50	0.48	0.48	0.48	0.50	0.49	0.51	0.495	10%	0.545
Assemble outwe,	Observed time	1.12	1.21	1.20	1.25	1.41	1.27	1.27	1.15	1.20	1.23			
fix and label	Rating	100	90	90	90	90	90	90	100	90	90			
	Basic time	1.12	1.09	1.08	1.13	1.27	1.14	1.14	1.15	1.08	1.21	1.138	12%	1.275

Raw standard time		3.817
Allowances for total job	5%	0.191
Standard time for job		4.01 SM

Figure S9.1 Time study of a packing task – standard time for the whole task calculated

Worked example

Two work teams in the Monrovian Embassy have been allocated the task of processing visa applications. Team A processes applications from Europe, Africa and the Middle East. Team B processes applications from North and South America, Asia and Australasia. Team A has chosen to organize itself in such a way that each of its three team members processes an application from start to finish. The four members of Team B have chosen to split themselves into two sub-teams. Two open the letters and carry out the checks for a criminal record (no one who has been convicted of any crime other than a motoring offence can enter Monrovia), while the other two team members check for financial security (only people with more than Monrovian $1,000 may enter the country). The head of consular affairs is keen to find out if one of these methods of organizing the teams is more efficient than the other. The problem is that the mix of applications differs region by region. Team A typically processes around two business applications to every one tourist application. Team B processes around one business application to every two tourist applications.

A study revealed the following data:

Average standard time to process a business visa = 63 standard minutes
Average time to process a tourist visa = 55 standard minutes

Average weekly output from Team A is:

85.2 business visas
39.5 tourist visas

Average weekly output from Team B is:

53.5 business visas
100.7 tourist visas

All team members work a 40-hour week.

The efficiency of each team can be calculated by comparing the actual output in standard minutes and the time worked in minutes.

So Team A processes:

$$(85.2 \times 63) + (39.5 \times 55) = 7{,}540.1 \text{ standard minutes of work}$$

$$\text{in } 3 \times 40 \times 60 \text{ minutes} = 7{,}200 \text{ minutes}$$

$$\text{So its efficiency} = \frac{7{,}540.1}{7{,}200} \times 100 = 104.72\%$$

Team B processes:

$$(53.5 \times 63) + (100.7 \times 55) = 8{,}909 \text{ standard minutes of work}$$

$$\text{in } 4 \times 40 \times 60 \text{ minutes} = 9{,}600 \text{ minutes}$$

$$\text{So its efficiency} = \frac{8{,}909}{9{,}600} \times 100 = 92.8\%$$

The initial evidence therefore seems to suggest that the way Team A has organized itself is more efficient.

PART THREE

Deliver

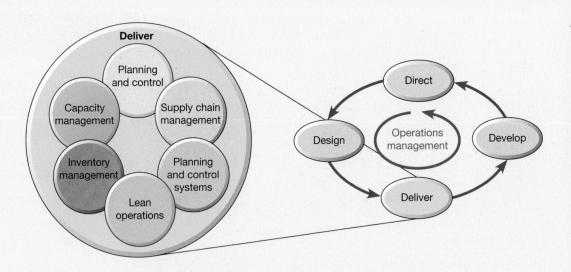

All the activities involved in the design of an operation should have provided the nature and shape of the transforming resources that are capable of satisfying customers' demands. Products and services then have to be created and delivered to customers. This is done by planning and controlling the activities of the transforming resources on a day-to-day basis to ensure the appropriate supply of products and services to meet the requirements of the market. This part of the book will look at six different aspects of planning and controlling the delivery of products and services as they flow through processes, operations and supply networks. The chapters in this part are:

▶ **Chapter 10 Planning and control**

This examines how operations organize the delivery of their products and services on an ongoing basis so that customers' demands are satisfied.

▶ **Chapter 11 Capacity management**

This explains how operations need to decide how to vary their capacity (if at all) as demand for their products and services fluctuates.

▶ **Chapter 12 Supply chain management**

This describes how operations relate to each other in the context of a wider network of suppliers and customers, and how these relationships can be managed.

▶ **Chapter 13 Inventory management**

This looks at how transformed resources accumulate as inventories as they flow through processes, operations or supply networks.

▶ **Chapter 14 Planning and control systems**

This describes how systems are needed to manage the very large amounts of information required to plan and control operations, and how enterprise resources planning (ERP) is used to do this.

▶ **Chapter 15 Lean operations**

This explains the concepts that underlie one of the most influential sets of ideas to impact operations management.

10 Planning and control

KEY QUESTIONS

What is planning and control?

What is the difference between planning and control?

How do supply and demand affect planning and control?

What are the activities of planning and control?

INTRODUCTION

The design of an operation determines the resources with which it creates its services and products, but then the operation has to deliver those services and products on an ongoing basis. And central to an operation's ability to deliver is the way it plans its activities and controls them so that customers' demands are satisfied. This chapter introduces and provides an overview of some of the principles and methods of planning and control. Later chapters in this part of the book develop some specific issues that are vital to an operation delivering its services and products. These issues start with managing capacity and move through managing inventory, providing an overview of supply chain management and looking at how planning and control systems, particularly enterprise resources planning (ERP), manage the information that ensures effective delivery. We then examine how 'lean' philosophy has influenced operations practice. Figure 10.1 shows where this topic fits into the activities of operations management.

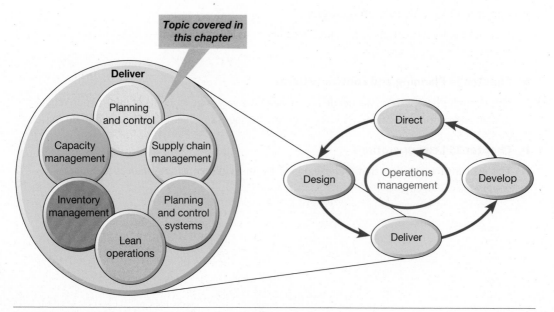

Figure 10.1 This chapter examines planning and control

What is planning and control?

Planning and control is concerned with the activities that attempt to reconcile the demands of the market and the ability of the operation's resources to deliver. It provides the systems, procedures and decisions which bring different aspects of supply and demand together. Consider, for example, the way in which routine surgery is organized in a hospital. When a patient arrives and is admitted to the hospital, much of the planning for the surgery will already have happened. The operating theatre will have been reserved, and the doctors and nurses who staff the operating theatre will have been provided with all the information regarding the patient's condition. Appropriate preoperative and postoperative care will have been organized. All this will involve staff and facilities in different parts of the hospital, all of whom must have been given the same information and their activities coordinated. Soon after the patient arrives, he or she will be checked to make sure that the condition is as expected (in much the same way as material is inspected on arrival in a factory). Blood, if required, will be cross-matched and reserved, and any medication will be made ready (in the same way that all the different materials are brought together in a factory). Any last-minute changes may require some degree of re-planning. For example, if the patient shows unexpected symptoms, observation may be necessary before the surgery can take place. Not only will this affect the patient's own treatment, but other patients' treatment may also have to be rescheduled (in the same way as machines will need rescheduling if a job is delayed in a factory). All these activities of scheduling, coordination and organization are concerned with the planning and control of the hospital.

Operations principle

Customers' perceptions of an operation will partially be shaped by the customer interface of its planning and control system.

OPERATIONS IN PRACTICE

Joanne manages the schedule[1]

Joanne Cheung is the Senior Service Adviser at a premier BMW dealership. She and her team act as the interface between customers who want their cars serviced and repaired, and the 16 technicians who carry out the work in their state-of-the-art workshop. *'There are three types of work that we have to organize,'* says Joanne. *'The first is performing repairs on customers' vehicles. They usually want this doing as soon as possible. The second type of job is routine servicing. It is usually not urgent so customers are generally willing to negotiate a time for this. The remainder of our work involves working on the pre-owned cars which our buyer has bought-in to sell on to customers. Before any of these cars can be sold they have to undergo extensive checks. To some extent we treat these categories of work slightly differently. We have to give good service to our internal car buyers, but there is some flexibility in planning these jobs. At the other extreme, emergency repair work for customers has to be fitted into our schedule as quickly as possible. If someone is desperate to have their car repaired at very short notice, we sometimes ask them to drop their car in as early as they can and* pick it up as late as possible. This gives us the maximum amount of time to fit it into the schedule.

There are a number of service options open to customers. We can book short jobs in for a fixed time and do it while they wait. Most commonly, we ask the customer to leave the car with us and collect it later. To help customers we have ten loan cars which are booked out on a first-come first-served basis. Alternatively, the vehicle can be collected from the customer's home and delivered back there when it is ready. Our four drivers who do this are able to cope with up to 12 jobs a day.

Most days we deal with 50 to 80 jobs, taking from half-an-hour up to a whole day. To enter a job into our process all Service Advisers have access to the computer-based scheduling system. On-screen it shows the total capacity we have day-by-day, all the jobs that are booked in, the amount of free capacity still available, the number of loan cars available, and so on. We use this to see when we have the capacity to book a customer in, and then enter all the customer's details. BMW have issued "standard times" for all the major jobs. However, you have to modify these standard times a bit to take account of circumstances. That is where the Service Adviser's experience comes in.

We keep all the most commonly used parts in stock, but if a repair needs a part which is not in stock, we can usually get it from the BMW parts distributors within a day. Every evening our planning system prints out the jobs to be done the next day and the parts which are likely to be needed for each job. This allows the parts staff to pick out the parts for each job so that the technicians can collect them first thing the next morning without any delay.

Every day we have to cope with the unexpected. A technician may find that extra work is needed, customers may want extra work doing, and technicians are sometimes ill, which reduces our capacity. Occasionally parts may not be available so we have to arrange with the customer for the vehicle to be rebooked for a later time. Every day up to four or five customers just don't turn up. Usually they have just forgotten to bring their car in, so we have to rebook them in at a later time. We can cope with most of these uncertainties because our technicians are flexible in terms of the skills they have and also are willing to work overtime when needed. Also, it is important to manage customers' expectations. If there is a chance that the vehicle may not be ready for them, it shouldn't come as a surprise when they try and collect it.'

The difference between planning and control

Notice that we have chosen to treat 'planning and control' together. This is because the division between 'planning' and 'control' is not clear, either in theory or in practice. However, there are some general features that help to distinguish between the two. Planning is a formalization of what is intended to happen at some time in the future. But a plan does not guarantee that an event will actually happen. Rather it is a statement of intention. Although plans are based on expectations, during their implementation things do not always happen as expected. Customers change their minds about what they want and when they want it. Suppliers may not always deliver on time, process technology may fail, or staff may be absent through illness. Control is the process of coping with these types of change. It may mean that plans need to be redrawn in the short term. It may also mean that an 'intervention' will need to be made in the operation to bring it back 'on track' – for example, finding a new supplier who can deliver quickly, getting process technology up and running again, or moving staff from another part of the operation to cover for the absentees. Control activities make the adjustments which allow the operation to achieve the objectives that the plan has set, even when the assumptions on which the plan was based do not hold true.

Operations principle

Planning and control are separate but closely related activities.

Long-, medium- and short-term planning and control

The nature of planning and control activities changes over time. In the very long term, operations managers make plans concerning what they intend to do, what resources they need, and what objectives they hope to achieve. The emphasis is on planning rather than control, because there is little to control as such. They will use forecasts of likely demand described in aggregated terms. For example, a hospital will make plans for '2,000 patients' without necessarily going into the details of the individual needs of those 2,000 patients. Similarly, the hospital might plan to have 100 nurses and 20 doctors but again without deciding on the specific attributes of the staff. Operations managers will focus mainly on volume and financial targets

Medium-term planning and control is more detailed. It looks ahead to assess the overall demand which the operation must meet in a partially disaggregated manner. By this time, for example, the hospital must distinguish between different types of demand. The number of patients coming as accident and emergency cases will need to be distinguished from those requiring routine operations. Similarly, different categories of staff will have been identified and broad staffing levels in each category set. Just as important, contingencies will have been put in place which allow for slight deviations from the plans. These contingencies will act as 'reserve' resources and make planning and control easier in the short term.

In short-term planning and control, many of the resources will have been set and it will be difficult to make large changes. However, short-term interventions are possible if things are not going to plan. By this time, demand will be assessed on a totally disaggregated basis, with all types of surgical procedures treated as individual activities. More importantly, individual patients will have been identified by name, and specific time slots booked for their treatment. In making short-term interventions and changes to the plan, operations managers will be attempting to balance the quality, speed, dependability, flexibility and costs of their operation dynamically on an *ad hoc* basis. It is unlikely that they will have the time to carry out detailed calculations of the effects of their short-term planning and control decisions on all these objectives, but a general understanding of priorities will form the background to their decision making. Figure 10.2 shows how the control aspects of planning and control increase in significance closer to the date of the event.

The volume–variety effect on planning and control

As we have found previously, the volume and variety characteristics of an operation will have an effect on its planning and control activities. Operations which produce a high variety of services or products in relatively low volume will have customers with different requirements and use different processes from operations which create standardized services or products in high volume (see Table 10.1).

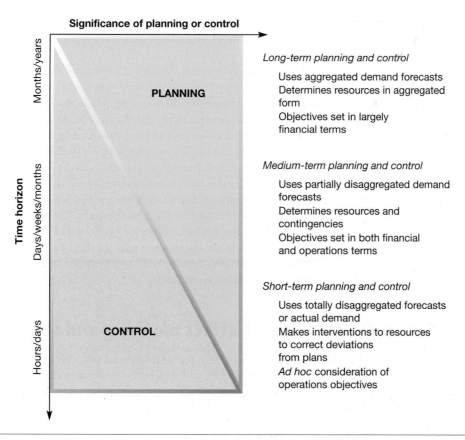

Figure 10.2 The balance between planning and control activities changes in the long, medium and short terms

Table 10.1 The volume–variety effects on planning and control

Volume	Variety	Customer responsiveness	Planning horizon	Major planning decision	Control decisions	Robustness
Low	High	Slow	Short	Timing	Detailed	High
↓	↓	↓	↓	↓	↓	↓
High	Low	Fast	Long	Volume	Aggregated	Low

Take two contrasting operations – an architects' practice and an electricity utility. The architects' high variety of customized services means they cannot produce designs in advance of customers requesting them. Because of this, the time it will take to finally deliver their services to customers will be relatively slow. Customers will understand this, but will expect to be consulted extensively as to their needs. The details and requirements of each job will emerge only as each individual building is designed to the client's requirements, so planning occurs on a relatively short-term basis. The individual decisions which are taken in the planning process will usually concern the timing of activities and events – for example, when a design is to be delivered, when building should start, when each individual architect will be needed to work on the design. Control decisions also will be at a relatively detailed level. A small delay in fixing one part of the design could have significant implications in many other parts of the job. For an architect, planning and control cannot be a totally routine matter; projects need managing on an individual basis. However, the robustness of the operation (that is, its vulnerability to serious disruption if one part of the operation fails) will be relatively high. There are probably plenty of other things to get on with if an architect is prevented from progressing one part of the job.

The electricity utility, on the other hand, is very different. Volume is high, production is continuous, and variety is non-existent. Customers expect instant 'delivery' whenever they plug in an appliance. The planning horizon in electricity generation can be very long. Major decisions regarding the capacity of power stations are made years in advance. Even the fluctuations in demand over a typical day can be forecast in advance. Popular television programmes can affect minute-by-minute demand and these are scheduled weeks or months ahead. The weather, which also affects demand, is more uncertain, but can to some extent be predicted. Individual planning decisions made by the electricity utility are not concerned with the timing, but rather the volume of output. Control decisions will concern aggregated measures of output such as the total kilowatts of electricity generated, because the product is more or less homogeneous. However, the robustness of the operation is very low because, if a generator fails, the operation's capability of supplying electricity from that part of the operation also fails.

> **Operations principle**
>
> The volume–variety characteristics of an operation will affect its planning and control activities.

How do supply and demand affect planning and control?

If planning and control is the process of reconciling demand with supply, then the nature of the decisions taken to plan and control an operation will depend on both the nature of demand and the nature of supply in that operation. In this section, we examine some differences in demand and supply which can affect the way in which operations managers plan and control their activities.

'In many ways a major airline can be viewed as one large planning problem which is usually approached as many independent, smaller (but still difficult) planning problems. The list of things which need planning seems endless: crews, reservation agents, luggage, flights, through trips, maintenance, gates, inventory, equipment purchases. Each planning problem has its own considerations, its own complexities, its own set of time horizons, its own objectives, but all are interrelated.'

Air France has 80 flight planners working 24-hour shifts in its flight planning office at Roissy, Charles de Gaulle. Their job is to establish the optimum flight routes, anticipate any problems such as weather changes, and minimize fuel consumption. Overall the goals of the flight planning activity are first, and most important, safety followed by economy and passenger comfort. Increasingly powerful computer programs process the mountain of data necessary to plan the flights, but in the end many decisions still rely on human judgement. Even the most sophisticated expert systems only serve as support for the flight planners. Planning Air France's schedule is a massive job. The following are just some of the considerations which need to be taken into account:

▶ *Frequency* – for each airport how many separate services should the airline provide?
▶ *Fleet assignment* – which type of plane should be used on each leg of a flight?
▶ *Banks* – at any airline hub where passengers arrive and may transfer to other flights to continue their journey, airlines like to organize flights into 'banks' of several planes which arrive close together, pause to let passengers change planes, and all depart close together. So, how many banks should there be and when should they occur?
▶ *Block times* – a block time is the elapsed time between a plane leaving the departure gate at an airport and arriving at its gate in the arrival airport. The longer the allowed block time, the more likely a plane will keep to schedule even if it suffers minor delays. However, longer block times also mean fewer flights can be scheduled.
▶ *Planned maintenance* – any schedule must allow for planes to have time at a maintenance base.
▶ *Crew planning* – pilot and cabin crew must be scheduled to allocate pilots to fly planes on which they are licensed and to keep within maximum 'on duty' times for all staff.
▶ *Gate plotting* – if many planes are on the ground at the same time, there may be problems in loading and unloading them simultaneously.
▶ *Recovery* – many things can cause deviations from any plan in the airline industry. Allowances must be built in to allow for recovery.

For flights within and between Air France's 12 geographic zones, the planners construct a flight plan that will form the basis of the actual flight only a few hours later. All planning documents need to be ready for the flight crew who arrive two hours before the scheduled departure time. Being responsible for passenger safety and comfort, the captain always has the final say and, when satisfied, co-signs the flight plan together with the planning officer.

Uncertainty in supply and demand

Uncertainty is important in planning and control because it makes it more difficult. Sometimes the supply of inputs to an operation may be uncertain. Local village carnivals, for example, rarely work to plan. Events take longer than expected, some of the acts scheduled in the programme may be delayed *en route*, and some traders may not even arrive. In other operations supply is relatively predictable, and the need for control is minimal. For example, cable TV services provide programmes to a schedule into subscribers' homes. It is rare to change the programme plan. Similarly demand may be unpredictable. A fast-food outlet inside a shopping centre does not know how many people will arrive, when they will arrive and what they will order. It may be possible to predict certain patterns, such as an increase in demand over the lunch and tea-time periods, but a sudden rainstorm that drives shoppers indoors into the centre could significantly and unpredictably increase demand in the very short term. Conversely, demand may be more predictable. In a school, for example, once classes are fixed and the term or semester has started, a teacher knows how many pupils are in the class. Both supply and demand uncertainty make planning and control more difficult, but a combination of supply *and* demand uncertainty is particularly difficult.

> **✔ Operations principle**
>
> Planning and control systems should be able to cope with uncertainty in demand.

Dependent and independent demand

Some operations can predict demand with relative certainty because demand for their services or products is dependent upon some other factor which is known. This is known as dependent demand. For example, the demand for tyres in an automobile factory is not a totally random variable. The process of demand forecasting is relatively straightforward. It will consist of examining the manufacturing schedules in the car plant and deriving the demand for tyres from these. If 600 cars are to be manufactured on a particular day, then it is simple to calculate that 3,000 tyres will be demanded by the car plant (each car has five tyres) – demand is dependent on a known factor, the number of cars to be manufactured. Because of this, the tyres can be ordered from the tyre manufacturer to a delivery schedule which is closely related to the demand for tyres from the plant (as in Figure 10.3). In fact, the demand for every part of the car plant will be derived from the assembly schedule for the finished cars. Other operations will act in a dependent-demand manner because of the nature of the service or product which they provide. For example, a custom-made dressmaker will not buy fabric and make up dresses in many different sizes just in case someone comes along and wants to buy one.

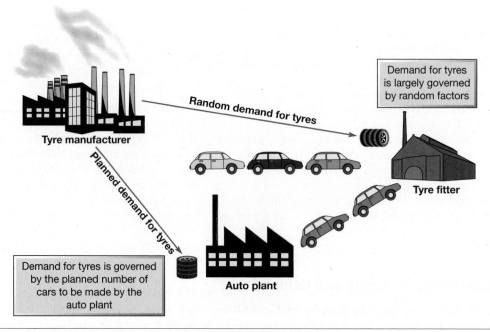

Figure 10.3 Dependent demand is derived from the demand for something else; independent demand is more random

Nor will a high-class restaurant begin to cook food just in case a customer arrives and requests it. In both these cases, a combination of risk and the perishability of the product or service prevent the operation from starting to create the goods or services until it has a firm order. Planning and control in dependent-demand situations is largely concerned with how the operation should respond when demand has occurred.

By contrast, some operations are subject to independent demand. They need to supply future demand without knowing exactly what that demand will be; or in the terminology of planning and control, they do not have firm 'forward visibility' of customer orders. For example, the Ace Tyre Company, which operates a drive-in tyre replacement service, will need to manage a stock of tyres. In that sense it is exactly the same task that faced the manager of tyre stocks in the car plant. However, demand is very different for Ace Tyres. It cannot predict either the volume or the specific needs of customers. It must make decisions on how many and what type of tyres to stock, based on demand forecasts and in the light of the risks it is prepared to run of being out of stock. This is the nature of *independent-demand planning and control*. It makes 'best guesses' concerning future demand, attempts to put the resources in place which can satisfy this demand, and attempts to respond quickly if actual demand does not match the forecast. Inventory planning and control, treated in Chapter 13, is typical of independent-demand planning and control.

> **Operations principle**
> Planning and control systems should distinguish between dependent and independent demand.

Responding to demand

It is clear then that the nature of planning and control in any operation will depend on how it responds to demand, which is in turn related to the type of services or products it produces. For example, an advertising agency will only start the process of planning and controlling the creation of an advertising campaign when the customer (or client as the agency will refer to them) confirms the contract with the agency. The creative 'design' of the advertisements will be based on a 'brief' from the client. Only after the design is approved are the appropriate resources (director, scriptwriters, actors, production company, etc.) contracted. The actual shooting of the advertisement and post-production (editing, putting in the special effects, etc.) then goes ahead, after which the finished advertisements are 'delivered' through television slots. This is shown in Figure 10.4 as a 'Design, resource, create and deliver to order' operation.

Other operations might be sufficiently confident of the nature of demand, if not its exact details, to keep 'in stock' most of the resources it requires to satisfy its customers. Certainly it will keep its transforming resources, if not its transformed resources. However, it will still make the actual service or product only when it receives a firm customer order. For example, a website designer will have most of its resources (graphic designers, software developers, specialist development software, etc.) in place, but must still design, create and deliver the website after it understands its customer's requirements. (See the 'Operations in practice' example of Torchbox, in Chapter 1.) This is shown in Figure 10.4 as a 'Design, create and deliver to order' operation.

Some operations offer relatively standard services or products, but do not create them until the customer has chosen which particular service or product to have. So a house builder who has standard designs might choose to build each house only when a customer places a firm order. Because the design of the house is relatively standard, suppliers of materials will have been identified, even if the building operation does not keep the items in stock itself. This is shown in Figure 10.4 as a 'Create and deliver to order' operation. In manufacturing it would be called a 'Make to order' operation.

Some operations have services or products that are so predictable that they can start to 'create' them before specific customer orders arrive. Possibly the best-known example of this is Dell Computers where customers can 'specify' their computer by selecting between various components through the company's website. These components will have already been created (usually by suppliers) but are assembled to a specific customer order. This is shown in Figure 10.4 as a 'Partially create and deliver to order' operation. In manufacturing it would be called an 'Assemble to order' operation.

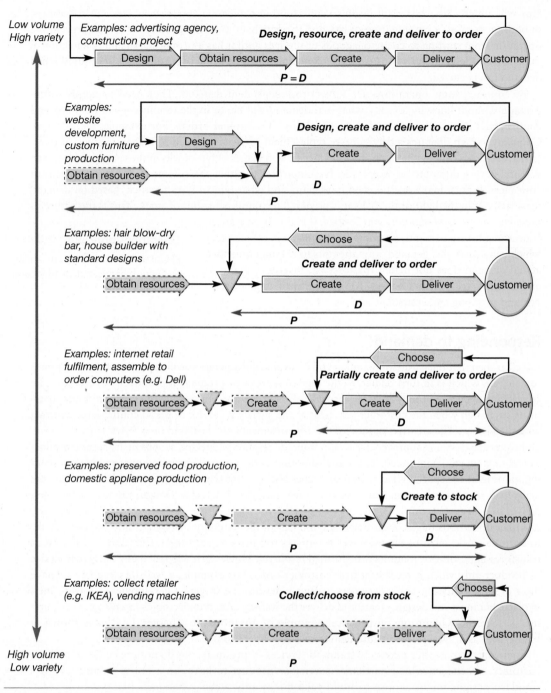

Figure 10.4 The *P:D* ratio of an operation indicates how long the customer has to wait for the service or product as compared with the total time needed to carry out all the activities to make the service or product available to the customer

Operations principle

The planning and control activity will vary depending on how much work is done before demand is known.

When an operation's services or products are standardized, there is the potential to create them entirely before demand is known. Almost all domestic products, for example, are 'Created to stock', or 'Make to stock' (shown in Figure 10.4), from which they are delivered to customers. Taking this evolving logic to its conclusion, some operations require their customers to collect their own services or products. This is the 'Choose/collect from stock' illustration in Figure 10.4. IKEA and most high-street retail operations are like this.

One point to note in the operations illustrated in Figure 10.4 is that there is a relationship between how operations respond to demand and their volume–variety characteristics. It is easy to see that 'Design, resource, create and deliver to order' operations are intended for low-volume and high-variety businesses. By definition, designing different services or products will result in high variety, and performing each activity for each customer would be too cumbersome for a high-volume business. Conversely, 'Create to stock' or 'Choose/collect from stock' clearly rely on standardized services or products.

P:D ratios[3]

Another way of characterizing the graduation between 'Design, resource, create and deliver to order' and 'Choose/collect from stock' planning and control is by using a P:D ratio. This contrasts the total length of time customers have to wait between asking for the service or product and receiving it, called the demand time, D, and the total throughput time from start to finish, P. Throughput time is how long the operation takes to design the service or product (if it is customized), obtain the resources, create and deliver it.

P and D times depend on the operation

P and D are illustrated for each type of operation in Figure 10.4. Generally the ratio of P to D gets larger as operations move from 'Design, resource, create and deliver to order' to 'Choose/collect from stock'. In other words, as one moves down this spectrum towards the 'Create to stock' and 'Choose/Collect from stock' end, the operation has anticipated customer demand and already created the services and products even though it has no guarantee that the anticipated demand will really happen. This is a particularly important point for the planning and control activity. The larger the P:D ratio, the more speculative the operation's planning and control activities will be. In its extreme form, the 'Choose/collect from stock' operation, such as a high-street retailer, has taken a gamble by designing, resourcing, creating and delivering (or more likely, paying someone else to do so) products to its shops before it has any certainty that customers will want them. Contrast this with a 'Design, resource, create and deliver to order' operation as in the advertising agency mentioned earlier. Here, D is the same as P and speculation regarding the volume of demand in the short term is eliminated because everything happens in response to a firm order So by reducing their P:D ratio operations reduce their degree of speculative activity and also reduce their dependence on forecasting (although bad forecasting will lead to other problems).

But do not assume that when the P:D ratio approaches 1, all uncertainty is eliminated. The volume of demand (in terms of the number of customer 'orders') may be known, but not the time taken to perform each 'order'. Take the advertising agency again: during each stage of the process, from design to delivery, it is common to have to seek the customer's approval and/or feedback many times. Moreover, there will almost certainly be some recycling back through stages as modifications are made. And, in a similar way to how simultaneous development works in new service and product design (see Chapter 5), a stage can be started before the previous one has been completed. So, for example, the video shoot director will have started prior to the artwork design being completed. This is illustrated in Figure 10.5. So here it is the timings that are uncertain.

Operations principle

The P:D ratio of an operation contrasts how long customers have to wait for a service or product with its total throughput time.

Sales and Operations Planning (S&OP)

One of the problems with traditional operations planning and control is that, although several functions were often routinely involved in the process, each function could have a very different set of objectives. For example, marketing could be interested in maximizing revenues and ensuring continuity of delivery to customers. Operations are likely to be under pressure to minimize cost (perhaps achieved through relatively long and stable operating levels). Finance will be interested in reducing working capital and inventory, and also reducing fixed costs. And so on. Yet

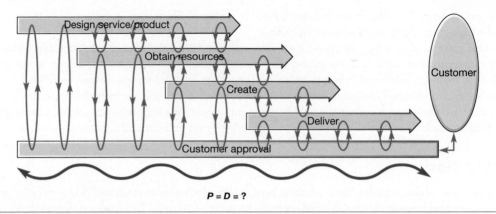

$P = D = ?$

Figure 10.5 The relationship between stages in some *'Design, resource, create and deliver to order'* operations, such as an advertising agency, can be complex with frequent consultation and unpredictable recycling

these, and other functions such as engineering or human resources management, are all impacted by operations planning decisions and are probably involved in their own planning processes that partly depend on the output from the operations planning process. Sales and Operations Planning (S&OP) was first promoted as an important element of planning as Manufacturing Resource Planning (see the supplement to Chapter 14) became a commonly used process. Early Manufacturing Resource Planning implementations were often made less effective by the system being driven by unachievable plans. This is the dilemma that S&OP is intended to address. It is a planning process that attempts to ensure that all tactical plans are aligned across the business's various functions and with the company's longer-term strategic plans.

It is a formal business process that looks over a period of 18 to 24 months ahead. In other words, it is not a purely short-term process. In fact, S&OP developed as an attempt to integrate short- and longer-term planning, as well as integrating the planning activities of key functions. It is an aggregated process that does not deal with detailed activities, but rather focuses on the overall (often aggregated) volume of output. Generally, it is a process that happens monthly, and tends to take place at a higher level, involving more senior management than traditional operations planning. S&OP also goes by many names. It can be called Integrated Business Planning, Integrated Business Management, Integrated Performance Management, Rolling Business Planning and Regional Business Management, to name a few. It has also been noted[4] that some organizations continue to use the phrase 'S&OP', although they may mean something quite different.

What are planning and control activities?

Planning and control requires the reconciliation of supply and demand in terms of volumes, timing and quality. In this chapter we will focus on an overview of the activities that plan and control volume and timing (most of this part of the book is concerned with these issues). There are four overlapping activities: loading, sequencing, scheduling, and monitoring and control (see Figure 10.6).

Some caution is needed when using these terms. Different organizations may use them in different ways, and even textbooks in the area adopt different definitions. For example, some authorities term what we have called planning and control as 'operations scheduling'. However, the terminology of planning and control is less important than understanding the basic ideas described in the remainder of this chapter.

> **Operations principle**
>
> Planning and control activities include loading, sequencing, scheduling, and monitoring and control.

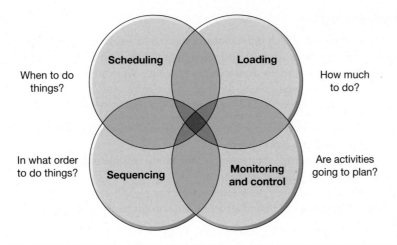

Figure 10.6 Planning and control activities

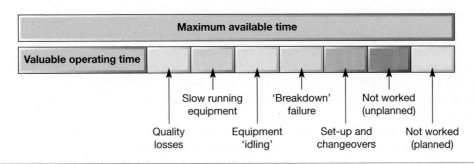

Figure 10.7 The reduction in the valuable operating time available

Loading

Loading is the amount of work that is allocated to a work centre. For example, a machine on the shop floor of a manufacturing business is available, in theory, 168 hours a week. However, this does not necessarily mean that 168 hours of work can be loaded onto that machine. Figure 10.7 shows what erodes this available time. For some periods the machine cannot be worked: for example, it may not be available on statutory holidays and weekends. Therefore, the load put onto the machine must take this into account. Of the time that the machine is available for work, other losses further reduce the available time. For example, time may be lost while changing over from making one component to another. If the machine breaks down, it will not be available. If machine reliability data are available, these must also be taken into account. Sometimes the machine may be waiting for parts to arrive or be 'idling' for some other reason. Other losses could include an allowance for the machine being run below its optimum speed (for example, because it has not been maintained properly) and an allowance for the 'quality losses' or defects which the machine may produce. Of course, many of these losses should be small or non-existent in a well-managed operation. However, the valuable operating time available for productive working, even in the best operations, can be significantly below the maximum time available. This idea is taken further in Chapter 11 when we discuss the measurement of capacity.

> **Operations principle**
>
> For any given level of demand, a planning and control system should be able to indicate the implications for the loading on any part of the operation.

Finite and infinite loading

Finite loading is an approach which only allocates work to a work centre (a person, a machine, or perhaps a group of people or machines) up to a set limit. This limit is the estimate of capacity for the work centre (based on the times available for loading). Work over and above this capacity is not accepted. Figure 10.8 first shows how the load on the work centres is not allowed to exceed the capacity limit. Finite loading is particularly relevant for operations where:

▶ *it is possible to limit the load* – for example, it is possible to run an appointment system for a general medical practice or a hairdresser;
▶ *it is necessary to limit the load* – for example, for safety reasons only a finite number of people and weight of luggage are allowed on aircraft;
▶ *the cost of limiting the load is not prohibitive* – for example, the cost of maintaining a finite order book at a specialist sports car manufacturer does not adversely affect demand, and may even enhance it.

Infinite loading is an approach to loading work which does not limit accepting work, but instead tries to cope with it. The second diagram in Figure 10.8 illustrates this loading pattern where capacity constraints have not been used to limit loading so the work is completed earlier. Infinite loading is relevant for operations where:

▶ *it is not possible to limit the load* – for example, an accident and emergency department in a hospital should not turn away arrivals needing attention;
▶ *it is not necessary to limit the load* – for example, fast-food outlets are designed to flex capacity up and down to cope with varying arrival rates of customers. During busy periods, customers accept that they must queue for some time before being served. Unless this is extreme, the customers might not go elsewhere;
▶ *the cost of limiting the load is prohibitive* – for example, if a retail bank turned away customers at the door because a set number were inside, customers would feel less than happy with the service.

In complex planning and control activities where there are multiple stages, each with different capacities and with a varying mix arriving at the facilities, such as a machine shop in an engineering

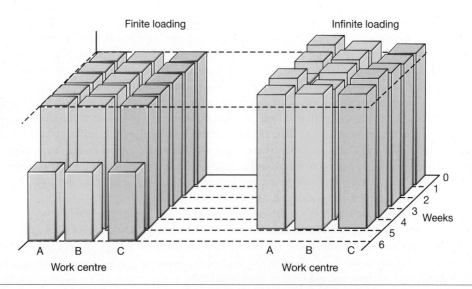

Figure 10.8 Finite and infinite loading of jobs on three work centres A, B and C. Finite loading limits the loading on each centre to their capacities, even if it means that jobs will be late. Infinite loading allows the loading on each centre to exceed their capacities to ensure that jobs will not be late

company, the constraints imposed by finite loading make loading calculations complex and not worth the considerable computational power which would be needed.

Sequencing

Whether the approach to loading is finite or infinite, when work arrives, decisions must be taken on the order in which the work will be tackled. This activity is termed sequencing. The priorities given to work in an operation are often determined by some predefined set of rules, some of which are relatively complex. Some of these are summarized below.

Physical constraints

The physical nature of the inputs being processed may determine the priority of work. For example, in an operation using paints or dyes, lighter shades will be sequenced before darker shades. On completion of each batch, the colour is slightly darkened for the next batch. This is because darkness of colour can only be added to and not removed from the colour mix. Sometimes the mix of work arriving at a part of an operation may determine the priority given to jobs. For example, when fabric is cut to a required size and shape in garment manufacture, the surplus fabric would be wasted if not used for another product. Therefore, jobs that physically fit together may be scheduled together to reduce waste. The sequencing issue described in the short case 'Can airline passengers be sequenced?' is of this type.

OPERATIONS IN PRACTICE

Can airline passengers be sequenced?[5]

Like many before him, Dr Jason Steffen, a professional astrophysicist, was frustrated by the time it took to load him and his fellow passengers onto the aircraft. He decided to devise a way to make the experience a little less tedious. So, for a while, he neglected his usual work of examining extra-solar planets, dark matter and cosmology, and experimentally tested a faster method of boarding aircraft. He found that, by changing the sequence in which passengers are loaded onto the aircraft, airlines could potentially save both time and money. Using a computer simulation and the arithmetic techniques routinely used in his day-to-day job, he was able to find what seemed to be a superior sequencing method. His simulations showed that the most common way of boarding passengers was the least efficient. This is called the 'block method' where blocks of seats are called for boarding, starting from the back. Previously other experts in the airline industry had suggested boarding those in window seats first followed by middle and aisle seats. This is called the Wilma method. But according to

Dr Steffen's simulations, two things slow down the boarding process. The first is that passengers may be required to wait in the aisle while those ahead of them store their luggage before they can take their seat. The second is that passengers already seated in aisle or middle seats frequently have to rise and move into the aisle to let others take seats nearer the window. So Dr Steffen

▶

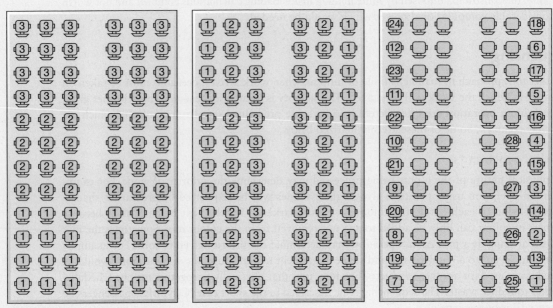

Block (conventional) method	Wilma method	Steffen method

Figure 10.9 The best way to sequence passengers onto an aircraft

suggested a variant of the Wilma method that minimized the first type of disturbance and eliminated the second. He suggested boarding in alternate rows, progressing from the rear forward, window seats first. Using this approach (now called the Steffen method), first, the window seats for every other row on one side of the plane are boarded. Next, alternate rows of window seats on the opposite side are boarded. Then, the window seats in the skipped rows are filled in on each side. The procedure then repeats with the middle seats and the aisles (see Figure 10.9).

Later, the effectiveness of the various approaches were tested using a mock-up of a Boeing 757 aircraft and 72 luggage-carrying volunteers. Five different scenarios were tested: 'block' boarding in groups of rows from back to front, one by one from back to front, the 'Wilma method', the Steffen method, and completely random boarding.

In all cases, parent–child pairs were allowed to board first. It was assumed that families were likely to want to stay together. As Dr Steffen had predicted, the conventional block approach came out as the slowest, with the strict back-to-front approach not much better. Completely random boarding (unallocated seating), which is used by several low-cost airlines, fared much better, most probably because it randomly avoids space conflicts. The times for fully boarding the 72 passengers using each method were as follows: 'block' boarding – 6:54 minutes, back-to-front – 6:11 minutes, random boarding – 4:44 minutes, Wilma method – 4:13 minutes, Steffen method – 3:36 minutes.

The big question is, 'would passengers really be prepared to be sequenced in this way as they queue to board the aircraft?' Some airlines argue that directing passengers on to a plane is a little like herding cats.

Customer priority

Operations will sometimes use customer priority sequencing, which allows an important or aggrieved customer, or item, to be 'processed' prior to others, irrespective of the order of arrival of the customer or item. This approach is typically used by operations whose customer base is skewed, containing a mass of small customers and a few large, very important customers. Some banks, for example, give priority to important customers. Similarly, in hotels, complaining customers will be treated as a priority because their complaint may have an adverse effect on the perceptions of other customers. More seriously, the emergency services often have to use their judgement in prioritizing the urgency of requests for service. For example, Figure 10.10 shows a typical triage system used in hospitals to prioritize patients (see the 'Operations in practice' example). However, customer priority sequencing, although giving a high level of service to some customers, may erode the service given

1	Immediate resuscitation	Patient in need of immediate treatment for preservation of life
2	Very urgent	Seriously ill or injured patients whose lives are not in immediate danger
3	Urgent	Patients with serious problems, but apparently stable conditions
4	Standard	Standard cases without immediate danger or distress
5	Non-urgent	Patients whose conditions are not true accidents or emergencies

Figure 10.10 A triage prioritization scale

to many others. This may lower the overall performance of the operation if work flows are disrupted to accommodate important customers.

Due date (DD)

Prioritizing by due date means that work is sequenced according to when it is 'due' for delivery, irrespective of the size of each job or the importance of each customer. For example, a support service, such as a printing unit, will often ask when copies are required, and then sequence the work according to that due date. Due date sequencing usually improves the delivery dependability and average delivery speed. It may not provide optimal productivity, as a more efficient sequencing of work may reduce total costs. However, it can be flexible when new, urgent work arrives at the work centre.

OPERATIONS IN PRACTICE

The hospital triage system

One of the hospital environments that is most difficult to schedule is the Accident and Emergency department, where patients arrive at random, without any prior warning, throughout the day. It is up to the hospital's reception and the medical staff to devise very rapidly a schedule which meets most of the necessary criteria. In particular, patients who arrive having had very serious accidents, or presenting symptoms of a serious illness, need to be attended to urgently. Therefore, the hospital will schedule these cases first. Less urgent cases – perhaps patients who are in some discomfort, but whose injuries or illnesses are not life-threatening – will have to wait until the urgent cases are treated. Routine non-urgent cases will have the lowest priority of all. In many circumstances, these patients will have to wait

for the longest time, which may be many hours, especially if the hospital is busy. Sometimes these non-urgent cases

Last in, first out (LIFO)

Last in, first out (LIFO) is a method of sequencing usually selected for practical reasons. For example, unloading an elevator is more convenient on a LIFO basis, as there is only one entrance and exit. However, it is not an equitable approach. Patients at hospital clinics may be infuriated if they see newly arrived patients examined first.

First in, first out (FIFO)

Some operations serve customers in exactly the sequence they arrive in. This is called first in, first out sequencing (FIFO), or sometimes 'first come, first served' (FCFS). For example, UK passport offices receive mail, and sort it according to the day when it arrived. They work through the mail, opening it in sequence, and process the passport applications in order of arrival. Queues in theme parks may be designed so that one long queue snakes around the lobby area until the row of counters is reached. When customers reach the front of the queue, they are served at the next free counter.

Longest operation time (LOT)

Operations may feel obliged to sequence their longest jobs first, called longest operation time sequencing. This has the advantage of occupying work centres for long periods. By contrast, relatively small jobs progressing through an operation will take up time at each work centre because of the need to change over from one job to the next. However, although longest operation time sequencing keeps utilization high, this rule does not take into account delivery speed, reliability or flexibility. Indeed, it may work directly against these performance objectives.

Shortest operation time first (SOT)

Most operations at some stage become cash constrained. In these situations, the sequencing rules may be adjusted to tackle short jobs first; this is called shortest operation time sequencing. These jobs can then be invoiced and payment received to ease cash-flow problems. Larger jobs that take more time will not enable the business to invoice as quickly. This has an effect of improving delivery performance, if the unit of measurement of delivery is jobs. However, it may adversely affect total productivity and can damage service to larger customers.

Judging sequencing rules

All five performance objectives, or some variant of them, could be used to judge the effectiveness of sequencing rules. However, the objectives of dependability, speed and cost are particularly important. So, for example, the following performance objectives are often used:

▶ meeting 'due date' promised to customer (dependability);
▶ minimizing the time the job spends in the process, also known as 'flow time' (speed);
▶ minimizing work-in-progress inventory (an element of cost);
▶ minimizing idle time of work centres (another element of cost).

Comparing the three sequencing rules described in the worked example, together with the two other sequencing rules described earlier and applied to the same problem, gives the results summarized in Table 10.2. The SOT rule results in both the best average time in process and the best (or least bad)

Steve Smith is a website designer in a business school. Returning from his annual vacation (he finished all outstanding jobs before he left), five design jobs are given to him upon arrival at work. He gives them the codes A to E. Steven has to decide in which sequence to undertake the jobs. He wants both to minimize the average time the jobs are tied up in his office and, if possible, to meet the deadlines (delivery times) allocated to each job.

His first thought is to do the jobs in the order they were given to him, i.e. first in, first out (FIFO):

Sequencing rule – first in, first out (FIFO)

Sequence of jobs	Process time (days)	Start time	Finish time	Due date	Lateness (days)
A	5	0	5	6	0
B	3	5	8	5	3
C	6	8	14	8	6
D	2	14	16	7	9
E	1	16	17	3	14
Total time in process	60		**Total lateness**		32
Average time in process (total/5)	12		**Average lateness (total/5)**		6.4

Alarmed by the average lateness, he tries the due date (DD) rule:

Sequencing rule – due date (DD)

Sequence of jobs	Process time (days)	Start time	Finish time	Due date	Lateness (days)
E	1	0	1	3	0
B	3	1	4	5	0
A	5	4	9	6	3
D	2	9	11	7	4
C	6	11	17	8	9
Total time in process			42	**Total lateness**	16
Average time in process (total/5)	8.4		**Average lateness (total/5)**		3.2

Better! But Steve tries out the shortest operation time (SOT) rule:

Sequencing rule – shortest operation time (SOT)

Sequence of jobs	Process time (days)	Start time	Finish time	Due date	Lateness (days)
E	1	0	1	3	0
D	2	1	3	7	0
B	3	3	6	5	1
A	5	6	11	6	5
C	6	11	17	8	9
Total time in process	38			**Total lateness**	16
Average time in process (total/5)	7.6		**Average lateness (total/5)**		3.2

This gives the same degree of average lateness but with a lower average time in the process. Steve decides to use the SOT rule.

Table 10.2 Comparison of five sequencing decision rules

Rule	Average time in process (days)	Average lateness (days)
FIFO	12	6.4
DD	8.4	3.2
SOT	7.6	3.2
LIFO	8.4	3.8
LOT	12.8	7.4

in terms of average lateness. Although different rules will perform differently depending on the circumstances of the sequencing problem, in practice the SOT rule generally performs well.

Scheduling

Having determined the sequence that work is to be tackled in, some operations require a detailed timetable showing at what time or date jobs should start and when they should end – this is scheduling. Schedules are familiar statements of volume and timing in many consumer environments. For example, a bus schedule shows that more buses are put on routes at more frequent intervals during rush-hour periods. The bus schedule shows the time each bus is due to arrive at each stage of the route. Schedules of work are used in operations where some planning is required to ensure that customer demand is met. Other operations, such as rapid-response service operations where customers

Sequencing and scheduling at London's Heathrow airport[6]

Heathrow is the UK's busiest airport, and the busiest two-runway airport in the world, welcoming around 1,300 combined take-offs and landings each day. Landing around 650 aircraft in a day, air traffic controllers have one of the most complex sequencing jobs to perform as they decide which aircraft to call down next from their waiting areas (known as 'stacks') to land on one of the two runways. Many airports use a sequencing policy based on 'first come, first served'. However, this does not always give the best airport performance, where performance is assessed by such measures as runway utilization, total aircraft throughput, passenger throughput and passenger waiting time. For very busy airports such as Heathrow, a more sophisticated sequencing approach is needed. For most of the time at Heathrow, one runway is solely used for take-offs and the other solely

for landings (known as a 'segregated' operating mode). However, at particularly busy times, both runways can be used for landings. Safety considerations are, of course, paramount in deciding on an appropriate sequence. There must be a minimum time and distance between aircraft when they take off or land. This is because of what is known as the 'wake vortex' – turbulence that is caused by the 'lift' component of flight (without which the aircraft could not fly). Lift is caused by the pressure difference between the upper and lower surfaces of the wing. Wake vortices can result in turbulent conditions if an aircraft follows too close to the previous one, which passengers would find uncomfortable, and possibly distressing. It could even cause possible damage to the following aircraft. The magnitude of a wake vortex depends on the size of the aircraft, large aircraft causing more air turbulence. So, following a large aircraft means leaving a (relatively) long time before another aircraft can land. Conversely, a light aircraft generates little air turbulence and therefore only a (relatively) small time delay is needed before other aircraft can land. In other words, the sequence in which aircraft are called to land will determine the total time taken to complete landing. But, in addition to deciding the sequence in which aircraft will land, controllers must also construct a schedule that determines a landing time for each aircraft. This schedule should:

▶ Allow sufficient time for an aircraft to fly safely from its current position in the stack to the runway so that it will land at the appropriate position in the sequence.
▶ Make sure that no aircraft run low on fuel whilst waiting to land.
▶ Ensure that aircraft do not land too close together.

To complicate the task further, weather can also complicate things. Aircraft have to take off and land against the wind, so the landing direction depends on the prevailing wind (which can change). This is why meteorological experts are constantly monitoring weather conditions prevailing at 30,000 feet. Also, the airport must try to minimize the noise nuisance caused to local communities, which means that no landings are allowed before 04.30 with a maximum of 16 flights before 06.00, preferably the quietest planes.

arrive in an unplanned way, cannot schedule the operation in a short-term sense. They can only respond at the time demand is placed upon them.

The complexity of scheduling

The scheduling activity is one of the most complex tasks in operations management. First, schedulers must deal with several different types of resource simultaneously. Machines will have different capabilities and capacities; staff will have different skills. More importantly, the number of possible schedules increases rapidly as the number of activities and processes increases. For example, suppose one machine has five different jobs to process. Any of the five jobs could be processed first and, following that, any one of the remaining four jobs, and so on. This means that there are:

$$5 \times 4 \times 3 \times 2 = 120 \text{ different schedules possible}$$

In other words, for n jobs there are $n!$ (factorial n) different ways of scheduling the jobs through a single process. But when there are (say) two machines, there is no reason why the sequence on machine 1 would be the same as the sequence on machine 2. If we consider the two sequencing tasks to be independent of each other, for two machines there would be

$$120 \times 120 = 14,400 \text{ possible schedules of the two machines and five jobs}$$

So a general formula can be devised to calculate the number of possible schedules in any given situation, as follows:

$$\text{Number of possible schedules} = (n!)^m$$

where n is the number of jobs and m is the number of machines.

In practical terms, this means that there are often many millions of feasible schedules, even for relatively small scheduling tasks. This is why scheduling rarely attempts to provide an 'optimal' solution but rather satisfies itself with an 'acceptable' feasible one.

Table 10.3 The effects of forward and backward scheduling

Task	Duration	Start time (backwards)	Start time (forwards)
Press	1 hour	3.00 pm	1.00 pm
Dry	2 hours	1.00 pm	11.00 am
Wash	3 hours	10.00 am	8.00 am

Forward and backward scheduling

Forward scheduling involves starting work as soon as it arrives. Backward scheduling involves starting jobs at the last possible moment to prevent them from being late. For example, assume that it takes six hours for a contract laundry to wash, dry and press a batch of overalls. If the work is collected at 8.00 am and is due to be picked up at 4.00 pm, there are more than six hours available to do it. Table 10.3 shows the different start times of each job, depending on whether they are forward or backward scheduled.

The choice of backward or forward scheduling depends largely upon the circumstances. Table 10.4 lists some advantages and disadvantages of the two approaches. In theory, both materials requirements planning (MRP, see Chapter 14) and lean, or just-in-time, planning (JIT, see Chapter 15) use backward scheduling, only starting work when it is required. In practice, however, users of MRP have tended to allow too long for each task to be completed, and therefore each task is not started at the latest possible time. In comparison, JIT is started, as the name suggests, just in time.

> **Operations principle**
>
> An operation's planning and control system should allow for the effects of alternative schedules to be assessed.

Gantt charts

One crude but simple method of scheduling is by use of the Gantt chart. This is a simple device which represents time as a bar, or channel, on a chart. The start and finish times for activities can be indicated on the chart and sometimes the actual progress of the job is also indicated. The advantage of Gantt charts is that they provide a simple visual representation both of what should be happening and of what actually is happening in the operation. Furthermore, they can be used to 'test out' alternative schedules. It is a relatively simple task to represent alternative schedules (even if it is a far from simple task to find a schedule which fits all the resources satisfactorily). Figure 10.11 illustrates a Gantt chart for a specialist software developer. It indicates the progress of several jobs as they are expected to move through five stages of the process. Gantt charts are not an optimizing tool, they merely facilitate the development of alternative schedules by communicating them effectively.

Table 10.4 Advantages of forward and backward scheduling

Advantages of forward scheduling	Advantages of backward scheduling
High labour utilization – workers always start work to keep busy	Lower material costs – materials are not used until they have to be, therefore delaying added value until the last moment
Flexible – the time slack in the system allows unexpected work to be loaded	Less exposed to risk in case of schedule change by the customer
	Tends to focus the operation on customer due dates

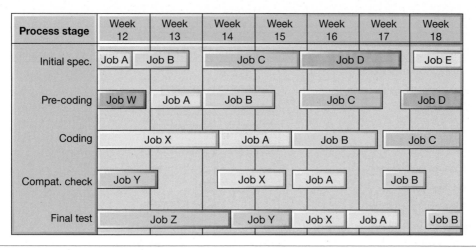

Process stage	Week 12	Week 13	Week 14	Week 15	Week 16	Week 17	Week 18
Initial spec.	Job A	Job B	Job C		Job D		Job E
Pre-coding	Job W	Job A	Job B		Job C		Job D
Coding	Job X		Job A		Job B		Job C
Compat. check	Job Y		Job X	Job A		Job B	
Final test	Job Z		Job Y	Job X	Job A		Job B

Figure 10.11 Gantt chart showing the schedule for jobs at each process stage

Scheduling work patterns

Where the dominant resource in an operation is its staff, then the schedule of work times effectively determines the capacity of the operation itself. The main task of scheduling, therefore, is to make sure that sufficient numbers of people are working at any point in time to provide a capacity appropriate

The life and times of a chicken salad sandwich (Part 1)[7]

Pre-packed sandwiches are a growth product around the world as consumers put convenience and speed above relaxation and cost. But if you have recently consumed a pre-packed sandwich, think about the schedule of events which has gone into its making. For example, take a chicken salad sandwich. Less than five days ago, the chicken was on the farm unaware that it would never see another weekend. The Gantt chart schedule shown in Figure 10.12 tells the story of the sandwich, and (posthumously) of the chicken.

From the forecast, orders for non-perishable items are placed for goods to arrive up to a week in advance of their use. Orders for perishable items will be placed daily, a day or two before the items are required. Tomatoes, cucumbers and lettuces have a three-day shelf life so may be received up to three days before production. Stock is held on a strict first-in, first-out (FIFO) basis. If today is (say) Wednesday, vegetables are processed that have been received during the last three days. This morning the bread arrived from a local bakery and the chicken arrived fresh, cooked and in strips ready to be placed directly in the sandwich during assembly. Yesterday (Tuesday) it had been killed, cooked, prepared and sent on its journey to the factory. By midday orders for tonight's production will have been received on the internet. From 2.00 pm until 10.00 pm the production lines are closed down for maintenance and a very thorough cleaning. During this time the production planning team

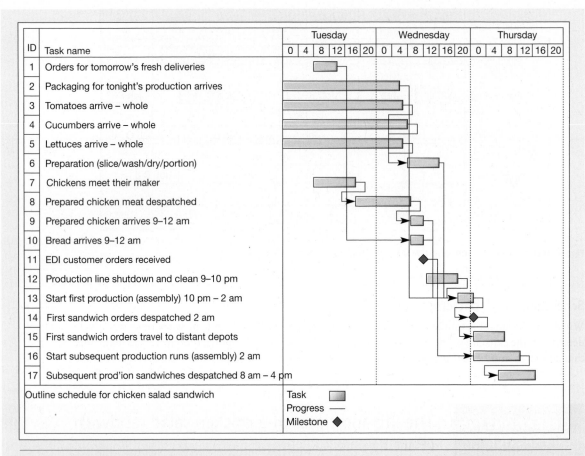

ID	Task name	Tuesday 0 4 8 12 16 20	Wednesday 0 4 8 12 16 20	Thursday 0 4 8 12 16 20
1	Orders for tomorrow's fresh deliveries			
2	Packaging for tonight's production arrives			
3	Tomatoes arrive – whole			
4	Cucumbers arrive – whole			
5	Lettuces arrive – whole			
6	Preparation (slice/wash/dry/portion)			
7	Chickens meet their maker			
8	Prepared chicken meat despatched			
9	Prepared chicken arrives 9–12 am			
10	Bread arrives 9–12 am			
11	EDI customer orders received			
12	Production line shutdown and clean 9–10 pm			
13	Start first production (assembly) 10 pm – 2 am			
14	First sandwich orders despatched 2 am			
15	First sandwich orders travel to distant depots			
16	Start subsequent production runs (assembly) 2 am			
17	Subsequent prod'ion sandwiches despatched 8 am – 4 pm			

Outline schedule for chicken salad sandwich

Task ▭
Progress —
Milestone ◆

Figure 10.12 Simplified schedule for the manufacture and delivery of a chicken salad sandwich

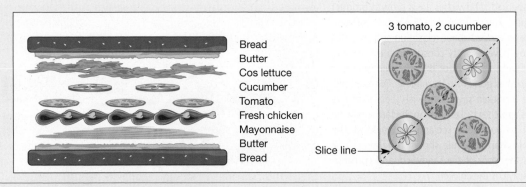

Bread
Butter
Cos lettuce
Cucumber
Tomato
Fresh chicken
Mayonnaise
Butter
Bread

3 tomato, 2 cucumber

Slice line →

Figure 10.13 Design for a chicken salad sandwich

is busy planning the night's production run. Production for delivery to customers furthest away from the factory will have to be scheduled first. By 10 pm production is ready to start. Sandwiches are made on production lines. The bread is loaded into a conveyor belt by hand and butter is spread automatically by a machine. Next the various fillings are applied at each stage according to the specified sandwich 'design' (see Figure 10.13). After the filling has been assembled the top slice of bread is placed on the sandwich and machine-chopped into two triangles, packed

and sealed by machine. It is now early Thursday morning and by 2.00 am the first refrigerated lorries are already departing on their journeys to various customers. Production continues through until 2.00 pm on the Thursday, after which once again the maintenance and cleaning teams move in. The last sandwiches are dispatched by 4.00 pm on the Thursday. There is no finished goods stock.

Part 2 of the life and times of a chicken salad sandwich is in Chapter 14.

for the level of demand at that point in time. This is often called staff rostering. Operations such as call centres, postal delivery, policing, holiday couriers, retail shops and hospitals will all need to schedule the working hours of their staff with demand in mind. This is a direct consequence of these operations having relatively high 'visibility' (we introduced this idea in Chapter 1). Such operations cannot store their outputs in inventories and so must respond directly to customer demand. For example, Figure 10.14 shows the scheduling of shifts for a small technical 'hot line' support service for a small software company. It gives advice to customers on their technical problems. Its service times are 4:00 hours to 20:00 hours on Monday, 4:00 hours to 22:00 hours Tuesday to Friday, 6:00 hours to 22:00 hours on Saturday, and 10:00 hurs to 20:00 hours on Sunday. Demand is heaviest on Tuesday to Thursday, starts to decrease on Friday, is low over the weekend and starts to increase again on Monday.

The scheduling task for this kind of problem can be considered over different time scales, two of which are shown in Figure 10.14. During the day, working hours need to be agreed with individual staff members. During the week, days off need to be agreed. During the year, vacations, training periods, and other blocks of time where staff are unavailable need to be agreed. All this has to be scheduled such that:

▶ capacity matches demand;
▶ the length of each shift is neither excessively long nor too short to be attractive to staff;
▶ working at unsocial hours is minimized;
▶ days off match agreed staff conditions – in this example, staff prefer two consecutive days off every week;
▶ vacation and other 'time-off' blocks are accommodated;
▶ sufficient flexibility is built into the schedule to cover for unexpected changes in supply (staff illness) and demand (surge in customer calls).

Scheduling staff times is one of the most complex of scheduling problems. In the relatively simple example shown in Figure 10.14 we have assumed that all staff have the same level and type of skill. In very large operations with many types of skill to schedule and uncertain demand (for example, a large hospital) the scheduling problem becomes extremely complex. Some mathematical techniques are available but most scheduling of this type is, in practice, solved using heuristics (rules of thumb), some of which are incorporated into commercially available software packages.

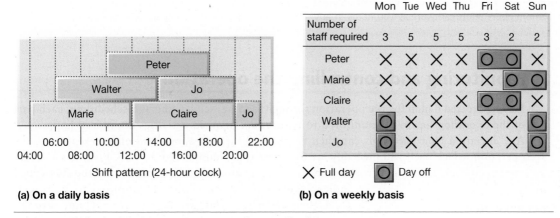

(a) On a daily basis

(b) On a weekly basis

Figure 10.14 Shift scheduling in a support service for a small software company

Ryanair cancels flights after 'staff scheduling' errors[8]

Ryanair, the largest European airline, is used to making the headlines for both good and bad reasons (see the 'Operations in practice' example in Chapter 17), but its announcement of multiple flight cancellations, potentially affecting up to 285,000 passengers, was not its finest hour. The cause, according to Ryanair Marketing Officer Kenny Jacobs, was that *'We have messed up in the planning of pilot holidays and we're working hard to fix that'*. It was unable to fix a pilot schedule that accommodated staff holidays, but left enough pilots to staff scheduled flights. Ryanair said that actually less than 2 per cent of its flights would be cancelled, and that it would not stop it hitting its annual punctuality target of 90 per cent. Yet this did not stop passengers complaining about the resulting uncertainty.

The root cause of the damaging staff shortage were two factors – annual holidays and flight time limitations (FTLs). Scheduling pilots' holidays was always problematic for European airlines, partly because of the seasonality of demand. Short-haul flying in Europe is highly seasonal, with demand between Easter and early September much higher than the rest of the year. This is an important time for airlines such as Ryanair, because it is when they make the majority of their profits. Because of this, most airlines prefer their pilots to take their holidays in one block of a month, somewhere between September and March. To complete the remainder of their holiday allocation, they can arrange to take 'ad hoc' days as and when the airline's plans permit. Complicating the scheduling task are FTLs. These stipulate the maximum hours pilots can work as 100 hours in any

28 days, 900 hours in a calendar year or 1,000 hours in any rolling 12-month period. Staff schedulers have to make sure their schedules conform to these limits. These rules are unbreakable. Ryanair's problem came when the Irish Aviation Authority told the airline that it had to change its calendar for the calculation of pilots' hours and leave from its previous April to March calendar, to one using the calendar year to keep it in line with the rules adopted by European regulators. Ryanair said the change meant it had to allocate annual leave to pilots (at relatively short notice) in September and October. Kenny Jacobs said, *'Most of the cancellations were due to a backlog of staff leave which has seen large numbers of the airline's staff book holidays towards the end of the year.'* The airline tried asking pilots to 'sell back' their annual leave. However, this was not always possible within the FTL rules, and some pilots were reluctant to change their holiday plans at short notice.

Monitoring and controlling the operation

Having created a plan for the operation through loading, sequencing and scheduling, each part of the operation has to be monitored to ensure that planned activities are indeed happening. Any deviation from the plans can then be rectified through some kind of intervention in the operation, which itself will probably involve some re-planning. Figure 10.15 illustrates a simple view of control. The output from a work centre is monitored and compared with the plan which indicates what the work centre is supposed to be doing. Deviations from this plan are taken into account through a re-planning activity and the necessary interventions made to the work centre which will (hopefully) ensure that the new plan is carried out. Eventually, however, some further deviation from planned activity will be detected and the cycle is repeated.

> **Operations principle**
>
> A planning and control system should be able to detect deviations from plans within a timescale that allows an appropriate response.

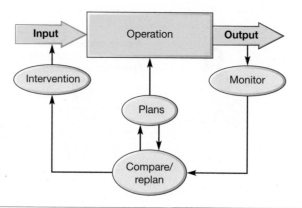

Figure 10.15 A simple model of control

Push and pull control

One element of control, then, is periodic intervention into the activities of the operation. An important decision is how this intervention takes place. The key distinction is between intervention signals which push work through the processes within the operation and those which pull work only when it is required. In a push system of control, activities are scheduled by means of a central system and completed in line with central instructions, such as an MRP system (see Chapter 14). Each work centre pushes out work without considering whether the succeeding work centre can make use of it. Work centres are coordinated by means of the central operations planning and control system. In practice, however, there are many reasons why actual conditions differ from those planned. As a consequence, idle time, inventory and queues often characterize push systems. By contrast, in a pull system of control, the pace and specification of what is done are set by the 'customer' workstation, which 'pulls' work from the preceding (supplier) workstation. The customer acts as the only 'trigger' for movement. If a request is not passed back from the customer to the supplier, the supplier cannot produce anything or move any materials. A request from a customer not only triggers production at the supplying stage, but also prompts the supplying stage to request a further delivery from its own suppliers. In this way, demand is transmitted back through the stages from the original point of demand by the original customer.

The inventory consequences of push and pull

Understanding the differing principles of push and pull is important because they have different effects in terms of their propensities to accumulate inventory in the operation. Pull systems are far less likely to result in inventory build-up and are therefore favoured by lean operations (see Chapter 15). To understand why this is so, consider an analogy: the 'gravity' analogy is illustrated in Figure 10.16. Here a push system is represented by an operation, each stage of which is on a lower level than the previous stage. When items are processed by each stage, gravity pushes them down the slope to the next stage. Any delay or variability in processing time at that stage will result in the items accumulating as inventory. In the pull system, items cannot naturally flow uphill, so they can only progress if the next stage along deliberately pulls them forward. Under these circumstances, inventory cannot accumulate as easily.

> **Operations principle**
> Pull control reduces the build-up on inventory between processes or stages.

Drum, buffer, rope

The drum, buffer, rope concept comes from the theory of constraints (TOC) and a concept called optimized production technology (opt) originally described by Eli Goldratt in his novel *The Goal*.[9] (We will deal more with his ideas in Chapter 15.) It is an idea that helps to decide exactly *where* in a process control should occur. Most do not have the same amount of work loaded onto each separate

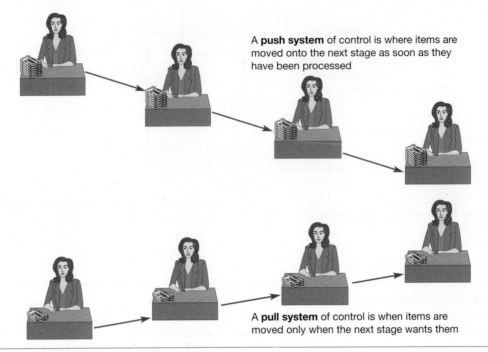

A **push system** of control is where items are moved onto the next stage as soon as they have been processed

A **pull system** of control is when items are moved only when the next stage wants them

Figure 10.16 Push versus pull: the gravity analogy

work centre (that is, they are not perfectly balanced). This means there is likely to be a part of the process which is acting as a bottleneck on the work flowing through the process. Goldratt argued that the bottleneck in the process should be the control point of the whole process. It is called the *drum* because it sets the 'beat' for the rest of the process to follow. Because it does not have sufficient capacity, a bottleneck is (or should be) working all the time. Therefore, it is sensible to keep a *buffer* of inventory in front of it to make sure that it always has something to work on. Because it constrains the output of the whole process, any time lost at the bottleneck will affect the output from the whole process. So it is not worthwhile for the parts of the process before the bottleneck to work to their full capacity. All they would do is produce work which would accumulate further along in the process up to the point where the bottleneck is constraining the flow. Therefore, some form of communication between the bottleneck and the input to the process is needed to make sure that activities before the bottleneck do not overproduce. This is called the *rope* (see Figure 10.17).

> **Operations principle**
>
> The constraints of bottleneck processes and activities should be a major input to the planning and control activity.

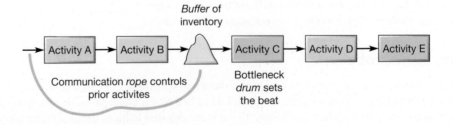

Figure 10.17 The drum, buffer, rope concept

Most of the perspectives on control taken in this chapter are simplifications of a far messier reality. They are based on models used to understand mechanical systems such as car engines. But anyone who has worked in real organizations knows that organizations are not machines. They are social systems, full of complex and ambiguous interactions. Simple models such as these assume that operations objectives are always clear and agreed, yet organizations are political entities where different and often conflicting objectives compete. Local government operations, for example, are overtly political. Furthermore, the outputs from operations are not always easily measured. A university may be able to measure the number and qualifications of its students, for example, but it cannot measure the full impact of its education on their future happiness. Also, even if it is possible to work out an appropriate intervention to bring an operation back into 'control', most operations cannot perfectly predict what effect the intervention will have. Even the largest of burger bar chains does not know *exactly* how a new shift allocation system will affect performance. Also, some operations never do the same thing more than once anyway. Most of the work done by construction operations are one-offs. If every output is different, how can 'controllers' ever know what is supposed to happen? Their plans themselves are mere speculation.

Controlling operations is not always routine

The simple monitoring control model in Figure 10.15 helps us to understand the basic functions of the monitoring and control activity. But, as the critical commentary box says, it is a simplification. Some simple routine processes may approximate to it, but many other operations do not. In fact, some of the specific criticisms cited in the critical commentary box provide a useful set of questions which can be used to assess the degree of difficulty associated with control of any operation. In particular:

▶ Is there consensus over what the operation's objectives should be?
▶ Are the effects of interventions into the operation predictable?
▶ Are the operation's activities largely repetitive?

Starting with the first question, are strategic objectives clear and unambiguous? It is not always possible (or necessarily desirable) to articulate every aspect of an operation's objectives in detail. Many operations are just too complex for that. Nor does every senior manager always agree on what the operation's objectives *should* be. Often the lack of a clear objective is because individual managers have different and conflicting interests. In social care organizations, for example, some managers are charged with protecting vulnerable members of society, others with ensuring that public money is now wasted, and yet others may be required to protect the independence of professional staff. At other times objectives are ambiguous because the strategy has to cope with unpredictable changes in the environment making the original objectives redundant. A further assumption in the simplified control model is that there is some reasonable knowledge of how to bring about the desired outcome. That is, when a decision is made, one can predict its effects with a reasonable degree of confidence. In other words, operational control assumes that any interventions which are intended to bring a process back under control will indeed have the intended effect. Yet, this implies that the relationships between the intervention and the resulting consequence within the process are predictable, which in turn assumes that the degree of process knowledge is high. For example, if an organization decides to relocate in order to be more convenient for its customers, it may or may not prove to be correct. Customers may react in a manner that was not predicted. Even if customers seem initially to respond well to the new location there may be a lag before negative reactions become evident. In fact, many operations decisions are taken about activities about which the cause–effect relationship is only partly understood. The final assumption about control is that control interventions are made in a repetitive way and occur frequently (for example, checking on a process, hourly or daily). This means that the operation has the opportunity to learn how its interventions affect the process, which considerably facilitates control. However, some control situations are non-repetitive; for example, those involving unique services or products. So because the intervention, or the deviation from plan that caused it, may not be repeated, there is little opportunity for learning.

Figure 10.18 illustrates how these questions can form a 'decision tree' type model that indicates how the nature of operations control may be influenced.[10] Operational control is relatively straightforward: objectives are unambiguous, the effects of interventions are known, and activities are repetitive. This type of control can be done using predetermined conventions and rules. There are, however, still some challenges to successful routine control. It needs operational discipline to make sure that control procedures are systematically implemented. The main point though is that any divergence from the conditions necessary for routine control implies a different type of control.

Operations principle

Planning and control is not always routine, especially when objectives are ambiguous, the effects of interventions into the operation are not predictable and activities not repetitive?

Expert control

If objectives are unambiguous, yet the effects of interventions relatively well understood, but the activity is not repetitive (for example, installing or upgrading software or IT systems) control can be delegated to an 'expert'; someone for whom such activities are repetitive because they have built their knowledge on previous experience elsewhere. Making a success of expert control requires that such experts exist and can be 'acquired' by the firm. It also requires that the expert takes advantage of the control knowledge already present in the firm and integrates his or her 'expert' knowledge with the support that potentially exists internally. Both of these place a stress on the need to 'network', in terms of both acquiring expertise and then integrating that expertise into the organization.

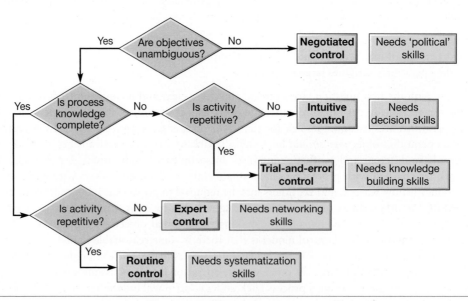

Figure 10.18 Control is not always routine, different circumstances require different types of control

Trial-and-error control

If strategic objectives are relatively unambiguous, but effects of interventions not known, yet the activity is repetitive, the operation can gain knowledge of how to control successfully through its own failures. In other words, although simple prescriptions may not be available in the early stages of making control interventions, the organization can learn how to do it through experience. For example, if a fast food chain is opening new stores into new markets, it may not be sure how best to arrange the openings at first. But if the launch is the first of several, the objective must be, not only to make a success of each launch, but equally (or more) important, it must learn from each experience. It is these knowledge building skills that will ultimately determine the effectiveness of trial and error control.

Intuitive control

If objectives are relatively unambiguous (so it is clear what the operation is trying to do), but effects of control interventions not known, and nor are they repetitive, learning by trial and error is not possible. Here control becomes more of an art than a science. And in these circumstances control must be based on the management team using its intuition to make control decisions. Many strategic operations processes fall into this category – for example, setting up a strategic supply partnership (see Chapter 13). Objectives are clear (jointly survive in the long term, make an acceptable return, and so on) but, not only are control interventions not repetitive an their effects not fully understood, but sometimes the supplier's interests may be in conflict with yours. Yet, simply stating that 'intuition' is needed in these circumstances is not particularly helpful. Instinct and feelings are, of course, valuable attributes in any management team, but they are the result, at least partly, of understanding how best to organize their shared understanding, knowledge, and decision-making skills. It requires thorough decision analysis, not to 'mechanistically' make the decision, but to frame it so that connections can be made, consequences understood, and insights gained.

Negotiated control

The most difficult circumstance for strategic control is when objectives are ambiguous. This type of control involves reducing ambiguity in some way by making objectives less uncertain. Sometimes this is done simply by senior managers 'pronouncing' or arbitrarily deciding what objectives *should* be irrespective of opposing views. For example, controlling the activities of a child care service can involve very different views amongst the professional social workers making day-to-day decisions. Often a negotiated settlement may be sought which then can become an unambiguous objective. Alternatively, outside experts could be used, either to help with the negotiations, or to remove control decisions from those with conflicting views. But, even within the framework of negotiation, there is almost always a political element when ambiguities in objectives exist. Negotiation processes will be, to some extent, dependent on power structures.

Summary answers to key questions

What is planning and control?

▶ Planning and control is the reconciliation of the potential of the operation to supply products and services, and the demands of its customers on the operation. It is the set of day-to-day activities that run the operation on an ongoing basis.

What is the difference between planning and control?

▶ A plan is a formalization of what is intended to happen at some time in the future. Control is the process of coping with changes to the plan and the operation to which it relates. Although planning and control are theoretically separable, they are usually treated together.

▶ The balance between planning and control changes over time. Planning dominates in the long term and is usually done on an aggregated basis. At the other extreme, in the short term, control usually operates within the resource constraints of the operation but makes interventions into the operation in order to cope with short-term changes in circumstances.

How does the nature of demand affect planning and control?

▶ The degree of uncertainty in demand affects the balance between planning and control. The greater the uncertainty, the more difficult it is to plan, and greater emphasis must be placed on control.

▶ This idea of uncertainty is linked with the concepts of dependent and independent demand. Dependent demand is relatively predictable because it is dependent on some known factor. Independent demand is less predictable because it depends on the chances of the market or customer behaviour.

▶ The different ways of responding to demand can be characterized by differences in the *P:D* ratio of the operation. The *P:D* ratio is the ratio of total throughput time of services or products to demand time.

What is involved in planning and control?

▶ In planning and controlling the volume and timing of activity in operations, four distinct activities are necessary:

  ▶ loading, which dictates the amount of work that is allocated to each part of the operation;

  ▶ sequencing, which decides the order in which work is tackled within the operation;

  ▶ scheduling, which determines the detailed timetable of activities and when activities are started and finished;

  ▶ monitoring and control, which involve detecting what is happening in the operation, replanning if necessary, and intervening in order to impose new plans. Two important types are 'pull' and 'push' control. Pull control is a system whereby demand is triggered by requests from a work centre's (internal) customer. Push control is a centralized system whereby control (and sometimes planning) decisions are issued to work centres which are then required to perform the task and supply the next workstation. In manufacturing, 'pull' schedules generally have far lower inventory levels than 'push' schedules.

▶ The ease with which control can be maintained varies between operations.

C.K. was clearly upset. Since he had founded *subText* in the fast-growing South East Asian computer-generated imaging (CGI) market, three years ago, this was the first time that he had needed to apologize to his clients. In fact, it had been more than an apology; he had agreed to reduce his fee, though he knew that didn't make up for the delay. He admitted that, up to that point, he hadn't fully realized just how much risk there was, both reputational and financial, in failing to meet schedule dates. It wasn't that either he or his team was unaware of the importance of reliability. On the contrary. 'Imagination', 'expertise' and 'reliability' all figured prominently in their promotional literature, mission statements, and so on. It was just that the 'imagination' and 'expertise' parts had seemed to be the things that had been responsible for their success so far. Of course, it had been bad luck that, after more than a year of perfect reliability (not one late job), the two that had been late in the first quarter of this year had been particularly critical. *'They were both for new clients,'* said CK, *'and neither of them indicated just how important the agreed delivery date was to them. We should have known, or found out, I admit. But it's always more difficult with new clients, because without a track record with them, you don't really like even to admit the possibility of being late.'*

The company

After studying computer science at the National University of Singapore, C.K. Ong had worked in CGI workshops in and around the Los Angeles area of California, after which he returned to Singapore to start *subText* Studios. At the heart of the company were the three 'core' departments that dealt sequentially with each job taken on. These three departments were 'Pre-production', 'Production' and 'Post-production'.

 Pre-production was concerned with taking and refining the brief as specified by the client, checking with and liaising with the client to iron out any ambiguities in the brief, story-boarding the sequences, and obtaining outline approval of the brief from the client. In addition, pre-production also acted as account liaison with the client and were also responsible for estimating the resources and timing for each job. They also had nominal responsibility for monitoring the job through the remaining two stages, but generally they only did this if the client needed to be consulted during the production and post-production processes.

▶ **Production** involved the creation of the imagery itself. This could be a complex and time-consuming process involving the use of state-of-the-art workstations and CGI software. Around 80 per cent of all production work was carried out in-house, but for some jobs other specialist workshops were contracted. This was only done for work that *subText* either could not do, or would find difficult to do.

▶ **Post-production** had two functions; the first was to integrate the visual image sequences produced by Production with other effects such as sound effects, music, voiceovers, etc., the second was to cut, edit and generally produce the finished 'product' in the format required by the client.

Each of the three department employed teams of two people. Pre-production had two teams, Production three teams, and Post-production two teams. For Pre-production and Post-production work, one team is always exclusively devoted to one job. *'We never allow either one team to be working on two jobs at the same time, or have both teams working on one job. It just doesn't work because of the confusion it creates. That doesn't apply to Production. Usually (but not always) the Production work can be parcelled up so that two or even all three of the teams could be working on different parts of it at the same time. Provided there is close coordination between the teams and provided that they are all committed to pulling it together at the end, there should be a more or less inverse relationship between the number of bodies working on the job and the length of time it takes. In fact, with the infamous 'fifty-three slash F' job that's exactly what we had to do. However, not withstanding what I just said about shortening the time, we probably did lose some efficiency there by having all three teams working on it. Our teams generally work until the job is finished. That level of work is factored in to the time estimates we make for each stage of the process. And, although we can be a little inaccurate sometimes, it's because this type of thing is difficult to estimate'* (C.K. Ong).

Table 10.5 *subText* Studios Singapore – Planning data for day 02 to day 58

Job (04)	Day in	Estimated total time	Actual total time	Due date	Actual delivery	Pre-prod		Prod		Post-prod	
						Est	Actual	Est	Actual	Est	Actual
06/A	−4	29	30	40	34	6	8	11	10	12	12
11/B	−4	22	24	42	31	4	5.5	7	7.5	11	11
04/C	2	31	30.5	43	40	9	9.5	12	13	10	9
54/D	5	28	34	55	58	10	12	12	17	6	5
31/E	15	34	25	68	57	10	11	12	14	12	-
53/F	18	32	49	50	53	6	10	18	28	8	11
24/G	25	26	20	70	-	9	11	9	9	8	-
22/H	29	32	26	70	-	10	12	14	14	8	-
22/I	33	30	11	75	-	10	11	12	-	8	-
09/J	41	36	14	81	-	12	14	14	-	10	-
20/K	49	40	-	89	-	12	-	14	-	14	-

The fifty-three slash F job

The fifty-three slash F job, recently finished (late) and delivered to the client (dissatisfied) had been the source of much chaos, confusion and recrimination over the last two or three weeks. Although the job was only three days late, it had caused the client to postpone a presentation to its own client. Worse, *subText* had given only five days' notice of late delivery, trying until the last to pull back onto schedule.

The full name of the job that had given it so much trouble was 04/53/F. Table 10.5 shows the data for all the jobs started

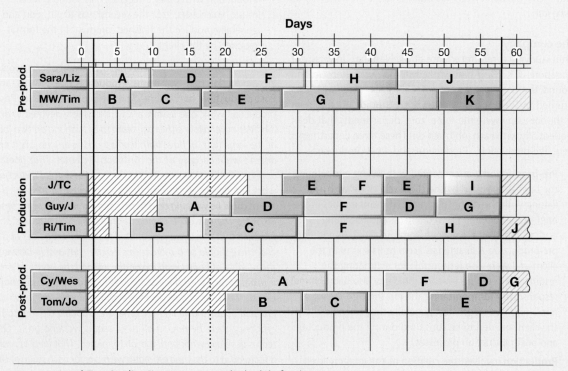

Figure 10.19 *subText* Studios Singapore – actual schedule for day

this year up to the current time (day 58; every working day was numbered throughout the year). Figure 10.19 shows the schedule for this period. The job had been accepted on day 18 and had seemed relatively straightforward, although it was always clear that it would be a long production job. It was also clear that time was always going to be tight. There were 32 days in which to finish a job that was estimated to take 30 days.

'In hindsight we underestimated how much having three teams working on the production stage of this job at one point or other would increase its complexity. OK, it was not an easy piece of CGI to carry off, but we probably would have been OK if we had organized the CGI stage better. It was also real bad luck that, in our efforts to deliver the fifty-three slash F job on time, we also disrupted the fifty-four slash D job that turned out to be the only other new client we have had this year' (C.K. Ong).

The job had proved difficult from the start. The pre-production stage took longer than estimated, mainly because the client's creative team changed just before the start of subText beginning the work. But it was the actual CGI itself that proved to be the major problem. Not only was the task intrinsically difficult, it was difficult to parcel it up into separate packages that could be coordinated for working on by the two teams allocated to the job. More seriously, it became apparent within two or three days of starting the production work that they would need the help of another studio for some of the effects. Although the other studio was a regular supplier at short notice, this time they were too busy with their own work to help out. Help eventually came from a specialist studio in Hong Kong. 'The subcontracting delay was clearly a problem, but it was only half way through the production phase that we first realized just how much difficulty the fifty-three slash F job was in. It was at that stage that we devoted all our production resources to finishing it. Unfortunately, even then, the job was late. The decision eventually to put all three teams on to the fifty-three slash F job was not easy because we knew that it would both disrupt other jobs and potentially cause more coordination problems.'

'No way will be doing that again'

'No way will be doing that again', said CK to the core teams when they met to pick over what had gone wrong. 'We are desperately in need of a more professional approach to keeping track of our activities. There is no point in me telling everyone how good we are if we then let them down. The problem is that I don't want to encourage a "command and control" culture in the studio. We depend on all staff feeling that they have the freedom to explore seemingly crazy options that may just lead to something real special. We aren't a factory. But we do need to get a grip on our estimating so that we have a better idea of how long each job really will take. After that each of the core departments can be responsible for their own planning.'

QUESTIONS

1 What went wrong with the fifty-three slash F job and how could the company avoid making the same mistakes again?

2 What would you suggest that subText does to tighten up its planning and control procedures?

Problems and applications

All chapters have 'Problems and applications' questions that will help you practise analysing operations. They can be answered by reading the chapter. Model answers for the first two questions can be found on the companion website for this book.

1 Re-read the 'Operations in practice' examples 'Joanne manages the schedule', and 'Operations control at Air France'. How do the planning and control tasks in these two operations compare?

2 Mark Key is an events coordinator for a small company. Returning from his annual holiday in France, he is given six events to plan. He gives them the codes A–F. He needs to decide upon the sequence in which to plan the events and wants to minimize the average time the jobs are tied up in the office and, if possible, meet the deadlines allocated. The six jobs are detailed in Table 10.6.

Determine a sequence based on using (a) the FIFO rule, (b) the due date rule, (c) the shortest operation time rule. (d) Which of these sequences gives the most efficient solution and which gives the least lateness?

Table 10.6 The six jobs that Mark has to sequence

Sequence of jobs	Process time (days)	Due date
A	4	12
B	3	5
C	1	7
D	2	9
E	2	15
F	5	8

3 It is week 35 of a busy year at Ashby Architects and Jo Ashby is facing a big problem. Both her two junior partners have been diagnosed with a serious illness contracted on a trip to scope out a prospective job in Lichtenstein. So Jo has to step in and complete the outstanding jobs that were being worked on by the two juniors. The outstanding jobs are shown in Table 10.7.

Jo has heard that a sequencing rule called the critical ratio (CR) will give efficient results. The priority of jobs using the CR rule is defined by an index computed as follows:

$$CR = \frac{\text{time remaining}}{\text{workdays remaining}} = \frac{\text{due date-today's date}}{\text{workdays remaining}}$$

Using this rule, in what priority should Jo give the jobs?

Table 10.7 Outstanding jobs that Jo will need to complete

Job	Due Date (week)	Weeks of work remaining
Ashthorpe lavatory block	40	2.0
Bubgwitch bus shelters	48	5.0
Crudstone plc HQ	51	3.0
Dredge sewage works	52	8.0

4 It takes 6 hours for a contract laundry to wash, dry and press (in that order) a batch of overalls. It takes 3 hours to wash the batch, 2 hours to dry it, and 1 hour to press it. Usually each day's batch is collected and ready for processing at 8.00 am and needs to be picked up at 4.00 pm. The two people who work in the laundry have different approaches to how they schedule the work. One schedules 'forward'. Forward scheduling involves starting work as soon as it arrives. The other schedules 'backwards'. Backward scheduling involves starting jobs at the last possible moment that will prevent them from being late. (a) Draw up a schedule indicating the start and finish time for each activity

(wash, dry and press) for both forward and backward approaches. (b) What do you think are the advantages and disadvantages of these two approaches?

5   Read the following descriptions of two cinemas.

Kinepolis in Brussels is one the largest cinema complexes in the world, with 28 screens, a total of 8,000 seats, and four showings of each film every day. It is equipped with the latest projection technology. All the film performances are scheduled to start at the same times every day: 4 pm, 6 pm, 8 pm and 10.30 pm. Most customers arrive in the 30 minutes before the start of the film. Each of the 18 ticket desks has a networked terminal and a ticket printer. For each customer, a screen code is entered to identify and confirm seat availability of the requested film. Then the number of seats required is entered, and the tickets are printed, though these do not allocate specific seat positions. The operator then takes payment by cash or credit card and issues the tickets. This takes an average of 19.5 seconds, and a further 5 seconds is needed for the next customer to move forward. An average transaction involves the sale of approximately 1.7 tickets.

The UCI cinema in Birmingham has eight screens. The cinema incorporates many 'state-of-the-art' features, including the high-quality THX sound system, fully computerized ticketing and a video games arcade off the main hall. In total the eight screens can seat 1,840 people; the capacity (seating) of each screen varies, so the cinema management can allocate the more popular films to the larger screens and use the smaller screens for the less popular films. The starting times of the eight films at UCI are usually staggered by 10 minutes, with the most popular film in each category (children's, drama, comedy, etc.) being scheduled to run first. Because the films are of different durations, and since the manager must try to maximize the utilization of the seating, the scheduling task is complex. Ticket staff are continually aware of the remaining capacity of each 'screen' through their terminals. There are up to four ticket desks open at any one time. The target time per overall transaction is 20 seconds. The average number of ticket sales per transaction is 1.8. All tickets indicate specific seat positions, and these are allocated on a first-come, first-served basis.

(a) What are the main differences between the two cinemas from the perspectives of their operations managers?

(b) What are the advantages and disadvantages of the two different methods of scheduling the films onto the screens?

(c) Find out the running times and classification of eight popular films. Try to schedule these onto the UCI Birmingham screens, taking account of what popularity you might expect at different times. Allow 20 minutes for emptying, cleaning, and admitting the next audience, and 15 minutes for advertising, before the start of the film.

6   Think through the following three brief examples. What type of control (according to Figure 10.18) do you think they warrant?

The Games Delivery Authority (GDA) was a public body responsible for developing and building the new venues and infrastructure for the 'International Games' and their use after the event. The GDA appointed a consortium responsible for the overall programme's quality, delivery and cost, in addition to health and safety, sustainability, equality and diversity targets. The Games Park was a large construction programme spreading across five separate local government areas, including transport developments, retail areas and local regeneration projects. Sustainability was central to the development. *'Sustainability' was ingrained into our thinking – from the way we planned, built and worked, to the way we play, socialise and travel.'* To ensure they stuck to commitments, the GDA set up an independent body to monitor the project. All potential contractors tendering for parts of the project were aware that a major underlying objective of the Games initiative was regeneration. The Games site was to be built on highly industrialized and contaminated land.

The supermarket's new logistics boss was blunt in his assessment of its radical supply chain implementation. *'Our rivals have watched in utter disbelief'*, he said. *'Competitors looked on in amazement as we poured millions into implementing new IT systems and replaced 21 depots with a handful of giant automated "fulfilment factories."* In hindsight, the heavy reliance on automation was a big mistake, especially for fast moving goods'*, said the company's CIO. *'When a conventional facility goes wrong, you have lots of options. You have flexibility to deal with issues. When an automated "fulfilment factory" goes wrong, frankly, you're buggered.'* Most damning was the way that the supermarket pressed on with the implementation of the automated facilities before proving that the concept worked at the first major site. *'I'd have at least proved that one of them worked before building the other three'*, he said. *'Basically, the whole company was committed to doing too much, too fast, trying to implement a seven-year strategy in a three-year timescale.'*

'It's impossible to overemphasise just how important this launch is to our future', said the CEO. *'We have been losing market share for seven quarters straight. However, we have very high hopes for the new XC10 unit.'* And most of the firm's top management team agreed with her. Clearly the market had been maturing for some time now, and was undoubtedly getting more difficult. New product launches from competitors had been eroding market share. Yet competitors' products, at best, simply matched the firm's offerings in all benchmark tests. *'Unless someone comes up with a totally new technology, which is very unlikely, it will be a matter of making marginal improvements in product performance and combining this with well-targeted and coordinated marketing. Fortunately, we are good at both of these. We know this technology, and we know these markets. We are also clear what role the new XC10 should play. It needs to consolidate our market position as the leader in this field, reduce the slide in market share by half, and re-establish our customers' faith in us. Margins, at least in the short term, are less important.'*

Selected further reading

Chapman, S.N. (2005) *Fundamentals of Production Planning and Control,* **Pearson, Harlow.**
A detailed textbook, intended for those studying the topic in depth.

Goldratt, E.Y. and Cox, J. (1984) *The Goal,* **North River Press, Croton-on-Hudson, NY.**
Don't read this if you like good novels, but do read it if you want an enjoyable way of understanding some of the complexities of scheduling. It particularly applies to the drum, buffer, rope concept described in this chapter and it also sets the scene for the discussion of OPT in Chapter 14.

Kehoe, D.F. and Boughton N.J. (2001) New paradigms in planning and control across manufacturing supply chains – The utilization of Internet technologies, *International Journal of Operations & Production Management,* **vol. 21, issue 5/6, 582–593.**
Academic, but interesting.

Pinedo, M.L. (2016) *Scheduling: Theory, Algorithms, and Systems,* **5th edn, Springer, NY.**
A very technical, but well-established text.

Vollmann, T.W., Berry, W.L., Whybark, D.C. and Jacobs, F.R. (2010) *Manufacturing Planning and Control Systems for Supply Chain Management: The Definitive Guide for Professionals,* **McGraw Hill Higher Education, New York.**
The latest version of the 'bible' of manufacturing planning and control.

11

Capacity management

KEY QUESTIONS

What is capacity management?

How is demand measured?

How is capacity measured?

How is the demand side managed?

How is the supply side managed?

How can operations understand the consequences of their capacity management decisions?

INTRODUCTION

Capacity management is the activity of understanding the nature of an operation's demand and supply, and coping with mismatches between them. It involves an attempt to forecast demand and measure the ability to supply products and services, followed by the selection of appropriate demand-side and supply-side responses based on performance objectives and long-term outlook. In doing this, operations managers must be able to understand and reconcile two competing requirements. On the one hand, is the importance of maintaining customer satisfaction by delivering products and services to customers reasonably quickly. On the other, is the need for operations (and their extended supply networks) to maintain efficiency by minimizing the costs of excess capacity. In this chapter, we look at these competing tensions at an aggregated level. At this level, managers do not discriminate between the different products and services that might be created by the operation. Instead, they aim to ensure that the overall ability to supply is in line with the overall demand placed on the operation. Figure 11.1 shows where this chapter fits in the structure of the book. At the end of the chapter is a supplement on queuing for those wishing to go into more detail on this important sub-topic of capacity management.

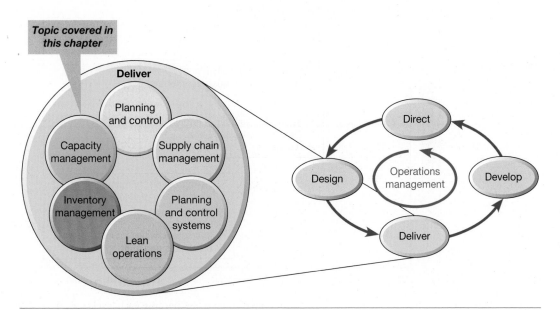

Figure 11.1 This chapter examines capacity management

What is capacity management?

Capacity management is the activity of understanding the nature of product or service demand, and effectively planning and controlling capacity. All this must be done while reconciling the competing demands of customer satisfaction and resource efficiency. Capacity decisions are taken across multiple time horizons – minute-by-minute, day-by-day, month-on-month and year-on-year. They are also made within the constraints of the operation, the ability of its suppliers to supply, the availability of staff, and so on. As such, each level of capacity decision is made within the constraints of a higher level. In the other direction, short-term decisions provide important feedback for planning over longer-term time horizons. This interaction effect between different time horizons is illustrated in Figure 11.2.

In Chapter 5, we examined long-term capacity decisions as they relate to the structure and scope of operations. In Chapter 10, we examined the more short-term capacity decisions around allocation, sequencing and resourcing of tasks. In this chapter, we focus on the medium-term aspects of capacity management, where decisions are being made largely within the constraints of the physical capacity set by the operation's long-term capacity strategy. Medium-term capacity management usually involves assessing demand forecasts with a time horizon of between 2 and 18 months, during which time planned output can be varied, for example, by changing the number of hours that resources are used. In practice, however, few forecasts are accurate, and most operations also need to respond to changes in demand that occur over an even shorter timescale – termed short-term capacity management. Hotels and restaurants have unexpected and apparently random changes in demand from night to night, but also know from experience that certain days are on average busier than others. So, operations managers also have to make short-term capacity adjustments, which enable them to flex output for a short period, either on a predicted basis (for example, bank checkouts are always busy at lunchtimes) or at short notice (for example, a sunny, warm day at a theme park).

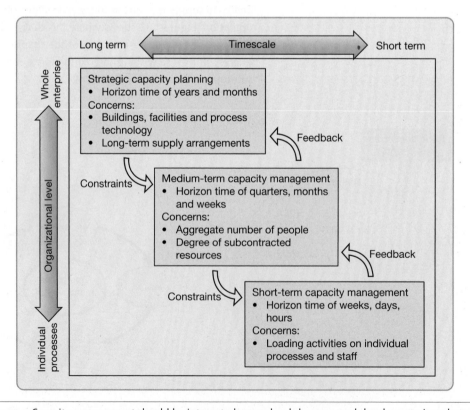

Figure 11.2 Capacity management should be integrated across levels because each level constrains what can be done in the level below and can provide feedback for the level above

The rise of the gig economy[1]

At one time, most people had one job and a permanent contract for life. But this is no longer the universal rule, which is because of the rise of the 'gig economy'. The gig economy describes the trend to employ sub-contractors and freelancers to perform an increasing proportion of activities rather than relying on full-time employees. As a method of flexing capacity, this is now employed across a wide range of industries, including arts and design, transportation, construction, accommodation, media, ICT, education and professional services. Here are three examples of companies at the forefront of the gig revolution.

▶ **Uber:** Uber has become, arguably, the most famous of all gig economy companies worldwide. It uses its technology platform to connect those wanting taxi rides, food delivery and transportation of small packages, with individuals who want to use their cars to provide the service. It gives sub-contracted drivers considerable flexibility over when and where they drive. Uber has also developed other operations in over 600 cities worldwide with extensions to its core ride-sharing service including UberBOAT (a water taxi service), UberMOTO (transportation by motorcycle), UberEats (a meal delivery service) and UberRUSH (a courier package service).

▶ **Udemy:** The online education provider Udemy is a peer-to-peer platform that hosts more than 65,000 courses developed by around 30,000 instructors and has a student base of over 20 million. Courses cover a wide variety of subjects including business, arts, health and fitness, languages and technology. And given the sheer scale of its user base, online content developers are able to generate returns on the time they invest – some are millionaires. Similar companies include Coursera, Kahn Institute, Canvas and Futurelearn, all enabling freelance experts to post content. Some, like Udemy, operate for profit, whereas others are not-for-profit platforms looking to 'democratize learning'.

▶ **Airbnb:** Airbnb operates in the hotel, catering and tourism sector. The company provides a peer-to-peer platform connecting customers with those wanting to lease lodgings, including houses, apartments, bedrooms, hotel rooms and hostels. They generate income by taking a commission on every transaction on their marketplace. It has over 4 million listings, in around 200 countries, and has facilitated over 300 million check-ins. In its efforts to increase trust between customers and suppliers of capacity, Airbnb uses a rating system and AirbnbPlus, which only features homes that have been vetted for quality and comfort. Those not wanting the hassle of preparing their property might instead choose OneFineStay, a competitor that, in addition to undertaking quality vetting, provides greeting services, key handling, insurance, cleaning and the provision of bed linen.

Other companies using platforms that act as intermediaries between demand (customers) and supply include ones for leasing vehicles, leasing aircraft, web development, graphic design, programming, finance and consulting advice, and chef services. From a capacity management perspective, the gig economy can maintain high levels of customer service, even in the face of changeable demand, while also achieving high levels of utilization. Operations do not have the fixed costs of employees or facilities when demand drops, yet can ramp up capacity when demand increases. However, to many, the idea of fluctuating the workforce to match demand, using 'gig workers', is unethical. 'Gig working' can offer poor conditions of service and can cause permanent anxiety to those employed in this way. In addition, the advantages of gig working to employers may diminish as legislation moves towards establishing greater legal rights for 'gig workers', such as sick pay, maternity leave and paid holidays.

Aggregate planning of demand and capacity

The important characteristic of capacity management, as we are treating it here, is that it is concerned with setting capacity levels over the medium and short terms in *aggregated* terms (in fact, what we call capacity management here is sometimes called 'aggregate planning'). That is, it is making overall, broad capacity decisions, but is not concerned with all of the detail of the individual products and services offered. This is what 'aggregated' means – different products and services are bundled together in order to get a broad view of demand and capacity. This may mean some degree of approximation, especially if the mix of products or services being created varies significantly (as we shall see later in this chapter). Nevertheless, as a first step in capacity management, aggregation is necessary. For example, a hotel might think of demand and capacity in terms of 'room nights per month'. This ignores the number of guests in each room and their individual requirements, but it is a good first approximation. A woollen knitwear factory might measure demand and capacity in the number of units (garments) it is capable of making per month, ignoring size, colour or style variations. The ultimate aggregation measure is money. For example, retail stores, which sell an exceptionally wide variety of products, use revenue per month, ignoring variation in spend, number of items bought, the gross margin of each item and the number of items per customer transaction.

> **Operations principle**
>
> Capacity is usually expressed in aggregated terms.

Capacity management performance objectives

The decisions taken by operations managers in devising their capacity plans will affect several different aspects of performance:

▶ *Costs* will be affected by the balance between demand and capacity. Capacity levels in excess of demand could mean under-utilization of capacity and therefore high units cost.

▶ *Revenues* will also be affected by the balance between demand and capacity, but in the opposite way. Capacity levels equal to or higher than demand at any point in time will ensure that all demand is satisfied and no revenue lost.

▶ *Working capital* will be affected if an operation decides to build up finished goods inventory prior to demand. This might allow demand to be satisfied, but the organization will have to fund the inventory until it can be sold.

▶ *Quality* of services might be affected by a capacity plan that involves large fluctuations in capacity levels, by hiring temporary staff for example. The new staff and the disruption to the routine working of the operation could increase the probability of errors being made.

▶ *Speed* of response to customer demand could be enhanced either by the deliberate provision of surplus capacity to avoid queuing, or through the build-up of inventories (allowing customers to be satisfied directly from the inventory rather than having to wait for items to be manufactured).

▶ *Dependability* of supply will also be affected by how close demand levels are to capacity. The closer demand gets to the operation's capacity ceiling, the less able it is to cope with any unexpected disruptions and the less dependable its deliveries of goods and services could be.

▶ *Flexibility*, especially volume flexibility, will be enhanced by surplus capacity. If demand and capacity are in balance, the operation will not be able to respond to any unexpected increase in demand.

A framework for capacity management

There are a series of activities involved in capacity management, which are shown in Figure 11.3. The most common first step is in on the demand side of the 'equation' measuring (forecasting) demand for products and services over different time periods. This involves selecting from a range of qualitative (panel, Delphi and scenario planning) and quantitative (time series and casual models) tools to support more accurate prediction of demand. It also requires balancing between investments in between better forecasts and investments in greater operations flexibility. The second step is typically on the supply side of the framework and involves measuring the capacity to deliver products and services. Here, the impacts of product or service mix, timeframe and output specification should

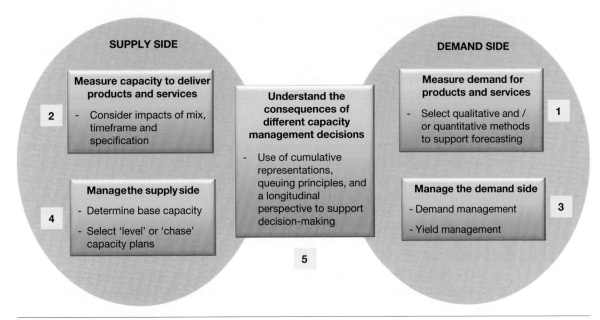

Figure 11.3 Capacity management framework

be considered. The third step is to consider if and how to manage demand using demand management and yield management techniques. The fourth step is to manage the supply side by determining the appropriate level of average capacity and then deciding whether to keep this constant of the timeframe (level capacity plan) or to adjust capacity in line with changing demand patterns (chase capacity plan). Finally, operations managers must understand the consequences of different capacity management decisions for both the demand side and supply side of the framework. Using cumulative representations, principles of queuing and a longitudinal perspective can all help in the decision-making process.

How is demand measured?

The first task of capacity management is to understand the patterns of demand for products and services. Importantly, knowing that demand may be rising or falling, whilst a useful start, is not enough in itself. Knowing the *rate of change* is often vital for business planning. A firm of lawyers may have to decide the point at which, in their growing business, they will have to take on another partner. Hiring a new partner could take months, so they need to be able to forecast when they expect to reach that point and then when they need to start their recruitment drive. The same applies to a plant manager who needs to respond rising demand. She may not want to commit to buying an expensive piece of machinery until absolutely necessary but in enough time to order the machine and have it built, delivered, installed and tested. Therefore, key questions when considering demand include: What is the overall demand for a product or service over a period of time? How much does demand change? Are the total requirements and/or the changes in demand easy or difficult to predict? In any period of time, how much does demand change, and how accurate is forecast demand likely to be? Although demand forecasting is often the responsibility of the sales and/or marketing functions, it is a very important input into the capacity management decisions, and so is of interest to operations managers. After all, without an estimate of future demand it is not possible to plan effectively for future events, only to react to them.

> **Operations principle**
>
> Understanding patterns of demand for products and services is critical for successful capacity management.

Qualitative approaches to forecasting

Managers sometimes use qualitative methods based on judgement, past experience, and even best guesses to forecast demand. There are a range of qualitative forecasting techniques available to help managers evaluate trends and causal relationships, and make predictions about the future. Three popular qualitative forecasting methods are the panel approach, Delphi method and scenario planning.

Panel approach

Just as panels of sports pundits gather to speculate about likely outcomes, so too do politicians, business leaders, stock market analysts, banks and airlines. The panel acts like a focus group allowing everyone to talk openly and freely. Although there is the great advantage of several brains being better than one, it can be difficult to reach a consensus, or sometimes the views of the loudest or highest status may emerge (the bandwagon effect). Although more reliable than one person's views, the panel approach still has the weakness that everybody, even the experts, can get it wrong.

Delphi method

Perhaps the best-known approach to generating forecasts using experts is the Delphi method. This is a more formal method which attempts to reduce the influences from procedures of face-to-face meetings. It employs a survey of experts where replies are analysed, and anonymous summaries are sent back to all experts. The experts are then asked to re-consider their original response in the light of the replies and arguments put forward by the other experts. This process is repeated several times to conclude with either a consensus or at least a narrower range of decisions. One refinement of this approach is to allocate weights to the individuals and their suggestions based on, for example, their experience, their past success in forecasting, and other people's views of their abilities. The obvious problems associated with this method include constructing an appropriate questionnaire, selecting an appropriate panel of experts, and trying to deal with their inherent biases.

Scenario planning

One method for dealing with situations of even greater uncertainty is scenario planning. This is usually applied to long-range forecasting again using a panel. The panel members are usually asked to devise a range of future scenarios. Each scenario can then be discussed and the inherent risks considered. Unlike the Delphi method, scenario planning is not necessarily concerned with arriving at a consensus but looking at a range of options and putting plans in place to try to avoid the ones that are least desired and taking action to follow the most desired.

Quantitative approaches to forecasting

Managers sometimes prefer to use quantitative methods to forecast demand. Two key approaches are time series analysis and causal modelling techniques. Time series examine the pattern of past behaviour of a single phenomenon, over time, taking into account reasons for variation in the trend, in order to use the analysis to forecast the phenomenon's future behaviour. Causal modelling is an approach which describes and evaluates the complex cause–effect relationships between the key variables.

Time series analysis

Simple time series plot a variable over time and then, by removing underlying variations with assignable causes, use extrapolation techniques to predict future behaviour. The key weakness with this approach is that it simply looks at past behaviour to predict the future ignoring causal variables, which are taken into account in other methods such as causal modelling or qualitative techniques. For example, suppose a company is attempting to predict the future service sales. The past three years' sales, quarter by quarter, are shown in Figure 11.4(a). This series of past sales may be analysed to indicate future sales. For instance, underlying the series might be a linear upward trend in sales. If this is taken out of the data, as in Figure 11.4(b), we are left with a cyclical seasonal variation.

The mean deviation of each quarter from the trend line can now be taken out, to give the average seasonality deviation. What remains is the random variation about the trends and seasonality lines, Figure 11.4(c). Future sales may now be predicted as lying within a band about a projection of the trend, plus the seasonality. The width of the band will be a function of the degree of random variation.

The random variations which remain after taking out trend and seasonal effects are without any known or assignable cause. This does not mean that they do not have a cause, however, just that we do not know what it is. Nevertheless, some attempt can be made to forecast it, if only on the basis that future events will, in some way, be based on past events. We will examine two of the more common approaches to forecasting which are based on projecting forward from past behaviour. These are:

Operations principle

Time series methods of forecasting use past patterns of demand to make predictions.

▶ moving-average forecasting;
▶ exponentially smoothed forecasting.

Moving-average forecasting

The moving-average approach to forecasting takes the previous n periods' actual demand figures, calculates the average demand over the n periods, and uses this average as a forecast for the next period's demand. Any data older than the n periods plays no part in the next period's forecast. The value of n can be set at any level, but is usually in the range 4 to 7. Table 11.1 shows the weekly demand for Eurospeed, a European-wide parcel delivery company. It measures demand, on a weekly basis, in terms of the number of parcels which it is given to deliver (irrespective of the size of each parcel). Each week, the next week's demand is forecast by taking the moving average of the previous

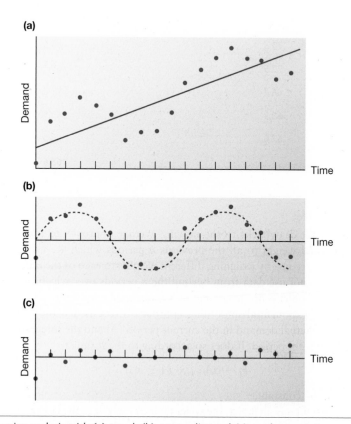

Figure 11.4 Time series analysis with (a) trend, (b) seasonality and (c) random variation

four weeks' actual demand. Thus, if the forecast demand for week t is F_t and the actual demand for week t is A_t, then:

$$F_t = \frac{A_{t-1} + A_{t-2} + A_{t-3} + A_{t-4}}{4}$$

For example, the forecast for week 35:

$$F_{35} = (72.5 + 66.7 + 68.3 + 67.0)/4$$

$$= 68.8$$

Table 11.1 Moving-average forecast calculated over a four-week period

Week	Actual demand (thousands)	Forecast
20	63.3	
21	62.5	
22	67.8	
23	66.0	
24	67.2	64.9
25	69.9	65.9
26	65.6	67.7
27	71.1	66.3
28	68.8	67.3
29	68.4	68.9
30	70.3	68.5
31	72.5	69.7
32	66.7	70.0
33	68.3	69.5
34	67.0	69.5
35		**68.6**

Exponential smoothing

There are two significant drawbacks to the moving-average approach to forecasting. First, in its basic form, it gives equal weight to all the previous n periods which are used in the calculations (although this can be overcome by assigning different weights to each of the n periods). Second, and more important, it does not use data from beyond the n periods over which the moving average is calculated. Both these problems are overcome by *exponential smoothing*, which is also somewhat easier to calculate. The exponential-smoothing approach forecasts demand in the next period by taking into account the actual demand in the current period (A) and the forecast (F) which was previously made for the current period. It does so according to the formula:

$$F_t = \alpha A_{t-1} + (1 - x)F_{t-1}$$

where α is the smoothing constant.

The smoothing constant α is, in effect, the weight which is given to the last (and therefore assumed to be most important) piece of information available to the forecaster. However, the other expression in the formula includes the forecast for the current period which included the previous period's actual demand, and so on. In this way, all previous data has an (albeit diminishing) effect on the next forecast. Table 11.2 shows the data for Eurospeed's parcels forecasts using this exponential-smoothing method, where $\alpha = 0.2$. For example, the forecast for week 35 is:

$$F_{35} = (0.2 \times 67.0) + (0.8 \times 68.3) = 68.04$$

The value of α governs the balance between the *responsiveness* of the forecasts to changes in demand, and the *stability* of the forecasts. The closer α is to 0, the more forecasts will be dampened by previous forecasts (not very sensitive but stable). Figure 11.5 shows the Eurospeed volume data plotted for a four-week moving average, exponential smoothing with $\alpha = 0.2$ and exponential smoothing with $\alpha = 0.3$.

Table 11.2 Exponentially smoothed forecast calculated with smoothing constant $\alpha = 0.2$

Week (t)	Actual demand (thousands) (A)	Forecast ($F_t = \alpha A_{t-1} + (1 - \alpha)F_{t-1}$) ($\alpha = 0.2$)
20	63.3	60.00
21	62.5	60.66
22	67.8	60.03
23	66.0	61.58
24	67.2	62.83
25	69.9	63.70
26	65.6	64.94
27	71.1	65.07
28	68.8	66.28
29	68.4	66.78
30	70.3	67.12
31	72.5	67.75
32	66.7	68.70
33	68.3	68.30
34	67.0	68.30
35		**68.04**

Seasonality in forecasting

Most organizations experience seasonal patterns in their demand. The causes of seasonality are sometimes climatic (holidays), sometimes festive (gift purchases), sometimes financial (tax processing), or social, or political. Most of us typically think of seasonality in annual terms. However, in forecasting the term is used to describe any regularly repeating changes in demand (quarterly, monthly, weekly, daily, or hourly). For example, utility companies may experience annual seasonality, but will also face seasonal patterns over the week and across the day. Similarly, repeating patterns of the daily and weekly demand patterns of a supermarket will fluctuate, with some degree of predictability. Demand might be low in the morning, higher in the afternoon, with peaks at lunchtime and after work in the evening. Demand might be low on Monday and Tuesday, build up during the latter part of the week and reach a peak on Friday and Saturday. A popular technique for incorporating seasonality in

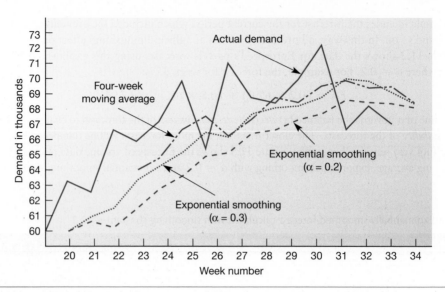

Figure 11.5 A comparison of a moving-average forecast and exponential smoothing with the smoothing constant $\alpha = 0.2$ and 0.3

forecasting is the multiplicative seasonal model, where seasonal factors are multiplied by an estimate of average demand to generate a seasonal forecast. For simplicity, here we assume that there is no other trend in the data, apart from seasonality. The seasonal model involves for following five steps.

1 Find the average demand for each 'season' by summing the demand for that season and dividing by the number of seasons available. For example, if in March, we have had sales of 80, 75 and 100 over the last three years, average March demand equals $(80 + 75 + 100)/3 = 85$.

2 Calculate average demand over all 'seasons' by dividing total average demand by the number of seasons. For example, if total average annual demand is 1,320 and there are 12 seasons (months), average demand equals $1,320/12 = 110$.

3 Compute the seasonal index by dividing average season demand (step 1) by average demand (step 2). For example, the March seasonal index equals $85/110 = 0.77$.

Operations principle

In demand forecasting, 'seasonality' refers to any repeating pattern of demand – annual, quarterly, monthly, weekly, daily or even hourly.

4 Estimate the next time period's (in this case, annual) total demand using one or more of the qualitative of quantitative methods described in this section.

5 Divide this estimate by the number of seasons (in this case, 12 months) and multiply by the seasonal index to provide a seasonal forecast.

Causal models

Causal models often employ complex techniques to understand the strength of relationships between the network of variables and the impact they have on each other. 'Simple regression' models try to determine the 'best fit' expression between two variables. For example, suppose an ice-cream company is trying to forecast its future sales. After examining previous demand, it figures that the main influence on demand at the factory is the average temperature of the previous week. To understand this relationship, the company plots demand against the previous week's temperatures. This is shown in Figure 11.6. Using this graph, the company can make a reasonable prediction of demand, once the average temperature is known, provided that the other conditions prevailing in the market are reasonably stable.

If they are not, then these other factors that have an influence on demand will need to be included in a 'multiple regression' model. These more complex networks comprise many variables and

Phoenix Consulting expects to have an annual demand for 7,500 hours of supply chain strategy consulting in 2018. Using the multiplicative seasonal model, we can forecast demand for June, July and August of that year.

Month	2015	2016	2017	Ave 20 15-17 demand	Ave monthly demand	Seasonal index
Jan	450	475	475	466.67	570.14	0.82
Feb	500	500	550	516.67	570.14	0.91
Mar	625	600	575	600.00	570.14	1.05
Apr	600	600	650	616.67	570.14	1.08
May	550	600	600	583.33	570.14	1.02
Jun	600	625	650	625.00	570.14	1.10
Jul	700	750	800	750.00	570.14	1.32
Aug	450	400	500	450.00	570.14	0.79
Sep	500	450	450	466.67	570.14	0.82
Oct	550	500	525	525.00	570.14	0.92
Nov	650	600	650	633.33	570.14	1.11
Dec	600	600	625	608.33	570.14	1.07
Total average annual demand				6,841.67		

$$\text{June 2018 forecast} = (7{,}500/12) \times 1.10 = 687.50$$

$$\text{July 2018 forecast} = (7{,}500/12) \times 1.32 = 825.00$$

$$\text{August 2018 forecast} = (7{,}500/12) \times 0.79 = 493.75$$

relationships, each with their own set of assumptions and limitations. While developing such models and assessing the importance of each of the factors is beyond the scope of this text, many techniques are available to help managers undertake this more complex modelling and also feedback data into the model to further refine and develop it, in particular structural equation modelling.

Operations principle

Causal models make predictions by examining the impact that one or more variables have on demand.

Making forecasts useful for operations managers

Without some attempt to understand future demand (and indeed supply fluctuations – see below), it is not possible to plan effectively for future events, only to react to them. Yet, some forecasts are much more useful than others. There are three key ways to assess the usefulness of a demand forecast from an operations manager's perspective – its level of accuracy, its ability to indicate relative uncertainty, and its expression in terms that are useful for capacity management.

It is as accurate as possible

Forecasts are (almost) always wrong – the economist John Kenneth Galbraith once said, '*the only function of economic forecasting is to make astrology look respectable*'. Yet clearly the process of capacity management is hugely aided if forecasts are as accurate as possible because, whereas demand can change instantaneously, there is usually a lag between deciding to change capacity and the change taking effect. Thus, many operations managers are faced with a dilemma. In order to attempt to meet demand, they must often decide output in advance, based on a forecast, which might change before the demand occurs, or worse, prove not to reflect actual demand at all.

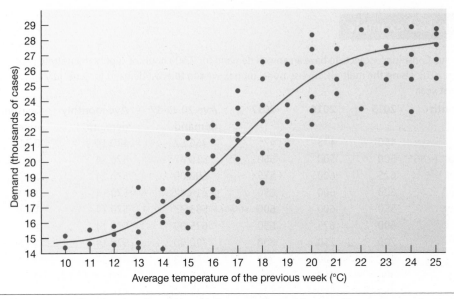

Figure 11.6 Regression line showing the relationship between the previous week's average temperature and demand

Demand forecasting in baseball[2]

Baseball remains to this day one of the most popular sports in America and going to a match is a national pastime. Still, some games are a great deal more popular than others. For the New York Mets, a Saturday night game against their crosstown rivals, the New York Yankees, will have a great deal more natural demand than a mid-week game against a low-performing team from the other side of the country. Yet, for years, the price of a ticket at most baseball matches was based solely on the location of the ticket in the stadium rather than what the actual demand for the game was. However, this is changing across Major League Baseball and nowhere more so than at Wrigley Field, home of the Chicago Cubs. Here, causal modelling has been used to help more accurately predict the demand for its games. Based on the new 'market factors' price model, there appear to be two key drivers of the Cubs' forecasting model – the day of the week and the opponent. Firstly, prices of tickets rise steadily through the week, with a Monday game averaging just $27 in the bleachers (the section of the stadium where analysis has been carried out), whilst a Saturday game ticket averages around

$76. On Sunday, the price falls back to $46. The opponent is also key in demand patterns. Games against the Boston Red Sox and the Chicago White Sox drive demand (and hence prices) up, given the prestige of the former and the local rivalry of the latter. Conversely, tickets for (apologies to their fans!) games against the Atlanta Braves and the Milwaukee Brewers averaged just $19 and $16. So, for those with limited resources, go to a mid-week game against lowly opposition; for those who can't skip work, go to a Sunday game; and for those where money is no object, enjoy Saturday night against the mighty Boston Red Sox!

Although no approach or technique will result in a perfect forecast, a combination of qualitative and quantitative approaches can be used to great effect by bringing together expert judgements and predictive models.

It gives an indication of relative uncertainty

Perhaps most importantly, good forecasts give an indication of relative uncertainty. Decisions to operate extra hours and recruit extra staff are usually based on forecast levels of demand, which could in practice differ considerably from actual demand, leading to unnecessary costs or unsatisfactory customer service. For example, a forecast of demand levels in a supermarket may show initially slow business that builds up to a lunchtime rush. After this, demand slows, only to build up again for the early evening rush, and it finally falls again at the end of trading. The supermarket manager can use this forecast to adjust checkout capacity throughout the day, for example. However, although this may be an accurate average demand forecast, no single day will exactly conform to predicted patterns. Of equal importance is an estimate of how much actual demand could differ from the average. This can be found by examining demand statistics to build up a distribution of demand at each point in the day. The importance of this is that the manager now has an understanding of when it will be important to have reserve staff, perhaps filling shelves, but on call to staff the checkouts should demand warrant it.

Generally, the advantage of probabilistic forecasts such as this is that they allow operations managers to make a judgement between possible plans that would virtually guarantee the operation's ability to meet actual demand, and plans that minimize costs. Ideally, this judgement should be influenced by the nature of the way the business wins orders: price-sensitive markets may require a risk-avoiding cost minimization plan that does not always satisfy peak demand, whereas markets that value responsiveness and service quality may justify a more generous provision of operational capacity.

It is expressed in terms that are useful for capacity management

Forecasts also need to be expressed in units that are useful for capacity planning. If forecasts are expressed only in money terms and give no indication of the demands that will be placed on an operation's capacity, they will need to be translated into realistic expectations of demand, expressed in the same units as the capacity (for example, operatives required, machine hours per year, space needed, etc.). Nor should forecasts be expressed in money terms, such as sales, when those sales are themselves a consequence of capacity planning. For example, some retail operations use sales forecasts to allocate staff hours throughout the day. Yet sales will also be a function of staff allocation. Better to use forecasts of 'traffic', the number of customers who potentially could want serving if there is sufficient staff to serve them.

Better forecasting or better operations responsiveness?

The degree of effort (and cost) to devote to forecasting is often a source of heated debate within organizations. This often comes down to two opposing arguments. One goes something like this. *'It's important for forecasts to be as accurate as possible. We cannot plan operations capacity otherwise. This invariably means we finish up with too much capacity (thereby increasing costs), or too little capacity (thereby losing revenue and dissatisfying customers).'* The counter argument is very different. *'Demand will always be uncertain, that is the nature of demand. Get used to it. The only way to satisfy customers is to make the operation sufficiently responsive to cope with demand, almost irrespective of what it is.'* Both these arguments have some merit, but both are extreme positions. In practice, operations must find some balance between having better forecasts and being able to cope without perfect forecasts.

Although forecasts can never be perfectly accurate all the time, sometimes forecast errors are particularly damaging. For example, if a process is operating at a level close to its maximum capacity, over-optimistic forecasts could lead the process to committing itself to unnecessary capital expenditure to increase its capacity.

Operations principle

Capacity management requires combining attempts to increase market knowledge with attempts to increase operations flexibility.

Inaccurate forecasts for a process operating well below its capacity limit will also result in extra cost, but probably not to the same extent. So, critically, the effort put into forecasting should reflect the varying sensitivity to forecast error. Trying to get forecasts right has particular value where the operation finds it difficult or impossible to react to unexpected demand fluctuations in the short term. Internet-based retailers at some holiday times, for example, find it difficult to flex the quantity of goods they have in stock in the short term. Customers may not be willing to wait. On the other hand, other types of operation working in intrinsically uncertain markets may develop fast and flexible processes to compensate for the difficulty in obtaining accurate forecasts. For example, fashion garment manufacturers try to overcome the uncertainty in their market by shortening their response time to new fashion ideas (cat walk to rack time) and the time taken to replenish stocks in the stores (replenishment time). Similarly, when the cost of not meeting demand is very high, processes also have to rely on their responsiveness rather than accurate forecasts. For example, accident and emergency departments in hospitals must be responsive even if it means underutilized resources at times.

How is capacity measured?

The second task of capacity management is to understand the nature of capacity or supply. The capacity of an operation is the *maximum level of value-added activity over a period of time* that the process can achieve under normal operating conditions. Critically, this definition reflects the scale of capacity but, more importantly, its *processing capabilities*. Suppose a pharmaceutical manufacturer invests in a new 1,000-litre capacity reactor or a property company purchases a 500-vehicle capacity car park. This information gives you a good sense of the *scale* of capacity but it is far from a useful measure of capacity for an operations manager. Instead, the pharmaceutical company will be concerned with the level of output (i.e. the processing capability) that can be achieved from the 1,000-litre reactor vessel. If a batch of standard products can be produced every hour, the planned processing capacity could be as high as 24,000 litres per day. If the reaction takes four hours, and two hours are used for cleaning between batches, the vessel may only produce 4,000 litres per day. Similarly, the car park may be fully occupied by office workers during the working day, 'processing' only 500 cars per day. Alternatively, it may be used for shoppers staying on average only one hour, and theatre-goers occupying spaces for three hours, in the evening. The processing capability would then be up to 5,000 cars per day.

> **Operations principle**
>
> Capacity is the maximum level of value-added activity over a period of time that the process or operation can achieve under normal operating conditions.

Measuring capacity may sound simple, but can in fact be relatively hard to define unambiguously unless the operation is standardized and repetitive. So if a television factory produces only one basic model, the weekly capacity could be described as 2,000 Model A televisions. A government office may have the capacity to print and post 500,000 tax forms per week. A fast ride at a theme park might be designed to process batches of 60 people every three minutes – a capacity to convey 1,200 people per hour. In each case, an *output capacity measure* is the most appropriate measure because the output from the operation does not vary in its nature. For many operations, however, the definition of capacity is not so obvious. When a much wider range of outputs places varying demands on the process, for instance, output measures of capacity are less useful. Here *input capacity measures* are frequently used to define capacity. Almost every type of operation could use a mixture of both input and output measures, but in practice, most choose to use one or the other (see Table 11.3).

> **Operations principle**
>
> Any measure of capacity should reflect the ability of an operation or process to supply demand.

The effect of activity mix on capacity measurement

How much an operation can do depends on what it is being required to do. For example, a hospital may have a problem in measuring its capacity because the nature of the products and service may vary significantly. If all its patients required relatively minor treatment with only short stays in hospital, it could

Next-generation signal technology expands railway capacity[3]

In many parts of the world, railway networks are at breaking point, struggling to deal with the demands placed on them daily. At peak times of the day, some commuter lines are near gridlock, and many commentators put the blame on capacity shortages. But recall our earlier definition – the capacity of an operation is the *maximum level of value-added activity over a period of time* that can be achieved under normal operating conditions. Therefore, for railway networks, as with airports, sea ports, and roads, and other transport infrastructure, it's not just about what resources you have (the scale of capacity), it's about what you can do with it (the processing capabilities of capacity). Herein lies the problem – increasing the scale of capacity is often difficult. It can be expensive, very slow and often politically sensitive. Therefore, while they wait for longer-term increments in capacity, railways (as with other operations) often have to make the best of what they have.

One way this can be achieved is through the digitization of railway signalling systems. Traditional signalling was developed over a century ago using an approach called 'block working' whereby only one train can be in a 'block' at any one time. However, the fixed position of signals means that it is impossible to increase capacity without risking safety. In addition, many railways around the world now combine a wide array of different systems to manage trains – in one area there may be advanced software automatically routing train pathways, in another signal workers continue to operate manual wire-systems to control semaphore arms on the side of the track. This makes for very complex, inefficient and often dysfunctional operations networks!

Then things started to change. Replacing the 'working block' method of managing train movements and its associated physical infrastructure of signals and signal boxes, came the European Train Control System (ETCS). This system created a digital 'moving block' by transmitting the actual location of trains via sensors placed close together along the track, in much the same way as aircraft transponders report the position of a plane to air traffic control. Large rail operating centres then used advanced software to calculate the optimum distance between trains, factoring in train speeds, braking distances, and stations on the route. The effect was to create a safety buffer zone around each train, while minimizing unnecessary distance between trains. Importantly, when implemented, the ETCS was expected to have a positive effect on safety and general reliability through improved co-ordination, and also create increases in effective capacity. Conventional railway networks have a mix of high-speed passenger trains and low-speed freight trains, which creates significant problems for the fixed position 'working block' system. The 'moving blocks' used by the ETCS could increase effective *processing* capacity by around 40 per cent.

The system was rolled out on a number of dedicated high-speed lines, such as the Wuhan–Guangzhou route in China and the TGV route in France. However, the bigger tests were expected to come as moving-block technology was implemented across more complex networks with many more legacy systems to replace. These included projects to install ETCS on trans-European 'corridor' routes connecting different EU countries, specific routes or regions in Australia, Hungry, Italy and New Zealand, and across the entire railways networks of Belgium, Denmark, Germany, Israel and the UK. But even these projects looked small when compared with the announcement in 2018 by Indian Railways of a ₹780 billion ($12 billion) ETCS roll-out across the country's enormous 67,368km railway network. Yet just a month later, the Prime Minister of India, Mr Narendra Modi, controversially delayed the proposal, citing cost–benefit concerns.

treat many people per week. Alternatively, if most of its patients required long periods of observation or recuperation, it could treat far fewer. Output depends on the mix of activities in which the hospital is engaged and, because most hospitals perform many different types of activities, output is difficult (although not impossible!) to predict. Some of the problems caused by variation mix can be

Operations principle

Capacity is a function of service/product mix, duration, and product/service specification.

Table 11.3 Input and output capacity measures for different operations

Operation	Input measure of capacity	Output measure of capacity
Hospital	**Beds available**	Number of patients treated per week
Air-conditioner plant	Machine hours available	**Number of units per week**
Theatre	**Number of seats**	Number of customers entertained per week
University	**Number of students**	Students graduated per year
Electricity company	Generator size	**Megawatts of electricity generated**
Retail store	**Sales floor area**	Number of items sold per day
Airline	**Number of seats available**	Number of passengers per week
Brewery	Volume of fermentation tanks	**Litres per week**

(Note: The most commonly used measure is shown in bold.)

partially overcome by using aggregated capacity measures. (Remember that 'aggregated' means that different products and services are bundled together in order to get a broad view of demand and capacity.)

The effect of time-frame on capacity measurement

The level of activity and output that may be achievable over short periods of time is not the same as the capacity that is sustainable on a regular basis. For example, a tax return processing office, during its peak periods at the end (or beginning) of the financial year, may be capable of processing 120,000 applications a week. It does this by extending the working hours of its staff, discouraging its staff from taking vacations during this period, avoiding any potential disruption to its IT systems, and maybe just by working hard and intensively. Nevertheless, staff do need vacations, nor can they work long hours continually, and eventually the information system will have to be upgraded. As such, when

Worked example

Suppose an air-conditioner factory produces three different models of air-conditioner unit: the deluxe, the standard and the economy. The deluxe model can be assembled in 1.5 hours, the standard in 1 hour and the economy in 0.75 hours. The assembly area in the factory has 800 staff hours of assembly time available each week.

If demand for deluxe, standard and economy units is in the ratio 2:3:2, the time needed to assemble $2 + 3 + 2 = 7$ units is:

$$(2 \times 1.5) + (3 \times 1) + (2 \times 0.75) = 7.5 \text{ hours}$$

The number of units produced per week is:

$$\frac{800}{7.5} \times 7 = 746.7 \text{ units}$$

If demand changes to a ratio of deluxe, economy, standard units of 1:2:4, the time needed to assemble $1 + 2 + 4 = 7$ units is:

$$(1 \times 1.5) + (2 \times 1) + (4 \times 0.75) = 6.5 \text{ hours}$$

Now the number of units produced per week is:

$$\frac{800}{6.5} \times 7 = 861.5 \text{ units}$$

measuring capacity, operations managers should consider three different measures of capacity as shown in Figure 11.7.

▶ *Design capacity*: the theoretical capacity of an operation – the one that its technical designers had in mind when they commissioned it. For example, a company coating photographic paper will have several coating lines which deposit thin layers of chemicals onto rolls of paper at high speed. Each line will be capable of running at a particular speed. Multiplying the maximum coating speed by the operating time of the plant gives the theoretical design capacity of the line.

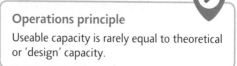
▶ *Effective capacity*: the capacity of an operation after planned losses are accounted for. For example, in the case above, the line cannot realistically be run continuously at its maximum rate. Different products will have different coating requirements, so the line will need to be stopped while it is changed over. Maintenance will need to be performed on the line, which will take out further productive time. Technical scheduling difficulties might mean further lost time. Not all of these losses are the operations manager's fault; they have occurred because of the market and technical demands on the operation.

▶ *Actual output*: the capacity of an operation after both planned and unplanned losses are accounted for. For example, quality problems, machine breakdowns, absenteeism and other avoidable problems all take their toll. This means that the *actual output* of the line will be even lower than the effective capacity. The ratio of the output actually achieved by an operation to its design capacity, and the ratio of output to effective capacity are called, respectively, the utilization and the efficiency of an operation:

$$\text{Utilization} = \frac{\text{Actual output}}{\text{Design capacity}}$$

$$\text{Efficiency} = \frac{\text{Actual output}}{\text{Effective capacity}}$$

Capacity 'leakage'

This reduction in capacity, caused by both predictable and unpredictable losses, is sometimes called 'capacity leakage' and one popular method of assessing this leakage is the overall equipment effectiveness (OEE) measure, which is calculated as follows:

$$\text{OEE} = a \times p \times q$$

where a is the availability of a process; p is the performance or speed of a process and q is the quality of products or services that the process creates. OEE works on the assumption that some capacity leakage occurs causing reduced availability. For example, availability can be lost through time losses such as set-up and changeover losses (when equipment, or people in a service context, are being prepared for the next activity), and breakdown failures (when the machine is being repaired or in a service context where employees are being trained/absent). Some capacity is lost through speed losses such as when equipment is idling (for example, when it is temporarily waiting for work from another process) and when equipment is being run below its optimum work rate. In a service context, the same principle can be seen when individuals are not working at an optimum

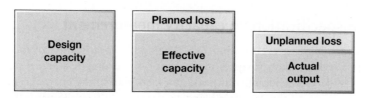

Figure 11.7 Design capacity, effective capacity and actual output

Suppose the photographic paper manufacturer has a coating line with a design capacity of 200 square metres per minute, and the line is operated on a 24-hour day, 7 days per week (168 hours per week) basis. Design capacity is $200 \times 60 \times 24 \times 7 = 2.016$ million square metres per week. The records for a week's production show the following lost production time:

1	Product changeovers (set-ups)	20 hours
2	Regular preventative maintenance	16 hours
3	No work scheduled	8 hours
4	Quality sampling checks	8 hours
5	Shift change times	7 hours
6	Maintenance breakdown	18 hours
7	Quality failure investigation	20 hours
8	Coating material stockouts	8 hours
9	Labour shortages	6 hours
10	Waiting for paper rolls	6 hours

During this week the actual output was only 582,000 square metres. The first five categories of lost production occur as a consequence of reasonably unavoidable, planned occurrences and amount to a total of 59 hours. The last five categories are unplanned, and avoidable, losses and amount to 58 hours. Measured in hours of production:

$$\text{Design capacity} = 168 \text{ hours per week}$$

$$\text{Effective capacity} = 168 - 59 = 109 \text{ hours}$$

$$\text{Actual output} = 168 - 59 - 58 = 51 \text{ hours}$$

$$\text{Utilization} = \frac{\text{Actual output}}{\text{Design capacity}} = \frac{51 \text{ hours}}{168 \text{ hours}} = 0.304 = 30\%$$

$$\text{Efficiency} = \frac{\text{Actual output}}{\text{Effective capacity}} = \frac{51 \text{ hours}}{109 \text{ hours}} = 0.468 = 47\%$$

rate: for example, mail order call centre employees in the quiet period after the winter holiday season. Finally, not everything processed by an operation will be error free. So some capacity is lost through quality losses (see Figure 11.8).

For processes to operate effectively, they need to achieve high levels of performance against all three dimensions – availability, performance (speed) and quality. Viewed in isolation, these individual metrics are important indicators of performance, but they do not give a complete picture of the process's *overall* effectiveness. And critically, all these losses in the calculation mean that OEE represents the valuable operating time as a percentage of the capacity something was designed to have.

The effect of specification on capacity measurement

Some operations can increase their output by changing the specification of the product or service (although this is more likely to apply to a service). For example, a parcel service may effectively reduce its delivery dependability at peak times. So, during the busy Christmas period, the number of parcels delivered the day after being sent may drop from 95 per cent to 85 per cent. Similarly, accounting firms may avoid long 'relationship building' meetings with clients during

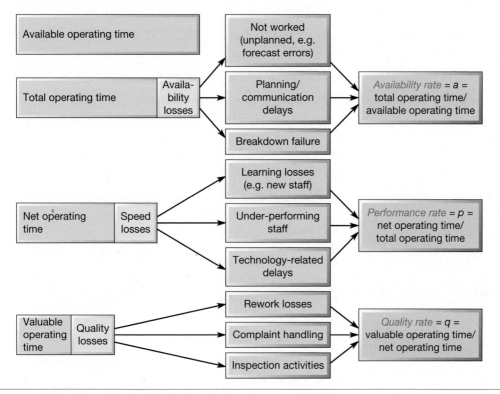

Figure 11.8 Overall equipment effectiveness (OEE)

Worked example

In a typical 7-day period, the planning department programmes a particular machine to work for 150 hours – its loading time. Changeovers and set-ups take an average of 10 hours and breakdown failures average 5 hours every 7 days. The time when the machine cannot work because it is waiting for material to be delivered from other parts of the process is 5 hours on average and during the period when the machine is running, it averages 90 per cent of its rated speed. Three per cent of the parts processed by the machine are subsequently found to be defective in some way.

$$\text{Maximum time available} = 7 \times 24 \text{ hours}$$

$$= 168 \text{ hours}$$

$$\text{Loading time} = 150 \text{ hours}$$

$$\text{Availability losses} = 10 \text{ hours (set-ups)} + 5 \text{ hours (breakdowns)}$$

$$= 15 \text{ hours}$$

$$\text{So, Total operating time} = \text{loading time} - \text{availability}$$

$$= 150 \text{ hours} - 15 \text{ hours}$$

$$= 135 \text{ hours}$$

$$\text{Speed losses} = 5\,\text{hours(idling)} + ((135 - 5) \times 0.1)(10\%\,\text{of remaining time})$$

$$= 18\,\text{hours}$$

$$\text{So, net operating time} = \text{Total operating time} - \text{speed losses}$$

$$= 135 - 18$$

$$= 117\,\text{hours}$$

$$\text{Quality losses} = 117\,(\text{Net operating time}) \times 0.03\,(\text{error rate})$$

$$= 3.51\,\text{hours}$$

$$\text{So, valuable operating time} = \text{Net operating time} - \text{quality losses}$$

$$= 117 - 3.51$$

$$= 113.49\,\text{hours}$$

$$\text{Therefore, availability rate} = a = \frac{\text{Total operating time}}{\text{Loading time}}$$

$$= \frac{135}{150} = 90\%$$

$$\text{and, performance rate, } p = \frac{\text{Net operating time}}{\text{Total operating time}}$$

$$= \frac{117}{135} = 86.67\%$$

$$\text{and quality rate, } q = \frac{\text{Valuable operating time}}{\text{Net operating time}}$$

$$= \frac{113.49}{117} = 97\%$$

$$\text{OEE}(a \times p \times q) = 75.6\%$$

busy periods. Important though these are, they can usually be deferred to less busy times. The important task is to distinguish between the 'must do' elements of the service that should not be sacrificed and the 'nice to do' parts of the service that can be omitted or delayed in order to increase capacity in the short term.

Understanding changes in capacity

While many operations are most concerned with dealing with changes in demand, some operations also have to cope with variation in *capacity* (if it is defined as 'the ability to supply'). For example, Figure 11.9 shows the demand and capacity variation of two businesses. The first is

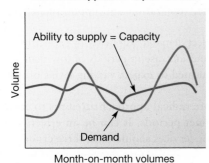

Domestic appliance repair service

Volume

Ability to supply = Capacity

Demand

Month-on-month volumes

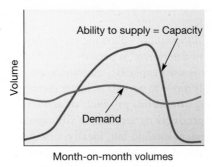

Frozen spinach

Volume

Ability to supply = Capacity

Demand

Month-on-month volumes

Figure 11.9 Volatility in demand versus volatility in capacity

a domestic appliance repair service. Both demand and capacity vary month on month. Capacity is relatively stable with only small variations caused by the field service operatives preferring to take their vacations at particular times of the year. Demand, by contrast, fluctuates more significantly, with peak demand being approximately twice the level of the low point in demand. The second business is a food manufacturer producing frozen spinach. The demand for this product is relatively constant throughout the year but the capacity of the business varies significantly. During the growing and harvesting season capacity to supply is high, but it falls off almost to zero for part of the year. Yet although the mismatch between demand and capacity is driven primarily by fluctuations in demand in the first case, and capacity in the second case, the essence of the capacity management activity is essentially similar for both.

Operations principle

Capacity management decisions should reflect both predictable and unpredictable variations in capacity and demand.

How is the demand side managed?

Earlier in the chapter, we discussed the value of improved forecasting in helping operations managers know what demand for its products and services to expect. Demand patterns clearly have a big influence on the way operations function and therefore many organizations will seek to influence them in some way. Referred to as demand management, this involves changing the pattern of demand to bring it closer to available capacity. Figure 11.10 illustrates how this achieved – either by stimulating off-peak demand or by constraining peak demand. There are a number of methods used to manage demand.

Operations principle

Demand management involves changing the pattern of demand by stimulating off-peak demand or constraining peak demand.

▶ *Price differentials* – adjusting price to reflect demand (see the 'Operations in practice' case on surge pricing): that is, increasing prices during periods of high demand and reducing prices during periods of low demand. For example, skiing and camping holidays are cheapest at the beginning and end of the season and are particularly expensive during school vacations, while ice cream is on offer in many supermarkets during the winter.

▶ *Scheduling promotion* – varying the degree of market stimulation through promotion and advertising in order to encourage demand during normally low periods. For example, turkey growers in the UK and the USA make vigorous attempts to promote their products at times other than Christmas and Thanksgiving.

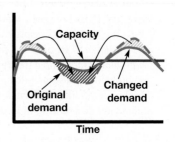

Figure 11.10 Demand management plan

- ► *Constraining customer access* – customers may only be allowed access to the operations products or services at particular times: for example, reservation and appointment systems in hospitals.
- ► *Service differentials* – allowing service levels to reflect demand (implicitly or explicitly), allowing service to deteriorate in periods of high demand and increase in periods of low demand. If this strategy is used explicitly, customers are being educated to expect varying levels of service and hopefully move to periods of lower demand.
- ► *Creating alternative products or services* – a more radical approach attempts to create alternative products or services to fill capacity in quiet periods. It can be an effective demand management method but, ideally, new products or services should meet three criteria: (a) they can be produced on the same processes, (b) they have different demand patterns to existing offerings, and (c) they are sold through similar marketing channels. For example, most universities fill their accommodation and lecture theatres with conferences and company meetings during vacations. Ski resorts may provide organized mountain activity holidays in the summer, and garden tractor companies may make snow movers in the autumn and winter. However, the apparent benefits of filling capacity in this way must be weighed against the risks of damaging the core product or service, and the operation must be fully capable of serving both markets.

OPERATIONS IN PRACTICE | ## Surge pricing

Surge (or dynamic) pricing is a demand management technique that relies on frequent adjustments in price to influence supply and (especially) demand so that they match each other. For example, some electricity suppliers charge different rates for energy depending on when it is consumed. Similarly, in countries with road charging, tolls are set at higher levels during peak times in an effort to keep traffic flowing. But perhaps the best-known example of surge pricing is the algorithm used by the taxi app Uber. During times of excessive demand or inadequate supply, when the number of people wanting a ride exceeds the number of available drivers, Uber applies a multiplier to increase its normal fares based on the scarcity of available drivers. Uber says that it does this, *'to make sure those who need a ride can get one* [and] *for riders, surge* [pricing] *helps ensure that pickup is available quickly and reliably . . . for driver-partners, surge means higher fares and a steady stream of ride requests.'* The problem with surge pricing is that it is efficient yet deeply unpopular with customers. Economists may understand and have faith in the power of supply and demand, but most of Uber's customers are not economists. In the press and on social media, customers complain that it seems that the company is taking advantage of them. But some marketing experts say it is, at least partly, a matter of perception. As well as perhaps capping its multiplier, Uber should make the way it calculates it more transparent, limit how often prices are adjusted, communicate the benefits of the technique, and change its name (certainty pricing and priority pricing have been suggested).

Yield management

In operations which have relatively inflexible capacities, such as airlines and hotels, it is important to use the capacity of the operation for generating revenue to its full potential. One approach used by such operations is called yield management. This is really a collection of methods, some of which we have already discussed, which can be used to ensure that an operation maximizes its potential to generate profit. Yield management is especially useful where: capacity is relatively fixed; the market can be fairly clearly segmented; the service cannot be stored in any way; the service is sold in advance; and the marginal cost of making a sale is relatively low.

Airlines, for example, fit all these criteria. They adopt a collection of methods to try to maximize the yield (i.e. profit) from their capacity. Over-booking capacity may be used to compensate for passengers who do not show up for the flight. However, if more passengers show up than they expect, the airline will have a number of upset passengers. By studying past data on flight demand, airlines try to balance the risks of over-booking and under-booking. Operations may also use price discounting at quiet times, when demand is unlikely to fill capacity. For example, hotels will typically offer cheaper room rates outside of holiday periods to try and increase naturally lower demand. In addition, many larger chains will sell heavily discounted rooms to third parties who in turn take on the risk (and reward) of finding customers for these rooms.

<table>
<tr><td>OPERATIONS IN
PRACTICE</td><td>Demand management through gaming[4]</td></tr>
</table>

In service settings, queues will build up when demand exceeds capacity. Nowhere is this more evident than during the daily rush hour. But in California, USA, a novel gaming approach may just offer an innovative solution to this age-old problem. Balaji Prabhakat, a Computer Science Professor, wanted to support Stanford's efforts to alleviate rush-hour traffic in the local Santa Clara County. First, he managed to persuade nearly half of the university's 8,000 parking permit holders to install tracking devices in their cars. Second, he created a simple system that awards points to a person each time they arrive or leave an hour before or after rush-hour. Third, these points can then be used in an online game of chance with random cash rewards from $2 to $50. Although the prizes are small, the idea has proved popular, with around 15 per cent of trips taken shifting out of the rush-hour periods. Students are tending to arrive and leave university later, whereas faculty are arriving and leaving earlier! The scheme is unlike classic peak load pricing schemes, where customers pay more to use capacity when there is naturally high demand for it. For example, Seattle's transit system charges a 75¢ excess to travel between 06.00 and 09.00. Rather, the gaming idea is that some participants will change their habits for little or no reward, whilst others gain a (relatively) much bigger reward. So, it is the randomness of the reward that makes this example a particularly interesting one. If the scheme can be rolled out to a wider population in the area, the effect of reducing load on stretched capacity by 15 per cent will be significant. The challenge, as with many improvement projects, is to retain the incentives for individuals to stick with the game even when they're not 'winning' and when their attention is on other things.

How is the supply side managed?

In addition to evaluating demand-side options in the capacity management framework, operations managers must also make important decisions on the *supply side*. These decisions include setting the base capacity level, and then using two key methods of managing supply – *level capacity plans*, where demand fluctuations are ignored and nominal capacity is kept constant; and *chase capacity plans*, where capacity is adjusted to 'chase' fluctuations in demand over time.

Operations principle

Managing the supply side involves setting base capacity and using 'level' or 'chase' plans to manage the supply of products or services.

United Airlines breaks passengers[5]

When footage shot by a fellow passenger showed a bloodied and unconscious man being pulled off of a flight at O'Hare international airport in Chicago, the clip caused a sensation on social media and later mainstream news outlets. It also called down a barrage of criticism on United Airlines, the offending carrier. The company's shares fell by around 4 per cent and wiped $770 million off its market capitalization. The incident began when United over-booked the flight (a problem made worse because at the last minute it decided to carry four crew members so they could staff another flight). The airline bumped four passengers to make way for them (common practice when a flight is overbooked). The first step was to offer passengers $400, overnight hotel accommodation and a flight the following day. No-one accepted and the offer was increased to $800. Still no-one accepted, so a manager announced that passengers would be selected to leave the flight, with frequent fliers and business-class passengers being given priority. The first two people selected agreed to leave the plane. The third person selected (as it happened, the wife of the man who was later dragged off forcibly) also agreed. However, when the fourth man was approached, he refused, saying that he was a doctor and had to see patients in the morning. Eyewitnesses said the man was 'very upset' and tried to call his lawyer. So, instead of selecting another passenger, or increasing its offer (it could have offered a maximum of $1,350), security staff were called. The encounter with the security staff concluded with the man being wrenched from his seat onto the floor, after which he was hauled down the aisle, blood covering his face.

It is not uncommon for airlines sell more tickets than they have seats under the assumption that some passengers will either fail to show or cancel at the last minute. It avoids flying with empty seats. As the incident gained publicity, the CEO of United Airlines, Oscar Munoz, said that employees 'followed established procedures', but 'he was 'upset to see and hear about what happened', although the passenger had been 'disruptive and belligerent'. When the passenger refused to voluntarily leave the plane, he said, the staff were 'left with no choice but to call Security Officers to assist in removing the customer from the flight'. Travel expert, Simon Calder, said that the airline was technically within its rights. *'The captain is in charge of the aircraft. And if he or she decides that someone needs to be offloaded, that command has to be obeyed. It appears from the evidence that the law was broken – by him, not by the airline. But I would be surprised if United pressed charges.'*

Setting base capacity

The most common starting point in managing the supply side is to decide the 'base level' of capacity and then adjust it periodically up or down to reflect fluctuations in demand. The base level of capacity in any operation is influenced by many factors, but should be related to three in particular:

▶ operation's performance objectives;
▶ perishability of the operation's outputs;
▶ variability in demand or supply.

Operation's performance objectives

Base levels of capacity should be set primarily to reflect an operation's performance objectives (see Figure 11.11). For example, setting the base level of capacity high compared to average demand will result in relatively high levels of underutilization of capacity and therefore high costs. This is especially true when an operation's fixed costs are high and therefore the consequences of underutilization are also high. Conversely, high base levels of capacity result in a capacity 'cushion' for much of the time, so the ability to flex output to give responsive customer service will be enhanced. When the output from the operation is capable of being stored, there may also be a trade-off between fixed capital and working capital in where base capacity level is set. A high level of base capacity can require considerable investment whilst a lower base level would reduce the need for capital investment but may require inventory to be built up to satisfy future demand, thus increasing working capital. For some operations, building up inventory is risky either because products have a short shelf-life (for example, perishable food, high-performance computers or fashion items) or because the output cannot be stored at all (most services).

Perishability of the operation's outputs

When either supply or demand is perishable, base capacity will need to be set at a relatively high level because inputs to the operation or outputs from the operation cannot be stored for long periods. For example, a factory that produces frozen fruit will need sufficient freezing, packing and storage

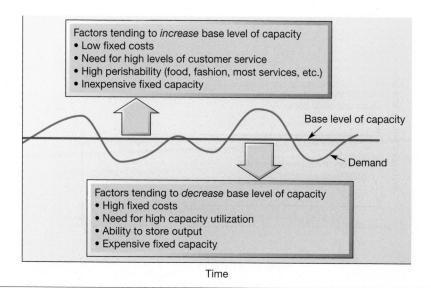

Figure 11.11 Base level of capacity should reflect the relative importance of the operation's performance objectives

capacity to cope with the rate at which the fruit crop is being harvested during its harvesting season. Similarly, a hotel cannot store its accommodation services. If an individual hotel room remains unoccupied, the ability to sell for that night has 'perished'. In fact, unless a hotel is fully occupied every single night, its capacity is always going to be higher than the average demand for its services.

Degree of variability in demand or supply

Variability in either demand or capacity will reduce the ability of an operation to process its inputs. That is, it will reduce its effective capacity. This effect was explained in Chapter 6 when the consequences of variability in individual processes were discussed. As a reminder, the greater the variability in arrival time (demand) or activity time (supply) at a process, the more the process will suffer both high throughput times *and* reduced utilization. This principle holds true for whole operations, and because long throughput times mean that queues will build up in the operation, high variability also affects inventory levels. This is illustrated in Figure 11.12.

The implication of this is that the greater the variability, the more extra capacity will need to be provided to compensate for the reduced utilization of available capacity. Therefore, operations with high levels of variability will tend to set their base level of capacity relatively high in order to provide this extra capacity. Of course, not all operations have the option of simply increasing capacity (see the 'Operations in practice' example of Heathrow airport).

Level capacity plan

Once base capacity is set, the first alternative supply-side approach is to keep this level fixed throughout the planning period regardless of the fluctuations in forecast demand. This is a called a 'level capacity plan'. It means that the same number of staff operate the same processes and should therefore be capable of producing the same aggregate output in each period. This results in stable employment patterns, high process utilization, and often high productivity with low unit costs. Unfortunately, it can create considerable inventory which has to be financed and stored. Where non-perishable materials are processed, but not immediately sold, they can be transferred to finished goods inventory in anticipation of sales at a later time. However, this involves speculating on future sales. Will sweaters knitted in July still be popular in October? Most firms operating this plan, therefore, give priority to creating inventory where future sales

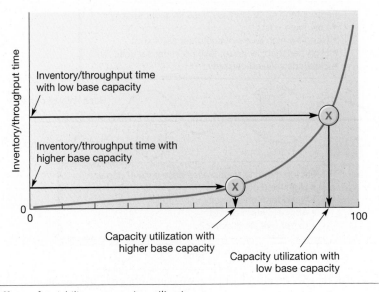

Figure 11.12 Effects of variability on capacity utilization

are relatively certain. Clearly, such plans are not suitable for 'perishable' products, such as foods, for products where fashion changes rapidly and unpredictably (for example, fashion garments), or for customized products.

A level capacity plan could also be used by services such as a hotel, although this could result in a waste of staff resources. Service cannot be stored as inventory, so a level capacity plan would involve running the operation at a uniformly high level of capacity availability. The hotel would employ sufficient staff to service all the rooms, to run a full restaurant, and to staff the reception even in months when demand was expected to be well below capacity. Generally, low utilization can make level capacity plans prohibitively expensive in many service operations, but may be considered appropriate where the opportunity costs of individual lost sales are very high: for example, in the high-margin retailing of jewellery and in (real) estate agents. It is also possible to set the capacity somewhat below the forecast peak demand level in order to reduce the degree of under-utilization. However, in the periods where demand is expected to exceed planned capacity, customer service may deteriorate. Customers may have to queue for long periods or may be 'processed' faster and less sensitively.

> **Operations principle**
>
> The higher the base level of capacity, the less capacity fluctuation is needed to satisfy demand.

Chase (demand) capacity plan

The opposite of a level capacity plan is one that attempts to match capacity closely to forecast demand. The difference between a chase capacity plan and level capacity plan is illustrated in Figure 11.13.

OPERATIONS IN PRACTICE

Heathrow's capacity crises[6]

London Heathrow is one of the busiest airports in the world. Its size and location give it powerful 'network effects'. This means that it can match incoming passengers with outgoing flights to hundreds of different cities. Yet, its attractiveness to the airlines is one of its main problems. On an average day, 60 per cent of arrivals, totalling over 55,000 customers, spend time in one of Heathrow's four 'holding stacks'. These delays range from 4–10 minutes, rising to 20 minutes in the late morning peak, when between 32 and 40 jets typically circle over London. The results of these delays include wasted fuel, additional CO_2 emissions, and frustration to customers. The problem is operating capacity, which currently stands at 98 per cent of demand compared to around 70 per cent at most other airports – '[When] *you have* [one of] *the most utilized pieces of infrastructure in the world, then one of the results is that you have airborne holding*', says Jon Proudlove, managing director of the national air traffic service (NATS) at Heathrow. With no spare capacity, the effect (as we have seen with the operations triangle in Chapter 6) is that any variations (such as poor weather or poor conditions on the ground) have an immediate impact on airplane processing

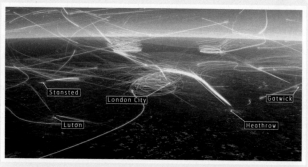

speeds. The lack of capacity meant that several airlines used alternative capacity in the UK and Europe to expand their operations. Yet, solutions to the problem all came with problems. Significant investment was made to air traffic systems to try to increase existing capacity, but the effects were limited. Similarly, improvements to boarding processes improved plane turn-around to some extent. Expanding runway capacity was the obvious 'solution' (Heathrow had two runways, compared with the four or five at its major European competitors), but faced political challenges from local residents and opposition from environmental lobbies.

Chase capacity strategies can be more difficult to achieve than level capacity plans, as different numbers of staff, different working hours and even different amounts of equipment may be necessary in each period. For this reason, pure chase plans are unlikely to appeal to operations that manufacture standard, non-perishable products. Also, where manufacturing operations are particularly capital-intensive, this approach would require a high level of physical capacity, much of which would only be used occasionally. A pure chase plan is more usually adopted by operations that are not able to store their output, such as customer-processing operations or manufacturers of perishable products. It avoids the wasteful provision of excess staff that occurs with a level capacity plan, and yet should satisfy customer demand throughout the planned period. Where output can be stored, the chase demand policy might be adopted in order to minimize or eliminate finished goods inventory, especially if the nature of future demand (in terms of volume or mix) is relatively unpredictable. There are a number of different methods for adjusting capacity, although they may not all be feasible for all types of operation. Some of these methods are shown in Table 11.4.

> **Operations principle**
>
> The 'chase' (demand) approach is most useful when output cannot be stored or when demand is both volatile and unpredictable.

How can operations understand the consequences of their capacity management decisions?

For many organizations, these 'pure' approaches on the demand or supply side do not match their required combination of competitive and operational objectives. Most operations managers are required simultaneously to reduce costs and inventory, to minimize capital investment, and yet to provide a responsive and customer-oriented approach at all times. For this reason, most organizations choose to follow a mixture of approaches. For example, an accounting firm may seek to bring forward some of its peak demand by offering discounts to selected clients (demand management plan). Capacity may also be increased through the use of outsourced suppliers during the busiest months of the year (chase capacity plan). However, some capacity may be constrained (for example, specialist advisory services offered by the firm) and therefore clients may still experience delays during high demand periods (level capacity plan).

> **Operations principle**
>
> Most organizations mix demand-side (demand management and yield management) and supply-side (level and chase plans) capacity management strategies to maximize performance.

Of critical importance in deciding on the most appropriate mix of capacity management strategies is an understanding of the balance between predictable and unpredictable variation in demand. When demand is stable and predictable, the life of an operations manager is relatively easy! If demand is changeable,

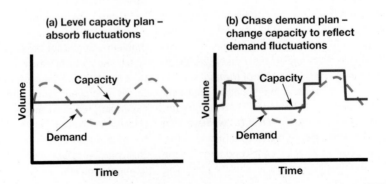

Figure 11.13 (a) 'Level' capacity plan versus (b) 'Chase' capacity plan

Table 11.4 Methods of executing a chase (demand) capacity plan

Method of adjusting capacity	Advantages	Disadvantages
Overtime – staff working longer than their normal working times.	Quickest and most convenient.	Extra payment and agreement from staff normally necessary. Can reduce productivity over long periods.
Annualized hours – staff contracting to work a set number of hours per year rather than a set number of hours per week.	Without many of the costs associated with overtime the number of staff available to an organization can be varied throughout the year to reflect demand.	When very large and unexpected fluctuations in demand are possible, all the negotiated annual working time flexibility can be used before the end of the year.
Staff scheduling – arranging working times (start and finish times) to vary the aggregate number of staff available for working at any time.	Staffing levels can be adjusted to meet demand without changing job responsibilities or hiring in new staff.	Providing start and finish (shift) times that both satisfy staff's need for reasonable working times and shift patterns as well as providing appropriate capacity can be difficult.
Varying the size of the workforce – hiring extra staff during periods of high demand and laying them off as demand falls, or hire and fire.	Reduces basic labour costs quickly.	Hiring costs and possible low productivity while new staff go through the learning curve. Lay-offs may result in severance payments and possible loss of morale in the operation and loss of goodwill in the local labour market.
Using part-time staff – recruit staff who work for less than the normal working day (at the busiest periods).	Good method of adjusting capacity to meet predictable short-term demand fluctuations.	Expensive if the fixed costs of employment for each employee (irrespective of how long he or she works) are high.
Skills flexibility – designing flexibility in job design and job demarcation so that staff can transfer across from less busy parts of the operation.	Fast method of reacting to short-term demand fluctuations.	Investment in skills training needed and may cause some internal disruption.
Sub-contracting/outsourcing – buying, renting or sharing capacity or output from other operations.	No disruption to the operation.	Can be very expensive because of sub-contractor's margin and sub-contractor may not be as motivated to give same service, or quality. Also a risk of leakage of knowledge.
Change output rate – expecting staff (and equipment) to work faster than normal.	No need to provide extra resources.	Can only be used as a temporary measure, and even then can cause staff dissatisfaction, a reduction in the quality of work, or both.

but this change is predictable, capacity adjustments may be needed, but at least they can be planned in advance. With unpredictable variation in demand, if an operation is to react to it at all, it must do so quickly; otherwise the change in capacity will have little effect on the operation's ability to deliver products and services as needed by its customers. Figure 11.14 illustrates how the objective and tasks of capacity management vary depending on the balance between predictable and unpredictable variation.

In addition, before an operation adopts one or more of the three 'pure' capacity management plans (demand management, level capacity or chase capacity), it should examine the likely consequences. Three methods are particularly useful in helping to assess the consequences of adopting particular capacity management plans:

▶ using cumulative representations to make capacity management decisions;
▶ using queuing principles to make capacity management decisions;
▶ using a longitudinal perspective to make capacity management decisions.

		Unpredictable variation	
		Low	**High**
Predictable variation	**High**	*Objective* – Adjust planned capacity as efficiently as possible *Capacity management tasks* • Evaluate optimum mix of methods for capacity fluctuation • Work on how to reduce cost of putting plan into effect	*Objective* – Adjust planned capacity as efficiently as possible and enhance capability for further fast adjustments *Capacity management tasks* • Combination of those for predictable and unpredictable variation
	Low	*Objective* – Make sure the base capacity is appropriate *Capacity management tasks* • Seek ways of providing steady capacity effectively	*Objective* – Adjust capacity as fast as possible *Capacity management tasks* • Identify sources of extra capacity and/or uses for surplus capacity • Work on how to adjust capacity and/or uses of capacity quickly

Figure 11.14 The nature of capacity management depends on the mixture of predictable and unpredictable demand and capacity variation

Using cumulative representations to make capacity management decisions

Figure 11.15 shows the forecast aggregated demand for a chocolate factory that makes confectionery products. Demand for its products in the shops is greatest at Christmas. To meet this demand and allow time for the products to work their way through the distribution system, the factory must supply a demand that peaks in September, as shown. One method of assessing whether a particular level of capacity can satisfy the demand would be to calculate the degree of over-capacity below the graph which represents the capacity levels (areas A and C) and the degree of under-capacity above the graph (area B). If the total over-capacity is greater than the total under-capacity for a particular level of capacity, then that capacity could be regarded as adequate to satisfy demand fully, the assumption being that inventory has been accumulated in the periods of over-capacity. However, there are two problems with this approach. The first is that each month shown in Figure 11.15 may not have the same amount of productive time. Some months (August, for example) may contain vacation periods that reduce the availability of capacity. The second problem is that a capacity level that seems adequate may only be able to supply products *after* the demand for them has occurred. For example, if the period of under-capacity occurred at the beginning of the year, no inventory could have accumulated to meet demand. A far superior way of assessing capacity plans is first to plot demand on a *cumulative* basis. This is shown as the thicker line in Figure 11.15.

The cumulative representation of demand immediately reveals more information. First, it shows that although total demand peaks in September, because of the restricted number of available productive days, the peak demand per productive day occurs a month earlier in August. Second, it shows that the fluctuation in demand over the year is even greater than it seemed. The ratio of monthly peak demand to monthly lowest demand is 6.5-to-1, but the ratio of peak to lowest demand per productive day is 10-to-1. Demand per productive day is more relevant to operations managers, because productive days represent the time element of capacity.

The most useful consequence of plotting demand on a cumulative basis is that, by plotting capacity on the same graph, the feasibility and consequences of a capacity plan can be assessed. Figure 11.16

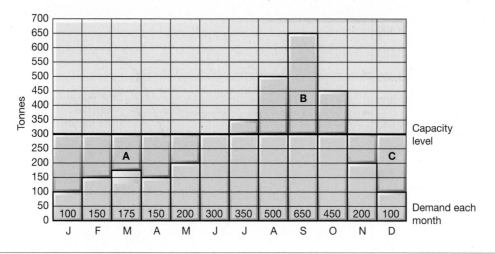

Figure 11.15 If the over-capacity areas (A + C) are greater than the under-capacity area (B), the capacity level seems adequate to meet demand. However, this may not necessarily be the case

also shows a level capacity plan which produces at a rate of 14.03 tonnes per productive day. This meets cumulative demand by the end of the year. It would also pass our earlier test of total over-capacity being the same or greater than under-capacity.

However, if one of the aims of the plan is to supply demand when it occurs, the plan is inadequate. Up to around day 168, the line representing cumulative production is above that representing cumulative demand. This means that at any time during this period, the factory has produced more products than has been demanded from it. In fact the vertical distance between the two lines is the level of inventory at that point in time. So, by day 80, 1,122 tonnes have been produced but only 575 tonnes have been demanded. The surplus of production above demand, or inventory, is therefore 547 tonnes. When the cumulative demand line lies above the cumulative production line, the reverse is true. The vertical distance between the two lines now indicates the shortage, or lack of supply. So, by day 198, around 3,025 tonnes have been demanded but only 2,778 tonnes produced. The shortage is therefore 247 tonnes.

For any capacity plan to meet demand as it occurs, its cumulative production line must always lie above the cumulative demand line. This makes it a straightforward task to judge the adequacy of a plan, simply by looking at its cumulative representation. An impression of the inventory implications can also be gained from a cumulative representation by judging the area between the cumulative production and demand curves. This represents the amount of inventory carried over the period. Figure 11.17 illustrates an adequate level capacity plan for the chocolate manufacturer, together with the costs of carrying inventory. It is assumed that inventory costs £2 per tonne per day to keep in storage. The average inventory each month is taken to be the average of the beginning- and end-of-month inventory levels, and the inventory carrying cost each month is the product of the average inventory, the inventory cost per day per tonne and the number of days in the month.

Operations principle

For any capacity plan to meet demand as it occurs, its cumulative production line must always lie above its cumulative demand line.

Comparing plans on a cumulative basis

Chase (demand) capacity plans can also be illustrated on a cumulative representation. Rather than the cumulative production line having a constant gradient, it would have a varying gradient representing the production rate at any point in time. If a pure demand chase plan were adopted, the cumulative production line would match the cumulative demand line.

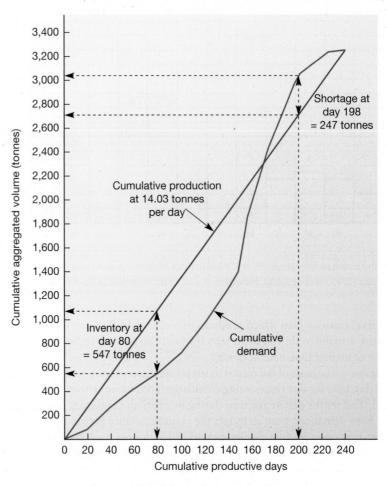

	J	F	M	A	M	J	J	A	S	O	N	D
Demand (tonnes/month)	100	150	175	150	200	300	350	500	650	450	200	100
Productive days	20	18	21	21	22	22	21	10	21	22	21	18
Demand (tonnes/day)	5	8.33	8.33	7.14	9.52	13.64	16.67	50	30.95	20.46	9.52	5.56
Cumulative days	20	38	59	80	102	124	145	155	176	198	219	237
Cumulative demand	100	250	425	575	775	1,075	1,425	1,925	2,575	3,025	3,225	3,325
Cumulative production (tonnes)	281	533	828	1,122	1,431	1,740	2,023	2,175	2,469	2,778	3,073	3,325
Ending inventory (tonnes)	181	283	403	547	656	715	609	250	(106)	(247)	(150)	0

Figure 11.16 A level capacity plan which produces shortages in spite of meeting demand at the end of the year

The gap between the two lines would be zero and hence inventory (or the queue if we were taking a service example) would be zero. Although this would eliminate inventory-carrying costs, as we discussed earlier, there would be costs associated with changing capacity levels. Usually, the marginal cost of making a capacity change increases with the size of the change. For example, if the chocolate manufacturer wishes to increase capacity by 5 per cent, this can be achieved by requesting its staff to work overtime – a simple, fast and relatively inexpensive option. If the change is 15 per cent, overtime cannot provide sufficient extra capacity and temporary staff will need to be employed – a more expensive solution which also would take

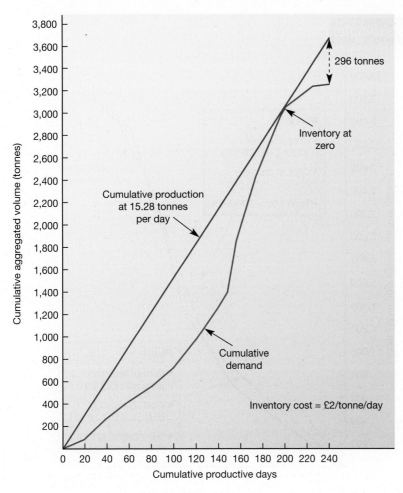

	J	F	M	A	M	J	J	A	S	O	N	D
Demand (tonnes/month)	100	150	175	150	200	300	350	500	650	450	200	100
Productive days	20	18	21	21	22	22	21	10	21	22	21	18
Demand (tonnes/day)	5	8.33	8.33	7.14	9.52	13.64	16.67	50	30.95	20.46	9.52	5.56
Cumulative days	20	38	59	80	102	124	145	155	176	198	219	237
Cumulative demand	100	250	425	575	775	1,075	1,425	1,925	2,575	3,025	3,225	3,325
Cumulative production (tonnes)	306	581	902	1,222	1,559	1,895	2,216	2,368	2,689	3,025	3,346	3,621
Ending inventory (tonnes)	206	331	477	647	784	820	791	443	114	0	121	296
Average inventory (tonnes)	103	270	404	562	716	802	806	617	279	57	61	209
Inventory cost for month (£)	4,120	9,720	16,968	23,604	31,504	35,288	33,852	12,340	11,718	2,508	2,562	7,524

Total inventory cost for year = £191,608

Figure 11.17 A level capacity plan which meets demand at all times during the year

more time. Increases in capacity of above 15 per cent might only be achieved by sub-contracting some work out. This would be even more expensive. The point from which the change is being made, as well as the direction of the change, will also affect the cost of the change. Usually, it is less expensive to change capacity towards what is regarded as the 'normal' capacity level than away from it.

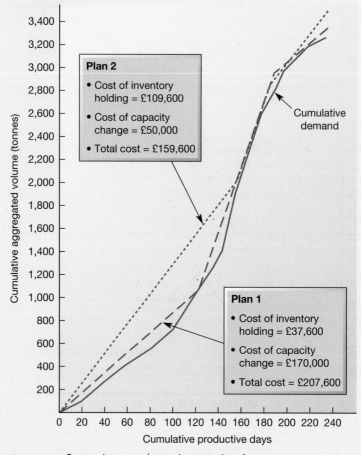

Figure 11.18 Comparing two alternative capacity plans

Suppose the chocolate manufacturer, which has been operating the level capacity plan shown in Figure 11.18, is unhappy with the inventory costs of this approach. It decides to explore two alternative plans, both involving some degree of demand chasing.

Plan 1

▶ Organize and staff the factory for a 'normal' capacity level of 8.7 tonnes per day.

▶ Produce at 8.7 tonnes per day for the first 124 days of the year, then increase capacity to 29 tonnes per day by heavy use of overtime, hiring temporary staff and some sub-contracting.

▶ Produce at 29 tonnes per day until day 194, then reduce capacity back to 8.7 tonnes per day for the rest of the year.

The costs of changing capacity by such a large amount (the ratio of peak to normal capacity is 3.33:1) are calculated by the company as being:

Cost of changing from 8.7 tonnes/day to 29 tonnes/day = £110,000

Cost of changing from 29 tonnes/day to 8.7 tonnes/day = £60,000

Plan 2

▶ Organize and staff the factory for a 'normal' capacity level of 12.4 tonnes per day.

▶ Produce at 12.4 tonnes per day for the first 150 days of the year, then increase capacity to 29 tonnes per day by overtime and hiring some temporary staff.

▶ Produce at 29 tonnes/day until day 190, then reduce capacity back to 12.4 tonnes per day for the rest of the year.

The costs of changing capacity in this plan are smaller because the degree of change is smaller (a peak to normal capacity ratio of 2.34:1), and they are calculated by the company as being:

Cost of changing from 12.4 tonnes/day to 29 tonnes/day $= £35,000$

Cost of changing from 29 tonnes/day to 12.4 tonnes/day $= £15,000$

Figure 11.18 illustrates both plans on a cumulative basis. Plan 1, which envisaged two drastic changes in capacity, has high capacity change costs but, because its production levels are close to demand levels, it has low inventory carrying costs. Plan 2 sacrifices some of the inventory cost advantage of Plan 1 but saves more in terms of capacity change costs.

Using queuing principles to make capacity management decisions

Cumulative representations of capacity plans are useful where the operation has the ability to store its finished goods as inventory. However, for operations where it is not possible to produce products and services *before* demand for them has occurred, a cumulative representation would tell us relatively little. At best, it could show when an operation failed to meets its demand. This is why, for operations which cannot store their output (such as most service operations) capacity management decisions are best considered using queuing theory (sometimes called 'waiting line' theory).

Treating capacity as a queuing problem assumes that, while demand may sometimes be satisfied instantly, at other times customers may have to wait. This is particularly true when the arrival of individual demands on an operation are difficult to predict, or the time to produce a product or service is uncertain, or both. These circumstances make providing adequate capacity at all points in time particularly difficult. Figure 11.19 shows the general form of this capacity issue. Customers arrive according to some probability distribution and wait to be processed (unless part of the operation is idle); when they have reached the front of the queue, they are processed by one of the *n* parallel 'servers' (their processing time also being described by a probability distribution), after which they leave the operation. There are many examples of this kind of system, some of which are illustrated in Table 11.5.

Operations principle

Using queuing principles to make capacity management decisions is useful for operations that cannot store their output.

▶ *The source of customers* – In queue management 'customers' are not always human. 'Customers' could for example be trucks arriving at a weighbridge, orders arriving to be processed or machines waiting to be serviced, etc. The source of customers for the queuing system can be either *finite* or *infinite*. A finite source has a known number of possible customers. For example, if one maintenance person serves four assembly lines, the number of customers for the maintenance person is known, i.e. four. There will be a particular probability that one of the assembly lines will break down and need repairing. However, if one line really does break down, the probability of another line needing repair is reduced because there are now only three lines to break down. So, with a finite source of customers the probability of a customer arriving depends on the number of customers already being serviced. By contrast, an infinite customer source assumes that there is a large number of potential customers so that it is always possible for another customer to arrive no matter how many are being serviced. Most queuing systems that deal with outside markets have infinite, or 'close-to-infinite', customer sources.

6 Unfair waits feel longer than equitable waits.

7 The more valuable the service, the longer the customer will 'happily' wait.

8 Solo waiting feels longer than group waiting.

9 Uncomfortable waits feel longer than comfortable waits.

10 New or infrequent users feel they wait longer than frequent users.

Using a longitudinal perspective to make capacity management decisions

Our emphasis so far has been on the planning aspects of capacity management. In practice, capacity management is a far more dynamic process, which involves controlling and reacting to *actual* demand and *actual* capacity as it occurs. The capacity control process can be seen as a sequence of partially reactive capacity decisions. At the beginning of each period, operations management considers its forecasts of demand, its understanding of current capacity and, if appropriate, how much inventory has been carried forward from the previous period. Based on all this information, it makes plans for the following period's capacity. During the next period, demand might or might not be as forecast and the actual capacity of the operation might or might not turn out as planned. But whatever the actual conditions during that period, at the beginning of the next period the same types of decisions must be made, in the light of the new circumstances.

Operations principle

The learning from managing capacity should be captured and used to refine both demand forecasting and capacity planning.

The success of capacity management is generally measured by some combination of costs, revenue, working capital and customer satisfaction (which goes on to influence revenue). This is influenced by the actual product or service and the capacity available to the operation in any period. However, capacity management is essentially a forward-looking activity. Overriding other considerations of what one or more capacity strategies to adopt is usually the difference between the long- and short-term outlook for the volume of demand. Figure 11.20 illustrates some appropriate capacity

Short-term outlook for volume

	Decreasing below current capacity	Level with current capacity	Increasing above current capacity
Decreasing below current capacity	Reduce capacity (semi) permanently. For example, reduce staffing levels; reduce supply agreements.	Plan to reduce capacity (semi) permanently. For example, freeze recruitment; modify supply agreements.	Increase capacity temporarily. For example, increase working hours, and/or hire temporary staff; modify supply agreements.
Level with current capacity	Reduce capacity temporarily. For example, reduce staff working hours; modify supply agreements.	Maintain capacity at current level.	Increase capacity temporarily. For example, increase working hours, and/or hire temporary staff; modify supply agreements.
Increasing above current capacity	Reduce capacity temporarily. For example, reduce staff working hours, but plan to recruit; modify supply agreements.	Plan to increase capacity above current level; plan to increase supply agreements.	Increase capacity (semi) permanently. For example, hire staff; increase supply agreements.

(Left axis label: **Long-term outlook for volume**)

Figure 11.20 Capacity management strategies are partly dependent on the long- and short-term outlook for volumes

management strategies depending on the comparison of long- and short-term outlooks. If long-term outlook for demand is 'good' (in the sense that it is higher than current capacity can cope with) then it is unlikely that even 'poor' (demand less than capacity) short-term demand would cause an operation to make large, or difficult to reverse, cuts in capacity. Conversely if long-term outlook for demand is 'poor' (in the sense that it is lower than current capacity) then it is unlikely that even 'good' (demand more than capacity) short-term demand would cause an operation to take on large, or difficult to reverse, extra capacity.

Summary answers to key questions

What is capacity management?

▶ Capacity management is the activity of understanding the nature of demand for products and services, and effectively planning and controlling capacity.

▶ Capacity decisions are taken across multiple time horizons and each level of capacity decision is made with the constraints of a higher level. In the other direction, short-term decisions provide important feedback for longer-term planning.

▶ Medium-term capacity management focuses on the medium-term aspects of capacity management, where decisions are being made largely within the constraints of the physical capacity set by the operation's long-term capacity strategy.

▶ The process of capacity management includes (1) measuring and forecasting changes in aggregate demand; (2) measuring capacity (ability to supply products and services); (3) managing the demand side; (4) managing the supply side; and (5) understanding the consequences of different capacity management decisions.

How is demand measured?

▶ Organizations can attempt to forecast demand using a mix of qualitative methods (panel, Delphi and scenario planning) and quantitative methods (time series and causal models).

▶ Good demand forecasts should: (1) be as accurate as possible; (2) give a clear indication of relative uncertainty; and (3) be expressed in terms that are useful for capacity management (e.g. units per hour, operatives per month, etc.).

▶ Operations must find some balance between having better forecasts and being able to cope without perfect forecasts. The resources invested in forecasting should reflect the varying sensitivity to forecast error.

How is capacity measured?

▶ The capacity of an operation is the *maximum level of value-added activity over a period of time* that the process can achieve under normal operating conditions.

▶ Capacity can be measured by the availability of its input resources or by the output that is created. Which of these measures is used partly depends on how stable is the mix of outputs. If it is difficult to aggregate the different types of output from an operation, input measures are usually preferred.

▶ The usage of capacity is measured by the factors 'utilization' and 'efficiency'. A useful measure of capacity leakage is overall operations effectiveness (OEE).

▶ Some operations can increase their output by changing the specification of the product or service (although this is more likely to apply to a service).

How is the demand side managed?

▶ 'Demand management' involves changing the pattern of demand to bring it closer to available capacity. This is achieved either by stimulating off-peak demand or by constraining peak demand.

▶ A number of methods are used to manage demand, including price differentials, scheduling promotion, constraining customer access, service differentials and creating alternative products or services.

▶ Yield management is a common method of coping with mismatches when outputs cannot be stored.

How is the supply side managed?

▶ Capacity planning often involves setting a base level of capacity and then planning capacity fluctuations around it. The level at which base capacity is set depends on three main factors: the relative importance of the operation's performance objectives, the perishability of the operation's outputs; and the degree of variability in demand or supply.

▶ 'Level capacity' plans involve no change in capacity and require that the operation absorb demand–capacity mismatches, usually through under or over-utilization of its resources, or the use of inventory.

▶ 'Chase' (demand) plans involve the changing of capacity to track demand as closely as possible. Methods include overtime, annualized hours, staff scheduling, varying workforce size, using part-time staff, increasing skills flexibility, sub-contracting and changing the output rate.

How can operations understand the consequence of their capacity management decisions?

▶ Most organizations choose to follow a mixture of capacity management approaches because single 'pure' approaches do not match their required combination of competitive and operational objectives.

▶ Understanding of the balance between predictable and unpredictable variation in demand is critical in deciding the most appropriate mix of capacity management strategies.

▶ Representing demand and output in the form of cumulative representations allows the feasibility of alternative capacity plans to be assessed.

▶ In many operations, especially service operations, a queuing approach can be used to explore the consequences of capacity strategies.

▶ Taking a longitudinal perspective, considering both long-term and short-term outlook for demand, allows further evaluation of alternative capacity management decisions.

Blackberry Hill Farm

'Six years ago, I had never heard of agri-tourism. As far as I was concerned, I had inherited the farm and I would be a farmer all my life' (Jim Walker, Blackberry Hill Farm).

The 'agri-tourism' that Jim was referring to is 'a commercial enterprise at a working farm, or other agricultural centre, conducted for the enjoyment of visitors that generates supplemental income for the owner'. *'Farming has become a tough business,'* says Jim. *'Low world prices, a reduction in subsidies, and increasingly uncertain weather patterns have made it a far riskier business than when I first inherited the farm. Yet, because of our move into the tourist trade we are flourishing. Also . . . I've never had so much fun in my life'.* But, Jim warns, agri-tourism isn't for everyone. *'You have to think carefully. Do you really want to do it? What kind of life style do you want? How open-minded are you to new ideas? How business-minded are you? Are you willing to put a lot of effort into marketing your business? Above all, do you like working with people? If you had rather be around cows than people, it isn't the business for you.'*

History

Blackberry Hill Farm was a 200-hectare mixed farm in the south of England when Jim and Mandy Walker inherited it 15 years ago. It was primarily a cereal growing operation with a small dairy herd, some fruit and vegetable growing and mixed woodland that was protected by local preservation laws. Six years ago, it had become evident to Jim and Mandy that they might have to rethink how the farm was being managed. *'We first started a pick-your-own (PYO) operation because our farm is close to several large centres of population. Also, the quantities of fruit and vegetables that we were producing were not large enough to interest the commercial buyers. Entering the PYO market was a reasonable success and in spite of making some early mistakes, it turned our fruit and vegetable growing operation from making a small loss to making a small profit. Most importantly, it gave us some experience of how to deal with customers face-to-face and of how to cope with unpredictable demand. The biggest variable in PYO sales is weather. Most business occurs at the weekends between late spring and early autumn. If rain keeps customers away during part of those weekends, nearly all sales have to occur in just a few days.'*

Within a year of opening up the PYO operation Jim and Mandy had decided to reduce the area devoted to cereals and increase their fruit and vegetable growing capability. At the same time, they organized a Petting Zoo that allowed children to mix with, feed and touch various animals.

'We already had our own cattle and poultry but we extended the area and brought in pigs and goats. Later we also introduced some rabbits, ponies and donkeys, and even a small bee keeping operation.' At the same time the farm started building up its collection of 'farm heritage' exhibits. These were static displays of old farm implements and 'recreations' of farming processes together with information displays. This had always been a personal interest of Jim's and it allowed him to convert two existing farm outbuildings to create a 'Museum of Farming Heritage'.

The year after, they introduced tractor rides for visitors around the whole farm and extended the petting zoo and farming tradition exhibits further. But the most significant investment was in the 'Preserving Kitchen'. *'We had been looking for some way of using the surplus fruits and vegetable that we occasionally accumulated and also for some kind of products that we could sell in a farm shop. We started the Preserving Kitchen to make jams and fruit, vegetables and sauces preserved in jars. The venture was an immediate success. We started making just 50 kilograms of preserves a week, within three months that had grown 300 kilograms a week and we are now producing around 1,000 kilograms a week, all under the "Blackberry Hill Farm" label.'* The following year the Preserving Kitchen was extended and a viewing area added. *'It was a great attraction from the beginning,'* says Mandy, *'We employed ladies from the local village to make the preserves. They are all extrovert characters, so when we asked them to dress up in traditional "farmers wives" type clothing they were happy to do it. The visitors*

Table 11.6(a) Number of visitors last year

Month	Total visitors
January	1,006
February	971
March	2,874
April	6,622
May	8,905
June	12,304
July	14,484
August	15,023
September	12,938
October	6,687
November	2,505
December	3,777
Total	88,096
Average	7,341.33

Table 11.6(b) Farm opening times*

January–Mid March: Wednesday–Sunday	10.00–16.00
Mid March–May: Tuesday–Sunday	9.00–18.00
May–September: All week	8.30–19.00
October–November: Tuesday–Sunday	10.00–16.00
December: Tuesday–Sunday	9.00–18.00

*Special evening events, easter, summer weekends and Christmas

love it, especially the good natured repartee with our ladies. The ladies also enjoy giving informal history lessons when we get school parties visiting us.'

Within the last two years the farm had further extended its Preserving Kitchen, farm shop, exhibits and Petting Zoo. It had also introduced a small adventure playground for the children, a café serving drinks and its own produce, a picnic area and a small bakery. The bakery was also open to view by customers and staffed by bakers in traditional dress. 'It's a nice little visitor attraction,' says Mandy, 'and it gives us another opportunity to squeeze more value out of our own products.' Table 11.6(a) shows last year's visitor numbers, Table 11.6(b) shows the farm's opening times.

Demand

The number of visitors to the farm was extremely seasonal (see Figure 11.21). From a low point in January and February, when most people just visited the farm shop, the spring and summer months could be very busy, especially on public holidays. The previous year Mandy had tracked the number of visitors arriving at the farm each day. 'It is easy to record the number of people visiting the farm attractions, because they pay the entrance charge. What we had not done before is include the people who just visited the farm shop and bakery that can be accessed both from within the farm and from the car park. We estimate that the number of people visiting the shop but not the farm ranges from 74 per cent in February down to around 15 per cent in August.' Figure 11.22 shows the number of visitors in the previous year's August. 'What our figures do not include are those people who visit the shop but don't buy anything. This is unlikely to be a large number.'

Mandy had also estimated the average stay at the farm and/ or farm shop. She reckoned that in winter time the average stay was 45 minutes, but in August it climbed to 3.1 hours.

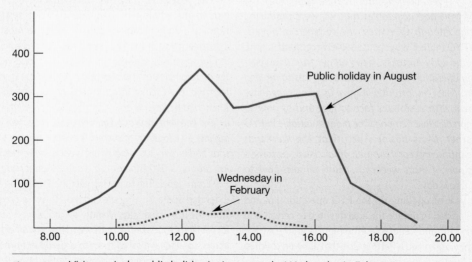

Figure 11.21 Visitor arrivals, public holiday in August and a Wednesday in February

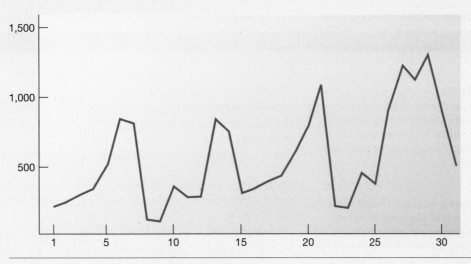

Figure 11.22 Daily numbers of visitors in August last year

Current issues

Both Jim and Mandy agreed that their lives had fundamentally changed over the last few years. Income from visitors and from the Blackberry Hill brand of preserves now accounted for 70 per cent of the farm's revenue. More importantly, the whole enterprise was significantly more profitable than it had ever been. Nevertheless, the farm faced a number of issues.

The first was the balance between its different activities. Jim was particularly concerned that the business remained a genuine farm. *'When you look at the revenue per hectare, visitor and production activities bring in far more revenue than conventional agricultural activities. However, if we push the agri-tourism too far, we become no better than a theme park. We represent something more than this to our visitors. They come to us partly because of what we represent as well as what we actually do. I am not sure that we would want to grow much more. Anyway, more visitors would mean that we have to extend the car park. That would be expensive, and although it would be necessary, it does not directly bring in any more revenue. There are already parking problems during peak period and we have had complaints from the police that our visitors park inappropriately on local roads.*

There is also the problem of complexity. Every time we introduce a new attraction, the whole business gets that little bit more complex to manage. Although we enjoy it tremendously, both Mandy and I are spreading ourselves thinly over an ever widening range of activities. Mandy was also concerned over this. *'I'm starting to feel that my time is being taken up in managing the day-to-day problems of the business. This does not leave time either for thinking about the overall direction in which we should be going, or spending time talking with the staff. That is why we both see this coming year as a time for consolidation and for smoothing out the day-to-day problems of managing the business, particularly the queuing, which is getting excessive at busy times. That is why this year we are limiting ourselves to just one new venture for the business.'*

Staff management was also a concern for Mandy. The business had grown to over 80 (almost all part-time and seasonal) employees. *'We have become a significant employer in the area. Most of our employees are still local people working part-time for extra income but we are also now employing 20 students during the summer period and, last year, 8 agricultural students from Eastern Europe. But now, labour is short in this part of the country and it is becoming more difficult to attract local people, especially to produce Blackberry Hill Farm Preserves. Half of the Preserving Kitchen staff work all year, with the other employed during the summer and autumn periods. But most of them would prefer guaranteed employment throughout the year.'*

Table 11.7 gives more details of some of the issues of managing the facilities at the farm, and Table 11.8 shows the preserve demand and production for the previous year.

Where next?

By the 'consolidation' and improvement of 'day-to-day' activities Jim and Mandy meant that they wanted to increase their revenue, while at the same time reducing the occasional queues that they knew could irritate their visitors, preferably without any significant investment in extra capacity. They also were concerned to be able to offer more stable employment to the Preserving Kitchen employees throughout the year, who would produce at a near constant rate. However, they were not sure if this could be done without storing the products for so long that their shelf life would be seriously affected. There was no problem with the supply of produce to keep production level – less than 2 per cent of the fruit and vegetables that go into the preserves were actually grown on the farm. The remainder were bought at wholesale markets, although this was not generally understood by customers.

Of the many ideas being discussed as candidates for the 'one new venture' for next year, two were emerging as particularly attractive. Jim liked the idea of developing a Maize

Table 11.7 The farm's main facilities and some of the issues concerned with managing them

Facility	Issues
Car park	85 car parking spaces, 4 × 40 − seater tour bus spaces
Fixed exhibits, etc. Recreation of old farmhouse kitchen, recreation of barnyard, old fashioned milking parlour, various small exhibits on farming past and present, adventure playground, ice-cream and snack stands	Most exhibits in, or adjacent to the farm museum At peak times have helpers dressed in period costume to entertain visitors Feedback indicates customers find exhibits more interesting than they thought they would Visitors free to look when they wish absorbs demand from busy facilities
Tractor rides One tractor towing decorated covered cart with maximum capacity of 30 people, tour takes around 20 minutes on average (including stops). Waits 10 minutes between tours except at peak times when tractor circulates continuously	Tractor acts as both transport and entertainment, approximately 60 per cent of visitors stay on for the whole tour, 40 per cent use it as 'hop-on, hop-off' facility Overloaded at peak times, long queues building Feedback indicates it is popular, except for queuing Jim reluctant to invest in further cart and tractor
Pick-your-own area Largest single facility on the farm. Use local press, dedicated telephone line (answering machine) and website to communicate availability of fruit and vegetables. Check-out and weighing area next to farm shop, also displays picked produce and preserves etc. for sale	Very seasonal and weather dependent, for both supply and demand Farm plans for a surplus over visitor demand, uses surplus in preserves Six weighing/paying stations at undercover checkout area. Queues develop at peak times. Feedback indicates some dissatisfaction with this Can move staff from farm shop to help with checkout in busy periods, but farm shop also tends to be busy at the same time Considering using packers at pay stations to speed up the process
Petting Zoo Accommodation for smaller animals including sheep and pigs. Large animals (cattle, horses) brought to viewing area daily. Visitors can view all animals and handle/stroke most animals under supervision	Approximately 50 per cent of visitors view Petting Zoo Number of staff in attendance varies between 0 (off-peak) and 5 (peak periods) The area can get congested during peak periods Staff need to be skilled at managing children
Preserving kitchen Boiling vats, mixing vats, jar sterilizing equipment, etc. Visitor viewing area can hold 15 people comfortably. Average length of stay 7 minutes in off-season, 14 minutes in peak season	Capacity of kitchen is theoretically 4,500 kilogrammes per month on a 5-day week and 6,000 kilograms on a 7-day week In practice, capacity varies with season because of interaction with visitors. Can be as low as 5,000 kilograms on a 7-day week in summer, or up to 5,000 kilograms on a 5-day week in winter Shelf-life of products is on average 12 months Current storage area can hold 16,000 kilograms
Bakery Contains mixing and shaping equipment, commercial oven, cooling racks, display stand, etc. Just installed doughnut-making machine. All pastries contain farm's preserved fruit	Starting to become a bottleneck since doughnut-making machine installed, visitors like watching it Products also on sale at farm shop adjacent to bakery. Would be difficult to expand this area because of building constraints
Farm shop and café Started by selling farm's own products exclusively. Now sells a range of products from farms in the region and wider. Started selling frozen menu dishes (lasagne, goulash, etc.) produced off-peak in the preserving kitchen	The most profitable part of the whole enterprise, Jim and Mandy would like to extend the retailing and café operation Shop includes area for cooking displays, cake decoration, fruit dipping (in chocolate), etc. Some congestion in shop at peak times but little visitor dissatisfaction More significant queuing for café in peak periods Considering allowing customers to place orders before they tour the farm's facilities and collect their purchases later Retailing more profitable per square metre than café

Table 11.8 Preserve demand and production (previous year)

Month	Demand (kg)	Cumulative demand (kg)	Production (kg)	Cumulative product (kg)	Inventory (kg)
January	682	682	4,900	4,900	4,218
February	794	1,476	4,620	9,520	8,044
March	1,106	2,582	4,870	14,390	11,808
April	3,444	6.026	5,590	19,980	13,954
May	4,560	10,586	5,840	25,820	15,234
June	6,014	16,600	5,730	31,550	14,950
July	9,870	26,470	5,710	37,260	10,790
August	13,616	40,086	5,910	43,170	3,084
September	5,040	45,126	5,730	48,900	3,774
October	1,993	47,119	1,570*	50,470	3,351
November	2,652	49,771	2,770*	53,240	3,467
December	6,148	55,919	4,560	57,800	1,881
Average demand	4,660			Average inventory	7,880

*Technical problems reduced production level

Maze, a type of attraction that had become increasingly popular in Europe and North America in the last five years. It involved planting a field of maize (corn) and, once grown, cutting through a complex series of paths in the form of a maze. Evidence from other farms indicated that a maze would be extremely attractive to visitors and Jim reckoned that it could account for up to an extra 10,000 visitors during the summer period. Designed as a separate activity with its own admission charge, it would require an investment of around £20,000, but generate more than twice that in admission charges as well as attracting more visitors to the farm itself.

Mandy favoured the alterative idea – that of building up their business in organized school visits. *'Last year we joined the National Association of Farms for Schools. Their advice is that we could easily become one of the top school attractions in this part of England. Educating visitors about farming tradition is already a major part of what we do. Many of our staff have developed the skills to communicate to children exactly what farm life used to be like. We would need to convert and extend one of our existing underused farm outbuildings to make a "school room" and that would cost between and £30,000 and £35,000. Although we would need to discount our admission charge substantially, I think we could break even on the investment within around two years.'*

QUESTIONS

1 How could the farm's day-to-day operations be improved?

2 What advice would you give Jim and Mandy regarding this year's 'new venture'?

Problems and applications

All chapters have 'Problems and applications' questions that will help you practise analysing operations. They can be answered by reading the chapter. Model answers for the first two questions can be found on the companion website for this book.

1   In March, a law firm predicted April demand for 360 client consultations. Actual April demand was 410. Using a smoothing constant chosen by management of $\alpha = 0.20$, what is the forecast May demand using the exponential smoothing model?

2   A German car manufacturer defines 'utilization' as the ratio of actual output for a process to its design capacity, where design capacity is the capacity of a process as it is designed to operate. However, it knows that it is rarely possible to achieve this theoretical level of capacity. This is why the company uses a measure that it calls 'effective capacity'. This is the actual capacity of a process, once maintenance, changeover, other stoppages and loading have been considered. The ratio of actual output for a process to its effective capacity is defined as its 'efficiency'.

   The company has a painting line with a design capacity of 100 square metres per minute and the line is operated 24 hour day, 7 days a week (168 hours). Records for a week show the following lost time in production:

1	Product changeovers (set-ups)	18 hours
2	Regular maintenance	12 hours
3	No work scheduled	6 hours
4	Quality sampling checks	8 hours
5	Shift change times	8 hours
6	Maintenance breakdown	16 hours
7	Quality failure investigation	12 hours
8	Paint stock-outs	6 hours
9	Labour shortages	6 hours
10	Waiting for paint	5 hours
	Total	100 hours

   During this week, production was only $100 \times 60 \times (168 - 100) = 408{,}000$ square metres per week. What is the painting line's 'utilization' and 'efficiency' according to the company's definitions?

3   In a typical 7-day period, the planning department of the pizza company programs its 'Pizzamatic' machine for 148 hours. It knows that changeovers and set-ups take 8 hours and breakdowns average 4 hours each week. Waiting for ingredients to be delivered usually accounts for 6 hours, during which the machine cannot work. When the machine is running, it averages 87 per cent of its design speed. An inspection has revealed that 2 per cent of the pizzas processed by the machine are not up to the company's quality standard. Calculate the OEE of the 'Pizzamatic' machine.

4   Revisit the example, 'United Airlines breaks passengers'. (a) How should the airline have handled the situation? (b) After the incident attracted so much negative publicity, United announced a new upper limit of $10,000 in compensation for passengers who agree to give up a seat on a flight where United needs to free space and that it would create a 'customer solutions team to provide agents with creative solutions' for getting inconvenienced customers to their destination. Do you think that these were sensible moves, and what else could it have done? (c) Within a few days another 'scandal' hit the airline. A 'potentially prize-winning' rabbit (called Simon) reportedly died while in transit from London Heathrow to O'Hare airport in Chicago. Why is this incident so important to United?

5 Seasonal demand is particularly important to the greetings card industry. Mother's Day, Father's Day, Halloween, Valentine's Day and other occasions have all been promoted as times to send (and buy) appropriately designed cards. Now, some card manufacturers have moved on to 'non-occasion' cards, which can be sent at any time. The cards include those intended to be sent from a parent to a child with messages such as 'Would a hug help?', 'Sorry I made you feel bad' and 'You're perfectly wonderful – it's your room that's a mess'. Other cards deal with more serious adult themes such as friendship ('you're more than a friend, you're just like family') or even alcoholism ('this is hard to say, but I think you're a much neater person when you're not drinking'). Some card companies have founded 'loyalty marketing groups' that 'help companies communicate with their customers at an emotional level'. They promote the use of greetings cards for corporate use, to show that customers and employees are valued. (a) What seem to be the advantages and disadvantages of these strategies? (b) What else could card companies do to cope with demand fluctuations?

6 A Pizza company has a demand forecast for the next 12 months that is shown in the table below. The current workforce of 100 staff can produce 1,500 cases of pizzas per month.
   (a) Prepare a production plan that keeps the output level. How much warehouse space would the company need for this plan?
   (b) Prepare a demand chase plan. What implications would this have for staffing levels, assuming that the maximum amount of overtime would result in production levels of only 10 per cent greater than normal working hours?

Pizza demand forecast

Month	Demand (cases per month)
January	600
February	800
March	1,000
April	1,500
May	2,000
June	1,700
July	1,200
August	1,100
September	900
October	2,500
November	3,200
December	900

Selected further reading

Gilliland, M., Tashman, L. and Sglavo, U. (2015) *Business Forecasting: Practical Problems and Solutions*, Wiley, Chichester.
A collection of papers focused on forecasting practitioners.

Gunther, N.J. (2007) *Guerrilla Capacity Planning*, Springer, New York.
This book provides a tactical approach for planning capacity in both product-based and service-based contexts. Particularly interesting for those new to the ideas of capacity planning as it covers basic and more advanced demand forecasting techniques as well as 'classic' capacity responses.

Kolassa, S. and Siemsen, E. (2016) *Demand Forecasting for Managers*, Business Expert Press, New York.

Manas, J. (2014) *The Resource Management and Capacity Planning Handbook: A Guide to Maximizing the Value of Your Limited People Resources*, McGraw-Hill Education, New York.
A practitioner's guide, particularly focused on managed human resource capacity to deliver better performance.

Ord, K., Fildes, R. and Kourentzes, N. (2017) *Principles of Business Forecasting*, 2nd edn. Wessex, New York.
A very detailed textbook covering demand in real depth.

INTRODUCTION

In the main part of Chapter 11, we described how the queuing approach (in the United States it would be called the 'waiting line approach') can be useful in thinking about capacity, especially in service operations. It is useful because it deals with the issue of variability, both in the arrival of customers (or items) at a process and in how long each customer (or item) takes to process. Where variability is present in a process (as it is in most processes, but particularly in service processes), the capacity required by an operation cannot easily be based on averages but must include the effects of the variation. Unfortunately, many of the formulae that can be used to understand queuing are extremely complicated, especially for complex systems, and are beyond the scope of this book. In fact, computer programs are almost always now used to predict the behaviour of queuing systems. However, studying queueing formulae can illustrate some useful characteristics of the way queueing systems behave.

Notation

Unfortunately, there are several different conventions in the notation used for different aspects of queueing system behaviour. It is always advisable to check the notation used by different authors before using their formulae. We shall use the following notation:

$$c_a = \text{coefficient of variation of arrival times}$$

$$c_e = \text{coefficient of variation of process time}$$

$$m = \text{number of parallel servers at a station}$$

$$r_a = \text{arrival rate (items per unit time)} = 1/t_a$$

$$r_e = \text{processing rate (items per unit time)} = m/t_e$$

$$t_a = \text{average time between arrival}$$

$$t_e = \text{mean processing time}$$

$$u = \text{utilization of station} = r_a/r_e = (r_a t_e)/m$$

$$W = \text{expected waiting time in the system (queue time + processing time)}$$

$$W_q = \text{expected waiting time in the queue}$$

$$\text{WIP} = \text{average work in progress (number of items) in the queue}$$

$$\text{WIP}_q = \text{expected work in progress (number of times) in the queue}$$

Some of these factors are explained later.

Variability

The concept of variability is central to understanding the behaviour of queues. If there were no variability, there would be no need for queues to occur because the capacity of a process could be relatively easily adjusted to match demand. For example, suppose one member of staff (a server) serves customers at a bank counter who always arrive exactly every five minutes (i.e. 12 per hour). Also suppose that every customer takes exactly five minutes to be served, then because,

(a) the arrival rate is $\leq$ processing rate, and
(b) there is no variation

no customer need ever wait because the next customer will arrive when, or before, the previous customer. That is, $\text{WIP}_q = 0$.

Also, in this case, the server is working all the time, again because exactly as one customer leaves the next one is arriving. That is, $u = 1$.

Even with more than one server, the same may apply. For example, if the arrival time at the counter is five minutes (12 per hour) and the processing time for each customer is now always exactly 10 minutes, the counter would need two servers, and because,

(a) arrival rate is $\leq$ processing rate m, and
(b) there is no variation

again, $\text{WIP}_q = 0$, and $u = 1$.

Of course, it is convenient (but unusual) if arrival rate/processing rate equals a whole number. When this is not the case (for this simple example with no variation):

$$\text{Utilization} = \text{processing rate}/(\text{arrival rate multiplied by} m)$$

$$\text{if arrival rate, } r_a = 5 \text{ minutes}$$

$$\text{processing rate, } r_e = 8 \text{ minutes}$$

$$\text{number of servers, } m = 2$$

$$\text{then, utilization, } u = 8/(5 \times 2) = 0.8 \text{ or } 80\%$$

Incorporating variability

The previous examples were not realistic because the assumption of no variation in arrival or processing times very rarely occurs (unless demand is carefully scheduled). We can calculate the average or mean arrival and process times but we also need to take into account the variation around these means. To do that we need to use a probability distribution – Figure S11.1 contrasts two

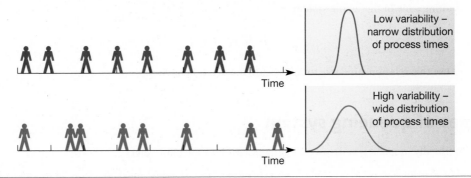

Figure S11.1 Low and high arrival variation

processes with different arrival distributions. The units arriving are shown as people, but they could be jobs arriving at a machine, trucks needing servicing, or any other uncertain event. The top example shows low variation in arrival time where customers arrive in a relatively predictable manner. The bottom example has the same average number of customers arriving but this time they arrive unpredictably with sometimes long gaps between arrivals and at other times two or three customers arriving close together. Of course, we could do a similar analysis to describe processing times. Again, some would have low variation, some higher variation and others somewhere in between.

In Figure S11.1, high arrival variation has a distribution with a wider spread (called 'dispersion') than the distribution describing lower variability. Statistically the usual measure for indicating the spread of a distribution is its standard deviation, σ. But variation does not only depend on standard deviation. For example, a distribution of arrival times may have a standard deviation of 2 minutes. This could indicate very little variation when the average arrival time is 60 minutes. But it would mean a very high degree of variation when the average arrival time is 3 minutes. Therefore, to normalize standard deviation, it is divided by the mean of its distribution. This measure is called the coefficient of variation of the distribution. So,

$$c_a = \text{coefficient of variation of arrival times} = \sigma_a / t_a$$

$$c_e = \text{coefficient of variation of processing times} = \sigma_e / t_e$$

Incorporating Little's law

In Chapter 6, we discussed one of the fundamental laws of processes that describes the relationship between the cycle time of a process (how often something emerges from the process), the work in progress within the process and the throughput time of the process (the total time it takes for an item, person or piece of information to move through the whole process including waiting time). It was called Little's law and it was denoted by the following simple relationship.

$$\text{Throughput time} = \text{Work in progress} \times \text{Cycle time}$$

Therefore, Work in progress = Throughput time/Cycle time
Or:

$$\text{WIP} = T/C$$

We can make use of Little's law to help understand queueing behaviour. Consider the queue in front of station.

Work in progress in the queue = the arrival rate at the queue (equivalent to 1/cycle time) × waiting time in the queue (equivalent to throughput time)

$$\text{WIP}_q = r_a \times W_q$$

and

waiting time in the whole system = the waiting time in the queue + the average process time at the station

$$W = W_q + t_e$$

We will use this relationship later to investigate queueing behaviour.

Types of queueing system

Conventionally, queueing systems are characterized by four parameters.

A – the distribution of arrival times (or more properly interarrival times, the elapsed times between arrivals)

B – the distribution of process times

m – the number of servers at each station

b – the maximum number of items (or people) allowed in the system

The most common distributions used to describe A or B are either:

(a) the exponential (or Markovian) distribution denoted by M.

(b) the general (for example normal) distribution denoted by G.

So, for example, an M/G/1/5 queueing system would indicate a system with exponentially distributed arrivals, process times described by a general distribution such as a normal distribution, with one server and a maximum number of items (or people) allowed in the system of 5. This type of notation is called Kendall's notation.

Queueing theory can help us investigate any type of queueing system, but in order to simplify the mathematics, we shall here deal only with the two most common situations, namely:

M/M/m - the exponential arrival and processing times with m servers and no maximum limit to the queue;

G/G/m - general arrival and processing distributions with m servers and no limit to the queue.

And first we will start by looking at the simple case when m (number of servers) $= 1$.

M/M/1 queueing systems

For M/M/1 queueing systems, the formulae are as follows:

$$\text{WIP} \frac{u}{1-u}$$

Using Little's law,

$$\text{WIP} = \text{Cycle time} \times \text{Throughput time}$$

$$\text{Throughput time} = \text{WIP/Cycle time}$$

Then:

$$\text{Throughput time} = \frac{u}{1-u} \times \frac{1}{r_a} \times \frac{t_e}{1-u}$$

and since,

Throughput time in the queue $=$ Total throughput time $-$ Average processing time

Then:

$$W_q = W - t_e$$

$$= \frac{t_e}{1-u} - t_e$$

$$= \frac{t_e - t_e(1-u)}{1-u} = \frac{t_e - t_e - ut_e}{1-u}$$

$$= \frac{u}{(1-u)} t_e$$

again, using little's law:

$$\text{WIP}_q = r_a \times W_q = \frac{u}{(1-u)} t_e r_a$$

and since,

$$u = \frac{r_a}{r_e} = r_a t_e$$

$$r_a = \frac{u}{t_e}$$

then,

$$\text{WIP}_q = \frac{u}{(1-u)} \times t_e \times \frac{u}{t_e}$$

$$= \frac{u^2}{(1-u)}$$

M/M/m systems

When there are m servers at a station the formula for waiting time in the queue (and therefore all other formulae) needs to be modified. Again, we will not derive these formulae but just state them.

$$W_q = \frac{u^{\sqrt{2(m+1)}-1}}{m(1-u)} t_e$$

From which the other formulae can be derived as before.

Worked example

A bank wishes to decide how many staff to schedule during its lunch period. During this period customers arrive at a rate of 9 per hour and the enquiries that customers have (such as opening new accounts, arranging loans, etc.) take on average 15 minutes to deal with. The bank manager feels that four staff should be on duty during this period but wants to make sure that the customers do not wait more than 3 minutes on average before they are served. The manager has been told that the distributions that describe both arrival and processing times are likely to be exponential. Therefore,

$$r_a = 9 \text{ per hour, therefore}$$

$$t_a = 6.67 \text{ minutes}$$

$$r_e = 4 \text{ per hour, therefore}$$

$$t_e = 15 \text{ minutes}$$

The proposed number of servers

$$m = 4$$

therefore, the utilization of the system, $u = 9/(4 \times 4) = 0.5625$.
From the formula for waiting time for a M/M/m system,

$$W_q = \frac{u^{\sqrt{2(m+1)}-1}}{m(1-u)} t_e$$

$$= \frac{0.5625^{\sqrt{10}-1}}{4(1-0.5625)} \times 0.25$$

$$= \frac{0.5625^{2.162}}{1.75} \times 0.25$$

$$= 0.042 \text{ hours}$$

$$= 2.52 \text{ minutes}$$

Therefore, the average waiting time with 4 servers would be 2.52 minutes, which is well within the manager's acceptable waiting tolerance.

G/G/1 systems

The assumptions of exponential arrival and processing times used in M/M/m systems above are convenient as far as mathematical derivation. However, in practice, process times in particular are rarely truly exponential. This is why it is important to have some idea of how a G/G/1 and G/G/m queue behaves, where it is assumed that arrivals and processing follow a normal distribution. However, exact mathematical relationships are not possible with such distributions. Therefore, some kind of approximation is needed. The one here is in common use, and although it is not always accurate, it is suitable for practical purposes. For G/G/1 systems the formula for waiting time in the queue is as follows.

$$W_q = \left(\frac{c_a^2 + c_e^2}{2} \right) \left(\frac{u}{(1 - u)} \right) t_e$$

There are two points to make about this equation. The first is that it is exactly the same as the equivalent equation for an M/M/1 system but with a factor to take account of the variability of the arrival and process times. The second is that this formula is sometimes known as the VUT formula because it describes the waiting time in a queue as a function of:

V – the variability in the queueing system

U – the utilization of the queueing system (that is, demand versus capacity), and

T – the processing times at the station.

In other words, we can reach the intuitive conclusion that queueing time will increase as variability, utilization or processing time increase.

For G/G/m systems

The same modification applies to queueing systems using general equations and m servers. The formula for waiting time in the queue is now as follows:

$$W_q = \left(\frac{c_a^2 + c_e^2}{2} \right) \left(\frac{u^{\sqrt{2(m+1)} - 1}}{m(1 - u)} \right) t_e$$

Worked example

'I can't understand it. We have worked out our capacity figures and I am sure that one member of staff should be able to cope with the demand. We know that customers arrive at a rate of around 6 per hour and we also know that any trained member of staff can process them at a rate of 8 per hour. So why is the queue so large and the wait so long? Have a look at what is going on there please.'

▶

Sarah knew that it was probably the variation, both in customers arriving and in how long it took each of them to be processed, that was causing the problem. Over a two-day period when she was told that demand was more or less normal, she timed the exact arrival times and processing times of every customer. Her results were as follows:

The coefficient of variation, c_a of customer arrivals $= 1$

The coefficient of variation, c_e of processing time $= 3.5$

The average arrival rate of customers, $r_a = 6$ per hour,

therefore, the average interarrival time $= 10$ minutes

The average processing rate, $r_e = 8$ per hour

therefore, the average processing time $= 7.5$ minutes

Therefore, the utilization of the single server, $u = 6/8 = 0.75$

Using the waiting time formula for a G/G/1 queueing system:

$$W_q = \frac{(1 + 12.25)}{2}\left(\frac{0.75}{1 - 075}\right)7.5$$

$$= 6.625 \times 3 \times 7.5 = 149.06 \text{ minutes}$$

$$= 2.48 \text{ hours}$$

Also because:

$$\text{WIP}_q = \text{Arrival rate}(r_a) \times \text{Waiting time in queue}(W_q)$$

$$\text{WIP}_q = 6 \times 2.48 = 14.68$$

So, Sarah had found out that the average wait that customers could expect was 2.48 hours and that there would be an average of 14.68 people in the queue.

'Ok, so I see that it's the very high variation in the processing time that is causing the queue to build up. How about investing in a new computer system that would standardize processing time to a greater degree? I have been taking with our technical people and they reckon that, if we invested in a new system, we could cut the coefficient of variation of processing time down to 1.5. What kind of a difference would this make?'

Under these conditions with $c_e = 1.5$:

$$W_q = \left(\frac{1 + 2.25}{2}\right)\left(\frac{0.75}{1 - 0.75}\right)7.5$$

$$= 1.625 \times 3 \times 7.5 = 36.56 \text{ minutes}$$

$$= 0.61 \text{ hours}$$

Therefore:

$$\text{WIP}_q = 6 \times 0.61 = 3.66$$

In other words, reducing the variation of the process time has reduced average queueing time from 2.48 hours down to 0.61 hours and has reduced the expected number of people in the queue from 14.68 down to 3.66.

KEY QUESTIONS

What is supply chain management?

How should supply chains compete?

How should relationships in supply chains be managed?

How is the supply side managed?

How is the demand side managed?

What are the dynamics of supply chains?

INTRODUCTION

How is it that businesses such as Apple, Toyota, Zara and Maersk achieve notable results in highly competitive markets? Partly, it is down to their products and services, but partly it is a matter of how they manage their supply chains. This is what supply chain management is concerned with – the way operations managers have to look beyond a purely internal view to also consider the performance of suppliers, and suppliers' suppliers, as well as customers, and customers' customers. In addition, increasingly operations are outsourcing many of their activities, buying more of their services and materials from outside specialists. So, the way they manage supplies to their operations becomes increasingly important, as does the integration of their distribution activities. In Chapter 5 we explored the structure and scope of operations; by contrast. This chapter is more concerned with how supply chains and networks are subsequently managed. Figure 12.1 shows where supply chain management fits in the overall model of operations management.

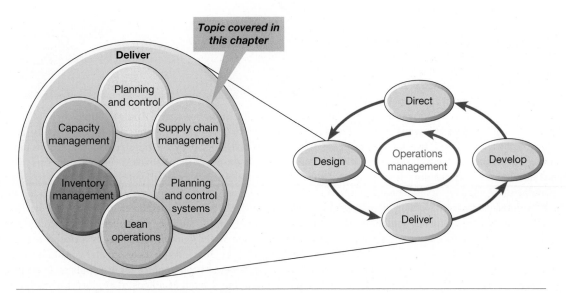

Figure 12.1 This chapter examines supply chain management

What is supply chain management?

Supply chain management (SCM) is the management of the relationships and flows between the 'string' (or chain) of operations and processes that produce value in the form of products and services to the ultimate consumer. It is a holistic approach to managing across the boundaries of companies and of processes. Technically, supply *chains* are different to supply *networks*. A supply network is *all* the operations that are linked together so as to provide products and services through to end customers. In large supply networks, there can be many hundreds of supply chains of linked operations passing through a single operation (see Figures 12.2 and 12.3). The same distinction holds within operations. Internal supply networks, and supply chains, management concerns flow between processes or departments. Confusingly, the terms 'supply network' and 'supply chain management' are often (mistakenly) used interchangeably. It is also worth noting that the 'flows' in supply chains are not restricted to the downstream flow of products and services from suppliers through to customers. Modern supply chain management is as much concerned with managing information flows (upstream and downstream) as it is with managing the flow of products and services.

Does Apple really have the best supply chain in the World?[1]

Every time Apple launches a new product it is worldwide news. It attracts the kind of attention and publicity that only the most famous celebrities can match. And it's similar (but lower key maybe) in the world of operations management, where Apple is often credited with having the 'best supply chain in the world'. It is a title that is especially impressive when one considers the complexity of Apple's products and the company's strategy of frequently introducing new, and technologically advanced, products. Yet there is a connection between Apple's products and its supply chain. Innovative products that combine advanced functionality, a

fast ramp-up of manufacturing capacity and customers who have a near-obsessive interest in the detail of design will typically require innovative approaches to the development of its supply chains. It integrates all its research and development, marketing, purchasing, outsourced manufacturing and logistics functions together, facilitating the detailed advanced planning that accelerated new product introduction requires, sometimes by acquiring exclusive rights from its suppliers to secure strategic raw materials and components. Early in its history the company established a formalized list of expectations for suppliers and quickly moved on to creating exclusivity agreements in exchange for volume guarantees. The relationship with suppliers is vital. Apple can use its financial muscle to guarantee sufficient supply capacity by placing large pre-orders with suppliers, which also prevents competitors from gaining access to the same

manufacturing resources. Apple's supply chain is structured to give the company maximum visibility and, essentially, control over the design and nature of its products, right down to the smallest components. This focus on control was reinforced when Apple started to refine its relationships with suppliers. Conventional outsourcing usually expects the outsourcer to arrange for its own supply (Apple's supplier's suppliers). But according to the *Wall Street Journal* (which keeps a close watch on Apple's activities), Apple takes greater control over the procurement of components for its suppliers. To do this, the company hired hundreds of engineers and supply-chain managers to its staff in Shanghai and Taipei to help its suppliers.

But as well as advantages, extensive outsourcing of production does not come without risk. It exposes any company to disruption caused by anything from natural disasters to changes in international trade agreements. There are also reputational risks. Apple has suffered from criticism of the work practices in its (or rather its suppliers') extended supply chain in Asia, including a large number of suicides at a giant factory in China of its major contract manufacturer Foxconn. This explains Apple's extensive efforts to report on what is happening in terms of improvements at its suppliers. Every year it issues a report on its progress that some see as a model for other companies. Apple says that it audits deep into its supply chain and holds its suppliers accountable to some of the industry's strictest standards. In fact, it cares as much about how its products are made as it does about how they're designed.

Internal and external supply chains

Although we often describe supply chains as an interconnection of 'organizations', this does not necessarily mean that these 'organizations' are distinctly separate entities belonging to and managed by different owners. Earlier in the book, we pointed out how the idea of networks can be applied, not just at the supply network level of 'organization-to-organization' relationships, but also at the 'process-to-process' within-operation level and even at the 'resource-to-resource' within-process level. We also introduced the idea of internal customers and suppliers. Put these two related ideas together and one can understand how some of the issues that we will be discussing in the context of 'organization-to-organization' supply chains can also provide insight into internal 'process-to-process' supply chains.

> **Operations principle**
>
> The supply chain concept applies to the internal relationships between processes as well as the external relationships between operations.

Tangible and intangible supply chains

Almost all the books, blogs and articles on supply chain management deal with relationships between what we called 'material transformation' operations: that is, operations concerned with the creation, movement, storage or sale of physical products. But, as we mentioned in Chapter 5, the idea of supply networks (and therefore, supply chains) applies equally to operations with

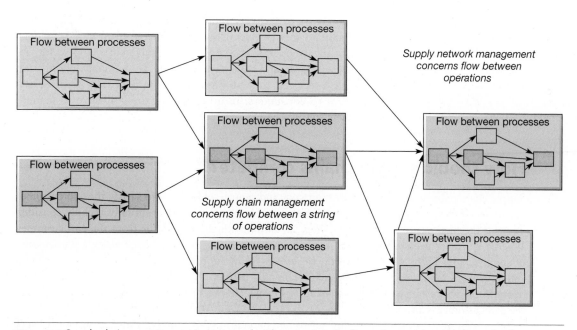

Figure 12.2 Supply chain management is concerned with managing the flow of materials and information between a string of operations that form the strands or 'chains' of a supply network

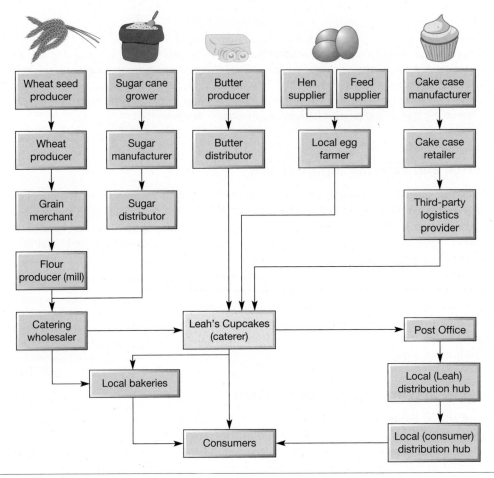

Figure 12.3 A simple supply network for a small catering company

largely or exclusively intangible inputs and outputs, such as financial services, retail shopping malls, insurance providers, healthcare operations, consultants, universities and so on. All these operations have suppliers and customers, they all purchase services, they all have to choose how they get their services to consumers: in other words, they all have to manage their supply chains.

How should supply chains compete?

Supply chain management shares one common, and central, objective – to satisfy the end customer. All stages in the various chains that form the supply network must eventually include consideration of the final customer, no matter how far an individual operation is from the end customer. When a customer decides to make a purchase, he or she triggers action back along a whole series of supply chains in the network. All the businesses in the supply network pass on portions of that end-customer's money to each other, each retaining a margin for the value it has added. Thus, each operation in each chain should be satisfying its own customer, but also making sure that eventually the end customer is also satisfied.

For a demonstration of how end customer perceptions of supply satisfaction can be very different from that of a single operation, examine the customer 'decision tree' in Figure 12.4.

It charts the hypothetical progress of 100 customers requiring service (or products) from a business (for example, a printer requiring paper from an industrial paper stockist). Supply performance, as seen by the core operation (the warehouse), is represented by the shaded part of the diagram. It has received 20 orders, 18 of which were 'produced' (shipped to customers) as promised (on time, and in full). However, originally 100 customers may have requested service, 20 of whom found the business did not have appropriate products (did not stock the right paper), 10 of whom could not be served because the products were not available (out of stock), 50 of whom were not satisfied with the price and/or delivery (of whom 10 placed an order notwithstanding). Of the 20 orders received, 18 were produced as promised (shipped) but 2 were not received as promised (delayed or damaged in transport). So what seems to be a 90 per cent supply performance is in fact an 8 per cent performance from the customer's perspective.

This is just one operation in a whole network. Include the cumulative effect of similar reductions in performance for all the operations in a chain, and the probability that the end customer is adequately served could become remote. The point here is not that all supply chains have unsatisfactory supply performances (although most supply chains have considerable potential for improvement). Rather it is that the performance both of the supply chain as a whole, and of its constituent operations, should be judged in terms of how all end customer needs are satisfied.

> **Operations principle**
>
> The performance of a single operation in a supply chain does not necessarily reflect the performance of the whole supply chain.

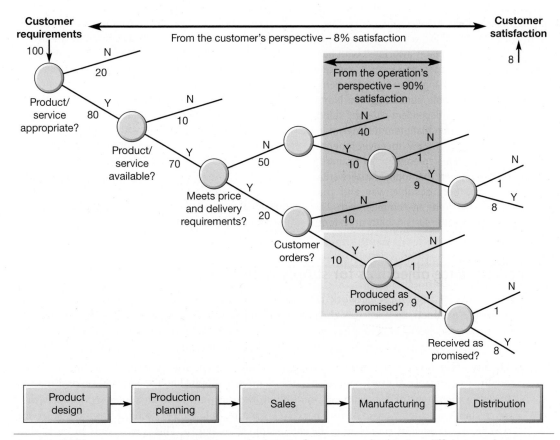

Figure 12.4 Taking a customer perspective to supply chain performance can lead to very different conclusions

North Face's sustainable purchasing

Few outdoor clothing brands have had the impact of The North Face since it was founded over 40 years ago in San Francisco. Now, The North Face is part of the VF Corporation, a $9 billion giant that dominates the leisurewear garment market. According to one influential blog, 'one of the brilliant things about The North Face jackets is that no matter whether you're off to battle with some sub-zero temperatures or just to chill out and take a load off there is always a North Face jacket to accompany you and keep you warm and snug'. Named for the coldest, most unforgiving side of northern hemisphere mountains, its range of high-performance outdoor apparel, equipment and footwear has developed a reputation for durability, fashionable styling and, increasingly, sustainable sourcing of its materials. VF Corporation's claim is that they 'responsibly manage the industry's most efficient and complex supply chain, which spans multiple geographies, product categories and distribution channels'.

In particular, The North Face is keen to promote sustainable purchasing in its supply chain management. Its commitment to sustainability, it says, comes from a desire to protect the natural places associated with how and where its products are used and from its concern about the effects of climate change. As a sign of its determination to pursue sustainable purchasing The North Face has partnered with the independent bluesign® standard, a Swiss-based organization that promotes maximum resource productivity with a view to environmental protection, health and safety, representing an assurance for manufacturers and retailers that today's quality criteria are fulfilled in the best possible way and that applicable regulations and limits are complied with. The idea of bluesign® is to tackle the sustainability at its roots and exclude substances and practices which are potentially hazardous to human health or the environment from all processes in the garment supply chain. So to be considered as a supplier to The North Face any factory must meet the rigorous, independent bluesign® standard which ensures that suppliers address harmful chemicals at the fabric level and meet demanding requirements for consumer and worker safety, efficient resource use and environmental protection. But it is not only the monitoring of suppliers that is important in meeting sustainability targets, says The North Face; product and process innovation is also vital. An example it gives of innovation going hand-in-hand with environmental sustainability is its Venture jacket. It reduced the synthetic compounds in the membrane by 50 per cent by incorporating castor oil, which is a renewable resource. The castor bean plant is widely grown throughout the tropics and produces oil that provides an effective substitute for half of the petroleum-derived materials in the waterproof membrane of the Venture product line.

Performance objectives for supply networks

The objective of any supply network is to meet the requirements of end customers by supplying appropriate products and services through its many supply chains, when they are needed at a competitive cost. Doing this requires the supply network to achieve appropriate levels of the five operations performance objectives, quality, speed, dependability, flexibility and cost.

▶ **Quality** – The quality of a product or service when it reaches the customer is a function of the quality performance of every operation in the chain that supplied it. The implication of this is that errors in each stage of the chain can multiply in their effect on end customer service (if each of seven stages in a supply chain has a 1 per cent error rate, only 93.2 per cent of products or services will be of good quality on reaching the end customer, i.e. 0.99^7). This is why, only by every stage taking some responsibility for its own *and its suppliers'* performance, can a supply chain achieve high end customer quality.

▶ **Speed** – This has two meanings in a supply chain context. The first is how fast customers can be served (the elapsed time between a customer requesting a product or service and receiving it in full), an important element in any business's ability to compete. However, fast customer response can be achieved simply by over-resourcing or over-stocking within the supply chain. For example, very large stocks in a retail operation can reduce the chances of stock-out to almost zero, so reducing customer waiting time virtually to zero. Similarly, an accounting firm may be able to respond quickly to customer demand by having a very large number of accountants on standby waiting for demand that may (or may not) occur. An alternative perspective on speed is the time taken for goods and services to move through the chain. So, for example, products that move quickly down a supply chain from raw material suppliers through to retailers will spend little time as inventory because to achieve fast throughput time, material cannot dwell for significant periods as inventory. This in turn reduces the working capital requirements and other inventory costs in the supply chain, so reducing the overall cost of delivering to the end customer. Achieving a balance between speed as responsiveness to customers' demands and speed as fast throughput (although they are not incompatible) will depend on how the supply chain is choosing to compete.

▶ **Dependability** – Dependability in a supply chain context is similar to speed in so much as one can almost guarantee 'on-time' delivery by keeping excessive resources, such as inventory, within the chain. However, dependability of throughput time is a much more desirable aim because it reduces uncertainty within the chain. If the individual operations in a chain do not deliver as promised on time, there will be a tendency for customers to over-order, or order early, in order to provide some kind of insurance against late delivery. The same argument applies if there is uncertainty regarding the *quantity* of products or services delivered. This is why delivery dependability is often measured as 'on time, in full' in supply chains.

▶ **Flexibility** – In a supply chain context, flexibility is usually taken to mean the chain's ability to cope with changes and disturbances. Very often this is referred to as supply chain agility. The concept of agility includes previously discussed issues such as focusing on the end customer and ensuring fast throughput and responsiveness to customer needs. But, in addition, agile supply chains are sufficiently flexible to cope with changes, either in the nature of customer demand or in the supply capabilities of operations within the chain.

▶ **Cost** – In addition to the costs incurred within each operation to transform its inputs into outputs, the supply chain as a whole incurs additional costs that derive from each operation in a chain doing business with each other. These transaction costs may include such things as the costs of finding appropriate suppliers, setting up contractual agreements, monitoring supply performance, transporting products between operations, holding inventories, and so on. Many of the recent developments in supply chain management, such as partnership agreements or reducing the number of suppliers, are an attempt to minimize transaction costs.

▶ **Sustainability** – Any organization that subscribes to environmentally responsible practices itself will want to make sure that it purchases its input products and services from suppliers that are similarly responsible. The concept is called 'sustainable procurement'. It is a process whereby organizations 'meet their needs for goods, services, works and utilities in a way that achieves value for money on a whole life basis in terms of generating benefits not only to the organization, but also to society and the economy, while minimising damage to the environment'.[2] Operations that try to follow sustainable purchasing often recommend practices such as buying from local vendors where possible, sourcing supplies from suppliers with ethical practices, choosing environmentally-friendly products and services, using minimal packaging, transporting products by ground transport rather than air, and so on.

Lean versus agile supply networks

A distinction is often drawn between supply networks that are managed to emphasize efficiency – *lean supply networks* – and those that emphasize responsiveness and flexibility – *agile supply networks*. These two modes of managing supply chains are reflected in an idea proposed by Professor Marshall Fisher[3] that supply chains serving different markets should be managed in different ways. Even companies that have seemingly similar products or services, in fact, may compete in different ways with different products. For example, shoe manufacturers may produce classics that change little over the years, as well as fashion shoes that last only one season. Chocolate manufacturers have stable lines that have been sold for 50 years, but also product 'specials' associated with an event or film release, the latter selling only for a matter of months. Hospitals have routine 'standardized' surgical procedures such as cataract removal, but also have to provide emergency post-trauma surgery. Demand for the former products will be relatively stable and predictable, but demand for the latter will be far more uncertain. Also, the profit margin commanded by the innovative product will probably be higher than that of the more functional product. However, the price (and therefore the margin) of the innovative product may drop rapidly once it has become unfashionable in the market. Figure 12.5 illustrates key differences between what are typically described as 'functional' and 'innovative' products.

> **✔ Operations principle**
>
> Supply chains with different end objectives need managing differently.

The supply chain policies that are seen to be appropriate for functional products and innovative products are termed efficient (or lean), and responsive (or agile) supply chain policies, respectively. Efficient supply chain policies include keeping inventories low, especially in the downstream parts of the network, so as to maintain fast throughput and reduce the amount of working capital tied up in the inventory. What inventory there is in the network is concentrated mainly in the manufacturing operation, where it can keep utilization high and therefore manufacturing costs low. Information must flow quickly up and down the chain from retail outlets back up to the manufacturer so that schedules can be given the maximum time to adjust efficiently. The chain is then managed to make sure that products flow as quickly as possible down the chain to replenish what few stocks are kept downstream.

By contrast, responsive supply chain policy stresses high service levels and responsive supply to the end customer. The inventory in the network will be deployed as closely as possible to the customer.

> **✔ Operations principle**
>
> Functional' products and services require lean supply chain management; 'innovative' products and service require agile supply chain management.

In this way, the chain can still supply even when dramatic changes occur in customer demand. Fast throughput from the upstream parts of the chain will still be needed to replenish downstream stocks. But those downstream stocks are needed to ensure high levels of availability to end customers. Figure 12.6 illustrates how the different supply chain policies match the different market requirements implied by functional and innovative products.

FUNCTIONAL ←——————————→ INNOVATIVE

Product	Bucket	Bread	Mobile phone	Fashion handbag
Time between new product/ service introductions	10 yr+	1 yr–10 yr+	1yr–18 months	3–6 months
Profit margins	Tiny	Small	Very high	High
Volume and variety	High/very low	High/low	Moderate/ moderate	Moderate/ moderate
Demand volatility and uncertainty	Very low	Very low	Moderate	Moderate–high

Figure 12.5 'Functional' versus 'innovative' products

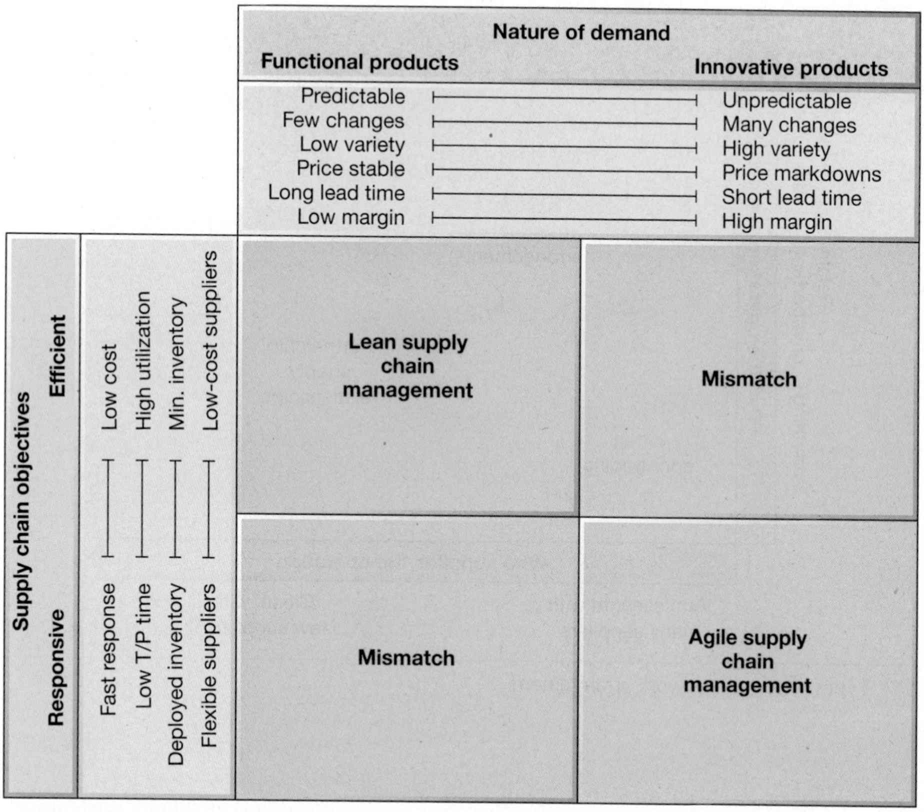

Figure 12.6 Matching the operations resources in the supply chain with market requirements

Source: Adapted from Fisher, M.C. (1997) What is the right supply chain for your product? *Harvard Business Review,* March–April, pp. 105–116.

How should relationships in supply chains be managed?

The 'relationship' between operations in a supply chain is the basis on which the exchange of products, services, information and money is conducted. Managing supply chains is about managing relationships, because relationships influence the smooth flow between operations and processes. Different forms of relationship will be appropriate in different circumstances. Two dimensions are particularly important – *what* the company chooses to outsource, and *who* it chooses to supply it. In terms of *what* is outsourced, key questions are 'how many activities are outsourced?' (from doing everything in-house at one extreme, to outsourcing everything at the other extreme) and 'how important are the activities outsourced?' (from outsourcing only trivial activities at one extreme, to outsourcing even core activities at the other extreme). We discussed these in detail in Chapter 5 when exploring the scope of supply networks.

When dealing with the question of *who* is chosen to supply products and services, again two questions are important, 'how many suppliers will be used by the operation?' (from using many suppliers to perform the same set of activities at one extreme, through to only one supplier for each activity at the other extreme), and 'how close are the relationships?' (from 'arm's length' relationships at one extreme, through to close and intimate relationships at the other extreme). Figure 12.7 illustrates this way of characterizing relationships.

Contracting and relationships

There are two basic ingredients of supply interactions that are connected to the horizontal axis of Figure 12.7; they are 'contracts' and 'relationships'. Whatever arrangement with its suppliers a firm chooses to have, it can be described by the balance between contracts and relationships

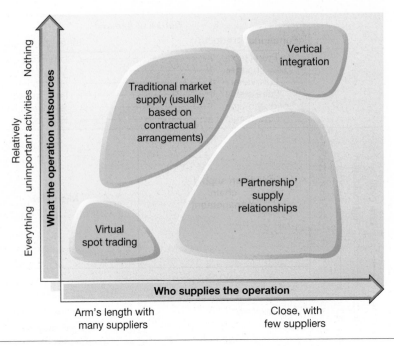

Figure 12.7 Types of supply network arrangement

(see Figure 12.8). They complement each other, but can cause major problems with suppliers if they are not balanced. The more a supply agreement is market-based with purchases based on relatively short-term arrangements, the more the agreement is likely to be defined in a detailed contract. By contracts we mean explicit, usually written and formal, documents that specify the legally binding obligations and roles of both parties in a relationship. The more a supply agreement is based on long-term, usually exclusive, agreements, the more a broad, trust-based, partnership agreement is appropriate. In any one operation a range of different approaches will be required. We will now examine contracts and relationships in more detail.

> **✓ Operations principle**
>
> All supply chain relationships can be described by the balance between their 'contractual' and 'partnership' elements.

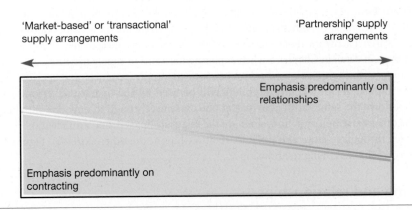

Figure 12.8 Supply arrangements are a balance between contracting and relationships

Contract-based 'transactional' relationships

Contract-based, transactional relationships involve purchasing goods and services in a 'pure' market fashion, often seeking the 'best' supplier every time it is necessary to make a purchase. Each transaction effectively becomes a separate decision and as such the orientation is short term. Often, price will dominate the decision-making process with minimal information sharing between the buyer and the supplier, and with no guarantee of further trading between the parties once the goods or services are delivered and payment is made. The *advantages* of contract-based 'transactional' relationships are usually seen as follows:

▶ They maintain competition between alternative suppliers. This promotes a constant drive between suppliers to provide best value.

▶ A supplier specializing in a small number of products or services, but supplying them to many customers, can gain natural economies of scale, enabling the supplier to offer the products and services at a lower price than if customers performed the activities themselves on a smaller scale.

▶ There is inherent flexibility in outsourced supplies. If demand changes, customers can simply change the number and type of suppliers; a faster and cheaper alternative to redirecting internal activities.

▶ Innovations can be exploited no matter where they originate. Specialist suppliers are more likely to come up with innovations that can be acquired faster and cheaper than developing them in-house.

There are, however, *disadvantages* of buying in a purely contractual manner:

▶ Suppliers owe little loyalty to customers. If supply is difficult, there is no guarantee of receiving supply.

▶ Choosing whom to buy from takes time and effort. Gathering sufficient information and making decisions continually are, in themselves, activities that need to be resourced.

Short-term contractual relationships of this type may be appropriate when new companies are being considered as more regular suppliers, or when purchases are one-off or very irregular (for example, the replacement of all the windows in a company's office block would typically involve this type of competitive-tendering market relationship).

Long-term 'partnership' relationships

Partnership relationships in supply chains are sometimes seen as a compromise between vertical integration on the one hand (owning the resources which supply you) and transactional relationships on the other. Partnership (or 'collaborative') relationships involve a longer-term commitment between buyers and suppliers. These relationships emphasize cooperation, frequent interaction, information sharing and joint problem solving (Figure 12.9). At their core, partnerships are *close* and *trusting* relationships, the degree to which is influenced by a number of factors.

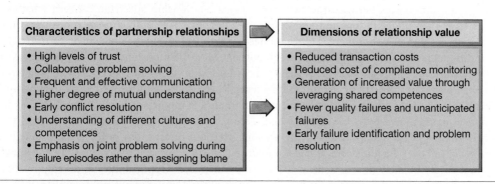

Characteristics of partnership relationships	⇨	Dimensions of relationship value
• High levels of trust • Collaborative problem solving • Frequent and effective communication • Higher degree of mutual understanding • Early conflict resolution • Understanding of different cultures and competences • Emphasis on joint problem solving during failure episodes rather than assigning blame	⇨	• Reduced transaction costs • Reduced cost of compliance monitoring • Generation of increased value through leveraging shared competences • Fewer quality failures and unanticipated failures • Early failure identification and problem resolution

Figure 12.9 The value of partnership relationships

- *Sharing success* – both partners jointly benefit from the cooperation rather than manoeuvring to maximize their own individual contribution. This may sometime involve formal profit-sharing arrangements.
- *Long-term expectations* - relatively long-term commitments, but not necessarily permanent ones.
- *Multiple points of contact* – communication not restricted to formal channels, but may take place between many individuals in both organizations.
- *Joint learning* – a relationship commitment to learn from each other's experience.
- *Few relationships* – a commitment on the part of both parties to limit the number of customers or suppliers with whom they do business.
- *Joint coordination of activities* – fewer relationships allow joint coordination of activities such as the flow of materials or service, payment, and so on.
- *Information transparency* – confidence is built through information exchange between the partners.
- *Joint problem solving* – jointly approaching problems can increase closeness over time.
- *Trust* – probably the key element in partnership relationships. In this context, trust means the willingness of one party to relate to the other on the understanding that the relationship will be beneficial to both, even though that cannot be guaranteed. Trust is widely held to be both the key issue in successful partnerships and also, by far, the most difficult element to develop and maintain.

Which type of relationship?

It is very unlikely that any business will find it sensible to engage exclusively in one type of relationship or another. Most businesses will have a portfolio of, possibly, widely differing relationships. The real question is: 'where, on the spectrum from transactional to partnership, should each relationship be positioned?' And, while there is no simple formula for choosing the 'ideal' form of relationship in each case, there are some important factors that can sway the decision. The most obvious issue will concern how a business intends to compete in its marketplace. If price is the main competitive factor then the relationship could be determined by which approach offers the highest potential savings. On one hand, market-based contractual relationships could minimize the actual price paid for purchased products and services, while partnerships could minimize the transaction costs of doing business. If a business is competing primarily on product or service innovation, the type of relationship may depend on where innovation is likely to happen. If innovation depends on close collaboration between supplier and customer, partnership relationships are needed. On the other hand, if suppliers are busily competing in terms of their innovations, and especially if the market is turbulent and fast growing (as with many software and internet-based industries), then it may be preferable to retain the freedom to change suppliers quickly using market mechanisms. However, if markets are very turbulent, partnership relationships may reduce the risks of being unable to secure supply.

> **Operations principle**
>
> All supply chain relationships can be described by the balance between their 'contractual' and 'partnership' elements.

The main differences between the two ends of this relationship spectrum concern whether a customer sees advantage in long-term or short-term relationships. Contractual relationships can be either long or short term, but there is no guarantee of anything beyond the immediate contract. They are appropriate when short-term benefits are important. Many relationships and many businesses are best concentrating on the short term (especially if, without short-term success, there is no long term). Partnership relationships are by definition long term. There is a commitment to work together over time to gain mutual advantage. The concept of mutuality is important here. A supplier does not become a 'partner' merely by being called one. True partnership implies mutual benefit, and often mutual sacrifice. Partnership means giving up some freedom of action in order to gain something more beneficial over the long term. If it is not in the culture of a business to give up some freedom of action, it is very unlikely to ever make a success of partnerships. Opportunities to develop relationships can be limited by the structure of the market itself. If the number of potential suppliers is small, there may be few opportunities to use market mechanisms to gain any kind of supply advantage and it would probably be sensible to develop a close relationship with at least one supplier. On the other hand, if there are many potential suppliers, and especially if it is easy to judge the capabilities of the suppliers, contractual relationships are likely to be best.

> **Operations principle**
>
> True 'partnership' relationships involve mutual sacrifice as well as mutual benefit.

How should the supply side be managed?

The ability of any process or operation to produce outputs is dependent on the inputs it receives. So good supply management is a necessary (but not sufficient) condition for effective operations management in general. Once a decision has been made to buy products or services (as opposed to make or do in-house), managers must decide on sourcing strategies for different products and services, select appropriate suppliers, manage on-going supply and improve suppliers' capabilities over time. These activities are usually the responsibility of the purchasing or procurement function within the business. Purchasing should provide a vital link between the operation itself and its suppliers. It should understand the requirements of all the processes within its own operation and also the capabilities of the suppliers who could potentially provide products and services for the operation.

Sourcing strategy

In Chapter 5, we outlined a number of issues concerning the configuration of a supply network. Changing the shape of the supply network may involve reducing the number of suppliers to the operation so as to develop closer relationships, and bypassing or disintermediating operations in the network. Here, we go a bit further by examining four key sourcing approaches – *multiple sourcing*, *single sourcing*, *delegated sourcing* and *parallel sourcing* (Figure 12.10).

Multiple sourcing (Figure 12.10(a)) involves obtaining a product or service component from more than one supplier. It is commonly seen in competitive markets where switching costs are low and performance objectives are primarily focused on price and dependability. Multiple sourcing can help maintain competition in the supply market, reduce supply risk and increase flexibility in the face of supplier failure or changes in customer demand. In addition, some firms like to multi-source to prevent supplier dependence, thus allowing for changes in purchase volumes without the risk of supplier bankruptcy. However, the disadvantage of multiple sourcing is that it becomes hard to encourage supplier commitment and as such limits the opportunity to develop a partnership approach to supply management.

Single sourcing (Figure 12.10(b)) involves buying all of one product or service component from a single supplier. Often these components represent a high proportion of total spend or are of strategic importance. In other cases, however, firms simply prefer the simplicity (and reduced transaction costs) of single sourcing. Many single-source arrangements have a longer-term focus than multiple-sourcing arrangements and focus on a wider range of performance objectives. However, single-source arrangements can carry an increased risk of lock-in and a reduction in the firm's bargaining power.

Delegated sourcing (FIgure 12.10(c)) involves a tiered approach to managing supplier relationships. This means that one supplier is responsible for delivering an entire sub-assembly as opposed to a single part, or a package of services as opposed to an individual service. This has the advantage of reducing the number of tier-one suppliers significantly whilst simultaneously allowing a focus on strategic partners. However, delegated sourcing can alter the dynamics of the supply market and risk creating 'mega-suppliers' with significant power in the network.

Parallel sourcing (FIgure 12.10(d)) has the aim of providing the advantages of both multiple sourcing and single sourcing simultaneously. It involves having single source relationships for components or services for different product models or service packages. If a supplier is deemd unsatisfactory, it is possible to switch to the alternative supplier who currently provides the *same* component but for a *different* model. The advantage of this sourcing approach is that it maintains competition and allows for switching. However, managing delegated sourcing arrangements is relatively complex.

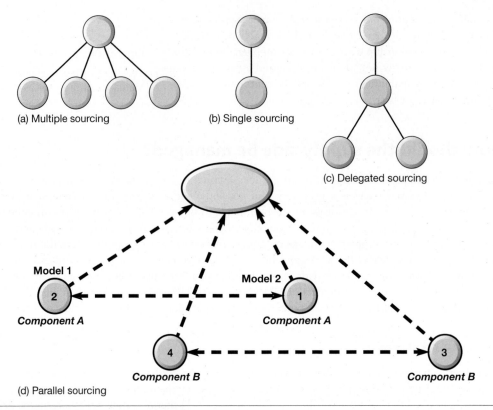

(a) Multiple sourcing

(b) Single sourcing

(c) Delegated sourcing

Model 1
2
Component A

Model 2
1
Component A

4
Component B

3
Component B

(d) Parallel sourcing

Figure 12.10 Four key sourcing approaches

Making the sourcing strategy decision

Given that each sourcing strategy has its advantages and disadvantages, a key challenge is to decide which is most suitable. Here, we can explore two key questions – *what is the risk in the supply market, and what is the criticality of the product or service to the business?* Considering risk, we can consider the number of alternative suppliers, how easy it is to switch from one supplier to another, exit barriers, and the cost of bringing operations back in-house. For criticality, managers may consider a product or service component's importance in terms of volume purchased, percentage of total purchase cost, or the impact on business growth. By looking at these two dimensions, it is possible to position product or service components broadly in one of four key quadrants – leverage, strategic, non-critical, or bottleneck[4] – and select appropriate sourcing strategies. Figure 12.11 shows this for a high-end bicycle manufacturer.

▶ *Non-critical:* The innertubes (A) account for a relatively low proportion of the total cost of the product and, with the large number of alternative suppliers, the supply risk is low. For the non-critical purchase category, multiple-sourcing strategies tend to be most common.

▶ *Bottleneck:* The tubing (B) on the bike frame is a particular grade of carbon and is specially moulded for different types of model. While this component accounts for a relatively low proportion of the total cost of the product, the limited supply alternatives and high switching costs increase risk. For products and services in the bottleneck category, single sourcing is common because of a lack of choice in the supply market.

▶ *Leverage:* The carbon fibre stem and bars (C) account for a high proportion of the cost of this bicycle but are relatively easy to source as there are a relatively large number of available suppliers. For leverage products and services, bundling of requirements allows a shift towards delegated sourcing in many cases.

▶ *Strategic:* The 'groupset' (D) refers to the gearing systems on the bicycle. These are complex to source and account for a high proportion of total spending. In addition, there are few suppliers capable of manufacturing these components to sufficient quality for high-end bicycles and so the cost of switching is high. For strategic products and services, single-sourcing approaches remain

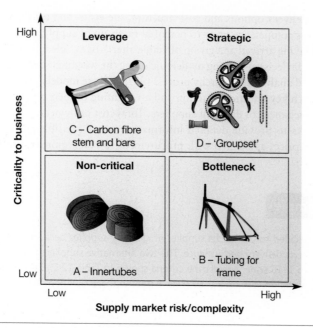

Figure 12.11 Key sourcing groups and strategies for a high-end bicycle manufacturer

popular. However, given the associated risks of single sourcing, many firms have moved to delegated or parallel approaches for this group of purchases.

Supplier selection

In conjunction with deciding on sourcing strategies for different products and services, organizations much select appropriate suppliers. Given the trends of outsourcing, supply base rationalization, supplier involvement in new product/service development, and longer-term supplier relationships, the selection process is all the more important to the success of organizations. Figure 12.12 outlines the four key steps in supplier selection.

▶ *Initial qualification:* This is aimed at reducing possible suppliers to a manageable set for subsequent assessment. Pre-qualification criteria often include financial viability, accreditation (such as ISO 9000), location (e.g. only considering suppliers located within a certain distance of a manufacturer) and scale.

▶ *Agree measurement criteria:* Determining the relative importance of key performance objectives (quality, speed, dependability, flexibility, cost, and others) is critical in the selection of suppliers. For key performance objectives, measurable criteria are then needed. For example, for cost a firm might consider unit price, pricing terms (e.g. volume discounts), exchange rate effects and so on.

▶ *Obtain relevant information:* As firms narrow down to a smaller group of potential suppliers, further information can be gathered to inform the selection decision. This may include additional

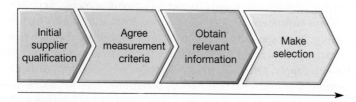

Figure 12.12 The supplier selection process

levels of detail in delivery options and cost structure, site visits, and tests (e.g. test orders in small quantities) to assess competence prior to potential ramp-up of supply.

▶ *Make selection:* Having arrived at a group of viable alternatives, selection may be supported using various multi-criteria decision-making models including the weighted score method (see the worked example below) and analytical hierarchy process (AHP). These models aim to provide quantifiable information for each key selection criterion and a weighting of their relative importance to allow for an objective assessment of different suppliers. Total cost of ownership (TCO) is an alternative approach that seeks to provide detailed information on all possible costs (rather than simply product or service price) associated with procurement to reach more 'rational' decisions during supplier selection.

Worked example

A hotel chain has decided to change its supplier of cleaning supplies because its current supplier has become unreliable in its delivery performance. The two alternative suppliers that it is considering have been evaluated, on a 1–10 scale, against the criteria shown in Table 12.1. This also shows the relative importance of each criterion, also on a 1–10 scale. Based on this evaluation, Supplier B has the superior overall score.

Table 12.1 Weighted supplier selection criteria for the hotel chain

Factor	Weight	Supplier A score	Supplier A score
Cost performance	10	$8(8 \times 10 = 80)$	$5(5 \times 10 = 50)$
Quality record	10	$7(7 \times 10 = 70)$	$9(9 \times 10 = 90)$
Delivery speed promised	7	$5(5 \times 7 = 35)$	$5(5 \times 7 = 35)$
Delivery speed achieved	7	$4(4 \times 7 = 28)$	$8(8 \times 7 = 56)$
Dependability record	8	$6(6 \times 8 = 48)$	$8(8 \times 8 = 64)$
Range provided	5	$8(8 \times 5 = 40)$	$5(5 \times 5 = 25)$
Innovation capability	4	$6(6 \times 4 = 24)$	$9(9 \times 4 = 36)$
Total weighted score		325	356

Managing on-going supply

Managing supply relationships is not just a matter of choosing the right suppliers and then leaving them to get on with day-to-day supply. It is also about ensuring that suppliers are given the right information and encouragement to maintain smooth supply and that internal inconsistency does not negatively affect their ability to supply. A basic requirement is that some mechanism should be set up that ensures the two-way flow of information between customer and supplier. It is easy for both suppliers and customers simply to forget to inform each other of internal developments that could affect supply. Customers may see suppliers as having the responsibility for ensuring appropriate supply 'under any circumstances'. Suppliers themselves may be reluctant to inform customers of any potential problems with supply because they see it as risking the relationship. Yet, especially if customer and supplier see themselves as 'partners', the free flow of information, and a mutually supportive tolerance of occasional problems, is the best way to ensure smooth supply. Often day-to-day supplier relationships are damaged because of internal inconsistencies. For example, one part of a business may be asking a supplier for some special service beyond the strict nature of their agreement, while another part of the business is not paying suppliers on time.

Service-level agreements

Some organizations bring a degree of formality to supplier relationships by encouraging (or requiring) all suppliers to agree service-level agreements (SLAs). SLAs are formal definitions of the dimensions of service and the relationship between operations: for example, between a supplier and its customer, or between in internal supplier of service and its internal customer. SLAs are also an important tool in quality management and are described more fully in Chapter 17.

Improving supplier capabilities

In any relationship other than pure market-based transactional relationships, it is in a customer's long-term interests to take some responsibility for developing supplier capabilities. Helping a supplier to improve not only enhances the service (and hopefully price) from the supplier; it may also lead to greater supplier loyalty and long-term commitment. This is why some particularly successful

---

OPERATIONS IN PRACTICE

The tsunami effect[5]

The volcanic ash from Iceland that disrupted air transport across Europe provided a preview of how natural disasters could throw global supply chains into disarray, especially those that had adopted the lean, low-inventory, just-in-time philosophy. That was in 2010. Yet the following year an even more severe disaster caused chaos in all supply chains with a Japanese connection; and that is a lot of supply chains. It was a quadruple disaster: an earthquake off Japan's eastern coast, one of the largest ever recorded, caused a tsunami that killed thousands of people and caused a meltdown at a nearby nuclear power plant, which necessitated huge evacuations and nationwide power shortages. The effect on global supply networks was immediate and drastic. Sony Corporation shut down some of its operations in Japan because of the on-going power shortages and announced that it was giving its staff time off during the summer (when air conditioning needs are high) to save energy. Japanese automobile companies' production was among the worst affected. Toyota suspended production at most of its Japanese plants, and reduced and then suspended output from its North American and European operations. Nissan said it would be suspending its UK production for three days at the end of the month due to a shortfall of parts from Japan. Honda announced that it was halving production at its factory in Swindon in the south of the UK. However, the disruption was not as severe as it might have been. Honda said that the vast majority of the parts used in Swindon are made in Europe, and added that its flexible working policy would allow it to make up for the lost production later in the year.

In the longer term, the disruption caused a debate amongst practitioners about how supply chains could be made more robust. One said, '*It is very important now to think the extreme. You have to have some buffers.*' Some commentators even drew parallels with financial meltdowns, claiming that just as some financial institutions proved 'too big to fail', some Japanese suppliers may be too crucial to do without. For example, at the time of the disruption, two companies, Mitsubishi Gas Chemical and Hitachi Chemical, controlled about 90 per cent of the market for a specialty resin used to make the microchips that go into smartphones and other devices. Both firms' plants were damaged and the effect was felt around the world. So maybe suppliers who have near-monopolies on vital components should spread their production facilities geographically. Similarly, businesses that rely on single suppliers may be more willing to split their orders between two or more suppliers.

businesses invest in supplier development teams whose responsibility is to help suppliers to improve their own operations processes. Of course, committing the resources to help suppliers is only worthwhile if it improves the effectiveness of the supply chain as a whole. Nevertheless, the potential for such enlightened self-interest can be significant.

How customers and suppliers see each other[6]

One of the major barriers to supplier development is the mismatch between how customers and suppliers perceive both what is required and how the relationship is performing. Exploring potential mismatches is often a revealing exercise, for both customers and suppliers. Figure 12.13 illustrates this. It shows that gaps may exist between four sets of ideas. As a customer, you (presumably) have an idea about what you really want from a supplier. This may, or may not, be formalized in the form of a service-level agreement (SLA). But no SLA can capture everything about what is required. There may be a gap between how you as a customer interpret what is required and how the supplier interprets it. This is the *requirements perception gap*. Similarly, as a customer, you (again presumably) have a view on how your supplier is performing in terms of fulfilling your requirements. That may not coincide with how your supplier believes it is performing. This is the *fulfilment perception gap*. Both these gaps are a function of the effectiveness of the communication between supplier and customer. But there are also two other gaps. The gap between what you want from your supplier and how it is performing indicates the type of development that, as a customer, you should be giving to your supplier. Similarly, the gap between your supplier's perceptions of your needs and its performance indicates how it should initially see itself improving its own performance. Ultimately, of course, its responsibility for improvement should coincide with its customers' views of requirements and performance.

> **Operations principle**
>
> Unsatisfactory supplier relationships can be caused by requirements and fulfilment perception gaps.

Global sourcing

One of the major supply chain developments of recent years has been the expansion in the proportion of products and (occasionally) services which businesses are willing to source from outside their home country. This is called global sourcing. It is the process of identifying, evaluating, negotiating and configuring supply across multiple geographies. Traditionally, even companies that exported their goods and services all over the world (that is, they were international on their demand side)

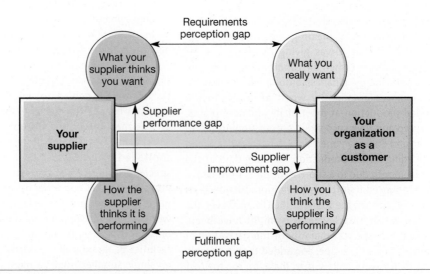

Figure 12.13 Potential perception mismatches to understand supplier development needs

still sourced the majority of their supplies locally (that is, they were not international on their supply side). This has changed – companies are now increasingly willing to look further afield for their supplies, and for very good reasons. There can be significant cost savings by sourcing from low-cost-country suppliers. And tougher world competition has forced companies to look to reducing their total costs. Given that in many industries bought-in items are the largest single part of operations costs, an obvious strategy is to source from wherever is cheapest. But it is not just cost that has driven the move towards global sourcing. Partly it is also because the barriers to sourcing outside one's own country have been lowered. The formation of trading blocks in different parts of the world has had the effect of lowering tariff barriers, at least within those blocks. Transportation infrastructures are considerably more sophisticated and cheaper than they once were. Super-efficient port operations in Rotterdam and Singapore, for example, integrated road–rail systems, jointly developed auto route systems and cheaper air freight have all reduced some of the cost barriers to international trade.

There are of course problems with global sourcing. The risks of increased complexity and increased distance need managing carefully. Suppliers that are a significant distance away need to transport their products across long distances. The risks of delays and hold-ups can be far greater than when sourcing locally (see the 'Operations in practice' example on the tsunami effect). Also negotiating with suppliers whose native language is different from one's own makes communication more difficult and can lead to misunderstandings over contract terms. Therefore, global sourcing decisions require businesses to balance cost, performance, service and risk factors, not all of which are obvious. These factors are important in global sourcing because of non-price or 'hidden' cost factors such as cross-border freight and handling fees, complex inventory stocking and handling requirements, and even more complex administrative, documentation and regulatory requirements.

Global sourcing and social responsibility

Although the responsibility of operations to ensure that they only deal with ethical suppliers has always been important, the expansion of global sourcing has brought the issue into sharper focus. Local suppliers can (to some extent) be monitored relatively easily. However, when suppliers are located around the world, often in countries with different traditions and ethical standards, monitoring becomes more difficult. Not only that, but there may be genuinely different views of what is regarded as ethical practice. Social, cultural and religious differences can easily make for mutual incomprehension regarding each other's ethical perspective. This is why many companies are putting significant effort into articulating and clarifying their supplier selection policies. The 'Operations in practice' example on 'Levi Strauss' global sourcing policy is typical of an enlightened organization's approach to global sourcing.

How should the demand side be managed?

As we noted in Chapter 10, not all operations have predictable demand. Some operations are subject to 'independent demand' that includes a random element virtually independent of any obvious factors. They, like their suppliers, are required to satisfy demand without having any firm forward visibility of customer orders. In Chapter 10 we used the example of a drive-in tyre replacement service. It cannot predict either the volume or the specific needs of customers. It must make decisions on how many and what type of tyres to stock, based on demand forecasts and in the light of the risks it is prepared to take of running out of stock. Managing internal process networks when external demand is independent involves making 'best guesses' concerning future demand, attempting to put the resources in place to satisfy this demand, and attempting to respond quickly if actual demand does not match the forecast. Inventory management, which we treat in Chapter 13, is a typical approach to this situation.

Logistics services

Logistics means moving products to customers. Sometimes the term 'physical distribution management' or simply 'distribution' is used as being analogous to logistics. An important decision is how much of the logistical process of organizing the movement of goods to trust to outside service providers. The extent and integration of this type of service provision is often referred to as first-,

Extracts from Levi Strauss' global sourcing policy[7]

Our Global Sourcing and Operating Guidelines help us to select business partners who follow workplace standards and business practices that are consistent with our company's values. These requirements are applied to every contractor who manufactures or finishes products for Levi Strauss & Co. Trained inspectors closely audit and monitor compliance among approximately 600 cutting, sewing, and finishing contractors in more than 60 countries. . . . The numerous countries where Levi Strauss & Co. has existing or future business interests present a variety of cultural, political, social and economic circumstances. . . . The Country Assessment Guidelines help us assess any issue that might present concern in light of the ethical principles we have set for ourselves. Specifically, we assess . . . the . . . Health and Safety Conditions, Human Rights Environment, the Legal System and the Political, Economic and Social Environment would protect the company's commercial interests and brand/corporate image. The company's employment standards state that they will only do business with partners who adhere to the following guidelines:

Child Labor: Use of child labor is not permissible. Workers can be no less than 15 years of age and not younger than the compulsory age to be in school. We will not utilize partners who use child labor in any of their facilities.

Prison Labor/Forced Labor: We will not utilize prison or forced labor in contracting relationships in the manufacture and finishing of our products. We will not utilize or purchase materials from a business partner utilizing prison or forced labor.

Disciplinary Practices: We will not utilize business partners who use corporal punishment or other forms of mental or physical coercion.

Working Hours: While permitting flexibility in scheduling, we will identify local legal limits on work hours and

seek business partners who do not exceed them except for appropriately compensated overtime. Employees should be allowed at least one day off in seven.

Wages and Benefits: We will only do business with partners who provide wages and benefits that comply with any applicable law and match the prevailing local manufacturing or finishing industry practices.

Freedom of Association: We respect workers' rights to form and join organizations of their choice and to bargain collectively. We expect our suppliers to respect the right to free association and the right to organize and bargain collectively without unlawful interference.

Discrimination: While we recognize and respect cultural differences, we believe that workers should be employed on the basis of their ability to do the job, rather than on the basis of personal characteristics or beliefs. We will favour business partners who share this value.

Health & Safety: We will only utilize business partners who provide workers with a safe and healthy work environment. Business partners who provide residential facilities for their workers must provide safe and healthy facilities.

---

second-, third- or fourth-party logistics (or 1PL, 2PL, 3PL, 4PL, for short). However, the distinction between the PL classifications can sometimes be blurred, with different firms using slightly different definitions.

▶ First-party logistics (1PL) is when, rather than outsourcing the activity, the owner of whatever is being transported organizes and performs product movements itself. For example, a manufacturing firm will deliver directly, or a retailer such as a supermarket will collect products from a supplier. The logistics activity is an entirely internal process.

- ▶ Second-party logistics (2PL) is when a firm decides to outsource or sub-contract logistics services over a specific segment of a supply chain. It could involve a road, rail, air or maritime shipping company being hired to transport, and if necessary store, products from a specific collection point to a specific destination.
- ▶ Third-party logistics (3PL) is when a firm contracts a logistics company to work with other transport companies to manage their logistics operations. It is a broader concept than 2PL and can involve transportation, warehousing, inventory management and even packaging or re-packaging products. Generally 3PL involves services that are scaled and customised to a customer's specific needs.
- ▶ Fourth-party logistics (4PL) is a yet broader idea than 3PL. Accenture, the consulting group, originally used the term '4PL'. Its definition of 4PL is: 'A 4PL is an integrator that assembles the resources, capabilities, and technology of its own organization and other organizations to design, build and run comprehensive supply chain solutions.' 4PL service suppliers pool transport capabilities, processes, technology support and coordination activities to provide customised supply chain services for part or all of a client's supply chain. 4PL firms can manage all aspects of a client's supply chain. They may act as a single interface between the client and multiple logistics service providers, and are often separate organizational entities founded on a long-term basis or as a joint venture between a client and one or more partners.
- ▶ 5PL? – you guessed it, almost inevitably, some firms are selling themselves as fifth-party logistics providers, mainly by defining themselves as broadening the scope further to e-business.

Logistics management and the internet

In fact, internet-based communication has had a significant impact on physical distribution management. Information can be made available more readily along the distribution chain, so that transport companies, warehouses, suppliers and customers can share knowledge of where goods are in the chain (and sometimes where they are going next). This allows the operations within the chain to coordinate their activities more readily. It also gives the potential for some significant cost savings. For example, an important issue for transportation companies is back-loading. When the company is contracted to transport goods from A to B, its vehicles may have to return from B to A, empty. Back-loading means finding a potential customer that wants its goods transported from B to A in the right timeframe. With the increase in information availability through the Internet, the possibility of finding a back-load increases. Companies that can fill their vehicles on both the outward and return journeys will have significantly lower costs per distance travelled than those whose vehicles are empty for half the total journey. Similarly, internet-based technology that allows customers visibility of the progress of distribution can be used to enhance the perception of customer service. 'Track-and-trace' technologies, for example, allow package distribution companies to inform and reassure customers that their service is being delivered as promised.

Perhaps the most significant recent development of internet-based technologies on logistics is the 'internet of things' (IoT), although IoT technology is not without its vulnerabilities (see Chapter 18 for a full explanation). Its use of 'automatic identification technologies' such as radio frequency identification (RFID) to trace the progress of items through a supply chain means that during every stage of manufacturing, distribution, storage and sale each product can be individually tracked and the information used to coordinate supply.

Customer relationship management (CRM)

There is a story (which may or may not be true) that is often quoted to demonstrate the importance of using information technology to analyse customer information. It goes like this: Wal-Mart, the huge US-based supermarket chain, did an analysis of customers' buying habits and found a statistically significant correlation between purchases of beer and purchases of diapers (nappies), especially on Friday evenings. The reason? Fathers were going to the supermarket to buy nappies for their

A nation panics as supply problems closes KFC outlets[8]

According to retail researchers Mintel, UK customers spend over £2bn a year in chicken restaurants such as KFC. Perhaps that explains the anguish of some KFC customers when the chain had to close more than half of its 900 UK outlets when delivery problems meant they ran out of chicken. Customers sometimes queued only to find that there was no chicken. One distraught customer apparently complained that they went on Saturday night to their local KFC and queued for about 20 minutes in the drive-thru, but when they arrived at the counter and asked for a family bucket, they were told there was no chicken. Other dissatisfied KFC customers took to Twitter to express their dismay. 'So, @KFC have run out of chicken. This is how the apocalypse starts 😩' tweeted one. KFC outlets posted apologetic notices on the doors of their closed restaurants and set up a web page where enthusiasts could find their nearest outlet that was still open. The cause of chicken famine? The previous week, KFC had transferred its delivery contract from one delivery firm, the South African-owned distribution group Bidvest, to another, DHL, part of Germany's Deutsche Post. DHL blamed 'operational issues' for the supply disruption. One commentator said that it was an example of a firm underestimating the complexity of running a smooth delivery operation. One cannot expect a new contractor to come in and, without the relevant experience, do the same job. A union official made a similar point, that Bidvest were specialists – a food distribution firm with years of experience. DHL simply undercut them. KFC was left with hundreds of restaurants closed while DHL tried to run the whole operation out of one distribution centre.

Samir Dani, professor of logistics and supply chain management at the University of Huddersfield, was quoted as saying: 'The situation now shows business continuity was not thought out very well.' When things started to go wrong, the single distribution centre 'becomes a major constraint to the delivery system'. Further, he said that because the product being delivered was perishable (KFC uses fresh, not frozen, chicken), and subject to strict food safety rules, he thought 'there should have been at least two sites'. That would have provided a back-up and helped deal with the potential for food safety problems, he said, but it would likely have been more

expensive. As another authority on fast-food distribution put it, 'frozen food is one thing, but chilled food is something else. You can't afford to make any mistakes. It's easy to move a can of beans; it's much more difficult to move chicken.' While its outlets were closed, KFC encouraged its workers to take their holiday, but did not require them to do so. The restaurants that were owned by the chain paid the average hours worked per day over the past 12 weeks to staff on short-term contracts, while those on salaries were paid as normal. Although 80 per cent of KFC outlets were franchised, they were encouraged to adopt the same policy.

Even amidst the problems, KFC's response did receive some praise. It was generally held to be informative, apologetic and humorous. 'To put it simply', KFC tweeted, 'we've got the chicken, we've got the restaurants, but we've just had issues getting them together.' It also tweeted, 'The chicken crossed the road, just not to our restaurants.' It ran a newspaper advert showing a photo of a chicken bucket with the KFC logo letters rearranged to read 'FCK'. The associated text read: 'WE'RE SORRY. A chicken restaurant without any chicken. It's not ideal . . . Thank you for bearing with us. Unfortunately, the very next week KFC admitted that some restaurants were also running low on gravy. One customer took to Twitter . . . 'KFC could survive no chicken but no gravy?? . . . it's curtains!' Shortly afterwards KFC (partially) reversed its decision to totally switch its distribution partners. Bidvest signed a new agreement with KFC to supply up to 350 of its 900 restaurants. Bidvest said it was 'delighted' to resume its partnership with KFC.

babies, and because fatherhood restricted their ability to go out for a drink as often, they would also buy beer. Supposedly this led the supermarket to start locating nappies next to the beer in their stores, resulting in increased sales of both.

Whether it is true or not, it does illustrate the potential of analysing data to understand customers. This is the basis of customer relationship management (CRM). It is a method of learning more about customers' needs and behaviours in order to develop stronger relationships with them. Although CRM usually depends on information technology, it is misleading to see it as a 'technology'. Rather it is a process that helps to understand customers' needs and develop ways of meeting those needs while maximizing profitability. CRM brings together all the disparate information about customers so as to gain insight into their behaviour and their value to the business. It helps to sell products and services more effectively and increase revenues by:

▶ providing services and products that are exactly what your customers want;
▶ retaining existing customers and discovering new ones;
▶ offering better customer service;
▶ cross-selling products more effectively.

CRM tries to help organizations understand who their customers are and what their value is over a lifetime. It does this by building a number of steps into its customer interface processes. First, the business must determine the needs of its customers and how best to meet those needs. For example, a bank may keep track of its customers' age and lifestyle so that it can offer appropriate products like mortgages or pensions to them when they fit their needs. Second, the business must examine all the different ways and parts of the organization where customer-related information is collected, stored and used. Businesses may interact with customers in different ways and through different people. For example, sales people, call centres, technical staff, operations and distribution managers may all, at different times, have contact with customers. CRM systems should integrate these data. Third, all customer-related data must be analysed to obtain a holistic view of each customer and identify where service can be improved.

Customer development

Earlier in the chapter, Figure 12.13 illustrated some of the gaps in perception and performance that can occur between customers and suppliers. The purpose then was to demonstrate the nature of supplier development. The same approach can be used to analyse the nature of requirements and performance with customers. In this case the imperative is to understand customer perceptions, both of their requirements and their view of your performance, and feed these into your own performance improvement plans. What is less common, but can be equally valuable, is to use these gaps (shown in Figure 12.14) to examine the question of whether customer requirements and perceptions of performance are either accurate or reasonable. For example, customers may be placing demands on suppliers without fully considering their consequences. It may be that slight modifications in what is demanded would not inconvenience customers and yet would provide significant benefits to suppliers that could then be passed on to customers. Similarly, customers may be incompetent at measuring supplier performance, in which case the benefits of excellent supplier service will not

Critical commentary

Despite its name, some critics of CRM argue that the greatest shortcoming is that it is insufficiently concerned with directly helping customers. CRM systems are sold to executives as a way to increase efficiency, force standardized processes and gain better insight into the state of the business. But they rarely address the need to help organizations resolve customer problems, answer customer questions faster, or help them solve their own problems. This may explain the shift in focus from automating internal front-office functions to streamlining processes such as online customer support.

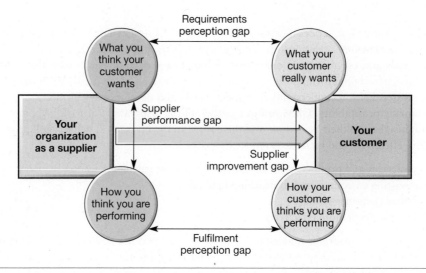

Figure 12.14 Potential perception mismatches to understand customer development needs

Operations principle

Unsatisfactory customer relationships can be caused by requirements and fulfilment perception gaps.

be recognized. So, just as customers have a responsibility to help develop their own suppliers' performance, in their own as well as their suppliers' interests, suppliers have a responsibility to develop their customers' understanding of how supply should be managed.

What are the dynamics of supply chains?

There are dynamics that exist between firms in supply chains that cause errors, inaccuracies and volatility, and these increase for operations further upstream in the supply chain. This effect is known as the bullwhip effect, so called because a small disturbance at one end of the chain causes increasingly large disturbances as it works its way towards the end. Its main cause is a perfectly understandable and rational desire by the different links in the supply chain to manage their levels

The 80,000 km journey of Wimbledon's tennis balls

The Wimbledon 'Grand Slam' tennis tournament is a quintessentially British occasion, and Slazenger the UK sports equipment manufacturer and has been the official ball supplier for Wimbledon since 1902. Yet those balls used at Wimbledon, and the materials from which they are made, will have travelled 81,385 km between 11 countries and across four continents before they reach Centre Court. Professor Mark Johnson, of Warwick Business School, said: *'It is one of the longest journeys I have seen for a product. On the face of it, travelling more than 80,000 kilometres to make a tennis ball does seem fairly ludicrous, but it just shows the global nature of production, and in the end, this will be the most cost-effective way of making tennis balls.'*

Slazenger is locating production near the primary source of its materials in Bataan in the Philippines, where labour is also relatively low cost.

The complex supply chain is illustrated in Figure 12.15. It sees clay shipped from South Carolina in the USA, silica from Greece, magnesium carbonate from Japan, zinc oxide from Thailand, sulphur from South Korea and rubber from Malaysia to Bataan where the rubber is vulcanized – a chemical process for making the rubber more durable. Wool is then shipped from New Zealand to Stroud in the UK, where it is weaved into felt and then flown back to Bataan in the Philippines. Meanwhile, petroleum naphthalene from

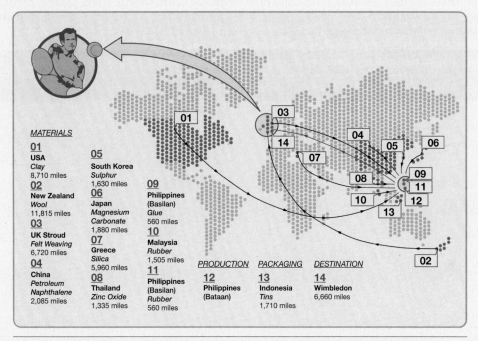

Figure 12.15 Wimbledon's tennis balls travel over 80,000 kilometres in their supply network

MATERIALS

01
USA
Clay
8,710 miles
02
New Zealand
Wool
11,815 miles
03
UK Stroud
Felt Weaving
6,720 miles
04
China
*Petroleum
Naphthalene*
2,085 miles

05
South Korea
Sulphur
1,630 miles
06
Japan
*Magnesium
Carbonate*
1,880 miles
07
Greece
Silica
5,960 miles
08
Thailand
Zinc Oxide
1,335 miles

09
Philippines
(Basilan)
Glue
560 miles
10
Malaysia
Rubber
1,505 miles
11
Philippines
(Basilan)
Rubber
560 miles

PRODUCTION
12
Philippines
(Bataan)

PACKAGING
13
Indonesia
Tins
1,710 miles

DESTINATION
14
Wimbledon
6,660 miles

Zibo in China and glue from Basilan in the Philippines are brought to Bataan where Slazenger manufactures the balls. Finally, the tins which contain the balls are shipped in from Indonesia and once the balls have been packaged they are sent to Wimbledon. *'Slazenger shut down the factory in the UK years ago and moved the* *equipment to Bataan in the Philippines',* says Professor Johnson. *'They still get the felt from Stroud, as it requires a bit more technical expertise. Shipping wool from New Zealand to Stroud and then sending the felt back to the Philippines adds a lot of miles, but they obviously want to use the best wool for the Wimbledon balls.'*

of activity and inventory sensibly. To demonstrate this, examine the production rate and stock levels for the supply chain shown in Table 12.2. This is a four-stage supply chain where an original equipment manufacturer (OEM) is served by three tiers of suppliers. The demand from the OEM's market has been running at a rate of 100 items per period, but in period 2, demand reduces to 95 items per period. All stages in the supply chain work on the principle that they will keep in stock one period's demand. This is a simplification but not a gross one. Many operations gear their inventory levels to their demand rate. The column headed 'stock' for each level of supply shows the starting stock at the beginning of the period and the finishing stock at the end of the period. At the beginning of period 2, the OEM has 100 units in stock (that being the rate of demand up to period 2). Demand in period 2 is 95 and so the OEM knows that it would need to produce sufficient items to finish up at the end of the period with 95 in stock (this being the new demand rate). To do this, it need only manufacture 90 items; these, together with five items taken out of the starting stock, will supply demand and leave a finished stock of 95 items. The beginning of period 3 finds the OEM with 95 items in stock. Demand is also 95 items and therefore its production rate to maintain a stock level of 95 will be 95 items per period. The original equipment manufacturer now operates at a steady rate of producing 95 items per period. Note, however, that a change in demand of only five items has produced a fluctuation of 10 items in the OEM's production rate.

Carrying this same logic through to the first-tier supplier, at the beginning of period 2, the second-tier supplier has 100 items in stock. The demand which it has to supply in period 2 is derived from the production rate of the OEM. This has dropped down to 90 in period 2. The first-tier supplier therefore has to produce sufficient to supply the demand of 90 items (or the equivalent) and leave one month's demand (now 90 items) as its finish stock. A production rate of 80 items per month will achieve this.

Table 12.2 Fluctuations of production levels along supply chain in response to small change in end-customer demand (Starting stock (a) + production (b) = finishing stock (c) + demand: that is, production in previous tier down (d): see explanation in text. Note all stages in the supply chain keep one period's inventory, c = d.)

Period	Third-tier supplier		Second-tier supplier		First-tier supplier		Original equipment mfr		Demand
	Prodn.	Stock	Prodn.	Stock	Prodn.	Stock	Prodn.	Stock	
1	100	100	100	100	100	100	100	100	100
		100		100		100		100	
2	20	100	60	100	80	100	90	100	95
		60		80		90		95	
3	180	60	120	80	100	90	95	95	95
		120		100		95		95	
4	60	120	90	100	95	95	95	95	95
		90		95		95		95	
5	100	90	95	95	95	95	95	95	95
		95		95		95		95	
6	95	95	95	95	95	95	95	95	95
		95		95		95		95	

It will therefore start period 3 with an opening stock of 90 items, but the demand from the OEM has now risen to 95 items. It therefore has to produce sufficient to fulfil this demand of 95 items and leave 95 items in stock. To do this, it must produce 100 items in period 3. After period 3 the first-tier supplier then resumes a steady state, producing 95 items per month. Note again, however, that the fluctuation has been even greater than that in the OEM's production rate, decreasing to 80 items a period, increasing to 100 items a period, and then achieving a steady rate of 95 items a period. Extending the logic back to the third-tier supplier, it is clear that the further back up the supply chain an operation is placed, the more drastic are the fluctuations.

> **Operations principle**
>
> Demand fluctuations become progressively amplified as their effects work back up the supply chain.

This relatively simple demonstration ignores any time lag in material and information flow between stages. In practice there will be such a lag, and this will make the fluctuations even more marked. Figure 12.16 shows the net result of all these effects in a typical supply chain. Note the increasing volatility further back in the chain.

Controlling supply chain dynamics

One of the reasons for the fluctuations in output described in the example earlier was that each operation in the chain reacted to the orders placed by its immediate customer. None of the operations had an overview of what was happening throughout the chain. If information had been available and shared throughout the chain, it is unlikely that such wild fluctuations would have occurred. It is

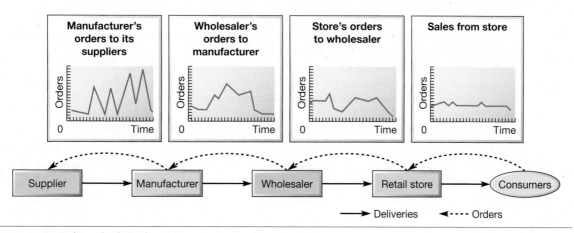

Figure 12.16 Typical supply chain dynamics

sensible therefore to try to transmit information throughout the chain so that all the operations can monitor true demand, free of these distortions. An obvious improvement is to make information on end customer demand available to upstream operations. Electronic point-of-sale (EPOS) systems used by many retailers attempt to do this. Sales data from checkouts or cash registers are consolidated and transmitted to the warehouses, transportation companies and supplier manufacturing operations that form its supply chain. Similarly, electronic data interchange (EDI) helps to share information and can affect the economic order quantities shipped between operations in the supply chain. The other rapidly developing approach to gaining a trusted overview of supply chains is the use of blockchain technology, described in the following section.

Blockchain technology in the supply chain

Many new technologies find particular applications for which they seem to have been designed – robots in manufacturing processing, face recognition in retail and security operations, and so on. Blockchain technology is slightly different. Its first and best-known application was as the accounting method for the virtual currency Bitcoin. As such, blockchain uses 'distributed ledger technology' (DLT), which was later developed in a variety of business applications.

What is a 'blockchain'?

A blockchain is a decentralized, digitized, public ledger (list) of transactions (movements, author-izations, payments, etc.). A 'block' is a record of new transactions. When each block is completed (verified) it is added to the chain, thus creating a chain of blocks, or 'blockchain'. There are five basic principles underlying the technology.[9]

1 *It uses distributed databases* – All participants on a blockchain have access to the entire database and its complete history. No single participant controls the data or the information. Every partic-ipant can verify the records of its transaction partners directly, without an intermediary.

2 *It uses peer-to-peer (P2P) transmission* – All communication occurs directly between peers (or rather their computers, known as nodes) rather than through a central node. Each node in the network stores and forwards information to all other nodes.

3 *It is transparent and can be used anonymously* – Every transaction is visible to anyone with access to the system. Each node (user) on a blockchain has a unique 30-plus-character alphanumeric address that identifies it. Users can either choose to remain anonymous, or alternatively provide proof of their identity to others. Transactions occur between blockchain addresses.

4 *Its records are irreversible* – Once a transaction is entered in the database (and the accounts updated) the records cannot be altered, because they're linked to every transaction record that

came before them (which is why it is called a 'chain'). Computational algorithms and approaches are used to ensure that the recording on the database is permanent, chronologically ordered and available to all others on the network.

5 *It uses computational logic* – Because the distributed ledgers are digital, all blockchain transactions can be tied to a known computational logic. This means that participants can set up algorithms and rules that automatically trigger transactions between nodes.

Why is blockchain technology so useful in supply chain management?

Why is blockchain technology so useful in supply chain management? Because it is good at the practical issues that face supply chain managers. First, supply chains are often complex with many operations involved in the network, and the larger the number of nodes in a distributed ledger network, the more secure it is, which is why it is good to have a large number of nodes running the blockchain. Second, a very large number of transactions necessary are for the smooth running of most supply chains. Especially if the supply chain crosses national boundaries, customs, certification and other documents are required by many regulatory authorities (see the 'Operations in practice' example, 'Maersk and IBM team up to develop blockchain potential in supply chains'). In a blockchain, every time the network makes an update to the database, it is automatically updated and downloaded to every computer on the network, saving considerable time and cost in managing supply. Third, blockchain technology is secure. Its cryptographic techniques make it close to impossible for hackers to make changes to it. The validation rules of blockchains mean that the only way to make changes would be to hack more than half of the nodes in the blockchain (which is why again it is more secure to have more nodes in the blockchain). Fourth, the security of blockchains means that all parties can trust the provenance (history) of supplies. This is particularly important when dealing with food supplies, luxury goods (that are frequently forged) or ethical goods ('blood diamonds', for example). Finally, supply chains are 'threads of operations through supply networks'. The key word is 'networks'. Blockchain technology is 'distributed' – the whole concept is based on how supply chains operate as parts of networks. Figure 12.17 illustrates how blockchains can be used in a supply chain context.

Reducing the bullwhip effect

The first step in improving supply chain performance involves attempting to reduce the bullwhip effect. This usually means coordinating the activities of the operations in the chain in several ways.[10]

Channel alignment in supply networks

Channel alignment means the adjustment of scheduling, material movements, stock levels, pricing and other sales strategies so as to bring all the operations in the chain into line with each other. This goes beyond the provision of information. It means that the systems and methods of planning and control decision making are harmonized through the chain. For example, even when using the same information, differences in forecasting methods or purchasing practices can lead to fluctuations in orders between operations in the chain. One way of avoiding this is to allow an upstream supplier to manage the inventories of its downstream customer. This is known as vendor-managed inventory (VMI). So, for example, a packaging supplier could take responsibility for the stocks of packaging materials held by a food manufacturing customer. In turn, the food manufacturer takes responsibility for the stocks of its products that are held in its customer's, the supermarket's warehouses.

Operational efficiency in supply networks

'Operational efficiency' in this context means the efforts that each operation in the chain makes to reduce its own complexity, the cost of doing business with other operations in the chain, and its throughput time. The cumulative effect of this is to simplify throughput in the whole chain. For example, imagine a chain of operations whose performance level is relatively poor: quality defects are frequent, the lead time to order products and services is long, delivery is unreliable and so on. The behaviour of the chain would be a continual sequence of errors and effort wasted in re-planning

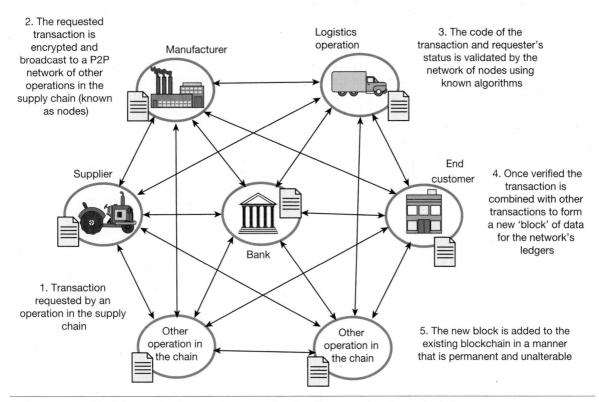

2. The requested transaction is encrypted and broadcast to a P2P network of other operations in the supply chain (known as nodes)

Manufacturer

Logistics operation

3. The code of the transaction and requester's status is validated by the network of nodes using known algorithms

Supplier

Bank

End customer

4. Once verified the transaction is combined with other transactions to form a new 'block' of data for the network's ledgers

1. Transaction requested by an operation in the supply chain

Other operation in the chain

Other operation in the chain

5. The new block is added to the existing blockchain in a manner that is permanent and unalterable

Figure 12.17 How blockchain technology works to record and verify transactions in supply chains

---

Maersk and IBM team up to develop blockchain potential in supply chains[11]

Although the technology was still very much in its infancy, the global shipping giant Maersk announced in January 2018 that, subject to receipt of regulatory approvals, it was teaming up with IBM to form a joint venture to provide more efficient and secure methods for conducting global trade using blockchain technology. General Motors and Procter & Gamble were among the multinationals to express interest in the new platform. IBM was already recognized as a leading provider of blockchain technology. An early member of Hyperledger, an open source collaborative effort created to advance cross-industry blockchain technologies, it had worked with other clients to implement blockchain applications, and operate a number of networks running live and in production. The aim of the new company, they said, would be to offer a jointly developed platform, built on open standards and designed for use by the entire global shipping ecosystem. According to commentators, joining up with Maersk made sense, because of the complexity of its integrated transport, container shipping, ports and logistics operations in 130 countries. With more than $4 trillion in goods shipped each year, more than 80 per cent of the goods consumers use daily are carried by the ocean shipping industry. But, traditionally, it had been a document-intensive business. The maximum cost of generating and processing all the required trade documentation to organize many of these shipments was estimated to be as high as one-fifth of the actual physical transportation costs. Blockchain technology was seen as ideally suited to large networks of disparate partners across complex supply chains. Maersk executives said that, with access to a shared, trusted record of transactions, the world's shipping companies would save money and be able to better compete on enhanced services.

The CEO of the joint venture, Michael J. White, said, *'Today, a vast amount of resources are wasted due to inefficient and error-prone manual processes. The pilots confirmed our expectations that, across the industry, there is considerable demand for efficiency gains and opportunities coming from streamlining and standardizing information flows using digital solutions. Our ambition is to apply these learnings to establish a fully open platform whereby all players in the global supply chain can participate and extract significant value. We look forward to further expanding our ecosystem of partners as we progress toward a global solution.'*

to compensate for the errors. Poor quality would mean extra and unplanned orders being placed, and unreliable delivery and slow delivery lead times would mean high safety stocks. Just as important, most operations managers' time would be spent coping with the inefficiency. By contrast, a chain whose operations had high levels of operations performance would be more predictable and have faster throughput, both of which would help to minimize supply chain fluctuations.

Forecasting in supply networks

Improved forecast accuracy also helps to reduce the bullwhip effect. Bullwhip is caused by the demand pattern, lead times, forecasting mechanisms and replenishment decisions used to order product from production facilities or suppliers. Improving the accuracy of your forecasts directly reduces the inventory holding requirements that will achieve customer service level targets. Reducing lead times means that you need to forecast less far into the future and thus lead times have a large impact on bullwhip and inventory costs. The exact nature of how bullwhip propagates in a supply chain is also dependent on the nature of the demand pattern. Negatively correlated demands require less inventory in the supply chain than positively correlated demand patterns, for example. But bullwhip is not unavoidable. By using sophisticated replenishment policies, designed using control engineering principles, many businesses have been able to eliminate bullwhip effects. Sometimes this comes at a cost. Extra inventory may be required in parts of the chain, or customer service levels reduce. But more often bullwhip avoidance creates a 'win-win'. It reduces inventory requirements and improves customer service.

Operations principle

The bullwhip effect can be reduced by information sharing, aligning planning and control decisions, improving flow efficiency, and better forecasting.

Summary answers to key questions

What is supply chain management?

▶ Supply chain management is the management of relationships and flows between operations and processes. Technically, it is different from supply network management, which looks at all the operations or processes in a network, but the two terms are often used interchangeably.

▶ Many of the principles of managing external supply chains (flow between operations) are also applicable to internal supply chains (flow between processes and departments).

How should supply chains compete?

▶ The central objective of supply chain management is to satisfy the needs of the end customer.

▶ So, each operation in the chain (and each chain in the supply network) should contribute to whatever mix of quality, speed, dependability, flexibility and cost that the end customer requires.

- Individual operations failure in any of these objectives can be multiplied throughout the chain. So, although each operation's performance may be adequate, the performance of the whole chain could be poor.
- An important distinction is between lean and agile supply chain performance. Broadly, lean (or efficient) supply chains are appropriate for stable 'functional' products and services, while agile (or responsive) supply chains are more appropriate for less predictable innovative products and services.

How should relationships in supply chains be managed?

- Supply chain relationships can be described on a spectrum from market-based, contractual, 'arm's length' relationships, through to close and long-term partnership relationships.
- The types of relationships adopted may be dictated by the structure of the market itself.

How is the supply side managed?

- Managing supply-side relationships involves determining sourcing strategy, selecting appropriate suppliers, managing on-going supply activity, and supplier development.
- Sourcing strategies include multiple sourcing, single sourcing, delegated sourcing and parallel sourcing. Their selection is influenced by the complexity and risk of the supply market and the criticality to the business.
- Supplier selection involves trading off different supplier attributes, often using scoring assessment methods.
- Managing on-going supply involves clarifying supply expectations, often using service-level agreements to manage the supply relationships.
- Supplier development can benefit both suppliers and customers, especially in partnership relationships. Very often barriers are the mismatches in perception between customers and suppliers.

How is the demand side managed?

- This will depend partly on whether demand is dependent on some known factor and therefore predictable, or independent of any known factor and therefore less predictable. Approaches such as materials requirements planning (MRP) are used in the former case, while approaches such as inventory management are used in the latter case.
- The increasing outsourcing of physical distribution and the use of new tracking technologies, such as RFID, have brought efficiencies to the movement of physical goods and customer service.

What are the dynamics of supply chains?

- Supply chains have a dynamic of their own that is often called the *bullwhip* effect. It means that relatively small changes at the demand end of the chain increasingly amplify into large disturbances as they move upstream.
- Blockchain technology is increasingly used to give a trusted overview of supply chain transactions.
- Four key methods can be used to reduce this effect. E-enabled supply chains can prevent over-reaction to immediate stimuli and give a better view of the whole chain. Channel alignment through standardized planning and control methods allows for easier coordination of the whole chain. Improving the operational efficiency of each part of the chain prevents local errors multiplying to affect the whole chain. Improved forecasts reduce the inventory holding requirements for supply chains while maintaining customer service levels.

Supplying fast fashion

Garment retailing has changed. No longer is there a standard look that all retailers adhere to for a whole season. Fashion is fast, complex and furious. Different trends overlap and fashion ideas that are not even on a store's radar screen can become 'must haves' within six months. Many retail businesses with their own brands, such as H&M and Zara, sell up-to-the-minute clothes at low prices, in stores that are clearly focused on one particular market. In the world of fast fashion, catwalk designs speed their way into high street stores at prices anyone can afford. The quality of the garment means that it may only last one season, but fast fashion customers don't want yesterday's trends. As *Newsweek* puts it, '. . . being a "quicker picker-upper" is what made fashion retailers H&M and Zara successful. [They] *thrive by practicing the new science of "fast fashion"; compressing product development cycles as much as six times.'* But the retail operations that customers see are only the end part of the supply chains that feed them. And these have also changed.

At its simplest level, the fast-fashion supply chain has four stages. First, the garments are designed, after which they are manufactured; they are then distributed to the retail outlets where they are displayed and sold in retail operations designed to reflect the businesses' brand values. In this short case we examine two fast-fashion operations, Hennes and Mauritz (known as H&M) and Zara, together with United Colours of Benetton (UCB), a similar chain, but with a different market positioning.

▶ **Benetton** – Almost 50 years ago, Luciano Benetton took the world of fashion by storm by selling the bright, casual sweaters designed by his sister across Europe (and later the rest of the world), promoted by controversial advertising. The Benetton Group is present in over 20 countries throughout the world. Selling casual garments, mainly under its United Colours of Benetton (UCB) and its more fashion-orientated Sisley brands, it produces 110 million garments a year, over 90 per cent of them in Europe. Its retail network of over 6,000 stores produces revenue of around €1.6 billion. Benetton products are seen as less 'high fashion' but of higher quality and durability, with higher prices, than H&M and Zara.

▶ **H&M** – Established in Sweden in 1947, it now sells clothes and cosmetics in over 1,000 stores in 20 countries around the world. The business concept is 'fashion and quality at the best price'. With more than 40,000 employees, and revenues of around SEK 60,000 million, its biggest market is Germany, followed by Sweden and the UK. H&M is seen by many as the originator of the fast-fashion concept. Certainly it has years of experience at driving down the price of up-to-the-minute fashions. '*We ensure the best price,'* H&M says, '*by having few middlemen, buying large volumes, having extensive experience of the clothing industry, having a great knowledge of which goods should be bought from which markets, having efficient distribution systems, and being cost-conscious at every stage.'*

▶ **Zara** – The first store opened almost by accident in 1975 when Amancio Ortega Gaona, a women's pyjama manufacturer, was left with a large cancelled order. The shop he opened was intended only as an outlet for cancelled orders. Inditex, the holding group that includes the Zara brand, currently has over 2,000 stores in over 100 countries and revenues of over €11.5 billion. The Zara brand accounts for over 75 per cent of the group's total retail sales, and is still based in north-west Spain. The Inditex group also has several other branded chains including Pull and Bear, and Massimo Dutti. In total it employs almost 40,000 people in a business that is known for a high degree of vertical integration compared with most fast-fashion companies. The company believes that its integration along the supply chain allows it to respond to customer demand fast and flexibly while keeping stock to a minimum.

Design

All three businesses emphasize the importance of design in this market. Although not *haute couture,* capturing design trends is vital to success. Even the boundary between high and fast fashion is starting to blur. In 2004 H&M recruited high-fashion designer Karl Lagerfeld, previously noted for his work with more exclusive brands. For H&M his designs were priced for value rather than exclusivity, *'Why do I work for H&M? Because I believe in inexpensive clothes, not "cheap" clothes,'* said Lagerfeld. Yet most of H&M's products come from over 100 designers in Stockholm who work with a team of 50 pattern designers, around 100 buyers and a number of budget controllers. The department's task is to find the optimum balance between the three components comprising H&M's business concept – fashion, price and quality. Buying volumes and delivery dates are then decided.

Zara's design functions are organized in a different way to most similar companies. Conventionally, the design input comes from three *separate* functions: the designers themselves, market specialists, and buyers who place orders on to suppliers. At Zara the design stage is split into three product areas: women's, men's and children's garments. In each area, designers, market specialists and buyers are co-located in design halls that also contain small workshops for trying out prototype designs. The market specialists in all three design halls are in regular contact with Zara retail stores, discussing customer reaction to new designs. In this way, the retail stores are not the end of the whole supply chain but the beginning of the design stage of the chain. Zara's around 300 designers, whose average age is 26, produce approximately 40,000 items per year of which about 10,000 go into production.

Benetton also has around 300 designers, who not only design for all its brands, but also are engaged in researching new materials and clothing concepts. Since 2000 the company has moved to standardize its range globally. At one time more than 20 per cent of its ranges were customized to the specific needs of each country; now only between 5 and 10 per cent of garments are customized. This reduced the number of individual designs offered globally by over 30 per cent, strengthening the global brand image and reducing production costs.

Both H&M and Zara have moved away from the traditional industry practice of offering two 'collections' a year, for spring/summer and autumn/winter. Their 'seasonless cycle' involves the continual introduction of new products on a rolling basis throughout the year. This allows designers to learn from customers' reactions to their new products and incorporate them quickly into more new products. The most extreme version of this idea is practised by Zara. A garment will be designed, and a batch manufactured and 'pulsed' through the supply chain. Often the design is never repeated; it may be modified and another batch produced, but there are no 'continuing' designs as such. Even Benetton has increased the proportion of what it calls 'flash' collections, small collections that are put into its stores during the season.

Manufacturing

At one time Benetton focused its production on its Italian plants. Then it significantly increased its production outside Italy to take advantage of lower labour costs. Non-Italian operations include factories in North Africa, eastern Europe and Asia. Yet each location operates in a very similar manner. A central, Benetton-owned, operation performs some manufacturing operations (especially those requiring expensive technology) and coordinates the more labour-intensive production activities that are performed by a network of smaller contractors (often owned and managed by ex-Benetton employees). These contractors may in turn sub-contract some of their activities. The company's central facility in Italy allocates production to each of the non-Italian networks, deciding what and how much each is to produce. There is some specialization: for example, jackets are made in eastern Europe while T-shirts are made in Spain. Benetton also has a controlling share in its main supplier of raw materials, to ensure fast supply to its factories. Benetton is also known for the practice of dying garments after assembly rather than using died thread or fabric. This postpones decisions about colours until late in the supply process so that there is a greater chance of producing what is needed by the market.

H&M does not have any factories of its own, but instead works with around 750 suppliers. Around half of production takes place in Europe and the rest mainly in Asia. It has 21 production offices around the world that between them are responsible for coordinating the suppliers which produce over half a billion items a year for H&M. The relationship between production offices and suppliers is vital, because it allows fabrics to be bought in early. The actual dyeing and cutting of the garments can then be decided at a later stage in the production. The later an order can be placed on suppliers, the less the risk of buying the wrong thing. Average supply lead times vary from three weeks up to six months, depending on the nature of the goods. However, 'The most important thing,' H&M says, 'is to find the optimal time to order each item. Short lead times are not always best. Some high-volume fashion basics, it is to our advantage to place orders far in advance. Trendier garments require considerably shorter lead times.'

Zara's lead times are said to be the fastest in the industry, with a 'catwalk to rack' time as little as 15 days. According to one analyst this is because they 'owned most of the manufacturing capability used to make their products, which they use as a means of exciting and stimulating customer demand.' About half of Zara's products are produced in its network of 20 Spanish factories, which, like at Benetton, tended to concentrate on the more capital-intensive operations such as cutting and dying. Sub-contractors are used for most labour-intensive operations like sewing. Zara buys around 40 per cent of its fabric from its own wholly-owned subsidiary, most of which is in undyed form for dying after assembly. Most Zara factories and their sub-contractors work on a single shift system to retain some volume flexibility.

Distribution

Both Benetton and Zara have invested in highly automated warehouses, close to their main production centres that store, pack and assemble individual orders for their retail networks. These automated warehouses represent a major investment for both companies. In 2001, Zara caused some press comment by announcing that it would open a second automated warehouse even though, by its own calculations, it was only using about half its existing warehouse capacity. More recently, Benetton caused some controversy by announcing that it was exploring the use of RFID tags to track its garments.

At H&M, while the stock management is primarily handled internally, physical distribution is sub-contracted.

A large part of the flow of goods is routed from production site to the retail country via H&M's transit terminal in Hamburg. Upon arrival the goods are inspected and allocated to the stores or to the centralized store stock room. The centralized store stock room, within H&M referred to as the 'Call-Off warehouse', replenishes stores on item level according to what is selling.

Retail

All H&M stores (average size, 1,300 square metres) are owned and solely run by H&M. The aim is to 'create a comfortable and inspiring atmosphere in the store that makes it simple for customers to find what they want and to feel at home'. This is similar to Zara stores, although they tend to be smaller (average size, 800 square metres). Perhaps the most remarkable characteristic of Zara stores is that garments rarely stay in the store for longer than two weeks. Because product designs are often not repeated and are produced in relatively small batches, the range of garments displayed in the store can change radically every two or three weeks. This encourages customers both to avoid delaying a purchase and to revisit the store frequently.

Since 2000 Benetton has been reshaping its retail operations. At one time the vast majority of Benetton retail outlets were small shops run by third parties. Now these small stores have been joined by several, Benetton-owned and operated, larger stores (1,500 to 3,000 square metres). These mega-stores can display the whole range of Benetton products and reinforce the Benetton shopping experience.

QUESTION

1. Compare and contrast the approaches taken by H&M, Benetton and Zara to managing their supply networks.

All chapters have 'Problems and applications' questions that will help you practise analysing operations. They can be answered by reading the chapter. Model answers for the first two questions can be found on the companion website for this book.

1 Re-read the 'Operations in practice' example, 'Extracts from Levi Strauss' global sourcing policy'. (a) What do you think motivates a company like Levi Strauss to draw up a policy of this type? (b) What other issues would you include in such a supplier selection policy?

2 A chain of women's apparel retailers had all its products made by Lopez Industries, a small but high-quality garment manufacturer. They worked on the basis of two seasons: spring/summer season and autumn/winter. *'Sometimes we are left with surplus items because our designers have just got it wrong'*, said the retailer's chief designer. *'It is important that we are able to flex our order quantities from Lopez during the season. Although they are a great supplier in many ways, they can't change their production plans at short notice.'* Lopez Industries was aware of this. *'I know that they are happy with our ability to make even the most complex designs to a high level of quality. I also know that they would like us to be more flexible in changing our volumes and delivery schedules. I admit that we could be more flexible within the season. Partly, we can't do this because we have to buy in cloth at the beginning of the season based on the forecast volumes from our customers. Even if we could change our production schedules, we could not get extra deliveries of cloth. We only deal with high-quality and innovative cloth manufacturers who are very large compared to us, so we do not represent much business for them.'* A typical cloth supplier said: *'We compete primarily on quality and innovation. Designing cloth is as much of a fashion business as designing the clothes into which it is made. Our cloth goes to tens of thousands of customers around the world. These vary considerably in their requirements, but presumably all of them value our quality and innovation.'* Use the supply network behavior (gap) model and its gaps to analyse the relationships between the players in this chain.

3 The example of the bullwhip effect shown in Table 12.2 shows how a simple 5 per cent reduction in demand at the end of supply chain causes fluctuations that increase in severity the further back an operation is placed in the chain. (a) Using the same logic and the same rules (i.e. all operations keep one period's inventory), what would the effect on the chain be if demand fluctuated period by period between 100 and 95? That is, period 1 had a demand of 100, period 2 a demand of 95, period 3 a demand of 100, period 4 a demand of 95, and so on? (b) What would happen if all operations in the supply chain decided to keep only half of the periods demand as inventory? (c) Find examples of how supply chains try to reduce this bullwhip effect.

4 If you were the owner of a small local retail shop, what criteria would you use to select suppliers for the goods that you wish to stock in your shop? Visit two or three shops that are local to you and ask the owners how they select their suppliers. In what way were their answers different from what you thought they might be?

5 Many companies devise a policy on ethical sourcing covering such things as workplace standards and business practices, Health and Safety conditions, human rights, legal systems, child labour, disciplinary practices, wages and benefits, etc. (a) What do you think motivates a company to draw up a policy of this type? (b) What other issues would you include in such a supplier selection policy?

6 Airline catering is a tough business. Meals must be of a quality that is appropriate for the class and type of flight, yet the airlines that are their customers are always looking to keep costs as low as possible, menus must change frequently and they must respond promptly to customer feedback. Forecasting passenger numbers is difficult. Suppliers are advised of likely numbers for each flight several days in advance, but the actual minimum number of passengers is only fixed six hours before take-off. Also, flight arrivals can be delayed, upsetting work schedules – even when on time, no more

than 40 minutes are allowed before the flight takes off again. Airline caterers usually produce food on, or near, airports using their own staff. Catering companies' suppliers are also usually airline specialists that are also located near the caterers. A consortium of Northern Foods, a leading food producer that normally supplies retailers, and DHL won a large contract at Heathrow airport against the traditional suppliers. DHL was already a large supplier to 'airside' caterers there with its own premises at the airport. Northern Foods made the food at its existing factories and delivered it to DHL, which assembled it onto airline catering trays and transferred them to the aircraft. (a) Why would an airline use a catering services company rather than organize its own on-board services? (b) What are the main operations objectives that a catering services company must achieve in order to satisfy its customers? (c) Why is it important for airlines to reduce turn-around time when an aircraft lands? (d) Why was the Northern Foods–DHL consortium a threat to more traditional catering companies?

Selected further reading

Akkermans, H. and Voss, C. (2013) The service bullwhip effect, *International Journal of Operations & Production Management,* **vol. 33, no. 6, 765–788.**
An academic paper that deals with the important issue of service supply.

Chopra, S. and Meindl, P. (2015) *Supply Chain Management,* **5th edition, Pearson, Harlow.**
One of the best of the specialist texts.

Christopher, M. (2011) *Logistics and Supply Chain Management: Creating Value-Adding Networks,* **Financial Times Prentice Hall, Harlow.**
Updated version of a classic that gives a comprehensive treatment on supply chain management from a distribution perspective by one of the gurus of supply chain management.

Johnsen, T., Howard, M. and Miemczyk, J. (2014) *Purchasing and Supply Chain Management: A Sustainability Perspective,* **Routledge, Milton.**
Focuses on the important topic of the longer-term implications of global sourcing and sustainability.

Inventory management

KEY QUESTIONS

What is inventory?

Why should there be any inventory?

How much to order? The volume decision

When to place an order? The timing decision

How can inventory be controlled?

INTRODUCTION

Operations managers often have an ambivalent attitude towards inventories. On the one hand, they are costly, sometimes tying up considerable amounts of working capital. They are also risky because items held in stock could deteriorate, become obsolete or just get lost, and, furthermore, they take up valuable space in the operation. On the other hand, they provide some security in an uncertain environment that one can deliver items in stock, should customers demand them. This is the dilemma of inventory management: in spite of the cost and the other disadvantages associated with holding stocks, they do facilitate the smoothing of supply and demand. In fact, inventories only exist because supply and demand are not exactly in harmony with each other.

Figure 13.1 shows where inventory management fits in the overall model of operations management.

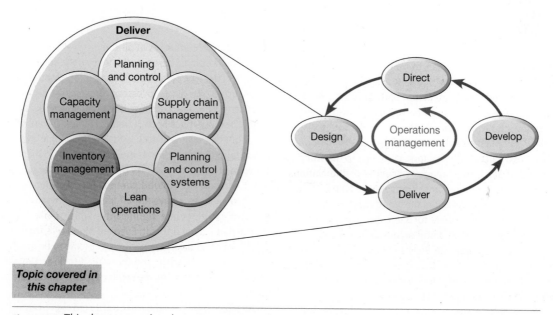

Topic covered in this chapter

Figure 13.1 This chapter examines inventory management

What is inventory?

Inventory is a term used to describe the accumulations of materials, customers or information as they flow through processes or networks. Occasionally the term is also used to describe transforming resources, such as rooms in hotels or automobiles in a vehicle hire firm, but here we use the term for the accumulation of the transformed resources that flow through processes, operations or supply networks. Physical inventory (sometimes called 'stock') is the accumulation of physical materials such as components, parts, finished goods or physical (paper) information records. Queues are accumulations of customers, physical as in a queuing line or people in an airport departure lounge, or waiting for service at the end of phone lines. Databases are stores for accumulations of digital information, such as medical records or insurance details. Managing these accumulations is what we call 'inventory management'. And it is important. Material inventories in a factory can represent a substantial proportion of cash tied up in working capital. Minimizing them can release large quantities of cash. However, reducing them too far can lead to customers' orders not being fulfilled. Customers held up in queues for too long can get irritated, angry, and possibly leave, so reducing revenue. Databases are critical for storing digital information and, while storage may be inexpensive, maintaining databases may not be.

OPERATIONS IN PRACTICE

The blood bank's 'perfect storm'[1]

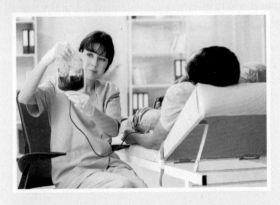

The first successful human-to-human blood transfusion took place 200 years ago. Today, it is a vital part of many aspects of medical treatment, but both the supply of blood and the demand for it can be uncertain. And when, in addition, the consequences of running out of stock can affect people's health, then inventory management becomes a particularly vital task. Welcome to the world of the Blood Stocks Management Scheme of the National Health Service Blood and Transplant (NHSBT) that manages blood stocks across the blood supply chain in the UK. NHSBT is responsible for the collection, processing, testing and issuing of blood across England and North Wales. Each year approximately 2 million blood donations are collected from 1.4 million donors to supply hospitals with all the blood needed for accident and emergency situations and regular medical treatment. Many people owe their lives to transfusions that were made possible by the efficient management of blood, stocked in a supply network that stretches from donation centres through to hospital blood banks. The blood supply chain has three main stages.

▶ *Collection,* which involves recruiting and retaining blood donors, encouraging them to attend donor sessions and transporting the donated blood.
▶ *Processing,* which breaks blood down into its constituent parts.
▶ *Distribution,* which transports blood from blood centres to hospitals in response to both routine and emergency requests.

Inventory accumulates at all three stages, as well as in individual hospitals' blood banks. Within the supply chain some, less than 10 per cent, of donated red blood cells are lost. Much of this is due to losses in processing, but around 5 per cent is not used because it has 'become unavailable', mainly because it has been stored for too long. Part of the inventory management task is to keep this 'time expired' loss to a minimum. In fact, most blood is lost when it is stored in hospital blood banks that are outside the service's direct control. Also, blood components will deteriorate over time. Platelets have a shelf life of only five days and demand can fluctuate significantly which makes stock control particularly difficult. Even red blood cells that have a shelf life of 35 days may not be acceptable to hospitals if they are close to their 'use-by date'. Stock accuracy is crucial. Giving a patient the wrong type of blood can be fatal.

At a local level demand can be affected significantly by accidents. One serious accident involving a cyclist used

750 units of blood, which completely exhausted the available supply (miraculously, he survived). Large-scale accidents usually generate a surge of offers from donors wishing to make immediate donations. There is also a more predictable seasonality to the donating of blood, however, with a low period during the summer vacation. During public holidays and sporting events blood donations drop. For example, on one day when the football World Cup quarter final and Andy Murray's (a British tennis player) Wimbledon semi-final coincided, there was a 12 per cent drop in donations compared with the previous year. Similarly, one summer when public holidays coincided with the Queen's Jubilee, European football events, the London Olympic Games and the Paralympics Games proved particularly difficult. Not only did these events reduce donations (supply), the increased number of visitors to London also increased demand. Before the period NHSBT said that the number of major events would create a 'perfect storm' and dramatically impact the number of blood donations coming in.

All processes, operations and supply networks have inventories

Most things that flow do so in an uneven way. Rivers flow faster down steep sections or where they are squeezed into a ravine. Over relatively level ground they flow slowly, and form pools or even large lakes where there are natural or man-made barriers blocking their path. It is the same in operations. Passengers in an airport flow from public transport or their vehicles then have to queue at several points including check-in, security screening and immigration. They then have to wait (a queue even if they are sitting) again in the departure lounge as they are joined (batched) with other passengers to form a group of several hundred people who are ready to board the aircraft. They are then squeezed down the air bridge as they file in one at a time to board the plane. Likewise, in a tractor assembly plant, stocks of components such as gearboxes, wheels, lighting circuits etc. are brought into the factory in 10s or 100s and are then stored next to the assembly line ready for use. Finished tractors will also be stored until the transporter comes to take them away in ones or 10s to the dealers or directly to the end customer. Similarly, a government tax department collects information about us and our finances from various sources, including our employers, our tax forms, information from banks or other investment companies, and stores this in databases until it is checked, sometimes by people, sometimes automatically, to create our tax codes and/or tax bills. In fact, because most operations involve flows of materials, customers and/or information, at some points they are likely to have material and information inventories and queues of customers waiting for goods or services (see Table 13.1).

Inventories are often the result of uneven flows. If there is a difference between the timing or the rate of supply and demand at any point in a process or network then accumulations will occur. A common analogy is the water tank shown in Figure 13.2. If, over time, the rate of supply of water to the tank differs from the rate at which it is demanded, a tank of water (inventory) will be needed to maintain supply. When the rate of supply exceeds the rate of demand, inventory increases; when the rate of demand exceeds the rate of supply, inventory decreases. So if an operation or process can match supply and demand rates, it will also succeed in reducing its inventory levels. But most organizations must cope with unequal supply and demand, at least at some points in their supply chain. Both the following organizations depend on the ability to manage supply and demand inequality through their inventory management.

There is a complication when using this 'water flow' analogy to represent flows and accumulations (inventories) of information. Inventories of information can either be stored because of uneven flow, in the same way as materials and people, or stored because the operation needs to use the information to process something in the future. For example, an internet retail operation will process each order it receives, and inventories of information may accumulate because of uneven flows as we have described. But, in addition, during order processing customer details could be permanently stored in a database. This information will then be used, not only for future orders from the same customer, but also for other processes, such as targeting promotional activities.

Table 13.1 Examples of inventory held in processes, operations or supply networks

Process, operation or supply network	'Inventories'		
	Physical inventories	Queues of customers	Information in databases
Hotel	Food items, drinks, toilet items	At check-in and check-out	Customer details, loyalty card holders, catering suppliers
Hospital	Dressings, disposable instruments, blood	Patients on a waiting list, patients in bed waiting for surgery, patients in recovery wards	Patient medical records
Credit card application process	Blank cards, form letters	Customers waiting on the phone	Customers' credit and personal information
Computer manufacturer	Components for assembly, packaging materials, finished computers ready for sale	Customers waiting for delivery of their computer	Customers' details, supplier information

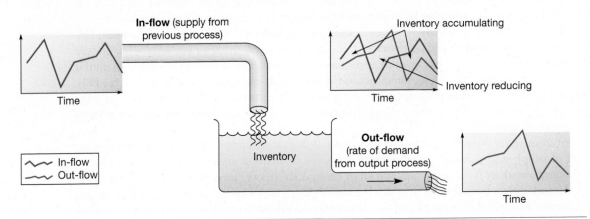

Figure 13.2 Inventory is created to compensate for the differences in timing between supply and demand

In this case the inventory of information has turned from a transformed resource into a transforming resource, because it is being used to transform other information rather than being transformed itself. So, whereas managing physical material concerns ordering and holding the right amounts of goods or materials to deal with the variations in flow, and managing queues is about the level of resources to deal with demand, a database is the accumulation of information but may not cause an interruption to the flow. Managing databases is about the organization of the data, its storage, security and retrieval (access and search).

An inventory of energy?[2]

Inventory exists to smooth out the differences over time between supply and demand. And the bigger the gap between supply and demand, the more useful inventory is. But for some industries there is a big problem – they deal in things that cannot be stored very easily. And probably the best illustration of this is the business of generating and supplying energy. First, demand can fluctuate wildly, especially in countries that use large amounts of energy for cooling or heating. Nor can generating capacity be planned purely on the basis of average demand. In electricity generation, aggregated demand and average usage don't count for much when demand can spike with little warning. Second, supply, especially of the most convenient or cleaner forms of energy is not always available at the right time.

For example, wind does not blow all the time. Worse than that, it tends to be at its strongest at night, when demand is low. Third, in most countries regulators require energy firms to preserve a safety margin over total estimated demand to safeguard a reliable supply to citizens. Finally, energy is not easy to store. It would be ideal if energy firms could easily store excess energy, such as that produced by wind turbines at night, for later use at peak times. This so-called 'time shifting' would counteract the irregular supply from 'green' sources such as wind and solar power, which would make them simpler to integrate into the grid. If energy could be stored it would also permit what energy companies call 'peak shaving', using stored energy instead of having to buy more expensive energy on the spot (short-term) market. So how can energy be stored? Batteries can deliver power for short periods, but are expensive for storing (or discharging) energy at high rates (hundreds of megawatts) or in huge quantities (thousands of megawatt hours). However, this is changing. *'You have seen prices fall through the floor,'* said Claire Curry, a senior analyst at Bloomberg New Energy Finance. *'Batteries have been very expensive,'* she says. *'However, because prices are falling so dramatically we are now seeing some cases where the utility or grid operators see value in a battery.'*

The most practical method of energy storage, and the most widely used, is pumped-storage hydropower (PSH). This method harnesses water and gravity to 'store' off-peak power and release it during periods of high demand by using off-peak electricity to pump water from one reservoir up to another higher one. The water is then released back down to the lower reservoir, when power is needed, through a turbine that produces electricity. The drawback to traditional PSH is that it requires the two reservoirs at different heights. This is why, if greener energy is to be stored, new methods need to be developed. Ideas include using wind turbines to pump water from a deep central reservoir out to sea, which is allowed to flow back into the reservoir through turbines that produce electricity, pumping water to raise a piston that sinks back down through a generator, using modified railway cars on a specially built track that utilize off-peak electricity to get to the top of a hill, and releasing the cars run back down the track so that their motion drives a generator. Other ideas include using compressed air to store the energy, using argon gas to transfer heat between two vast tanks filled with gravel, and storing energy in molten salt. And these are just a few of the different approaches being explored. But for whichever method proves the most effective at creating energy inventories, there will be rewards, both in terms of the potential market and in enabling the better use of sustainable energy.

Why should there be any inventory?

There are plenty of reasons to avoid accumulating inventory where possible. Table 13.2 identifies some of these, particularly those concerned with cost, space, quality and operational/organizational issues.

Table 13.2 Some reasons to avoid inventories

	'Inventories'		
	Physical inventories	Queues of customers	Digital information in databases
Cost	Ties up working capital and there could be high administrative and insurance costs	Primarily time-cost to the customer, i.e. wastes customers' time.	Cost of set-up, access, update and maintenance
Space	Requires storage space	Requires areas for waiting or phone lines for held calls	Requires memory capacity. May require secure and/or special environment
Quality	May deteriorate over time, become damaged or obsolete	May upset customers if they have to wait too long. May lose customers	Data may be corrupted or lost or become obsolete
Operational/ organizational	May hide problems (see Chapter 15 on lean production)	May put undue pressure on the staff and so quality is compromised for throughput	Databases need constant management; access control, updating and security

So why have inventory?

On the face of it, it may seem sensible to have a smooth and even flow of materials, customers and information through operational processes and networks and thus not have any accumulations. In fact, inventories provide many advantages for both operations and their customers. If a customer has to go to a competitor because a part is out of stock or because they have had to wait too long or because the company insists on collecting all their personal details each time they call, the value of inventories seems undisputable. The task of operations management is to allow inventory to accumulate only when its benefits outweigh its disadvantages. The following are some of the benefits of inventory.

▶ **Physical inventory is an insurance against uncertainty** – Inventory can act as a buffer against unexpected fluctuations in supply and demand. For example, a retail operation can never forecast demand perfectly over the lead time. It will order goods from its suppliers such that there is always a minimum level of inventory to cover against the possibility that demand will be greater than expected during the time taken to deliver the goods. This is buffer, or safety inventory. It can also compensate for the uncertainties in the process of the supply of goods into the store. The same applies with the output inventories, which is why hospitals always have a supply of blood, sutures and bandages for immediate response to accident and emergency patients. Similarly, auto servicing services, factories and airlines may hold selected critical spare parts inventories so that maintenance staff can repair the most common faults without delay. Again, inventory is being used as an 'insurance' against unpredictable events.

Operations principle

Inventory should only accumulate when the advantages of having it outweigh its disadvantages.

▶ **Physical inventory can counteract a lack of flexibility** – Where a wide range of customer options is offered, unless the operation is perfectly flexible, stock will be needed to ensure supply when it is engaged on other activities. This is sometimes called cycle inventory. For example, Figure 13.3 shows the inventory profile of a baker who makes three types of bread. Because of the nature of the mixing and baking process, only one kind of bread can be produced at any time. The baker will have to produce each type of bread in batches large enough to satisfy the demand for each kind of bread between the times when each batch is ready for sale. So, even when demand is steady and predictable, there will always be some inventory to compensate for the intermittent supply of each type of bread.

▶ **Physical inventory allows operations to take advantage of short-term opportunities** – Sometimes opportunities arise that necessitate accumulating inventory, even when there is no immediate demand for it. For example, a supplier may be offering a particularly good deal on selected items for a limited time period, perhaps because it wants to reduce its own finished goods inventories. Under these circumstances a purchasing department may opportunistically take advantage of the short-term price advantage.

▶ **Physical inventory can be used to anticipate future demands** – Medium-term capacity management (covered in Chapter 11) may use inventory to cope with demand–capacity differences. Rather than trying to make a product (such as chocolate) only when it is needed, it is produced throughout the year ahead of demand and put into inventory until it is needed. This type of inventory is called anticipation inventory and is most commonly used when demand fluctuations are large but relatively predictable.

▶ **Physical inventory can reduce overall costs** – Holding relatively large inventories may bring savings that are greater than the cost of holding the inventory. This may be when bulk-buying gets the lowest possible cost of inputs, or when large order quantities reduce both the number of orders placed and the associated costs of administration and material handling. This is the basis of the 'economic order quantity' (EOQ) approach that will be treated later in this chapter.

▶ **Physical inventory can increase in value** – Sometimes the items held as inventory can increase in value and so become an investment. For example, dealers in fine wines are less reluctant to hold inventory than dealers in wine that does not get better with age. (However, it can be argued that keeping fine wines until they are at their peak is really part of the overall process rather than inventory as such.) A more obvious example is inventories of money. The many financial processes within most organizations will try to maximize the inventory of cash they hold because it is earning them interest.

▶ **Physical inventory fills the processing 'pipeline'** – 'Pipeline' inventory exists because transformed resources cannot be moved instantaneously between the point of supply and the point of demand. When a retail store places an order, its supplier will 'allocate' the stock to the retail store in its own warehouse, pack it, load it onto its truck, transport it to its destination, and unload it into the retailer's inventory. From the time that stock is allocated (and therefore it is unavailable to any other customer) to the time it becomes available for the retail store, it is pipeline inventory. Especially in geographically dispersed supply networks, pipeline inventory can be substantial.

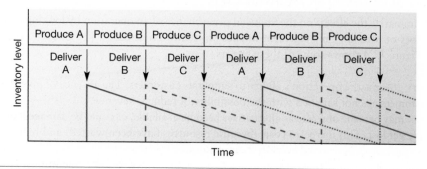

Figure 13.3 Cycle inventory in a bakery

▶ **Queues of customers help balance capacity and demand** – This is especially useful if the main service resource is expensive: for example, doctors, consultants, lawyers or expensive equipment such as CAT scans. By waiting a short time after their arrival, and creating a queue of customers, the service always has customers to process. This is also helpful where arrival times are less predictable: for example, where an appointment system is not used or not possible.

▶ **Queues of customers enable prioritization** – In cases where resources are fixed and customers are entering the system with different levels of priority, the formation of a queue allows the organization to serve urgent customers while keeping other less urgent ones waiting. In some circumstances it is not usual to have to wait 3–4 hours for treatment in an accident and emergency ward, with more urgent cases taking priority.

▶ **Queuing gives customers time to chose** – Time spent in a queue gives customers time to decide what products/services they require: for example, customers waiting in a fast food restaurant have time to look at the menu so that when they get to the counter they are ready to make their order without holding up the server.

▶ **Queues enable efficient use of resources** – By allowing queues to form customers can be batched together to make efficient use of operational resources. For example, a queue for an elevator makes better use of its capacity; in an airport by calling customers to the gate, staff can load the aircraft more efficiently and quickly.

▶ **Databases provide efficient multi-level access** – Databases are relatively cheap ways of storing information and providing many people with access, although there may be restrictions or different levels of access. The doctor's receptionist will be able to call up a patient's records to check name and address and make an appointment, the doctor will then be able to call up the appointment and the patient's records, the pharmacist will be able to call up the patient's name and prescriptions and cross check for other prescriptions and known allergies etc.

▶ **Databases of information allow single data capture** – There is no need to capture data at every transaction with a customer or supplier, though checks may be required.

▶ **Databases of information speed the process** – Amazon, for example, stores, if you agree, your delivery address and credit card information so that purchases can be made with a single click, making it fast and easy for the customer.

Reducing physical inventory

For the remainder of this chapter we will focus on physical inventory largely because this is what most operations managers assume is meant by the term 'inventory'. Moreover, we assume that the objective of those who manage physical inventories is to reduce the overall level (and/or cost) of inventory whilst maintaining an acceptable level of customer service. Table 13.3 identifies some of the ways in which physical inventory may be reduced.

The effect of inventory on return on assets

One can summarize the effects on the financial performance of an operation by looking at how some of the factors of inventory management impact on 'return on assets', a key financial performance measure. Figure 13.4 shows some of these factors.

▶ Inventory governs the operation's ability to supply its customers. The absence of inventory means that customers are not satisfied with the possibility of reduced revenue.

▶ Inventory may become obsolete as alternatives become available, or could be damaged, deteriorate, or simply get lost. This increases costs (because resources have been wasted) and reduces revenue (because the obsolete, damaged or lost items cannot be sold).

▶ Inventory incurs storage costs (leasing space, maintaining appropriate conditions, etc.). These could be high if items are hazardous to store (for example, flammable solvents, explosives, chemicals) or difficult to store requiring special facilities (for example, frozen food).

▶ Inventory involves administrative and insurance costs. Every time a delivery is ordered, time and costs are incurred.

Table 13.3 Some ways in which physical inventory may be reduced

Reason for holding inventory	Example	How inventory could be reduced
As an insurance against uncertainty	Safety stocks for when demand or supply is not perfectly predictable	▶ Improve demand forecasting ▶ Tighten supply, e.g. through service level penalties
To counteract a lack of flexibility	Cycle stock to maintain supply when other products are being made	▶ Increase flexibility of processes, e.g. by reducing changeover times (see Chapter 15) ▶ Using parallel processes producing output simultaneously (see Chapter 6)
To take advantage of relatively short-term opportunities	Suppliers offer 'time limited' special low-cost offers	▶ Persuade suppliers to adopt 'everyday low prices' (see Chapter 12)
To anticipate future demands	Build up stocks in low-demand periods for use in high-demand periods	▶ Increase volume flexibility by moving towards a 'chase demand' plan (see Chapter 11)
To reduce overall costs	Purchasing a batch of products in order to save delivery and administration costs	▶ Reduce administration costs through purchasing process efficiency gains ▶ Investigate alternative delivery channels that reduce transport costs
To fill the processing 'pipeline'	Items being delivered to customer	▶ Reduce process time between customer request and dispatch of items ▶ Reduce throughput time in the downstream supply chain (see Chapter 12)

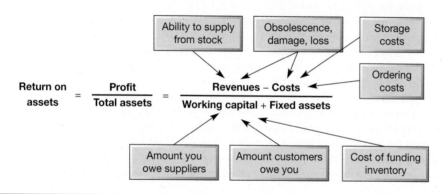

Figure 13.4 Inventory management has a significant effect on return on assets

▶ Inventory ties up money, in the form of working capital, which is therefore unavailable for other uses, such as reducing borrowings or making investment in productive fixed assets (we shall expand on the idea of working capital later).

▶ Inventory contracts with suppliers can dictate the timing of when suppliers need to be paid. If they require paying before the operation receives payment from *its* customers (as is normal), the difference between the amount the operation owes suppliers and the amount suppliers owe the operation adds to working capital requirements.

Operations principle

Inventory management can have a significant effect on return on assets.

Sometimes the cost of too much stock is total destruction[3]

No forecast is (ever) perfect. No inventory decision process is (ever) error-free. Occasionally (usually) businesses end up with either too little or too much inventory to serve their markets. Too little inventory will result in reduced customer service. But too much can be even more problematic, particularly for some businesses that trade in high- value, 'brand integrity' goods. What does a business do, when demand slows and you can't sell any surplus stock without affecting your brand? In 2016, Burberry, the up-market fashion brand, had to defend its decision to destroy £19 million of its products that it could not sell through its discount outlet stores. At its annual meeting in London, the company said that

it was looking to reduce the amount of wasted stock 'every single season', but also said that destroying surplus stock was a common practice among luxury goods companies. The company's outgoing chief executive said: 'We have a process where we have a sale, then packs go to [a discount] outlet . . . There are some raw materials at the end of that process that we do have to destroy because of intellectual property. It is a common practice but it is something we're enormously mindful of. Every single season we look at how we can reduce, and we have reduced it over the years.'

Burberry is not alone. When sales of Cartier and Montblanc products slowed sharply, partly because of a crackdown on corruption in China, the overstocking by dealers, and an uncertain outlook for growth, the Swiss luxury group Richemont that owns the brands bought back stock from some of its Hong Kong dealers. The watches that were bought back were either reallocated to other regions or, in

the case of older models which were no longer selling, were dismantled and recycled. With some luxury goods, the tax rules in some countries actively encourage scrapping surplus stock. For example, if a company makes a bottle of perfume, its cost is a relatively tiny amount (the value comes through advertising and the effect it has on public perception). But the tax loss that the company can claim comes from destroying the product is based on its retail price not production cost. Of course, there are perfectly legitimate reasons for destroying surplus stock. Any business is responsible for protecting its intellectual property and its brand. However, stock destruction as a means of maintaining 'brand integrity' can backfire. After bags of slashed and cut clothing were found outside one of its New York stores, the clothing retailer H&M had to promise that it would stop destroying new, unworn clothing that it could not sell, and would instead donate the garments to charities.

Day-to-day inventory decisions

Wherever inventory accumulates operations managers need to manage the day-to-day tasks of managing inventory. Orders will be received from internal or external customers; these will be dispatched and demand will gradually deplete the inventory. Orders will need to be placed for replenishment of the stocks; deliveries will arrive and require storing. In managing the system, operations managers are involved in three major types of decision:

▶ *How much to order.* Every time a replenishment order is placed, how big should it be (sometimes called the *volume decision*)?
▶ *When to order.* At what point in time, or at what level of stock, should the replenishment order be placed (sometimes called the *timing decision*)?
▶ *How to control the system.* What procedures and routines should be installed to help make these decisions? Should different priorities be allocated to different stock items? How should stock information be stored?

How much to order? The volume decision

To illustrate this decision, consider again the example of the food and drinks we keep at our home. In managing this inventory, we implicitly make decisions on *order quantity,* which is how much to purchase at one time. In making this decision we are balancing two sets of costs: the costs associated with going out to purchase the food items and the costs associated with holding the stocks. The option of holding very little or no inventory of food and purchasing each item only when it is needed has the advantage that it requires little money since purchases are made only when needed. However, it would involve purchasing provisions several times a day, which is inconvenient. At the very opposite extreme, making one journey to the local superstore every few months and purchasing all the provisions we would need until our next visit reduces the time and costs incurred in making the purchase but requires a very large amount of money each time the trip is made – money which could otherwise be in the bank and earning interest. We might also have to invest in extra cupboard units and a very large freezer. Somewhere between these extremes there will lie an ordering strategy which will minimize the total costs and effort involved in the purchase of food.

Inventory costs

The same principles apply in commercial order-quantity decisions as in the domestic situation. In making a decision on how much to purchase, operations managers must try to identify the costs which will be affected by their decision. Earlier we examined how inventory decisions affect some of the important components of return on assets. Here we take a cost perspective and re-examine these components in order to determine which costs go up and which go down as the order quantity increases. In the following list, the first three costs will decrease as order size is increased, whereas the next four generally increase as order size is increased.

1 *Cost of placing the order.* Every time that an order is placed to replenish stock, a number of transactions are needed which incur costs to the company. These include preparing the order, communicating with suppliers, arranging for delivery, making payment, and maintaining internal records of the transaction. Even if we are placing an 'internal order' on part of our own operation, there are still likely to be the same types of transaction concerned with internal administration.

2 *Price discount costs.* Often suppliers offer discounts for large quantities and cost penalties for small orders.

3 *Stockout costs.* If we misjudge the order-quantity decision and our inventory runs out of stock, there will be lost revenue (opportunity costs) of failing to supply customers. External customers may take their business elsewhere, internal customers will suffer process inefficiencies.

4 *Working capital costs.* After receiving a replenishment order, the supplier will demand payment. Of course, eventually, after we supply our own customers, we in turn will receive payment. However, there will probably be a lag between paying our suppliers and receiving payment from our customers. During this time we will have to fund the costs of inventory. This is called the *working capital* of inventory. The costs associated with it are the interest we pay the bank for borrowing it, or the opportunity costs of not investing it elsewhere.

5 *Storage costs.* These are the costs associated with physically storing the goods. Renting, heating and lighting the warehouse, as well as insuring the inventory, can be expensive, especially when special conditions are required such as low temperature or high security.

6 *Obsolescence costs.* When we order large quantities, this usually results in stocked items spending a long time stored in inventory. This increases the risk that the items might either become obsolete (in the case of a change in fashion, for example) or deteriorate with age (in the case of most food-stuffs, for example).

7 *Operating inefficiency costs.* According to just-in-time philosophies, high inventory levels prevent us seeing the full extent of problems within the operation. This argument is fully explored in Chapter 15.

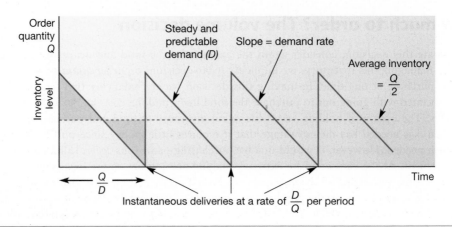

Figure 13.5 Inventory profiles chart the variation in inventory level

It is worth noting that it may not be the same organization that incurs the costs. For example, sometimes suppliers agree to hold consignment stock. This means that they deliver large quantities of inventory to their customers to store but will only charge for the goods as and when they are used. In the meantime, they remain the supplier's property so do not have to be financed by the customer, who does, however, provide storage facilities.

Inventory profiles

An inventory profile is a visual representation of the inventory level over time. Figure 13.5 shows a simplified inventory profile for one particular stock item in a retail operation. Every time an order is placed, Q items are ordered. The replenishment order arrives in one batch instantaneously. Demand for the item is then steady and perfectly predictable at a rate of D units per month. When demand has depleted the stock of the items entirely, another order of Q items instantaneously arrives, and so on. Under these circumstances:

OPERATIONS IN
PRACTICE

Mountains of grit[4]

Students of operations management from Singapore to Saudi Arabia might not have a full appreciation of how important this decision is in the colder parts of the world, but, believe it or not, road gritting is big news every winter where snow and ice can cause huge disruption to everyday life. But not every time it snows and, more interestingly, not everywhere it snows. The local government authorities around northern Europe and America differ significantly in how well they cope with freezing weather, usually by spreading grit (actually rock salt, a mixture of salt and grit) on the roads. So how do the authorities decide how much grit to stock up in preparation for winter, and when to spread it on the roads?

For example, in the UK, when snow is forecast, potential trouble spots are identified by networks of sensors embedded in the road surface to measure climatic conditions. Each sensor is connected by cable or mobile phone technology to an automatic weather station by the roadside. The siting of the sensors is important. They must be sited either on a representative stretch of road (no nearby trees, buildings or bridges, which offer some protection from the cold), or traditional cold spots. The weather stations then beam back data about air and road temperatures, wind speed and direction, and the wetness of roads. Salt levels are also measured to ensure that grit already spread has not been blown away by wind or washed away by rain. It has been known for cold weather to be forecast and the gritting trucks to be dispatched, only for the weather to change, with snow turning to rain, which washed away the grit. Then when temperatures suddenly drop again the rain freezes on the road. But forecasting how much grit will be needed is even more difficult. Long-range weather forecasts are notoriously inaccurate, so no one knows just how bad a coming winter will be. To make matters worse, the need for road grit depends on more than just the total volume of snow. Local authorities can use the same amount of salt on one 30 cm snowfall as one 5 cm snowfall. Furthermore, the number of snowy days is important in determining how much grit will be needed. In the skiing areas of central Europe, most winter days will have snow predictably, while parts of the UK could have little or no snow one winter and many weeks of snow the next.

Supplies of road grit can also vary, as can its price. There are many reasons for this. Mainly of course, if a bad winter is forecast, all authorities in an area will want to buy the same grit, which will reduce supply and put prices up. Also salt mines can flood, especially in winter. Nor is it cheap to transport grit from one area to another; it is a low-value but heavy material. As a consequence, some authorities organize purchasing groups to get better prices before the season starts. Getting more salt during the season may be possible but prices are higher and supply is not guaranteed. In addition, an authority has do decide how fast to use up its inventory of grit. At the start of the winter period, authorities may be cautious about gritting because, once used, the grit cannot be used again, and who knows what the weather will be like later in the season. But in the final analysis the decision of how large an inventory of grit to buy and how to use it is a balance between risks and consequences. Build up too big an inventory of grit and it may not all be used with the cost of carrying it over to next year being borne by local taxpayers. Build up too small an inventory and incur the wrath of local voters when the roads are difficult to negotiate. Of course, a perfect weather forecast would help!

The average inventory $= \dfrac{Q}{2}$ (because the two shaded areas in Figure 13.5 are equal)

The time interval between deliveries $= \dfrac{Q}{D}$

The frequency of deliveries $=$ the reciprocal of the time interval $= \dfrac{D}{Q}$

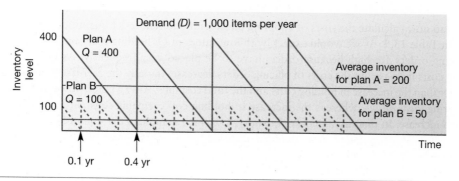

Figure 13.6 Two alternative inventory plans with different order quantities (Q)

The economic order quantity (EOQ) formula

The most common approach to deciding how much of any particular item to order when stock needs replenishing is called the economic order quantity (EOQ) approach. This approach attempts to find the best balance between the advantages and disadvantages of holding stock. For example, Figure 13.6 shows two alternative order-quantity policies for an item. Plan A, represented by the unbroken line, involves ordering in quantities of 400 at a time. Demand in this case is running at 1,000 units per year. Plan B, represented by the dotted line, uses smaller but more frequent replenishment orders. This time only 100 are ordered at a time, with orders being placed four times as often. However, the average inventory for plan B is one-quarter of that for plan A.

To find out whether either of these plans, or some other plan, minimizes the total cost of stocking the item, we need some further information, namely the total cost of holding one unit in stock for a period of time (C_h) and the total costs of placing an order (C_o). Generally, holding costs are taken into account by including:

▶ working capital costs;
▶ storage costs;
▶ obsolescence risk costs.

Order costs are calculated by taking into account:

▶ cost of placing the order (including transportation of items from suppliers if relevant);
▶ price discount costs.

In this case the cost of holding stocks is calculated at £1 per item per year and the cost of placing an order is calculated at £20 per order.

We can now calculate total holding costs and ordering costs for any particular ordering plan as follows:

$$\text{Holding costs} = \text{Holding cost/unit} \times \text{Average inventory}$$

$$= C_h \times \frac{Q}{2}$$

$$\text{Ordering costs} = \text{Ordering cost} \times \text{Number of orders per period}$$

$$= C_o \times \frac{D}{Q}$$

So, total cost,

$$C_t = \frac{C_h Q}{2} + \frac{C_o D}{Q}$$

We can now calculate the costs of adopting plans with different order quantities. These are illustrated in Table 13.4. As we would expect, with low values of Q, holding costs are low but the costs of placing orders are high because orders have to be placed very frequently. As Q increases, the holding costs increase but the costs of placing orders decrease. Initially the decrease in ordering costs is greater than the increase in holding costs and the total cost falls. After a point, however, the decrease in ordering costs slows, whereas the increase in holding costs remains constant and the total cost starts to increase. In this case the order quantity, Q, which minimizes the sum of holding and order costs, is 200. This 'optimum' order quantity is called the *economic order quantity (EOQ)*. This is illustrated graphically in Figure 13.7.

A more elegant method of finding the EOQ is to derive its general expression. This can be done using simple differential calculus as follows. From before:

Table 13.4 Costs of adoption of plans with different order quantities

Demand (D) = 1,000 units per year Order costs (C₀) = £20 per order			Holding costs (Cₕ) = £1 per item per year		
Order quantity (Q)	Holding costs (0.5Q × Cₕ)	+	Order costs((D/Q) × C₀)	=	Total costs
50	25		20 × 20 = 400		425
100	50		10 × 20 = 200		250
150	75		6.7 × 20 = 134		209
200	100		5 × 20 = 100		200*
250	125		3.4 × 20 = 80		205
300	150		2.3 × 20 = 66		216
350	175		9 × 20 = 58		233
400	200		2.5 × 20 = 50		250

* Minimum total cost.

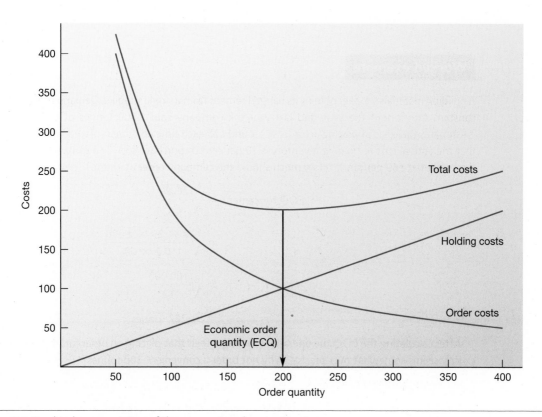

Figure 13.7 Graphical representation of the economic order quantity

$$\text{Total cost} = \text{Holding cost} + \text{Order cost}$$

$$C_t = \frac{C_h Q}{2} + \frac{C_o D}{Q}$$

The rate of change of total cost is given by the first differential of C_t with respect to Q:

$$\frac{dC_t}{dQ} = \frac{C_h}{2} + \frac{C_o D}{Q^2}$$

The lowest cost will occur when $\frac{dC_t}{dQ} = 0$, that is:

$$0 = \frac{C_h}{2} + \frac{C_o D}{Q_o^2} 0 =$$

where Q_o = the EOQ. Rearranging this expression gives:

$$Q_o = EOQ = \sqrt{\frac{2C_o D}{C_h}}$$

When using the EOQ:

$$\text{Time between orders} = \frac{EOQ}{D}$$

$$\text{Order frequency} = \frac{D}{EOQ} \text{ per period}$$

Worked example

A building materials supplier obtains its bagged cement from a single supplier. Demand is reasonably constant throughout the year, and last year the company sold 2,000 tonnes of this product. It estimates the costs of placing an order at around £25 each time an order is placed, and calculates that the annual cost of holding inventory is 20 per cent of purchase cost. The company purchases the cement at £60 per tonne. How much should the company order at a time?

$$EOQ \text{ for cement} = \sqrt{\frac{2C_o D}{C_h}}$$

$$= \sqrt{\frac{2 \times 25 \times 2,000}{0.2 \times 60}}$$

$$= \sqrt{\frac{100,000}{12}}$$

$$= 91.287 \text{ tonnes}$$

After calculating the EOQ the operations manager feels that placing an order for 91.287 tonnes *exactly* seems somewhat over-precise. Why not order a convenient 100 tonnes?

Total cost of ordering plan for $Q = 91.287$:

$$= \frac{C_h Q}{2} + \frac{C_o D}{Q}$$

$$= \frac{(0.2 \times 60) \times 91.287}{2} + \frac{25 \times 2,000}{91.287}$$

$$= £1,095.454$$

Total cost of ordering plan for Q = 100:

$$= \frac{(0.2 \times 60) \times 100}{2} + \frac{25 \times 2{,}000}{100}$$

$$= £1{,}100$$

The extra cost of ordering 100 tonnes at a time is £1,100 − £1,095.45 = £4.55. The operations manager therefore should feel confident in using the more convenient order quantity.

Sensitivity of the EOQ

Examination of the graphical representation of the total cost curve in Figure 13.7 shows that, although there is a single value of Q which minimizes total costs, any relatively small deviation from the EOQ will not increase total costs significantly. In other words, costs will be near-optimum provided a value of Q which is reasonably close to the EOQ is chosen. Put another way, small errors in estimating either holding costs or order costs will not result in a significant deviation from the EOQ. This is a particularly convenient phenomenon because, in practice, both holding and order costs are not easy to estimate accurately.

Operations principle

For any stock replenishment activity there is a theoretical 'optimum' order quantity that minimizes total inventory-related costs.

Gradual replacement – the economic batch quantity (EBQ) model

Although the simple inventory profile shown in Figure 13.5 made some simplifying assumptions, it is broadly applicable in most situations where each complete replacement order arrives at one point in time. In many cases, however, replenishment occurs over a time period rather than in one lot. A typical example of this is where an internal order is placed for a batch of parts to be produced on a machine. The machine will start to produce the parts and ship them in a more or less continuous stream into inventory, but at the same time demand is continuing to remove parts from the inventory. Provided the rate at which parts are being made and put into the inventory (P) is higher than the rate at which demand is depleting the inventory (D) then the size of the inventory will increase. After the batch has been completed the machine will be reset (to produce some other part), and demand will continue to deplete the inventory level until production of the next batch begins. The resulting profile is shown in Figure 13.8. Such a profile is typical for cycle inventories supplied by batch processes, where items are produced internally and intermittently. For this reason, the minimum-cost batch quantity for this profile is called the economic batch quantity (EBQ). It is also sometimes known as the economic manufacturing quantity (EMQ), or the production order quantity (POQ). It is derived as follows:

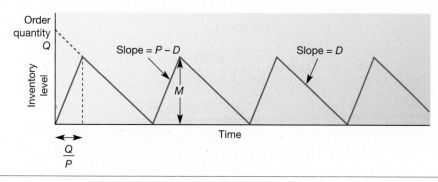

Figure 13.8 Inventory profile for gradual replacement of inventory

$$\text{Maximum stock level} = M$$

$$\text{Slope of inventory build-up} = P - D$$

Also, as is clear from Figure 13.8:

$$\text{Slope of inventory build-up} = M \div \frac{Q}{P}$$

$$= \frac{MP}{Q}$$

So,

$$\frac{MP}{Q} = P - D$$

$$M = \frac{Q(P - D)}{P}$$

$$\text{Average inventory level} = \frac{M}{2}$$

$$= \frac{Q(P - D)}{2P}$$

As before:

$$\text{Total cost} = \text{Holding cost} + \text{Order cost}$$

Worked example

The manager of a bottle-filling plant which bottles soft drinks needs to decide how long a 'run' of each type of drink to process. Demand for each type of drink is reasonably constant at 80,000 per month (a month has 160 production hours). The bottling lines fill at a rate of 3,000 bottles per hour, but take an hour to clean and reset between different drinks. The cost (of labour and lost production capacity) of each of these changeovers has been calculated at £100 per hour. Stock-holding costs are counted at £0.1 per bottle per month.

$$D = 80,000 \text{ per month}$$

$$= 500 \text{ per hour}$$

$$EBQ = \sqrt{\frac{2C_oD}{C_h(1 - (D/P))}}$$

$$= \sqrt{\frac{2 \times 100 \times 80,000}{0.1(1 - (500/3,000))}}$$

$$EBQ = 13,856$$

▶

The staff who operate the lines have devised a method of reducing the changeover time from 1 hour to 30 minutes. How would that change the EBQ?

$$\text{New } C_o = £50$$

$$\text{New EBO} = \sqrt{\frac{2 \times 50 \times 80{,}000}{0.1\left(1\left(500/3{,}000\right)\right)}}$$

$$= 9{,}798$$

$$C_t = \frac{C_h Q (P - D)}{2P} + \frac{C_o}{D}$$

$$\frac{dC_t}{dQ} = \frac{C_h (P - D)}{2P} - \frac{C_o D}{Q^2}$$

Again, equating to zero and solving Q gives the minimum-cost order quantity EBQ:

$$\text{EBQ} = \sqrt{\frac{2C_o D}{C_h (1 - (D/P))}}$$

Critical commentary

The approach to determining order quantity which involves optimizing costs of holding stock against costs of ordering stock, typified by the EOQ and EBQ models, has always been subject to criticisms. Originally these concerned the validity of some of the assumptions of the model; more recently they have involved the underlying rationale of the approach itself. The criticisms fall into four broad categories, all of which we shall examine further.

▶ The assumptions included in the EOQ models are simplistic.

▶ The real costs of stock in operations are not as assumed in EOQ models.

▶ The models are really descriptive, and should not be used as prescriptive devices

▶ Cost minimization is not an appropriate objective for inventory management.

Responding to the criticisms of EOQ

In order to keep EOQ-type models relatively straightforward, it was necessary to make assumptions. These concerned such things as the stability of demand, the existence of a fixed and identifiable ordering cost, that the cost of stock-holding can be expressed by a linear function, shortage costs were identifiable, and so on. While these assumptions are rarely strictly true, most of them can approximate to reality. Furthermore, the shape of the total cost curve has a relatively flat optimum point which means that small errors will not significantly affect the total cost of a near-optimum order quantity. However, at times the assumptions do pose severe limitations to the models. For example, the assumption of steady demand (or even demand which conforms to some known probability distribution) is untrue for a wide range of the operation's inventory problems. For example, a bookseller might be very happy to adopt an EOQ-type ordering policy for some of its most regular and stable products such as dictionaries and popular reference books. However, the demand patterns for many other books could be highly erratic, dependent on critics' reviews and word-of-mouth recommendations. In such circumstances it is simple inappropriate to use EOQ models.

Cost of stock

Other questions surround some of the assumptions made concerning the nature of stock-related costs. For example, placing an order with a supplier as part of a regular and multi-item order might be relatively inexpensive, whereas asking for a special one-off delivery of an item could prove far more costly. Similarly with stock-holding costs – although many companies make a standard percentage charge on the purchase price of stock items, this might not be appropriate over a wide range of stock-holding levels. The marginal costs of increasing stock-holding levels might be merely the cost of the working capital involved. On the other hand, it might necessitate the construction or lease of a whole new stock-holding facility such as a warehouse. Operations managers using an EOQ-type approach must check that the decisions implied by the use of the formulae do not exceed the boundaries within which the cost assumptions apply. In Chapter 15 we explore the 'lean' approach that sees inventory as being largely negative. However, it is useful at this stage to examine the effect on an EOQ approach of regarding inventory as being more costly than previously believed. Increasing the slope of the holding cost line increases the level of total costs of *any* order quantity, but more significantly, shifts the minimum cost point substantially to the left, in favour of a lower economic order quantity. In other words, the less willing an operation is to hold stock on the grounds of cost, the more it should move towards smaller, more frequent ordering.

Using EOQ models as prescriptions

Perhaps the most fundamental criticism of the EOQ approach again comes from the Japanese-inspired 'lean' and JIT philosophies. The EOQ tries to optimize order decisions. Implicitly the costs involved are taken as fixed, in the sense that the task of operations managers is to find out what are the true costs rather than to change them in any way. EOQ is essentially a reactive approach. Some critics would argue that it fails to ask the right question. Rather than asking the EOQ question of 'What is the optimum order quantity?' operations managers should really be asking, 'How can I change the operation in some

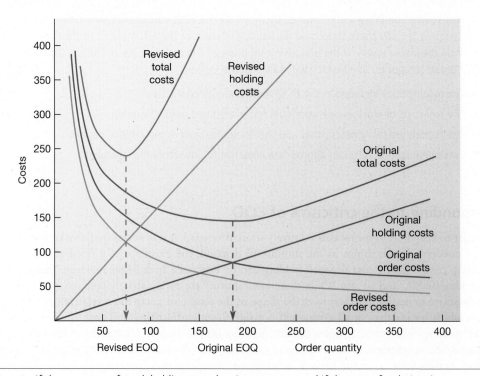

Figure 13.9 If the true costs of stock holding are taken into account, and if the cost of ordering (or changeover) is reduced, the economic order quantity (EOQ) is much smaller

way so as to reduce the overall level of inventory I need to hold?' The EOQ approach may be a reasonable description of stock-holding costs but should not necessarily be taken as a strict prescription over what decisions to take. For example, many organizations have made considerable efforts to reduce the effective cost of placing an order. Often they have done this by working to reduce changeover times on machines. This means that less time is taken changing over from one product to the other, and therefore less operating capacity is lost, which in turn reduces the cost of the changeover. Under these circumstances, the order cost curve in the EOQ formula reduces and, in turn, reduces the effective economic order quantity. Figure 13.9 shows the EOQ formula represented graphically with increased holding costs (see the previous discussion) and reduced order costs. The net effect of this is to significantly reduce the value of the EOQ.

Should the cost of inventory be minimized?

Many organizations (such as supermarkets and wholesalers) make most of their revenue and profits simply by holding and supplying inventory. Because their main investment is in the inventory, it is critical that they make a good return on this capital, by ensuring that it has the highest possible 'stock turn' (defined later in this chapter) and/or gross profit margin. Alternatively, they may also be concerned to maximize the use of space by seeking to maximize the profit earned per square metre. The EOQ model does not address these objectives. Similarly for products that deteriorate or go out of fashion, the EOQ model can result in excess inventory of slower-moving items. In fact, the EOQ model is rarely used in such organizations, and there is more likely to be a system of periodic review (described later) for regular ordering of replenishment inventory. For example, a typical builders' supply merchant might carry around 50,000 different items of stock (SKUs). However, most of these cluster into larger families of items such as paints, sanitary ware or metal fixings. Single orders are placed at regular intervals for all the required replenishments in the supplier's range, and these are then delivered together at one time. For example, if such deliveries were made weekly, then on average, the individual item order quantities will be for only one week's usage. Less popular items, or ones with erratic demand patterns, can be individually ordered at the same time, or (when urgent) can be delivered the next day by carrier.

If customers won't wait – the news vendor problem

A special case of the inventory order-quantity decision is when an order quantity is purchased for a specific event or time period, after which the items are unlikely to be sold. A simple example of this is the decision taken by a newspaper vendor of how many newspapers to stock for the day. If the news vendor should run out of papers, customers will either go elsewhere or decide not to buy a paper that day. Newspapers left over at the end of the day are worthless and demand for the newspapers varies day-by-day. In deciding how many newspapers to carry, the newsvendor is in effect balancing the risk and consequence of running out of newspapers against that of having newspapers left over at the end of the day. Retailers and manufacturers of high-class leisure products, such as some books and popular music CDs, face the same problem. For example, a concert promoter needs to decide how many concert T-shirts to order emblazoned with the logo of the main act. The profit on each T-shirt sold at the concert is £5 and any unsold T-shirts are returned to the company that supplies them, but at a loss to the promoter of £3 per T-shirt. Demand is uncertain but is estimated to be between 200 and 1,000. The probabilities of different demand are as follows:

Demand level	200	400	600	800
Probability	0.2	0.3	0.4	0.1

How many T-shirts should the promoter order? Table 13.5 shows the profit which the promoter would make for different order quantities and different levels of demand.

Inventory management at Flame Electrical

Inventory management in some operations is more than just a part of their responsibility; it is their very reason for being in business. Flame Electrical is South Africa's largest independent supplier and distributor of lamps. It stocks almost 3,000 different types of lamp, which are sourced from 14 countries and distributed to customers through-out the country. *'In effect our customers are using us to manage their stocks of lighting sources for them,'* said Jeff Schaffer, the Managing Director of Flame Electrical. *'They could, if they wanted to, hold their own stock but might not want to devote the time, space, money or effort to doing so. Using us they get the widest range of products to choose from, and an accurate, fast and dependable service.'*

Orders for the replenishment of stocks in the warehouse are triggered by a re-order point system. The re-order point for each stocked item takes into account the likely demand for the product during the order lead time (forecast from the equivalent period's orders the previous year), the order lead time for the item (which varies from 24 hours to four months) and the variability of the lead time (from previous experience). Flame prefers most orders to its suppliers to be for a whole number of container loads (the shipping costs for part-container loads being more expensive). However, lower order quantities of small or expensive lamps may be used. The order quantity for each lamp is based on its demand, its value and the cost of transporta-tion from the suppliers. However, all this could be overridden in an emergency. If a customer, such as a hospi-tal, urgently needs a particular lamp which is not in stock, the company will even use a fast courier to fly the item in from overseas – all for the sake of maintaining its reputa-tion for high service levels.

'We have to get the balance right,' says Jeff Schaffer. 'Excellent service is the foundation of our success. But we could not survive if we did not control stocks tightly. After all we are carrying the cost of every lamp in our warehouse until the customer eventually pays for it. If stock levels were too high, we just could not operate profitably. It is for that reason that we go as far as to pay incentives to the relevant staff based on how well they keep our working capital and stocks under control.'

We can now calculate the expected profit which the promoter will make for each order quantity by weighting the outcomes by their probability of occurring.

If the promoter orders 200 T-shirts:

$$\text{Expected profit} = 1{,}000 \times 0.2 + 1{,}000 \times 0.3 + 1{,}000 \times 0.4 + 1{,}000 \times 0.1$$

$$= \pounds1{,}000$$

If the promoter orders 400 T-shirts:

$$\text{Expected profit} = 400 \times 0.2 + 2{,}000 \times 0.3 + 2{,}000 \times 0.4 + 2{,}000 \times 0.1$$

$$= \pounds1{,}680$$

Table 13.5 Pay-off matrix for T-shirt order quantity (profit or loss in £s)

Demand level	200	400	600	800
Probability	0.2	0.3	0.4	0.1
Promoter orders 200	1,000	1,000	1,000	1,000
Promoter orders 400	400	2,000	2,000	2,000
Promoter orders 600	−200	1,400	3,000	3,000
Promoter orders 800	−800	800	2,400	4,000

If the promoter orders 600 T-shirts:

$$\text{Expected profit} = -200 \times 0.2 + 1{,}400 \times 0.3 + 3000 \times 0.4 + 3{,}000 \times 0.1$$

$$= £1{,}880$$

If the promoter orders 800 T-shirts:

$$\text{Expected profit} = -800 \times 0.2 + 800 \times 0.3 + 2{,}400 \times 0.4 + 4{,}000 \times 0.1$$

$$= £1{,}440$$

The order quantity which gives the maximum profit is 600 T-shirts, which results in a profit of £1,880.

The importance of this approach lies in the way it takes a probabilistic view of part of the inventory calculation (demand). We will return to this later in the chapter.

Mr Ruben's bakery[5]

Be careful about treating the newsvendor problem on a product-by-product basis. It is a powerful idea, but needs to be seen in context. Take the famous (in New York) City Bakery, in Manhattan. It is run by Maury Rubin, a master baker, who knows the economics of baking fresh products. Ingredients and rent are expensive. It costs Mr Rubin $2.60 to make a $3.50 croissant. If he makes 100 and sells 70, he earns $245 but his costs are $260, and because all goods are sold within a day (his quality standards mean that he won't sell leftovers), he loses money. Nor can he raise his prices. In his competitive market, he says, shoppers bristle when the cost of baked goods passes a certain threshold. However, Mr Ruben has two 'solutions'. First, he can subsidize his croissants by selling higher-margin items such as fancy salads and sandwiches. Second, he uses data to cut waste, by studying sales so that he can detect demand trends and fine-tune supply. He monitors the weather carefully (demand drops away when it rains) and carefully inspects

school calendars so he can reduce the quantities he bakes during school holidays. Each day in the morning, he makes sure that pastries are prepared, but then he checks sales every 60 × 90 minutes before making the decision to adjust supply or not. Only when the numbers are in do the pastries go into the oven. Having no croissants left by the end of the day is a sign of success.

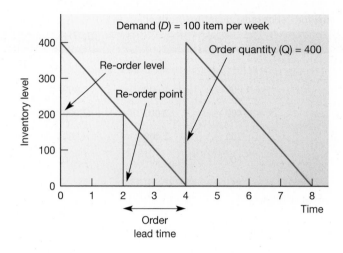

Figure 13.10 Re-order level (ROL) and re-order point (ROP) are derived from the order lead time and demand rate

When to place an order? The timing decision

When we assumed that orders arrived instantaneously and demand was steady and predictable, the decision on when to place a replenishment order was self-evident. An order would be placed as soon as the stock level reached zero. This would arrive instantaneously and prevent any stock-out occurring. If replenishment orders do not arrive instantaneously, but have a lag between the order being placed and it arriving in the inventory, we can calculate the timing of a replacement order as shown in Figure 13.10. The lead time for an order to arrive is in this case two weeks, so the re-order point (ROP) is the point at which stock will fall to zero minus the order lead time. Alternatively, we can define the point in terms of the level which the inventory will have reached when a replenishment order needs to be placed. In this case this occurs at a re-order level (ROL) of 200 items.

However, this assumes that both the demand and the order lead time are perfectly predictable. In most cases, of course, this is not so. Both demand and the order lead time are likely to vary to produce a profile which looks something like that in Figure 13.11. In these circumstances it is necessary to make the replenishment order somewhat earlier than would be the case in a purely deterministic situation. This will result in, on average, some stock still being in the inventory

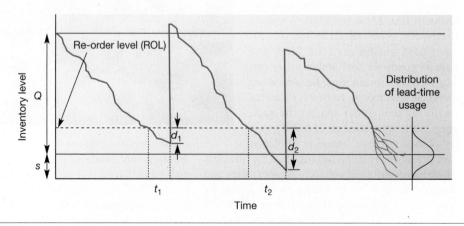

Figure 13.11 Safety stock (s) helps to avoid stockouts when demand and/or order lead time are uncertain

when the replenishment order arrives. This is buffer (safety) stock. The earlier the replenishment order is placed, the higher will be the expected level of safety stock (s) when the replenishment order arrives. But because of the variability of both lead time (t) and demand rate (d), there will sometimes be a higher-than-average level of safety stock and sometimes lower. The main consideration in setting safety stock is not so much the average level of stock when a replenishment order arrives but rather the probability that the stock will not have run out before the replenishment order arrives.

The key statistic in calculating how much safety stock to allow is the probability distribution which shows the lead-time usage. The lead-time usage distribution is a combination of the distributions

Worked example

A company which imports running shoes for sale in its sports shops can never be certain of how long, after placing an order, the delivery will take. Examination of previous orders reveals that out of 10 orders: one took one week, two took two weeks, four took three weeks, two took four weeks and one took five weeks. The rate of demand for the shoes also varies between 110 pairs per week and 140 pairs per week. There is a 0.2 probability of the demand rate being either 110 or 140 pairs per week, and a 0.3 chance of demand being either 120 or 130 pairs per week. The company needs to decide when it should place replenishment orders if the probability of a stockout is to be less than 10 per cent.

Both lead time and the demand rate during the lead time will contribute to the lead-time usage. So the distributions which describe each will need to be combined. Figure 13.12 and Table 13.6 show how this can be done. Taking lead time to be either one, two, three, four or five weeks, and demand rate to be either 110, 120, 130 or 140 pairs per week, and also assuming the two variables to be independent, the distributions can be combined as shown in Table 13.6. Each element in the matrix shows a possible lead-time usage with the probability of its occurrence. So if the lead time is one week and the demand rate is 110 pairs per week, the actual lead-time usage will be

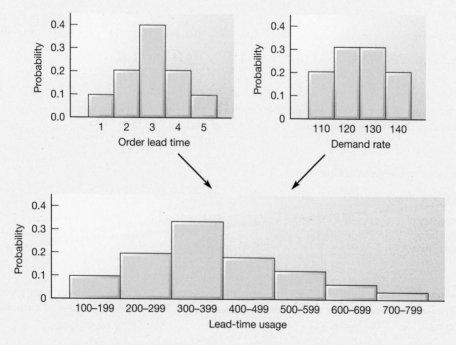

Figure 13.12 The probability distributions for order lead time and demand rate combine to give the lead-time usage distribution

Table 13.6 Matrix of lead-time and demand-rate probabilities

			Lead-time probabilities				
			1	2	3	4	5
			0.1	0.2	0.4	0.2	0.1
	110	0.2	110	220	330	440	550
			(0.02)	(0.04)	(0.08)	(0.04)	(0.02)
Demand-rate probabilities	120	0.3	120	240	360	480	600
			(0.03)	(0.06)	(0.12)	(0.06)	(0.03)
	130	0.3	130	260	390	520	650
			(0.03)	(0.06)	(0.12)	(0.06)	(0.03)
	140	0.2	140	280	420	560	700
			(0.02)	(0.04)	(0.08)	(0.04)	(0.02)

$1 \times 110 = 110$ pairs. Since there is a 0.1 chance of the lead time being one week, and a 0.2 chance of demand rate being 110 pairs per week, the probability of both these events occurring is $0.1 \times 0.2 = 0.02$.

We can now classify the possible lead-time usages into histogram form. For example, summing the probabilities of all the lead-time usages which fall within the range 100–199 (all the first column) gives a combined probability of 0.1. Repeating this for subsequent intervals results in Table 13.7.

Table 13.7 Combined probabilities

Lead-time usage	100–199	200–299	300–399	400–499	500–599	600–699	700–799
Probability	0.1	0.2	0.32	0.18	0.12	0.06	0.02

This shows the probability of each possible range of lead-time usage occurring, but it is the cumulative probabilities that are needed to predict the likelihood of stockout (see Table 13.8).

Table 13.8 Combined probabilities

Lead-time usage X	100	200	300	400	500	600	700	800
Probability of usage being greater than X	1.0	0.9	0.7	0.38	0.2	0.08	0.02	0

Setting the re-order level at 600 would mean that there is only a 0.08 chance of usage being greater than available inventory during the lead time, i.e. there is a less than 10 per cent chance of a stockout occurring.

which describe lead-time variation and the demand rate during the lead time. If safety stock is set below the lower limit of this distribution then there will be shortages every single replenishment cycle. If safety stock is set above the upper limit of the distribution, there is no chance of stockouts occurring. Usually, safety stock is set to give a predetermined likelihood that stockouts will not occur. Figure 13.11 shows that, in this case, the first replenishment order arrived after t_1, resulting in a lead-time usage of d_1. The second replenishment order took longer, t_2, and demand rate was also higher, resulting in a lead-time usage of d_2. The third order cycle shows several possible inventory profiles for different conditions of lead-time usage and demand rate.

Operations principle

For any stock replenishment activity, the timing of replenishment should reflect the effects of uncertain lead time and uncertain demand during that lead time.

Continuous and periodic review

The approach we have described to making the replenishment timing decision is often called the continuous review approach. This is because, to make the decision in this way, there must be a process to review the stock level of each item continuously and then place an order when the stock level reaches its re-order level. The virtue of this approach is that, although the timing of orders may be irregular (depending on the variation in demand rate), the order size (Q) is constant and can be set at the optimum economic order quantity. Such continual checking on inventory levels can be time consuming, especially when there are many stock withdrawals compared with the average level of stock, but in an environment where all inventory records are computerized, this should not be a problem unless the records are inaccurate.

An alternative and far simpler approach, but one which sacrifices the use of a fixed (and therefore possibly optimum) order quantity, is called the periodic review approach. Here, rather than ordering at a predetermined re-order level, the periodic approach orders at a fixed and regular time interval. So the stock level of an item could be found, for example, at the end of every month and a replenishment order placed to bring the stock up to a predetermined level. This level is calculated to cover demand between the replenishment order being placed and the following replenishment order arriving. Figure 13.13 illustrates the parameters for the periodic review approach.

At time T_1 in Figure 13.13 the inventory manager would examine the stock level and order sufficient to bring it up to some maximum, Q_m. However, that order of Q_1 items will not arrive until a further time of t_1 has passed, during which demand continues to deplete the stocks. Again, both demand and lead time are uncertain. The Q_1 items will arrive and bring the stock up to some level lower than Q_m (unless there has been no demand during t_1). Demand then continues until T_2, when again an order Q_2 is placed which is the difference between the current stock at T_2 and Q_m. This order arrives after t_2, by which time demand has depleted the stocks further. Thus the replenishment order placed at T_1 must be able to cover for the demand which occurs until T_2 and t_2. Safety stocks will need to be calculated, in a similar manner to before, based on the distribution of usage over this period.

The time interval

The interval between placing orders, t_1, is usually calculated on a deterministic basis, and derived from the EOQ. So, for example, if the demand for an item is 2,000 per year, the cost of placing an order £25, and the cost of holding stock £0.5 per item per year:

$$EOQ = \sqrt{\frac{2C_oD}{C_h}} = \sqrt{\frac{2 \times 2,000 \times 25}{0.5}} = 447$$

The optimum time interval between orders, t_f, is therefore:

$$t_f = \frac{EOQ}{D} = \frac{447}{2,000} \text{ years}$$

$$= 2.68 \text{ mouths}$$

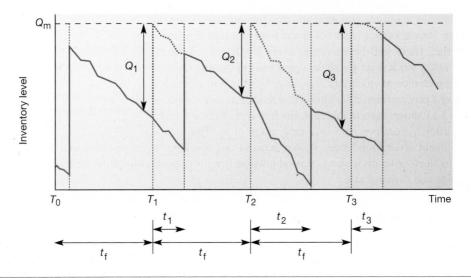

Figure 13.13 A periodic review approach to order timing with probabilistic demand and lead time

It may seem paradoxical to calculate the time interval assuming constant demand when demand is, in fact, uncertain. However, uncertainties in both demand and lead time can be allowed for by setting Q_m to allow for the desired probability of stockout based on usage during the period t_f + lead time.

Two-bin and three-bin systems

Keeping track of inventory levels is especially important in continuous review approaches to re-ordering. A simple and obvious method of indicating when the re-order point has been reached is necessary, especially if there are a large number of items to be monitored. The two- and three-bin systems illustrated in Figure 13.14 are such methods. The simple two-bin system involves storing the re-order point quantity plus the safety inventory quantity in the second bin and using parts from the first bin. When the first bin empties, that is the signal to order the next re-order quantity. Sometimes the safety inventory is stored in a third bin (the three-bin system), so it is clear when demand is exceeding that which was expected. Different 'bins' are not always necessary to operate this type of system. For example, a common practice in retail operations is to store the second 'bin' quantity upside-down behind or under the first 'bin' quantity. Orders are then placed when the upside-down items are reached.

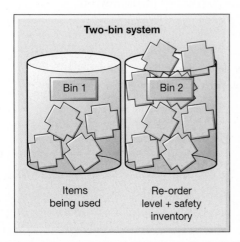
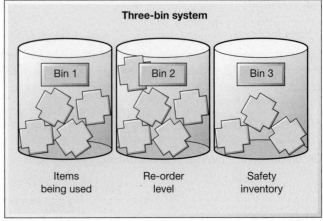

Figure 13.14 The two-bin and three-bin systems of re-ordering

Amazon's 'anticipatory shipping'[6]

Forecast accuracy and time to deliver are related. Poor forecasts mean that the wrong items will be stored, which in turn means that delivery will be delayed until the right items are received. But what if a supplier could know what its customers were going to order, even before they do? That is the ambition of Amazon's online retail operation. It filed a patent to protect the technology that aims to predict what its customers will buy, even before they have clicked the 'order' button. The company, which is the world's largest online retailer, calls its new system 'anticipatory shipping' and perceives it as a way to speed up its delivery times. Amazon's patient application reveals the thinking behind the system. Its application says that: *'One substantial disadvantage to the virtual storefront model is that in many instances, customers cannot receive their merchandise immediately upon purchase, but must instead wait for product to be shipped to them. The availability of expedited shipping methods from various common carriers may mitigate the delay in shipment, but often at substantial additional cost that may rival the price paid for the merchandise. Such delays may dissuade customers from buying items from online merchants,*

particularly if those items are more readily available locally.' The approach is reported as using several elements to predict what purchases a person may make. Factors to be taken into account could include age, income, previously purchased items, searched-for items, 'wish lists' and maybe even the time a user's cursor lingers over a product. Armed with this information, Amazon could ship items that are likely to be ordered to the inventory 'hub' nearest to the customer. So, when a customer really does order the item it can be delivered far faster.

How can inventory be controlled?

The models we have described, even the ones which take a probabilistic view of demand and lead time, are still simplified compared with the complexity of real stock management. Coping with many thousands of stocked items, supplied by many hundreds of different suppliers, with possibly tens of thousands of individual customers, makes for a complex and dynamic operations task. In order to control such complexity, operations managers have to do two things. First, they have to discriminate between different stocked items, so that they can apply a degree of control to each item which is appropriate to its importance. Second, they need to invest in an information-processing system which can cope with their particular set of inventory control circumstances.

Inventory priorities – the ABC system

In any inventory which contains more than one stocked item, some items will be more important to the organization than others. Some, for example, might have a very high usage rate, so if they ran out many customers would be disappointed. Other items might be of particularly high value, so excessively high inventory levels would be particularly expensive. One common way of discriminating between different stock items is to rank them by the usage value (their usage rate multiplied by their individual value). Items with a particularly high usage value are deemed to warrant the most careful control, whereas those with low usage values need not be controlled quite so rigorously. Generally, a relatively small proportion of the total range of items contained in an inventory will account for a large proportion of the total usage value. This phenomenon is known as the Pareto law (after the person who described it), sometimes referred to as the 80/20 rule. It is called this because, typically, 80 per cent of an operation's sales are accounted for by only 20 per cent of all stocked item types. The Pareto law is also used elsewhere in operations management (see, for example, Chapter 16). Here the relationship can be used to classify the different types of items kept in an inventory by their usage value. ABC inventory control allows inventory managers to concentrate their efforts on controlling the more significant items of stock.

▶ *Class A items* are those 20 per cent or so high-usage value items which account for around 80 per cent of the total usage value.

Worked example

Table 13.9 shows all the parts stored by an electrical wholesaler. The 20 different items stored vary in terms of both their usage per year and cost per item, as shown. However, the wholesaler has ranked the stock items by their usage value per year. The total usage value per year is £5,569,000. From this it is possible to calculate the usage value per year of each item as a percentage of the total usage value, and from that a running cumulative total of the usage value, as shown. The wholesaler can then plot the cumulative percentage of all stocked items against the cumulative percentage of their value. So, for example, the part with stock number A/703 is the highest-value part and accounts for 25.14 per cent of the total inventory value. As a part, however, it is only one-twentieth or 5 per cent of the total number of items stocked. This item and the next highest-value item (D/012) account for only 10 per cent of the total number of items stocked, yet account for 47.37 per cent of the value of the stock, and so on.

This is shown graphically in Figure 13.15. Here the wholesaler has classified the first four part numbers (20 per cent of the range) as Class A items and will monitor the usage and ordering of these items very closely and frequently. A few improvements in order quantities or safety stocks for these items could bring significant savings. The six next part numbers C/375 through to A/138 (30 per cent of the range) are to be treated as Class B items with slightly less effort devoted to their control. All other items are classed as Class C items whose stocking policy is reviewed only occasionally.

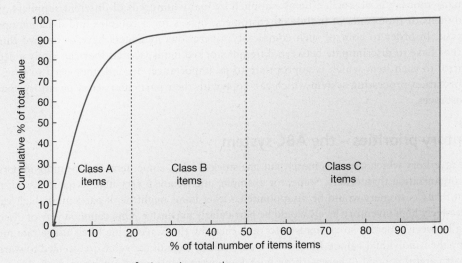

Figure 13.15 Pareto curve for items in a warehouse

Table 13.9 Warehouse items ranked by usage value

Stock no.	Usage (items/year)	Cost (£/item)	Usage value (£000/year)	% of total value	Cumulative % of total value
A/703	700	20.00	1,400	25.14	25.14
D/012	450	2.75	1,238	22.23	47.37
A/135	1,000	0.90	900	16.16	63.53
C/732	95	8.50	808	14.51	78.04
C/375	520	0.54	281	5.05	83.09
A/500	73	2.30	168	3.02	86.11
D/111	520	0.22	114	2.05	88.16
D/231	170	0.65	111	1.99	90.15
E/781	250	0.34	85	1.53	91.68
A/138	250	0.30	75	1.34	93.02
D/175	400	0.14	56	1.01	94.03
E/001	80	0.63	50	0.89	94.92
C/150	230	0.21	48	0.86	95.78
F/030	400	0.12	48	0.86	96.64
D/703	500	0.09	45	0.81	97.45
D/535	50	0.88	44	0.79	98.24
C/541	70	0.57	40	0.71	98.95
A/260	50	0.64	32	0.57	99.52
B/141	50	0.32	16	0.28	99.80
D/021	20	0.50	10	0.20	100.00
Total			5,569	100.00	

▶ *Class B items* are those of medium usage value, usually the next 30 per cent of items, which often account for around 10 per cent of the total usage value.

▶ *Class C items* are those low usage value items which, although comprising around 50 per cent of the total types of items stocked, probably only account for around 10 per cent of the total usage value of the operation.

Although annual usage and value are the two criteria most commonly used to determine a stock classification system, other criteria might also contribute towards the (higher) classification of an item:

▶ *Consequence of stockout.* High priority might be given to those items which would seriously delay or disrupt other operations, or the customers, if they were not in stock.

▶ *Uncertainty of supply.* Some items, although of low value, might warrant more attention if their supply is erratic or uncertain.

▶ *High obsolescence or deterioration risk.* Items which could lose their value through obsolescence or deterioration might need extra attention and monitoring.

Some more complex stock classification systems might include these criteria by classifying on an A, B, C basis for each. For example, a part might be classed as A/B/A, meaning it is an A category item by value, a class B item by consequence of stockout and a class A item by obsolescence risk.

Critical commentary

This approach to inventory classification can sometimes be misleading. Many professional inventory managers point out that the Pareto law is often misquoted. It does not say that 80 per cent of the SKUs (stock keeping units) account for only 20 per cent of inventory value. It accounts for 80 per cent of inventory 'usage' or throughput value; in other words, sales value. In fact, it is the slow-moving items (the C category items) that often pose the greatest challenge in inventory management. Often these slow-moving items, although only accounting for 20 per cent of sales, require a large part (typically between one-half and two-thirds) of the total investment in stock. This is why slow-moving items are a real problem. Moreover, if errors in forecasting or ordering result in excess stock in 'A class' fast-moving items, it is relatively unimportant in the sense that excess stock can be sold quickly. However, excess stock in slow-moving C items will be there a long time. According to some inventory managers, it is the A items that can be left to look after themselves; it is the B and even more the C items that need controlling.

Measuring inventory

In our example of ABC classifications, we used the monetary value of the annual usage of each item as a measure of inventory usage. Monetary value can also be used to measure the absolute level of inventory at any point in time. This would involve taking the number of each item in stock, multiplying it by its value (usually the cost of purchasing the item) and summing the value of all the individual items stored. This is a useful measure of the investment that an operation has in its inventories but gives no indication of how large that investment is relative to the total throughput of the operation. To obtain this we must compare the total number of items in stock against their rate of usage. There are two ways of doing this. The first is to calculate the amount of time the inventory

Worked example

Table 13.10 Stock, cost and demand for three stocked items

Item	Average number in stock	Cost per item (£)	Annual demand
Chateau A	500	3.00	2,000
Chateau B	300	4.00	1,500
Chateau C	200	5.00	1,000

A small specialist wine importer holds stocks of three types of wine, Chateau A, Chateau B and Chateau C. Current stock levels are 500 cases of Chateau A, 300 cases of Chateau B, and 200 cases of Chateau C. Table 13.10 shows the number of each held in stock, their cost per item and the demand per year for each.

$$\text{The total value of stock} = \Sigma(\text{average stock level} \times \text{cost per item})$$

$$= (500 \times 3) + (300 \times 4) + (200 \times 5)$$

$$= 3{,}700$$

The amount of *stock cover* provided by each item stocked is as follows (assuming 50 sales weeks per year):

$$\text{Chateau A, stock cover} = \frac{\text{Stock}}{\text{Demand}} = \frac{500}{2{,}000} \times 50 = 12.5 \text{ weeks}$$

$$\text{Chateau B, stock cover} = \frac{\text{Stock}}{\text{Demand}} = \frac{300}{1{,}500} \times 50 = 10 \text{ weeks}$$

$$\text{Chateau C, stock cover} = \frac{\text{Stock}}{\text{Demand}} = \frac{200}{1{,}000} \times 50 = 10 \text{ weeks}$$

The *stock turn* for each item is calculated as follows:

$$\text{Chateau A, stock turn} = \frac{\text{Demand}}{\text{Stock}} = \frac{2{,}000}{500} = 4 \text{ times/year}$$

$$\text{Chateau B, stock turn} = \frac{\text{Demand}}{\text{Stock}} = \frac{1{,}500}{300} = 5 \text{ times/year}$$

$$\text{Chateau C, stock turn} = \frac{\text{Demand}}{\text{Stock}} = \frac{1{,}000}{200} = 5 \text{ times/year}$$

To find the average stock cover or stock turn for the total items in the inventory, the individual item measures can be weighted by their demand levels as a proportion of total demand (4,500). Thus:

$$\text{Average stock cover} = \left(12.5 \times \frac{2{,}000}{4{,}500}\right) + \left(10 \times \frac{1{,}500}{4{,}500}\right) + \left(10 \times \frac{1{,}000}{4{,}000}\right)$$

$$= 11.11$$

$$\text{Average stock turn} = \left(4 \times \frac{2{,}000}{4{,}500}\right) + \left(5 \times \frac{1{,}500}{4{,}500}\right) + \left(5 \times \frac{1{,}000}{4{,}500}\right)$$

$$= 4.56$$

would last, subject to normal demand, if it were not replenished. This is sometimes called the number of weeks' (or days', months', years' etc.) *cover* of the stock. The second method is to calculate how often the stock is used up in a period, usually one year. This is called the stock turn or turnover of stock and is the reciprocal of the stock-cover figure mentioned earlier.

Inventory information systems

Most inventories of any significant size are managed by computerized systems. The many relatively routine calculations involved in stock control lend themselves to computerized support. This is especially so since data capture has been made more convenient through the use of bar-code readers and the point-of-sale recording of sales transactions. Many commercial systems of stock control are available, although they tend to share certain common functions.

Updating stock records

Every time a transaction takes place (such as the sale of an item, the movement of an item from a warehouse into a truck, or the delivery of an item into a warehouse) the position, status and possibly value of the stock will have changed. This information must be recorded so that operations managers can determine their current inventory status at any time.

Generating orders

The two major decisions we have described previously, namely how much to order and when to order, can both be made by a computerized stock control system. The first decision, setting the value of how much to order (Q), is likely to be taken only at relatively infrequent intervals. Originally almost all computer systems automatically calculated order quantities by using the EOQ formulae covered earlier. Now more sophisticated algorithms are used, often using probabilistic data and based on examining the marginal return on investing in stock. The system will hold all the information which goes into the ordering algorithm but might periodically check to see if demand or order lead times, or any of the other parameters, have changed significantly and recalculate Q accordingly. The decision on when to order, on the other hand, is a far more routine affair which computer systems make according to whatever decision rules operations managers have chosen to adopt: either continuous review or periodic review. Furthermore, the systems can automatically generate whatever documentation is required, or even transmit the re-ordering information electronically through an electronic data interchange (EDI) system.

Generating inventory reports

Inventory control systems can generate regular reports of stock value for the different items stored, which can help management monitor its inventory control performance. Similarly, customer service performance, such as the number of stockouts or the number of incomplete orders, can be regularly

---

Toilet roll delay[7]

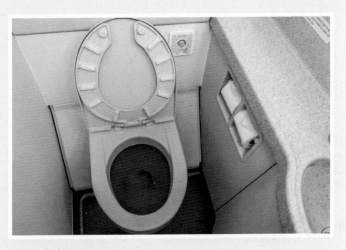

Inventory management systems should not only get order quantities and timing right, they also need to make sure that stocks are in the right place. British Airways found this out when a shortage of toilet paper and 'the wrong kind of headphones' delayed a London to Barbados flight for five hours. The Boeing 777 flight was due to leave the London airport at 1.40 pm on Sunday but was delayed until 6.51 pm. It eventually arrived at Bridgetown five-and-a-half hours later than scheduled. The problem, apparently, was that a newly appointed supply company had failed to load the right supplies on board, and by the time the supplies arrived, the outbound crew was 'out of hours'. This meant that they could not operate the service within predetermined time limits. It then took three more hours to find another crew. Not only was it embarrassing for the airline, it put them in danger of having to face an almost £300,000 bill for compensation. European rules on flight delays entitle each passenger to compensation of €600. Even worse, the delay to the outbound flight meant that the return service was also delayed by almost six hours, pushing up the compensation bill even further.

monitored. Some reports may be generated on an exception basis. That is, the report is only generated if some performance measure deviates from acceptable limits.

Forecasting

Inventory replenishment decisions should ideally be made with a clear understanding of forecast future demand. The inventory control system can compare actual demand against forecast and adjust the forecast in the light of actual levels of demand. Control systems of this type are treated in more detail in Chapter 14.

Common problems with inventory systems

Our description of inventory systems has been based on the assumption that operations (a) have a reasonably accurate idea of costs such as holding cost, or order cost, and (b) have accurate information that really does indicate the actual level of stock and sales. But data inaccuracy often poses one of the most significant problems for inventory managers. This is because most computer-based inventory management systems are based on what is called the perpetual inventory principle. This is the simple idea that stock records are (or should be) automatically updated every time that items are recorded as having been received into an inventory or taken out of the inventory. So,

$$\text{Opening stock level} + \text{Receipts in} - \text{Dispatches out} = \text{New stock level}$$

Any errors in recording these transactions and/or in handling the physical inventory can lead to discrepancies between the recorded and actual inventory, and these errors are perpetuated until physical stock checks are made (usually quite infrequently). In practice there are many opportunities for errors to occur, if only because inventory transactions are numerous. This means that it is surprisingly common for the majority of inventory records to be in inaccurate. The underlying causes of errors include:

Operations principle

The maintenance of data accuracy is vital for the day-to-day effectiveness of inventory management systems.

- ► keying errors – entering the wrong product code;
- ► quantity errors – a miscount of items put into or taken from stock;
- ► damaged or deteriorated inventory not recorded as such, or not correctly deleted from the records when it is destroyed;
- ► the wrong items being taken out of stock, but the records not being corrected when they are returned to stock;
- ► delays between the transactions being made and the records being updated;
- ► items stolen from inventory (common in retail environments, but also not unusual in industrial and commercial inventories).

Summary answers to key questions

What is inventory?

- ► Inventory, or stock, is the stored accumulation of the transformed resources in an operation. Sometimes the words 'stock' and 'inventory' are also used to describe transforming resources, but the terms *stock control* and *inventory control* are nearly always used in connection with transformed resources.
- ► Almost all operations keep some kind of inventory, most usually of materials but also of information and customers (customer inventories are normally called queues).

Why should there be any inventory?

▶ Inventory occurs in operations because the timing of supply and the timing of demand do not always match. Inventories are needed, therefore, to smooth the differences between supply and demand.

▶ There are five main reasons for keeping physical inventory:

— to cope with random or unexpected interruptions in supply or demand (buffer inventory);

— to cope with an operation's inability to make all products simultaneously (cycle inventory);

— to allow different stages of processing to operate at different speeds and with different schedules (de-coupling inventory);

— to cope with planned fluctuations in supply or demand (anticipation inventory);

— to cope with transportation delays in the supply network (pipeline inventory).

▶ Inventory is often a major part of working capital, tying up money which could be used more productively elsewhere.

▶ If inventory is not used quickly, there is an increasing risk of damage, loss, deterioration or obsolescence.

▶ Inventory invariably takes up space (for example, in a warehouse), and has to be managed, stored in appropriate conditions, insured, and physically handled when transactions occur. It therefore contributes to overhead costs.

How much to order? – The volume decision

▶ This depends on balancing the costs associated with holding stocks against the costs associated with placing an order. The main stock-holding costs are usually related to working capital, whereas the main order costs are usually associated with the transactions necessary to generate the information to place an order.

▶ The best-known approach to determining the amount of inventory to order is the economic order quantity (EOQ) formula. The EOQ formula can be adapted to different types of inventory profile using different stock behaviour assumptions.

▶ The EOQ approach, however, has been subject to a number of criticisms regarding the true cost of holding stock, the real cost of placing an order, and the use of EOQ models as prescriptive devices.

▶ One approach to this problem, the newsvendor problem, includes the effects of probabilistic demand in determining order quantity.

When to place an order? – The timing decision

▶ Partly this depends on the uncertainty of demand. Orders are usually timed to leave a certain level of average safety stock when the order arrives. The level of safety stock is influenced by the variability of both demand and the lead time of supply. These two variables are usually combined into a lead-time usage distribution.

▶ Using re-order level as a trigger for placing replenishment orders necessitates the continual review of inventory levels. This can be time consuming and expensive. An alternative approach is to make replenishment orders of varying size but at fixed time periods.

How can inventory be controlled?

▶ The key issue here is how managers discriminate between the levels of control they apply to different stock items. The most common way of doing this is by what is known as the ABC classification of stock. This uses the Pareto principle to distinguish between the different values of, or significance placed on, types of stock.

▶ Inventory is usually managed through sophisticated computer-based information systems which have a number of functions: the updating of stock records, the generation of orders, the generation of inventory status reports and demand forecasts. These systems critically depend on maintaining accurate inventory records.

Supplies4medics.com

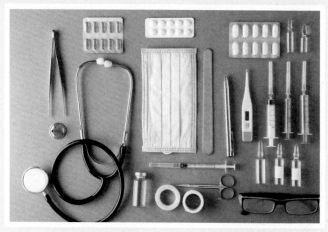

Founded almost 20 years ago, supplies4medics.com has become one of Europe's most successful direct mail suppliers of medical hardware and consumables to hospitals, doctors' and dentists' surgeries, clinics, nursing homes and other medical-related organizations. Its physical and online catalogues list just over four thousand items, categorized by broad applications such as 'hygiene consumables' and 'surgeons' instruments'. Quoting their website: *'We are the pan-European distributors of wholesale medical and safety supplies . . . We aim to carry everything you might ever need; from nurses' scrubs to medical kits, consumables for operations, first aid kits, safety products, chemicals, fire-fighting equipment, nurse and physicians' supplies, etc. Everything is at affordable prices – and backed by our very superior customer service and support – supplies4medics is your ideal source for all medical supplies. Orders are normally despatched same-day, via our European distribution partner, the Brussels Hub of DHL. You should therefore receive your complete order within one week, but you can request next day delivery if required, for a small extra charge. You can order our printed catalogue on the link at the bottom of this page, or shop on our easy-to-use on-line store.'*

Last year turnover grew by over 25 per cent to about €120 million, a cause for considerable satisfaction in the company. However, profit growth was less spectacular; and market research suggested that customer satisfaction, although generally good, was slowly declining. Most worrying, inventory levels had grown faster than sales revenue, in percentage terms. This was putting a strain on cash flow, requiring the company to borrow more cash to fund the rapid growth planned for the next year. Inventory holding is estimated to be costing around 15 per cent per annum, taking account of the cost of borrowing, insurance and all warehousing overheads.

Pierre Lamouche, the Head of Operations, summarized the situation faced by his department: *'As a matter of urgency, we are reviewing our purchasing and inventory management systems! Most of our existing re-order levels (ROL) and re-order quantities (ROQ) were set several years ago, and have never been recalculated. Our focus has been on rapid growth through the introduction of new product lines. For more recently introduced items, the ROQs were based only on forecast sales, which actually can be quite misleading. We estimate that it costs us, on average, €50 to place and administer every purchase order, since most suppliers are still not able to take orders over the Internet or by EDI. In the meantime, sales of* some products have grown fast, whilst others have declined. *Our average inventory (stock) cover is about 10 weeks, but . . . amazingly . . . we still run out of critical items! In fact, on average, we are currently out of stock of about 500 SKUs (Stock Keeping Units) at any time. As you can imagine, our service level is not always satisfactory with this situation. We really need help to conduct a review of our system, so have employed a mature intern from the local business school to review our system. He has first asked my team to provide information on a random, representative sample of twenty items from the full catalogue range, which is copied below'* (see Table 13.11).

QUESTIONS

1 Prepare a spreadsheet-based ABC analysis of usage value. Classify as follows:

  A items: top 20 per cent of usage value
  B items: next 30 per cent of usage value
  C items: remaining 50 per cent of usage value

2 Calculate the inventory weeks for each item, for each classification, and for all the items in total. Does this suggest that the operational manager's estimate of inventory weeks is correct?

3 If so, what is your estimate of the overall inventory at the end of the base year, and how much might that have increased during the year?

4 Based on the sample, analyse the underlying causes of the availability problem described in the text.

5 Calculate the EOQs for the A items.

6 What recommendations would you give to the company?

Table 13.11 Representative sample of 20 catalogue items

Sample number	Catalogue reference number*	Sales unit description**	Sales unit cost (euro)	Last 12 months' sales (units)	Inventory as at last year end (units)	Re-order quantity (units)
1	11036	Disposable aprons (10pk)	2.40	100	0	10
2	11456	Ear-loop masks (box)	3.60	6,000	1,200	1,000
3	11563	Drill type 164	1.10	220	420	250
4	12054	Incontinence pads large	3.50	35,400	8,500	10,000
5	12372	150 ml syringe	11.30	430	120	100
6	12774	Rectal speculum 3 prong	17.40	65	20	20
7	12979	Pocket organizer blue	7.00	120	160	500
8	13063	Oxygen trauma kit	187.00	40	2	10
9	13236	Zinc oxide tape	1.50	1260	0	50
10	13454	Dual head stethoscope	6.25	10	16	25
11	13597	Disp. latex catheter	0.60	3560	12	20
12	13999	Roll-up wheelchair ramp	152.50	12	44	50
13	14068	WashClene tube	1.40	22,500	10,500	8,000
14	14242	Cervical collar	12.00	140	24	20
15	14310	Head wedge	89.00	44	2	10
16	14405	Three-wheel scooter	755.00	14	5	5
17	14456	Neonatal trach. tube	80.40	268	6	100
18	14675	Mouldable strip paste	10.20	1250	172	100
19	14854	Sequential comp. pump	430.00	430	40	50
20	24943	Toilet safety frame	25.60	560	18	20

* Reference numbers are allocated sequentially as new items are added to catalogue

** All quantities are in sales units (e.g. item, box, case, pack)

Problems and applications

All chapters have 'Problems and applications' questions that will help you practise analysing operations. They can be answered by reading the chapter. Model answers for the first two questions can be found on the companion website for this book.

1 A supplier makes monthly shipments to 'House & Garden Stores, in average lot sizes of 200 coffee tables. The average demand for these items is 50 tables per week, and the lead time from the supplier is 3 weeks. 'House & Garden Stores' must pay for inventory from the moment the supplier ships the products. If they are willing to increase their lot size to 300 units, the supplier will offer a lead time of 1 week. What will be the effect on cycle and pipeline inventories?

2   A local shop has a relatively stable demand for tins of sweetcorn throughout the year, with an annual total of 1,400 tins. The cost of placing an order is estimated at £15 and the annual cost of holding inventory is estimated at 25 per cent of the product's value. The company purchases tins for 20p. How much should the shop order at a time, and what is the total cost of the plan?

3   A fruit canning plant has a single line for three different fruit types. Demand for each type of tin is reasonably constant at 50,000 per month (a month has 160 production hours). The tinning process rate is 1,200 per hour, but it takes 2 hours to clean and re-set between different runs. The cost of these changeovers (C_o) is calculated at £250 per hour. Stock-holding is calculated at $0.1 per tin per month. How big should the batch size be?

4   'Our suppliers often offer better prices if we are willing to buy in larger quantities. This creates a pressure on us to hold higher levels of stock. Therefore, to find the best quantity to order we must compare the advantages of lower prices for purchases and fewer orders with the disadvantages of increased holding costs. This means that calculating total annual inventory-related costs should now not only include holding costs and ordering costs, but also the cost of purchased items themselves' (Manager, Tufton Bufton Port Importers Inc.). One supplier to Tufton Bufton Port Importers Inc. (TBPI) has introduced quantity discounts to encourage larger order quantities. The discounts are show below:

Order quantity	Price per bottle
0–100	€15.00
101–250	€13.50
250+	€11.00

TBPI estimates that its annual demand for this particular wine is 1,500 bottles, its ordering costs are €30 per order, and its annual holding costs are 20 per cent of the bottle's price. (a) How should TBPI go about deciding how many to order? (b) How many should it order?

5   Revisit the 'Operations in practice' example on the Blood and Transplant service at the beginning of the chapter. (a) What are the factors which constitute inventory holding costs order costs, and stockout costs in a National Blood Service? (b) What makes this particular inventory planning and control example so complex? (c) How might the efficiency with which a National Blood Service controls its inventory affect its ability to collect blood?

6   Re-read the 'Operations in practice' example on 'An inventory of energy'. It mentions the potential of battery storage of energy, but stresses the cost of this method. What do you think would be the implications for energy distribution if batteries become both cheaper and more effective?

Selected further reading

Axsäter, S. (2015) *Inventory Control,* **3rd edn, Springer, New York.**
A traditional, but comprehensive textbook that takes an 'operational research' quantitative approach.

Bragg, S.M. (2015) *Inventory Management,* **2nd edn, Accounting Tools.**
A supply chain and financial approach to the subject.

Emmett, S. and Granville, D. (2007) *Excellence in Inventory Management: How to Minimise Costs and Maximise Service,* **Cambridge Academic, Cambridge.**
Practical guide.

Muller, M. (2011) *Essentials of Inventory Management,* **2nd edn, Amacom, New York.**
Straightforward treatment.

Relph, G. and Milner, C. (2015) *Inventory Management: Advanced Methods for Managing Inventory within Business Systems,* **Kogan Page, London.**
An advanced book that covers most topics in the subject, including the 'k-curve' that is not included in this chapter.

Silver, E.A., David, F., Pyke, D. and Thomas, J. (2016) *Inventory and Production Management in Supply Chains,* **4th edn, CRC Press, New York.**
Current and practical. Strong on managing inventory in multiple locations.

Waters, D. (2003) *Inventory Control and Management,* **Wiley, Chichester.**
Conventional but useful coverage of the topic.

Wild, T. (2017) *Best Practice in Inventory Management,* **Butterworth-Heinemann, Oxford.**
A straightforward and readable practice-based approach to the subject.

Planning and control systems

KEY QUESTIONS

What are planning and control systems?

What is enterprise resource planning, and how did it develop into the most common planning and control system?

How should planning and control systems be implemented?

INTRODUCTION

One of the most important issues in planning and controlling operations is managing the sometimes vast amounts of information generated by the activity. It is not just the operations function that is the author and recipient of this information; almost every other function of a business will be involved. So, it is important that all relevant information that is spread throughout the organization is brought together, and that, based on this information, appropriate decisions are taken. This is the function of planning and control systems. They bring information together, help to make decisions (with or without human intervention), then inform the relevant parts of the operation about decisions such as when activities should take place, where they should happen, who should be doing them, how much capacity will be needed, and so on. In this chapter we shall also look at what has become the dominant form of planning and control system – enterprise resource planning (ERP). It grew out of a set of calculations known as materials requirements planning (MRP), which is described in the supplement to this chapter. Figure 14.1 shows where this topic fits in our overall model of operations activities.

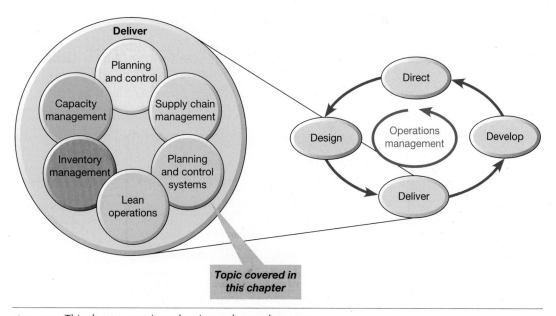

Topic covered in this chapter

Figure 14.1 This chapter examines planning and control systems

What are planning and control systems?

Before treating this question, it is worth reminding ourselves what planning and control is by looking again at what we covered in Chapter 10. The activity of planning and control is concerned with managing the ongoing allocation of resources and activities to ensure that the operation's processes are both efficient and reflect customer demand for products and services. Planning and control activities are distinct but often overlap. Formally, planning determines what is *intended* to happen at some time in the future, while control is the process of *coping* when things do not happen as intended. Control makes the adjustments that help the operation to achieve the objectives that the plan has set, even when the assumptions on which the plan was based do not hold true.

Planning and control systems

Planning and control systems are the information processing, decision support and execution mechanisms that support the operations planning and control activity. Although planning and control systems can differ they tend to have a number of common elements. These are: a customer interface that forms a two-way information link between the operation's activities and its customers; a supply interface that does the same thing for the operation's suppliers; a set of overlapping 'core' mechanisms that perform basic tasks such as loading, sequencing, scheduling, and monitoring and control; a decision mechanism involving both operations staff and information systems that makes or confirms planning and control decisions. It is important that all these elements are effective in their own right and work together. Figure 14.2 illustrates the elements that should be present in all planning and control systems. In more sophisticated systems they may even be extended to include the integration of this core operations resource planning and control task with other functional areas of the firm such as finance, marketing and personnel. We deal with this cross-functional perspective when we discuss enterprise resource planning (ERP) later.

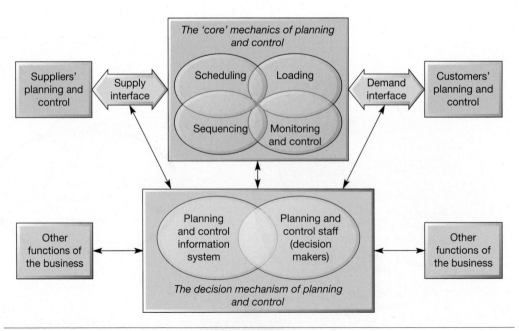

Figure 14.2 Planning and control systems interface with the internal planning and control mechanisms, customers, suppliers and the other functions of the business

Butcher's Pet Care coordinates its ERP[1]

It may not be a glamorous business, but pet food is certainly big business. It is also competitive with smaller suppliers battling against the giants like Nestlé. One of the most successful of the smaller European producers of dog food is Butcher's Pet Care located in the Midlands of the UK that takes a positive moral and ethical approach towards the dog food it produces. It also needs to be super-efficient at coordinating its production and distribution if it is to compete with larger rivals. Listen to how Butcher's IT manager, Malcolm Burrows, explains his vision of how its planning and control system helps it do this.

Why implement a new planning and control system?

'There were specific goals that needed to be achieved, as the legacy systems created long processes, and it was an issue to find out what was in the warehouse, etc. A lot of manual planning tasks took place outside of the system, whereas now the planning, the enterprise resource planning (ERP), and the scheduling of material coming in is a lot better.'

What were the benefits of the new system?

'We're definitely getting a better view of what stock we're holding, and a much quicker response in being able to change product fore-ordering. As you can probably guess, within an environment whereby we are supplying to supermarkets and supply chains, there are regularly promotions that affect the manufacturing we produce to, and it's a fairly quick turnaround. So from that point of view, the system does have a core value in that we can respond and meet requirements much quicker and easier.'

What were the challenges in implementing the system?

'It was a very big cultural change for the staff . . . As with any ERP [planning and control, see later] system, business and process mapping is crucial. The interesting challenges were working out how we needed to change to get the best out of the system, and that we had agreed a timeline for its implementation.'

How did you train staff to use the system?

'We had a core project team, and they were the "champions" who had to go out and then work within their areas. [The] IT [department] really cannot dictate that; [users] need to be able to have that autonomy to say "this is how we want to operate it". We will get involved if there are technical queries, but otherwise the "champions" [are in charge].'

How does the system interface with customers?

The part of the resource planning and control system that manages the way customers interact with the business on a day-to-day basis is called the 'customer interface' or sometimes 'demand management'. This is a set of activities that interface with both individual customers and the market more broadly. Depending on the business, these activities may include customer negotiation, order entry, demand forecasting, order promising, updating customers, keeping customer histories, post-delivery customer service and physical distribution.

Customer interface defines the customer experience

The customer interface is important because it defines the nature of the customer experience. It is the public face of the operation (the 'line of visibility' as it was called in Chapter 6). Therefore, it needs to be managed like any other 'customer processing' process, where the quality of the service, as the

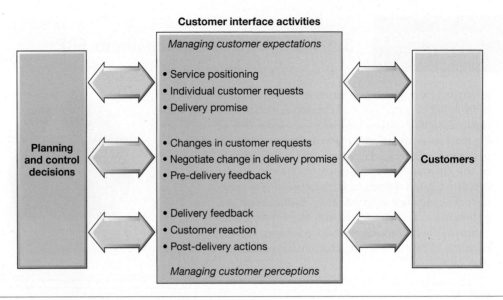

Customer interface activities

Managing customer expectations

- Service positioning
- Individual customer requests
- Delivery promise

- Changes in customer requests
- Negotiate change in delivery promise
- Pre-delivery feedback

- Delivery feedback
- Customer reaction
- Post-delivery actions

Managing customer perceptions

Planning and control decisions

Customers

Figure 14.3 The customer interface as a 'customer experience'

customer sees it, is defined by the gap between customers' expectations and their perceptions of the service they receive. Figure 14.3 illustrates a typical customer experience of interacting with a planning and control customer interface. The experience itself will start before any customer contact is initiated. Customer expectations will have been influenced by the way the business presents itself through promotional activities, the ease with which channels of communication can be used (for example, design of the website), and so on. The question is, 'Does the communication channel give any indication of the kind of service response (for example, how long will we have to wait?) that the customer can expect?' At the first point of contact when an individual customer requests services or products, their request must be understood, delivery possibly negotiated, and a delivery promise made. Prior to the delivery of the service or product, the customer may or may not change their mind, which in turn may or may not involve renegotiation delivery promises. Similarly, customers may require or value feedback as to the progress of their request. At the point of delivery, not only are the products and services handed over to the customer, but there may also be an opportunity to explain the nature of the delivery and gauge customers' reactions. Following the completion of the delivery there may also be some sort of post-delivery action, such as a phone call to confirm that all is well.

> ✓ **Operations principle**
>
> Customers' perceptions of an operation will partially be shaped by the customer interface of its planning and control system.

As is usual with such customer experiences, the managing of customer expectations is particularly important in the early stages of the experience. For example, if there is a possibility that a delivery may be late (perhaps because of the nature of the service being requested) then that possibility is established as an element in the customer's expectations. As the experience continues, various interactions with the customer interface service to build up customer perceptions of the level of support and care exhibited by the operation. (We shall deal with this idea of customer perceptions and expectations further in Chapter 17.)

The customer interface should reflect the operation's objectives

In managing a customer's experience, the customer interface element of the planning and control system is, in effect, operationalizing the business's operations objectives. It may have to prioritize one type of customer over another. It may have to encourage some types of customer to transact business more than other (possibly less profitable) types of customer. It will almost certainly have to trade off elements of customer service against the efficiency and utilization of the operations resources. No matter how sophisticated the customer interface technology, or how skilled the customer interface staff, this part of the planning and control system cannot operate effectively without clear priorities derived from the operation's strategic objectives.

The customer interface acts as a trigger function

Acceptance of an order should prompt the customer interface to trigger the operation's processes. Exactly what is triggered will depend on the nature of the business. For example, some building and construction companies, because they are willing to build almost any kind of construction, will keep relatively few of their own resources within the business, but rather hire them in when the nature of the job becomes evident. This is a 'resource-to-order' operation where the customer interface triggers the task of hiring in the relevant equipment (and possibly labour) and purchasing the appropriate materials. If the construction company confined itself to a narrower range of construction tasks, thereby making the nature of demand slightly more predictable, it would be likely to have its own equipment and labour permanently within the operation. Here, accepting a job would only need to trigger the purchase of the materials to be used in the construction, and the business is a 'produce to order' operation. Some construction companies will construct pre-designed standard houses or apartments ahead of any firm demand for them. If demand is high, customers may place requests for houses before they are started or during their construction. In this case, the customer will form a backlog of demand and must wait. However, the company is also taking the risk of holding a stock of unsold houses. Operations of this type 'produce ahead of order'.

How does the system interface with suppliers?

The supplier interface provides the link between the activities of the operation itself and those of its suppliers. The timing and level of activities within the operation or process will have implications for the supply of products and services to the operation. Suppliers need to be informed so that they can make products and services available when needed. In effect this is the mirror image of the customer interface. As such, the supplier interface is concerned with managing the supplier experience to ensure appropriate supply. Because the customer is not directly involved in this does not make it any less important. Ultimately, customer satisfaction will be influenced by supply effectiveness because that in turn influences delivery to customers. Using the expectations–perception gap to judge the quality of the supplier interface function may at first seem strange. After all, suppliers are not customers as such. Yet, it is important to be a 'quality customer' to suppliers because this increases the chances of receiving high-quality service from them. This means that suppliers fully understand expectations because they have been made clear and unambiguous.

> **Operations principle**
>
> An operation's planning and control system can enhance or inhibit the ability of its suppliers to support delivery effectiveness.

The supplier interface has both a long- and short-term function. It must be able to cope with different types of long-term supplier relationship, and also handle individual transactions with suppliers. To do the former it must understand the requirements of all the processes within the operation and also the capabilities of the suppliers (in large operations, there could be thousands of suppliers). Figure 14.4 shows a simplified sequence of events in the management of a typical supplier–operation interaction that the supplier interface must facilitate. When the planning and control activity requests supply, the supplier interface must have identified potential suppliers and might also be able to suggest alternative materials or services if necessary. Formal request for quotations may be sent to potential suppliers if no supply agreement exists. These requests might be sent to several suppliers or a smaller group, which may be 'preferred' suppliers. Just as it was important to manage customer expectations, it is important to manage supplier expectations, often prior to any formal supply of products or services. This issue was discussed in Chapter 12 as supplier development. To handle individual transactions, the supplier interface will need to issue formal purchase orders. These may be stand-alone documents or, more likely, electronic orders. Whatever the mechanisms, it is an important activity because it often forms the legal basis of the contractual relationship between the operation and its supplier. Delivery promises will need to be formally confirmed. Whilst waiting for delivery, it may be necessary to negotiate changes in supply

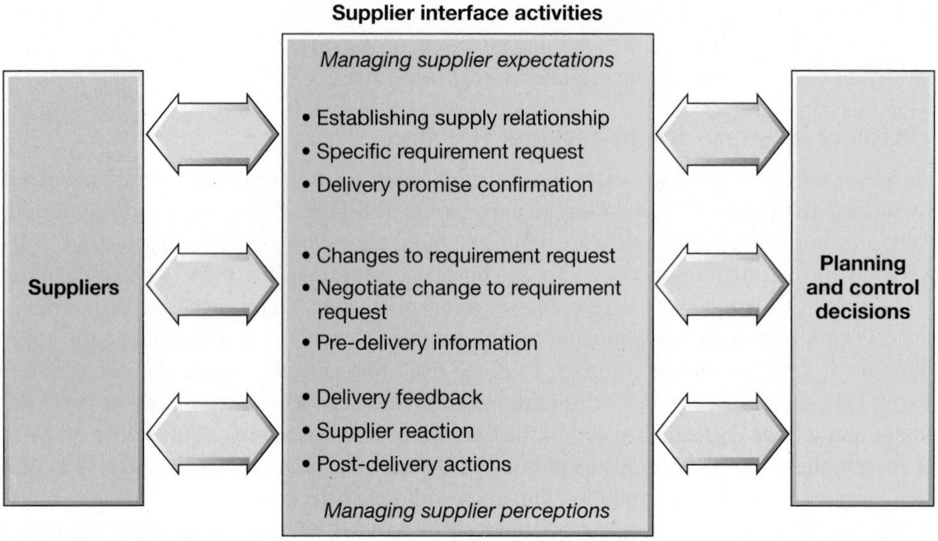

Supplier interface activities

Figure 14.4 The supplier interface as a 'customer' experience

and track progress to get early warning of potential changes to delivery. Also, delivery supplier performance needs to be established and communicated with follow-up as necessary.

Hierarchical planning and control[2]

The activity of operations planning and control is a complicated process. Demand for products and services is usually uncertain, supply can be problematic, and the composition of products and services is often complex with many components and sub-components. And to add to the difficulty, the cumulative lead times for sourcing components and for production itself are usually longer than customers are prepared to wait (see Chapter 10).

The 'hierarchical approach' to operations planning recognizes these difficulties and tries to bring some order to the complexity by dividing up the many interrelated planning and control decisions into sub-problems to reflect the organizational hierarchy. So, decisions at a high level link with decisions at lower levels in an effective manner. Decisions that are made at the higher level will of course impose some constraints on the lower-level decisions. And the execution of detailed decisions at the lower level will provide the necessary feedback so that the quality of higher-level decision making can be judged. In this way the hierarchical approach separates different kinds of decisions at different levels in the organization and over different time periods. It allows a degree of stability in the planning process so that relatively complex operations are, to some extent, protected against too many short-term changes. In addition, it gives a certain amount of independence to the planners at different levels. Figure 14.5 illustrates this hierarchical approach. This shows a general structure of the approach. In practice, different operations will interpret this structure in different ways, probably using different terms, incorporating different decisions, and having different numbers of levels. How well the hierarchical approach works will depends largely on how effectively and consistently the boundaries between the levels of the hierarchy are managed. Each hierarchical level is likely to have its own set of decision rules and methods with different planning horizons, levels of detail of information and forecasts, scope of the planning activity and managerial authority, all of which can lead to problems in translating the decisions at one level to another. This hierarchical approach is closely associated with enterprise resource planning, which we shall deal with later in this chapter.

> **Operations principle**
>
> Hierarchical planning and control systems separate different kinds of decisions at different levels in the organization and over different time periods.

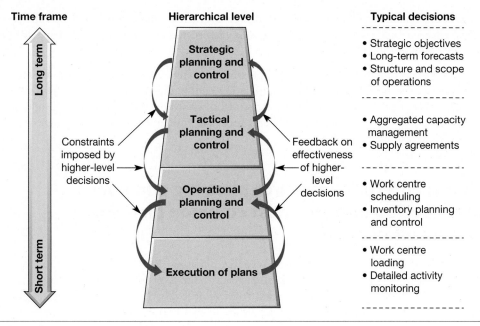

Figure 14.5 The general structure of hierarchical production planning and control

Does the system integrate human with 'automated' decision making?

Although computer-based resource planning and control systems are now widespread in many industries, much of the decision making is still carried out partially by people. This is always likely to be the case because some elements of the task, such as negotiating with customers and suppliers, are difficult to automate. Yet the benefits of computer-aided decision making are difficult to ignore. Unlike humans, computer-based planning and control can cope with immense complexity, both in terms of being able to model the inter-relationship between decisions and in terms of being able to store large quantities of information. However, humans are generally better at many of the 'soft' qualitative tasks that can be important in planning and control. In particular, humans are good at the following.

▶ *Flexibility, adaptability and learning.* Humans can cope with ambiguous, incomplete, inconsistent and redundant goals and constraints. In particular they can deal with the fact that planning and control objectives and constraints may not be stable for longer than a few hours.

▶ *Communication and negotiation.* Humans are able to understand and sometimes influence the variability inherent in an operation. They can influence job priorities and sometimes processing times. They can negotiate between internal processes and communicate with customers and suppliers in a way that could minimize misunderstanding.

Critical commentary[3]

Hierarchical planning and control looks to be both rational and straightforward; however, making it work in practice can be problematic. Several questions need to be addressed. How many levels are needed? What should constrain what and how tightly? What should one plan in advance? Does a hierarchical approach reduce the speed of decision making by requiring continual upward referral? How much autonomy and local control should be devolved to lower levels or to distributed production facilities? Is stability achieved by rigidity and at the expense of speed and responsiveness? In addition, data must be accurate, timely and in common formats. Effective transition between the levels also requires a significant degree of managerial discipline.

▶ *Intuition.* Humans can fill in the blanks of missing information that is required to plan and control. They can accumulate the tacit knowledge about what is, and what may be, really happening with the operation's processes.

These strengths of human decision making versus computer decision making provide a clue as to what should be the appropriate degree of automation built into decision making in this area. When planning and controlling stable and relatively straightforward processes that are well understood, decision making can be automated to a greater degree than with processes that are complex, unstable and poorly understood.

What is enterprise resource planning and how did it develop into the most common planning and control system?

An easy way of thinking about enterprise resource planning (ERP) is to imagine that you have decided to hold a party in two weeks' time and expect about 40 people to attend. As well as drinks, you decide to provide sandwiches and snacks. You will probably do some simple calculations, estimating guests' preferences and how much people are likely to drink and eat. You may already have some food and drink in the house that you will use, so you will take into account when making your shopping list. If any of the food is to be cooked from a recipe, you may have to multiply up the ingredients to cater for 40 people. Also, you may wish to take into account the fact that you will prepare some of the food the week before and freeze it, while you will leave the rest to either the day before or the day of the party. So, you will need to decide when each item is required so that you can shop in time. In fact, planning a party requires a series of interrelated decisions about the volume (quantity) and timing of the *materials* needed. This is the basis of the foundation concept for ERP called materials requirements planning (MRP). It is a process that helps companies make volume and timing calculations (similar to those in the party, but on a much larger scale, and with a greater degree of complexity). But your planning may extend beyond 'materials'. You may want to hire in a sound system from a local supplier – you will have to plan for this. The party also has financial implications. You may have to agree a temporary increase to your credit card limit. Again, this requires some forward planning and calculations of how much it is going to cost, and how much extra credit you require. Both the equipment and financial implications may vary if you increase the number of guests. But, if you postpone the party for a month, these arrangements will change. Also, there are other implications of organizing the party. You will need to give friends, who are helping with the organization, an idea of when they should come and for how long. This will depend on the timing of the various tasks to be done (making sandwiches etc.).

So, even for this relatively simple activity, the key to successful planning is how we generate, integrate and organize all the information on which planning and control depends. Of course, in business operations it is more complex than this. Companies usually sell many different products to many hundreds of customers who are likely to vary their demand for the products. This is a bit like organizing 200 parties one week, 250 the next and 225 the following week, all for different groups of guests with different requirements who keep changing their minds about what they want to eat and drink. This is what an ERP system does; it automates and integrates core business processes such as customer demand, scheduling operations, ordering items, keeping inventory records and updating financial data. it helps companies 'forward plan' these types of decisions and understand all the implications of any changes to the plan.

> **Operations principle**
> ERP systems automate and integrate core business processes.

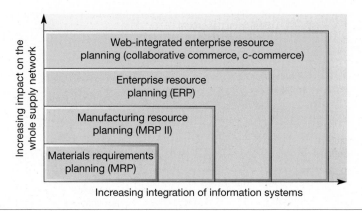

Figure 14.6 The development of ERP

How did ERP develop?

Enterprise resource planning is the latest, and the most significant, development of the original MRP philosophy. The (now) large companies which have grown almost exclusively on the basis of providing ERP systems include SAP and Oracle. Yet to understand ERP, it is important to understand the various stages in its development, summarized in Figure 14.6. The original MRP became popular during the 1970s, although the planning and control logic that underlies it had, by then, been known for some time. What popularized MRP was the availability of computer power to drive the basic planning and control mathematics. We will deal with MRP in detail in the supplement to this chapter; it uses product information in the form of a bill of material (BOM) that is similar to the 'component structure' that was discussed in Chapter 4, together with demand information in the form of a master production schedule (MPS).

Manufacturing resource planning (MRP II) expanded out of MRP during the 1980s. Again, it was a technology innovation that allowed the development. Connected networks together with increasingly powerful desktop computers allowed a much higher degree of processing power and communication between different parts of a business. Also, MRP II's extra sophistication allowed the forward modelling of 'what-if' scenarios. The strength of MRP and MRP II lay always in the fact that it could explore the *consequences* of any changes to what an operation was required to do. So, if demand changed, the MRP system would calculate all the 'knock-on' effects and issue instructions accordingly. This same principle also applies to ERP, but on a much wider basis. ERP has been defined as:

> 'a complete enterprise wide business solution. The ERP system consists of software support modules such as: marketing and sales, field service, product design and development, production and inventory control, procurement, distribution, industrial facilities management, process design and development, manufacturing, quality, human resources, finance and accounting, and information services. Integration between the modules is stressed without the duplication of information.'[4]

Some authorities caution against taking a naive view of ERP. Look at this view:

> 'Enterprise resource planning software, or ERP, doesn't live up to its acronym. Forget about planning – it doesn't do much of that – and forget about resource, [it is] a throwaway term. But remember the enterprise part. This is ERP's true ambition. It attempts to integrate all departments and functions across a company onto a single computer system that can serve all those different departments' particular needs.'[5]

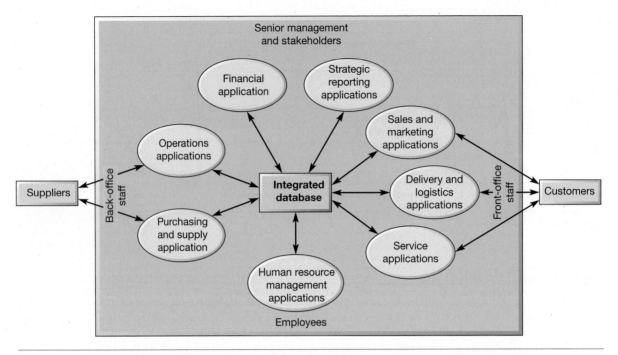

Figure 14.7 ERP integrates information from all parts of the organization

So ERP systems allow decisions and databases from all parts of the organization to be integrated so that the consequences of decisions in one part of the organization are reflected in the planning and control systems of the rest of the organization (see Figure 14.7). ERP is the equivalent of the organization's central nervous system, sensing information about the condition of different parts of the business and relaying the information to other parts of the business that need it. The information is updated in real time by those who use it and yet is always available to everyone connected to the ERP system.

Also, the potential of internet-based communication has provided a further boost to ERP development. Many companies have suppliers, customers and other businesses with which they collaborate, which themselves have ERP-type systems. An obvious development is to allow these systems to communicate. However, the technical, as well organizational and strategic consequences of this can be formidable. Nevertheless, many authorities believe that the true value of ERP systems is only fully exploited when such web-integrated ERP (known by some people as 'collaborative commerce', or c-commerce) becomes widely implemented.

The benefits of ERP

ERP is generally seen as having the potential to very significantly improve the performance of many companies in many different sectors. This is partly because of the very much enhanced visibility that information integration gives, but it is also a function of the discipline that ERP demands. Yet this discipline is itself a 'double-edged' sword. On one hand, it 'sharpens up' the management of every process within an organization, allowing best practice (or at least common practice) to be implemented uniformly through the business. No longer will individual idiosyncratic behaviour by one part of a company's operations cause disruption to all other processes. On the other hand, it is the rigidity of this discipline that is both difficult to achieve and (arguably) inappropriate for all parts of the business. Nevertheless, the generally accepted benefits of ERP are usually held to be the following:

The growth of SAP, the largest European software company, based in Walldorf, Germany, over the years has matched the popularity of the ERP systems that are still the foundation of its success. Founded by five former IBM engineers in 1972, SAP launched its ground-breaking SAP R/1 system one year later. This was followed by SAP R/2 in 1979 and R/3 in 1992. Now its SAP S/4HANA Business Suite products offer cloud, on-premise and hybrid deployment options to provide, it says, more choice to customers.

With almost 300,000 customers in more than 130 countries, a wide variety of businesses run SAP 'business software' applications. These range, as the company phrases it, from distinct solutions addressing the needs of small businesses and midsize companies to suite offerings for global organizations. SAP defines 'business software' as comprising enterprise resource planning and related applications such as supply chain management, customer relationship management, product life-cycle management, and supplier relationship management.

SAP is well known for developing a network of 'business partners' to develop new products, sell its 'solutions', implement them into customers' operations, provide service, educate end users, and several other activities. There are various categories of partnerships.

▶ *Global Alliances.* SAP global alliance partners are themselves global leaders and are therefore strategic partners with significant global presence. Membership is by invitation only.

▶ *Original Equipment Manufacturers (OEM).* This is for independent software vendors that integrate SAP technologies with their own products. OEM partners may add on, bundle, host or embed SAP software.
▶ *Solution Providers.* These partners offer customized solutions (a combination of business, technical or application expertise) that include SAP software.
▶ *Complementary Technology Partners.* These partners provide complete, technically verified turnkey (out-of-the-box) software solutions that extend and add value to SAP solutions.
▶ *Volume Resellers.* These partners resell all or part of the SAP software portfolio and derive their primary revenue from licence sales.
▶ *Authorized Education.* These partners are authorized by SAP to provide official training and education services to ensure that customers' employees gain optimal training.

▶ Because software communicates across all functions, there is absolute visibility of what is happening in all parts of the business.
▶ The discipline of forcing business process-based changes is an effective mechanism for making all parts of the business more efficient.
▶ There is better 'sense of control' of operations that will form the basis for continuous improvement (albeit within the confines of the common process structures).
▶ It enables far more sophisticated communication with customers, suppliers and other business partners, often giving more accurate and timely information.
▶ It is capable of integrating whole supply chains including suppliers' suppliers and customers' customers.

In fact, although the integration of several databases lies at the heart of ERP's power, it is nonetheless difficult to achieve in practice. This is why ERP installation can be particularly expensive. Attempting to get new systems and databases to talk to old (sometimes called *legacy*) systems can be very problematic. Not surprisingly, many companies choose to replace most, if not all, their existing systems simultaneously. Common systems and relational databases help to ensure the smooth transfer of data between different parts of the organization. In addition to the integration of systems, ERP usually includes other features that make it a powerful planning and control tool.

ERP changes the way companies do business

Arguably the most significant issue in many company's decision to buy an off-the-shelf ERP system is its compatibility with the company's current business processes and practices. The advice that is emerging from the companies that have adopted ERP (either successfully or unsuccessfully) is that

The life and times of a chicken salad sandwich (Part 2)[7]

In Chapter 10 we looked at the schedule for the manufacture of a chicken salad sandwich. This concentrated on the lead times for the ordering of the ingredients and the manufacturing schedule for producing the sandwiches during the afternoon and night time of each day for delivery during the evening and the night time, and the morning of the following day. But that is only one half of the story, the half that is concerned with planning and controlling the timing of events. The other half concerns how the sandwich company manages the *quantity* of ingredients to order, the quantity of sandwiches to be made, and the whole chain of implications for the whole company. In fact, this sandwich company uses an ERP system that has at its core an MRP II package. This MRP II

system has the two normal basic drivers of, first, a continually updated sales forecast, and, second, a product structure database. In this case the product structure and/or bill of materials is the 'recipe' for the sandwich, and within the company this database is called the 'Recipe Management System'. The 'recipe' for the chicken sandwich (its bill of materials) is shown in Table 14.1.

Figure 14.8 shows the ERP system used by this sandwich company. Orders are received from customers electronically through the EDI system. These orders are then checked through what the company calls a 'Validation System' that checks the order against current

product codes and expected quantities to make sure that the customer has not made any mistakes, such as forgetting to order some products (this happens surprisingly often). After validation the orders are transferred through the central database to the MRP II system that performs the main requirements breakdown. Based on these requirements and forecasted requirements for the next few days, orders are placed to the company's suppliers for raw materials and packaging. Simultaneously, confirmation is sent to customers, accounts are updated, staffing schedules are finalized for the next two weeks (on a rolling basis), customers are invoiced, and all this information

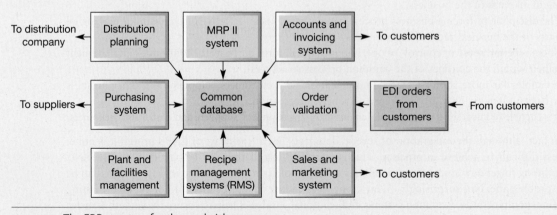

Figure 14.8 The ERP structure for the sandwich company

Table 14.1 Bill of materials for a chicken salad sandwich

FUNCTION: MBIL		MULTI-LEVEL BILL INQUIRY					
PARENT: BTE80058 RV: PLNR: LOU		UM:EA	DESC: RUNLT: PLN POL: N		HE CHICKEN SALAD TRY 0 FIXED LT: 0 DRWG: WA1882		LA
LEVEL 1 . . . 5 . . . 10	PT USE	SEQN	COMPONENT	C T	PARTIAL DESCRIPTION	QTY	UM
1	PACK	010	FTE80045	P	H.E. CHICKENS	9	EA
2	ASSY	010	MBR–0032	P	BREAD HARVESTE	2	SL
3	HRPR	010	RBR–0023	N	BREAD HARVESTE	.4545455	EA
2	ASSY	020	RDY–0001	N	SPREAD BUTTER	.006	KG
2	ASSY	030	RMA–0028	N	MAYONNAISE MYB	.01	KG
2	ASSY	040	MFP–0016	P	CHICKEN FRESH	.045	KG
3	HRPR	010	RFP–0008	N	CHICKEN FRESH	1	KG
	ASSY	050	MVF–0063	P	TOMATO SLICE 4	3	SL
3	ALTI	010	RVF–0026	P	TOMATOES PRE–S	.007	KG
4	HRPR	010	RVF–0018	N	TOMATOES	1	KG
2	ASSY	060	MVF–0059	P	CUCUMBER SLICE	2	SL
3	ALTI	010	RVF–0027	P	CUCUMBER SLICE	.004	KG
4	TRAN	010	RVF–0017	N	CUCUMBER	1	KG
2	ASSY	070	MVF–0073	P	LETTUCE COS SL	.02	KG
3	HRPR	010	RVF–0015	N	LETTUCE COS	1	KG
2	ASSY	080	RPA–0070	N	WEBB BASE GREY	.00744	KG
2	ASSY	090	RPA–0071	N	WEBB TOP WHITE	.0116	KG
2	ASSY	100	RLA–0194	N	LABEL SW H	1	EA
2	ASSY	110	RLA–0110	N	STICKER NE	1	EA
1	PACK	010	RPA–0259	N	SOT LABELL	1	EA
1	PACK	030	RPA–0170	N	TRAY GREEN	1	EA

is made available both to the customers' own ERP systems and the transportation company's planning system.

Interestingly, the company, like many others, found it difficult to implement its ERP system. 'It was a far bigger job than we thought', according to the company's operations director. *'We had to change the way we organized our processes so that they would fit in with the ERP system that we bought. But that was relatively easy compared to making sure that the system integrated with our customers', suppliers' and distributors' systems.* *Because some of these companies were also implementing new systems at the time, it was like trying to hit a moving target.'* However, three years after the start of implementation, the whole process was working relatively smoothly.

it is extremely important to make sure that their current way of doing business will fit (or can be changed to fit) with a standard ERP package. In fact, one of the most common reasons for companies to decide not to install ERP is that they cannot reconcile the assumptions in the software of the ERP system with their core business processes. If, as most businesses find, their current processes do not fit, they can do one of two things. They could change their processes to fit the ERP package. Alternatively, they could modify the software within the ERP package to fit their processes. Both of these options involve costs and risks. Changing business practices that are working well will involve reorganization costs as well introducing the potential for errors to creep into the processes. Adapting the software will both slow down the project and introduce potentially dangerous software 'bugs' into the system. It would also make it difficult to upgrade the software later on.

> **Operations principle**
>
> ERP systems are only fully effective if the way a business organizes its processes is aligned with the underlying assumptions of its ERP system.

Why do companies invest in ERP?

If one accepts only some of the criticisms of ERP outlined in the critical commentary box overleaf, it does pose the question as to why companies have invested such large amounts of money in it. Partly it was the attraction of turning the company's information systems into a 'smooth-running and integrated machine'. The prospect of such organizational efficiency is attractive to most managers, even if it does presuppose a very simplistic model of how organizations work in practice. After a while, although organizations could now see the formidable problems in ERP implementation, the investments were justified on the basis that 'even if we gain no significant advantage by investing in ERP, we will be placed at a disadvantage by *not* investing in it because all our competitors are doing so'. There is probably some truth in this; sometimes businesses have to invest just to stand still.

Web-integrated ERP

Perhaps the most important justification for embarking on ERP is the potential it gives the organization to link up with the outside world. For example, it is much easier for an operation to move into internet-based trading if it can integrate its external internet systems into its internal ERP systems. However, as has been pointed out by some critics of the ERP software companies, ERP vendors were not prepared for the impact of e-commerce and had not made sufficient allowance in their products for the need to interface with internet-based communication channels. The result of this has been that whereas the internal complexity of ERP systems was designed only to be intelligible to systems experts, the internet has meant that customers and suppliers (who are non-experts) are demanding access to the same information. So, important pieces of information such as the status of orders, whether products are in stock, the progress of invoicing, etc., need to be available, via the ERP system, on a company's website.

One problem is that different types of external company often need different types of information. Customers need to check the progress of their orders and invoicing, whereas suppliers and other partners want access to the details of operations planning and control. Not only that, but they want

Far from being the magic ingredient that allows operations to fully integrate all their information, ERP is regarded by some as one of the most expensive ways of getting zero or even negative return on investment. For example, the American chemicals giants, Dow Chemical, spent almost half a billion dollars and seven years implementing an ERP system which became outdated almost as soon as it was implemented. One company, FoxMeyer Drug, claimed that the expense and problems that it encountered in implementing ERP eventually drove it into bankruptcy. One problem is that ERP implementation is expensive. This is partly because of the need to customize the system, understand its implications for the organization, and train staff to use it. Spending on what some call the *ERP ecosystem* (consulting, hardware, networking and complementary applications) has been estimated as being twice the spending on the software itself. But it is not only the expense that has disillusioned many companies, it is also the returns they have had for their investment. Some studies show that the vast majority of companies implementing ERP are disappointed with the effect it has had on their businesses. Certainly many companies find that they have to (sometimes fundamentally) change the way they organize their operations in order to fit in with ERP systems. This organizational impact of ERP (which has been described as the corporate equivalent of root-canal work) can have a significantly disruptive effect on the organization's operations.

access all the time. The internet is always there, but web-integrated ERP systems are often complex and need periodic maintenance. This can mean that every time the ERP system is taken off-line for routine maintenance or other changes, the website also goes off-line. To combat this some companies configure their ERP and e-commerce links in such a way that they can be decoupled, so that ERP can be periodically shut down without affecting the company's web presence.

Supply chain ERP

The step beyond integrating internal ERP systems with immediate customers and suppliers is to integrate all the ERP and similar systems along a supply chain. Of course, this can never be straightforward and is often exceptionally complicated. Not only do different ERP systems have to communicate together, they have to integrate with other types of system. For example, sales and marketing functions often use systems such as customer relationship management (CRM) that manage the complexities of customer requirements, promises and transactions. Getting ERP and CRM systems to work together is itself often difficult. Sometimes the information from ERP systems has to be translated into a form that CRM and other e-commerce applications are able to understand. Nevertheless, such web-integrated ERP, or c-commerce (collaborative commerce), applications are emerging and starting to make an impact on the way companies do business. Although implementing supply chain ERP is a formidable task, the benefits are potentially great. The costs of communicating between supply chain partners could be dramatically reduced and the potential for avoiding errors as information and products move between partners in the supply chain is significant. Yet as a final warning note, it is as well to remember that although integration can bring all the benefits of increased transparency in a supply chain, it may also transmit systems failure. If the ERP system of one operation within a supply chain fails for some reason, it may block the effective operation of the whole integrated information system throughout the chain.

> **Operations principle**
> The effectiveness of ERP systems depends partly on suppliers' and customers' ERP systems.

How should planning and control systems be implemented?

By their nature, planning and control systems are designed to address problems of information having to be obtained from different parts of a business. It is not surprising then that any planning and control system will be complex and difficult to get right. Implementing this type of system will necessarily involve crossing organizational boundaries and integrating internal processes that cover many, if not all, functional areas of a business. Building a single system that simultaneously satisfies the requirements of operations managers, marketing and sales managers, finance managers and everyone else in the organization is never going to be easy. It is likely that each function will have its own set of processes and well-understood system that has been designed for its specific needs. Moving everyone onto a single, integrated system that runs off a single database is going to be potentially very unpopular. Furthermore, few people like to change, and planning and control systems, particularly ERP, ask almost everyone to change how they do their jobs. If planning and control system implementation were not difficult there would not be so many reports of the failure of ERP implementations, or even the complete abandonment of systems.

The particular challenges of information technology (IT) implementation

Surprisingly, given the ubiquity of IT systems, such as planning and control systems, the cost effectiveness of investment in IT is not altogether straightforward. Generally research recognizes a plain and positive connection between investment in IT and increased operations effectiveness, even if the benefits can vary widely. As one authority put it, *'there's no bank where companies can deposit IT investment and withdraw an 'average' return . . . [A] strategy of blindly investing in IT and expecting productivity to automatically rise is sure to fail.'*[8] Moreover, there is a high failure rate for IT projects (often cited as between 35 per cent and 75 per cent, although the definition of 'failure' is debated). Yet there is extensive agreement that the most common reasons for failure are connected in some way with managerial, implementation or organizational factors. And of these managerial, implementation or organizational factors, one of the main issues was the degree of alignment and integration between a firm's overall IT strategy and the general strategy of the firm. This is a particularly important point for operations strategy. It reinforces the idea that IT strategy must be regarded as an integral part of overall operations strategy.

Of course, different kinds of IT pose different kinds of challenge. The impact of some IT is limited to a defined and (relatively) limited part of the operation. This type of IT is sometimes called 'function IT' because it facilitates a single function or task.[9] Examples include computer-aided design (CAD), spreadsheets and simple decision support systems. The organizational challenges for this type of technology can usually be treated separately from the technology itself. Put another way, function IT can be adopted with or without any changes to other organizational structures. Yet this does not mean that no organizational, cultural or development challenges will be faced. Often the effectiveness of the technology can be enhanced by appropriate changes to other aspects of the operation. By contrast, 'enterprise IT' extends across much of, or even the entire organization. Because of this, enterprise IT will need potentially extensive changes to the organization. And the most common (and problematic) enterprise IT systems are ERP systems. The third IT category is 'network IT'. Network IT facilitates exchanges between people and groups inside and/or outside the organization. However, it does not necessarily pre-define how these exchanges should work. For example, simple e-mail is a network IT. It has brought significant changes to how operations and supply networks function, but the changes are not imposed by the technology itself; rather they emerge over time as people gain experience of using the technology. The challenge with this type of technology is to learn how to exploit its emergent potential. This is the challenge for many operations as they extend their ERP systems to encompass the whole, or even a part, of their supply chain.

Implementation critical success factors

One of the key issues in ERP implementation is what critical success factors (CSFs) should be managed to increase the chances of a successful implementation. In this case, CSFs are those things that the organization must 'get right' in order for the ERP system to work effectively. Much of the research in this area has been summarized by Finney and Corbett[10] who distinguish between the broad, organization-wide, or strategic, factors, and the more project specific, or tactical, factors. These are shown in Table 14.2.

Of course, some of these CSFs could be appropriate for any kind of complex implementation, whether of an ERP system, or some other major change to an operation. But that is the point. ERP implementation certainly has some specific technical requirements, but good ERP implementation practice is very similar to other complicated and sensitive implementation. Again, what is different about ERP is that it is enterprise-wide, so implementation should always be considered on an enterprise-wide level. Therefore there will at all times be many different stakeholders to consider, each with their own concerns. That is why implementing an ERP system is always going to be an exercise in change management. Only if the anxieties of all relevant groups are addressed effectively will the prospect of achieving superior system performance be high.

Table 14.2 Strategic and tactical critical success factors (CSF) related to successful ERP implementation.

Strategic critical success factors	Tactical critical success factors
▶ Top management commitment and support – strong and committed leadership at the top management level is essential to the success of an ERP implementation	▶ Balanced team – the need for an implementation team that spans the organization, as well as one that possesses a balance of business and IT skills
▶ Visioning and planning – articulating a business vision to the organization, identifying clear goals and objectives, and providing a clear link between business goals and systems strategy	▶ Project team – there is a critical need to put in place a solid, core implementation team that comprises the organization's 'best and brightest' individuals. These individuals should have a proven reputation and there should be a commitment to 'release' these individuals to the project on a full-time basis
▶ Project champion – the individual should possess strong leadership skills as well as business, technical and personal managerial competences	▶ Communication plan – planned communication among various functions and organizational levels (specifically between business and IT personnel) is important to ensure that open communication occurs within the entire organization, as well as with suppliers and customers
▶ Implementation strategy and timeframe – implement the ERP under a time-phased approach	
▶ Project management – the ongoing management of the implementation plan	▶ Project cost planning and management – it is important to know up front exactly what the implementation costs will be and dedicate the necessary budget
▶ Change management – this concept refers to the need for the implementation team to formally prepare a change management programme and be conscious of the need to consider the implications of such a project. One key task is to build user acceptance of the project and a positive employee attitude. This might be accomplished through education about the benefits and need for an ERP system. Part of this building of user acceptance should also involve securing the support of opinion leaders throughout the organization. There is also a need for the team leader to effectively negotiate between various political turfs. Some authorities also stress that in planning the ERP project, it must be looked upon as a change management initiative not an IT initiative	▶ IT infrastructure – it is critical to assess the IT readiness of the organization, including the architecture and skills. Infrastructure might need to be upgraded or revamped
	▶ Selection of ERP – the selection of an appropriate ERP package that matches the businesses processes
	▶ Consultant selection and relationship – some authorities advocate the need to include an ERP consultant as part of the implementation team
	▶ Training and job redesign – training is a critical aspect of an implementation. It is also necessary to consider the impact of the change on the nature of work and the specific job descriptions
	▶ Troubleshooting/crisis management – it is important to be flexible in ERP implementations and to learn from unforeseen circumstances, as well as be prepared to handle unexpected crisis situations. Troubleshooting skills will be an ongoing requirement of the implementation process

Source: Based on Sherry Finney and Martin Corbett (2007) ERP implementation: a compilation and analysis of critical success factors, *Business Process Management Journal*, vol. 13 no. 3, 2007, 329–347.

What a waste[11]

Not only can ERP implementation go wrong, even when undertaken by experienced professionals, sometimes it can end up in the law courts. Waste Management, Inc. is the leading provider of waste and environmental services in North America. So when it announced that it was suing SAP (see earlier 'Operations in practice' example) over the failure of an ERP implementation, planning and control systems practitioners took notice. Waste Management said that it was seeking the recovery of more than $100 million in project expenses as well as *'the savings and benefits that the SAP software was promised to deliver to Waste Management'.* It said that SAP promised that the software could be fully implemented throughout all of Waste Management within 18 months, and that its software was an 'out-of-the-box' solution that would meet Waste Management's needs without any customization or enhancements.

Waste Management signed a sales pact with SAP in October 2005, but according to Waste Management, *'Almost immediately following execution of the agreements, the SAP implementation team discovered significant "gaps" between the software's functionality and Waste* Management's business requirements. Waste Management has discovered that these gaps were already known to the product development team in Germany even before the SLA (service-level agreement) was signed.' But members of SAP's implementation team had reportedly blamed Waste Management for the functional gaps and had submitted change orders requiring that Waste Management pay for fixing them.

Five years later, the dispute was settled when SAP made a one-time cash payment to Waste Management.

At a purely practical level, many consultants who have had to live through the difficulties of implementing ERP have summarized their experiences. The following list of likely problems with an ERP implementation is typical (and really does reflect reality).[12]

▶ The total cost is likely to be underestimated.
▶ The time and effort to implement it is likely to be underestimated.
▶ The resourcing from both the business and the IT function is likely to be higher than anticipated.
▶ The level of outside expertise required will be more than anticipated.
▶ The changes required to business processes will be greater than expected.
▶ Controlling the scope of the project will be more difficult than expected.
▶ There will never be enough training.
▶ The need for change management is not likely to be recognized until it is too late, and the changes required to corporate culture are likely to be grossly underestimated. (This is the single biggest failure point for ERP implementations.)

What are planning and control systems?

▶ Planning and control systems are the information processing, decision support and execution mechanisms that support the operations planning and control activity.

▶ Planning and control systems can take various forms, but usually have some common elements such as customer and supplier interfaces, an information system, a set of decision rules and functions to schedule, sequence, load and monitor operations activities.

▶ Hierarchical planning and control systems separate different kinds of decisions at different levels in the organization and over different time periods

What is ERP and how did it develop into the most common planning and control system?

▶ ERP is an enterprise-wide information system that integrates all the information from many functions, which is needed for planning and controlling operations activities. This integration around a common database allows for transparency.

▶ It often requires very considerable investment in the software itself, as well as its implementation. More significantly, it often requires a company's processes to be changed to bring them in line with the assumptions built into the ERP software.

▶ ERP can be seen as the latest development from the original planning and control approach known as MRP.

▶ Although ERP is becoming increasingly competent at the integration of internal systems and databases, there is the even more significant potential of integration with other organizations' ERP (and equivalent) systems.

▶ In particular, the use of Internet-based communication between customers, suppliers and other partners in the supply chain has opened up the possibility of wider integration.

How should planning and control systems be implemented?

▶ Because planning and control systems are designed to address problems of information fragmentation, implementation will be complex and cross organizational boundaries.

▶ There are a number of critical success factors (CSFs) that the organization must 'get right' in order for the ERP system to work effectively. Some of these are broad, organization-wide, or strategic, factors. Others are more project specific, or tactical, factors.

CASE STUDY   Psycho Sports Ltd

Peter Townsend knew that he would have to make some decisions pretty soon. His sports goods manufacturing business, Psycho Sports, had grown so rapidly over the last two years that he would soon have to install some systematic procedures and routines to manage the business. His biggest problem was in manufacturing control. He had started making specialist high-quality table tennis bats but now made a wide range of sports products, including tennis balls, darts and protective equipment for various games. Furthermore, his customers, once limited to specialist sports shops, now included some of the major sports retail chains.

'We really do have to get control of our manufacturing. I keep getting told that we need what seems to be called an MRP system. I wasn't sure what this meant and so I have bought a specialist production control book from our local bookshop and read all about MRP principles. I must admit, these academics seem to delight in making simple things complicated. And there is so much jargon associated with the technique, I feel more confused now than I did before.

'Perhaps the best way forward is for me to take a very simple example from my own production unit and see whether I can work things out manually. If I can follow the process through on paper then I will be far better equipped to decide what kind of computer-based system we should get, if any!'

Peter decided to take as his example one of his new products: a table tennis bat marketed under the name of the 'high-resolution' bat, but known within the manufacturing unit more prosaically as Part Number 5654. Figure 14.9 gives

the product structure for this table tennis bat, showing the table tennis bat made up of two main assemblies: a handle assembly and a face assembly. In order to bring the two main assemblies together to form the finished bat, various fixings are required, such as nails, connectors, etc.

The gross requirements for this particular bat are shown below. The bat is not due to be launched until Week 13 (it is now Week 1), and sales forecasts have been made for the first 23 weeks of sales:

Weeks 13–21 inclusive, 100 per week
Weeks 22–29 inclusive, 150 per week
Weeks 30–35 inclusive, 200 per week.

Peter also managed to obtain information on the current inventory levels of each of the parts which made up the

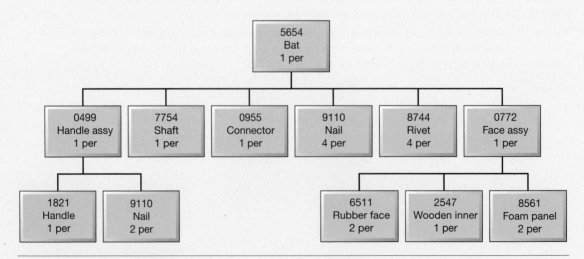

Figure 14.9 Product structure for bat 5654

Table 14.3 Inventory, cost and lead-time information for parts

Part no.	Description	Inventory	EQ	LT	Std cost
5645	Bat	0	500	2	12.00
0499	Handle assy	0	400	3	4.00
7754	Shaft	15	1,000	5	1.00
0955	Connector	350	5,000	4	0.02
9110	Nail	120	5,000	4	0.01
8744	Rivet	3,540	5,000	4	0.01
0772	Face assy	0	250	4	5.00
1821	Handle	0	500	4	2.00
6511	Rubber face	0	2,000	10	0.50
2547	Wooden inner	10	300	7	1.50
8561	Foam panel	0	1,000	8	0.50

LT = lead time for ordering (in weeks); EQ = economic quantity for ordering; Std cost = standard cost in £.

finished bat, together with cost data and lead times. He was surprised, however, how long it took him to obtain this information. 'It has taken me nearly two days to get hold of all the information I need. Different people held it, nowhere was it conveniently put together, and sometimes it was not even written down. To get the inventory data, I actually had to go down to the stores and count how many parts were in the boxes.' The data Peter collected were as shown in Table 14.3.

Peter set himself six exercises which he knew he would have to master if he was to understand fully the basics of MRP.

Exercise 1

Draw up:

(a) the single-level bill of materials for each level of assembly;
(b) a complete indented bill of materials for all levels of assembly.

Exercise 2

(a) Create the materials requirements planning records for each part and sub-assembly in the bat.
(b) List any problems that the completed MRP records identify.
(c) What alternatives are there that the company could take to solve any problems? What are their relative merits?

Exercise 3

Based on the first two exercises, create another set of MRP records, this time allowing one week's safety lead time for each item: that is, ensuring the items are in stock the week prior to when they are required.

Exercise 4

Over the time period of the exercise, what effect would the imposition of a safety lead time have on average inventory value?

Exercise 5

If we decided that our first task was to reduce inventory costs by 15 per cent, what action would we recommend? What are the implications of our action?

Exercise 6

How might production in our business be smoothed?

QUESTIONS

1 Why did Peter have such problems getting to the relevant information?

2 Perform all the exercises which Peter set for himself. Do you think he should now fully understand MRP?

All chapters have 'Problems and applications' questions that will help you practise analysing operations. They can be answered by reading the chapter. Model answers for the first two questions can be found on the companion website for this book.

1   Rolls-Royce is one of the world's largest manufacturers of gas turbines. They are exceptionally complex products, typically with around 25,000 parts, and hundreds of sub-assemblies, and their production is equally complex with over 600 external suppliers. This makes planning a complex task, which is why Rolls-Royce was one of the earliest users of ERP to help with the task. Up to that point, the company had developed its own software, which had become increasingly expensive. It was also risky because customized and complex software could be difficult to update and often could not exchange or share data. So, the company decided to implement a standard ERP system from SAP. Because it was a 'commercial' off-the-shelf system it would force the company to adopt a standardized approach. Also it would fully integrate all the company's systems, and updates would be made available by SAP. Finally, the whole organization would be able to use a single database, reducing duplication and errors. The database modules included product information, resource information (plant assets, capacities of machines, all human resource data, etc.), inventory, external suppliers, order processing information, and external sales. Yet the company knew that many ERP implementations had been expensive disasters. *'We were determined to ensure that this did not happen in Rolls-Royce,'* said Julian Goulder, who led the implementation. *'The project was too important to us; it was the largest single element within our strategic investment plan. So, we had a core technical team that led the design of the systems, and a large implementation team that was spread around the businesses. We always made sure that we communicated the changes throughout the company and used extensive education, and training. We also phased the implementation to avoid any risky "big-bang" approach. There was an extensive data "clean up" to ensure accuracy and integrity of existing information, and all existing processes were reviewed and standardized. In fact, this implementation forced us to re-examine all of our processes, to make sure that they fitted the SAP system. Within operations we have already seen a significant reduction in inventory, improved customer service, and substantially improved business information and controls.'* What decisions did Rolls-Royce take in adopting its ERP system?

2   Re-read the 'Operations in practice' example, 'SAP and its partners'. If you were managing SAP's strategic partner programme, how would you ensure their long-term collaboration?

3   Re-read the 'Operations in practice' example, 'The life and times of a chicken salad sandwich (Part 2)'. Why do you think that integrating an ERP system with those of suppliers and customers is so difficult?

4   Re-read the operations in practice example, ''What a waste'. Why did things go wrong with the relationship between SAP and Waste Management?

5   *It is advised that you read the supplement to this chapter before attempting this question.* Your company has developed a simple, but amazingly effective mango peeler. It is constructed from a blade and a supergrip handle that has a top piece and a bottom piece. The assembled mango peeler is packed in a simple recycled card pack. All the parts simply clip together and are bought in from suppliers, which can deliver the parts within one week of orders being placed. Given enough parts, your company can produce products within a day of firm orders being placed. Initial forecasts indicate that demand will be around 500 items per week. You and your suppliers all work 5-day weeks. (a) Draw the component structure for the product. (b) Draw up an MRP table (similar to Figure S14.4 in the supplement to this chapter) assuming that the economic order quantity (EOQ) for all parts is 500. (c) Develop a schedule indicating when and how many of each component should be ordered (your scheduler tells you that, actually, the EOQ for all parts is 1,500).

6 A lunch kiosk serves two meals every day: veggie fritters and mushroom stroganoff, the recipes for which are as follows.

Veggie fritters (serves 10) – Prepare the 'veggie mix' by grating 500 g of carrots, 500 g of courgettes (zucchini), and chopping 300 g of mushrooms, 100 g of onions and 50 g of parsley. Prepare the batter by beating together 4 eggs, 500 g of flour and 500 ml of cream. Combine the veggie mix with the batter and fry as small disks of approximately 10 cm in 100 ml of oil. Keep warm and serve.

Mushroom stroganoff (serves 10) – Gently fry 400 g of finely chopped onions and 10 g of crushed garlic in 20 ml of oil. When cooled, mix with 1,000 ml of cream and gently heat until reduced slightly to make the 'cream base'. Fry 2,000 g of mushrooms in 100 ml of oil until soft. Mix the mushrooms with the cream base and cover with 50 g of chopped parsley.

(a) Draw the component structures for these two 'products'. (b) If the kiosk sells 50 portions of veggie fritters and 30 portions of mushroom stroganoff every day, how much of each ingredient should it order every day?

Selected further reading

Akhtar, J. (2016) *Production Planning and Control with SAP ERP,* **2nd edn, SAP Press.**
A good practical treatment.

Atkinson, R. (2013) *Enterprise Resource Planning (ERP) The Great Gamble: An Executive's Guide to Understanding an ERP Project,* **Xlibris, Bloomington, IN.**
A basic book. Don't look for great depth, but it is a good introduction.

Bradford, M. (2010) Modern ERP: Select, implement & use today's advanced business systems, lulu.com.
A good solid class text.

Davenport, T.H. (1998) Putting the enterprise into the enterprise system, *Harvard Business Review,* **July–August.**
Covers some of the more managerial and strategic aspects of ERP.

Koch, C. and Wailgum, T. (2007) ERP definition and solutions, www.cio.com.
CIO.com has some really useful articles, of which this is one of the most thought provoking.

MacCarthy, B.L. (2006) Organizational, systems and human issues in production planning, scheduling and control, in Hermann, J. (ed.) *Handbook of Production Scheduling,* **International Series in Operations Research and Management Science, Springer, New York.**
This is an academic paper, but don't be put off. It's a good and sensible overview of the topic by one of the best authorities in the area.

Srivastava, D. and Batra, A. (2010) *ERP Systems,* **I K International Publishing House, New Delhi.**
An in-depth study of ERP systems and their benefits including implementation.

Turbit, N. (2005) ERP Implementation – The Traps, The Project Perfect White Paper Collection, www .projectperfect.com.au.
Practical (and true).

Vollmann, T., Berry, W., Whybark, D.C. and Jacobs, F.R. (2004) *Manufacturing Planning and Control Systems for Supply Chain Management: The Definitive Guide for Professionals,* **McGraw Hill Higher Education, New York.**
The latest version of the 'bible' of manufacturing planning and control. Explains the 'workings' of MRP and ERP in detail.

Supplement to Chapter 14
Materials requirements planning (MRP)

INTRODUCTION

Materials requirements planning (MRP) is an approach to calculating how many parts or materials of particular types are required and what times they are required. This requires data files which, when the MRP program is run, can be checked and updated. Figure S14.1 shows how these files relate to each other. The first inputs to materials requirements planning are customer orders and forecast demand. MRP performs its calculations based on the combination of these two parts of future demand. All other requirements are derived from, and dependent on, this demand information.

Master production schedule

The master production schedule (MPS) forms the main input to materials requirements planning and contains a statement of the volume and timing of the end products to be made. It drives all the production and supply activities that eventually will come together to form the end products. It is the basis for the planning and utilization of labour and equipment, and it determines the provisioning of materials and cash. The MPS should include all sources of demand, such as spare parts, internal production promises, etc. For example, if a manufacturer of earth excavators plans an exhibition of its products and allows a project team to raid the stores so that it can build two pristine examples to be exhibited, this is likely to leave the factory short of parts. MPS can also be used in service organizations. For example, in a hospital theatre there is a master schedule that contains a statement of which operations are planned and when. This can be used to provision materials for the operations, such as the sterile instruments, blood and dressings. It may also govern the scheduling of staff for operations.

The master production schedule record

Master production schedules are time-phased records of each end product, which contain a statement of demand and currently available stock of each finished item. Using this information, the available inventory is projected ahead in time. When there is insufficient inventory to satisfy forward demand, order quantities are entered on the master schedule line. Table S14.1 is a simplified example of part of a master production schedule for one item. In the first row the known sales orders and any forecast are combined to form 'Demand'. The second row, 'Available', shows how much inventory of this item is

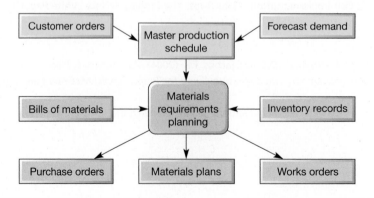

Figure S14.1 Materials requirements planning (MRP) schematic

Table S14.1 Example of a master production schedule

		Week number								
		1	2	3	4	5	6	7	8	9
Demand		10	10	10	10	15	15	15	20	20
Available		20	10	0	0	0	0	0	0	0
MPS		0	0	10	10	15	15	15	20	20
On hand	30									

expected to be in stock at the end of each weekly period. The opening inventory balance, 'On hand', is shown separately at the bottom of the record. The third row is the master production schedule, or MPS; this shows how many finished items need to be completed and available in each week to satisfy demand.

Chase or level master production schedules

In the example in Table S14.1, the MPS increases as demand increases and aims to keep available inventory at 0. The master production schedule is 'chasing' demand (see Chapter 11) and so adjusting the provision of resources. An alternative 'levelled' MPS for this situation is shown in Table S14.2. Level scheduling involves averaging the amount required to be completed to smooth out peaks and troughs; it generates more inventory than the previous MPS.

Available to promise (ATP)

The master production schedule provides the information to the sales function on what can be promised to customers and when delivery can be promised. The sales function can load known sales orders against the master production schedule and keep track of what is available to promise (ATP) (see Table S14.3). The ATP line in the master production schedule shows the maximum that is still available in any one week, against which sales orders can be loaded.

The bill of materials (BOM)

From the master schedule, MRP calculates the required volume and timing of assemblies, sub-assemblies and materials. To do this it needs information on what parts are required for each product. This is called the 'bill of materials'. Initially it is simplest to think about these as a product structure. The product structure in Figure S14.2 is a simplified structure showing the parts required to make a simple board game. Different 'levels of assembly' are shown with the finished product (the boxed game) at level 0, the parts and sub-assemblies that go into the boxed game at level 1, the parts that go into the sub-assemblies at level 2, and so on.

Table S14.2 Example of a 'level' master production schedule

		Week number								
		1	2	3	4	5	6	7	8	9
Demand		10	10	10	10	15	15	15	20	20
Available		31	32	33	34	30	26	22	13	4
MPS		11	11	11	11	11	11	11	11	11
On hand	30									

Table S14.3 Example of a level master production schedule including available to promise

		Week number								
		1	**2**	**3**	**4**	**5**	**6**	**7**	**8**	**9**
Demand		10	10	10	10	15	15	15	20	20
Sales orders		10	10	10	8	4				
Available		31	32	33	34	30	26	22	13	4
ATP		31	1	1	3	7	11	11	11	11
MPS		11	11	11	11	11	11	11	11	11
On hand	30									

A more convenient form of the product structure is the 'indented bill of materials'. Table S14.4 shows the whole indented bill of materials for the board game. The term 'indented' refers to the indentation of the level of assembly, shown in the left-hand column. Multiples of some parts are required; this means that MRP has to know the required number of each part to be able to multiply up the requirements. Also, the same part (for example, the TV label, part number 10062) may be used in different parts of the product structure. This means that MRP has to cope with this commonality of parts and, at some stage, aggregate the requirements to check how many labels in total are required.

Inventory records

MRP calculations need to recognize that some required items may already be in stock. So, it is necessary, starting at level 0 of each bill, to check how much inventory is available of each finished product, sub-assembly and component, and then to calculate what is termed the 'net' requirements:

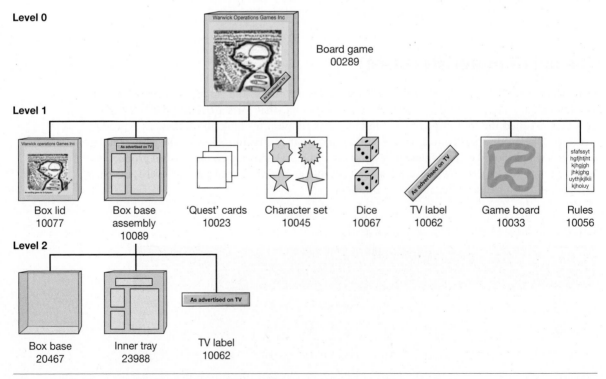

Figure S14.2 Product structure for the Treasure Hunt game

Table S14.4 Indented bill of materials for board game

Part number: 00289 **Description: Board game** **Level: 0**			
Level	**Part number**	**Description**	**Quantity**
0	00289	Board game	1
. 1	10077	Box lid	1
. 1	10089	Box base assy	1
. . 2	20467	Box base	1
. . 2	10062	TV label	1
. . 2	23988	Inner tray	1
. 1	10023	Quest cards set	1
. 1	10045	Character set	1
. 1	10067	Die	2
. 1	10062	TV label	1
. 1	10033	Game board	1
. 1	10056	Rules booklet	1

that is, the extra requirements needed to supplement the inventory so that demand can be met. This requires that three main inventory records are kept: the item master file, which contains the unique standard identification code for each part or component, the transaction file, which keeps a record of receipts into stock, issues from stock and a running balance, and the location file, which identifies where inventory is located.

The MRP netting process

The information needs of MRP are important, but they are not the 'heart' of the MRP procedure. At its core, MRP is a systematic process of taking this planning information and calculating the volume and timing requirements which will satisfy demand. The most important element of this is the MRP netting process. Figure S14.3 illustrates the process that MRP performs to calculate the volumes of materials required. The master production schedule is 'exploded', examining the implications of the schedule through the bill of materials, checking how many sub-assemblies and parts are required. Before moving down the bill of materials to the next level, MRP checks how many of the required parts are already available in stock. It then generates 'works orders', or requests, for the net requirements of items. These form the schedule which is again exploded through the bill of materials at the next level down. This process continues until the bottom level of the bill of materials is reached.

Back-scheduling

In addition to calculating the volume of materials required, MRP also considers when each of these parts is required: that is, the timing and scheduling of materials. It does this by a process called back-scheduling which takes into account the lead time (the time allowed for completion of each stage of the process) at every level of assembly. Again using the example of the board game, assume that 10 board games are required to be finished by a notional planning day which we will term day 20. To determine when we need to start work on all the parts that make up the game, we need to know all the lead times that are stored in MRP files for each part (see Table S14.5).

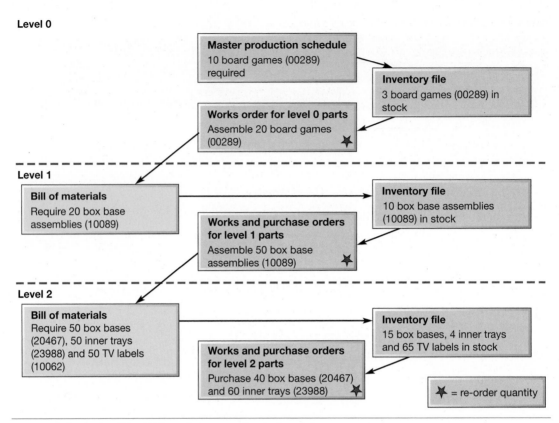

Level 0

Master production schedule
10 board games (00289) required

Inventory file
3 board games (00289) in stock

Works order for level 0 parts
Assemble 20 board games (00289) ✦

Level 1

Bill of materials
Require 20 box base assemblies (10089)

Inventory file
10 box base assemblies (10089) in stock

Works and purchase orders for level 1 parts
Assemble 50 box base assemblies (10089) ✦

Level 2

Bill of materials
Require 50 box bases (20467), 50 inner trays (23988) and 50 TV labels (10062)

Inventory file
15 box bases, 4 inner trays and 65 TV labels in stock

Works and purchase orders for level 2 parts
Purchase 40 box bases (20467) and 60 inner trays (23988) ✦

✦ = re-order quantity

Figure S14.3 Example of the MRP netting process for the board game

Using the lead-time information, the programme is worked backwards to determine the tasks that have to be performed and the purchase orders that have to be placed. Given the lead times and inventory levels shown in Table S14.5, the MRP records shown in Figure S14.4 can be derived.

Table S14.5 Back-scheduling of requirements in MRP

Part no.	Description	Inventory on-hand day 0	Lead time (days)	Re-order quantity
00289	Board game	3	2	20
10077	Box lid	4	8	25
10089	Box base assy	10	4	50
20467	Box base	15	12	40
23988	Inner tray	4	14	60
10062	TV label	65	8	100
10023	Quest cards set	4	3	50
10045	Character set	46	3	50
10067	Die	22	5	80
10033	Game board	8	15	50
10056	Rules booklet	0	3	80

00289: Treasure Hunt game Assembly lead time = 2 Re-order quantity = 20

Day Number:	0	1	2	3	4	5	6	7	8	9	10	11	12	13	14	15	16	17	18	19	20
Requirements Gross																					10
Scheduled Receipts																					
On-hand Inventory	3	3	3	3	3	3	3	3	3	3	3	3	3	3	3	3	3	3	3	3	13
Planned Order Release																			20		

10077: Box lid Purchase lead time = 8 Re-order quantity = 25

Day Number:	0	1	2	3	4	5	6	7	8	9	10	11	12	13	14	15	16	17	18	19	20
Requirements Gross																			20		
Scheduled Receipts																					
On-hand Inventory	4	4	4	4	4	4	4	4	4	4	4	4	4	4	4	4	4	4	9	9	9
Planned Order Release											25										

10089: Box base assembly Assembly lead time = 4 Re-order quantity = 50

Day Number:	0	1	2	3	4	5	6	7	8	9	10	11	12	13	14	15	16	17	18	19	20
Requirements Gross																			20		
Scheduled Receipts																					
On-hand Inventory	10	10	10	10	10	10	10	10	10	10	10	10	10	10	10	10	10	10	40	40	40
Planned Order Release															50						

20467: Box base Purchase lead time = 12 Re-order quantity = 40

Day Number:	0	1	2	3	4	5	6	7	8	9	10	11	12	13	14	15	16	17	18	19	20
Requirements Gross															50						
Scheduled Receipts																					
On-hand Inventory	15	15	15	15	15	15	15	15	15	15	15	15	15	15	5	5	5	5	5	5	5
Planned Order Release		40																			

23988: Inner tray Purchase lead time = 14 Re-order quantity = 60

Day Number:	0	1	2	3	4	5	6	7	8	9	10	11	12	13	14	15	16	17	18	19	20
Requirements Gross															50						
Scheduled Receipts																					
On-hand Inventory	4	4	4	4	4	4	4	4	4	4	4	4	4	4	14	14	14	14	14	14	14
Planned Order Release	60																				

10062: TV label Purchase lead time = 8 Re-order quantity = 100

Day Number:	0	1	2	3	4	5	6	7	8	9	10	11	12	13	14	15	16	17	18	19	20
Requirements Gross															50				20		
Scheduled Receipts																					
On-hand Inventory	65	65	65	65	65	65	65	65	65	65	65	65	65	65	15	15	14	15	95	95	95
Planned Order Release											100										

10023: Quest card set Purchase lead time = 3 Re-order quantity = 50

Day Number:	0	1	2	3	4	5	6	7	8	9	10	11	12	13	14	15	16	17	18	19	20
Requirements Gross																			20		
Scheduled Receipts																					
On-hand Inventory	4	4	4	4	4	4	4	4	4	4	4	4	4	4	4	4	4	4	34	34	34
Planned Order Release															50						

10045: Character set Purchase lead time = 3 Re-order quantity = 50

Day Number:	0	1	2	3	4	5	6	7	8	9	10	11	12	13	14	15	16	17	18	19	20
Requirements Gross																			20		
Scheduled Receipts																					
On-hand Inventory	46	46	46	46	46	46	46	46	46	46	46	46	46	46	46	46	46	46	26	26	26
Planned Order Release																					

10067: Die Purchase lead time = 5 Re-order quantity = 80

Day Number:	0	1	2	3	4	5	6	7	8	9	10	11	12	13	14	15	16	17	18	19	20
Requirements Gross																			40		
Scheduled Receipts																					
On-hand Inventory	3	3	3	3	3	3	3	3	3	3	3	3	3	3	3	3	3	3	3	3	13
Planned Order Release														80							

10033: Game board Purchase lead time = 15 Re-order quantity = 50

Day Number:	0	1	2	3	4	5	6	7	8	9	10	11	12	13	14	15	16	17	18	19	20
Requirements Gross																			20		
Scheduled Receipts																					
On-hand Inventory	8	8	8	8	8	8	8	8	8	8	8	8	8	8	8	8	8	8	38	38	38
Planned Order Release				50																	

10056: Rules booklet Purchase lead time = 3 Re-order quantity = 80

Day Number:	0	1	2	3	4	5	6	7	8	9	10	11	12	13	14	15	16	17	18	19	20
Requirements Gross																			20		
Scheduled Receipts																					
On-hand Inventory	0	0	0	0	0	0	0	0	0	0	0	0	0	0	0	0	0	0	60	60	60
Planned Order Release															80						

Figure S14.4 Extract of the MRP records for the board game

MRP capacity checks

The MRP process needs a feedback loop to check whether a plan was achievable and whether it has actually been achieved. Closing this planning loop in MRP systems involves checking production plans against available capacity and, if the proposed plans are not achievable at any level, revising them. All but the simplest MRP systems are now closed-loop systems. They use three planning routines to check production plans against the operation's resources at three levels.

- Resource requirements plans (RRPs) involve looking forward in the long term to predict the requirements for large structural parts of the operation, such as the numbers, locations and sizes of new plants.
- Rough-cut capacity plans (RCCPs) are used in the medium to short term, to check the master production schedules against known capacity bottlenecks, in case capacity constraints are broken. The feedback loop at this level checks the MPS and key resources only.
- Capacity requirements plans (CRPs) look at the day-to-day effect of the works orders issued from the MRP on the loading individual process stages.

Summary

▶ MRP stands for materials requirements planning, which is a dependent demand system that calculates materials requirements and production plans to satisfy known and forecast sales orders. It helps to make volume and timing calculations based on an idea of what will be necessary to supply demand in the future.

▶ MRP works from a master production schedule which summarizes the volume and timing of end products or services. Using the logic of the bill of materials (BOM) and inventory records, the production schedule is 'exploded' (called the MRP netting process) to determine how many sub-assemblies and parts are required, and when they are required.

▶ Closed-loop MRP systems contain feedback loops which ensure that checks are made against capacity to see if plans are feasible.

▶ MRP II systems are a development of MRP. They integrate many processes that are related to MRP, but which are located outside the operation's function.

15 Lean operations

INTRODUCTION

The focus of lean is to achieve a flow of materials, information or customers that delivers exactly what customers want (perfect quality), in exact quantities (neither too much nor too little), exactly when needed (not too early nor too late), exactly where required (in the right location) and at the lowest possible cost. The principles of lean were once a radical departure from traditional operations practice, but have now become orthodox in promoting the synchronization of flow through processes, operations and supply networks. In addition, despite the pioneering role of Toyota in its development, lean is no longer seen as a manufacturing phenomenon and is found in a wide range of industries. In this chapter, we examine: the key characteristics of lean; the ways that lean eliminates waste; the application of lean across supply networks; and how lean compares to other approaches. Figure 15.1 places lean in the overall model of operations management.

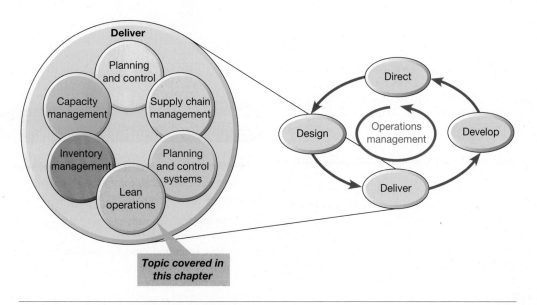

Figure 15.1 This chapter examines lean operations

What is lean?

Lean aims to meet demand for products and services instantaneously, with perfect quality, no waste, and at low cost. It is a concept that is almost synonymous with terms such as 'just-in-time' (JIT), the 'Toyota Production System' (TPS), 'stockless production' and 'lean synchronization'. It results in materials, information and customers flowing rapidly and smoothly through processes, operations and supply networks. The central idea is that this not only ensures reduced throughput time, but also avoids the negative effects of in-process inventory or queues. Inventories and queues are seen as obscuring the problems that exist within processes and therefore inhibiting process improvement.

In this chapter, we provide examples of organizations in a wide range of sectors that apply aspects of lean to their operations and supply networks. Many of the examples of lean philosophy and lean techniques in service industries are directly analogous to those found in manufacturing because physical items are being moved or processed in some way. For example, supermarkets usually replenish their shelves only when customers have taken sufficient products off the shelf. The movement of goods from the 'back office' store to the shelf is triggered by the 'empty-shelf' demand signal. Construction companies increasingly make a rule of only calling for material deliveries to their sites the day before they are needed. This reduces clutter and the chances of theft. Both are examples of the application of *pull control* principles. Other examples of lean concepts and methods apply even when most of the service elements are intangible. For example, new publishing technologies allow professors to assemble printed and e-learning course material customized to the needs of individual courses or even individual students. Here, we see the lean principles of flexibility and small batch sizes allowing customization and rapid delivery.

OPERATIONS IN PRACTICE — Lean construction[1]

Lean can be found across a wide range of settings, including finance, healthcare, IT, retailing, professional services, energy, agriculture and the public sector. Now the construction industry has become the latest to embrace lean principles (sometime referred to in construction as 'integrated project delivery'). With its emphasis on waste reduction and maximization of customer value, lean has strong appeal to many in the construction industry. Construction remains notoriously ineffective in delivering good value for its customers. At present, an estimated 70 per cent of all construction projects are over budget and delivered late, labour productivity is still very low and every year there are thousands of deaths and injuries caused by poor safety standards and lack of adherence to procedures.

Over the past decade, an increasing number of firms in Australia, Germany, Scandinavia, the USA and UK have attempted to introduce lean thinking to construction. The aim has been to apply continuous improvement to the complete project lifecycle including design, procurement, manufacture and construction of infrastructure. It also involves stronger collaboration between key stakeholders in these projects, including clients, architects, engineers, sub-contractors, builders on-site, and planning authorities, with an important shift in emphasis – delivering *value* (as seen by the end customer)

as opposed to delivering *low cost*. Some of the activities that have been implemented by construction companies seeking to adopt lean principles include:

▶ greater emphasis on early planning to avoid expensive changes to projects later on;

▶ pre-fabrication and modular building to reduce the amount of activity being carried out on-site and to increase predictability in scheduling work;

▶ Kaizen practices to ensure improvement ideas are transitioned from one project to another (see Chapter 18 for more on project learning);

- value stream mapping to identify non-value-added activities that cause delays in the completion of construction projects;
- more advanced project monitoring software and daily review meetings to flag potential issues with projects *before* they create delays rather than responding to problems after they occur;
- visual management techniques on-site to help different sub-contractors 'see the bigger picture' of a project and where bottlenecks in work may be forming;
- just-in-time deliveries of materials onto construction sites, to support a 'clean site' and minimize both costs of holding and on-site materials movement;
- reduction in human movement through re-positioning of material and tools on construction sites;
- decentralized decision making through the use of information systems that improve visibility and the empowerment of individuals to take action as needed;
- reduced overproduction, by avoiding working on tasks earlier than scheduled or before the next task in the sequence can be started;

- talent-matching to ensure that the skills of workers are more carefully aligned with task requirements, so knowledge doesn't go to waste;
- benchmarking against other lean construction firms as well as those in other project-based sectors, such as events management, consultancy firms and research labs.

Where firms have actively engaged in lean, improvements have been significant. More projects are being delivered on-time, on-budget and to specification, resulting in improved client satisfaction. Lean construction firms report reduced materials waste, higher labour productivity, lower inventory and fewer work-based injuries. However, some firms have only just started to engage with lean whilst many others argue that the innate characteristics of construction – low volume, high variety – make the principles of lean difficult or even impossible to implement. Other barriers include organizational resistance, unrealistic expectations (especially around the pace of improvement), and a lack of senior management sponsorship for lean implementation.

Three perspectives of lean

Defining lean is not entirely straightforward. In many ways lean can be viewed as three related, but distinct things: a philosophy, a method of planning and control with useful prescriptions of how to manage day-to-day operations, and a set of improvement tools. A short video clip of lean applied to a food bank gives a nice idea of these three elements.[2]

- **Lean is a philosophy of how to run operations.** It is a coherent set of principles that are founded on smoothing flow through processes by doing all the simple things well, gradually doing them better, meeting customer needs exactly, and squeezing out waste every step of the way. Three key issues define the lean philosophy – the involvement of staff in the operation, the drive for continuous improvement, and the elimination of waste. Other chapters look at the first two issues, so we devote much of this chapter to the central idea of waste elimination.
- **Lean is a method of planning and controlling operations.** Many lean ideas are concerned with how items (materials, information, customers) flow through operations; and more specifically, how operations managers can manage this flow. For this reason lean can be viewed as a method of planning and control. Yet it is planning and control in pursuit of lean's philosophical aims. Uncoordinated flow causes unpredictability, and unpredictability causes waste because people hold inventory, capacity or time, to protect themselves against it. So lean planning and control uses several methods to achieve synchronized flow and reduce waste. Above all it uses 'pull' control, which was described in Chapter 10 (in contrast to MRP, described in Chapter 14, which relies on 'push' control). This is usually achieved using some sort of kanban system (described later). In addition, the other lean planning and control methods which promote smooth flow include levelled scheduling and delivery, and mixed modelling (again described later in this chapter).
- **Lean is a set of tools that improve operations performance.** The 'engine room' of the lean philosophy is a collection of improvement tools and techniques that are the means for cutting out waste. What is important to understand is how the

Operations principle

Lean can be viewed as a philosophy of how to run operations, a method of planning and controlling operations, and a set of tools that improve operations performance.

Seen as the leading practitioner and the main originator of the lean approach, the Toyota Motor Company has progressively synchronized all its processes simultaneously to give high-quality, fast throughput and exceptional productivity. It has done this by developing a set of practices that has largely shaped what we now call 'lean' or 'just-in-time' but which Toyota calls the Toyota Production System (TPS). In recent years, Toyota has expanded the application of lean principles from its manufacturing into purchasing, finance, logistics and its dealership network. The TPS has two themes, 'just-in-time' and 'jidoka'. Just-in-time is defined as the rapid and coordinated movement of parts throughout the production system and supply network to meet customer demand. It is operationalized by means of *heijunka* (levelling and smoothing the flow of items), *kanban* (signalling to the preceding process that more parts are needed) and *nagare* (laying out processes to achieve smoother flow of parts throughout the production process). *Jidoka* is described as 'humanizing the interface between operator and machine'. Toyota's philosophy is that the machine is there to serve the operator's purpose. The operator should be left free to exercise his/her judgement. Jidoka is operationalized by means of fail-safing (or machine jidoka), line-stop authority (or human jidoka) and visual control (at-a-glance status of production processes and visibility of process standards).

Toyota believes that both just-in-time and jidoka should be applied ruthlessly to the elimination of waste, where waste is defined as 'anything other than the minimum amount of equipment, items, parts and workers that are absolutely essential to production'. Arguably, Toyota's strength lies in understanding the differences between the tools used within its operations and the overall philosophy. Activities and processes are constantly being challenged and pushed to a higher level of performance, enabling the company to continually innovate and improve. Improvement ideas are ideally simple and low cost, allowing for a high degree of trial and error. While some adopters of lean principles may think they have 'done lean', Toyota simply changes the goal to constantly challenge improvement. As such, we see a key distinction between those that see lean as a specific end-point to be achieved through the application of a series of improvement tools, and those such as Toyota who treat lean as a philosophy that defines a way of conducting business. This perspective may also explain Toyota's heavy investment in its mentorship programme to support those within its supply network in successfully embedding lean principles.

introduction of lean as a philosophy helped to shift the focus of operations management generally towards viewing improvement as its main purpose. In addition, the rise of lean ideas gave birth to techniques that have now become mainstream in operations management. Some of these tools and techniques are well known outside the lean sphere and are covered in other chapters of this book.

How lean operations considers flow

The best way to understand how lean differs from more traditional approaches to managing flow is to contrast the two simple processes in Figure 15.2. The traditional approach assumes that each stage in the process will place its output in an inventory that 'buffers' that stage from the next one downstream in the process. The next stage down will then (eventually) take outputs from the inventory, process them, and pass them through to the next buffer inventory. These buffers are there to 'insulate' each stage from its neighbours, making each stage relatively independent so that if, for example, stage A stops operating for some reason, stage B can continue, at least for a time. The larger the buffer inventory, the greater the degree of insulation between the stages. This insulation has to be paid for in terms of inventory or queues and slow throughput times because products, customers or information will spend time waiting between stages in the process.

The main argument against this traditional approach lies in the very condition it seeks to promote, namely the insulation of the stages from one another. When a problem occurs at one stage, the problem will not immediately be apparent elsewhere in the system. The responsibility for solving the problem will be centred largely on the people within that stage, and the consequences of the problem will be prevented from spreading to the whole system. However, contrast this with the lean process illustrated in Figure 15.2. Here, products, customers or information are processed and then passed directly to the next stage in a

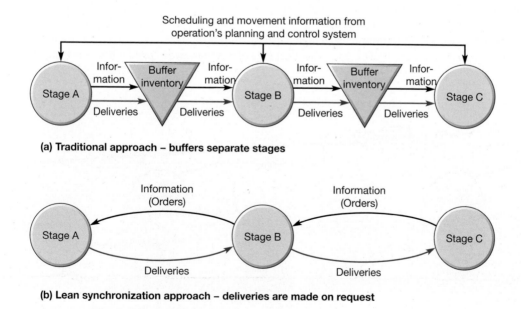

(a) Traditional approach – buffers separate stages

(b) Lean synchronization approach – deliveries are made on request

Figure 15.2 (a) Traditional flow versus (b) lean flow between stages synchronized manner 'just-in-time' for them to be processed further. The aim is to match demand perfectly – neither too much nor too little, only when it is needed. Problems at any stage have a very different effect in such a system. Now if stage A stops processing, stage B will notice immediately and stage C very soon after. Stage A's problem is now quickly exposed to the whole process, which is immediately affected by the problem. This means that the responsibility for solving the problem is no longer confined to the staff at stage A. It is now shared by everyone, considerably improving the chances of the problem being solved, if only because it is now too important to be ignored. In other words, by preventing items accumulating between stages, the operation has increased the chances of the intrinsic efficiency of the plant being improved. Non-synchronized approaches seek to encourage efficiency by protecting each part of the process from disruption. The lean approach takes the opposite view. Exposure of the system (although not suddenly, as in our simplified example) to problems can both make them more evident and change the 'motivation structure' of the whole system towards solving the problems. Lean sees accumulations of inventory, be they product, customer or information inventories, as a 'blanket of obscurity' that lies over the system and prevents problems being noticed.

How lean operations consider inventory

The idea of obscuring effects of inventory is often illustrated diagrammatically, as in Figure 15.3. The many problems of the operation are shown as rocks in a riverbed that cannot be seen because of the depth of the water. The water in this analogy represents the inventory (materials, customers or information) in the operation. Yet, even though the rocks cannot be seen, they slow the progress of the river's flow and cause turbulence. Gradually reducing the depth of the water (inventory) exposes the worst of the problems which can be resolved, after which the water is lowered further, exposing more problems, and so on. The same argument also applies to the flow between whole processes, or whole operations. For example, stages A, B and C in Figure 15.2 could be a supplier operation, a manufacturer and a customer's operation, respectively.

How lean operations considers capacity utilization

Lean has many benefits but these come at the cost of capacity utilization. Return to the process shown in Figure 15.2. When stoppages occur in the traditional system, the buffers allow each stage to continue working and thus achieve high capacity utilization. However, the high utilization does not necessarily make the process as a whole deliver more. Often extra 'production' goes into buffer

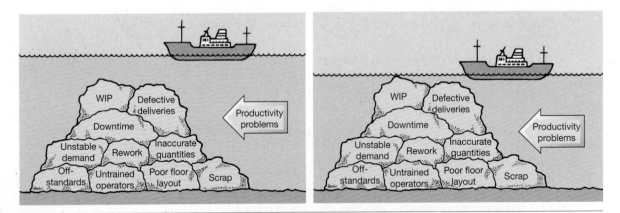

Figure 15.3 Reducing the level of materials, customers or information inventories (the water) allows operations management (the ship) to see the problems in the operation (the rocks) and work to reduce them

inventories or queues of customers. By contrast, any stoppages in a lean process affect the whole process. This will necessarily lead to lower capacity utilization, at least in the short term. In organizations that place a high value on the utilization of capacity this can prove particularly difficult to accept. However, there is no point in producing output just for its own sake. In fact, producing just to keep utilization high is not only pointless, it is counter-productive, because the extra inventory produced merely serves to make improvements less likely. Figure 15.4 illustrates the two approaches to capacity utilization.

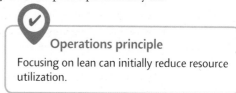

Operations principle

Focusing on lean can initially reduce resource utilization.

How lean operations considers the role of people

Lean proponents frequently stress the behavioural change required to make lean work. The Japanese origins of lean are very much in evidence when considering the role of people in lean operations. It encourages (and often requires) team-based problem-solving, job enrichment (by including maintenance and setup tasks in operators' jobs), job rotation and multi-skilling. The intention is to encourage a high degree of personal responsibility, engagement and 'ownership' of the job. Similarly, what are called 'basic working practices' are sometimes used to implement the 'involvement of everyone' principle. These include the following:

▶ **Discipline** – Work standards that are critical for the safety of staff, the environment and quality must be followed by everyone all the time.
▶ **Flexibility** – It should be possible to expand responsibilities to the extent of people's capabilities. This applies as equally to managers as it does to shop-floor personnel. Barriers to flexibility, such as grading structures and restrictive practices, should be removed.
▶ **Equality** – Unfair and divisive personnel policies should be discarded. Many companies implement the egalitarian message through to company uniforms, consistent pay structures that do not differentiate between full-time staff and hourly-rated staff, and open-plan offices.
▶ **Autonomy** – Delegate responsibility to people involved in direct activities so that management's task becomes one of supporting processes. Delegation includes giving staff the responsibility for stopping processes in the event of problems, scheduling work, gathering performance monitoring data and general problem solving.

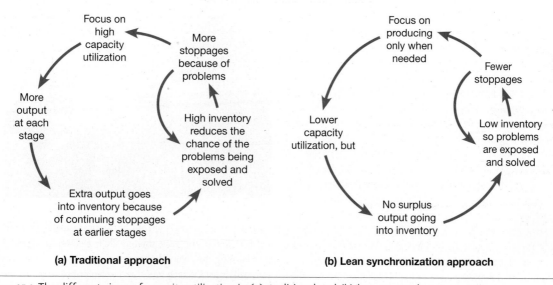

(a) Traditional approach

(b) Lean synchronization approach

Figure 15.4 The different views of capacity utilization in (a) traditional and (b) lean approaches to operations

- ▶ **Development of personnel** – Over time, the aim is to create more company members who can support the rigours of being competitive.
- ▶ **Quality of working life (QWL)** – This may include, for example, involvement in decision making, security of employment, enjoyment and working area facilities.
- ▶ **Creativity** – This is one of the indispensable elements of motivation. Creativity in this context means not just doing a job, but also improving how it is done, and building the improvement into the process.
- ▶ **Total people involvement** – Staff take on more responsibility to use their abilities to the benefit of the company as a whole. They are expected to participate in activities such as the selection of new recruits, dealing directly with suppliers and customers over schedules, quality issues and delivery information, spending improvement budgets, and planning and reviewing work done each day through communication meetings.

How lean operations consider improvement

Lean objectives are often expressed as ideals, such as our definition: 'to meet demand instantaneously with perfect quality and no waste'. While any operation's current performance may be far removed from such ideals, a fundamental lean belief is that it is possible to get closer to them over time. Without such beliefs to drive progress, lean proponents argue that improvement is more likely to be transitory than continuous. This is why the concept of continuous improvement is such an important part of the lean philosophy. If its aims are set in terms of ideals which individual organizations may never fully achieve, then the emphasis must be on the way in which an organization moves closer to the ideal state. The Japanese word for continuous improvement is *kaizen,* and it is a key part of the lean philosophy. It is explained fully in Chapter 17.

How does lean eliminate waste?

Arguably the most significant part of the lean philosophy is its focus on the elimination of all forms of waste. Waste can be defined as any activity that does not add value. For example, studies often show that as little as 5 per cent of total throughput time is actually spent directly adding value. This means

---

OPERATION IN PRACTICE

Autonomy at Amazon[3]

Amazon is a strong believer in delegating responsibility to those on the front line of its service centres. Every day, service agents at Amazon receive calls from customers who are unhappy with some aspect of the product delivered to them. Employees dealing with these complaints are now empowered to make judgements on the extent to which such complaints may be systemic. In cases where they suspect it's a repetitive defect, service agents can 'stop the line' for a particular product ('pulling the andon chord', as will described later in the chapter). This involves taking the product off the website while the problem is fully investigated. According to Amazon, the improved visibility of the system has eliminated tens of thousands of defects a year and has also given service agents a strong sense of being able to deal effectively with customer complaints. Now an agent can not only refund the individual customer, they are also able to tell the customer that others won't receive products until the problem has been properly investigated. Amazon

claims that around 98 per cent of the times when the product is pulled in this way, there really is a systemic problem, highlighting the value of giving its service agents autonomy to make decisions as to when and when not to stop the line.

Critical commentary

Not all commentators see lean-influenced people-management practices as entirely positive. Probably the biggest criticism of lean is the potentially damaging effect on workers that a constant focus on improvement can have. In addition, the emphasis on waste reduction tends to ignore other important performance indicators such as corporate social responsibility and quality of work life. While less autocratic than some Japanese management practices dating from earlier times, lean is certainly not in line with some of the job design philosophies which place a high emphasis on contribution and commitment, as described in Chapter 9. Finally, as we explore in Chapter 18 in the face of increased uncertainty, lean operations may face higher levels of exposure to failure events.

that for 95 per cent of its time, an operation is adding cost to the service or product, not adding value. Such calculations can alert even relatively efficient operations to the enormous waste which is dormant within all operations. This same phenomenon applies as much to service processes as it does to manufacturing ones. Relatively simple requests, such as applying for a driving licence, may only take a few minutes to actually process, yet take days (or weeks) to be returned.

> **Operations principle**
>
> Simple, transparent flow exposes sources of waste.

OPERATIONS IN PRACTICE

Pixar adopts lean

It seems that lean principles (or some lean principles) can be applied even to the most unlikely of processes. None less likely than Pixar Animation Studios, the Academy Award winning computer animation studio and makers of feature films that have resulted in an unprecedented streak of both critical and box office success including *Toy Story* (1, 2 and 3), *A Bug's Life, Monsters, Inc., Inside Out, Finding Nemo, The Incredibles, Ratatouille, WALL-E* and *Up*. Since its incorporation, Pixar has been responsible for many important breakthroughs in the application of computer graphics (CG) for filmmaking. So, the company has attracted some of the world's finest technical, creative and production talent in the area. And such 'knowledge-based' talent is notoriously difficult to manage; certainly not the type of processes that are generally seen as being appropriate for lean. Managing creativity involves a difficult trade-off, between encouraging the freedom to produce novel ideas, yet making sure that people work within an effective overall structure.

Nevertheless, Pixar did get the inspiration from Toyota and the way it uses lean production, especially the way Toyota has encouraged continuous advice and criticism from its production line workers to improve its performance. Pixar realized that it could do the same with producing cartoon characters. Adopting constant feedback surfaces problems before they become crises, and provides creative teams with inspiration and challenge. Pixar also devotes a great deal of effort to persuading its creative staff to work together. In similar companies, people may collaborate on specific projects, but are less good at focusing on what's going on elsewhere in the business. Pixar, however, tries to cultivate a sense of collective responsibility. Staff even show unfinished work to one another in daily meetings, so get used to giving and receiving constructive criticism.

Causes of waste – muda, mura, muri

The terms muda, mura, and muri are Japanese words conveying three causes of waste that should be reduced or eliminated.

▶ *Muda* are activities in a process that are wasteful because they do not add value to the operation or the customer. The main causes of these wasteful activities are likely to be poorly communicated objectives (including not understanding the customer's requirements), or the inefficient use of resources. The implication of this is that, for an activity to be effective, it must be properly recorded and communicated to whoever is performing it.

▶ *Mura* means 'lack of consistency' or unevenness that results in periodic overloading of staff or equipment. So, for example, if activities are not properly documented so that different people at different times perform a task differently, then not surprisingly, the result of the activity may be different. The negative effects of this are similar to a lack of dependability (see Chapter 2).

▶ *Muri* means absurd or unreasonable. It is based on the idea that unnecessary or unreasonable requirements put on a process will result in poor outcomes. The implication of this is that appropriate skills, effective planning, accurate estimation of times and schedules will avoid this 'muri' form of waste. In other words, waste can be caused by failing to carry out basic operations planning tasks such as prioritizing activities (sequencing), and understanding the time (scheduling) and resources (loading) needed to perform activities. All these issues are discussed in Chapter 10.

These three causes of waste are obviously related. When a process is inconsistent (mura), it can lead to the overburdening of equipment and people (muri), which, in turn, will cause all kinds of non-value-adding activities (muda).

Types of waste

Muda, mura and muri are three *causes* of waste. Now we turn to *types* of waste, which apply in many different types of operations – both service and manufacturing – and which form the core of lean philosophy. Here we consolidate these into four broad categories.

Waste from irregular flow

Perfect synchronization means smooth and even flow through processes, operations and supply networks. Barriers that prevent streamlined flow include the following:

▶ *Waiting time* – machine efficiency and labour efficiency are two popular measures that are widely used to measure machine and labour waiting time, respectively. Less obvious is the time when products, customers or information wait as inventory or queues, there simply to keep operators busy.

▶ *Transportation* – moving items or customers around the operation, together with double and triple handling, does not add value. Layout changes that bring processes closer together, and improvements in transport methods and workplace organization can all reduce waste.

▶ *Process inefficiencies* – the process itself may be a source of waste. Some operations may only exist because of poor component design, or poor maintenance, and so could be eliminated.

▶ *Inventory* – regardless of type (product, customer, information) all inventories should become a target for elimination. However, it is only by tackling the causes of inventory or queues, such as irregular flow, that it can be reduced.

▶ *Motion* – an operator may look busy but sometimes no value is being added by the work. Simplification of work is a rich source of reduction in the waste of motion.

Waste from inexact supply

Lean also means supplying exactly what is wanted, exactly when it is needed. Any under or over supply and any early or late delivery will result in waste, something we have already explored in Chapter 11. Barriers to achieving an exact match between supply an demand include the following:

- *Over-production or under-production* – supplying more than, or less than, is immediately needed by the next stage, process or operation. (This is the greatest source of waste according to Toyota.)
- *Early or late delivery* – items should only arrive exactly when they are needed. Early delivery is as wasteful as late delivery.
- *Talent* – misaligning individual talents, skills, creativity, and knowledge relative to task generates waste. Examples include having skilled workers completing unskilled tasks or limiting decision-making authority to a high level within a business.
- *Inventory* – again, all inventories should become a target for elimination. However, it is only by tackling the causes of inventory, such as inexact supply, that it can be reduced.

Waste from inflexible response

Customer needs can vary, in terms of what they want, how much they want and when they want it. However, processes usually find it more convenient to change what they do relatively infrequently, because every change implies some kind of cost. That is why hospitals schedule specialist clinics only at particular times, and why machines often make a batch of similar products together. Yet responding to customer demands exactly and instantaneously requires a high degree of process flexibility. Symptoms of inadequate flexibility include the following:

- *Large batches* – sending batches of materials, customers, or information through a process inevitably increases inventory as the batch moves through the whole process.
- *Delays between activities* – the longer the time (and the cost) of changing over from one activity to another, the more difficult it is to synchronize flow to match customer demand instantaneously.
- *More variation in activity mix than in customer demand* – if the mix of activities in different time periods varies more than customer demand varies, then some 'batching' of activities must be taking place.

Waste from variability

Lean implies exact levels of quality. If there is variability in quality levels then customers will not consider themselves as being adequately supplied. Variability therefore is an important barrier to achieving synchronized supply. Symptoms of poor variability include the following:

- *Poor reliability of equipment or staff* – unreliable equipment or staff usually indicates a lack of conformance in quality levels. It also means that there will be irregularity in supplying customers. Either way, it prevents synchronization of supply.
- *Defective products or services* – waste caused by poor quality is significant in most operations. Errors in the service or product cause both customers and processes to waste time until they are corrected.

Looking for waste (and kaizen opportunities) – the 'Gemba walk'

Gemba (also sometimes called 'ganba'), when roughly translated from the Japanese, means 'the actual place' where something happens. It is a term often used in lean philosophy or in improvement generally, to convey the idea that, if you really want to understand something, you go to where it actually takes place. Only then can a true appreciation of the realities of improvement opportunities be gained. Lean improvement advocates often use the idea of 'the gemba walk' to make problems visible. By this they mean that managers should regularly visit the place where the job is done to seek out waste (the Western idea of 'Management by Walking Around' is similar). The concept of Gemba is also used in new service or product development to mean that designers should go to where the service happens, or where the product is used, to develop their ideas.

Operations principle

There is no substitute for seeing the way processes actually operate in practice.

Eliminating waste through streamlined flow

The smooth flow of materials, information and people in the operation is a central idea of lean. Long process routes provide opportunities for delay and inventory build-up, add no value, and slow down throughput time. So, the first contribution any operation can make to streamline flow is to reconsider the basic layout of its processes. Primarily, reconfiguring the layout of a process to aid lean involves moving it down the 'natural diagonal' of process design that was discussed in Chapter 6. Broadly speaking, this means moving from functional layouts towards cell-based layouts, or from cell-based layouts towards line layouts. Either way, it is necessary to move towards a layout that brings more systematization and control to the process flow. At a more detailed level, typical layout techniques include placing workstations close together so that inventories of products or customers simply have no space to build up, and arranging workstations in such a way that all those who contribute to a common activity are in sight of each other and can provide mutual help. For example, at the Virginia Mason Medical Centre, Seattle, USA, a leading proponent of lean in healthcare, many of the waiting rooms have been significantly reduced in their capacity or removed entirely. This forces a focus on the flow of the whole process because patients have literately nowhere to be stored.

Throughput time is often taken as a surrogate measure for waste in a process. The longer that items being processed are held in inventory, moved, checked or subject to anything else that does not add value, the longer they take to progress through the process. So, looking at exactly what happens to items within a process is an excellent method of identifying sources of waste.

<table>
<tr><td>OPERATIONS IN PRACTICE</td><td>Waste reduction in airline maintenance[4]</td></tr>
</table>

Aircraft maintenance is important. Planes have a distressing tendency to fall out of the sky unless they are checked, repaired and generally maintained regularly! So the overriding objective of the operations that maintain aircraft must be the quality of maintenance activities. But it is not the only objective. Improving maintenance turnaround time can reduce the number of aircraft an airline needs to own, because they are not out of action for as long. Also, the more efficient the maintenance process, the more profitable is the activity and the more likely a major airline with established maintenance operations can create additional revenue streams by doing maintenance for other airlines. Figure 15.5 shows the path taken by maintenance staff before and after lean analysis. The objectives of the lean analysis were to preserve, or even improve, quality levels while at the same time improving the cost of maintaining airframes and increasing the availability of airframes by reducing turnaround time.

The lean analysis focused on identifying waste in the maintenance process. Two findings emerged from this. First, the sequence of activities on the airframe itself was being set by the tasks identified in the technical manuals supplied by the engine, body, control system and other suppliers. No one had considered all the individual activities together to work out a sequence that would save maintenance staff time and effort. The overall sequence of activities was defined and allocated with structured work preparation of tools, materials and equipment. Second, maintenance staff would often be waiting until the airframe became available. Yet some of the preparatory work and set-ups did not need to be done while the airframe was present. Therefore why not get maintenance staff to do these tasks when they would otherwise be waiting before the airframe became available? The result of these changes was a substantial improvement in cost and availability. In addition, work preparation was

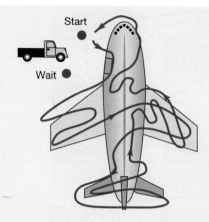

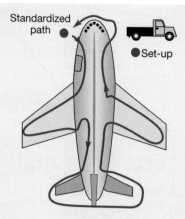

Before:
- Maintenance staff follow the steps as detailed in the technical documentation.
- The overall sequence of tasks is not optimized.
- Preparation work and set-ups included as part of the task.

After:
- The overall sequence of tasks is defined and allocated to minimize non-value-added.
- Preparation work and set-ups may be done ahead of time to minimize aircraft contact time.
- Increased productivity and reduced aircraft waiting time.

Figure 15.5 Aircraft maintenance procedures subject to waste reduction analysis

conducted in a more rigorous and routine manner and maintenance staff were more motivated because many minor frustrations and barriers to their efficient working were removed.

Value stream mapping

Value stream mapping (also known as 'end-to-end' system mapping) is a simple but effective approach to understanding the flow of people, information and materials as they move through the entire process, operation or supply network. It records not only the direct activities of creating products and services, but also the 'indirect' information systems that support the direct process. It is called 'value stream' mapping because it focuses on distinguishing between value-adding and non-value-adding activities. It is similar to process mapping (see Chapter 6) but different in three ways:

▶ It uses a broader range of information than most process maps.
▶ It is usually at a higher level (5–10 activities) than most process maps.
▶ It often has a wider scope, frequently taking a supply network perspective.

A value stream perspective involves working on (and improving) the 'big picture', rather than just optimizing individual processes. Value stream mapping is seen by many practitioners as a starting point to help recognize waste and identify its causes. It is a four-step technique that identifies waste and suggests ways in which activities can be streamlined. First, it involves identifying the value stream (the process, operation or supply chain) to map. Second, it involves physically mapping a process, then above it mapping the information flow that enables the process to occur. This is the so-called 'current state' map. Third, problems are diagnosed and changes suggested, making a future state map that represents the improved process, operation or supply chain. Finally, the changes are implemented. Figure 15.6 shows a value stream map for an industrial air conditioning installation service. The service process itself is broken down into five relatively large stages and various items of data for each stage is marked on the chart. The type of data collected here does vary, but all types of value stream map compare the total throughput time with the amount of value-added time within the larger process. In this case, only 8 of the 258 hours of the process are value adding.

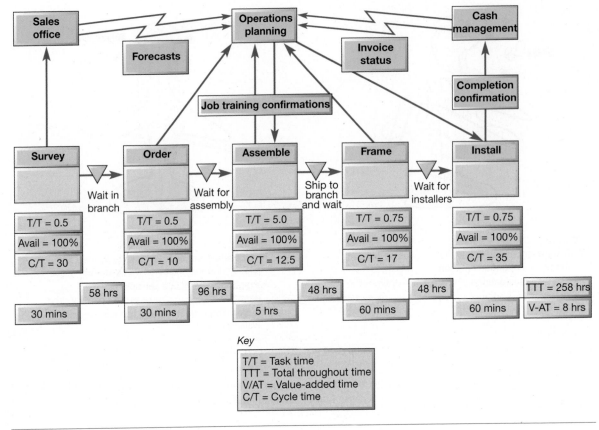

Figure 15.6 Value stream map for an industrial air conditioning installation service

Adopting visual management

Visual management is one of the lean techniques designed to make the current and planned state of the operation or process transparent to everyone, so that anyone (whether working in the process or not) can very quickly see what is going on. It usually employs some kind of visual sign, such as a notice board, computer screen, or simply lights or other signals, which convey what is happening. Although a seemingly trivial and usually simple device, visual management has several benefits. It:

▶ acts as a common focus for team meetings;
▶ demonstrates methods for safe and effective working practice;
▶ communicates to everyone how performance is being judged;
▶ assesses at a glance the current status of the operation;
▶ increases understanding of tasks and work priorities;
▶ judges your and others' performance;
▶ identifies the flow of work, what has been and is being done;
▶ identifies when something is not going to plan;
▶ shows what agreed standards should be;
▶ provides real-time feedback on performance to everyone involved;
▶ reduces the reliance on formal meetings.

An important technique used to ensure flow visibility is the use of simple, but highly visual signals to indicate that a problem has occurred, together with operational authority to stop the process. For example, on an assembly line, if an employee detects some kind of quality problem, he or she could activate a signal that illuminates a light (called an 'andon' light) above the work station and stops the line. Although this may seem to reduce the efficiency of the line, the idea is that this loss of efficiency in the short term is less than the accumulated losses of allowing defects to continue on in the process

Visual mapping at KONKEPT

The finance operation of KONKEPT, the online toy retailer based in Singapore, was having problems. Service levels were low, and complaints high, as the office attempted to deal with payments from customers, invoices from suppliers and requests for information from its distribution centre; all while demand was increasing. It was agreed that the office's processes were chaotic and poorly managed, with little understanding of priorities or how each member of staff was contributing. To remedy this state of affairs, the manager responsible for the office first tried to bring clarity to the process by defining individual and team roles and started establishing visual management. Collectively the staff mapped processes and set performance objectives. These objectives were shown on a large board placed so everyone in the office could see it. At the end of each day, process supervisors updated the board with each process's performance for the day. Also indicated on the board were visual representations of various improvement projects being carried out by the teams. Every morning, staff gathered in what was called 'the morning huddle' to discuss the previous day's performance,

identify how it could be improved, review the progress of on-going improvement projects, and plan for the upcoming day's work. For the staff at KONKEPT, the experience illustrated the three main functions of visual management:

▶ to act as a communication mechanism;
▶ to encourage commitment to agreed goals;
▶ to facilitate cooperation between team members.

(see the 'Operations in practice' case of 'Autonomy at Amazon' earlier). Unless problems are tackled immediately, they may never be corrected.

Using small-scale simple process technology

Lean often involves moving towards smaller-scale process technology to reduce fluctuations in flow volume. For example, in Figure 15.7 one large machine produces a batch of A, followed by a batch of B, followed by a batch of C. However, if three smaller machines are used, they can each produce A, B or C simultaneously. The system is also more robust. If one large machine breaks down, the whole system ceases to operate. If one of the three smaller machines breaks down, it is still operating at two-thirds effectiveness. Small machines are also easily moved, so that layout flexibility is enhanced, and the risks of making errors in investment decisions are reduced. However, investment in capacity may increase in total because parallel facilities are needed, so utilization may be lower (see the earlier arguments).

Eliminating waste through matching supply and demand exactly

The value of the supply of services or products is always time dependent. Something that is delivered early or late often has less value than something that is delivered exactly when it is needed. For example, parcel delivery companies charge more for guaranteed faster delivery. This is because we often need delivery to be as fast as possible. The closer to instantaneous delivery we can get, the more value the delivery has for us and the more

Operations principle

Delivering only and exactly what is needed, and when it is needed, smooths flow and exposes waste.

 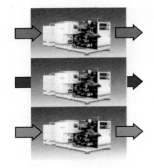

Figure 15.7 Using several small machines rather than one large one allows simultaneous processing, is more robust, and is more flexible

we are willing to pay for it. In fact, delivery of information earlier than it is required can be even more harmful than late delivery because it results in information inventories that serve to confuse flow through the process.

Using pull control

The exact matching of supply and demand is often best served by using 'pull control' wherever possible (discussed in Chapter 10). At its simplest, consider how some fast-food restaurants cook and assemble food and place it in the warm area only when the customer-facing server has sold an item. Production is being triggered only by real customer demand. The essence of pull control is to let the downstream stage in a process, operation or supply network pull items (product, customers or information) through the system rather than have the items 'pushed' to it by the supplying stage.

Using kanbans

The most common method to support pull control in lean operations is the use of kanbans – simple signalling devices that prevent the accumulation of material, customer and information inventories. The word '*kanban*' is the Japanese for card or signal. It is sometimes called the 'invisible conveyor' that controls the transfer of items between the stages of an operation. In its simplest form, it is a card used by a customer stage to instruct its supplier stage to send more items. In some companies, kanbans remain physical – solid plastic markers or even coloured ping-pong balls; in others, electronic point of sales (EPOS) systems generate digital kanbans for further 'production' (delivery of stock). Whichever kind of kanban is being used, the principle is always the same: the receipt of a kanban triggers the movement, production or supply of one unit of product or one standard amount of service activity. If two kanbans are received, two units of work are 'produced', and so on. Some companies use 'kanban squares' – marked spaces on the shop floor to fit one or more work pieces or containers. Only the existence of an empty square triggers production at the stage that supplies the square. Likewise 'kanban' whiteboards are increasingly used to 'pull' activity through many service process. The kanban serves three purposes:

▶ It is an instruction for the preceding process to send more.
▶ It is a visual control tool to show up areas of over-production and lack of synchronization.
▶ It is a tool for kaizen (continuous improvement). Toyota's rules state that 'the number of kanbans should be reduced over time'.

Eliminating waste through flexible processes

Responding exactly and instantaneously to customer demand implies that operations resources need to be sufficiently flexible to change both what they do and how much they do of it without incurring high cost or long delays. In fact, flexible processes (often with flexible technologies) can significantly enhance smooth and synchronized flow. For example, a firm of lawyers used to take ten days to prepare its bills for customers. This meant that customers were not asked to pay until ten days after the work had been done. Now it uses a system that, every day, updates each customer's account. So, when a bill is sent it includes all work up to the day before the billing date. The principle here is that process inflexibility also delays cash flow.

Reducing changeover times

Responding to demand only when it is needed usually requires a degree of flexibility in processes, both to cope with unexpected demand and to allow quick changeover between one activity and another. Changeover time can often be reduced significantly – compare, for example, the time it takes you to change a car tyre with the sub-3 seconds taken by a Formula 1 team! Changeover time reduction can be achieved by a variety of methods such as the following:

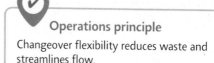

Operations principle

Changeover flexibility reduces waste and streamlines flow.

▶ *Measure and analyse changeover activities* – Sometimes simply measuring the current changeover times, recording them and analysing exactly what activities are performed can help to improve changeover times.

▶ *Separate external and internal activities* – 'External' activities are simply the activities that can be carried out while the process is continuing. For example, processes could be getting ready for the next customer or job while waiting for the next one (see the example of aircraft maintenance described earlier). 'Internal' activities are those that cannot be carried out while the process is going on (e.g. interviewing the customer while completing a service request for the previous customer). By identifying and separating internal and external activities, the intention is to do as much as possible while the step/process is continuing

▶ *Convert internal to external activities* – The other common approach to changeover time reduction is to convert work which was previously performed during the changeover to work that is performed outside the changeover period. There are three major methods of achieving the transfer of internal set-up work to external work:

— Pre-prepare activities or equipment instead of having to do it during changeover periods.
— Make the changeover process intrinsically flexible and capable of performing all required activities without any delay.
— Speed up any required changes of equipment, information or staff, for example by using simple devices.

▶ *Practise changeover routines* – Not surprisingly, the constant practice of changeover routines and the associated learning curve effect tends to reduce changeover times.

Eliminating waste through minimizing variability

One of the biggest causes of the variability is variation in the quality of items. This is why a discussion of lean should always include an evaluation of how quality conformance is ensured within processes, which was referred to as 'mura' earlier. In particular, the principles of statistical process control (SPC) can be used to understand quality variability. Chapter 17 and its supplement on SPC examine this subject, so in this section we shall focus on other causes of variability. The first of these is variability in the mix of items moving through processes operations or supply networks.

Rapid changeover for Boeing and Airbus[5]

Fast changeovers are particularly important for airlines because they can't make money from aircraft that are sitting idle on the ground. It is called 'running the aircraft hot' in the industry. For many airlines, the biggest barrier to running hot is that their markets are not large enough to justify passenger flights during the day and night. So, in order to avoid aircraft being idle over night, they must be used in some other way. That was the motive behind Boeing's 737 'Quick Change' (QC) aircraft. With this aircraft, airlines have the flexibility to use it for passenger flights during the day and, with less than a one-hour changeover (set-up) time, use it as a cargo aeroplane throughout the night. Boeing engineers designed frames that hold entire rows of seats that could smoothly glide on and off the aircraft, allowing twelve seats to be rolled into place at once. When used for cargo, the seats are simply rolled out and replaced by special cargo containers designed to fit the curve of the fuselage and prevent damage to the interior. Before reinstalling the seats, the sidewalls are thoroughly cleaned so that, once the seats are in place, passengers cannot tell the difference between a QC aircraft and a normal 737.

The rapid changeover concept has also been developed by Airbus. It announced that in future it intends to introduce new 'living area' options on its A330 family of aircraft . . . positioned in the cargo hold! There will be a variety of different pod types, including family sleeping areas, meeting rooms, a children's play area and gym space. Each pod has been designed to be taken in and out of the cargo holds quickly (as with Boeing's 'Quick Change') to allow rapid changeover in capacity use depending on the needs of the market and route at any given time.

Levelling product or service schedules

Levelled scheduling (or heijunka) means keeping the mix and volume of flow between stages at an even rate over time. The move from conventional to levelled scheduling is illustrated in Figure 15.8. Conventionally, if a mix of items were required in a time period (usually a month), a batch size would be calculated for each item and the batches produced in some sequence. Figure 15.8(a) shows three items that are produced in a 20-day time period in an operation.

Quantity of item A required = 3,000
Quantity of item B required = 1,000
Quantity of item C required = 1,000

Batch size of item A = 600
Batch size of item B = 200
Batch size of item C = 200

Starting at day 1, the unit commences producing item A. During day 3, the batch of 600 As is finished and dispatched to the next stage. The batch of Bs is started but is not finished until day 4. The remainder of day 4 is spent making the batch of Cs and both batches are dispatched at the end of that day. The cycle then repeats itself. The consequence of using large batches is, first, that relatively large amounts of inventory accumulate within and between the units, and second, that most days are different from one another in terms of what they are expected to produce (in more complex circumstances, no two days would be the same).

Now suppose that the flexibility of the unit could be increased to the point where the batch sizes for the items were reduced to a quarter of their previous levels without loss of capacity (see Figure 15.8(b)):

Batch size of item A = 150
Batch size of item B = 50
Batch size of item C = 50

A batch of each item can now be completed in a single day, at the end of which the three batches are dispatched to their next stage. Smaller batches of inventory are moving between each stage, which will reduce the overall level of work-in-progress in the operation. Just as significant, however, is the effect on the regularity and rhythm of production at the unit. Now every day in the month is the same in terms of what needs to be processed. This makes planning and control of each stage in the operation much easier. For example, if on day 1 of the month the daily batch of As was finished by 11.00 am, and all the batches were successfully completed in the day, then the following day the unit will know that, if it again completes all the As by 11.00 am, it is on schedule. When every day is different, the simple question 'Are we on schedule to complete our processing today?' requires some investigation before it can be answered.

> **Operations principle**
>
> Variability in product or service quality, or quantity, or timing, acts against smooth flow and waste elimination.

Levelling delivery schedules

A similar concept to levelled scheduling can be applied to many transportation processes (illustrated in Figure 15.9). For example, a chain of convenience stores may need to make deliveries of all the different types of products it sells every week. Traditionally it may have dispatched a truck loaded

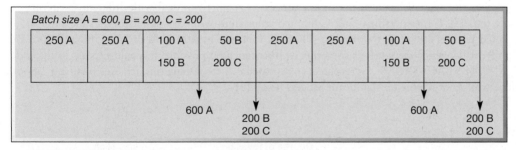

(a) Scheduling in large batches

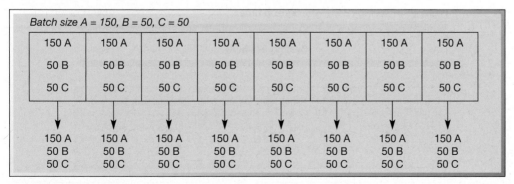

(b) Levelled scheduling

Figure 15.8 Levelled scheduling equalizes the mix of products/services delivered each day

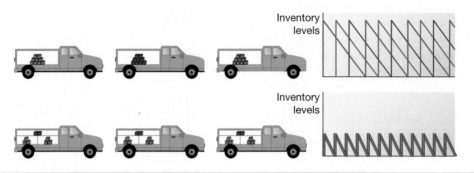

Figure 15.9 Delivering smaller quantities more often can reduce inventory levels

with one particular product around all its stores so that each store received the appropriate amount of the product that would last them for one week. This is equivalent to the large batches discussed in the previous example. An alternative would be to dispatch smaller quantities of all products in a single truck more frequently. Then, each store would receive smaller deliveries more frequently, inventory levels would be lower and the system could respond to trends in demand more readily because more deliveries means more opportunity to change the quantity delivered to a store.

Adopting mixed modelling

The principle of levelled scheduling can be taken further to give mixed modelling – repeating the mix of outputs. Suppose that the machines in the production unit or employees in a service operation can be made so flexible that they achieve the JIT ideal of a batch size of one. The sequence of individual products or services emerging from the process could be reduced progressively as illustrated in Figure 15.10. This would create a steady stream flowing continuously from the unit. However, the sequence does not always fall as conveniently as in Figure 15.10. The working times needed for different products or services are rarely identical and the ratios of required volumes are less convenient. For example, a small business tax return process is required to deal with different tax returns A (sole traders), B (partnerships) and C (limited companies with 0–3 employees) in the ratio 8:5:4. It could process 800 of A, followed by 500 of B, followed by 400 of A; or 80A, 50B and 40C. But ideally, to sequence the work as smoothly as (theoretically) possible, it would process in the order BACABACABACABACAB . . . repeated. . . repeated . . . etc. Doing this achieves relatively smooth flow, whilst not relying on significant process flexibility.

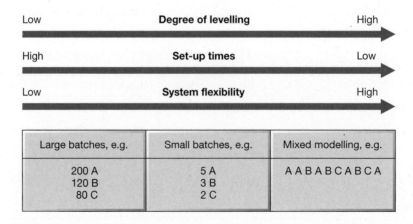

Figure 15.10 Levelled scheduling and mixed modelling: mixed modelling becomes possible as the batch size approaches 1

Jamie's 'lean' cooking[6]

Most people do not have the time to devote long hours to cooking. This might be why the celebrity chef Jamie Oliver has written a book *Jamie's 30-Minute Meals,* whose philosophy is that cooking a delicious dinner should be as quick and cheap as a take-away. The book presents 50 ready-made menus with three to four courses per menu designed to take no more than 30 minutes to prepare. To achieve this performance Jamie has, perhaps inadvertently, applied the principles and methods of lean to the everyday activity of cooking.

Let's imagine that your family is coming over for dinner and you want to surprise them with a new Indian multi-course meal with chicken, rice, salad on the side and of course a dessert. Traditionally, you would search and look up four different recipes, one for each dish. Because all recipes come from different places, you need to figure out the quantity of food to buy, doing the maths in the case of shared ingredients across the dishes, how to allocate pots, pans and other equipment to the different ingredients, and most importantly, you need to figure out in what order to prepare things, especially if you want all your dishes ready at the same time. Jamie's approach significantly reduces this complexity by ensuring dishes are prepared right when the next step in the process needs it, regardless of which dish it is. In other words, dishes are not cooked in sequence, one after another, but they are prepared and completed simultaneously.

If we identify all the tasks related to preparing the salad (e.g., chopping the vegetables) with the letter A, cooking the rice (e.g., blending) with letter B, cooking the chicken with letter C, and finally making the dessert with the letter D, then in the traditional way of cooking our task scheduling would look something like AAAA BBBBBBB CCCCCCC DDDD. This results in batching, waiting time and causing dishes to be ready before the dinner is supposed to be served. Conversely, Jamie Oliver's 30-minute cooking involves scheduling tasks in a sequence like ABCDACBADCBABDC, where single tasks

related to different dishes follow smoothly, as the chef chops a salad ingredient, then blends the rice, then chops some more salad ingredients while the chicken is being roasted in the oven and a part of the desert is being prepared. This way, all dishes are ready at the same time, just in time, and nothing is prepared before it has to be, avoiding any form of waste. Such a levelled approach to scheduling is called heijunka (mixed modelling) in the lean approach.

In addition, Jamie's lean cooking builds on reduced set-up times. At the beginning of each recipe, the equipment needed to prepare the menu is presented under the headline 'To Start'. Other necessary preparations, such as heating the oven, are also specified. Having all equipment ready from the start saves time in the process, and is, according to Jamie, a prerequisite for getting done in thirty minutes. The use of simple equipment that is suitable for many different purposes also makes the process quicker as changeovers are minimized. The rationale is to make the most out of the time available, eliminating the 'faffing around' in cooking (non-value-added activity in OM language) and leaving only what is strictly 'good, fast cooking', without compromising on quality.

Keeping things simple – the 5Ss

The **5S terminology** comes originally from Japan, and although the translation into English is approximate, they are generally taken to represent the following.

▶ **Sort** (*seiri*). Eliminate what is not needed and keep what is needed.
▶ **Straighten** (*seiton*). Position things in such a way that they can be easily reached whenever they are needed.
▶ **Shine** (*seiso*). Keep things clean and tidy; no refuse or dirt in the work area.

- ▶ **Standardize** (*seiketsu*). Maintain cleanliness and order – perpetual neatness.
- ▶ **Sustain** (*shitsuke*). Develop a commitment and pride in keeping to standards.

The 5Ss can be thought of as a simple housekeeping methodology to organize work areas that focuses on visual order, organization, cleanliness and standardization. It helps to eliminate all types of waste relating to uncertainty, waiting, searching for relevant information, creating variation and so on. By eliminating what is unnecessary, and making everything clear and predictable, clutter is reduced, needed items are always in the same place and work is made easier and faster.

Adopting total productive maintenance (TPM)

Total productive maintenance aims to eliminate the variability in operations processes caused by the effect of breakdowns. This is achieved by involving everyone in the search for maintenance improvements. Process owners are encouraged to assume ownership of their equipment and to undertake routine maintenance and simple repair tasks. These principles apply equally to service operations. For example, at a car wash, service employees regularly maintain their power-hoses to prevent unnecessary downtime, while university employees may be encouraged to regularly 'clean' e-mail inboxes, delete old files on their computers, and update software with the aim of maintaining system availability speed and protecting from viruses. By doing so, maintenance specialists can then be freed to develop higher-order skills for improved maintenance systems. TPM is discussed in more detail in Chapter 18 on risk and recovery.

How does lean apply throughout the supply network?

Although most of the concepts and techniques discussed in this chapter are devoted to the management of stages *within* processes and processes *within* an operation, the same principles can apply to the whole supply network. In this context, the stages in a process are the whole businesses, operations or processes between which products flow. And as any business starts to approach lean it will eventually come up against the constraints imposed by the lack of synchronization of the other operations in its supply network. So, achieving further gains must involve trying to spread lean practice outward to its partners. Ensuring entire supply networks are lean is clearly a far more demanding task than doing the same within a single process. The nature of the interaction between whole operations is far more complex than between individual stages within a process. A far more complex mix of products and services is likely to be being provided and the whole network is likely to be subject to a less predictable set of potentially disruptive events. To make a supply network lean means more than making each operation in the network lean. Rather one needs to apply the lean philosophy to the supply chain *as a whole*, something that is extremely challenging in practice.

Essentially, the principles of lean are the same for a supply network as they are for a process. Fast throughput throughout is still valuable and will save cost. Lower levels of inventory will still make it easier to achieve lean. Waste is just as evident (and even larger) at the level of the supply network and reducing waste is still a worthwhile task. Streamlined flow, exact matching of supply and demand, enhanced flexibility, and minimizing variability are all still tasks that will benefit the whole network. The principles of pull control can work between whole operations in the same way as they can between stages within a single process. In fact, the principles and the techniques of lean are essentially the same no matter what level of analysis is being used. In addition, because lean is being implemented on a larger scale, the benefits will also be proportionally greater.

> **Operations principle**
>
> The advantages of lean apply at the level of the process, the operation and the supply network.

One of the weaknesses of lean is that it is difficult to achieve when conditions are subject to unexpected disturbance. This is especially a problem with applying lean principles in the context of the whole supply network. Whereas unexpected fluctuations and disturbances do occur within operations, local management has a reasonable degree of control that it can exert in order to reduce them. Outside the operation, within the supply network, it is far more difficult. Nevertheless, it is generally

Remember the section on supply chain vulnerability in Chapter 13, where it was argued that lean principles can be taken to an extreme. When just-in-time ideas first started to have an impact on operations practice, some authorities advocated the reduction of between-process inventories to zero. While in the long term this provides the ultimate in motivation for operations managers to ensure the efficiency and reliability of each process stage, it does not admit the possibility of some processes always being intrinsically less than totally reliable. An alternative view is to allow inventories (albeit small ones) around process stages with higher than average uncertainty. This at least allows some protection for the rest of the system. The same ideas apply to just-in-time delivery between factories. Severe disruption to supply chains, as from the effects of the Japanese tsunami caused many overseas Japanese factories to close down for a time because of a shortage of key parts.

Another key issue is the way lean appears to downplay the idea of capacity underutilization in the short term. It is true that fast throughput time and smooth flow *are* more important than high utilization, which can result in the build-up of inventory or queues. However, this criticism is not really valid in the long term. Remember the relationship between capacity utilization and process throughput time (or inventory of products, customers or information), discussed earlier in the book and shown in Figure 15.11 below. The improvement path envisaged by adopting lean is shown as moving from the state that most businesses find themselves in (high utilization but long throughput times) towards the lean ideal of short throughput time. Although, inevitably, this means moving towards a position of lower capacity utilization, lean also stresses a reduction in all types of process variability. As this begins to become reality, the improvement path moves towards the point where throughput time is short and capacity utilization high. It manages to do this because of the reduction in process variability.

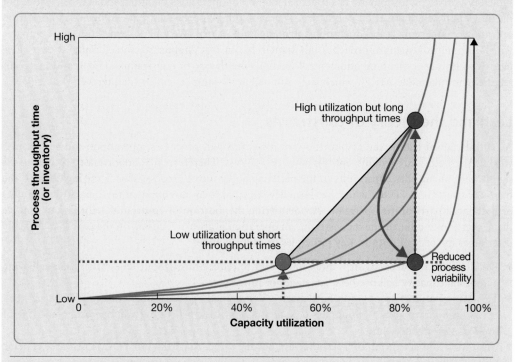

Figure 15.11 Developing lean processes can mean accepting lower utilization in the short to medium term

held that, although the task is more difficult and although it may take longer to achieve, the aim of lean is just as valuable for the supply network as a whole as it is for an individual operation.

Lean supply chains are like an air traffic control system

The concept of the lean supply chain has been likened to an air traffic control system, in that it attempts to provide continuous 'real-time visibility and control' to all elements in the chain. This is the secret of how the world's busiest airports handle thousands of departures and arrivals daily. All aircraft are given an identification number that shows up on a radar map. Aircraft approaching an airport are detected by the radar and contacted. The control tower positions the aircraft precisely in an approach pattern, which it coordinates. The radar detects any small adjustments that are necessary, which are communicated to the aircraft. This real-time visibility and control can optimize airport throughput while maintaining extremely high safety and reliability.

Contrast this to how most supply chains are coordinated. Information is captured only periodically, probably once a day, output levels at the various operations in the supply chain are adjusted, and plans are rearranged. But imagine what would happen if this was how the airport operated, with only a 'radar snapshot' once a day. Coordinating aircraft with sufficient tolerance to arrange take-offs and landings every two minutes would be out of the question. Aircraft would be jeopardized, or alternatively, if aircraft were spaced further apart to maintain safety, throughput would be drastically reduced. Yet this is how most supply chains have traditionally operated. They use a daily 'snapshot' from their ERP systems (see Chapter 14 for an explanation of ERP). This limited visibility means operations must either space their work out to avoid 'collisions' (i.e. missed customer orders), thereby reducing output, or they must 'fly blind', thereby jeopardizing reliability.

How does lean compare with other approaches?

Either as a broad philosophy or as a practical method of operations planning and control, lean is not the only approach that is used in practice. There are other approaches that can be used to underpin operations improvement and operations planning and control. We will describe how lean compares with other improvement approaches in Chapter 16. In this chapter we look briefly at two alternatives to lean as a planning and control method: the theory of constraints (TOC), and materials requirements planning (MRP), which we examined in the supplement to Chapter 14.

Lean and the theory of constraints

A central idea of lean is the smooth flow of items through processes, operations and supply networks. Any bottleneck will disrupt this smooth progress. Therefore, it is important to recognize the significance of capacity constraints to the planning and control process. This is the idea behind the theory of constraints (TOC) which has been developed to focus attention on the capacity constraints or bottleneck parts of the operation. By identifying the location of constraints, working to remove them, then looking for the next constraint, an operation is always focusing on the part that critically determines the pace of output. Key principles of TOC include:

► Balance flow, not capacity. It is more important to reduce throughput time rather than achieving a notional capacity balance between stages or processes.
► The level of utilization of a non-bottleneck is determined by some other constraint in the system, not by its own capacity. This applies to stages in a process, processes in an operation, and operations in a supply network.
► Utilization and activation of a resource are not the same. According to TOC, a resource is being utilized only if it contributes to the entire process or operation creating more output. A process or stage can be activated in the sense that it is working, but it may only be creating stock (of products, customers or information) or performing other non-value-added activity.

- An hour lost (not used) at a bottleneck is an hour lost forever out of the entire system. The bottleneck limits the output from the entire process or operation, and therefore the underutilization of a bottleneck affects the entire process or operation.
- An hour saved at a non-bottleneck is a mirage. Non-bottlenecks have spare capacity anyway. Why bother making them even less utilized?
- Bottlenecks govern both throughput and inventory in the system. If bottlenecks govern flow, then they govern throughput time, which in turn governs inventory.
- You do not have to transfer batches in the same quantities as you create them. Flow will probably be improved by dividing large batches of work into smaller ones for moving through a process.
- The size of the process batch should be variable, not fixed. Again, from the EBQ model, the circumstances that control batch size may vary between different products.
- Fluctuations in connected and sequence-dependent processes add to each other rather than averaging out. So, if two parallel processes or stages are capable of a particular average output rate, in parallel, they will never be able to achieve the same average output rate.
- Schedules should be established by looking at all constraints simultaneously. Because of bottlenecks and constraints within complex systems, it is difficult to work out schedules according to a simple system of rules. Rather, all constraints need to be considered together.

TOC uses the terminology of 'drum, buffer, rope' to explain its planning and control approach. We explained this idea in Chapter 10. The bottleneck work centre becomes a 'drum', beating the pace for the rest of the operation. This 'drum beat' determines the schedules in non-bottleneck areas, pulling through work (the rope) in line with the bottleneck capacity, not the capacity of the work centre. A bottleneck should never be allowed to be working at less than full capacity; therefore, inventory buffers should be placed before it to ensure that it never runs out of work.

Table 15.1 shows some of the differences between the theory of constraints and lean operations. Arguably, the main contribution of TOC to smooth, synchronized flow is its inclusion of the idea that the effects of bottleneck constraints (a) must be prioritized, and (b) can 'excuse' inventory, if it means maximizing the utilization of the bottleneck. Nor (unlike ERP / MRP, for example) does it necessarily require large investment in new information technology. Further, because it attempts to improve the flow, it can release inventory (of products, customers or information), which in turn releases invested capital.

Lean and MRP

The operating philosophies of lean and MRP do seem to be fundamentally opposed. Lean encourages a 'pull' system of planning and control, whereas MRP is a 'push' system. Lean has aims that are wider than the operations planning and control activity, whereas MRP is essentially a planning

Table 15.1 Theory of constraints compared with lean operations[7]

	Theory of constraints	Lean operations
Overall objectives	To increase profit by increasing the throughput of a process or operation	To increase profit by adding value from the customers' perspective
Measures of effectiveness	- Throughput - Inventory - Operating expense	- Cost - Throughput time - Value-added efficiency
Achieve improvement by . . .	Focusing on the constraints (the 'weakest links') in the process	Eliminating waste and adding value by considering the entire process, operation or supply network
How to implement	A four-step repeated cycle of identification of system constraint, exploitation of constraint, sub-ordination of non-constraint elements to the constraint element, and elimination of constraint	Continuous improvement emphasizing the whole supply network

and control 'calculation mechanism'. Yet the two approaches can reinforce each other in the same operation, provided their respective advantages are preserved. The irony is that lean and MRP have similar objectives. JIT scheduling aims to connect the new network of internal and external supply processes by means of invisible conveyors so that parts only move in response to coordinated and synchronized signals derived from end-customer demand. MRP seeks to meet projected customer demand by directing that items be only produced as needed to meet that demand. However, there are differences. MRP is driven by the master production schedule, which identifies future end-item demand. It models a fixed lead-time environment, using the software to calculate how many, and when, each part should be made. Its output is in the form of time-phased requirements plans that are centrally calculated and coordinated. Parts are made in response to central instructions. Day-to-day disturbances, such as inaccurate stock records, undermine MRP authority and can make the plans unworkable. While MRP is excellent at planning, it is weak at control. On the other hand, lean scheduling aims to meet demand instantaneously through simple control systems based on kanban. If the total throughput time (P) is less than the demand lead time (D), then lean systems should be capable of meeting that demand. But if the $P{:}D$ ratio is greater than 1, some speculative production will be needed. And if demand is suddenly far greater than expected for certain products, the JIT system may be unable to cope. Pull scheduling is a reactive concept that works best when independent demand has been levelled and dependent demand synchronized. As such, while lean may be good at control, it is weak on planning.

MRP is also better at dealing with complexity, as measured by numbers of items being processed. It can handle detailed requirements even for 'strangers'. Lean, by contrast is less capable of responding instantaneously to changes in demand as product or service complexity increases. Therefore, lean systems favour designs based on simpler structures with high levels of commonality.

When to use lean, MRP and combined systems

Figure 15.12 distinguishes between the complexity of product and service structures and the complexity of the flow-path routings through which they must pass.[8] Simple structures with high repeatability are prime candidates for pull control. Lean can easily cope with their relatively straightforward requirements. However, as structures and routings become more complex, and activities become more irregular, so the opportunities for using pull scheduling decrease. Very complex structures require network-planning methods (see Chapter 19) for planning and control.

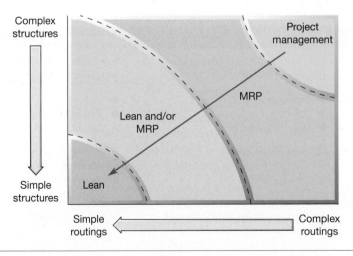

Figure 15.12 Complexity as a determinant of an appropriate planning and control system
Source: Adapted from Voss, C.A. and Harrison, A.

Summary answers to key questions

What is lean?

▶ Lean is an approach to operations that seeks to achieve a flow of materials, information or customers that delivers exactly what customers want (perfect quality), in exact quantities (neither too much nor too little), exactly when needed (not too early nor too late), exactly where required (in the right location), and at the lowest possible cost. It can be viewed in three related ways – as a philosophy, as a method of planning and control and as a set of improvement tools.

▶ Lean uses a 'pull system' to manage flow of products and services as opposed to a 'push system' in traditional operations.

▶ Lean focuses on the removal of inventory in order to expose operations problems. It places less emphasis on maximizing capacity utilization given there is little value in producing products or processing customers if the next stage in the process is not ready to receive them.

▶ Behavioural change is at the centre of lean philosophy, with particular emphasis on the involvement of all staff in driving improvement on an on-going basis (kaizen).

How does lean eliminate waste?

▶ Lean identifies three causes of waste – muda (poorly communicated processes or inefficient resource use), mura (lack of consistency) and muri (unnecessary or unreasonable requests placed on the process).

▶ Lean identifies eight types of waste that, together, form four barriers to achieving lean. They are waste from irregular flow (waiting time, transportation, process inefficiencies, inventory and wasted motion), waste from inexact supply (over-production, under-production, early or late delivery, talent misalignment and inventory), waste from inflexible response (large batches, delays, more variation than is demanded by the customer), and waste from variability (poor staff or equipment reliability, defective products or services).

How does lean apply throughout the supply network?

▶ Most of the concepts and techniques of lean, although usually described as applying to individual processes and operations, also apply to the whole supply networks.

▶ The concept of the lean supply chain has been likened to an air traffic control system, in that it attempts to provide continuous, 'real-time visibility and control' to all elements in the chain.

How does lean compare with other approaches?

▶ In this chapter, we have examined theory of constraints (TOC) and materials requirements planning as two alternatives to lean operations.

▶ TOC focuses attention on the capacity constraints or bottlenecks within the operation. By identifying the location of constraints, working to remove them, then looking for the next constraint, an operation is always focusing on the part that critically determines the pace of output.

▶ MRP is a 'push' system of planning and control as opposed to 'pull' system. As such, it is seen as useful when greater levels of planning are needed and when system complexity is very high.

▶ The way in which these different approaches can be combined depends on the complexity of product or service structures, the complexity of routing, volume–variety characteristics of the operation, and the level of control required.

Saint Bridget's Hospital[9]

When Denize Ahlgren arrived at St Bridget's, one of the main hospitals in the Götenborg area, she knew that it had gained a reputation for fresh thinking on how healthcare could be organized to give superior levels of public care at lower cost to the taxpayer. In fact, that was one of the reasons she had taken the job of its Chief of Administration (COA). In particular Denize had been reading about St Bridget's 'Quality Care' (QC) initiative. 'Yes, QC is obviously important', explained Dr Pär Solberg who, in addition to his clinical duties, also headed the QC initiative, 'but don't think that it is only about "quality". We don't just throw money at improving the quality of care; we also want to improve efficiency. Any money saved by improving efficiency can then be invested in improving clinical outcomes.'

'It all started with quality'

Although run by a private company, St Bridget's is little different from any other Swedish hospital. To its patients, treatment is free, after a minimal charge that is universal in Sweden. St Bridget's gets virtually all its revenue from the government. However, in terms of how it organizes itself, it is at the forefront of implementing ides that are more common in private business. 'It all started with our efforts a few years ago to be systematic in how we measured quality', said Pär Solberg. 'We felt that quality must be reported on a systematic and logical basis if it is going to be meaningful. It should also be multi-faceted, and not just focus on one aspect of quality. We measure three aspects, "reported patient experience"(RPE), what the patient thinks about the total experience of receiving treatment, "reported patient outcome" (RPO), how the patient views the effectiveness of the treatment received, and most importantly "reported clinical outcome" (RCO), how the clinicians view the effectiveness of the treatment. Of course these three measures are interconnected. So, RPO eventually depends on the medical outcome (RCO) and how much discomfort and pain the treatment triggers. But it is also influenced by the patient's experience (RPE), for example, how well we keep the patient informed, how empathetic our staff are, and so on.'

'Measuring quality led naturally to continuous improvement'

The hospital's quality measurement processes soon developed into a broader approach to improvement in general. In particular the idea of continuous improvement began to be discussed. 'Measuring quality led naturally to continuous improvement', explained Pär Solberg. 'Once we had measurable indicators of quality, we could establish targets, and most importantly we could start to think about what was preventing us improving quality. This, in turn, led to an understanding of all the processes that affected quality indicators. It was a shift to seeing the hospital as a whole set of processes that governed a set of

flows – flows of patients through their treatment stages, flows of clinical staff, flows of information, flows of pharmaceuticals, flows of equipment, and so on. It was a revolution in our thinking. We started examining these flows and looking at how they impacted on our performance and how we could improve the working methods that we considered significant for the quality indicators that we wanted to influence. That was when we discovered the concept of "lean".'

'Continuous improvement introduced us to lean'

It was an 'Improving European Healthcare' conference that was attended by Pär and another colleague that first introduced St Bridget's to the idea of 'lean'. 'We were talking to some representatives from the UK's National Health Service Institute, who had been involved in introducing lean principles in UK hospitals. They explained that lean was an improvement approach that improved flow and eliminated waste that had been used successfully in some hospitals to build on continuous improvement. Lean, they said, as developed by Toyota was about getting the right things to the right place, at the right time, in the right quantities, while minimizing waste and being flexible and open to change. It sounded worth following up. However, they admitted that not every attempt to introduce lean principles had met with success.'

'It can easily all get political'

Intrigued by the conversation, Pär contacted one of the hospitals in the UK that had been mentioned, and talked to Marie Watson who had been the 'Head of Lean' and had initiated several lean projects. She said that one of the problems she had faced was her Chief Executive's insistence on bringing in several firms of consultants to implement lean ideas. To make matters more confusing, when a new Chief Executive was appointed, he brought in his own preferred consultants in addition to those already operating in the hospital. Marie had not been happy with the change. 'Before the change of executives we had a very clear way of how we were going to move forward and spread lean throughout the organization, then we became far less clear. The emphasis shifted to get some quick results. But that wasn't why we were set up. Originally it was about having a positive impact, getting people involved in lean, engaging and empowering them towards continuous improvement. There were things that were measurable but then it changed to "show us some quick results". People were forgetting the cultural side of it. Also it can easily all get "political". The different consultancy teams and the internal lean initiatives all had their own territories. For example, we [Marie's internal team] were about to start a study of A&E activities, when they were told to keep away from A&E so as not to "step on the toes" of the firm of consultants working there.'

'We're not making cars, people are different'

Pär was determined not to make the same mistakes that Marie's hospital had, and consulted widely before attempting any lean improvements with his colleagues. Some were sceptical: 'We're not making cars, people are different and the processes that we put people through repeatedly are more complicated than the processes that you go through to make a car.' Also, some senior staff were dubious about changes that they perceived to threaten their professional status. Instead of doctors and nurses maintaining separate and defined roles that focused solely on their field of medical expertise, they were encouraged to work (and sit) together in teams. The teams were also made responsible for suggesting process improvements. But most could be converted. One senior clinician, at first claimed that 'This is all a load of rubbish. There's no point in mapping this process, we all know what happens: the patient goes from there to there and this is the solution and that's what we need to do.' Yet only a few days later he was saying 'I never realized this is what really happens, that won't work now will it, actually this has been great because I never understood, I only saw my bit of it, now I understand all of the process'.

'It works, it makes things better for the patients'

Over time, most (although not quite all) scepticism was overcome, mainly because, in the words of one doctor, 'It works, it makes things better for the patients.' As more parts of the hospital became convinced of the effectiveness of the lean approach, the improvements to patient flow and quality started to accumulate. Some of the first improvements were relatively simple, such as a change of signage (to stop patients getting lost). Another simply involved a roll of yellow tape. Rather than staff wasting precious time looking for equipment such as defibrillators, the yellow tape was used to mark a spot on the floor where the machines were always kept. Another involved using magnetic dots on a progress chart to follow each patient's progress and indicate which beds were free. Some were even simpler: for example, discharging patients throughout the day rather than all at the same time, so that they can easily find a taxi. Other improvements involved more analysis, such as reducing the levels of stock being held (for example, 25,000 pairs of surgical gloves from 500 different suppliers). Some involved a complete change in assumptions, such as the effectiveness of the Medical Records department. 'It was amazing. We just exploded the myth that when you didn't get case notes in a clinical area it was Medical Records' fault. But it never was. Medics had notes in their cars, they had them at home, we had a thousand notes in the secretaries' offices, there were notes in wards, drawers and cupboards, they were all over the place. And we wondered why we couldn't get case notes! Two people walked 7 miles a day to go and find case notes!' (Pär Solberg)

'We need to go to the next level'

Denize Ahlgren was understandably impressed by the improvements that Pär had outlined to her; however, Pär was surprisingly downbeat about the future. 'OK, I admit that we have had some impressive gains from continuous improvement and latterly from the adoption of lean principles. I am especially impressed with Toyota's concept of the eight types of waste. It is both a conceptually powerful and a very practical idea for identifying where we could improve. Also the staff like it. But it's all getting like a box-ticking exercise. Looking for waste is not exactly an exciting or radical idea. The more that I study how lean got going in Toyota and other manufacturing plants, the more I see that we haven't really embraced the whole philosophy. Yet, at the same time, I'm not totally convinced that we can. Perhaps some of the doubters were right, a hospital isn't a car plant, and we can apply only some lean ideas.'

Ironically, as Pär was having doubts some of colleagues were straining to do more. One clinician in particular, Fredrik Olsen, chief physician at St Bridget's lower back pain clinic, thought that his clinic could benefit from a more radical approach. 'We need to go to the next level. The whole of Toyota's philosophy is concerned with smooth synchronous flow, yet we haven't fully got our heads round that here. I know that we are reluctant to talk about "inventories" of patients, but that is exactly what waiting rooms are. They are "stocks" of people, and we use them in exactly the same way as pre-lean manufacturers did – to buffer against short-term mismatches between supply and demand. What we should be doing is tackling the root causes of the mismatch. Waiting rooms are stopping us from moving towards smooth, value-added, flow for our patients.'

Fredrik went on to make what Denize thought was an interesting, but radical, proposal. He proposed scrapping the current waiting room for the lower back pain clinic and replacing it with two extra consulting rooms to add to the two existing consulting rooms. Patients would be given appointments for specific times rather than being asked to arrive 'on the hour' (effectively in batches) as at present. A nurse would take the patents' details and perform some preliminary tests, after which they would call in the specialist physician. Staffing levels during clinic times would be controlled by a nurse, who would also monitor patient arrival, direct them to consulting rooms and arrange any follow-up appointments (for MRI scans, for example).

Denize was not sure about Fredrik's proposal. 'It seems as though it might be a step too far. Patients expect to wait until a doctor can see them, so I'm not sure what benefits would result from the proposal. And what is the point of equipping two new consulting rooms if they are not going to be fully utilized?'

QUESTIONS

1 What benefits did St Bridget's get from adopting first a continuous improvement, then a lean, approach?

2 Do you think that Pär Solberg is right in thinking that there is a limit to how far a hospital can go in adopting lean ideas?

3 On the St Bridget's website there are several references to its 'Quality Care' programme, but none to its lean initiatives, even though lean is regarded as important by most clinicians and administrators in the hospital. Why do you think this might be?

4 Denize cannot see the benefits of Fredrik's proposal. What do you think they might be?

5 Are any benefits of scrapping the waiting room in the clinic worth the underutilization of the four consulting rooms that Fredrik envisages?

All chapters have 'Problems and applications' questions that will help you practise analysing operations. They can be answered by reading the chapter. Model answers for the first two questions can be found on the companion website for this book.

1 What elements of lean are described in the Toyota Production System (TPS)?

2 The Zucchero mail-order clothing company in Milan receives order forms, types in the customer details, checks the information provided from the customers and that the products are in stock, confirms payment and processes the order. During an average eight-hour day, 150 orders are processed. Generally, 225 orders are waiting to be processed or 'in progress'. It takes 20 minutes for all activities required to process an order. What is the throughput efficiency of the process?

3 Consider this record of an ordinary flight. *'Breakfast was a little rushed but left the house at 6.15. Had to return a few minutes later, forgot my passport. Managed to find it and leave (again) by 6.30. Arrived at the airport 7.00, dropped Angela off with bags at terminal and went to the long-term car park. Eventually found a parking space after 10 minutes. Waited 8 minutes for the courtesy bus. Six-minute journey back to the terminal, we start queuing at the check-in counters by 7.24. Twenty-minute wait. Eventually get to check-in and find that we have been allocated seat at different ends of the plane. Staff helpful but takes 8 minutes to sort it out. Wait in queue for security checks for 10 minutes. Security decide I look suspicious and search bags for 3 minutes. Waiting in lounge by 8.05. Spend 1 hour and 5 minutes in lounge reading computer magazine and looking at small plastic souvenirs. Hurrah, flight is called 9.10, takes 2 minutes to rush to the gate and queue for further 5 minutes at gate. Through the gate and on to air bridge, there is continuous queue going onto plane, takes 4 minutes but finally in seats by 9.21. Wait for plane to fill up with other passengers for 14 minutes. Plane starts to taxi to runway at 9.35. Plane queues to take off for 10 minutes. Plane takes off 9.45. Smooth flight to Amsterdam, 55 minutes. Stacked in queue of planes waiting to land for 10 minutes. Touch down at Schiphol Airport 10.50. Taxi to terminal and wait 15 minutes to disembark. Disembark at 11.05 and walk to luggage collection (calling at lavatory on way), arrive luggage collection 11.15. Wait for luggage 8 minutes. Through customs (not searched by Netherlands security who decide I look trustworthy) and to taxi rank by 11.26. Wait for taxi 4 minutes. Into taxi by 11.30, 30 minutes ride into Amsterdam. Arrive at hotel 12.00.'*

(a) Analyse the journey in terms of value-added time (actually going somewhere) and non-value-added time (the time spent queuing etc.).

(b) Visit the websites of two or three airlines and examine their business-class and first-class services to look for ideas that reduce the non-value-added time for customers who are willing to pay the premium.

(c) Next time you go on a journey, time each part of the journey and perform a similar analysis.

4 An insurance underwriting process consists of the following separate stages.

Stage	Processing time per application (minutes)	Average work in progress before the stage
Data entry	30	250
Retrieve client details	5	1,500
Risk assessment	18	300
Inspection	15	150
Policy assessment	20	100
Dispatch proposal	10	100

What is the 'value-added percentage for the process? (Hint – use Little's law to work out how long applications have to wait at each stage before they are processed. Little's law is covered in Chapter 6.)

5   Examine the *marking process* of an assignment you are currently working on. What is the typical elapsed time between handing the assignment in and receiving it back with comments? How much of this elapsed time do you think is value-added time?

6   A production process is required to produce 980 of product X, 560 of product Y, and 280 of product Z in a 4-week period. If the process works 7 hours per day and 5 days per week, devise a mixed model schedule per hour that would meet this demand.

Selected further reading

Bicheno, J. and Holweg, M. (2016) *The Lean Toolbox: The Essential Guide to Lean Transformation,* **5th edn, PICSIE Books, Buckingham.**
A practical guide from two of the European authorities on all matters lean.

Mann, D. (2010) *Creating a Lean Culture,* **2nd edn, Productivity Press, New York.**
Treats the behavioural side of lean.

Modig, N. and Ahlstrom, P. (2012) *This is Lean: Resolving the Efficiency Paradox,* **Rheologica Publishing, Stockholm.**
This book provides a very practical guide to what lean is and its application in a variety of sectors. Not only does the book demonstrate a clear understanding of how the various aspects of lean come together, it does it in a very readable way.

Womack, J.P., Jones, D.T. and Roos, D. (1990) *The Machine that Changed the World,* **Rawson Associates, New York.**
One of the most influential books on operations management practice of the last fifty years. Firmly rooted in the automotive sector but did much to establish lean/JIT.

Womack, J.P. and Jones, D.T. (2003) *Lean Thinking: Banish Waste and Create Wealth in Your Corporation,* **Free Press, New York.**
Some of the lessons from *The Machine that Changed the World* but applied in a broader context.

PART FOUR

Development

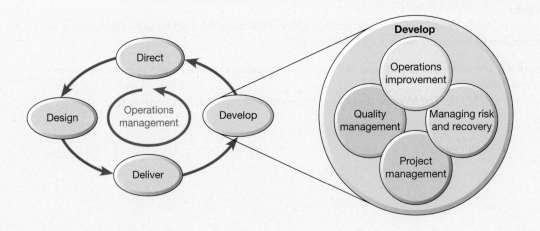

E ven when an operation's direction is set, its design finalized and its deliveries planned and controlled, the operations manager's task is not finished. Even the best operation will need to improve and develop, partly because customers' expectations are likely to be rising, and partly because the operation's competitors will also be improving. This part of the book looks at four key issues for operation development. The chapters in this part are:

▶ **Chapter 16 Operations improvement**

This examines how managers can make their operation perform better through the use of the many elements of new (and not so new) improvement approaches.

▶ **Chapter 17 Quality management**

This identifies some of the ideas of quality management and how they can be used to facilitate improvement.

▶ **Chapter 18 Managing risk and recovery**

This examines how operations managers can reduce the risk of things going wrong and how they can recover when they do.

▶ **Chapter 19 Project management**

This looks at how they can project manage improvement (among other activities) to organize the changes that improvement inevitably requires.

Operations improvement

KEY QUESTIONS

Why is improvement so important in operations management?

What are the key elements of operations improvement?

What are the broad approaches to improvement?

What techniques can be used for improvement?

How can the improvement process be managed?

INTRODUCTION

Improvement means to make something better. And all operations, no matter how well managed, are capable of being better. Of course, in one sense, all of operations management is concerned with being better, but there are some issues that relate specifically to the activity of improvement itself. Yet, at one time improvement was not central to operations managers, who were expected simply to 'run the operation', 'keep the show on the road', and 'maintain current performance'. No longer. In fact, in recent years the emphasis has shifted markedly towards making improvement one of the main responsibilities of operations managers. Moreover, the study of improvement as a specific activity has attracted significant attention from both academics and practitioners. Some of this attention focuses on specific techniques and prescriptions while some looks at the underlying philosophy of improvement. Both aspects are covered in this chapter, because both aspects of improvement have their place in effective improvement. Figure 16.1 shows where this topic fits into our overall model of operations management.

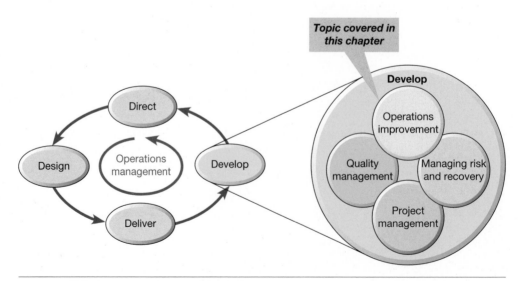

Figure 16.1 This chapter examines operations improvement

Why is improvement so important in operations management?

Why is operations improvement so important? Well, who doesn't want to get better? And businesses are (or should be) just the same as people – they generally want to get better. Not just for the sake of their own excellence, although that may be one factor, but mainly because improving operations performance has such an impact on what any organization is there to do. Emergency services want to reach distressed people faster and treat them better because by doing so they are fulfilling their role more effectively. Package delivery businesses want to deliver more reliably, at lower cost and reducing emissions because it means happier customers, higher profits and less pollution. Development charities want to target their aid and campaign for improvement in human conditions as wisely and efficiently as possible because more money will find its way to beneficiaries rather than be wasted or consumed in administration. It is not surprising then that the whole emphasis of operations management has shifted towards emphasizing improvement. Operations managers are judged not only on how they meet their ongoing responsibilities of producing products and services to acceptable levels of quality, speed, dependability, flexibility and cost, but also on how they improve the performance of the operations function overall.

> **Operations principle**
>
> Performance improvement is the ultimate objective of operations and process management.

Why the focus on improvement?

Various reasons have been suggested to explain the shift towards a focus on improvement in professional operations managers' activities.

▶ There is a perceived increase in the intensity of competitive pressures (or 'value for money' in not-for-profit or public sector operations). In fact, economists argue about whether markets are really getting more competitive. As far as improvement is concerned it doesn't matter; there is a *perception* of increased competitive pressure, and certainly the owners of operations (shareholders or governments) are less likely to tolerate poor returns or value for money.

▶ The nature of world trade is changing. Emerging economies are becoming important as both producers and consumers. This has introduced cost pressures in countries with relatively expensive labour and infrastructure costs; it has introduced new challenges for global companies, such as managing complex supply chains; and it has accelerated demand for resources (materials, food, energy), pushing up (or destabilizing) prices for these commodities.

▶ New technology has both introduced opportunities to improve operations practice and disrupted existing markets.

▶ The interest in operations improvement has resulted in the development in many new ideas and approaches to improving operations. The more ways there are to improve operations, the more operations will be improved.

▶ The scope of operations management has widened from a subject associated largely with manufacturing to one that embraces all types of enterprise and processes in all functions of the enterprise. Because of this extended scope, operations managers have seen how they can learn from each other.

The Red Queen effect

The scientist Leigh Van Valen was looking to describe a discovery that he had made while studying marine fossils. He had established that, no matter how long a family of animals had already existed, the probability that the family will become extinct is unaffected. In other words, the struggle for survival never gets easier. However well a species fits with its environment, it can never relax. The analogy that Van Valen drew came from *Through the Looking Glass*, by Lewis Carroll. In the book, Alice had encountered living chess pieces and, in particular, the 'Red Queen'. '*Well, in our country*', said Alice, still panting a little, '*you'd generally get to somewhere else – if you ran very fast for a long*

(Adapted, with permission, from an original case by Professors Rui Soucasaux Sousa and Sofia Salgado Pinto, Católica Porto Business School, Portugal.)

The retail industry may not seem to be the most likely setting for the use of improvement approaches more usually associated with manufacturing, but Sonae Corporation's Continente supermarkets' 22,500 employees in its 170 stores and two distribution centres have demonstrated that any type of business can benefit. The operations improvement programme was originally a response to Portuguese labour laws requiring a minimum of 35 hours of training per year, per worker. Jaime Maia, Sonae's Human Resource Director, was keen that the training should be 'on-the-job' and asked a consulting firm, The Kaizen Institute (KI), to help, first by observing daily operations at several retail stores. The results were surprising. KI uncovered a significant amount of waste (or 'muda' in lean terminology, see Chapter 15). However, when Jaime Maia and KI presented their ideas to the chief operations officer (COO), their photographs showing examples of waste caused some discomfort; after all, they were the most successful retailer in Portugal. Yet the programme went ahead, despite several managers arguing that lean principles would not work in retail.

Within a store, 'back-office' processes include unloading trucks, routing goods to sales areas or the warehouses, cleaning, shelf replenishment and store decoration. 'Front-office' processes include sales areas and their supporting checkout and customer service areas. Key operational goals include the efficient use of space, increasing sales per square metre of store space and customer satisfaction. The first stage of the programme focused on 'goods reception' and 'shelf replenishment'. Simple lean tools such as 5S and visual management (see Chapter 15) were used, as was the idea of 'Gemba', or working out improvements in the workplace. After a seminar, store managers returned to work with their teams to develop training based on a 'lean manual', define an action plan, identify problem areas, and select the lean tools to be applied. As Jaime Maia explained, *'Improvements were suggested by Store Managers, top down. But those ideas were immediately enriched and put into action by the teams in the stores, bringing about further improvements in a continuous fashion.'*

After just one year there had been an 'explosion of creativity' in the stores. Productivity increased; inventory and stockouts were reduced; and customer satisfaction increased. As Jaime Maia put it, '[continuous

improvement] *stimulates a good attitude and a constant sense of critique'*. A typical improvement project concerned the company's shelf replenishing policy. Initially, stock was continuously replenished as sales took place during the day. However, this meant that product movements were constrained by customer flows and the need to keep the store clean and tidy. So a new method was tested. *'The store is fully loaded before the morning opening. From then on, we just need to perform minimal stock maintenance during the day. There is a time of the day at which a shelf may appear to be quite empty. However, typically, there is no need to replenish the shelf, but simply bring the products from the back to the front of the shelf, or from the upper shelves to the eye level shelves'*, explained Nuno Almeida, Regional Operations Manager. Only a few fast-moving goods needed to be replenished during the day with the store open.

With the success of the programme it was expanded by involving all employees. A formal steering group was created with monthly general meetings and a videoconference meeting every two weeks to assess progress. Substantial improvements in performance continued, but progress was not uniform. Stores ranged from 87 per cent implementation, down to 37 per cent implementation. So, the steering group decided to place more emphasis on benchmarking and learning.

And the future? *'One challenge'*, said Jaime Maia, *'is to sustain the motivation for the programme across the organization, after years of continuous successes.'* He also felt the programme was reaching a new turning point and needed to be reinvented. Until now, lean principles had been applied mainly to materials flows and workplace organization. Could lean principles be extended to customer flows?

time, as we've been doing'. 'A slow sort of country!' said the Queen. *'Now, here, you see, it takes all the running you can do, to keep in the same place. If you want to get somewhere else, you must run at least twice as fast as that!'*[1]

In many respects this is like business. Improvements and innovations may be imitated or countered by competitors. For example, in the automotive sector, the quality of most firms' products is very significantly better than it was two decades ago. This reflects the improvement in those firms' operations processes. Yet their relative competitive position has in many cases not changed. Those firms that have improved their competitive position have improved their operations performance *more than* competitors. Where improvement has simply matched competitors, survival has been the main benefit. The implications for operations improvement are clear. It is even more important, especially when competitors are actively improving their operations.

An important distinction in the approach taken by individual operations is that between radical or 'breakthrough' improvement, on one hand, and continuous or 'incremental' improvement, on the other.

Radical or breakthrough change

Radical, breakthrough improvement (or 'innovation'-based improvement as it is sometimes called) is a philosophy that assumes that the main vehicle of improvement is major and dramatic change in the way the operation works. The introduction of a new, more efficient machine in a factory, the total redesign of a computer-based hotel reservation system, and the introduction of an improved degree programme at a university are all examples of breakthrough improvement. The impact of these improvements is relatively sudden, abrupt and represents a step change in practice (and hopefully performance). Such improvements are rarely inexpensive, usually calling for high investment of capital, often disrupting the ongoing workings of the operation, and frequently involving changes in the product/service or process technology. The solid line in Figure 16.2(a) illustrates the pattern of performance with several breakthrough improvements. The improvement pattern illustrated by the dashed line in Figure 16.2(a) is regarded by some as being more representative of what really occurs when operations rely on pure breakthrough improvement. Breakthrough improvement places a high value on creative solutions. It encourages free thinking and individualism. It is a radical philosophy insomuch as it fosters an approach to improvement which does not accept many constraints on what is possible. 'Starting with a clean sheet of paper', 'going back to first principles' and 'completely rethinking the system' are all typical breakthrough improvement principles.

> **Operations principle**
> Performance improvement sometimes requires radical change.

Continuous or incremental improvement

Continuous improvement, as the name implies, adopts an approach to improving performance which assumes many small incremental improvement steps. For example, modifying the way a product is fixed to a machine to reduce changeover time, simplifying the question sequence when taking a hotel reservation, and rescheduling the assignment completion dates on a university course so as to smooth the students' workload are all examples of incremental improvements. Although there is no guarantee that such small steps towards better performance will be followed by other steps, the whole philosophy of continuous improvement attempts to ensure that they will be. Continuous improvement is not concerned with promoting small improvements *per se*. It does view small improvements, however, as having one significant advantage over large ones – they can be followed relatively painlessly by other small improvements (see Figure 16.2(b)). Continuous improvement is also known as kaizen. Kaizen is a Japanese word, the definition of which is given by Masaaki Imai[2] (who has been one of the main proponents of continuous improvement) as follows: *'Kaizen means improvement. Moreover, it means improvement in personal life, home life, social life and work life. When*

> **Operations principle**
> Performance improvement almost always benefits from continuous improvement.

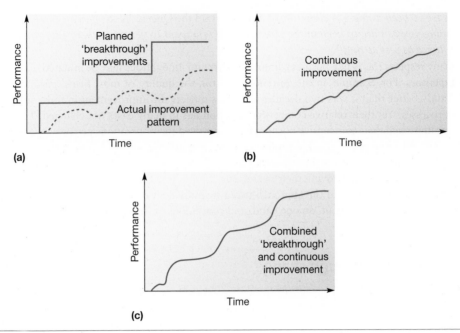

Figure 16.2 (a) 'Breakthrough' improvement (b) 'Continuous' improvement and (c) combined improvement patterns

applied to the work place, kaizen means continuing improvement involving everyone – managers and workers alike.'

In continuous improvement, it is not the *rate* of improvement which is important; it is the *momentum* of improvement. It does not matter if successive improvements are small; what does matter is that every month (or week, or quarter, or whatever period is appropriate) some kind of improvement has actually taken place.

The checklist manifesto[3]

Improvement methodologies are often associated with repetitive operations. Performing the same task repeatedly means that there are plenty of opportunities to 'get it right'. The whole idea behind continuous improvement derives from this simple idea. By contrast, operations that have to perform more difficult activities, especially those that call for expert judgement and diagnostic ability, must call for equally complex improvement approaches, no? Well no, according to Atul Gawande, a physician at the prestigious Johns Hopkins Hospital. Mr Gawande thinks that the very opposite is true. Although medicine is advancing at an astounding rate and medical journals produce learned papers adding the results of advanced research to an ever-expanding pool of knowledge, medics are less good at the basics. Surgeons carry out over 200 major operations a year, unfortunately not all of them successful, but the medical profession overall does not always have a

reliable method for learning from its mistakes. Atul Gawande's idea is that his and similar 'knowledge-based' professions are in danger of sinking under the weight of facts.

Scientists are accumulating more and more information and professions are fragmenting into ever narrower specialisms. Mr Gawande tells the story of Peter Pronovost, a specialist in critical care at Johns Hopkins Hospital who in 2001 tried to reduce the number of patients who were becoming infected on account of the use of intravenous central lines. There are five steps that medical teams can take to reduce the chances of patients contracting such infections. Initially Pronovost simply asked nurses to observe whether doctors took the five steps. What they found was that, at least a third of the time, they missed one or more of the steps. So nurses were authorized to stop doctors who had missed out any of the steps, and, as a matter of course, ask whether existing intravenous central lines should be reviewed. As a result of applying these simple checklist-style rules, the ten-day line-infection rates went down from 11 per cent to zero. In one hospital, it was calculated that, over a year, this simple method had prevented 43 infections, eight deaths and saved about $2 million. Using the same checklist approach, the hospital identified and applied the method to other activities. For example, a check in which nurses asked patients about their pain levels led to untreated pain reducing from 41 per cent to 3 per cent. Similarly, the simple checklist method helped the average length of patient stay in intensive care to fall by half. When Pronovost's approach was adopted by other hospitals, within 18 months, 1,500 lives and $175 million had been saved.

Mr Gawande's describes checklists, used in this way, as a 'cognitive net' – a mechanism that can help prevent experienced people from making errors due to flawed memory and attention, and ensure that teams work together. Simple checklists are common in other professions. Civil engineers use them to make certain that complicated structures are assembled on schedule. Chefs use them to make sure that food is prepared exactly to the customers' taste. Airlines use them to make sure that pilots take off safely and also to learn from, now relatively rare, crashes. Indeed, Mr Gawande is happy to acknowledge that checklists are not a new idea. He tells the story of the prototype of the Boeing B17 Flying Fortress that crashed after take-off on its trial flight in 1935. Most experts said that the bomber was 'too complex to fly'. Facing bankruptcy, Boeing investigated and discovered that, confronted with four engines rather than two, the pilot forgot to release a vital locking mechanism. But Boeing created a pilot's checklist, in which the fundamental actions for the stages of flying were made a mandated part of the pilot's job. In the following years, B17s flew almost two million miles without a single accident. Even for pilots, many of whom are rugged individualists, says Mr Gawande, it is usually the application of routine procedures that saves planes when things go wrong, rather than 'hero-pilotry' so fêted by the media. It is discipline rather than brilliance that preserves life. In fact, it is discipline that leaves room for brilliance to flourish.

Exploitation or exploration

A closely related distinction to that between continuous and breakthrough improvement is the one that management theorists draw between what they call 'exploitation' and 'exploration'. Exploitation is the activity of enhancing processes (and products) that already exist within a firm. The focus of exploitation is on creating efficiencies rather than radically changing resources or processes. Its emphasis is on tight control of the improvement process, standardizing processes, clear organizational structures, and organizational stability. The benefits from exploitation tend to be relatively immediate, incremental and predictable. They also are likely to be better understood by the firm and fit into its existing strategic framework. Exploration, by contrast, is concerned with the exploration of new possibilities. It is associated with searching for and recognizing new mindsets and ways of doing things. It involves experimentation, taking risks, simulation of possible consequences, flexibility and innovation. The benefits from exploration are principally long term but can be relatively difficult to predict. Moreover, any benefits or discoveries that might come may be so different from what the firm is familiar with that it may not find it easy to take advantage of them.

Organizational 'ambidexterity'

It is clear that the organizational skills and capabilities to be successful at exploitation are likely to be very different from those that are needed for the radical exploration of new ideas. Indeed, the two views of improvement may actively conflict. A focus on thoroughly exploring for totally novel choices may consume managerial time and effort and the financial resources that could otherwise be used for refining existing ways of doing things, reducing the effectiveness of improving existing processes. Conversely, if existing processes are improved over time, there may be less motivation to experiment with new ideas. So, although both exploitation and exploration can be beneficial, they may compete both for resources and for management attention. This is where the concept of 'organizational ambidexterity' becomes important. Organizational ambidexterity means the ability of a firm to both exploit and explore as it seeks to improve; to be able to compete in mature markets where efficiency is important, by improving existing resources and processes, while also competing in new technologies and/or markets where novelty, innovation and experimentation are required.

> **Operations principle**
>
> Organizational ambidexterity is the ability to both exploit existing capabilities and explore new ones as the organization seeks to improve.

The structure of improvement ideas

There have been hundreds of ideas relating to operations improvement that have been proposed over the last few decades. To understand how these ideas relate to each other it is important to distinguish between four aspects of improvement.

▶ The *elements* contained within improvement approaches – These are the fundamental ideas of what improves operations. They are the 'building blocks' of improvement.

▶ The broad *approaches* to improvement – These are the underlying sets of beliefs that form a coherent philosophy and shape how improvement should be accomplished. Some improvement approaches have been used for over a century (for example, some work study approaches – see Chapter 9), others are relatively recent (for example, Six Sigma, explained later). But do not think that approaches to improvement are different in all respects; there are many elements that are common to several approaches.

▶ The improvement *techniques* – There are many 'step-by-step' techniques, methods and tools that can be used to help find improved ways of doing things; some of these use quantitative modelling and others are more qualitative.

▶ The *management* of improvement – How the process of improvement is managed is as important as, if not more important than, understanding the elements and approaches to improvement. The improvement activity must be organized, resources deployed and generally controlled for it to be effective at actually achieving demonstrable improvement.

The rest of this chapter will treat each of these aspects of improvement. The best way to understand improvement is to deal with the elements contained within improvement approaches first, then see how they come together to form broad approaches to improvement, and then examine some typical improvement techniques, before looking briefly at how operations improvement can be managed. Figure 16.3 illustrates the structure of the four aspects of improvement.

What are the key elements of operations improvement?

> **Operations principle**
>
> The various approaches to improvement draw from a common group of elements.

The elements of improvement are the individual basic fundamental ideas of improvement. Think of these elements of improvement as the building blocks of the various improvement approaches that we shall look at later. Here we explain some, but not all (there are lots), of the more common elements in use today.

Improvement cycles

An important element within some improvement approaches is the use of a literally never-ending process of repeatedly questioning and re-questioning the detailed working of a process or activity. This repeated and cyclical questioning is usually summarized by the idea of the improvement cycle, of which there are many, but two are widely used models – the PDCA (or PDSA) cycle (sometimes called the Deming cycle, named after the famous quality 'guru', W.E. Deming) and the DMAIC (pronounced 'De-Make') cycle, made popular by the Six Sigma approach (see later).

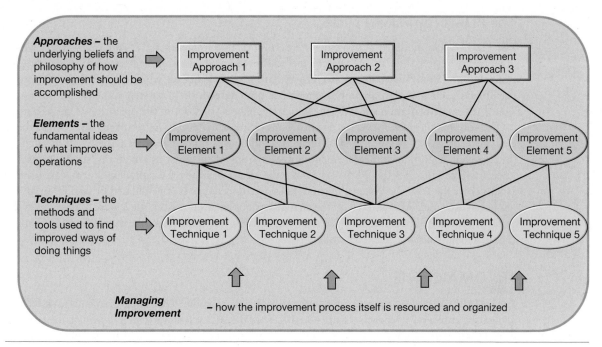

Figure 16.3 How the four aspects of improvement – approaches, elements, techniques and management – relate

---

Anarchy at 6Wonderkinder[4]

It's a problem every creative firm faces – how do you organize yourself so you can keep some kind of control over what's happening in the firm while not inhibiting the creativity of the people whom you are paying to be creative? When 6Wonderkinder, a Berlin-based developer of 'Wunderlist', the task management tool, was founded in 2010 with only six people, it was relatively easy to foster a creative and innovative atmosphere. But by the time the company had grown tenfold, it was more difficult to preserve the 'start-up spirit'. Chad Fowler, the company's chief technology officer, understands the importance of keeping the innovative culture: *'Probably every single company wants to maintain the feeling of being in a start-up, no matter how big they get.'* As the company grew it used several mechanisms to preserve the 'start-up spirit', such as the yearly 'Wunderkamp', when all staff spend a week away in Bavarian forest cabins or on the Baltic coast, and 'Sexy Friday' when developers get a day a week to pursue their own passions, the aim being to challenge established patterns of working and encourage novel thinking. Christian Reber, the German chief executive and co-founder, says: *'On an assembly line you always get the work you expect. People do the stuff you tell them to do. What we, here, try to achieve is that*

we regularly get the "wow" factor . . . if everyone acts like a CEO, they make the decisions, [if] they are responsible for their own projects, then it completely changes [the] dynamics.' The relatively flat hierarchy is also an advantage in retaining skilled staff in a sector where the competition for the best developers can be fierce. *'The talent pool is extremely limited. People choose the workplace, especially developers, based more on the working atmosphere – the culture, rather than the salary,'* says Christian Reber.

The PDCA (or PDSA) cycle

The PDCA cycle model is shown in Figure 16.4(a). It starts with the P (for plan) stage, which involves an examination of the current method or the problem area being studied. This involves collecting and analysing data so as to formulate a plan of action which is intended to improve performance. Once a plan for improvement has been agreed, the next step is the D (for do) stage. This is the implementation stage during which the plan is tried out in the operation. This stage may itself involve a mini-PDCA cycle as the problems of implementation are resolved. Next comes the C (for check) stage where the new implemented solution is evaluated to see whether it has resulted in the expected performance improvement. Some versions of this idea use the term 'study' instead of 'check' and call the idea the 'PDSA' cycle, but the idea is basically the same. Finally, at least for this cycle, comes the A (for act) stage. During this stage, the change is consolidated or standardized if it has been successful. Alternatively, if the change has not been successful, the lessons learned from the 'trial' are formalized before the cycle starts again. You may also find this cycle called the Deming cycle, Deming wheel or Shewhart cycle.

The DMAIC cycle

The DMAIC cycle is in some ways more intuitively obvious than the PDCA cycle in so much as it follows a more 'experimental' approach (Figure 16.4(b)). The DMAIC cycle starts with (D) defining the problem or problems, partly to understand the scope of what needs to be done and partly to define exactly the requirements of the process improvement. Often at this stage a formal goal or target for the improvement is set. After definition comes (M) the measurement stage. This stage involves validating the problem to make sure that it really is a problem worth solving, using data to refine the problem and measuring exactly what is happening. Once these measurements have been established, they can be (A) analysed. The analysis stage is sometimes seen as an opportunity to develop hypotheses as to what the root causes of the problem really are. Such hypotheses are validated (or not) by the analysis and the main root causes of the problem identified. Once the causes of the problem are identified, work can begin on (I) improving the process. Ideas are developed to remove the root causes of problems, solutions are tested and those solutions that seem to work are implemented, formalized and results measured. The improved process needs then to be continually monitored and (C) controlled to check that the improved level of performance is sustaining. After this point, the cycle starts again and defines the problems which are preventing further improvement. Remember though, it is the last point about both cycles that is the most important – the cycle starts again. In a continuous improvement philosophy these cycles quite literally never stop and improvement becomes part of every person's job.

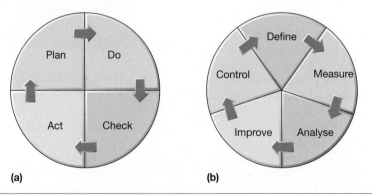

Figure 16.4 (a) The plan-do-check-act, or 'Deming' improvement cycle, and (b) the define–measure–analyse–improve–control, or DMAIC Six Sigma improvement cycle

A process perspective

Even if some improvement approaches do not explicitly or formally include the idea that taking a process perspective should be central to operations improvement, almost all do so implicitly. This has two major advantages. First, it means that improvement can be focused on what actually happens rather than which part of the organization has responsibility for what happens. In other words, if improvement is not reflected in the process of creating products and services, then it is not really improvement as such. Second, as we have mentioned before, all parts of the business manage processes. This is what we call operations as activity rather than operations as a function. So, if improvement is described in terms of how processes can be made more effective, those messages will have relevance for all the other functions of the business in addition to the operations function.

End-to-end processes

Some improvement approaches take the process perspective further and prescribe exactly how processes should be organized. One of the more radical prescriptions of business process re-engineering (BPR, see later), for example, is the idea that operations should be organized around the total process which adds value for customers, rather than the functions or activities which perform the various stages of the value-adding activity. We have already pointed out the difference between conventional processes within a specialist function, and an end-to-end business process in Chapter 1. Identified customer needs are entirely fulfilled by an 'end-to-end' business process. In fact, the processes are designed specifically to do this, which is why they will often cut across conventional organizational boundaries. Figure 16.5 illustrates this idea.

Evidence-based problem solving

In recent years there has been a resurgence of the use of quantitative techniques in improvement approaches. Six Sigma (see later) in particular promotes systematic use of (preferably quantitative) evidence. Yet Six Sigma is not the first of the improvement approaches to use quantitative methods (some of the total quality management (TQM) gurus promoted statistical process control, for example), although it has done a lot to emphasize the use of quantitative evidence. In fact, much of the considerable training required by Six Sigma consultants is devoted to mastering quantitative analytical techniques. However, the statistical methods used in improvement activities do not always reflect conventional academic statistical knowledge as such. They emphasize observational methods of collecting data and the use of experimentation to examine hypothesis. Techniques include graphical

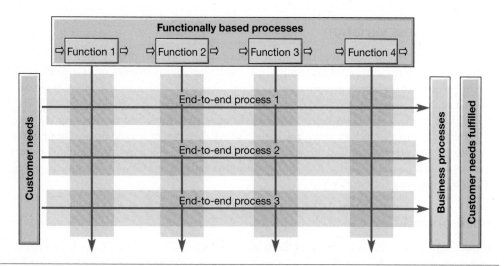

Figure 16.5 BPR advocates reorganizing (re-engineering) micro operations to reflect the natural customer-focused business processes

methods, analysis of variance, and two-level factorial experiment design. Underlying the use of these techniques is an emphasis on the scientific method, responding only to hard evidence, and using statistical software to facilitate analysis.

Customer centricity

There is little point in improvement unless it meets the requirements of the customers. However, in most improvement approaches, meeting the expectations of customers means more than this. It involves the whole organization in understanding the central importance of customers to its success and even to its survival. Customers are seen not as being external to the organization but as the most important part of it. However, the idea of being customer centric does not mean that customers must be provided with everything that they want. Although 'What's good for customers' may frequently be the same as 'What's good for the business', it is not always. Operations managers are always having to strike a balance between what customers would like and what the operation can afford (or wants) to do.

Voice of the customer (VOC)

The 'voice of the customer' (VOC) is an idea that is closely related to the idea of customer centricity. The term means capturing a customer's requirements, expectations, perceptions and preferences in some depth. Sometimes a VOC exercise is done as part of new service and product development as part of quality function deployment (QFD), which was explained in Chapter 4. Sometimes it is part of a more general improvement activity. There are several ways to do this, but it usually involves using market research to derive a comprehensive set of customer requirements, which is ordered into a hierarchical structure, often prioritized to indicate the relative importance of different aspects of operations performance.

Systems and procedures

Improvement is not something that happens simply by getting everyone to 'think improvement'. Some type of system that supports the improvement effort may be needed. An improvement system (sometimes called a 'quality system') is defined as: *'the organizational structure, responsibilities, procedures, processes and resources for implementing quality management'.*[5] It should *'define and cover all facets of an organization's operation, from identifying and meeting the needs and requirements of customers, design, planning, purchasing, manufacturing, packaging, storage, delivery and service, together with all relevant activities carried out within these functions. It deals with organization, responsibilities, procedures and processes. Put simply [it] is good management practice.'*[6]

Reduce process variation

Processes change over time, as does their performance. Some aspect of process performance (usually an important one) is measured periodically (either as a single measurement or as a small sample of measurements). These are then plotted on a simple time-scale. This has a number of advantages. The first is to check that the performance of the process is, in itself, acceptable (capable). They can also be used to check if process performance is changing over time, and to check on the extent of the variation in process performance. In Chapter 17 we illustrate how random variation in the performance of any process can obscure what is really happening within the process. So a potentially useful method of identifying improvement opportunities is to try and identify the sources of random variation in process performance.

Synchronized flow

This is another idea that we have seen before – in Chapter 15, as part of the lean philosophy. Synchronized flow means that items in a process, operation or supply network flow smoothly and with even velocity from start to finish. This is a function of how inventory accumulates within the operation. Whether inventory is accumulated in order to smooth differences between demand and supply, or as a contingency against unexpected delays, or simply to batch for purposes of processing or movement, it all means that flow becomes asynchronous. It waits as inventory rather than progressing smoothly on. Once this state of perfect synchronization of flow has been achieved, it becomes easier to expose any irregularities of flow which may be the symptoms of more deep-rooted underlying problems.

Improvement at Heineken[7]

Heineken International produces and sells beer around the world with growing sales, especially in its Heineken and Amstel brands. However, sales growth can put pressure on any company's operations. For example, Heineken's Zoeterwoude facility, a packaging plant that fills bottles and cans in The Netherlands, had to increase its volume by between 8 and 10 per cent per year on a regular basis. The company faced two challenges. First, it needed to improve its operations processes to reduce its costs. Second, because it would have taken a year to build a new packaging line, it needed to improve the efficiency of its existing lines in order to increase its capacity. So, improving line efficiency was vital if the plant was to cut its costs and create the extra capacity it needed to delay investment in a new packaging line.

The objective of the improvement project was to improve the equipment efficiency of the operation. Setting a target of 20 per cent improvement was seen as important because it was challenging yet achievable as well as meeting cost and capacity objectives. It was also decided to focus the improvement project around two themes. First: first, obtaining accurate operational data that could be converted into useful business information on which improvement decisions could be based; and second, changing the culture of the operation to promote fast and effective decision making. Having access to accurate and up-to-date information would help people at all levels in the plant, as well as encouraging staff to focus on the *improvement* of how they do their job rather than just 'doing the job'. Before the improvement, project staff at the Zoeterwoude plant had approached problem solving as an ad hoc activity, only to be done when circumstances made it unavoidable. The improvement initiative taught the staff to use various problem-solving techniques such as cause–effect and Pareto diagrams (discussed later in this chapter). Other techniques included the analysis of improved equipment maintenance and failure mode and effective analysis (FMEA). (Both are discussed in Chapter 18.)

'Until we started using these techniques,' says Wilbert Raaijmakers, Heineken Netherlands Brewery Director, 'there was little consent regarding what was causing any

problems. There was poor communication between the various departments and job grades. For example, maintenance staff believed that production stops were caused by operating errors, while operators were of the opinion that poor maintenance was the cause.' The use of better information, analysis and improvement techniques helped the staff to identify and treat the root causes of problems. With many potential improvements to make, staff teams were encouraged to set priorities that would reflect the overall improvement target. There was also widespread use of benchmarking performance against targets periodically so that progress could be reviewed.

At the end of 12 months, the improvement project had achieved its objectives of a 20 per cent improvement in all the plant's packaging lines. This allowed it to increase the volume of its exports and cut its costs significantly. Not only that, but other aspects of the plant's performance improved. Up to that point, the plant had gained a reputation for poor delivery dependability. After the project it was seen by the other operations in its supply chain as a much more reliable partner. Yet Wilbert Raaijmakers still sees room for improvement: 'The optimization of an organization is a never-ending process. If you sit back and do the same thing tomorrow as you did today, you'll never make it. We must remain alert to the latest developments and stress the resulting information to its full potential.'

Emphasize education/training

Several improvement approaches stress the idea that structured training and organization of improvement should be central to improvement. Not only should the techniques of improvement be fully understood by everyone engaged in the improvement process, the business and organizational context of improvement should also be understood. After all, how can one improve without knowing what kind of improvement would best benefit the organization and its customers? Furthermore, education and training have an important part to play in motivating all staff towards seeing improvement as a worthwhile activity. Some improvement approaches in particular place great emphasis on formal education. Six Sigma, for example (see later), and its proponents often mandate a minimum level of training (measured in hours) that they deem necessary before improvement projects should be undertaken.

Perfection is the goal

Almost all organization-wide improvement programmes will have some kind of goal or target that the improvement effort should achieve. And while targets can be set in many different ways, some improvement authorities hold that measuring process performance against some kind of absolute target does most for encouraging improvement. By an 'absolute target' one literally means the theoretical level of perfection: for example, zero errors, instant delivery, delivery absolutely when promised, infinite flexibility, zero waste, etc. Of course, in reality such perfection may never be achievable. That is not the point. What is important is that current performance can be calibrated against this target of perfection in order to indicate how much more improvement is possible. Improving (for example) delivery accuracy by 5 per cent may seem good until it is realized that only an improvement of 30 per cent would eliminate all late deliveries.

Waste identification

All improvement approaches aspire to eliminate waste. In fact any improvement implies that some waste has been eliminated, where waste is any activity that does not add value. But the identification and elimination of waste is sometimes a central feature. For example, as we discussed in Chapter 15, it is arguably the most significant part of the lean philosophy.

Include everybody

Harnessing the skills and enthusiasm of every person and all parts of the organization seems an obvious principle of improvement. The phrase 'quality at source' is sometimes used, stressing the impact that each individual has on improvement. The contribution of all individuals in the organization may go beyond understanding their contribution as 'not making mistakes'. Individuals are expected to bring something positive to improving the way they perform their jobs. The principles of 'empowerment' are frequently cited as supporting this aspect of improvement. When Japanese improvement practices first began to migrate in the late 1970s, this idea seemed even more radical. Yet now it is generally accepted that individual creativity and effort from all staff represents a valuable source of development. However, not all improvement approaches have adopted this idea. Some authorities believe that a small number of internal improvement consultants or specialists offer a better method of organizing improvement. However, these two ideas are not incompatible. Even with improvement specialists used to lead improvement efforts, the staff who actually operate the process can still be a valuable source of information and improvement ideas.

Develop internal customer–supplier relationships

One of the best ways to ensure that external customers are satisfied is to establish the idea that every part of the organization contributes to external customer satisfaction by satisfying its own internal customers. This idea was introduced in Chapter 17, as was the related concept of service level agreements (SLAs). It means stressing that each process in an operation has a responsibility to manage these internal customer–supplier relationships. They do this primarily by defining as clearly as possible what their own and their customers' *requirements* are. In effect this means defining what constitutes 'error-free' service – the quality, speed, dependability and flexibility required by internal customers.

What are the broad approaches to improvement?

By the broad approaches to improvement we mean the underlying sets of beliefs that form a coherent philosophy and shape how improvement should be accomplished. But do not think that approaches to improvement are different in all respects; there are many elements that are common to several approaches. Some of these approaches have been, or will be, described in other chapters. For example, both lean operations (Chapter 15) and TQM (in Chapter 17) are discussed in some detail. So, in this section we will only briefly examine TQM and lean operations, specifically from an improvement perspective, and also add two further approaches – business process re-engineering (BPR) and Six Sigma.

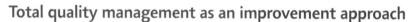

Operations principle

There is no single universal approach to improvement.

Total quality management as an improvement approach

Total quality management was one of the earliest management 'fashions'. Its peak of popularity was in the late 1980s and early 1990s. As such it has suffered from something of a backlash in recent years. Yet the general precepts and principles that constitute TQM are still hugely relevant. Few, if any, managers have not heard of TQM and its impact on improvement. Indeed, TQM has come to be seen as an approach to the way operations and processes should be managed and improved, generally. Even if TQM is not the label given to an improvement initiative, many of its elements will almost certainly have become routine. It is best thought of as a philosophy of how to approach improvement. This philosophy, above everything, stresses the 'total' of TQM. It is an approach that puts quality (and indeed improvement generally) at the heart of everything that is done by an operation. As a reminder, this totality can be summarized by the way TQM lays particular stress on the following elements (see Chapter 17):

- ▶ meeting the needs and expectations of customers;
- ▶ improvement covers all parts of the organization (and should be group-based);
- ▶ improvement includes every person in the organization (and success is recognized);
- ▶ including all costs of quality;
- ▶ getting things 'right first time', i.e. designing-in quality rather than inspecting it in;
- ▶ developing the systems and procedures which support improvement.

Lean as an improvement approach

The idea of 'lean' spread beyond its Japanese roots and became fashionable in the West at about the same time as TQM. And although its popularity has not declined to the same extent as TQM, over 25 years of experience have diminished the excitement once associated with the approach. But, unlike TQM, it was seen initially as an approach to be used exclusively in manufacturing. Now, lean has become fashionable as an approach that can be applied in service operations. As a reminder (see Chapter 15), the lean approach aims to meet demand instantaneously, with perfect quality and no waste'. The key elements of the lean when used as an improvement approach are as follows:

- ▶ customer-centricity;
- ▶ internal customer–supplier relationships;
- ▶ the goal of perfection;

- synchronized flow;
- reduced variation;
- including all people;
- waste elimination.

Some organizations, especially now that lean is being applied more widely in service operations, view waste elimination as the most important of all the elements of the lean approach. In fact, they sometimes see the lean approach as consisting almost exclusively of waste elimination. What they fail to realize is that effective waste elimination is best achieved through changes in behaviour. It is the behavioural change brought about through synchronized flow and customer triggering that provides the window onto exposing and eliminating waste.

Business process re-engineering (BPR)

The idea of business process re-engineering originated in the early 1990s when Michael Hammer proposed that rather than using technology to automate work, it would be better applied to doing away with the need for the work in the first place ('don't automate, obliterate'). In doing this he was warning against establishing non-value-added work within an information technology system where it would be even more difficult to identify and eliminate. All work, he said, should be examined for whether it adds value for the customer and, if not, processes should be redesigned to eliminate it. In doing this BPR was echoing similar objectives in both scientific management and more recently lean approaches. But BPR, unlike those two earlier approaches, advocated radical changes rather than incremental changes to processes. Shortly after Hammer's article, other authors developed the ideas, again the majority of them stressing the importance of a radical approach to elimination of non-value-added work.

BPR has been defined as: '*the fundamental rethinking and radical redesign of business processes to achieve dramatic improvements in critical, contemporary measures of performance, such as cost, quality, service and speed*'.[8] But there is far more to it than that. In fact, BPR was a blend of a number of ideas which had been current in operations management for some time. Lean concepts, process flow charting, critical examination in method study, operations network management and customer-focused operations all contribute to the BPR concept. It was the potential of information technologies to enable the fundamental redesign of processes, however, which acted as the catalyst in bringing these ideas together. It was information technology that allowed radical process redesign, even if many of the methods used to achieve the redesign had been explored before. The main principles of BPR can be summarized in the following points.

- Rethink business processes in a cross-functional manner which organizes work around the natural flow of information (or materials or customers).
- Strive for dramatic improvements in performance by radically rethinking and redesigning the process.
- Have those who use the output from a process, perform the process. Check to see if all internal customers can be their own supplier rather than depending on another function in the business to supply them (which takes longer and separates out the stages in the process).
- Put decision points where the work is performed. Do not separate those who do the work from those who control and manage the work.

Example

We can illustrate this idea of reorganizing (or re-engineering) around business processes through the following simple example. Figure 16.6(a) shows the traditional organization of a trading company which purchases consumer goods from several suppliers, stores them, and sells them on to retail outlets. At the heart of the operation is the warehouse which receives the goods, stores them, and packs and dispatches them when they are required by customers. Orders for more stock are placed by Purchasing, which also takes charge of materials planning and stock control. Purchasing buys the goods based on a forecast which is prepared by Marketing, which takes advice from the Sales department, which is processing customers' orders. When a customer does place an order, it is the Sales department's job to instruct the warehouse to pack and dispatch the order and tell the Finance department to invoice the customer for the goods. So, traditionally, five departments (each a micro operation) have between them organized the flow of materials and information within the total operation. But at each interface between the departments there is the possibility of errors and miscommunication arising. Furthermore, *who is responsible for looking after the customer's needs?* Currently, three separate departments all have dealings with the customer. Similarly, *who is responsible for liaising with suppliers?* This time two departments have contact with suppliers.

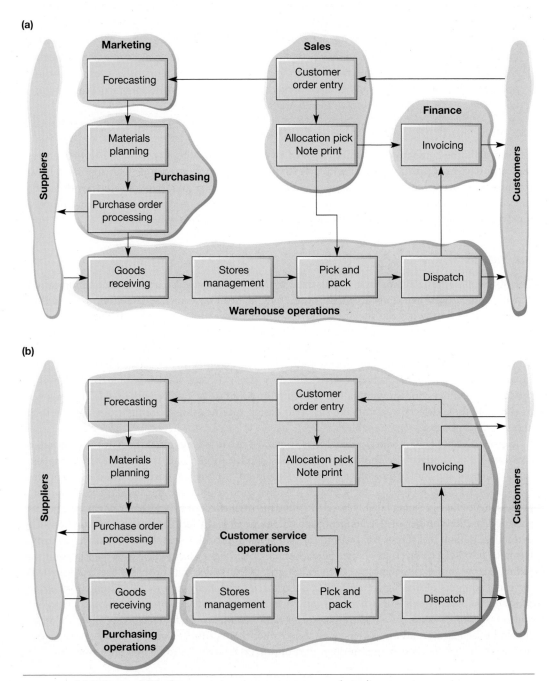

Figure 16.6 (a) Before and (b) after re-engineering a consumer goods trading company

BPR has aroused considerable controversy, mainly because BPR sometimes looks only at work activities rather than at the people who perform the work. Because of this, people become 'cogs in a machine'. Many critics equate BPR with the much earlier principles of scientific management, pejoratively known as 'Taylorism'. Generally these critics mean that BPR is overly harsh in the way it views human resources. Certainly there is evidence that BPR is often accompanied by a significant reduction in staff. Studies at the time when BPR was at its peak often revealed that the majority of BPR projects could reduce staff levels by over 20 per cent.[9] Often BPR was viewed as merely an excuse for getting rid of staff. Companies that wished to 'downsize' were using BPR as the pretext, putting the short-term interests of the shareholders of the company above either their longer-term interests or the interests of the company's employees. Moreover, a combination of radical redesign together with downsizing could mean that the essential core of experience was lost from the operation. This left it vulnerable to any marked turbulence since it no longer possessed the knowledge and experience of how to cope with unexpected changes.

Eventually the company reorganized around two essential business processes. The first process (called purchasing operations) dealt with everything concerning relationships with suppliers. It was this process's focused and unambiguous responsibility to develop good working relationships with suppliers. The other business process (called customer service operations) had total responsibility for satisfying customers' needs. This included speaking 'with one voice' to the customer.

Six Sigma

The Six Sigma approach was first popularized by Motorola, the electronics and communications systems company. When it set its quality objective as 'total customer satisfaction' in the 1980s, it started to explore what the slogan would mean to its operations processes. It decided that true customer satisfaction would only be achieved when its products were delivered when promised, with no defects, with no early-life failures and when the product did not fail excessively in service. To achieve this, Motorola initially focused on removing manufacturing defects. However, it soon came to realize that many problems were caused by latent defects, hidden within the design of its products. These may not show initially but eventually could cause failure in the field. The only way to eliminate these defects was to make sure that design specifications were tight (i.e. narrow tolerances) and its processes very capable.

Motorola's Six Sigma quality concept was so named because it required the natural variation of processes (± 3 standard deviations) to be half their specification range. In other words, the specification range of any part of a product or service should be ± 6 the standard deviation of the process (see Chapter 17). The Greek letter sigma (σ) is often used to indicate the standard deviation of a process, hence the Six Sigma label. Figure 16.7 illustrates the effect of progressively narrowing process variation on the number of defects produced by the process, in terms of defects per million. The defects per million measure is used within the Six Sigma approach to emphasize the drive towards a virtually zero-defect objective.[9] Now the definition of Six Sigma has widened to well beyond this rather narrow statistical perspective. General Electric (GE), which was probably the best known of the early adopters of Six Sigma, defined it as '*A disciplined methodology of defining, measuring, analysing, improving, and controlling the quality in every one of the company's products, processes, and transactions – with the ultimate goal of virtually eliminating all defects*'. So, now Six Sigma should be seen as a broad improvement concept rather than a simple examination of process variation, even though this is still an important part of process control, learning and improvement.

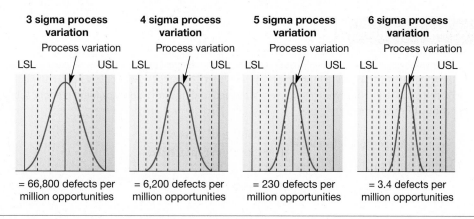

3 sigma process variation	4 sigma process variation	5 sigma process variation	6 sigma process variation
= 66,800 defects per million opportunities	= 6,200 defects per million opportunities	= 230 defects per million opportunities	= 3.4 defects per million opportunities

Figure 16.7 Process variation and its impact on process defects per million

Measuring performance

The Six Sigma approach uses a number of related measures to assess the performance of operations processes.

▶ **A defect** – a failure to meet customer required performance (defining performance measures from a customer's perspective is an important part of the Six Sigma approach).

▶ **A defect unit or item** – any unit of output that contains a defect (i.e. only units of output with no defects are not defective; defective units will have one or more than one defects).

▶ **A defect opportunity** – the number of different ways a unit of output can fail to meet customer requirements (simple products or services will have few defect opportunities, but very complex products or services may have hundreds of different ways of being defective).

▶ **Proportion defective** – the percentage or fraction of units that have one or more defect.

▶ **Process yield** – the percentage or fraction of total units produced by a process that are defect free (that is, 1 – proportion defective).

▶ **Defect per unit (DPU)** – the average number of defects on a unit of output (the number of defects divided by the number of items produced).

▶ **Defects per opportunity** – the proportion or percentage of defects divided by the total number of defect opportunities (the number of defects divided by (the number items produced $\times$ the number of opportunities per item)).

▶ **Defects per million opportunities (DPMO)** – the number of defects which the process will produce if there were one million opportunities to do so.

▶ **The Sigma measurement**[10] – derived from the DPMO, this is the number of standard deviations of the process variability that will fit within the customer specification limits.

Although the scope of Six Sigma is disputed, among elements frequently associated with Six Sigma are the following:

▶ Customer-driven objectives – Six Sigma is sometimes defined as 'the process of comparing process outputs against customer requirements'. It uses a number of measures to assess the performance of operations processes. In particular, it expresses performance in terms of defects per million opportunities (DPMO).

▶ Use of evidence – Although Six Sigma is not the first of the new approaches to operations to use statistical methods, it has done a lot to emphasize the use of quantitative evidence.

▶ Structured improvement cycle – The structured improvement cycle used in Six Sigma is the DMAIC cycle.

▶ Process capability and control – Not surprisingly, given its origins, process capability and control are important within the Six Sigma approach.

An insurance process checks details of insurance claims and arranges for customers to be paid. It samples 300 claims at random at the end of the process. It finds that 51 claims had one or more defects and there were 74 defects in total. Four types of error were observed: coding errors, policy conditions errors, liability errors and notification errors.

$$\text{Proportion defective} = \frac{\text{Number of defects}}{\text{Number of units processed}}$$

$$= \frac{51}{300} = 0.17 \ (17\% \text{ defective})$$

$$\text{Yield} = 1 - \text{proportion of defectives}$$

$$= 1 - 0.17 = 0.83 \text{ or } (83\% \text{ yield})$$

$$\text{Defects per unit} = \frac{\text{Number of defects}}{\text{Number of units processed}}$$

$$= \frac{74}{300} = 0.247 \ (\text{or } 24.7) \text{ DPO}$$

$$\text{Defects per opportunity} = \frac{\text{Number of defects}}{\text{Number of units produced} \times \text{Number of opportunities}}$$

$$= \frac{74}{300 \times 4} = 0.062 \text{ DPO}$$

$$\text{Defects per million opportunities} = \text{DPO} \times 10^6$$

$$= 62{,}000 \text{ DPMO}$$

▶ Process design – Latterly Six Sigma proponents also include process design into the collection of elements that define the Six Sigma approach.

▶ Structured training and organization of improvement – The Six Sigma approach holds that improvement initiatives can only be successful if significant resources and training are devoted to their management.

The 'marshal arts' analogy

The terms that have become associated with Six Sigma experts (and denote their level of expertise) are Master Black Belt, Black Belt and Green Belt. Master Black Belts are experts in the use of Six Sigma tools and techniques as well as how such techniques can be used and implemented. Primarily Master Black Belts are seen as teachers who can not only guide improvement projects, but also coach and mentor Black Belts and Green Belts who are closer to the day-to-day improvement activity. They are expected to have the quantitative analytical skills to help with Six Sigma techniques and also the organizational and interpersonal skills to teach and mentor. Given their responsibilities, it is expected that Master Black Belts are employed full time on their improvement activities. Black Belts can take a direct hand in organizing improvement teams. Like Master Black Belts, Black Belts are expected to develop their quantitative analytical skills and also act as coaches for Green Belts. Black Belts are dedicated full time to improvement, and although opinions vary on how many Black Belts should be employed in an operation, some organizations recommend one Black Belt for every 100 employees. Green Belts work within improvement teams, possibly as team leaders. They have significant amounts of training, although less than Black Belts. Green Belts are not full-time positions; they have normal day-to-day process responsibilities but are expected to spend at least 20 per cent of their time on improvement projects.

Differences and similarities

In this chapter we have chosen to very briefly explain four improvement approaches. It could have been more. Enterprise resource planning (ERP, see Chapter 14), total preventive maintenance (TPM, see Chapter 18), Lean Sigma (a combination of lean and Six Sigma), and others could have been added. But these four constitute a representative sample of the most commonly used approaches. Nor do we have the space to describe them fully. But there are clearly some common elements between some of these approaches that we have described. Yet there are also differences between them in

---

Six Sigma at Wipro[11]

There are many companies that have benefited from Six Sigma-based improvement, but few have gone on to be able to sell the expertise that they gathered from applying it to themselves. Wipro is one of these. Wipro is a global information technology, consulting and outsourcing company with 145,000 employees serving over 900 clients in 60 countries. It provides a range of business services from 'business process outsourcing' (doing processing for other firms) to 'software development', and from 'Information Technology consulting' to 'cloud computing'. (Surprisingly for a global IT services giant Wipro was actually started in 1945 in India as a vegetable oil company.) Wipro also has one of the most developed Six Sigma programmes in the IT and consulting industries, especially in its software development activities where key challenges included reducing the data transfer time within the process, reducing the risk of failures and errors, and avoiding interruption due to network downtime. For Wipro, Six Sigma simply means a measure of quality that strives for near perfection. It means:

▶ having products and services that meet global standards;
▶ ensuring robust processes within the organization;
▶ Consistently meeting and exceeding customer expectations;
▶ establishing a quality culture throughout the business.

Individual Six Sigma projects were selected on the basis of their probability of success and were completed relatively quickly. This gave Wipro the opportunity to assess the success and learn from any problems that had occurred. Projects were identified on the basis of the problem areas under each of the critical Business Processes that could adversely impact business performance. Because Wipro took a customer-focused definition of quality, Six Sigma

implementation was measured in terms of progress towards what the customer finds important (and what the customer pays for). This involved improving performance through a precise quantitative understanding of the customer's requirements. Wipro says that its adoption of Six Sigma has been an unquestionable success, whether in terms of customer satisfaction, improvement in internal performance, or the improvement of shareowner value.

However, as the pioneers of Six Sigma in India, Wipro's implementation of Six Sigma was not without difficulties – and, they stress, opportunities for learning from them. To begin with, it took time to build the required support from the higher-level managers, and to restructure the organization to provide the infrastructure and training to establish confidence in the process. In particular, the first year of deployment was extremely difficult. Resourcing the stream of Six Sigma projects was problematic, partly because each project required different levels and types of resource.

Also, the company learned not to underestimate the amount of training that would be required. To build a team of professionals and train them for various stages of Six Sigma was a difficult job. (In fact this motivated Wipro to start its own consultancy that could train its own people.) Nevertheless, regular and timely reviews of each project proved particularly important in ensuring the success of a project and Wipro had to develop a team of experts for this purpose.

Critical commentary

One common criticism of Six Sigma is that it does not offer anything that was not available before. Its emphasis on improvement cycles comes from TQM, its emphasis on reducing variability comes from statistical process control, its use of experimentation and data analysis is simply good quantitative analysis. The only contribution that Six Sigma has made, argue its critics, is using the rather gimmicky martial arts analogy of Black Belt etc. to indicate a level of expertise in Six Sigma methods. All Six Sigma has done is package pre-existing elements together in order for consultants to be able to sell it to gullible chief executives. In fact, it is difficult to deny some of these points. Maybe the real issue is whether it is really a criticism. If bringing these elements together really does form an effective problem-solving approach, why is this is a problem? Six Sigma is also accused of being too hierarchical in the way it structures its various levels of involvement in the improvement activity (as well as in the dubious use of martial arts derived names such as Black Belt). It is also expensive. Devoting such a large amount of training and time to improvement is a significant investment, especially for small companies. Nevertheless, Six Sigma proponents argue that the improvement activity is generally neglected in most operations and if it is to be taken seriously, it deserves the significant investment implied by the Six Sigma approach. Furthermore, they argue, if operated well, Six Sigma improvement projects run by experienced practitioners can save far more than their cost. There are also technical criticisms of Six Sigma. Most notably, in purely statistical terms the normal distribution which is used extensively in Six Sigma analysis does not actually represent most process behaviour. Other technical criticisms (that are not really the subject of this book) imply that aiming for the very low levels of defects per million opportunities, as recommended by Six Sigma proponents, is far too onerous.

that each approach includes a different set of elements and therefore a different emphasis, and these differences need to be understood. For example, one important difference relates to whether the approaches emphasize a gradual, continuous approach to change, or whether they recommend a more radical 'breakthrough' change. Another difference concerns the aim of the approach. What is the balance between the approach emphasizing *what* changes should be made and *how* changes should be made? Some approaches have a firm view of what is the best way to organize the operation's processes and resources. Other approaches hold no particular view on what an operation should do but rather concentrate on how the management of an operation should decide what to do. Indeed, we can position each of the elements and the approaches that include them. This is illustrated in Figure 16.8. The approaches differ in the extent that they prescribe appropriate operations practice. BPR, for example, is very clear in what it is recommending. Namely, that all processes should be organized on an end-to-end basis. Its focus is *what* should happen rather than *how* it should happen. To a slightly lesser extent, lean is the same. It has a definite list of things that processes should or should not be – waste should be eliminated, inventory should be reduced, technology should be flexible, and so on. Contrast this with both Six Sigma and TQM, which focus to a far greater extent on *how* operations should be improved. Six Sigma in particular has relatively little to say about what is good or bad in the way operations resources are organized (with the possible exception of emphasizing the negative effects of process variation). Its concern is largely the way improvements

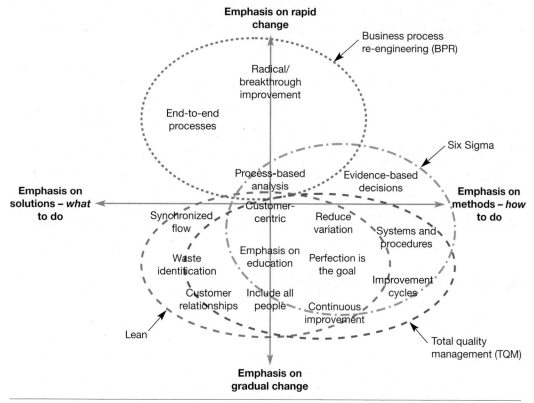

Figure 16.8 The four approaches on the two dimensions of improvement

should be made: using evidence, using quantitative analysis, using the DMAIC cycle, and so on. They also differ in terms of whether they emphasize gradual or rapid change. BPR is explicit in its radical nature. By contrast TQM and lean both incorporate ideas of continuous improvement. Six Sigma is relatively neutral on this issue and can be used for small or very large changes.

> **Operations principle**
>
> There is significant overlap between the various approaches to improvement in terms of the improvement elements they contain.

Lean Sigma[12]

As if to emphasize the shared elements of the various approaches to operations improvement, some organizations are blending two or more approaches to form hybrids that try and combine their best characteristics. The best known of these is Lean Sigma (also called Lean Six Sigma or Six Sigma Lean). As its name suggests, Lean Six Sigma is a combination of lean methods and Six Sigma concepts. It attempts to build on the experience, methods and tools that have emerged from the several decades of operational improvement and implementation using lean and Six Sigma approaches separately. Lean Sigma combines the waste reduction, fast throughput time and impact of lean with the data-driven rigour and variation control of Six Sigma. Some organizations also include other elements from other approaches. For example, the continuous improvement and error-free quality orientation of TQM is frequently included in the concept.

What techniques can be used for improvement?

Improvement techniques are the 'step-by-step' methods and tools that can be used to help find improved ways of doing things. Some of these use quantitative modelling and others are more qualitative. All the techniques described in this book and its supplements can be regarded as 'improvement' techniques. However, some

> **Operations principle**
>
> Improvement is facilitated by relatively simple analytical techniques.

techniques are particularly useful for improving operations and processes generally. Here we select some techniques which either have not been described elsewhere or need to be reintroduced in their role of helping operations improvement particularly.

Scatter diagrams

Scatter diagrams provide a quick and simple method of identifying whether there is evidence of a connection between two sets of data: for example, the time at which you set off for work every morning and how long the journey to work takes. Plotting each journey on a graph which has departure time on one axis and journey time on the other could give an indication of whether departure time and journey time are related, and if so, how. Scatter diagrams can be treated in a far more sophisticated manner by quantifying how strong the relationship between the sets of data is. But, however sophisticated the approach, this type of graph only identifies the existence of a relationship, not necessarily the existence of a cause–effect relationship. If the scatter diagram shows a very strong connection between the sets of data, it is important evidence of a cause–effect relationship, but not proof positive. It could be coincidence!

Example: Kaston Pyral Services Ltd (A)

Kaston Pyral Services Ltd (KPS) installs and maintains environmental control, heating and air conditioning systems. It has set up an improvement team to suggest ways in which it might improve its levels of customer service. The improvement team had completed its first customer satisfaction survey. The survey asked customers to score the service they received from KPS in several ways. For example, it asked customers to score services on a scale of 1 to 10 on promptness, friendliness, level of advice, etc. Scores were then summed to give a 'total satisfaction score' for each customer – the higher the score, the greater the satisfaction. The spread of satisfaction scores puzzled the team and they considered what factors might be causing such differences in the way their customers viewed them. Two factors were put forward to explain the differences:

(a) the number of times in the past year the customer had received a preventive maintenance visit;
(b) the number of times the customer had called for emergency service.

All these data were collected and plotted on scatter diagrams as shown in Figure 16.9. It shows that there seems to be a clear relationship between a customer's satisfaction score and the number of times the customer was visited for regular servicing. The scatter diagram in Figure 16.9(b) is less clear. Although all customers who had very high satisfaction scores had made very few emergency calls, so had some customers with low satisfaction scores. As a result of this analysis, the team decided to survey customers' views on its emergency service.

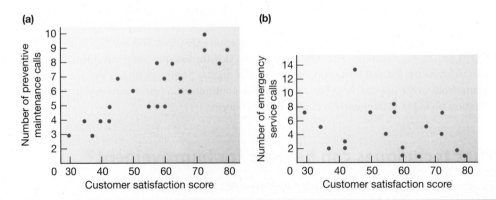

Figure 16.9 Scatter diagrams for customer satisfaction versus (a) number of preventive maintenance calls and (b) number of emergency service calls

Process maps (flow charts)

Process maps (sometimes called flow charts in this context) can be used to give a detailed understanding prior to improvement. They were described in Chapter 6 and are widely used in improvement activities. The act of recording each stage in the process quickly shows up poorly organized flows. Process maps can also clarify improvement opportunities and shed further light on the internal mechanics or workings of an operation. Finally, and probably most importantly, they highlight problem areas where no procedure exists to cope with a particular set of circumstances.

Example: Kaston Pyral Services Ltd (B)

As part of its improvement programme the team at KPS is concerned that customers are not being served well when they phone in with minor queries over the operation of their heating systems. These queries are not usually concerned with serious problems, but often concern minor irritations which can be equally damaging to the customers' perception of KPS's service. Figure 16.10 shows the process map for this type of customer query. The team found the map illuminating. The procedure had never been formally laid out in this way before, and it showed up three areas where information was not being recorded. These are the three points marked with question marks on the process map in Figure 16.10. As a result of this investigation, it was decided to log all customer queries so that analysis could reveal further information on the nature of customer problems.

Cause–effect diagrams

Cause–effect diagrams are a particularly effective method of helping to search for the root causes of problems. They do this by asking what, when, where, how and why questions, but also add some possible 'answers' in an explicit way. They can also be used to identify areas where further data are needed. Cause–effect diagrams (which are also known as Ishikawa diagrams) have become extensively used in improvement programmes. This is because they provide a way of structuring group brainstorming sessions. Often the structure involves identifying possible causes under the (rather old-fashioned) headings of: machinery, manpower, materials, methods and money. Yet in practice, any categorization that comprehensively covers all relevant possible causes could be used.

Example: Kaston Pyral Services Ltd (C)

The improvement team at KPS was working on a particular area which was proving a problem. Whenever service engineers were called out to perform emergency servicing for a customer, they took with them the spares and equipment which they thought would be necessary to repair the system. Although engineers could never be sure exactly what materials and equipment they would need for a job, they could guess what was likely to be needed and take a range of spares and equipment which would cover most eventualities. Too often, however, the engineers would find that they needed a spare that they had not brought with them. The cause–effect diagram for this particular problem, as drawn by the team, is shown in Figure 16.11.

Pareto diagrams

In any improvement process, it is worthwhile distinguishing what is important and what is less so. The purpose of the Pareto diagram (which was first introduced in Chapter 13) is to distinguish between the 'vital few' issues and the 'trivial many'. It is a relatively straightforward technique which involves arranging items of information on the types of problem or causes of problem into their order of importance (usually measured by 'frequency of occurrence'). This can be used to highlight areas where further decision-making will be useful. Pareto analysis is based on the phenomenon of relatively few causes explaining the majority of effects. For example, most revenue for any company is likely to come from relatively few of the company's customers. Similarly, relatively few of a doctor's patients will probably occupy most of his or her time.

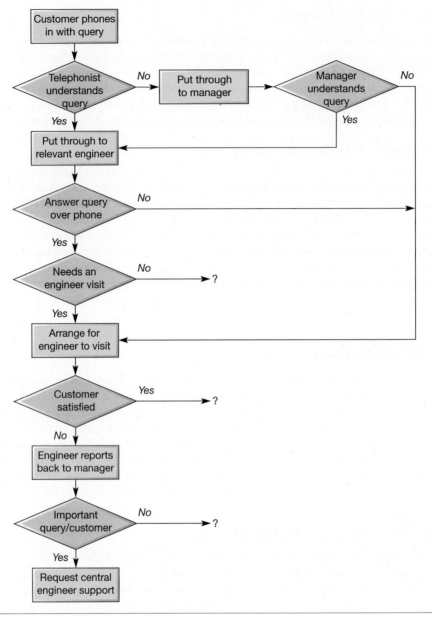

Figure 16.10 Process map for customer query

Example: Kaston Pyral Services Ltd (D)

The KPS improvement team which was investigating unscheduled returns from emergency servicing (the issue which was described in the cause–effect diagram in Figure 16.11) examined all occasions over the previous 12 months on which an unscheduled return had been made. They categorized the reasons for unscheduled returns as follows:

1 The wrong part had been taken to a job because, although the information which the engineer received was sound, he or she had incorrectly predicted the nature of the fault.
2 The wrong part had been taken to the job because there was insufficient information given when the call was taken.

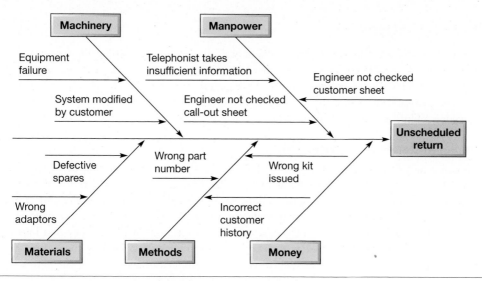

Figure 16.11 Cause–effect diagram of unscheduled returns at KPS

3 The wrong part had been taken to the job because the system had been modified in some way not recorded on KPS's records.
4 The wrong part had been taken to the job because the part had been incorrectly issued to the engineer by stores.
5 No part had been taken because the relevant part was out of stock.
6 The wrong equipment had been taken for whatever reason.
7 Any other reason.

The relative frequency of occurrence of these causes is shown in Figure 16.12. About a third of all unscheduled returns were due to the first category, and more than half the returns were accounted for by the first and second categories together. It was decided that the problem could best be tackled by concentrating on how to get more information to the engineers that would enable them to predict the causes of failure accurately.

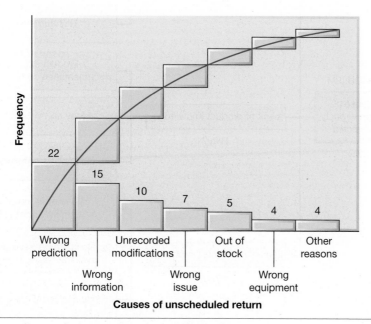

Figure 16.12 Pareto diagram for causes of unscheduled returns

Why–why analysis

Why–why analysis starts by stating the problem and asking *why* that problem has occurred. Once the reasons for the problem occurring have been identified, each of the reasons is taken in turn and again the question is asked *why* those reasons have occurred, and so on. This procedure is continued until either a cause seems sufficiently self-contained to be addressed by itself or no more answers to the question 'Why?' can be generated.

Example: Kaston Pyral Services Ltd (E)

The major cause of unscheduled returns at KPS was the incorrect prediction of reasons for the customer's system failure. This is stated as the 'problem' in the why–why analysis in Figure 16.13. The question is then asked, why was the failure wrongly predicted? Three answers are proposed: first, that the engineers were not trained correctly; second, that they had insufficient knowledge of the particular product installed in the customer's location; and third, that they had insufficient knowledge of the customer's particular system with its modifications. Each of these three reasons is taken in turn, and the questions are asked, why is there a lack of training, why is there a lack of product knowledge, and why is there a lack of customer knowledge? And so on.

How can the improvement process be managed?

Improvement does not just happen. It needs organizing and it needs implementing. It also needs a purpose that is well thought through and clearly articulated. In the final part of this chapter we examine some of the managerial issues associated with how improvement can be organized. Not all the issues concerned with managing the improvement process are easily defined, and many are

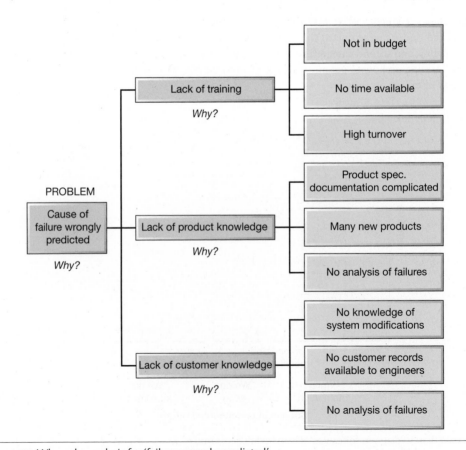

Figure 16.13 Why–why analysis for 'failure wrongly predicted'

outside the traditional scope of an operations management text, but they are important. Many of the issues could be described as the 'soft' side of improvement. But do not dismiss this as in any way less important. In practice it is often the 'soft' stuff that determines the success or failure of improvement efforts. Moreover, the 'soft' stuff can be more difficult to get right than the 'hard', more technique-based, aspects of improvement. The 'hard' stuff is hard, but the 'soft' stuff is harder!

Improvement is a cultural issue

It is generally held by most organizational theorists that the ability to improve its operations performance depends to a large extent on its 'culture'. We discussed what is meant by culture in Chapter 9. It is 'the way we do things around here' or 'the organization's climate'.[13] So, organizational culture and improvement are clearly related. A receptive organizational culture that encourages a constant search for improved ways to do things nurtures improvement. It is an important issue, if only because not all of the improvement initiatives which are launched by organizations, often with high expectations, will go on to fulfil their potential of having a major impact on performance. Estimates of the failure of improvement efforts range from half to 80 per cent. Many aspects of exactly how organizations can develop an appropriate improvement culture, although important, are beyond the scope of this text. However, there are some issues that fall very clearly within the scope of operations management.

Top-management support

The importance of top-management support goes far beyond the allocation of resources to the programme; it sets the priorities for the whole organization. If the organization's senior managers do not understand and show commitment to the programme, it is only understandable that others will ask why they should do so. Usually this is taken to mean that top management must:

▶ understand and believe in the benefits of the improvement approach;
▶ communicate the principles and techniques of improvement;
▶ participate in the improvement process;
▶ formulate and maintain a clear 'improvement strategy'.

This last point is particularly important. Without thinking through the overall purpose and long-term goals of improvement it is difficult for any organization to know where it is going. An improvement strategy is necessary to provide the goals and guidelines which help to keep improvement efforts in line with strategic aims. Specifically, the improvement strategy should have something to say about the competitive priorities of the organization, the roles and improvement responsibilities of all parts of the organization, the resources available for improvement, and its overall improvement philosophy.

It is also important that all senior managers fully understand the underlying principles of whatever improvement approach is adopted. Each of the improvement approaches that we described earlier in this chapter have been the subject of several books that describe them in great detail. There is no shortage of advice from consultants and academics as to how they should be used. Yet it is not difficult to find examples of where senior management have used one or more of these approaches without fully understanding them. The details of Six Sigma or lean, for example, are not simply technical matters. They are fundamental to how appropriate the approach could be in different contexts. Not every approach fits every set of circumstances. So understanding in detail what each approach means must be the first step in deciding whether it is appropriate.

Another responsibility of senior management is to avoid excessive 'hype'. Operations improvement has, to some extent, become a fashion industry with new ideas and concepts continually being introduced as offering a novel way to improve business performance. There is nothing intrinsically wrong with this. Fashion stimulates and refreshes, through introducing novel ideas. Without it, things would stagnate. The problem lies not with new improvement ideas, but rather with some managers becoming a victim of the process, where some new idea will entirely displace whatever went before. Most new ideas have something to say, but jumping from one fad to another will not only generate a backlash against any new idea, but also destroy the ability to accumulate the experience that comes from experimenting with each one. Avoiding becoming an improvement fashion victim is not easy.

Sourcing improvement ideas

When we examined the elements of, and approaches to, improvement, earlier, they focused on generating improvement ideas that originated within the organization. Yet to ignore the improvements that other companies are deploying is to ignore a potentially huge source of innovation. Whether they are competitors, suppliers, customers, or simply other firms with similar challenges, external firms can provide solutions to internal problems. But some commentators argue that (legally) 'copying' from outsiders can be an effective, if underused, approach to improvement. Oded Shenkar, an authority on international management, claims that although to argue *'imitation can be strategic seems almost blasphemous in the current scholarly climate'*, it can *'be strategic and should be part of the strategic repertoire of any agile firm'*.[14] In fact, *'imitation can be a differentiating factor and has the potential to deliver unique value'*. He identifies three 'strategic types' of imitators.

> **Operations principle**
>
> Many improvement ideas can originate from outside an organization.

- ▶ The pioneer importer – an imitator that is the pioneer in another place (another country, industry, or product market). This is what Ryanair did in Europe when it imported the Southwest model.
- ▶ The fast second – a rapid mover arriving quickly after an innovator or pioneer, but before they have had an opportunity to establish an unassailable lead, and before other potentially rival imitators take a large share of the market.
- ▶ The come from behind – a late entrant or adopter that has deliberately delayed adopting a new idea. Samsung did this with its chip-making business, by using its manufacturing capability and knowledge to halve the time it takes to build a semiconductor plant. It then established a lead over competitors by exploiting its key technical, production and quality skills.

Benchmarking

Benchmarking is clearly related to the idea of finding inspiration from outside the organization. It is 'the process of learning from others' and involves comparing one's own performance or methods against other comparable operations. It is a broader issue than setting performance targets, and includes investigating other organizations' operations practice in order to derive ideas that could contribute to performance improvement. Its rationale is based on the idea that (a) problems in managing processes are almost certainly shared by processes elsewhere, and (b) that there is probably another operation somewhere that has developed a better way of doing things. For example, a bank might learn some things from a supermarket about how it could cope with demand fluctuations during the day. Benchmarking is essentially about stimulating creativity in improvement practice.

> **Operations principle**
>
> Improvement is aided by contextualizing processes and operations performance through some kind of benchmarking.

Types of benchmarking

There are many different types of benchmarking (which are not necessarily mutually exclusive), some of which are listed below:

- ▶ *Internal benchmarking* is a comparison between operations or parts of operations which are within the same total organization.
- ▶ *External benchmarking* is a comparison between an operation and other operations which are part of a different organization.
- ▶ *Non-competitive benchmarking* is benchmarking against external organizations which do not compete directly in the same markets.

- *Competitive benchmarking* is a comparison directly between competitors in the same, or similar, markets.
- *Performance benchmarking* is a comparison between the levels of achieved performance in different operations.
- *Practice benchmarking* is a comparison between an organization's operations practices, or way of doing things, and those adopted by another operation.

Benchmarking as an improvement tool

Although benchmarking has become popular, some businesses have failed to derive maximum benefit from it. Partly this may be because there are some misunderstandings as to what benchmarking actually entails. First, it is not a 'one-off' project. It is best practised as a continuous process of comparison. Second, it does not provide 'solutions'. Rather, it provides ideas and information that can lead to solutions. Third, it does not involve simply copying or imitating other operations. It is a process of learning and adapting in a pragmatic manner. Fourth, it means devoting resources to the activity. Benchmarking cannot be done without some investment, but this does not necessarily mean allocating exclusive responsibility to a set of highly paid managers. In fact, there can be advantages in organizing staff at all levels to investigate and collate information from benchmarking targets.

Improvement as learning

Many of the abilities and behaviours often associated with the successful management of improvement are directly or indirectly related to learning in some way. This is not surprising given that operations improvement implies some kind of intervention or change to the operation, and change

---

OPERATIONS IN PRACTICE

Triumph motorcycles resurrected through benchmarking[15]

Triumph motorcycles once built the coolest bikes in the world. In the classic prisoner-of-war film, *The Great Escape'* Steve McQueen memorably jumped across the wire on a Triumph motorcycle. In the 1960s its larger motorcycles were selling well, in both the UK and America. But competition was catching up on the company, and just like the UK auto industry, Triumph declined from the 1970s onwards as better designed and better produced (mainly Japanese) products started to dominate the market. Within a few years the company had gone into receivership, and a property developer, John Bloor, bought the rights to the Triumph name relatively cheaply. He believed that there was a future for the company, yet he did not restart production immediately. Instead he spent years rethinking how the company's operations could be designed and run to compete in the modern motorcycle market. With his new team of managers, he went on an in-depth benchmarking study tour of Japan to analyse the production methods of those competitors that had driven the original Triumph into insolvency. *'We learned a lot,'* says Nick Bloor, John's son, who now runs the company. It soon became clear to the

management team that the original old factory in the West Midlands of the UK was not up to the task of producing world-class products. It was demolished and a new plant built in the UK that utilized the modern equipment and production methods learned on the Japanese visits. Now the company's plants in the UK and Thailand produce record numbers of bikes with styling that reflects the original bike's heritage, but with standards of engineering and reliability that match the operations that it learned from.

It can be argued that there is a fundamental flaw in the whole concept of benchmarking. Operations that rely on others to stimulate their creativity, especially those that are in search of 'best practice', are always limiting themselves to currently accepted methods of operating or currently accepted limits to performance. In other words, benchmarking leads companies only as far as others have gone. 'Best practice' is not 'best' in the sense that it cannot be bettered, it is only 'best' in the sense that it is the best one can currently find. Indeed, accepting what is currently defined as 'best' may prevent operations from ever making the radical breakthrough or improvement that takes the concept of 'best' to a new and fundamentally improved level. This argument is closely related to the concept of breakthrough improvement discussed later in this chapter. Furthermore, methods or performance levels that are appropriate in one operation may not be in another. Because one operation has a set of successful practices in the way it manages its process does not mean that adopting those same practices in another context will prove equally successful. It is possible that subtle differences in the resources within a process (such as staff skills or technical capabilities) or the strategic context of an operation (for example, the relative priorities of performance objectives) will be sufficiently different to make the adoption of seemingly successful practices inappropriate.

> **Operations principle**
>
> There can be no intentional improvement without learning.

will be evaluated in terms of whatever improvement occurs. This evaluation adds to our knowledge of how the operation really works, which in turn increases the chances that future interventions will also result in improvement. This idea of an improvement cycle was discussed earlier. What is important is to realize that it is a learning process, and it is crucial that improvement is organized so that it encourages, facilitates and exploits the learning that occurs during improvement. This requires us to recognize that there is a distinction between single- and double-loop learning.[16]

Single- and double-loop learning

Single-loop learning occurs when there is a repetitive and predictable link between cause and effect. This is similar to the idea of 'routine control' that we discussed in Chapter 10. Some kind of output characteristic from a process is measured and associated with the input conditions that caused it. Every time an operational error or problem is detected, it is corrected and, in doing so, more is learned about the process. However, this happens without questioning or altering the underlying values and objectives of the process, which may, over time, create an unquestioning inertia that prevents it adapting to a changing environment. Double-loop learning, by contrast, questions the fundamental objectives, service or even underlying culture of the operation. This kind of learning implies an ability to challenge existing operating assumptions in a fundamental way. It seeks to re-frame competitive assumptions and remain open to any changes in the competitive environment. But being receptive to new opportunities sometimes requires abandoning existing operating routines, which may be difficult to achieve in practice, especially as many operations reward experience and past achievement (rather than potential) at both an individual and group level. Figure 16.14 illustrates single- and double-loop learning.

Knowledge management

Central to the idea of learning how to do things better is the idea of 'knowledge', where knowledge is defined as: *'facts, information, and skills acquired through experience or education; the theoretical or practical understanding of a subject'*.[17] But note how this definition distinguishes between two sources of knowledge – experience (doing things) and education (explaining or describing what experience has taught you for the benefit of other people). Doing something may lead to you knowing more about it, but having to articulate it or explain it makes your knowledge more valuable because it can be shared with others. It is this process of formalizing experience that distinguishes between 'tacit' knowledge and 'explicit' knowledge.

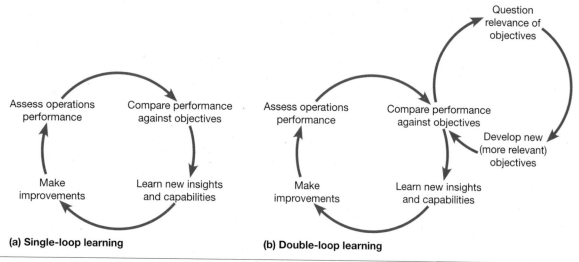

Figure 16.14 Single- and double-loop learning

▶ Tacit knowledge is knowledge that is in people's heads rather than written or formally articulated or described. An example of tacit knowledge that is often used is the knowledge of how to ride a bicycle. If you can do it, it is easy to understand, but explaining how to do it in precise terms is very difficult.

▶ Explicit knowledge is that which is set out in definite form. It can be transmitted in formal, organized language. It has been 'codified', i.e. arranged into systematic language. It is probably included in manuals, records or process maps. Explicit knowledge can be relatively easily communicated between individuals formally and systematically.

Learning from Formula 1[18]

As driving jobs go, there could be no bigger difference than between Formula 1 racing drivers weaving their way through some of the fastest competitors in the world and a supermarket truck driver quietly delivering beans, beer and bacon to distribution centres and stores. But they have more in common than one would suspect. Both Formula 1 and truck drivers want to save fuel, either to reduce pit-stops (Formula 1) or keep delivery costs down (Heavy Goods Vehicles). And although grocery deliveries in the suburbs do not seem as thrilling as racing round the track at Monza, the computer-assisted simulation programs developed by the Williams Formula 1 team are being deployed to help Sainsbury's (a British supermarket group) drivers develop the driving skills that could potentially cut its fuel bill by up to 30 per cent. The simulator technology, which allows realistic advanced training to be conducted in a controlled environment, was developed originally for the advanced training of Formula 1 drivers and was developed and extended at the Williams Technology Centre in Qatar. It can now train drivers to a high level of professional driving skills and road safety applications.

Williams F1's Chief Executive, Alex Burns, commented, 'Formula 1 is well recognized as an excellent technology incubator. It makes perfect sense to embrace some of the new and emerging technologies that the Williams Technology Centre in Qatar is developing from this incubator to help Sainsbury's mission to reduce its energy consumption and enhance the skills and safety of those supporting its crucial logistics operation.' Sainsbury's energy-related improvement programmes tackle energy

Improvement (at least as far as operations managers are concerned) relies on the continual transformation of experience (tacit knowledge) into a formal, recognized 'better way of doing things' (explicit knowledge). The activity of managing how knowledge is formalized in this way is called 'knowledge management' (often abbreviated to KM). It is an idea that became popular in the early 1990s and means *'the process of capturing, distributing, and effectively using knowledge'.*[19]

KM is a way of not having to 'reinvent the wheel', and of building on previous experience. It is also a way of supporting improvement activities because of its potential to combine ideas from all parts of an organization and its external contacts. KM has two distinct, but connected, functions, as shown in Figure 16.15.

▶ It *collects* knowledge together, often codifying tacit into explicit knowledge, allowing anyone with access to the knowledge base to search for, and use, the knowledge whenever and wherever it is needed. This requires the building of large information repositories such as databases.

▶ It *connects* individual staff (who themselves are holders of tacit knowledge) with the formal codified knowledge that has been collected, and to each other. Connecting individuals together is particularly important because it is not always possible to completely codify tacit knowledge into explicit knowledge. People need to interact with the tacit knowledge that is embodied in the people who have the understanding derived from direct experience in order to gain the insights that may not be obvious in its formal codified form.

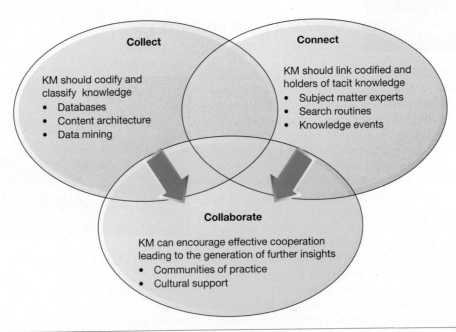

Figure 16.15 Knowledge management systems exploit the ability of e-technologies to collect knowledge and connect individuals and knowledge in order to encourage collaboration

Schlumberger's InTouch technology for knowledge management[20]

Schlumberger is a global company working in the oilfield services industry, supplying the latest technology to *'optimize reservoir performance for customers working in the oil and gas industry'*. The company often operates in difficult and challenging environments, so deploying technology to manage its knowledge base is vital for Schlumberger's continued success. It describes knowledge management (KM) as the *'development and deployment of processes and technology to improve organizational performance and reduce costs for Schlumberger and its customers by enabling individuals to capture, share and apply their overall knowledge – in real time'*. Or, as the company sometimes puts it more simply, *'apply everywhere what you learn anywhere'*. According to Susan Rosenbaum, Schlumberger's director of knowledge management, *'Knowledge is respected as an important asset at Schlumberger. We've had technological solutions internally to capture knowledge since before the term "knowledge management" entered the popular business lexicon. But, while such systems are essential, the key is in how we make use of these tools. It's the sustained interaction between our people that makes the difference.'*

As is normal in KM, technology is important. Schlumberger's proprietary InTouch system is central for knowledge capture and sharing, and has a direct impact on its customers' experience. The InTouch database, which contains more than 1 million knowledge items and receives 8 million views per year, is typically the first recourse for field engineers experiencing a persistent technical problem. It also comprises a team of 125 dedicated InTouch engineers available to help solve field issues one on one. These specialists, who 'sleep with beepers and cell phones', have at least five years of field experience and are drawn

from all of the company's product and domain segments. Their location within the company's research and technology centres gives them immediate access to the scientists and engineers involved in developing the products and services in the first place. Schlumberger also supports internal Eureka technical bulletin boards, many of which log 20 or more discussion threads per week. *'You have field and InTouch engineers interacting through the InTouch system'*, says Rosenbaum. *'But you also have field engineers helping other field engineers on the bulletin boards. InTouch engineers routinely scan these discussion threads to glean information and spot experienced contacts.'* Increasingly, the flow of knowledge is cyclical, making it more robust than ever. *'Field engineers can flag content on the InTouch database that they feel is outdated, to ensure it gets checked'*, says Rosenbaum. *'We're using the power of the people to keep our information up to date.'*

Summary answers to key questions

Why is improvement so important in operations management?

▶ Improvement is now seen as the prime responsibility of operations management. Furthermore, all operations management activities are really concerned with improvement in the long term. Also, companies in many industries are having to improve simply to retain their position relative to their competitors. This is sometimes called the 'Red Queen' effect.

▶ A common distinction is between radical or breakthrough improvement on one hand, and continuous or incremental improvement on the other.

▶ This distinction is closely associated with the distinction between the exploitation of existing capabilities and the exploration of new ones. The ability to do both is called 'organizational ambiguity'.

What are the key features of operations improvement?

▶ There are many 'elements' that are the building blocks of improvement approaches. The ones described in this chapter are:

— improvement cycles;

— a process perspective;

— end-to-end processes;

— radical change;

— evidence-based problem solving;

— customer centricity;

— systems and procedures;

— reducing process variation;

— synchronized flow;

— emphasizing education/training;

— perfection is the goal;

— waste identification;

— including everybody;

— developing internal customer–supplier relationships.

What are the broad approaches to managing improvement?

▶ What we have called 'the broad approaches to improvement' are relatively coherent collections of some of the 'elements' of improvement. The four most common are TQM, lean, business process re-engineering (BPR) and Six Sigma.

▶ There are differences between these improvement approaches. Each includes a different set of elements and therefore has a different emphasis. They can be positioned on two dimensions. The first is whether the approaches emphasize a gradual, continuous approach to change or a more radical 'breakthrough' change. The second is whether the approach emphasizes *what* changes should be made or *how* changes should be made.

What techniques can be used for improvement?

▶ Many of the techniques described throughout this book could be considered improvement techniques, for example statistical process control (SPC).

▶ Techniques often seen as 'improvement techniques' include: scatter diagrams, flow charts, cause–effect diagrams, Pareto diagrams and why–why analysis.

How can the improvement process be managed?

▶ Improvement does not just happen by itself. It needs organizing, information must be gathered so that improvement is treating the most appropriate issues, responsibility for looking after the improvement effort must be assigned, and resources must be allocated. It must also be linked to the organization's overall strategy.

▶ The process of benchmarking is often used as a means of obtaining competitor performance standards.

▶ An organization's ability to improve its operations performance depends to a large extent on its 'culture': that is, *'the pattern of shared basic assumptions . . . that have worked well enough to be considered valid . . . '*. A receptive organizational culture that encourages a constant search for improved ways to do things can encourage improvement.

▶ Many of the abilities and behaviours related to an improvement culture concern learning in some way. They involve two types of learning, single- and double-loop learning.

Ferndale Sands Conference Centre[21]

You may want to remind yourself of the principles behind the importance–performance matrix, described in Chapter 3, when considering this case.

Mario Romano, the owner and General Manager of Ferndale Sands Conference Centre, had just seen an article in *The Conference Centre Journal,* and he was furious. The excellent reputation that he had worked so hard to build up over the last ten years was being threatened by one unreasonable customer and a piece of sloppy, sensationalist journalism. *'It really is unfair. Why do they let one mistake dictate the whole story? I'll tell you why, it's because they are more interested in a damning headline than they are in representing the truth.'*

Ferndale Sands Conference Centre is a conference venue of 52 rooms in Victoria State, Australia, about 20 km outside Melbourne. Established by Mario's father, initially as a hotel, it was re-launched as a conference centre 4 years ago and Mario was broadly pleased with the business he had attracted so far. The centre had managed to establish a presence in the fast-growing and profitable conference market. Specifically it aimed at the 'executive retreat', rather than the 'company meeting' market. These events could be anything from one day's duration through two weeks. He had also negotiated deals with three higher education institutions to accommodate their Executive Education programmes. With its traditional 'Victorian' architecture, tranquil setting and excellent kitchen, Ferndale Sands offered a *'. . . . supremely comfortable setting in which to work on those important decisions that will shape the future of your organization'* (Ferndale Sands brochure).

What had infuriated Marco was an article in a journal that had claimed to uncover administrative complacency and inefficiency at some of the State's conference centres (see the extract in Figure 16.16). Yet in the same edition, another piece had, generally, given a good rating to Ferndale Sands. This article had compared four conference centre facilities in and around Melbourne, and although the editorial comment had been neutral, the details included in the survey had quite clearly shown Ferndale Sands in a favourable light. Table 16.1 shows the summary of the four conference centres reviewed.

Both Mario and his front-of-house manager Robyn Wells disputed the article's rating of their administrative capabilities. However, they also were aware that administrative support was seen as being fairly important when they surveyed their clients (see Table 16.2 for Ferndale Sands' latest survey results).

Mario was determined to do something about the negative publicity. He called a meeting between himself, Nick Godfrey who was in charge of catering and recreational facilities, and Robyn Wells, the front-of-house manager, who also was in charge of all client relations.

Nick – *'OK Mario, I know you're not pleased, but I think you are in danger of overreacting. The best way to respond is just to ignore it. It's the survey that will be saved by potential clients, not a minor article at the front of the journal. And it's the survey that reflects what we really are.'*

Mario – *'Yeah, but even that gets it wrong. It shows administration and support as uneven. What do they mean uneven?'*

Robin – *'I don't know, I guess they must have talked to a couple of clients with some kind of grudge. But look, two things always come out as the most important things for our customers: quality of service and the flexibility to accommodate their needs in different configurations of rooms. We're great at service quality. We're always getting extravagant praise; it's a real winner for us. I've got files full of compliments.'*

Shambles behind the grandeur?

Alison Peraway

Even the grandest of Victorian conference centres can fall from grace, it seems. Recent complaints that Ferndale Sands may look like a Governor's palace, but can't get the basics right, were supported in hard hitting comments from the State's leading reservations agency. *"Ferndale Sands may not be the only venue to get complacent"* said Charles.

Figure 16.16 Extract from *The Conference Centre Journal*

Table 16.1 Extract from *The Conference Centre Journal's* survey of conference venues in and around Melbourne

	Ferndale Sands Conference Centre	Collins International	The Yarrold Conference Centre	St Kildan Conference Centre
Price ($$$$$ = very expensive, $$$ = average, $ = budget)	$$$$	$$$$$	$$$	$
Size of menu	Extensive	Standard	Standard	Limited
Decor	Traditional, luxurious and tasteful	Modern, very luxurious and stylish	Modern but basic	Needs renovation
Style and quality of food	Modern, best in the State	International modern, slightly standardized	Varies, undistinguished but acceptable	Varies, very basic
Quality of service	Excellent, friendly and relaxed	Good	Limited	Enthusiastic but limited
Administration and support	Variable, some problems recently	Good	Good	OK
Flexibility of accommodation	Poor	Very good	Acceptable	OK
Off-peak price discounts	None offered	Some in summer, none in winter	Willing to negotiate	Willing to negotiate
Equipment	Normal range	Normal range	Normal range	Requires notice for 'anything unusual'
Recreational facilities	Full range, gym, tennis, golf, swimming pool, etc.	Gym, swimming pool	Gym only	Gym only
Ease of access	Good, will pick up from airport and city	City centre, no airport shuttle to hotel, but bus service, taxies, etc.	Close to city center	10 km from city center

It's room flexibility that's our problem. Most clients accept that you can't mess around with a historic building like this, but that doesn't get round the fact that we can't reconfigure our rooms like you could in a modern hotel with sliding room partitions.'

Mario – 'Well, maybe that's something we could minimize by making it clear to clients what we can and can't do when they make a reservation.'

Robyn – 'True, and we do that when demand is very high. But you can't ask us to turn away business by stressing what we can't do during quiet periods.'

Mario – 'Well, maybe we should. But that's not my main concern right now. What worries me are the things that always show up as mid-range factors in our customer surveys. We tend to forget about these. They may not be the most important things in the clients' eyes but there not unimportant either. I'm talking about things like the quality of our food and the decor of the rooms, and also, Robyn, the administrative support we offer. If we get these things wrong it can almost cause us as many problems as the really important things. That's why I'm upset about the poor administrative score we get in the journal. We score 5 for decor, and really good for food, but poor for administration.'

Robyn – 'But as we said, that's just unfortunate. I still have every confidence in my administrative staff.'

Nick – 'Before we get into that again, can I raise the question of our recreation facilities? It's one of our best assets yet it never rates as important with clients. It's the same with the choice we offer on our menus. Both these things are expensive to provide, and yet we don't seem to get the benefit. Why don't we make a real effort to really promote both of these things? You know, really convince the clients that great facilities and a wide choice on the menu are things that are worth paying a little more for.'

Table 16.2 Percentage of Ferndale Sands clients reporting factor as important or very important

	Percentage of customers reporting factor as important or very important
Price	72
Size of menu	16
Decor	55
Style and quality of food	58
Quality of service	89
Administration and support	56
Flexibility of accommodation	85
Off-peak price discounts	16
Equipment	72
Recreational facilities	21
Ease of access	73

Mario – 'It's not our pricing that's the problem. Although it's a fairly important issue with most clients, we can command relatively high prices. It's out costs that worry me more. Our general running costs are higher than they should be. Talking to the guys over at Parramatta Pacific in New South Wales, they are very similar to us, but their costs are a good 10 per cent less than ours.'

Robyn – 'So, what is more important, raising our revenue our cutting our costs?'

Mario – 'They are both equally important, of course. The point is, what do we do about attracting more business and keeping our costs down?'

Robyn – 'OK, we've got to do something, but remember we've also got the centre to run. Our busy period is just coming up and I don't want everyone distracted by lots of little improvement initiatives.'

Nick – 'Absolutely. We have to limit ourselves to one or two actions that will have a noticeable impact.'

Mario – 'I think you're probably right. But I would also add a further comment. And that is that if what we choose to do requires investment, then it must be guaranteed to have an impact. I need to go now, but why don't you two draw up a list of things that we could do. I'll review them later. OK, thanks everyone.'

Robyn and Nick's suggestions

In fact, Robyn and Nick decided to draw up their individual lists of potential improvement initiatives. They also decided that, to begin with, only two of these improvement initiatives should be chosen.

Robyn's suggestions:

▶ Increase prices – 'Why not? Although demand is variable, the general trend is rising as the conference market expands. At this top end of the market I don't think we are that price sensitive. It would also bring in the revenue that we need to make further reinvestments to the centre.'

▶ Reduce menu choice – 'This really is a left-over from what menus used to be like. It goes back to the time when "more" was considered "better" instead of just "more". It is also very expensive to maintain that range of food while still maintaining quality.'

▶ Close the golf course – 'The golf course is probably the most expensive facility we have outside the house. It isn't rated by customers, so why do we keep it on?'

▶ Renovate outbuildings to provide flexible conference rooms – 'We can't easily change the inside of the house, but we do have outbuildings that could be converted into conference suites. They could be equipped with moveable partitions that would enable the space to be configured however our clients wanted it. OK, it would be expensive, but in the long term it's necessary.'

Nick's suggestions:

▶ Promote food and facilities more effectively – 'We have a great reputation for food and for having marvellous facilities. Ferndale Sands is just a beautiful place, yet we're not exploiting it fully. A campaign from a good public relations company could really establish us as the premier conference centre, not just in the state, but in the whole of Australia.'

▶ Cut in-house staff numbers and replace part-time staff with a smaller number of full-time staff – 'Having so many part-time staff is expensive. We pay them the same hourly rate as full-time staff yet there are all the extra personnel costs. Also, I think we are over-staffed in the house. Staff costs are a major part of our expenditure. It's the obvious area to look for cuts.'

▶ Invest in more equipment, both relaxation equipment and presentation equipment – 'We have great sporting facilities but they could be better. If we are going to exploit them more it may not be a bad thing to invest even more heavily in them. Also, we could make sure that we were ahead of the game in terms of the very latest audio-visual equipment. Both these things would help us to promote ourselves as the premier conference centre in Australia.'

QUESTIONS

1 What factors would you use to judge the operations performance of Ferndale Sands'?

2 What improvement priority would you give to each of these performance measures?

3 Which two suggestions put forward by Robyn and Nick would you recommend?

Problems and applications

All chapters have 'Problems and applications' questions that will help you practise analysing operations. They can be answered by reading the chapter. Model answers for the first two questions can be found on the companion website for this book.

1   Sophie was sick of her daily commute. *'Why',* she thought, *'should I have to spend so much time in the morning stuck in traffic listening to some babbling halfwit on the radio? We can work flexi-time, after all. Perhaps I should leave the apartment at some other time?'* So resolved, Sophie deliberately varied her time of departure from her usual 8.30. Also, being an organized soul, she recorded her time of departure each day and her journey time. Her records are shown in Table 16.3. (a) Draw a scatter diagram that will help Sophie decide on the best time to leave her apartment. (b) How much time per (5-day) week should she expect to be saved from having to listen to a babbling halfwit?

2   *'Everything we do can be broken down into a process'*, said Lucile, chief operating officer of an outsourcing business for the 'back office' functions of a range of companies. *'It may be more straightforward in a manufacturing business, but the concept of process improvement is just as powerful in service operations. Using this approach our team of Black Belts has achieved 30 per cent productivity improvements in 6 months. I think Six Sigma is powerful because it is the process of comparing process outputs against customer requirements. To get processes operating at less than 3.4 defects per million opportunities means that you must strive to get closer to perfection and it is the customer that defines the goal. Measuring defects per opportunity means that you can actually compare the process of, say, a human resources process with a billing and collection process.'*
(a)   What are the benefits of being able to compare the number of defects in a human resources process with those of collection or billing?
(b)   Why is achieving defects of less than 3.4 per million opportunity seen as important by Lucile?
(c)   What do you think are the benefits and problems of training Black Belts and taking them off their present job to run the improvement projects rather than the project being run by a member of the team that has responsibility for actually operating the process?

3   Develop cause–effect diagrams for the following types of problem:
   ▶ staff waiting too long for their calls to be answered at their IT helpdesk;
   ▶ poor food in the company restaurant;
   ▶ poor lecturing from teaching staff at a university;
   ▶ customer complaints that the free plastic toy in their breakfast cereal packet is missing;
   ▶ staff having to wait excessively long periods to gain access to the coffee machine.

4   For over 10 years a hotel group had been developing self-managed improvement groups within its hotels. At one hotel reception desk, staff were concerned about the amount of time the reception

Table 16.3 Sophie's journey times (in minutes)

Day	Leaving time	Journey time	Day	Leaving time	Journey time	Day	Leaving time	Journey time
1	7.15	19	6	8.45	40	11	8.35	46
2	8.15	40	7	8.55	32	12	8.40	45
3	7.30	25	8	7.55	31	13	8.20	47
4	7.20	19	9	7.40	22	14	8.00	34
5	8.40	46	10	8.30	49	15	7.45	27

Table 16.4 Reasons for staff time away from the reception desk

Reason for being away from reception desk	Total number of minutes away
Checking files in back office	150
Providing glasses for night drinks	120
Providing extra key cards	90
Providing medication	20
Providing extra stationery	70
Providing misc. items to rooms	65
Providing night drinks	40
Making photocopies	300
Carrying messages to meeting rooms	125
Locking and unlocking meeting rooms	80
Providing extra linen	100

desk was left unattended. To investigate this the staff began keeping track of the reasons they were spending time away from the desk and how long each absence kept them away. Everyone knew that reception desk staff often had to leave their post to help or give service to a guest. However, no one could agree what was the main cause of absence. Collecting the information was itself not easy because the staff had to keep records without affecting customer service. After three months the data were presented in the form of a Pareto diagram, which is shown in Table 16.4. It came as a surprise to reception staff and hotel management that making photocopies for guests was the main reason for absence. Fortunately, this was easily remedied by moving the photocopier to a room adjacent to the reception area, enabling staff to keep a check on the reception desk while they were making copies.

(a) Do you think it was wise to spend so much time on examining this particular issue? Isn't it a trivial issue?

(b) Should this information be used to reflect improvement priorities? In other words, was the group correct to put priority on avoiding absence through photocopying, and should its next priority be to look at the time checking files in the back office?

5   A transport services company provides a whole range of services to railway operators. Its reputation for quality is a valuable asset in its increasingly competitive market. *'We are continually looking for innovation in the way we deliver our services because the continuous improvement of our processes is the only way to make our company more efficient,'* said the company's CEO. *'We use a defined set of criteria to identify critical processes, each of which is allocated a "process owner" by our quality steering committee. This is helped by the company's "process excellence index" (EPI) which is an indicator of the way a process performs, particularly how it is designed, controlled and improved. The EPI score, which is expressed on a scale of 1 to 100, is calculated by the process owner and registered with the quality department. With this one figure we can measure the cost, reliability and quality of each process so that we can compare performance. If you don't measure, you can't improve. And if you don't measure in the correct way, how can you know where you are? Employee recognition is also an important. Our suggestion scheme is designed to encourage staff to submit ideas that are evaluated and rated. No individual suggestion is finally evaluated until it has been fully implemented. Where a team of employees puts ideas forward, the score is divided between them, either equally or according to the wishes of the team itself. These employee policies are supported by the company's training schemes, many of which are designed to ensure all employees are customer-focused.'*

(a) What seem to be the key elements in this company's approach to improvement?

(b) Do you think this approach is appropriate for all operations?

6   Step 1 – As a group, identify a class of 'high-visibility' operations that you all are familiar with. This could be a type of quick service restaurant, record stores, public transport systems, libraries, etc.

Step 2 – Once you have identified the broad class of operation, visit a number of them and use your experience as customers to identify:

(a) the main performance factors that are of importance to you as customers, and

(b) how each store rates against each other in terms of their performance on these same factors.

Step 3 – Draw an importance–performance diagram for one of the operations that indicates the priority they should be giving to improving their performance.

Step 4 – Discuss the ways in which such an operation might improve its performance and try to discuss your findings with the staff of the operation.

Selected further reading

Ahlstrom, J. (2015) *How to Succeed with Continuous Improvement: A Primer for Becoming the Best in the World,* **McGraw-Hill Professional, New York.**
This is very much a practical guide. Slightly evangelical, but it gets the message over.

George, M.L., Rowlands, D. and Kastle, B. (2003) *What Is Lean Six Sigma?* **McGraw-Hill, New York.**
A quick introduction to what Lean Six Sigma is and how to use it.

Goldratt, E.M. and Cox, J. (2004) *The Goal: A Process of Ongoing Improvement,* **Gower Publishing Limited, Aldershot.**
Updated version of a classic.

Hendry, L. and Nonthaleerak, P. (2004) Six Sigma: Literature review and key future research areas, Lancaster University Management School, Working Paper, 2005/044 http://www.lums.lancs.ac.uk/ publications/
Good overview of the literature on Six Sigma.

Hindo, B. (2007) At 3M, a struggle between efficiency and creativity: How CEO George Buckley is managing the yin and yang of discipline and imagination, *Business Week,* **11 June.**
Readable article from the popular business press.

Pande, P.S., Neuman, R.P. and Cavanagh, R. (2002) *Six Sigma Way Team Field Book: An implementation guide for project improvement teams,* **McGraw Hill, New York.**
Obviously based on the Six Sigma principle and related to the book by the same author team recommended in Chapter 17, this is an unashamedly practical guide to the Six Sigma approach.

Xingxing Zu, Fredendall, L.D. and Douglas, T.J. (2008) The evolving theory of quality management: The role of Six Sigma, *Journal of Operations Management,* **vol. 26, 630–650.**
As it says . . .

Quality management

KEY QUESTIONS

What is quality and why is it so important?

What steps lead towards conformance to specification?

What is total quality management (TQM)?

INTRODUCTION

Quality management has always been an important part of operations management, but its position and role within the subject have changed. At one time it was seen largely as an essential, but 'routine,' activity that prevented errors having an impact on customers (and would have been located unambiguously in the 'Deliver' section of this book). And that function is still there. But increasingly quality management is viewed as also having a part to play in how operations improve. Quality management can contribute to improvement by making the changes to operations processes that lead better outcomes for customers. In fact, in most organizations, quality management is one of the main drivers of improvement. It is also the only one of the five 'operations performance objectives' to have its own dedicated chapter in this book. Partly this is because of this central role of 'quality' in improvement. Some operations managers believe that, in the long run, quality is the most important single factor affecting an organization's performance relative to its competitors. But it is also because in many organizations a separate function is devoted exclusively to the management of quality. Figure 17.1 shows where quality management fits into the model of operations activities.

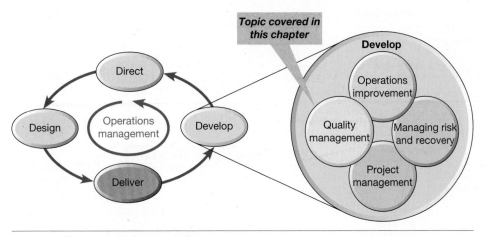

Figure 17.1 This chapter examines quality management

What is quality and why is it so important?

It is worth revisiting some of the arguments which were presented in Chapter 2 regarding the benefits of high levels of quality. It will help to explain why quality is seen as being so important by most operations. Figure 17.2 illustrates the various ways in which quality improvements can affect other aspects of operations performance. Revenues can be increased by better sales and enhanced prices in the market. At the same time, costs can be brought down by improved efficiencies, productivity and the use of capital. So, a key task of the operations function must be to ensure that it provides quality goods and services, both to its internal and external customers.

The operation's view of quality

There are many definitions of quality; here we define it as *consistent conformance to customers' expectations*.

The use of the word 'conformance' implies that there is a need to meet a clear specification. Ensuring a service or product conforms to specification is a key operations task. 'Consistent' implies that conformance to specification is not an ad hoc event but that the service or product meets the specification because quality requirements are used to design and run the processes that produce services or products. The use of 'customers' expectations' recognizes that the service or product must take the views of customers into account, which may be influenced by price. Also note the use of the word 'expectations' in this definition, rather than needs or wants.

Customers' view of quality

Past experiences, individual knowledge and history will all shape customers' expectations. Furthermore, customers may each *perceive* a service or product in different ways. One person may perceive a long-haul flight as an exciting part of a holiday; the person on the next seat may see it as a necessary chore to get to a business meeting. So quality needs to be understood from a customer's point of view because, to the customer, the quality of a particular service or product is whatever he

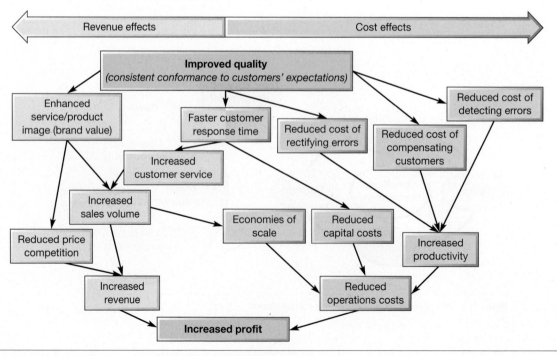

Figure 17.2 Higher quality has a beneficial effect on both revenues and costs

or she perceives it to be. If the passengers on a skiing charter flight perceive it to be of good quality, despite long queues at check-in or cramped seating and poor meals, then the flight really is of good perceived quality.[1] Also customers may be unable to judge the 'technical' specification of the service or product and so use surrogate measures as a basis for their perception of quality. For example, a customer may find it difficult to judge the technical quality of dental treatment, except insofar as their teeth do not give any more trouble. The customer may therefore perceive quality in terms the demeanour of the dentist and technician and how they were treated.

> **Operations principle**
>
> Quality is multi-faceted and its individual elements differ for different operations.

OPERATIONS IN PRACTICE	Quality at two operations: Victorinox and Four Seasons

Victorinox and the Swiss Army Knife[2]

The famous Swiss Army Knife is made by the Victorinox Company in its factory in the Swiss town of Ibach. The company has numerous letters from its customers testifying to their product's quality and durability. For example, *'I was installing a new piece of equipment in a sewage treatment plant . . . The knife slipped out of my hand and fell into the aeration tank . . . that is extremely corrosive to metals. Four years later, I received a small parcel with a note from the supervisor of the plant. They had emptied the aeration tank and found my knife . . . it was in astonishingly good condition. I can assure you that very few products could have survived treatment like this, the components would have dissolved or simply disappeared.'*

Today, the Victorinox factory assembles 27,000 knives a day (plus nearly 100,000 other items). More than 450 steps are required in its manufacture. But a major threat to sales that has been growing is the appearance on the market of fake 'Swiss Army' knives, made mostly in China. Many of them look similar to the original; they even have the familiar Swiss cross on the handle. So what is their defence against these fakes? *'Quality'*, says CEO Carl Elsener. *'We have exhausted all legal means for the brand protection of our popular products. Our best means of protection is quality which remains unsurpassed and speaks louder than words.'* It is the 'Victorinox quality control system' that is at the heart of this defence.

First, receiving inspection ensures that incoming materials conform to quality specifications. This includes precisely measuring all aspects of incoming quality. The Victorinox laboratory conforms to the latest standard of engineering and guarantees that only steel and plastic that comply with their rigorous quality standards are used in the manufacturing of the products. The steel consists of special alloys, which possess those material characteristics that are most important for the respective field of application. All alloys are tested for composition by means of spectrum analysis that uses an electric arc on the material under protective gas, so that parts of its surface melt and evaporate. From the spectrometric analysis of the arc, the alloy composition of the various metals can be calculated. Metallurgical inspection is also used by polishing samples, casting them in plastic and etching with an acid. This allows faults in materials to be easily detected. The laboratory also has an 'edge retention test', using special equipment to test the ability of material to retain its edge during a series of cutting tests. During the production of the knives, process control is employed at all stages of the production process, and is the responsibility of the company's employees, who use it to maintain, implement and improve the quality of products. They are also responsible for following the company's quality procedures and for continuous, measurable improvement. At the end of the production process, the 'Final Inspection Department' employs 50–60 people who are responsible for ensuring that all products conform to requirements. Any nonconforming products are isolated and identified. Non-conforming parts are repaired or replaced at the repair department.

▶

Four Seasons Canary Wharf[3]

The first Four Seasons Hotel opened over 50 years ago and the hotel group has now grown to 100 properties all over the world. Famed for its quality of service, it has won countless awards for the quality of its service. From its inception the group has had the same guiding principle, *'to make the quality of our service our competitive advantage'*. The company has what it calls its Golden Rule: *'Do to others (guests and staff) as you would wish others to do to you.'* It is a simple rule, but it guides the whole organization's approach to quality. *'Quality service is our distinguishing edge and the company continues to evolve in that direction. We are always looking for better, more creative and innovative ways of serving our guests,'* says Michael Purtill, the General Manager of the Four Seasons Hotel Canary Wharf in London. *'We have recently refined all of our operating standards across the company enabling us to further enhance the personalized, intuitive service that all our guests receive. All employees are empowered to use their creativity and judgement in delivering exceptional service and making their own decisions to enhance our guests' stay. For example, one morning an employee noticed that a guest had a flat tyre on their car and decided on his own accord to change it for them, which was very much appreciated by the guest.*

'The golden rule means that we treat our employees with dignity, respect and appreciation. This approach encourages them to be equally sensitive to our guests' needs and offer sincere and genuine service that exceeds expectations. Just recently one of our employees accompanied a guest to the hospital and stayed there with him for entire afternoon. He wanted to ensure that the guest wasn't alone and was given the medical attention he needed. The following day that same employee took the initiative to return to the hospital (even though it was his day off) to visit and made sure that that guest's family in America was kept informed about his progress.

'We ensure that we have an on-going focus on recognizing these successes and publicly praise and celebrate all individuals who deliver these warm, spontaneous, thoughtful touches.

'At Four Seasons, we believe that our greatest asset and strength are our people. We pay a great deal of

attention to selecting the right people with an attitude that takes great pride in delivering exceptional service. We know that motivated and happy employees are essential to our service culture and are committed to developing our employees to their highest potential. Our extensive training programmes and career development plans are designed with care and attention to support the individual needs of our employees as well as operational and business demands. In conjunction with traditional classroom-based learning, we offer tailor-made web-based learning featuring exceptional quality courses for all levels of employee. Career wise, the sky is the limit and our goal is to build lifelong, international careers with Four Seasons.

'Our objective is to exceed guest expectations and feedback from our guests and our employees is an invaluable barometer of our performance. We have created an in-house database that is used to record all guest feedback (whether positive or negative). We also use an online guest survey and guest comment cards which are all personally responded to and analysed to identify any potential service gaps.

'We continue to focus on delivering individual personalized experiences and our Guest History database remains vital in helping us to achieve this. All preferences and specific comments about service experience are logged on the database. Every comment and every preference is discussed and planned for, for every guest, for every visit. It is our culture that sets Four Seasons apart; the drive to deliver the best service in the industry that keeps our guests returning again and again.'

Reconciling the operation's and the customer's views of quality

The operation's view of quality is concerned with trying to meet customer expectations The customer's view of quality is what he or she *perceives* the service or product to be. To create a unified view, quality can be defined as the degree of fit between customers' expectations and customer perception of the service or product.[4] Using this idea allows us to see the customers' view of quality of (and, therefore, satisfaction with) the service or product as the result of the customers comparing their expectations of the service or product with their perception of how it performs. If the service or product experience was better than expected then the customer is satisfied and quality is perceived to be high. If the service or product was less than his or her expectations then quality is low and the customer may be dissatisfied. If the service or product matches expectations then the perceived quality of the service or product is seen to be acceptable. These relationships are summarized in Figure 17.3.

Both customers' expectations and perceptions are influenced by a number of factors, some of which cannot be controlled by the operation and some of which, to a certain extent, can be managed. Figure 17.4 shows some of the factors that will influence the gap between expectations and perceptions. This model of customer-perceived quality can help us understand how operations can manage quality and identifies some of the problems in so doing. The bottom part of the diagram represents the operation's 'domain' of quality and the top part the customer's 'domain'. These two domains meet in the actual service or product, which is provided by the organization and experienced by the customer. Within the operation's domain, management is responsible for designing the service or product and providing a specification of the quality to which the service or product has to be created. Within the customer's domain, his or her expectations are shaped by such factors as previous experiences with the particular service or product, the marketing image provided by the organization and word-of-mouth information from other users. These expectations are internalized as a set of quality characteristics.

Operations principle

Perceived quality is governed by the magnitude and direction of the gap between customers' expectations and their perceptions of a product or service.

How can quality problems be diagnosed?[5]

Figure 17.4 also shows how quality problems can be diagnosed. If the perceived quality gap is such that customers' perceptions of the service or product fail to match their expectations of it, then the reason (or reasons) must lie in other gaps elsewhere in the model as follows.

Gap 1: The customer's specification–operation's specification gap. Perceived quality could be poor because there may be a mismatch between the organization's own internal quality specification and the specification which is expected by the customer. For example, a car may be designed to need servicing every 10,000 kilometres but the customer may expect 15,000 kilometre service intervals.

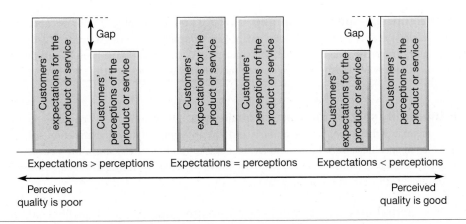

Figure 17.3 Perceived quality is governed by the magnitude and direction of the gap between customers' expectations and their perceptions of the service or product

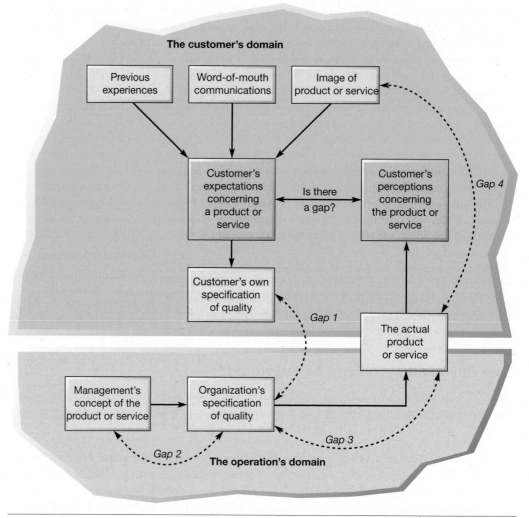

The customer's domain

Previous experiences

Word-of-mouth communications

Image of product or service

Customer's expectations concerning a product or service

Is there a gap?

Customer's perceptions concerning the product or service

Gap 4

Customer's own specification of quality

Gap 1

The actual product or service

Management's concept of the product or service

Organization's specification of quality

Gap 2

Gap 3

The operation's domain

Figure 17.4 The customer's domain and the operations domain in determining the perceived quality, showing how the gap between customers' expectations and their perception of a service or product could be explained by one or more gaps elsewhere in the model

Source: Adapted from Parasuraman, A. *et al.* (1985) 'A Conceptual Model of Service Quality and Implications for Future Research', *Journal of Marketing,* Vol. 49, Fall.

Gap 2: The concept–specification gap. Perceived quality could be poor because there is a mismatch between the service or product concept (see Chapter 5) and the way the organization has specified quality internally. For example, the concept of a car might have been for an inexpensive, energy-efficient means of transportation, but the inclusion of a climate control system may have both added to its cost and made it less energy-efficient.

Gap 3: The quality specification–actual quality gap. Perceived quality could be poor because there is a mismatch between actual quality and the internal quality specification (often called 'conformance to specification'). For example, the internal quality specification for a car may be that the gap between its doors and body, when closed, must not exceed 7 mm. However, because of inadequate equipment, the gap in reality is 9 mm.

Gap 4: The actual quality–communicated image gap. Perceived quality could be poor because there is a gap between the organization's external communications or market image and the actual quality delivered to the customer. This may be because the marketing function has set unachievable expectations or operations is not capable of the level of quality expected by the customer. For example, an advertising campaign for an airline might show a cabin attendant offering to replace a customer's shirt on which food or drink has been spilt, whereas such a service may not in fact be available should this happen.

'Quality', 'Quality of service' and 'quality of experience'

The definition of quality that we use here (the *consistent conformance to customers' expectations*) is useful because it can be used to describe 'quality' for either physical products, or intangible services, or any offering that combines both tangible and intangible elements. However, not all authorities or individual operations view 'quality' in this way, which can lead to some confusion. For example, the term 'quality of service' (QoS) is often used to describe how an operation serves its customers by combining what we have called 'quality' with some or all of 'speed', 'dependability' and 'flexibility'. So in Chapter 2 we described the 'quality' of a supermarket as including such factors as the quality of the goods stocked, the cleanliness of the facilities and the courtesy of its staff. But, in assessing its QoS, the supermarket would probably want to include other factors such as the speed of service, the predictability of opening times, stockouts, the range of goods available, and so on.

The limitation of QoS is that it may not capture the overall satisfaction with the service as perceived by the users. More useful, claim some providers of service, is to try and assess 'quality of experience' (QoE). Quality of experience is the overall acceptability of the service, *as perceived subjectively by the end-user.* More formally it has been defined as *'the degree of delight or annoyance of the user of an application or service. It results from the fulfillment of his or her expectations with respect to the utility and/or enjoyment of the application or service in the light of the user's personality and current state.'*[6] QoE is clearly related to, but differs from, QoS in that it expresses, and focuses on, user satisfaction *both objectively and subjectively.* QoS generally includes the aspects of a service that are under the control of the operation creating the service, whereas QoE involves both the aspects governed by the operation and those that are a function of the individual customer and the context in which the service is consumed. Figure 17.5 illustrates the relationship between these ideas, and Table 17.1 shows some typical factors that could be included in assessing the 'quality', 'quality of service' and 'quality of experience' of a supermarket operation and an online education service.

The QoE concept originated in, and has found its most extensive application in, telecommunications operations, information technology (IT) and consumer electronics. Yet its underlying principles

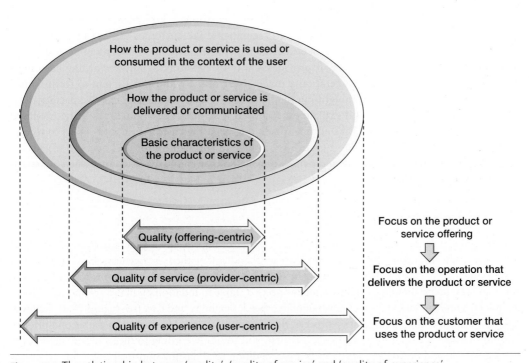

Figure 17.5 The relationship between 'quality', 'quality of service' and 'quality of experience'

Table 17.1 Examples of typical factors that could be included in assessing the 'quality', 'quality of service' and 'quality of experience' of a supermarket operation and an online education service

Operation	Quality	Quality of service (QoS) 'Quality' plus the following . . .	Quality of experience (QoE) 'Quality' plus 'Quality of service' plus the following . . .
Supermarket	Quality of goods Cleanliness Staff courtesy	Speed of service Stockouts Predictability of service (hours of opening) Range of goods stocked	Open when I want to use the service? Perception of speed of service Is what I want available? Nature of other users of the service
Online education service	Quality/accuracy of the lesson content Quality of production values	Various technical measures of network performance (such as throughput, packet loss, delay and jitter)	Relevance of content to me How the content works on the device I am using (display fidelity, transport/stalling quality, etc.) How easy is it for me to navigate the content?

have a far wider application. The QoE idea can be applied to any consumer-related business or service where the end user of a service or product could assess its quality subjectively and partly dependent on the context in which it is consumed. But the dependence of this judgement on the individual subjectivity of the user, and on the context of its consumption (which is beyond the influence of the operation) is both a strength and a weakness for the concept of QoE. An obvious strength is that it focuses operations on the richness of how their offerings are experienced by users. A practical weakness is that it is difficult idea to operationalize. Subjective metrics of QoE are difficult to design, expensive and time-consuming.

Service guarantees

One method of formalizing quality standards from a customer's viewpoint is called a 'service guarantee'. A service guarantee is a promise to recompense the customer for service that fails to meet a defined quality level. It is a way of ensuring quality standards, and of overcoming customers' potential doubts regarding a service. It provides a way of encouraging and rewarding customers who report problems, so that the operation is made aware of them and can attempt to rectify them. A good guarantee should be meaningful, in the sense that it is based on customers' expectations. It should be easy to understand, and explain exactly what level and type of quality is being promised and what the operation will do if it's not met (including what the customer should expect to receive in compensation). It should include a clear 'easy to invoke' mechanism for customers to trigger the guarantee and appropriate training and empowerment, so that employees can cope when a guarantee is invoked by a customer.[7]

The sandcone theory

An endorsement of the importance of quality as a driver of improvement generally comes from what is known as the 'sandcone theory'.[8] It comes from the idea that there is a generic 'best' sequence of improvement. It is called called the sandcone theory because the sand is analogous to management effort and resources. Building a stable sandcone needs a stable foundation of quality, claims the theory, upon which one can build layers of dependability, speed, flexibility and cost (see Figure 17.6). Building up improvement is thus a cumulative process, not a sequential one. Moving on to the second priority for improvement does not mean dropping the first, and so on. According to the sandcone theory, the first priority should be *quality*, since this is a precondition to all lasting improvement. Only when the

Virgin Atlantic offers a service guarantee for aviophobes[9]

According to market research firm YouGov, nearly one in six people have a fear of flying. This is clearly an issue for airlines, which do not want a sixth of their potential market reluctant to use their services. That's why the airline Virgin Atlantic made an offer to its customers that if they booked a flight on one particular day, they would will be offered a free place on its 'Flying Without Fear' course. Better still, if they were not cured in time for their trip, the money they spent on their plane ticket would be returned. Shai Weiss, Chief Commercial Officer at Virgin Atlantic, said: *'We want everyone to be able to say "screw it, let's do it" and try something different, fly*

somewhere new. Hopefully by guaranteeing to cure people of one of the main things holding them back, we can inspire Britain to choose something more positive. Nothing should hold anyone back from seizing the day.' The Virgin Atlantic 'Flying Without Fear' programme has become, according to the airline, the leading course in the industry, having helped 2,000–3,000 people every year to overcome their fear of flying. They say that they *'want to reassure you that you are not alone in your fear of flying, millions of people suffer similar anxieties. This course has been designed to help you conquer your fears of flying. Our aim is for you to take that holiday or business trip and actually enjoy it. Fear of flying is a phobia that many never, ever face. Now that you are here, we are the best people to help you to get rid of your fear'.* People from 4 years old up to 87 (oldest so far) with fears ranging from mild anxiety to complete terror have all been helped by the programme and are now flying. They say that they have a 98 per cent success rate. The programme runs courses more than 20 times a year, and claims to 'help you to learn new ways to think about flying.' And the guarantee? The airline states: *'If you can provide sufficient evidence that your fear of flying is not cured, we will provide a full refund for the flight purchased. This will be determined by our professionals who administer the Flying Without Fear programme.'*

operation has reached a minimally acceptable level in quality should it then tackle the next issue, that of internal *dependability*. Importantly though, moving on to include dependability in the improvement process will actually require further improvement in quality. Once a critical level of dependability is reached, enough to provide some stability to the operation, the next stage is to improve the *speed* of

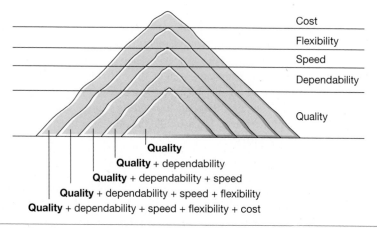

Figure 17.6 The sandcone model of improvement; cost reduction relies on a cumulative foundation of improvement in the other performance objectives

internal throughput, but again only while continuing to improve quality and dependability further. Soon it will become evident that the most effective way to improve speed is through improvements in response *flexibility,* which is changing things within the operation faster. Again, including flexibility in the improvement process should not divert attention from continuing to work further on quality, dependability and speed. Only now, according to the sandcone theory, should *cost* be tackled head on.

Conformance to specification

Conformance to specification means providing a service or producing a product to its design specification. It is usually seen as the most important contribution that operations management can make to the customer's perception of quality. We shall examine how it can be achieved in the remainder of this chapter by describing quality management as six sequential steps.

What steps lead towards conformance to specification?

Achieving conformance to specification requires the following steps.

Step 1 Define the quality characteristics of the service or product.

Step 2 Decide how to measure each quality characteristic.

Step 3 Set quality standards for each quality characteristic.

Step 4 Control quality against those standards.

Step 5 Find and correct causes of poor quality.

Step 6 Continue to make improvements.

Step 1 – Define the quality characteristics

Much of the 'quality' of a service or product will have been specified in its design and can be summarized by a set of quality characteristics. Table 17.2 shows a list of the quality characteristics which are generally useful. Also many services have several elements, each with their own quality characteristics, and to understand the quality characteristics of the whole service it is necessary to understand the individual characteristics within and between each element of the whole service.

Step 2 – Decide how to measure each characteristic

These characteristics must be defined in such a way as to enable them to be measured and then controlled. This involves taking a very general quality characteristic such as 'appearance' and breaking it down, as far as one can, into its constituent elements. 'Appearance' is difficult to measure as such, but 'colour match', 'surface finish' and 'number of visible scratches' are all capable of being described in a more objective manner. They may even be quantifiable. Other quality characteristics pose more difficulty. The 'courtesy' of airline staff, for example, has no objective quantified measure. Yet operations with high customer contact, such as airlines, place a great deal of importance on the need to ensure courtesy in their staff. In cases like this, the operation will have to attempt to measure customer *perceptions* of courtesy.

Variables and attributes

The measures used by operations to describe quality characteristics are of two types: variables and attributes. Variable measures are those that can be measured on a continuously variable scale (for example, length, diameter, weight or time). Attributes are those which are assessed by judgement and are dichotomous, i.e. have two states (for example, right or wrong, works or does not work, looks OK or not OK). Table 17.3 categorizes some of the measures which might be used for the quality characteristics of the automobile and the airline journey.

Table 17.2 Quality characteristics for an automobile, a bank loan and an air journey

Quality characteristic	Automobile (Material transformation process)	Bank loan (Information transformation process)	Air journey (Customer transformation process)
Functionality – how well the service or product does its job	Speed, acceleration, fuel consumption, ride quality, road-holding, etc.	Interest rate, terms and conditions	Safety and duration of journey, onboard meals and drinks, car and hotel booking services
Appearance – the sensory characteristics of the service or product: its aesthetic appeal, look, feel, etc.	Aesthetics, shape, finish, door gaps, etc.	Aesthetics of information, website, etc.	Decor and cleanliness of aircraft, lounges and crew
Reliability – the consistency of the product's or service's performance over time	Mean time to failure	Keeping promises (implicit and explicit)	Keeping to the published flight times
Durability – the total useful life of the service or product	Useful life (with repair)	Stability of terms and conditions	Keeping up with trends in the industry
Recovery – the ease with which problems with the service or product can be resolved	Ease of repair	Resolution of service failures	Resolution of service failures
Contact – the nature of the person-to-person contact which might take place	Knowledge and courtesy of sales staff	Knowledge and courtesy of branch and call centre staff	Knowledge, courtesy and sensitivity of airline staff

Quality at Magic Moments

Magic Moments is a small, but successful wedding photography business. Its owner, Richard Webber, has seen plenty of changes over the last 20 years. 'In the past, my job involved taking a few photos during the wedding ceremony and then formal group shots outside. I was rarely at a wedding for more than two hours. Clients would select around 30 photos to go in a standard wedding album. It was important to get the photos right, because that was really the only thing I was judged on. Now it's different. I usually spend all day at a wedding, and sometimes late into the evening as well. This creates a very different dynamic with the wedding party, as you're almost like another guest. Whilst the bride and groom are still my primary concern, other guests at the wedding are also important. The challenge is to find the right balance between getting the best photos possible whilst being as discreet as possible. I could spend hours getting the perfect picture, but annoy everyone in the process. It's difficult, because clients judge you on both the technical quality of your work and the way you interact with everyone on the day. The product has changed too. Clients receive a CD or memory stick with *around 500 photos taken during the day. Also I can give them a choice of 10 albums in different sizes, ranging from 30 to 100 photos. This year, I have started offering photo books which allow a much greater level of customization and have proved popular for younger couples. For the future, I'm considering offering albums with wedding items such as invitations, confetti and menus; and individual paintings created from photographs. Obviously I would have to outsource the paintings. I'm also going to upgrade our website, so wedding guests can order photos and related products online. This will generate revenue and act as a good marketing tool. My anxiety is that advertising this additional service at the wedding will be seen as being too commercial, even if it's actually of benefit to guests.*

One of the biggest problems for the business is the high level of demand in the summer months. Weekends in June, July and August are often booked up two years in advance. One option is to take on additional photographers during busy periods. However, the best ones are busy themselves. The concern is that the quality of the service I offer would deteriorate. A large part of the business is about how one relates to clients and that's hard to replicate. Having been to so many weddings, I often offer clients advice on various aspects of their wedding, such as locations, bands, caterers and florists. However, with development, wedding planning is clearly an area that could be profitable to the business. Of course, another option is to move beyond weddings into other areas, such as school photos, birthdays, celebrations or studio work.'

Step 3 – Set quality standards

When operations managers have identified how any quality characteristic can be measured, they need a quality standard against which it can be checked; otherwise they will not know whether it indicates good or bad performance. The quality standard is that level of quality which defines the boundary between acceptable and unacceptable. Such standards may well be constrained by operational factors such as the state of technology in the factory, and the cost limits of making the product. At the same time, however, they need to be appropriate to the expectations of customers. But quality judgements can be difficult. If one airline passenger out of every 10,000 complains about the food, is that good because 9,999 passengers out of 10,000 are satisfied? Or is it bad because, if one passenger complains, there must be others who, although dissatisfied, did not bother to complain? And if that level of complaint is similar to other airlines, should it regard its quality as satisfactory?

Step 4 – Control quality against those standards

After setting up appropriate standards the operation will then need to check that the products or services conform to those standards; doing things right, first time, every time. This involves three decisions:

1 Where in the operation should it check that it is conforming to standards?
2 Should it check every service or product or take a sample?
3 How should the checks be performed?

Where should the checks take place?

At the start of the process incoming resources may be inspected to make sure that they are to the correct specification. For example, a car manufacturer will check that components are of the right specification. A university will screen applicants to try to ensure that they have a high chance of getting through the programme. During the process checks may take place before a particularly costly process, prior to 'difficult to check', immediately after a process with a high defective rate, before potential damage or distress might be caused, and so on. Checks may also take place after the process itself to ensure that customers do not experience non-conformance.

Check every product and service or take a sample?

While it might seem ideal to check every single service or product, a sample may be more practical for a number of reasons.

Table 17.3 Variable and attribute measures for quality characteristics

Quality characteristic	Automobile		Airline journey	
	Variable	Attribute		Attribute
Functionality	Acceleration and braking characteristics from test bed	Is the ride quality satisfactory?	Number of journeys which actually arrived at the destination (i.e. didn't crash!)	Was the food acceptable?
Appearance	Number of blemishes visible on car	Is the colour to specification?	Number of seats not cleaned satisfactorily	Is the crew dressed smartly?
Reliability	Average time between faults	Is the reliability satisfactory?	Proportion of journeys which arrived on time	Were there any complaints?
Durability	Life of the car	Is the useful life as predicted?	Number of times service innovations lagged competitors	Generally, is the airline updating its services in a satisfactory manner?
Recovery	Time from fault discovered to fault repaired	Is the serviceability of the car acceptable?	Proportion of service failures resolved satisfactorily	Do customers feel that staff deal satisfactorily with complaints?
Contact	Level of help provided by sales staff (1 to 5 scale)	Did customers feel well served (yes or no)?	The extent to which customers feel well treated by staff (1 to 5 scale)	Did customers feel that the staff were helpful (yes or no)?

▶ It might be dangerous to inspect everything. A doctor, for example, checks just a small sample of blood rather than taking all of a patient's blood! The characteristics of this sample are taken to represent those of the rest of the patient's blood.

▶ Checking everything might destroy the product or interfere with the service. Not every light bulb is checked for how long it lasts; it would destroy every bulb. Waiters do not check that customers are enjoying the meal every 30 seconds.

▶ Checking everything can be time-consuming and costly. It may not be feasible to check all output from a high-volume machine or to check the feelings of every bus commuter every day.

Also 100 per cent checking may not guarantee that all defects will be identified. Sometimes it is intrinsically difficult. For example, although a physician may undertake the correct testing procedure, he or she may not necessarily diagnose a (real) disease. Nor is it easy to notice everything. For example, try counting the number of 'e's on this page. Count them again and see if you get the same score.

Type I and type II errors

Although it reduces checking time, using a sample to make a decision about quality does have its own inherent problems. Like any decision activity, we may get the decision wrong. Take the example of a pedestrian waiting to cross a street. He or she has two main decisions: whether to continue waiting or to cross. If there is a satisfactory break in the traffic and the pedestrian crosses then a correct decision has been made. Similarly, if that person continues to wait because the traffic is too dense then he or she has again made a correct decision. There are two types of incorrect decisions or errors, however. One incorrect decision would be if he or she decides to cross when there is not an adequate break in the traffic,

Testing cars (close) to destruction[10]

Away from the public eye, at Millbrook Proving Ground, one of Europe's leading independent technology centres for the design, engineering, test and development of automotive and propulsion systems, they treat cars really badly. But all in a good cause. It is where auto manufacturers send their new vehicles to be tested, so that any glitches, from irritating rattles to more serious safety problems, can be exposed and corrected before the product reaches the market. The site, in Bedfordshire in the UK, is hidden away behind security fences and high embankments to discourage automobile paparazzi taking pictures of new models as they are put through their paces. Auto manufacturers also test their new models out on public roads, usually with stick-on panels to disguise them, but for repeatable, carefully measured conditions, a facility like the Millbrook Proving Ground is needed. The site has been called 'an automotive time machine', where a gleaming new model drives in, and about 20 weeks later it drives out (if it can) having been exposed to the equivalent of ten years of severe weather and wear-and-tear comparable to being driven around 160,000 miles. During this time it will have been driven on straight and twisty roads, up and down hills, slowly and very fast, through salt-water baths (to accelerate rusting) and along gravel roads that damage its paintwork. But that's not all. It will be roasted at high temperatures, frozen at down to Arctic conditions, and drenched in water to expose any leaks. Also, it will be subjected to the infamous 'Belgian Pavé'. This is a mile-long track made from blocks of paving with rough sections and random depressions. The suspension takes such a beating that after five laps on the track vehicles need to be dowsed in a water trough to cool their dampers down. And during all this wrecking treatment engineers periodically examine the vehicles for signs of wear or damage. This allows carmakers to fine-tune their designs or manufacturing processes to avoid failures which would be expensive and reputationally damaging if they occurred after product launch.

resulting in an accident – this is referred to as a type I error. Another incorrect decision would occur if he or she decides not to cross even though there was an adequate gap in the traffic – this is called a type II error. In crossing the road, therefore, there are four outcomes, which are summarized in Table 17.4.

Type I errors are those which occur when a decision was made to do something and the situation did not warrant it. Type II errors are those which occur when nothing was done, yet a decision to do something should have been taken as the situation did indeed warrant it. For example, if a school's inspector checks the work of a sample of 20 out of 1,000 pupils and all 20 of the pupils in the sample have failed, the inspector might draw the conclusion that all the pupils have failed. In fact, the sample just happened to contain 20 out of the 50 students who had failed the course. The inspector, by assuming a high fail rate, would be making a type I error. Alternatively, if the inspector checked 20 pieces of work, all of which were of a high standard, he or she might conclude that all the pupils' work was good despite having been given, or having chosen, the only pieces of good work in the whole school. This would be a type II error. Although these situations are not likely, they are possible. Therefore any sampling procedure has to be aware of these risks.

How should the checks be performed?

In practice most operations will use some form of sampling to check the quality of their services or products. The most common approach for checking the quality of a sample service or product so as to make inferences about all the output from an operation is called statistical process control (SPC). SPC is concerned with sampling the process during the production of the goods or the delivery of service. Based on this sample, decisions are made as to whether the process is 'in control': that is, operating as it should be. A key aspect of SPC is that it looks at the

Table 17.4 Type I and type II errors for a pedestrian crossing the road

Decision	Road conditions	
	Unsafe	Safe
Cross	Type I error	Correct decision
Wait	Correct decision	Type II error

variability in the performance of processes to check whether the process is operating as it should do (known as the process being 'in control'). In fact variability (or more specifically, reducing variability) is one of the most important objectives of quality improvement. For an illustration of this, see the 'Operations in practice' example 'What a giveaway'. SPC is explained in detail in the supplement to this chapter.

Steps 5 and 6 Find and correct causes of poor quality and continue to make improvements

The final two steps in our list of quality management activities are, in some ways, the most important yet also the most difficult. They also blend into the general area of operations improvement. The material that we covered in Chapter 16 has contributed to these two steps. Nevertheless, there

---

OPERATIONS IN PRACTICE

What a giveaway[11]

Go round any supermarket and look at all the products that are packaged, bottled or otherwise 'filled' into containers. Bottled drinks, detergent, bags of vegetables, cans of paint; they are all put in their containers in the manufacturing operations that produce them. And this filling or packing process is, in most countries, governed by strict government regulations. When a package claims to have a certain amount of product, customers have a right to expect that it really does include that amount; otherwise they are paying for something that they are not getting. On any product sold that has an 'e' after its claimed weight printed on the container, the law states that the average weight must be greater than the declared weight on the container, with the average weight being determined by sampling. The problem is that the technology used to fill packages is not always totally consistent. There is always some degree of variation in the amount 'dispensed'. So, if packers or fillers want to conform to legal weights and measures stipulations on minimum fill levels, they must build a margin of safety into filling levels in order to overcome the variation of the filling technology. This margin of safety is known as 'giveaway' or 'over-fill'. Experts in this technology estimate that this kind of routine over-filling can mean that 3

per cent of an operation's output is literally given away. This idea is illustrated in Figure 17.7.

Typical of the type of operation that has benefited from reducing the amount of variation in its processes, and therefore the amount of giveaway, is the food producer Quick Food Products. Founded in 1988 by immigrants from the Caribbean, it specializes in producing Jamaican patties with a range of meat, vegetable and fish fillings. Now it has expanded its range to include producing patties for the British-based Nigerian community, as well as patties certified to carry the Halal label, indicating compliance with Muslim religious requirements. However,

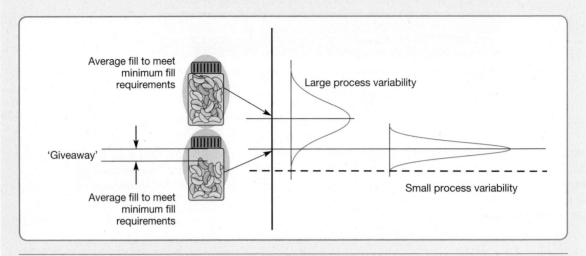

Figure 17.7 Average fill to meet minimum fill requirements has to be larger when process variability is large, resulting in 'giveaway'

the firm had a problem – it needed extra capacity to manufacture and fill the new patties, but it was reluctant to spend the large sums that would be necessary to install new filling lines. To help it solve the problem, Quick Food Products called in operations improvement consultants. The consultants soon realized that there was too much variation in the weight of filling in the patties, and that reducing the variation in filling quantities could make significant savings – both in terms of reducing cost and in freeing up capacity. Maxine Chapman, one of the consultants, says, *'It wasn't a big technical problem, but more a question of agreeing best operating-practices, and then using them.'* And the improvement at Quick Foods is not a one-off. *'Time and again'*, she says, *'significant improvements in the performance of filling and packing lines can be achieved by applying simple tools consistently, and through a better understanding of the parameters of the equipment that you're dealing with.'*

is an aspect of quality management that has been particularly important in shaping how quality is improved and the improvement activity made self-sustaining. This is total quality management (TQM). The remainder of the main body of this chapter is devoted to TQM.

What is total quality management (TQM)?

Total quality management (TQM) was one of the earliest of the current wave of management 'fashions'. Its peak of popularity was in the late 1980s and early 1990s. As such it has suffered from something of a backlash in recent years and there is little doubt that many companies adopted TQM in the simplistic belief that it would transform their operations performance overnight. Yet the general precepts and principles that constitute TQM are still the dominant mode of organizing operations improvement. The approach we take here is to stress the importance of the 'total' in total quality management and how it can guide the agenda for improvement.

TQM as an extension of previous practice

TQM can be viewed as a logical extension of the way in which quality-related practice has progressed (see Figure 17.8). Originally quality was achieved by inspection – screening out defects before they were noticed by customers. The quality control (QC) concept developed a more systematic approach

Augmented reality technology adds to IKEA's service quality[12]

A technological revolution swept through retailing operations when online shopping began to take an increasing share of customers' spending. But so-called 'bricks and mortar' retailers – those with a physical presence on the high street or in out-of-town sites – are using technology to provide the quality of service that their online rivals find difficult to match. It is an important issue for retailers because quality of service is a key factor in promoting customer loyalty. (See the case study at the end of Chapter 2.) And, to customers, an important element of quality of service in retailing is how they can interact with staff and products, particularly to answer their questions or 'solve problems'.[13] This is why augmented reality (AR) is seen by IKEA as an ideal way for its customers to interact with their products. AR is defined by Gartner, the research and advisory company, as the 'real-time use of information in the form of text, graphics, audio and other virtual enhancements integrated with real-world objects. It is this "real world" element that differentiates AR from virtual reality.'

The objective is to let customers visualize IKEA's furniture to get a realistic impression of how it would look in their home. They do this by using the 'IKEA Place' on their smartphones, an app that uses Apple's ARKit technology. Customers can view 3D representations (from a wide range of angles) of products before deciding which one they want. The app then directs them to the IKEA site to finalize their purchase. Using the app lets customers make a 'reliable buying' decision, says Michael Valdsgaard, who is in charge of digital transformation at Inter IKEA, the holding company for IKEA. *'Most people postpone a purchase of a new sofa because they're not comfortable making the decision if they aren't sure the colour is going to match* [the rest of the room] *or it fits the style,'* he said. *'Now, we can give them* [those answers] *in their hands, while letting them have fun with home furnishing for free and with no effort. The most important thing for us is that we're not a tech company,* [but] *in order to sell furniture, we have to understand technology and try to move in the direction it's moving. The first* [augmented reality] *experience we had was more like a picture. You could put in a 3D object, but you couldn't really move around it or trust the size of it.'* But the later versions achieved 98 per cent accuracy, with true-to-life representations of the texture, fabric, lighting and shadows.

to not only detecting, but also treating quality problems. Quality assurance (QA) widened the responsibility for quality to include functions other than direct operations. It also made increasing use of more sophisticated statistical quality techniques. TQM included much of what went before but developed its own distinctive themes to make quality both more strategic and more widespread in the organization. We will use some of these themes to describe how TQM represents a clear shift from traditional approaches to quality.

What is TQM?

TQM is *'an effective system for integrating the quality development, quality maintenance and quality improvement efforts of the various groups in an organization so as to enable production and service at the most economical levels which allow for full customer satisfaction'*.[14] However, it was the Japanese who first made the concept work on a wide scale and subsequently popularized the approach and the term 'TQM'. It was then developed further by several so-called 'quality gurus'. Each 'guru' stressed a different set of issues, from which emerged the TQM approach. It is best thought of as a philosophy of how to approach quality improvement. This philosophy, above everything, stresses the 'total' of TQM. It is an approach that puts quality at the heart

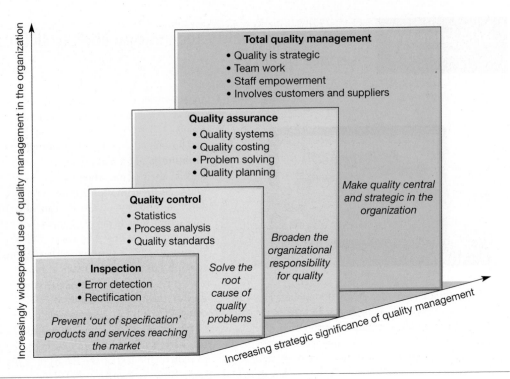

Figure 17.8 TQM as an extension of previous views of quality

of everything that is done by an operation and includes all activities within an operation. This totality can be summarized by the way TQM lays particular stress on the following:

► meeting the needs and expectations of customers;
► covering all parts of the organization;
► including every person in the organization;
► examining all costs which are related to quality, especially failure costs and getting things 'right first time'
► developing the systems and procedures which support quality and improvement;
► developing a continuous process of improvement (this was treated in Chapter 16).

Not surprisingly, several researchers have tried to establish how much of a relationship there is between adopting total quality management and the performance of the organization. One of the best-known studies[15] found that there was a positive relationship between the extent to which companies implement TQM and its overall performance. It found that TQM practices did indeed have a direct effect on operating performance but that managers should implement TQM as a whole set of ideas rather than simply picking a few techniques to implement. The same study also suggests that where TQM does not prove successful in improving performance the problems could be the result of poor implementation rather than the TQM practices themselves and that a serious commitment on the part of top management to TQM is a prerequisite for success.

TQM means meeting the needs and expectations of customers

Earlier in this chapter we defined quality as 'consistent conformance to customers' expectations'. Therefore, any approach to quality management must necessarily include the customer perspective. In TQM, this customer perspective is particularly important. It may be referred to as 'customer centricity' (discussed briefly in Chapter 16) or the 'voice of the customer'. Whatever it is called, TQM stresses the importance of starting with an insight into customer needs, wants, perceptions and preferences. This can then be translated into quality objectives and used to drive quality improvement.

TQM means covering all parts of the organization

For an organization to be truly effective, every single part of it, each department, each activity, and each person and each level, must work properly together, because every person and every activity affects and in turn is affected by others. One of the most powerful concepts that has emerged from various improvement approaches is the concept of the internal customer/supplier. This is recognition that everyone is a customer within the organization and consumes goods or services provided by other internal suppliers, and everyone is also an internal supplier of goods and services for other internal customers. The implication of this is that errors in the service provided within an organization will eventually affect the service or product which reaches the external customer.

<table>
<tr><td>OPERATIONS IN PRACTICE</td><td><h2>Ryanair reforms its view of service quality[16]</h2></td></tr>
</table>

Ryanair is arguably the best-known, and certainly the most successful, budget airline in Europe, but it was not the first to focus its operations strategy on very low operating costs. The idea was born when Southwest Airlines in the USA found that, if it organized its airline operations ruthlessly around providing a low-cost 'no frills' service, it could both grow its customer base and do so profitably. To some extent the strategy included trading off certain aspects of quality of service for reduced costs. Complimentary in-flight services were kept to a minimum, secondary and sometimes less convenient airports were used, and one standard class of travel was offered. Some critics said that Ryanair went too far in its attitude towards service quality. However, the boss of the airline, Michael O'Leary's policy on customer service was both straightforward and clear. *'Our customer service',* he said, *'is about the most well defined in the world. We guarantee to give you the lowest air fare. You get a safe flight. You get a normally on-time flight. That's the package. We don't, and won't, give you anything more. Are we going to say sorry for our lack of customer service? Absolutely not. If a plane is cancelled, will we put you up in a hotel overnight? Absolutely not. If a plane is delayed, will we give you a voucher for a restaurant? Absolutely not.'* And Ryanair's customer satisfaction ratings were high, with over 90 per cent of customers surveyed expressing satisfaction with their overall flight experience, according to the airline. In 2018 Ryanair announced an environmental plan which included a commitment to eliminate all non-recyclable plastics from its operations over a five-year period. Yet, said Ryanair, *'while we continue to innovate, the one thing that won't change will be our low fares'.*

However, one attempt by Ryanair to cut costs prompted something of a backlash when it was criticized by the UK's Office of Fair Trading (OFT). John Fingleton, the OFT's boss, criticized the company for adding extra fees when customers use anything but a MasterCard prepaid card to pay for flights. Although this practice was within the law, Mr Fingleton was reported as saying that the company were using a legal loophole to justify charging the extra fee. Stephen McNamara, Ryanair's Head of Communications, retorted that *'What the OFT must realise is that passengers prefer Ryanair's model as it allows them to avoid costs, such as baggage charges, which are still included in the high fares of high-cost, fuel-surcharging . . . airlines.'* But the backlash against Ryanair's policy continued, perhaps encouraged by the airline's reluctance to apologize, or sometimes even comment. Then, after a drop in its hitherto rapid profit growth and some shareholders voicing concern, Ryanair announced that it was to reform its 'abrupt culture, and try to eliminate things that unnecessarily annoy customers'. Included in these annoying practices were fines for small luggage size transgressions and an unpopular €70 fee for issuing boarding passes at the airport when customers had not printed them out at home (it was lowered to €10). Ryanair did insist that such charges had not been money-spinning schemes, but were designed to encourage the type of operational efficiency that kept fairs low. In fact fewer than ten passengers a day had to pay for forgotten boarding passes.

Operations principle

An appreciation of, involvement in, and commitment to quality should permeate the entire organization.

Service-level agreements

Some organizations bring a degree of formality to the internal customer concept by encouraging (or requiring) different parts of the operation to agree service-level agreements (SLAs) with each other. SLAs are formal definitions of the dimensions of service and the relationship between two parts of an organization. The type of issues which would be covered by such an agreement could include response times, the range of services, dependability of service supply, and so on. Boundaries of responsibility and appropriate performance measures could also be agreed. For example, an SLA between an information systems support unit and a research unit in the laboratories of a large company could define such performance measures as:

▶ the types of information network services which may be provided as 'standard';
▶ the range of special information services which may be available at different periods of the day;
▶ the minimum 'up time', i.e. the proportion of time the system will be available at different periods of the day;
▶ the maximum response time and average response time to get the system fully operational should it fail;
▶ the maximum response time to provide 'special' services, and so on.

TQM means including every person in the organization

Every person in the organization has the potential to contribute to quality and TQM was amongst the first approach to stress the centrality of harnessing everyone's potential contribution to quality. There is scope for creativity and innovation even in relatively routine activities, claim TQM proponents. The shift in attitude which is needed to view employees as the most valuable intellectual and creative resource which the organization possesses can still prove difficult for some organizations. Yet most advanced organizations do recognize that quality problems are almost always the results of human error.

TQM means all costs of quality are considered

The costs of controlling quality may not be small, whether the responsibility lies with each individual or a dedicated quality control department. It is therefore necessary to examine all the costs and benefits associated with quality (in fact 'cost of quality' is usually taken to refer to both costs and benefits of quality). These costs of quality are usually categorized as *prevention costs, appraisal costs, internal failure costs* and *external failure costs*.

▶ **Prevention costs** are those costs incurred in trying to prevent problems, failures and errors from occurring in the first place. They include such things as:
— identifying potential problems and putting the process right before poor quality occurs;

Critical commentary

While some see the strength of SLAs as the degree of formality they bring to customer–supplier relationships, there are also some clear drawbacks. The first is that the 'pseudo-contractual' nature of the formal relationship can work against building partnerships (see Chapter 12). This is especially true if the SLA includes penalties for deviation from service standards. Indeed, the effect can sometimes be to inhibit rather than encourage joint improvement. The second and related problem is that SLAs, again because of their formal documented nature, tend to emphasize the 'hard' and measurable aspects of performance rather than the 'softer' but often more important aspects. So a telephone may be answered within four rings, but how the caller is treated, in terms of 'friendliness', may be far more important.

Feeling sleepy one day, a German bank worker briefly fell asleep on his keyboard when processing a €64 debit (withdrawal) from a pensioner's account, repeatedly pressing the number 2. The result was that the pensioner's account had €222 million withdrawn from it instead of the intended €64. Fortunately the bank spotted the error before too much damage was done (and before the account-holder noticed). More seriously, the supervisor who should have checked his junior colleague's work was sacked for failing to notice the blunder (unfairly, a German labour tribunal later ruled). It is known as 'fat finger syndrome' – a term used to describe a person who makes keyboard errors when chatting, tired or over-stressed. And for some people, like traders working in fast-moving electronic financial markets, if they press the wrong button on their keyboard, it means a potential fortune could be lost.

Fat finger trading mistakes are not uncommon. In 2009, Swiss bank UBS mistakenly ordered 3 trillion yen (instead of 30 million yen) of bonds in a Japanese video games firm. In 2005 a Japanese trader tried to sell one share of a recruitment company at 610,000 yen per share. But he accidentally sold 610,000 shares at one yen each, despite this being 41 times the number of shares available. Unlike the German example, the error was not noticed and the Tokyo Stock Exchange processed the order. It resulted in Mizuho Securities losing 27 billion yen. The head of the Exchange later resigned. But what is believed to be the biggest fat finger error on record occurred in 2014, when share trades worth more than the size of Sweden's economy had to be cancelled in Tokyo. The error briefly sparked panic after a trader accidentally entering a trade worth nearly 68 trillion yen in several of the Asian country's largest blue-chip companies. The Japan Securities Dealers Association said the trader had in error put together the volume and price of a series of transactions instead of the volume alone. However, the transactions were cancelled 17 minutes after they were made and no permanent (financial) damage was done.

— designing and improving the design of products and services and processes to reduce quality problems;
— training and development of personnel in the best way to perform their jobs;
— process control through SPC.

▶ **Appraisal costs** are those costs associated with controlling quality to check to see if problems or errors have occurred during and after the creation of the service or product. They might include such things as:
— the setting up of statistical acceptance sampling plans;
— the time and effort required to inspect inputs, processes and outputs;
— obtaining processing inspection and test data;
— investigating quality problems and providing quality reports;
— conducting customer surveys and quality audits.

▶ **Internal failure costs** are failure costs associated with errors which are dealt with inside the operation. These costs might include such things as:
— the cost of scrapped parts and material;
— reworked parts and materials;
— the lost production time as a result of coping with errors;
— lack of concentration due to time spent troubleshooting rather than improvement.

▶ **External failure costs** are those which are associated with an error going out of the operation to a customer. These costs include such things as:
— loss of customer goodwill affecting future business;

— aggrieved customers who may take up time;

— litigation (or payments to avoid litigation);

— guarantee and warranty costs;

— the cost to the company of providing excessive capability (too much coffee in the pack or too much information to a client).

The relationship between quality costs

In traditional quality management it was assumed that failure costs reduce as the money spent on appraisal and prevention increases. Furthermore, it was assumed that there is an *optimum* amount of quality effort to be applied in any situation, which minimizes the total costs of quality. The argument is that there must be a point beyond which diminishing returns set in – that is, the cost of improving quality gets larger than the benefits which it brings. Figure 17.9(a) sums up this idea. As quality effort is increased, the costs of providing the effort – through extra quality controllers, inspection procedures and so on – increases proportionally. At the same time, however, the cost of errors, faulty products and so on decreases because there are fewer of them. However, TQM proponents believe that this logic is flawed. First, it implies that failure and poor quality are acceptable. Why, TQM proponents argue, should any operation accept the *inevitability* of errors? Some occupations seem to be able to accept a zero-defect standard. No one accepts that pilots are allowed to crash a certain proportion of their aircraft, or that nurses will drop a certain proportion of the babies they deliver. Second, it assumes that costs are known and measurable. In fact putting realistic figures to the cost of quality is not a straightforward matter. Third, it is argued that failure costs in the traditional model are greatly underestimated. In particular, all the management time wasted by failures and the loss of concentration it causes are rarely accounted for. Fourth, it implies that prevention costs are inevitably high because it involves expensive inspection. But why should quality not be an integral part of everyone's work rather than employing extra people to inspect? Finally, the 'optimum-quality level' approach, by accepting compromise, does little to challenge operations managers and staff to find ways of improving quality. Put these corrections into the optimum-quality effort calculation and the picture looks very different (see Figure 17.9(b)). If there is an 'optimum', it is a lot further to the right, in the direction of putting more effort (but not necessarily cost) into quality.

Operations principle

Effective investment in preventing quality errors can significantly reduce appraisal and failure costs.

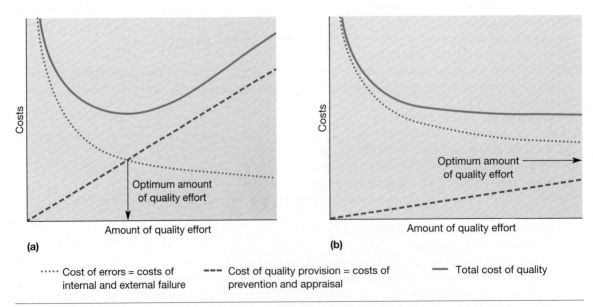

(a)

(b)

····· Cost of errors = costs of internal and external failure

--- Cost of quality provision = costs of prevention and appraisal

— Total cost of quality

Figure 17.9 (a) The traditional cost of quality model, and (b) the traditional cost of quality model with adjustments to reflect TQM criticisms

The TQM quality cost model

TQM rejects the optimum-quality-level concept and strives to reduce all known and unknown failure costs by preventing errors and failure taking place. Rather than looking for 'optimum' levels of quality effort, TQM stresses the relative balance between different types of quality cost. Of the four cost categories, two (costs of prevention and costs of appraisal) are open to managerial influence, while the other two (internal costs of failure and external costs of failure) show the consequences of changes in the first two. So, rather than placing most emphasis on appraisal (so that 'bad products and service don't get through to the customer') TQM emphasizes prevention (to stop errors happening in the first place). That is because the more effort that is put into error prevention, the more internal and external failure costs are reduced. Then, once confidence has been firmly established, appraisal costs can be reduced. Eventually even prevention costs can be stepped down in absolute terms, though prevention remains a significant cost in relative terms. Figure 17.10 illustrates this idea. Initially total quality costs may rise as investment in some aspects of prevention – mainly training – is increased. However, a reduction in total costs can quickly follow.

Getting things 'right first time'

Accepting the relationships between categories of quality cost as illustrated in Figure 17.10 has a particularly important implication for how quality is managed. It shifts the emphasis from *reactive* (waiting for something to happen) to *proactive* (doing something before anything happens). This change in the view of quality costs has come about with a movement from an inspect-in (appraisal-driven) approach to a design-in (getting it right first time) approach.

TQM means developing the systems and procedures which support quality and improvement

The emphasis on highly formalized systems and procedures to support TQM has declined in recent years, yet one aspect is still active for many companies. This is the adoption of the ISO 9000 standard. And although ISO 9000 can be regarded as a stand-alone issue, it is very closely associated with TQM.

Deliberate defectives

A story that illustrates the difference in attitude between a TQM and a non-TQM company has become almost a legend among TQM proponents. It concerns a plant in Ontario, Canada, of IBM, the computer company. It ordered a batch of components from a Japanese manufacturer and specified that the batch should have an acceptable quality level (AQL) of three defective parts per thousand. When the parts arrived in Ontario they were accompanied by a letter which expressed the supplier's bewilderment at being asked to supply defective parts as well as good ones. The letter also explained that they had found it difficult to make parts which were defective, but had indeed managed it. These three defective parts per thousand had been included and were wrapped separately 'for the convenience of the customer'.

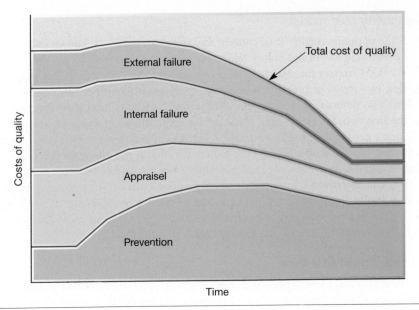

Figure 17.10 Increasing the effort spent on preventing errors occurring in the first place brings a more than equivalent reduction in other cost categories

The ISO 9000 approach

The ISO 9000 series is a family of standards compiled by the International Organization for Standardization (ISO) which is the world's largest developer and publisher of international standards, based in Geneva, Switzerland. According to the ISO, *'the standards represent an international consensus on good quality management practices. It consists of standards and guidelines relating to quality management systems and related supporting standards.'* To be precise, it is the 'ISO 9001:2008' standard that provides the set of standardized requirements for a quality management system which should apply to any organization, regardless of size, or whether it is in the private, or public sector. It is the only standard in the family against which organizations can be certified – although certification is not a compulsory requirement of the standard. Its purpose when it was first framed was to provide an assurance to the purchasers of products or services that they have been produced in such a way that they meet their requirements. The best way to do this, it was argued, was to define the procedures, standards and characteristics of the management control system which governs the operation. Such a system would help to ensure that quality was 'built into' the operation's transformation processes. Rather than using different standards for different functions within a business, it takes a 'process' approach that focuses on outputs from any operation's process rather than detailed procedures. This process orientation requires operations to define and record core processes and sub-processes (in a manner very similar to the 'hierarchy of processes' principle that was outlined in Chapter 1). In addition, processes are documented using the process mapping approach that was described in Chapter 4. It also stresses four other principles.

▶ Quality management should be customer focused. Customer satisfaction should be measured through surveys and focus groups and improvement against customer standards should be documented.
▶ Quality performance should be measured. In particular, measures should relate both to processes that create products and services and to customer satisfaction with those products and services. Furthermore, measured data should be analysed in order to understand processes.
▶ Quality management should be improvement driven. Improvement must be demonstrated in both process performance and customer satisfaction.

▶ Top management must demonstrate their commitment to maintaining and continually improving management systems. This commitment should include communicating the importance of meeting customer and other requirements, establishing a quality policy and quality objectives, conducting management reviews to ensure the adherence to quality policies, and ensuring the availability of the necessary resources to maintain quality systems.

The ISO illustrates the benefits of the standard as follows. '*Without satisfied customers, an organization is in peril! To keep customers satisfied, the organization needs to meet their requirements. The ISO 9001:2008 standard provides a tried and tested framework for taking a systematic approach to managing the organization's processes so that they consistently turn out product that satisfies customers' expectations.*' In addition it is also seen as providing benefits both to the organizations adopting it (because it gives them detailed guidance on how to design their control procedures) and especially to customers (who have the assurance of knowing that the products and services they purchase are produced by an operation working to a defined standard). Further, it may also provide a useful discipline to stick to 'sensible' process-oriented procedures which lead to error reduction, reduced customer complaints and reduced costs of quality, and may even identify existing procedures which are not necessary and can be eliminated. Moreover, gaining the certificate demonstrates that the company takes quality seriously; it therefore has a marketing benefit.

Quality awards

Various bodies have sought to stimulate improvement through establishing 'quality' awards. The three best-known awards are the Deming Prize, the Malcolm Baldrige National Quality Award and the European Quality Award.

The Deming Prize

The Deming Prize was instituted by the Union of Japanese Scientists and Engineers in 1951 and is awarded to those companies, initially in Japan, but more recently opened to overseas companies, which have successfully applied 'company-wide quality control' based upon statistical quality control. There are 10 major assessment categories: policy and objectives, organization and its operation, education and its extension, assembling and disseminating of information, analysis, standardization, control, quality assurance, effects and future plans. The applicants are required to submit a detailed description of quality practices. This is a significant activity in itself and some companies claim a great deal of benefit from having done so.

Critical commentary

Notwithstanding its widespread adoption (and its revision to take into account some of its perceived failing), ISO 9000 is not seen as beneficial by all authorities, and is still subject to some specific criticisms. These include the following:

▶ The continued use of standards and procedures encourages 'management by manual' and over-systematized decision making.

▶ The whole process of documenting processes, writing procedures, training staff and conducting internal audits is expensive and time consuming.

▶ Similarly, the time and cost of achieving and maintaining ISO 9000 registration are excessive.

▶ It is too formulaic. It encourages operations to substitute a 'recipe' for a more customized and creative approach to managing operations improvement.

Quality systems only work if you stick to them[18]

When passengers on the Hakata to Tokyo express, one of Japan's famous bullet trains, noticed a burning smell and an unusual sound, they were ordered off the train. The cause turned out to be cracks in the chassis and it marked the latest episode in a long line of quality scandals that had rocked the country, and caused serious reputational risk to the world's image of 'Japanese quality'. The previous months had seen public admissions by some of Japan's most prestigious names — including Kobe Steel, Mitsubishi Materials, Nissan Motor and Subaru – that their quality tests had been falsified or the results had been fabricated, all to sell products of a lower quality than officially stated. Quality systems had been in place, but often ignored. Quality records had been doctored on materials that had been shipped to make a wide range of products, including the Boeing 787 Dreamliner, nuclear plants and space rockets. It was the shock announcement from Kobe Steel that focused the world's attention on the problem. It confessed that 'improper conduct' had led to the falsification of data relating to 19,300 tonnes of aluminium sheets and poles; 19,400 aluminium components; 2,200 tonnes of copper products and an unspecified amount of iron powder that was supplied to over 200 customers. All these items had been falsely certified as conforming to specifications concerning properties such as tensile strength. Kobe admitted that for up to ten years its employees had falsified quality checks on tens of thousands of tonnes of metal products, including the aluminium used by Boeing to make the parts that held the 787 together. However, Boeing made it clear that it had been conducting comprehensive inspections and analysis of affected shipments since it was told about Kobe Steel's data falsification. '*Nothing in our review to date leads us to conclude that this issue presents a safety concern, and we will continue to work diligently with our suppliers to complete our investigation*', it said. And, notwithstanding the falsification, no deaths or accidents seem to have resulted from the under-specification products. Also, officials at Japan's Ministry of Economy, Trade and Industry said Kobe Steel's products did not fall below industry minimum standards. It was, it said, an issue between Kobe and its customers because it had not met specifications that they had demanded.

Nevertheless, Kobe Steel demoted three executives from the aluminium and copper divisions who had been aware of the data tampering. Two executives had apparently known of the falsification problems for eight years. The company said that they were relieved from their duties and reassigned to lower-ranking roles. Also, the government-backed Japan Industrial certification was revoked at one of its factories owing to 'improper quality management'. But, it was the nation-wide inquest as to why so many problems had occurred in so many Japanese companies that was followed closely by quality professionals. Some commentators claimed that it was because of increased pressure to produce profits. When Toray Industries, the chemical company, disclosed data falsification on tyre material, Akihiro Nikkaku, its president, chief executive and chief operating officer, blamed the '*pressure to meet productivity targets*'. Other observers pointed to Japanese corporate culture and the reluctance of middle managers to bring quality mistakes to their superiors' attention. Yet others say that the reason that so many scandals have emerged relatively recently is that, amongst younger employees, revealing bad practice has become more acceptable. Moreover, social media provided a forum and an environment for whistleblowing and airing such grievances, which previously did not exist.

The Malcolm Baldrige National Quality Award

In the early 1980s the American Productivity and Quality Center recommended that an annual prize, similar to the Deming Prize, should be awarded in America. The purpose of the award was to stimulate American companies to improve quality and productivity, to recognize achievements, to establish criteria for a wider quality effort and to provide guidance on quality improvement. The main examination categories are: leadership, information and analysis, strategic quality planning, human resource utilization, quality assurance of products and services, quality results and customer satisfaction. The process, like that of the Deming Prize, includes a detailed application and site visits.

The EFQM Excellence Model

Over 20 years ago, western European companies formed the European Foundation for Quality Management (EFQM). Since then the importance of quality excellence has become far more accepted. According to the EFQM, '*Whilst there are numerous management tools and techniques commonly used, the EFQM Excellence Model provides an holistic view of the organisation and it can be used to determine how these different methods fit together and complement each other. The Model . . . . [is] . . . an overarching framework for developing sustainable excellence. Excellent organisations achieve and sustain outstanding levels of performance that meet or exceed the expectations of all their stakeholders. The EFQM Excellence Model allows people to understand the cause and effect relationships between what their organisation does and the Results it achieves.*'[19]

The model is based on the idea that it is important to understand the cause and effect relationships between what an organization does (what it terms 'the Enablers') and its results. The EFQM excellence model is shown in Figure 17.11. There are five enablers:

▶ Leadership – that looks to the future, acts as a role model for values and ethics, inspires trust, is flexible, enables anticipation and so can react in a timely manner.
▶ Strategy – that implements the organization's mission and vision by developing and deploying a stakeholder-focused strategy.
▶ People – organizations should value their people, creating a culture that allows mutually beneficial achievement of both organizational and personal goals, develops the capabilities of people, promotes fairness and equality, cares for, communicates, rewards and recognizes people, in a way that motivates and builds commitment.
▶ Partnership and resources – organizations should plan and manage external partnerships, suppliers and internal resources in order to support strategy and policies and the effective operation of processes.
▶ Processes, products and services – organizations should design, manage and improve processes to ensure value for customers and other stakeholders.

Results are assessed using four criteria. They are:

▶ Customer results – meeting or exceeding the needs and expectations of customers.
▶ People results – meeting or exceeding the needs and expectations of employees.

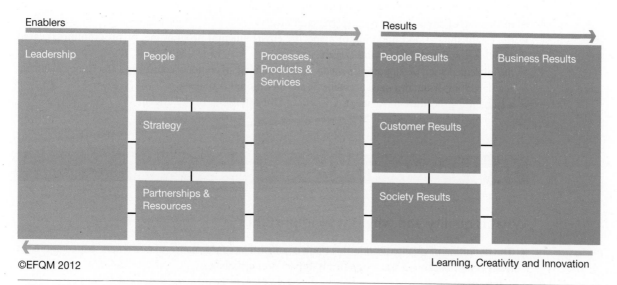

©EFQM 2012

Learning, Creativity and Innovation

Figure 17.11 The EFQM Excellence Model (reproduced with the permission of the EFQM)

The similarity of ISO 14000 to the quality procedures of ISO 9000 is a bit of a giveaway. ISO 14000 can contain all the problems of ISO 9000 (management by manual, obsession with procedures rather than results, a major expense to implement it, and, at its worst, the formalization of what was bad practice in the first place). But ISO 14000 also has some further problems. The main one is that it can become a 'badge for the smug'. It can be seen as 'all there is to do to be a good environmentally sensitive company'. At least with quality standards like ISO 9000 there are real customers continually reminding the business that quality does matter. Pressures to improve environmental standards are far more diffuse. Customers are not likely to be as energetic in forcing good environmental standards on suppliers as they are in forcing the good quality standards from which they benefit directly. Instead of this type of procedure-based system, surely the only way to influence a practice that has an effect at a societal level is through society's normal mechanism – legal regulation. If quality suffers, individuals suffer and have the sanction of not purchasing goods and services again from the offending company. With bad environmental management, however, we all suffer. Because of this, the only workable way to ensure environmentally sensitive business policies is by insisting that our governments protect us. Legislation, therefore, is the only safe way forward.

▶ Society results – achieving and sustaining results that meet or exceed the needs and expectations of the relevant stakeholders within society.

▶ Business results – achieving and sustaining results that meet or exceed the needs and expectations of business stakeholders.

Green reporting and ISO 14000[20]

Until recently, relatively few companies around the world provided information on their environmental practices and performance. Now environmental reporting is increasingly common. Another emerging issue has been the introduction of the ISO 14000 standard. It has a three-section environmental management system which covers initial planning, implementation and objective assessment. Although it has had some impact, it is largely limited to Europe.

ISO 14000 makes a number of specific requirements, including the following:

▶ a commitment by top-level management to environmental management;
▶ the development and communication of an environmental policy;
▶ the establishment of relevant and legal and regulatory requirements;
▶ the setting of environmental objectives and targets;
▶ the establishment and updating of a specific environmental programme, or programmes, geared to achieving the objectives and targets;
▶ the implementation of supporting systems such as training, operational control and emergency planning;
▶ regular monitoring and measurement of all operational activities;
▶ a full audit procedure to review the working and suitability of the system.

Summary answers to key questions

What is quality and why is it so important?

▶ The definition of quality used in this book is 'consistent conformance to customers' expectations'. It is important because it has a significant impact on profitability.

- At a broad level, quality is best modelled as the gap between customers' expectations concerning the service or product and their perceptions concerning the service or product.
- Modelling quality this way will allow the development of a diagnostic tool that is based around the perception–expectation gap. Such a gap may be explained by four other gaps:
  — the gap between a customer's specification and the operation's specification;
  — the gap between the service or product concept and the way the organization has specified it;
  — the gap between the way quality has been specified and the actual delivered quality;
  — the gap between the actual delivered quality and the way the service or product has been described to the customer.
- Some operations that produce primarily intangible services often use the term 'quality of service' to include elements of speed, dependably and flexibility. Also, increasingly the term 'quality of experience' is used to denote a more user-centric view of quality.
- The 'sandcone' theory of improvement holds that it is generally better to start with improving quality rather than other performance objectives, but then to keep improving quality even as other performance objectives are pursued.

What steps lead towards conformance to specification?

- There are six steps:
  — define quality characteristics;
  — decide how to measure each of the quality characteristics;
  — set quality standards for each characteristic;
  — control quality against these standards;
  — find and correct the causes of poor quality;
  — continue to make improvements.
- Most quality planning and control involves sampling the operations performance in some way. Sampling can give rise to erroneous judgements which are classed as either type I or type II errors. Type I errors involve making corrections where none are needed. Type II errors involve not making corrections where they are in fact needed.

What is total quality management (TQM)?

- TQM is 'an effective system for integrating the quality development, quality maintenance and quality improvement efforts of the various groups in an organization so as to enable production and service at the most economical levels which allow for full customer satisfaction'.
- It is best thought of as a philosophy that stresses the 'total' of TQM and puts quality at the heart of everything that is done by an operation.
- Total in TQM means the following:
  — meeting the needs and expectations of customers;
  — covering all parts of the organization;
  — including every person in the organization;
  — examining all costs which are related to quality, and getting things 'right first time';
  — developing the systems and procedures which support quality and improvement, potentially including 'quality awards'.

Turnround at the Preston plant[21]

Introduction

'Before the crisis, production monitoring was done to please the client, not for problem solving. Data read-outs were brought to Production meetings, we would all look at it, but none of us were looking behind it' (Chief Operating Officer (COO), Preston Plant).

The Preston plant was located in Preston, Vancouver. Precision coated papers for specialist printing uses accounted for the majority of the plant's output. The plant used state-of-the-art coating machines that allowed very precise coatings to be applied to bought-in rolls of paper. After coating, the coated rolls were cut into standard sizes.

The curl problem

In the spring of 2008 Hewlett Packard (the plant's main customer) informed the plant of problems it had encountered with paper curling under conditions of low humidity. There had been no customer complaints, but HP's own personnel had noticed the problem. The Preston plant took the problem seriously. Over the next eight months the plant's Production staff worked to isolate the cause of the problem and improve systems that monitored processing metrics. By January 2009 the process was producing acceptable product, yet it had not been a good year for the plant. Although volumes were buoyant, the plant was making a loss of around $10 million a year. In October 2008, Tom Branton was appointed as COO.

Slipping out of control

Although the curl project was solved, productivity, scrap and re-work levels were poor. In response to this, operations managers increased the speed of the line in order to raise productivity. *'Looking back, changes were made without any proper discipline, there was no real concept of control and the process was allowed to drift. Our culture said, "If it's within specification then it's OK", and we were very diligent in making sure that the product which was shipped*

was in specification. However, Hewlett Packard gets "process data" which enables them to see exactly what is happening right inside your operation. We were also getting all the data but none of it was being internalized. By contrast, HP has a "capability mentality". They say, "You might be capable of making this product but we are thinking two or three product generations forward and asking ourselves, do we want to invest in this relationship for the future?"' (Tom Branton)

The spring of 2009 was eventful. First, Hewlett Packard asked the plant to carry out preliminary work for a new paper to supply its next generation of printers, known as the Viper project. Second, the plant was acquired by the Rendall Group, which was not impressed by what it found. The plant had been making a loss for two years and had incurred HP's disapproval over the curl issue. The group made it clear that, if the plant did not get the Viper contract, its future looked bleak. Meanwhile, in the plant, the chief concern was plant productivity, but HP was starting to make complaints about quality levels. Yet HP's attitude caused bewilderment in the Production team. *'When HP asked questions about our process the operations guys would say, "Look we're making roll after roll of paper, it's within specification and we've got 97 per cent up-time. What's the* problem?"' (COO, Preston Plant). But it was not until summer that the full extent of HP's disquiet was made clear. *'I will never forget that day in June of 2009. I was with HP in Chicago and during the meeting one of their engineers handed me some of the process data that we had to supply with every batch of product, and said, "Here's your latest data. We think you're out of control and you don't know that you're out of control and we think that HP is looking at this data more than you are." He was absolutely right'.* (Tom Branton)

The crisis

Tom immediately set about the task of bringing the plant back under control. He first of all decided to go back to the conditions which the monitoring system indicated had prevailed in January, when the curl problem had been solved and before productivity pressures had caused the process to be adjusted. At the same time Production worked on ways of implementing unambiguous 'shut-down rules' which would indicate to operators when a line should be halted if they were in doubt about operating quality. *'At one point in May of 2009 we had to throw away 64 jumbo rolls of out-of-specification product. That's over $400,000 of product scrapped in one run. That was because operators had been afraid to shut the line down. Either that or they had tried to tweak the line while it was running to get rid of the defect. The shut-down system says, "We are not going to operate when we are not in a state of control." Prior to that, our operators just couldn't win. If they failed to keep the process running we would say, "You've got to keep productivity up." If they kept the machines running but had quality problems as a result, we criticized them for making garbage. Now you get into far more trouble for violating process procedures than for not meeting productivity targets. We did two further things. First, each production team started holding daily reviews of processing data and some "first pass" analysis of the data. Second, one day a month we brought all three shifts together, looked at the processing data and debated the implications of production data. Some people got nervous because we were not producing anything. But for the first time you got operators from the three shifts, together with the Production team, talking about operating issues. We also invited HP up to attend these meetings. Remember these weren't staged meetings, it was the first time these guys had met together and there was plenty of heated discussion, all of which the Hewlett Packard representatives witnessed'* (Engineer, Preston plant).

In spite of the changes, morale on the shop floor was good. At last something positive was happening. By September 2009 the process was coming under control and the efficiency of the plant was improving, as was its outgoing quality level, its on-time delivery, its responsiveness to customer orders and its inventory levels. Yet the Preston team did not have time to enjoy their emerging success. In September of 2009 Hewlett Packard announced that the plant would not get the Viper project because of HP's discomfort about quality levels, and Rendall formally made its decision on the future of the plant. *'We lost ten million dollars in 2009. We had also lost the Viper project. It was no surprise when they made the decision to shut the plant down. I told the senior management team that we would announce it, in April of 2010. The irony was that we knew that we had already turned the corner. It would take perhaps three or four months, but we were convinced that we would become profitable'* (Tom Branton).

Convincing the rest of the world

Notwithstanding the closure decision, the management team in Preston set about the task of convincing both HP and Rendall that the plant could be viable. They figured it would take three things. First, it was vital that they continue to improve quality. Second, costs had to be brought down further. Third, the plant had to create a portfolio of new product ideas.

Improving quality further involved establishing full statistical process analysis in the process monitoring system. It also meant establishing quality consciousness and problem-solving tools throughout the plant. *'We had people out there, technologists and managers, who saw themselves as concerned with investment projects rather than the processes that were affected. But taking time out and discussing process performance and improvement, we got used to discussing the basic capabilities that we needed to improve'* (Tom Branton).

Working on cost reduction was inevitably going to be painful. The first task was to get an understanding of what should be an appropriate level of operating costs. *'We went through a zero-based assessment to decide what ideal processes would look like. By the way, in hindsight, cutting numbers had a greater impact on cost than the payroll saving figures seems to suggest. If you really understand your process, when you cut people it cuts complexity and makes things clearer to understand. Although most staff had not been told about the closure decision, they were left in no doubt that the plant had its back to the wall. We were careful to be very transparent. We made sure that everyone knew whether they would be affected or not. I did lots of walking around explaining the company's position. There were tensions and some negative reactions from the people who* had to leave. Yet most accepted the business logic of what we were doing' (Tom Branton).

By December of 2009 there were 40 per cent fewer people in the plant than two months earlier. All departments were affected. Surprisingly the quality department shrank more than most, moving from 22 people down to nine. *'When the plant was considering down-sizing they asked me, "How can we run a lab with six technicians?" Remember that at this time we had 22 technicians. I said, "Easy. We get production to make good product in the first place, and then we don't have to control all the garbage"'* (Quality Manager, Preston plant).

Several new product ideas were investigated, including some that were only possible because of the plant's enhanced capability. The most important of these became known as 'Ecowrap', a recyclable protective wrap, aimed at the Japanese market. It was technically difficult, but the plant's new capabilities allowed it to develop appropriate coatings at a cost that made the product attractive.

Out of the crisis

In spite of their trauma in the fall, the plant's management team faced Christmas of 2009 with increasing satisfaction, if not optimism for the plant's future. In December they made an operational profit for the first time for over two years. By spring of 2010 even HP, at a corporate level, was starting to look more favourably on the Preston plant. More significantly, HP had asked the plant to start work on trials for a new product – 'heavyweight' paper. April 2010 was a good month for the plant. It had chalked up three months of profitability and HP formally gave the heavyweight ink-jet paper contract to Preston, and was generally more up-beat about

the future. At the end of April, Rendall reversed its decision to close the plant.

The future

The year 2010 was profitable for the plant, by the end of which it had captured 75 per cent of Hewlett Packard's US printing paper business and was being asked to work on several other large projects. *'Hewlett Packard now seems very keen to work with us. It has helped us with our own suppliers also. We have already given considerable assistance to our main paper supplier to improve their own internal process control procedures. Recently we were in a meeting with people from all different parts of HP. There were all kinds of confidential information going around. But you could never tell that there was an outsider (us) in the room. They were having arguments amongst themselves about certain issues and no one could have been there without feeling that basically we were a part of that company. In the past they've always been very close with some information. Basically the change is all down to their new found trust in our capabilities'* (Tom Branton).

QUESTIONS

1 **What are the most significant events in the story of how the plant survived because of its adoption of quality-based principles?**

2 **The plant's processes eventually were brought under control. What were the main benefits of this?**

3 **SPC is an operational-level technique for ensuring quality conformance. How many of the benefits of bringing the plant under control would you class as strategic?**

Problems and applications

All chapters have 'Problems and applications' questions that will help you practise analysing operations. They can be answered by reading the chapter. Model answers for the first two questions can be found on the companion website for this book.

(Read the supplement on Statistical Process Control, before attempting problems 7 and 8.)

1 Human error is a significant source of quality problems. Think through the times that you have (with hindsight) made an error and answer the following questions. (a) How do you think that human error causes quality problems? (b) What could one do to minimize human error?

2   Re-read the 'Operations in practice' example 'Quality at Magic Moments'.
    (a) How has the business changed over time?
    (b) What do you think are the key quality challenges facing the business?
    (c) What do you think should be done to ensure the business maintains quality levels in the future?

3   Re-read the 'Operations in practice' example 'Ryanair reforms its view of service quality'. What does this example tell us about the trade-off between service quality and cost?

4   Understanding type I and type II errors is essential for surgeons' quality planning. For example, in the case of appendicitis, removal of the appendix is necessary because of the risk of its bursting, causing potentially fatal poisoning of the blood. The surgical procedure is relatively simple but there is always a small risk with any invasive surgery. It is also expensive; in the USA around $4,500 per operation. Unfortunately, appendicitis is difficult to diagnose: diagnosis is only 10 per cent accurate. However, a new technique claims to be able to identify 100 per cent of true appendicitis cases prior to surgery. The new technique costs less than $250, which means that one single avoided surgery pays for around 20 tests.
    (a) How does this new test change the likelihood of type I and type II errors?
    (b) Why is this important?

5   'Tea and Sympathy' (not a made-up name) was a British restaurant and café in the heart of New York's West Village. It became fashionable not only with expatriate Brits but also with native New Yorkers, who were willing to queue to get in. One reason it become famous was for the unusual nature of its service. *'Everyone is treated in the same way'*, said Nicky Perry, one of the two ex-Londoners who ran it. *'We have a firm policy that we don't take any shit.'* This robust attitude to the treatment of customers is reinforced by 'Nicky's Rules' which are printed on the menu.
    1 Be pleasant to the waitresses – remember Tea and Sympathy girls are always right.
    2 You will have to wait outside the restaurant until your entire party is present: no exceptions.
    3 Occasionally, you may be asked to change tables so that we can accommodate all of you.
    4 If we don't need the table you may stay all day, but if people are waiting it's time to naff off.
    5 These rules are strictly enforced. Any argument will incur Nicky's wrath. You have been warned.
       Nicky's Rules were strictly enforced. If customers objected, they were thrown out. Nicky said that she has had to train 'her girls' to toughen up. *'I've taught them that when people cross the line they can tear their throats out as far as I'm concerned. What we've discovered over the years is that if you are really sweet, people see it as a weakness.'* People were thrown out about twice a week and yet customers still queued for the food (and of course the service).
    (a) Why do you think 'Nicky's Rules' help to make the Tea and Sympathy operation more efficient?
    (b) The restaurant's approach to quality of service seems very different to most restaurants. Why do you think it seems to work here?

6   Look again at the 'Operations in practice' example that includes a description of the Four Seasons Canary Wharf. (a) The company has what it calls its Golden Rule: 'Do to others (guests and staff) as you would wish others to do to you'. Why is this important in ensuring high-quality service? (b) What do you think the hotel's guests expect from their stay? (b) How do staff using their own initiative contribute to quality?

7   An animal park in Amsterdam has decided to sample 50 visitors each day (n) to see how many visitors are from overseas. The data below are for the last 7 days. If it decided to continue recording these data and plot them on a control chart for attributes, what should the upper and lower control limits be?

Day	Number of overseas visitors
1	7
2	8
3	12
4	5
5	5
6	4
7	8

8 The manager of a sweet shop decides to sample batches of sweets to check that the weight is reasonably consistent. She takes nine samples, each with 10 bags. The data below show the average mean weight for each sample and the weight range. What control limits would a control chart for variables use?

Sample	Weight average in grams $\bar{x}$	Range (R)
1	10	1.50
2	8	2.00
3	9	3.00
4	9	2.50
5	8	1.50
6	9	1.00
7	11	2.00
8	14	2.50
9	12	2.00

Selected further reading

ASQ Quality Press (2010) *Seven Basic Quality Tools,* **ASQ Quality Press, Milwaukee, WI.**
Very much a 'how to do it' handbook.

Dale, B.G, van der Wiele, T. and van Iwaarden, J. (2007) *Managing Quality,* **5th edn, Wiley-Blackwell, Oxford.**
The latest version of a long-established, comprehensive and authoritative text.

Garvin, D.A. (1988) *Managing Quality,* **Free Press, New York.**
Somewhat dated now but relates to our discussion at the beginning of this chapter.

Kiran, D.R. (2016) *Total Quality Management: Key Concepts and Case Studies,* **Butterworth-Heinemann, Oxford.**
A good blend of basic principles and examples.

Oakland, J.S. (2014) *Total Quality Management and Operational Excellence: Text with Cases,* **4th edn, Routledge, Milton.**
A classic text from one of the founders of TQM in Europe.

Webber, L. (2007) *Quality Control for Dummies,* **Wiley, Hoboken, NJ.**
Not just for dummies (though they might like it too).

INTRODUCTION

Statistical process control (SPC) is concerned with checking a service or product during its creation. If there is reason to believe that there is a problem with the process, then it can be stopped and the problem can be identified and rectified. For example, an international airport may regularly ask a sample of customers if the cleanliness of its restaurants is satisfactory. If an unacceptable number of customers in one sample are found to be unhappy, airport managers may have to consider improving its procedures. Similarly, an automobile manufacturer will periodically check whether a sample of door panels conforms to its standards so it knows whether the machinery which produces them is performing correctly.

Control charts

The value of SPC is not just to make checks of a single sample but to monitor the quality over a period of time. It does this by using control charts[1], to see if the process seems to be performing as it should, or alternatively if it is 'out of control'. If the process does seem to be going out of control, then steps can be taken *before* there is a problem. Actually, most operations chart their quality performance in some way. Figure S17.1, or something like it, could be found in almost any operation. The chart could, for example, represent the percentage of customers in a sample of 1,000 who, each month, were dissatisfied with the restaurant's cleanliness. While the amount of dissatisfaction may be acceptably small, management should be concerned that it has been steadily increasing over time and may wish to investigate why this is so. In this case, the control chart is plotting an attribute measure of quality (satisfied or not). Looking for trends is an important use of control charts. If the trend suggests the process is getting steadily worse, then it will be worth investigating the process. If the trend is

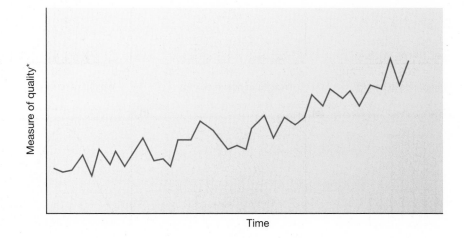

*e.g. A *variable* such as average impact resistance of samples of door panels
or
An *attribute* such as percentage of customer sample who are dissatisfied with cleanliness

Figure S17.1 Charting trends in quality measures

steadily improving, it may still be worthy of investigation to try to identify what is happening that is making the process better. This information might then be shared with other parts of the organization, or, on the other hand, the process might be stopped as the cause could be adding unnecessary expense to the operation.

Variation in process quality

Common causes

The processes charted in Figure S17.1 showed an upwards trend. But the trend was neither steady nor smooth; it varied, sometimes up, sometimes down. All processes vary to some extent. No machine will give precisely the same result each time it is used. People perform tasks slightly differently each time. Given this, it is not surprising that the measure of quality will also vary. Variations which derive from these *common causes* can never be entirely eliminated (although they can be reduced). For example, if a machine is filling boxes with rice, it will not place *exactly* the same weight of rice in every box it fills. When the filling machine is in a stable condition (that is, no exceptional factors are influencing its behaviour) each box could be weighed and a histogram of the weights could be built up. Figure S17.2 shows how the histogram might develop. The first boxes weighed could lie anywhere within the natural variation of the process but are more likely to be close to the average weight (see Figure S17.2(a)). As more boxes are weighed they clearly show the tendency to be close to the process average (see Figure S17.2(b) and (c)). After many boxes have been weighed they form a smoother distribution (Figure S17.2(d)), which can be drawn as a histogram (Figure S17.2(e)), which will approximate to the underlying process variation distribution (Figure S17.2(f)).

Usually this type of variation can be described by a normal distribution with 99.7 per cent of the variation lying within ± 3 standard deviations. In this case the weight of rice in the boxes is described by a distribution with a mean of 206 grams and a standard deviation of 2 grams. The obvious question for any

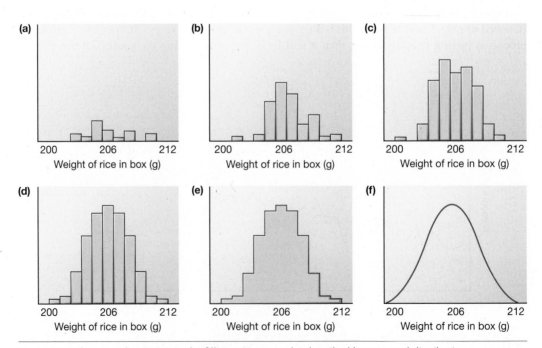

Figure S17.2 The natural variation in the filling process can be described by a normal distribution

---

[1]control charts

operations manager would be: 'Is this variation in the process performance acceptable?' The answer will depend on the acceptable range of weights which can be tolerated by the operation. This range is called the **specification range**.[2] If the weight of rice in the box is too small then the organization might infringe labelling regulations; if it is too large, the organization is 'giving away' too much of its product for free.

Process capability

Process capability[3] is a measure of the acceptability of the variation of the process. The simplest measure of capability (C_p) is given by the ratio of the specification range to the 'natural' variation of the process (i.e. ± 3 standard deviations):

$$C_p = \frac{UTL - LTL}{6s}$$

where

$$UTL = \text{the upper tolerance limit}$$
$$LTL = \text{the lower tolerance limit}$$
$$s = \text{the standard deviation of the process variability.}$$

Generally, if the C_p of a process is greater than 1, it is taken to indicate that the process is 'capable', and a C_p of less than 1 indicates that the process is not 'capable', assuming that the distribution is normal (see Figure S17.3(a), (b) and (c)).

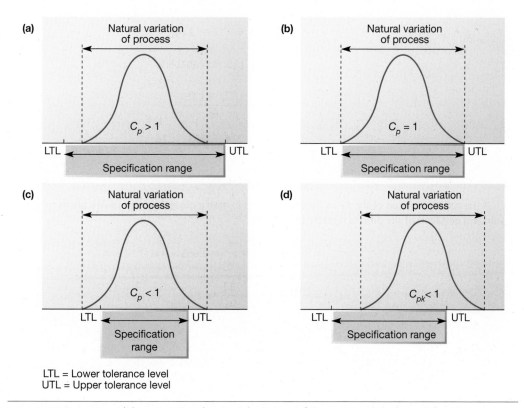

LTL = Lower tolerance level
UTL = Upper tolerance level

Figure S17.3 Process capability compares the natural variation of the process with the specification range which is required

---

[2]specification range
[3]process capability

The simple C_p measure assumes that the average of the process variation is at the mid-point of the specification range. Often the process average is offset from the specification range, however (see Figure S17.3(d)). In such cases, *one-sided* capability indices are required to understand the capability of the process:

$$\text{Upper one-sided index } C_{pu} = \frac{\text{UTL} - X}{3s}$$

$$\text{Lower one-sided index } C_{pl} = \frac{X - \text{LTL}}{3s}$$

where X = the process average.

Sometimes only the lower of the two one-sided indices for a process is used to indicate its capability (C_{pk}):

$$C_{pk} = \min(C_{pu}, C_{pl})$$

Worked example

In the case of the process filling boxes of rice, described previously, process capability can be calculated as follows:

$$\text{Specification range} = 214 - 198 = 16\text{ g}$$

$$\text{Natural variation of process} = 6 \times \text{standard deviation}$$

$$= 6 \times 2 = 12\text{ g}$$

$$C_p = \text{process capability}$$

$$= \frac{\text{UTL} - \text{LTL}}{6s}$$

$$= \frac{214 - 198}{6 \times 2} = \frac{16}{12}$$

$$= 1.333$$

If the natural variation of the filling process changed to have a process average of 210 grams but the standard deviation of the process remained at 2 grams:

$$C_{pu} = \frac{214 - 210}{3 \times 2} = \frac{4}{6} = 0.666$$

$$C_{pl} = \frac{210 - 198}{3 \times 2} = \frac{12}{6} = 2.0$$

$$C_{pk} = \min(0.666, 2.0)$$

$$= 0.666$$

Assignable causes of variation

Not all variation in processes is the result of common causes. There may be something wrong with the process which is assignable to a particular and preventable cause. Machinery may have worn or

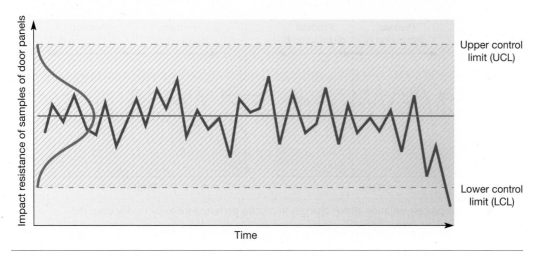

Figure S17.4 Control chart for the impact resistance of door panels, together with control limits

been set up badly. An untrained person may not be following prescribed procedures. The causes of such variation are called *assignable causes*. The question is whether the results from any particular sample, when plotted on the control chart, simply represent the variation due to common causes or due to some specific and correctable, *assignable* cause. Figure S17.4, for example, shows the control chart for the average impact resistance of samples of door panels taken over time. Like any process the results vary, but the last three points seem to be lower than usual. So, is this a natural (common cause) variation, or the symptom of some more serious (assignable) cause?

To help make this decision, **control limits**[4] can be added to the control chart (the red dotted lines) which indicate the expected extent of 'common-cause' variation. If any points lie outside these control limits (the shaded zone) then the process can be deemed out of control in the sense that variation is likely to be due to assignable causes. These control limits could be set intuitively by examining past variation during a period when the process was thought to be free of any variation which could be due to assignable causes. But control limits can also be set in a more statistically revealing manner. For example, if the process which tests door panels had been measured to determine the normal distribution which represents its common-cause variation, then control limits can be based on this distribution. Figure S17.4 also shows how control limits can be added; here put at ± 3 standard deviations (of the population of sample means) away from the mean of sample averages. It shows that the probability of the final point on the chart being influenced by an assignable cause is very high indeed. When the process is exhibiting behaviour which is outside its normal 'common-cause' range, it is said to be 'out of control'. Yet there is a small but finite chance that the (seemingly out of limits) point is just one of the rare but natural results at the tail of the distribution which describes perfectly normal behaviour. Stopping the process under these circumstances would represent a type I error because the process is actually in control. Alternatively, ignoring a result which in reality is due to an assignable cause is a type II error (see Table S17.1).

Table S17.1 Type I and type II errors in SPC

Decision	Actual process state	
	In control	Out of control
Stop process	Type I error	Correct decision
Leave alone	Correct decision	Type II error

[4]control limits

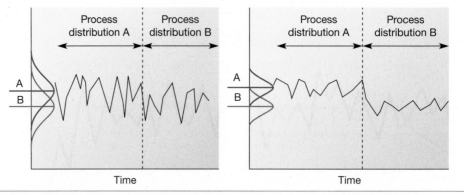

Figure S17.5 Low process variation allows changes in process performance to be readily detected

Control limits are usually set at three standard deviations either side of the population mean. This would mean that there is only a 0.3 per cent chance of any sample mean falling outside these limits by chance causes (that is, a chance of a type I error of 0.3 per cent). The control limits may be set at any distance from the population mean, but the closer the limits are to the population mean, the higher the likelihood of investigating and trying to rectify a process which is actually problem-free. If the control limits are set at two standard deviations, the chance of a type I error increases to about 5 per cent. If the limits are set at one standard deviation then the chance of a type I error increases to 32 per cent. When the control limits are placed at ± 3 standard deviations away from the mean of the distribution which describes 'normal' variation in the process, they are called the **upper control limit**[5] (UCL) and **lower control limit**[6] (LCL).

Why variability is a bad thing

Assignable variation is a signal that something has changed in the process which therefore must be investigated. But normal variation is itself a problem because it masks any changes in process behaviour. Figure S17.5 shows the performance of two processes, both of which are subjected to a change in their process behaviour at the same time. The process on the left has such a wide natural variation

> ### Critical commentary
>
> When its originators first described SPC more than half a century ago, the key issue was only to decide whether a process was 'in control' or not. Now, we expect SPC to reflect common sense as well as statistical elegance and promote continuous operations improvement. This is why two (related) criticisms have been levelled at the traditional approach to SPC. The first is that SPC seems to assume that any values of process performance which lie within the control limits are equally acceptable, while any values outside the limits are not. However, surely a value close to the process average or 'target' value will be more acceptable than one only just within the control limits. For example, a service engineer arriving only 1 minute late is a far better 'performance' than one arriving 59 minutes late, even if the control limits are 'quoted time $\pm$ one hour'. Also, arriving 59 minutes late would be almost as bad as 61 minutes late! Second, a process always within its control limits may not be deteriorating, but is it improving? So rather than seeing control limits as fixed, it would be better to view them as a reflection of how the process is being improved. We should expect any improving process to have progressively narrowing control limits.

[5]upper control limit
[6]lower control limit

that it is not immediately apparent that any change has taken place. Eventually it will become apparent because the likelihood of process performance violating the lower (in this case) control limit has increased, but this may take some time. By contrast, the process on the right has a far narrower band of natural variation. Because of this, the same change in average performance is more easily noticed (both visually and statistically). So, the narrower the natural variation of a process, the more obvious are changes in the behaviour of that process. And the more obvious are process changes, the easier it is to understand how and why the process is behaving in a particular way. Accepting any variation in any process is, to some degree, admitting to ignorance of how that process works.

> **Operations principle**
>
> High levels of variation reduce the ability to detect changes in process performance

Control charts for attributes

Attributes have only two states – 'right' or 'wrong', for example – so the statistic calculated is the proportion of wrongs (p) in a sample. (This statistic follows a binomial distribution.) Control charts using p are called 'p-charts'. In calculating the limits, the population mean ($\bar{p}$) – the actual, normal or expected proportion of 'defectives' or wrongs to rights – may not be known. Who knows, for example, the actual number of city commuters who are dissatisfied with their journey time? In such cases the population mean can be estimated from the average of the proportion of 'defectives' ($\bar{p}$), from m samples each of n items, where m should be at least 30 and n should be at least 100:

$$\bar{p} = \frac{p^1 + p^2 + p^3 \ldots p^n}{m}$$

One standard deviation can then be estimated from:

$$\sqrt{\frac{\bar{p}(1 - \bar{p})}{n}}$$

The upper and lower control limits can then be set as:

$$\text{UCL} = \bar{p} + 3 \text{ standard deviations}$$

$$\text{LCL} = \bar{p} - 3 \text{ standard deviations}$$

Of course, the LCL cannot be negative, so when it is calculated to be so it should be rounded up to zero.

Worked example

A credit card company deals with many hundreds of thousands of transactions every week. One of its measures of the quality of service it gives its customers is the dependability with which it mails customers' monthly accounts. The quality standard it sets itself is that accounts should be mailed within two days of the 'nominal post date' which is specified to the customer. Every week the company samples 1,000 customer accounts and records the percentage which was not mailed within the standard time. When the process is working normally, only 2 per cent of accounts are mailed outside the specified period: that is, 2 per cent are 'defective'.

Control limits for the process can be calculated as follows:

Mean proportion defective, $\bar{p} = 0.02$

Sample size $n = 1,000$

$$\text{Standard deviation } s = \sqrt{\frac{\bar{p}(1-\bar{p})}{n}}$$

$$= \sqrt{\frac{0.02(0.98)}{1000}}$$

$$= 0.0044$$

With the control limits at $\bar{p} \pm 3s$:

$$\text{Upper control limit (UCL)} = 0.02 + 3(0.0044) = 0.0332$$

$$= 3.32\%$$

$$\text{and lower control limit (LCL)} = 0.02 - 3(0.0044) = 0.0068$$

$$= 0.68\%$$

Figure S17.6 shows the company's control chart for this measure of quality over the last few weeks, together with the calculated control limits. It also shows that the process is in control. Sometimes it is more convenient to plot the actual number of defects (c) rather than the proportion (or percentage) of defectives, on what is known as a c-chart. This is very similar to the p-chart but the sample size must be constant and the process mean and control limits are calculated using the following formulae:

$$\text{Process mean } \bar{c} = \frac{c_1 + c_2 + c_3 \ldots c_m}{m}$$

$$\text{Control limits} = \bar{c} \pm 3\sqrt{\bar{c}}$$

$$\text{where } c = \text{number of defects}$$

$$m = \text{number of samples}$$

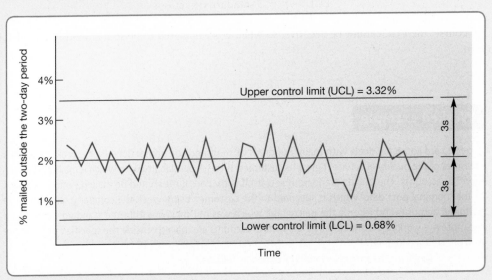

Figure S17.6 Control chart for the percentage of customer accounts which are mailed outside their two-day period

Control chart for variables

The most commonly used type of control chart employed to control variables is the $\overline{X}-R$ *chart*. In fact this is really two charts in one. One chart is used to control the sample average or mean ($\overline{X}$). The other is used to control the variation within the sample by measuring the range (R). The range is used because it is simpler to calculate than the standard deviation of the sample.

The means ($\overline{X}$) chart can pick up changes in the average output from the process being charted. Changes in the means chart would suggest that the process is drifting generally away from its supposed process average, although the variability inherent in the process may not have changed (see Figure S17.7).

The range (R) chart plots the range of each sample: that is, the difference between the largest and the smallest measurement in the samples. Monitoring sample range gives an indication of whether the variability of the process is changing, even when the process average remains constant (see Figure S17.7).

Control limits for variables control chart

As with attributes control charts, a statistical description of how the process operates under normal conditions (when there are no assignable causes) can be used to calculate control limits. The first task in calculating the control limits is to estimate the grand average or population mean ($\overline{\overline{X}}$) and average range ($\overline{R}$) using m samples each of sample size n.

The population mean is estimated from the average of a large number (m) of sample means:

$$\overline{\overline{X}} = \frac{\overline{X_1} + \overline{X_2} + \dots \overline{X_m}}{m}$$

The average range is estimated from the ranges of the large number of samples:

$$\overline{R} = \frac{R_1 + R_2 + \dots R_m}{m}$$

The control limits for the sample means chart are:

$$\text{Upper control limit (UCL)} = \overline{\overline{X}} + A_2\overline{R}$$

$$\text{Lower control limit (LCL)} = \overline{\overline{X}} - A_2\overline{R}$$

The control limits for the range charts are:

$$\text{Upper control limit (UCL)} = D_4\overline{R}$$

$$\text{Lower control limit (LCL)} = D_3\overline{R}$$

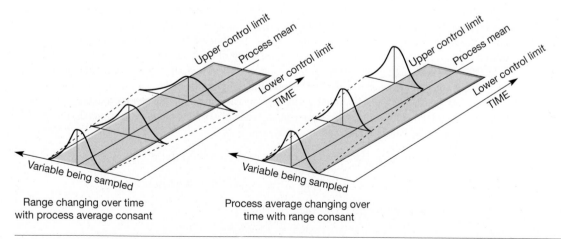

Range changing over time with process average consant

Process average changing over time with range consant

Figure S17.7 The process mean or the process range (or both) can change over time

Table S17.2 Factors for the calculation of control limits

Sample size n	A_2	D_3	D_4
2	1.880	0	3.267
3	1.023	0	2.575
4	0.729	0	2.282
5	0.577	0	2.115
6	0.483	0	2.004
7	0.419	0.076	1.924
8	0.373	0.136	1.864
9	0.337	0.184	1.816
10	0.308	0.223	1.777
12	0.266	0.284	1.716
14	0.235	0.329	1.671
16	0.212	0.364	1.636
18	0.194	0.392	1.608
20	0.180	0.414	1.586
22	0.167	0.434	1.566
24	0.157	0.452	1.548

The factors A_2, D_3 and D_4 vary with sample size and are shown in Table S17.2.

The LCL for the means chart may be negative (for example, temperature or profit may be less than zero) but it may not be negative for a range chart (or the smallest measurement in the sample would be larger than the largest). If the calculation indicates a negative LCL for a range chart then the LCL should be set to zero.

Worked example

GAM (Groupe As Maquillage) is a contract cosmetics company, based in France but with plants around Europe, which manufactures and packs cosmetics and perfumes for other companies. One of its plants, in Ireland, operates a filling line which automatically fills plastic bottles with skin cream and seals the bottles with a screw-top cap. The tightness with which the screw-top cap is fixed is an important part of the quality of the filling line process. If the cap is screwed on too tightly, there is a danger that it will crack; if screwed on too loosely, it might come loose when packed. Either outcome could cause leakage of the product during its journey between the factory and the customer. The Irish plant had received some complaints of product leakage which it suspected was caused by inconsistent fixing of the screw-top caps on its filling line. The 'tightness' of the screw tops could be measured by a simple test device which recorded the amount of turning force (torque) that was required to unfasten the tops. The company decided to take samples of the bottles coming out of the filling-line process, test them for their unfastening torque and plot the results on a control chart. Several samples of four bottles were taken during a period when the process was regarded as being in control. The following data were calculated from this exercise:

$$\text{The grand average of all samples } \overline{\overline{X}} = 812 \text{ g/cm}^3$$

$$\text{The average range of the samples } \overline{R} = 6 \text{ g/cm}^3$$

Control limits for the means ($\overline{X}$) chart were calculated as follows:

$$\text{UCL} = \overline{\overline{X}} + A_2\overline{R}$$

$$= 812 + (A_2 \times 6)$$

From Table S17.2, we know, for a sample size of four, $A_2 = 0.729$. Thus:

$$UCL = 812 + (0.729 \times 6)$$

$$= 816.37$$

$$LCL = \bar{\bar{X}} - (A_2\bar{R})$$

$$= 812 - (0.729 \times 6)$$

$$= 807.63$$

Control limits for the range chart (R) were calculated as follows:

$$UCL = D_4 \times \bar{R}$$

$$= 2.282 \times 6$$

$$= 13.69$$

$$LCL = D_3\bar{R}$$

$$= 0 \times 6$$

$$= 0$$

After calculating these averages and limits for the control chart, the company regularly took samples of four bottles during production, recorded the measurements and plotted them as shown in Figure S17.8. The control chart revealed that only with difficulty could the process average be kept in control.

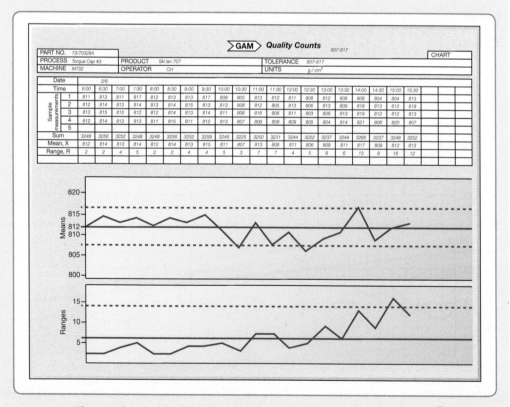

Figure S17.8 The completed control form for GAM's torque machine showing the mean ($\bar{X}$) and range ($\bar{R}$) charts

Occasional operator interventions were required. Also the process range was moving towards (and once breaking) the upper control limit. The process seemed to be becoming more variable. After investigation it was discovered that, because of faulty maintenance of the line, skin cream was occasionally contaminating the torque head (the part of the line which fitted the cap). This resulted in erratic tightening of the caps.

Interpreting control charts

Plots on a control chart which fall outside control limits are an obvious reason for believing that the process might be out of control, and therefore for investigating the process. This is not the only clue which could be revealed by a control chart, however. Figure S17.9 shows some other patterns which could be interpreted as behaviour sufficiently unusual to warrant investigation.

Process control, learning and knowledge

In recent years the role of process control, and SPC in particular, has changed. Increasingly, it is seen not just as a convenient method of keeping processes in control, but also as an activity which is fundamental to the acquisition of competitive advantage. This is a remarkable shift in the status

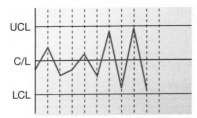

(a) Alternating behaviour – Investigate

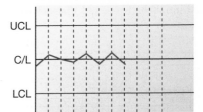

(d) Suspiciously average behaviour – Investigate

(b) Two points near control limit – Investigate

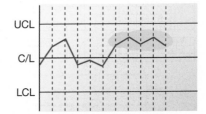

(e) Five points one side of centre line – Investigate

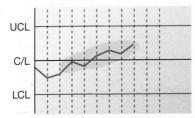

(c) Apparent trend in one direction – Investigate

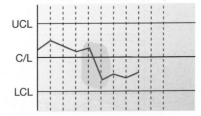

(f) Sudden change in level – Investigate

Figure S17.9 In addition to points falling outside the control limits, other unlikely sequences of points should be investigated

of SPC. Traditionally it was seen as one of the most *operational*, immediate and 'hands-on' operations management techniques. Yet it is now being connected with an operation's *strategic* capabilities. This is how the logic of the argument goes:

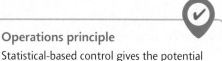

Operations principle

Statistical-based control gives the potential to enhance process knowledge

1 SPC is based on the idea that process variability indicates whether a process is in control or not.

2 Processes are brought into *control* and improved by progressively reducing process variability. This involves eliminating the assignable causes of variation.

3 One cannot eliminate assignable causes of variation without gaining a better understanding of how the process operates. This involves *learning* about the process, where its nature is revealed at an increasingly detailed level.

4 This learning means that **process knowledge**[7] is enhanced, which in turn means that operations managers are able to predict how the process will perform under different circumstances. It also means that the process has a greater capability to carry out its tasks at a higher level of performance.

5 This increased *process capability* is particularly difficult for competitors to copy. It cannot be bought 'off-the-shelf'. It only comes from time and effort being invested in controlling operations processes. Therefore, process capability leads to strategic advantage.

In this way, process control leads to learning which enhances process knowledge and builds difficult-to-imitate process capability.

Summary of supplement

▶ Statistical process control (SPC) involves using control charts to track the performance of one or more quality characteristics in the operation. The power of control charting lies in its ability to set control limits derived from the statistics of the natural variation of processes. These control limits are often set at ± 3 standard deviations of the natural variation of the process samples.

▶ Control charts can be used for either attributes or variables. An attribute is a quality characteristic which has two states (for example, right or wrong). A variable is one which can be measured on a continuously variable scale.

▶ Process control charts allow operations managers to distinguish between the 'normal' variation inherent in any process and the variations which could be caused by the process going out of control.

Selected further reading

Woodall, W.H. (2000) Controversies and Contradictions in Statistical Process Control, Paper presented at the Journal of Quality Technology Session at the 44th Annual Fall Technical Conference of the Chemical and Process Industries Division and Statistics Division of the American Society for Quality and the Section on Physical & Engineering Sciences of the American Statistical Association in Minneapolis, Minnesota, 12–13 October, 2000. *Academic but interesting.*

---

[7]process knowledge

Managing risk and recovery

KEY QUESTIONS

What is risk management?

How can operations assess the potential causes and consequences of failure?

How can failures be prevented?

How can operations mitigate the effects of failure?

How can operations recover from the effects of failure?

INTRODUCTION

No matter how much effort is put into improvement, all operations will face risk and occasionally experience failures. Some risks emerge from poor operations management practice, such as poor quality control. Some risks come from the operation's supply network, for example relying on unreliable suppliers. Other risks come from broader environmental forces, such as political unrest, and environmental disasters. An increasingly important source of risk comes from failures in cyber security. In the face of such risks, a 'resilient' operation is one that can identify likely sources of risk, prevent failures occurring, minimize their effects and learn how to recover from them. In a world where the sources of risk and the consequences of failure are becoming increasingly difficult to handle, managing risk is a vital task. From sudden changes in demand to the bankruptcy of a key supplier, from terrorist attacks to cybercrime, the threats to normal smooth running of operations are rising. And the consequences of such events are becoming more serious. Paring down costs, cutting inventories and striving for higher levels of capacity utilization can all result in higher vulnerability. At the same time, more regulation, and attentive media, can make operations failure more damaging. In this chapter, we examine both the dramatic and the more routine risks that can prevent operations working as they should. Figure 18.1 shows how this chapter fits into the operation's improvement activities.

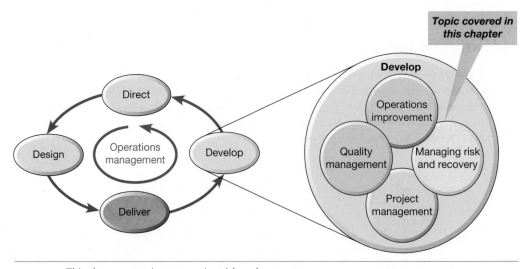

Figure 18.1 This chapter examines managing risk and recovery

What is risk management?

Risk management is about identifying things that could go wrong, stopping them going wrong, reducing the consequences when things do go wrong, and recovering after things have gone wrong. Things happen in operations, or to operations, that have negative consequences; this is failure. But accepting that failure occurs is not the same thing as tolerating or ignoring it. Although operations managers do generally attempt to minimize both the likelihood of failure and the effect it will have, the methods of coping with failure will depend on how serious its consequences are, and how likely it is to occur. At the lower end of the scale, the whole area of quality management is concerned with identifying and reducing every small error in the creation and delivery of products and services. Other failures will have more impact on the operation, even if they do not occur very frequently. For example, a server failure can seriously affect service and therefore customers, which is why system reliability is such an important measure of performance for IT service providers. Some failures, although much less likely, are so serious in terms of negative consequences that we class them as disasters. Examples may include major floods, earthquakes, hurricanes, wars and acts of terrorism, and financial collapses such as a stock market crash.

Operations principle

Failure will always occur in operations. Recognizing this does not imply accepting or ignoring it.

This chapter is concerned with all types of failure other than those with relatively minor consequences. This is illustrated in Figure 18.2. Some of these failures are irritating, but relatively unimportant, especially those close to the bottom left-hand corner of the matrix in Figure 18.2. Other failures, especially those close to the top right-hand corner of matrix, are normally avoided by all business because embracing such risks would be clearly foolish. In between these two extremes is where most operations-related risks occur. In this chapter will shall be treating various aspects of these types of failure, and in particular how they can be moved in the direction of the red arrows in Figure 18.2.

Obviously, some operations have to work in a more risky environment than others. Those operations with a high likelihood of failure and/or serious consequences deriving from that failure will need to give it more attention. But managing risk and recovery is relevant to all organizations and generally involves four sets of activities. The first is concerned with understanding what failures could

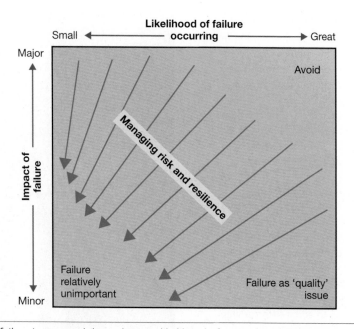

Figure 18.2 How failure is managed depends on its likelihood of occurrence and the negative consequences of failure

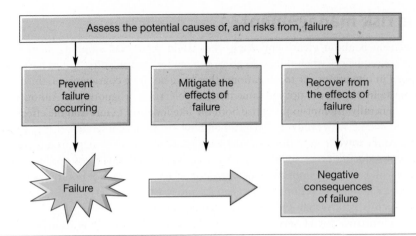

Assess the potential causes of, and risks from, failure

Prevent failure occurring

Mitigate the effects of failure

Recover from the effects of failure

Failure

Negative consequences of failure

Figure 18.3 Risk management involves failure prevention, mitigating the negative consequences of failure, and failure recovery

Operations principle

Resilience is governed by the effectiveness of failure prevention, mitigation and recovery.

potentially occur in the operation and assessing their seriousness. The second task is to examine ways of preventing failures occurring. The third is to minimize the negative consequences of failure – called failure or risk 'mitigation'. The final task is to devise plans and procedures that will help the operation to recover from failures when they do occur. The remainder of this chapter deals with these four tasks (see Figure 18.3).

OPERATIONS IN PRACTICE

Rollercoaster tragedy drags Merlin down[1]

What should have been a fun day out turned into tragedy for 16 people caught up in a devastating crash at the 'Smiler' rollercoaster, at the Alton Towers attraction in Staffordshire in the UK. Amongst the injuries, two young women, aged 17 and 19, were airlifted to hospital to undergo leg amputations after sustaining serious injuries in the crash. Merlin, the group that operated over 100 attractions around the world, suffered a £40 million dent in its earnings, 150 of its staff were laid off and later at the court hearing was fined £5 million. Merlin described it as 'without doubt' the most difficult year in its history.

So, what happened to cause the crash?

On the day of the crash, the Smiler was operating in 46 mph winds (despite guidance saying it should not operate in wind speeds over 34 mph) when an operator noticed a warning light, which indicated a fault on the ride. She immediately removed visitors from the ride and called for help from the theme park's engineers.

The ride had been operating with four passenger carriages, but staff had been told to add a fifth carriage because of the level of demand. It was decided that,

because the ride was currently empty of passengers, it was a good time to put the extra carriage on the tracks. While this was being added, staff sent an empty carriage around the track to check that the ride was operating normally. However, the empty train failed to make it up an incline and a warning system was activated. The two engineers arrived to fix the problem. They were told (incorrectly) that the fifth train had already been added. After they got the empty train working again, the process to restart the ride began again. While staff prepared to allow visitors back onto the ride, they sent another empty train onto the track, which failed to make the climb and rolled back down the track, eventually coming to rest in a valley of the track. Fatefully, the staff were not aware of this and the ride was handed back to an operator who allowed passengers to board, and with operators unaware that the empty test carriage was on the track, the car full of passengers was sent around the track. However, as it climbed the ride's first incline its computer system stopped it from moving ahead, indicating that a section of the track ahead was occupied. The carriage, with its passengers, was stopped while engineers again looked at why the warning alert had activated. The engineers, apparently under pressure to get

to the ride back working quickly, did not see the empty carriage sitting on the track. The official report on the incident said that *'the evidence provided . . . indicated that management had set targets for downtime on rides, with bonuses linked to achieving acceptable low levels. There were also "clocks" in the ride control cabins showing the current performance on downtime.'* Thinking the ride was safe again, the engineer simultaneously pressed a button with a colleague which overrode the safety device that had blocked the carriage from moving ahead. This resulted in the packed train moving ahead with staff unaware it was hurtling towards the empty carriage. The packed carriage slammed into the stranded car, causing devastating injuries to those on board. The impact was equivalent to a car crash at 135 km per hour.

At the subsequent court case, the judge described the incident as a 'catastrophic failure', and the court heard how there was an 'obvious shambles' of systems. Merlin Attractions Operations Ltd later admitted breaching Health and Safety rules. After sentencing, Merlin Entertainment's chief executive Nick Varney apologized, saying the company had *'let people down with devastating consequences'*.

How can operations assess the potential causes and consequences of failure?

The first stage of risk management is to understand the potential sources of risk. This means assessing where failure might occur and what the consequences of failure might be. Often it is a 'failure to understand failure' that results in unacceptable risk. Each potential cause of failure needs to be assessed in terms of how likely it is to occur and the impact it may have. Only then can measures be taken to prevent or minimize the effect of the more important potential failures. The classic approach to assessing potential failures is to inspect and audit operations activities. Unfortunately, inspection and audit cannot, on their own, provide complete assurance that undesirable events will be avoided. The content of any audit has to be appropriate, the checking process has to be sufficiently frequent and comprehensive, and the inspectors have to have sufficient knowledge and experience. But whatever approach to risk is taken, it can only be effective if the organizational culture that it is set in fully supports a 'risk-aware' attitude.

Identify the potential causes of failure

The causes of some failures are purely random, like lightning strikes, and are difficult, if not impossible, to predict. However, the vast majority of failures are caused by something that could have been avoided. So, as a minimum starting point, a simple checklist of failure causes is useful. Figure 18.4 illustrates how this might be done. Here, failure sources are classified as: (1) failures of supply; (2) internal failures such as those deriving from human organizational and technological sources; (3) cyber-security failures that can 'open up' an operation to external threats; (4) failures deriving from the design of products and services; (5) failures deriving from customer failures; and (6) general environmental (or institutional) failures.

Operations principle

A 'failure to understand failure' can be the root cause of a lack of resilience.

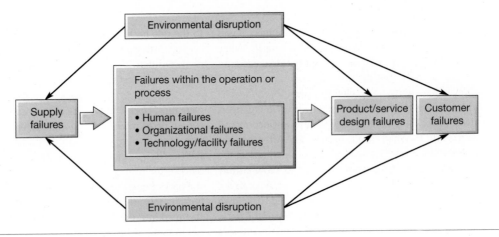

Figure 18.4 The sources of potential failure in operations

Supply failure

Supply failure is any failure in the timing or quality of goods and services delivered into an operation: for example, suppliers delivering the wrong or faulty components, outsourced call centres suffering a telecoms failure, disruption to power supplies and so on. It can be an important source of failure because of increasing dependence on outsourced activities in most industries. The more an operation relies on suppliers for materials or services, the more it is at risk from failure caused by missing or sub-standard inputs. It is an important source of failure because of the increasing dependence on outsourced activities in many industries, and the emphasis on keeping supply chains 'lean' in order to cut costs. Other factors have also increased exposure to supply failure in recent years. For example, the rise of global sourcing usually means that parts are shipped around the world on their journey through the supply chain. Microchips manufactured in Taiwan could be assembled to printed circuit boards in Shanghai that are then assembled into a computer in Ireland and sold in the United States. At the same time, many industries are suffering increased volatility and uncertainty in demand. This may be as a result of market fragmentation, where small customer segments have to be accommodated. Or it may be as a result of faster changes in products, services or the supply base. Perhaps most significantly there tends to be far less inventory in supply chains that could buffer interruptions to supply. According to one authority on supply chain management, *'Potentially the risk of disruption has increased dramatically as the result of a too-narrow focus on supply chain efficiency at the expense of effectiveness.'*[2]

Human failures

There are two broad types of human failure. The first is where key personnel leave, become ill, die, or in some way cannot fulfil their role. The second is where people are doing their job but are making mistakes. Understanding risk in the first type of failure involves identifying the key people without whom operations would struggle to operate effectively. These are not always the most senior individuals, but rather those fulfilling crucial roles that require special skills or tacit knowledge. Human failure through 'mistakes' also comes in two types: errors and violations. 'Errors' are mistakes in judgement, where a person should have done something different: for example, if the manager of a sports stadium fails to anticipate dangerous crowding during a championship event. 'Violations' are acts that are clearly contrary to defined operating procedure. For example, if a maintenance engineer fails to clean a filter in the prescribed manner, it is eventually likely to cause failure. Catastrophic failures are often caused by a combination of errors and violations.

Organizational failure

Organizational failure is usually taken to mean failures of procedures and processes and failures that derive from a business's organizational structure and culture. This is a huge potential source of failure and includes almost all operations and process management. In particular, failure in the design of processes (such as bottlenecks causing system overloading) and failures in the resourcing of processes (such as insufficient capacity being provided at peak times) need to be investigated. But there are also many other procedures and processes within an organization that can make failure more likely. For example, remuneration policy may motivate staff to work in a way that, although increasing the financial performance of the organization, also increases the risk of failure. Examples of this can range from sales people being so incentivized that they make promises to customers that cannot be fulfilled, through to investment bankers being more concerned with profit than the risks of financial overexposure. This type of risk can derive from an organizational culture that minimizes consideration of risk, or it may come from a lack of clarity in reporting relationships.

Technology/facilities failures

By 'technology and facilities' we mean all the IT systems, machines, equipment and buildings of an operation. All are liable to failure, or breakdown. The failure may be only partial: for example, a machine that has an intermittent fault. Alternatively, it can be what we normally regard as a 'breakdown – a total and sudden cessation of operation. Either way, its effects could bring a large part of the operation to a halt. For example, a computer failure in a supermarket chain could paralyse several large stores until it is fixed. Such IT failures have occurred for several leading banks over recent years. The route cause of these failures can often be traced back to inadequate maintenance of exceptionally complex information systems. In other cases, cyber attacks on corporate information systems create a new, or at least increased, threat to operations.

Cyber security

Any advance in processes or technology creates risks. No real advance comes without risk, threats and even danger. A specific type of technological failure is a failure of an operation's technology leading to exposure to cyber-risk, which the Institute of Risk Management defines as *'any risk of financial loss, disruption or damage to the reputation of an organization from some sort of failure of its information technology systems'*. With the increased reliance on internet-based communication in all types of business, it has become a major risk factor. The Internet is by design an open, non-secure medium. Since the original purpose of the Internet was not commercial, it is not designed to handle secure transactions. So, there is a trade-off between providing wider access through the Internet, and the security concerns it generates. Three developments have amplified cyber security concerns. First, increased connectivity means that everyone has at least the potential to 'see' everyone else. Organizations want to make enterprise systems and information more available to internal employees, business partners and customers (see Chapter 14 on planning and control systems). Second, there is reduced 'perimeter' security as more people work from home or through mobile communications. Hackers can exploit lower levels of security in home computers to burrow into corporate networks. Third, it takes time to discover all possible sources of risk, especially as new technologies are introduced.

Cyber risk includes hacker attacks, data breaches, virus transmission, cyber extortion, and network downtime. Any of these could be the result of:

▶ deliberate unauthorized breaches of security firewalls;
▶ unintentional/accidental breaches of security (which could still constitute a risk);
▶ poor systems integrity in the design of IT systems;
▶ unsecure use of cloud usage or storage;
▶ unpoliced use of 'bring your own device' (BYOD) policies.

Most authorities on cyber security stress that, stripped of its technological terminology, cyber risk is just another sort of risk which should be treated using the same identify, prevent, mitigate, recover framework that we are using here in this chapter. The UK government security services maintain that about 80 per cent of cyber-attacks would be defeated by using these basic security controls.

Product/service design failures

In its design stage, a product or service might look fine on paper; only when it has to cope with real circumstances might inadequacies become evident. An example of this is Heathrow's Terminal 5, which reported that it had not been able to replace a single light bulb in five years since its opening. The reason? When designing it, no one thought to examine how its many light fittings would be maintained when they reached the end of their life. After several failed attempts at finding a solution, Heathrow Airport Holdings announced it would be hiring the services of a specialist high-level rope-work company to carry out the work – it declined to state what the cost of such skilled operators would be! One could argue that during the design process, this should have been identified and 'designed out'. But one only has to look at the number of 'product recalls' or service failures to understand that design failures are far from uncommon.

Customer failures

Not all failures are (directly) caused by the operation or by its suppliers. Customers may 'fail' in that they misuse products and services. For example, an IT system might have been well designed, yet the user could treat it in a way that causes it to fail. Customers are not 'always right'; they can be inattentive and incompetent. However, merely complaining about customers is unlikely to reduce the chances of this type of failure occurring. Most organizations will accept that they have a responsibility to educate and train customers, and to design their products and services so as to minimize the chances of failure.

Environmental disruption

Environmental disruption includes all the causes of failure that lie outside of an operation's direct influence. Typically, such disasters include major political upheaval, hurricanes, floods, earthquakes, temperature extremes, fire, corporate crime, theft, fraud, sabotage, terrorism, other security attacks and the contamination of products or processes. This source of potential failure has risen to near the top of many firms' agenda due to a series of major events over recent years. As operations become increasingly integrated (and increasingly dependent on integrated technologies such as information technologies), businesses are more aware of the critical events and malfunctions that have the potential to interrupt normal business activity and even stop the entire company.

OPERATIONS IN PRACTICE	**The threats from new technology – the Internet of Things[3]**

All new technology poses some kind of risk. Financial risk certainly – will the investment in the technology bring a return? Operational risk sometimes – will the technology enhance operational performance, or will implementation problems disrupt the smooth running of the operation? Even physical risk – for example, can we trust autonomous vehicles with our safety? But one particular technology, the Internet of Things (IoT), poses unique security issues, largely because (a) it is complex, (b) it is not always obvious that security has been breached, and (c) it is based on its ability to network, with many potential points of vulnerability. Ensuring that a single Internet-connected device is secure and safe is not a trivial problem, but as the number and connectivity of devices increases, managing these networks of devices becomes exponentially more difficult. One estimate of the total economic impact of

▶

networked devices is 10 trillion dollars by 2025. Yet, according to one school of thought, 'if one thing can prevent the Internet of Things from transforming the way we live and work, it will be a breakdown in security'. It was the arrival of IoT botnets that alerted users to their vulnerabilities, specifically their susceptibility to cyber-criminal activity. (A botnet is a collection of Internet-connected devices that are infected and controlled by a common type of malware.) It has exposed two different issues: (a) a large number of IoT devices are accessible through the public Internet; (b) if security is considered at all, it is often an afterthought in the design of many IoT devices. In 2016, the largest ever (at the time of writing) Distributed Denial of Service (DDoS) attack was launched on Dyn, the service provider, using an IoT botnet. In a DDoS attack a hacker temporarily enslaves a number of Internet-enabled devices into a botnet and then make simultaneous requests to a server, or an array of servers, thus overpowering the server, which ignores legitimate requests from its end-users. The result of this was large parts of the internet going down, affecting Twitter, the Guardian, Netflix, Reddit and CNN. Worse, the IoT botnet involved in the attack was enabled by malware called Mirai. Once infected with Mirai malware, a computer

would persistently search the Internet for susceptible IoT devices. It then used known default usernames and passwords to login and infect them with malware.

After the attack, *PC Magazine* recommended four measures that IoT users could take.

▶ Never use devices that cannot have their software, passwords or firmware updated.
▶ Change the default username and password for the installation of any device on the Internet.
▶ Passwords for IoT devices should be unique per device.
▶ Always patch IoT devices with the latest software and firmware updates.

Post-failure analysis

Although sources of failure can often be identified in advance of their occurrence, it is also valuable to use previous failures to learn about sources of potential risk. This activity is called post-failure analysis. It is used to uncover the root cause of failures. This includes such activities as the following:

▶ **Accident investigation:** Large-scale national disasters such as oil tanker spillages and aeroplane accidents are investigated using specifically trained staff. The reason so much attention goes into examining these kinds of failures is not only because of the damaging consequences of failure, but also because their infrequency makes it relatively hard to identify new sources of risks in advance of an event.

▶ **Failure traceability:** Some businesses adopt traceability procedures to ensure that all their failures (such as contaminated food products) are traceable. Any failures can be traced back to the process which produced them, the components from which they were produced, or the suppliers who provided them. Bio-tagging in pharmaceuticals is one example of this approach. If a medical product is found or suspected to have a problem, all other products in the batch can be recalled.

▶ **Complaint analysis:** Complaints (and compliments) are a valuable source for detecting the root causes of failures of customer service. The prime function of complaint analysis involves analysing the number and 'content' of complaints over time to understand better the nature of the failure, as the customer perceives it (see later).

▶ **Fault-tree analysis:** Here a logical procedure starts with a failure or a potential failure and works backwards to identify all the possible causes and therefore the origins of that failure. Fault tree analysis is made up of branches connected by two types of nodes: AND nodes and OR nodes. The branches below an AND node all need to occur for the event above the node

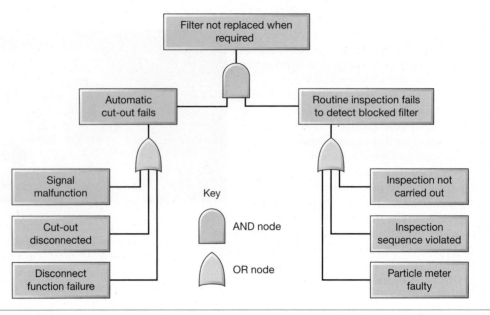

Figure 18.5 Fault-tree analysis for failure to replace filter when required

to occur. Only one of the branches below an OR node needs to occur for the event above the node to occur. Figure 18.5 shows a simple tree identifying the possible reasons for a filter in a heating system not being replaced when it should have been.

Likelihood of failure

The difficulty of estimating the chance of a failure occurring varies greatly. Some failures are well understood through a combination of rational causal analysis and historical performance. For example, a mechanical component may fail between 10 and 17 months after its installation in 99 per cent of cases. Other types of failure are far more difficult to predict. The chances of a fire in a supplier's plant are (hopefully) low, but how low? There will be some data concerning fire hazards in this type of plant, but the estimated probability of failure will be subjective.

'Objective' estimates

Estimates of failure based on historical performance can be measured in three main ways:

▶ **failure rates** – how often a failure occurs;
▶ **reliability** – the chances of a failure occurring;
▶ **availability** – the amount of available useful operating time.

Failure rate

Failure rate (FR) is calculated as the number of failures over a period of time. For example, the security of an airport can be measured by the number of security breaches per year, and the failure rate of an engine can be measured in terms of the number of failures divided by its operating time. It can be measured either as a percentage of the total number of products tested or as the number of failures over time:

$$FR = \frac{\text{Number of failures}}{\text{Total number of products tested}} \times 100$$

or

$$FR = \frac{\text{Number of failures}}{\text{Operating time}}$$

Worked example

A batch of 50 electronic components is tested for 2,000 hours. Four of the components fail during the test as follows:

Failure 1 occurred at 12:00 hours

Failure 2 occurred at 14:50 hours

Failure 3 occurred at 17:20 hours

Failure 4 occurred at 19:05 hours

$$\text{Failure rate (as a percentage)} = \frac{\text{Number of failures}}{\text{Numbers tested}} \times 100 = \frac{4}{50} \times 10 = 8\%$$

The total time of the test $= 50 \times 2,000 = 100,000$ component hours

But:

one component was not operating $2,000 - 1,200 = 800$ hours

one component was not operating $2,000 - 1,450 = 550$ hours

one component was not operating $2,000 - 1,720 = 280$ hours

one component was not operating $2,000 - 1,905 = 95$ hours

Thus:

Total non-operating time $= 1,725$ hours

$$\text{Operating time} = \text{Total time} - \text{Non-operating time}$$

$$= 100,000 - 1,725 = 98,275 \text{ hours}$$

$$\text{Failure rate (in time)} = \frac{\text{Number of failures}}{\text{Operating time}} = \frac{48}{98,725}$$

$$= 0.000041$$

Bath-tub curves Sometimes failure is a function of time. For example, the probability of an electric lamp failing is relatively high when it is first used, but if it survives this initial stage, it could still fail at any point, and the longer it survives, the more likely its failure becomes. The curve that describes failure probability of this type is called the bath-tub curve. It comprises three distinct stages: the 'infant-mortality' or 'early-life' stage where early failures occur caused by defective parts or improper use; the 'normal-life' stage when the failure rate is usually low and reasonably constant, and caused by normal random factors; the 'wear-out' stage when the failure rate increases as the part approaches the end of its working life and failure is caused by the ageing and deterioration of parts. Figure 18.6 illustrates three bath-tub curves with slightly different characteristics. Curve A shows a part of the

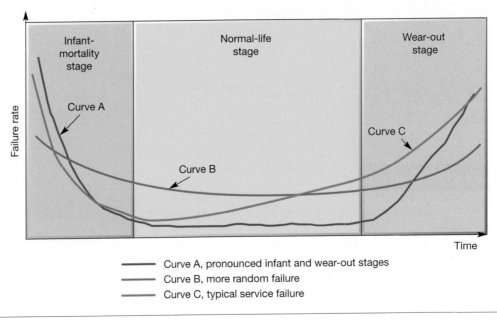

Figure 18.6 Bath-tub curves for three types of process

Legend in figure:
Curve A, pronounced infant and wear-out stages
Curve B, more random failure
Curve C, typical service failure

operation which has a high initial infant-mortality failure but then a long, low-failure, normal life followed by the gradually increasing likelihood of failure as it approaches wear-out. Curve B is far less predictable. The distinction between the three stages is less clear, with infant-mortality failure subsiding only slowly and a gradually increasing chance of wear-out failure. Failure of the type shown in curve B is far more difficult to manage in a planned manner. The failure of operations that rely more on human resources than on technology, such as some services, can be closer to curve C. They may be less susceptible to component wear-out but more so to staff complacency as the service becomes tedious and repetitive.

OPERATIONS IN PRACTICE

It's the exception that proves the rule[4]

Those 'bath-tub' curves show how long something lasts – no? Well, they give a good indication, but they indicate probabilities, not certainties. Take the household appliances that an elderly couple bought more than 50 years ago. They bought the tumble dryer, water boiler, cooker and washing machine when they got married in 1956 and have been using most of them ever since. They (the appliances) have been working, almost incident-free, for far longer than one would expect from average life statistics. They (the couple) decided to eventually replace them when they decided to have a clear out. They say they are 'not interested' in money and 'hope a museum or collector will take them'. But the record for longevity possibly goes to a light bulb in the men's lavatories of an electrical firm in Suffolk, England. When it finally burnt out it was at least 60 years old. It had survived traumas that should have caused it to fail much earlier. Bombs dropped in the Second World War had devastated buildings in neighbouring streets, shaking buildings in the whole area but leaving the bulb intact and working. During the 1950s the army regularly fired its field guns in the neighbouring park land. It was not even affected by the less-than-quiet punk rock bands that played at an adjacent venue and caused residents to complain that their windows were being shaken by the noise. Brian Stopher, a manager at the firm, said, '*It is actually a little bit sad. Over the years, when you went into the toilet, you'd occasionally look up, look at the bulb and think how long it had been there.*' When the bulb did eventually fail, the firm had it mounted on a stand and gave it a place of honour.

Reliability Reliability measures the ability to perform as expected over time. Usually the importance of any particular failure is determined partly by how interdependent the other parts of the system are. With interdependence, a failure in one component will cause the whole system to fail. So, if an inter-dependent system has n components each with their own reliability, $R_1, R_2 \ldots R_n$, the reliability of the whole system, R_s, is given by:

$$R_s = R_1 \times R_2 \times R_2 \times \ldots R_n$$

where

R_1 = reliability of component 1

R_2 = reliability of component 2
etc.

Worked example

An automated pizza-making machine in a food manufacturer's factory has five major components, with individual reliabilities (the probability of the component not failing) as follows:

Dough mixer	Reliability = 0.95
Dough roller and cutter	Reliability = 0.99
Tomato paste applicator	Reliability = 0.97
Cheese applicator	Reliability = 0.90
Oven	Reliability = 0.98

If one of these parts of the production system fails, the whole system will stop working. Thus the reliability of the whole system is:

$$R_s = 0.95 \times 0.99 \times 0.97 \times 0.90 \times 0.98$$
$$= 0.805$$

The number of components In the example, the reliability of the whole system was only 0.8, even though the reliability of the individual components was significantly higher. If the system had been made up of more components, then its reliability would have been even lower. The more inter-dependent components an operation or process has, the lower its reliability will be. For one composed of components which each have an individual reliability of 0.99, with 10 components the system reliability will shrink to 0.9, with 50 components it is below 0.8, with 100 components it is below 0.4, and with 400 components it is down below 0.05. In other words, with a process of 400 components (not unusual in a large automated operation), even if the reliability of each individual component is 99 per cent, the whole system will be working for less than 5 per cent of its time.

Mean time between failures An alternative (and common) measure of failure is the mean time between failures (MTBF) of a component or system. MTBF is the reciprocal of failure rate (in time). Thus:

$$\text{MTBF} = \frac{\text{Operating hours}}{\text{Number of failures}}$$

In the previous worked example which was concerned with electronic components, the failure rate (in time) of the electronic components was 0.000041. For that component:

$$\text{MTBF} = \frac{1}{0.000041} = 24{,}390.24 \text{ hours}$$

That is, a failure can be expected once every 24,390.24 hours on average.

Availability Availability is the degree to which the operation is ready to work. An operation is not available if it has either failed or is being repaired following failure. There are several different ways of measuring it depending on how many of the reasons for not operating are included. Lack of availability because of planned maintenance or changeovers could be included, for example. However, when 'availability' is being used to indicate the operating time excluding the consequence of failure, it is calculated as follows:

$$\text{Availability } (A) = \frac{\text{MTBF}}{\text{MTBF} + \text{MTTR}}$$

where

MTBF = the mean time between failures of the operation

MTTR = the mean time to repair, which is the average time taken to repair the operation, from the time it fails to the time it is operational again.

A company which designs and produces display posters for exhibitions and sales promotion events competes largely on the basis of its speedy delivery. One particular piece of equipment which the company uses is causing some problems. This is its large platform colour laser printer. Currently, the mean time between failures of the printer is 70 hours and its mean time to repair is six hours. Thus:

$$\text{Availability} = \frac{70}{70 + 6} = 0.92$$

The company has discussed its problem with the supplier of the printer, which has offered two alternative service deals. One option would be to buy some preventive maintenance (see later for a full description of preventive maintenance) which would be carried out each weekend. This would raise the MTBF of the printer to 90 hours. The other option would be to subscribe to a faster repair service which would reduce the MTTR to 4 hours. Both options would cost the same amount. Which would give the company the higher availability?

With MTBF increased to 90 hours:

$$\text{Availability} = \frac{90}{90 + 6} = 0.938$$

With MTTR reduced to 4 hours:

$$\text{Availability} = \frac{70}{70 + 4} = 0.946$$

Availability would be greater if the company took the deal which offered the faster repair time.

'Subjective' estimates Failure assessment, even for subjective risks, is increasingly a formal exercise that is carried out using standard frameworks, often prompted by health and safety, environmental or other regulatory reasons. These frameworks are similar to the formal quality inspection methods

The rise of the MicroMort[5]

Calculating risk is far from easy. However, two authorities on risk, Michael Blastand and David Spiegelhalter, try to untangle the nature of risk and probability through the concept of the 'MicroMort'. The MicroMort is defined as a one-in-a-million chance of death and its use allows for some interesting comparisons to be made. For example, the chance of dying on a return motorbike trip from Edinburgh to London in the UK is around 120 MicroMorts (i.e. a 120-in-a-million chance). This is comparable to the risk faced by mothers giving birth in Britain or a soldier spending 2.5 days during the most dangerous period of the Afghanistan conflict. The concept also allows us to examine how risks have changed over time. For example, aircrews involved in bombing raids during the Second World War were 'exposed' to 25,000 MicroMorts – a depressing 2.5 per cent chance of death – per mission. Soldiers in Afghanistan in the recent conflict faced 47 Micromorts – or 0.0047 per cent chance of death – per day on the ground. What is perhaps most interesting about the work is that it explores just how irrational humans are

when attempting to calculate risk. Typically high impact / low probability risk is over-emphasized, while low impact / high probability risk is under-emphasized. For organizations, appreciating the innate irrationality and cognition biases of most of their managers and employees can be a important step towards developing better assessments of various potential sources of failure.

associated with quality standards like ISO 9000 (see Chapter 17) that often implicitly assume unbiased objectivity. However, individual attitudes to risk are complex and subject to a wide variety of influences. In fact many studies have demonstrated that people are generally very poor at making risk-related judgements. Consider the success of state and national lotteries. The chances of winning, in nearly every case, are so low as to make the financial value of the investment entirely negative. If a player has to drive their car in order to purchase a ticket, they may be more likely to be killed or seriously injured than they are to win the top prize. But, although people do not always make rational decisions, this does not mean abandoning the attempt. Even when 'objective' evaluations of risks are used, they may still cause negative consequences. For example, when the oil giant Royal-Dutch Shell took the decision to employ deep-water disposal in the North Sea for its Brent Spar Oil Platform, it felt that it was making a rational operational decision based upon the best available scientific evidence concerning environmental risk. Unfortunately Greenpeace disagreed and put forward an alternative 'objective analysis' showing significant risk from deep-water disposal. Eventually Greenpeace admitted its evidence was flawed but by that time Shell had lost the public relations battle and had altered its plans.

Operations principle

Subjective estimates of failure probability are better than no estimates at all.

Critical commentary

The idea that failure can be detected through in-process inspection is increasingly seen as only partially true. Although inspecting for failures is an obvious first step in detecting them, it is not even close to being 100 per cent reliable. Accumulated evidence from research and practical examples consistently indicates that people, even when assisted by technology, are not good at detecting failure and errors. This applies even when special attention is being given to inspection. For example, airport security was significantly strengthened after 11 September 2001, yet one in ten lethal weapons that were entered into airports' security systems (in order to test them) were not detected. *'There is no such thing as 100 per cent security, we are all human beings,'* said one airport security expert. No one is advocating abandoning inspection as a failure detection mechanisms. Rather it is seen as one of a range of methods of preventing failure.

Failure mode and effect analysis

Having identified potential sources of failure (either in advance of an event or through post-failure analysis) and having then examined the likelihood of these failures occurring through some combination of objective and subjective analysis, managers can move to assigning relative priorities to risk. The most well-known approach for doing this is failure mode and effect analysis (FMEA). Its objective is to identify the factors that are critical to various types of failure as a means of identifying failures before they happen. It does this by providing a 'checklist' procedure built around three key questions for each possible cause of failure:

▶ What is the likelihood that failure will occur?
▶ What would the consequence of the failure be?
▶ How likely is such a failure to be detected before it affects the customer?

Based on a quantitative evaluation of these three questions, a risk priority number (RPN) is calculated for each potential cause of failure. Corrective actions, aimed at preventing failure, are then applied to those causes whose RPN indicates that they warrant priority (see Figure 18.7).

How can failures be prevented?

Failure prevention is an important responsibility for operations managers. The obvious way to do this is to systematically examine any processes involved and 'design out' any failure points. Many of the approaches used in Chapter 4 on product/service innovation, Chapter 6 on process design and Chapter 17 on quality management can be used to do this. In this section, we will look at three further approaches to reducing risk by trying to prevent failure: building redundancy into a process in case of failure, 'fail-safeing' some of the activities in the process, and maintaining the physical facilities in the process.

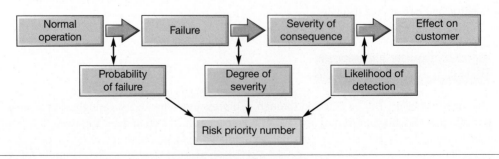

Figure 18.7 Procedure for failure modes effects analysis (FMEA)

Worked example

Part of an FMEA exercise at a transportation company has identified three failure modes associated with the failure of 'goods arriving damaged' at the point of delivery:

▶ Goods not secured (failure mode 1)

▶ Goods incorrectly secured (failure mode 2)

▶ Goods incorrectly loaded (failure mode 3).

The improvement group which is investigating the failures allocates scores for the probability of the failure mode occurring, the severity of each failure mode, and the likelihood that they will be detected, using the rating scales shown in Table 18.1, as follows:

Probability of occurrence

Failure mode 1	5
Failure mode 2	8
Failure mode 3	7

Severity of failure

Failure mode 1	6
Failure mode 2	4
Failure mode 3	4

Probability of detection

Failure mode 1	2
Failure mode 2	6
Failure mode 3	7

The RPN of each failure mode is calculated:

Failure mode 1 (goods not secured)	$5 \times 6 \times 2 = 60$
Failure mode 2 (goods incorrectly secured)	$8 \times 4 \times 5 = 160$
Failure mode 3 (goods incorrectly loaded)	$7 \times 4 \times 7 = 196$

Priority is therefore given to failure mode 3 (goods incorrectly loaded) when attempting to eliminate the failure.

Table 18.1 Rating scales for FMEA

A. Occurrence of failure		
Description	*Rating*	*Possible failure occurrence*
Remote probability of occurrence	1	0
It would be unreasonable to expect failure to occur		
Low probability of occurrence	2	1:20,000
Generally associated with activities similar to previous ones with a relatively low number of failures	3	1:10,000
Moderate probability of occurrence	4	1:2,000
Generally associated with activities similar to previous	5	1:1,000
ones which have resulted in occasional failures	6	1:200
High probability of occurrence	7	1:100

▶

A. Occurrence of failure		
Description	Rating	Possible failure occurrence
Generally associated with activities similar to ones which have traditionally caused problems	8	1:20
Very high probability of occurrence	9	1:10
Near certainty that major failures will occur	10	1:2

B. Severity of failure	
Description	Rating
Minor severity	1
A very minor failure which would have no noticeable effect on system performance	
Low severity	2
A minor failure causing only slight customer annoyance	3
Moderate severity	4
A failure which would cause some customer dissatisfaction, discomfort or annoyance, or would cause noticeable deterioration in performance	5
	6
High severity	7
A failure which would engender a high degree of customer dissatisfaction	8
Very high severity	9
A failure which would affect safety	
Catastrophic	10
A failure which may cause damage to property, serious injury or death	

C. Detection of failure		
Description	Rating	Probability of detection
Remote probability that the defect will reach the customer	1	0 to 5%
(It is unlikely that such a defect would pass through inspection, test or assembly)		
Low probability that the defect will reach the customer	2	6 to 15%
	3	16 to 25%
Moderate probability that the defect will reach the customer	4	26 to 35%
	5	36 to 45%
	6	46 to 55%
High probability that the defect will reach the customer	7	56 to 65%
	8	66 to 75%
Very high probability that the defect will reach the customer	9	76 to 85%
	10	86 to 100%

Redundancy

Building in redundancy to an operation means having back-up systems or components in case of failure. It can be expensive and is generally used when the breakdown could have a critical impact. Redundancy means doubling or even tripling some parts of a process or system in case one component fails. Nuclear power stations, spacecraft and hospitals all have auxiliary systems in case of an emergency. Some organizations also have 'back-up' staff held in reserve in case someone does not turn up for work. Spacecraft have several back-up computers on board that will not only monitor the main computer but also act as a back-up in case of failure.

One response to the threat of large failures, such as terrorist activity, has been a rise in the number of companies (known as 'business continuity' providers) offering 'replacement office' operations, fully equipped with normal internet and telephone communications links, and often with access to a company's current management information. Should a customer's main operation be affected by a disaster, business can continue in the replacement facility within days or even hours.

The effect of redundancy can be calculated by the sum of the reliability of the original process component and the likelihood that the back-up component will both be needed and be working.

$$R_{a+b} = R_a + (R_b \times P(\text{failure}))$$

> **Operations principle**
> Redundancy is an important failure prevention method, especially when the consequences of failure could be serious.

where

R_{a+b} = reliability of component a with its back-up component b

R_a = reliability of a alone

R_b = reliability of back-up component b

$P(\text{failure})$ = the probability that component a will fail and therefore component b will be needed

Redundancy is often used for servers, where system availability is particularly important. In this context, the industry uses three main types of redundancy.

▶ Hot standby – where both primary and secondary (backup) systems run simultaneously. The data are copied to the secondary server in real time so that both systems contain identical information.
▶ Warm standby – where the secondary system runs in the background to the primary system. Data are copied to the secondary server at regular intervals, so there are times when both servers do not contain exactly the same data.
▶ Cold standby – where the secondary system is only called upon when the primary system fails. The secondary system receives scheduled data backups, but less frequently than a warm standby, so cold standby is mainly used for non-critical applications.

Worked example

An e-auction provider has two servers, one of which will come online if the first server fails. If each server has a reliability of 90 per cent, the two working together will have a reliability of:
$$0.9 + [0.9 \times (1 - 0.09)] = 0.99$$

Fail-safeing

The concept of fail-safeing has emerged since the introduction of Japanese methods of operations improvement. Called poka-yoke in Japan (from *yokeru* (to prevent) and *poka* (inadvertent errors)), the idea is based on the principle that human mistakes are to some extent

> **Operations principle**
> Simple methods of fail-safeing can often be the most cost effective.

OVH regrets its lack of redundancy[6]

In the aggressively competitive cloud services market a reputation for service reliability is vital. So, when OHV, the quickly growing French cloud provider, suffered a power outage that brought down its entire Strasbourg campus, it was a serious blow to the company's reputation. The outage caused prolonged disruption to customer applications, and lasted throughout the day and well into the evening. The Strasbourg site was without power for three and a half hours. But even after power was restored, it took OVH staff many hours to restart servers and restore applications.

OVH servers, which the company builds itself, apparently experienced hardware failure as a result of the outage. Almost immediately, a team in the company's base in Roubaix (500 km from Strasbourg) loaded a truck with spare parts and sent it to Strasbourg, with technicians working well into the night to replace parts and boot up computers. The company's founder and CEO Octave Klaba said, '*This is probably the worst-case scenario that could have happened to us.*' He admitted that OVH was ultimately responsible for the outage by not being 'paranoid' enough. '*Uptime is a matter of design that must consider every eventuality, including when nothing else works. OVH must make sure to be even more paranoid than it already is in every system that it designs.*' Data centres usually minimize the chances of power failures by building in redundancy in their power supply. But on the Strasbourg site, the entire site was fed by one 20KV utility feed, as opposed to the standard practice of having two redundant feeds, often from two separate electrical grids. In fact, OVH uses redundant utility feeds and separate power grids for individual data centres on its other campuses, but not in Strasbourg, where two of the buildings are on the same grid. After the incident OVH decided to install a second utility feed for the campus and put buildings on separate power grids.

inevitable. What is important is to prevent them becoming defects. Poka-yokes are simple (preferably inexpensive) devices or systems which are incorporated into a process to prevent inadvertent mistakes by those providing service as well as customers receiving a service. Examples of poka-yokes include:

▶ trays used in hospitals with indentations shaped to each item needed for a surgical procedure – any item not back in place at the end of the procedure might have been left in the patient;
▶ checklists which have to be filled in, either in preparation for, or on completion of, an activity, such as a maintenance checklist for a plane during turnaround;
▶ gauges placed on machines through which a part has to pass in order to be loaded onto, or taken off, the machine – an incorrect size or orientation stops the process;
▶ the locks on aircraft lavatory doors, which must be turned to switch the light on;
▶ beepers on ATMs to ensure that customers remove their cards or in cars to remind drivers to take their keys with them;
▶ limit switches on machines which allow the machine to operate only if the part is positioned correctly;
▶ height bars on amusement rides to ensure that customers do not exceed size limitations.

Maintenance

Maintenance is how organizations try to avoid failure by taking care of their physical facilities. It is an important part of most operations' activities particularly in operations dominated by their physical facilities such as power stations, hotels, airlines and petrochemical refineries. The benefits of effective maintenance include enhanced safety, increased reliability, higher quality (badly maintained equipment is more likely to cause errors), lower operating costs (because regularly serviced process technology is more efficient), a longer life span for process technology, and higher 'end value' (because well-maintained facilities are generally easier to dispose of into the second-hand market).

The three basic approaches to maintenance

In practice an organization's maintenance activities will consist of some combination of the three basic approaches to the care of its physical facilities. These are run to breakdown (RTB), preventive maintenance (PM) and condition-based maintenance (CBM).

▶ *Run to breakdown maintenance (RTB)* – As its name implies, this involves allowing the facilities to continue operating until they fail. Maintenance work is performed only after failure has taken place. For example, the televisions, bathroom equipment and telephones in a hotel's guest rooms will probably only be repaired when they fail. The hotel will keep some spare parts and the staff available to make any repairs when needed. Failure in these circumstances is neither catastrophic (although perhaps irritating to the guest) nor so frequent as to make regular checking of the facilities appropriate.

▶ *Preventive maintenance (PM)* – This attempts to eliminate or reduce the chances of failure by servicing (cleaning, lubricating, replacing and checking) the facilities at pre-planned intervals. For example, the engines of passenger aircraft are checked, cleaned and calibrated according to a regular schedule after a set number of flying hours. Taking aircraft away from their regular duties for preventive maintenance is clearly an expensive option for any airline. The consequences of failure while in service are considerably more serious, however. The principle is also applied to facilities with less catastrophic consequences of failure. The regular cleaning and lubricating of machines, even the periodic painting of a building, could be considered preventive maintenance.

▶ *Condition-based maintenance (CBM)* – This attempts to perform maintenance only when the facilities require it. For example, continuous process equipment, such as that used in coating photographic paper, is run for long periods in order to achieve the high utilization necessary for cost-effective production. Stopping the machine to change, say, a bearing when it is not strictly necessary to do so would take it out of action for long periods and reduce its utilization. Here condition-based maintenance might involve continuously monitoring the vibrations, for example, or some other characteristic of the line.

How much maintenance?

The balance between preventive and breakdown maintenance is usually set to minimize the total cost of breakdown. Infrequent preventive maintenance will cost little to provide but will result in a high likelihood (and therefore cost) of breakdown maintenance. Conversely, very frequent preventive maintenance will be expensive to provide but will reduce the cost of having to provide breakdown maintenance (see Figure 18.8(a)). The total cost of maintenance appears to minimize at an 'optimum' level of preventive maintenance. However, the cost of providing preventive maintenance may not increase quite so steeply as indicated in Figure 18.8(a). The curve assumes that it is carried out by a separate set of people (skilled maintenance staff) from the 'operators' of the facilities. Furthermore, every time preventive maintenance takes place, the facilities cannot be used productively. This is why the slope of the curve increases, because the maintenance episodes start to interfere with the normal working of the operation. But in many operations some preventive maintenance can be performed by the operators themselves (which reduces the cost of providing it) and at times which are convenient for the operation (which minimizes the disruption to the operation). The cost of breakdowns could also be higher than is indicated in Figure 18.8(a). Unplanned breakdowns may do more than necessitate a repair and stop the operation; they can take away stability from the operation which prevents it being able to improve itself. Put these two ideas together and the minimizing total curve and maintenance cost curve look more like Figure 18.8(b). The emphasis is shifted more towards the use of preventive maintenance than run-to-breakdown maintenance.

Total productive maintenance

Total productive maintenance (TPM) is 'the productive maintenance carried out by all employees through small group activities', where productive maintenance is *maintenance management which recognizes the importance of reliability, maintenance and economic efficiency in plant design'.*[7] In Japan, where TPM originated, it is seen as a natural extension in the evolution from run-to-breakdown to preventive maintenance. TPM adopts some of the team-working and empowerment principles discussed in Chapter 9, as well as a continuous improvement approach to failure prevention as discussed in Chapter 16. It also sees maintenance as an organization-wide issue, to which staff can contribute in some way. It is analogous to the total quality management approach discussed in Chapter 17.

The five goals of TPM

TPM aims to establish good maintenance practice in operations through the pursuit of 'the five goals of TPM':

1 Improve equipment effectiveness by examining all the losses which occur.
2 Achieve autonomous maintenance by allowing staff to take responsibility for some of the maintenance tasks and for the improvement of maintenance performance.
3 Plan maintenance with a fully worked-out approach to all maintenance activities.
4 Train all staff in relevant maintenance skills so that both maintenance and operating staff have all the skills to carry out their roles.
5 Achieve early equipment management by 'maintenance prevention' (MP), which involves considering failure causes and the maintainability of equipment during its design, manufacture, installation and commissioning.

How can operations mitigate the effects of failure?

Even when a failure has occurred, its impact on the customer can, in many cases, be minimized through mitigation actions. Failure (or risk) mitigation means isolating a failure from its negative consequences. It is an admission that not all failures can be avoided. Mitigation can be vital when used in conjunction with prevention to reduce overall risk. One way of thinking about mitigation is as a series of decisions under conditions of uncertainty.

> **Operations principle**
>
> Failure (or risk) mitigation means isolating a failure from its negative consequences.

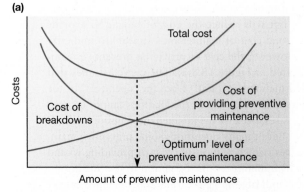
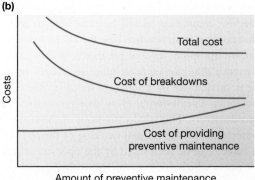

Figure 18.8 Two views of maintenance costs. (a) One model of the costs associated with preventive maintenance shows an optimum level of maintenance effort. (b) If routine preventive maintenance tasks are carried out by operators and if the real cost of breakdowns is considered, the 'optimum' level of preventive maintenance shifts toward higher levels

Critical commentary

Table 18.2 The cost per life saved of various safety (failure prevention) investments

Safety investment	Cost per life (€M)
Advanced train protection system	30
Train protection warning systems	7.5
Implementing recommended guidelines on rail safety	4.7
Implementing recommended guidelines on road safety	1.6
Local authority spending on road safety*	0.15

As previously discussed, being human, managers often respond to the perception of risk rather than its reality. For example, Table 18.2 shows the cost of each life saved by investment in various road and rail transportation safety (in other words, failure prevention) investments. The table shows that investing in improving road safety is very much more effective than investing in rail safety. And while no one is arguing for abandoning efforts on rail safety, it is noted by some transportation authorities that actual investment reflects more the public perception of rail deaths (low) compared with road deaths (very high).

Failure mitigation actions

The nature of the action taken to mitigate failure will obviously depend on the nature of the risk. In most industries technical experts have established a classification of failure mitigation actions that are appropriate for the types of failure likely to be suffered. So, for example, in agriculture, government agencies and industry bodies have published mitigation strategies for such risks as the outbreak of crop disease, contagious animal infections and so on. Likewise, governments have different contingency plans in place to deal with the spread of major health risks such as the H1N1 and H7Np influenza viruses and an Ebola outbreak in West Africa. Such documents will outline the various mitigation actions that can be taken under different circumstances and detail exactly who are responsible for each action. Although these classifications tend to be industry specific, the following generic categorization gives a flavour of the types of mitigation actions that may be generally applicable.

▶ *Mitigation planning* – This is the activity of ensuring that all possible failure circumstances have been identified and the appropriate mitigation actions identified. It is the overarching activity that encompasses all subsequent mitigation actions, and may be described in the form of a decision tree or guide rules. It is worth noting that mitigation planning, as well as being an overarching action, also provides mitigation action in its own right. For example, if mitigation planning has identified appropriate training, job design, emergency procedures and so on, then the financial liability of a business for any losses should a failure occur will be reduced. Certainly, businesses that have not planned adequately for failures will be more liable in law for any subsequent losses.
▶ *Economic mitigation* – This includes actions such as insurance against losses from failure, spreading the financial consequences of failure, and 'hedging' against failure. Insurance is the best known of these actions and is widely adopted, although ensuring appropriate insurance and effective claims management is a specialized skill in itself. Hedging often takes the form of financial instruments: for example, a business may purchase a financial 'hedge' against the price risk of a vital raw material deviating significantly from a set price.
▶ *Containment (spatial)* – This means stopping the failure physically spreading to affect other parts of an internal or external supply network. Preventing contaminated food from spreading through

the supply chain, for example, will depend on real-time information systems that provide traceability data.

▶ *Containment (temporal)* – This means containing the spread of a failure over time. It particularly applies when information about a failure or potential failure needs to be transmitted without undue delay. For example, systems that give advanced warning of hazardous weather such as snow storms must transmit such information to local agencies such as the police and road clearing organizations in time for them to stop the problem causing excessive disruption.

▶ *Loss reduction* – This covers any action that reduces the catastrophic consequences of failure by removing the resources that are likely to suffer those consequences. For example, the road signs that indicate evacuation routes in the event of severe weather, or the fire drills that train employees in how to escape in the event of an emergency, may not reduce all the consequences of failure, but can help in reducing loss of life or injury.

▶ *Substitution* – This means compensating for failure by providing other resources that can substitute for those rendered less effective by the failure. It is a little like the concept of redundancy that was described earlier, but does not always imply excess resources if a failure has not occurred. For example, in a construction project, the risk of encountering unexpected geological problems may be mitigated by the existence of a separate work plan that is invoked only if such problems are found.

How can operations recover from the effects of failure?

Failure recovery is the set of actions that are taken to reduce the impact of failure once the customer has experienced its negative effects. Recovery needs to be planned and procedures put in place that can discover when failures have occurred, guide appropriate action to keep everyone informed, capture the lessons learnt from the failure, and plan to absorb lessons into any future recovery. All types of operation can benefit from well-planned recovery. For example, a construction company whose mechanical digger breaks down can have plans in place to arrange a replacement from a hire company. The breakdown might be disruptive, but not as much as it might have been if the operations manager had not worked out what to do. Recovery procedures will also shape customers' perceptions of failure.

Even where the customer sees a failure, it may not necessarily lead to dissatisfaction. Indeed, in many situations, customers may well accept that things do go wrong. If there is a metre of snow on the train lines, or if the restaurant is particularly popular, we may accept that the product or service does not work. It is not necessarily the failure itself that leads to dissatisfaction but often the organization's response to the breakdown. While mistakes may be inevitable, dissatisfied customers are not. A failure may even be turned into a positive experience. A good recovery can turn angry, frustrated customers into loyal ones.

> **Operations principle**
>
> Successful failure recovery can yield more benefits than if the failure had not occurred.

The complaint value chain

The complaint value chain, shown in Figure 18.9, helps us to visualize the potential value of good recovery at different stages. In Figure 18.9(a) an operation provides service to 5,000 customers, but 20 per cent experience some form of failure. Of these 1,000 customers, 40 per cent decide not to complain, perhaps because it seems like more trouble than it's worth or because the complaint processes are too convoluted. Evidence suggests that around 80 per cent of these non-complainers will switch to an alternative service provider. (Of course, the precise switching percentage will depend on the number of alternatives in the market and the ease of switching.) Another group of the 1,000 customers who experienced a failure do decide to complain, in this case 60 per cent. Some will be satisfied (in this case, 75 per cent) and others will not be (in this case, 25 per cent). Dissatisfied complainers will generally leave the organization (in this case, 80 per cent), while satisfied complainers will tend to remain loyal (in this case, 80 per cent). So, assuming these percentages are correct, for every 5,000 customers processed by this particular service operation, 530 will switch.

Now let us assume that the operations manager decides to invest in small improvements to all stages in the complain value chain. In Figure 18.9(b) the company has reduced its failures from 20 to 18 per cent (still very poor of course!); and has encouraged more customers who experienced a failure to come forward and complain. So the percentage complaining has risen from 60 per cent to 70 per cent. It has also made sure that a higher proportion (in this case, up from 75 to 83 per cent) of those who do make the effort to complain are satisfied. The end result is that the number of lost customers falls from 530 to 406. Assuming that the extra 124 customers retained have a value that is equal to, or more than, the costs of improvements, the organization is making a good investment in its recovery and prevention efforts. What is important to understand here is how a relatively small improvement across the failure and complaint process can have such a significant impact on customer loyalty and switching.

Operations principle

The complaint value chain helps to visualize the potential value of good recovery at different stages.

Failure planning

Organizations need to design appropriate responses to failure that are suitably aligned with the cost and the inconvenience caused by the failure to their customers. Such recovery processes need to be carried out either by empowered front-line staff or by trained personnel who are available to deal with recovery in a way which does not interfere with day-to-day service activities. Figure 18.10 illustrates a typical recovery sequence. It is often represented by stage models, one of which is represented in Figure 18.10. We shall follow it through from the point where failure is recognized.

▶ **Discover** – The first thing any manager needs to do when faced with a failure is to discover its exact nature. Three important pieces of information are needed: first of all, what exactly has

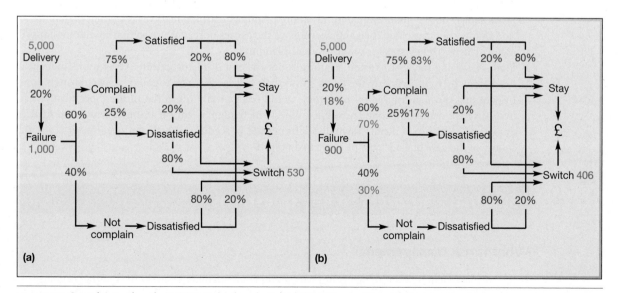

Figure 18.9 Complaint value chain (a) initial value chain and (b) with small improvements to each step

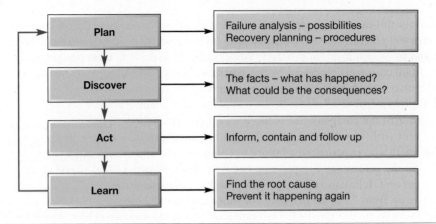

Figure 18.10 Recovery sequence for minimizing the impact from failure

happened; second, who will be affected by the failure; and, third, why did the failure occur? This last point is not intended to be a detailed inquest into the causes of failure (that comes later) but it is often necessary to know something of the causes of failure in case it is necessary to determine what action to take.

▶ **Act** – The discover stage might only take minutes or even seconds, depending on the severity of the failure. If the failure is a severe one with important consequences, we need to move on to doing something about it quickly. This means carrying out three actions, the first two of which could be carried out in reverse order, depending on the urgency of the situation. First, tell the significant people involved what you are proposing to do about the failure. In service operations this is especially important where customers need to be kept informed, both for their peace of mind and to demonstrate that something is being done. Second, the effects of the failure need to be contained in order to stop the consequences spreading and causing further failures. The precise containment actions will depend on the nature of the failure. Third, there needs to be some kind of follow-up to make sure that the containment actions really have contained the failure.

▶ **Learn** – As discussed earlier in this chapter, the benefits of failure in providing learning opportunities should not be underestimated. In failure planning, learning involves revisiting the failure to find out its root cause and then engineering out the causes of the failure so that it will not happen again. This is the key stage for much failure planning.

▶ **Plan** – Learning the lessons from a failure is not the end of the procedure. Operations managers need formally to incorporate the lessons into their future reactions to failures. This is often done by working through 'in theory' how they would react to failures in the future. Specifically, this involves first identifying all the possible failures which might occur (in a similar way to the FMEA approach). Second, it means formally defining the procedures which the organization should follow in the case of each type of identified failure.

Summary answers to key questions

What is risk management?

▶ Risk management is about things going wrong and what operations can do to stop things going wrong. Or, more formally, 'the process which aims to help organizations understand, evaluate and take action on all their risks with a view to increasing the probability of their success and reducing the likelihood of failure'.

- It consists of four broad activities:
  - Understanding what failures could occur.
  - Preventing failures occurring.
  - Minimizing the negative consequences of failure (called risk 'mitigation').
  - Recovering from failures when they do occur.

How can operations assess the potential causes and consequences of failure?

- There are several causes of failure including design failures, facilities failure, staff failure, supplier failure, cyber failure, customer failure and environmental disruption.

- There are three ways of measuring failure. 'Failure rates' indicate how often a failure is likely to occur. 'Reliability' measures the chances of a failure occurring. 'Availability' is the amount of available and useful operating time left after taking account of failures.

- Failure over time is often represented as a failure curve. The most common form of this is the so-called 'bath-tub curve' which shows the chances of failure as being greater at the beginning and end of the life of a system or part of a system.

- Failure analysis mechanisms include accident investigation, product liability, complaint analysis, critical incident analysis, and failure mode and effect analysis (FMEA).

How can failures be prevented?

- There are four major methods of improving reliability: designing out the fail points in the operation, building redundancy into the operation, 'fail-safeing' some of the activities of the operation, and maintenance of the physical facilities in the operation.

- Maintenance is the most common way operations attempt to improve their reliability, with three broad approaches. The first is running all facilities until they break down and then repairing them, the second is regularly maintaining the facilities even if they have not broken down, and the third is to monitor facilities closely to try to predict when breakdown might occur.

- Total productive maintenance, where all employees carry out maintenance in small groups, is a particularly useful approach to managing maintenance.

How can operations mitigate the effects of failure?

- Risk, or failure, mitigation means isolating a failure from its negative consequences.

- Risk mitigation actions include:
  - Mitigation planning
  - Economic mitigation
  - Containment (spatial and temporal)
  - Loss reduction
  - Substitution.

How can operations recover from the effects of failure?

- Recovery can be enhanced by a systematic approach to discovering what has happened to cause failure, acting to inform, contain and follow up the consequences of failure, learning to find the root cause of the failure and preventing it taking place again, and planning to avoid the failure occurring in the future.

Slagelse Industrial Services (SIS)

Slagelse Industrial Services (SIS) had become one of Europe's most respected die casters of zinc, aluminium and magnesium parts for hundreds of companies in many industries, especially automotive and defence. The company cast and engineered precision components by combining the most modern production technologies with precise tooling and craftsmanship. SIS began life as a classic family firm run by Erik Paulsen, who opened a small manufacturing and die-casting business in his hometown of Slagelse, a town in east Denmark, about 100 km southwest of Copenhagen. He had successfully leveraged his skills and passion for craftsmanship over many years while serving a variety of different industrial and agricultural customers. His son, Anders, had spent nearly 10 years working as a production engineer for a large automotive parts supplier in the UK, but eventually returned to Slagelse to take over the family firm. Exploiting his experience in mass manufacturing, Anders spent years building the firm into a larger- scale industrial component manufacturer but retained his father's commitment to quality and customer service. After 20 years he sold the firm to a UK-owned industrial conglomerate and within ten years it had doubled in size again and now employed in the region of 600 people and had a turnover approaching £200 million. Throughout this period the firm had continued to target its products into niche industrial markets where its emphasis upon product quality and dependability meant they it was vulnerable to price and cost pressures. However, in 2009, in the midst of difficult economic times and widespread industrial restructuring, it had been encouraged to bid for higher volume, lower margin work. This process was not very successful but eventually culminated in a tender for the design and production of a core metallic element of a child's toy (a 'transforming' robot).

Interestingly the client firm, Alden Toys, was also a major customer for other businesses owned by SIS's corporate parent. It was adopting a preferred supplier policy and intended to have only one or two purchase points for specific elements in its global toy business. It had a high degree of trust in the parent organization and on visiting the SIS site was impressed by the firm's depth of experience and commitment to quality. In 2010, it selected SIS to complete the design and begin trial production.

'Some of us were really excited by the prospect . . . but you have to be a little worried when volumes are much greater than anything you've done before. I guess the risk seemed okay because in the basic process steps, in the type of product if you like, we were making something that felt very similar to what we'd been doing for many years' (SIS Operations Manager).

'Well obviously we didn't know anything about the toy market but then again we didn't really know all that much about the auto industry or the defence sector or any of our traditional customers before we started serving them. Our key competitive advantage, our capabilities, call it what you will, they are all about keeping the customer happy, about meeting and sometimes exceeding specification' (SIS Marketing Director).

The designers had received an outline product specification from Alden Toys during the bid process and some further technical detail afterwards. Upon receipt of this final brief, a team of engineers and managers confirmed that the product could and would be manufactured using an up-scaled version of current production processes. The key operational challenge appeared to be accessing sufficient (but not too much) capacity. Fortunately, for a variety of reasons, the parent company was very supportive of the project and promised to underwrite any sensible capital expenditure plans. Although this opinion of the nature of the production challenge was widely accepted throughout the firm (and shared by Alden Toys and SIS'sparent group), it was left to one specific senior engineer to actually sign both the final bid and technical completion documentation. By early 2011, the firm had begun a trial period of full volume production. Unfortunately, as would become clear later, during this design validation process SIS had effectively sanctioned a production method that would prove to be entirely inappropriate for the toy market but it was not until 12 months later that any indication of problems began to emerge.

Throughout both North America and Europe, individual customers began to claim that their children had been 'poisoned' whilst playing with the end product. The threat of litigation was quickly levelled at Alden Toys and the whole issue rapidly became a 'full-blown' child health scare. A range of pressure groups and legal damage specialists supported and acted to aggregate the individual claims. Although similar accusations had been made before, the litigants and their supporters focused in on the recent changes made to the production process at SIS and particular the role of Alden Toys in managing its suppliers. '. . . .It's all very well claiming that you trust your suppliers but you simply cannot have the same level of control over another firm in another country. I am afraid that this all comes down to simple economics, that Alden Toys put its profits before children's health. Talk about trust . . . parents trusted this firm to look out for them and their families and have every right to be angry that boardroom greed was more important!' (legal spokesperson for US litigants when being interviewed on a UK TV consumer rights show).

Under intense media pressure, Alden Toys rapidly convened a high-profile investigation into the source of the contamination. It quickly revealed that an 'unauthorized' chemical had been employed in an apparently trivial metal cleaning and preparation element of the SIS production process. Although when interviewed by the US media, the parent firm's legal director emphasized there was 'no causal link established or any admission of liability by either party', Alden Toys immediately withdrew its order and began to signal an intent to bring legal action against SIS and its parent. This action brought an immediate end to production in this part of the operation and the inspection (and subsequent official and legal visits) had a crippling impact upon the productivity of the whole site. The competitive impact of the failure was extremely significant. After over a year of production, the new product accounted for more than a third (39 per cent) of the factory's output. In addition to major cash-flow implications, the various investigations took up lots of managerial time and the reputation of the firm was seriously affected. As the site operations manager explained, even their traditional customers expressed concerns. 'It's amazing but people we had been supplying for thirty or forty years were calling me up and asking '[Manager's name] what's going on?" and that they were worried about what all this might mean for them . . . these are completely different markets!'

QUESTIONS

1 What operational risks did SIS face when deciding to become a strategic supplier for Alden Toys?

2 What control problems did it encounter in implementing this strategy (pre and post investigation)?

Problems and applications

All chapters have 'Problems and applications' questions that will help you practise analysing operations. They can be answered by reading the chapter. Model answers for the first two questions can be found on the companion website for this book.

1   Although rare, air crashes do happen. Predominantly, the reason for this is human failure such as pilot fatigue. One kind of accident which is known as 'controlled flight into terrain', where the aircraft appears to be under control and yet still flies into the ground, has a chance of happening less than once in two million flights. To occur, a whole chain of minor failures must happen. The pilot at the controls has to be flying at the wrong altitude (one chance in a thousand). The co-pilot would have to fail to cross-check the altitude (one chance in a hundred). The air traffic controllers would have to miss the fact that the plane was at the wrong altitude (one-in-ten chance). Finally, the pilot would have to ignore the ground proximity warning alarm in the aircraft (which can be prone to give false alarms, a one-in-two chance). (a) What are your views on the quoted probabilities of each failure

described above occurring? (b) How would you try to prevent these failures occurring? (c) If the probability of each failure occurring could be reduced by a half, what would be the effect on the likelihood of this type of crash occurring?

2 Wyco is a leading international retailer selling clothing and accessories with stores throughout the world. The countries from which it sources its products include Sri Lanka, Bangladesh, India and Vietnam. It was shocked when a British newspaper reported that an unauthorized sub-contractor had used child workers to make some of its products at a factory in Delhi. In response Wyco immediately issued a statement.

   'Earlier this week, the company was informed about an allegation of child labour at a facility in India that was working on one product for Wyco. An investigation was immediately launched. The company noted that a very small portion of a particular order placed with one of its vendors was apparently sub-contracted to an unauthorized sub-contractor without the company's knowledge or approval. This is in direct violation of the company's agreement with the vendor under its Code of Vendor Conduct.'

   Wyco's CEO said, *'We strictly prohibit the use of child labour. This is a non-negotiable for us. Wyco has a history of addressing challenges like this head-on. Wyco ceased business with 20 factories due to code violations. We have 90 people located around the world whose job is to ensure compliance with our Code of Vendor Conduct. As soon as we were alerted, we stopped the work order and prevented the product from being sold in stores. While such violations are extremely rare, we have called an urgent meeting with our suppliers to reinforce our policies. Wyco has one of the industry's most comprehensive programmes in place to fight for workers' rights. We will continue to work with stakeholder organizations in an effort to end the use of child labour.'*

   (a) 'Being an ethical company isn't enough any more. These days, leading brands are judged by the company they keep.' What does this mean for Wyco? (b) When Wyco found itself with this supply chain problem, did it respond in the right way?

3 An Airbus A320 would not turn left no matter what the pilot tried. Eventually he made an emergency landing. Fortunately, no one was hurt. The cause of the near-disaster was that engineers had forgotten to reactivate four of the five spoilers on the right wing that help the plane to turn. The investigation blamed 'a chain of human errors', by the engineers and by the pilots who had failed to notice the problem before take-off. The A320 is a 'fly-by-wire' aircraft where computer-controlled electrical impulses activate the hydraulically powered spoilers and surfaces which control the movement of the plane. When the aircraft went for repair to a damaged flap, the engineers had put the spoilers into 'maintenance mode' to block them off from the controls. They had then forgotten to reactivate. According to the official report, the engineers were not guilty of *'simple acts of neglect or ignorance. Their approach implied that they believed there were benefits to the organization if they could successfully deliver the aircraft on time. With more complex aircraft, it is no longer possible for maintenance staff to understand all the consequences of any deviation. The avoidance of future accidents with high-technology aircraft depends on total compliance. If a check has been carried out numerous times without any fault being present, it is human nature to anticipate no fault when next the check is carried out.'* (a) Why should fly-by-wire aircraft pose a more complex maintenance problem than conventional aircraft which have a physical link between the control and the flaps? (b) If you were the accident investigator, what questions would you want to ask in order to understand why this failure occurred?

4 Re-read the 'Operations in practice' example 'It's the exception that proves the rule'. Do these examples invalidate the use of failure data in estimating component life?

5   An automated sandwich-making machine in a food manufacturer's factory has six major components, with individual reliabilities as shown in Table 18.3.

Table 18.3 Individual reliabilities of major components

Component	Reliability
Bread slicer	0.97
Butter applicator	0.96
Salad filler	0.94
Meat filler	0.92
Top slice of bread applicator	0.96
Wrapper	0.91

(a) What is the reliability of the whole system?
(b) If it is decided that the wrapper in the automated sandwich making machine is too unreliable and a second wrapper is needed which will come into action if the first one fails, what will happen to the reliability of the machine?

6   Every time we enter an elevator we are trusting our lives to the people who designed, made and maintain it. Without effective maintenance, elevators would literally be death traps. Otis, the elevator company, has its 'Otis Maintenance Management System' (OMMS), a programme that takes into account its clients' elevators' maintenance needs. Otis can customize inspection and maintenance schedules for up to 12 years of operation or 5 million trips in advance. Maintenance procedures are determined by each elevator's individual pattern of use, such as frequency of trips, loads carried and conditions of use. Otis also monitors the life cycle characteristics of all its elevators' components. This information on wear and failure is made available to its customers, and is used to update maintenance schedules. When an elevator has a problem, a technician can be on their way to a customer within minutes, 24 hours a day, 7 days a week. The service can get the elevators back in service on average within two and half hours. Otis monitors, collects, records, analyses and communicates hundreds of different system functions. If it detects a problem, it calls out a technician. 'Around-the-clock response is important,' says Otis, 'because problems, don't keep office hours. The remote sensing system identifies most potential problems before they occur.' (a) What could be the effects of failure in elevator systems? How does this explain the maintenance service that Otis offers its customers? (b) What approach(es) to maintenance are implied by the services that Otis offers? (c) How would you convince potential customers for these services that they are worthwhile?

7   Carlsberg, the brewing company, learnt of its crisis late one Friday afternoon. Something appeared to have gone wrong with the 'widget' (the device which gives some canned beer its creamy characteristic) in one of its cans of beer. One customer had found a piece of plastic in his mouth. He had complained to an environmental health official who had contacted the Carlsberg. The company's pre-planned crisis management procedure immediately swung into action. A crisis control group of 12 members, with experts on insurance, legal affairs, quality control and public relations, took control. This group had everyone's telephone number, so any relevant person in the company could be contacted. It also had a control room at one of the company's sites. By the Tuesday they had issued a press release, set up a hotline and taken out national advertising to

announce the recall decision. Even though the problem had originated in only one of its six brands, the company decided to recall all of them (a total of one million cans) and all production using the suspect widget was halted. (a) What seem to be the essential elements of this successful recovery from failure? (b) How do the advantages and disadvantages of deciding whether or not to recall products in a case such as this depend on the likelihood of another potential failure being out there in the market? (c) Relate this issue to the concept of type I and type II errors dealt with in Chapter 17.

Selected further reading

Hopkin, P. (2017) *Fundamentals of Risk Management: Understanding, Evaluating and Implementing Effective Risk Management,* 4th edn, Kogan Page, London.
A comprehensive introduction to risk with good coverage of many core frameworks.

Hubbard, D.W. (2009) *The Failure of Risk Management: Why It's Broken and How to Fix It,* Wiley, Chichester.
An interesting read, particularly for those who like the critical commentaries in this book! A polemic, but one that is clearly written.

Smith, D.J. (2011) *Reliability, Maintainability and Risk,* Butterworth-Heinemann, Oxford.
A comprehensive and excellent guide to all aspects of maintenance and reliability. The book has a good mix of qualitative and quantitative perspectives on the subject.

Waters, D. (2012) *Supply Chain Risk Management: Vulnerability and Resilience in Logistics,* 2nd edn, Chartered Institute of Logistics and Transportation, Corby.
Provides a very detailed and practical guide to considering risks within operations and supply chains.

19 Project management

INTRODUCTION

Recent years have seen a significant increase in the proportion of operations managers' time that is spent working on discrete projects as opposed to 'steady-state' activities – a trend sometimes referred to as 'projectification'. Yet, despite the increase in project-based activity for many operations and their supply networks, many projects are only partially successful. Not all projects are the same – they come in all shapes and sizes, with differences in scale, uncertainty, complexity, novelty, technology and pace. However, projects share key characteristics that make their management tasks broadly universal. First, managers must understand the fundamental characteristics of a project and their implications for successfully executing projects. Second, they must understand the project environment and manage key project stakeholders. Third, they must be able to define, plan and control projects through their life cycle, while balancing competing performance objectives and different (internal and external) stakeholder requirements. In this chapter, we examine: what projects are; the important role of project management for contemporary organizations; the different environments within which projects take place; and the way that projects are defined, planned, controlled and learnt from.
Figure 19.1 shows where project management fits in the overall model of operations management.

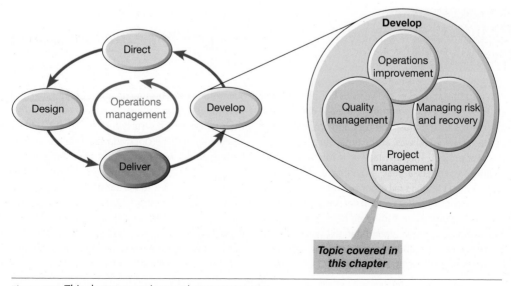

Figure 19.1 This chapter examines project management

What are projects?

A project is a set of activities with a defined start point and a defined end state, which pursues a defined goal and uses a defined set of resources. Technically many small-scale operations management endeavours, taking minutes or hours, conform to this definition of a project. However, in this chapter we will mainly focus on larger-scale projects, lasting months, years or even several decades. Although all projects have a defined goal, some of these will be part of a larger purpose. So, most operations improvement (even continuous improvement) can be seen as a series of overlapping 'mini-projects' that cumulatively contribute to a never-ending development effort. Likewise, organizational change projects often are contributing to a larger purpose. Research and development (R&D) projects sometimes have a specific application or product in mind, but often, if the research is more 'blue-sky', they won't. Capital goods and infrastructure projects, such as new buildings, railways, sports stadia and airports, do contribute to a larger social purpose (such as 'improving communications') but can be so large that they seem to stand alone. By contrast, some projects are relatively stand-alone in the sense that they are a 'one-off' in themselves. These are often projects that are focused on delivering a specific event, such as the Olympics. Naturally, these types of projects draw on other projects, such as capital goods and infrastructure, and organizational change.

It is also worth pointing out the distinction between 'projects' and 'programmes'. A programme, such as a continuous improvement programme, has no defined end point. Rather it is an on-going process of change. Individual projects may be individual subsections of an overall programme, but 'programme management' will overlay and integrate the individual projects. Generally, it is a more difficult task in the sense that it requires resource coordination, particularly when multiple projects share common resources.

Common features of projects

Projects have a number of common features. All projects are mission focused – that is, they are dedicated to achieving a specific goal that should be delivered within a set timeframe, to certain specifications, using a defined group of resources. The result is that project outcomes are unique or at least highly customized, involve many non-routine and complex tasks, and therefore face relatively high levels of risk and uncertainty when contrasted with higher-volume and lower-variety operations. It is these features that go some way to explaining why so many projects are only partially successful at best, with changed specifications (quality), severe delays (time), cost escalation (cost) and major disputes between key stakeholders being commonplace.

OPERATIONS IN PRACTICE | ## Crossrail – Europe's biggest infrastructure project[1]

It was an idea that took over 100 years to be approved and 10 years to complete – not surprisingly, the £14.8bn Crossrail project was one of the most complex and ambitious that London had known, and was, at the time, Europe's biggest infrastructure project. The new railway is forecast to carry 200 million passengers a year, providing a 10 per cent increase in central London's rail capacity, and more frequent and reliable train journeys for London's growing population. It will serve 40 stations, including eight new subsurface stations and two new above-ground stations, with 42 km of new tunnels, and using 200m-long new trains. Crossrail's eight tunnel boring machines, each weighing 1,000 tonnes,

spent three years burrowing under London to construct the new tunnels. It was a huge technical challenge. To construct the tunnels, which were completed in 2015, the machines worked around the clock, moving through ground already honeycombed with networks of sewer lines, water and gas mains, building foundations and London Underground tunnels dating back to the 1860s.

But the idea was not new. It first emerged during the 1880s when the UK government gave permission for the Regents Canal & Railway Company to create a surface line between west London and the busy dockland area in east London. The plan was discarded, but a similar idea

▶

control, and making sure the reporting regime was a true reflection of what was really happening. A succession of 'gateways' were also agreed. These were deadlines by which Crossrail Ltd was required to demonstrate it had met stages of completion. As the project progressed and gateways were passed, Crossrail was given more power to award large contracts itself.

Notwithstanding its management structure, the project was late and did exceed its original budget. But many did hale it as a technical success. However, others are more critical. Professor Gil of Manchester Business School argues that the project's governance structure failed to prevent the spending of £5bn of contingency funding that had been included in the budget (later reduced to £4bn). *'The spending of contingencies becomes a self-fulfilling prophecy that politicians and managers can't prevent. If there was less money for a project available at the beginning, it might focus the stakeholders' minds better.'* Some have suggested that the lesson from the decision to separate the sponsor group from the delivery company is that, for such large and complex infrastructure projects, civil servants should be kept well away from delivery. But that is not totally true, said James Stewart, chairman of global infrastructure at consultancy KPMG. *'The competencies required within Whitehall are not to run the day-to-day commercial procurements and project management, it is true. But there is a lot of skill in being a good client. You are monitoring the performance of the delivery body and not relying on their assurances that everything is fine. You are also managing the politics and policy environment.'*

re-emerged in 1944, only to be abandoned again. Through the 1990s the project was the subject of several policy changes and cost–benefit discussions, but it was not until 2008 that the project was finally approved, with construction starting in 2009.

The governance of the project was always seen as important. Responsibility for delivering the final project was given to Crossrail Ltd, an independent company with all of its shares owned by Transport for London (TfL). It reported to a 'sponsor group' that included representatives of TfL and government departments. The sponsor group was responsible for defining the scope of the project and holding the budget for the project. Crossrail Ltd had to work within the budget and manage the details of the project including scheduling and control activities, cost

Differentiating between projects

So far, we have described the *commonalities* of projects – temporary activities, with specific and highly customized goals, within time, cost and quality requirements, usually involving many non-routine and complex tasks. However, it is also critical to understand *differences* between projects. This is important because these differences play a critical role in subsequent project management challenges. We illustrate three complementary methods of distinguishing between different types of project:

▶ the volume and variety characteristics of a project;
▶ the scale, complexity and degree of uncertainty in the project;
▶ the novelty, complexity, nature of technology (if any) and 'pace' of the project.

We will deal with these methods in turn.

Operations principle

The difficulty of managing a project is a function of (a) its volume and variety characteristics; (b) its scale, complexity and uncertainty characteristics; and (c) its novelty, technology, complexity and pace characteristics.

Differentiating by projects' volume and variety characteristics

At a simple level, we can use the 'product–process' matrix, already explored in Chapter 6 of this book, to distinguish between projects based on their volume and variety characteristics. This is shown in Figure 19.2. Of course, all project processes are, by definition, in the top left corner of the matrix. But within that end of the 'natural diagonal' projects do vary. At the very top left-hand part of the matrix

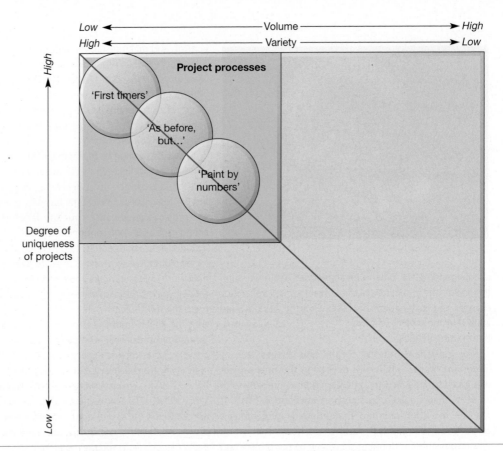

Figure 19.2 Differentiating projects using their volume and variety characteristics

are projects that are genuinely '*first timers*' with a very high degree of uniqueness, a volume of one and infinite variety. With less uniqueness, higher volume and less variety, '*as before, but. . .*' projects may in many ways share some of the attributes of previous projects, but may have new features where project managers have little or no previous experience to help guide them. With higher volume (therefore a greater degree of repetition) and lower variety, so-called '*paint by numbers*' projects are relatively routine and predictable, and therefore (generally) more straightforward to manage.

Differentiating by projects' scale, complexity and uncertainty characteristics

An alternative approach to distinguishing between projects is by considering their scale, complexity and uncertainty. This is shown in Figure 19.3. For example, a wedding planning project has (relatively) low levels of scale, complexity and uncertainty. The effect is that the management challenges of such a project are significantly different to developing the Airbus A380, which exhibited much higher levels of all three dimensions. The scale, complexity and uncertainty of such 'ground-breaking' projects demand far more sophisticated planning, greater and more flexible resources, and careful control if they are to be successful.

> **Operations principle**
>
> The difficulty of managing a project is a function of its scale, complexity and uncertainty.

Differentiating using novelty, technology, complexity and pace

Yet another alternative (and very useful) way to distinguish between projects is to consider their relative novelty, technology, complexity and pace. Using the scales and terminology developed by Aaron Shenhar and Dov Dvir,[2] Figure 19.4 illustrates the profile of two projects – the development of the Airbus A380 and the World Health Organization (WHO) malaria project.

▶ *The novelty dimension* – This is concerned with how new the outcome of the project is to the customers or users (i.e. the market). On this scale, a derivative project is one that extends or improves

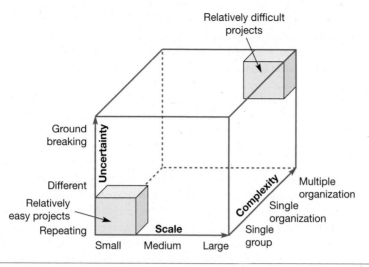

Figure 19.3 Differentiating projects by scale, complexity and uncertainty

an existing product, service or process: for example, developing a new version of a phone app. A platform project is one that develops or produces new generations of existing products, services or processes to serve existing markets: for example, building a new generation of car. A breakthrough project is one that introduces a totally new product or service, uses a new idea, or uses a product or service in a way that customers have never seen before: for example, introducing the very first iPad.

▶ *The technology dimension* – This is concerned with how much new technology is being used within the project. Low-technology projects have almost no new technology integrated, so designs can be 'frozen' (i.e. fixed) early on in the project. Medium-technology projects typically involve the integration of a single new technology, for example, the improvement of an existing product. This allows early design-freezes, but some testing, evaluation and corrections may be required as the project progresses. High-technology projects involve the integration of several new technologies and therefore must be flexible for a longer period of time to allow for integration and optimization. Finally, super high-technology projects involve the integration of several (currently) non-existing technologies. This takes extended periods to develop and prove new technologies, so design-freeze typically occurs very late in the project.

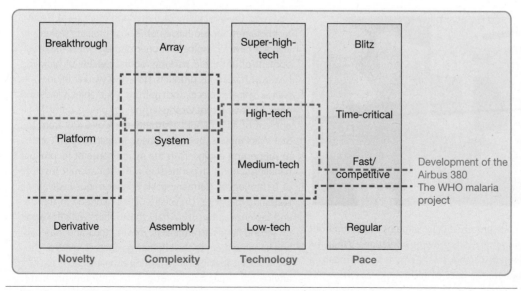

Figure 19.4 Differentiating projects using novelty, technology, complexity and pace (using example of the development of the Airbus 380 and the WHO malaria projects)

▶ *The complexity dimension* – This is concerned with how complex the system and its subsystems are. At the lowest level are 'assembly' projects, with self-contained 'components', or sub-projects that perform a function within a larger system. Examples may include developing a next-generation smartphone, creating a new undergraduate operations and process management module, or putting on a new play in a theatre. 'System' projects involve a collection of interactive elements and sub-elements. Examples include developing a new aircraft, constructing a new research and development facility, or developing a new portfolio of post-experience education within a university. Whilst the sub-elements of the project have a common goal, the added complexity creates significantly higher coordination and integration problems. Finally, 'array' projects are 'systems of systems' – with each system having an independent function, but each with a common goal. Heathrow's Terminal 5 project, with its 16 major projects and 147 sub-projects, is a good example of an array project. Another is the South-to-North water diversion project in China, a multi-decade infrastructural mega-project expected to be completed in 2050 at a cost of $62bn.

▶ *The pace dimension* – This is concerned with how critical the time frame of the project is. Pace is not simply about speed – some projects have urgency but last for many years; others are not urgent but last a few weeks. For example, in May 1961, President John F. Kennedy delivered a speech to the US Congress in which he stated, '*I believe that this nation should commit itself to achieving the goal, before this decade is out, of landing a man on the moon and returning him safely to the earth.*' In doing so, he set a time frame that was to be critical to the ambitions of the moon-landing project. Some projects are regular pace in that they are not time critical. Many public works and internal projects fall into this category. Others are fast/competitive in that the completion on time is important for competitive advantage and leadership. Many business-related projects, such as new product/service introductions and new capacity development in the face of market growth, fall into this category. Time-critical projects have a specific window of opportunity and delays mean project failure. The space launch and the Olympic games are examples of this kind of project. Finally, 'blitz' projects have the utmost urgency and often occur through crises such as war, response to natural disasters, and fast response to business surprises.

<table>
<tr><td>OPERATIONS IN
PRACTICE</td><td>Artificial intelligence project at Ocado[3]</td></tr>
</table>

Ocado, the online grocery retailer, remains at the forefront of technology to support its growing operations. While the use of automated warehouse systems is by no means a new phenomenon, the pace of technology adoption has risen sharply in recent years as a result of both rising labour costs and the availability of better and more cost-effective technologies. Ocado has a number of projects seeking to leverage new technological opportunities. One is the development of advanced packing robots, capable of handling heavy or hazardous products (to avoid worker injuries) as well as delicate objects, such as fruits, vegetables, salads and eggs. Another recent Ocado technology project is the development of a humanoid assistant (think of C_3PO from the Star Wars movies, but with wheels instead of legs!) aimed at supporting engineers in the maintenance of its product handling systems. In partnership with the Karlsruhe Institute of Technology in Germany, Ecole Polytechnique Fédérale de Lausanne in France, University College London in the UK, and Sapienza University in Italy, these robots will offer a pair of 'second hands' to engineers, moving tools and materials, and handing them to their human partners as needed. They will also be capable of interrupting human actions to offer advice on alternative solutions to common problems. According to Ocado, the aim is to create a '*fluid and natural*

interaction between robot and technician'. The project points to the continually changing nature of the workplace, as technology is increasingly integrated within most tasks.

It also highlights the value (and challenges) of bringing different areas of expertise from geographically dispersed partners in order to deliver project success.

What is project management?

It is not only the innate complexity of projects that leads to many failing, it is also the lack of effective project management. Project management is the activity of defining, planning and executing projects of any type. The key stages in this process include:

Stage 1 Understanding the project environment – internal and external factors which may influence the project.

Stage 2 Defining the project – setting the objectives, scope and strategy for the project.

Stage 3 Project planning – deciding how the project will be executed.

Stage 4 Technical execution – performing the technical aspects of the project.

Stage 5 Project control – ensuring that the project is carried out according to plan.

Stage 6 Learning – reviewing project performance in order to improve future projects.

In the following sections of this chapter, we deal with each of these stages in turn with the exception of Stage 4. The technical execution of the project is determined by the specific technicalities of individual projects, so is beyond the remit of the chapter. While these stages are presented sequentially, it is important to understand that project management is essentially an *iterative* process. Problems or changes that become evident in project control, for example, may require re-planning and may even cause modifications to the original project definition.

Going beyond the 'life cycle perspective' described above, project management is also concerned with effectively balancing quality/deliverables, time and cost objectives within the so-called 'iron triangle' (of quality, time and cost). Finally, from an organizational perspective, project management involves managing these life cycles and performance objectives across multiple functions within an organization. The activity of project management is very broad in so much as it could encompass almost all the operations management tasks described in this book. Partly because of this, it could have been treated almost anywhere within its direct, design, delivery, develop structure. We have chosen to place it in the context of operations development because the majority of projects that managers will be engaged in are essentially improvement projects. Of course, many projects are vast enterprises with very high levels of resourcing, complexity and uncertainty that will extend over many years. Look around you at the civil engineering, social, political and environmental successes (and failures) to see the evidence of major projects. Such projects require professional project management involving high-level technical expertise and management skills. But, so do the smaller, yet important, projects that implement the many and continuous improvements that will determine the strategic impact of operations development. This is why it is equally important to take a rigorous and systematic approach to managing projects regardless of their size and type.

In order to coordinate the efforts of many people in different parts of the organization (and often outside it as well), all projects need a project manager. Many of a project manager's activities are concerned with managing human resources. The people working in the project team need a clear understanding of their roles in the (usually temporary) organization. Controlling an uncertain project environment requires the rapid exchange of relevant information with the project stakeholders, both within and outside the organization. People, equipment and other resources must be identified and allocated to the various tasks. Undertaking these tasks successfully makes the management of a project a particularly challenging operations activity. Over the last decade, there have been significant moves towards professionalising project management. More of those leading projects hold professional qualifications and many organizations now treat the activity as a critical function for success.

Halting the growth of malaria[4]

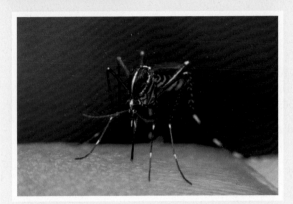

In 2000 the World Health Organization (WHO) set a challenging objective – to halt the growth of malaria. At the time, there were an estimated 300–500 million cases of malaria each year, with between 1.1 and 2.7 million deaths, and the largest proportion of these children under 5 years old. The WHO faced a hugely complex project management climate, with major political, economic, climatic, and cultural impediments to success. And yet, by 2013 the reported number of malaria cases was down to 198 million and the number of deaths down to 580,000. At the heart of its success was a clear overriding vision that gained buy-in from the project's diverse set of stakeholders. Building on this, the WHO spent significant time understanding the project environment – the internal and external factors that might influence the success or failure of its various malaria projects worldwide. It also committed significant resources to objective setting, scoping, and planning of its projects. Finally, in technically executing different malaria-related projects, focused both on preventing incidence of malaria and on curing those infected, the WHO and its partners relied heavily on careful project monitoring, milestones and continuing stakeholder engagement to ensure that they were on track. The fight against malaria is far from over, but at least this preventable and curable disease is in decline.

How is the project environment understood?

The project environment comprises all the factors that may affect the project during its life. It is the context and circumstances in which the project takes place. Understanding the project environment is important because the environment affects the way in which a project will need to be managed and (just as important) the possible dangers that may cause the project to fail. Environmental factors can be considered under the following four headings:

▶ Geo-social environment – geographical, climatic and cultural factors that may affect the project.
▶ Econo-political environment – the economic, governmental and regulatory factors affecting the project.
▶ The business environment – industrial, competitive, supply network and customer expectation factors that shape the likely objectives of the project.
▶ The internal environment – the individual company's or group's strategy and culture, the resources available, and the interaction with other projects that will influence the project.

The role of stakeholders in the project environment

Once managers have understood the fundamental characteristics of a project, they must consider the stakeholders or agents who are likely to interact with the project, and who could play a critical role in its success or failure. Project stakeholders (also called 'agents') are those individuals, groups or entities that have an interest in the project process or outcome. In other words, they affect, or are affected by, the project. Internal stakeholders include the client, the project sponsor, the project team, functional managers, contractors and project support. External stakeholders (i.e. those outside of the core project, rather than outside of the organization) include end users, suppliers, competitors, lobby groups, shareholders, government agencies and employees.

All projects will have stakeholders – complex projects will have many stakeholders. They are likely to have different views on a project's objectives that may conflict with other stakeholders. At the very least, different stakeholders are likely to stress different aspects of a project. So, as well there being an ethical imperative to include as many people as possible in a project from an early stage, it is often useful in preventing objections and problems later in the project. Moreover, there can be significant direct benefits from using a stakeholder-based approach. Project managers can use the opinions of powerful stakeholders to shape the project at an early stage. This makes it more likely that they will support the project, and also can improve its quality. Communicating with stakeholders early and frequently can ensure that they fully understand the project and understand potential benefits. Stakeholder support may even help to win more resources, making it more likely that projects will be successful. Perhaps most important, one can anticipate stakeholder reaction to various aspects of the project, and plan the actions that could prevent opposition, or build support.

Operations principle

All projects have stakeholders with different interests and priorities.

Some (even relatively experienced) project managers are reluctant to include stakeholders in the project management process, preferring to 'manage them at a distance' rather than allow them to interfere with the project. Others argue that the benefits of stakeholder management are too great to ignore. Emphasizing the responsibilities as well as the rights of project stakeholders can moderate many of the risks of stakeholder involvement. For example, one information technology company formally identifies the rights and responsibilities of project stakeholders as shown in Table 19.1.

Operations principle

Project stakeholders have responsibilities as well as rights.

Understanding stakeholders and their motivations

Think of all the people who are affected by your work, who have influence or power over it, or have an interest in its successful or unsuccessful conclusion. Although stakeholders may be both organizations and people, ultimately you must communicate with people, so look to identify key individuals within a stakeholder organization. In addition, even if one decides not to attempt to manage every identified stakeholder, the process of stakeholder mapping is still useful because it gets those working on a project to see the variety of competing forces at play in many complex projects.

Once all stakeholders have been identified, it is important to understand how they are likely to feel about and react to the project, and how best to communicate with them. One method is to position key stakeholders in relation to their positive and negative 'energy' towards a project (also called the level of synergy and antagonism), in order to understand likely attitudes and behaviours towards

Table 19.1 The rights and responsibilities of stakeholders in one IT company

The rights of stakeholders	The responsibilities of project stakeholders
1 To expect developers to learn and speak their language	1 Provide resources (time, money, . . .) to the project team
2 To expect developers to identify and understand their requirements	2 Educate developers about their business
3 To receive explanations of artefacts that developers use as part of working with project stakeholders, such as models they create with them (e.g. user stories or essential UI prototypes), or artefacts that they present to them (e.g. UML deployment diagrams)	3 Spend the time to provide and clarify requirements
	4 Be specific and precise about requirements
	5 Make timely decisions
	6 Respect a developer's assessment of cost and feasibility
	7 Set requirement priorities
4 To expect developers to treat them with respect	8 Review and provide timely feedback regarding relevant work artefacts of developers
5 To hear ideas and alternatives for requirements	9 Promptly communicate changes to requirements
6 To describe characteristics that make the product easy to use	10 Own your organization's software processes: to both follow them and actively help to fix them when needed
7 To be presented with opportunities to adjust requirements to permit reuse, reduce development time, or reduce development costs	
8 To be given good-faith estimates	
9 To receive a system that meets their functional and quality needs	

projects. Figure 19.5 illustrates this 'socio-dynamic' perspective, pioneered by Jean-Christian Fauvet. *Zealots* have high levels of positive energy towards the project and are almost always in agreement with the project leader. They often fail to understand a lack of commitment in others and so may find it hard to compromise. *Golden Triangles* also have relatively high levels of positive energy towards the project, but their slight antagonism (or negative energy) can be useful in providing a critical perspective on a project and makes it easier for such stakeholders to understand any opposition to some or all of the project components. *Waverers* are stakeholders who have a balance of positive and negative energy towards a project. While they are sometimes considered to be time-wasters or ditherers, their doubts often reflect the 'passive majority', and they may be important in influencing others stakeholders. *Passive* stakeholders are those that do not hold strong positive or negative attitudes towards the project, but like to be kept informed and to ratify change. Zealot stakeholders will often dislike passive stakeholders because of their lack of any 'energy', either positive or negative! *Moaners* hold low levels of positive energy towards a project, but are more negative than passive stakeholders. These stakeholders are typically more active and can often act as an early warning of the views of *opponent* stakeholders. *Opponents,* as one might expect, are strongly opposed to the project and will look to ensure it fails. Unlike stakeholders with either higher levels of positive energy (e.g. waverers) or lower levels of negative energy (e.g. passives or moaners), the minds of opponent stakeholders are very hard to change and so methods of overcoming opposition are critical. *Mutineers* are stakeholders who are fervently opposed to the project. They represent a very small minority of all stakeholders but are extremely active in their opposition. Finally, *schismatic* stakeholders are rare in that they have very high levels of both positive *and* negative energy towards a project. An example might be an entrepreneur who has built up a business but is now retired and is on the board of directors. She or he may be strongly in favour of the organization and its overall project objectives, but feel that the decisions being made are completely wrong (academics are often considered to be schismatic stakeholders in universities!).

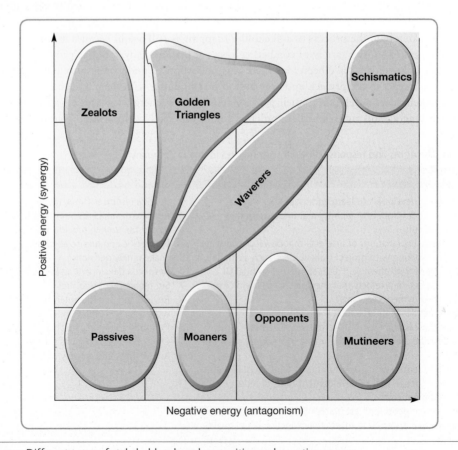

Figure 19.5 Different types of stakeholders based on positive and negative energy

Vasa's first and last voyage[5]

Don't think that projects going wrong are a recent phenomenon! Project specification changes, bad communication, schedule delays and simple bad luck are nothing new and have always been able to bring down even the most high-profile projects. In 1628, the *Vasa*, the most magnificent warship ever built for the Royal Swedish Navy, was launched in front of an excited crowd. It had sailed less than a few thousand metres during its maiden voyage in the waters of the Stockholm harbour when, suddenly, after a gun salute was shot in celebration, the *Vasa* heeled over and,

as water gushed in through the gun ports, vanished beneath the surface, killing 53 of the 150 passengers. Shocked officials were left questioning how such a disaster could happen.

Yet, as a project, the story of the *Vasa* displayed many of the signs of potential failure. When her construction began in 1625, the *Vasa* was designed as a small traditional warship, similar to many others previously built by the experienced shipbuilder Henrik Hybertsson. Soon after, the Swedish king Gustav II Adolphus, at that time fighting the Polish Navy in the Baltic Sea, started ordering a series of changes to the shape and the size of the warship, making its design much longer and bigger than originally envisaged. Also, his spies informed the king that the Danes had started building warships with two gun decks, instead of the customary one. This would give the Danes a great advantage in terms of superior firepower from a longer distance. From the battle-front the king mailed his order to add a second gun deck to the *Vasa*. The message caused consternation when it reached the shipbuilder several months later, but they attempted to comply with the change even though it caused wasteful reworking and complex patching up, as no one had ever seen or built such a revolutionary design before. Yet more pressure was put on the project when a catastrophic storm in the Baltic Sea destroyed ten of the king's ships, making the commissioning of the *Vasa* even more urgent. Then, as a final piece of bad luck (especially for him) the shipbuilder, Hybertsson, died. Nevertheless, just before the ship's completion, a Navy representative, Admiral Fleming, conducted a stability test to assess the seaworthiness of the ship. Notwithstanding the strong signals of instability during the test, the *Vasa* was launched on its maiden voyage – with disastrous results for the king, for the Swedish Navy and for the passengers.

Prioritizing and managing stakeholders

Once the nature of key stakeholders, in terms of their positive and negative energy towards a project, has been determined, managers must prioritize different stakeholders and identify suitable methods of stakeholder engagement. One approach to discriminating between different stakeholders, and more important, how they should be managed, is to distinguish between their power to influence the project and their interest in doing so. Stakeholders who have the power to exercise a major influence over the project should never be ignored. At the very least, the nature of their interest, and their motivation, should be well understood. But not all stakeholders who have the power to exercise influence over a project will be interested in doing so, and not everyone who is interested in the project has the power to influence it. The power–interest grid, shown in Figure 19.6, classifies stakeholders simply in terms of these two dimensions. Although there will be graduations between them, the two dimensions are useful in providing an indication of how stakeholders can be managed in terms of four categories.

High-power, interested groups must be fully engaged, with the greatest efforts made to satisfy them. High-power, less interested

Operations principle

Different stakeholder groups will need managing differently.

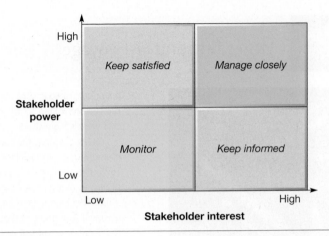

Figure 19.6 The stakeholder power–interest grid

groups require enough effort to keep them satisfied, but not so much that they become bored or irritated with the message. Low-power, interested groups need to be kept adequately informed, with checks to ensure that no major issues are arising. These groups may be very helpful with the detail of the project. Low-power, less interested groups need monitoring though without excessive communication. Some key questions that can help to understand high-priority stakeholders include the following:.

▶ What financial or emotional interest do they have in the outcome of the project? Is it positive or negative?
▶ What motivates them most of all?
▶ What information do they need?
▶ What is the best way of communicating with them?
▶ What is their current opinion of the project?
▶ Who influences their opinions? Do some of these influencers therefore become important stakeholders in their own right?
▶ If they are not likely to be positive, what will win them around to support the project?
▶ If you don't think you will be able to win them

How are projects defined?

Before starting the complex task of planning and executing a project, it is necessary to be clear about exactly what the project is – its definition. This is not always straightforward, especially in projects with many stakeholders. Three different elements define a project:

▶ its objectives: the end state that project management is trying to achieve;
▶ its scope: the exact range of the responsibilities taken on by project management;
▶ its strategy: how project management is going to meet its objectives.

Project objectives

Objectives help to provide a definition of the end point that can be used to monitor progress and identify when success has been achieved. They can be judged in terms of the five performance objectives – quality, speed, dependability, flexibility and cost. However, flexibility is regarded as a 'given' in most projects that, by definition, are to some extent one-offs, and speed and dependability are typically compressed to one composite objective – 'time'. This results in what are known as the 'iron triangle of project management' – cost, time and quality. Figure 19.7 shows the 'project objectives triangle' with three types of project marked.

The relative importance of each objective will differ for different projects. Some aerospace projects, such as the development of a new aircraft, which impact on passenger safety, will place a very high

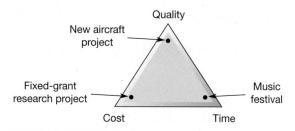

Figure 19.7 The iron triangle of project management

emphasis on quality objectives. With other projects, for example a research project that is being funded by a fixed government grant, cost might predominate. Other projects emphasize time: for example, the organization of an open-air music festival has to happen on a particular date if the project is to meet its objectives. In each of these projects, although one objective might be particularly important, the other objectives can never be totally forgotten.

Good objectives are those which are clear, measurable and, preferably, quantifiable. Clarifying objectives involves breaking down project objectives into three categories – the purpose, the end results and the success criteria. For example, a project that is expressed in general terms as 'improve the budgeting process' could be broken down into:

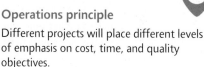

Operations principle

Different projects will place different levels of emphasis on cost, time, and quality objectives.

▶ Purpose – to allow budgets to be agreed and confirmed prior to the annual financial meeting.
▶ End result – a report that identifies the causes of budget delay, and which recommends new budgeting processes and systems.
▶ Success criteria – the report should be completed by 30 June, meet all departments' needs and enable integrated and dependable delivery of agreed budget statements. Cost of the recommendations should not exceed $200,000.

Project scope

The scope of a project identifies its work content and its products or outcomes. It is a boundary-setting exercise that attempts to define the dividing line between what each part of the project will do and what it won't do. Project scoping is critical and failure to scope appropriately or constantly changing scopes is one of the key reasons projects fail. Defining scope is particularly important when part of a project is being outsourced. A supplier's scope of supply will identify the legal boundaries within which the work must be done. Sometimes the scope of the project is articulated in a formal 'project specification'. This is the written, pictorial and graphical information used to define the output, and the accompanying terms and conditions. The project scope will also outline limits or exclusions to the project. This is critical, because perceptions of project success or failure often originate from the extent to which deliverables, limits and exclusions have been clearly stated and understood by all parties during the scoping phase.

Project strategy

The third part of a project's definition is the project strategy, which defines, in a general rather than a specific way, how the project is going to meets its objectives. It does this in two ways: by defining the phases of the project, and by setting milestones and/or 'stagegates'. Milestones are important events during the project's life. Stagegates are the decision points that allow the project to move onto its next phase. A stagegate often launches further activities and therefore commits the project to additional costs etc. Milestone is a more passive term, which may herald the review of a part-complete project or mark the completion of a stage, but does not necessarily have more significance than a measure of achievement or completeness. At this stage, the actual dates for each milestone are not necessarily determined. It is useful, however, to at least identify the significant milestones and stagegates, either to define the boundary between phases or to help in discussions with the project's customer.

How are projects planned?

All projects, even the smallest, need some degree of planning. The planning process fulfils four distinct purposes:

▶ It determines the cost and duration of the project. This enables major decisions to be made – such as the decision whether to go ahead with the project at the start.
▶ It determines the level of resources that will be needed.
▶ It helps to allocate work and to monitor progress. Planning must include the identification of who is responsible for what.
▶ It helps to assess the impact of any changes to the project.

Planning is not a one-off process. It may need repeating several times during the project's life as circumstances change. Nor is re-planning a sign of project failure or mismanagement. As discussed earlier, projects can and should be differentiated based on their characteristics – in our case, we examined three alternative approaches of volume–variety; uncertainty–complexity–scale; and novelty–technology–complexity–pace. And when managing particularly difficult projects, it is a normal occurrence to repeat planning throughout the project's life. Figure 19.8 shows the five steps involved in the process of project planning.

Failure to launch – Berlin Brandenburg Airport[6]

Originally intended to replace the German capital's three ageing airports, the Berlin Brandenburg Airport became a major source of embarrassment for a country renowned for delivering things on-time and on-budget. The infrastructure project, one of the country's largest for decades, had an initial budget of €2 billion, was expected to receive 27 million passengers per year, and was due to open in 2011. However, after several delays and failures, the project's expected completion was pushed back to 2020, and its expected budget increased to over €7 billion. It was estimated that it cost €20 million per month just to run the (empty) terminal building, plus €13 million in lost rental income. So, what went so badly wrong? First, the growing popularity of Berlin as a destination meant that the original demand forecasts, made in 2006, were too low. This meant that additional investment was needed to increase planned terminal space (especially around security, check-in and luggage reclaim). It also prompted calls for a third runway to be developed. Hatmut Mehdorn, the industrial trouble-shooter brought in to save the failing project, suggested keeping open one of the old airports that had been intended for closure so the projected excess demand could be accommodated. Other problems include implementing the airport's novel fire safety systems. These incorporated an innovative technology that, in the event of fire, pumped smoke under the terminal building rather than through the roof. However, there were delays in the system gaining regulatory approval. In addition, over a thousand automatic doors in the terminal building needed to be re-jigged to ensure that they closed properly in the event of a fire breaking out. Other unplanned costs came in at between €1.7 and €2.3 billion. These included €80 million for additional parking, check-in counters and aircraft gates, €1.25 million for rebuilding the airport's entrance hall, €1.1 million for extending luggage facilities, and other cost overruns caused by cracking concrete in car parks, re-fitting of pipes and cables, missing conveyor belts, and problems with fire safety walls between the train station and terminal building. To add to these problems, the decision by airport bosses to cancel the contracts of the original consortium of architects and engineering firms led to significant re-work in planning, as many of the original documents and construction expertise became unavailable.

Identify activities – the work breakdown structure

Most projects are too complex to be planned and controlled effectively unless they are first broken down into manageable portions. This is achieved by structuring the project into a 'family tree' that specifies major tasks or sub-projects. These in turn are divided up into smaller tasks until a defined, manageable series of tasks, called a *work package,* is arrived at. Each work package can be allocated its own objectives in terms of time, cost and quality. Typically, work packages do not exceed 10 days, should be independent from each other, should belong to one sub-deliverable, and should constantly be monitored. The output from this is called the work breakdown structure (WBS). The WBS brings clarity and definition to the project planning process. It shows 'how the jigsaw fits together'. It also provides a framework for building up information for reporting purposes.

Example project

As a simple example to illustrate the application of each stage of the planning process, let us examine the following domestic project. The project definition is:

▶ *purpose:* to make breakfast in bed;
▶ *end result:* breakfast in bed of boiled egg, toast and orange juice;
▶ *success criteria:* plan uses minimum staff resources and time, and product is high quality (egg freshly boiled, warm toast, etc.);
▶ *scope:* project starts in kitchen at 6.00 am, and finishes in bedroom; needs one operator and normal kitchen equipment.

The work breakdown structure is based on the above definition and can be constructed as shown in Figure 19.9.

Estimate times and resources

The second stage in project planning is to identify the time and resource requirements of the work packages. Without some idea of how long each part of a project will take and how many resources it will need, it is impossible to define what should be happening at any time during the execution of the project. Estimates are just that, however – a systematic best guess, not a perfect forecast of reality. Estimates may never be perfect but they can be made with some idea of how accurate they might be.

Example project

Returning to our very simple example, the 'breakfast-in-bed' project, the activities were identified and times estimated as in Table 19.2. While some of the estimates may appear generous, they take into account the time of day and the state of the operator.

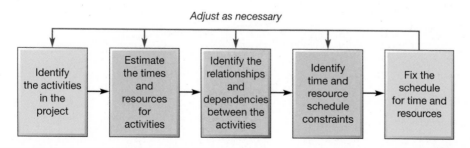

Figure 19.8 Stages in the planning process

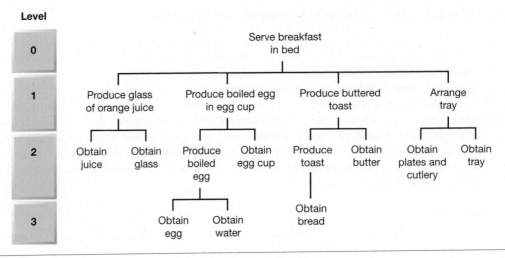

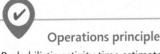

Figure 19.9 A work breakdown structure for a simple domestic project

Probabilistic estimates

The amount of uncertainty in a project has a major bearing on the level of confidence that can be placed on an estimate. The impact of uncertainty on estimating times leads some project managers to use a probability curve to describe the estimate. In practice, this is usually a positively skewed distribution, as in Figure 19.10. The greater is the risk, the greater the range of the distribution. The natural tendency of some people is to produce *optimistic* estimates, but these will have a relatively low probability of being correct because they represent the time that would be taken if *everything* went well. *Most likely* estimates have the highest probability of proving correct. Finally, *pessimistic* estimates assume that almost everything that could go wrong does go wrong. Because of the skewed nature of the distribution, the expected time for the activity will not be the same as the most likely time.

> **Operations principle**
>
> Probabilistic activity time estimates facilitate the assessment of a project being completed on time.

Identify the relationships and dependencies between the activities

The third stage of planning is to understand the interactions between different project work packages. All the work packages (or activities) that are identified as comprising a project will have some relationship with one another that will depend on the logic of the project. Some activities will, by

Table 19.2 Time and resources estimates for a 'breakfast-in-bed' project

Activity	Effort (person-min)	Duration (min)
Butter toast	1	1
Pour orange juice	1	1
Boil egg	0	4
Slice bread	1	1
Fill pan with water	1	1
Bring water to boil	0	3
Toast bread	0	2
Take loaded tray to bedroom	1	1
Fetch tray, plates, cutlery	1	1

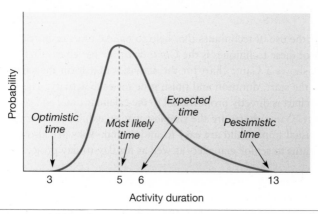

$$\text{Expected activity time} = t_e = \frac{t_o + 4t_l + t_p}{6}$$

$$\text{Variance} = V = \frac{(t_p - t_o)^2}{36}$$

where,

t_o = optimistic activity time

t_l = most likely activity time

t_p = pessimistic activity time

Figure 19.10 Probability distribution of time estimates

necessity, need to be executed in a particular order. For example, in the construction of a house, the foundations must be prepared before the walls are built, which in turn must be completed before the roof is put in place. These activities have a dependent or series relationship. Other activities do not have any such dependence on each other. The rear garden of the house could probably be prepared totally independently of the garage being built. These two activities have an independent or parallel relationship.

The BBC's Digital Media Initiative[7]

The BBC is one of the best-known broadcasters in the world, with an unrivalled reputation for the quality of some of its programmes. Sadly, its reputation for introducing new technology is less exemplary. Among its more spectacular failures was its Digital Media Initiative (DMI). It was an endeavour by the BBC to dispense with video-tapes and create a kind of 'internal YouTube' of archive content that staff could access, upload, edit and then air from their computers. When the project was originally envisaged, creating a single TV programme could involve 70 individual video-handling processes. DMI was meant to halve that. The project cost almost £100 million and lasted

five years before it was scrapped due to failures of governance and delayed delivery. The flaws in the technology were exposed during the BBC's coverage of the State funeral of Margaret Thatcher, a well-known ex-prime minister. The DMI was supposed to create a production system linked to the BBC's huge broadcasting archive, but instead of streamlining access to old video footage video editors were unable to access archive footage to use in news reports from their computers in central London. They had to transport videotapes there using taxis and the underground network from the archive storage facility in northwest London. Admitting that to continue with the project would be 'throwing good money after bad', the BBC suspended its chief technology officer. One BBC manager called the DMI project 'the axis of awful', while another said, 'The scale of the project was just too big, and it got out of hand.' Tony Hall, the BBC's Director General, said that off-the-shelf tools 'that simply didn't exist five years ago', had now become available and they could do the same job as some elements of the DMI. Experts, commenting on the BBC DMI case, said, 'it is not the biggest or the worst IT project failure in the public or private sectors and, without organizations' implementing measures to guard against them, it will almost certainly not be the last.' Others put many of the problems down to 'scope creep' where users kept changing their requirements.

Gantt charts

Project planning is greatly aided by the use of techniques that help to handle time, resource and relationships complexity. The simplest of these techniques is the *Gantt chart* (or bar chart) that we introduced in Chapter 10. Figure 19.11 shows a Gantt chart for the activities that form the sales system interface project. The bars indicate the start, duration and finish time for each activity. The length of the bar for each activity on a Gantt chart is directly proportional to the calendar time, and so indicates the relative duration of each activity. Gantt charts are the simplest way to exhibit an overall project plan, because they have excellent visual impact and are easy to understand. They are also useful for communicating project plans and status to senior managers as well as for day-to-day project control.

Network analysis

As project complexity increases, it becomes more necessary to identify clearly the relationships between activities, and show the logical sequence in which activities must take place. This is commonly done using the *critical path method* (CPM) to clarify the relationships between activities diagrammatically. Though there are alternative methods of carrying out critical path analysis, by far the most common, and also the one used in most project management software packages, is the 'activity on node' (AoN) method. For example, Table 19.3 shows the activities, time estimates, precedence relationships and resources needed (in terms of the number of IT developers) for one phase of a new sales knowledge management system that is being installed in an insurance company. The project is a cooperation between the company's IT systems department and its sales organization.

Figure 19.12 shows the critical path analysis for the new sales knowledge management system. Activities are drawn as boxes, and arrows are used to define the relationships between them. In the centre of each box is the description of the activity (in this case, 'activity a', 'activity b' and so on). Above the description is the duration (D) of the activity (or work package), the earliest start time (EST) and earliest finish time (EFT). Below the description is the latest start time (LST), the latest finish time (LFT) and the 'float' (F) (the number of extra days that the activity could take without slowing down the overall project. The diagram shows that there are a number of chains of events that must be completed before the project can be considered as finished (event 5). In this case, activity chains a–c–f, and a–d–e–f, and b–e–f, must all be completed before the project can be considered as finished. The longest (in duration) of these chains of activities is called the 'critical path' because it represents the shortest time in which the project can be finished, and therefore dictates the project timing. In this case b–e–f is the longest path and the earliest the project can finish is after 57 days.

Activities that lie on the critical path will have the same earliest and latest start times and earliest and latest finish times. That is why these activities are critical. Non-critical activities, however, have some flexibility as to when they start and finish. This flexibility is quantified into a figure that is known either as 'float' or 'slack'. So, activity c, for example, is only of 5 days' duration and it can

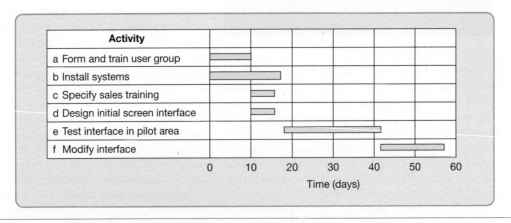

Figure 19.11 Gantt chart for the project to design an information interface for a new sales knowledge management system in an insurance company

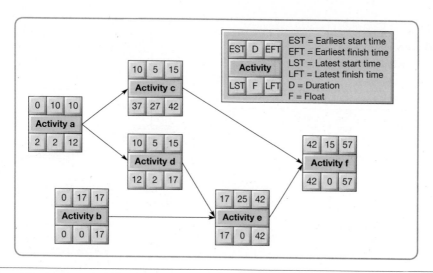

Figure 19.12 Critical path analysis for the project to design an information interface for a new sales knowledge management system in an insurance company

start any time after day 10 (when activity a is completed) and must finish any time before day 42 (when activities a, b, c and d are completed). Its 'float' is therefore $(42 - 10) - 5 = 27$ days (i.e. latest finish time minus earliest start time minus activity duration). Obviously, activities on the critical path have no float; any change or delay in these activities would immediately affect the whole project. In addition to a critical path (or network) diagram, the idea of float or slack can be shown diagrammatically on a Gantt chart, as in Figure 19.13. Here, the Gantt chart for the project has been revisited, but this time the time available to perform each activity (the duration between the earliest start time and the latest finish time for the activity) has been shown.

Identify time and resource schedule constraints

Once estimates have been made of the time and effort involved in each activity, and their dependencies identified, it is possible to compare project requirements with the available resources. The finite nature of critical resources – such as staff with special skills – means that they should be taken into account in the planning process. This often has the effect of highlighting the need for more detailed re-planning.

The logic that governs project relationships, as shown in the critical path analysis (or network diagram), is primarily derived from the technical details, but the availability of resources may also

Table 19.3 Time, resource and relationships for the sales system interface design project

Code	Activity	Immediate predecessor(s)	Duration (days)	Resources (developers)
a	Form and train user group	None	10	3
b	Install systems	None	17	5
c	Specify sales training	A	5	2
d	Design initial screen interface	A	5	3
e	Test interface in pilot area	b, d	25	2
f	Modify interface	c, e	15	3

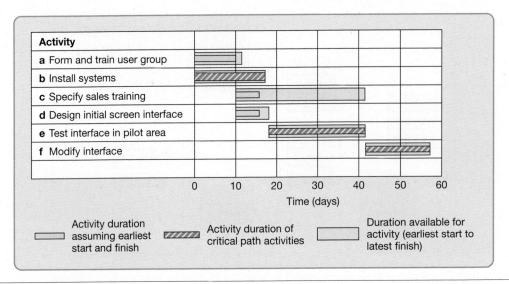

Figure 19.13 Gantt chart for the project to design an information interface for a new sales knowledge management system in an insurance company with latest and earliest start and finish times indicated

impose its own constraints, which can materially affect the relationships between activities. Returning to the sales system interface design project, Figure 19.14 shows the resource profile under two different assumptions. The critical path activities (b–e–f) form the initial basis of the project's resource profile. These activities have no float and can only take place as shown. However, activities a, c and d are not on the critical path, so project managers have some flexibility as to when these activities occur, and therefore when the resources associated with these activities will be required. From Figure 19.14 if one schedules all activities to start as soon as possible, the resource profile peaks between days 10 and 15 when 10 IT development staff are required. However, if the project managers exploit the float that activity c possesses and delay its start until after activity b has been completed (day 17), the number of IT developers required by the project does not exceed 8. In this way, float can be used to smooth out resource requirements or make the project fit resource constraints. However, it does impose further resource constrained logic on the relationship between the activities. So, for example, in this project moving activity c as shown in Figure 19.14 results in a further constraint of not starting activity c until activity b has been completed.

Fix the schedule for time and resources

Project planners should ideally have a number of alternatives to choose from. The one which best fits project objectives can then be chosen or developed. While it can be challenging to examine several alternative schedules, especially in very large or very uncertain projects, computer-based software packages such as Bitrix24, Trello, 2-Plan PMS, Asana, MS project and Producteev make critical path optimization more feasible. The rather tedious computation necessary in network planning can relatively easily be performed by project planning models. All they need are the basic relationships between activities together with timing and resource requirements for each activity. Earliest and latest event times, float and other characteristics of a network can be presented, often in the form of a Gantt chart. More significantly, the speed of computation allows for frequent updates to project plans. Similarly, if updated information is both accurate and frequent, such computer-based systems can also provide effective project control data.

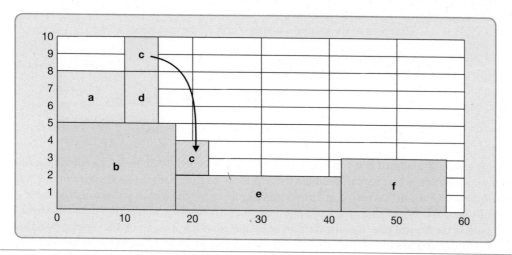

Figure 19.14 Resource profiles for the sales knowledge system interface design, assuming that all activities are started as soon as possible, and assuming that the float in activity c is used to smooth the resource profile

Program evaluation and review technique (PERT)

While it is beyond the scope of this book to enter into much more detail of the various ways that critical path analysis can be made more sophisticated, program evaluation and review technique is worth noting as it represents an enrichment of the basic network approach. PERT, as it is universally known, originated in the planning and controlling of major defence projects in the US Navy, with its most spectacular gains in the highly uncertain environment of space and defence projects. The technique recognizes that activity durations and costs in project management are not deterministic (fixed), and that probability theory can be applied to estimates. In this type of network the duration of each activity is estimated on an optimistic, a most likely and a pessimistic basis, as shown in Figure 19.15. If it is assumed that these time estimates are consistent with a beta probability distribution, the mean and variance of the distribution can be estimated as follows:

$$t_e \frac{t_o = 4t_l = t_p}{6}$$

where

t_e = the expected time for the activity

t_o = the optimistic time for the activity

t_l = the most likely time for the activity

t_p = the pessimistic time for the activity

The variance of the distribution (V) can be calculated as follows:

$$V = \frac{(t_p - t_o)^2}{6^2} = \frac{(t_p - t_o)^2}{36}$$

The time distribution of any path through a network will have a mean which is the sum of the means of the activities that make up the path, and a variance which is a sum of their variances. In Figure 19.15:

$$\text{The mean of the first activity (a)} = \frac{2 + (4 \times 3) + 5}{6} = 3.17$$

$$\text{The variance of the first activity (a)} = \frac{(5 - 2)^2}{36} = 0.25$$

$$\text{The mean of the second activity} = \text{(b)} \ \frac{3 + (4 \times 4) + 7}{6} = 4.33$$

$$\text{The variance of the second activity (b)} = \frac{(7 - 3)^2}{36} = 0.44$$

$$\text{The mean of the network distribution} = 3.17 + 4.33 = 7.5$$

$$\text{The variance of the network distribution} = 0.25 + 0.44 = 0.69$$

It is generally assumed that the whole path will be normally distributed. The advantage of this extra information is that we can examine the 'riskiness' of each path through a network as well as its duration. Given the increased attention on risk management within project management over recent years, this is essential. For example, Figure 19.16 shows a simple two-path network. The top path is the critical one; the distribution of its duration has a mean of 14.5 with a variance of 0.22. The distribution of the non-critical path has a lower mean of 12.66 but a far higher variance of 2.11. The implication of this is that there is a chance that the non-critical path could in reality be critical. Although we will not discuss the probability calculations here, it is possible to determine the probability of any sub-critical path turning out to be critical when the project actually takes place. However, on a practical level, even if the probability calculations are judged not to be worth the effort involved, it is useful to be able to make an approximate assessment of the riskiness of each part of a network.

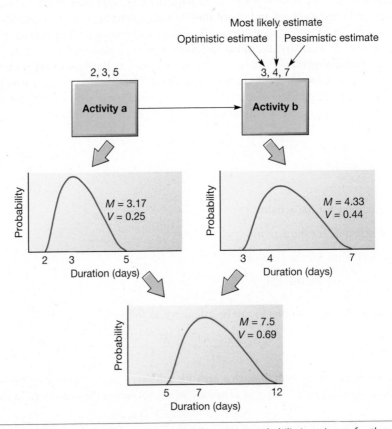

Figure 19.15 Probabilistic time estimates can be summed to give a probabilistic estimate for the whole project

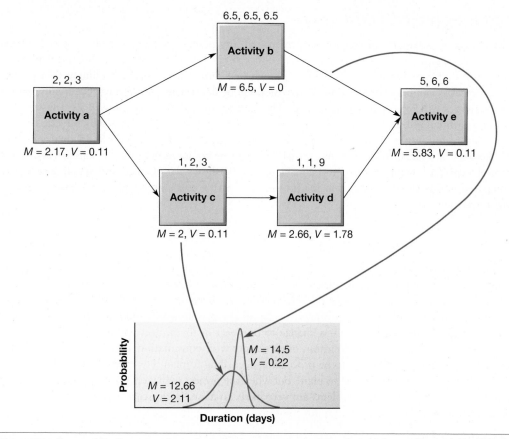

Figure 19.16 One path in the network can have the longest expected duration while another path has the greater variance

How are projects controlled and learnt from?

Understanding the project environment, project definition, and project planning stages of project management largely take place before the actual project begins. By contrast, project control and learning deals with the management activities that take place during the execution of the project and after it ends. It involves five key challenges:

▶ how to *monitor* the project in order to check on its progress;
▶ how to *assess the performance* of the project by comparing monitored observations of the project with the project plan;
▶ how to *intervene* in the project in order to make the changes that will bring it back to plan;
▶ how to *manage matrix tensions* in the project in order to reconcile the interests of both the project and different organizational functions;
▶ how to *learn* from the project in order to improve performance in subsequent projects.

Project monitoring

Project managers have first to decide what they should be looking for as the project progresses. Usually a variety of measures are monitored. To some extent, the measures used will depend on the nature of the project. However, common measures include current expenditure to date, supplier price changes, amount of overtime authorized, technical changes to project, inspection failures, number and length of delays, activities not started on time, missed milestones, etc. Some of these monitored measures affect mainly cost, some mainly time. However, when something affects the quality of the project, there are also time and cost implications. This is because quality problems in project planning and control usually have to be solved in a limited amount of time.

Assessing project performance

The monitored measures of project performance at any point in time need to be assessed so that project management can make a judgement concerning overall performance. A typical planned cost profile of a project through its life is shown in Figure 19.17. At the beginning of a project some activities can be started, but most activities will be dependent on finishing. Eventually, only a few activities will remain to be completed. This pattern of a slow start followed by a faster pace with an eventual tail-off of activity holds true for almost all projects, which is why the rate of total expenditure follows an S-shaped pattern, even when the cost curves for the individual activities are linear. It is against this curve that actual costs can be compared in order to check whether the project's costs are being incurred to plan. Figure 19.17 shows the planned and actual cost figures compared in this way. It shows that the project is incurring costs, on a cumulative basis, ahead of what was planned.

Intervention in projects

If the project is obviously out of control in the sense that its costs, quality levels or times are significantly different from those planned, then some kind of intervention is almost certainly likely to be required. The exact nature of the intervention will depend on the technical characteristics of the project, but it is likely to need the advice of all the people who would be affected. Given the interconnected nature of projects – a change to one part of the project will have knock-on effects elsewhere – this means that interventions often require wide consultation. Sometimes intervention is needed even if the project looks to be proceeding according to plan. For example, the schedule and cost for a project may seem to be 'to plan', but when the project managers project activities and cost into the future, they see that problems are very likely to arise. In this case it is the *trend* of performance which is being used to trigger intervention.

Crashing or accelerating activities

Crashing activities is the process of reducing time spans on critical path activities so that the project is completed in less time. Usually, crashing activities incur extra cost. This can be as a result of:

▶ overtime working;
▶ additional resources, such as manpower;
▶ sub-contracting.

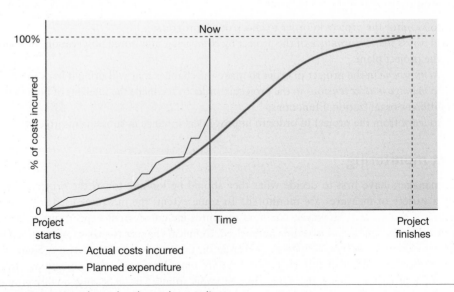

Figure 19.17 Comparing planned and actual expenditure

The Scottish Parliament Building[8]

The Scottish Parliament Building, which opened in 2004, divides opinions like few other projects in the world. To some, it is an architectural masterstroke that is without parallel in a hundred years, described by one critic as '*A Celtic-Spanish cocktail to blow both minds and budgets . . . energetically mining a new seam of National Romanticism refined and reinterpreted for the twenty-first century*'. To others, it is an example of appalling cost estimation and lack of control. The project timeline makes for interesting reading:

▶ July 1999: A budget of £10–£40m set.
▶ September 1997: Indicative estimates between £54m and £71m.
▶ June 1998: Five designers submit bids between £58m and £90m.
▶ July 1998: The bid of EnricMiralles, the Spanish architect, is chosen within a cost range of £50m to £55m.

▶ June 1999: Provisional cost estimate at £109m including consulting fees, site costs, demolition, VAT, archaeology work, risk and contingencies.
▶ November 2001: Cost estimate rises to £241m due to increase in space and major design change.
▶ December 2002: Cost estimate rises to £295m due to increased security needs and 'hidden extras' in the construction process.
▶ June 2003: Cost estimate rises to £374m due to higher than expected consultancy fees now up to £50m.
▶ February 2004: Cost rises to £430m due to construction problems.

At one level, the Scottish Parliament is still a success story, with around 400,000 visitors every year coming to a building that pushed the boundaries of architecture. Yet, from a project management perspective, it should be viewed as a failure. Ultimately, the project was delivered at cost of £414.6 million, 10–40 times the original budget of £10–£40 million, and was opened three years late. Several causes have been identified for the failure of the project, including: the approved design being more complex than envisaged at the feasibility stage; increases in construction cost estimates, almost half of which were attributable to a 47 per cent increase in the total area of the building; additional costs for landscaping and road re-alignment work; poor cost reporting; and inadequate risk allowance. Yet, the Scottish Parliament project is not alone in failing to accurately predict or effectively manage its costs. The Wembley Stadium Project cost £900 million compared to the original forecast of £757 million and was delivered a year late, while the 2014 Brazil football world cup was originally estimated at $2.05 billion and had a final approximate cost of $4.25 billion.

Figure 19.18 shows an example of crashing a simple network. For each activity the duration and normal cost are specified, together with the (reduced) duration and (increased) cost of crashing them. Not all activities are capable of being crashed; here activity e cannot be crashed. The critical path is the sequence of activities a, b, c, e. If the total project time is to be reduced, one of the activities on the critical path must be crashed. In order to decide which activity to crash, the 'cost slope' of each is calculated. This is the cost per time period of reducing durations. The most cost-effective way of shortening the whole project then is to crash the activity on the critical path which has the lowest cost slope. This is activity a, the crashing of which will cost an extra €2,000 and will shorten the project by one week. After this, activity c can be crashed, saving a further two weeks and costing an extra €5,000. At this point all the activities have become critical and further time savings can only be achieved by crashing two activities in parallel.

The shape of the time–cost curve in Figure 19.18 is entirely typical. Initial savings come relatively inexpensively if the activities with the lowest cost slope are chosen. Later in the crashing sequence the more expensive activities need to be crashed and eventually two or more paths become jointly critical. Inevitably by that point, savings in time can only come from crashing two or more activities on parallel paths.

> **Operations principle**
> Only accelerating activities on the critical path(s) will accelerate the whole project.

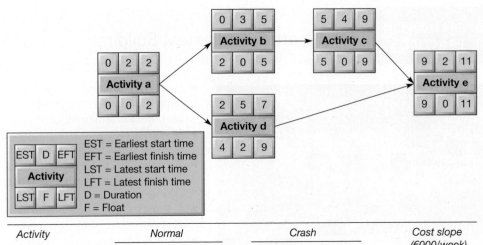

Activity	Normal		Crash		Cost slope (€000/week)
	Cost (€000)	Time (weeks)	Cost (€000)	Time (weeks)	
a	6	2	8	1	2
b	5	3	8	2	3
c	10	4	15	2	2.5
d	5	5	9	4	4
e	7	2	Not possible		–

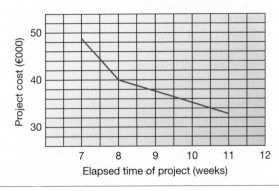

Figure 19.18 Crashing activities to shorten project time becomes progressively more expensive

Managing matrix tensions

In all but the simplest project, project managers usually need to reconcile the interests of both the project itself and the departments contributing resources to the project. When calling on a variety of resources from various departments, projects are operating in a 'matrix management' environment, where projects cut across organizational boundaries and involve staff that are required to report to their own line manager as well as to the project manager. Figure 19.19 illustrates the type of reporting relationship that usually occurs in matrix management structures running multiple projects. A person in department 1, assigned part-time to projects A and B, will be reporting to three different managers all of whom will have some degree of authority over their activities. This is why matrix management requires a high degree of cooperation and communication between all individuals and departments. Although decision-making authority will formally rest with either the project or departmental manager, most major decisions will need some degree of consensus. Arrangements need to be made that reconcile potential differences between project managers and

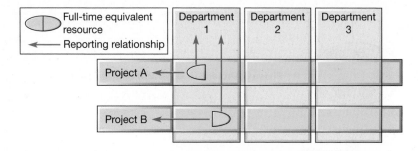

Figure 19.19 Matrix management structures often result in staff reporting to more than one project manager as well as their own department

departmental managers. To function effectively, matrix management structures should have the following characteristics:

▶ There should be effective channels of communication between all managers involved, with relevant departmental managers contributing to project planning and resourcing decisions.
▶ There should be formal procedures in place for resolving the management conflicts that do arise.
▶ Project staff should be encouraged to feel committed to their projects as well as to their own department.
▶ Project management should be seen as the central coordinating role, with sufficient time devoted to planning the project and securing the agreement of the line managers to deliver on time and within budget.

Managing project learning

The activity of project management doesn't stop when a project comes to an end – managing the process of project learning is key to future project success. Yet, within the majority of projects, there remains very little formalized learning. This can partly be explained by the key performance objectives for individuals involved in projects – typically focused on the success of an individual project (in terms of quality, time, cost) as opposed to longer-term learning effects and the development of organizational capability building. As a result, when the project ends, there may be little incentive for stakeholders to spend time reviewing aspects of the project's execution that could have been improved. In addition, when things go wrong, those involved often prefer to move on rather than go back and examine failures. However, not making learning a key part of all projects is a huge missed opportunity. Remember, most projects fail in some way – failure to fully understand the project environment and manage key stakeholders; failure to accurately define the project in terms of objectives and scope; failure in time and resource estimation, scheduling or constraint identification; failure in performance monitoring and intervention during project delivery; or failure to manage the interests of different organizational functions involved in a project. Conversely, when failures *are* actively learned from, they can provide significant performance benefits over time, as illustrated in Figure 19.20.

In phase 1, 'Vanguard' projects are typically separate from the mainstream business, involve significant departures from existing project capabilities, and as a result require a high degree of exploration and experimentation in developing new routines. In phase 2, insights and experiences from the vanguard project are captured and transferred to new projects. Project-to-project learning can be achieved through project accounts, team discussions, project guides, intranet discussion boards, and stories shared by project members. In addition, key participants in the vanguard project are often involved in these new projects to assist in the transfer of project learning. In phase 3, project-to-organization learning occurs when there have been enough projects undertaken to institutionalize new project routines and processes based on the

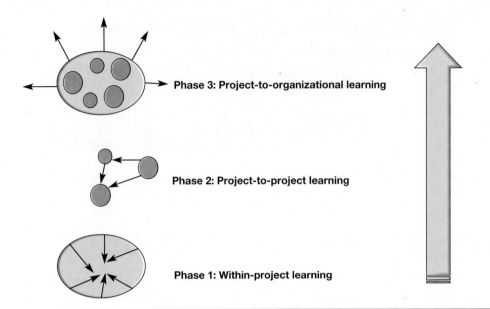

Figure 19.20 Improving project performance over time

systematic consolidation of learning across different projects. As such, we see a steady transition from 'exploration' towards 'exploitation' of learning over time, an idea initially described by Professor James March of Stanford Business School in his seminal research on organizational learning.

Summary answers to key questions

What are projects?

▶ A project is a set of activities with a defined start point and a defined end state, which pursues a defined goal and uses a defined set of resources.

▶ While projects share similarities, they can also be differentiated by volume and variety characteristics, their scale, complexity, the degree of uncertainty in the project, how much novelty is involved, the nature of technology (if any), and the 'pace' of the project.

What is project management?

▶ Project management is the activity of understanding the project environment, defining, planning, controlling and finally learning from projects.

▶ Beyond the 'life cycle' perspective, project management is also concerned with effectively balancing quality/deliverables, time and cost objectives within the so-called 'iron triangle' (of quality, time and cost).

- From an organizational perspective, project management involves managing these life cycles and performance objectives across multiple functions within an organization.

How is the project environment understood?

- The project environment comprises all the factors that may affect the project during its life. These factors include geo-social environment, econo-political environment, business environment and internal environment.
- Stakeholder management is a key role for project managers. This involves identifying stakeholders, understanding their motivations and prioritizing and managing different stakeholders.

How are projects defined?

- Project definition involves (1) determining objectives (the end state that project management is trying to achieve), (2) scoping (the exact range of the responsibilities taken on by project management), and strategy (how project management is going to meet the project objectives).

How are projects planned?

- Project planning helps to determine the cost and duration of the projects, determines resource requirements, helps allocate work, and helps assess the impact of changes to the project.
- Project planning involves five stages:
  - identifying the activities within a project;
  - estimating times and resources for the activities;
  - identifying the relationships and dependencies between the activities;
  - identifying time and resource schedule constraints;
  - fixing the schedule for time and resources.

How are projects controlled and learnt from?

- Project control deals with the management activities that take place during the execution of the project and involves five key challenges:
  - how to *monitor* the project in order to check on its progress;
- how to *assess the performance* of the project by comparing monitored observations of the project with the project plan;
- how to *intervene* in the project in order to make the changes that will bring it back to plan, including crashing or accelerating activities;
- how to *manage matrix tensions* in the project in order to reconcile the interest of both the project and different organizational functions;
- how to *learn* from the project in order to improve performance in subsequent projects.

Introduction

AnuarKamaruddin, COO of United Photonics Malaysia (UPM), was conscious that the project in front of him was one of the most important he had handled for many years. The number and variety of the development projects underway within the company had risen sharply in the last few years, and although they had all seemed important at the time, this one – the 'Laz-skan' project – clearly justified the description given it by the President of United Photonics Corporation, the US parent of UPM, '. . . *the make or break opportunity to ensure the division's long-term position in the global instrumentation industry'.*

The United Photonics Group

United Photonics Corporation had been founded over 70 years ago (as the Detroit Gauge Company), a general instrument and gauge manufacturer for the engineering industry. By expanding its range into optical instruments, it eventually moved also into the manufacture of high-precision and speciality lenses, mainly for the photographic industry. Its reputation as a specialist lens manufacturer led to such a growth in sales that soon the optical side of the company accounted for about 60 per cent of total business and it ranked as one of the top two or three optics companies of its type in the world. Although its reputation for skilled lens making had not diminished since then, the instrument side of the company came to dominate sales as the market for microchip-making equipment expanded.

UPM product range

UPM's product range on the optical side included lenses for inspection systems that were used mainly in the manufacture of microchips. These lenses were sold both to the inspection system manufacturers and to the chip manufacturers themselves. They were very high-precision lenses; however, most of the company's optical products were specialist photographic and cinema lenses. In addition, about 15 per cent of the company's optical work was concerned with the development and manufacture of 'one- or two-off' extremely high-precision lenses for defence contracts, specialist scientific instrumentation, and other optical companies. The group's instrument product range consisted largely of electromechanical assemblies with an increasing emphasis on software-based recording, display and diagnostic abilities. This move towards more software-based products had led the instrument side of the business towards accepting some customized orders. The growth of this part of the instrumentation had resulted in a special development unit being set up: the Customer Services Unit (CSU), which modified, customized, or adapted products for those customers who required an unusual product. Often CSU's work involved incorporating the company's products into larger systems for a customer.

Some years earlier United Photonics Corporation had set up its first non-North American facility just outside Kuala Lumpur in Malaysia. United Photonics Malaysia Sdn Bhd (UPM) had started by manufacturing subassemblies for Photonics instrumentation products, but soon had developed into a laboratory for the modification of United Photonics products for customers throughout the Asian region. This part of the Malaysian business was headed by T.S. Lim, a Malaysian engineer who had taken his post-graduate qualifications at Stanford and three years ago moved back to his native KL to head up the Malaysian outpost of the CSU, reporting directly to Bob Brierly, the Vice-President of Development, who ran the main CSU in Detroit. Over the last three years, T.S. Lim and his small team of engineers had gained quite a reputation for innovative development. Bob Brierly was delighted with their enthusiasm. *'Those guys really do know how to make things happen. They are giving us all a run for our money.'*

The Laz-skan project

The idea for Laz-skan had come out of a project which T.S. Lim's CSU had been involved with. CSU had successfully installed a high-precision Photonics lens into a character recognition system for a large clearing bank. The enhanced capability that the lens and software modifications had given had enabled the bank to scan documents even when they were not correctly aligned. This had led to CSU proposing the development of a 'vision metrology' device that could optically scan a product at some point in the manufacturing process, and check the accuracy of up to 20 individual dimensions. The geometry of the product to be scanned, the dimensions to be gauged, and the tolerances to be allowed, could all be programmed into the control-logic of the device. The T.S. Lim team were convinced that the idea could have considerable potential. The proposal, which the CSU team had called the Laz-skan project, was put forward to Bob Brierly, who both saw the potential value of the idea and was again impressed by the CSU team's enthusiasm. '*To be frank, it was their evident enthusiasm that influenced me as much as anything. Remember that the Malaysian CSU had only been in existence for two years at this time – they were a group of keen but relatively young engineers. Yet their proposal was well thought out and, on reflection, seemed to have considerable potential.*'

In the November following their proposal to Brierly, Lim and his team were allocated funds (outside the normal budget cycle) to investigate the feasibility of the Laz-skan idea. Lim was given one further engineer and a technician, and a three-month deadline to report to the board. In this time he was expected to overcome any fundamental technical problems, assess the feasibility of successfully developing the concept into a working prototype and plan the development task that would lead to the prototype stage.

The Lim investigation

T.S. Lim, even at the start of his investigation, had some firm views as to the appropriate 'architecture' for the Laz-skan project. By 'architecture' he meant the major elements of the system, their functions, and how they related to each other. The Laz-skan system architecture would consider five major subsystems: the lens and lens mounting, the vision support system, the display system, the control logic software and the documentation.

T.S. Lim's first task, once the system's overall architecture was set, was to decide whether the various components in the major subsystems would be developed in-house, developed by outside specialist companies from UPM's specifications, or bought in as standard units and if necessary modified in-house. Lim and his colleagues made these decisions themselves, while recognizing that a more consultative process might have been preferable. '*I am fully aware that ideally we should have made more use of the expertise within the company to decide how units were to be developed. But within the time available we just did not have the time explain the product concept, explain the choices, and wait for already busy people to come up with a recommendation. Also, there was the security aspect to think of. I'm sure our employees are to be trusted but the more people who know about the project, the more chance there is for leaks. Anyway, we did not see our decisions as final. For example, if we decided that a component was to be bought in and modified for the prototype building stage it does not mean that we can't change our minds and develop a better component in-house at a later stage.*' By February, TS's small team had satisfied themselves that the system could be built to achieve their original technical performance targets. Their final task before reporting to Brierly would be to devise a feasible development plan.

Planning the Laz-skan development

As a planning aid the team drew up a network diagram for all the major activities within the project from its start through to completion, when the project would be handed over to Manufacturing Operations. A simplified network diagram is shown in Figure 19.21. The duration of all the activities in the project was estimated either by T.S. Lim or (more often) by him consulting a more experienced engineer back in Detroit. While he was reasonably confident in the estimates, he was keen to stress that they were just that – estimates.

1) The lens

The lens was particularly critical since the shape was complex and precision was vital if the system was to perform up to its intended design specification. T.S. Lim was relying heavily upon the skill of the Group's expert optics group in Pittsburgh to produce the lens to the required high tolerance. Since what in effect was a trial and error approach was involved in their manufacture, the exact time to manufacture would be uncertain. T.S. Lim realized this. '*The lens is going to be a real problem. We just*

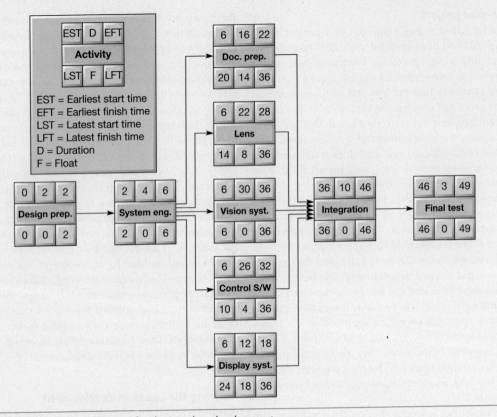

Figure 19.21 Network diagram for the Laz-skan development

don't know how easy it will be to make the particular geometry and precision we need. The optics people won't commit themselves even though they are regarded as some of the best optics technicians in the world. If the development goes wrong it could overrun substantially. It is a relief that lens development is not amongst the "critical path" activities.'

2) Vision support system

The vision support system included many components that were commercially available, but considerable engineering effort would be required to modify them. Although the development, design and testing of the vision support system was complicated, there was no great

uncertainty in the individual activities, or therefore the schedule of completion. If more funds were allocated to their development, some tasks might even be completed ahead of time.

3) The control software

The control software represented the most complex task, and the most difficult to plan and estimate. In fact, the software development unit had little experience of this type of work but (partly in anticipation of this type of development) had recently recruited a young software engineer with some experience of the type of work that would be needed for Laz-skan. He was confident that any technical problems could be solved even though the system needs were novel, but completion times would be difficult to predict with confidence.

4) Documentation

A relatively simple subsystem, 'documentation' included specifying and writing the technical manuals, maintenance routines, online diagnostics, and 'help desk' information. It was a relatively predictable activity, part of which could be sub-contracted to technical writers and translation companies in Kuala Lumpur.

5) Display system

The simplest of the subsystems to plan, the display system, would need to be manufactured entirely outside the company and tested and calibrated on receipt.

Market prospects

In parallel with T.S. Lim's technical investigation, Sales and Marketing had been asked to estimate the market potential of Laz-skan. In a very short time, the Laz-skan project had aroused considerable enthusiasm within the function, to the extent that Halim Ramli, the Asian Marketing Vice President, had taken personal charge of the market study. The major conclusions from this investigation were:

a) The global market for Laz-skan type systems was unlikely to be less than 50 systems per year in 2 years' time, climbing to more than 200 per year after 5 years.

b) The volume of the market in financial terms was more difficult to predict, but each system sold was likely to represent around US$300,000 of turnover.

c) Some customization of the system would be needed for most customers. This would mean greater emphasis on commissioning and post-installation service than was necessary for UPM's existing products.

d) Timing the launch of Laz-skan would be important. Two 'windows of opportunity' were critical. The first and most important was the major world trade show in Geneva in almost exactly a year's time (the following April). This show, held every two years, was the most prominent showcase for new products such as Laz-skan. The second related to the development cycles of the original equipment manufacturers that would be the major customers for Laz-skan. Critical decisions were generally taken in the fall. If Laz-skan was to be incorporated into these products it would have to be available within 18 months (the September of the following year).

The Laz-skan go-ahead

At the end of February UPM considered both the Lim and the Ramli reports. In addition, estimates of Laz-skan's manufacturing costs had been sought from George Hudson, the head of Instrument Development. His estimates indicated that Laz-skan's operating contribution would be far higher than the company's existing products. The board approved the immediate commencement of the Laz-skan development through to prototype stage, with an initial development budget of US$4.5m. The objective of the project was to '. . . build three prototype Laz-skan systems to be "up and running" for April'.

The decision to go ahead was unanimous. Exactly how the project was to be managed provoked far more discussion. The Laz-skan project posed several problems. First, engineers had little experience of working on such a major project. Second, the crucial deadline for the first batch of prototypes meant that some activities might have to be accelerated, an expensive process that would need careful judgement. Finally, no one could agree either whether there should be a single project leader, which function he or she should come from, or how senior the project leader should be. AnuarKamaruddin knew that these decisions could affect the success of the project, and possibly the company, for years to come.

QUESTIONS

1 Who do you think should manage the Laz-skan development project?

2 What are the major dangers and difficulties that will be faced by the development team as they manage the project towards its completion?

3 What can they do about these dangers and difficulties?

Problems and applications

All chapters have 'Problems and applications' questions that will help you practise analysing operations. They can be answered by reading the chapter. Model answers for the first two questions can be found on the companion website for this book.

1 Revisit the Crossrail project example at the start of this chapter. Using the three methods of distinguishing between projects that are described in the chapter (their volume and variety characteristics; their scale, complexity and degree of uncertainty; their novelty, complexity, nature of technology and 'pace'), analyse this project.

2 The activities, their durations and precedences for designing, writing and installing a bespoke computer database are shown in Table 19.4 below. Draw a network diagram (activity-on-node) for the project and calculate the fastest time in which the operation might be completed.

Table 19.4 Bespoke computer database activities

Activity	Duration (weeks)	Activities that must be completed before it can start
1 Contract negotiation	1	–
2 Discussions with main users	2	1
3 Review of current documentation	5	1
4 Review of current systems	6	2
5 Systems analysis (A)	4	3,4
6 Systems analysis (B)	7	5
7 Programming	12	5
8 Testing (prelim)	2	7
9 Existing system review report	1	3,4
10 System proposal report	2	5,9
11 Documentation preparation	19	5,8
12 Implementation	7	7,11
13 System test	3	12
14 Debugging	4	12
15 Manual preparation	5	11

3 'Funding comes from a variety of sources to restore the literally irreplaceable buildings we work on. We try to reconcile historical integrity with commercial viability, and rely on the support of volunteers. So, we need to involve all stakeholders all the way through the project' (Janine Walker, chief project manager, Happy Heritage, a not-for-profit restoration organization). Her latest project was the restoration of a 200-year-old 'poorhouse' as a visitor attraction, originally built to house local poor. Janine's team drew up a list of stakeholders and set out to win them over with their enthusiasm

for the project. They invited local people to attend meetings, explained the vision and took them to look round the site. Also before work started Janine took all the building staff on the same tour of the site as they had the other groups and the VIPs who provided the funding. *'Involving the builders in the project sparked a real interest in the project and the archaeological history of the site. Often, they would come across something interesting, tell the foreman who would involve an archae-ologist and so preserve an artefact that might otherwise have been destroyed. They took a real interest in their work, they felt involved.'* (a) Who do you think would be the main stakeholders for this project? (b) How might not involving them damage the project, and how would involving them benefit the project?

4 Some (even relatively experienced) project managers neglect stakeholders in the project manage-ment process, preferring to 'manage them at a distance' rather than allow them to interfere with the project. Others argue that the benefits of stakeholder management are too great to ignore. It has been suggested that emphasizing the *responsibilities* as well as the rights of project stakeholders can moderate many of the risks of stakeholder involvement. If you were in charge of drawing up a general list of the rights and responsibilities of project stakeholders in an information technology company, what would you include?

5 In the oil industry, project teams are increasingly using virtual reality and visualization models of offshore structures that allow them to check out not only the original design but any modifications that have to be made during construction.
   (a) Why do you think a realistic picture of a completed project helps the process of project management?
   (b) Why are such visualizations becoming more important?

Table 19.5 Time and resources estimates for a 'breakfast-in-bed' project

Activity	Effort (person-min)	Duration (min)
a) Butter toast	1	1
b) Pour orange juice	1	1
c) Boil egg	0	4
d) Slice bread	1	1
e) Fill pan with water	1	1
f) Bring water to boil	0	3
g) Toast bread	0	2
h) Take loaded tray to bedroom	1	1
i) Fetch tray, plates, cutlery	1	1

6 Examine this simple domestic project. The project definition is to make breakfast in bed consisting of a boiled egg, toast and orange juice, using the minimum staff resources and time, and to a high quality (egg freshly boiled, warm toast, etc.). The project starts in the kitchen at 6.00 am, and finishes in the bedroom. The activities involved in the project, resources and times, are shown in Table 19.5.

Selected further reading

There are hundreds of books on project management. They range from the introductory to the very detailed, and from the managerial to the highly mathematical. Here are four general (as opposed to mathematical) books, which are worth a look, plus a more detailed paper looking at megaprojects.

Cole, R. and Scotcher, E. (2015) *Brilliant Agile Project Management: A Practical Guide to Using Agile, Scrum and Kanban,* **Pearson Business, London.**
A practical and modern take on project management.

Flyvbjerg, B. (2014). What you should know about megaprojects and why: An overview. *Project Management Journal,* **vol. 45, no. 2, 6–19.**

Lock, D. (2013) *Project Management,* **Routledge, London.**
A classic text.

Maylor, H. (2018) *Project Management,* **5th edn, Pearson, Harlow.**
A good basic text on the subject.

Pinto, J.K. (2015) *Project Management: Achieving Competitive Advantage,* **4th edn, Pearson, Harlow.**
Long-running text with comprehensive coverage.

NOTES ON CHAPTERS

Chapter 1

1. For more information, see: Pret website, http://www.pret.co.uk/en-gb
2. From our discussions with Tom Dyson and Olly Willans of Torchbox, to whom we are grateful for their advice and assistance.
3. For further information, see: MSF website (2018), http://www.msf.org.uk
4. Definition from Professor Andy Neeley of Cambridge University, http://andyneely.blogspot.co.uk/2013/11/what-is-servitization.html
5. Thanks to Tom Avery for his help in this example.
6. For further information, see: HP website, http://www8.hp.com/us/en/hp-information/environment/product-recycling.html

Chapter 2

1. For more information, see: Novozymes annual report, https://www.novozymes.com/en/about-us
2. Source: https://www.gov.uk
3. Source: https://corporate.marksandspencer.com/?intid=gft_company
4. The phrase 'the triple bottom line' was first used in 1994 by John Elkington, the founder of a British consultancy called SustainAbility. Read Elkington, J. (1997) *Cannibals with Forks: the Triple Bottom Line of 21st Century Business,* Capstone, Oxford. Also recommended is: Savitz, A.W. and Weber, K. (2006) *The Triple Bottom Line: How Today's Best-Run Companies Are Achieving Economic, Social and Environmental Success – and How You Can Too,* Jossey-Bass, San Francisco.
5. For more information, see: Patagonia website, http://www.patagonia.com
6. See: https://openknowledge.worldbank.org/handle/10986/27445
7. Jensen, M.C. (2001) Value maximization, stakeholder theory, and the corporate objective function, *Journal of Applied Corporate Finance,* vol. 14, no. 3, 7–21.
8. For further information, see: Nestlé Press Release (2015) Expect the unexpected: why food safety depends on staying one step ahead, 30 March, http://www.nestle.com/media/newsandfeatures/; Nestlé Corporate website (2014), Nestlé quality policy, March.
9. For further information, see: London's Air Ambulance Service (2015) Our services, https://londonsairambulance.co.uk
10. For further information, see: McCurry, J. (2017) Japanese rail company apologises after train leaves 20 seconds early, *The Guardian,* 17 November; The Local (2017) SBB remains most punctual train company in Europe, news@thelocal.ch, 21 March 2017.
11. For further information, see: mymuesli website, http://uk.mymuesli.com/muesli/

12. For further information, see: Miles, A. and Baldwin, T. (2002) Spidergram to check on police forces, *The Times,* 10 July.
13. Kaplan, R.S. and Norton, D.P. (1993) *The Balanced Scorecard,* Harvard Business School Press, Boston, MA.
14. Skinner, W. (1985) *Manufacturing: The Formidable Competitive Weapon,* John Wiley, Chichester.
15. For further information, see, for example: IKEA website (accessed 2018); Matlack, C. (2018) The tiny Ikea of the future, without meatballs or showroom mazes, *Bloomberg Businessweek,* 10 January; Milne, R. (2018) What will Ikea build next? *Financial Times,* 1 February; Frictionless furnishing; IKEA undertakes some home improvements, *Economist,* 2 November 2017; Hipwell, D. (2017) This is no time to sit back and relax – we must deliver, says IKEA's UK boss, *The Times,* 10 February; Gerschel-Clarke, A.T. (2016) 'Peak Stuff': Why IKEA is shifting towards new business models, Sustainablebrands.com, 17 February; Milne, R. (2017) Ikea turns to ecommerce sites in online sales push, *Financial Times,* 9 October; Hope, K. (2017) Ikea: why we have a love-hate relationship with the Swedish retailer, BBC News, 17 October; Armstrong, A. (2017) Revealed: How after 30 years, Ikea is undergoing a radical overhaul, *The Telegraph,* 15 October.

Chapter 3

1. For a more thorough explanation, see Slack, N. and Lewis, M. (2017) *Operations Strategy,* 5th edn, Pearson, Harlow.
2. Based on an example from Slack, N. (2017) *The Operations Advantage,* Kogan Page, London. Used by permission.
3. Hayes, R.H. and Wheelwright, S.C. (1984) *Restoring our Competitive Edge,* John Wiley, Chichester.
4. For a more thorough explanation, see Slack, N. and Lewis, M. (2015) *Operations Strategy,* 4th edn, Pearson Education, Harlow.
5. For further information, see: Cookson, C. (2015) Guildford's SSTL leads world in small satellite supply, *Financial Times,* 12 June; The pioneer of small satellites is laying plans for the infrastructure and services needed for travel to other planets, *Economist* 30 May 2015; SSTL (2015) Corporate brochure, Changing the economics of space – SSTL is the world's premier provider of small satellite missions and services.
6. Based on an idea in Slack, N. (2017) *The Operations Advantage,* Kogan Page, London.
7. Osterwalder, A. (2005) What is a business model? http://business-model-design.blogspot.com/2005/11/what-is-business-model.html
8. Based on the definitions developed by Cap Gemini.
9. The Micraytech examples have had names and some details changed to preserve commercial confidentiality.
10. For further information, see: Vandevelde, M. (2016) Tesco ditches global ambitions with retreat to UK, *Financial Times,* 21 June; Clark, M.A. and Ralph, A. (2014) Tesco boss defiant amid 4% plunge in sales, *The Times,* 4 June.

11. Mintzberg, H. and Waters, J.A. (1995) Of strategies: deliberate and emergent, *Strategic Management Journal,* July/Sept.

12. For a full explanation of this concept, see: Slack, N. and Lewis, M. (2017) *Operations Strategy,* 5th edn, Pearson, Harlow.

13. An idea proposed by Jay Barney. See Barney, J.B. (2001) Is the resource-based theory a useful perspective for strategic management research? Yes. *Academy of Management Review,* vol. 26, no. 1, 41–56.

14. Barney, J. (1991) The resource-based model of the firm: origins, implications and prospect, *Journal of Management,* vol. 17, no. 1, 97–98.

15. For further information, see: Birkinshaw, J. (2013) Why corporate giants fail to change, CNN Money, 8 May; Magazine, A. (2013) Two lessons learned from Nokia's downfall, Techwell.com, 24 October; Hessman, T. (2013) The Road to Failure: Nokia, Blackberry and. . . Apple, *Industry Week,* 6 September.

16. Adapted from Slack, N. and Lewis, M.A. (2017) *Operations Strategy,* 5th edn, Pearson Education, Harlow.

17. For further information, see: Whipp, L. (2015) McDonald's to slim down in home market, *Financial Times,* 18 June: Smith, T. (2015) Where's the beef, *Financial Times,* 22 May; Whipp, L. (2015) McDonald's may struggle to replicate British success, *Financial Times,* 5 May; McDonald's Annual Report, 2017; Kroc, R.A. (1977) *Grinding it Out: The Making of McDonald's,* St. Martin's Press, New York; Cooper, L. (2015) At McDonald's the burgers have been left on the griddle far too long, *The Times,* 24 August.

Chapter 4

1. For further information, see: https://www.theverge.com/2018/2/14/17013694/dyson-electric-car-lineup; https://jalopnik.com/dysons-plan-to-build-three-electric-cars-from-scratch-i-1823052977; https://www.telegraph.co.uk/business/2016/04/27/james-dyson-launches-299-hair-dryer-in-shock-move-into-beauty-ind/; https://www.thememo.com/2017/03/27/dyson-supersonic-hair-dryer-blew-away-the-competition-in-2016/

2. For further information, see: https://www.ft.com/content/030feb32-7c7d-11e3-b514-00144feabdc0

3. For further information, see: Jervell, E. (2013) The long, slow process of IKEA design, *Wall Street Journal,* 14 October.

4. For further information, see: Goodwin, L. (2015) How to bust the biggest myths about the circular economy, *Guardian,* 12 March; Clegg, A. (2015) Sustainable innovation: shaped for the circular economy, *Financial Times,* 26 August; Company website, Newlife Paints, http://newlifepaints.com

5. For further information, see: Heisler, Y. (2013) Apple's iPhone: The untold story, Network World, 1 September; Vogelstein, F. (2013) And Then Steve Said, 'Let There Be an iPhone', *New York Times Magazine,* 4 October; Ahmed, M. (2012) Apple nearly ditched the iPhone, designer admits, *The Times,* 31 July; Breillatt, A. (2012) You Can't Innovate Like Apple, http://www.pragmaticmarketing.com

6. Christensen, C.M. (1997) *The Innovator's Dilemma: When New Technologies Cause Great Firms to Fail,* Harvard Business School Press, Boston, MA.

7. Coppinger, R. (2016) Digital twins: CAD design through the looking glass, *Engineering and Technology Magazine,* 9 November.

8. Volkmann, D. (2016) The rise of digital twins, Linkedin blog, linkedin.com/pulse, 7 November.

Chapter 5

1. For further information, see: Dutch flower auction, long industry's heart, is facing competition. Christopher Schuetze, *New York Times,* 16 December 2014; https://www.royalfloraholland.com/en/about-floraholland, accessed 20 May 2018.

2. For further information, see: 'Dubai airport retains position as world's No.1' *Gulf News,* 5 February 2108, see https://gulf-news.com/business/aviation/aviation-in-uae-a-continuing-success-story-1.2224997; Dubai is the world's busiest airport for international travellers, *Traveller,* 8 February 2018, http://www.traveller.com.au/dubai-again-tops-ranking-as-worlds-busiest-international-airport-despite-slower-growth-h0vqzx

3. For further information, see: Arlidge, J. (2013) Rolls finds its Derby in the east, *Sunday Times,* 27 October; Raghuvanshi, G. (2013) Rolls-Royce pushes focus on Singapore, *Wall Street Journal,* 15 September; Syed, S. (2013) Rolls-Royce gears up for Singapore production, BBC News website, 21 February.

4. For further information, see: Butler, S. (2014) Rana Plaza disaster marked by Oxford Street demonstration, *Guardian,* 24 April; Disaster at Rana Plaza – a gruesome accident should make all bosses think harder about what behaving responsibly means, *Economist,* 4 May 2013; Bangladesh's clothing industry – bursting at the seams, *Economist,* 26 October 2013.

5. For further information, see: Burton, G. (2013) ARM vs Intel: a battle of business models, *Computing,* 29 May; Turley, J. (2014) Intel vs. ARM: Two titans' tangled fate, InfoWorld.com Created 2014-02-27

6. Brandon-Jones, E., Dutordoir, M., Quariguasi Frota Neto, J. and Squire, B. (2017) The impact of re-shoring decisions on shareholder wealth, *Journal of Operations Management,* vol. 49–51, March, 31–36.

7. Definition from techtarget.com, see searchdatacenter.techtarget.com

Chapter 6

1. Takt time was originated by Toyota, the automobile company. It is their adaptation of the German word *taktzeit,* originally meaning 'clock cycle'.

2. Associated Press (2012) Standardised bed chart 'could prevent hundreds of hospital deaths', *Guardian,* 27 July.

3. For further information, see: Ecover website, http://www.ecover.com

4. For more information, see: Sand Films website, http://www.sandsfilms.co.uk

5. The idea of the product–process matrix was originally presented in a different form in Hayes, R.H. and Wheelwright, S.C. (1984) *Restoring our Competitive Edge,* John Wiley, Chichester.

6. One note of caution regarding this idea: although logically coherent, it is a conceptual model rather than something that can be 'scaled'. Although it is intuitively obvious that deviating from the diagonal increases costs, the precise amount by which costs will increase is very difficult to determine.

7. For more information, see: https://www.persimmonhomes.com/corporate/about-us/our-brands/space4

8. Shostack, L.G. (1984). Designing services that deliver. *Harvard Business Review,* vol. 62, no. 1, 133–139.

Chapter 7

1. For more information, see for example: Urry, J. (2017) Inside Ducati: MCN walk around the Bologna factory, *Motorcycle News,* 21 September; Blain, L. (2014) Inside the Ducati factory: Building the 1199 Panigale from the ground up, Newatlas.com, 23 January; Segran, E. (2015) Designing a happier office on the super cheap, Fast Company, 30 March; Hickey, S. (2014) Death of the desk: the architects shaping offices of the future, *Guardian,* 14 September.

2. There are many studies and surveys that examine the effect of workplace design on staff performance, not all of which agree on specific details. For example, start with Gensler (2013) The Gensler Workplace Survey, gensler.com

3. For further information, see for example: Booth, R. (2017) Francis Crick Institutes £700m building too noisy to concentrate, *Guardian,* 21 November.

4. For further information, see: Carr-Brown, J. (2005) French factory surgeon cuts NHS queues, *Sunday Times,* 23 October.

5. Koontz, C. (2012) Retail Interior Layout for Libraries, Info Today, 27 January, http://www.infotoday.com/mls/jan05/koontz.shtml

6. Schein, E.M. (1999). *The Corporate Culture Survival Guide: Sense and Nonsense about Culture Change,* Jossey-Bass, San Francisco.

7. Savage, M. (2014) *Workplace Aesthetics – Not Just Perks & Paint,* J Walter Thompson Inside, 28 July.

8. Herman Miller (2008) *Home Sweet Office Comfort in the Workplace,* Herman Miller.com

9. AGSM (2010) *Workspace Design: Will Aesthetics Give Your Business the Edge,* University of New South Wales, 5 October.

10. Montessori management: The backlash against running firms like progressive schools has begun, *Economist,* 7 September 2013.

11. There are many histories of the origin of the office cubicle. For example, see: Saval, N. (2014) A brief history of the dreaded office cubicle, *Wall Street Journal,* 9 May; Inside the box: How workers ended up in cubes—and how they could break free, *Economist,* 3 January 2015.

12. Waber, B., Magnolfi, J. and Lindsay, G. (2014) Workspaces that move people, *Harvard Business Review*, October.

13. The idea of 'servicescapes was originally explored by Bitner, M.J. (1992) Servicescapes: the impact of physical surroundings on customers and employees. *Journal of Marketing,* vol. 56, 57–71.

Chapter 8

1. For further information, see: OECD (2018) Automation, skills use and training, OECD Social, Employment and Migration Working Papers, OECD, ISSN: 1815199X; The future of jobs: Previous technological innovation has always delivered more long-run employment, not less. But things can change, *Economist,* 18 January 2014; Schumpeter – The age of smart machines, *Economist,* 25 May 2013; Finkelstein, D. (2013) Machines are becoming cheaper than labour, *The Times,* 6 November; Groom, B. (2014) Automation and the threat to jobs, *Financial Times,* 26 January; Benedikt Frey, C. and Osborne, M.A. (2013) The future of employment: how susceptible are jobs to computerisation?, Oxford Martin School Working Paper, 17 September; Brynjolfsson, E. and McAfee, A. (2014) *The Second Machine Age: Work, Progress, and Prosperity in a Time of Brilliant Technologies,* W. W. Norton, New York.

2. Duhigg, C. (2012) *The Power of Habit: Why We Do What We Do in Life and Business.* Random House, New York. For further information, see: qb house website, http://www.qbhouse.com

3. Techopedia.

4. For more information, see for example: Artificial intelligence and Go, *Economist,* 12 March 2016; Koch, C. (2016) How the computer beat the go master, *Scientific American,* 19 March.

5. 'SAP IOT Definition'. SAP Research. internet.eu/images/1/16/A4_Things_Haller.pdf.

6. For more information, see: Unilever's sustainable living report (2018) http://www.unilever.co.uk/sustainable-living/

7. Time value of money.

8. Sources include: High tech meets low finance, Buttonwood blog, *Economist,* 12 March 2016; The fintech revolution, *Economist,* 9 May 2015; Wilkins, C. (2016) Fintech and the Financial Ecosystem: Evolution or Revolution? Bank of Canada, Remarks issued 17 June 2016.

9. For further information, see: Walsh, D. (2015) Irregular parcels put UK Mail out of shape, *The Times,* 8 August; UK Mail website.

10. Dosi, G., Teece, D. and Winter, S.G., (1992) Towards a theory of corporate coherence, in Dosi, G., Giametti, R. and Toninelli, P.A. (eds) *Technology and Enterprise in a Historical Perspective,* Oxford University Press, Oxford.

11. Walley, P. and Amin, V. (1994) Automation in a customer contact environment, *International Journal of Operations and Production Management,* vol. 14, no. 5, 86–100.

12. For further information, see: Deng, B. (2016) Security robot runs over toddler at shopping centre, *The Times,* 15 July; Times Leader (2016) They, Robots – Accelerating progress in robotics demands advances in ethics and economics, *The Times,* 1 January; Hall, A. (2015) Factory robot grabs worker and kills him, *The Times,* 3 July.

13. Chew, W.B., Leonard-Barton, D. and Bohn, R.E. (1991) Beating Murphy's law, *Sloan Management Review,* vol. 5, Spring.

Chapter 9

1. Schein, E.M. (1999) *The Corporate Culture Survival Guide: Sense and Nonsense about Culture Change,* Jossey-Bass, San Francisco.

2. For more information, see: Company website, https://www.gore.com; Roberts, D. (2015) At W.L. Gore, 57 years of authentic culture, Fortune.com, 5 March.

3. Slack, N. (2017) *The Operations Advantage,* Kogan Page, London.

4. Morgan describes these and other metaphors in Morgan, G. (1986) *Images of Organization,* Sage, London.

5. Hoxie, R.F. (1915) *Scientific Management and Labour,* D. Appleton, Washington, DC.

6. For further information, see: Byers, D. (2017) Bionic suits to make tools feel weightless, *The Times,* 24 July; Coxworth, B. (2017) Exoskeleton helps Ford workers reach up, newatlas, https://newatlas.com/ford-eksovest/52166/; Goode, L. (2017) Are exoskeletons the future of physical labour?, The Verge, 5 December, https://www.theverge.com

7. Hackman, J.R. and Oldham, G. (1975) A new strategy for job enrichment, *California Management Review,* vol. 17, no. 3, 57–71.

8. For further information, see: Hill, A. (2017) Power to the workers: Michelin's great experiment, *Financial Times,* 11 May; Hill, A. (2017) Michelin chief Jean-Dominique Senard devolves power to workers, *Financial Times,* 14 May; 2016 Michelin Annual Report (2017).

9. Bowen, D.E. and Lawler, E.E. (1992) The empowerment of service workers: what, why, how and when, *Sloan Management Review,* vol. 33, no. 3,. 31–39.

10. For further information, see: Lavey-Heaton, M. (2014) Working from home: how Yahoo, Best Buy and HP are making moves, *The Guardian,* 10 March; Surowiecki, J. (2013) Face Time, *The New Yorker,* 18 March; Mayer culpa, *Economist,* 2 March 2013.

11. The Health and Safety Executive (HSE) of the UK government.

12. Beauregard, T. Alexandra and Henry, Lesley C. (2009) Making the link between work-life balance practices and organizational performance, *Human Resource Management Review,* vol. 19, 9–22. ISSN 1053-4822.

13. For further information, see: Bone, J., Robertson, D. and Pavia, W. (2010) Plane rumpus puts focus on crews' growing revolution in the air, *The Times,* 12 August.

14. For further information, see: Jones, A. (2015) The riff: Dangers of music at work, *Financial Times,* 5 August; Ciotti, G. (2014) How music affects your productivity, *FastCompany,* 11 July; BBC (2013) Does music in the workplace help or hinder? *Magazine Monitor,* 9 September.

15. For further information, see: Clark, P. (2017) How office snooping boosts the bottom line, *Financial Times,* 26 November; Derousseau, R. (2017) The tech that tracks your movements at work, bbc.com/capital, 14 June; Solon, O. (2017) Big Brother isn't just watching: workplace surveillance can track your every move, *The Guardian,* 6 November; Staats, B.R., Dai, H.,Hofmann, D. and Milkman, K.L. (2016) Motivating process compliance through individual electronic monitoring: an empirical examination of hand hygiene in healthcare, *Management Science,* vol. 63, no. 5, 1563–1585; Webster, B. (2018) CCTV to monitor hygiene in meat factories, *The Times,* 3 March.

16. Samaranayake, V. and Gamage, C. (2012) Employee perception towards electronic monitoring at work place and its impact on job satisfaction of software professionals in Sri Lanka, *Telematics and Informatics,* vol. 29, no. 2, 233–244.

Chapter 10

1. With thanks to Joanne Cheung, Steve Deeley and other staff at Godfrey Hall, BMW Dealership, Coventry.

2. For further information, see: Farman, J. (1999) 'Les Coulisses du Vol', Air France. Talk presented by Richard E. Stone, North-West Airlines at the IMA Industrial Problems Seminar, 1998.

3. The concept of *P:D* ratios comes originally from Shingo, S. (1981) *Study of Toyota Production Systems,* Japan Management Association, Tokyo, and was extended by Mather, K. (1988) *Competitive Manufacturing,* Prentice Hall, Upper Saddle River, NJ.

4. Coldrick, A., Ling, D. and Turner, C. (2003) Evolution of Sales and Operations Planning, StrataBridge Working Paper.

5. Sources include: Please be seated: A faster way of boarding planes could save time and money, *Economist,* 3 September 2011; Palmer, J. (2011) Tests show fastest way to board passenger planes, BBC Website, BBC News, 31 August.

6. For more information, see: Heathrow website, https://www.heathrow.com; for a technical explanation of the aircraft landing algorithm, see Beasley, J.E., Sonander, J. and Havelock, P. (2001) Scheduling aircraft landings at London Heathrow using a population heuristic, *Journal of the Operational Research Society,* vol. 52, 483–493.

7. Thanks to Lawrence Wilkins for this example.

8. For further information, see: Calder, S. (2017) Ryanair cancellations: The truth behind why 2,000 flights are due to be scrapped, *Independent,* 18 September.

9. Goldratt, E.Y. and Cox, J. (1984) *The Goal,* North River Press.

10. Based on an original model described in Hofstede,G. (1981) Management control of public and not-for-profit activities accounting, *Organizations and Society,* vol. 6, no. 3, 193–211.

Chapter 11

1. For further information, see: https://www.nytimes.com/2018/05/07/opinion/new-york-uber-problem.html; https://www.nytimes.com/2018/02/22/travel/new-airbnb-plus.html;https://www.nytimes.com/2012/03/05/education/moocs-large-courses-open-to-all-topple-campus-walls.html

2. For further information, see: Levenson, E. (2012) SeatGeek 'Bleacher Bum Economics: A fan guide to dynamic pricing at Wrigley Field, operationsroom.files.wordpress.com

3. For further information, see: http://www.railtechnologymagazine.com/Rail-News/network-rail-awards-landmark-150m-etcs-signalling-contract; https://www.railwaypro.com/wp/india-install-etcs-level-2-entire-broad-gauge-network/; http://www.railjournal.com/index.php/signalling/modi-blocks-indian-railways-etcs-plan.html

4. For further information, see: Wessel, D. (2013) Gaming the system to beat rush-hour traffic, *Wall Street Journal,* 31 August.

5. For further information, see: Airline price war means you could be dragged off your next flight, *The Times,* 11 April; BBC (2017) United CEO says removed passenger was 'disruptive and belligerent', BBC News site, 11 April; Gunter, J. (2017) United Airlines incident: Why do airlines overbook?, BBC News, 10 April; Hill A (2017) United's reputational repair job mixes sense and nonsense, *Financial Times,* 27 April.

6. For further information, see: Heathrow Airport Holdings Company (2014) Heathrow Airport Holdings Company Information, Retrieved 12 October 2014; https://www.independent.co.uk/travel/news-and-advice/heathrow-airport-third-runway-expansion-plans-glory-project-british-airways-boss-willie-walsh-iag-a7998631.html

Chapter 12

1. For further information, see Bajarin, T. (2016) Apple's little-known (and somewhat unsexy) secret to success, recode.nat, posted 30 August; Williams, R. (2014) Apple's supply chain in trouble? *The Telegraph,* 23 March; Ellinor, R. (2013)

Apple named world's best supply chain, supplymamagement .com, 24 May; Tate, R. (2014) 'Apple tightens grip on worldwide supply chain with Asia hiring spree', *Wired Magazine,* 3 March.

2. The UK government Department for Environment, Food and Rural Affairs (2006) Procuring the Future – report of the Sustainable Procurement Task Force.

3. Fisher, M.L. (1997) What is the right supply chain for your product, *Harvard Business Review,* March–April.

4. Adapted from Kraljic (1983) Purchasing must become supply management, *Harvard Business Review,* September.

5. For more information, see: The Economist (2011) Broken links - The disruption to manufacturers worldwide from Japan's disasters will force a rethink of how they manage production, *Economist* print edition, 31 March; BBC (2011) Sony considers two-week shutdown due to power shortages Production at some of Japan's biggest companies has been affected by power shortages, BBC News Website, 11 April; BBC (2011) Toyota motors has suspended production at most of its plants in Japan and also reduced output at its North American and European factories, BBC News Website, 11 April.

6. Harland, C.M. (1996) Supply chain management relationships, chains and networks, *British Journal of Management,* vol. 1, no. 7.

7. For more information, see: www.levistrauss.com/responsibility/ conduct/guidelines

8. For further information, see: Rutter Pooley, C. (2018) KFC's UK chicken run caused by too many eggs in one basket, *Financial Times,* 23 February; Rutter Pooley, C. (2018) KFC runs out of chicken in logistics fiasco, *Financial Times,* 19 February.

9. Iansiti, M. and Lakhani, K.R. (2017) The truth about blockchain, *Harvard Business Review,* January–February.

10. Thanks to Stephen Disney at Cardiff Business School, UK, for help with this section.

11. For more information, see: del Castillo, M. (2018) Shipping blockchain: Maersk spinoff aims to commercialize trade platform, Coindesk.com, Jan 16; Slocum, H. (2018) Maersk and IBM to form joint venture applying blockchain to improve global trade and digitize supply chains, Press release, Maersk, 18 January.

Chapter 13

1. For further information, see: Stanger, S.H.W., Wilding, R., Yates, N. and Cotton, S. (2012) What drives perishable inventory management performance? Lessons learnt from the UK blood supply chain, *Supply Chain Management: An International Journal,* vol. 17, no. 2, 107–123.

2. For further information, see: Gosden, E (2017) Power shift brings energy market closer to holy grail, *The Times,* 17 April; Energy storage, *Economist Technology Quarterly,* 3 March 2012.

3. Sources include: Leroux, M. (2016) Burberry boss defends stock destruction, *The Times,* 15 July; Atkins, R. (2016) Richemont buys back and destroys stock as sales fall, *Financial Times,* 20 May; Dwyer, J. (2010) A clothing clearance where more than just the prices have been slashed, *New York Times,* 5 January.

4. For further information, see: Grimm, E. (2009) Prepare for winter, *Daily Chronicle,* 30 November.

5. For more information, see: Croissantonomics – lessons in managing supply and demand for perishable products, *Economist,* 29 August 2015.

6. For more information, see: Duke, S. (2014) He knows what you want – before you even want it, *Sunday Times,* 2 February; Ahmed, M. (2014) Amazon will know what you want before you do, *The Times,* 27 January.

7. For more information, see: Calder, S. (2017) British Airways faces £300,000 bill for flight to Barbados without enough toilet paper, *The Independent,* 7 March; Morris, H. (2017) British Airways faces £290,000 bill after running out of toilet roll, *The Telegraph,* 8 March.

Chapter 14

1. For further information, see: Allan, K. (2009) Butcher's Pet Care relies on IT that can co-ordinate its ERP, *Engineering & Technology Magazine,* 21 July; Company website.

2. For a good explanation of this and similar issues, see: MacCarthy, B.L. (2006) Organizational, systems and human issues in production planning, scheduling and control, in Herman, J. (ed.) *Handbook of Production Scheduling,* International Series in Operations Research and Management Science, Springer, New York.

3. For further discussion of this topic, see MacCarthy, op. cit.

4. Wight, O. (1984) *Manufacturing Resource Planning: MRP II,* Oliver Wight Ltd.

5. Koch, C. and Wailgum, T. (2007) ERP definition and solutions, www.cio.com

6. For further information, see company website, www.sap.com

7. Source: Thanks to Lawrence Wilkins for this example.

8. Brynjolfsson, E. (1994) Technology's true payoff, *Information Week,* October.

9. This categorization is described in McAffee, A. (2007) Managing in the Information Age, *Harvard Business School,* Teaching note 5-608-011.

10. Based on a review of the research in this area by Finney, S. and Corbett, M. (2007) ERP implementation: a compilation and analysis of critical success factors, *Business Process Management Journal,* vol. 13, no. 3, 329–347.

11. For further information, see: Kanaracus, C. (2008) Waste Management sues SAP over ERP implementation, *InfoWorld,* 27 March.

12. Turbit, N. (2005) ERP Implementation – The Traps, The Project Perfect White Paper Collection, www.projectperfect.com.au

Chapter 15

1. For further information, see: https://blog.kainexus.com/ improvement-disciplines/lean/lean-construction/6-principles-of-lean-constrcution; https://www.designingbuildings.co .uk/wiki/Lean_construction; https://www.leanconstruction. org/about-us/what-is-lean-design-construction/; Banawi, A. and Bilec, M.M. (2014) A framework to improve construction processes: integrating lean, green and six sigma, *International Journal of Construction Management,* vol. 14, no. 1, 45–55.

2. See http://www.youtube.com/watch?v=EedMmMedj3M.

3. For further information, see: When Toyota met e-commerce: lean at Amazon, Mckinsey Quarterly (2014), no. 2; Liker, J. (2004) *The Toyota Way,* McGraw-Hill, New York.

4. Corbett, S. (2004) Applying lean in offices, hospitals, planes, and trains, Presentation at the Lean Service Summit, Amsterdam, 24 June.

5. For further information, see: http://www.wired.co.uk/article/airbus-sleeping-pods-naps-cargo-hold-zodiac-330

6. Example written and supplied by Janina Aarts and Mattia Bianchi, Department of Management and Organization, Stockholm School of Economics.

7. Based on: Rattner, S. (2009) What is the theory of constraints, and how does it compare to lean thinking?, The Lean Enterprise Institute, at http://www.leanvs.com/tocvsleanthinking.pdf

8. Voss, C.A. and Harrison, A. (1987) Strategies for implementing JIT, in Voss, C.A. (ed.) *Just-In-Time Manufacture,* IFS/Springer-Verlag, Berlin.

9. This case is based on the work of several real hospitals, in Scandinavia and the rest of the world, that have used the concepts of lean operations to improve their performance. However, all names and places are fictional and no connection is intended to any specific hospital.

Chapter 16

1. Carroll, L. (1871) *Through the Looking Glass,* Macmillan, London.

2. Imai, M. (1986) *Kaizen – The Key to Japan's Competitive Success,* McGraw-Hill, New York.

3. For a full explanation, see: Gawande, A. (2010)*The checklist manifesto: how to get things right,* Metropolitan. Aaronovitch, D. (2010) The checklist manifesto: review, *The Times* (of London), 23 January.

4. For more information, see: Vasagar, J. (2014) Experiment with a bit of anarchy, *Financial Times,* 28 January.

5. International Standards Organization (1986) ISO 8402.

6. Dale, B.G. (1994) Quality management systems, in Dale, B.G. (ed.) *Managing Quality,* Prentice Hall, Upper Saddle River, NJ.

7. For more information, see: Company website, http://www.heinekeninternational.com

8. Davenport, T. (1995) 'Reengineering – The fad that forgot people', Fast Company, November.

9. These Defects per Million (DPM) figures assume that the mean and/or SD may vary over the long term so the 3 sigma DPM is actually based on 1.5 sigma and 6 sigma on 4.5 sigma. These distributions are assumed to be 'one-tailed' as the shift is usually in one direction.

10. The Defects per Million (DPM) figures assume that the mean and/or SD may vary over the long term so the 3 sigma DPM is actually based on 1.5 sigma and 6 sigma on 4.5 sigma. These distributions are assumed to be 'one-tailed' as the shift is usually in one direction.

11. For more information, see: Sharma, M., Pandla, K. and Gupta, P. (2014) A case study on Six Sigma at Wipro Technologies: Thrust on Quality, Working Paper, The Jaipuria Institute of Management; Wipro website, www.wipro.com

12. There are many books and publications that explain the benefits of combining lean and Six Sigma. For example, see Byrne, G., Lubowe, D. and Blitz, A. (2007) *Driving Operational Innovation using Lean Six Sigma,* IBM Institute for Business Value; Brue, G. (2005) *Six Sigma for Managers: 24 Lessons to Understand and Apply Six Sigma Principles in Any Organization,* McGraw-Hill Professional Education Series, New York.

13. Schein, E.M. (1999). *The Corporate Culture Survival Guide: Sense and Nonsense about Culture Change,* Jossey-Bass, San Francisco.

14. Shenkar, O. (2010) *Copycats: How Smart Companies Use Imitation to Gain a Strategic Edge,* Harvard Business Review Press, Boston, MA.

15. For further information, see: The great escape: What other makers can learn from the revival of Triumph motorcycles, *Economist*, 23 January 2016.

16. Argyris, C. and Schon, D. (1978) *Organizational Learning,* Addison-Wesley, Reading, MA.

17. *The New Oxford Dictionary of English,* Oxford University Press, Oxford.

18. For further information, see: West, K. (2011) Formula One trains van drivers, *The Times,* 1 May; f1network.net,http://www.f1network.net/main/s107/st164086.htm

19. Davenport, T.H. (1994) Saving its soul: human centered information management. *Harvard Business Review,* March–April, vol. 72, no. 2, 119–131. Duhon, B. (1998), It's all in our heads, *Inform,* September, vol. 12, no. 8.

20. For further information, see: Schlumberger Press Release (2010) Schlumberger Cited for Knowledge Management, Schlumberger Press Office Date: 03/12/2010; Deltour, F., Ple, L. and Roussel, C.S. (2013) Eureka! Developing Online Communities of Practice to Facilitate Knowledge Sharing at Schlumberger, IESEG School of Management, LEM, Case Study 313-122-1.

21. This case is based on several residential conference centres but does not reflect the concerns of any particular one.

Chapter 17

1. Parasuraman, A., Zeithaml, V.A. and Berry, L.L. (1985) A conceptual model of service quality and implications for future research, *Journal of Marketing,* vol. 49, Fall, 41–50; and Gummesson, E. (1987) Lip service: a neglected area in services marketing, *Journal of Services Marketing,* vol. 1, no. 1, 19–23.

2. For more information, see: Vitaliev, V. (2009) The much-loved knife, *Engineering and Technology Magazine,* 21 July; Zuber, F. (2015) The Victorinox Quality System, Victorinox website.

3. Interview with Michael Purtill, the General Manager of the Four Seasons Hotel Canary Wharf in London. We are grateful for Michael's cooperation (and for the great quality of service at his hotel!).

4. Berry, L.L. and Parasuraman, A. (1991) *Marketing Services: Competing Through Quality,* Free Press, New York.

5. Based on Parasuraman et al., op cit.

6. Qualinet (2012) White Paper on Definitions of Quality of Experience, Qualinet.

7. The idea of service guarantees was first popularised in Hart, C.W. (1988) The power of unconditional service guarantees, *Harvard Business Review,* July.

8. For further information, see: Millington, A. (2018) Virgin Atlantic is offering a full refund on flights booked today if it can't cure a passenger's fear of flying, uk.businessinsider.com, 9 January; Edwards, J. (2018) Why you should book a flight today if you've got a fear of flying, *Cosmopolitan,* 9 January.

9. Ferdows, K. and de Meyer, A. (1990) Lasting improvement in manufacturing, *Journal of Operations Management,* vol. 9, no. 2, 168–184.

10. For further information, see: Markillie, P. (2011) They trash cars, don't they? *Intelligent lifeMagazine,* Summer.

11. For further information, see: Wheatley, M. (2010) Filling time on the production line, *Engineering and Technology Magazine,* 8 November.

12. For further information, see: Pardesarielle, A. (2017) Ikea's new app flaunts what you'll love most about AR, Wired, 20 September; Joseph, S. (2017) How Ikea is using augmented reality, Digiday UK, 4 October; D. Y. Sha, Guo-Liang Lai (2012) Exploring the intention of customers to use innovative digital content information technology, *Industrial Engineering and Engineering Management* (IEEM) 2012 IEEE International Conference on, pp. 1065–1069.

13. Euphemia, F.T. and YuenSian S.L. Chan (2010) The effect of retail service quality and product quality on customer loyalty, *Journal of Database Marketing & Customer Strategy Management,* September 2010, vol. 17, no. 3–4, 222–240.

14. Feigenbaum, A.V. (1986) *Total Quality Control,* McGraw-Hill, New York.

15. Kaynak, H. (2003) The relationship between total quality management practices and their effects on firm performance, *Journal of Operations Management,* vol. 21, 405–435.

16. For further information, see for example: Ryanair's future – Oh really, O'Leary?, *Economist*, 19 October 2013.

17. For further information, see for example: Overtired, and overdrawn, *Economist,* 15 June 2013; Wilson, H. (2014) Fat-fingered trader sets Tokyo alarms ringing, *The Times,* 2 October.

18. For further information, see for example: Wells, P. and Lewis, L. (2018) Japan Inc: a corporate culture on trial after scandals, *Financial Times,* 3 January; Parry, R.L. (2017) Japan's failed corporate culture at root of Kobe Steel scandal, *The Times,* 16 October; Kobe Steel admits falsifying data on 20,000 tonnes of metal, *Economist,* 12 October 2017; Wells, P. (2017) Kobe Steel demotes three executives over cheating scandal, *Financial Times,* 21 December; Wells, P. and Terazono, E. (2017) Five questions on Kobe Steel and quality controls, *Financial Times,* 11 October.

19. Source: The EFQM Website, www.efqm.org

20. Based on Kolk, A. (2000) *The Economics of Environmental Management,* Financial Times, Prentice Hall Upper Saddle River, NJ. Also see www.globalreporting.org

21. This case is based on a real situation, but data have been changed for reasons of commercial confidentiality.

Chapter 18

1. For further information, see: Bond, A. and Rodger, J. (2017) What happened on The Smiler crash at Alton Towers? Birmingham Live, 28 June; Walsh, D. (2016) Merlins roller coaster tragedy in 'toughest ever year' takes its toll, *The Times,* 20 May.

2. Christopher, M. (2002) Business is failing to manage supply chain vulnerability, *Odyssey,* Issue 16, June.

3. For further information, see: Fu, K., Kohno, T., Lopresti, D., Mynatt, E., Nahrstedt, K., Patel, S., Richardson, D. and Zorn, B. (2017) Safety, Security, and Privacy Threats Posed by Accelerating Trends in the Internet of Things. http://cra.org/ccc/resources/ccc-led-whitepapers/; Writer, G. (2017) The 5 Worst Examples of IoT Hacking and Vulnerabilities in Recorded History, iot for all, 10 May.

4. For further information, see: Exeter couple finally ditch 1950s appliances, BBC News, 19 November 2017.

5. For further information, see: Blastland, M. and Spiegehalter, D. (2013) The norm chronicles; stories and numbers about danger, *Profile*; Spiegelhalter, D. (2014) The power of the Micro-Mort, *British Journal of Obstetrics and Gynaecology,* vol. 121, 662–663; Making sense of the statistics that riddle our days, *Economist,* 22 June 2013.

6. For more information, see: Sverdlik, Y. (2017) OVH to disassemble container data centers after epic outage in Europe, Data Center Knowledge, 11 November.

7. Nahajima, S. (1988) *Total Productive Maintenance,* Productivity Press.

Chapter 19

1. Sources include: Bechtel report, Better train lines for London commuters, http://www.bechtel.com/projects/crossrail-london/, accessed 1 May 2017; Marrs, C. (2016) Crossrail: on time and on budget, is this how to get a major infrastructure project right?, *Civil Service World,* 8 February.

2. Shenhar, A.J. and Dvir, D. (2007) *Reinventing Project Management: The Diamond Approach to Successful Growth and Innovation,* Harvard Business School Press, Boston, MA.

3. For further information, see https://secondhands.eu/ ; http://www.wired.co.uk/article/ocado-humanoid-armar-6-secondhands; https://www.theguardian.com/business/2018/jan/11/ocado-to-wheel-out-c3po-style-robot-to-lend-a-hand-at-warehouses

4. Sources include raconteur.net 'Project Management' 02/08/2015; World Health Organization malaria programme, http://www.who.int/topics/malaria/en/

5. This example was written and kindly supplied by Mattia Bianchi, Department of Management and Organization, Stockholm School of Economics.

6. For more information, see: Why Berlin's new airport keeps missing its opening date, *Economist,* 25 January 2017; Berlin's new airport is too small even before take-off, *The Times,* December 2014; Berliner Flaughafen erst 2021 [Berlin airport opening 2021?] *Frankfurter Allgemeine Zeitung,* 23 November 2017.

7. For more information, see: Gilick, B. (2014) The BBC DMI project – what went wrong?, *Computer Weekly,* 5 February.

8. For more information, see: The Scottish Parliament website (www.scottish.parliament.uk; 'Holyrood price tag rise to £430 million', BBC News, 24 February 2004, http://news.bbc.co.uk/1/hi/scotland/3517225.stm

3D printing: also known as additive manufacturing, a 3D printer produces a three-dimensional object by laying down layer upon layer of material until the final form is obtained.

5 Ss: a simple housekeeping methodology to organize work areas. Originally translated from the Japanese, they are generally taken to mean sort, strengthen, shine, standardized and sustain. The aim is to reduce clutter in the workplace.

ABC inventory control: an approach to inventory control that classes inventory by its usage value and varies the approach to managing it accordingly.

Acceptance sampling: a technique of quality sampling that is used to decide whether to accept a whole batch of products (and occasionally services) on the basis of a sample; it is based on the operation's willingness to risk rejecting a 'good' batch and accepting a 'bad' batch.

Activity: as used in project management, it is an identifiable and defined task, used together with event activities to form network planning diagrams.

Aggregated planning and control: a term used to indicate medium-term capacity planning that aggregates different products and services together in order to get a broad view of demand and capacity.

Agility: the ability of an operation to respond quickly and at low cost as market requirements change.

Algorithmic decision making: where decisions are made automatically using a predefined sequence of instructions, or rules.

Allen Curve: a relationship that shows a powerful negative correlation between the physical distance between colleagues and their frequency of communication.

Allowances: term used in work study to indicate the extra time allowed for rest, relaxation and personal needs.

Alpha testing: essentially an *internal* process where the developers or manufacturers (or sometimes an outside agency that they have commissioned) examine the product for errors. Generally, it is also a private process, not open to the market or potential customers.

Andon: a light above a workstation that indicates its state, whether working, waiting for work, broken down, etc.; andon lights may be used to stop the whole line when one station stops.

Annual hours: a type of flexitime working that controls the amount of time worked by individuals on an annual rather than a shorter basis.

Anthropometric data: data that relate to people's size, shape and other physical abilities, used in the design of jobs and physical facilities.

Anticipation inventory: inventory that is accumulated to cope with expected future demand or interruptions in supply.

Appraisal costs: those costs associated with checking, monitoring and controlling quality to see if problems or errors have occurred, an element within quality-related costs.

Approaches to improvement: the underlying sets of beliefs that form a coherent philosophy and shape how improvement should be accomplished.

Artificial intelligence (AI): an 'area of computer science that emphasizes the creation of intelligent machines that work and react like humans.

Attributes of quality: measures of quality that can take one of two states: for example, right or wrong, works or does not work, etc.

Augmented reality: technologies that show an enhanced version of reality where live views of physical real-world environments are augmented with overlaid computer-generated images.

Automated guided vehicle (AGV): a materials-handling system that uses automated vehicles programmed to move between different stations without a driver.

B Corps: an abbreviation for Benefit Corporations; those that have a clear and unequivocal social benefit.

B2B: abbreviation of Business to Business operation, meaning those that provide their products or services to other businesses.

B2C: abbreviation of Business to Consumer operation, meaning those that provide their products or services direct to the consumers who (generally) are the ultimate users of the outputs from the operation.

Back-office: the low-visibility part of an operation.

Backward scheduling: starting jobs at such a time that they should be finished exactly when they are due, as opposed to forward scheduling.

Balanced scorecard (BSC): in addition to financial performance, the balanced scorecard also includes assessment of customer satisfaction, internal processes and innovation and learning.

Balancing loss: the quantification of the lack of balance in a production line, defined as the percentage of time not used for productive purposes as a proportion of the total time invested in making a product.

Bar code: a unique product code that enables a part or product type to be identified when read by a bar-code scanner.

Basic time: the time taken to do a job without any extra allowances for recovery.

Batch processes: processes that treat batches of products together, and where each batch has its own process route.

Bath-tub curve: a curve that describes the failure probability of a product, service or process and indicates relatively high probabilities of failure at the beginning and at the end of the life cycle.

Behavioural job design: an approach to job design that considers individuals' desire to fulfil their needs for self-esteem and personal development.

Benchmarking: the activity of comparing methods and/or performance with other processes in order to learn from them and/or assess performance.

Beta testing: when the product or service is released for testing by selected customers. It is an *external* 'pilot-test' that takes place in the 'real world' (or near real world, because it is still a relatively short trial with a small sample) before commercial production.

Big data: a large volume of both structured and unstructured data whose analysis can reveal hidden patterns, correlations and other insights.

Bill of materials (BOM): a list of the component parts required to make up the total package for a product or service together with information regarding their level in the product or component structure and the quantities of each component required.

Blockchain: a decentralized, digitized, public ledger (list) of transactions (movements, authorizations, payments, etc.), where a 'block' is a record of new transactions. When each block is completed (verified) it is added to the chain, thus creating a chain of blocks, or 'blockchain'.

Blueprinting: a term often used in service design to mean process mapping.

Bottleneck: the capacity-constraining stage in a process; it governs the output of the whole process.

Bottom-up: the influence of operational experience on operations decisions.

Brainstorming: an improvement technique where small groups of people put forward ideas in a creative free-form manner.

Break-even analysis: the technique of comparing revenues and costs at increasing levels of output in order to establish the point at which revenue exceeds cost: that is, the point at which it 'breaks even'.

Breakthrough improvement: an approach to improving operations performance that implies major and dramatic change in the way an operation works; for example, business process re-engineering (BPR) is often associated with this type of improvement, also known as innovation-based improvement, contrasted with continuous improvement.

Broad definition of operations: all the activities necessary for the fulfilment of customer requests.

Buffer inventory: an inventory that compensates for unexpected fluctuations in supply and demand; can also be called safety inventory.

Bullwhip effect: the tendency of supply chains to amplify relatively small changes at the demand side of a supply chain such that the disruption at the supply end of the chain is much greater.

Business continuity: the procedures adopted by businesses to mitigate and recover from the effects of major failures.

Business ecosystem: an idea that is closely related to that of co-opetition. Like supply networks, business ecosystems include suppliers and customers. However, they also include stakeholders that may have little or no direct relationship with the main supply network yet interact with it by complementing or contributing significant components of the value proposition for customers.

Business model: the plan that is implemented by a company to generate revenue and make a profit (or fulfil its social objectives if a not-for-profit enterprise).

Business process outsourcing (BPO): the term that is applied to the outsourcing of whole business processes; this need not mean a change in location of the process, sometimes it involves an outside company taking over the management of processes that remain in the same location.

Business process re-engineering (BPR): the philosophy that recommends the redesign of processes to fulfil defined external customer needs.

Business processes: processes, often that cut across functional boundaries, which contribute some part to fulfilling customer needs.

Business strategy: the strategic positioning of a business in relation to its customers, markets and competitors, a subset of corporate strategy.

Capacity lagging: the strategy of planning capacity levels such that they are always less than or equal to forecast demand.

Capacity leading: the strategy of planning capacity levels such that they are always greater than or equal to forecast demand.

Capacity: the maximum level of value-added activity that an operation, or process, or facility is capable of over a period of time.

Causal modelling: a quantitative approach to demand forecasting, which describes and evaluates the complex cause–effect relationships between the key variables.

Cause–effect diagrams: a technique for searching out the root cause of problems; it is a systematic questioning technique, also known as Ishikawa diagrams.

Cell layout: locating transforming resources with a common purpose such as processing the same types of product, serving similar types of customer, etc., together in close proximity (a cell).

Centre-of-gravity method of location: a technique that uses the physical analogy of balance to determine the geographical location that balances the weighted importance of the other operations with which the one being located has a direct relationship.

Chase demand: an approach to medium-term capacity management that attempts to adjust output and/or capacity to reflect fluctuations in demand.

Circular economy: an alternative to the traditional linear economy (or make-use-dispose as it is termed). The idea is to keep products in use for as long as possible, extract the maximum value from them whilst in use, and then recover and regenerate products and materials at the end of their service life.

Closed-loop economy: *see* 'Circular economy'.

Cluster analysis: a technique used in the design of cell layouts to find which process groups fit naturally together.

Clusters: where similar companies with similar needs locate relatively close to each other in the same geographical area.

Co-creation: where the customer or customers play an important part in the character of the product or service offering.

Combinatorial complexity: the idea that many different ways of processing products and services at many different locations or points in time combine to result in an exceptionally large number of feasible options; the term is often used in facilities layout and scheduling to justify non-optimal solutions (because there are too many options to explore).

Commonality: the degree to which a range of products or services incorporate identical components (also called 'parts commonality').

Community factors: those factors that are influential in the location decision that relate to the social, political and economic environment of the geographical position.

Competitive factors: the factors such as delivery time, product or service specification, price, etc. that define customers' requirements.

Component structure: *see* 'Product structure'.

Computer-aided design (CAD): a system that provides the computer ability to create and modify product, service or process drawings.

Computer-integrated manufacturing (CIM): a term used to describe the integration of computer-based monitoring and control of all aspects of a manufacturing process, often using a common database and communicating via some form of computer network.

Concept generation: a stage in the product and service design process that formalizes the underlying idea behind a product or service.

Concurrent engineering: *see* 'Simultaneous development'.

Condition-based maintenance: an approach to maintenance management that monitors the condition of process equipment and performs work on equipment only when it is required.

Content of strategy: the set of specific decisions and actions that shape the strategy.

Continuous improvement: an approach to operations improvement that assumes many, relatively small, incremental improvements in performance, stressing the momentum of improvement rather than the rate of improvement; also known as 'kaizen', often contrasted with breakthrough improvement.

Continuous processes: processes that are high volume and low variety; usually products made on a continuous process are produced in an endless flow, such as petrochemicals or electricity.

Continuous review: an approach to managing inventory that makes inventory-related decisions when inventory reaches a particular level, as opposed to period review.

Contracting relationships: relationship between operations in a supply network that rely on formal and/or legal contracts that specify obligations and roles.

Control charts: the charts used within statistical process control to record process performance.

Control limits: the lines on a control chart used in statistical process control that indicate the extent of natural or common-cause variations; any points lying outside these control limits are deemed to indicate that the process is likely to be out of control.

Control: the process of monitoring operations activity and coping with any deviations from the plan; usually involves elements of replanning.

Co-opetition: an approach to supply networks that defines businesses as being surrounded by suppliers, customers, competitors and complementors.

Core functions: the functions that manage the three core processes of any business: marketing, product/service development and operations.

Corporate social responsibility: how business takes account of its economic, social and environmental impacts.

Corporate strategy: the strategic positioning of a corporation and the businesses within it.

CRAFT: Computerized Relative Allocation of Facilities Technique, a heuristic technique for developing good, but non-optimal, solutions.

Crashing: a term used in project management to mean reducing the time spent on critical path activities so as to shorten the whole project.

Create-to-order: *see* 'Make-to-order'.

Critical path: the longest sequence of activities through a project network, it is called the critical path because any delay in any of its activities will delay the whole project.

Critical path method (CPM): a technique of network analysis.

Crowdsourcing: the act of taking an activity traditionally performed by a designated agent and outsourcing it to a large group of people in the form of an open call.

Customer contact skills: the skills and knowledge that operations staff need to meet customer expectations.

Customer relationship management (CRM): a method of learning more about customers' needs and behaviours by analysing sales information.

Customization: the variation in product or service design to suit the specific need of individual customers or customer groups.

Cyber security: activity that attempts to protect an operation from exposure to any risk of financial loss, disruption or damage to the reputation of an organization from some sort of failure of its information technology systems.

Cycle inventory: inventory that occurs when one stage in a process cannot supply all the items it produces simultaneously and so has to build up inventory of one item while it processes the others.

Cycle time: the average time between units of output emerging from a process.

Decision support system (DSS): a management information system that aids or supports managerial decision-making; it may include both databases and sophisticated analytical models.

De-coupling inventory: the inventory that is used to allow work centres or processes to operate relatively independently.

Delegated sourcing: involves a tiered approach to managing supplier relationships, where one supplier is responsible for delivering an entire sub-assembly as opposed to a single part, or a package of services as opposed to an individual service.

Delivery: the activities that plan and control the transfer of products and services to customers.

Delivery flexibility: the operation's ability to change the timing of the delivery of its services or products.

Delphi method: the best-known approach to generating forecasts using experts. It employs a survey of experts where replies are analysed, and anonymous summaries are sent back to all experts. The experts are then asked to re-consider their original response in the light of the replies and arguments put forward by the other experts. This process is repeated several times to conclude either with a consensus or at least a narrower range of decisions.

Demand management: an approach to medium-term capacity management that attempts to change or influence demand to fit available capacity.

Demand side: the chains of customers, customers' customers, etc. that receive the products and services produced by an operation.

Dependability: delivering, or making available, products or services when they were promised to the customer.

Dependent demand: demand that is relatively predictable because it is derived from some other known factor.

Design acceptability: the attractiveness to the operation of a process, product or service.

Design capacity: the capacity of a process or facility as it is designed to be, often greater than effective capacity.

Design concept: the set of expected benefits to the customer encapsulated in a product or service design.

Design feasibility: the ability of an operation to produce a process, product or service.

Design for manufacture and assembly (DFMA) software: an extension of CAD that allows those involved in the innovation process to integrate their designs prior to manufacture. Examples include 3-D object modelling and the use of virtual reality technologies.

Design funnel: a model that depicts the design process as the progressive reduction of design options from many alternatives down to the final design.

Design package: the component products, services and parts within a product or service design that provide the benefits to the customer.

Design screening: the evaluation of alternative designs with the purpose of reducing the number of design options being considered.

Development: a collection of operations activities that improve products, services and processes.

Digital twins: powerful digital 'replicas' that can be used instead of the physical reality of a product. For example, digital twins could monitor and simulate possible future scenarios and predict the need for repairs and other problems before they occur.

Directing: operations activities that create a general understanding of an operation's strategic purpose and performance.

Disaster recovery: a term used in a similar way to business continuity, but which is concerned largely with action plans and procedures for the recovery of critical information technology and systems after a natural or human-induced disaster.

Diseconomies of scale: a term used to describe the extra costs that are incurred in running an operation as it gets larger.

Disintermediation: the emergence of an operation in a supply network that separates two operations that were previously in direct contact.

Disruptive technologies: technologies which in the short term cannot match the performance required by customers but may improve faster than existing technology to make that existing technology redundant.

Distributed processing: a term used in information technology to indicate the use of smaller computers distributed around an operation and linked together so that they can communicate with each other; the opposite of centralized information processing.

Division of labour: an approach to job design that involves dividing a task down into relatively small parts, each of which is accomplished by a single person.

DMAIC cycle: an increasingly used improvement cycle model, popularized by the Six Sigma approach to operations improvement. DMAIC stands for defining the problem, measuring data to refine the problem, analysing to detect the root causes of the problem, improving the process, and controlling to check that the improved level of performance is sustaining.

Do or buy: the term applied to the decision of whether to own a process that contributes to a product or service, or, alternatively, outsource the activity performed by the process to another operation.

Downstream: the other operations in a supply chain between the operation being considered and the end customer.

Drum, buffer, rope: an approach to operations control that comes from the theory of constraints (TOC) and uses the bottleneck stage in a process to control materials movement.

Dynamic pricing: *see* 'Surge pricing'.

Earned-value control: a method of assessing performance in project management by combining the costs and times achieved in the project with the original plan.

E-business: the use of Internet-based technologies either to support existing business processes or to create entirely new business opportunities.

E-commerce: the use of the Internet to facilitate buying and selling activities.

Economic batch quantity (EBQ): the number of items to be produced by a machine or process that supposedly minimizes the costs associated with production and inventory holding.

Economic bottom line: the part of the triple bottom line that assesses an organization's economic performance, usually in financial terms.

Economic order quantity (EOQ): the quantity of items to order that supposedly minimizes the total cost of inventory management, derived from various EOQ formulae.

Economy of scale: the manner in which the costs of running an operation decrease as it gets larger.

Effective capacity: the useful capacity of a process or operation after maintenance, changeover and other stoppages and loading have been accounted for.

Efficient frontier: the convex line which describes current performance trade-offs between (usually two) measures of operations performance.

EFQM excellence model: a model that identifies the categories of activity that supposedly ensure high levels of quality; now used by many companies to examine their own quality-related procedures.

Electronic marketplaces: also sometimes called infomediaries or cybermediaries, websites that offer services to both buyers and sellers, usually in B2B markets.

Elements of improvement: the fundamental ideas of what improves operations.

Emergent strategy: a strategy that is gradually shaped over time and based on experience rather than theoretical positioning.

Emotional mapping: charting how customers' emotions could be engaged (positively and negatively) at each stage of a process.

Empowerment: a term used in job design to indicate increasing the authority given to people to make decisions within the job or changes to the job itself.

End-to-end business processes: processes that totally fulfil a defined external customer need.

Enterprise project management (EPM): software that integrates all the common activities in project management.

Enterprise resource planning (ERP): the integration of all significant resource planning systems in an organization that, in an operations context, integrates planning and control with the other functions of the business.

Environmental bottom line: the element of the triple bottom line that assesses an organization's performance in terms of how it affects the natural environment.

E-procurement: the use of the Internet to organize purchasing; this may include identifying potential suppliers and auctions as well as the administrative tasks of issuing orders etc.

Ergonomics: a branch of job design that is primarily concerned with the physiological aspects of job design, with how the human body fits with process facilities and the environment; can also be referred to as human factors, or human factors engineering.

Ethernet: a technology that facilitates local-area networks that allows any device attached to a single cable to communicate with any other devices attached to the same cable; also now used for wireless communication that allows mobile devices to connect to a local-area network.

European Quality Award (EQA): a quality award organized by the European Foundation for Quality Management (EFQM), it is based on the EFQM excellence model.

Events: points in time within a project plan; together with activities, they form network planning diagrams.

Evidence-based problem solving: using statistical methods and hard data as a basis for improvement.

Expert systems (ES): computer-based problem-solving systems that, to some degree, mimic human problem-solving logic.

External failure costs: those costs that are associated with an error or failure reaching a customer, an element within quality-related costs.

External neutrality: the second stage of Hayes and Wheelwright's four-stage model of operations contribution, where the operations function begins comparing itself with similar companies or organizations in the outside market.

Externally supportive: the final stage of Hayes and Wheelwright's four-stage model of operations contribution, where the operations function is the foundation for an organization's competitive success.

Extranets: computer networks that link organizations together and connect with each organization's internal network.

Facilitating products: products that are produced by an operation to support its services.

Facilitating services: services that are produced by an operation to support its products.

Fail-safeing: building in, often simple, devices that make it difficult to make the mistakes that could lead to failure; also known by the Japanese term 'poka-yoke'.

Failure analysis: the use of techniques to uncover the root cause of failures; techniques may include accident investigation, complaint analysis, etc.

Failure mode and effect analysis (FMEA): a technique used to identify the product, service or process features that are crucial in determining the effects of failure.

Failure rate: a measure of failure that is defined as the number of failures over a period of time.

Fault tree analysis: a logical procedure that starts with a failure or potential failure and works backwards to identify its origins.

Finite loading: an approach to planning and control that only allocates work to a work centre up to a set limit (usually its useful capacity).

First-tier: the description applied to suppliers and customers that are in immediate relationships with an operation with no intermediary operations.

Fixed cost break: the volumes of output at which it is necessary to invest in operations facilities that bear a fixed cost.

Fixed-position layout: locating the position of a product or service such that it remains largely stationary, while transforming resources are moved to and from it.

Flexibility: the degree to which an operation's process can change what it does, how it is doing it, or when it is doing it.

Flexible manufacturing systems (FMS): manufacturing systems that bring together several technologies into a coherent system, such as metal cutting and material handling technologies; usually their activities are controlled by a single governing computer.

Flexi-time working: increasing the possibility of individuals varying the time during which they work.

Focus group: a group of potential product or service users, chosen to be typical of its target market, who are formed to test their reaction to alternative designs.

Forward scheduling: loading work onto work centres as soon as it is practical to do so, as opposed to backward scheduling.

Four-stage model of operations contribution: model devised by Hayes and Wheelwright that categorizes the degree to which operations management has a positive influence on overall strategy.

Front-office: the high-visibility part of an operation.

Functional layout: layout where similar resources or processes are located together (sometimes called process layout).

Functional operations: the idea that every function in an organization uses resources to produce products and services for (internal) customers, therefore all functions are, to some extent, operations.

Functional strategy: the overall direction and role of a function within the business; a subset of business strategy.

Gantt chart: a scheduling device that represents time as a bar or channel on which activities can be marked.

Gartner hype cycle: an idea created by Gartner, the information technology research and consultancy company, that attempts to illustrate how perceptions of a technology's usefulness develop over time.

Gemba: also sometimes called Gamba, a term used to convey the idea of going to where things actually take place as a basis for improvement.

Gig economy: the trend of organizations to employ sub-contractors and freelancers to do a greater proportion of their activities rather than relying on full-time employees. This flexing of capacity is now employed across a wide range of industries, including arts and design, transportation, construction, accommodation, media, ICT, education, and professional services.

Globalization: the extension of operations' supply chain to cover the whole world.

Heijunka: *see* 'Levelled scheduling'.

Henderson–Clark Model: innovation theory that distinguishes between knowledge of the components of an idea and knowledge of how the components fit together.

Heuristics: 'rules of thumb' or simple reasoning short cuts that are developed to provide good but non-optimal solutions, usually to operations decisions that involve combinatorial complexity.

Hierarchy of operations: the idea that all operations processes are made up of smaller operations processes.

High-level process mapping: an aggregated process map that shows broad activities rather than detailed activities (sometimes called an 'outline process map').

Hire and fire: a (usually pejorative) term used in medium-term capacity management to indicate varying the size of the workforce through employment policy.

House of quality: *see* 'Quality function deployment'.

Human factors engineering: an alternative term for ergonomics.

Human resource strategy: the overall long-term approach to ensuring that an organization's human resources provide a strategic advantage.

Immediate supply network: the suppliers and customers that have direct contact with an operation.

Importance–performance matrix: a technique that brings together scores that indicate the relative importance and relative performance of different competitive factors in order to prioritize them as candidates for improvement.

Improvement cycles: the practice of conceptualizing problem solving as used in performance improvement in terms of a never-ending cyclical model: for example, the PDCA cycle or the DMAIC cycle.

Independent demand: demand that is not obviously or directly dependent on the demand for another product or service.

Indirect process technology: technology that assists in the management of processes rather than directly contributes to the creation of products and services: for example, information technology that schedules activities.

Indirect responsibilities of operations management: the activities of collaborating with other functions of the organization.

Industry 4.0: cyber-physical systems that comprise smart machines, storage systems and production facilities capable of autonomously exchanging information, triggering actions and controlling each other independently.

Infinite loading: an approach to planning and control that allocates work to work centres irrespective of any capacity or other limits.

Information technology (IT): any device, or collection of devices, that collects, manipulates, stores or distributes information, nearly always used to mean computer-based devices.

Infrastructural decisions: the decisions that concern the operation's systems, methods and procedures and shape its overall culture.

Innovation: the act of introducing new ideas to products, services or processes.

Innovation S-Curve: the curve that describes the impact of an innovation over time.

Input resources: the transforming and transformed resources that form the input to operations.

Intangible resources: the resources within an operation that are not immediately evident or tangible, such as relationships with suppliers and customers, process knowledge, new product and service development.

Interactive design: the idea that the design of products and services on one hand, and the processes that create them on the other, should be integrated.

Internal customers: processes or individuals within an operation that are the customers for other internal processes or individuals' outputs.

Internal failure costs: the costs associated with errors and failures that are dealt with inside an operation but cause disruption; an element within quality-related costs.

Internal neutrality: the first stage of Hayes and Wheelwright's four-stage model of operations contribution, where the operations function performance harms the organization's ability to compete effectively.

Internal suppliers: processes or individuals within an operation that supply products or services to other processes or individuals within the operation.

Internally supportive: the third stage of Hayes and Wheelwright's four-stage model of operations contribution, where the operations functions have typically reached the 'first division' of their markets.

Internet of Things: the integration of physical objects into an information network where the physical objects become active participants in business processes.

Inventory: also known as stock, the stored accumulation of transformed resources in a process; usually applies to material resources but may also be used for inventories of information; inventories of customers or customers of customers are usually queues.

ISO 14000: an international standard that guides environmental management systems and covers initial planning, implementation and objective assessment.

ISO 9000: a set of worldwide standards that established the requirements for companies' quality management systems; last revised in 2000, there are several sets of standards.

Job design: the way in which we structure the content and environment of individual staff members' jobs within the workplace and the interface with the technology or facilities that they use.

Job enlargement: a term used in job design to indicate increasing the amount of work given to individuals in order to make the job less monotonous.

Job enrichment: a term used in job design to indicate increasing the variety and number of tasks within an individual's job; this may include increased decision-making and autonomy.

Job rotation: the practice of encouraging the movement of individuals between different aspects of a job in order to increase motivation.

Jobbing processes: processes that deal with high variety and low volumes, although there may be some repetition of flow and activities.

Just-in-time (JIT): a method of planning and control and an operations philosophy that aims to meet demand instantaneously with perfect quality and no waste.

Kaizen: Japanese term for continuous improvement.

Kanban: Japanese term for card or signal; it is a simple controlling device that is used to authorize the release of materials in pull control systems such as those used in JIT.

Keiretsu: a Japanese term used to describe a coalition of companies which form a supply network around a large manufacturer and can include service companies such as banks as well as conventional suppliers.

Knowledge management: the management of facts, information and skills acquired through experience or education; the theoretical or practical understanding of a subject.

Lead-time usage: the amount of inventory that will be used between ordering replenishment and the inventory arriving, usually described by a probability distribution to account for uncertainty in demand and lead time.

Lead user: users who are ahead of the majority of the market on a major market trend, and who also have a high incentive to innovate. As these lead users will be familiar with both the positives and negatives of the early versions of products and services, they are a particularly valuable source of potential innovative ideas.

Lean Sigma: a blend of improvement elements from lean and Six Sigma.

Lean: (also known as Lean Synchronization) an approach to operations management that emphasizes the continual elimination of waste of all types, often used interchangeably with just-in-time (JIT); it is more an overall philosophy whereas JIT is usually used to indicate an approach to planning and control that adopts lean principles.

Less important factors: competitive factors that are neither order-winning nor qualifying; performance in them does not significantly affect the competitive position of an operation.

Level capacity plan: an approach to medium-term capacity management that attempts to keep output from an operation or its capacity constant, irrespective of demand.

Levelled scheduling: the idea that the mix and volume of activity should even out over time so as to make output routine and regular, sometimes known by the Japanese term 'heijunka'.

Life-cycle analysis: a technique that analyses all the production inputs, life-cycle use of a product and its final disposal in terms of total energy used and wastes emitted.

Line balancing: the activity of attempting to equalize the load on each station or part of a line layout or mass process.

Line layout: a more descriptive term for what is technically a product layout.

Line of fit: an alternative name for the 'natural' diagonal of the product process matrix.

Line of visibility: the boundary between the parts of the process visible to the customer and those that are not.

Little's law: the mathematical relationship between throughput time, work-in-process and cycle time (throughput time equals work-in-process $\times$ cycle time).

Loading: the amount of work that is allocated to a work centre.

Local-area network (LAN): a communications network that operates, usually over a limited distance, to connect devices such as PCs, servers, etc.

Location: the geographical position of an operation or process.

Logistics: a term in supply chain management broadly analogous to physical distribution management.

Long thin process: a process designed to have many sequential stages, each performing a relatively small part of the total task; the opposite of short fat process.

Long-term capacity management: the set of decisions that determine the level of physical capacity of an operation in whatever the operation considers to be long term; this will vary between industries, but is usually in excess of one year.

MacLeamy curve: a model that conveys the idea that, as projects move forward, the cost of making changes to the original project plan increases but the ability of project managers to influence the project goes down.

Maintenance: the activity of caring for physical facilities so as to avoid or minimize the chance of those facilities failing.

Make-to-order: operations that produce products only when they are demanded by specific customers.

Make-to-stock: operations that produce products prior to their being demanded by specific customers.

Management information systems (MIS): information systems that manipulate information so that it can be used in managing an organization.

Manufacturing resource planning (MRP II): an expansion of materials requirement planning to include greater integration with information in other parts of the organization and often greater sophistication in scheduling calculations.

Market requirements: the performance objectives that reflect the market position of an operation's products or services, also a perspective on operations strategy.

Mass customization: the ability to produce products or services in high volume, yet vary their specification to the needs of individual customers or types of customer.

Mass processes: processes that produce goods in high volume and relatively low variety.

Mass services: service processes that have a high number of transactions, often involving limited customization: for example, mass transportation services, call centres, etc.

Master production schedule (MPS): the important schedule that forms the main input to material requirements planning, it contains a statement of the volume and timing of the end products to be made.

Materials requirement planning (MRP): a set of calculations embedded in a system that helps operations make volume and timing calculations for planning and control purposes.

Matrix organizational forms: hybrids of M-form and U-form organizations.

Mean time between failures (MTBF): operating time divided by the number of failures; the reciprocal of failure rate.

Method study: the analytical study of methods of doing jobs with the aim of finding the 'best' or an improved job method.

M-form organization: an organizational structure that groups together either its resources needed to produce a product or service group, or those needed to serve a particular geographical area in separate divisions.

Milestones: term used in project management to denote important events at which specific reviews of time, cost and quality can be made.

Mitigation: a term used in risk management to mean isolating a failure from its negative consequences.

Mix flexibility: the operation's ability to produce a wide range of products and services.

Modular design: the use of standardized sub-components of a product or service that can be put together in different ways to create a high degree of variety.

MRP netting process: the process of calculating net requirements using the master production schedule and the bills of materials.

Muda: all activities in a process that are wasteful because they do not add value to the operation or to the customer.

Multi-skilling: increasing the range of skills of individuals in order to increase motivation and/or improve flexibility.

Multi-sourcing: the practice of obtaining the same type of product, component, or service from more than one supplier in order to maintain market bargaining power or continuity of supply.

Mura: a term meaning lack of consistency or unevenness that results in periodic overloading of staff or equipment.

Muri: waste because of unreasonable requirements placed on a process that will result in poor outcomes.

Network analysis: overall term for the use of network-based techniques for the analysis and management of projects; for example, includes critical path method (CPM) and programme evaluation and review technique (PERT).

N-form organization: networked organizational structures where clusters of resources have delegated responsibility for the strategic management of those resources.

Off-shoring: sourcing products and services from operations that are based outside one's own country or region.

Open sourcing: products or services developed by an open community, including users.

Operating model: a high-level design of the organization that defines the structure and style which enables it to meet its business objectives.

Operations function: the arrangement of resources that are devoted to the production and delivery of products and services.

Operations management: the activities, decisions and responsibilities of managing the production and delivery of products and services.

Operations managers: the staff of the organization who have particular responsibility for managing some or all of the resources which compose the operation's function.

Operations resource capabilities: the inherent ability of operations processes and resources; also a perspective on operations strategy.

Operations strategy: the overall direction and contribution of the operation's function with the business; the way in which market requirements and operations resource capabilities are reconciled within the operation.

Optimized production technology (OPT): software and concept originated by Eliyahu Goldratt to exploit his theory of constraints (TOC).

Order fulfilment: all the activities involved in supplying a customer's order, often used in e-retailing but now also used in other types of operation.

Order-winners: the competitive factors that directly and significantly contribute to winning business.

Organizational ambidexterity: the ability of an operation to both exploit and explore as they seek to improve.

Outline process map: see 'High-level process mapping'.

Outsourcing: the practice of contracting out to a supplier work previously done within the operation.

Overall equipment effectiveness (OEE): a method of judging the effectiveness of how operations equipment is used.

P:D ratio: a ratio that contrasts the total length of time customers have to wait between asking for a product or service and receiving it (*D*) and the total throughput time to produce the product or service (*P*).

Panel approach: Qualitative method of forecasting using a panel of experts to discuss and agree on likely future demand (or other future events).

Parallel sourcing: involves having single source relationships for components or services for different product models or service packages in order to provide the advantages of both multiple sourcing and single sourcing simultaneously.

Pareto law: a general law found to operate in many situations that indicates that 20 per cent of something causes 80 per cent of something else, often used in inventory management (20 per cent of products produce 80 per cent of sales value) and improvement activities (20 per cent of types of problems produce 80 per cent of disruption).

Partnership: a type of relationship in supply chains that encourages relatively enduring co-operative agreements for the joint accomplishment of business goals.

Parts commonality: see 'Commonality'.

Parts family coding: the use of multi-digit codes to indicate the relative similarity between different parts, often used to determine the process route that a part takes through a manufacturing operation.

PDCA cycle: stands for Plan, Do, Check, Act cycle, perhaps the best known of all improvement cycle models.

Performance management: similar but broader to performance measurement but also attempts to influence decisions behaviour and skills development so that individuals and processes are better equipped to meet objectives.

Performance measurement: the activity of measuring and assessing the various aspects of a process or whole operation's performance.

Performance objectives: the generic set of performance indicators that can be used to set the objectives or judge the performance of any type of operation; although there are alternative lists proposed by different authorities, the five performance objectives as used in this book are quality, speed, dependability, flexibility and cost.

Performance standards: a defined level of performance against which an operation's actual performance is compared; performance standards can be based on historical performance, some arbitrary target performance, the performance of competitors, etc.

Periodic review: an approach to making inventory decisions that defines points in time for examining inventory levels and then makes decisions accordingly, as opposed to continuous review.

Perpetual inventory principle: a principle used in inventory control that inventory records should be automatically updated every time items are received or taken out of stock.

Physical distribution management: organizing the integrated movement and storage of materials.

Pipeline inventory: the inventory that exists because material cannot be transported instantaneously.

Planning: the formalization of what is intended to happen at some time in the future.

Plant-within-a-plant: a similar term to a cell layout but sometimes used to indicate a larger clustering of resources; *see also* 'Shop-within-a-shop'.

Poka-yoke: Japanese term for fail-safeing.

Polar diagram: a diagram that uses axes, all of which originate from the same central point, to represent different aspects of operations performance.

Predetermined motion–time systems (PMTS): a work measurement technique where standard elemental times obtained from published tables are used to construct a time estimate for a whole job.

Preliminary design: the initial design of a product or service that sets out its main components and functions, but does not include many specific details.

Prevention costs: those costs that are incurred in trying to prevent quality problems and errors occurring, an element within quality-related costs.

Preventive maintenance: an approach to maintenance management that performs work on machines or facilities at regular intervals in an attempt to prevent them breaking down.

Principles of motion economy: a checklist used to develop new methods in work study that is intended to eliminate elements of the job, combine elements together, simplify the activity or change the sequence of events so as to improve efficiency.

Process capability: an arithmetic measure of the acceptability of the variation of a process.

Process design: the overall configuration of a process that determines the sequence of activities and the flow of transformed resources between them.

Process distance: the degree of novelty required by a process in the implementation of a new technology.

Process hierarchy: the idea that a network of resources form processes, networks of processes form operations, and networks of operations form supply networks.

Process layout: alternative (misleading) name for functional layout.

Process mapping: describing processes in terms of how the activities within the process relate to each other (may also be called 'process blueprinting' or 'process analysis').

Process mapping symbols: the symbols that are used to classify different types of activity; they usually derive either from scientific management or from information-systems flow-charting.

Process mining: a technique used for processes at the 'high variety–low volume' end of the volume–variety spectrum that uses statistical analysis, algorithms and artificial intelligence tools together with database management to understand how a process is actually performed in practice.

Process of operations strategy: how operations strategies are put together, often divided into formulation, implementation, monitoring and control.

Process outputs: the mixture of goods and services produced by processes.

Process technology: the machines and devices that create and/or deliver goods and services.

Process types: terms that are used to describe a particular general approach to managing processes; in manufacturing these are generally held to be project, jobbing, batch, mass and continuous processes; in services they are held to be professional services, service shops and mass services.

Process variability: the degree to which activities vary in their time or nature in a process.

Processes: an arrangement of resources that produces some mixture of products and services.

Product layout: locating transforming resources in a sequence defined by the processing needs of a product or service.

Product structure: a diagram that shows the constituent component parts of a product or service package and the order in which the component parts are brought together (often called components structure).

Product technology: the embedded technology within a product or service, as distinct from process technology.

Product/service flexibility: the operation's ability to introduce new or modified products and services.

Product/service life cycle: a generalized model of the behaviour of both customers and competitors during the life of a product or service; it is generally held to have four stages: introduction, growth, maturity and decline.

Production flow analysis (PFA): a technique that examines product requirements and process grouping simultaneously to allocate tasks and machines to cells in cell layout.

Productivity: the ratio of what is produced by an operation or process to what is required to produce it: that is, the output from the operation divided by the input to the operation.

Product–process matrix: a model derived by Hayes and Wheelwright that demonstrates the natural fit between volume and variety of products and services produced by an operation on one hand, and the process type used to produce products and services on the other.

Professional services: service processes that are devoted to producing knowledge-based or advice-based services, usually involving high customer contact and high customization; examples include management consultants, lawyers, architects, etc.

Programme: as used in project management, it is generally taken to mean an ongoing process of change comprising individual projects.

Programme evaluation and review technique (PERT): a method of network planning that uses probabilistic time estimates.

Project: a set of activities with a defined start point and a defined end state which pursue a defined goal using a defined set of resources.

Project manager: competent project managers are vital for project success.

Project processes: processes that deal with discrete, usually highly customized, products.

Projectification: a term describing the increasing proportion of individuals' time spent working on projects as opposed to 'steady-state' activities.

Prototyping: an initial design of a product or service devised with the aim of further evaluating a design option.

Pull control: a term used in planning and control to indicate that a workstation requests work from the previous station only when it is required, one of the fundamental principles of just-in-time planning and control.

Purchasing: the organizational function, often part of the operations function, that forms contracts with suppliers to buy in materials and services.

Push control: a term used in planning and control to indicate that work is being sent forward to workstations as soon as it is finished on the previous workstation.

Qualified worker: term used in work study to denote a person who is accepted as having the necessary physical attributes, intelligence, skill, education and knowledge to perform the task.

Qualifiers: the competitive factors that have a minimum level of performance (the qualifying level) below which customers are unlikely to consider an operation's performance satisfactory.

Quality: there are many different approaches to defining this. We define it as consistent conformance to customers' expectations.

Quality characteristics: the various elements within the concept of quality, such as functionality, appearance, reliability, durability, recovery, etc.

Quality function deployment (QFD): a technique used to ensure that the eventual design of a product or service actually meets the needs of its customers (sometimes called 'house of quality').

Quality loss function (QLF): a mathematical function devised by Genichi Taguchi that includes all the costs of deviating from a target performance.

Quality of experience: the overall acceptability of the service, as perceived subjectively by the end-user.

Quality sampling: the practice of inspecting only a sample of products or services produced rather than every single one.

Quality variables: measures of quality that can be measured on a continuously variable scale: for example, length, weight, etc.

Quality-related costs: an attempt to capture the broad cost categories that are affected by, or affect, quality, usually categorized as prevention costs, appraisal costs, internal failure costs and external failure costs.

Queuing theory: a mathematical approach that models random arrival and processing activities in order to predict the behaviour of queuing systems (also called 'waiting line theory').

Radical improvement: *see* 'Breakthrough improvement'.

Rating: a work study technique that attempts to assess a worker's rate of working relative to the observer's concept of standard performance – controversial and now accepted as being an ambiguous process.

Received variety: the variety that occurs because the process is not designed to prevent it.

Recovery: the activity (usually a predetermined process) of minimizing the effects of an operation's failure.

Red Queen effect: the idea that improvement is relative; a certain level of improvement is necessary simply to maintain one's current position against competitors.

Redundancy: the extent to which a process, product or service has systems or components that are used only when other systems or components fail.

Relationship chart: a diagram used in layout to summarize the relative desirability of facilities to be close to each other.

Reliability: when applied to operations performance, it can be used interchangeably with 'dependability'; when used as a measure of failure it means the ability of a system, product or service to perform as expected over time; this is usually measured in terms of the probability of it performing as expected over time.

Reliability-centred maintenance: an approach to maintenance management that uses different types of maintenance for different parts of a process depending on their pattern of failure.

Remainder cell: the cell that has to cope with all the products that do not conveniently fit into other cells.

Re-order level: the level of inventory at which more items are ordered, usually calculated to ensure that inventory does not run out before the next batch of inventory arrives.

Re-order point: the point in time at which more items are ordered, usually calculated to ensure that inventory does not run out before the next batch of inventory arrives.

Repeatability: the extent to which an activity does not vary.

Repetitive strain injury (RSI): damage to the body because of repetition of activities.

Research and development (R&D): the function in the organization that develops new knowledge and ideas and operationalizes the ideas to form the underlying knowledge on which product, service and process designs are based.

Re-shoring: the action of moving business activities that had been moved overseas back to the country from which they were originally relocated (also referred to as 'back-shoring', 'home-shoring' and 'on-shoring').

Resource distance: the degree of novelty required of an operation's resources during the implementation of a new technology or process.

Resource-based view (RBV): the perspective on strategy that stresses the importance of capabilities (sometimes known as core competences) in determining sustainable competitive advantage.

Resource-to-order: operations that buy in resources and produce only when products are demanded by specific customers.

Reverse engineering: the taking apart or deconstruction of a product or service in order to understand how it has been produced (often by a competing organization).

RFID (radio frequency identification): technologies that use radio waves to automatically identify objects and often collect data about them.

Robots: automatic manipulators of transformed resources whose movement can be programmed and reprogrammed.

Rostering: a term used in planning and control, usually to indicate staff scheduling, the allocation of working times to individuals so as to adjust the capacity of an operation.

Run-to-breakdown maintenance: an approach to maintenance management that only repairs a machine or facility when it breaks down.

Sales and Operations Planning (S&OP): a formal business process that looks over a period of 18 to 24 months ahead in an attempt to integrate short- and longer-term planning, as well as integrating the planning activities of key functions.

SAP: a German company which is the market leader in supplying ERP software, systems and training.

Scheduling: a term used in planning and control to indicate the detailed timetable of what work should be done, when it should be done and where it should be done.

Scientific management: a school of management theory dating from the early twentieth century; more analytical and systematic than 'scientific' as such, sometimes referred to (pejoratively) as Taylorism, after Frederick Taylor who was influential in founding its principles.

SCOR model: a broad but highly structured and systematic framework of supply chain improvement developed by the Supply Chain Council.

Second-tier: the description applied to suppliers and customers who are separated from the operation only by first-tier suppliers and customers.

Sequencing: the activity within planning and control that decides on the order in which work is to be performed.

Service guarantee: a promise to recompense a customer for service that fails to meet a defined quality level.

Service shops: service processes that are positioned between professional services and mass services, usually with medium levels of volume and customization.

Service-level agreements (SLAs): formal definitions of the dimensions and levels of service that should be provided by one process or operation to another.

Servicescape: a term used to describe the look and feel of the environment within an operation.

Servitization: involves (often manufacturing) firms developing the capabilities they need to provide services and solutions that supplement their traditional product offerings.

Set-up reduction: the process of reducing the time taken to change over a process from one activity to the next; also called 'single-minute exchange of dies' (SMED) after its origins in the metal pressing industry.

Seven types of waste: types of waste identified by Toyota; they are overproduction, waiting time, transport, process waste, inventory, motion and defectives.

Shop-within-a-shop: an operations layout that groups facilities that have a common purpose together; the term was originally used in retail operations but is now sometimes used in other industries, very similar to the idea of a cell layout.

Short fat processes: processes designed with relatively few sequential stages, each of which performs a relatively large part of the total task; the opposite of long thin processes.

Simulation: the use of a model of a process, product or service to explore its characteristics before the process, product or service is created.

Simultaneous development: overlapping the stages in the design process so that one stage in the design activity can start before the preceding stage is finished, the intention being to shorten time to market and save design cost (also called 'simultaneous engineering' or 'concurrent engineering').

Single-minute exchange of dies (SMED): alternative term for set-up reduction.

Single-sourcing: the practice of obtaining all of one type of input product, component or service from a single supplier, as opposed to multi-sourcing.

Six Sigma: an approach to improvement and quality management that originated in the Motorola Company but which was widely popularized by its adoption in the GE Company in America. Although based on traditional statistical process control, it is now a far broader 'philosophy of improvement' that recommends a particular approach to measuring, improving and managing quality and operations performance generally.

Skunkworks: a small, focused development team who are taken out of their normal working environment.

Social bottom line: the element of the triple bottom line that assesses the performance of a business in relation to the people and the society with which it has contact; and/or an environmental mission and a legal responsibility to respect the interests of workers, the community and the environment as well as shareholders.

Social responsibility: the incorporation of the operation's impact on its stakeholders into operations management decisions.

Spatially variable costs: the costs that are significant in the location decision that vary with geographical position.

Speed: the elapsed time between customers requesting products or services and their receiving them.

Stakeholders: the people and groups of people who have an interest in the operation and who may be influenced by, or influence, the operation's activities.

Standard performance: a term used in work measurement to indicate the rate of output that qualified workers will achieve without over-exertion as an average over the working day provided they are motivated to apply themselves, now generally accepted as a very vague concept.

Standard time: a term used in work measurement indicating the time taken to do a job and including allowances for recovery and relaxation.

Standardization: the degree to which processes, products, or services are prevented from varying over time.

Statistical process control (SPC): a technique that monitors processes as they produce products or services and attempts to distinguish between normal or natural variation in process performance and unusual or 'assignable' causes of variation.

Stock: alternative term for inventory.

Strategic decisions: those which are widespread in their effect, define the position of the organization relative to its environment and move the organization closer to its long-term goals.

Strategic level of operations performance: the five aspects of performance that contribute to the 'economic' aspect of the triple bottom line: cost, revenue, investment, risk and capabilities.

Structural decisions: the strategic decisions which determine the operation's physical shape and configuration, such as those concerned with buildings, capacity, technology, etc.

Sub-contracting: when used in medium-term capacity management, it indicates the temporary use of other operations to perform some tasks, or even produce whole products or services, during times of high demand.

Subscription model: where an operation's customers pay a fixed amount each agreed time period, for which they receive a pre-agreed service.

Supplier quality assurance (SQA): the activity of monitoring and improving levels of quality of the products and services delivered by suppliers; also used to assess supply capability when choosing between alternative suppliers.

Supply chain dynamics: the study of the behaviour of supply chains, especially the level of activity and inventory levels at different points in the chain; its best known finding is the bullwhip effect.

Supply chain risk: a study of the vulnerability of supply chains to disruption.

Supply chain: a linkage or strand of operations that provides goods and services through to end-customers; within a supply network several supply chains will cross through an individual operation.

Supply network: the network of supplier and customer operations that have relationships with an operation.

Supply side: the chains of suppliers, suppliers' suppliers, etc. that provide parts, information or services to an operation.

Support functions: the functions that facilitate the working of the core functions: for example, accounting and finance, human resources, etc.

Surge pricing: surge (or dynamic) pricing is a demand management technique that relies on frequent adjustments in price to influence supply and (especially) demand so that they match each other. For example, some electricity suppliers charge different rates for energy depending on when it is consumed.

Sustainability: the ability of a business to create acceptable profit for its owners as well as minimizing the damage to the environment and enhancing the existence of the people with whom it has contact.

Synthesis from elemental data: a work measurement technique for building up a time from previously timed elements.

Systemization: the extent to which standard procedures are made explicit.

Taguchi method: a design technique that uses design combinations to test the robustness of a design.

Take-back economy: *see* 'Circular economy'.

Takt time: (similar to cycle time) the time between items emerging from a process, usually applied to 'paced' processes.

Tangibility: the main characteristic that distinguishes products (usually tangible) from services (usually intangible).

Telemedicine: the ability to provide interactive healthcare utilizing modern telecommunications technology.

Teleworking: the ability to work from home using telecommunications and/or computer technology.

Theory of constraints (TOC): philosophy of operations management that focuses attention on capacity constraints or bottleneck parts of an operation; uses software known as 'optimized production technology' (OPT).

Three-D printing: also known as additive manufacturing, a technology that produces three-dimensional objects by laying down layer upon layer of material.

Throughput efficiency: the work content needed to produce an item in a process expressed as a percentage of total throughput time.

Throughput time: the time for a unit to move through a process.

Time series analysis: a quantitative approach to forecasting that examines the pattern of past behaviour of a single phenomenon over time, considering reasons for variation in the trend, in order to use the analysis to forecast the phenomenon's future behaviour.

Time study: a term used in work measurement to indicate the process of timing (usually with a stopwatch) and rating jobs; it involves observing times, adjusting or normalizing each observed time (rating) and averaging the adjusted times.

Time to market (TTM): the elapsed time taken for the whole design activity, from concept through to market introduction.

Top-down: the influence of the corporate or business strategy on operations decisions.

Total productive maintenance (TPM): an approach to maintenance management that adopts a similar holistic approach to total quality management (TQM).

Total quality management (TQM): a holistic approach to the management of quality that emphasizes the role of all parts of an organization and all people within an organization to influence and improve quality; heavily influenced by various quality 'gurus', it reached its peak of popularity in the 1980s and 1990s.

Total supply network: all the suppliers and customers who are involved in supply chains that 'pass through' an operation.

Touch-points: the points in a high-visibility process that are the points of contact between a process and customers.

Trade-off theory: the idea that the improvement in one aspect of operations performance comes at the expense of deterioration in another aspect of performance, now substantially modified to include the possibility that in the long term different aspects of operations performance can be improved simultaneously.

Transactional relationships: involve purchasing goods and services in a 'pure' market fashion, often seeking the 'best' supplier every time it is necessary to make a purchase.

Transformation process model: a model that describes operations in terms of their input resources, transforming processes and outputs of goods and services.

Transformed resources: the resources that are treated, transformed or converted in a process, usually a mixture of materials, information and customers.

Transforming resources: the resources that act upon the transformed resources, usually classified as facilities (the buildings, equipment and plant of an operation) and staff (the people who operate, maintain and manage the operation).

Triple bottom line: (also known as people, plants and profit) the idea that organizations should measure themselves on social and environmental criteria as well as financial ones.

Two-handed process chart: a type of micro-detailed process map that shows the motion of each hand used in an activity on a common timescale.

U-form organization: an organizational structure that clusters its resources primarily by their functional purpose.

Upstream: the other operations in a supply chain that are towards the supply side of the operation.

Usage value: a term used in inventory control to indicate the quantity of items used or sold multiplied by their value or price.

Utilization: the ratio of the actual output from a process or facility to its design capacity.

Valuable operating time: the amount of time at a piece of equipment or work centre that is available for productive working after stoppages and inefficiencies have been accounted for.

Value engineering: an approach to cost reduction in product design that examines the purpose of a product or service, its basic functions and its secondary functions.

Value stream map: a mapping process that aims to understand the flow of material and information through a process or series of processes; it distinguishes between value-added and non-value-added times in the process.

Value-added throughput efficiency: the amount of time an item spends in a process having value added to it expressed as a percentage of total throughput time.

Vanguard projects: typically separate from the mainstream business, involving significant departures from existing project capabilities. As a result, they require a high degree of exploration and experimentation in developing new routines.

Variation: the degree to which the rate or level of output varies from a process over time, a key characteristic in determining process behaviour.

Variety: the range of different products and services produced by a process; a key characteristic that determines process behaviour.

Vertical integration: the extent to which an operation chooses to own the network of processes that produce a product or service; the term is often associated with the 'do or buy' decision.

Virtual operation: an operation that performs few, if any, value-adding activities itself; rather it organizes a network of supplier operations, seen as the ultimate in outsourcing.

Virtual prototype: a computer-based model of a product, process or service that can be tested for its characteristics before the actual process, product or service is produced.

Virtual reality: uses entirely computer-generated simulations, with which humans can interact in a seemingly real manner using special helmets and gloves fitted with sensors.

Visibility: the amount of value-added activity that takes place in the presence (in reality or virtually) of the customer, also called 'customer contact'.

Visual management: an approach to making the current and planned state of an operation or process transparent to everyone.

Voice of the customer (VOC): capturing a customer's requirements, expectations and perceptions and using them as improvement targets within an operation.

Volume: the level or rate of output from a process, a key characteristic that determines process behaviour.

Volume flexibility: the operation's ability to change its level of output or activity to produce different quantities or volumes of products and services over time.

VRIO framework: a model, based on ideas of Jay Barney, to explain what resources need to generate competitive advantage – they should be *valuable, rare, costly to imitate, and organized to capture the value of the resource.*

Waiting line theory: an alternative term for queuing theory.

Web-integrated ERP: enterprise resource planning that is extended to include the ERP-type systems of other organizations such as customers and suppliers.

Weighted-score method of location: a technique for comparing the attractiveness of alternative locations that allocates a score to the factors that are significant in the decision, and weights each score by the significance of the factor.

Wide-area networks (WANs): similar to local-area networks (LANs) but with a greater reach, usually involving elements outside a single operation.

Work breakdown structure: the definition of, and the relationship between, the individual work packages in project management; each work package can be allocated its own objectives that fit in with the overall work breakdown structure.

Work content: the total amount of work required to produce a unit of output, usually measured in standard times.

Work measurement: a branch of work study that is concerned with measuring the time that should be taken for performing jobs.

Work study: the term generally used to encompass method study and work measurement, derived from the scientific management school.

Workflow: process of design of information-based processes.

Work-in-progress (WIP): the number of units within a process waiting to be processed further (also called 'work-in-process').

Work–life balance: the imperative to achieve an appropriate split between work and personal life so that work should not interfere unreasonably with family obligations and personal interests.

World Wide Web (WWW): the protocols and standards that are used on the Internet for formatting, retrieving, storing and displaying information.

Yield management: a collection of methods that can be used to ensure that an operation (usually with a fixed capacity) maximizes its potential to generate profit.

Zero defect: the idea that quality management should strive for perfection as its ultimate objective even though in practice this will never be reached.

INDEX